Global Business Dictionary

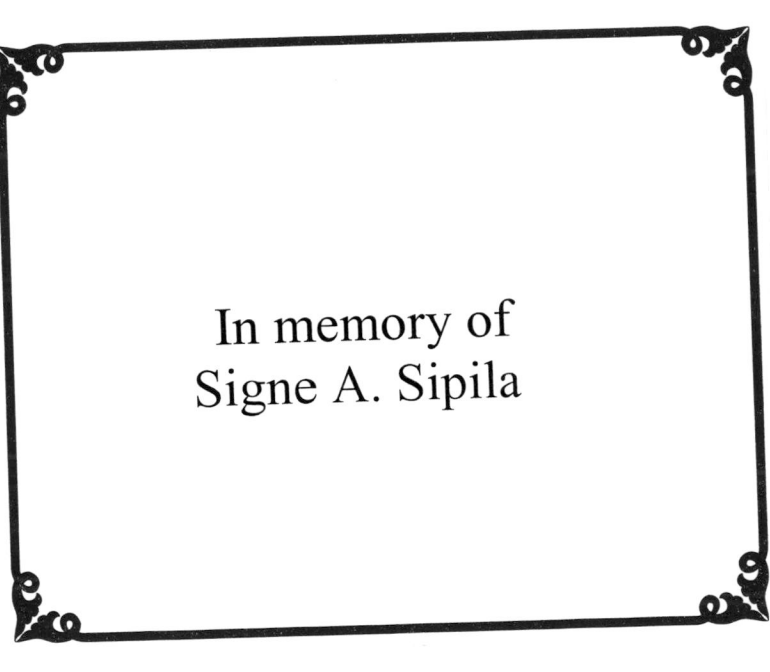

In memory of
Signe A. Sipila

Global Business Dictionary

English-Chinese-French-German-Japanese-Russian

Edited by
Morry Sofer

Schreiber Publishing
Rockville, Maryland

Global Business Dictionary
Morry Sofer, Editor

Published by:

Schreiber Publishing
Post Office Box 4193
Rockville, MD 20849 USA
e-mail: books@schreiberpublishing.com
www.schreiberpublishing.com

Library of Congress Cataloging-in-Publication Data

Sofer, Morry.
  Global business dictionary : English-French-German-Russian-Chinese-Japanese / Morry Sofer.
       p. cm.
   Includes bibliographical references and index.
   ISBN-13 : 978-0-88400-309-0 (alk. paper)
   ISBN-10 : 0-88400-309-4 (alk. paper)
   1. Business- -Dictionaries. 2. Commerce- -Dictionaries. 3.
Business- -Dictionaries- -Polyglot. 4. Commerce- -Dictionaries- -Polyglot. 5.
English language- -Dictionaries- -Polyglot. I. Title.

HF1002.S56 2005
650' .03- -dc22

                                        2005022194

Printed in the United States of America

Introduction

Business language around the world in the twenty-first century is in a state of rapid change. This creates the need for new business dictionaries that are not tied to the past but rather reflect the new global economy. This is particularly true in regard to the major business languages of the world, namely, English, Chinese, French, German, Japanese, and Russian. Two of those languages, namely, Chinese and Russian, represent two nations whose economy changed radically in recent years. Both made a major shift from a closed socialist economy to an open free market one. As a result, both have had to coin new business terms, and continue to do so.

Additionally, business has become totally dependent on digital data and its transmission. Since this is a field that changes practically from day to day, new words appear regularly, and have to be added to any current business dictionary.

Many of the English business terms in this dictionary are very American-specific. As such, they do not always have equivalent terms in other languages and therefore are explained in some detail.

This dictionary covers many areas of business, such as banking, insurance, real estate, export-import, stock market, and more. In addition, several hundred business-related computer and internet terms have been included.

Many of the business terms used today around the world are directly copied from American English. As a result, more than a few terms have both English-derived equivalents and original ones. This too is reflected in this dictionary.

The user of this dictionary is advised not to look upon all the terms herein included as cast in stone. Some may be questioned by business professionals. But it goes without saying that the need for this kind of dictionary is urgent and it should go a long way in contributing to better trade relations between English-speaking and other business partners.

The editors of this dictionary are open to suggestions, and will be glad to hear from you (you can e-mail us using the address on the copyright page).

A note about the French *entries:*

We have included French terms and translations from both France and Canada. Most of the terms used in Canada are the same as the ones used in

France. Those Canadian terms that are not commonly used in France are preceded by the designator (C).

A

abandonment
(CHIN) 放弃、报废
(FRE) abandon
(GER) Abandon *m* (Versicherung);
Verzicht *m*, Entäußerung *f*, Preisgabe *f*,
Stilllegung *f*, Außerbetriebnahme *f*
(Anlagevermögen); Nichtannahme *f*
(Lieferung); Optionsverzicht *f* (Börse)
(JAP) 放棄
(RUS) ДОБРОВОЛЬНЫЙ ОТКАЗ (ОТ ПРАВ,
ПРИТЯЗАНИЙ); ОСТАВЛЕНИЕ;
АБАНДОНИРОВАНИЕ

abandonment clause
(CHIN) 放弃条款
(FRE) clause d'abandon
(GER) Abandonerklärung *f*,
Verzichtklausel *f*
(JAP) 委付条項
(RUS) ПОЛОЖЕНИЕ (ПУНКТ) ОБ ОТКАЗЕ
(ОТ ПРАВ, ПРИТЯЗАНИЙ)

abatement
(CHIN) 冲销、减免、注销
(FRE) Diminution, réduction,
(C) défalcation
(GER) Kürzung *f* (Ausgaben); Abschlag *m*,
Minderung *f*, Ermäßigung *f*, Nachlass *m*,
Herabsetzung *f* (Preis)
(JAP) 排除、失効
(RUS) ОТМЕНА; ПРЕКРАЩЕНИЕ;
СНИЖЕНИЕ; УМЕНЬШЕНИЕ

ABC method
(CHIN) ABC 库存管理方法、
价值分类库存管理法
(FRE) méthode ABC
(GER) ABC-Methode *f*,
Prozesskosten- *f*,
Aktivitätskostenrechnung *f*
(JAP) ABC 方式
(RUS) МЕТОД УПРАВЛЕНИЯ ЗАПАСАМИ,
ОСНОВАННЫЙ НА РАЗДЕЛЕ ВСЕХ
ЗАПАСОВ НА ТРИ КАТЕГОРИИ:
НАИБОЛЕЕ ЦЕННЫЕ (A), СРЕДНЕЙ
ЦЕННОСТИ (B) И МЕНЕЕ ЦЕННЫЕ (C)

ability to pay
(CHIN) 支付能力
(FRE) capacité à payer, solvabilité
(GER) Zahlungsfähigkeit *f*, Solvenz *f*,
Liquidität *f*; steuerliche
Leistungsfähigkeit *f* (Steuer)
(JAP) 担税力、支払能力
(RUS) ПЛАТЕЖЕСПОСОБНОСТЬ

abort
(CHIN) 异常终止，放弃
(FRE) abandonner, suspender
(GER) abbrechen *v*
(JAP) 中止（する）、アボート
(RUS) 1. ПРЕЖДЕВРЕМЕННОЕ
ПРЕКРАЩЕНИЕ ПРОЦЕССА 2. АВАРИЙНО
ЗАВЕРШАТЬСЯ 3. ПРЕРВАТЬ
ВЫПОЛНЕНИЕ ПРОГРАММЫ В СВЯЗИ С
ОШИБКОЙ

above the line
(CHIN)（资产负债表或损益表上的）
线上项目
(FRE) au-dessus de la ligne
(GER) zum ordentlichen Haushalt gehörig
m (Finanzwesen); normale
Werbemaßnahmen *f*, klassische
Verkaufsstrategie *f* (Marketing); eingestellt
in die Gewinn- und Verlustrechnung des
Unternehmens (Wirtschaft, Finanzwesen)
(JAP) 一定の標準以上の、
経常支出の
(RUS) "НАД ЛИНИЕЙ" СУММА,
ВЫЧИТАЕМАЯ ИЗ ВАЛОВОГО ДОХОДА
ДЛЯ ПОЛУЧЕНИЯ
СКОРЕКТИРОВАННОГО ВАЛОВОГО
ДОХОДА ПРИ ЗАПОЛНЕНИИ
НАЛОГОВОЙ ДЕКЛАРАЦИИ

abrogate
(CHIN) 废除、废止
(FRE) abroger
(GER) kündigen, aufheben, außer Kraft
setzen, für ungültig erklären, abschaffen *v*
(RUS) ОТМЕНИТЬ; АННУЛИРОВАТЬ;
УПРАЗДНИТЬ

absence rate, absenteeism
(CHIN) 缺勤率
(FRE) taux d'absentéisme
(GER) Fehlzeitenquote *f*,
Abwesenheitsrate *f*
(JAP) 欠勤率、常習欠勤、（地主の）
長期不在、不在地主制度
(RUS) ЧАСТОТА НЕЯВКИ НА РАБОТУ,
ПРОГУЛОВ;
УКЛОНЕНИЕ ОТ УЧАСТИЯ ИЛИ
ПРИСУТСТВИЯ; АБСЕНТЕИЗМ

absentee owner
(CHIN) 缺勤业主
(FRE) propriétaire non gérant
(GER) abwesender Eigentümer*m*
(JAP) 不在地主、無機能資本家
(RUS) ВЛАДЕЛЕЦ СОБСТВЕННОСТИ
(ОБЫЧНО, НЕДВИЖИМОСТИ),
ПОСТОЯННО ПРОЖИВАЮЩИЙ ЗА ЕЁ
ПРЕДЕЛАМИ

absolute advantage
(CHIN) 绝对优势、绝对利益
(FRE) avantage absolu
(GER) absoluter (Kosten) vorteil *m*
(Kosten)vorteil *m*
(JAP) 絶対優位
(RUS) АБСОЛЮТНОЕ ПРЕИМУЩЕСТВО,
(В МИРОВОЙ ЭКОНОМИКЕ)
СПОСОБНОСТЬ ОДНОГО
ПРОИЗВОДИТЕЛЯ ПРОИЗВОДИТЬ
КОНКРЕТНЫЙ ТОВАР С МЕНЬШИМИ
ЗАТРАТАМИ, ЧЕМ КОНКУРЕНТЫ

absolute liability
(CHIN) 完全责任
(FRE) responsabilité absolue, (C) obligation
inconditionnelle
(GER) volle Haftung *f*, strenge Haftpflicht
f; unbedingte Verbindlichkeit *f*
(JAP) 絶対責任、無過失責任
(RUS) АБСОЛЮТНАЯ, ПОЛНАЯ
(ЮРИДИЧЕСКАЯ) ОТВЕТСТВЕННОСТЬ

absolute sale
(CHIN) 完全出售
(FRE) vente irrevocable
(GER) endgültiger Verkauf *m*
(JAP) 無条件売買
(RUS) ОКОНЧАТЕЛЬНАЯ
(АБСОЛЮТНАЯ) ПРОДАЖА

absorbed
(CHIN) 归入、合并
(FRE) absorbé, (C) impute
(GER) aufgenommen *adj*; verrechnet *adj*
(Kosten); umgelegt *adj* (Lasten)
(JAP) 吸収された、併合された
(RUS) ПОГЛОЩАТЬ; БСОРБИРОВАТЬ

absorption costing
(CHIN) 全额成本计算
(FRE) méthode du coût de revient
(GER) Vollkostenrechnung *f*, Umlegung *f*
der Kosten *pl*, Kostenaufteilungsverfahren *n*,
Durchschnittskostenrechnung *f*
(JAP) 全部原価計算
(RUS) ОТНЕСЕНИЕ ИЗДЕРЖЕК НА СЧЁТ
ПРОИЗВОДСТВА

absorption rate
(CHIN) 占有率
(FRE) coefficient d'imputation des coûts
indirects
(GER) Absorptionsgeschwindigkeit *f*;
Sättigungsgeschwindigkeit *f* (Markt)
(JAP) 吸収率
(RUS) ЁМКОСТЬ РЫНКА

abstract of record
(CHIN) 案件摘要
(FRE) extrait, (C) document cadastral d'un
immeuble
(GER) Zusammenfassung *f* eines
Dokumentes *n*
(JAP) 登記書
(RUS) ВЫПИСКА ИЗ ПРОТОКОЛА

abstract of title
(CHIN) 所有权摘要
(FRE) relevé chronologique d'un titre de
propriété
(GER) Eigentumsnachweis *m*
(JAP) 権利証明要約書
(RUS) документ на право владения

abusive tax shelter
(CHIN) 税务滥用保护条款
(FRE) abri fiscal abusive
(GER) mißbräuchliche Steuerzuflucht *f* bzw.
Steueroase*f*

(JAP) 税金避難手段の乱用
(RUS) НЕЗАКОННЫЙ МЕТОД СНИЖЕНИЯ НАЛОГОВ

accelerated cost recovery system (ACRS)

(CHIN) 成本加速恢复系统(ACRS)
(FRE) système de récupération accélérée des coûts
(GER) beschleunigte Abschreibung *f* (US-Abschreibungssystem)
(JAP) 加速原価回収方式
(RUS) СИСТЕМА УСКОРЕННОГО ВОЗМЕЩЕНИЕ ЗАТРАТ

accelerated depreciation

(CHIN) 加速折旧
(FRE) amortissement accéléré
(GER) erhöhte Abschreibung *f*, Sonderabschreibung *f*
(JAP) 加速償却
(RUS) УСКОРЕННАЯ АМОРТИЗАЦИЯ

acceleration

(CHIN) 提前偿付
(FRE) acceleration
(GER) Beschleunigung *f*; Akzeleration *f*; Vorverlegung *f* (Fälligkeitstermin); vorzeitige Fälligkeit *f*
(JAP) 加速、加速度、促進
(RUS) УСКОРЕНИЕ

acceleration clause

(CHIN) 提前偿付条款
(FRE) clause accélératrice,
(C) clause d'exigibilité anticipée
(GER) Vorfälligkeitsklausel *f*, Klausel *f* über die Vorverlegung *f* der Fälligkeit *f*
(JAP) 利益喪失条項、
弁済期日繰上日条項
(RUS) ОГОВОРКА В КОНТРАКТЕ, ПОЗВОЛЯЮЩАЯ ЗАИМОДАТЕЛЮ ПРИ ОПРЕДЕЛЁННЫХ ОБСТОЯТЕЛЬСТВАХ ТРЕБОВАТЬ ОТ ЗАЁМЩИКА ДОСРОЧНОЙ ВЫПЛАТЫ ЗАЙМА

accelerator, accelerator principle

(CHIN) 加速因子，加速比
(FRE) accélérateur, principe de l'accélérateur
(GER) Akzelerator *m* (Wirtschaft), Akzeleratorprinzip *n*
(JAP) 加速度因子、加速度原理
(RUS) УСКОРИТЕЛЬ, ПРИНЦИП УСКОРЕНИЯ, ВЗАИМОСВЯЗЬ МЕЖДУ ИЗМЕНЕНИЕМ ОБЪЁМА ПРОИЗВОДСТВА И УРОВНЕМ ИНВЕСТИЦИЙ

acceptance

(CHIN) 接受，同意，承兑
(FRE) acceptation
(GER) Annahme *f*, Entgegennahme *f* (Vertrag, Güter); Einwilligung *f*, Akzeptanz *f*; Abnahme *f* (Inspektion); Akzept n, akzeptierter Wechsel *m*; Handelswechsel *m*
(JAP) 受領、手形の引受け
(RUS) ПРИНЯТИЕ; АКЦЕПТ, АКЦЕПТОВАНИЕ

acceptance sampling

(CHIN) 验收采样
(FRE) échantillonnage pour acceptation
(GER) Stichprobenentnahme *f* für Annahmeprüfung *f*
(JAP) 受入れ抜き取り検査
(RUS) СТАТИСТИЧЕСКИЙ ПОДХОД ПРОВЕРКИ КАЧЕСТВА, ПРИ КОТОРОМ АНАЛИЗИРУЕТСЯ НАЛИЧИЕ ОПРЕДЕЛЁННЫХ АТРИБУТОВ У СПЕЦИАЛЬНО ОТОБРАННОЙ ПАРТИИ ИЗДЕЛИЙ

access

(CHIN) 存取，访问
(FRE) accès
(GER) Zugriff *m*
(JAP) アクセスする、接続する
(RUS) 1. ДОСТУП 2. ОБРАЩЕНИЕ 2. ОСУЩЕСТВЛЯТЬ ДОСТУП

accession

(CHIN) 增加，取得
(FRE) accession, enregistrement,
(C) accroissement du personnel
(GER) Neuanschaffung *f*; Zugang *m*; Beitritt *m*, Akzession *f*; Vermögenszuwachs *m*
(JAP) 登録、受入、符合
(RUS) ВСТУПЛЕНИЕ (В ДОЛЖНОСТЬ, В ПРАВА); ПРИСОЕДИНЕНИЕ (К ДОГОВОРУ); ПРИРАЩЕНИЕ (ИМУЩЕСТВА)

access right
(CHIN) 出入权，使用权
(FRE) droit d'accès
(GER)Zugangsrecht *n*;
Zugriffsberechtigung *f* (Computer)
(JAP) アクセス権
(RUS) ПРАВО ДОСТУПА

access time
(CHIN) 存取时间
(FRE) temps d'accès
(GER) Zugriffszeit *f*
(JAP) アクセスタイム，
呼出し時間
(RUS) ВРЕМЯ,ТРЕБУЕЩЕЕСЯ
КОМПЬЮТЕРУ ДЛЯ ПОИСКА
ИНФОРМАЦИИ В ПАМЯТИ

accommodation endorser, maker or party
(CHIN) 通融票据背书人，
出票人或当事人
(FRE)endosseur par complaisance
(GER) Indossant oderAussteller *m* eines
Gefälligkeitsakzepts *n*,
Gefälligkeitszeichner *m*
(JAP) 融通手形裏書人、
融通手形振出人
(RUS) ЛИЦО (ИЛИ СТОРОНА),
УТВЕРЖДАЮЩЕЕ СОГЛАСОВАНИЕ ИЛИ
РАЗРЕШЕНИЕ СПОРА

accommodation paper
(CHIN) 通融票据
(FRE) effet de complaisance
(GER) Gefälligkeitspapier *n*
(JAP) 融通手形
(RUS) ДОКУМЕНТ О СОГЛАСОВАНИИ
ИЛИ РАЗРЕШЕНИИ СПОРА

accord and satisfaction
(CHIN) 债务替代清偿协议，
协议与补偿
(FRE) accord et satisfaction
(GER) vergleichsweise Erfüllung *f*
(JAP) 代物弁済
(RUS) ВЫПЛАТА ДЕНЕГ ИЛИ ДРУГИХ
ЦЕННОСТЕЙ (ОБЫЧНО В МЕНЬШЕМ
РАЗМЕРЕ) В ОБМЕН НА ПОГАШЕНИЕ
ЗАДОЛЖЕННОСТИ

account
(CHIN) 帐，帐户，会计科目
(FRE) compte
(GER) Konto *n*; Rechnung *f*
(JAP) 会計、勘定、計算書、口座、
報告（書）、説明、理由、評価、利益
(RUS) СЧЕТ

accountability
(CHIN) 计责任，经管责任，受托责任
(FRE) obligation de rendre compte,
responsabilité, responsabilisation
(GER) Rechenschafts-, Nachweis-,
Rechnungslegungspflicht *f*;
Verantwortlichkeit *f*, Haftung *f*
(JAP) 執行責任、職責
(RUS) ПОДОТЧЕТНОСТЬ; ОТЧЕТНОСТЬ

accountancy
(CHIN) 会计专业，会计工作
(FRE) comptabilité
(GER) Rechnungswesen *n*; Buchhaltung *f*,
-führung *f*, Rechnungsführung *f*;
ontenführung *f*
(JAP) 会計業務、会計学、会計制度
(RUS) БУХГАЛТЕРСКИЙ УЧЕТ

accountant
(CHIN) 会计，会计师，会计员
(FRE) comptable, expert-comptable
(GER) Buchhalter *m*, Kontenführer *m*;
Buch- *m*, Wirtschaftsführer *m*;
Rechnungsführer *m*
(JAP) 会計士、計理士
(RUS) БУХГАЛТЕР

accountant's opinion
(CHIN) 查帐意见书
(FRE) opinion de l'expert-comptable
(GER) Prüfungsbericht *m*;
Bestätigungsvermerk *m*
(JAP) 会計士の意見
(RUS) ЗАКЛЮЧЕНИЕ БУХГАЛТЕРА

account executive
(CHIN) 营业经理
(FRE) responsable de budget,
(C) représentant, (C) chef de publicité
d'agence, (C) relationniste-conseil

(GER) Kontakter *m* (Marketing); Sachbearbeiter *m* eines Werbeetats *m*; Kundenbetreuer *m*
(JAP) アカウント・エグゼクティブ、顧客会計主任
(RUS) ЛИЦО, УПОЛНОМОЧЕННОЕ НА ОПЕРАЦИИ СО СЧЕТОМ; ЗАРЕГИСТРИРОВАННЫЙ ПРЕДСТАВИТЕЛЬ (БИРЖ.)

accounting change
(CHIN) 会计变更
(FRE) changement de méthode comptable, modification comptable
(GER) Bilanzierungsänderung *f*
(JAP) 会計方針変更
(RUS) ИЗМЕНЕНИЕ СИСТЕМЫ БУХГ. УЧЕТА

accounting cycle
(CHIN) 会计循环，会计周期
(FRE) cycle comptable
(GER) Buchungsperiode *f*, Buchungszyklus *m*; Umschlagzyklus *m*; Buchungsdurchlauf *m*
(JAP) 会計周期
(RUS) ПЕРИОДИЧНОСТЬ БУХГ. ОТЧЕТНОСТИ (НАПРИМЕР, НАЛОГОВОЙ)

accounting equation
(CHIN) 会计方程式
(FRE) équation comptable, (C) identité fondamentale
(GER) Bilanzgleichung *f*
(JAP) 会計等式
(RUS) ФОРМУЛА БУХГ. УЧЕТА, ПО КОТОРОЙ АКТИВЫ ДОЛЖНЫ РАВНЯТЬСЯ СУММЕ ПАССИВОВ И СОБСТВЕННЫХ СРЕДСТВ

accounting error
(CHIN) 会计差错
(FRE) erreur comptable
(GER) Falschbuchung *f*, Buchungsfehler *m*
(JAP) 会計ミス
(RUS) ОШИБКА В БУХГ. УЧЕТЕ

accounting method
(CHIN) 核算方法，会计方法
(FRE) méthode comptable

(GER) Rechnungslegungsmethode *f*; Bilanzierungsweise *f*, Buchführungsmethode *f*; Gewinnermittlungsmethode *f* (Steuer)
(JAP) 会計方法、会計手続き
(RUS) МЕТОДИКА ВЕДЕНИЯ БУХГ. УЧЕТА

accounting period
(CHIN) 会计期间，会计结算期
(FRE) exercice financier
(GER) Rechnungsperiode *f*, Bilanzierungsperiode *f*, Buchungs- *m*, Abrechnungszeitraum *m*
(JAP) 会計期間、会計年度
(RUS) ПЕРИОД ОФОРМЛЕНИЯ БУХГ. ОТЧЕТНОСТИ; ФИНАНСОВЫЙ ГОД

accounting principles, accounting standards
(CHIN) 会计原则，会计标准
(FRE) normes comptables, principes comptables
(GER) Buchführungsrichtlinien *fpl*, -grundsätze *mpl*; Bilanzierungsrichtlinien *mpl*
(JAP) 会計原則、会計基準
(RUS) ПРИНЦИПЫ, НОРМЫ ВЕДЕНИЯ БУХГ. УЧЕТА

accounting procedure
(CHIN) 会计程序
(FRE) procédure comptable
(GER) Buchhaltungsverfahren *n*; Bilanzierungsverfahren *n*
(JAP) 会計手続き
(RUS) ПОРЯДОК ВЕДЕНИЯ БУХГ. УЧЕТА

accounting rate of return
(CHIN) 会计收益率，投资报酬率
(FRE) taux de rendement comptable, (C) rendement nominal
(GER) rechnerische Rendite *f*; Gewinnvergleichsrechnung *f*
(JAP) 会計的利益率
(RUS) МЕТОД ОПРЕДЕЛЕНИЯ НОРМЫ ПРИБЫЛИ ПО БУХГАЛТЕРСКОЙ ОТЧЁТНОСТИ

accounting records
(CHIN) 会计帐册，会计记录
(FRE) états comptables
(GER) Geschäftsbücher *npl*, Buchführungs-*fpl*, Buchungsunterlagen *fpl*
(JAP) 会計帳簿、会計記録
(RUS) БУХГАЛТЕРСКАЯ ОТЧЕТНОСТЬ

accounting software
(CHIN) 会计软件
(FRE) logiciel de comptabilité,
(C) logiciel comptable
(GER) Buchführungs- *f*,
Buchhaltungssoftware *f*
(JAP) 財務会計ソフト
(RUS) ПРОГРАМНОЕ ОБЕСПЕЧЕНИЕ
БУХГАЛТЕРСКОГО УЧЕТА

accounting system
(CHIN) 会计制度，会计系统
(FRE) système comptable, plan comptable
(GER) Buchführungs- *n*,
Buchhaltungssystem *n*
(JAP) 会計システム、会計制度
(RUS) СИСТЕМА ВЕДЕНИЯ БУХГ. УЧЕТА

account number
(CHIN) 帐号，帐户编号
(FRE) numéro de compte
(GER) Kontonummer *f*
(JAP) 課金番号、勘定番号
(RUS) НОМЕР СЧЕТА

accounts payable
(CHIN) 应付帐款
(FRE) comptes fournisseurs
(GER) Verbindlichkeiten *fpl*, Buchschulden *fpl*; Kreditoren *mpl*, Passiva *npl*;
Schuldposten *mpl*
(JAP) 買掛金、未払金
(RUS) СЧЕТА К ОПЛАТЕ

accounts payable ledger
(CHIN) 应付款分类帐
(FRE) grand livre des comptes fournisseurs
(GER) Lieferanten- *n*, Kreditorenbuch *n*
(JAP) 仕入先元帳
(RUS) КНИГА КРЕДИТОВЫХ
ПРОВОДОК

accounts receivable
(CHIN) 应收帐款
(FRE) comptes clients
(GER) Forderungen *fpl*, Außenstände *pl*;
Debitoren *mpl*
(JAP) 売掛金（勘定）受取勘定
(RUS) СЧЕТА К ПОЛУЧЕНИЮ

accounts receivable financing
(CHIN) 应收帐款融资
(FRE) financement des comptes clients
(GER) Finanzierung *f* durch
Forderungsabtretung *f*
(JAP) 売掛金担保融資
(RUS) КРАТКОСРОЧНОЕ
ФИНАНСИРОВАНИЕ, ПРИ КОТОРОМ
СЧЕТА К ПОЛУЧЕНИЮ СЛУЖАТ
ЗАЛОГОМ

accounts receivable ledger
(CHIN) 应收帐款分类帐
(FRE) grand livre des comptes clients
(GER) Kontokorrentbuch *n*;
Debitorenbuch *n*
(JAP) 得意先元帳
(RUS) КНИГА ЗАДОЛЖЕННОСТЕЙ
ОТДЕЛЬНЫХ КЛИЕНТОВ

accounts receivable turnover
(CHIN) 应收款周转率
(GER) Debitoren-Umschlag *m*
(JAP) 売掛金回転率
(RUS) ОБОРОТ ДЕБЕТОВАНИЯ

account statement
(CHIN) 对帐单
(FRE) relevé de compte
(GER) Kontoauszug *m*; Kontenblatt *n*
(JAP) 計算書、預金取引明細書
(RUS) ВЫПИСКА С БАНКОВСКОГО СЧЕТА

accredited investor
(CHIN) 受信投资人
(FRE) investisseur accrédité
(GER) zugelassener Anleger *m*
(JAP) 公認投資家
(RUS) АККРЕДИТОВАННЫЙ ИНВЕСТОР

accretion
(CHIN) 自然增值
(FRE) accroissement
(GER) Wertzuwachs *m*, -steigerung *f*
(JAP) 増大、増加物、付加価値、

価値増加
(RUS) ПРИРАЩЕНИЕ; УВЕЛИЧЕНИЕ
ФОНДОВ ЗА СЧЁТ РОСТА ОСНОВНОГО
КАПИТАЛА И ПРОЦЕНТОВ, АККРЕЦИЯ

accrual method
(CHIN) 应计方法
(FRE) méthode d'exercice',
(C) méthode du report d'impôts variable
(GER) Prinzip *n* der Periodenabgrenzung *f*;
Gewinnermittlung *f* durch
Vermögensvergleich *m*
(JAP) 発生主義
(RUS) БУХГАЛТЕРСКИЙ УЧЁТ ПО
МЕТОДУ НАЧИСЛЕНИЙ

accrue
(CHIN) 增值，应计
(FRE) accumuler
(GER) auflaufen, zurückstellen, abgrenzen
v; anfallen, auflaufen, ansammeln *v*
(Zinsen);
zufließen *v*
(JAP) 利子がつく
(RUS) НАКАПЛИВАТЬ
(ПРИЧИТАЮЩИЙСЯ ДОХОД, ПРОЦЕНТЫ)

accrued interest
(CHIN) 应计利息，应付利息
(FRE) intérêts courus, intérêts échus
(GER) aufgelaufene Zinsen *mpl*
(JAP) 未払利息、未払利子
(RUS) НАКОПЛЕННЫЙ ПРОЦЕНТНЫЙ
ДОХОД

accrued liabilities
(CHIN) 应计负债，应付债务
(FRE) charge à payer, passif couru
(GER) aufgelaufene Verbindlichkeiten *fpl*,
antizipative Passiva *npl*
(JAP) 未払債務、見越負債
(RUS) НАКОПЛЕННЫЕ ПАССИВЫ

accrued taxes
(CHIN) 应计税款
(FRE) impôts courus
(GER) Steuerrückstellungen *fpl*; angefallene
Steuern *fpl*, Steuerschulden *fpl*, fällige
Steuerforderungen *fpl*
(JAP) 未収税金、未収租税
(RUS) НАКОПЛЕННЫЕ НАЛОГОВЫЕ

ОБЯЗАТЕЛЬСТВА

accumulated depletion
(CHIN) 累积折耗
(FRE) provision pour épuisement
(GER) kumulierte Wertberichtigung *f*,
kumulierter Substanzverlust *m*
(JAP) 累積減耗償却
(RUS) КУМУЛЯТИВНОЕ ИСТОЩЕНИЕ

accumulated depreciation
(CHIN) 累积折旧
(FRE) amortissement cumuli
(GER) aufgelaufene (planmäßige)
Abschreibungen *fpl*
(JAP) 減価償却引当金、累積減価償却額
(RUS) КУМУЛЯТИВНАЯ
(НАКАПЛИВАЕМАЯ) АМОРТИЗАЦИЯ

accumulated dividend
(CHIN) 累积股息
(FRE) dividende cumulé
(GER) aufgelaufene Dividende *f*, noch nicht
ausgeschüttete Dividende *f*
(JAP) 未払配当、未払配当金
(RUS) КУМУЛЯТИВНЫЙ
(НАКОПЛЕННЫЙ) ДИВИДЕНД

**accumulated earnings tax or
accumulated profits**
(CHIN) 累积收益税或累积利润
(FRE) impôt sur les bénéfices cumulés,
réserves, (C) impôt sur les reserves
(GER) Sondersteuer *f* auf nicht
ausgeschütteten, thesaurierten Gewinn *m*
oder Steuer *f* bei überhöhter
Gewinnthesaurierung *f*
(JAP) 留保収益税、留保利益金
(RUS) НАКОПЛЕННЫЙ НАЛОГ НА
ПОСТУПЛЕНИЯ ИЛИ НАКОПЛЕННАЯ
ПРИБЫЛЬ

acid test ratio
(CHIN) 酸性试验比率
(FRE) ratio de liquidité immédiate,
(C) ratio de liquidité relative
(GER) Liquidität *f* ersten Grades *m*
(JAP) 当座比率
(RUS) НАИБОЛЕЕ СУРОВОЕ ИСПЫТАНИЕ
НАДЁЖНОСТИ

acknowledgment

(CHIN) 承认，回执
(FRE) reconnaissance
(GER) Bestätigung *f*; notarielle
Beglaubigung *f*, Bescheinigung *f*;
Empfangsbestätigung *f*
(JAP) 承認、確認、領収書
(RUS) ПОДТВЕРЖДЕНИЕ

acquisition

(CHIN) 买进，收购
(FRE) acquisition
(GER) Erwerb *m*; Übernahme *f*,
Aufkauf *m* (Unternehmen); Zukauf *m*,
Beteiligungserwerb *m*;
Akquisition *f* (Versicherung)
(JAP) 取得、買収、（企業の）吸収
(RUS) ПРИОБРЕТЕНИЕ; ПОГЛОЩЕНИЕ

acquisition cost

(CHIN) 购置成本，取得成本
(FRE) coût d'achat
(GER) Anschaffungs- *pl*,
Erwerbskosten *pl*; Akquisitionskosten *pl*,
Abschlussaufwendungen *pl* (Versicherung)
(JAP) 取得原価
ЗАТРАТЫ НА ПРИОБРЕТЕНИЕ

acre

(CHIN) 英亩
(FRE) acre
(GER) Acre (Flächeneinheit) *m* (= 4046.856
m²)
(JAP) エーカー、土地
(RUS) АКР

acreage

(CHIN) 英亩制土地
(FRE) acreage
(GER) Anbau- *f*, Nutz- *f*, Bodenfläche *f*
(JAP) エーカー数で計った面積
(RUS) ЗЕМЕЛЬНАЯ ПЛОЩАДЬ

across the board

(CHIN) 全面
(FRE) général, (C) général et uniforme
(GER) allgemein, pauschal,
durchgängig *adj*
(JAP) 一律に、全体的に
(RUS) ПО ВСЕМУ ДИАПАЗОНУ

activate

(CHIN) 激活，启动
(FRE) activer
(GER) aktivieren, einschalten, starten *v*
(JAP) 起動する
(RUS) 1. АКТИВИЗИРОВАТЬ 2. ВЫЗЫВАТЬ

activate a file

(CHIN) 启动文件
(FRE) activer un fichier
(GER) Datei *f* aufrufen *v*
(JAP) ファイルを起動する、
ファイルを作動させる
(RUS) ОТКРЫТЬ ФАЙЛ

activate a macro

(CHIN) 启动宏(功能，指令)
(FRE) activer une macro
(GER) Makrobefehl *m* aufrufen *v*
(JAP) マクロを起動する
(RUS) АКТИВИЗИРОВАТЬ
МАКРОКОМАНДУ

active cell

(CHIN) 当前数据单元
(FRE) cellule active
(GER) aktive Zelle *f*
(JAP) （表計算ソフトの）
アクティブセル
(RUS) АКТИВНАЯ ЯЧЕЙКА

active income

(CHIN) 主动收入
(FRE) revenus actifs
(GER) aktives Einkommen *n*; Einkünfte *pl*
aus aktiver gewerblicher Tätigkeit *f*
(JAP) 能動所得
(RUS) (В НАЛОГООБЛОЖЕНИИ) СТАТЬЯ
ДОХОДОВ, ВКЛЮЧАЮЩАЯ
ЗАРАБОТНУЮ ПЛАТУ И
КОМИССИОННЫЕ

active market

(CHIN) 活跃市场，流通市场
(FRE) marché actif
(GER) aktiver Markt *m*; lebhafte Umsätze
mpl
(JAP) 好況市場、好況市況
(RUS) АКТИВНЫЙ РЫНОК, АКТИВНАЯ
ТОРГОВЛЯ НА БИРЖЕ

act of bankruptcy

(CHIN) 破产法

(FRE) acte de faillite

(GER) Konkursgrund *n*, Tatbestand *m*, der zum Konkursantrag *m* berechtigt

(JAP) 破産法

(RUS) ОСНОВАНИЕ ДЛЯ ДЕЛА О БАНКРОТСТВЕ

act of god

(CHIN) 不可抗力，天灾

(FRE) catastrophe naturelle, cas fortuity

(GER) höhere Gewalt *f*, Naturereignis *n*

(JAP) 不可抗力、天災

(RUS) ФОРС-МАЖОРНОЕ ОБСТОЯТЕЛЬСТВО, СТИХИЙНОЕ БЕДСТВИЕ

actual cash value

(CHIN) 实际现金价值

(FRE) valeur vénale, valeur de remplacement vétusté déduite

(GER) tatsächlicher bzw. gegenwärtiger Barwert *m*; Istwert *m* (Versicherung)

(JAP) 取替え価額、現金換価価値

(RUS) ФАКТИЧЕСКАЯ ДЕНЕЖНАЯ ЦЕННОСТЬ

actual cost

(CHIN) 实际成本

(FRE) prix de revient, prix d'achat, (C) coût réel

(GER) Effektiv- *pl*, Ist- *pl*, Realkosten *pl*

(JAP) 実費、実際原価

(RUS) ФАКТИЧЕСКАЯ СТОИМОСТЬ (СЕБЕСТОИМОСТЬ)

actual damages

(CHIN) 实际损失

(FRE) dommages-intérêts compensatoires

(GER) echter Schadensersatz *m*; tatsächliche Schäden *mpl*; tatsächliche Vermögenseinbuße *f*

(JAP) 現実的損害賠償金

(RUS) ФАКТИЧЕСКИЙ УЩЕРБ

actuarial science

(CHIN) 保险统计计算科学

(FRE) science actuariale, science des actuaires, (C) actuariat

(GER) Versicherungswissenschaft *f*

(JAP) 数理科学、保険統計科学

(RUS) ДЕЛОПРОИЗВОДСТВО

actuary

(CHIN) 理算师，精算师，保险统计员

(FRE) actuaire

(GER) Versicherungsmathematiker *m*, -statistiker *m*

(JAP) 保険数理士

(RUS) СЕКРЕТАРЬ СУДА; АКТУАРИЙ

addendum

(CHIN) 附约，附录

(FRE) addenda

(GER) Anhang *m*, Beiblatt *n*, Nachtrag *m*, Zusatz *m*

(JAP) 補遺、付録

(RUS) ПРИЛОЖЕНИЕ; ДОПОЛНЕНИЕ

additional first-year depreciation (tax)

(CHIN) 第一年的（税务）补提折旧

(FRE) déduction supplémentaire d'amortissement

(GER) Sondererstjahresabschreibung *f*, Sondersteuerbegünstigung *f* (Steuer)

(JAP) 初年度割増償却（税）

(RUS) ДОПОЛНИТЕЛЬНАЯ АМОРТИЗАЦИЯ ПЕРВОГО ГОДА (НАЛ.)

additional mark-on

(CHIN) 额外加成

(FRE) marge supplémentaire sur coût 'achat

(GER) zusätzlicher Aufschlag *m*

(JAP) 追加値入、追加マークアップ

(RUS) ДОПОЛНИТЕЛЬНАЯ НАЦЕНКА

additional paid-in capital

(CHIN) 溢缴资本

(FRE) capital d'apport, capital verse

(GER) Eigenkapitalzuwachs *m* aus sonstigen Quellen *fpl*; Agiorücklage *f*; zusätzlich eingebrachtes Kapital *n*

(JAP) 追加払込資本金

(RUS) СУММА, УПЛАЧЕННАЯ ЗА АКЦИИ ВЫШЕ ИХ ПАРИТЕТА

add-on interest

(CHIN) 追加利息

(FRE) taux d'intérêt majoré

(GER) Zinszuschlag *m*

9

(JAP) アドオン金利
(RUS) ДОБАВЛЕННЫЙ ПРОЦЕНТ

adequacy of coverage
(CHIN) 投保条款充分
(FRE) couverture suffisante
(GER) Angemessenheit *f* des
Versicherungsschutzes *m* bzw. der
Deckung *f*
(JAP) 険担保の妥当性、
適用範囲の妥当性
(RUS) АДЕКВАТНОСТЬ СТРАХОВОГО
ПОКРЫТИЯ

adhesion contract
(CHIN) 服从契约
(FRE) contrat d'adhésion
(GER) Knebelungsvertrag *m*, diktierter
Vertrag *m*
(JAP) 附合契約、附従契約
(RUS) ТИПОВОЙ ДОГОВОР МЕЖДУ
ПРОДАВЦОМ И ПОТРЕБИТЕЛЕМ,
ИСКЛЮЧАЮЩИЙ ВОЗМОЖНОСТЬ
ТОРГОВАТЬСЯ

adhesion insurance contract
(CHIN) 服从保险契约
(FRE) contrat d'assurance
(GER) Versicherungsvertragsbedingungen
fpl
(JAP) 附合保険契約
(RUS) ТИПОВОЙ СТРАХОВОЙ ДОГОВОР

ad infinitum
(CHIN) 无限制
(FRE) à l'infini
(GER) unbegrenzt, unbeschränkt *adj*
(JAP) 無限に、永久に、無限の、永久の
(RUS) БЕЗ ОГРАНИЧЕНИЯ

ad item
(CHIN) 附加项目
(FRE) par poste
(GER) Anzeigeneinzelteil
(JAP) アド・アイテム、同じ点について
(RUS) КОМПЛЕКТУЮЩИЕ
ПРИНАДЛЕЖНОСТИ

ad valorem
(CHIN) 从价，按价

(FRE) ad valorem, (C) selon la valeur
(GER) wertmäßig *adj*, dem Wert
entsprechend, im Wert von
(JAP) 価格に従って、価格に準じた
(RUS) ПО ФАКТИЧЕСКОЙ СТОИМОСТИ

adjective law
(CHIN) 程序法，程序规则
(FRE) droit judicataire, (C) procedure
(GER) formelles Recht *n*, Verfahrensrecht *n*
(JAP) 手続形式法
(RUS) ПРОЦЕДУРНОЕ ПРАВО

adjoining
(CHIN) 毗连，贴近
(FRE) attenant
(GER) angrenzend, benachbart *adj*
(JAP) 近接の、隣接する
(RUS) ПРИЛЕГАЮЩИЙ; ПРИМЫКАЮЩИЙ

adjudication
(CHIN) 判决，宣告
(FRE) jugement, arrêt, (C) déclaration,
C) publication, (C) jugement déclaratif
(GER) Eröffnung *f* (eines
Konkursverfahrens); Beschluss *m* (über
Konkurseröffnung); gerichtliche
Entscheidung *f*
(JAP) 判決、破産宣告、裁定
(RUS) ПРИЗНАНИЕ, ОБЪЯВЛЕНИЕ
(В СУДЕБНОМ ПОРЯДКЕ)

adjustable life insurance
(CHIN) 可调整人寿保险
(FRE) assurance vie variable
(GER) offene bzw. anpassbare
Lebensversicherung *f*
(JAP) 調整可能生命保険
(RUS) СТРАХОВАНИЕ ЖИЗНИ С
ВАРЬИРУЕМЫМИ УСЛОВИЯМИ

adjustable margin
(CHIN) 可调节边际
(FRE) marge adjustable
(GER) einstellbarer Rand *m*
(JAP) 調節可能なマージン（欄外）
(RUS) РЕГУЛИРУЕМЫЙ РАЗМЕР ПОЛЯ

adjustable mortgage loan (AML)
(CHIN) 可调整抵押贷款（AML）

(FRE) prêt hypothécaire variable
(GER) variabel verzinsliches
Hypothekendarlehen *n*
(JAP) 調整金利抵当ローン
(RUS) ИПОТЕКА С ИЗМЕНЯЕМЫМИ
УСЛОВИЯМИ

adjustable-rate mortgage (ARM)
(CHIN) 利率可调抵押贷款（ARM）
(FRE) prêt hypothécaire à taux variable, (C)
prêt hypothécaire à taux reference
(GER) variabel verzinsliche Hypothek *f*,
Hypothek *f* mit variablem Zinssatz *m*
(JAP) 変動金利住宅ローン、
利率変動型抵当
(RUS) ИПОТЕКА С ПЛАВАЮЩЕЙ
СТАВКОЙ

adjusted basis or adjusted tax basis
(CHIN) 调整制或税款调整制
(FRE) assiette fiscale rectifiée
(GER) angepasste Grundlage *f* oder
berichtigte Steuerbemessungsgrundlage *f*
(RUS) СКОРРЕКТИРОВАННАЯ БАЗА ИЛИ
СКОРРЕКТИРОВАННАЯ БАЗА ДЛЯ
НАЛОГООБЛОЖЕНИЯ
(JAP) 修正基礎額、修正課税基準

adjusted gross income
(CHIN) 调整后总收入
(FRE) revenu brut rectifié
(GER) berichtigtes Bruttoeinkommen *n*
(JAP) 調整済総収入、修正総所得
(RUS) СКОРРЕКТИРОВАННЫЙ ВАЛОВОЙ
ДОХОД

adjuster
(CHIN) 理算人，理算师
(FRE) Inspecteur, (C) expert répartiteur
(GER) Schadenregulierer *m*;
Schadensachverständiger *m*
(JAP) 損害（海損）査定人、海損精算人
(RUS) ОЦЕНЩИК

adjusting entry
(CHIN) 整理帐，调整分录
(FRE) écriture de régularisation,
(C) écriture de rajustement, (C) écriture de
correction
(GER) Berichtigungsbuchung *f*
(JAP) 修正仕分、修正記入

(RUS) КОРРЕКТИРУЮЩАЯ ПОЗИЦИЯ

administer
(CHIN) 管理，支配，执行
(FRE) administrer
(GER) verwalten *v;* führen *v* (Konto);
durchführen *v* (Gesetz)
(JAP) 経営する、管理する
(RUS) УПРАВЛЯТЬ

administered price
(CHIN) 管制价格，受控价格
(FRE) prix administré, prix fixé par le
procureur, (C) prix collusoire, (C) prix
impose
(GER) administrierter Preis *m*, amtlich
geregelter Preis *m*; Richtpreis *m* (EU)
(JAP) 管理価格
(RUS) РЕГУЛИРУЕМАЯ ЦЕНА

administrative expense
(CHIN) 管理费用，行政费用
(FRE) frais d'administration, frais de
gestion
(GER) Verwaltungskosten *pl*, -ausgaben *pl*,
-aufwand *m*
(JAP) 経営費、管理費
(RUS) АДМИНИСТРАТИВНЫЕ
РАСХОДЫ

administrative law
(CHIN) 行政法
(FRE) droit administrative
(GER) Verwaltungsrecht *n*
(JAP) 行政法
(RUS) ЗАКОНОДАТЕЛЬСТВО О
ДЕЯТЕЛЬНОСТИ АДМИНИСТРАТИВНЫХ
ОРГАНОВ

administrative management society
(CHIN) 行政管理学会
(FRE) organisme de gestion dministrative
(GER) Gesellschaft *f* für
nternehmensleitung *f*
(JAP) 経営管理学会
(RUS) ОБЩЕСТВО
АДМИНИСТРАТИВНЫХ
РУКОВОДИТЕЛЕЙ

administrative services only (ASO)
(CHIN) 唯行政服务（ASO）

(FRE) services administratifs seulement
(GER) nur Verwaltungsdienste *mpl*
(JAP) 政職種限定、一般管理サービス
のみ
(RUS) ТОЛЬКО АДМИНИСТРАТИВНЫЕ
УСЛУГИ, СИСТЕМА, ПРИ КОТОРОЙ
РАБОТОДАТЕЛЬ НАНИМАЕТ ТРЕТЬЕ
ЛИЦО ДЛЯ АДМИНИСТРАТИВНОЙ
ОБРАБОТКИ ЛЬГОТ И ПОСОБИЙ
РАБОТНИКАМ

administrator

(CHIN) 主管，经理，行政人员
(FRE) administrateur
(GER) Verwalter *m*; Nachlassverwalter *m*
(Erbschaft); Sachverwalter *m*;
Konkursverwalter *m*
(JAP) 行政官、管理人、管財人
(RUS) АДМИНИСТРАТОР; ПОПЕЧИТЕЛЬ;
РУКОВОДИТЕЛЬ

administrator's deed

(CHIN) 管理人契约
(FRE) acte d'administrateur
(GER) Auflassung *f* durch den
Nachlassverwalter *m*
(JAP) 遺産管理人の捺印証書
(RUS)ДОКУМЕНТ , РАСПОРЯЖАЮЩИЙСЯ
СОБСТВЕННОСТЬЮЛИЧНОСТИ,
УМЕРШЕЙ БЕЗ ЗАВЕЩАНИЯ

advance

(CHIN) 改进，提高，提前，预付，贷款
(FRE) avance, prêt
(GER) Vorauszahlung *f*; Vorschuss *m*
(Gehalt); Kursbefestigung *f*, -anstieg *m*, -
anzug, -gewinn *m* (Börse)
(JAP) 立替金、前払い
(RUS) АВАНС; ПРЕДОПЛАТА

advanced funded pension plan

(CHIN) 预收资金养老金计划
(FRE) régime de retraite financé par
anticipation
(GER) kapitalkräftige Pensionskasse *f* (bzw.
Rentenversicherung *f*, Altersversorgung *f*)
(JAP) 事前積立年金制度
(RUS) СХЕМА НАЧИСЛЕНИЯ ПЕНСИИ С
ПРЕДОПЛАТОЙ

adversary

(CHIN) 反方当事人
(FRE) adversaire

(GER) Gegner *m*; Prozessgegner *m*,
Gegenpartei *f*
(JAP) 相手方、相手方当事者
(RUS) ПРОТИВНАЯ СТОРОНА

adverse opinion

(CHIN) 反对意见
(FRE) opinion défavorable
(GER) ablehnendes Gutachten *n* (EU)
(JAP) 反対意見
(RUS) ОТРИЦАТЕЛЬНОЕ МНЕНИЕ

adverse possession

(CHIN) 非法占有
(FRE) occupation sans titre appropriation
par occupation, (C) prescription
acquisitive, (C) possession adversative
(GER) bestrittener Besitz *m*, Ersitzung *f*
(JAP) 不法占有
(RUS) МЕТОД ПРИОБРЕТЕНИЯ ПРАВА НА
ЗЕМЛЮ ПУТЁМ ПОСТОЯННОГО И
ОТКРЫТОГО НА НЕЙ ПРОЖИВАНИЯ
ОПРЕДЕЛЁННЫЙ ОТРЕЗОК ВРЕМЕНИ
ВОПРЕКИ ЕЁ ЗАКОННОМУ ВЛАДЕЛЬЦУ

advertising

(CHIN) 广告，广告业，广告学
(FRE) publicité
(GER) Werbung *f*, Reklame *f*
(JAP) 広告、広告業
(RUS) РЕКЛАМА

advertising appropriation

(CHIN) 广告拨款
(FRE) fixation de budget de publicité,
(C) budget de publicité
(GER) Bewilligung *f* des Werbeetats *m*
(JAP) 広告費、広告充当金
(RUS) АССИГНОВАНИЯ НА РЕКЛАМУ

affective behavior

(CHIN) 奉承行为
(FRE) comportement affectif
(GER) affektives Verhalten *n*
(JAP) 感情的行動
(RUS) ПОВЕДЕНИЕ, НАПРАВЛЕННОЕ НА
ДОСТИЖЕНИЕ ОПРЕДЕЛЁННОГО
РЕЗУЛЬТАТА

affidavit

(CHIN) 宣誓书

(FRE) Affidavit, (C) déclaration écrite sous serment
(GER) eidesstattliche Versicherung *f*, Erklärung *f* unter Eid *m*, beeidete Aussage *f*
(JAP) （宣誓）供述書、口述書、宣誓書
(RUS) ПОКАЗАНИЕ ПОД ПРИСЯГОЙ; АФФИДЕВИТ

affiliated chain
(CHIN) 联营连锁店
(FRE) chaîne affiliée
(GER) angegliederter bzw. verbundener Filialbetrieb *n*
(JAP) チェーン加盟店
(RUS) ДОЧЕРНЯЯ (АФФИЛИИРОВАННАЯ) ЦЕПЬ; ФИЛИАЛЫ

affiliated company
(CHIN) 附属公司
(FRE) société affiliée
(GER) angegliedertes bzw. verbundenes Unternehmen *n*, Konzerngesellschaft *f*
(JAP) 従属会社、関連会社
(RUS) ДОЧЕРНЯЯ КОМПАНИЯ

affiliated retailer
(CHIN) 连锁零售商
(FRE) détaillant affilié
(GER) angegliederter bzw. verbundener Einzelhändler *m*
(JAP) 関連小売業者、加盟小売業者
(RUS) РОЗНИЧНЫЙ ТОРГОВЕЦ – ДОЧЕРНЯЯ КОМПАНИЯ

affirmative action
(CHIN) 反优先雇用行动
(FRE) mesure, (C) action positive
(GER) Affirmative Action *f*; active Fördermaßnahmen *fpl* bzw. Quotenpolitik *f* zugunsten von Minderheiten *fpl*, Politik *f* der Chancengleichheit *f*
(JAP) アファーマティブ・アクション、マイノリティー優遇措置
(RUS) ОБЯЗАТЕЛЬНЫЕ ДЕЙСТВИЯ ВО ИЗБЕЖАНИЕ ДИСКРИМИНАЦИИ

affirmative relief
(CHIN) 确认赔偿
(FRE) exonération positive
(GER) beantragte Rechtshilfe *f*, aktiver Rechtsbehelf *m*

(JAP) 被告に与えられる救済
(RUS) ЛЬГОТА ИЛИ КОМПЕНСАЦИЯ, ПРИСУЖДАЕМАЯ ОТВЕТЧИКУ

after-acquired clause
(CHIN) 后得财产条款
(FRE) clause relative aux biens acquis après la date
(GER) Nacherwerbsklausel *f*, -verpfändungsklausel *f*
(JAP) 事後取得条項
(RUS) ОГОВОРКА «ПО ПРИОБРЕТЕНИИ»

after-acquired property
(CHIN) 后得财产
(FRE) biens acquis après la date
(GER) Nacherwerbsgut *n*, -verpfändungsgut *n*
(JAP) 事後取得財産
(RUS) СОБСТВЕННОСТЬ ПОСЛЕДУЮЩЕГО ПРИОБРЕТЕНИЯ

after market
(CHIN) 销售后市场，闭市后市场
(FRE) marché secondaire
(GER) Anschlussmarkt *m* (Marketing); Sekundärmarkt *m* (Börse); Nach- *f*, Abendbörse *f*
(JAP) アフターマーケット、第二次市場
(RUS) ВТОРИЧНЫЙ РЫНОК

after-tax basis
(CHIN) 税后制
(FRE) après impôt, net d'impôts
(GER) Basis *f* nach Steuerabzug *m*
(JAP) 税引後ベース
(RUS) УЧЕТ «ПОСЛЕ НАЛОГОВ»

after-tax cash flow
(CHIN) 税后资金流动
(FRE) flux monétaire après impôt Cashflow *m* nach Steuern *fpl*
(JAP) 税引キャッシュフロー
(RUS) ПОТОК СРЕДСТВ ПОСЛЕ УПЛАТЫ НАЛОГОВ

after-tax real rate of return
(CHIN) 税后实际收益率
(FRE) rendement réel après impôt

(GER) effektive Rendite *f* nach Steuern *fpl*,
reale Nachsteuerrendite *f*
税引後実質利回り
(RUS) РЕАЛЬНАЯ ОКУПАЕМОСТЬ
(ДОХОДНОСТЬ) ПОСЛЕ УПЛАТЫ
НАЛОГОВ

against the box
(CHIN) 以保险箱为抵押
(FRE) vente à découvert
(GER) Leerverkauf *m* eines Haussiers *m*
(JAP) 空売りで
(RUS) «КОРОТКАЯ» ПРОДАЖА
ВЛАДЕЛЬЦА «ДЛИННОЙ» ПОЗИЦИИ ПО
ТЕМ ЖЕ АКЦИЯМ (БИРЖ.); «ПРОТИВ
СЕЙФА»

age discrimination
(CHIN) 年龄歧视
(FRE) discrimination fondée sur l'âge
(GER) Altersdiskriminierung *f*
(JAP) 年齢差別
(RUS) ДИСКРИМИНАЦИЯ ПО ВОЗРАСТУ

agency
(CHIN) 代理商，代理权，代理机构
(FRE) Organisme, agence, mandat
(GER) Agentur *f*; Zweigstelle *f*, Filiale *f*;
Dienststelle *f* (Verwaltung)
(JAP) 代理店、（政府の）機関
(RUS) ПОСРЕДНИЧЕСТВО; АГЕНСТВО

agency by necessity
(CHIN) 必需代理
(FRE) mandat d'urgence
(GER) Vertretung *f* (im Notfall) ohne
Auftrag *m*; Geschäftsführung *f* ohne
Auftrag *m*
(JAP) 必要代理店
(RUS) ПОСРЕДНИЧЕСТВО ИЛИ
ПРЕДСТАВИТЕЛЬСТВО «ПО
НЕОБХОДИМОСТИ», Т. Е. ПРИЗНАНЫЕ
СУДОМ ОТНОШЕНИЯ, ПОЗВОЛЯЮЩИЕ
ОДНОМУ ИЗ СУПРУГОВ ВЗЫСКИВАТЬ С
ДРУГОГО СУПРУГА (ИЛИ ИЖДИВЕНЦУ С
РОДИТЕЛЕЙ) НЕОБХОДИМЫЕ К
ПРОЖИВАНИЮ СРЕДСТВА

agent
(CHIN) 代理人，经纪人
(FRE) représentant, agent, mandataire

(GER) Vertreter *m*; Beauftragter *m*,
Bevollmächtigter *m*; Makler *m*
(JAP) 代理人、代理店
(RUS) ПРЕДСТАВИТЕЛЬ; АГЕНТ

agglomeration
(CHIN) 经营集中化，企业集团
(FRE) agglomeration
(GER) Agglomeration *f*; Ballungsgebiet *n*,
raum *m*
(JAP) 集団、アグロメレーション
(RUS) УКРУПНЕНИЕ (КОМПАНИЙ),
АГЛОМЕРАЦИЯ

agglomeration diseconomies
(CHIN) 集约劣势
(FRE) déséconomies agglomérées
(GER) Agglomerationsnachteile *mpl*
(JAP) 集団の不経済性
(RUS) ЭКОНОМИЧЕСКИЕ ИЗДЕРЖКИ
УКРУПНЕНИЯ

aggregate demand
(CHIN) 总需求，总需求量
(FRE) demande globale
(GER) gesamtwirtschaftliche Nachfrage *f*,
Gesamtnachfrage *f*
(JAP) 総需要
(RUS) СОВОКУПНЫЙ СПРОС

aggregate income
(CHIN) 收入总额，总收入
(FRE) revenus totalizes
(GER) Volkseinkommen *n*;
Gesamteinkommen *n*
(JAP) 総所得
(RUS) СОВОКУПНЫЙ ДОХОД

aggregate indemnity (aggregate limit)
(CHIN) 总赔偿（总限额）
(FRE) indemnité globale
(GER) maximale Schadensersatzleistung *f*
(Gesamtlimit einerVersicherung)
(JAP) 総責任限度額、総損害賠償限度額
(RUS) СОВОКУПНОЕ ВОЗМЕЩЕНИЕ
(СОВОКУПНЫЙ ПРЕДЕЛ)

aggregate supply
(CHIN) 总供给，总供应量
(FRE) approvisionnement global

(GER) gesamtwirtschaftliches Angebot *n*, Gesamtangebot *n*
(JAP) 総供給
(RUS) СОВОКУПНОЕ ПРЕДЛОЖЕНИЕ

aging of accounts receivable or aging schedule

(CHIN) 应收账款分期或定期分析表
(FRE) classement chronologique des comptes clients
(GER) Einteilung der Außenstände nach Fälligkeiten *f* oder Terminliste *f*
(JAP) 売掛金の経過期間調査または経過期間表
(RUS) ХРОНОЛОГИЧЕСКАЯ ОРГАНИЗАЦИЯ ДЕБЕТА ИЛИ СЧЕТОВ

agreement

(CHIN) 协议书，和约
(FRE) convention, accord, contrat
(GER) Abrede *f*, Vereinbarung *f*, Übereinkunft *f*, Übereinkommen *n*, Abmachung *f*, Absprache *f*; Vertrag *m*; Einwilligung *f*; Vertragswerk *n*
(JAP) 合意（書）、契約（書）
(RUS) СОГЛАШЕНИЕ; ДОГОВОР

agreement of sale

(CHIN) 销售协议
(FRE) contrat de vente
(GER) Verkaufsabkommen *n*, Kaufvertrag *m*
(JAP) 売買契約
(RUS) ДОГОВОР О ПРОДАЖЕ

agribusiness

(CHIN) 农工联合企业
(FRE) « agribusiness », industrie agricole, chaîne agroalimentaire
(GER) Agrarindustrie *f*, Agrarmittelindustrie *f*, Agrargeschäft *n*
(JAP) アグリビジネス、農業関連産業
(RUS) АГРОБИЗНЕС

air bill

(CHIN) 空运单，空运提单
(FRE) lettre de transport aérien
(GER) Luftfrachtbrief *m*
(JAP) 航空貨物輸送状
(RUS) НАКЛАДНАЯ НА СРОЧНУЮ ДОСТАВКУ

airfreight

(CHIN) 空运费，空运
(FRE) fret aérien
(GER) Luftfracht *f*
(JAP) 航空貨物（の）、空輸する
(RUS) ИСПОЛЬЗОВАНИЕ ВОЗДУШНОГО ТРАНСПОРТА ДЛЯ ПЕРЕВОЗКИ ГРУЗОВ

air rights

(CHIN) 空运法权
(FRE) droits aériens, (C) droits de construction au-dessus d'un terrain
(GER) Flugrechte *npl*; Rechte *npl* am Luftraum *m*
(JAP) 空中権
(RUS) ПРАВА ИСПОЛЬЗОВАНИЯ И КОНТРОЛЯ ВОЗДУШНОГО ПРОСТРАНСТВА НАД ЗЕМЕЛЬНОЙ СОБСТВЕННОСТЬЮ

aleatory contract

(CHIN) 保险单，投机性合同
(FRE) contrat aléatoire
(GER) aleatorischer Vertrag *m*
(JAP) 偶発事契約、射倖契約
(RUS) РИСКОВЫЙ, АЛЕАТОРНЫЙ ДОГОВОР

alienation

(CHIN) 让度，转让
(FRE) alienation
(GER) Veräußerung *f* (Immobilien); Abwerbung *f* (Marketing); Entfremdung *f*; Übertragung *f*
(JAP) 割譲、譲渡、疎外
(RUS) ОТЧУЖДЕНИЕ; ДОБРОВОЛЬНАЯ ПЕРЕДАЧА ПРАВА СОБСТВЕННОСТИ НА НЕДВИЖИМОСТЬ ДРУГОМУ ЛИЦУ

alien corporation

(CHIN) 外国公司
(FRE) société étrangère
(GER) ausländische Kapitalgesellschaft *f*
(JAP) 外国企業
(RUS) КОРПОРАЦИЯ, СОЗДАННАЯ ПО ЗАКОНАМ ДРУГОЙ СТРАНЫ

alimony

(CHIN) 生活费，赡养费
(FRE) pension alimentaire
(GER) Unterhaltszahlung *f*, -leistung *f*, Alimente *pl*

(JAP) 別居手当、離婚手当
(RUS) АЛИМЕНТЫ; СОДЕРЖАНИЕ

allegation

(CHIN) 声明，宣告
(FRE) allegation
(GER) Behauptung *f*, tatsächliches
Vorbringen *f*
(JAP) 申立て、陳述
(RUS) УТВЕРЖДЕНИЕ

allocate

(CHIN) 分配，拨款
(FRE) affecter
(GER) zuteilen, zuweisen, umlegen,
zuordnen, zurechnen *v*
(JAP) 割り当てる、配分する
(RUS) ВЫДЕЛЕНИЕ; АССИГНОВАНИЕ

allocated benefits

(CHIN) 已分配福利
(FRE) avantages répartis
(GER) Zugewiesene bzw. zugeteilte
Leistungen *fpl*
(JAP) 表定給付
(RUS) ВЫПЛАТЫ В ПЕНСИОННЫЙ ФОНД

allocation of resources

(CHIN) 资源配置
(FRE) répartition des resources
(GER) Zuweisung *f* von Ressourcen *pl*,
Mittelzuteilung *f*
(JAP) 資源配分
(RUS) ВЫДЕЛЕНИЕ, РАСПРЕДЕЛЕНИЕ
РЕСУРСОВ

allodial

(CHIN) 自主拥有
(FRE) franc
(GER) allodial, erbeigen, zinsfrei *adj*
(JAP) 自由保有地の、完全私有地の
(RUS) ВЛАДЕНИЕ ПО БЕЗУСЛОВНОМУ
ПРАВУ СОБСТВЕННОСТИ

allodial system

(CHIN) 自主拥有体系
(FRE) terre allodiale, alleu
(GER) Allodsystem *n*
(JAP) 私有地制度
(RUS) СИСТЕМА ВЛАДЕНИЯ БЕЗ
ПОВИННОСТЕЙ, АЛЛОДИАЛЬНАЯ
СИСТЕМА

allowance

(CHIN) 折扣，减价
(FRE) provision, moins-value, allocation,
(C) réfaction
(GER) zulässige Abweichung *f*;
Preisnachlass *m*, Ermäßigung *f*;
Wertberichtigungsposten *m*;
Steuerfreibetrag *m*; Abschreibungsquote *f*;
Zuschuss *m*, Zulage *f*
(JAP) 割当額、手当、給与、割引
(RUS) РАЗРЕШЕНИЕ, ДОПУЩЕНИЕ;
СОДЕРЖАНИЕ, ПОСОБИЕ;
СНИЖЕНИЕ ЦЕНЫ

allowance for depreciation

(CHIN) 折旧提存
(FRE) provision pour depreciation
(GER) Wertberichtigung *f*,
Abschreibungsbetrag *m*
減価償却引当金
(RUS) СКИДКА НА АМОРТИЗАЦИЮ

allowed time

(CHIN) 放宽时间
(FRE) temps alloué
(GER) Vorgabezeit *f*, Frist *f*
(JAP) 有給時間、許容時間
ВЫДЕЛЕННОЕ, НАЗНАЧЕННОЕ ВРЕМЯ

all risk/all peril

(CHIN) 全险，一切险
(FRE) tous risques
(GER) gegen alle Gefahren/Risiken *fpl*
(JAP) 全危険担保の
(RUS) СТРАХОВОЙ ПОЛИС,
ПОКРЫВАЮЩИЙ ВСЕ РИСКИ КРОМЕ
СПЕЦИАЛЬНО ОГОВОРЕННЫХ

alternate coding key (alt key)

(CHIN) 替用编码键 （alt键）
(FRE) touche double fonction, touche
alt
(GER) Alt-Taste *f*
(JAP) alt キー
(RUS) РЕГИСТРОВАЯ КЛАВИША ALT

alternative hypothesis

(CHIN) 替换性假设
(FRE) hypothèse alternative
(GER) Alternativ- *f*, Gegenhypothese *f*
(JAP) 対立仮説、代替仮説
(RUS) АЛЬТЕРНАТИВНАЯ ГИПОТЕЗА

alternative minimum tax

(CHIN) 替换最小课税
(FRE) impôt minimum de remplacement
(GER) Alternative Mindeststeuer f
(JAP) 中低所得層税減免の１つ
(RUS) АЛЬТЕРНАТИВНЫЙ
МИНИМАЛЬНЫЙ НАЛОГ, Т. Е.
ЕДИНООЬРАЗНАЯ АЛОГОВАЯ СТАВКА,
ПОЗВОЛЯЮЩАЯ ВЗЫСКИВАТЬ НАЛОГИ
С КРУПНЫХ КОРПОРАЦИЙ НЕСМОТРЯ
НА ИХ НАЛОГОВЫЕ ДЕРЖАНИЯ

alternative mortgage instrument (AMI)

(CHIN) 可选择抵押证书(AMI)
(FRE) effet hypothécaire alternatif
(GER) alternatives ypothekeninstrument n
(JAP) 代替抵当手段
(RUS) АЛЬТЕРНАТИВНЫЙ ИПОТЕЧНЫЙ
ИНСТРУМЕНТ, Т. Е. ОТЛИЧНЫЙ ОТ
ЗАЙМА С ФИКСИРОВАННЫМ
ПРОЦЕНТОМ И РАВНОМЕРНОЙ
ВЫПЛАТОЙ

amass

(CHIN) 囤积
(FRE) amasser
(GER) anhäufen, zusammentragen,
ansammeln v
(JAP) 蓄積する、集める
(RUS) НАКОПИТЬ,
СКОПИТЬ

amend

(CHIN) 修改，订正
(FRE) amender, modifier
(GER) abändern, v; novellieren, ergänzen v
(Vertrag, Gesetz)
(JAP) 修正する、補正する
(RUS) ИЗМЕНИТЬ, ИСПРАВИТЬ

amended tax return

(CHIN) 修正的税款申报书
(FRE) déclaration de revenus modifiée
(GER) abgeänderte Steuererklärung f
(JAP) （税金の）修正申告
(RUS) СКОРРЕКТИРОВАННАЯ
НАЛОГОВАЯ ДЕКЛАРАЦИЯ

amendment

(CHIN) 修改，更正

(FRE) rectification
(GER) Abänderung f, Novellierung f,
Ergänzung f, Gesetzesänderung f;
Zusatzartikel m (Grundrecht, Verfassung)
(JAP) 改正、修正（条項）、補正書
(RUS) ИЗМЕНЕНИЕ; ПОПРАВКА

amenities

(CHIN) 舒适，适意
(FRE) agréments, (C) aménités
(GER) Annehmlichkeiten fpl;
Gebrauchsvorteil m, Einrichtungen fpl
(JAP) 生活を便利にする施設・
設備アメニティ
(RUS) УДОБСТВАКОЭФФИЦИЕНТ
ГОДОВОЙ ВЫПЛАТЫ, РЕНТЫ

American Stock Exchange (AMEX)

(CHIN) 美国证券交易所（AMEX）
(FRE) bourse américaine (AMEX)
(GER) American Stock Exchange f
(AMEX)
(JAP) アメリカ株式取引所
(RUS) АМЕРИКАНСКАЯ ФОНДОВАЯ
БИРЖА

amortization

(CHIN) 分期摊还，摊销
(FRE) amortissement
(GER) Amortisation f; planmäßige
Tilgung f
(JAP) 年賦償還、割賦償却（金）
(RUS) АМОРТИЗАЦИЯ; СПИСАНИЕ
СТОИМОСТИ АКТИВА; ПОСТЕПЕННОЕ
ПОГАШЕНИЕ КРЕДИТА

amortization schedule

(CHIN) 摊销表
(FRE) plan d'amortissement
(GER) Tilgungs- m, Amortisationsplan m
(JAP) 債務償還計画（表）
(RUS) ГРАФИК СПИСАНИЯ ПО
АМОРТИЗАЦИИ; ГРАФИК ПОГАШЕНИЯ
КРЕДИТА

analysis

(CHIN) 分析
(FRE) analyse
(GER) Analyse f
(JAP) 分析、解析
(RUS) АНАЛИЗ

analysis of variance (ANOVA)
(CHIN) 方差分析 （ANOVA）
(FRE) analyse de (la) variance
(GER) Varianzanalyse *f*,
Streuungszerlegung *f*
(JAP) 分散分析法
(RUS) СТАТИСТИЧЕСКАЯ МОДЕЛЬ,
АНАЛИЗИРУЮЩАЯ НАЛИЧИЕ СХОДСТ И
РАЗЛИЧИЙ ОТДЕЛЬНЫХ ГРУПП

analysts
(CHIN) 分析员
(FRE) analystes
(GER) Analysten *mpl*
(JAP) アナリスト、分析者
(RUS) АНАЛИТИКИ

analytic process
(CHIN) 分析过程
(FRE) processus analytique
(GER) analytischer Prozess *m*
(JAP) 分析過程
(RUS) АНАЛИТИЧЕСКИЙ ПРОЦЕСС

analytical review
(CHIN) 分析检查
(FRE) examen analytique
(GER) analytische Prüfung *f*
(JAP) 分析的研究 （レビュー）
(RUS) АНАЛИТИЧЕСКИЙ ОБЗОР

anchor tenant
(CHIN) 主要租户
(FRE) locomotive
(GER) Haupt- *m*, Schlüsselmieter *m*
(JAP) アンカーテナント
(RUS) ОСНОВНОЙ (БАЗОВЫЙ) СЪЕМЩИК

animate
(CHIN) 活动的，动画制作
(FRE) animer
(GER) animieren *v*
(JAP) 〜を活発にさせる、動かす
(RUS) МУЛЬЦИПЛИЦИРОВАТЬ

annexation
(CHIN) 兼并，并吞
(FRE) annexion
(GER) Annektierung *f*, Annexion *f*,
Einverleibung *f*

(JAP) 付加物、併合
(RUS) ПРИСОЕДИНЕНИЕ; АННЕКСИЯ

annual basis
(CHIN) 年度基准
(FRE) annuellement
(GER) Jahresbasis *f*, Jahresgrundlage *f*
(JAP) 年次ベース、年間ベース
(RUS) ЕЖЕГОДНАЯ ОСНОВА

annual debt service
(CHIN) 按年支付债务本息
(FRE) service annuel de la dette
(GER) jährlicher Schuldendienst *m*,
jährliche Bedienung *f* eines Kredits *m*
(JAP) 年間未払金サービス
(RUS) ТРЕБУЕМОЕ ЕЖЕГОДНОЕ
ПОГАШЕНИЕ ДОЛГА

annual earnings
(CHIN) 年收益
(FRE) revenu annuel, (C) gains annuels
(GER) Jahresgewinn *m* (Unternehmen);
Jahresverdienst *m*, -einkommen *n*,
-bezüge *pl*
(JAP) 年間所得、年間収入
(RUS) ГОДОВОЙ ДОХОД, ЗАРАБОТОК

annualized rate
(CHIN) 按年率计算
(FRE) taux annualize
(GER) auf das Jahr umgerechneter Satz *m*
(RUS) ПЕРЕСЧЕТ В ГОДОВОЕ
ИСЧИСЛЕНИЕ

annual meeting
(CHIN) 年度会议
(FRE) réunion annuelle
(GER) Hauptversammlung *f* (Aktionäre),
Generalversammlung *f*, Jahrestagung *f*
(JAP) 年次総会、年次会合
(RUS) ЕЖЕГОДНОЕ СОБРАНИЕ

annual mortgage constant
(CHIN) 年度抵押贷款常数
(FRE) constante hypothécaire annuelle
(GER) Jahreshypothekenkonstante *f*, -
festwert *m*
(JAP) 年間抵当貸付定数
(RUS) ГОДОВАЯ ИПОТЕЧНАЯ
КОНСТАНТА. Т. Е. ОТНОШЕНИЕ СУММЫ

ТРЕБУЕМОГО ЕЖЕГОДНОГО
ПОГАШЕНИЯ ДОЛГА К СУММЕ ДОЛГА

annual percentage rate (APR)
(CHIN) 年百分利率（APR）
(FRE) pourcentage annuel
(GER) effektiver Jahreszins *m*
(JAP) 年率
(RUS) ГОДОВАЯ СТАВКА ПРОЦЕНТА

**annual renewable term
insurance**
(CHIN) 年度可展期人寿保险
(FRE) assurance avec reconduction
utomatique annuelle
(GER) jährlich erneuerbare
Risikoversicherung *f*
(RUS) СТРАХОВОЙ ПОЛИС С
ЕЖЕГОДНЫМ ОБНОВЛЕНИЕМ

annual report
(CHIN) 年度报告
(FRE) rapport annuel
(GER) Jahresabschluss *m*
(JAP) 年次報告書、年報
(RUS) ГОДОВОЙ ОТЧЕТ

annual wage
(CHIN) 年度工资
(FRE) salaire annuel
(GER) Jahresverdienst *m*, -lohn *m*
(JAP) 年間賃金
(RUS) ГОДОВАЯ ЗАРПЛАТА

annuitant
(CHIN) 年度受益人
(FRE) rentier viager, (C) rcstatairc, (C)
pensionnaire
(GER) Rentenempfänger *m*, Empfänger
einer Jahresrente *m*
(JAP) 年金受取人、年金受給者
(RUS) ПОЛУЧАТЕЛЬ ГОДОВОЙ РЕНТЫ,
АННУИТЕТА

annuity
(CHIN) 年金，年金保险
(FRE) annuité, versement périodique, rente
(GER) Jahresrente *f*; Leibrente *f*;
Rentenzahlungen *fpl*
(JAP) 年金、年金収受権

(RUS) ЕЖЕГОДНАЯ РЕНТА, АННУИТЕТ

annuity due
(CHIN) 到期年金
(FRE) rente payable d'avance
(GER) fällige Annuität *f*
(JAP) 期首払込金
(RUS) РАВНОМЕРНАЯ РЕНТА, КОТОРАЯ
ВЫПЛАЧИВАЕТСЯ В КОНЦЕ
ОПРЕДЕЛЁННОГО ПЕРИОДА

annuity factor
(CHIN) 年金因子
(FRE) facteur d'actualisation
(GER) Annuitätenfaktor *m*
(JAP) 年金係数
(RUS) КОЭФФИЦИЕНТ ГОДОВОЙ
ВЫПЛАТЫ, РЕНТЫ

annuity in advance
(CHIN) 预付年金(
FRE) versement de début de
période
(GER) vorausbezahlte Jahresrente *f*, im
voraus fällige Jahresrente *f*
(JAP) 前払い年金
(RUS) РАВНОМЕРНАЯ РЕНТА, КОТОРАЯ
ВЫПЛАЧИВАЕТСЯ В ПАЧАЛЕ
ОПРЕДЕЛЁННОГО ПЕРИОДА

annuity in arrears
(CHIN) 拖欠年金
(FRE) versement de fin de période
(GER) Jahresrente *f* im Verzug *m* bzw. Im
Rückstand *m*
(JAP) 未払い年金
(RUS) CM. ANNUITY DUE

answer
(CHIN) 答辩
(FRE) réponse
(GER) Antwort *f*; Bescheid *m*
(JAP) 解決策、対策
(RUS) ОТВЕТ; РЕАГИРОВАНИЕ;
АРГУМЕНТИРОВАННОЕ ОТРИЦАНИЕ
ОТВЕТЧИКОМ ОБВИНЕНИЙ,
ПРЕДЪЯВЛЕННЫЙ ИСТЦОМ

anticipated holding period
(CHIN) 预期持有期间

(FRE) période d'attente anticipée
(GER) voraussichtliche Eigentumsdauer *f*;
voraussichtliche Sperrfrist *f*
(JAP) 予想資産保有期限
(RUS) ОЖИДАЕМЫЙ СРОК ВЛАДЕНИЯ
ФИН. АКТИВОМ

anticipatory breach
(CHIN) 先期违约
(FRE) rupture anticipée, (C) violation
anticipée
(GER) vorweggenommener Vertragsbruch
m, Erfüllungsverweigerung *f*
(JAP) 期限前の契約違反
(RUS) НАРУШЕНИЕ УСЛОВИЙ
КОНТРАКТА ДО ВРЕМЕНИ ЕГО
ИСТЕЧЕНИЯ

antitrust acts
(CHIN) 反托拉斯法案
(FRE) lois antitrust
(GER) Antitrustgesetze *fpl*;
Kartellgesetzgebung *f*
(JAP) 独占禁止法，反トラスト法
(RUS) АНТИМОНОПОЛЬНОЕ
АКОНОДАТЕЛЬСТВО

antitrust laws
(CHIN) 反托拉斯法
(FRE) lois antitrust
(GER) Antitrustgesetze *npl* (US-
Rechtgebung gegen Monopole und
Wettbewerbsbeschränkungen)
(JAP) 独占禁止法、反トラスト法

apparent authority
(CHIN) 当然权力
(FRE) autorité apparente
(GER) Anscheinsvollmacht *f*,
Scheinvollmacht *f*
(JAP) 表見的権限
(RUS) УТВЕРЖДЕНИЕ, ЧТО ПРИНЦИПАЛ
НЕСЁТ ОТВЕТСТВЕННОСТЬ ЗА
ДЕЙСТВИЯ СВОЕГО ТОРГОВОГО АГЕНТА

appeal bond
(CHIN) 申诉保证金
(FRE) cautionnement d'appel
(GER) Sicherheitsleistung *f* des
Berufungsklägers
(JAP) 上訴供託金

(RUS) ОБЯЗАТЕЛЬСТВО ВОЗМЕЩЕНИЯ
ИЗДЕРЖЕК ПО АПЕЛЛЯЦИИ

appellate court (appeals court)
(CHIN) 受理上诉的法院（上诉法院）
(FRE) cour d'appel, tribunal d'appel
(GER) Rechtsmittelinstanz *f*,
Berufungsgericht *n*
(JAP) 上訴裁判所、控訴裁判所
(RUS) АПЕЛЛЯЦИОННЫЙ СУД

applet
(CHIN) 小应用程序
(FRE) applet
(GER) Applet *n*
(JAP) アプレット
(RUS) ПРОГРАММА, НАПИСАННАЯ НА
ЯЗЫКЕ JAVAБ КОТОРАЯ ВСТАВЛЯЕТСЯ В
HTML СТРАНИЦУ НА ПОДОБИИ
ИЗОБРАЖЕНИЯ

application of funds
(CHIN) 资金申请
(FRE) utilisation des fonds, affectation des
fonds
(GER) Mittelverwendung *f*,
Verwendungszweck *m* von Geldmitteln *npl*
(JAP) 資金の運用、資金の使途
(RUS) РАСХОДОВАНИЕ (РАЗМЕЩЕНИЕ)
СРЕДСТВ

application program
(CHIN) 应用程序
(FRE) programme applicatif, programme
d'application
(GER) Anwender- *n*, Anwendungs- *n*,
Benutzerprogramm *n*
(JAP) アプリケーションプログラム
(RUS) ПРИКЛАДНАЯ ПРОГРАММА

application software
(CHIN) 应用软件
(FRE) logiciel d'application, logiciel licatif
(GER) Anwender- *f*, Anwendungssoftware *f*
(JAP) アプリケーションソフトウエア
(RUS) ПРИКЛАДНОЕ ПРОГРАМНОЕ
ОБЕСПЕЧЕНИЕ

application window
(CHIN) 应用程序窗口
(FRE) fenêtre d'application

(GER) Anwendungsfenster *n*
(JAP) アプリケーションウィンドウ
ПРИКЛАДНОЕ ОКНО

applied economics
(CHIN) 应用经济学
(FRE) économie appliquée
(GER) angewandte Volkswirtschaftslchre *f*,
angewandte Wirtschaftswissenschaften *fpl*
(JAP) 応用経済学
(RUS) ПРИКЛАДНАЯ
ЭКОНОМИКА

applied overhead
(CHIN) 已分摊间接费
(FRE) coûts indirects imputés, frais
généraux imputés
(GER) verrechnete Gemeinkosten *pl*
(JAP) 応用間接費
(RUS) ПРИМЕНЕННЫЕ НАКЛАДНЫЕ
РАСХОДЫ

applied research
(CHIN) 应用研究
(FRE) recherche appliquée
(GER) angewandte Forschung *f*,
Zweckforschung *f*
(JAP) 応用研究
(RUS) ПРИКЛАДНЫЕ
ИССЛЕДОВАНИЯ   .

apportionment
(CHIN) 分担，分摊
(FRE) répartition, (C) imputation,
(C) ventilation
(GER) Mittelzuweisung *f*, Repartierung *f*;
Zu-,Ver-, Aufteilung *f*, Zurechnung *f*;
Umlage *f*; Aufteilung *f* der
Steuereinnahmen *fpl* (Steuer);
(JAP) 割当、分配、配当
(RUS) СОРАЗМЕРНОЕ
РАСПРЕДЕЛЕНИЕ

appraisal
(CHIN) 估价，评估
(FRE) estimation, évaluation
(GER) Bewertung *f*, Schätzung *f*,
Wertermittlung *f*, Schätzungsbericht *m*
(JAP) 評価、（資産の）査定
(RUS) ОЦЕНКА СТОИМОСТИ

appraisal rights
(CHIN) 估价权
(FRE) droits d'évaluation
(GER) Barabfindungsrechte *npl* (Aktionäre)
(JAP) 鑑定権
(RUS) ПРАВА ОЦЕНКИ СТОИМОСТИ

appraise
(CHIN) 估价，评定，鉴定
(FRE) estimer, priser, évaluer
(GER) bewerten, schätzen *v*;
veranschlagen *v*
(JAP) 鑑定する
(RUS) ОЦЕНИВАТЬ СТОИМОСТЬ

appraiser
(CHIN) 估价师，鉴定人
(FRE) évaluateur, estimateur
(GER) Schätzer *m*, Taxator *m*
(JAP) 鑑定人、（税関の）査定官
(RUS) ОЦЕНЩИК

appreciate
(CHIN) 增值，赞赏
(FRE) fixer, apprécier
(GER) an Wert gewinnen, im Wert steigen
v; aufwerten *v* (Währung)
(JAP) 価値が上がる、値上がりする
(RUS) ВОЗРАСТАТЬ В СТОИМОСТИ;
ОЦЕНИВАТЬ

appreciation
(CHIN) 升值，增值
(FRE) augmentation de la dette, (C) plus-
value, (C) appreciation
(GER) Wertzuwachs *m*, -steigerung *f*,
-gewinn *m* (Anlagevermögen);
Kurssteigerung *f*, Aufwertung *f* (Währung)
(JAP) （価格の）騰貴、増加
(RUS) РОСТ ЦЕННОСТИ,
СТОИМОСТИ

appropriate
(CHIN) 预算拨款
(FRE) affecter
(GER) sich aneignen, Besitz ergreifen von
v; bewilligen, zuweisen, bereitstellen,
zuteilen *v*
(JAP) （予算を）計上する、充当する

(RUS) ОБРАЩАТЬ В СОБСТВЕННОСТЬ;
ПРИСВАИВАТЬ; АССИГНОВАТЬ

appropriated expenditure
(CHIN) 拨定支出
(FRE) dépense affectée
(GER) Bewilligte bzw. zweckgebundene
Ausgaben *fpl*
(JAP) 特殊割当支出金
(RUS) ВЫДЕЛЕНИЕ СРЕДСТВ НА
РАСХОДЫ

appropriation
(CHIN) 拨款，挪用
(FRE) affectation, imputation
Bewilligung *f*; Bereitstellung *f*;
buchmäßige Gewinnverteilung *f*;
Investitionsgenehmigung *f*; Zweckbindung
f; Inbesitznahme *f*, Aneignung *f*; Emission *f*
von Fondanteilen *mpl*
(JAP) 支出充当、（予算の）承認、予算
割当額
(RUS) АССИГНОВАНИЕ;
РАСПРЕДЕЛЕНИЕ ПРИБЫЛИ

approved list
(CHIN) 核准单
(FRE) liste approuvée
(GER) genehmigte Liste *f*
(JAP) 承認リスト
(RUS) УТВЕРЖДЕННЫЙ СПИСОК,
ПЕРЕЧЕНЬ; СПИСОК ИНВЕСТИЦИЙ,
КОТОРЫЕ МОЖЕТ СДЕЛАТЬ
ОПРЕДЕЛЁННЫЙ ИНВЕСТИЦИОННЫЙ
ФОНД ИЛИ ДРУГОЕ ФИНАНСОВОЕ
УЧРЕЖДЕНИЕ

appurtenant
(CHIN) 附属的
(FRE) annexe, (C) rattaché à
(GER) zugehörig *adj*
(JAP) 一に従属して、従属している、
他物付属の
(RUS) ПРИНАДЛЕЖАЩИЙ

appurtenant structures
(CHIN) 附属结构
(FRE) ouvrages annexes
(GER) Nebenanlagen *fpl*, zugehörige
Anlagen *fpl*

(JAP) 付属建築
(RUS) ВСТРОЕННЫЕ СТРУКТУРЫ,
УСЛОВИЯ

a priori statement
(CHIN) 外因报告
(FRE) rapport a priori
(JAP) 直感的声明、推測的報告書
(RUS) УТВЕРЖДЕНИЕ, СДЕЛАННОЕ НА
ОСНОВЕ УМОЗАКЛЮЧЕНИЙ, НО НЕ
ОСНОВАННОЕ НА ФАКТАХ

arbiter
(CHIN) 仲裁人
(FRE) arbitre
(GER) Schiedsrichter *m*, Schlichter *m*
(JAP) 裁決者、仲裁人
(RUS) НАЗНАЧЕННЫЙ СУДОМ
ТРЕТЕЙСКИЙ СУДЬЯ, РЕШЕНИЯ
КОТОРОГО ДОЛЖНЫ УТВЕРЖДАТЬСЯ
СУДОМ

arbitrage
(CHIN) 套汇，套利
(FRE) arbitrage,
 (C) opération d'arbitrage
(GER) Arbitrage *f*, Arbitragegeschäft *n*
(JAP) 鞘取引，鞘売買，裁定取引
(RUS) ТРЕТЕЙСКИЙ СУД, АРБИТРАЖ

arbitrage bond
(CHIN) 套汇债券
(FRE) cautionnement d'arbitrage
(GER) Anleihenarbitrage *f*
(JAP) 裁定取引契約、鞘取引約定
(RUS) АРБИТРАЖНАЯ
ОБЛИГАЦИЯ

arbitration
(CHIN) 仲裁
(FRE) arbitrage
(GER) Schlichtung *f*,
Schiedsgerichtsverfahren *n*;
Schiedsgerichtsbarkeit *f*
(JAP) 仲裁、仲裁裁判、裁定
(RUS) РАССМОТРЕНИЕ В ТРЕТЕЙСКОМ
СУДЕ, АРБИТРАЖЕ

arbitrator
(CHIN) 仲裁人，公断人

22

(FRE) arbiter
(GER) Schiedsrichter *m*, Schlichter *m*,
Vermittler *m*
(JAP) 仲裁人
(RUS) ТРЕТЕЙСКИЙ СУДЬЯ, АРБИТР,
СПОСОВНЫЙ ПРИНЯТЬ
ОКОНЧАТЕЛЬНОЕ РЕШЕНИЕ В СПОРЕ

archive storage
(CHIN) 档案保管
(FRE) archivage,
(C) entreposage d'archives
(GER) Archivierung *f*, Archivlagerung *f*
(JAP) アーカイブ・ストレージ、公文書
（保管所）
(RUS) АРХИВНЫЕ ДОКУМЕНТЫ; АРХИВ

arm's length transaction
(CHIN) 正常交易，公平交易
(FRE) transaction dans les conditions
normales de la concurrence, (C) transaction
sans lien de dépendance
(GER) Geschäft *m* wie mit
Außenstehenden, Transaktion *f* zwischen
rechtlich selbständigen Geschäftspartnern
mpl
(JAP) 独立当事者間の互いに対等な立場
での取引
(RUS) СДЕЛКА «НА РАССТОЯНИИ
ВЫТЯНУТОЙ РУКИ», Т. Е. СДЕЛКА, В
КОТОРОЙ ВСЕ УЧАВСТВУЮЩИЕ
СТОРОНЫ ДЕЙСТВУЮТ, ИСХОДЯ ИЗ
СОБСТВЕННЫХ ИНТЕРЕСОВ

array
(CHIN) 阵列，整列，一批
(FRE) tableau, matrice, (C) appel nominal
(GER) Anordnung *f*, Reihe *f*, Schema *n*
(JAP) 配列、配列する
(RUS) СЕРИЯ; АССОРТИМЕНТ

arrearage
(CHIN) 欠款，拖欠数
(FRE) fait d'avoir des arriérés, (C) arrérages
(GER) Rückstände *mpl*
(JAP) 滞り、未払金、
予備に保存したもの
(RUS) СУММА ПРОСРОЧЕННОГО
ДОЛГОВОГО ОБЯЗАТЕЛЬСТВА;
НЕВЫПЛАЧЕННЫЕ ПРОЦЕНТЫ И
ДИВИДЕНТЫ

arrears
(CHIN) 欠款
(FRE) arriéré
(GER) Rückstände *mpl*, Verzugsummen *fpl*
(JAP) 滞納、滞納金
(RUS) ЗАДОЛЖЕННОСТЬ; В КОНЦЕ
СРОКА (В ОТЛИЧАЕ ОТ IN ADVANCE)

articles of incorporation
(CHIN) 公司条例，公司章程
(FRE) statuts, (C) statuts constitutifs
(GER) Statuten *npl*; Gründungsurkunde *f*
einer Aktiengesellschaft *f*, Satzung *f*,
Gesellschaftsvertrag *m*
(JAP) 会社定款
(RUS) УСТАВ КОРПОРАЦИИ

artificial intelligence (AI)
(CHIN) 人工智能（AI）
(FRE) intelligence artificielle
(GER) künstliche Intelligenz *f*
(JAP) 人工知能
(RUS) ИСКУССТВЕННЫЙ РАЗУМ

as is
(CHIN) 按货样，概不保证，现状如此
(FRE) en l'état, (C) sans garantie
(GER) wie die Ware liegt und steht *adj*
(JAP) 現状有姿（で）、現品限り、
正札どおり
(RUS) «КАК ЕСТЬ»

asked
(CHIN) 卖方报价
(FRE) demandé
(GER) Brief *m*, Briefkurs *m*
(JAP) 請求された、提示された
(RUS) ЗАПРОШЕНО

asking price
(CHIN) 索价，要价
(FRE) prix demandé, prix de départ
(GER) Briefkurs *m*; Preisforderung *f*
(JAP) 提示価格
(RUS) ЗАПРАШИВАЕМАЯ ЦЕНА

assemblage
(CHIN) 组装，装配
(FRE) montage, assemblage,

(C) groupement
(GER) Menge *f*; Ansammlung *f*
(JAP) 組立て
(RUS) СБОРКА; ОБЪЕДИНЕНИЕ

assembly line

(CHIN) 装配线，流水作业
(FRE) chaîne de montage
(GER) Fließ- *n*, Montageband *n*,
Fertigungs- *f*, Produktionsstraße *f*
(JAP) 組立ライン、アセンブリーライン
(RUS) СБОРОЧНЫЙ КОНВЕЙЕР

assembly plant

(CHIN) 装配厂
(FRE) usine d'assemblage
(GER) Montagewerk *n*
(JAP) 組立工場
(RUS) СБОРОЧНЫЙ ЗАВОД

assess

(CHIN) 估价，评估
(FRE) évaluer, estimer, (C) calculer
(GER) bewerten, veranschlagen *v*;
festsetzen, bemessen *v*; prüfen *v*; schätzen *v*;
veranlagen *v*; feststellen *v*
(JAP) 査定する、賦課する
(RUS) ОПРЕДЕЛЯТЬ; ОЦЕНИВАТЬ

assessed valuation

(CHIN) 估定价值
(FRE) valeur estimée, (C) valeur imposable,
(C) valeur cotisée
(GER) Bewertung *f*; festgesetzter Wert *m*
(JAP) 鑑定額、査定価額
(RUS) ОЦЕНЕННАЯ СТОИМОСТЬ

assessment

(CHIN) 资产评估，税款评定
(FRE) evaluation, (C) appréciation,
 (C) appels de fonds
(GER) Schätzung *f*, Wertfeststellung *f*;
steuerliche Veranlagung *f*
(JAP) 賦課（金）、査定（額）
(RUS) ОЦЕНКА; ОПРЕДЕЛЕНИЕ

assessment of deficiency

(CHIN) 亏损评估
(FRE) évaluation de l'insuffisance

(GER) Bemessung *f* des Fehlbestandes *m*,
Mankoberechnung *f*
(RUS) СУММА НАЛОГА К ВЫПЛАТЕ
ПОСЛЕ АППЕЛЯЦИИ В НАЛОГОВОМ
СУДЕ

assessment ratio

(CHIN) 估价比
(FRE) ratio d'évaluation
(GER) Veranlagungs-,
Bemessungsverhältnis *n*
(JAP) 評価額比率
(RUS) СООТНОШЕНИЕ МЕЖДУ
ОЦЕНЕННОЙ СТОИМОСТЬЮ И
РВНОЧНОЙ СТОИМОСТЬЮ

assessment role

(CHIN) 摊派税捐清册，课税清册
(FRE) rôle d'évaluation
(GER) Veranlagungs-, Bemessungsrolle *f*
(RUS) ОБЩЕДОСТУПНЫЙ ПРОТОКОЛ
ОЦЕНКИ СТОИМОСТИ СОБСТВЕННОСТИ
НАЛОГОВОЙ ЮРИСДИКЦИЕЙ

assessor

(CHIN) 估算员，审查员
(FRE) expert, (C) assesseur, (C) évaluateur,
(C) noteur
(GER) Schätzer *m*; Sachverständiger
(Versicherung); Grundstücksbewerter *m*
(Immobilien)
(JAP) (財産)評価人、（課税）査定人、
（損害）鑑定人
(RUS) ОЦЕНЩИК, В ЧАСТНОСТИ
ЕДВИЖИМОСТИ

asset

(CHIN) 资产
(FRE) actif, (C) élément d'actif
(GER) Vermögenswert *m*; Rechtsgut *n*;
Aktivposten *m*; Kapital *n*, Guthaben *n*
(JAP) 資産、資産の一項目
(RUS) АКТИВ

asset depreciation range (ADR)

(CHIN) 固定资产折旧幅度（ADR）
(FRE) fourchette d'amortissement de l'actif,
(C) fourchette de dépréciation de l'actif
(GER) betriebsgewöhnliche Nutzungsdauer
f, (Abschreibungssystem *n*, das
Nutzungsrichtwerte für Anlagegüter enthält)

(JAP) 資産償却限度
(RUS) ДИАПАЗОН АМОРТИЗАЦИИ
АКТИВОВ

assign

(CHIN) 转让
(FRE) assigner, (C) ayant droit
(GER) abtreten (Recht, Anspruch) *v*
übereignen *v*; zuweisen,
zuteilen *v* (Kostenrechnung)
(JAP) 譲渡する、割当てる
(RUS) ПЕРЕДАТЬ, ПЕРЕУСТУПИТЬ
ПРАВА; НАЗНАЧИТЬ

assignee

(CHIN) 受让人，代理人
(FRE) cessionnaire, (C) ayant cause
(GER) Abtretungsempfänger *m*; Zessionär
m; Rechtsnachfolger *m*; Abwickler *m*,
Liquidator *m*
(JAP) 譲受人、管財人
(RUS) ПРАВОПРАВОПРЕЕМНИК

assignment

(CHIN) 转让，分配，指定(FRE)
attribution, (C) délégation de dette,
(C) affectation, (C) cession
(GER) Abtretung *f*; Vermögensübertragung
f; Zurechnung *f* (Kostenrechnung);
Zession *f*
(JAP) 譲渡、譲渡証書
(RUS) ПЕРЕДАЧА, ПЕРЕУСТУПКА ПРАВ;
НАЗНАЧЕНИЕ, ЗАДАНИЕ

assignment of income

(CHIN) 收益转让
(FRE) cession de revenues
(GER) Einkommensübertragung *f*
(JAP) 収入を抵当にした借金、収入譲渡
（証書）
(RUS) ПЕРЕДАЧА
НАЛОГОПЛАТЕЛЬЩИКОМ СВОЕГО
ДОХОДА ДРУГОМУ ЛИЦУ (ЧТОБЫ
ПОСЛЕДНИЙ ОБЛАГАЛСЯ
ФЕДЕРАЛЬНЫМ НАЛОГОМ)

assignment of lease

(CHIN) 转租
(FRE) cession de bail
(GER) Weiterübertragung der Rechte aus

einem Miets- bzw. Pachtvertrag *m*; Miet-,
Pachtabtretung *f*
(JAP) 賃借権の譲渡
(RUS) ПЕРЕДАЧА ПРАВА НА АРЕНДУ

assignor

(CHIN) 转让人，指定人
(FRE) cédant
(GER) Abtretender *m*; Zedent *m*
(JAP) 譲渡人
(RUS) ЛИЦО, ПЕРЕДАЮЩЕЕ ИЛИ
УСТУПАЮЩЕЕ ПРАВО

assimilation

(CHIN) 融合
(FRE) assimilation
(GER) Angleichung *f*; Assimilation *f*,
Einverleibung *f*
(JAP) 同化、同化作用、混成作用
(RUS) ПРИВЛЕЧЕНИЕ; ОСВОЕНИЕ

association

(CHIN) 协会，公会，商会
(FRE) association
(GER) Personenvereinigung *f*;
Interessenverband *m*; Partnerschaft *f*,
Vereinigung *f*, Verband *m*, Verein *m*,
Gesellschaft *f*
(JAP) 連合、組合，協会、提携
(RUS) АССОЦИАЦИЯ; ОБЪЕДИНЕНИЕ

assumption of mortgage

(CHIN) 承担抵押贷款
(FRE) prise en charge de prêt hypothécaire
(GER) Hypothekenübernahme *f*
(JAP) 抵当の引き受け
(RUS) ПРИНЯТИЕ НА СЕБЯ ИПОТЕЧНОЙ
ЗАДОЛЖЕННОСТИ ПРЕДЫДУЩЕГО
ВЛАДЕЛЬЦА

asterisk

(CHIN) 星号
(FRE) astérisque
(GER) Sternchen *n*, Asterisk *m*
(JAP) アステリスク、星印
(RUS) ВСПОМОГАТЕЛЬНЫЙ ФАЙЛ

asynchronous

(CHIN) 不同步

(FRE) asynchrone
asynchron *adj*
(JAP) 非同期（式）の、異時性の、非同期性、非同期
(RUS) АСИНХРОННЫЙ; НЕОДНОВРЕМЕННЫЙ

at par

(CHIN) 按照票面价格，按平价
(FRE) au pair
(GER) zu pari, zum Nennwert *adv*
(JAP) 額面価格で、払込額で、割引なしで、
(RUS) ПО НОМИНАЛЬНОЙ СТОИМОСТИ

at risk

(CHIN) 担风险
(FRE) à risqué
(GER) risikobehaftet
(JAP) 危険な状態で、危険にさらされて
(RUS) НА УСЛОВИЯХ РИСКА

at the close

(CHIN) 最后价格，收市价格
(FRE) au dernier cours
(GER) bei Schluss *m* (Börsenschluss)
(JAP) 大引けに
(RUS) ПРИ ЗАВЕРШЕНИИ; ИСТРУКЦИИ БРОКЕРУ, ПРЕДПИСЫВАЮЩИЕ ПОКУПКУ ЦЕННЫХ БУМАГ В ПОСЛЕДНИЕ МИНУТЫ РАБОТЫ БИРЖИ

at the opening

(CHIN) 开始价格，开盘平价
(FRE) au premier cours
(GER) bei Eröffnung *f* Börseneröffnung)
(JAP) 寄り付き注文
(RUS) ПРИ НАЧАЛЕ; ИСТРУКЦИИ БРОКЕРУ, ПРЕДПИСЫВАЮЩИЕ ПОКУПКУ ЦЕННЫХ БУМАГ В ПЕРВЫЕ МИНУТЫ РАБОТЫ БИРЖИ

attachment

(CHIN) 查封，扣押，附件
(FRE) pièce jointe
(GER) dinglicher Arrest *m*, Beschlagnahme *f*
(JAP) 添付書類、差押、差押令状

(RUS) ПРИЛОЖЕНИЕ; СКРЕПЛЕНИЕ ПЕЧАТЬЮ; ЗАКЛЮЧЕНИЕ ПОД СТРАЖУ

attained age

(CHIN) 永久保险年龄
(FRE) âge atteint
(GER) erreichtes Alter *n*
(JAP) 現在の年齢
(RUS) ДОСТИГНУТЫЙ ВОЗРАСТ (СРОК)

attention

(CHIN) 引人注意，收件人
(FRE) attention
(GER) Beachtung *f*; zu Händen von
(JAP) 〜宛て
(RUS) ВНИМАНИЕ

attention line

(CHIN) 收件人书写处
(FRE) ligne d'attention
(GER) 'zu Händen von' Zeile *f*
(JAP) 名宛人記載欄、アテンションライン
(RUS) СТРОКА НА КОНВЕРТЕ, ГДЕ УКАЗЫВАЕТСЯ ИМЯ ПРЕДНАЗНАЧЕННОГО ПОЛУЧАТЕЛЯ

attest

(CHIN) 作证，证明
(FRE) attester
(GER) Bescheinigung *f*, Attest *n*; bestätigen, bezeugen, beglaubigen *v*
(JAP) 証言する、証明する、誓言する
(RUS) УДОСТОВЕРЯТЬ, СВИДЕТЕЛЬСТВОВАТЬ

attorney-at-law

(CHIN) 律师
(FRE) avocat, avoué
(GER) Rechtsanwalt *m*, Jurist *m*
(JAP) 弁護士
(RUS) АДВОКАТ

attorney-in-fact

(CHIN) 代理人
(FRE) avocat de droit, (C) avocat en fait
(GER) Beauftragter *m*, Bevollmächtigter *m*
(JAP) 代理人
(RUS) УПОЛНОМОЧЕННОЕ ЛИЦО

attribute sampling
(CHIN) 属性抽样，特性抽样法
(FRE) échantillonnage attributif,
(C) sondage d'attribut
(GER) Stichprobennahme *f* für qualitative
Merkmale *npl*
(JAP) アトリビュートサンプリング
(RUS) ВЫБОРКА АТРИБУТОВ,
СТАТИСТИЧЕСКИЙ МЕТОД ИЗУЧЕНИЯ
ОСОБЫХ ХАРАКТЕРИСТИК
СОВОКУПНОСТИ

attrition
(CHIN) 磨损，消耗，减员
(FRE) attrition
(GER) bar ausgezahlter Teil *m* einer
Emission *f;* (natürlicher)
Arbeitskräfteabgang *m,*
Personalabbau *m*
(JAP) 自然減（耗）、消耗
(RUS) ИСТОЩЕНИЕ; НОРМАЛЬНОЕ
СОКРАЩЕНИЕ РАБОЧЕЙ СИЛЫ В СВЯЗИ
С УХОДОМ ПЕНСИЮ, СМЕРТЬЮ,
БОЛЕЗНЬЮ И ИЗМЕНЕНИЕМ МЕСТА
ЖИТЕЛЬСТВА

auction or auction sale
(CHIN) 拍卖
(FRE) enchères, (C) vente par inscriptions
(GER) Auktion *f,* (öffentliche)
Versteigerung *f,*
Auktionsverkauf *m*
(JAP) オークション、競売
(RUS) АУКЦИОН ИЛИ АУКЦИОННАЯ
ПРОДАЖА

audience
(CHIN) 听众
(FRE) audience, (C) assistance
(GER) Publikum *n,* Zielgruppe *f*
(JAP) 観客、聴衆、視聴者、聞き手、
読者
(RUS) АУДИТОРИЯ

audit
(CHIN) 审计，查账，核数
(FRE) vérification, audit comptable
(GER) Buch-, Bilanzprüfung *f,* Revision *f,*
Rechnungsprüfung *f;*
Haushaltskontrolle *f*

(JAP) 会計監査、決算、（会計を）監査
する
(RUS) БУХГАЛТЕРСКАЯ РЕВИЗИЯ; АУДИТ

auditing standards
(CHIN) 查账标准，审计规则
(FRE) normes de verification
(GER) Prüfungs-, Revisionsvorschriften *fpl,*
Prüfungs-, Revisionsrichtlinien *fpl*
(JAP) 監査基準
(RUS) НОРМЫ АУДИТА

auditor
(CHIN) 审计师，核数师
(FRE) vérificateur des comptes,
commissaire aux comptes, (C) vérificateur
(GER) Rechnungs-, Bilanz-,
Wirtschaftsprüfer *m,* Revisor *m*
(JAP) 監査役、会計監査人
(RUS) АУДИТОР, РЕВИЗОР

auditor's certificate
(CHIN) 审计师证明书
(FRE) rapport du vérificateur, certificat du
vérificateur
(GER) Bestätigungs-, Prüfungsvermerk *m*
(Kurzform); Prüfungsbericht *m* (Langform)
(JAP) 監査役証明書
(RUS) УДОСТОВЕРЕНИЕ,
СВИДЕТЕЛЬСТВО АУДИТОРА

auditor's certificate, opinion, or report
(CHIN) 计师证明书，意见书，或报告书
(FRE) rapport du commissaire aux comptes,
(C) certificat, avis ou rapport du vérificateur
(GER) Bestätigungsvermerk *m* (Kurzform);
Prüfungs-, Revisions-, Rechnungsbericht *m*
(Langform), Prüfungsprotokoll *n*
(JAP) 監査役証明書、監査意見書、監査
（人）報告書
(RUS) СВИДЕТЕЛЬСТВО, ЗАКЛЮЧЕНИЕ
ИЛИ ОТЧЕТ АУДИТОРА

audit program
(CHIN) 审计计划，审计程序
(FRE) programme d'audit
(GER) Prüfungsprogramm *n,*
Prüfungsplan *m*
(JAP) 監査計画、監査計画書
(RUS) ПОСЛЕДОВАТЕЛЬНОСТЬ АУДИТА,
РЕВИЗИИ

audit trail

(CHIN) 查账索引
(FRE) trace d'audit, (C) piste de verification
(GER) Prüfungsweg *m*; Prüfspfad *m*,
Belegnachweis *m*, Prüfliste *f*;
Buchungskontrolle *f*
(JAP) 監査証跡、監査の手がかり
(RUS) ПОЭТАПНАЯ ДОКУМЕНТАЦИЯ
ПОЛУЧЕНИЯ БУХГАЛТЕСКОЙ
ИНФОРМАЦИИ

authentication

(CHIN) 验证，认证，鉴定
(FRE) authentication, certification, (C)
légalisation, (C) vérification,
(C) validation
(GER) Beglaubigung *f*; Beurkundung *f*,
Bescheinigung *f*; Echtheitsprüfung *f*
(JAP) （文書）の真正性証明、認証
(RUS) УДОСТОВЕРЕНИЕ ПОДЛИННОСТИ

authorized shares or authorized stock

(CHIN) 核定股份，额定股本
(FRE) capital autorisé
(GER) genehmigte Aktienanteile *fpl*;
genehmigtes Kapital *n*
(JAP) 授権株式数、授権株式
(RUS) РАЗРЕШЁННЫЙ КАПИТАЛ

automatic checkoff

(CHIN) 自动扣除
(FRE) retenue obligatoire, (C) précompte
obligatoire, (C) retenue obligatoire des
cotisations syndicales
(GER) automatische Einziehung *f* der
Gewerkschaftsbeiträge *mpl* durch den
Arbeitgeber *m*
(JAP) 自動天引き
(RUS) АВТОМАТИЧЕСКИЙ
ЗАЧЕТ

automatic (fiscal) stabilizers

(CHIN) 自动（财政）稳
定功能
(FRE) stabilisateurs fiscaux
(GER) automatische
(Konjuktur)stabilisatoren *mpl*
(JAP) 自動（財政）安定装置
(RUS) АВТОМАТИЧЕСКИЕ (НАЛОГОВО-
БЮДЖЕТНЫЕ) ФАКТОРЫ
СТАБИЛИЗАЦИИ

automatic merchandising

(CHIN) 自动推销
(FRE) vente par distributeur automatique
(GER) automatische Absatz-
,Verkaufsförderung *f*; automatisches
Merchandising *n*
(JAP) 自動販売機による販売
(RUS) АВТОМАТИЧЕСКАЯ РЕАЛИЗАЦИЯ
(ЧЕРЕЗ ТОРГОВЫЕ АВТОМАТЫ)

automatic reinvestment

(CHIN) 自动再投资
(FRE) réinvestissement automatique
(GER) automatische Reinvestition *f*
(JAP) 自動再投資
(RUS) АВТОМАТИЧЕСКАЯ
РЕИНВЕСТИЦИЯ

automatic withdrawal

(CHIN) 自动提款
(FRE) prélèvement automatique
(GER) automatische Abhebung *f*;
automatische Abbuchung *f*
(JAP) 預金自動引出し
(RUS) АВТОМАТИЧЕСКОЕ СНЯТИЕ
СРЕДСТВ

average

(CHIN) 平均数，平均指数
(FRE) moyenne
(GER) Durchschnitt *m*, Mittelwert *m*
(JAP) 平均（値）、平均株価
(RUS) СРЕДНИЙ; В СРЕДНЕМ

average cost

(CHIN) 平均成本
(FRE) coût moyen
(GER) Durchschnittskosten *pl*
(JAP) 平均費用
(RUS) СРЕДНЯЯ
СЕБЕСТОИМОСТЬ

average (daily) balance

(CHIN) （日）平均余额
(FRE) solde moyen quotidian
(GER) Durchschnitts(tages)saldo *m* (für
Zinsberechnung)
(JAP) 平均（一日）残高
(RUS) СРЕДНИЙ (ДНЕВНОЙ)
БАЛАНС

average down
(CHIN) 低于平均价,
低于正常价
(FRE) moyenne inférieure
(GER) Durchschnitt *m* gefallen
(JAP) 難平買い
(RUS) СРЕДНЕЕ СНИЖЕНИЕ; СТРАТЕГИЯ
СНИЖЕНИЯ СРЕДНЕЙ ЦЕНЫ ПОКУПКИ
АКЦИЙ КОМПАНИИ

average fixed cost
(CHIN) 平均固定成本
(FRE) frais fixes moyens
(GER) durchschnittliche Fixkosten *pl*,
(JAP) 平均固定費用
(RUS) СРЕДНИЕ ФИКСИРОВАННЫЕ
ИЗДЕРЖКИ

average tax rate
(CHIN) 平均税率
(FRE) taux d'imposition moyen
(GER) durchschnittlicher Steuersatz *m*
(JAP) 平均税率
(RUS) СРЕДНЯЯ СТАВКА НАЛОГА

avoirdupois
(CHIN) 常衡
(FRE) avoirdupois
(GER) Handelsgewicht *n*
(JAP) 常衡
(RUS) СИСТЕМА ВЕСОВ (16 УНЦИЙ НА
ФУНТ)

avulsion
(CHIN) 因河水改道后土地的转移
(FRE) avulsion
(GER) Abschwemmen *n*, plötzliche
Strombettverlagerung *f*
(JAP) (土地の)自然分離、突然の転
(RUS) ВНЕЗАПНОЕ ИЗМЕНЕНИЕ
(ЗЕМЛЯНОГО) НАДЕЛА

B

baby bond
(CHIN) 小额债券
(FRE) mini-obligation, obligation de faible
montant
(GER) Babybond *m*, Kleinobligation *f*
(JAP) 少額債券
(RUS) ОБЛИГАЦИИ НОМИНАЛОМ МЕНЕЕ
1 ТЫС. ДОЛЛ.

baby boomers
(CHIN) 婴儿潮人群
(FRE) enfant du baby boom, (C) baby-
boomers
(GER) Baby Boomer *pl*
(JAP) 1945年から60年代に生まれた人、
ベビーブーマー、
ベビーブーム世代の人
(RUS) ПОСЛЕВОЕННОЕ ПОКОЛЕНИЕ,
(РОДИВШИЕСЯ В ГОДЫ ПОСЛЕ 2-ОЙ
МИРОВОЙ ВОЙНЫ)

backdating
(CHIN) 倒填日期
(FRE) antidatation
(GER) rückdatieren *v*
(JAP) 日付を遡らせること、前の日付け
に遡って発効すること
(RUS) ДАТИРОВАНИЕ ЛЮБОГО
ДОКУМЕНТА ЗАДНИМ ЧИСЛОМ

background investigation
(CHIN) 背景调查
(FRE) examen de curriculum vitae,
(C) enquête sur les antécédents
(GER) Hintergrundermittlung *f*
(JAP) 背後事情の調査、経歴・
履歴調査
(RUS) АНАЛИЗ КВАЛИФИКАЦИИ
ПРЕТЕНДЕНТА НА ДОЛЖНОСТЬ

background check
(CHIN) 背景支票
(FRE) vérification des antecedents
(GER) Beschaffung *f* von
Hintergrundinformation *f*

(JAP) 背後事情の調査、経歴・履歴調査
(RUS) ПРОВЕРКА ПРЕДЫСТОРИИ;
КВАЛИФИКАЦИИ

back haul
(CHIN) 回程
(FRE) retour a charge, (C) frais de retour
(GER) Transport *m* von Rückfracht *f*
(JAP) 帰路、復路、逆送
(RUS) ДОСТАВКА ПОРОЖНЯКА

backlog
(CHIN) 积压未交付
(FRE) accumulation, réserve, retard, (C)
travail en retard, (C) carnet de commandes
(GER) Auftragsrückstand *m*;
Arbeitsrückstand *m*
(JAP) 注文残高、売残品
(RUS) НЕВЫПОЛНЕННАЯ РАБОТА или
ЗАКАЗЫ

back office
(CHIN) 事务部门，后勤人员
(FRE) département de contrôle, (C) travail
en retard, (C) carnet de commandes, post-
marché, services administratifs, (C) service
de post-marché
(GER) Abwicklungsstelle *f*
(Devisenhandel); Back Office *n*
(JAP) 窓際、非営業部門
(RUS) «С ЧЕРНОГО ВХОДА»

back pay
(CHIN) 欠薪，欠付工资
(FRE) rappel de salaire, (C) arriéré de
salaire, (C) salaire (FRE) rétroactif
(GER) Lohn-, Gehaltsnachzahlung *f*,
rückständiger Lohn *m*
(JAP) 未払給料、遡及的給与
(RUS) ВЫПЛАТА ПРИЧИТАЮЩЕЙСЯ
РАЗНИЦЫ ЗА ПРЕЖНИЙ ПЕРИОД

backslash
(CHIN) 反斜杠，反斜线符号
(FRE) barre de fraction inverse,
antislash

30

(GER) nach vorn geneigter Schrägstrich *m*,
Gegenschräger *m*, Backslash *m*
(JAP) バックスラッシュ、逆スラッシュ
(RUS) ОБРАТНАЯ КОСАЯ ЧЕРТА

backspace key
(CHIN) 退格键
(FRE) touche de rappel arrière
(GER) Rücktaste *f*
(JAP) バックスペースキー
(RUS) КЛАВИША ВОЗВРАТА

back up
(CHIN) 备份
(FRE) sauvegarder
(GER) sichern *v*
(JAP) バックアップ
(RUS) РЕЗЕРВ

backup file
(CHIN) 备份文件
(FRE) fichier de sauvegarde
(GER) Sicherungsdatei *f*,
Datensicherungskopie *f*
(JAP) バックアップ・ファイル
(RUS) ФАЙЛ РЕЗЕРВА

back up withholding
(CHIN) 备用扣交
(FRE) retenue d'impôt, retenue à la source,
(C) retenue automatique à la source
(GER) Anschlussquellensteuer *m*(US)
(JAP) 予備
(RUS) УДЕРЖАНИЕ 31% С ВЫПЛАТ
ПРОЦЕНТОВ, ДИВИДЕНТОВ И Т.П. В
ПОЛЬЗУ ФЕДЕРАЛЬНОГО
ПРАВИТЕЛЬСТВА В СЛУЧАЕ ЕСЛИ
ПОЛУЧАТЕЛЬ НЕ ПРЕДСТАВЛЯЕТ СВОЙ
СОЦИАЛЬНЫЙ НОМЕР

backward-bending supply curve
(CHIN) 向后弯曲的供给曲线
(FRE) courbe d'offre de travail « backward-
bending » (croissante au début, elle devient
décroissante à partir d'un certain niveau de
salaire), courbe d'offre de travail coudée,
(C) courbe d'offre à rebours
(GER) rückwärts geneigte Angebotskurve *f*
(JAP) 後方屈伸供給曲線
(RUS) КРИВАЯ ПРЕДЛОЖЕНИЯ С

ОТРИЦАТЕЛЬНЫМ НАКЛОНОМ

backward vertical integration
(CHIN) 后向垂直合并
(FRE) intégration verticale, intégration en
amont, (C) intégration verticale en
amont
(GER) vertikale Rückwärtsintegration *f*
(JAP) 後方垂直統合
(RUS) ОБРАТНАЯ ВЕРТИКАЛЬНАЯ
ИНТЕГРАЦИЯ

bad debt
(CHIN) 坏账，呆账
(FRE) créances irrécouvrables, créances
douteuses, (C) créance radiée
(GER) zweifelhafte Forderungen *fpl*,
uneinbringliche Schuld *f*, Risikokredite *mpl*
(Bank)
(JAP) 不良債権、貸倒金
(RUS) БЕЗНАДЁЖНЫЙ ДОЛГ

bad debt recovery
(CHIN) 收回坏账
(FRE) recouvrement des créances douteuses
(GER) Einziehung *f* bzw. Eintreibung *f* von
zweifelhaften Forderungen *fpl*
(JAP) 不良債権回復
(RUS) ВЗЫСКАНИЕ БЕЗНАДЁЖНОГО
ДОЛГА

bad debt reserve
(CHIN) 坏账准备金
(FRE) provision pour créances
douteuses, réserve pour créances
douteuses
(GER) Rücklage *f* für zweifelhafte
Forderungen *fpl*; Dubiosenreserve *f*
(JAP) 貸倒引当金、貸倒準備金
(RUS) РЕЗЕРВЫ ПО БЕЗНАДЁЖНЫМ
ДОЛГАМ

bad title
(CHIN) 失效产权
(FRE) titre non valide, (C) titre douteux
(GER) mangelhaftes Eigentumsrecht *n*,
fehlerhafter Besitzanspruch *m*
(JAP) 欠陥のある権原、不良権原
(RUS) НЕЗАКОННЫЙ ПРАВОВОЙ
ТИТУЛ

bail bond

(CHIN) 保释保证书

(FRE) cautionnement en garantie d'exécution, engagement signé par la caution

(GER) Bürgschaftsschein *m*, Kaution *f*

(JAP) 保釈金、保釈保証書

(RUS) ЗАЛОГ ЗА ЯВКУ ОТВЕТЧИКА В СУД

bailee

(CHIN) 委托人，受寄人

(FRE) dépositaire

(GER) Verwahrer *m*, Bürgschaftsempfänger *m*, treuhänderischer Besitzer *m* der Kaution *f*

(JAP) 受託者、受寄者

(RUS) ЗАВИСИМЫЙ ДЕРЖАТЕЛЬ; ДЕПОЗИТАРИЙ

bailment

(CHIN) 寄托，委托

(FRE) acte de dépôt, (C) titre douteux, contrat de depot

(GER) Hinterlegung *f*, Verwahrung *f*; treuhänderischer Besitz an beweglichen Sachen *f*; Kaution *f*

(JAP) 寄託、保釈、保釈金

(RUS) ЗАВИСИМОЕ ДЕРЖАНИЕ

bait and switch advertising

(CHIN) 诱销广告

(FRE) publicité appât, (C) dérive des ventes

(GER) Lockvogelwerbung *f*, Lockartikelwerbung *f*

(JAP) おとり広告、誇大広告

(RUS) СТРАТЕГИЯ РЕКЛАМИРОВАНИЯ ОДНОГО ТОВАРА ДЛЯ ПРИВЛЕЧЕНИЯ КЛИЕНТОВ, С ПОСЛЕДУЮЩЕЙ ЕГО ЗАМЕНОЙ ДРУГИМ ТОВАРОМ

bait and switch pricing

(CHIN) 诱销定价

(FRE) prix (n, m) mensonger, (C) tablissement des prix par dérive

(GER) Lockvogelpreisgebung *f*, Sonderangebote *npl*

(JAP) おとり商法の価格設定

(RUS) ЦЕНООБРАЗОВАНИЕ ДЛЯ «ЗАМАНИВАНИЯ» (см. выше)

balance

(CHIN) 差额，余数，平衡

(FRE) solde, balance

(GER) Saldo *m*, Kontostand *m*, Guthaben *n*

(JAP) 差額、差引残高

(RUS) БАЛАНС; РАВНОВЕСИЕ

balanced mutual fund

(CHIN) 平衡互助资金

(FRE) fonds commun de placement équilibré

(GER) ausgewogener Investmentfonds *m*, Stabilitätsfonds *m*, Mischfonds *m*

(JAP) 均衡投資信託

(RUS) СБАЛАНСИРОВАННЫЙ ИНВЕСТИЦИОННЫЙ ФОНД

balance of payments

(CHIN) 国际收支，国际收支差额

(FRE) balance des paiements, (C) balance des comptes

(GER) Zahlungsbilanz *f*

(JAP) 国債収支、支払残高

(RUS) ПЛАТЕЖНЫЙ БАЛАНС

balance of trade

(CHIN) 贸易平衡，贸易差额

(FRE) balance commerciale

(GER) Handelsbilanz *f*

(JAP) 貿易収支

(RUS) ТОРГОВЫЙ БАЛАНС

balance sheet

(CHIN) 资产负债表，决算表，平衡表

(FRE) bilan

(GER) Bilanz *f*, Bilanzrechnung *f*; Geschäftsbilanz *f*

(JAP) 貸借対照表、バランスシート

(RUS) БАЛАНС КОМПАНИИ

balance sheet reserve

(CHIN) 资产负债准备

(FRE) provision pour le bilan, (C) réserve pour le bilan

(GER) Bilanzrücklagen *fpl*

(JAP) 貸借対照表予備金

(RUS) РЕЗЕРВЫ ПО БАЛАНСУ КОМПАНИИ

balloon payment

(CHIN) 漂浮式付款

(FRE) paiement du solde d'un prêt
hypothécaire arrivé a échéance, versement
forfaitaire et final, règlement final, (C)
paiement gonflé
(GER) überdurchschnittlich hohe
Tilgungszahlung *f* bei Kreditfälligkeit *f*
(JAP) 最終残額一括払い、バルーン返済、
風船式支払
(RUS) БОЛЬШОЙ ОДНОРАЗОВЫЙ
ПЛАТЕЖ

ballot
(CHIN) 选票，投票
(FRE) scrutin, tour de scrutin, voter au
scrutiny
(GER) Wahlgang *m*, Stimmabgabe *f*;
Stimmzettel *m*; Urabstimmung *f*
(JAP) 投票用紙、投票、投票総数
(RUS) ГОЛОСОВАНИЕ, ИЗБИРАТЕЛЬНЫЙ
БЮЛЛЕТЕНЬ; ЖЕРЕБЬЕВКА

bandwidth
(CHIN) 带宽
(FRE) bande passante, largeur de bande
(GER) Bandbreite *f*
(JAP) （周波数）帯域幅
(RUS) ШИРОТА ДИАПАЗОНА

bank
(CHIN) 银行
(FRE) banque
(GER) Bank *f*, Geld- *n*, Kreditinstitut *n*
(JAP) 銀行、銀行に預ける
(RUS) БАНК

banker's acceptance
(CHIN) 银行承兑
(FRE) acceptation bancaire
(GER) Bankwechsel *m*, Bankakzept *n*
(JAP) 銀行引受手形
(RUS) БАНКОВСКИЙ АКЦЕПТ; ВЕКСЕЛЬ,
АКЦЕПТОВАННЫЙ БАНКОМ

bank holding company
(CHIN) 银行持股公司
(FRE) compagnie financière, (C) société
de ortefeuille bancaire
(GER) Bankholding *f*; Finanz-,
Bankgesellschaft *f*, Finanz-
Holdinggesellschaft *f*

(JAP) 銀行持株会社
(RUS) БАНК КАК ХОЛДИНГОВАЯ
КОМПАНИЯ

bank line
(CHIN) 银行授信额度
(FRE) ligne de crédit, ligne de écouvert
(GER) Kreditlinie *f* einer Bank *f*
(JAP) 銀行信用供与限度額、
銀行与信限度額
(RUS) КРЕДИТНАЯ ЛИНИЯ

bankruptcy
(CHIN) 破产，倒闭
(FRE) faillite
(GER) Konkurs *m*, Insolvenz *f*, Pleite *f*,
Bankrott *m*
(JAP) 倒産，破産，破綻
(RUS) БАНКРОТСТВО;
НЕСОСТОЯТЕЛЬНОСТЬ

bank trust department
(CHIN) 商业银行信托部门
(FRE) service bancaire de gestion financière
(GER) Vermögensverwaltungsstelle *f* einer
Bank, Treuhandabteilung *f*
(JAP) 銀行信託部門
(RUS) ТРАСТОВЫЙ ОТДЕЛ БАНКА

bar
(CHIN) 阻止，律师界
(FRE) barre
(GER) Rechtsanwaltskammer *f*
(JAP) 弁護士業、弁護士団、法曹（団）
阻却事由
(RUS) ЮРИДИЧЕСКАЯ КОЛЛЕГИЯ

bar code
(CHIN) 条形码
(FRE) code barre, (C) code à barres
(GER) Strich- *m*, Balken- *m*, Streifencode *m*
(JAP) バーコード、統一商品コード
(RUS) ШТРИХОВОЙ КОД

bar code label
(CHIN) 条码标号
(FRE) étiquette à code barre
(GER) Balkenetikett *n*, Strichcode- *n*,
Barcode-Etikett *n*

(JAP) バーコードラベル
(RUS) МЕТКА ШТРИХОВОГО КОДА

bargain and sale
(CHIN) 无保证交易
(FRE) vente parfaite
(GER) Grundstückskaufvertrag *m* ohne
Garantie *m*, (Grundstücksübertragung-
smethode)
(JAP) 大安売り、特売
(RUS) ПОТОРГОВАТЬСЯ И
ПРОДАТЬ

bargain hunter
(CHIN) 买便宜货的人
(FRE) chineur, investisseur à l'affut,
(C) chasseur d'aubaines
(GER) Käufer *m* auf der Suche nach
Billigangeboten *npl*, Schnäppchenjäger *m*
(JAP) 特売品あさり、
割安株狙いの投資家
(RUS) ИСКАТЕЛЬ ВЫГОДНЫХ
ПРИОБРЕТЕНИЙ ПО НИЗКОЙ ЦЕНЕ

bargaining agent
(CHIN) 谈判机构，交易代理人
(FRE) agent négociateur
(GER) ausschließlicher gewerkschaftlicher
Tarifverhandlungsführer *m*, Tarifpartner *m*
(JAP) 交渉代表権者
(RUS) ПРЕДСТАВИТЕЛЬ В ПЕРЕГОВОРАХ
ПО ЦЕНЕ

bargaining unit
(CHIN) 谈判单位，有独立交涉权的工会
单位
(FRE) groupement négociateur, unité de
négociation
(GER) gewerkschaftliche
Verhandlungsgruppe *f*,
Tarifpartei *f*
(JAP) 交渉単位、交渉団体
(RUS) ПРЕДМЕТ ТОРГА

barometer
(CHIN) 晴雨表，指标
(FRE) baromètre
(GER) Barometer *n*
(JAP) バロメーター、指標
(RUS) БАРОМЕТР; ПОКАЗАТЕЛЬ

barter
(CHIN) 物物交换，以货易货
(FRE) échange de marchandise, troc, (C)
échange-marchandises
(GER) Güter-,Waren-, Naturaltausch *m*,
Tauschhandel *m*; Bartergeschäft *n*
(JAP) 物々交換、バーター、
物々交換する
(RUS) БАРТЕР

base rate pay
(CHIN) 基本时薪
(FRE) taux de salaire de base
(GER) Grundlohn *m*, Grundlohnsatz *m*
(JAP) 基本給与
(RUS) ОПЛАТА ПО БАЗОВОЙ СТАВКЕ

base period
(CHIN) 基准期
(FRE) période de référence, période de
base, (C) époque de reference
(GER) Basis-, Bezugs-,Grund-, Vergleichs-,
Referenzzeitraum *m*
(JAP) 基準年次
(RUS) БАЗОВЫЙ СРОК

base rent
(CHIN) 基本租金
(FRE) loyer de base
(GER) Grundmiete *f*
(JAP) 基準賃貸料
(RUS) БАЗОВАЯ АРЕНДНАЯ СТАВКА

base-year analysis
(CHIN) 基年分析
(FRE) analyse d'après année de référence,
analyse d'après année de base
(GER) Vergleichs-, Bezugs-, Referenz-
Basisjahranalyse *f*
(JAP) 基準年次分析
(RUS) АНАЛИЗ ПО БАЗОВОМУ ГОДУ

basic input-output system (BIOS)
(CHIN) 基本输入-输出系统 （BIOS）
(FRE) système de gestion de base des
entrées sorties
(GER) Basiseingabe-Ausgabesystem *n*
(JAP) バイオス、
基本入出力システム

(RUS) БАЗОВАЯ СИСТЕМА ВВОДА-ВЫВОДА

basic limits of liability
(CHIN) 基本责任限额
(FRE) limites de base de la responsabilité
(GER) grundsätzliche
Haftungsbegrenzung *f*
(JAP) 基本的責任限度額
(RUS) БАЗОВЫЙ ПРЕДЕЛ
ТВЕТСТВЕННОСТИ

basic module
(CHIN) 基本模块
(FRE) module de base
(GER) Grundbaustein *m*
(JAP) 基本モジュール
(RUS) БАЗОВЫЙ МОДУЛЬ

basic operating system
(CHIN) 基本操作系统
(FRE) système d'exploitation de base
(GER) Grundbetriebssystem *n*
(JAP) 基本オペレーティングシステム
(RUS) БАЗОВАЯ ОПЕРАЦИОННАЯ
ИСТЕМА

basis
(CHIN) 基础，基数，标准
(FRE) base
(GER) Grundlage *f*; Basis *f* (Börse);
Bemessungsgrundlage *f*
(JAP) 基礎、基本、基準、原則
(RUS) БАЗИС

basis point
(CHIN) 基点
(FRE) point de base, point décimal, (C)
point d'assiette
(GER) Basispunkt *m*
(JAP) 基準ポイント（１％の１００分の１）
(RUS) ОТПРАВНОЙ ПУНКТ

batch application
(CHIN) 成批处理应用程序
(FRE) application par lots
(GER) Stapelanwendung *f*
(JAP) バッチアプリケーション

(RUS) СИСТЕМА ПАКЕТНОЙ ОБРАБОТКИ
ДАННЫХ

batch file
(CHIN) 批处理文件
(FRE) lot de traitement fichier batch
(GER) Stapeldatei *f*, Batch-Datei *f*
(JAP) バッチファイル
(RUS) (BAT) КОМАНДНЫЙ ФАЙЛ

batch processing
(CHIN) 分批加工，成批处理
(FRE) traitement par lots, (C) traitement par
lots
(GER) Stapelverarbeitung *f*, Stapelbetrieb
m, Batch-Verarbeitung *f*
(JAP) 一括処理（作業）
(RUS) ПАКЕТНАЯ ОБРАБОТКА

battery
(CHIN) 殴打，电池
(FRE) batterie, (C) pile
(GER) Körperverletzung *f*
(JAP) バッテリー、電池
(RUS) АККУМУЛЯТОРНАЯ БАТАРЕЯ

baud
(CHIN) 波特
(FRE) baud
(GER) Baud *n*, Baudrate *f*, Baudzahl *f*
(JAP) 変調速度
(RUS) БОД (единица скорости передачи)

baud rate
(CHIN) 波特率
(FRE) débit (en bauds)
(GER) Baudübertragungsrate *f*,
Baud-Zahl *f*,
(JAP) ボーレート
(RUS) СКОРОСТЬ ПЕРЕДАЧИ
ИНФОРМАЦИИ В БОДАХ

bear
(CHIN) 卖空，空头，负担
(FRE) baissier, à la baisse
(GER) Baissier *m*, Baissespekulant *m*
(JAP) 弱気筋、売方、売りたたく
(RUS) «МЕДВЕДЬ» (бирж.), СПЕКУЛЯНТ,
ИГРАЮЩИЙ НА ПОНИЖЕНИЕ

bearer bond
(CHIN) 无记名债券
(FRE) obligation au porteur
(GER) Inhaberschuldverschreibung *f*, -obligation *f*
(JAP) 無記名公債
(RUS) ОБЛИГАЦИЯ НА ПРЕДЪЯВИТЕЛЯ

bear hug
(CHIN) 熊抱式开价
(FRE) communiqué d'information, nnonçant une opa immédiate, (C) baiser de l'ours
(GER) Übernahmeangebot *n* ohne Vorverhandlungen *fpl*
(JAP) ベアハッグ、強く抱きしめること
(RUS) «МЕДВЕЖЬЕ ОБЪЯТИЕ», Т. Е. СТРАТЕГИЯ ПОГЛОЩЕНИЯ КОМПАНИИ ПУТЕМ ПРЕДЛОЖЕНИЯ ЗАВЫШЕННОЙ ЦЕНЫ НА ЕЁ АКЦИИ

bear market
(CHIN) 熊市，淡市
(FRE) marché baissier, (C) marché à la baisse
(GER) Baisse *f*, Baissemarkt *m*, Aktien- *f*, Effektenbaisse *f*, gedrückter Markt *m*
(JAP) 売相場、弱気市場
(RUS) «РЫНОК МЕДВЕДЕЙ» (бирж.)ДЛИТЕЛЬНЫЙ ПЕРИОД ПАДЕНИЯ ЦЕН НА БИРЖЕ

bear raid
(CHIN) 卖空浪潮
(FRE) attaque du découvert, attaque des baissiers
(GER) Baissemanöver *n*; Leerverkäufe *mpl* der Baissespekulation *f*
(JAP) 弱気筋の市場攪乱
(RUS) «НАЛЕТ МЕДВЕДЕЙ» (бирж.), Т. Е. НЕЛЕГАЛЬНАЯ ПОПЫТКА ИНВЕСТОРОВ МАНИПУЛИРОВАТЬ ЦЕНЫ АКЦИЙ В СТОРОНУ ИХ ПОНИЖЕНИЯ

before-tax cash flow
(CHIN) 税前现金流量
(FRE) flux de trésorerie avant impôts, cash flow avant impôts, (C) flux de l'encaisse en liquidités
(GER) Cashflow *m* vor Steuern *fpl*

(RUS) ПОТОК СРЕДСТВ ДО УПЛАТЫ НАЛОГОВ

bellwether
(CHIN) 指针性债券
(FRE) indicateur, précurseur (C) valeur indice
(GER) Leithammel
(JAP) 先導者、先行指標、先導指数
(RUS) ЦЕННЫЕ БУМАГИ, СЛУЖАЩИЕ ИНДИКАТОРАМИ СОСТОЯНИЯ РЫНКА

below par
(CHIN) 低于票面价值
(FRE) en dessous du pair, au-dessous de la parité
(GER) unter pari, unter Nennwert
(JAP) 額面以下で、割り引きで、
(RUS) НИЖЕ НОМИНАЛЬНОЙ СТОИМОСТИ

benchmark
(CHIN) 水准基点，基准
(FRE) test d'évaluation, mise au banc d'essai, phare, (C) point de référence, (C) chiffre repère
(GER) Benchmark *n*, Bezugsmarke *f*, -punkt *m*, Richt- *m*, Bezugswert *m*; Orientierungs- *m*, Vergleichswert *m*
(JAP) ベンチマーク、規準点
(RUS) ВЕХА; ОРИЕНТИР; БАЗА

beneficial interest
(CHIN) 受益权，受益人利益
(FRE) droit bénéficiaire, droit de participation bénéficiaire, droit à titre bénéficiaire (C) droit d'usufruit
(GER) Nießbrauch *m*; materieller Eigentumsanspruch *m* Treuhandbegünstigung *f*; Versicherungsanspruch *m*
(JAP) 受益的権利、（信託の）受益権 ВЫГОДА, ПОЛУЧАЕМАЯ БЕНЕФИЦИАРОМ

beneficial owner
(CHIN) 受益所有人
(FRE) usufruitier, propriétaire reel
(GER) materieller Rechtsinhaber, Nießbraucher, verfügungsberechtigter

Eigentümer *m*, Nutzungsberechtigter *m*;
Nutznießer *m*
(JAP) 受益株主、使用収益権者
(RUS) ПОДЛИННЫЙ ВЛАДЕЛЕЦ

beneficiary
(CHIN) 受益人，受款人
(FRE) bénéficiaire, ayant droit
(GER) Begünstigter *m*, Leistungsempfänger
m, Bezugsberechtigter *m*; Nutznießer *m*;
Anspruchsberechtigter *m*
(JAP) 受益者、（保険金などの）受取人
(RUS) БЕНЕФИЦИАРИЙ; ПОЛУЧАТЕЛЬ

benefit
(CHIN) 效益，利润，利益，津贴
(FRE) avantage, bénéfice prestation,
allocation
(GER) Nutzen *m*, Gewinn *m*, Leistung *f*;
Beihilfe *f*, Zuschuss *m*;
Versorgungsleistung *f*
(JAP) 給付金、年金
(RUS) ВЫГОДА; ЛЬГОТА; ПОСОБИЕ;
ПРИВИЛЕГИЯ

benefit-based pension plan
(CHIN) 公司担保的养老金计划
(FRE) régime de retraite basé sur les
avantages, plan de retraite basé sur
l'allocation, (C) régime de retraite à
prestations déterminées
(GER) auf Leistungen *fpl* basierender
Rentenplan *m*, leistungsorientierte
Altersversorgung *f*
(JAP) 手当に基ずく年金制度
(RUS) ПЕНСИОННЫЙ ПЛАН НА ОСНОВЕ
ЛЬГОТНЫХ ВЫПЛАТ

benefits, fringe
(CHIN) 附加利益，额外津贴
(FRE) avantages, (C) avantages sociaux,
(C) charges sociales
(GER) Lohnnebenleistungen *fpl*,
Lohnzuschläge *mpl*; Neben- *fpl*,
Zusatzleistungen *fpl*
(JAP) 付加給付、福利厚生給付
(RUS) ДОПОЛНИТЕЛЬНЫЕ ВЫПЛАТЫ,
ЛЬГОТЫ

benefit principle
(CHIN) 利益原则

(FRE) principe des avantages
(GER) Nutzenprinzip *n*; Leistungsprinzip *n*
(JAP) 利益原則、応益原則
(RUS) ПРИНЦИП , СОГЛАСНО КОТОРОГО
ТЕ, КТО ПОЛУЧАЮТ ФЕДЕРАЛЬНЫЕ
ЛЬГОТУ ФИНАНСИРУЕМЫЕ НАЛОГАМИ,
ТОЖЕ ДОЛЖНЫ ПЛАТИТЬ НАЛОГИ

bequeath
(CHIN) 遗赠，遗产
(FRE) léguer, donner par testament
(GER) (testamentarisch) vermachen,
hinterlassen, vererben *v*
(JAP) 遺贈する、遺譲する
(RUS) ЗАВЕЩАТЬ (ИМУЩЕСТВО)

bequest
(CHIN) 遗产，遗物
(FRE) legs
(GER) Vermächtnis *n*, Erbe *n*, Legat *n*
(JAP) 遺贈、遺産
(RUS) ЗАВЕЩАТЕЛЬНЫЙ ОТКАЗ
(ИМУЩЕСТВА)

best's rating
(CHIN) 最佳评级
(FRE) meilleure tarification, meilleurs
(GER) Best-Einstufung *f*, Best-Rating *n*,
Best-Bewertung *f*
(JAP) 格付け会社ベストによる評価
(RUS) РЕЙТИНГ ФИНАНСОВОГО
СОСТОЯНИЯ СТРАХОВЫХ КОМПАНИЙ

beta coefficient
(CHIN) 贝塔系数
(FRE) coefficient beta
(GER) Beta-Koeffizient *m*
(JAP) ベータ係数
(RUS) КОЭФФИЦИЕНТ «БЕТА» (показатель
неустойчивости цен акций)

betterment
(CHIN) 固定资产改良
(FRE) amélioration, accroissement,
développement
(GER) Wertzuwachs *m*, -steigerung *f*;
Qualitätsverbesserung *f*
(JAP) 改良、（不動産の）価格騰貴
(RUS) УЛУЧШЕНИЕ;
ОВЕРШЕНСТВОВАНИЕ

biannual

(CHIN) 一年两次的，半年一次的

(FRE) semi-annuel, (C) semestriel

(GER) halbjährlich *adj*

(JAP) 半期の、年 2 回の

(RUS) ПРОИСХОДЯЩИЙ ДВА РАЗА В ГОД

bid and asked

(CHIN) 喊价，要价

(FRE) cours d'achat et de vente, (C) l'offre et la demande

(GER) Geld *n* und Brief *m*

(JAP) 買呼値と売呼値

(RUS) РАЗНОСТЬ МЕЖДУ ЦЕНАМИ ПРОДАВЦА И ПОКУПАТЕЛЯ

bid bond

(CHIN) 投标押金

(FRE) garantie de soumission, cautionnement de l'offre

(GER) Bietungs- *f*, Aussschreibungsgarantie *f*, Submissionsgarantie *f*

(JAP) 入札保証状

(RUS) ГАРАНТИЯ ПРЕДЛОЖЕНИЯ

bidding up

(CHIN) 哄抬标价

(FRE) offre à la hausse, (C) surenchère

(GER) künstliches Hochbieten *n*

(JAP) せり上げ

НАБАВИТЬ ЦЕНУ

biennial

(CHIN) 两年一次的

(FRE) bisannuel, (C) biennal

(GER) alle zwei Jahre, zweijährlich *adj*

(JAP) 隔年の、 2 年に 1 回の、 2 年ごとの

(RUS) ПРОИСХОДЯЩИЙ РАЗ В ДВА ГОДА

big board

(CHIN) 纽约证券交易所

(FRE) bourse de New York

(GER) New York Stock Exchange (NYSE), New Yorker Börse *f*

(JAP) ニューヨーク証券取引所

(RUS) НЬЮ-ЙОРКСКАЯ ФОНДОВАЯ БИРЖА («БОЛЬШОЕ ТАБЛО»)

big-ticket items

(CHIN) 高价商品

(FRE) biens a prix unitaire élevé,

(C) produits coûteux

(GER) teure Konsumgüter *npl*

(JAP) 高価な商品

(RUS) ДОРОГОЙ ПОТРЕБИТЕЛЬСКИЙ ТОВАР (длительного пользования)

bilateral contact

(CHIN) 双边合约

(FRE) contact bilateral

(GER) bilateraler Vertrag *m*

(RUS) ДВУСТОРОННИЙ КОНТАКТ

bilateral mistake

(CHIN) 双边错失

(FRE) erreur bilatérale

(GER) bilateraler Fehler *m*

(JAP) 双方過失、当事者双方による錯誤

(RUS) ОБОЮДНАЯ ОШИБКА

bill

(CHIN) 汇票，票据，账单，钞票，证券

(FRE) facture

(GER) Frachtbrief *m*; Rechnung *f*; Banknote *f*; Urkunde *f*, Dokument *n*; Wechsel *m*, Quittung *f*; Gesetzesvorlage *f*; -entwurf *m*, Regierungsvorlage *f*

(JAP) 手形、勘定書、請求書

(RUS) СЧЕТ; НАКЛАДНАЯ; ПЕРЕВОДНОЙ ВЕКСЕЛЬ (ТРАТТА); БАНКНОТА; ЗАКОНОПРОЕКТ

billing cycle

(CHIN) 开单周期

(FRE) cycle de facturation

(GER) Abrechnungszeitraum *m*, -periode *f*

(JAP) 支払請求周期、 請求書作成周期

(RUS) ПЕРИОДИЧНОСТЬ ВЫСТАВЛЕНИЯ СЧЕТОВ

bill of exchange

(CHIN) 汇票

(FRE) effet de change, lettre de change

(GER) Wechsel *m*

(JAP) （外国）為替手形、輸出手形

(RUS) ПЕРЕВОДНОЙ ВЕКСЕЛЬ, ТРАТТА

bill of lading
(CHIN) 提单，提货单
(FRE) connaissement
(GER) Konnossement *n*
(JAP) 船荷証券
(RUS) КОНОСАМЕНТ

binder
(CHIN) 承保协议，暂保单
(FRE) classeur
(GER) Deckungszusage *f*, vorläufige Versicherungspolice *f*; vorläufiger Vertrag *m*, Vorverkaufsvertrag *m*
(JAP) 仮契約、仮保険証、手付金
(RUS) СКОРОСШИВАТЕЛЬ; ВРЕМЕННЫЙ СТРАХОВОЙ ДОКУМЕНТ

bit error rate
(CHIN) 误码率
(FRE) taux d'erreurs sur les bits
(GER) Bitfehlerrate *f*
(JAP) ビット誤り率
(RUS) ЧАСТОТА ПОЯВЛЕНИЯ ОШИБОК В БИТ/СЕК

bit map
(CHIN) 位图 ；位映象
(FRE) mode point
(GER) Bitmap *f*
(JAP) ビットマップ
(RUS) 1) БИТОВЫЙ МАССИВ, ПОРАЗРЯДНОЕ ПРЕДСТАВЛЕНИЕ; РАСТР ИЗОБРАЖЕНИЯ) СООТВЕТСТВУЕТ РАЗРЯД ПАМЯТИ
2) БУФЕР ИЗОБРАЖЕНИЯ

black list
(CHIN) 黑名单
(FRE) liste noire
(GER) schwarze Liste *f*, Sperrliste *f*
(JAP) ブラックリスト
(RUS) «ЧЕРНЫЙ» СПИСОК

black market
(CHIN) 黑市
(FRE) marché noir
(GER) Schwarzer Markt *m*, Schwarzhandel *m*,
(JAP) 闇市場、闇取引
(RUS) «ЧЕРНЫЙ» РЫНОК

blank cell
(CHIN) 空白单元格
(FRE) cellule vide
(GER) Leerzelle *f*
(JAP) ブランクセル、空白セル
(RUS) ПУСТАЯ ЯЧЕЙКА

blanket contract
(CHIN) 总合同
(FRE) contrat de couverture, (C) convention de branche
(GER) Generalvertrag *m*; Pauschalvertrag *m*
(JAP) 一括契約、包括的契約
(RUS) АККОРДНОЕ СОГЛАШЕНИЕ

blanket insurance
(CHIN) 统括保险
(FRE) police globale, (C) garantie globale
(GER) Pauschalversicherung *f*
(JAP) 総合保険、包括保険
(RUS) ГРУППОВОЕ СТРАХОВАНИЕ

blanket mortgage
(CHIN) 统括抵押
(FRE) hypothèque générale, (C) hypothèque englobante
(GER) General- *f*, Globalhypothek *f*
(JAP) 一括担保、包括的抵当
(RUS) СОВОКУПНАЯ ЗАКЛАДНАЯ

blanket recommendation
(CHIN) 统括建议
(FRE) recommandation générale
(GER) General- *f*, Pauschalempfehlung *f*
(JAP) 全面的推薦
(RUS) ОБЩАЯ РЕКОМЕНДАЦИЯ (БРОКЕРА) (бирж.)

bleed
(CHIN) 榨取
(FRE) à fond perdu
(GER) schröpfen, zur Ader lassen *v*
(JAP) 赤字を出す
(RUS) ОБОБРАТЬ; ВЫКАЧАТЬ ДЕНЬГИ

blended rate
(CHIN) 综合费率
(FRE) taux mixte, (C) taux moyen, (C) taux moyen pondéré

(GER) Misch(zins)satz *m*
(JAP) 混合料率
(RUS) СМЕШАННАЯ СТАВКА

blended value
(CHIN) 平均价值
valeur mixte, (C) valeur moyenne
(GER) Gesamtnutzen *m*
(JAP) 混合価額
(RUS) СМЕШАННАЯ СТОИМОСТЬ

blighted area
(CHIN) 衰落区
(FRE) quartier insalubre
(GER) Sanierungsgebiet *n*, verwahrloster Stadtteil *n*
(JAP) 胴枯れ地帯、荒廃地区
(RUS) ПОРАЖЕННАЯ ЗОНА

blind pool
(CHIN) 委任同盟
(FRE) fonds d'investissement dans une start-up sans droit de regard des investisseurs, (C) fonds d'investissement à fin indéterminée
(GER) Blindpool *m*, Blindpool-Fonds *m*
(JAP) 安全運用委任型資金連合委任企業同盟
(RUS) ТОВАРИЩЕСТВО С ОГРАНИЧЕННОЙ ОТВЕТСТВЕННОСТЬЮ, НЕ РАСКРЫВАЮЩЕЕ ЗАРАНИЕ ОБЪЕКТ ИНВЕСТИЦИЙ

blind trust
(CHIN) 保密委托，盲目信托
(FRE) fiducie sans droit de regard, blind trust
(GER) Blind Trust *m*, (US-Modell der Treuhandverwaltung, bei dem der Besitzer keinen Einfluss nehmen kann)
(JAP) 白紙委任信託
(RUS) «СЛЕПОЙ» ТРАСТ

blister packaging
(CHIN) 发泡（塑料）包装，薄膜包装
(FRE) emballage-bulle, (C) plaquette, (C) emballage-coque
(GER) Blisterverpackung *f*
(JAP) ブリスター包装
(RUS) БЛИСТЕРНАЯ УПАКОВКА

block
(CHIN) 巨额证券，大宗股票
(FRE) bloc
(GER) Block *m*; (Wertpapier)paket *n*
(JAP) ブロック（株券取引単位）
(RUS) БЛОК; ПАКЕТ; КВАРТАЛ; ЛОКИРОВАТЬ

blockbuster
(CHIN) 畅销书/影片
(FRE) superproduction
(GER) Marktrenner *m*, Kassenschlager *m*, Knüller *m*
(JAP) 圧倒的な影響力を与える人・物、悪徳不動産業者、立ち退かせ屋
(RUS) ПРОГРАММА, ПРЕДМЕТ, ФИЛЬМ И Т. П. ИМЕЮЩИЙ НЕОЖИДАННО ВЫСОКИЙ УСПЕХ

blockbusting
(CHIN) 房屋唉卖生意
(FRE) « blockbusting », (C) vente sous pression à une minorité ethnique
(GER) heiß, begehrt *adj*
(JAP) ブロックバスティング、ブロック破壊商法、不動産屋の悪徳商法
(RUS) ОСНОВАННАЯ НА РАССОВОЙ ДИСКРИМИНАЦИИ НЕЛЕГАЛЬНАЯ ТАКТИКА СНИЖЕНИЯ ЦЕН НА ДОМА В ОПРЕДЕЛЁННОМ РАЙОНЕ ПУТЁМ ПОСЕЛЕНИЯ ТАМ ПРЕДСТАВИТЕЛЕЙ "НЕЖЕЛАТЕЛЬНОЙ" НАЦИОНАЛЬНОСТИ

block policy
(CHIN) 成组货保单
(FRE) police multirisque, (C) police tous risques
(GER) Pauschalsachversicherung *f*; Generalpolice *f*
(JAP) 包括保険証券、予定保険証書
(RUS) БЛОК-ПОЛИС

block sampling
(CHIN) 区域采样
(FRE) échantillonnage (n, m) par bloc
(GER) Blockstichprobennahme *f*
(JAP) ブロックのサンプリング、一区画抜き取り見本
(RUS) БЛОКОВАЯ ВЫБОРКА

blowout

(CHIN) 贱价甩卖，销售一空

(FRE) liquidation

(GER) Blowout *m*, Supersonderangebot *n*

(JAP) 新規発行債券の即完売、どんちゃん騒ぎ度を超す行為

(RUS) БЫСТРАЯ ПРОДАЖА (АКЦИЙ НОВОГО ВЫПУСКА)

blue-chip stock

(CHIN) 蓝筹码股票，热门股票

(FRE) action de premier ordre, valeur de premier ordre, valeur de père de famille

(GER) Blue-Chip-Aktie *f*, erstklassiges Wertpapier *n*; Spitzenwert *m*, -papier *n*

(JAP) 花形株

(RUS) АКЦИИ НАИБОЛЕЕ ИЗВЕСТНЫХ КРУПНЫХ КОМПАНИЙ, ИМЕЮЩИХ СТАБИЛЬНЫЙ РОСТ ПРИБЫЛИ И ВЫПЛАТЫ ДИВИДЕНТОВ

blue collar

(CHIN) 蓝领，蓝领工人

(FRE) col bleu, ouvrier

(GER) Arbeiter *m*

(JAP) ブルーカラー、肉体労働者

(RUS) "СИНИЙ ВОРОТНИЧОК", РАБОЧИЙ

blue laws

(CHIN) 蓝法

(FRE) blue laws (lois sur l'observation du repos dominical), (C) lois bleues

(GER) Blue Laws, (Gesctze zu Sonntagsaktivitäten)

(JAP) 清教徒的厳法、日曜厳守法

(RUS) ОТМЕНЁННЫЕ ЗАКОНЫ, РЕГУЛИРОВАВШИЕ РАЗРЕШЕННУЮ ДЕЯТЕЛЬНОСТЬ ПО ВОСКРЕСЕНЬЯМ

blueprint

(CHIN) 蓝图

(FRE) minute, ferro, schéma, directeur, (C) modèle

(GER) Blaupause *f*; Entwurf *m;* Plan *m;* Musterkopie *f*

(JAP) 青写真、詳細な計画

(RUS) ПЛАН; ПРОЕКТ; ПРОГРАММА

blue-sky law

(CHIN) 蓝天法，股票发行控制法

(FRE) reglementation administrative régissant la négociation des valeurs mobilières, (C) loi sur l'émission des valeurs mobilières

(GER) Blue-Sky Laws *pl*, (US-Gesetzgebung gegen Missbrauch im Wertpapierhandel zum Schutz der Öffentlichkeit)

(JAP) ブルースカイ法、青空法

(RUS) ЗАКОНЫ «ГОЛУБОГО НЕБА» ДЛЯ ЗАЩИТЫ ОТ МОШЕННИЧЕСТВА С ЦЕННЫМИ БУМАГАМИ

board of directors

(CHIN) 董事会，理事会

(FRE) conseil d'administration

(GER) Verwaltungsrat *m*, Vorstand *m;* Börsenvorstand *m*

(JAP) 取締役会、役員会、理事会

(RUS) СОВЕТ (КОЛЛЕГИЯ) ДИРЕКТОРОВ; ПРАВЛЕНИЕ

board of equalization

(CHIN) 税率调查委员会

(FRE) board of equalization

(GER) Behörde *f* zur Vereinheitlichung *f* örtlicher Steuersätze *mpl*

(JAP) 平等化委員会

(RUS) МЕСТНЫЙ ОРГАН ПО РАВНОМУ НАЛОГООБЛОЖЕНИЮ НЕДВИЖИМОСТИ

boardroom

(CHIN) 证券交易人经纪行情室，董事会会议室

(FRE) salle du conseil, chambre du conseil, salle de réunion, (C) salle du conseil d'administration

(GER) Vorstandszimmer *n*; Chefetage *f*

(JAP) 役員会議室、理事会議室、立会所

(RUS) ЗАЛ ЗАСЕДАНИЙ ПРАВЛЕНИЯ

boilerplate

(CHIN) 标准协议，公式化语言

(FRE) paragraphe passe-partout, (C) passe-partout

(GER) vorformulierter Satz *m*; umständliche Juristensprache *f*

(JAP) 共通記事、決まり文句、共通条項

(RUS) СТАНДАРТНЫЕ ФОРМУЛИРОВКИ В ДОКУМЕНТАХ; СТАНДАРТНЫЕ СОГЛАШЕНИЯ

bona fide

(CHIN) 真正的，真诚的

(FRE) de bonne foi

(GER) in gutem Glauben, ohne Missbrauchsabsicht redlich, gutgläubig *adj*

(JAP) 真実に（の）、真正に（の）

(RUS) ДОБРОСОВЕСТНО

bona fide purchaser

(CHIN) 真诚的买家

(FRE) acheteur de bonne foi

(GER) gutgläubiger Erwerber *m*

(JAP) 善意の購買者

(RUS) ПОДЛИННЫЙ ПОКУПАТЕЛЬ

bond

(CHIN) 债券，公债，证券，保证金

(FRE) obligation

(GER) Schuldverschreibung *f*, Obligation *f*; Bürgschaft *f*, Schuldschein *m*; Anleihe *f*; Kaution *f*; Rentenfonds-Anteil *m*, Rentenfonds-Titel *m*

(JAP) 債券、公債証書、債務証書

(RUS) ОБЛИГАЦИЯ; ДОЛГОВОЕ ОБЯЗАТЕЛЬСТВО

bond broker

(CHIN) 债券经纪人

(FRE) courtier en obligation/valeur

(GER) Makler *m* für festverzinsliche Wertpapiere *npl*

(JAP) 債券ブローカー

(RUS) ОБЛИГАЦИОННЫЙ БРОКЕР

bond discount

(CHIN) 债券折价

(FRE) décote de l'obligation, (C) escompte d'émission d'obligations

(GER) Emissionsdisagio *n*, Anleiheabschlag *m*

(JAP) 債券割引、社債発行差金

(RUS) ПРОДАЖА ОБЛИГАЦИЙ ПО ЦЕНЕ НИЖЕ НОМИНАЛА

bonded debt

(CHIN) 债券负债，公债借款

(FRE) dette obligataire, (C) emprunt obligataire

(GER) Anleihe- *f*, Obligationsschuld *f*;

Anleiheverbindlichkeiten *fpl*, -verschuldung *f*

(JAP) 公債発行（による）借入金、社債発行（による）借入金

(RUS) ОБЛИГАЦИОННАЯ ЗАДОЛЖЕННОСТЬ КОМПАНИИ ИЛИ ГОСУДАРСТВА

bonded goods

(CHIN) 保税货物

(FRE) marchandises entreposées, marchandises en douane

(GER) Zolllagergut *n*, Waren *fpl* unter Zollverschluss *m*, Zollverschlussware *f*

(JAP) 保税貨物、保税品

(RUS) НАХОДЯЩИЕСЯ В ЗАЛОГЕ НА ТАМОЖЕННОМ СКЛАДЕ ТОВАРЫ

bond premium

(CHIN) 债券溢价

(FRE) prime pour titre de cautionnement, (C) prime d'émission d'obligations

(GER) Anleiheaufschlag *m*, -agio *n*, Schuldverschreibungsagio *n*

(JAP) 社債発行差金、社債発行プレミアム

(RUS) ПРЕВЫШЕНИЕ ЦЕНЫ ОБЛИГАЦИЙ НАД НОМИНАЛОМ

bond rating

(CHIN) 债券评级

(FRE) cotation de l'obligation, (C) notation des obligations

(GER) Rating *n*, Rangskala *f*, Ordinalskala *f*; Anleihe- *f*, Schuldverschreibungsbewertung *f*

公社債の格付け

(RUS) РЕЙТИНГ ОБЛИГАЦИИ

book

(CHIN) 账簿，记录，簿记

(FRE) registre, livre

(GER) bestellen; buchen, reservieren (Reise); verbuchen (Transaktion) *v*; (Kredit)portefeuille einer Bank *f*; Bestände *mpl* eines Wertpapier- *m*, Devisen- *m*, Options- *m*, Swap-Händlers *m*

(JAP) 会計簿、帳簿

(RUS) КНИГА; БУХГАЛТЕРСКАЯ КНИГА

book-entry securities

(CHIN) 记账债券

(FRE) titres relevés, titres financiers informatisés

(GER) buchmäßig verwaltete Wertpapiere *npl*; Schuldbuchforderungen *fpl*; stückelose Wertpapiere *npl*

(JAP) 帳簿記入証券

(RUS) ЦЕННЫЕ БУМАГИ ТОЛЬКО В ФОРМЕ БУХГ. ЗАПИСЕЙ

book inventory

(CHIN) 账面盘存

(FRE) stock comptable

(GER) Buchinventar *n*, -bestand *m*

(JAP) 帳簿棚卸

(RUS) ПЕРЕЧЕНЬ АКТИВОВ ПО ГРОССБУХУ

bookkeeper

(CHIN) 簿记员，账房

(FRE) aide-comptable

(GER) Buchhalter *m*, -führer *m*, Rechnungsführer *m*

(JAP) 簿記係、記帳係

(RUS) БУХГАЛТЕР; УЧЕТЧИК

bookmark

(CHIN) 书签

(FRE) signet

(GER) Lesezeichen *n*,

(JAP) ブックマーク、しおり

(RUS) ЗАКЛАДКА; В СИСТЕМАХ ПОДГОТОВКИ ТЕКСТОВ - СРЕДСТВО, ПОЗВОЛЯЮЩЕЕ ОТМЕТИТЬ ПОЗИЦИЮ В ТЕКСТЕ И ВЕРНУТЬСЯ К НЕЙ ВПОСЛЕДСТВИИ

book value

(CHIN) 账面价值

(FRE) valeur comptable, (C) valeur 'inventaire

(GER) Buch- *m*, Rest- *m*; Papierwert *m*, Bilanzkurs *m* (Aktie)

(JAP) 帳簿価額

(RUS) БАЛАНСОВАЯ СТОИМОСТЬ ПО БУХГ. КНИГАМ

boondoggle

(CHIN) 无价值的事

(FRE) projet aussi futile que coûteux,

(C) projet inutile

(GER) wertloses Programm *n*

(JAP) 役に立たない仕事、無用な仕事をする

(RUS) НАДУМАННАЯ, БЕСПОЛЕЗНАЯ ДЕЯТЕЛЬНОСТЬ (иногда с нечестными намерениями)

boot

(CHIN) 补价，附加利益，引导程序；启动，自举

(FRE) initialiser, amorcer, initialisation, (C) complément d'échange

(GER) Entlassung *f* (Arbeit); zusätzliche Leistung *f*; urladen, booten, starten *v*

(JAP) 利益；ブートする、コンピューターを起動する、システムを立ち上げる (computer)

(RUS) ДЕНЬГИ ИЛИ СОБСТВЕННОСТЬ, НЕ ВКЛЮЧАЕМЫЕ В ОПРЕДЕЛЕНИЕ ИСКЛЮЧЕНИЙ ИЗ НАЛОГООБЛОЖЕНИЯ; ВКЛЮЧИТЬ КОМПЬЮТЕР; (RUS) 1) НАЧАЛЬНАЯ ЗАГРУЗКА; 2) ЗАГРУЖАТЬ(СЯ), ЗАПУСКАТЬ(СЯ

boot record

(CHIN) 引导记录

(FRE) enregistrement d'initialisation

(GER) Startprogramm *n*

(JAP) 起動記録、ブート記録

(RUS) ПРОТОКОЛ ЗАГРУЗКИ

borrowed reserve

(CHIN) 借入准备金

(FRE) réserve empruntée

(GER) aufgenommene Reserve *n*; gclichene Währungsreserve *f*

(JAP) 借入準備金

(RUS) ЗАИМСТВОВАННЫЕФОНДЫ (банк.)

borrowing power of securities

(CHIN) 证券借入能力

(FRE) pouvoir d'emprunt des valeurs, (C) capacité d'emprunt des valeurs

(GER) Beleihungswert *m* von Wertpapieren *npl*

(JAP) 証券借入能力

(RUS) ЗАЕМНАЯ СИЛА ЦЕННЫХ БУМАГ

bottom

(CHIN) 底价，谷底，最低市场价
(FRE) du bas, en bas, de fond, (C) creux
(GER) Tiefstand *m*, -punkt *m*;
Konjunkturtief *n*, Talsohle *f* (Wirtschaft)
(JAP) 底、景気の谷底、市況の底値
(RUS) НИЖНИЙ ПРЕДЕЛ

bottom fisher

(CHIN) 探底投资者
(FRE) bottom fisher, investisseur à la
recherche de titres à faible multiple cours-
bénéfices, (C) chasseur d'aubaines
(GER) Schnäppchenjäger *m*
(JAP) 底値株専門に狙う投資家、
ボトムフィッシャー
(RUS) ИНВЕСТОР, ИЩУЩИЙ ЦЕННЫЕ
БУМАГИ С ЦЕНАМИ, ДОСТИГШИМИ
«ДНА»

bottom line

(CHIN) 净损益
(FRE) solde final, résultat financier,
(C) résultat net, (C) bénéfices nets après
impost
(GER) Endergebnis *n*; Ergebnis *n* unterm
Strich *m*
(JAP) 結論、本音、純損益
(RUS) КОНЕЧНЫЙ РЕЗУЛЬТАТ; ЧИСТЫЙ
ДОХОД ИЛИ УБЫТОК ПОСЛЕ УПЛАТЫ
НАЛОГОВ (бухг.)

Boulewarism

(CHIN) 布里瓦主义
(FRE) boulewarisme
(GER) Boulewarismus *m*, (US-Anti-
Gewerkschaftsbewegung der 1950er und
1960er Jahre)
(JAP) ブーレワリズム
　（反差別法に関する）
(RUS) НЕЛЕГАЛЬНАЯ ТАКТИКА
ВЕДЕНИЯ ПЕРЕГОВОРОВ ПО ТРУДОВЫМ
СОГЛАШЕНИЯМ

boycott

(CHIN) 抵制
(FRE) boycottage, boycott
(GER) Boykott *m*
(JAP) ボイコット、不買同盟
(RUS) БОЙКОТ

bracket creep

(CHIN) 收入等级上升
(FRE) passage a la tranche d'imposition
supérieure, (C) élasticité de la tranche
d'imposition
(GER) schleichende Steuerprogression *f*
(RUS) ПЕРЕХОД В БОЛЕЕ ВЫСОКИЙ
НАЛОГОВЫЙ РАЗРЯД В РЕЗУЛЬТАТЕ
ИНФЛЯЦИИ

brainstorming

(CHIN) 智囊
(FRE) brainstorming, remue-méninges
(GER) Brainstorming *n*,
Gedankenaustausch *m*
(JAP) ブレーンストーミング
(RUS) "МОЗГОВАЯ АТАКА",
КОЛЛЕКТИВНОЕ ОБСУЖДЕНИЕ
ПРОБЛЕМЫ

branch office manager

(CHIN) 分支机构经理
(FRE) directeur d'agence, (C) directeur de
succursale, (C) gérant de succusale
(GER) Zweigstellenleiter *m*; Filialleiter *m*
(JAP) 支店長
(RUS) РУКОВОДИТЕЛЬ ФИЛИАЛА

brand

(CHIN) 商标，品牌
(FRE) marque
(GER) Markenartikel *m*; Handelsname *m*,
Marke *f*
(JAP) 銘柄、商標、品種
(RUS) ТОВАРНАЯ МАРКА

brand association

(CHIN) 品牌联系
(FRE) association de marque
(GER) Markengemeinschaft *f*
(JAP) ブランド連想、ブランド関連
(RUS) АССОЦИАТИВНОЕ ВОСПРИЯТИЕ
ПОТРЕБИТЕЛЕМ ТОВАРНОЙ МАРКИ

brand development

(CHIN) 品牌开发
(FRE) développement de
marque
(GER) Markenentwicklung *f*
(JAP) 銘柄開発

(RUS) РАЗВИТИЕ УЗНАВАЕМОСТИ, ПРИВЛЕКАТЕЛЬНОСТИ ТОВАРНОЙ МАРКИ

brand development index (BDI)
(CHIN) 品牌开发指数
(FRE) indice du développement de la marque
(GER) Marken(waren)konsumindex *m*
(JAP) 銘柄開発指数
(RUS) ПОКАЗАТЕЛЬ РАЗВИТИЯ ТОВАРНОЙ МАРКИ

brand extension
(CHIN) 品牌扩展
(FRE) extension de la marque
(GER) Markenerweiterung *f*
(JAP) JAP) ブランド拡充
(RUS) РАСШИРЕНИЕ АССОРТИМЕНТА ТОВАРНОЙ МАРКИ

brand image
(CHIN) 品牌形象
(FRE) image de marque
(GER) Markenprofil *n*, Markenimage *n*
(JAP) 商標イメージ、ブランドイメージ
(RUS) «ИМИДЖ» ТОВАРНОЙ МАРКИ

brand loyalty
(CHIN) 品牌忠诚度
(FRE) fidélité à la marque
(GER) Markentreue *f*
(JAP) ブランド名使用料
(RUS) ПРИВЕРЖЕННОСТЬ ТОВАРНОЙ МАРКЕ

brand manager
(CHIN) 品牌营销经理
(FRE) responsable du développement de la marque
(GER) Produktmanager *m*, Produktleiter *m*, Markenbetreuer *m*
(JAP) ブランドマネージャー
(RUS) ОТВЕТСТВЕННЫЙ ЗА ТОВАРНУЮ МАРКУ

brand name
(CHIN) 商标名称
(FRE) nom de marque

(GER) Marken- *m*, Produktname *m*, Handelsbezeichnung *f*
(JAP) 商標名、有名ブランド
(RUS) ФИРМЕННОЕ НАЗВАНИЕ

brand potential index (BPI)
(CHIN) 品牌潜力指数 (BPI)
(FRE) indice du potentiel de la marque
(GER) Markenpotenzialindex *m*
(JAP) 銘柄潜在性指数
(RUS) ПОКАЗАТЕЛЬ ПОТЕНЦИАЛА ТОВАРНОЙ МАРКИ

brand share
(CHIN) 品牌市场占有率
(FRE) partage de la marque, (C) part de marché de la marque
(GER) Markenanteil *m*
(JAP) ブランドシェア、商標占有率
(RUS) ДОЛЯ ТОВАРНОЙ МАРКИ

breach
(CHIN) 违反
(FRE) manquement, rupture, violation
(GER) Bruch *m*, Übertretung *f*, Verstoß *m*, Verletzung *f*, Zuwiderhandlung *f*
(JAP) 不履行、（法律・約束などを）破る
(RUS) НАРУШЕНИЕ

breach of contract
(CHIN) 违约，违反合同
(FRE) rupture de contrat, (C) inexécution de contrat , (C) violation de contrat
(GER) Vertragsverletzung *f*, -bruch *m*, Verletzung *f* der Vertragspflicht *f*
(JAP) 契約違反、契約不履行、協定違反、違約、破約
(RUS) НАРУШЕНИЕ ДОГОВОРА

breach of warranty
(CHIN) 违反保证
(FRE) rupture de garantie,
(C) inobservation de la garantie
(GER) Garantie- *f*, Gewährleistungsverletzung *f*, Verletzung *f* der Gewährleistungspflicht *f*
(JAP) 保証違反、保証不履行
(RUS) НАРУШЕНИЕ ГАРАНТИИ

breadwinner
(CHIN) 养家糊口的人
(FRE) soutien de famille
(GER) Ernährer *m* der Familie *f*,
Geldverdiener *m*
(JAP) （一家の）稼ぎ手、財源
(RUS) «КОРМИЛЕЦ»; РАБОТАЮЩИЙ
ЧЛЕН СЕМЬИ

break
(CHIN) 违约，物价暴跌，倒闭，停顿
(FRE) pause
(GER) Bruch *m*; Pause *f*, Unterbrechung *f*;
Wende *f*, Umschwung *m*; Kurseinbruch *m*
(JAP) 急激な変化、相場の暴落
(RUS) НАРУШЕНИЕ; ПЕРЕРЫВ;
ПРЕДСТАВИВШАЯСЯ ВОЗМОЖНОСТЬ

break-even analysis
(CHIN) 保本分析，盈亏平衡分析
(FRE) analyse de point mort
(GER) Break-Even-Analyse *f*;
Deckungsrechnung *f*;
Gewinnschwellenanalyse *f*;
Deckungspunktanalyse *f*
(JAP) 損益分岐分析
(RUS) АНАЛИЗ ПО БЕЗУБЫТОЧНОСТИ

break-even point
(CHIN) 损益两平点，保本点，
盈亏临界点
(FRE) seuil de rentabilité, point mort,
niveau d'indifférence
(GER) Break-Even-Punkt *m*; Gewinn- und
Verlustschwelle *f*; Rentabilitätsschwelle *f*;
Deckungspunkt *m*
(JAP) 損益分岐点，収支分岐点
(RUS) СОСТОЯНИЕ БЕЗУБЫТОЧНОСТИ

breakup
(CHIN) 拆售
(FRE) dissolution, scission
(GER) Aufteilung *f*, Auflösung *f*, Abbruch
m, Beendigung *f*
(JAP) 分解、分散、解散
(RUS) РАЗДЕЛЕНИЕ; РАЗУКРУПНЕНИЕ

bridge loan
(CHIN) 过渡性贷款，临时性贷款

prêt-relais, (C) crédit de relais
(GER) Überbrückungsdarlehen *n*,
Zwischenkredit *m*
(JAP) ブリッジローン、つなぎ融資
(RUS) КРАТКОСРОЧНЫЙ ЗАЁМ ДО
ПОЛУЧЕНИЯ ФИНАНСИРОВАНИЯ ИЗ
ДРУГОГО ИСТОЧНИКА

brightness (computer)
(CHIN) 亮度
(FRE) luminosité
(GER) Helligkeit *f*
(JAP) 輝度
(RUS) ЯРКОСТЬ

broken lot
(CHIN) 散批货物
(FRE) lot de taille normale
(GER) nicht handelsübliche Losgröße *f*
(JAP) 端株
(RUS) НЕПОЛНЫЙ ЛОТ

broker
(CHIN) 经纪人，掮客
(FRE) agent de change, courtier, broker
(GER) Makler *m*, Broker *m*; Person *f* mit
Börsenzulassung *f*; Agent *m*,
Versicherungsvermittler *m*
(JAP) 仲買人、ブローカー
(RUS) БРОКЕР; МАКЛЕР

brokerage
(CHIN) 经纪业，经纪费
(FRE) courtage
(GER) Maklergewerbe *n*, -tätigkeit *f*, -
gebühr *f*, Courtage *f*, Provision *f*
(JAP) 仲買、仲買業，仲買手数料
(RUS) БРОКЕРСКАЯ ДЕЯТЕЛЬНОСТЬ;
БРОКЕРСКИЕ КОМИССИОННЫЕ

brokerage allowance
(CHIN) 经纪人佣金
(FRE) indemnité de courtage
(GER) Maklerzulage *f*
(JAP) 仲介手数料割引
(RUS) БРОКЕРСКАЯ НАДБАВКА

broker loan rate
(CHIN) 经纪人贷款利率

(FRE) taux de prêt aux courtiers, (C) taux d'avances sur titres
(GER) Maklerkreditsatz *m*; Maklerlombardsatz *m*
(JAP) 証券担保貸付金利
(RUS) ПРОЦЕНТНАЯ СТАВКА ПО ССУДАМ БАНКОВ БРОКЕРАМ

browser
(CHIN) 浏览程序，浏览器
(FRE) navigateur
(GER) Browser *m*, Suchprogramm *n*
(JAP) ブラウザ、閲覧ソフト
(RUS) ОКНО ПРОСМОТРА; В СИСТЕМАХ ПРОГРАММИРОВАНИЯ С МНОГООКОННЫМ ДОСТУПОМ - СРЕДСТВА, ПОЗВОЛЯЮЩИЕ ПРОСМАТРИВАТЬ В ГРУППЕ ВЫДЕЛЕННЫХ ОКОН ТЕКСТОВЫЕ ПРЕДСТАВЛЕНИЯ ПРОГРАММ И ДАННЫХ

bucket shop
(CHIN) 黑市买空炎空小交易所
(FRE) officine douteuse
(GER) Schwindelmakler *m*, unreelle Maklerfirma *f*
(JAP) 闇証券業者、場外取引店
(RUS) НЕЗАКОННАЯ БРОКЕРСКАЯ ФИРМА

budget
(CHIN) 预算，安排
(FRE) budget
(GER) Budget *n*; Haushalts- *m*, Finanzplan *m*; Etat *m*, Staatshaushalt *m*
(JAP) 予算、予算案
(RUS) БЮДЖЕТ; СМЕТА

budget mortgage
(CHIN) 预算抵押贷款
(FRE) nantissement du budget
(GER) günstige Hypothek *f*
(JAP) バジェットモーゲージ
(RUS) ИПОТЕЧНЫЙ КРЕДИТ, В ВЫПЛАТУ КОТОРОГО ВКЛЮЧАЮТСЯ НАЛОГИ И СТРАХОВКА

buffer stock
(CHIN) 缓冲存货
(FRE) matelas stock tampon

(GER) Sicherheits- *m*, Pufferbestand *m*; Ausgleichslager *n*, -vorrat *m*, Reservelager *n*
(JAP) 緩衝在庫
(RUS) БУФЕРНЫЕ ЗАПАСЫ

building code
(CHIN) 建筑法律，建筑条例
(FRE) code de la construction, code du bâtiment
(GER) Bauvorschriften *fpl*; Bauordnung *f*
(JAP) 建築基準法
(RUS) СТРОИТЕЛЬНЫЕ НОРМЫ

building line
(CHIN) 建筑线
(FRE) limite de construction,
(C) enlignement des bâtiments
(GER) Bebauungsgrenze *f*; Fluchtlinie *f*, Baulinie *f*
(JAP) 建築境界線
(RUS) УСТАНОВЛЕННАЯ ЛИНИЯ ФАСАДОВ ЗДАНИЙ

building loan agreement
(CHIN) 建筑贷款协议
(FRE) contrat de prêt immobilier,
(C) accord de prêt à la construction
(GER) Baudarlehens- *m*, Baukredit- *m*, Baufinanzierungsvertrag *m*
(JAP) 建築融資契約
(RUS) КРЕДИТ, СРЕДСТВА КОТОРОГО ПОСТУПАЮТ ПОЛУЧАТЕЛЮ НА ОПРЕДЕЛЁННЫХ ОГОВОРЕННЫХ СТАДИЯХ СТРОИТЕЛЬСТВА

building permit
(CHIN) 建筑执照，建筑许可证
(FRE) permis de construire
(GER) Baugenehmigung *f*, -bewilligung *f*
(JAP) 建築許可（証）
(RUS) РАЗРЕШЕНИЕ НА СТРОИТЕЛЬСТВО

built-in stabilizer
(CHIN) 内在稳定因素
(FRE) stabilisateur intégré/incorporé
(GER) automatischer (Konjunktur)stabilisator *m*, automatischer Regelmechanismus *m*
(JAP) 内蔵スタビライザー自動安定装置

(RUS) «ВСТРОЕННЫЙ» СТАБИЛИЗАТОР

bull
(CHIN) 多头，灾方，哄抬价格
(FRE) haussier, à la hausse
(GER) Haussier *m*, Haussespekulant *m*
(JAP) 強気市場、強気筋
(RUS) «БЫК» (бирж.), СПЕКУЛЯНТ,
ИГРАЮЩИЙ НА ПОВЫШЕНИЕ

bulletin
(CHIN) 布告，公告
(FRE) bulletin
(GER) Bulletin *m*, Bekanntmachungsblatt *n*
(JAP) 告示する、掲示する
(RUS) БЮЛЛЕТЕНЬ

bulletin board system (BBS)
(CHIN) 布告板系统（BBS）
(FRE) serveur télématique, (C) babillard
électronique
(GER) Bulletinboardsystem *n*
(JAP) 電子掲示板システム
(RUS) «СИСТЕМА ТАБЛО»

bull market
(CHIN) 牛市，好市
(FRE) marché haussier
(GER) Haussemarkt *m*, Hausse *f*, steigende
Kurse *mpl*
(JAP) 強気相場、強気市場
(RUS) «РЫНОК БЫКОВ» (бирж.),
ДЛИТЕЛЬНЫЙ ПЕРИОД ПОВЫШЕНИЯ
ЦЕН НА БИРЖЕ

bunching
(CHIN) 年度相混收入
(FRE) groupement, concentration
(GER) Ballung *f*, Häufung *f*,
Konzentration *f*
(JAP) 集群、束、束ねること
(RUS) СКОПЛЕНИЕ, НАКОПЛЕНИЕ

bundle-of-rights theory
(CHIN) 整体权利理论
(FRE) théorie sur « l'ensemble des droits »
(GER) Theorie *f* des Bündels *n* von
Rechten *npl*
(JAP) 諸権利の束理論

(RUS) ТЕОРИЯ «СОВОКУПНОСТИ ПРАВ»

burden of proof
(CHIN) 举证责任
(FRE) fardeau de la preuve, charge de la
prevue
(GER) Beweislast *f*, Beweisführungslast *f*
(JAP) 挙証責任、立証責任
(RUS) БРЕМЯ ДОКАЗЫВАНИЯ

bureau
(CHIN) 局，处，所
(FRE) bureau
(GER) Behörde *f*, Amt *n*
(JAP) 局、省
(RUS) БЮРО; СТОЛ ДЛЯ ДЕЛОВЫХ
БУМАГ

bureaucrat
(CHIN) 官僚
(FRE) bureaucrate
(GER) Bürokrat *m*, Aktenmensch *m*
(JAP) 官僚
(RUS) БЮРОКРАТ

burnout
(CHIN) 透支，用尽
(FRE) usure, épuisement), (C) syndrome
d'épuisement professionnel
(GER) Burnout *n*, Ausgebranntsein *n*
(JAP) ストレスによる肉体的・
精神的疲労
(RUS) НЕУДАЧНАЯ ОПЕРАЦИЯ; КРАХ

business
(CHIN) 商业，企业，营业，业务
(FRE) affaires, entreprise, exploitation,
business; d'entreprise, d'exploitation,
professionnel, commercial (adj)
(GER) Geschäft *n*; Betriebswirtschaft *f*
(JAP) ビジネス、事業、業務
(RUS) ДЕЛО; БИЗНЕС

business combination
(CHIN) 企业合并
(FRE) combinaison d'entreprise,
(C) regroupement d'entreprises
(GER) Firmenzusammenschluss *m*
(JAP) 企業合同、合併
(RUS) ДЕЛОВОЕ СОЧЕТАНИЕ

business conditions
(CHIN) 商业状况，行情
(FRE) conditions commerciales,
(C) conjoncture
(GER) Geschäftslage f;
Geschäftsbedingungen fpl
(JAP) 商況、景気
(RUS) УСЛОВИЯ ВЕДЕНИЯ ДЕЛ

business cycle
(CHIN) 经济周期
(FRE) cycle économique, cycle des affaires
(GER) Konjunkturzyklus m,
Wirtschaftskreislauf m
(JAP) 景気循環
(RUS) ЦИКЛ ДЕЛОВЫХ ОПЕРАЦИЙ

business day
(CHIN) 营业日
(FRE) jour ouvrable
(GER) Geschäftstag m, -tag m
(JAP) 営業日、平日
(RUS) РАБОЧИЙ ДЕНЬ

business ethics
(CHIN) 商业道德，企业道德
(FRE) éthique commerciale, (C) éthique des
affaires
(GER) Geschäftsethik f, -moral f
(JAP) ビジネス倫理、商業倫理
(RUS) ЭТИКА ВЕДЕНИЯ ДЕЛ

business etiquette
(CHIN) 商业礼节
(FRE) déontologie commerciale
(GER) Geschäftsetikette f, Business-
Etikette f
(JAP) ビジネス・エチケット、商売上の
礼儀作法
(RUS) ЭТИКЕТ В ВЕДЕНИИ ДЕЛ

business interruption
(CHIN) 营业中断
(FRE) arrêt d'exploitation, (C) interruption
d'exploitation
(GER) Geschäfts- f,
Betriebsunterbrechung f
(JAP) 事業中断

(RUS) ПРЕРЫВАНИЕ ДЕЛОВЫХ
ОПЕРАЦИЙ

business reply card
(CHIN) 商务回信卡
(FRE) carte-réponse d'affaires, (C) carte-
réponse d'affaires
(GER) Antwortkarte f
(JAP) 切手不用返信はがき、
商用返信はがき
(RUS) ПРЕДОПЛАЧЕННАЯ
ОТПРАВИТЕЛЕМ ОТКРЫТКА ДЛЯ
ОТВЕТА НА ПРЕДЛОЖЕНИЕ ТОВАРА,
УСЛУГИ

business reply envelope
(CHIN) 商业回信信封
(FRE) enveloppe-réponse d'affaires
(GER) Rückumschlag m
(JAP) 切手不用返信封筒、商用返信封筒
(RUS) ПРЕДОПЛАЧЕННЫЙ КОНВЕРТ ДЛЯ
ОТВЕТА НА ПРЕДЛОЖЕНИЕ ТОВАРА,
УСЛУГИ

business reply mail
(CHIN) 商业回复邮件
(FRE) courrier réponse d'affaires
(GER) Werbeantwortpost f
(JAP) 商用［業務用］返信郵便物、
返信用郵便
(RUS) ПРЕДОПЛАЧЕННАЯ
ОТПРАВИТЕЛЕМ ОТКРЫТКА ИЛИ
КОНВЕРТ ДЛЯ ОТВЕТА НА
ПРЕДЛОЖЕНИЕ ТОВАРА, УСЛУГИ

business risk exclusion
(CHIN) 商业风险规避
(FRE) exclusion des risques de l'entreprise,
(C) exclusion des risques commerciaux
(GER) Ausschluss m des Geschäfts-,
Investitionsriskos n
(JAP) 事業リスク排除
(RUS) ПОЛОЖЕНИЕ СТРАХОВОГО
КОНТРАКТА, ИСКЛЮЧАЮЩЕЕ
ПОКРЫТИЕ ИЗДЕРЖЕК В СЛУЧАЕ, ЕСЛИ
ПРОДУКЦИЯ СТРАХУЮЩЕГОСЯ
ПРОИЗВОДИТЕЛЯ НЕ ВЫПОЛНЯЕТ СВОИ
ФУНКЦИИ

business-to-business adverting
(CHIN) 企业对企业广告宣传

(FRE) publicité business to business
publicité interentreprises
(GER) zwischengeschäftliche Werbung *f*,
B2B-Werbung *f*, Business-to-Business
Fachwerbung *f*
(JAP) 企業向け広告
(RUS) РЕКЛАМА МЕЖДУ ДЕЛОВЫМИ
ПРЕДПРИЯТИЯМИ

bust-up acquisition
(CHIN) 破产并购
(FRE) acquisition partielle d'actifs
(GER) zerstörerische Akquisition *f* bzw.
Übernahme *f*
(JAP) 解体買収、破産買収
(RUS) АГРЕССИВНОЕ ПРИОБРЕТЕНИЕ

buy
(CHIN) 购买
(FRE) acheter
(GER) kaufen, anschaffen, erwerben,
beziehen, *v*
(JAP) 買収する、購入する
(RUS) ПОКУПКА; ПОКУПАТЬ

buy-and-sell aggreeement
(CHIN) 买卖协议
(FRE) convention de rachat de parts,
(C) convention de rachat
(GER) Kauf- und Verkaufsvereinbarung *f*
(JAP) 相互売買協定
(RUS) ДОГОВОР ОПРЕДЕЛЯЮЩИЙ КАК
БУДЕТ ВЫКУПАТЬСЯ ДОЛЯ УМЕРШЕГО
ИЛИ ИНАЧЕ УШЕДШЕГО ИЗ БИЗНЕСА
ПАРТНЁРА ОСТАВШИМИСЯ ЧЛЕНАМИ
ТОВАРИЩЕСТВА ИЛИ АКЦИОНЕРНОГО
ОБЩЕСТВА ЗАКРЫТОГО ТИПА

buy-back agreement
(CHIN) 回购协议
(FRE) accord de rachat, accord de reprise,
(C) pension sur titres
(GER) Rückkaufvereinbarung *f*, -vertrag *m*
(JAP) 買戻し約定
(RUS) ДОГОВОР ОБ ОБРАТНОЙ
ПОКУПКЕ

buy down
(CHIN) 买低利率
(FRE) rachat de taux

(GER) mit hohem Disagio *n* (z.B.
Hypothek); Grundschuld *f* mit hohem
Disagio *n* aufnehmen
(JAP) （頭金を多く払って買う）バイダ
ウン方式
(RUS) СИТАЦИЯ, КОГДА ПРОАДАЮЩИЙ
БРОКЕР НЕ МОЖЕТ ВОВРЕМЯ
ПРЕДОСТАВИТЬ ЦЕННЫЕ БУМАГИ И
ТЕМ ВЫНУЖДАЕТ ПОКУПАЮЩЕГО
БРОКЕРА ПОКУПАТЬ ИХ ИЗ ДРУГИХ
ИСТОЧНИКОВ

buyer
(CHIN) 买方，买家
(FRE) acheteur
(GER) Käufer *m*, Kunde *m*, Abnehmer *m*
(JAP) 買手、バイヤー
(RUS) ПОКУПАТЕЛЬ

buyer behavior
买方行为
(FRE) comportement de l'acheteur
(GER) Käuferverhalten *n*
(JAP) 購買行動
(RUS) ПОВЕДЕНИЕ ПОКУПАТЕЛЯ

buyer's market
(CHIN) 买方市场
(FRE) marché des acheteurs
(GER) Käufermarkt *m*,
nachfragebegünstigter Markt *m*
(JAP) 買手市場
(RUS) «РЫНОК ПОКУПАТЕЛЕЙ»,
СИТУАЦИЯ НА РЫНКЕ, КОГДА
ПРЕДЛОЖЕНИЕ ПРЕВЫШАЕТ СПРОС

buy in
(CHIN) 买进，补进
(FRE) acheter, (C) couvrir
(GER) Deckungskäufe *mpl*; Rückkauf *m*
eigener Aktien *fpl*; sich einkaufen, *v*
(JAP) 処分買い、買戻し、自己落札
(RUS) ПОКУПКА УЧАСТИЯ В КАПИТАЛЕ

buying on margin
(CHIN) 边际购买，以差价购买
(FRE) achat sur marge
(GER) kreditfinanzierter Effektenkauf *m*
(JAP) 思惑買い，信用買い
(RUS) ПОКУПКА «НА МАРЖЕ»

buy order

(CHIN) 债券定单

(FRE) ordre d'achat

(GER) Kaufauftrag *m*, -order *f*

(JAP) 買注文

(RUS) ЗАКАЗ (ПОРУЧЕНИЕ) НА ПОКУПКУ

buyout

(CHIN) 买下全部股权或产权

(FRE) rachat

(GER) Aufkauf *m*, Buyout *n*, Aktienübernahme *f*, Spekulationserwerb *m*

(JAP) 買収、買占め

(RUS) ВЫКУП (КОМПАНИИ)

buzz words

(CHIN) 术语，专门用语

(FRE) jargonnerie, mot a la mode

(GER) Modewörter *npl*

(JAP) 専門的な響きを持つ流行語、もったいぶった専門用語

(RUS) ВЫСПРЕННИЕ СЛОВА (чтобы произвести впечатление)

bylaws

(CHIN) 公司章程，细则

(FRE) règlement, statuts

(GER) Satzung *f*, Statuten *npl*, Gesellschaftsvertrag *m*

(JAP) (会社の）付随定款、規則、内規、細則、付則

(RUS) УСТАВНЫЕ НОРМЫ; ВНУТРЕННИЕ ПРАВИЛА

bypass trust

(CHIN) 过继信托

(FRE) fiducie familiale, (C) fiducie de contournement

(GER) Bypass-Trust *m*, (ein Instrument nach US-Trust-Recht zur Erbschaftss teuerersparnis)

(RUS) ТРАСТ для снижения налогов на наследство

by-product

(CHIN) 副产品

(FRE) sous-produit

(GER) Nebenprodukt *n*, -erzeugnis *n*; Abfallprodukt *n*

(JAP) 副産物、副製品

(RUS) ПОБОЧНЫЙ ПРОДУКТ

by the book

(CHIN) 照章办事

(FRE) à la letter

(GER) sich an die Vorschriften *fpl* haltend

(JAP) 正確に、正式に、定石どおりに

(RUS) «ПО ВСЕМ ПРАВИЛАМ»

C

cable transfer
(CHIN) 电汇
(FRE) transmission par câble, (C) mandat
télégraphique
(GER) telegrafische Überweisung *f*
(JAP) 電信為替
(RUS) ТЕЛЕГРАФНЫЙ ПЕРЕВОД

cache
(CHIN) 高速缓冲存储器
(FRE) mémoire cache
(JAP) キャッシュ、貯蔵所、貯蔵物
(RUS) СВЕРХОПЕРАТИВНАЯ ПАМЯТЬ;
КЕШ

cadastre
(CHIN) 地籍簿，不动产估价清单
(FRE) cadastre
(GER) Grundsteuerregister *n*, Grundbuch *n*,
Flurbuch *n*, (Liegenschafts)kataster *n*
(JAP) 土地台帳
(RUS) КАДАСТР

cafeteria benefit plan
(CHIN) 自助餐馆式福利计划
(FRE) régime au choix, régime à la carte,
(C) avantages sociaux à la carte
(GER) Cafeteria Benefit Plan *m*,
(Vergütungssystem, bei dem leitende
Angestellte das Verhältnis von Grundgehalt
zu Nebenleistungen in bestimmtem
Umfang selbst wählen können)
(JAP) カフェテリアプラン（保険・
退職年金などの）
(RUS) СИСТЕМА ПРИ КОТОРОЙ
РАБОТНИКИ САМИ ВЫБИРАЮТ
СТРУКТУРУ ЛЬГОТ, ПРЕДЛАГАЕМЫХ
РАБОТОДАТЕЛЕМ

calendar year
(CHIN) 日历年度，自然年度
(FRE) année civile exercice civil
(GER) Kalenderjahr *n*
(JAP) 暦年
(RUS) КАЛЕНДАРНЫЙ ГОД

call
(CHIN) 催缴，要求偿还，买入，收回
(FRE) appel, (C) appel de fonds, (C) option
d'achat, (C) clause de remboursement
anticipé
(GER) Kaufoption *m* (Börse)
Zahlungsaufforderung *f*, Abruf *m*,
Einforderung *f* (von Geldern);
Einlösungsaufforderung *f*; Kündigung *f*
(Kredit, Anleihe)
(JAP) 買付選択権、コール(短期資金)
(RUS) ЗВОНОК; ТРЕБОВАНИЕ БАНКА К
ЗАЕМЩИКУ

callable
(CHIN) 可赎回
(FRE) remboursable sur demande,
remboursable avant échéance, révocable,
(C) rachetable
(GER) abrufbar, einziehbar, kündbar;
rückzahlbar, einlösbar; einforderbar;
kündigungsreif *adj*
(JAP) 請求次第支払われる、
(債権)償還請求できる
(RUS) ОБЛИГАЦИЯ, ПОГАШАЕМАЯ
ЭМИТЕНТОМ ДОСРОЧНО

call feature
(CHIN) 提前兑回条款
(FRE) clause de rachat clause de
remboursement anticipé
(GER) Rufmerkmal *n*
(JAP) 繰り上げ償還条項
(RUS) (ПРИ ВЫПУСКЕ ОБЛИГАЦИЙ)
ОГОВОРКА О ПРАВЕ ДОСРОЧНОГО
ВЫКУПА

call option
(CHIN) 购买选择权，买进约定权
(FRE) option d'achat
(GER) Kaufoption *f*; Kündigungsrecht
(Anleihe) *n*
(JAP) コール・オプション(コールは買
付選択権、オプションは選択権付取引)
(RUS) ОПЦИОН С ПРАВОМ ПОКУПКИ ПО
ФИКСИРОВАННОЙ ЦЕНЕ В ТЕЧЕНИЕ
ОГОВОРЕННОГО ВРЕМЕНИ

call premium
(CHIN) 赎回溢价
(FRE) prime de remboursement, (C) prime
de remboursement anticipé
(GER) Kaufoptionsprämie *f*; Rückkaufagio
n; Rückzahlungsprämie *f*, (Aufschlag, zu
dem die Rückzahlung einer Anleihe bei
vorzeitiger Kündigung crfolgt)
(JAP) 償還プレミアム
(RUS) ПРЕМИЯ, ВЫПЛАЧИВАЕМАЯ
ЭМИТЕНТОИ ДЕРЖАТЕЛЮ ОБЛИГАЦИЙ
В СЛУЧАЕ ИХДОСРОЧНОГО
ПОГАШЕНИЯ

call price
(CHIN) 赎回价格
(FRE) prix de rachat, (C) prix de
remboursement
(GER) Kündigungskurs *m*;
Rückkauf *m*, Rücknahmekurs *m*;
Abrufpreis *m*
(JAP) 買入価格、買入値段
(RUS) ЦЕНА ДОСРОЧНОГО ВЫКУПА
(ОБЛИГАЦИЙ)

call report
(CHIN) 报表，要求提供报表
(FRE) registre des visites, (C) rapport de
visite
(GER) Call Report *m*, (Bilanzen und
Vermögensaufstellungen, die US-
Kreditinstitute bei
Bankenaufsichtsbehörden einreichen
müssen)
(JAP) 販売訪問報告書、当局宛報告
(RUS) ПРОТОКОЛ О СОВЕЩАНИЯХ
МЕЖДУ ПРЕДСТАВИТЕЛЯМИ
РЕКЛАМНОГО АГЕНСТВА И ИХ
КЛИЕНТАМИ

cancel
(CHIN) 取消
(FRE) annuler, (C) révoquer, (C) résilier
(GER) annullieren, stornieren, kündigen,
absagen, streichen, auflösen, aufheben,
zurücktreten *v* (Vertrag); für kraftlos
erklären (Wechsel) *v*
(JAP) 解約する、取消す
(RUS) ОТМЕНА; АННУЛИРОВАНИЕ

cancellation clause
(CHIN) 撤消条款，解约条款
(FRE) clause d'annulation, (C) clause de
résiliation

(GER) Stornierungs- *f*, Rücktritts- *f*,
Kündigungs- *f*, Nichtigkeitsklausel *f*
(JAP) 解除約款、解約条項
(RUS) УСЛОВИЕ АННУЛИРОВАНИЯ
КОНТРАКТА
(RUS) ОГОВОРКА ОБ АННУЛИРОВАНИИ
СТРАХОВОГО КОНТРАКТА

cancellation provision clause
(CHIN) 撤消条件条款
(FRE) clause de disposition d'annulation
(GER) Rücktrittsbestimmungsklausel *f*
(JAP) 解約規定約款、解除規定条項

capacity
(CHIN) 容量，设备能力，生产率
(FRE) capacité, (C) capacité de production,
(C) potentiel productif, (C) dimension
(GER) Kapazität *f*; Geschäftsfähigkeit *f*;
Stellung *f*, Funktion *f*; Eignung *f*,
Kompetenz *f*; Höchsthaftungsbetrag *m*
(Versicherung)
(JAP) 資格、能力、容量
(RUS) МОЩНОСТЬ; ВОЗМОЖНОСТИ;
ФУНКЦИИ УЧАСТНИКА (РЫНКА)

capital
(CHIN) 资本，资金，股本，本金，资方
(FRE) capital, (C) capitaux propres,
(C) capital social
(GER) Kapital *n*, finanzielle Mittel *npl*
(JAP) 資本、元金
(RUS) КАПИТАЛ

capital account
(CHIN) 资本账户
(FRE) compte de capital, (C) compte
d'apport
(GER) Kapitalkonto *n*;
Kapitalverkehrsbilanz *f*;
Vermögensveränderungskonto *n*;
Kapitalaufstellung *f*, Kapital- *f*,
Vermögensrechnung *f*
(JAP) 資本的資金勘定、資本(金)勘定
(RUS) БАЛАНС ДВИЖЕНИЯ КАПИТАЛА

capital assets
(CHIN) 资本资产，固定资产
(FRE) immobilisations, (C) actif
immobilisé corporel

(GER) Geldkapital *m*, Kapitalvermögen *m*,
Wirtschaftsgüter *npl*; Anlagegüter *npl*, -
vermögen *n*, Kapitalanlagen *fpl*, -vermögen
n, Anlagenbestand *m*
(JAP) 固定資産、資本資産
(RUS) ОСНОВНОЙ КАПИТАЛ

capital budget

(CHIN) 资本预算，基本建设预算
(FRE) budget des investissements
(GER) Investitionsplan *m*; Kapital- *n*,
Finanzbudget *n*; Investitionshaushalt *m*;
Vermögenshaushalt *m*
(JAP) 資本予算
(RUS) БЮДЖЕТ ДОЛГОСРОЧНЫХ
РАСХОДОВ

capital consumption allowance

(CHIN) 折旧费，资本消耗的补偿
(FRE) provision pour consommation du
capital
(GER) Kapitalverschleiß *m*,
(verbrauchsbedingte) Abschreibungen *fpl*
(JAP) 資本(資産)減耗引当、
資本消耗引当金
(RUS) ПОПРАВКА НА АММОРТИЗАЦИЮ
КАПИТАЛА

capital contributed in excess of par value

(CHIN) 超票面值缴入资本，溢收资本
(FRE) apport en capital dépassant la valeur
nominale
(GER) über den Nennwert *m* hinaus
eingebrachte Kapital- *f*,
Stammeinlage *f*
(JAP) 額面価額超過分出資資本
(RUS) КАПИТАЛ, ВНЕСЕННЫЙ СВЕРХ
НОМИНАЛЬНОЙ ЦЕННОСТИ АКЦИЙ

capital expenditure

(CHIN) 资本开支，基本建设费
(FRE) dépense d'investissement,
(C) dépense en immobilisations,
(C) dépenses en capital
(GER) Investitionsausgaben *fpl*,
Kapitalkosten *pl*, Kapital- *m*,
Investitionsaufwand *m*
(JAP) 資本支出
(RUS) КАПИТАЛОВЛОЖЕНИЕ

capital formation

(CHIN) 资本形成，资本积累
(FRE) formation de capital
(GER) Kapitalbildung *f*,
Vermögensbildung *f*
(JAP) 資本形成
(RUS) ФОРМИРОВАНИЕ КАПИТАЛА

capital gain (loss)

(CHIN) 资本收益（损失）
(FRE) plus-value de capitaux, gain (perte)
en capital, (C) profit (perte) sur règlement
de dettes
(GER) Veräußerungsgewinne *mpl* (-verluste
mpl); Wert-, Vermögenszuwachs *m* (-
verlust *m*) aus Veräußerungen *fpl*; realisierte
Kapitalgewinne, -erträge *mpl* (-verluste *fpl*)
(JAP) 資本売却所得(損失)、資本売却差
益(差損)
(RUS) ВЫИГРЫШ (ПОТЕРЯ) ПРИ
ПРОДАЖЕ ОСНОВНОГО КАПИТАЛА

capital goods

(CHIN) 资本货物，固定资产
(FRE) biens d'investissement, (C) biens
d'équipement, (C) matériel
d'immobilisation,, (C) bien de production
(GER) Kapital- *npl*, Anlagegüter *npl*;
Investitionsgüter *npl*, Produktionsmittel *npl*;
Sachkapital *n*
(JAP) 資本財
(RUS) ВЫИГРЫШ (ПОТЕРЯ) ПРИ
ПРОДАЖЕ ОСНОВНОГО КАПИТАЛА

capital improvement

(CHIN) 改进生产设备
(FRE) amélioration du capital,
(C) amélioration des immobilisations
(GER) Kapitalverbesserung *f*;
Erweiterungsinvestition *f*,
Substanzverbesserung (Investition) *f*
(JAP) 資本的支出とみられる改良、
設備改良
(RUS) ПРИРАЩЕНИЕ КАПИТАЛА

capital intensive

(CHIN) 资本密集型
(FRE) capitalistique
(GER) kapitalintensiv *adj*
(JAP) 資本集中的
(RUS) КАПИТАЛОЕМКИЙ

capital inestment
(CHIN) 资本投资，基建投资
(FRE) capital investi, (C) mise de fonds, (C) placement de capitaux
(GER) Kapital- *f*, Geldanlage *f*; Investitionsausgaben *fpl*; Anlagekapital *n*; Anlageinvestitionen *fpl*; Kapitalaufwand *m*
(JAP) 設備投資、資本投資
(RUS) КАПИТАЛОВЛОЖЕНИЕ

capitalism
(CHIN) 资本主义
(FRE) capitalisme
(GER) Kapitalismus *m*
(JAP) 資本主義
(RUS) КАПИТАЛИЗМ

capitalization rate
(CHIN) 资本化率
(FRE) taux d'actualisation, (C) taux de capitalisation
(GER) Kapitalisierungsfaktor *m*, -zinsfuß *m*
(JAP) 資本化率
(RUS) УРОВЕНЬ КАПИТАЛИЗАЦИИ

capitalize
(CHIN) 资本化
(FRE) capitaliser
(GER) mit Kapital *n* ausstatten, aktivieren, in Kapital *n* umwandeln, kapitalisieren *v*; Wertpapiere *npl* emittieren *v*
(JAP) 資本化する、資本に組入れる
(RUS) КАПИТАЛИЗИРОВАТЬ

capitalized value
(CHIN) 核定资本值，资本化价值
(FRE) valeur de rendement, (C) valeur actualisée, (C) valeur capitalisée
(GER) kapitalisierter Wert *m*; Ertragswert *m*
(JAP) 資本還元価值、資本化価值
(RUS) КАПИТАЛИЗИРОВАННАЯ СТОИМОСТЬ

capital lease
(CHIN) 资本租赁
(FRE) contrat de location-acquisition
(GER) Finanzierungs-Leasingvertrag *m*
(JAP) 資本リース契約
(RUS) КАПИТАЛЬНАЯ АРЕНДА

capital market
(CHIN) 资本市场
(FRE) marché des capitaux, (C) marché financier
(GER) Kapital- *m*, Geld- *m*, Finanzmarkt *m*
(JAP) 資本市場、長期金融市場
(RUS) РЫНОК КАПИТАЛОВ

capital rationing
(CHIN) 资本配额
(FRE) rationnement du capital, (C) limite des investissements
(GER) Kapitalrationierung *f*; (Begrenzung der Kapitalbeschaffungsmöglichkeiten)
(JAP) 資本割当、資本制限、資本不足
(RUS) ДОЗИРОВАНИЕ КАПИТАЛА

capital requirement
(CHIN) 资本需求量
(FRE) besoin en immobilisations, exigence en immobilisation, (C) besoin de capitaux
(GER) Kapitalbedarf *m*, Kapitalanforderungen *fpl*
(JAP) 資金需要、必要資本量
(RUS) ПОТРЕБНОСТЬ В ПОСТОЯННОМ ФИНАНСИРОВАНИИ

capital resource
(CHIN) 资本来源
(FRE) ressource en immobilisation, (C) fonds propre
(GER) Kapitalausstattung *f*, -fonds *m*; das gesamte haftende Eigenkapital *n* der Bank *m*
(JAP) 資本資源
(RUS) КАПИТАЛЬНЫЕ РЕСУРСЫ

capital stock
(CHIN) 股本，基金，股金总额
(FRE) stock de capital, (C) capital social
(GER) Grund- *n*, Aktienkapital *n*, gezeichnetes Stammkapital *n*, Stammvermögen *n* (AG)
(JAP) 資本金、資本株式、総株数
(RUS) АКЦИОНЕРНЫЙ КАПИТАЛ; ОСНОВНЫЕ ФОНДЫ ЗА ВЫЧЕТОМ АММОРТИЗАЦИИ И СПИСАНИЙ

capital structure
(CHIN) 资本结构，资本构成

(FRE) structure du capital, (C) structure financière, (C) composition du capital
(GER) Kapitalstruktur *f,* Kapitalzusammensetzung *f*
(JAP) 資本構造、資本構成
(RUS) СТРУКТУРА КАПИТАЛА

capital surplus
(CHIN) 资本盈余
(FRE) excédent de capital, (C) surplus d'apport
(GER) Rücklagen (US) *fpl,* Kapitalreserve *f*
(JAP) 資本余剰金
(RUS) ИЗБЫТОЧНЫЙ КАПИТАЛ

capital turnover
(CHIN) 资本周转，资本周转率
(FRE) rentabilité du capital, (C) ratio de rotation des capitaux
(GER) Kapitalumschlag *m,* (Verhältnis von Umsatz zu investiertem Kapital); Kapitalumschlaghäufigkeit *f*
(JAP) 資本の回転、資本回転率
(RUS) ОБОРОТ КАПИТАЛА

caps
(CHIN) 上限，限额
(FRE) majuscules, (C) actions privilégiées convertibles à taux variable
(GER) Begrenzung *f,* Schwellen *fpl*
(JAP) 上限、最高限度
(RUS) ПРЕДЕЛЫ СТАВОК

caps lock key
(CHIN) 大写锁定键
(FRE) touche vérr. maj., (C) touche verrouillage des majuscules
(JAP) キャップスロックキー
(RUS) КЛАВИША ФИКСИРОВАНИЯ ПЕЧАТОНИЯ ЗАГЛАВНЫМИ БУКВАМИ

captive finance company
(CHIN) 控股金融公司
(FRE) société financière (de financement) captive, (C) société filiale de crédit
(GER) konzerneigene Finanzierungsgesellschaft *f*
(JAP) 専属金融会社
(RUS) дочерняя компания, СОЗДАННАЯ для финансирования ПОКУПКИПРОДУКЦИИ МАТЕРИНСКОЙ КОМПАНИИ

cargo
(CHIN) 货物，船货，物品
(FRE) cargo, (C) chargement, (C) facultés
(GER) Fracht *f,* Ladung *f;* Lade- *n,* Frachtgut *n*
(JAP) 積荷、船荷、貨物
(RUS) ГРУЗ

cargo insurance
(CHIN) 货物保险
(FRE) assurance cargo, (C) assurance sur facultés
(GER) Kargo- *f,* Güterversicherung *f*
(JAP) 積荷保険、貨物保険
(RUS) СТРАХОВАНИЕ ГРУЗА

carload rate
(CHIN) 整车运费
(FRE) tarif (barème) par wagon, (C) prix de transport par wagon complet, (C) tarif par plein wagon
(GER) Waggonfracht- *m,* Wagenladungssatz *m*
(JAP) 貸切扱運賃率
(RUS) УРОВЕНЬ ЗАГРУЗКИ АВТОМАШИН

carrier
(CHIN) 运输行，货运商，承运人
(FRE) transporteur
(GER) Beförderungs- *n,* Transportunternehmen *m;* Fluggesellschaft *f;* Verfrachter *m;* Spediteur *m,* Frachtführer *m,* Versicherungsträger *m*
(JAP) 運送業者、運搬設備
(RUS) ПЕРЕВОЗЧИК

carrier's lien
(CHIN) 承运人留置权
(FRE) droit de rétention du transporteur, (C) privilège du transporteur
(GER) Pfandrecht *n* des Transportunternehmens bzw. *m,* Frachtführers
(RUS) ПРАВО НА ЗАДЕРЖАНИЕ ГРУЗА ДО ОПЛАТЫ

carrot and stick

(CHIN) 胡萝卜加大棒，奖赏和处分
(FRE) la carotte et le bâton
(GER) Zuckerbrot *n* und Peitsche *f*
(JAP) ニンジンと鞭、飴と鞭
(RUS) «КНУТ И ПРЯНИК»

carryback

(CHIN) 转入以前年度
(FRE) report en arrière, (C) report rétrospectif
(GER) Rücktrag *m*; steuerlicher Verlustrücktrag *m*
(JAP) 貸越し分
(RUS) ВОЗМОЖНОСТЬ ПОКРЫВАТЬ УБЫТКИ ЗА СЧЕТ ПРОШЛОЙ ПРИБЫЛИ

carrying charge

(CHIN) 置存资产费用，存货囤积费用
(FRE) coût de détention des capitaux, (C) frais de possession, (C) frais afférents à des titres achetés à terme, (C) frais de couverture, (C) frais sur marge
(GER) Speditionskosten *pl*; Aufwand *m* für ungenutzte Anlagen *fp*; Lagerhaltungskosten *pl*; Nebenkosten *pl* für Teilzahlungskredit *m*
(JAP) 保管費、諸掛、前払経費
(RUS) СТОИМОСТЬ ХРАНЕНИЯ ТОВАРА

carryover

(CHIN) 移后扣减
(FRE) report du résultat, (C) report
(GER) Übertrag *m*; Prolongation *f* (Börse) ; Vortrag *m*
(JAP) 繰延、繰越(金)
(RUS) ПЕРЕХОДЯЩИЙ ОСТАТОК

cartage

(CHIN) 货运费，搬运费
(FRE) camionnage, (C) frais de camionnage, (C) frais de transport
(GER) Abrollkosten *pl*, Rollgeld *n*, Frachtlohn *m*, Transportkosten *pl*, Zustellgebühr *f*
(JAP) (荷車)運賃、運搬費
(RUS) СТАВКА ОПЛАТЫ ЗА ПЕРЕВОЗКУ АВТОМОБИЛЬНЫМИ СРЕДСТВАМИ

cartel

(CHIN) 卡特尔
(FRE) cartel, (C) entente
(GER) Kartell *n*; Horizontalabrede *f*
(JAP) 連合企業、カルテル
(RUS) КАРТЕЛЬ

case-study method

(CHIN) 案例分析法
(FRE) méthode d'étude de cas, (C) méthode des cas
(GER) Fallstudienmethode *f*
(JAP) 事例研究法
(RUS) МЕТОД ОСНОВАННЫЙ НА АНАЛИЗЕ ГИПОТЕТИЧЕСКИХ ИЛИ РЕАЛЬНЫХ ПРОИЗВОДСТВЕННЫХ СИТУАЦИЙ

cash

(CHIN) 现金，现款
(FRE) liquidité, au comptant, espèces, caisse, trésorerie, (C) encaisse, espèces, (C) comptant
(GER) Bargeld *n*; Kasse *f*, Kassenguthaben *n*, -bestand *m*; Barvermögen *n*; liquide bzw. flüssige Mittel *npl*
(JAP) 現金、現金化する
(RUS) ДЕНЕЖНЫЕ СРЕДСТВА; НАЛИЧНОСТЬ

cash acknowledgement

(CHIN) 现金回执
(FRE) reçu de paiement
(GER) Bestätigung *f* einer Bargeldzahlung *f*
(JAP) 現金受領書、現金受取証明書
(RUS) ПОДТВЕРЖДЕНИЕ ПОЛУЧЕНИЯ НАЛИЧНОСТИ

cash basis

(CHIN) 现金交易条件，现收现付制
(FRE) base des encaissements/décaissements, (C) méthode de la comptabilité de caisse
(GER) Einnahmen- *f*, Ausgabenrechnung *f*; gegen Nachnahme *f*; Grundbestand *m* an Zahlungsmitteln *pl*; Kassenbasis *f*
(JAP) 現金主義
(RUS) НАЛИЧНАЯ ОСНОВА (бухг.)

cashbook
(CHIN) 现金出纳账
(FRE) registre/livre des encaissements/décaissements, (C) journal de caisse
(GER) Kassenbuch *n*, Kassenjournal *n*
(JAP) 現金出納帳
(RUS) КАССОВАЯ КНИГА (бухг.)

cash budget
(CHIN) 现金预算
(FRE) budget de caisse, budget de trésorerie
(GER) Einnahmen-Ausgaben-Plan *m*, Zahlungsplan *m*; Liquiditäts- *n*, Kassenbudget *n*
(JAP) 現金予算
(RUS) НАЛИЧНЫЙ БЮДЖЕТ

cash buyer
(CHIN) 现金买入方
(FRE) acheteur au comptant
(GER) Bareinkäufer *m*
(JAP) 現金購入者
(RUS) ПОКУПАТЕЛЬ ЗА НАЛИЧНЫЕ

cash cow
(CHIN) 摇钱树
(FRE) vache à lait (pop)
(GER) lukratives Unternehmen *n*; Dukatenesel *m*
(JAP) 黒字部門、財源、ドル箱部門、儲かる商品優良株
(RUS) «ДОЙНАЯ КОРОВА» (бизнес, дающий непрерывный приток наличности)

cash disbursement
(CHIN) 现金支出
(FRE) déboursés, (C) décaissement
(GER) Zahlungsausgang *m*, Barauszahlung *f*, Kassenausgänge *mpl*
(JAP) 現金支払い、現金払い
(RUS) НАЛИЧНЫЕ РАСХОДЫ

cash dicount
(CHIN) 现金折扣
(FRE) escompte de caisse
(GER) Skonto *n*; Kassaskonto *n*; Barrabatt *m*; Barzahlungsnachlass *m*, -rabatt *m*
(JAP) 現金割引

(RUS) СКИДКА ЗА ОПЛАТУ НАЛИЧНЫМИ

cash dividend
(CHIN) 现金股息
(FRE) dividende en espèces
(GER) Bardividende *f*, -ausschüttung *f*
(JAP) 現金配当
(RUS) НАЛИЧНЫЙ ДИВИДЕНД

cash earnings
(CHIN) 现金收益
(FRE) revenus/gains en espèces, (C) profit en espèces
(GER) Bareinnahmen *fpl*, Kassengewinn *m*
(JAP) 現金収入
(RUS) НАЛИЧНЫЕ ДОХОДЫ

cash equivalence
(CHIN) 相当现金价值
(FRE) équivalence en espèces
(GER) Barwert *m*
(JAP) 現金等価
(RUS) ФАКТИЧЕСКАЯ СТОИМОСТЬ

cash flow
(CHIN) 现金流动，现金流量
(FRE) flux de trésorerie, cash flow, marge brute d'autofinancement, (C) décaissement, (C) flux de l'encaisse en liquidités, (C) mouvements de trésorerie
(GER) Cashflow *m*, Bargeld- *m*, Kapitalfluss *m*, Liquidität *f*, Finanzstrom *m*
(JAP) キャッシュ・フロー、現金流出入
(RUS) ПОТОК ДЕНЕЖНЫХ СРЕДСТВ (НАЛИЧНОСТИ)

cashier
(CHIN) 出纳员，司库
(FRE) caissier
(GER) Kassierer *m*, Kassenverwalter *m*, -führer *m*
(JAP) 出納係
(RUS) КАССИР

cashier's check
(CHIN) 本票，银行本票
(FRE) chèque de caisse, chèque de banque, (C) traite de banque
(GER) Bankscheck (US) *m*

(JAP) 銀行小切手、支払人小切手
(RUS) КАССИРСКИЙ ЧЕК; ЧЕК,
ВЫПИСАННЫЙ БАНКОМ

cash market

(CHIN) 现金交易市场
(FRE) marché au comptant
(GER) Kassamarkt *m*, -handel *m*,
Geldmarkt *m*
(JAP) 現金市場
(RUS) НАЛИЧНЫЙ РЫНОК

cash on delivery (COD)

(CHIN) 货到付款（COD）
(FRE) paiement à la livraison, (C) contre
remboursement
(GER) per Nachnahme *f*, Barzahlung *f* bei
Licferung *f*; Warennachnahme *f*
(JAP) 貨物引換払い、代金引替渡し
RUS) ОПЛАТА В МОМЕНТ ПОСТАВКИ

cash order

(CHIN) 现付票，现金票据
(FRE) ordre au comptant, (C) commande à
paiement comptant
(GER) Zahlungsanweisung *f*, Kassaorder *m*;
Warenbezugsanweisung *f* bei
Abzahlungsvereinbarungen *fpl*
(JAP) 要求払為替手形、現金支払票、
現金注文
(RUS) КАССОВЫЙ ОРДЕР

cash payment journal

(CHIN) 现金支出日记账
(FRE) registre des paiements en espèce,
(C) journal des paiements au comptant
(GER) Kassenausgangsbuch *n*
(JAP) 現金支払帳
(RUS) КНИГА ЗАПИСИ НАЛИЧНЫХ
РАСХОДОВ

cash position

(CHIN) 现金头寸，现金状况
(FRE) position de la trésorerie, (C) argent
en caisse
(GER) Barliquidität *f*; Kassen-,
Liquiditätsposition *f* (Börse), Geldmittel- *m*,
Kassen- *m*, Barbestand *m*, liquide Mittel *npl*
(JAP) 現金持ち高、資金繰り
(RUS) НАЛИЧНАЯ ПОЗИЦИЯ

cash ratio

(CHIN) 现金比率
(FRE) ration de trésorerie, (C) ratio de
liquidité immédiate
(GER) Liquidität *f* ersten Grades *m*,
Deckungsgrad *m*; Bar- *f*,
Kassenliquidität *f*
(JAP) 現金比率、現金準備(預金)率
(RUS) ОТНОШЕНИЕ НАЛИЧНОСТИ И
ДРУГИХ АКТИВОВ К СУММЕ
ОБЯЗАТЕЛЬСТВ

cash register

(CHIN) 现金出纳机
(FRE) caisse enregistreuse
(GER) Registrierkasse *f*
(JAP) 金銭登録機、キャッシュ・
レジスター
(RUS) КАССОВЫЙ АППАРАТ

cash reserve

(CHIN) 现金储备，准备金
(FRE) réserve en espèces, (C) réserve
liquide, réserve en espèces
(GER) Bar- *f*, Liquiditäts- *f*,
Kassenreserve *f*
(JAP) 現金準備、支払準備
(RUS) НАЛИЧНЫЙ РЕЗЕРВ

cash surrender value

(CHIN) 现金解约价值，退保金额
(FRE) valeur de rachat, (C) valeur de
rachat au comptant
(GER) Rückkaufswert *m* (Versicherung);
Barablösungswert *m*
(JAP) 解約払戻金
(RUS) НАЛИЧНАЯ СУММА,
ВОЗВРАЩАЕМАЯ СТРАХОВОЙ
КОМПАНИЕЙ ВЛАДЕЛЬЦУ ПОЛИСА
ПРИ АННУЛИРОВАНИИ ПОСЛЕДНЕГО

casual laborer

(CHIN) 临时工
(FRE) travailleur occasionnel, (C) ouvrier
auxiliaire
(GER) Gelegenheitsarbeiter *m*,
Tagelöhner *m*
(JAP) 日雇労働者、自由労働者
(RUS) НЕПОСТОЯННО ЗАНЯТЫЙ
РАБОТНИК

casuality insurance

(CHIN) 意外伤亡保险

(FRE) assurance accidents et risques divers

(GER) Unfall(schadens)versicherung *f*

(JAP) 災害保険

(RUS) СТРАХОВАНИЕ ОТ НЕСЧАСТНОГО СЛУЧАЯ

casuality loss

(CHIN) 意外损失

(FRE) victimes d'accidents, (C) sinistre accidents

(GER) Unfallschaden *m*; Zufallsschaden *m*

(RUS) УБЫТОК В РЕЗУЛЬТАТЕ НЕСЧАСТНОГО СЛУЧАЯ

catastrophe hazard

(CHIN) 巨灾危险

(FRE) risques de catastrophe

(GER) Katastrophenrisiko *n*

(JAP) 大災害による危険

(RUS) РИСК КАТАСТРОФИЧЕСКИХ СОБЫТИЙ

catastrophe policy

(CHIN) 巨灾医疗险

(FRE) police catastrophe, (C) assurance catastrophe

(GER) Katastrophenversicherungspolice *f*

(JAP) 大災害保険証券

(RUS) СТРАХОВАНМЕ КРУПНЫХ МЕДИЦИНСКИХ ЗАТРАТ

cats and dogs

(CHIN) 可疑证券，投机性证券

(FRE) chats et chiens, (C) actions de valeur spéculative

(GER) Spekulationspapiere *npl*

(JAP) がらくた株、くだらぬ商品

(RUS) СПЕКУЛЯТИВНЫЕ АКЦИИ; «КОШКИ И СОБАКИ»

cause of action

(CHIN) 起诉原因

(FRE) cause de l'action, (C) cause d'action

(GER) Klagegrund *m*

(JAP) 訴因、訴権

(RUS) ОСНОВАНИЕ ДЛЯ СУДЕБНОГО ИСКА

CD-writer/CD-burner

(CHIN) CD 写入器/CD 烧录机

(FRE) graveur de CD

(GER) CD-Schreiber/CD-Brenner *m*

(JAP) CD ライター／CD バーナー

(RUS) УСТРОЙСТВО ЗАПИСИ НА КОМПАКТНОМ ДИСКЕ

cell definition

(CHIN) 单元格定义

(FRE) définition de cellule

(GER) Feldinhaltsfestlegung *f*

(JAP) セルの定義

(RUS) ОПИСАНИЕ ЯЧЕЙКИ

cell format

(CHIN) 单元格式

(FRE) format de cellule, (C) définition de cellule

(GER) Feldgrösse *f*

(JAP) セルの形式

(RUS) ФОРМАТ ЯЧЕЙКИ

censure

(CHIN) 谴责，批评

(FRE) censure

(GER) Tadel *m*, Rüge *f*, Verweis *m*; Zensur *f*

(JAP) 非難(する)、不信任、

(RUS) ПОРИЦАНИЕ; ОСУЖДЕНИЕ; ЦЕНЗУРА

central bank

(CHIN) 中央银行

(FRE) banque centrale

(GER) Zentralbank *f*, Notenbank *f*

(JAP) 中央銀行

(RUS) ЦЕНТРАЛЬНЫЙ БАНК

central business district (CBD)

(CHIN) 中心商业区（CBD）

(FRE) centre d'affaires, (C) hypercentre

(GER) Hauptgeschäftsbezirk *m*, -viertel *n*

(JAP) 商業中心地区

(RUS) ЦЕНТРАЛЬНЫЙ ДЕЛОВОЙ РАЙОН

central buying

(CHIN) 集中购买

(FRE) achat central, (C) centrale d'achats
(GER) Zentraleinkauf *m*
(JAP) 一括仕入れ
(RUS) ЦЕНТРАЛИЗОВАННЫЕ ЗАКУПКИ

centralizaion
(CHIN) 集中
(FRE) centralisation
(GER) Zentralisierung *f*, Zentralisation *f*
(JAP) 集権化、中央集権
(RUS) ЦЕНТРАЛИЗАЦИЯ

central planning
(CHIN) 集中计划策略
(FRE) planification centrale
(GER) zentrale Planung *f*
(JAP) 集権的計画、中央計画
(RUS) ЦЕНТРАЛЬНОЕ ПЛАНИРОВАНИЕ

central processing unit (CPU)
(CHIN) 中央处理单元（CPU）
(FRE) unité centrale de traitement (UCT),
(C) unité centrale
(JAP) 中央処理装置、
中央演算処理装置、CPU
(RUS) ЦЕНТРАЛЬНЫЙ ПРОЦЕССОР

central tendency
(CHIN) 集中趋势
(FRE) tendance centrale, (C) centrisme
(GER) zentrale Tendenz *f*
(JAP) 中心傾向
(RUS) ПОКАЗАТЕЛЬ ТИПИЧНОЙ
СРЕДИННОЙ ВЕЛИЧИНЫ ДИСТРИБУЦИИ

certificate of deposit (CD)
(CHIN) 存款单，存单
(FRE) certificat de dépôt
(GER) Depositen- *n*, Einlagenzertifikat *n*,
Einlagebrief *m*; Hinterlegungsurkunde *f*
(JAP) 預金証書、有価証券預証
(RUS) ДЕПОЗИТНЫЙ СЕРТИФИКАТ

certificate of incorporation
(CHIN) 公司注册证书，公司执照
(FRE) certificat d'enregistrement de société,
(C) certificat de constitution, (C) charte
(GER) Gründungsurkunde (US) *f*

(JAP) 会社設立許可証、法人設立許可証
(RUS) ДОКУМЕНТ О СОЗДАНИИ
КОРПОРАЦИИ

certificate of occupancy
(CHIN) 居住证书
(FRE) certificat d'occupation
(GER) Bezugsfähigkeitsbescheinigung *f*
(JAP) 居住証明、建物使用許可証
(RUS) ДОКУМЕНТ О СООТВЕТСТВИИ
ЗДАНИЯ С НОРМАМИ СТРОИТЕЛЬСТВА
И БЕЗОПАСТНОСТИ

certificate of title
(CHIN) 产权证书
(FRE) certificat de titre, (C) titre
(GER) Eigentumsbescheinigung *f*;
Grundbuchauszug *m*
(JAP) 権利証書
(RUS) УДОСТОВЕРЕНИЕ О ПРАВЕ
СОБСТВЕННОСТИ

certificate of use
(CHIN) 使用证书
(FRE) certificat d'utilisation
(GER) Nutzungsbescheinigung *f*
(JAP) 使用許可書
(RUS) СЕРТИФИКАТ ИСПОЛЬЗОВАНИЯ

certification
(CHIN) 合格证，证明
(FRE) certification
(GER) Zertifizierung *f*, Beurkundung *f*,
Beglaubigung *f*, Bestätigung *f*,
Bescheinigung *f*, Zulassung *f*
(JAP) 証明、保証、証明書(RUS)
СЕРТИФИКАЦИЯ
(RUS) СЕРТИФИКАЦИЯ

certified check
(CHIN) 保付支票
(FRE) chèque certifié, (C) chèque visé
(GER) von der Bank *f* bestätigter und
garantierter Scheck *m*
(JAP) 支払保証小切手
(RUS) ЧЕК КЛИЕНТА,
ГАРАНТИРОВАННЫЙ БАНКОМ

certified financial statement
(CHIN) 已证明财务报表

(FRE) état financier certifié
(GER) Abschluss *m* mit
Bestätigungsvermerk *m*, testierter
Abschluss *m*, Bilanz *f* mit Prüfvermerk *m*
(JAP) 監査証明済み財務諸表
(RUS) СЕРТИФИЦИРОВАННЫЙ
ФИНАНСОВЫЙ ОТЧЕТ

certified mail
(CHIN) 登记信(保证递送,
但不保证赔偿)
(FRE) lettre certifiée
(GER) Einschreiben *n*,
Einschreibesendung *f*
(JAP) 受取証明郵便、書留郵便
(RUS) ЗАКАЗНОЕ ПОЧТОВОЕ
ОТПРАВЛЕНИЕ

C&F
(CHIN) 成本及运费
(FRE) coût et fret (C et F)
(GER) (Verlade)kosten *pl* und (See)fracht *f*
bezahlt (bis Bestimmungshafen *m*)
(JAP) 運賃込み値段(条件)
(RUS) СТОИМОСТЬ ДОСТАВКИ

chain of command
(CHIN) 控制跨度, 指挥系统
(FRE) voie hiérarchique
(GER) Dienstweg *m*, Befehlskette *f*
(JAP) 指揮系統、命令系統
(RUS) ИЕРАРХИЯ УПРАВЛЕНИЯ

chain feeding
(CHIN) 链式供应
(FRE) alimentation de la chaîne
(GER) Massenfütterung *f*
(JAP) 連鎖的補給 （供給）
(RUS) ПОСЛЕДОВАТЕЛЬНАЯ ПОДАЧА

chain store
(CHIN) 连锁店
(FRE) grand magasin, grande surface,
magasin à succursales multiples,
(C) entreprise à succursales
(GER) Filialkette *f*; Filialgeschäft *n*
(JAP) チェーンストア
(RUS) МАГАЗИН В СЕТИ ОБЩЕГО
ПОДЧИНЕНИЯ

chairman of the board
(CHIN) 董事长
(FRE) président du conseil
(GER) Vorstands-,
Verwaltungsratsvorsitzender *m*, Chairman
of the Board
(JAP) 取締役会長
(RUS) ПРЕДСЕДАТЕЛЬ ПРАВЛЕНИЯ

chancery
(CHIN) 平衡法院
(FRE) chancellerie
(GER) Kanzlei *f*, Gerichtshof *m*,
Kanzleigericht *n*
(JAP) 衡平法裁判所、エクイティ裁判所
(RUS) КАНЦЛЕРСКИЙ СУД; КАНЦЕЛЯРИЯ

change
(CHIN) 零钱, 兑换, 修改, 变动
(FRE) changer, (C) modifier
(GER) Änderung *f*, Wechsel- *n*, Kleingeld *n*
(JAP) 変動、変更、換算、両替賃、
両替する
(RUS) ПЕРЕМЕНА; ИЗМЕНЕНИЕ

change of beneficiary provision
(CHIN) 受益人条款变更
(FRE) modification de la disposition sur le
bénéficiaire
(GER) Klausel *f* zur Änderung *f* des
Begünstigten *m*, Bestimmung *f* zur
Änderung des Bezugsberechtigten *m*
(JAP) 受益者条項の変更
(RUS) ИЗМЕНЕНИЕ БЕНЕФИЦИАРИЯ

channel of distribution
(CHIN) 分销系统, 销售网
(FRE) circuits de distribution
(GER) Vertriebs- *m*, Absatzweg *m*;
Vertriebs- *m*, Absatzkanal *m*
(JAP) 流通経路、
ディストリビューション・チャンネル
(RUS) КАНАЛ СБЫТА

channel of sales
(CHIN) 销售渠道
(FRE) circuits de vente
(GER) Verkaufs- *m*, Absatzweg *m*;
Verkaufs- *m*, Absatzkanal *m*

(JAP) 販売経路
(RUS) ПУТИ ПОСТУПЛЕНИЯ НОВЫХ
ПОДПИСОК (В ИЗДАТЕЛЬСКОМ ДЕЛЕ)

character
(CHIN) 字符
(FRE) caractère
(GER) Schriftzeichen *n*
(JAP) 文字、キャラクター、字
(RUS) СИМВОЛ

charge
(CHIN) 主管，要价，收费，借项，充电
(FRE) frais, facturer
(GER) Preis *m*, Gebühr *f*; Last *f*, Kosten *pl*;
Belastung *f*, Abbuchung *f* (Konto);
Lastschrift *f* (Konto); Abgabe *f*
(Finanzwesen)
(JAP) 請求する、請求代金、
(RUS) ПЛАТА; ДЕНЕЖНЫЙ СБОР;
ПРЕДПИСАНИЕ; ОБВИНЕНИЕ

charge buyer
(CHIN) 信用购买人
(FRE) facturer l'acheteur
(GER) Kreditkäufer *m*, -kunde *m*
(JAP) 掛け買い客、信用取引客
(RUS) ПОКУПАТЕЛЬ ПО КРЕДИТНОМУ
ДОКУМЕНТУ

chart
(CHIN) 表，图表
(FRE) graphique, (C) tableau
(GER) Diagramm *n*, Grafik *f*
(JAP) 図、チャート、図表
(RUS) КАРТА, ДИАГРАММА, СХЕМА,
ЧЕРТЕЖ, ТАБЛИЦА

charter
(CHIN) 特许，特权，租赁契约，许可证，
宪章
(FRE) charte
(GER) Gründungsurkunde *f*; Charter *f*,
Konzession *f*, Verleihungsurkunde *f*;
Gesellschaftssatzung (US) *f*
(JAP) 設立免許状、基本定款、用船契約
(証券)、借上げ使用する(自動車など)
(RUS) УСТАВ; УСТАВНЫЕ ДОКУМЕНТЫ;
ФРАХТ; ЧАРТЕР

chartist
(CHIN) 图解专家，证券行情分析家
(FRE) chartiste
(GER) Chart-Analyst *m*, Chartist *m*,
(Anleger, der Anlageentscheidungen aus
Chartanalysen ableitet)
(JAP) チャーティスト、
株式チャート作成・分析者
(RUS) ЭКОНОМИСТ-АНАЛИТИК,
специалист по анализу рыночной
конъюнктуры

chart of accounts
(CHIN) 会计科目表
(FRE) plan comptable
(GER) Kontenplan *m*, -rahmen *m*
(JAP) 勘定科目一覧表
(RUS) ПЛАН СЧЕТОВ (бухг.)

chat forum
(CHIN) 闲谈论坛
(FRE) forum de discussion, (C) forum de
clavardage
(GER) Chatforum *n*
(JAP) チャット広場、
チャットフォーラム
(RUS) ИНТЕРНЕТ-КОНФЕРЕНЦИЯ

chattel
家财，动产
(FRE) biens meubles
(GER) bewegliche Sache *f*, Mobiliar *n*, Hab
und Gut *n*
(JAP) 家財、動産
(RUS) ДВИЖИМОЕ ИМУЩЕСТВО

chattel mortgage
(CHIN) 动产抵押
(FRE) nantissement de biens meubles,
hypothèque mobilière
(GER) Mobiliarhypothek *f*, Pfandrecht *n* an
beweglichen Sachen *fpl*,
Mobiliarpfändung *f*
(JAP) 動産抵当、動産担保
(RUS) ИПОТЕЧНЫЙ КРЕДИТ ПОД
ДВИЖИМОЕ ИМУЩЕСТВО

chattle paper
(CHIN) 动产文件

(FRE) nantissement de biens meubles
(GER) Verpfändungserklärung *f*,
Beleihung *f* beweglichen Vermögens *n*
(JAP) 動産抵当証券
(RUS) ДОКУМЕНТ О КРЕДИТНОМ
СОСТОЯНИИ ДВИЖИМОГО ИМУЩЕСТВА

check
(CHIN) 账单，支票，核对，校正，
盘货
(FRE) chèque, vérifier, contrôle, contrôler
(GER) Scheck *m*
(JAP) 小切手、小切手を振出す
(RUS) ЧЕК; ПЕРЕВОДНОЙ ВЕКСЕЛЬ;
СДЕРЖИВАТЬ; ОГРАНИЧИВАТЬ

check digit
(CHIN) 校验数据
(FRE) chiffre de contrôle
(GER) Prüf- *f*, Kontrollziffer *f*
(JAP) 検査数字
(RUS) КОНТРОЛЬНАЯ ЦИФРА

check-kiting
(CHIN) 支票骗空
(FRE) jeu de chèques
(GER) Scheckreiterei *f*; Schreiben eines
ungedeckten Schecks *m*
(JAP) 空手形を振り出す、手形詐欺
(RUS) ВЫПИСЫВАНИЕ
НЕОБЕСПЕЧЕННЫХ ЧЕКОВ ДЛЯ
ПОЛУЧЕНИЯ КРЕДИТА

check protector
(CHIN) 支票保护器
(FRE) protection des chèques
(GER) Schecksicherung *f*,
-schutz *m*
(JAP) チェック・プロテクター
(RUS) ЗАЩИТА ЧЕКОВ ОТ
ПОДДЕЛКИ

check register
(CHIN) 支票登记账
(FRE) registre de contrôle
(GER) Scheckregister *n*
(JAP) チェック・レジスター、小切手振
出し記録簿
(RUS) РЕГИСТР ПЛАТЕЖНЫХ
ДОКУМЕНТОВ

check stub
(CHIN) 支票存根
(FRE) souche de chèque
(GER) Scheckbeleg- *m*, Kontrollabschnitt *m*
(JAP) 小切手の控え
(RUS) КОРЕШОК ЧЕКА

chief executive officer (CEO)
(CHIN) 总裁，首席执行长
(FRE) président directeur général, (C) chef
de la direction
(GER) CEO, Chief Executive Officer *m*,
Hauptgeschäftsführer *m*
(RUS) ГЛАВНЫЙ ИСПОЛНИТЕЛЬНЫЙ
ДИРЕКТОР

chief financial officer (CFO)
(CHIN) 财务长
(FRE) directeur général des finances,
(C) chef de l'exploitation financière
(GER) CFO, Chief Financial Officer *m*,
oberster Finanzdirektor *m*
(JAP) 最高財務責任者
(RUS) ГЛАВНЫЙ ФИНАНСОВЫЙ
ДИРЕКТОР

chief operating officer (COO)
(CHIN) 业务长
(FRE) directeur général d'exploitation,
(C) chef de l'exploitation
(GER) COO, Chief Operating Officer *m*,
oberster Betriebsdirektor *m*
(JAP) 最高（業務）執行責任者
（社長）
(RUS) ГЛАВНЫЙ ОПЕРАЦИОННЫЙ
ДИРЕКТОР

child and dependent care credit
(CHIN) 儿童及家属照顾费用税务减免额
(FRE) crédit pour enfants et personnes
dépendantes
(GER) Freibetrag *m* für Kinder- und
Familienangehörigenbetreuung *f*
(JAP) 児童・扶養家族養護控除
(RUS) НАЛОГОВАЯ СКИДКА ПО УХОДУ
ЗА ДЕТЬМИ И ИЖДИВЕНЦАМИ

chi-square test
(CHIN) 交叉平方检验
(FRE) test du chi carré
(GER) Chi-Quadrat-Test *m*

(JAP) カイ二乗分布
(RUS) СТАТИСТИЧЕСКИЙ МЕТОД
ПРОВЕРКИ ТОГО, ЯВЛЯЮТСЯ ЛИ
ВЕЛИЧИНЫ НЕЗАВИСИМЫМИ ИЛИ
ГОМОГЕННЫМИ

chose in action
(CHIN) 诉讼产，权利上的财产
(FRE) choisir en action
(GER) obligatorischer Anspruch *m*,
Forderung *f*; unkörperlicher
Rechtsgegenstand *m*
(JAP) 債権、無体動産、無体財産
(RUS) ПРАВО ВОЗБУЖДЕНИЯ ИСКА или
ВОСТРЕБОВАНИЯ ДОЛГА

churning
(CHIN) 反复买卖
(FRE) multiplication des opérations
(GER) Überspekulation *f*,
(Vertrauensmissbrauch des Börsenmaklers
durch hohe Einsätze)
(JAP) 過度な売買勧誘、不当な回転商い
(RUS) ЧРЕЗМЕРНОЕ КОЛИЧЕСТВО КУПЛЬ
И ПРОДАЖ БРОКЕРОМ АКЦИЙ СВОИХ
КЛИЕНТОВ

CIF
(CHIN) 到岸价格
(FRE) coût assurance fret (CAF)
(GER) CIF *n*; Kosten *pl*, Versicherung *f*,
Fracht *f*
(JAP) 保険料運賃込み値段
(RUS) СТОИМОСТЬ, СТРАХОВАНИЕ И
ФРАХТ

cipher
(CHIN) 密码
(FRE) chiffrer
(GER) Chiffre *f*, Code *m*;
Ziffer *f*
(JAP) 暗号、暗号文
(RUS) ЗАКОДИРОВАННОЕ
СООБЩЕНИЕ

circuit
(CHIN) 电路，线路，循环，流通
(FRE) circuit
(GER) Kreis *m*; (lokaler) Gerichtsbezirk
(US) *m*

(JAP) 巡回、迂回、回路
(RUS) ОКРУГ (СУДА)

circuit board
(CHIN) 电路板
(FRE) circuit imprimé, (C) carte de circuit
imprimé
(GER) Leiterplatte *f*
(JAP) 回路基板
(RUS) МОНТАЖНАЯ ПЛАТА

civil law
(CHIN) 民法，大陆法
(FRE) droit civil
(GER) Zivilrecht *n*, bürgerliches Recht *n*
(JAP) 民法
(RUS) ГРАЖДАНСКОЕ ПРАВО

civil liability
(CHIN) 民事责任
(FRE) responsabilité civile
(GER) zivilrechtliche Haftung *f*
(JAP) 市民的責任義務
(RUS) ГРАЖДАНСКАЯ
ОТВЕТСТВЕННОСТЬ

civil penalty
(CHIN) 民事惩罚
(FRE) peine civile
(GER) Bußgeld *n*
(JAP) 民事刑罰
(RUS) ДЕНЕЖНЫЕ ВЫПЛАТЫ В
КАЧЕСТВЕ НАКАЗАНИЯ

claim
(CHIN) 索赔，债权，要求，申请
(FRE) réclamation
(GER) Anspruch *m*, Rechtsanspruch *m*;
Forderung *f*; Schadensfall *m*
(Versicherung); Behauptung *f*; Anspruch *m*
(Versicherung)
(JAP) 請求(権)、損害賠償を請求する
(RUS) ПРИТЯЗАНИЕ; ТРЕБОВАНИЕ;
РЕКЛАМАЦИЯ; ПУНКТ (патентной
формулы)

class
(CHIN) 类别，等级
(FRE) classe, catégorie

(GER) Klasse *f*, Gruppe *f*, Gattung *f*;
(soziale) Schicht *f*
(JAP) 集合、集団
(RUS) КЛАСС

class action B shares

(CHIN) 乙类活跃股
(FRE) parts du recours collectif B
(GER) Class A/Class B-Aktien *fpl*,
(Aufteilung des Stammaktienkapitals einer
Gesellschaft in zwei Kategorien, wobei
Stimmrechte nur mit einer Klasse
verbunden sind)
(JAP) B株クラスアクション、B株集団
代表訴訟
(RUS) АКЦИИ «Б» ПО КОЛЛЕКТИВНОМУ
ИСКУ

classification

(CHIN) 分类，分级
(FRE) classification
(GER) Klassifikation *f*, Klassifizierung *f*
(JAP) 分類、各付け
(RUS) КЛАССИФИКАЦИЯ

classified stock

(CHIN) 分类股票
(FRE) action classée
(GER) Aktiengattungen *fpl* mit
unterschiedlichen Rechten *npl* (siehe Class
A/B-Aktien)
(JAP) 発行別分類株、選別株
(RUS) КЛАССИФИЦИРОВАННЫЕ
АКЦИИ

clause

(CHIN) 条款，条例，科目，项目
(FRE) clause
(GER) Klausel *f*, Bestimmung *f*,
Vertragsartikel *m*
(JAP) 条項
(RUS) СТАТЬЯ; ПУНКТ;
ОГОВОРКА

clean

(CHIN) 不附保留条件的，清洁的
(FRE) propre, net
(GER) rein, sauber, einwandfrei *adj*
(JAP) きれいな、間違いのない、完全な

(RUS) ЧИСТЫЙ; СВОБОДНЫЙ ОТ
ДОЛГОВ; БЕЗ ПРИЛОЖЕНИЯ
ДОКУМЕНТОВ

clean hands

(CHIN) 清白，诚实
(FRE) droiture
(GER) redlich *adj*; mit sauberen Händen
fpl (fig)
(JAP) 潔白、汚れなき手の原則
(RUS) «ЧИСТЫЕ РУКИ», ЧЕСТНОЕ И
ПРОФЕССИОНАЛЬНОЕ ПОВЕДЕНИЕ

cleanup fund

(CHIN) 后事处理基金
(FRE) fonds de liquidation
(GER) Sanierungsfonds *m*
(JAP) 諸ζ整理資金、最終処理費基金
(RUS) ФОНД НА ПРЕОДОЛЕНИЕ
НЕПРЕДВИДЕННЫХ ЗАТРУДНЕНИЙ

clear

(CHIN) 支票兑现，结清，脱售
(FRE) clair, effacer
(GER) räumen; ausverkaufen; Kosten
decken; abrechnen, verrechnen
(Finanzwesen); tilgen (Darlehen); netto
verdienen; verzollen *v*; unbelastet *adj*
(JAP) 清算する、皆済する、一掃する、
見切売りする
(RUS) ВЫПЛАТИТЬ ПО ЧЕКУ; ПОЛУЧИТЬ
ПРИБЫЛЬ; ПРОЙТИ ПРОВЕРКУ

clearance sale

(CHIN) 清仓拍卖
(FRE) vente de liquidation
(GER) Ausverkauf *m*,
Räumungsverkauf *m*
(JAP) 残品見切販売、在庫一掃セール、
クリアランスセール
(RUS) РАСПРОДАЖА ПРИ ЛИКВИДАЦИИ
ИНВЕНТАРНЫХ ЗАПАСОВ

clearinghouse

(CHIN) 票据交换所，清算机构
(FRE) chambre de compensation
(GER) Clearing House *n*; Clearingstelle *f*;
Abrechnung- *f*, Abwicklungs- *f*,
Verrechnungsstelle *f*;
Effektenbuchungsstelle *f*

(JAP) クリアリングハウス、
手形交換所
(RUS) РАСЧЕТНАЯ ПАЛАТА

clear title
(CHIN) 明晰产权
(FRE) titre incontesté
(GER) einwandfreier Rechtsanspruch *m*,
unbelastetes Eigentum *n*; uneingeschränkte
Eigentumsurkunde *f*
(JAP) 無傷の権利
(RUS) ЧИСТЫЙ ПРАВОВОЙ
ТИТУЛ

clerical error
(CHIN) 笔误，纪录错误
(FRE) erreur d'écriture
(GER) Schreibfehler *m*
(JAP) 記帳ミス、誤記
(RUS) ТЕХНИЧЕСКАЯ ОШИБКА

clerk
(CHIN) 职员，办事员
(FRE) greffier
(GER) Büroangestellter *m*, Sachbearbeiter
m, Urkundsbeamter *m* (Gericht)
(JAP) 事務員、裁判所書記官
(RUS) КОНТОРСКИЙ РАБОТНИК; КЛЕРК;
СУДЕБНЫЙ СЕКРЕТАРЬ

client
(CHIN) 客户，顾客，买方
(FRE) client
(GER) Kunde *m*; Klient *m*, Mandant *m*,
Auftraggeber *m* (Rechtswesen);
Bauherr *m*
(JAP) 依頼人、クライアント
(RUS) КЛИЕНТ

clipboard
(CHIN) 剪贴板
(FRE) presse-papier, (C) tablette
électronique
(GER) Zwischenablage *f*
(JAP) クリップボード
(RUS) БУФЕР ВЫРЕЗАННОГО
ИЗОБРАЖЕНИЯ; В СИСТЕМАХ
НЕПОСРЕДСТВЕННОГО
ВЗАИМОДЕЙСТВИЯ - БУФЕР ДЛЯ
ЫРЕЗАННОГО ИЗОБРАЖЕНИЯ, КОТОРОЕ

МОЖЕТ БЫТЬ ПРЕОБРАЗОВАНО И
ВСТАВЛЕНО В ТО ЖЕ ОКНО ИЛИ ОКНО,
УПРАВЛЯЕМОЕ ДРУГОЙ ПРИКЛАДНОЙ
ПРОГРАММОЙ

close
(CHIN) 关闭，接近，达成，结清
(FRE) fermer
(GER) amtlicher Börsenschluss *m*
(JAP) 非公開の、限られた
(RUS) ЗАКРЫТЬ; ЗАКРЫТИЕ;
ЗАВЕРШЕНИЕ

close corporation plan
(CHIN) 股份不公开的公司计划
(FRE) plan de société fermée à peu
d'actionnaires, (C) plan de société privée
(GER) (Konzept einer Kapitalgesellschaft
mit geschlossenem Gesellschafterkreis,
ähnlich einer GmbH; Gesellschaft, die sich
im Besitz von weniger als 5 Aktionären
befindet)
(JAP) 株式非公開会社方式、
閉鎖会社方式
(RUS) ДОГОВОР ОПРЕДЕЛЯЮЩИЙ КАК
БУДЕТ ВЫКУПАТЬСЯ ДОЛЯ УМЕРШЕГО
ДЕРЖАТЕЛЯ АКЦИЙ ОСТАВШИМИСЯ
ЧЛЕНАМИ КОРПОРАЦИИ

closed account
(CHIN) 已结账，已结清账户
(FRE) compte clôturé
(GER) abgeschlossenes Konto *n*,
glattgestellte Position *f*
(JAP) 締切済み勘定
(RUS) ЗАКРЫТЫЙ СЧЕТ

closed economy
(CHIN) 封闭性经济
(FRE) économie fermée
(GER) geschlossene Volkswirtschaft *f*
(JAP) 封鎖経済、
クローズドエコノミー
(RUS) ЗАКРЫТАЯ ЭКОНОМИКА

closed-end mortgage
(CHIN) 限额型抵押
(FRE) hypothèque close
(GER) Hypothek *f* ohne
Erhöhungsmöglichkeit *f*, (Hypothek, die

weitere Belastung des zugrunde liegenden Gegenstands ausschließt)
(JAP) 閉鎖担保（モーゲージ）
(RUS) «ЗАКРЫТАЯ» ИПОТЕКА

closed-end mutual fund
(CHIN) 封闭式共同基金
(FRE) fonds de placement fermé
(GER) geschlossener Investmentfonds *m*
(JAP) 閉鎖型投資信託、クローズドエンド型投資信託
(RUS) «ЗАКРЫТЫЙ» ВЗАИМНЫЙ ФОНД

closed stock
(CHIN) 限额股份
(FRE) action fermée
(GER) geschlossene Aktie *f*
(JAP) セット品
(RUS) «ЗАКРЫТЫЕ» АКЦИИ

closely held corporation
(CHIN) 被少数人控制的公司
(FRE) société fermée à peu d'actionnaires
(GER) (Gesellschaft mit beschränkter Mitgliederzahl bzw. beschränktem Aktionärskreis)
(JAP) 閉鎖的所有会社
(RUS) АКЦИОНЕРНОЕ ОБЩЕСТВО ОТКРЫТОГО ТИПА С НЕБОЛЬШИМ КОЛИЧЕСТВОМ АКЦИОНЕРОВ, ИЛИ СОСТОЯНИЕ, КОГДА 5 ИЛИ МЕНЬШЕ АКЦИОНЕРОВ КОНТРОЛИРУЮТ БОЛЕЕ 50 % КОРПОРАЦИИ

close out
(CHIN) 出清存货
(FRE) liquidation, clôture
(GER) Glattstellung *f*, Kontenabschluss *m*
(JAP) 閉鎖、店仕舞
(RUS) ЛИКВИДАЦИЯ ТОВАРНЫХ ЗАПАСОВ ПУТЁМ ПРОДАЖИ

closing
(CHIN) 结束，结账，决算
(FRE) fermeture
(GER) Abschluss *m*; Schließung *f*; Auflösung *f*; Valutierung *f*; Termin *m* der Übertragung von Eigentums- bzw. Grundbesitzrechten
(JAP) 終結、取引終了

(RUS) ОКОНЧАТЕЛЬНОЕ ОФОРМЛЕНИЕ сделки

closing agreement
(CHIN) 税务结清协议
(FRE) accord final
(GER) Grundbesitzübertragungsvereinbarung *f*, -vertrag *m*; endgültige Vereinbarung *f*
(JAP) 最終的合意
(RUS) СОГЛАШЕНИЕ ОБ ОКОНЧАТЕЛЬНОМ ОФОРМЛЕНИИ СДЕЛКИ

closing cost
(CHIN) 成交价
(FRE) coût final
(GER) Grundbesitzübertragungskosten *pl*; Abschlusskosten *pl*
(JAP) 不動産売買手数料
(RUS) ЗАТРАТЫ НА ОКОНЧАТЕЛЬНОЕ ОФОРМЛЕНИЕ СДЕЛКИ(сверх продажной цены недвижимости – на осмотр, страхование и т.п.)

closing date
(CHIN) 截止日期
(FRE) date limite, date finale
(GER) Grundbesitzübertragungstermin *m*; Anmelde- *m*; Ausschreibungsterminschluss *m*; Einreichungsfrist *f*; Stich- *n*; Schlusstag *m*
(JAP) 決算日、締切日
(RUS) ДАТА ОКОНЧАТЕЛЬНОГО ОФОРМЛЕНИЯ СДЕЛКИ

closing entry
(CHIN) 结账分录
(FRE) écriture de fermeture
(GER) Abschluss- *f*, Ausbuchung *f*
(JAP) 決算記入、決算仕訳
(RUS) ВЫВЕДЕНИЕ ОСТАТКА; ЗАКРЫТИЕ СЧЁТА

closing inventory
(CHIN) 期末存货
(FRE) stock final
(GER) End- *m*, Schlussbestand *m*; Endbestand *m* am Ende *n* einer Rechnungsperiode *f*
(JAP) 期末棚卸(高)、期末在庫

(RUS) ИНВЕНТАРНЫЙ ЗАПАС НА КОНЕЦ УЧЁТНОГО ГОДА

closing price or closing quote
(CHIN) 收盘价或收盘行市
(FRE) cours de clôture ou cotation finale
(GER) Schlusskurs *m*, -notierung *f*, -wert *m*
(RUS) ЦЕНА ЗАКРЫТИЯ или ПОСЛЕДНЯЯ КОТИРОВКА (перед закрытием биржи)

closing statement
(CHIN) 结清报告
(FRE) déclaration finale, conclusion
(GER) Abschlussrechnung *m*, Kontoabschluss *m*, End- *f*, Schlussabrechnung *f*
(JAP) 最終陳述、最終報告書
(RUS) ЗАКЛЮЧИТЕЛЬНЫЙ ОТЧЁТ

cloud on title
(CHIN) 产权缺陷
(FRE) titre contesté, titre suspect
(GER) Beeinträchtigung *f* eines Eigenstumsrechts *n*, Eigentumsbeschränkung *f*, Eigentum *n* mit potentiellen Altlasten *fpl*
(JAP) 権原の瑕疵、権原への疑義
(RUS) ИЗЪЯН ПРАВОВОГО ТИТУЛА

cluster analysis
(CHIN) 群组分析
(FRE) analyse d'agrégats, analyse en grappes
(GER) Clusteranalyse *f*, Sammelanalyse *f*
(JAP) クラスター分析、集団化分析
(RUS) ГРУППОВОЙ АНАЛИЗ

cluster housing
(CHIN) 集中建筑群
(FRE) regroupement
(GER) geballtes Wohngebiet *n*
(JAP) 集合住宅，集合家屋
(RUS) ТЕСНАЯ ГРУППОВАЯ ЖИЛАЯ ЗАСТРОЙКА

cluster sample
(CHIN) 成群抽样样本
(FRE) échantillons en grappes
(GER) Klumpenstichprobe *f*
(JAP) クラスターサンプル、集落標本

(RUS) ГРУППОВАЯ ВЫБОРКА

cluster sampling
(CHIN) 成群抽样分析
(FRE) échantillonnage en grappes
(GER) Stichprobennahme *f* mit Klumpenauswahl *f*, Klumpenstichprobenziehung *f*
(JAP) 集落標本抽出

code
(CHIN) 代码，密码，符号，标记，规章，标准
(FRE) code
(GER) Code *m*, Schlüssel *m f*, Gesetzbuch *n*, Gesctzessammlung *f*, Kodex *m*
(JAP) 規則、慣例
(RUS) КОДЕКС, НОРМЫ, КОД

code of ethics
(CHIN) 行为准则，道德准则
(FRE) code de déontologie
(GER) Ehrenkodex *m*, Standesordnung *f*
(JAP) 倫理規範
(RUS) ЭТИЧЕСКИЙ КОДЕКС

codicil
(CHIN) 遗嘱更改
(FRE) codicille
(GER) Testamentsnachtrag *m*, -zusatz *m*, -anhang *m*
(JAP) 遺言補足書、追加条項
(RUS) ДОПОЛНЕНИТЕЛЬНОЕ РАСПОРЯЖЕНИЕ К ЗАВЕЩАНИЮ; КОДИЦИЛЬ

coding of accounts
(CHIN) 账户代码，科目代号
(FRE) codage des comptes
(GER) Kontierung *f*, Codierung *f* von Konten *npl*
(JAP) 会計用語の符号化、勘定符号法
(RUS) «КОДИРОВАНИЕ» СЧЕТОВ

coefficient of determination
(CHIN) 决定系数
(FRE) coefficient de détermination

(GER) Bestimmtheitsmaß *n*
(JAP) 決定係数
(RUS) ДЕТЕРМИНАНТНЫЙ
КОЭФФИЦИЕНТ (СТАТ.)

coinsurance
(CHIN) 共同保险，联保
(FRE) coassurance
(GER) gemeinsame Versicherung *f*;
proportionale Risikobeteiligung *f* des
Versicherten *m*, Selbstbehalt *m*
(JAP) 共同保険
(RUS) СОСТРАХОВАНИЕ; РАЗДЕЛЕНИЕ
РИСКА ПРИ СТРАХОВАНИИ

cold canvass
(CHIN) 兜售
(FRE) sollicitation au hazard　.
(GER) ungezielte Kundenwerbung *f*
(JAP) 飛び込み訪問
(RUS) АКТИВНЫЙ ПОИСК ЗАКАЗОВ

collapsible corporation
(CHIN) 可随时进行清理的公司
(FRE) société qui s'effondre
(GER) vorübergehend bestehende
Gesellschaft *f*
(JAP) 泡沫法人、泡沫会社
(RUS) «СВОРАЧИВАЕМАЯ» КОРПОРАЦИЯ
(на один проект)

collateral
(CHIN) 附属，担保
(FRE) garantie, collateral
(GER) Sicherungsgegenstand *m*, Pfand *n*,
Kreditsicherheit *f*, akzessorische Sicherheit *f*
(JAP) 担保物件
(RUS) ОБЕСПЕЧЕНИЕ КРЕДИТА

colatteral assignment
(CHIN) 间接转让，担保转让
(FRE) attribution collatérale, affectation
collatérale
(GER) Sicherungsforderungsabtretung *f*, -
übereignung *f*
(JAP) 担保の譲渡
(RUS) ВЫДЕЛЕНИЕ СТРАХОВОГО
ПОЛИСА В ОБЕСПЕЧЕНИЕ КРЕДИТА

collateralize
(CHIN) 提供抵押

(FRE) gager
(GER) besichern, Sicherheit beistellen,
lombardieren, mit Sicherheit unterlegen *v*
(JAP) 担保として使う、
担保により保証する
(RUS) ОБЕСПЕЧИВАТЬ, ГАРАНТИРОВАТЬ
(заем, кредит)

**collateralized mortgage obligation
(CMO)**
(CHIN) 附属抵押品贷款义务（CMO）
(FRE) obligation de nantissement avec
garantie
(GER) CMO-Emission *f*, durch Hypotheken
fpl gesicherte US-Schuldverschreibung *f*
(JAP) 不動産抵当証書担保債券、抵当付
きモーゲージ証書
(RUS) ОБЛИГАЦИЯ, ОБЕСПЕЧЕННАЯ
ПУЛОМ ИПОТЕК

colleague
(CHIN) 同事
(FRE) collègue
(GER) Kollege *m*, Mitarbeiter *m*
(JAP) 同僚、同業者
(RUS) КОЛЛЕГА

collectible
(CHIN) 可收回的
(FRE) encaissable
(GER) inkassofähig, einziehfähig,
einlösbar, einkassierbar *adj*
(JAP) 取り立てできる、収集可能な、
収集品
(RUS) ПОДЛЕЖАЩИЙ ВЗЫСКАНИЮ;
ПРЕДМЕТ КОЛЛЕКЦИОНИРОВАНИЯ

collection
(CHIN) 收兑，收款，托收
(FRE) encaissement, recouvrement
(GER) Steuererhebung *f*; Inkasso *n*; Einzug
m, Einnahme *f*, Einziehung *f*; Sammlung *f*;
Auswahl *f*, Sortiment *n*; Erfassung *f*,
Erhebung *f* (Daten)
(JAP) 徴収、集金、収集物
(RUS) ИНКАССАЦИЯ; ВЗЫСКАНИЕ;
СБОР

collection ratio
(CHIN) 收款比率

(FRE) taux de recouvrement
(GER) Forderungsumschlag *m*;
Tilgungskoeffizient *m*; Einzugsrate *f*,
-quote *f*
(JAP) 代金回収率
(RUS) СРЕДНИЙ СРОК ИНКАССАЦИИ
ПОСТУПЛЕНИЙ

collective bargaining
(CHIN) 集合议价，集体谈判
(FRE) négociation collective
(GER) Tarifvertragsverhandlungen *fpl*
(JAP) 団体交渉
(RUS) ВЫДВИЖЕНИЕ НАЁМНЫМИ
РАБОТНИКАМИ СВОИХ
ПРЕДСТАВИТЕЛЕЙ ДЛЯ РЕШЕНИЯ С
РАБОТОДАТЕЛЕМ

collusion
(CHIN) 共谋，串通舞弊
(FRE) collusion
(GER) geheimes Einverständnis *n*, geheime
Abmachung *f*, (heimliche) Absprache *f*, ;
Kollusion *f n*
(JAP) 共謀、通謀、馴れ合い訴訟
(RUS) СГОВОР (суд.)

collusive oligopoly
(CHIN) 串通性寡头垄断
(FRE) oligopole collusoire
(GER) verbotene Oligopolabsprache *f*
(JAP) 共謀寡占
(RUS) СГОВОР МЕЖДУ
ПРОИЗВОДИТЕЛЯМИ В ОЛИГОПОЛИИ

column chart/graph
(CHIN) 柱形图/柱形表
(FRE) graphique en colonnes,
(C) graphique en tuyaux d'orgue
(GER) Säulendiagramm *n*, -grafik *f*
(JAP) カラム図表／グラフ、縦列図表／
グラフ
СТОЛБИКОВАЯ ДИАГРАММА

combinations
(CHIN) 联合，合并，联合体
(FRE) combinaisons
(GER) Zusammenschlüsse *mpl* (von
Unternehmen)
(JAP) 組合わせ、連合体

(RUS) КОМБИНАЦИИ

comfort letter
(CHIN) 安抚信，安慰信
(FRE) lettre administrative de classement
(GER) Bericht *m* über begrenzte
Abschlussprüfung *f*; Verwaltungsschreiben
n; Patronatserklärung *f*; Prüfungsbericht *m*
(für Börsenzulassungsstelle *f*)
(RUS) ПОЛОЖИТЕЛЬНОЕ ЗАКЛЮЧЕНИЕ
НЕЗАВИСИМОГО АУДИТОРА

command
(CHIN) 控制权，指令，支配
(FRE) commande, ordonner
(GER) Befehl *m*, Gebot *n*,
Anweisung *f*
(JAP) 命令(する)、指揮(する)
(RUS) ПРИКАЗ; РАСПОРЯЖЕНИЕ

command economy
(CHIN) 控制经济，中央集权经济
(FRE) économie dirigiste
(GER) zentrales Planwirtschaftssystem *n*,
Plan- *f*, Befehls- *f*, Kommandowirtschaft *f*,
staatlich gelenkte Wirtschaft *f*
(JAP) 指令経済
(RUS) КОМАНДНАЯ ЭКОНОМИКА

commencement of coverage
(CHIN) 保险责任开始
(FRE) début de la couverture
(GER) Beginn *m* des Versicherungsschutzes
m, Versicherungs- *m*, Deckungsbeginn *m*
(JAP) （保険契約）適用の開始
(RUS) НАЧАЛО ПОКРЫТИЯ

commercial
(CHIN) 商业的
(FRE) message publicitaire
commercial
(GER) kaufmännisch, geschäftlich;
wirtschaftlich, Wirtschafts-; gewerblich;
kommerziell; handelsüblich *adj*
(JAP) 商業の、貿易の
(RUS) КОММЕРЧЕСКИЙ

commercial bank
(CHIN) 商业银行
(FRE) banque commerciale

(GER) Geschäfts- *f*, Handels- *f*,
Gewerbebank *f*
(JAP) 商業銀行
(RUS) КОММЕРЧЕСКИЙ БАНК

commercial blanket bond
(CHIN) 商业诚信保证
(FRE) obligation générale commerciale
(GER) Vertrauenschadensversicherung *f*
(JAP) 商業包括債券
(RUS) КОММЕРЧЕСКАЯ ОБЩАЯ
ОБЛИГАЦИЯ

commercial broker
(CHIN) 商业经纪人
(FRE) courtier commercial
(GER) Handelsmakler *m*
(JAP) 商業ブローカー
(RUS) КОММЕРЧЕСКИЙ БРОКЕР

commercial credit insurance
(CHIN) 商业信用保险
(FRE) assurance crédit commercial
(GER) Wirtschaftsdarlehensversicherung *f*,
Handels- *f*, Geschäftskreditversicherung *f*
(JAP) 商業信用保険
(RUS) СТРАХОВАНИЕ КОММЕРЧЕСКОГО
КРЕДИТА

commercial forgery policy
(CHIN) 伪造商业保险单
(FRE) politique de contrefaçon
commerciale
(GER) Warenfälschungspolice *f*,
Versicherungsschein *m* zum Schutz gegen
Warenfälschung *f*
(JAP) 商業偽造保険
(RUS) СТРАХОВАНИЕ ОТ ПОДДЕЛЬНЫХ
ЧЕКОВ

commercial forms
(CHIN) 保险单
(FRE) forme marchande
(GER) handelsübliche Formulare *npl*
(JAP) 商業書式
(RUS) КОММЕРЧЕСКИЕ БЛАНКИ

commercial health insurance
(CHIN) 商业医疗保险

(FRE) assurance maladie commerciale
(GER) (auf dem Markt erhältliche)
Krankenversicherung *f*
(JAP) 商業健康保険
(RUS) КОММЕРЧЕСКОЕ МЕДИЦИНСКОЕ
СТРАХОВАНИЕ

commercial law
(CHIN) 商法
(FRE) droit commercial
(GER) Wirtschafts- *n*, Handels- *n*,
Gewerberecht *n*; Handelsgesetz *n*
(JAP) 商法
(RUS) КОММЕРЧЕСКОЕ ПРАВО

commercial loan
(CHIN) 商业贷款
(FRE) prêt commercial
(GER) gewerblicher bzw. kommerzieller
Kredit *m*, Geschäftskredit *m*
(JAP) 銀行貸付、商業融資
(RUS) КОММЕРЧЕСКАЯ ССУДА

commercial paper
(CHIN) 商业票据，商业文件
(FRE) billet de trésorerie
(GER) Commercial Paper *n*; Wertpapier *n*;
Handelspapier *n*; Handels- *m*,
Warenwechsel *m*
(JAP) 商業手形
(RUS) КОММЕРЧЕСКИЙ ВЕКСЕЛЬ

commercial property
(CHIN) 商业财产
(FRE) propriété commerciale
(GER) gewerblich genutzte Immobilie *fpl*,
Gewerbeimmobilie *f*, gewerblich genutztes
Grundstück *n*, Gewerbeobjekt *n*;
kommerzielles Eigentum *n*
(JAP) 営業用不動産
(RUS) НЕДВИЖИМОСТЬ ИСПОЛЬЗУЕМАЯ
В КОММЕРЧЕСКИХ ЦЕЛЯХ

commercial property policy
(CHIN) 商业财产保单
(FRE) politique de propriété
commerciale
(GER) Versicherungsschein *m* bzw. Police *f*
für Gewerbeobjekt *n*
(JAP) 営利損害保険

(RUS) СТРАХОВАНИЕ КОММЕРЧЕСКОЙ
СОБСТВЕННОСТИ

commingling of funds

(CHIN) 资金混用

(FRE) amalgame des fonds

(GER) Vermischen von Fremdmitteln *npl*

(JAP) ファンドの合同運用

(RUS) СМЕШЕНИЕ ФОНДОВ
ДОВЕРЕННОГО ЛИЦА И ЕГО КЛИЕНТОВ

commission

(CHIN) 佣金，委员会

(FRE) commission

(GER) Kommission *f*, Ausschuss *m*;
Provision *f*, Courtage *f*, Vermittlungs-, *f*;
Maklergebühr *f*; Auftrag *m*, Bestellung *f*
Inauftraggabe *f*

(JAP) 手数料、コミッション

(RUS) КОМИССИЯ; КОМИССИОННЫЙ
СБОР; КОМИССИОННЫЕ

commission broker

(CHIN) 经纪人

(FRE) courtier à commission

(GER) Aktienmakler *m* auf
Provisionsbasis *f*

(JAP) 仲買人

(RUS) БРОКЕР-КОМИССИОНЕР

commitment

(CHIN) 承诺，保证

(FRE) engagement

(GER) Verpflichtung *f*; Engagement *n*
(Börse); Zusage *f*, Zusicherung *f*

(JAP) 約束、公約、売買約定

(RUS) ОБЯЗАТЕЛЬСТВО, ОБЯЗАННОСТЬ

commodities futures

(CHIN) 商品期货

(FRE) contrats à termes de marchandises

(GER) Warentermingeschäfte *npl*;
Terminkontrakte *mpl*

(JAP) 商品先物取引き

(RUS) ТОВАРНЫЕ ФЬЮЧЕРСЫ

commodity

(CHIN) 商品

(FRE) marchandise

(GER) Handelsobjekt *n*, Wirtschaftsgut *n*;
an der Warenbörse *f* gehandeltes Produkt *n*;
Bedarfsgegenstand *m*, -artikel *m*,
Gebrauchsgegegenstand *m*, -artikel *m*; Ware
f, Erzeugnis *n*, Produkt *n*; Rohstoff *m*

(JAP) 商品、物品、必需品、貨物

(RUS) ТОВАР

commodity cartel

(CHIN) 商品卡特尔

(FRE) cartel de marchandise

(GER) Rohstoffkartell *n*

(JAP) 商品カルテル

(RUS) ТОВАРНЫЙ КАРТЕЛЬ

common area

(CHIN) 共同领域

(FRE) zone commune

(GER) gemeinsamer Bereich *m*

(JAP) 共通範囲、共通域

(RUS) ОБЩАЯ ПЛОЩАДЬ, ЗОНА

common carrier

(CHIN) 承运商，公共运输企业

(FRE) transporteur

(GER) Spediteur *m*, Transportunternehmen
n; Fluggesellschaft *f*; öffentliches
Verkehrsunternehmen *n*; Frachtführer *m*

(JAP) 運送業者、運送会社、
公衆通信業者

(RUS) ПЕРЕВОЗЧИК НА ОБЩИХ
ОСНОВАНИЯХ

**common disaster clause or survivorship
clause**

(CHIN) 共同灾难条款或生存条款

(FRE) clause désastre ou clause de
survie

(GER) Klausel *f* über gleichzeitige
Todesvermutung *f*; Überlebensklausel *f*

(JAP) 共通災害条項、生存者取得権条項、
同時災害条項

(RUS) ОГОВОРКА ОБ ОДНОВРЕМЕННОЙ
ГИБЕЛИ ЗАВЕЩАТЕЛЯ И
БЕНЕФИЦИАРИЯ (с назначением
альтернативного бенефициара)

common elements

(CHIN) 共用设施

(FRE) éléments ordinaires, éléments
communs
(JAP) 共通ブロック要素
(RUS) (В КОНДОМИНИУМЕ) ЧАСТИ
СОБСТВЕННОСТИ, НЕ
ПРИНАДЛЕЖАЩИЕ НИКАКОМУ
КОНКРЕТНОМУ ЖИЛЬЦУ, НО
НАХОДЯЩИЕСЯ В ОБЩЕМ
ПОЛЬЗОВАНИИ

common law
(CHIN) 普通法
(FRE) droit commun
(GER) Common Law *n*,
Gewohnheitsrecht *n*
(JAP) 慣習法、判例法
(RUS) ОБЩЕЕ ПРАВО

common stock
(CHIN) 普通股
(FRE) action ordinaire
(GER) Stammaktien *fpl*
(JAP) 通常株、普通株
(RUS) ОБЫКНОВЕННЫЕ АКЦИИ

common stock equivalent
(CHIN) 等同普通股，准普通股
(FRE) équivalant à de l'action ordinaire,
(C) titres équivalant à des actions
(GER) Stammaktien-Äquivalent *n*;
Gegenwert *m* in Stammaktien *fpl*
(JAP) 普通株等価物、準普通株式
(RUS) ПРИВИЛЛЕГИРОВАННЫЕ АКЦИИ И
ВЕКСЕЛЯ, ОБРАТИМЫЕ В
ОБЫКНОВЕННЫЕ АКЦИИ

common stock fund
(CHIN) 普通股信托投资基金
(FRE) fonds d'actions ordinaires
(GER) Wachstumsfonds *m* (aus
Stammaktien), Aktieninvestmentfonds *m*
(JAP) 普通株ファンド
(RUS) ИНВЕСТИЦИОННЫЙ ФОНД
ОБЫКНОВЕННЫХ АКЦИЙ

common stock ratio
(CHIN) 普通股比率
(FRE) taux d'actions ordinaire
(GER) Verhältnis *n* der Stammaktien *fpl*
 zur Summe *f* aller Aktien *fpl* und
Obligationen *fpl*

(JAP) 通常株率、普通株率
(RUS) ОТНОШЕНИЕ СУММ
ОБЫКНОВЕННЫХ АКЦИЙ И ОБЩЕЙ
КАПИТАЛИЗАЦИИ (корпорации)

communications network
(CHIN) 通信网络，交通网
(FRE) réseau de communication
(GER) Kommunikationsnetz *n*
(JAP) 通信網、通信ネットワーク
(RUS) СЕТЬ СВЯЗИ

communism
(CHIN) 共产主义
(FRE) communisme
(GER) Kommunismus *m*
(JAP) 共産主義
(RUS) КОММУНИЗМ

community association
(CHIN) 社区组织
(FRE) association d'animation sociale
(GER) Gemeinde- *m*,
Einwohnerverband *m*
(JAP) 地域自治会
(RUS) АССОЦИАЦИЯ, ОБЪЕДИНЕНИЕ
ЖИЛЬЦОВ ИЛИ ЗЕМЛЕВЛАДЕЛЬЦЕВ

community property
(CHIN) 共有财产
(FRE) biens communs, biens de la
communauté
(GER) (eheliche)
Gütergemeinschaft *f*; Gesamtgut *n*,
Gemeinschaftsbesitz *m*
(JAP) 夫婦共有財産
(RUS) СОБСТВЕННОСТЬ
ПРИОБРЕТЁННАЯ В БРАКЕ

commutation right
(CHIN) 折偿权利
(FRE) droit de commutation
(GER) Umwandlungsrecht *n*, (Recht auf
Umwandlung einer Zeitrente in eine
Barabfindung)
(JAP) 金納化権、(生産物地代から貨幣
地代への転化)、(支払方法などの)振替
(RUS) ПРАВО ЗАМЕНЫ
ПЕРИОДИЧЕСКОГО ПЛАТЕЖА
ЕДИНОВРЕМЕННОЙ ВЫПЛАТОЙ

commuter

(CHIN) 月票旅客

(FRE) personne qui fait la navette entre son domicile et son lieu de travail, (C) navetteur

(GER) Pendler *m*

(JAP) 通勤者

(RUS) ЛИЦО, СОВЕРШАЮЩЕЕ ПОЕЗДКИ МЕЖДУ ПРИГОРОДОМ И ГОРОДОМ

commuter tax

(CHIN) 跨区工作税

(FRE) taxes sur les résidences secondaires

(GER) Gemeindebesteuerung *f* von Pendlern *mpl*

(JAP) 通勤税

(RUS) НАЛОГ НА ПОЕЗДКИ МЕЖДУ ПРИГОРОДОМ И ГОРОДОМ

co-mortgagor (co-mortgager)

(CHIN) 共同抵押贷款人

(FRE) codébiteur hypothécaire

(GER) Mit-Hypothekenschuldner *m*

(JAP) 共同抵当権設定者

(RUS) УЧАСТНИК СОВМЕСТНОГО ИПОТЕЧНОГО ЗАЛОГА

company

(CHIN) 公司，商行

(FRE) société, entreprise

(GER) Gesellschaft *f*, Kapitalgesellschaft *f*; Unternehmen *n*; Firma *f*

(JAP) 企業、会社

(RUS) КОМПАНИЯ

company benefits

(CHIN) 公司福利

(FRE) bénéfices de la société

(GER) betriebliche Nebenleistungen *fpl*

(JAP) 会社給付(金)

(RUS) ЛЬГОТЫ РАБОТНИКА КОМПАНИИ

company car

(CHIN) 公司车

(FRE) voiture de fonction

(GER) Firmen- *m*, Dienstwagen *m*, Firmen- *n*, Dienstfahrzeug *n*

(JAP) 社用車

(RUS) СЛУЖЕБНЫЙ АВТОМОБИЛЬ

company union

(CHIN) 公司工会

(FRE) syndicat d'entreprise

(GER) Betriebsgewerkschaft *f*

(JAP) 御用組合、企業別組合

(RUS) ПРОФСОЮЗ, НАХОДЯЩИЙСЯ В ТЁПЛЫХ ОТНОШЕНИЯХ С РУКОВОДСТВОМ КОМПАНИИ

comparables

(CHIN) 可比的，可比拟的

(FRE) comparable

(GER) vergleichbare Werte *mpl* bzw. Daten *pl*

(JAP) 匹敵物、比較できる物

(RUS) СРАВНИМЫЕ ОБЪЕКТЫ СОБСТВЕННОСТИ ДЛЯ ОЦЕНКИ КОНКРЕТНОЙ СОБСТВЕННОСТИ

comparable worth

(CHIN) 可比价值

(FRE) valeur comparable

(GER) vergleichbares Besitztum *n*; Vergleichswert *m*

(JAP) 男女同一賃金原則

(RUS) ПРИНЦИП, СОГЛАСНО КОТОРОГО ТРУД ДОЛЖЕН ОПЛАЧИВАТЬСЯ ИСХОДЯ ИЗ КОНЕЧНОГО РЕЗУЛЬТАТА, А НЕ ЛИЧНОСТИ РАБОТНИКА

comparitive finacial statements

(CHIN) 比较财务报表

(FRE) état/bilan financier comparatif

(GER) (Finanz)abschluss *m* mit Vergleichszahlen *fpl*

(JAP) 比較財務諸表

(RUS) СОПОСТАВИМАЯ ФИНАНСОВАЯ ОТЧЕТНОСТЬ

comparitive negligence

(CHIN) 共同疏忽责任

(FRE) négligence comparative

(GER) anspruchsminderndes Mitverschulden *n*

(JAP) 過失相殺、比較過失

(RUS) ВИНА УЧАСТНИКОВ НЕСЧАСТНОГО СЛУЧАЯ В ОТНОСИТЕЛЬНОМ (процентном) ВЫРАЖЕНИИ

comparison shopping
(CHIN) 采购条件的比较调查
(FRE) lèche-vitrines comparatifs
(GER) vergleichende Warenprüfung *f*
(JAP) 競争品調査
(RUS) СБОР КАК МОЖНО БОЛЬШЕГО КОЛИЧЕСТВА ИНФОРМАЦИИ О ТОВАРЕ ДО ЕГО ПОКУПКИ

compensating balance
(CHIN) 补偿余额
(FRE) balance compensatrice
(GER) Deckungsguthaben *n*, Ausgleichsguthaben *n*, -saldo *m*
(JAP) 相殺残金、補償預金
(RUS) КОМПЕНСАЦИОННЫЙ ОСТАТОК

compensating error
(CHIN) 补偿误差
(FRE) erreur compensatrice
(GER) sich gegenseitig aufhebende Buchungsfehler *mpl*; Gegenfehler *m*
(JAP) 相殺誤差
(RUS) КОМПЕНСИРУЮЩАЯ ОШИБКА

compensation
(CHIN) 补偿
(FRE) compensation, indemnisation
(GER) Entschädigung *f*; Abfindung *f*; Ausgleich *m*, Kompensation *f*; Vergütung *f*, Bezahlung *f*, Arbeitsentgelt *n*;
(JAP) 補償、賠償金、報酬、
(RUS) КОМПЕНСАЦИЯ; ВОЗМЕЩЕНИЕ

compensatory stock options
(CHIN) 补偿性股票选购权
(FRE) options d'action compensatrice
(GER) Abfindungsaktienoptionen *fpl*; kompensatorisches Aktienoptionssystem *n*
(JAP) 補整的自社株購入権
(RUS) КОМПЕНСАЦИОННЫЙ ОПЦИОНЫ

compensatory time
(CHIN) 补偿时间
(FRE) temps compensatoire
(GER) Überstundenausgleich *m*
(JAP) 代休
(RUS) КОМПЕНСАЦИОННЫЙ ПЕРИОД

competent party
(CHIN) 主管部门
(FRE) partie compétente
(GER) geschäftsfähige Partei *f*
(JAP) 適格当事者
(RUS) ДЕЕСПОСОБНАЯ, ПРАВОМОЧНАЯ СТОРОНА

competition
(CHIN) 竞争，比赛
(FRE) concurrence
(GER) Wettbewerb *m*, Konkurrenz *f*; Konkurrenzkampf *m*
(RUS) КОНКУРЕНЦИЯ; СОРЕВНОВАНИЕ

competitive bid
(CHIN) 公开招标，竞标
(FRE) offre concurrentielle, offre competitive
(GER) konkurrenz-, wettbewerbsfähiges Gebot *n*
(JAP) 競争入札
(RUS) КОНКУРЕНТНАЯ ЗАЯВКА

competitive party
(CHIN) 竞争方
(FRE) partie concurrentielle
(GER) Wettbewerbspartei *f* (Politik); Gegenbieter *m*
(JAP) 競争当事者
(RUS) КОНКУРИРУЮЩАЯ СТОРОНА

competitive party method
(CHIN) 竞争方方法
(FRE) méthode de la partie concurrentielle
(GER) System *n* der Wettbewerbspartei *f* (Politik)
(JAP) 競争当事者方法
(RUS) МЕТОД УСТАНОВЛЕНИЯ РАСХОДОВ НА РЕКЛАМУ НА УРОВНЕ КОНКУРИРУЮЩЕЙ СТОРОНЫ

competitive strategy
(CHIN) 竞争战略
(FRE) stratégie concurrentielle
(GER) Wettbewerbsstrategie *f*
(JAP) 競争戦略
(RUS) СТРАТЕГИЯ РЕКЛАМЫ, ОСНОВАННАЯ НА СОРЕВНОВАНИИ С КОНКУРЕНЦИЕЙ

competitor
(CHIN) 竞争对手
(FRE) concurrent
(GER) Konkurrent *m*; Konkurrenzbetrieb
m, -unternehmen *n*; Mitbewerber *m*
(JAP) 競争相手、競争企業
(RUS) КОНКУРЕНТ

compilation
(CHIN) 编制
(FRE) compilation
(GER) Erfassung *f*, Kompilation *f*;
Zusammenstellung *f*
(JAP) 編集、編纂、編纂著作物
(RUS) КОМПИЛЯЦИЯ;

compiler
(CHIN) 编译程序
(FRE) compilateur
(GER) Compiler *m*, Kompilierer *m*;
Verfasser *m*
(JAP) 編集者、コンパイラー（コンピュ
ーターの機械語翻訳プログラム）
(RUS) КОМПИЛЯТОР

compliant
(CHIN) 应允的，服从的
(FRE) conforme
(GER) Beschwerde *f*, Mängelrüge *f*,
Reklamation *f*; Klage(schrift) *f*;
Strafanzeige *f*
(JAP) 申し立て、告訴状、訴状
(RUS) УДОВЛЕТВОРЯЮЩИЙ
ТРЕБОВАНИЕ;
СООТВЕТСТВУЮЩИЙ

complete audit
(CHIN) 全部查账，全面审计
(FRE) audit complet, vérification complete
(GER) zum Jahresende *n* durchgeführte
Prüfung *f*; lückenlose Prüfung *f*
(JAP) 完全監査
(RUS) ПОЛНЫЙ АУДИТ

completed contract method
(CHIN) 完成合同法，全部完工法
(FRE) méthode de l'achèvement des
travaux
(GER) (Gewinn- bzw. Verlustermittlung
erst bei Abschluss langfristiger

Verträge)
(JAP) 完成契約方法
(RUS) МЕТОД УЧЕТА ПО ВЫПОЛНЕНИЮ
КОНТРАКТА (бухг.)

completed operations insurance
(CHIN) 完工保险
(FRE) opérations achevées
(GER) Versicherung *f* für
Montagefolgeschäden *mpl*
(JAP) 完成工事保険
(RUS) СТРАХОВАНИЕ ЗАВЕРШЕНИЯ
ОПЕРАЦИЙ

completion bond
(CHIN) 完工保证
(FRE) garantie de parfait achèvement
(GER) Leistungsgarantie *f*,
Erfüllungsgarantie *f*,
Vollendungsgarantie *f*
(JAP) 完成保証債券
(RUS) ГАРАНТИЯ ЗАВЕРШЩЕНИЯ
ПРОЕКТА

complex capital structure
(CHIN) 复合资本结构
(FRE) structure du capital complet
(GER) komplexe Kapitalstruktur *f*
(RUS) ПОЛНАЯ СТРУКТУРА КАПИТАЛА

complex trust
(CHIN) 复合信托
(FRE) trust complexe, (C) fiducie complexe
(GER) wohltätige Stiftung *f*
(JAP) 複合信託
(RUS) ТРАСТ, ИМЕЮЩИЙ ПРАВО ЛИБО
РАСПРЕДЕЛЯТЬ, ЛИБО УДЕРЖИВАТЬ
ДОХОД

compliance audit
(CHIN) 依法审计
(FRE) audit de conformité, vérification de
la conformité, (C) vérification du respect de
dispositions contractuelles
(GER) Audit *m* zur Überprüfung *f* der
Einhaltung *f* von Forderungen *fpl*
(JAP) 準拠性監査、
コンプライアンス監査
(RUS) АУДИТ ВЫПОЛНЕНИЯ
ОПРЕДЕЛЁННЫХ ТРЕБОВАНИЙ

component part

(CHIN) 构成部分，成分

(FRE) constituant

(GER) Teil *n*, Einzel- *n*, Bestandteil *n*

(JAP) 構成要素、構成部分

(RUS) СОСТАВНАЯ ДЕТАЛЬ; ЧАСТЬ

composite depreciation

(CHIN) 综合折旧

(FRE) dépréciation des matériaux composites

(GER) Pauschal- *f*, Sammel- *f*, Gruppenabschreibung *f*

(JAP) 包括減価償却、総合償却

(RUS) ОБОБЩЕННАЯ АМОРТИЗАЦИЯ

composition

(CHIN) 和解，组成，构成

(FRE) composition

(GER) Vergleich *m*, gütliche Regelung *f*, Kompromiss *m*; vergleichsweise Einigung *f*

(JAP) 一部返済金、和解

(RUS) СОСТАВ

compound growth rate

(CHIN) 复合增长率

(FRE) taux de croissance composée

(GER) kumulative Wachstumsrate *f*, kumulative Zuwachs- *f* bzw. Steigerungsrate *f*

(JAP) 複合成長率

(RUS) СОСТАВНОЙ ТЕМП РОСТА

compound interest

(CHIN) 复利

(FRE) intérêt composé

(GER) Zinseszins *m*

(JAP) 複利

(RUS) СЛОЖНЫЕ ПРОЦЕНТЫ

compound journal entry

(CHIN) 复合分录

(FRE) écriture complexe

(GER) Sammelbuchung *f*

(JAP) 複合仕訳記入

(RUS) СОСТАВНАЯ БУХГАЛТЕРСКАЯ ЗАПИСЬ

comprehensive annual financial report (CAFR)

(CHIN) 综合年度财务报告（CAFR）

(FRE) rapport annuel financier complet

(GER) Gesamtjahresabschluss *m*, Jahreshaushalts- *m*, Jahresfinanzbericht *m*

(JAP) 総合年次財務報告書

(RUS) КОМПЛЕКСНЫЙ ГОДОВОЙ ФИНАНСОВЫЙ ОТЧЕТ

comprehensive Insurance

(CHIN) 综合保险

(FRE) assurance multirisque

(GER) General- *f*, Universal- *f*, Pauschalversicherung *f*, Kombination *f* verschiedener Versicherungsdeckungen *fpl*

(JAP) 総合保険

(RUS) ОБЩЕЕ СТРАХОВАНИЕ

compress

(CHIN) 压缩

(FRE) compresser

(GER) komprimieren, verdichten *v*

(JAP) 圧縮、短縮する

(RUS) СЖИМАТЬ, СДАВЛИВАТЬ

comptroller

(CHIN) 主管会计

(FRE) assistant général de gestion

(GER) Controller *m*, Rechnungs- *m*, Bilanzprüfer *m*, Revisor *m*

(JAP) 財務部長、会計検査官、監査官

(RUS) КОНТРОЛЕР; ГЛАВНЫЙ БУХГАЛТЕР-КОНТРОЛЁР

compulsory arbitration

(CHIN) 强制仲裁

(FRE) arbitrage obligatoire

(GER) Zwangsschlichtung *f*, -schiedsverfahren *n* Schiedsgerichtszwang *m*

(JAP) 強制裁定、強制仲裁

(RUS) ПРИНУДИТЕЛЬНЫЙ АРБИТРАЖ

compulsory insurance

(CHIN) 强制保险

(FRE) assurance obligatoire

(GER) Pflichtversicherung *f*, Zwangsversicherung *f*, Versicherungspflicht *f*

(JAP) 強制保険
(RUS) ОБЯЗАТЕЛЬНОЕ СТРАХОВАНИЕ

compulsory retirement
(CHIN) 强制退休
(FRE) retraite obligatoire
(GER) Zwangspensionierung *f*
(JAP) 強制退職
(RUS) ОБЯЗАТЕЛЬНЫЙ ВЫХОД НА ПЕНСИЮ

computer
(CHIN) 计算机，电脑
(FRE) ordinateur
(GER) Computer *m*; Rechner *m*
(JAP) コンピューター、電子計算機
(RUS) КОМПЬЮТЕР; ЭВМ

computer-aided
(CHIN) 计算机辅助的
(FRE) assisté par ordinateur
(GER) computer-, rechnerunterstützt, computer-, rechnergestützt *adj*
(JAP) コンピューターに補助された
(RUS) ОСУЩЕСТВЛЁННЫЙ С ПОМОЩЬЮ КОМПЬЮТЕРА

concealment
(CHIN) 隐瞒，匿报
(FRE) dissimulation
(GER) Verschweigen *n*, Verschleierung *f*, Nichtangabe *f*; Unterschlagung *f*
(JAP) 隠蔽、隠匿、告知義務違反
(RUS) СОКРЫТИЕ; УТАИВАНИЕ

concentration banking
(CHIN) 集中银行处理业务
(FRE) activités bancaires de concentration
(GER) Transaktionssammlung *f* (einer Bank *f*)
(JAP) 集中的預金
(RUS) КОНЦЕНТРАЦИЯ БАНКОВСКИХ ОПЕРАЦИЙ

concept test
(CHIN) 概念测试
(FRE) test de concept
(GER) Akzeptanztest *m* (einer Produktidee *f*)

(JAP) コンセプト・テスト
(RUS) ПРОВЕРКА ОБЩЕГО ЗАМЫСЛА, КОНЦЕПЦИИ

concern
(CHIN) 公司，行号，企业，关注，难点
(FRE) inquiétude
(GER) Konzern *m*, (Firmen)gruppe *f*
(JAP) 利害関係、会社、企業
(RUS) КОНЦЕРН; ОБЕСПОКОЕННОСТЬ

concession
(CHIN) 承认，关税减让，特许，核准，让与
(FRE) concession
(GER) Konzession *f*, Einräumung *f*; behördliche Zulassung *f*, Gewerbeerlaubnis *f*; Genehmigung *f*, Bewilligung *f*
(JAP) 譲与、特権、利権
(RUS) КОНЦЕССИЯ; УСТУПКА

conciliation
(CHIN) 调解，调停
(FRE) conciliation
(GER) Schlichtung *f*, Vermittlung *f*
(JAP) 斡旋、調停
(RUS) ПРИМИРЕНИЕ

conciliator
(CHIN) 调停人
(FRE) conciliateur
(GER) Schlichter *m*, Vermittler *m*
(JAP) 調停者
(RUS) МИРОВОЙ ПОСРЕДНИК

condemnation
(CHIN) 征用
(FRE) condamnation
(GER) Verdammung *f*, Verurteilung *f*; Abbruch- *f*, Abrissverfügung *f*
(JAP) 土地収用・接収・没収、有罪の判決
(RUS) ОСУЖДЕНИЕ; ОТКАЗ В ИСКЕ

conditional contract
(CHIN) 有条件合同
(FRE) contrat conditionnel
(GER) bedingter Vertrag *m*
(JAP) 条件付契約

(RUS) ДОГОВОР НА ОСОБЫХ УСЛОВИЯХ

condition precedent
(CHIN) 先决条件
(FRE) condition suspensive
(GER) aufschiebende Bedingung *f*
(JAP) 先行条件
(RUS) ПРЕЦЕДЕНТ СИТУАЦИИ

conditional sale
(CHIN) 有条件销售
(FRE) vente conditionnelle
(GER) (Ver)kauf *m* unter
Eigentumsvorbehalt *m*,
Vorbehalts(ver)kauf *m*
(JAP) 条件付販売、条件付売約
(RUS) ПРОДАЖА НА ОСОБЫХ УСЛОВИЯХ

conditional-use permit
(CHIN) 有条件使用许可
(FRE) autorisation d'utilisation
conditionnelle
(GER) Genehmigung *f* zur beschränkten
Nutzung *f*
(RUS) РАЗРЕШЕНИЕ НА
ИСПОЛЬЗОВАНИЕ НА ОСОБЫХ
УСЛОВИЯХ

condition subsequent
(CHIN) 后续条件，解约文件
(FRE) condition résolutive/résolutoire
(GER) auflösende Bedingung *f*
(JAP) 後行条件
(RUS) ПОСЛЕДУЮЩАЯ СИТУАЦИЯ

conference call
(CHIN) 电话会议
(FRE) conversation multiple
(GER) Konferenzgespräch *n*, -schaltung *f*
(JAP) 会議通話
(RUS) МНОГОСТОРОННИЙ ТЕЛЕФОННЫЙ
РАЗГОВОР

confidence game
(CHIN) 骗取信用
(FRE) jeu de confiance
(GER) Bauernfängerei *f*
(JAP) （人の信頼につけこむ）詐欺、信
用詐欺

(RUS) МОШЕННИЧЕСТВО, ОСНОВАННОЕ
НА ИСПОЛЬЗОВАНИИ ДОВЕРИЯ

confidence interval
(CHIN) 置信区间
(FRE) intervalle de confiance
(GER) Konfidenzbereich *m*,
Vertrauensintervall *n*
(JAP) 信頼区間
(RUS) ИНТЕРВАЛ МЕЖДУ САМЫМ
НИЖНИМ И САМЫМ ВЕРХНИМ
ВЗОМОЖНЫМ ЗНАЧЕНИЕМ, В КОТОРОМ
ВЕРОЯТНО НАХОДИТСЯ ЗНАЧЕНИЕ
РАССМАТРИВАЕМОЙ ВЕЛИЧИНЫ (СТАТ)

confidence level
(CHIN) 置信度
(FRE) niveau de confiance
(GER) Konfidenz- *n*, Vertrauensniveau *n*
(JAP) 信頼水準、信頼性のレベル
(RUS) ВЕРОЯТНОСТЬ ТОГО, ЧТО
РАССМАТРИВАЕМАЯ ВЕЛИЧИНА
НАХОДИТСЯ В ВЫШЕУПОМЯНУТОМ
ИНТЕРВАЛЕ

confidential
(CHIN) 保密
(FRE) confidential
(GER) vertraulich, geheim *adj*
(JAP) 秘密の、機密の
(RUS) КОНФИДЕНЦИАЛЬНЫЙ

confirmation
(CHIN) 确认，证实，证明，批准
(FRE) confirmation
(GER) Bestätigung *f*
(JAP) 確定、確認
(RUS) ПОДТВЕРЖДЕНИЕ

conflict of interest
(CHIN) 利益冲突
(FRE) conflit d'intérêts
(GER) Interessenkonflikt *m*
(JAP) 利害の不一致、利害の衝突
(RUS) КОНФЛИКТ ИНТЕРЕСОВ

conformed copy
(CHIN) 一致的复印件
(FRE) photocopie conforme
(GER) angepasste Kopie *f*

(JAP) 正式な写し、合法の写し
(RUS) КОПИЯ ДОКУМЕНТА, ГДЕ
ПОДПИСЬ И ПЕЧАТЬ НАПЕЧАТАНЫ ИЛИ
ОПИСАНЫ

confusion
(CHIN) 混淆，混杂
(FRE) confusion
(GER) Verwirrung *f*; Unklarheit *f*
(JAP) 混同、混乱
(RUS) ЗАМЕШАТЕЛЬСТВО;
НЕДОПОНИМАНИЕ

conglomerate
(CHIN) 联合大企业
(FRE) conglomérat
(GER) Konglomerat *n*, Mischkonzern *m*
(JAP) 複合企業、コングロマリット
(RUS) КОНГЛОМЕРАТ

conservatism, conservative
(CHIN) 保守主义，谨慎
(FRE) conservatisme, conservateur
(GER) Konservatismus *m*, konservativ *adj*
(JAP) 保守主義、保守的な
(RUS) КОНСЕРВАТИЗМ;
КОНСЕРВАТИВНЫЙ (ОСТОРОЖНЫЙ)

consideration
(CHIN) 互相履行义务，补偿，审议，
考虑
(FRE) considération
(GER) Gegenleistung *f*; Tauschwert *m*
(JAP) 報酬、対価、約因
(RUS) СООБРАЖЕНИЕ

consignee
(CHIN) 承销人，收货人，受托人
(FRE) destinataire
(GER) (Waren)empfänger *m*, Destinatar *m*;
Konsignatar *m*
(JAP) 引受人、荷受人、受託者
(RUS) ГРУЗОПОЛУЧАТЕЛЬ; АДРЕСАТ;
КОНСИГНАТОР

consingment
(CHIN) 托运，寄销，交付，委托
(FRE) envoi, expédition
(GER) Konsignation *f*; Konsignationsware *f*

(JAP) 委託、委託販売、委託貨物、委託
販売品
(RUS) ПАРТИЯ ТОВАРА; ГРУЗ;
КОНСИГНАЦИЯ

consignment insurance
(CHIN) 收货人保险
(FRE) assurance envoi de marchandises
(GER) Kommissionsversicherung *f*
(JAP) 委託（品）保険
(RUS) СТРАХОВАНИЕ ГРУЗА

consignor
(CHIN) 委托人，托运人，发货人，货主
(FRE) expéditeur
(GER) Absender *m*; Versender *m*;
Verlader *m*; Konsignant *m*
(JAP) 荷送人、委託者、荷主
(RUS) ГРУЗООТПРАВИТЕЛЬ;
КОНСИГНАНТ

consistency
(CHIN) 一致性
(FRE) cohérence
(GER) Folgerichtigkeit *f*,
Widerspruchsfreiheit *f*; Beständigkeit *f*,
Konsistenz *f*, Konsequenz *f*, Stetigkeit *f*
(JAP) 一貫性、無矛盾性
(RUS) СОГЛАСОВАННОСТЬ;
ПОСЛЕДОВАТЕЛЬНОСТЬ

console
(CHIN) 控制面板
(FRE) console/panneau
(GER) Konsole *f*, Schalt- *n*, Steuerpult *n*
(JAP) コンソール
(RUS) КОНСОЛЬ; УСТРОЙСТВО,
ПОЗВОЛЯЮЩЕЕ НАПРЯМУЮ
СВЯЗЫВАТЬСЯ С КОМПЬЮТЕРОМ

consolidated financial statement
(CHIN) 合并决算表
(FRE) situation financière
consolidée
(GER) konsolidierter Abschluss *m*,
Konzernrechnung *f*;
-abschluss *m*
(JAP) 連結財務諸表
(RUS) КОНСОЛИДИРОВАННАЯ
ОТЧЕТНОСТЬ КОРПОРАЦИИ

consolidated tax return
(CHIN) 综合所得税报表
(FRE) déclaration d'impôts unifiée
(GER) konsolidierte Steuererklärung *f*
(JAP) 総合納税申告書
(RUS) СВОДНАЯ НАЛОГОВАЯ
ОТЧЕТНОСТЬ ГРУППЫ
АФФИЛИИРОВАННЫХ КОМПАНИЙ

consolidation loan
(CHIN) 统一贷款
(FRE) prêt de consolidation
(GER) Konsolidierungsdarlehen *n*,
-kredit *m*
(JAP) 総合ローン、合併融資、
併合ローン
(RUS) КОНСОЛИДИРУЮЩИЙ
КРЕДИТ

consolidator
(CHIN) 集装业者
(FRE) groupeur
(GER) Konsolidator *m*,
Konsolidierungsdienst *m*;
Sammelladungsagent *m*, -spediteur *m*
(JAP) コンソリデータ、混載業者、
統合整理者
(RUS) КОНСОЛИДИРУЮЩАЯ
ОРГАНИЗАЦИЯ

consortium
(CHIN) 国际财团
(FRE) consortium
(GER) Konsortium *n*,
Arbeitsgemeinschaft *f*,
Unternehmensgruppe *f*,
-zusammenschluss *m*
(JAP) コンソーシアム、共同事業体、
配偶者権
(RUS) КОНСОРЦИУМ

constant
(CHIN) 常数
(FRE) constant
(GER) Konstante *f*, Festwert *m*; stetig,
konstant *adj*
(JAP) 一定の、変わらない、定数
(RUS) ПОСТОЯННАЯ ВЕЛИЧИНА;
КОНСТАНТА

constant dollars
(CHIN) 定值美元
(FRE) dollars constants
(GER) Konstante *f* in US-Dollar *m* vom
(Jahr XXXX)
(JAP) 恒常ドル、不変ドル
(RUS) ПОКУПАТЕЛЬНАЯ СПОСОБНОСТЬ
ДОЛЛАРА В БАЗОВОМ ГОДУ

constant-payment loan
(CHIN) 定偿贷款
(FRE) prêt à paiements constants
(GER) Amortisationsdarlehen *n*,
Tilgungsdarlehen *n*, Darlehen *n* mit
gleichbleibenden Tilgungsbeträgen *mpl*
(JAP) 等支払ローン
(RUS) КРЕДИТ , ПОГАШАЕМЫЙ
РАВНЫМИ ПЕРИОДИЧЕСКИМИ
ВЫПЛАТАМИ

constituent company
(CHIN) 分公司，子公司
(FRE) société constituante
(GER) verbundenes Unternehmen *n*,
Konzernunternehmen *n*, -gesellschaft *f*
(JAP) 構成会社
(RUS) КОМПАНИЯ, ВХОДЯЩАЯ В
СОСТАВ ГРУППЫ АФФИЛИИРОВАННЫХ
ИЛИ СЛИВШИХСЯ КОРПОРАЦИЙ

constraining (limiting) factor
(CHIN) 限制因素
(FRE) facteur contraignant (limitant)
(GER) Engpassfaktor *m*
(JAP) 制約要素
(RUS) ОГРАНИЧИВАЮЩИЙ,
(ЛИМИТИРУЮЩИЙ) ФАКТОР

construction loan
(CHIN) 基建贷款，工程贷款
(FRE) prêt construction
(GER) Baudarlehen *n*,
Baufinanzierungskredit *m*
(JAP) 建築ローン、建設融資
(RUS) СТРОИТЕЛЬНЫЙ КРЕДИТ

constructive notice
(CHIN) 推定通知
(FRE) connaissance présumée

(GER) zurechenbare Kenntnis *f*, schuldhafte
Nichtkenntnis *f*
(JAP) 擬制悪意
(RUS) ДАННОЕ КОСВЕННЫМ ПУТЁМ
ИЗВЕЩЕНИЕ, КОТОРОЕ СУД СЧИТАЕТ
ПОЛУЧЕННЫМ АДРЕСАТОМ

constructive receipt of income
(CHIN) 推定收入
(FRE) doctrine selon laquelle une personne
est présumée avoir reçu et bénéficié d'une
somme alors même qu'elle n'a pas encaissé
le paiement, (C) recette réputée
(GER) konstruierter Einkommenszufluss *m*,
angenommenes Einkommen *n*
(JAP) 推定所得受領 （学説）
(RUS) ПРИНЦИП НАЛОГООБЛОЖЕНИЯ,
ТРЕБУЮЩИЙ, ЧТОБЫ
ДЕКЛАРИРОВАЛИСЬ КАК РЕАЛЬНО
ПОЛУЧЕННЫЕ ДОХОДЫ, ТАК И ТЕ,
КОТОРЫЕ СЧИТАЮТСЯ ПОЛУЧЕННЫМИ

consultant
(CHIN) 顾问，咨询
(FRE) consultant, conseiller
(GER) Berater *m*, Unternehmensberater *m*
(JAP) コンサルタント、顧問、相談役
(RUS) КОНСУЛЬТАНТ

consumer
(CHIN) 消费者，顾客
(FRE) consommateur
(GER) Verbraucher *m*, Konsument *m*
(JAP) 消費者
(RUS) ПОТРЕБИТЕЛЬ

consumer behavior
(CHIN) 消费行为
(FRE) comportement des consommateurs
(GER) Verbraucherverhalten *n*, Kunden-,
Käuferverhalten *n*
(JAP) 消費者行動
(RUS) ПОВЕДЕНИЕ, РЕАКЦИЯ
ПОТРЕБИТЕЛЯ

consumer goods
(CHIN) 消费品
(FRE) biens de consommation
(GER) Konsum- *npl*; Verbrauchsgüter *npl*,
Verbrauchsartikel *mpl*

(JAP) 消費財、消費物資
(RUS) ПОТРЕБИТЕЛЬСКИЕ ТОВАРЫ

consumerism
(CHIN) 消费主义
(FRE) consumérisme
(GER) Verbraucherschutzbewegung *f*,
Konsumentenschutz *m*, Konsumerismus *m*
(JAP) 消費者(優先)主義、消費者運動
(RUS) ОБЕСПОКОЕННОСТЬ
ОБЩЕСТВЕННОСТИ ПРАВАМИ
ПОТРЕБИТЕЛЕЙ, КАЧЕСТВОМ ТОВАРОМ
И ПРАВДИВОСТЬЮ РЕКЛАМЫ

consumer price index (CPI)
(CHIN) 消费物价指数
(FRE) index de prix à la consommation
(IPC)
(GER) Index *m* der Verbraucherpreise *mpl*,
Lebenshaltungskostenindex *m*
(JAP) 消費者物価指数
(RUS) ИНДЕКС ПОТРЕБИТЕЛЬСКИХ ЦЕН

consumer protection
(CHIN) 消费者保障
(FRE) protection des consommateurs
(GER) Verbraucherschutz *m*
(JAP) 消費者保護
(RUS) ЗАЩИТА ПОТРЕБИТЕЛЯ

consumer research
(CHIN) 消费研究
(FRE) recherche en consommation
(GER) Verbraucher- *f*, Konsumforschung *f*
(JAP) 消費者調査
(RUS) ИЗУЧЕНИЕ ПОТРЕБИТЕЛЕЙ

consumption function
(CHIN) 消费函数
(FRE) fonction de la consommation
(GER) Konsum- *f*,
Verbrauchsfunktion *f*
(JAP) 消費関数
(RUS) ФУНКЦИЯ ПОТРЕБЛЕНИЯ

container ship
(CHIN) 集装箱船
(FRE) navire porte-conteneurs
(GER) Containerschiff *n*

contestable clause

(CHIN) 可抗辩条款
(FRE) clause contestable
(GER) Anfechtungsklausel *f*
(JAP) 問題条項、異議条項
(RUS) ОСПАРИВАЕМОЕ
УСЛОВИЕ

contingencey fund

(CHIN) 意外开支准备金
(FRE) fonds de reserve
(GER) Not- *f*, Sicherheitsrücklage *f*;
Rückstellungen *fpl* für unvorhergesehene
Ausgaben *fpl*
(JAP) 臨時資金、危険準備金、偶発損失
積立金、緊急用積立金
(RUS) ФОНД НА НЕПРЕДВИДЕННЫЕ
РАСХОДЫ

contingency planning

(CHIN) 应急计划
(FRE) élaboration d'un plan de secours
(GER) Alternativplanung *f*;
Eventualplanung *f*; Vorausplanung *f* für den
Bedarfsfall *m*
(JAP) 非常事態計画、
不測事態対応計画
(RUS) ПЛАНИРОВАНИЕ
НЕПРЕДВИДЕННЫХ ОБСТОЯТЕЛЬСТВ

contingency table

(CHIN) 质量管理相依表
(FRE) table de contingence
(GER) Kontingenztafel *f*
(JAP) 分割表
(RUS) ТАБЛИЦА ПРЕДСТАВЛЯЮЩАЯ
КЛАССИФИКАЦИЮ ОБЪЕКТОВ
НАБЛЮДЕНИЯ ПО ДВУМ И БОЛЕЕ
ПАРАМЕТРАМ

contingent fee

(CHIN) 应急费
(FRE) honoraires conditionnels
(GER) Erfolgshonorar *n*, erfolgsabhängiges
Honorar *n*
(JAP) 全面成功報酬
(RUS) ГОНОРАР АДВОКАТА НА
УСЛОВИИ ВЫИГРЫША ДЕЛА

contingent liability

(CHIN) 不确定债务
(FRE) passif eventual
(GER) Ausfallhaftung *f*,
Eventualverbindlichkeit *f*
(JAP) 偶発債務、不確定責任

contingent liability (vicarious liability)

(CHIN) 不确定责任（转承责任）
(FRE) engagement conditionnel
(responsabilité du cautionnement)
(GER) Haftung *f* für fremdes Verschulden
n, stellvertretende Haftung *f*,
Repräsentationshaftung *f*
(JAP) 偶発債務　（代位責任）
(RUS) УСЛОВНАЯ ОТВЕТСТВЕННОСТЬ
КОМПАНИИ ЗА ПОСТУПКИ ЛИЦ, НЕ
ЯВЛЯЮЩИХСЯ ЕЁ РАБОТНИКАМИ

continuing education

(CHIN) 继续教育
(FRE) formation continue
(GER) Fort- *f*, Weiterbildung *f*
(JAP) 継続教育、生涯教育
(RUS) КУРСЫ ПОВЫШЕНИЯ
КАЛИФИКАЦИИ

continuity

(CHIN) 连续性
(FRE) continuité
(GER) Kontinuität *f*, Fortbestand *m*,
-dauer *f*
(JAP) 継続性、連続性
(RUS) ПРЕЕМСТВЕННОСТЬ

continous audit

(CHIN) 连续审计
(FRE) audit en continu
(GER) Dauerprüfung *f*, permanente
Prüfung *f*
(JAP) 継続監査
(RUS) НЕПРЕРЫВНЫЙ АУДИТ

continous process

(CHIN) 流水作业
(FRE) procédure en continu
(GER) Fließprozess *m*, dynamischer
Prozess *m*, kontinuierlicher Vorgang *m*
(JAP) 連続工程

(RUS) НЕПРЕРЫВНЫЙ ПРОЦЕСС

continous production
(CHIN) 连续生产
(FRE) production en continu
(GER) Kontinuierliche bzw. laufende Produktion *f*, Fließ(band)fertigung *f*
(JAP) 連続生産
(RUS) НЕПРЕРЫВНОЕ ПРОИЗВОДСТВО

contra-asset account
(CHIN) 资产抵消账户
(FRE) compte d'actif de contre-partie
(GER) Wertberichtigungskonto *n* (Aktivseite/Aktiva), Gegenkonto *n* (Aktivseite/Aktiva)
(JAP) 資産控除科目、資産対照勘定
(RUS) КОНТРСЧЕТ

contract
(CHIN) 合同，契约
(FRE) contrat
(GER) Vertrag *m*
(JAP) 契約、請負
(RUS) КОНТРАКТ; ДОГОВОР

contract carrier
(CHIN) 契约承运人
(FRE) transporteur sous contrat
(GER) Vertragsfrachtführer *m*; -spediteur *m*, -reederei *f*
(JAP) 契約輸送業者、契約輸送業
(RUS) ПЕРЕВОЗЧИК ПО КОНТРАКТУ

contraction
(CHIN) 萎缩，订约，签约
(FRE) contraction
(GER) Abschwung *m*, Abschwächung *f*, Rezession *f* (Konjunktur); Schrumpfung *f*, Rückgang *m*; Verknappung *f* (Angebot, Geld)
(JAP) 縮小、制限、短縮
(RUS) СЖАТИЕ; СОКРАЩЕНИЕ

contract of indemnity
(CHIN) 赔偿契约
(FRE) contrat d'indemnisation
(GER) Schadensersatz- *m*, Entschädigungsvertrag *m*
(JAP) 損害填補契約

(RUS) СТРАХОВАНИЕ ОТ ПОНЕСЕНИЯУБЫТКОВ

contractor
(CHIN) 承包商，签约人
(FRE) contractant, entrepreneur, (C) sous-traitant
(GER) (Sub)unternehmer *m*; Auftragnehmer *m*
(JAP) 請負人、請負会社
(RUS) ПОДРЯДЧИК

contract price (tax)
(CHIN) 合同价格
(FRE) prix contractual
(GER) Vertrags- *m*, Liefer- *m*, Festpreis *m*
(JAP) 契約価格(税)、協定価格（税）
(RUS) ЦЕНА ПРОДАЖИ ЗА ВЫЧЕТОМ ИПОТЕЧНОЙ ЗАДОЛЖЕННОСТИ, ПРИНЯТОЙ ОТ ПРЕДЫДУЩЕГО ВЛАДЕЛЬЦА (НАЛОГ)

contract rate
(CHIN) 约定费率
(FRE) tarif contractuel
(GER) vertraglich festgesetzte Gebühren *fpl*; Kontraktrate *f*; Kontraktfrachten *fpl*
(JAP) 契約運賃、契約料金
(RUS) НОМИНАЛЬНАЯ ПРОЦЕНТНАЯ СТАВКА

contract rent
(CHIN) 约定地租
(FRE) loyer contractuel
(GER) vertraglich festgesetzte Miete *f* bzw. Pacht *f*
(JAP) 契約家賃
(RUS) ДОГОВОРНАЯ АРЕНДА

contrarian
(CHIN) 反向投资人
(FRE) investisseur à contre courant
(GER) Contrarian *m*, Value-Manager *m*, antizyklischer Anleger *m*
(JAP) 逆張り投資家、
人と逆の行動を取る人
(RUS) ЛИЦО, ПОКУПАЮЩЕЕ АКЦИИ, КОГДА ДРУГИЕ ПРОДАЮТ, И НАОБОРОТ; НЕСОГЛАСНОЕ ЛИЦО

contribution

(CHIN) 捐献，贡献，分配，分担

(FRE) apport, cotisation, contribution

(GER) Kostenbeitrag *m*; Beitragsleistung *f*;
Einlage *f*; Kapital- *m*, Deckungsbeitrag *m*

(JAP) 寄付金、保険料

(RUS) ВЗНОС; СОДЕЙСТВИЕ;
УЧАСТИЕ

contribution profit, margin

(CHIN) 边际利润贡献

(FRE) revenu marginal

(GER) Deckungsbeitrag *m*,
Bruttogewinn *m*; Einschuss *m*

(JAP) 貢献利益、貢献マージン

(RUS) РАЗНИЦА МЕЖДУ ЦЕНОЙ И
ПЕРЕМЕННЫМИ ИЗДЕРЖКАМИ

(RUS) ВСТРЕЧНАЯ ВИНА; НЕБРЕЖНОСТЬ
ИСТЦА

contributory negligence

(CHIN) 共同过失，互有疏忽

(FRE) imprudence concurrente, négligence
concurrente, (C) négligence concourante de
la victime, (C) faute de la
victime

(GER) Mitverschulden *n*
(des Geschädigten *m*)

(JAP) 寄与過失

(RUS) ВСТРЕЧНАЯ ВИНА; НЕБРЕЖНОСТЬ
ИСТЦА

contributory pension plan

(CHIN) 分担退休基金办法

(FRE) régime de retraite contributif

(GER) Gruppenversicherung *f*,
beitragspflichtige Rentenversicherung *f*
bzw. Altersversorgung *f*

(JAP) 拠出年金制

(RUS) ПЕНСИОННАЯ СХЕМА, ПО
КОТОРОЙ И РАБОТОДАТЕЛЬ, И
РАБОТНИК ДЕЛАЮТ ВЗНОСЫ

control

(CHIN) 管制，控制，监督，检查，核对

(FRE) contrôle

(GER) Einfluss *m*; Leitung *f*, Lenkung *f*,
Steuerung *f*; Überwachung *f*, Kontrolle *f*,
Aufsicht *f*, Prüfung *f*

(JAP) 管理、支配

(RUS) УПРАВЛЕНИЕ; КОНТРОЛЬ

control account

(CHIN) 统制账户

(FRE) compte collectif, compte général

(GER) Sammel- *n*, Kontroll- *n*,
Kollektivkonto *n*

(JAP) 統轄勘定、統制勘定

(RUS) КОНТРОЛЬНЫЙ СЧЕТ

control key (ctrl)

(CHIN) 控制键（ctrl）

(FRE) touche contrôle (ctrl)

(GER) Strg-Taste *f*, Steuerungstaste *f*

(JAP) コンロトールキー、Ctrl キー

(RUS) КЛАВИША УПРАВЛЕНИЯ

controllable costs

(CHIN) 可控制成本

(FRE) coûts contrôlables

(GER) beeinflussbare Kosten *pl*

(JAP) 管理可能費、管理内経費、
統制可能原価

(RUS) КОНТРОЛИРУЕМЫЕ РАСХОДЫ

controlled company

(CHIN) 受控制公司，分公司，附属公司

(FRE) société dominée

(GER) beherrschte Gesellschaft *f*, Unter-,
Tochtergesellschaft *f*, kontrolliertes
Unternehmen *n*

(JAP) 子会社、被支配会社

(RUS) КОНТРОЛИРУЕМАЯ
КОМПАНИЯ

controlled economy

(CHIN) 统制经济

(FRE) économie dirigée

(GER) gelenkte Wirtschaft *f*, Plan- *f*,
Kommando- *f*, Verwaltungswirtschaft *f*

(JAP) 統制経済

(RUS) КОНТРОЛИРУЕМАЯ ЭКОНОМИКА

controller

(CHIN) 总监，审计长

(FRE) assistant général de gestion

(GER) Controller *m*, Leiter *m* des
Rechnungswesens *n*

(JAP) 監査役、コントローラー、
会計検査官

(RUS) КОНТРОЛЕР; РЕВИЗОР

controlling interest
(CHIN) 控股权，控制权
(FRE) contrôle direct, participation de contrôle
(GER) Mehrheitsbeteiligung *f*, (Kapital)mehrheit *f*
(JAP) 経営支配権、会社支配に十分な持ち株
(RUS) КОНТРОЛЬНЫЙ ПАКЕТ АКЦИЙ

convenience sampling
(CHIN) 便利抽样法
(FRE) échantillonnage de commodité
(GER) Ermessensauswahl *f*
(JAP) 便宜標本法、簡易標本法
(RUS) ПРОИЗВОЛЬНАЯ ВЫБОРКА

conventional mortgage
(CHIN) 约定抵押，常规抵押
(FRE) hypothèque traditionnelle
(GER) konventionelle bzw. gewöhnliche Hypothek *f*, Hypothekar- *m*, Realkredit *m*
(JAP) 無保証抵当貸付け
(RUS) ОБЫЧНАЯ ИПОТЕКА

conversion
(CHIN) 转化，变换，汇兑，交换
(FRE) conversion
(GER) Umtausch *m* von Wertpapieren *npl*; Währungsumtausch, -eintausch *m*; Konversion *f*, Umwandlung *f*, Konvertierung *f*
(JAP) 換算、現金化、転換
(RUS) ПРЕОБРАЗОВАНИЕ; КОНВЕРСИЯ; КОНВЕРТИРОВАНИЕ

conversion cost
(CHIN) 转换成本，换算成本
(FRE) coût de la conversion
(GER) Konvertierungs- *f*, Umwandlungskosten *f*
(JAP) 加工費
(RUS) ЗАТРАТЫ НА КОНВЕРТИРОВАНИЕ

conversion factor for employee contributions
(CHIN) 员工贡献换算因子
(FRE) facteur (taux) de conversion pour les cotisations des salariés
(GER) Umrechnungsfaktor *m* für Arbeitnehmerbeiträge *mpl*
(JAP) 従業員拠出換算係数
(RUS) КОЭФФИЦИЕНТ ПЕРЕСЧЕТА ВОЗНАГРАЖДЕНИЯ ЗА ВКЛАД РАБОТНИКА

conversion parity
(CHIN) 兑换平价
(FRE) parité de conversion
(GER) Wandelverhältnis *n*
(JAP) 転換平価
(RUS) КОНВЕРСИОННЫЙ ПАРИТЕТ

conversion price
(CHIN) 兑换价格，调换价格，汇价
(FRE) prix de conversion
(GER) Konvertierungs- *m*, Wandlungs- *m*, Umrechnungskurs *m*, Umrechnungspreis *m*
(JAP) 切換価格、転換価格
(RUS) ЦЕНА КОНВЕРСИИ ЗАЙМА

conversion ratio
(CHIN) 换算比率，兑换比率
(FRE) rapport de conversion
(GER) Konvertierungs- *n*, Umrechnungs- *n*, Wandelverhältnis *n*
(JAP) 換算率(通貨の)、転換比率
(RUS) СООТНОШЕНИЕ, ОПРЕДЕЛЯЮЩЕЕ СКОЛЬКО ОБЫКНОВЕННЫХ АКЦИЙ БУДЕТ ПОЛУЧЕНО В ОБМЕН НА ВЕКСЕЛЯ И ПРИВИЛЛЕГИРОВАННЫЕ АКЦИИ

convertibles
(CHIN) 可兑换证券
(FRE) titres convertibles, valeurs convertibles
(GER) Wandelschuldverschreibungen *fpl*, Wandelanleihen *fpl*, Wandelobligationen *fpl*
(RUS) КОНВЕРТИРУЕМЫЕ ЦЕННЫЕ БУМАГИ

convetible term life insurance
(CHIN) 可转换定期人寿保险
(FRE) assurance vie transformable
(GER) Risikoumtauschlebensversicherung *f*, Risikolebensversicherung *f* mit Umtauschrecht *n*

(JAP) 転換可能定期生命保険
(RUS) ВРЕМЕННОЕ СТРАХОВАНИЕ
ЖИЗНИ С ВОЗМОЖНОСТЬЮ ЕГО
КОНВЕРСИИ НА ПОЖИЗНЕННОЕ
СТРАХОВАНИЕ

convey
(CHIN) 运送，转让，搬运，传达
(FRE) transporter
(GER) befördern, transportieren (Güter);
übermitteln (Nachricht); übertragen,
abtreten, übereignen (Eigentum) *v*
(JAP) 運搬する、（財産・権利を）
譲渡する
(RUS) ПЕРЕДАВАТЬ ПРАВОВОЙ ТИТУЛ

conveyance
(CHIN) 转让，运输，转让证书
(FRE) aliénation, acte d'aliénation, moyen
de transport
(GER) Beförderung *f*, Transport *m* (Güter);
Übertragung *f*, Abtretung *f*, Überschreibung
f (Eigentum)
(JAP) 運搬、譲渡
(RUS) ПЕРЕДАЧА ПРАВОВОГО ТИТУЛА

cooling-off period
(CHIN) 等待期，冷却期
(FRE) délai de réflexion, délai de
renonciation
(GER) Abkühlungs- *f*, Beruhigungszeit *f*
(JAP) 冷却期間、クーリングオフ期間
(RUS) ПЕРИОД ОТКАЗА ОТ ДЕЙСТВИЙ
(профс.)

co-op
(CHIN) 消费合作社
(FRE) cooperative
(GER) Genossenschaft *f*, Kooperative *f*,
Co-Op *f*
(JAP) 生活協同組合、生活協同組合売店
(RUS) ДОГОВОРЁННОСТЬ АГЕНТОВ ПО
НЕДВИЖИМОСТИ О РАЗДЕЛЕ
КОМИССИОННЫХ; ЖИЛИЩНЫЙ
КООПЕРАТИВ

cooperative
(CHIN) 合作的，合作商店
(FRE) coopérative
(GER) Genossenschaft *f*; kooperativ,

gemeinsam *adj*
(JAP) 協同組合の、共同の、協同組合
(RUS) КООПЕРАТИВ; КООПЕРАТИВНЫЙ

cooperative advertising
(CHIN) 合作广告，联合广告
(FRE) publicité collective
(GER) Gemeinschaftswerbung *f*, Verbund-
f, Sammel- *f*, Kollektivwerbung *f*
(JAP) 共同広告、協同広告
(RUS) СОВМЕСТНАЯ РЕКЛАМА

cooperative apartment
(CHIN) 共管公寓
(FRE) appartement collectif
(GER) Eigentumswohnung *f*
(JAP) 共同住宅マンション
(RUS) КООПЕРАТИВНАЯ КВАРТИРА

copy-protected
(CHIN) 拷贝保护的，复制保护的
(FRE) interdit de copie
(GER) kopiergeschützt *adj*
(JAP) コピー防止（機能付き）の
(RUS) ЗАЩИЩЁННЫЙ ОТ КОПИРОВАНИЯ

copyright
(CHIN) 版权，著作权
(FRE) droit d'auteur, droit de reproduction,
copyright
(GER) Urheber- *n*, Eigentumsrecht *n*,
Copyright *n*, Verlagsrecht *n*, Nachdruck- *n*,
Vervielfältigungsrecht *n*
(JAP) 版権、著作権
(RUS) АВТОРСКОЕ ПРАВО

cornering the market
(CHIN) 垄断市场，囤积居奇
(FRE) réduire volontairement l'offre d'un
produit
(GER) den Markt *m* monopolisieren,
aufkaufen, unter Kontrolle
bekommen *v*
(JAP) 買い占め、市場独占
(RUS) МАНИПУЛИРОВАНИЕ РЫНКОМ

corporate bond
(CHIN) 公司债
(FRE) obligation de société

(GER) Industrieschuldverschreibung *f*, -anleihe *f*, -obligation *f*
(JAP) 社債、法人債券
(RUS) КОРПОРАЦИОННАЯ ОБЛИГАЦИЯ

corporate campaign
(CHIN) 公司公关活动
(FRE) campagne de société
(GER) Unternehmenskampagne *f*
(JAP) 企業キャンペーン
(RUS) РЕКЛАМНАЯ КАМПАНИЯ, НАПРАВЛЕННАЯ НА УЛУЧШЕНИЕ ИМИДЖА КОМПАНИИ

corporate equivalent yield
(CHIN) 公司约当收益率
(FRE) rendement équivalent à celui de la société
(GER) mit Industrieanleihen *fpl* vergleichbare Ertragsrate *f* bzw. Rendite *f* (einer Regierungsanleihe *f*)
(JAP) 社債等価利回り

corporate strategic planning
(CHIN) 公司战略计划
(FRE) planification stratégique de l'entreprise
(GER) strategische Unternehmensplanung *f*
(JAP) 企業戦略計画
(RUS) СТРАТЕГИЧЕСКОЕ ПЛАНИРОВАНИЕ КОРПОРАЦИИ

corporate veil
(CHIN) 以公司作掩护
(FRE) voile corporatif
(GER) Haftungsbeschränkung *f*
(JAP) 企業ベール
(RUS) ИСПОЛЬЗОВАНИЕ КОРПОРАЦИИ ДЛЯ МАСКИРОВКИ ДЕЙСТВИЙ ОТДЕЛЬНОЙ ЛИЧНОСТИ

corporation
(CHIN) 公司，有限公司，股份公司
(FRE) société anonyme
(GER) Kapital- *f*, Aktiengesellschaft *f*; Konzern *m*, Unternehmen *n*
(JAP) 企業、株式会社、法人

(RUS) КОРПОРАЦИЯ

corporeal
(CHIN) 物质的，有形的，标的物的
(FRE) corporel
(GER) körperlich, leiblich, materiell *adj*
(JAP) 物質的な、有形の
(RUS) МАТЕРИАЛЬНЫЙ (об имуществе)

corpus
(CHIN) 基金本金，主体财产
(FRE) corpus
(GER) Kapital *n* eines Vermögens *m*
(JAP) 元金、元本、資本金
(RUS) СОБРАНИЕ, СВОД (норм)

correction
(CHIN) 市价上涨后的回落，调整，修正，纠正
(FRE) correction
(GER) Korrektur *f*, Berichtigung *f*
(JAP) 修正、補正
(RUS) ИСПРАВЛЕНИЕ; КОРРЕКЦИЯ

correlation coefficient
(CHIN) 相关系数
(FRE) coefficient de correlation
(GER) Korrelationskoeffizient *m*
(JAP) 相関係数
(RUS) КОЭФФИЦИЕНТ КОРРЕЛЯЦИИ

correspondent
(CHIN) 顾客，往来客户，代理商行
(FRE) correspondant
(GER) Korrespondent *m*; Journalist *m*, Berichterstatter *m*
(JAP) 通信者、取引先
(RUS) КОРРЕСПОНДЕНТ

corrupted
(CHIN) 被破坏的
(FRE) corrompu
(GER) beschädigt *adj*
(JAP) 破損した、原形が失われた
(RUS) ИСПОРЧЕННЫЙ, ИСКАЖЁННЫЙ

cosign
(CHIN) 联署

(FRE) co-signer
(GER) mitunterzeichnen *v*
(JAP) 共同署名者
(RUS) ПОДПИСАТЬ СОВМЕСТНО

cost
(CHIN) 成本，费用，价格
(FRE) coût, frais, charge
(GER) Kosten *pl*, Preis *m*
(JAP) 原価、費用
(RUS) ЗАТРАТА; ИЗДЕРЖКА;
СЕБЕСТОИМОСТЬ

cost accounting
(CHIN) 成本会计，成本核算
(FRE) décompte des frais, (C) comptabilité
analytique d'exploitation
(GER) Kostenrechnung *f*,
Betriebskalkulation *f*, -abrechnung *f*
(JAP) 原価会計、原価計算
(RUS) УЧЕТ ИЗДЕРЖЕК; КОММЕРЧЕСКИЙ
РАСЧЕТ

cost application
(CHIN) 成本摊派，成本分配
(FRE) application de coûts
(GER) Zuteilung *f* von Kosten *pl*;
Kostenzurechnung *f*
(JAP) 費用配分
(RUS) УЧЕТ СЕБЕСТОИМОСТИ

cost approach
(CHIN) 成本计算法
(FRE) approce des coûts, (C) technique du
coût
(GER) Kostenansatz *m*, -methode *f*
(JAP) 費用的アプローチ
(RUS) ЗАТРАТНЫЙ ПОДХОД ОЦЕНКИ
СОБСТВЕННОСТИ

cost basis
(CHIN) 成本基础
(FRE) base des coûts
(GER) Kostengrundlage *f*
(JAP) 原価主義、原価基準
(RUS) ПЕРВОНАЧАЛЬНАЯ ЦЕНА АКТИВА

cost-benefit analysis
(CHIN) 成本效益分析

(FRE) analyse coût-rendement
(GER) Kosten-Nutzen-Analyse *f*
(JAP) 費用・便益分析
(RUS) АНАЛИЗ ИЗДЕРЖЕК И ПРИБЫЛИ

cost center
(CHIN) 成本中心
(FRE) section des frais
(GER) Kostenstelle *f*, -träger *m*
(JAP) 原価中心点、原価部門
(RUS) КАЛЬКУЛЯЦИОННЫЙ ОТДЕЛ

cost containment
(CHIN) 成本限制
(FRE) maîtrise des coûts
(GER) Kosteneindämmung *f*, -dämpfung *f*
(JAP) 費用抑制
(RUS) СОКРАЩЕНИЕ РАСХОДОВ

cost-effectiveness
(CHIN) 成本效益，成本效用
(FRE) rapport coût-efficacite
(GER) Kostenwirksamkeit *f*
(JAP) 費用有効度、費用効果
(RUS) ЭФФЕКТИВНОСТЬ ЗАТРАТ

cost method
(CHIN) 成本估计法
(FRE) méthode des coûts
(GER) Kostenmethode *f*, -verfahren *n*
(JAP) コスト主義、原価法
(RUS) МЕТОД ОЦЕНКИ ОТ
СЕБЕСТОИМОСТИ

cost objective
(CHIN) 成本对象，成本目标
(FRE) objectif des coûts
(GER) Kostenvorgabe *f*, -ziel *n*
(JAP) 費用目標
(RUS) ЦЕЛИ ПО СНИЖЕНИЮ РАСХОДОВ,
ДОСТИЖЕНИЮ СТОИМОСТИ

cost of capital
(CHIN) 资本成本
(FRE) coût de l'investissement
(GER) Kapitalkosten *fpl*
(JAP) 資本コスト
(RUS) СТОИМОСТЬ
КАПИТАЛА

cost of carry

(CHIN) 附加成本，折旧成本

(FRE) coût de portage

(GER) Carrykosten *pl*, Cost-of-Carry; Lagerhaltungskosten *pl*

(JAP) 持越し費用

(RUS) ИЗДЕРЖКИ ПО ПОДДЕРЖАНИЮ ИНВЕСТИЦИОННОЙ ПОЗИЦИИ

cost of goods manufactured

(CHIN) 制成品成本

(FRE) coût des biens manufactures

(GER) Kosten *pl* der Erzeugnisse *npl*, Kosten *pl* der hergestellten Waren *fpl*

(JAP) 製造原価

(RUS) СЕБЕСТОИМОСТЬ ПРОИЗВОДИМЫХ ТОВАРОВ

cost of goods sold

(CHIN) 销售成本，销货成本

(FRE) coût des biens vendus, (C) coût d'achat des marchandises vendues

(GER) Kosten *pl* der verkauften Erzeugnisse *npl* bzw. verkauften Waren *fpl*, Umsatzaufwendungen *fpl*

(JAP) 売上原価、販売原価

(RUS) СЕБЕСТОИМОСТЬ ПРОДАННЫХ ТОВАРОВ

cost-of-living adjustment (COLA)

(CHIN) 生活费用调整(COLA)

(FRE) majoration du coût de la vie

(GER) Lebenshaltungskostenausgleich *m*, Teuerungsausgleich *m*, Lebenshaltungskostenangleichung *f*

(JAP) 生計費調節、

(賃金の)生活費調節

(RUS) КОРРЕКТИРОВКА С УЧЕТОМ РОСТА СТОИМОСТИ ЖИЗНИ (индекса потребительских цен)

cost overrun

(CHIN) 超额费用

(FRE) dépassement des coûts

(GER) Kostenüberschreitung *f*, Mehrkosten *fpl*

(JAP) 予算超過、（原価）見積超過

(RUS) ПРЕВЫШЕНИЕ ПЛАНИРУЕМЫХ ИЗДЕРЖЕК

cost-plus contract

(CHIN) 成本附加合同

(FRE) contrat

(GER) Kostenzuschlagsvertrag *m*, Vertrag *m* auf der Grundlage *f* von Istkosten *pl* plus vereinbartem Gewinnzuschlag *m*, Vertrag *m* mit Preisgleitklausel *f*

(JAP) 利益加算契約、

原価加算契約

(RUS) ДОГОВОР С УЧЕТОМ ФАКТИЧЕСКИХ ИЗДЕРЖЕК

cost-push inflation

(CHIN) 成本推动型通货膨胀

(FRE) inflation par les coûts, (C) inflation par poussée sur les coûts

(GER) Kostendruckinflation *f*, kosteninduzierte Inflation *f*, durch Kostensteigerung *f* bedingte Inflation *f*

(JAP) コストインフレ、

費用圧力インフレ

(RUS) РОСТ ИНФЛЯЦИИ, ВЫЗВАННЫЙ РОСТОМ ЦЕН ИЗ-ЗА РОСТА ИЗДЕРЖЕК

cost records

(CHIN) 成本记录，成本登记

(FRE) enregistrement des coûts

(GER) Kostenerfassung *f*, -ermittlung *f*, -belege *mpl*

(JAP) 原価記録

(RUS) УЧЕТ ИЗДЕРЖЕК

co-tenancy

(CHIN) 共有物业

(FRE) copropriété

(GER) gemeinsames Pacht- *n* bzw. Mietrecht *n*

(JAP) 共同借地（借家）、

不動産共同保有

(RUS) СОВМЕСТНОЕ ПРОЖИВАНИЕ; СОВМЕСТНАЯ АРЕНДА

cottage industry

(CHIN) 家庭手工业

(FRE) industrie artisanale

(GER) Heimindustrie *f*, -gewerbe *n*

(JAP) 家内工業

(RUS) КУСТАРНАЯ ПРОМЫШЛЕННОСТЬ

counsel

(CHIN) 辩护人，出庭律师，法律顾问

(FRE) conseil, avocat consultant

(GER) Rechtanwalt *m*; Prozessvertreter *m*

(JAP) 弁護士、法律顧問、弁護団、助言

(RUS) ЮРИДИЧЕСКИЙ КОНСУЛЬТАНТ; АДВОКАТ В СУДЕ

counterclaim

(CHIN) 反诉

(FRE) demande reconventionnelle

(GER) Gegenforderung *f*, -anspruch *m*; Gegen- *f*, Widerklage *f*

(JAP) 反訴、反対要求

(RUS) ВСТРЕЧНАЯ ПРЕТЕНЗИЯ; ВСТРЕЧНЫЙ ИСК

countercyical policy

(CHIN) 反周期财政政策

(FRE) politique contrecyclique

(GER) antizyklische Politik *f*, konjunkturdämpfende Politik *f*

(JAP) 逆景気循環政策、景気対策

(RUS) ПОЛИТИКА ПРАВИТЕЛЬСТВА ПО СМЯГЧЕНИЮ ВЛИЯНИЯ ДЕЛОВЫХ ЦИКЛОВ НА ЭКОНОМИКУ СТРАНЫ

counterfeit

(CHIN) 伪造的，假冒的，伪币

(FRE) contrefaire, contrefaçon

(GER) Fälschung *f*, Imitation *f*

(JAP) 偽造（の）、模造品

(RUS) ПОДДЕЛЬНЫЙ, ПОДЛОЖНЫЙ

countermand

(CHIN) 取消，撤回，止付

(FRE) contremander

(GER) stornieren, sperren (Scheck), widerrufen *v*

(JAP) 取消命令、反対命令（を出す）、命令撤回（をする）、(注文の)取り消し

(RUS) ОТМЕНА; ОТМЕНЯТЬ

counteroffer

(CHIN) 反要约，还价

(FRE) surenchère

(GER) Gegenangebot *n*, -offerte *f*

(JAP) カウンターオファー、返し申込み、修正申込み

(RUS) ВСТРЕЧНОЕ ПРЕДЛОЖЕНИЕ

coupon bond

(CHIN) 附息票债券

(FRE) obligation à coupons

(GER) Inhaberschuldverschreibung *f*, -obligation *f*

(JAP) 利札付債権、利札付社債

(RUS) КУПОННАЯ ОБЛИГАЦИЯ

court of record

(CHIN) 法庭记录

(FRE) tribunal d'archives

(GER) ordentliches bzw. staatliches Gericht *n*

(JAP) 記録裁判所

(RUS) СУД ПИСЬМЕННОГО ПРОИЗВОДСТВА

covariance

(CHIN) 协方差

(FRE) covariance

(GER) Kovarianz *f*

(JAP) 共分散、共変量

(RUS) КОВАРИАНТНОСТЬ

covenant

(CHIN) 契约，条款，保护条款

(FRE) engagement formel

(GER) Vertrag *m*; Nebenvereinbarung *f*, vertraglich bindende Verpflichtung *f*

(JAP) 契約(書)、捺印証書による契約

(RUS) ДОГОВОР; ОБЯЗАТЕЛЬСТВО

covenant not to compete

(CHIN) 保证不竞争条款

(FRE) engagement à ne pas concurrencer

(GER) Nichtwettbewerbsvereinbarung *f*, -klausel *f*

(JAP) 非競争約款

(RUS) ОБЯЗАТЕЛЬСТВО НЕ КОНКУРИРОВАТЬ

cover

(CHIN) 保险，承保，弥补，抵偿，包括

(FRE) couvrir

(GER) decken; versichern; zuständig sein für; bestreiten (Kosten) *v*; Deckung *f*; Verhältnis *n* Gewinn *m* zu Dividende *f*

(JAP) 保証金、補償範囲、保険をかける
(RUS) ПОКРЫВАТЬ; ПОКРЫТИЕ (денежное)

covered option
(CHIN) 有保证期权
(FRE) option couverte
(GER) gedeckte Option *f*
(JAP) 担保オプション
(RUS) ПОКРЫТЫЙ ОПЦИОН

cracker
(CHIN) 换钞人，推销员
(FRE) saboteur de réseaux pirate
(GER) Knallkörper *m*
(JAP) クラッカー（コンピューターネットワークに不法侵入しデータの悪用やシステム破壊等をする者）
(RUS) НАРУШИТЕЛЬ СИСТЕМ БЕЗОПАСНОСТИ

craft union
(CHIN) 行业工会
(FRE) syndicat de métier
(GER) Berufsgewerkschaft *f*
(JAP) 職種別組合、職業別組合
(RUS) ПРОФЕССИОНАЛЬНЫЙ СОЮЗ

crash
(CHIN) 大跌，崩溃，破产;系统性故障，崩溃，失效
(FRE) krash, panne, (C) effondrement des cours, (C) plantage
(GER) Crash *m*, Kurseinbruch *m*, Börsenkrach *m*; Zusammenbruch *m*; Ruin *m*, Pleite *f*
(JAP) 失敗、破産、崩壊
(JAP) 故障、クラッシュする、機能が停止する
(RUS) КРАХ (биржевой); ФАТАЛЬНЫЙ СБОЙ; АВАРИЙНОЕ ЗАВЕРШЕНИЕ РАБОТЫ СИСТЕМЫ

creative black book
(CHIN) 创新型供应商黑皮书
(FRE) creative black book, (C) livre noir
(GER) Black Book *n* der schöpferischen Industrie *f*
(JAP) 創造的ブラックリスト

(RUS) «ЧЁРНАЯ КНИГА», Т. Е. МИРОВОЙ СПРАВОЧНИК ТВОРЧЕСКИХ ДЕЯТЕЛЕЙ (ФОТОГРАФОВ, ИЛЛЮСТРАТОРОВ И Т. П.)

creative financing
(CHIN) 创造性融资安排
(FRE) financement novateur
(GER) kreative Finanzierung *f*
(JAP) 工夫した金融、例外的なローン
(RUS) ФИНАНСИРОВАНИЕ ОТЛИЧНОЕ ОТ ТРАДИЦИОННОГО

credit
(CHIN) 信贷，信用，贷方，信用证
(FRE) crédit
(GER) Kredit *m*, Darlehen *n*; Akkreditiv *n*; Bonität *f*, Kreditwürdigkeit *f*; Zahlungsziel *n*; Freibetrag *m* (Steuer); Guthaben *n*; Gutschrift *f*; Habensaldo *n*; kreditieren, auf Kredit verkaufen; anrechnen, gutschreiben; anerkennen *v*
(JAP) 信用、貸方、債権
(RUS) КРЕДИТ; ССУДА

credit analyst
(CHIN) 信用分析师
(FRE) analyste en credit
(GER) Kreditanalyst *m*
(JAP) 信用分析家
(RUS) АНАЛИТИК ПО КРЕДИТАМ

credit balance
(CHIN) 贷方节余，结欠
(FRE) solde créditeur
(GER) Kontoguthaben *n*, Haben- *n*, Aktivsaldo *n*
(JAP) 貸方残高、預金尻
(RUS) КРЕДИТОВЫЙ (положительный) ОСТАТОК НА СЧЕТЕ

credit bureau
(CHIN) 征信所，信用咨询公司
(FRE) société de renseignements commerciaux, (C) agence d'évaluation du crédit
(GER) (Kredit)Auskunftei *f*
(JAP) 商業興信所、信用調査機関
(RUS) БЮРО КРЕДИТНОЙ ИНФОРМАЦИИ

credit card

(CHIN) 信用卡，转账卡
(FRE) carte de crédit
(GER) Kreditkarte *f*
(JAP) クレジットカード
(RUS) КРЕДИТНАЯ КАРТОЧКА

creditor

(CHIN) 债权人
(FRE) créancier
(GER) Gläubiger *m*, Kreditor *m*
(JAP) 債権者、貸主
(RUS) КРЕДИТОР; ЗАИМОДАТЕЛЬ

credit order

(CHIN) 信用定单
(FRE) ordre de crédit
(GER) Kredit- *m*, Gutschriftsauftrag *m*
(JAP) 掛け買い注文
(RUS) ПОРУЧЕНИЕ НА КРЕДИТ

credit rating

(CHIN) 信用评级，信用定额
(FRE) conditions de crédit, cote de crédit,
degré de solvabilité, estimée
(GER) Kreditwürdigkeit *f*, Bonität *f*,
Kreditbeurteilung *f*, Rating *n*
(JAP) 信用格付け、信用等級
(RUS) ПОКАЗАТЕЛЬ
КРЕДИТОСПОСОБНОСТИ

credit requirements

(CHIN) 信贷要求
(FRE) exigences de crédit
(GER) Kreditanforderungen *fpl*
(JAP) 資金需要、信用必要条件
(RUS) ТРЕБОВАНИЯ КРЕДИТОВАНИЯ

credit risk

(CHIN) 信用风险
(FRE) risque lié au credit
(GER) Kreditrisiko *n*
(JAP) 信用リスク
(RUS) КРЕДИТНЫЙ РИСК

credit union

(CHIN) 信用合作社
(FRE) coopérative de crédit

(GER) Kreditgenossenschaft *f*, -verein *m*,
Genossenschaftsbank *f*
(JAP) 信用組合
(RUS) КРЕДИТНЫЙ СОЮЗ

creeping inflation

(CHIN) 潜行通货膨胀
(FRE) inflation rampante
(GER) schleichende Inflation *f*
(JAP) 忍び寄るインフレ
(RUS) «ПОЛЗУЧАЯ» ИНФЛЯЦИЯ

critical path method (CPM)

(CHIN) 统筹法（CPM）
(FRE) méthode du chemin critique,
méthode CPM
(GER) CPM-Methode *f*,
Netzwerkplanungsmethode *f* mit
(zeit)kritischer Planung *f*
(JAP) 臨界経路法
(RUS) МЕТОД КОНТРОЛЯ ИЗДЕРЖЕК
ПУТЁМ ОПТИМИЗАЦИИ
ПОСЛЕДОВАТЕЛЬНОСТИ ЭТАПОВ
ПРОИЗВОДСТВА)

critical region

(CHIN) 临界区域
(FRE) région critique
(GER) kritischer Bereich *m*,
Ablehnungsbereich *m*
(JAP) 危険域、臨界領域
(RUS) КРИТИЧЕСКАЯ ЗОНА (СТАТ.)

crop

(CHIN) 修剪，剪切
(FRE) rognage
(GER) zuschneiden *v*
(JAP) (不必要な部分を)切り取る、
トリミングする

cross

(CHIN) 交叉，跨越
(FRE) croiser
(GER) privater Verkauf *m* eines
Aktienpakets *n*
(JAP) (不必要な部分を)切り取る、
トリミングする
(RUS) ОПЕРАЦИЯ С ЦЕННЫМИ
БУМАГАМИ, В КОТОРОЙ ОДИН БРОКЕР

94

ВЫСТУПАЕТ АГЕНТОМ КА ПРОДАЮЩЕЙ,
ТАК И ПОКУПАЮЩЕЙ СТОРОНЫ

cross-footing
(CHIN) 交叉总计
(FRE) opération horizontale
(GER) Querrechnen *n*, -rechnung *f*
(JAP) クロスフッティング

cross merchandising
(CHIN) 交叉商品摆放
(FRE) vente avec prime, (C) étalage jumelé,
(C) agencement de produits
complémentaires
(GER) Crossmerchandising *n*
(JAP) クロスマーチャンダイジング、
相互取引
(RUS) ПЕРЕКРЕСТНОЕ СОДЕЙСТВИЕ
ПРОДВИЖЕНИЮ ТОВАРА НА РЫНКЕ

cross purchase plan
(CHIN) 交叉购买计划
(FRE) plan d'achat croisé
(GER) Teilhaberversicherung *f*,
Gesellschaftsversicherungsvereinbarung,
bei der sich die Teilhaber verpflichten, ihren
Anteil nur an Mitgesellschafter zu
veräußern wie oft mit Mitteln aus der
Lebensversicherung des verstorbenen
Mitglieds)
(JAP) 相互買入れ制度
(RUS) СТРАХОВАНИЕ НА СЛУЧАЙ
СМЕРТИ ИЛИ БОЛЕЗНИ ДЕЛОВОГО
ПАРТНЁРА

cross tabulation
(CHIN) 交叉列表
(FRE) tableau combinatoire tableau à
multiples entrées
(GER) Kombinationstabelle *f*;
Kreuztabulierung *f*
(JAP) 組合せ分類、クロス集計
(RUS) ПЕРЕКРЕСТНЫЙ ИТОГ

crowd
(CHIN) 到场参加交易的伙伴
(FRE) foule
(GER) Menschenmenge *f*, Gedränge *n*
(JAP) 中間、グループ
(RUS) СКОПЛЕНИЕ (бирж.)

crowding out
(CHIN) 挤出，推出
(FRE) eviction
(GER) Verdrängungswettbewerb *m*, -effekt
m, Verdrängung *f*
(JAP) 追し出し、締め出し
(RUS) «ВЫТЕСНЕНИЕ» (бирж.)

crown jewels
(CHIN) 最值钱部分
(FRE) les joyaux de la couronne
(GER) Kronjuwelen *fpl*
(JAP) 重要部門、目玉、高採算部門
(RUS) «ЖЕМЧУЖИНЫ» , Т. Е. НАИБОЛЕЕ
ЦЕННЫЕ ДОЧЕРНИЕ КОМПАНИИ

crown loan
(CHIN) 克朗贷款
(FRE) prêt crown
(GER) Crown-Darlehen *n*, (benannt nach
Harry Crown, wobei das Darlehen aus
Steuergründen an die Eltern bzw. Kinder
des Kreditgebers geht)
(JAP) クラウン貸付サービス
(RUS) ЗАЁМ КРОУНЛ

**cum dividend, cum rights or cum
warrant**
(CHIN) 有股息，附有权利或附带权利
(FRE) avec droit à, droits attachés ou, (C)
coupons attachés
(GER) einschließlich Dividende *f*, mit
Bezugsrechten *npl*
(JAP) 配当付、権利付またはカムワラン
ト
(RUS) «ВКЛЮЧАЯ ДИВИДЕНД И ПРАВО
НА ПОКУПКУ» , АКЦИИ, ВЛАДЕЛЬЦЫ
КОТОРЫХ ИМЕЮТ ПРАВО НА
ПОЛУЧЕНИЕ ДИВИДЕНТОВ

cumulative dividend
(CHIN) 累积股息
(FRE) dividende cumulative
(GER) kumulative Dividende *f*,
Mehrfachdividende *f*
(JAP) 累加配当、累積配当
(RUS) КУМУЛЯТИВНЫЙ ДИВИДЕНД

cumulative liability
(CHIN) 累积责任

(FRE) responsabilité cumulative
(GER) kumulative Haftung *f*
(JAP) 重複責任
(RUS) СОВОКУПНАЯ
ОТВЕТСТВЕННОСТЬ

cumulative preferred stock
(CHIN) 累积优先股
(FRE) action cumulative privilégiée
(GER) kumulative Vorzugsaktien *fpl*,
Vorzugsaktie *f* mit kumulativem
Dividendenanspruch *m*
(JAP) 累積優先株、累加的優先株
(RUS) КУМУЛЯТИВНАЯ
ПРИВИЛЕГИРОВАННАЯ АКЦИЯ

cumulative voting
(CHIN) 累积投票权
(FRE) vote cumulé
(GER) Stimmhäufung *f*, kumulative
Stimmabgabe *f*, Mehrstimmrecht *n*
(JAP) 累積投票
(RUS) КУМУЛЯТИВНОЕ ГОЛОСОВАНИЕ
(акционеров)

curable depreciation
(CHIN) 可挽回的贬值
(FRE) dépréciation curable, dévalorisation
curable
(GER) korrigierbare Abschreibung *f*
(JAP) 回復可能な減価
(RUS) ИСПРАВИМАЯ
АМОРТИЗАЦИЯ

currency futures
(CHIN) 货币期货
(FRE) contrat à terme sur devise, contrat
financier à terme sur devises
(GER) Devisen- *mpl*,
Währungsterminkontrakte *mpl*
(JAP) 通貨先物
(RUS) ВАЛЮТНЫЕ ФЬЮЧЕРСЫ

currency in circulation
(CHIN) 流通中的货币
(FRE) devises en circulation
(GER) Währungsumlauf *m*
(JAP) 流通通貨、通貨流通高
(RUS) ДЕНЕЖНАЯ МАССА (банкноты и
монеты) В ОБРАЩЕНИИ

current
(CHIN) 活期，通用的，本期的，当前的
(FRE) actuel, en cours
(GER) gegenwärtig, aktuell, momentan;
umlaufend, zirkulierend; gängig;
marktgängig; verkehrs-, marktfähig *adj*
(JAP) 流通、流動
(RUS) ТЕКУЩИЙ

current asset
(CHIN) 流动资产
(FRE) actif circulant, actif réalisable
(GER) (kurzfristiges) Umlaufvermögen *n*;
Gegenstand *m* des Umlaufvermögens *n*,
flüssige Aktiva *pl*, kurzfristiger
Vermögenswert *m*; kurzfristige Forderung *f*
(Bilanz)
(JAP) 流動資産
(RUS) ТЕКУЩИЕ ОБОРОТНЫЕ АКТИВЫ

current assumption whole life insurance
(CHIN) 当前假定全寿命期保险
(FRE) assurance vie entiére d'après les
hypothèses actuelles
(GER) Todesfallversicherung *f* unter
aktuellen Annahmen *fpl*
(JAP) 現行引受け終身保険
(RUS) ПОЖИЗНЕННОЕ СТРАХОВАНИЕ НА
СЛУЧАЙ СМЕРТИ С ЕЛЕМЕНТАМИ
СБЕРЕЖЕНИЙ НА ОСНОВЕ ТЕКУЩЕЙ
ПРОЦЕНТНОЙ СТАВКИ

current cost
(CHIN) 时价，本期成本
(FRE) coût courant
(GER) laufende Kosten *pl*;
Wiederbeschaffungskosten *pl*
(JAP) 現行費用、現在の費用
(RUS) ТЕКУЩАЯ СТОИМОСТЬ

current dollars
(CHIN) 现值美元
(FRE) dollars courants
(GER) aktueller Dollarbetrag *m*,
gegenwärtiger Dollarwert *m*
(JAP) 経常ドル
(RUS) СТОИМОСТЬ АКТИВОВ В
СЕГОДНЯШНИХ ЦЕНАХ

current liabilities
(CHIN) 流动负债
(FRE) passif à court terme

(GER) kurzfristige Verbindlichkeiten *fpl*
bzw. Verpflichtungen *fpl*, kurzfristige
Passiva *pl*
(JAP) 流動負債、当座負債、
(RUS) ТЕКУЩИЕ ОБЯЗАТЕЛЬСТВА

current market value
(CHIN) 当叶市价
(FRE) cours du jour
(GER) Markt- *m*, Tageswert *m*, Tageskurs
m, Handelswert *m*
(JAP) 現行市場価格(価額)
(RUS) ТЕКУЩАЯ РЫНОЧНАЯ
СТОИМОСТЬ

current ratio
(CHIN) 现行比率
(FRE) taux de liquidité
(GER) Liquidität *f* zweiten Grades *m*,
Umlaufvermögen *n* in Prozent der
kurzfristigen Verbindlichkeiten *fpl*
(JAP) 流動比率
(RUS) ОТНОШЕНИЕ ТЕКУЩИХ
АКТИВОВ К ТЕКУЩИМ
ПАССИВАМ

current valu accounting
(CHIN) 现值会计法
(FRE) méthode du bilan actualize
(GER) Rechnungslegung *f* mit Bewertung *f*
zum Zeitwert *m*, Zeitwert- *n*,
Gegenwartswertprinzip *n*
(JAP) 時価会計
(RUS) УЧЕТ В ТЕКУЩИХ ЦЕНАХ

current yield
(CIIN) 本期收益
(FRE) rendement actualisé
(GER) Umlaufrendite *f*
(JAP) 現在収益、
現在利回り

cursor
(CHIN) 光标
(FRE) curseur
(GER) Cursor *m*, Positionsanzeiger *m*,
Schreib-, Positionsmarke *f*
(JAP) カーソル
(RUS) КУРСОРОГРАПИЧЕНИЕ
ПЕНСИОННОЙ СХЕМЫ

curtailment in pension plan
(CHIN) 削减养老金计划
(FRE) compression du plan de
retraite
(GER) Kürzung *f* der Pensionskasse bzw.
Rentenversicherung *f*
(JAP) 年金制度の縮小
(RUS) УРЕЗАНИЕ ПЕНСИОННОГО ФОНДА,
ПЛАНА

curtesy
(CHIN) 鳏夫产权
(GER) Nießbrauch *m* (des Witwers *m* am
Grundvermögen *n* der Frau *f*)
(JAP) 鳏夫産、かん夫権

curtilage
(CHIN) 庭园，宅地
(FRE) marge d'isolement (of building)
(GER) abgegrenzter Bauraum *m*; Baulücke *f*
(JAP) 住宅付属庭地、宅地
(RUS) ЗЕМЛЯ И СТРОЕНИЯ,
ПРИМЫКАЮЩИЕ К ЖИЛОМУ ДОМУ

custodial account
(CHIN) 保管账户
(FRE) compte de garde, (C) compte de
depot
(GER) Treuhandkonto *n*
(JAP) 保管口座、保管勘定
(RUS) ПОПЕЧИТЕЛЬСКИЙ СЧЕТ; СЧЕТ,
ОТКРЫТЫЙ НА
НЕСОВЕРШЕННОЛЕТНЕГО

custodian
(CHIN) 保管人，管理人
(FRE) dépositaire
(GER) Treuhänder *n*, Verwahrer *m*,
Vermögensverwalter *m*;
Hinterlegungsstelle *f*, Depotbank *f*
(JAP) 管理人、保管人
(RUS) ПОПЕЧИТЕЛЬ;
ОПЕКУН

custody
(CHIN) 保管，保护
(FRE) dépôt, garde
(GER) Verwahrung *f*, Obhut *f*, Verwaltung
f; Aufsicht *f*, Gewahrsam *m*, Haft *f*;
Sorgerecht *n*

(JAP) 保管、管理、保護、監護権
(RUS) ОПЕКА; СОДЕРЖАНИЕ ПОД
СТРАЖЕЙ

customer
(CHIN) 顾客，买方
(FRE) client
(GER) Kunde m, Käufer m, Abnehmer m;
Auftraggeber m
(RUS) ПОКУПАТЕЛЬ; КЛИЕНТ

customer profile
(CHIN) 顾客群组特征
(FRE) profil du client
(GER) Sonderprofil n; personalisiertes
Profil n
(JAP) 顧客のプロフィール、顧客情報
(RUS) «НА ЗАКАЗ»

customer service
(CHIN) 顾客服务
(FRE) service à la clientèle
(GER) Kundendienst m, -betreuung f, -
service m
(JAP) 顧客サービス
(RUS) ОБСЛУЖИВАНИЕ ПОКУПАТЕЛЕЙ

customer service representative
(CHIN) 顾客服务代表
(FRE) responsable du service clientèle
(GER) Kundendienstmitarbeiter m, -berater
m, -betreuer m
(JAP) 顧客サービス担当者
(RUS) ПРЕДСТАВИТЕЛЬ ПО
ОБСЛУЖИВАНИЮ ПОКУПАТЕЛЕЙ

customs
(CHIN) 海关，关税
(FRE) douanes
(GER) Zollbehörde f; Zollwesen n
(JAP) 関税
(RUS) ТАМОЖНЯ

customs court
(CHIN) 海关法院
(FRE) tribunal douanier
(GER) Zollgericht n
(JAP) 関税裁判所
(RUS) ТАМОЖЕННЫЙ СУД

cutoff point
(CHIN) 停止供应点，投资截点
(FRE) seuil de reclassement
(GER) Ausscheidungsrate f,
Mindestverzinsung f; Sperrpunkt m
(Werbung); Grenzpunkt m;
Schwelleneinkommen n (Steuer);
Schlussziffer f; Ober- bzw. Untergrenze f
(JAP) カットオフポイント、決算日
(RUS) «ТОЧКА ОТСЕЧЕНИЯ»

cyberspace
(CHIN) 电脑空间
(FRE) cyberespace
(GER) Cyberspace m
(JAP) サイバースペース、サイバー空間、
仮想空間
(RUS) «КИБЕР-ПРОСТРАНСТВО»

cycle billing
(CHIN) 分期开列账单
(FRE) facturation périodique
(GER) periodische Abrechnung f
(JAP) 周期請求方式、循環請求方式
(RUS) ПЕРИОДИЧЕСКОЕ ВЫСТАВЛЕНИЕ
СЧЕТОВ

cyclical demand
(CHIN) 周期性需求
(FRE) demande conjoncturelle
(GER) zyklische Nachfrage f
(JAP) 循環的需要
(RUS) ЦИКЛИЧЕСКИЙ СПРОС

cyclical industry
(CHIN) 周期性产业
(FRE) économie conjoncturelle
(GER) konjunkturabhängiger
Wirtschaftszweig m
(JAP) 循環産業
(RUS) ПРОМЫШЛЕННОСТЬ С
ПРОИЗВОДСТВЕННЫМ ЦИКЛОМ

cyclical stock
(CHIN) 周期性产业股票
(FRE) stock conjoncturel
(GER) Aktien fpl konjunkturempfindlicher
Unternehmen npl, konjunkturempfindliche
Aktie f, zyklischer Wert m

(JAP) 循環株
(RUS) «ЦИКЛИЧЕСКИЕ» ЦЕННЫЕ
БУМАГИ

cyclical unemployment
(CHIN) 周期性失业
(FRE) chômage conjoncturel
(GER) konjunkturbedingte
Arbeitslosigkeit *f*
(JAP) 循環的失業、周期的失業

(RUS) ЦИКЛИЧЕСКАЯ
БЕЗРАБОТИЦА

cyclic variation
(CHIN) 周期性变化
(FRE) évolution conjoncturelle
(GER) periodische Schwankung *f*
(JAP) 循環的変動、循環変動
(RUS) ЦИКЛИЧЕСКИЕ
ИЗМЕНЕНИЯ

D

daily trading limit

(CHIN) 每日交易极限

(FRE) limite de transactions quotidiennes, limite de fluctuation quotidienne

(GER) zulässiges Schwankungslimit *n*, maximal zulässige Kursfluktuation *f*

(JAP) 一日取引限度

(RUS) МАКСИМАЛЬНО РАЗРЕШЕННОЕ ДВИЖЕНИЕ ЦЕНЫ В ТЕЧЕНИЕ ОДНОГО ДНЯ ЛИМИТЫ ТОРГОВЛИ; МАКСИМУМ ТОВАРОВ

daisy chain

(CHIN) 连接器，联手操盘托市

(FRE) guirlande de marguerites, connexion en guirlande

(GER) undurchsichtiger Unternehmenskomplex *m*; Verkettung *f*

(JAP) 連鎖、一連の取引活動、見せ掛けの活況取引、デージーチェーン

(RUS) ТОРГОВЛЯ МЕЖДУ БРОКЕРАМИ С ЦЕЛЬЮ СОЗДАНИЯ ВИДИМОСТИ СПРОСА НА ОПРЕДЕЛЁННЫЕ АКЦИИ

damages

(CHIN) 损害，损失，赔偿金

(FRE) dommages et intérêts

(GER) Schadensersatz *m*

(JAP) 損害賠償金

(RUS) УЩЕРБ; ПОТЕРИ

data

(CHIN) 资料，数据，事实，知识

(FRE) données

(GER) Daten *pl*, Informationen *fpl*, Angaben *fpl*

(JAP) データ、資料

(RUS) ДАННЫЕ

database

(CHIN) 数据库

(FRE) base de données

(GER) Datenbank *f*

(JAP) データベース

(RUS) БАЗА ДАННЫХ

database management

(CHIN) 数据库管理

(FRE) gestion de base de données,

(C) gestion de banque de données

(GER) Datenbankverwaltung *f*

(JAP) データベース管理

(RUS) УПРАВЛЕНИЕ БАЗОЙ ДАННЫХ

data collection

(CHIN) 数据收集

(FRE) collecte des données

(GER) Datenerfassung *f*, -erhebung *f*, -sammlung *f*

(JAP) データ収集

(RUS) СБОР ДАННЫХ

data maintenance

(CHIN) 数据维护

(FRE) maintenance des données

(GER) Datenpflege *f*, -verwaltung *f*

(JAP) データ保守

(RUS) ХРАНЕНИЕ И ОБРАБОТКА ДАННЫХ

data processing insurance

(CHIN) 数据处理保险

(FRE) assurance de traitement des données,

(C) assurance de traitement des données

(GER) Datenverarbeitungsanlagenversicherung *f*

(JAP) データ処理保険

(RUS) СТРАХОВАНИЕ ОБРАБОТКИ ДАННЫХ

data retrieval

(CHIN) (CHIN) 数据检索

(FRE) récupération des données

(GER) Datenwiedergewinnung *f*, -wiederfindung *f*, -beschaffung *f*

(JAP) データ検索

(RUS) ВЫЗОВ ДАННЫХ

data transmission

(CHIN) 数据传送

(FRE) transmission des données

(GER) Datenübertragung *f*, -übermittlung *f*

(JAP) データ伝送
(RUS) ПЕРЕДАЧА ДАННЫХ

date of issue
(CHIN) 发行日期，签发日期
(FRE) date d'émission
(GER) Ausstellungs- *n*,
Ausfertigungsdatum *n*; Emissions- *m*,
Begebungs- *m*, Auflegungstag *m*
(Wertpapiere)
(JAP) 振出日、発行日
(RUS) ДАТА ВЫДАЧИ; ДАТА ЭМИССИИ;
ДАТА ИЗДАНИЯ

date of record
(CHIN) 记录日期，过广日期
(FRE) date du registre, (C) date de clôture
des registres
(GER) Bezugsrechts- *m*,
Dividendenstichtag *m*, Stopptag *m*
(JAP) 権利確定期日、記録日
(RUS) ДАТА, ФИКСИРУЮЩАЯ НАЧАЛО
ОФИЦИАЛЬНОГО ВЛАДЕНИЯ ЦЕННЫМИ
БУМАГАМИ, ДАЮЩЕГО ПРАВА НА
ПОЛУЧЕНИЕ ДИВИДЕНДА

dating
(CHIN) 填日期，注明日期
(FRE) datation
(GER) Festsetzung *f* der Laufzeit *f*,
Verlängerung *f* des Zahlungsziels *n* durch
(Rechnungs)vordatierung *f*,
Rechnungsausgleich *m*; Datierung *f*
(JAP) 日付記入
(RUS) ПРОДЛЕНИЕ КРЕДИТА СВЕРХ
ОБЫЧНОГО СРОКА

deadbeat
(CHIN) 故意赖账者
(FRE) mauvais payeur
(GER) nicht zahlungsfähig *adj*
(JAP) 資産の無い人、一文無し
(RUS) НЕПЛАТЕЛЬЩИК ДОЛГОВ

dead-end job
(CHIN) 没有出路的工作
(FRE) mploi sans possibilité d'avancement
(GER) Arbeitsplatz *m* ohne
Aufstiegsmöglichkeiten *fpl*, -chancen *fpl*
(JAP) 将来性の無い職

(RUS) ДОЛЖНОСТЬ БЕЗ ВОЗМОЖНОСТИ
ПРОДВИЖЕНИЯ

deadhead
(CHIN) 免费乘客，免费入场者
(FRE) course à vide
(GER) Leerfracht *f*, -fahrt *f*; blinder
Passagier *m*; Schwarzfahrer *m*
(JAP) 能なし、役立たず者、
やる気のない奴
(RUS) БЕЗБИЛЕТНИК; ПОРОЖНИЙ РЕЙС

deadline
(CHIN) 截止日期
(FRE) date limite, délai, date d'expiration,
(C) échéance
(GER) Schlusstermin *m*, Anmelde- *m*,
Einsendeschluss *m*, Stichtag *m*,
Terminvorgabe *f*
(JAP) 締切日、最終期限、準備金限界線
(RUS) КРАЙНИЙ СРОК

dead stock
(CHIN) 滞销货，呆滞资金
(FRE) capital improductif, (C) stock
dormant
(GER) totes Inventar *n*, unverkäufliche
Bestände *mpl*
(JAP) 売残り品、不良在庫、死蔵品
(RUS) ТОВАР, НЕ ПОЛЬЗУЮЩИЙСЯ
СПРОСОМ

dead time
(CHIN) 窝工工时，
停工时间
(FRE) temps mort
(GER) Stillstands- *f*, Ausfallzeit *f*;
Verlust- *f*, Totzeit *f*
(JAP) 不動時間、不感時間
(RUS) ПРОСТОЙ

dealer
(CHIN) 贩子，商人，经纪人
(FRE) marchand dc titres, négociant,
agent de contrepartie, dealer,
(C) contrepartiste ,(C) crieur
(GER) Händler *m*, Kaufmann *m*;
Makler *m*
(JAP) 商人、卸売業者
(RUS) ДИЛЕР

death benefit
(CHIN) 死亡抚恤金
(FRE) capital-décès, (C) prestation de
décès
(GER) Versicherungsleistung *f* im Todesfall
m, Sterbegeld *n*,
Hinterbliebenenversorgung *f*
(JAP) 死亡見舞金、死亡給付金
(RUS) ВЫПЛАТА ПО СТРАХОВАНИЮ В
СЛУЧАЕ СМЕРТИ

debasement
(CHIN) 降低品质，贬值，变质
(FRE) adultération, (C) amenuisement
(GER) Entwertung *f*, Wertminderung *f*,
Abwertung *f*
(JAP) (貨幣の)価値低下、品質低下
(RUS) УМЕНЬШЕНИЕ СОДЕРЖАНИЯ
ДРАГМЕТАЛЛА В МОНЕТАХ

debenture
(CHIN) 债券，公司债券，退税凭单
(FRE) reconnaissance de dette, émission
obligataire, (C) obligation non garantie
(GER) Schuldverschreibung *f*, -schein *m*,
Obligation *f*, Pfandbrief *m*, Rentenwert *m*
(JAP) 社債、債権、債務証書
(RUS) НЕОБЕСПЕЧЕННАЯ ССУДА

debit
(CHIN) 借方，借入，欠债
(FRE) débit
(GER) Soll *n*; Sollseite *f*; Belastung *f*,
Lastschrift *f*, Kontobelastung *f*, Abbuchung
f; Schuld- *m*, Lastposten *m*
(JAP) 借方
(RUS) ДЕБЕТ; ПРОВОДКА РАСХОДА
(бухг.)

debit memorandum
(CHIN) 借项凭单，欠款通知单
(FRE) note de débit
(GER) Lastschrift- *f*,
Belastungsanzeige *f*
(JAP) 貸方票、貸方メモ
(RUS) ДЕБЕТОВАЯ СПРАВКА

debt
(CHIN) 债，欠债，欠款
(FRE) dette

(GER) Schuld *f*, Verbindlichkeit *f*;
Verschuldung *f*
(JAP) 借金、負債、債務
(RUS) ДОЛГ; ЗАДОЛЖЕННОСТЬ

debt coverage ratio
(CHIN) 偿债能力系数
(FRE) (C) ratio de couverture de la dette,
taux de couverture de la dette
(GER) Schuldendeckungsverhältnis *n*,
Schuldendienstdeckungsgrad *m*, -quote *f*
(JAP) 債務回収比率
(RUS) СООТНОШЕНИЕ ЧИСТОГО
ОПЕРАЦИОННОГО ДОХОДА К СУММЕ
ЕЖЕГОДНЫХ ВЫПЛАТ ПО КРЕДИТАМ

debt instrument
(CHIN) 债券
(FRE) (C) titre de créance, instrument de
dette
(GER) Schuldurkunde *f*, Schuldschein, -titel
m, -instrument *n*
(JAP) 債務証書
(RUS) ДОЛГОВОЕ ОБЯЗАТЕЛЬСТВО

debtor
(CHIN) 债务人
(FRE) débiteur
(GER) Schuldner *m*; Kredit- *m*,
Darlehensnehmer *m*, Debitor *m*
(JAP) 借主、債務者、負債者
(RUS) ДОЛЖНИК

debt retirement
(CHIN) 偿债，偿还债务
(FRE) (C) remboursement d'un emprunt,
amortissement de la dette
(GER) Schuldenrückzahlung *f*,
(Schulden)tilgung *f*, -abbau *m*
(JAP) 債券償還
(RUS) ВЫПЛАТА (ПОГАШЕНИЕ) ДОЛГА

debt security
(CHIN) 债券
(FRE) titre de dette, titre d'emprunt, cédule,
(C) titre de créance
(GER) schuldrechtliches Wertpapier *n*,
Anleihepapier *n*; Schuldverschreibung *f*,
Schuldschein *m*, -titel *m*
(JAP) 債務証券

(RUS) ЦЕННАЯ БУМАГА, ЯВЛЯЮЩАЯСЯ
ДОЛГОВЫМ СВИДЕТЕЛЬСТВОМ

debt service
(CHIN) 偿债，债务还本付息
(FRE) service de la dette
(GER) Schuldendienst *m*, Bedienung *f* eines
Darlehens *n*
(JAP) 債務元利未払金
(RUS) ОБСЛУЖИВАНИЕ ДОЛГА,
ПОГАШЕНИЕ ДОЛГА

debt-to-equity ratio
(CHIN) 负债与股东权益比率
(FRE) ratio capitaux, empruntés/fonds
propres, rapport d'endettement général
(GER) Verschuldungsgrad *m*, -koeffizient
m; Fremdkapitalquote *f*
(JAP) 負債比率
(RUS) СООТНОШЕНИЕ СОБСТВЕННЫХ И
ЗАЕМНЫХ СРЕДСТВ

debug
(CHIN) 调试，除错
(FRE) déboguer
(GER) austesten, Fehler *mpl* beseitigen
bzw. bereinigen *v*
(JAP) デバッグ、バグを取る
(RUS) ОТЛАЖИВАТЬ

decentralization
(CHIN) 分制权，分权管理，分散
(FRE) décentralisation
(GER) Dezentralisierung *f*,
Dezentralisation *f*
(JAP) 分散（化）、分権（化）、
地方分権
(RUS) ДЕЦЕНТРАЛИЗАЦИЯ

deceptive advertising
(CHIN) 欺骗性广告
(FRE) publicité mensongère
(GER) irreführende Werbung *f*,
Falschwerbung *f*
(JAP) 詐欺広告、誇大広告
(RUS) ВВОДЯЩАЯ В ЗАБЛУЖДЕНИЕ
РЕКЛАМА

deceptive packaging
(CHIN) 欺骗性包装

(FRE) emballage trompeur, trompe l'œil,
(C) conditionnement trompeur
(GER) Mogelpackung *f*
(JAP) 詐欺包装
(RUS) ВВОДЯЩАЯ В ЗАБЛУЖДЕНИЕ
УПАКОВКА

decision model
(CHIN) 决策模型
(FRE) modèle décisionnel
(GER) Entscheidungsmodell *n*
(JAP) 決定モデル
(RUS) МОДЕЛЬ ПРИНЯТИЯ РЕШЕНИЙ

decision package
(CHIN) 决策组，决策单元
(FRE) dossier décisionnel, (C) devis
décisionnel
(GER) Entscheidungspaket *n*
(RUS) КОМПЛЕКСНОЕ РЕШЕНИЕ

decision support system (DSS)
(CHIN) 决策支持系统
(FRE) systèmes interactifs d'aide à la
décision (SIAD), (C) système d'aide à la
décision
(GER) Entscheidungsunterstützungssystem
n, -findungssystem *n*
(JAP) コンピュータによる意思決定支援
システム
(RUS) СИСТЕМА ОБЕСПЕЧЕНИЯ
(ВЫПОЛНЕНИЯ) ПРИНЯТЫХ РЕШЕНИЙ

decision tree
(CHIN) 决策树，决策体系
(FRE) arbre décisionnel, schéma
décisionnel
(GER) Entscheidungsbaum *m*
(JAP) 決定樹
(RUS) ДИАГРАММА, ПОКАЗЫВАЮЩАЯ
ВСЕВОЗМОЖНЫЕ ПОСЛЕДСТВИЯ
ОПРЕДЕЛЁННОГО РЕШЕНИЯ

declaration
(CHIN) 申请，申报，声明，宣布
(FRE) déclaration
(GER) Stellungsnahme *f*, unbeeidigte
Aussage *f*, Feststellung *f*; Willenserklärung
f, Deklaration *f*, Zollerklärung *f*;
Anmeldung *f* (Versicherung)
(JAP) 公表、申告

(RUS) ДЕКЛАРАЦИЯ; ЗАЯВЛЕНИЕ

declaration of estimated tax

(CHIN) 估计税额申报
(FRE) déclaration de revenus estimés,
(C) déclaration de revenus approximatifs
(GER) geschätzte
Steuervorauszahlungserklärung *f*, Erklärung
f über geschätzte Steuerschulden *fpl*
(JAP) 見積税申告
(RUS) УПЛАТА НАЛОГОВ НА ОСНОВЕ
ПРЕДПОЛАГАЕМОГО ДОХОДА

declaration of trust

(CHIN) 信托声明
(FRE) déclaration de fiducie,
(C) déclaration de dépöt
(GER) Treueerklärung *f*
(JAP) 信託宣言
(RUS) ДЕКЛАРАЦИЯ ОБ УЧРЕЖДЕНИИ
ТРАСТА

declare

(CHIN) 申报，宣布，声明，表示，报关
(FRE) déclarer
(GER) erklären, bekanntmachen; feststellen,
deklarieren *v*; verzollen, angeben (beim
Zoll), (zur Verzollung) anmelden *v*
(JAP) 公表する、申告する
(RUS) ЗАЯВЛЯТЬ; ДЕКЛАРИРОВАТЬ

declining-balance method

(CHIN) 余额递减法
(FRE) amortissement dégressif,
(C) méthode de l'amortissement dégressif à
taux constant
(GER) degressive bzw. fallende
Abschreibungsmethode *f*;
Buchwertabschreibung *f*
(JAP) 定率法
(RUS) МЕТОД УСКОРЕННОЙ
АММОРТИЗАЦИИ

decryption

(CHIN) 解密，解码
(FRE) décryptage
(GER) Entschlüsselung *f*, Dechiffrierung *f*,
Decodierung *f*
(JAP) 暗号解読
(RUS) РАСШИФРОВКА

dedicated line

(CHIN) 专用线路
(FRE) ligne dédiée
(GER) Standleitung *f*, Standverbindung *f*
(JAP) 専用回線、専用ライン
(RUS) ТЕЛЕФОННАЯ ЛИНИЯ,
ПРЕДНАЗНАЧЕННАЯ ДЛЯ
ОПРЕДЕЛЁННОЙ ЦЕЛИ, НАПРИМЕР,
СВЯЗИ С ИНТЕРНЕТОМ

dedication

(CHIN) 献地
(FRE) affectation
(GER) Widmung *f*; Einweihung *f*
(RUS) ПЕРЕДАЧА ЗЕМЕЛЬНОГО УЧАСТКА
ЗЕМЛЕВЛАДЕЛЬЦЕМ В ОБЩЕСТВЕННОЕ
ПОЛЬЗОВАНИЕ

deductibility of employee contributions

(CHIN) 员工摊付款的可扣除性
(FRE) droit à la déduction des cotisations
salariales, (C) cotisation salariale
(GER) steuerliche Abzugsfähigkeit *f* von
Arbeitnehmerbeiträgen *mpl*
(JAP) 従業員負担金控除性
(RUS) ВОЗМОЖНОСТЬ ВЫЧЕТА
(УДЕРЖАНИЯ) ВЗНОСОВ РАБОТНИКОВ

deduction

(CHIN) 扣除额，减免额，演绎
(FRE) déduction retenue
(GER) Abzug *m*; Nachlass *m*, Rabatt *m*;
Lohnabzug *m*; Absetzung *f* von der
Einkommenssteuer *f*, Abzugsposten *m*
(RUS) ВЫЧЕТ (УДЕРЖАНИЕ)

deductive reasoning

(CHIN) 演绎推理
(FRE) raisonnement par déduction
(GER) schlussfolgerndes Denken *n*
(JAP) 演繹法、演繹的推理・論証
(RUS) ДЕДУКТИВНОЕ ДОКАЗАТЕЛЬСТВО

deed

(CHIN) 契据，证书，契约
(FRE) acte
(GER) beurkundeter Vertrag *m*, Rechtstitel
m; Übertragungsurkunde *f*; Urkunde *f*
(JAP) 捺印証書、譲渡証書
(RUS) ЮРИДИЧЕСКИЙ ДОКУМЕНТ С
ПОДПИСЬЮ И ПЕЧАТЬЮ,

ОПРЕДЕЛЯЮЩИЙ ПРАВА И
ОБЯЗАННОСТИ СТОРОН; АКТ

deed in lieu of foreclosure

(CHIN) 替代没收的土地返还行为

(FRE) acte faisant foi de saisie

(GER) Übertragungsurkunde *f* anstatt
Zwangsvollstreckung *f*

(RUS) ПЕРЕДАЧА СОБСТВЕННОСТИ
КРЕДИТОРУ В СИТУАЦИИ, КОГДА
ЛИШЕНИЕ ПРАВА ВЫКУПА
ЗАЛОЖЕННОГО ИМУЩЕСТВ
НЕИЗБЕЖНО

deed of trust

(CHIN) 信托契约

(FRE) acte fiduciaire

(GER) Treuhand- *m*, Treuhändervertrag *m*,
Stiftungsurkunde *f*; treuhänderische
Grundstücksübertragung *f* (als
Grundpfandrecht)

(JAP) 信託証書

(RUS) ДОКУМЕНТ ОБ УЧРЕЖДЕНИИ
ДОВЕРИТЕЛЬНОЙ СОБСТВЕННОСТИ

deed restriction

(CHIN) 契约限制条款

(FRE) restriction de l'acte

(GER) beschränkte dingliche Rechte *npl*

(JAP) 捺印証書による不動産の使用権制限

(RUS) ОГРАНИЧЕНИЯ ПРАВ
ИСПОЛЬЗОВАНИЯ ЗЕМЛИ, ЗАЛОЖЕННЫЕ
В АКТ ЕЁ ПЕРЕДАЧИ НОВОМУ
ВЛАДЕЛЬЦУ

deep discount bond

(CHIN) 大幅度贴现债券

(FRE) obligation émise à décote,

(C) obligation à fort escompte,

(C) obligation à bas taux d'intérêt

(GER) stark abgezinste
Schuldverschreibung *f*,
Disagio-Obligation *f*

(RUS) ОБЛИГАЦИЯ ГЛУБОКОГО
ДИСКОНТА (по низкой цене по сравнению с
номиналом)

de facto corporation

(CHIN) 实际公司

(FRE) société de fait

(GER) de fakto Gesellschaft *f*

(JAP) 事実上の会社

(RUS) КОРПОРАЦИЯ, СУЩЕСТВУЮЩАЯ
«ДЕ-ФАКТО»

defalcation

(CHIN) 盗用公款，侵吞

(FRE) détournement de fonds

(GER) Unterschlagung *f*, Veruntreuung *f*

(JAP) 使い込み、金銭不当流用、横領

(RUS) РАСТРАТА

default

(CHIN) 违约，不履行，缺省

(FRE) défaillance, par défaut (adv.), mise
en demeure

(GER) Insolvenz *f*, Zahlungsunfähigkeit *f*, -
verzug *m*, -versäumnis *n*; Fahrlässigkeit *f*,
Vertragswidrigkeit *f*, Unterlassung *f*,
Nichterfüllung *f*; Leistungsverzug *m*,
Vertragsverletzung *f*; Standard *m*,
Vorgabe *f*

(JAP) 不履行、債務不履行、滞納;
デフォルト、省略値（時）

(RUS) НЕВЫПОЛНЕНИЕ УСЛОВИЙ,
ОБЯЗАТЕЛЬСТВ (ИСПОЛЬЗУЕМЫЙ) ПО
УМОЛЧАНИЮ; О ЗНАЧЕНИИ ИЛИ
ДЕЙСТВИИ, ИСПОЛЬЗУЕМОМ ИЛИ
ВЫПОЛНЯЕМОМ, ЕСЛИ НЕ УКАЗАНО
ИНАЧЕ

default judgment

(CHIN) 缺席判决

(FRE) jugement de mise en demeure,

(C) jugement par défaut

(GER) (Ver)säumnisurteil *n*

(JAP) 欠席裁判、欠席判決

(RUS) РЕШЕНИЕ СУДА В ПОЛЬЗУ ИСТЦА
ПРИ УКЛОНЕНИИ ОТ ЗАЩИТЫ

defeasance

(CHIN) 作废，废除契约的条款

(FRE) défaisance, acte résolutoire,

(C) désendettement

(GER) Finanzierungsmethode *f* zur
Reduzierung *f* von Buchverbindlichkeiten
fpl; Annullierung *f*, Aufhebung *f*

(JAP) 契約の無効化、契約解除条件

(RUS) АННУЛИРОВАНИЕ (условия);
ОТМЕНА

defective

(CHIN) 有缺陷的，亏损的

(FRE) défectueux
(GER) fehlerhaft, defekt, schadhaft *adj*
(JAP) 瑕疵ある権限
(RUS) ДЕФЕКТНЫЙ; НЕПОЛНОЦЕННЫЙ

defective title
(CHIN) 有缺陷的产权
(FRE) titre défectueux, titre invalide
(GER) mangelhaftes Eigentumsrecht *n*,
fehlerhafter Rechtstitel *m*, fehlerhafter
Anspruch *m*,
(JAP) 不完全な、不良品
(RUS) ДЕФЕКТНЫЙ ПРАВОВОЙ ТИТУЛ

defendant
(CHIN) 被告
(FRE) défendeur, accusé, inculpé
(GER) Beklagter *m* (Zivilrecht);
Angeklager *m*, Beschuldigter *m* (Strafrecht);
Antragsgegner *m* (Scheidung)
(JAP) 被告（人）
(RUS) ОТВЕТЧИК; ПОДСУДИМЫЙ

defense of suit against insured
(CHIN) 针对被保险人的诉讼辩护
(FRE) défense lors d'un procès à l'encontre
de l'assuré, (C) défense en cas de poursuite
contre les assures
(GER) Einrede *f* der Klage *f* gegen
Versicherungsnehmer *m*
(JAP) 被保険者（物）訴訟の弁護
(RUS) ЗАЩИТА ПО ИСКУ
ЗАСТРАХОВАННОГО

defensive securities
(CHIN) 防护性证券
(FRE) titres/valeurs de placement, (C) titre
défensif
(GER) risikoarme Wertpapiere *npl*,
defensive Anlagetitel *mpl*
(JAP) 防衛的証券、
価格安定性の高い証券
(RUS) СТАБИЛЬНЫЕ ЦЕННЫЕ БУМАГИ,
ЯВЛЯЮЩИЕСЯ ОТНОСИТЕЛЬНО
НАДЁЖНЫМИ ИНВЕСТИЦИЯМИ

deferred account
(CHIN) 延期账，递延账户
(FRE) compte reporté

(GER) Ratenprämienvertrag *m*; Konto *n*
zwecks späterer Gutschrift *f*
(JAP) 繰延勘定
(RUS) СЧЕТА С ОТСРОЧЕННОЙ УПЛАТОЙ
НАЛОГОВ

deferred billing
(CHIN) 延期开单
(FRE) facturation reportée
(GER) aufgeschobene Abrechnung *f* bzw.
Rechnungsstellung *f*, spätere
Inrechnungstellung *f*
(JAP) 繰延請求
(RUS) ОТСРОЧЕННОЕ ВЫСТАВЛЕНИЕ
СЧЕТА

deferred charge
(CHIN) 延期费
(FRE) charges différées
(GER) aktive Rechnungsabgrenzungsposten
mpl, Kostenabgrenzungen *mpl*, (Beträge,
die im voraus entrichtet wurden, jedoch erst
der nächsten Wirtschaftsperiode als
Aufwendungen zuzurechnen sind)
(JAP) 据置失費、繰延費用
(RUS) ОТСРОЧЕННЫЕ РАСХОДЫ

deferred compensation
(CHIN) 递延补偿
(FRE) indemnisation/compensation différée
(GER) aufgeschobene Abfindung *f*,
Vergütung *f*, Leistung *f*
(JAP) 繰延補償
(RUS) ОТСРОЧЕННАЯ КОМПЕНСАЦИЯ

deferred compensation plan
(CHIN) 延期补偿计划
(FRE) plan d'indemnisation différé,
(C) régime d'indemnisation différé
(GER) aufgeschobener Bezahlungs- bzw.
Vergütungsplan *m*
(JAP) 繰延補償制度
(RUS) ПЕНСИОННАЯ СХЕМА
ОТСРОЧЕННОЙ КОМПЕНСАЦИИ

deferred contribution plan
(CHIN) 延期摊付计划
(FRE) plan de cotisation différé
(GER) aufgeschobener Einlage- *m* bzw.
Beitragsplan *m*

(JAP) 繰延負担金制度
(RUS) СХЕМА ОТСРОЧЕННЫХ ВЗНОСОВ

deferred credit
(CHIN) 递延贷款
(FRE) crédit reporté
(GER) transitorische Passiva *npl*,
Rechnungsabgrenzungsposten *mpl*
(JAP) 繰延貸方項目
(RUS) ЗАЧИСЛЕНИЕ СРЕДСТВ НА
ТЕКУЩИЙ СЧЕТ С ОТСРОЧКОЙ

deferred group annuity
(CHIN) 递延集体年金
(FRE) rente collective différée
(GER) aufgeschobene Rentenversicherung
f, aufgeschobene Annuität *f*;
Anwartschaftsrente *f*
(JAP) 据置グループ年金
(RUS) ОТСРОЧЕННАЯ ГРУППОВАЯ РЕНТА

deferred interest bond
(CHIN) 递延利息债券
(FRE) obligation à intérêt différé
(GER) Anleihe *f* bzw. Obligation *f* mit
antizipatorischer Verzinsung *f*, Obligation *f*
mit Zinszahlung *f* bei Fälligkeit *f*
(JAP) 据置利子債券
(RUS) ОБЛИГАЦИЯ С ОТСРОЧЕННЫМИ
ВЫПЛАТАМИ

deferred maintenance
(CHIN) 递延维持费
(FRE) réparation/maintenance différée
(GER) aufgeschobene
Instandhaltungsmaßnahme *f*
(JAP) 繰延維持費、据置保守
(RUS) ОТЛОЖЕННЫЙ РЕМОНТ

deferred-payment annuity
(CHIN) 延期付款年金
(FRE) rente avec paiement reporté
(GER) Rente *f* bzw. Annuität *f* mit
aufgeschobener Zahlung *f*
(JAP) 延払い年金
(RUS) РЕНТА С ОТСРОЧЕННЫМИ
ВЫПЛАТАМИ

deferred payments
(CHIN) 延期付款

(FRE) paiements reportés
(GER) aufgeschobene Zahlungen *fpl*,
Zahlungsaufschub *m*, Stundung *f*;
Terminzahlung *f*
(JAP) 延払い、据置払い
(RUS) ОТСРОЧЕННЫЕ ПЛАТЕЖИ

deferred profit-sharing
(CHIN) 延期利润分享
(FRE) participation différée aux bénéfices
(GER) aufschobene Gewinnbeteiligung *f*
(JAP) 据置利益分配型退職年金
(RUS) ОТСРОЧЕННОЕ РАЗДЕЛЕНИЕ
ПРИБЫЛИ

deferred retirement
(CHIN) 递延退休
(FRE) retraite reportée
(GER) aufgeschobener Ruhestand *m*,
hinausgeschobene Pensionierung *f*
(JAP) 延期退職
(RUS) ОТСРОЧЕННЫЙ ВЫХОД НА
ПЕНСИЮ

deferred retirement credit
(CHIN) 递延贷款
(FRE) crédit reporté de retraite
(GER) aufgeschobener Rentenbeitrag *m*,
aufgeschobene Altersgutschrift *f*
(JAP) 据置退職金支払猶予

deferred wage increase
(CHIN) 递延工资增长
(FRE) hausse différée des salaires
(GER) aufgeschobene Lohn- *f*,
Tariferhöhung *f*
(JAP) 据置昇給
(RUS) ОТСРОЧЕННОЕ ПОВЫШЕНИЕ
ЗАРАБОТНОЙ ПЛАТЫ

deficiency
(CHIN) 亏损，不足额，缺少
(FRE) insuffisance
(GER) Fehlbestand *m*, Fehlbetrag *m*,
Manko
(JAP) 不足、不足額、欠損
(RUS) НЕДОСТАТОК; ДЕФИЦИТ

deficiency judgment
(CHIN) 补正判决

107

(FRE) jugement pour déficit, (C) jugement par insuffisance
(GER) Ausfallurteil *n*
(JAP) 不足金判決
(RUS) РЕШЕНИЕ СУДА О ВЗЫСКАНИИ ОСТАТКА ДОЛГА С ЗАЁМЩИКА

deficiency letter
(CHIN) 补正通知单
(FRE) demande de révision, (C) lettre d'insuffisance
(GER) erläuterndes Schreiben *n* des SEC (zum Registration Statement)
(JAP) 不備通知書
(RUS) ИЗВЕЩЕНИЕ ЭМИТЕНТУ О НЕПОЛНОТЕ ЕГО ПРОСПЕКТА

deficit
(CHIN) 亏损，亏空，逆差，赤字
(FRE) déficit
(GER) Defizit *n*; Verlust *m*, Manko *n*, Fehlbetrag *m*; Passivsaldo *n*
(JAP) 欠損(金)、赤字
(RUS) ДЕФИЦИТ

deficit financing
(CHIN) 赤字金融
(FRE) financement par le déficit
(GER) Defizitfinanzierung *f*
(JAP) 赤字財政、赤字財政策
(RUS) ДЕФИЦИТНОЕ ФИНАНСИРОВАНИЕ (из бюджета)

deficit net worth
(CHIN) 赤字资产净值
(FRE) valeur nette du déficit
(GER) negatives Reinvermögen *n*, negatives Nettovermögen *n*
(JAP) 負の純資産
(RUS) ИЗБЫТОК ПАССИВОВ СВЕРХ АКТИВОВ И КАПИТАЛА КОМПАНИИ

deficit spending
(CHIN) 赤字开支，超支
(FRE) financement par l'emprunt, (C) financement au découvert
(GER) Defizitfinanzierung *f*; konjunkturbedingte defizitäre Ausgaben *fpl* der öffentlichen Hand *f*
((JAP) 財政による)超過支出、赤字支出

(RUS) ДЕФИЦИТНОЕ РАСХОДОВАНИЕ

defined-benefit pension plan
(CHIN) 确定福利养老金计划
(FRE) système de retraite par répartition, (C) régime de retraite à prestations déterminées
(GER) Pensionsplan *m* mit definierten Leistungen *fpl*
(JAP) 確定給付年金制度
(RUS) ПЕНСИЯ С ФИКСИРОВАННОЙ ВЫПЛАТОЙ ПОСЛЕ ОГОВОРЕННОЙ ВЫСЛУГИ ЛЕТ

defined contributuion pension plan
(CHIN) 确定养老金方案
(FRE) système de retraite par capitalisation, (C) régime de retraite à cotisation déterminée
(GER) Pensionsplan *m* mit definierten Beitragsleistungen *fpl*; beitragsspezifischer Altersversorgungsplan *m*
(JAP) 定額負担年金制度
(RUS) ПЕНСИОННАЯ ПРОГРАММА С ФИКСИРОВАННЫМИ ВЗНОСАМИ

deflation
(CHIN) 通货紧缩
(FRE) déflation
(GER) Deflation *f*
(JAP) デフレ、通貨収縮
(RUS) ДЕФЛЯЦИЯ

deflator
(CHIN) 减缩指数，通货膨胀扣除率
(FRE) déflateur, (C) coefficient d'actualisation
(GER) Deflator *m*, Deflationierungsfaktor *m*, Deflationsfaktor *m*
(JAP) デフレータ-、価格修正因子
(RUS) ДЕФЛЯТОР

defunct company
(CHIN) 已停业公司
(FRE) société dissoute, (C) société conservatoire
(GER) erloschene Gesellschaft *f*, im Handesregister *n* gelöschte Firma *f*
(JAP) 抹消会社
(RUS) ПРЕКРАТИВШАЯ ДЕЯТЕЛЬНОСТЬ КОМПАНИЯ

108

degression

(CHIN) 递减

(FRE) dégression

(GER) Degression *f*

(JAP) 下降、(税率の)逓減

(RUS) УБЫВАНИЕ

deindustrialization

(CHIN) 非工业化

(FRE) désindustrialisation

(GER) De-Industrialisierung *f*,
Entindustrialisierung *f*, Industrieabbau *m*

(JAP) 逆工業化、重工業退化、
産業の空洞化

(RUS) ДЕИНДУСТРИАЛИЗАЦИЯ

delegate

(CHIN) 代表，委托，委任

(FRE) déléguer

(GER) Delegierter *m*, Abgeordneter *m*

(JAP) 代表、派遣委員

(RUS) ДЕЛЕГИРОВАТЬ, ПЕРЕДАВАТЬ
ПОЛНОМОЧИЯ; ДЕЛЕГАТ

delete

(CHIN) 删除

(FRE) supprimer

(GER) löschen, streichen, ausfügen *v*

(JAP) 削除、抹消、削除する

(RUS) ИСКЛЮЧИТЬ, УДАЛИТЬ

delete key (del)

(CHIN) 删除键 （del）

(FRE) touche supprimcr
(suppr)

(GER) Löschtaste （Entf） *f*

(JAP) 削除キー、Del キー

(RUS) КЛАВИША УДАЛЕНИЯ

delinquency

(CHIN) 拖欠债务，失职

(FRE) arriéré

(GER) Nichtzahlung *f* bei Fälligkeit *f*;
überfällige Forderung *f*; Zahlungsverzug *m*,
Säumnis *n*

(JAP) 義務不履行、職務怠慢、
滞納

(RUS) НЕВЫПОЛНЕНИЕ
ОБЯЗАННОСТЕЙ; НАРУШЕНИЕ;
ПРАВОНАРУШЕНИЕ

delinquent

(CHIN) 拖欠的，违约的，失职的

(FRE) contrevenant

(GER) überfällig, säumig, rückständig *adj*

(JAP) 義務不履行の、職務怠慢の、

(RUS) НАРУШИТЕЛЬ;
ПРАВОНАРУШИТЕЛЬ

delisting

(CHIN) 除牌

(FRE) retrait de marques de catalogue,
(C) déréférencement, (C) radiation de la
cote

(GER) Aufhebung *f* der Börsenzulassung *f*,
Streichung *f* der amtlichen Notierung *f*;
Herausnahme *f* (von Produkten *npl* aus dem
Sortiment *n*)

(JAP) 銘柄表から外すこと、上場廃止

(RUS) ЛИШЕНИЕ КОТИРОВКИ (бирж.)

delivery

(CHIN) 交货，递交，投递

(FRE) livraison

(GER) Lieferung *f*; Überbringung *f*;
Zustellung *f*, Zusendung *f*

(JAP) 引渡し、受渡し、交付

(RUS) ПОСТАВКА; ДОСТАВКА;
ВЫПОЛНЕНИЕ

delivery date

(CHIN) 交货期，交货日期

(FRE) date de livraison

(GER) Lieferdatum *n*, -termin *m*

(JAP) 引渡日、交付日、決済日

(RUS) ДАТА ПОСТАВКИ, ДОСТАВКИ

demand

(CHIN) 要求，需求，申请

(FRE) demande

(GER) Nachfrage *f*; Bedarf *m*; Anspruch *m*,
Forderung *f*

(JAP) 需要、要求、督促

(RUS) СПРОС

demand curve

(CHIN) 需求曲线

(FRE) courbe de la demande

(GER) Nachfragekurve *f*

(JAP) 需要曲線

(RUS) КРИВАЯ СПРОСА

demand deposit

(CHIN) 即期存款，活期存款
(FRE) dépôt à vue
(GER) Sichteinlage *f*, Tagesgeld *n*, täglich
fälliges Guthaben *n*, Sichtguthaben *n*
(JAP) 要求支払預金、別段預金
(RUS) СЧЕТ (ВКЛАД) ДО
ВОСТРЕБОВАНИЯ

demand loan

(CHIN) 活期贷款
(FRE) prêt à vue
(GER) täglich kündbares Darlehen *n*,
kurzfristiges Darlehen *n*, Tagesgeld *n*
(JAP) 要求払貸付、コール貸付金
(RUS) ССУДА ДО ВОСТРЕБОВАНИЯ

demand note

(CHIN) 即期票据
(FRE) bon à vue, billet à demande
(GER) Zahlungsaufforderung *f*,
Schuldschein *m*, Sichtpapier *n*
(JAP) 一覧払約束手形、要求払約束手形
(RUS) ДОЛГОВОЕ ОБЯЗАТЕЛЬСТВО С
ПОГАШЕНИЕМ ПО ТРЕБОВАНИЮ

demand price

(CHIN) 需求价格
(FRE) prix à vue
(GER) Geldkurs *m*
(JAP) 需要価格、付値
(RUS) ЦЕНА СПРОСА

demand-pull inflation

(CHIN) 需求扩大型通货膨胀
(FRE) inflation par la demande
(GER) Nachfrageinflation *f*,
nachfrageinduzierte Inflation *f*
(JAP) 需要インフレ
(RUS) ИНФЛЯЦИЯ ПОД ВОЗДЕЙСТВИЕМ
СПРОСА

demand schedule

(CHIN) 需求表
(FRE) courbe de la demande, (C) horaire à
la demande
(GER) Nachfragetabelle *f*
(JAP) 需要表
(RUS) ТАБЛИЦА ВЗАИМООТНОШЕНИЯ
СПРОСА И ЦЕНЫ

demarketing

(CHIN) 低行销，反倾销
(FRE) demarketing, (C) publicité de
dissuasion
(GER) Anti-Marketing *n*, Reduktions-
Marketing *n*, leise Werbung *f*
(JAP) 需要を抑制するための宣伝活動、
逆拡販運動
(RUS) УСИЛИЯ, НАПРАВЛЕННЫЕ НА
УМЕНЬШЕНИЕ ПОТРЕБЛЕНИЯ ИЛИ
УХОДА С РЫНКА ОПРЕДЕЛЁННОГО
ТОВАРА

demised premises

(CHIN) 已租让房产
(FRE) lieux loués
(GER) vermietetes bzw. verpachtetes
Betriebsobjekt *n* bzw. -gebäude *n*
(JAP) 譲渡家屋（土地）
(RUS) ПЛОЩАДЬ, СДАВАЕМАЯ В НАЕМ

demographics

(CHIN) 人口统计
(FRE) démographie
(GER) Demografie *f*, demografische
Daten *pl*
(JAP) 実体的人口統計
(RUS) ДЕМОГРАФИЯ

demolition

(CHIN) 拆除
(FRE) démolition
(GER) Abbruch *m*, Abriss *m*, Demolierung *f*
(JAP) 取壊し、破棄
(RUS) РАЗРУШЕНИЕ; СНОС

demonetization

(CHIN) 非货币化
(FRE) démonétisation
(GER) De- *f*, Entmonetisierung *f*,
Außerkurssetzung *f*, Einziehung *f*,
Entwertung *f*
(JAP) 廃貨、本位貨幣資格喪失
(RUS) ДЕМОНЕТИЗАЦИЯ; ИЗЪЯТИЕ ИЗ
ОБОРОТА ПОЛНОЦЕННЫХ ДЕНЕГ

demoralize

(CHIN) 使消沉，使道德败坏
(FRE) démoraliser
(GER) demoralisieren *v*

(JAP)（秩序・機能を）乱す、混乱させ
る、士気をくじく
(RUS) ДЕМОРАЛИЗАЦИЯ

demurrage
(CHIN) 滞留期，延期停泊
(FRE) surestaries
(GER) Überliegezeit *f*; Liegegeld *n*,
Überliegegebühr *f*, Wagenstandsgeld *n*
(JAP) 滞船料、貨車留置料
(RUS) ПЛАТА ЗА ПРОСТОЙ СУДНА ПРИ
ПОГРУЗКЕ/РАЗГРУЗКЕ; ДЕМЕРРЕДЖ

demurrer
(CHIN) 抗辩，异议
(FRE) exception pralable, (C) fin de non-
recevoir
(GER) Einrede *f*, Einwand *m*, Einspruch *m*,
Rechtseinwand *m*
(JAP) 異議、妨訴抗弁
(RUS) ПРОЦЕССУАЛЬНЫЙ ОТВОД (суд.)

denomination
(CHIN) 票面金额
(FRE) dénomination
(GER) Denominierung *f*, Nennwert *m*
(GER) Denominierung *f*, Nennwert *m*
(JAP)（度量衡の）単位、（貨幣の)呼称
(RUS) ДЕНОМИНАЦИЯ; НОМИНАЛ

density
(CHIN) 密度，浓度
(FRE) densité
(GER) Dichte *f*
(JAP) 密度、比率
(RUS) ПЛОТНОСТЬ

density zoning
(CHIN) 密度分区限制
(FRE) zonage par densité
(GER) Zonungseinteilung *f*;
Flächennutzung *f* nach Dichte *f*
(JAP) 密度区分
(RUS) ЗОНИРОВАНИЕ ПО ПЛОТНОСТИ
ЗАСЕЛЕНИЯ

department
(CHIN) 部门
(FRE) service
(GER) Abteilung *f*, Fachbereich *m*,

Ressort *n*
(JAP) 省、局、部門
(RUS) ОТДЕЛ; ДЕПАРТАМЕНТ;
МИНИСТЕРСТВО

dependent
(CHIN) 依靠的，相关的，从属的
(FRE) personne à charge, personne
dépendante
(GER) Abhängiger *m*,
Unterhaltsberechtigter *m*
(JAP) 扶養家族
(RUS) ИЖДИВЕНЕЦ

dependent coverage
(CHIN) 受赡养人保险
(FRE) couverture des personnes à charge
(GER) Versicherungsschutz *m* von
Unterhaltsberechtigten *mpl*
(JAP) 扶養家族補償
(RUS) СТРАХОВОЕ ПОКРЫТИЕ
ИЖДИВЕНЦЕВ

depletion
(CHIN) 折耗
(FRE) épuisement, (C) amortissement
(GER) Substanzverringerung *f*, -verzehr *m*,
Kapitalschwund *m*, -verzehr *m*; Wertabbau
m, -erschöpfung *f*
(JAP)（資源などの）消耗・減少・枯渇、
減耗償却(費)
(RUS) ИСТОЩЕНИЕ; УБЫВАНИЕ

deposit
(CHIN) 存款，押金，存放
(FRE) dépôt
(GER) Anzahlung *f*, Einlage *f*; Hinterlegung
f, Deponierung *f*, Pfandgeld *n*
(JAP) 銀行預金、保証金
(RUS) ДЕПОЗИТ; ВКЛАД

deposit administration plan
(CHIN) 存款管理计划
(FRE) plan de gestion des dépôts
(GER) Depotverwaltungsprogramm *n*
(JAP) 預託管理制度、預託管理方式
(RUS) ПЛАН ГРУППОВОГО АННУИТЕТА

deposit in transit
(CHIN) 在途存款

111

(FRE) dépôt en circulation
(GER) noch nicht verbuchte Einzahlung *f*,
transitorisches Guthaben *n*
(JAP) 未達預金
(RUS) ДЕПОЗИТ «В ПУТИ»

deposition
(CHIN) 宣誓，作证
(FRE) déposition
(GER) (Niederschrift einer
außergerichtlichen eidlichen Aussage),
etwa: eidesstattliche Erklärung *f*
(JAP) 証言録取(書)
(RUS) ПОКАЗАНИЯ (суд.)

depositors forgery insurance
(CHIN) 存款人虚假保险
(FRE) assurance contre la falsification des
déposants
(GER) Einlegerversicherung *f* gegen
Fälschung *m* (von Schecks *mpl*, Wechseln
mpl, etc.)
(JAP) 預金者文書偽造保険
(RUS) СТРАХОВАНИЕ ДЕПОЗИТАРИЯ ОТ
ФАЛЬСИФИКАЦИИ

depository trust company (DTC)
(CHIN) 保管人信托公司（DTC）
(FRE) compagnie de fiducie dépositaire,
(C) fiducie dépositaire
(GER) Depository Trust Company (DTC) *f*,
(zentrale Wertpapierhinterlegungsstelle, bei
der Aktien- und Rentenzertifikate
elektronisch ausgetauscht werden können)
(JAP) 投資信託会社
(RUS) ТРАСТОВАЯ КОМПАНИЯ –
ДЕПОЗИТАРИЙ

depreciable life
(CHIN) 应折旧年限
(FRE) vie amortissable
(GER) Abschreibungsdauer *f*
(JAP) 減価償却期間
(RUS) ПЕРИОД ПОЛНОЙ АМОРТИЗАЦИИ

depreciable real estate
(CHIN) 应折旧不动产
(FRE) biens immobiliers amortissables
(GER) abschreibungsfähige Immobilie *f*
(JAP) 減価償却不動産

(RUS) АМОРТИЗИРУЕМАЯ
НЕДВИЖИМОСТЬ

depreciate
(CHIN) 折旧，贬值
(FRE) déprécier, dévaloriser, (C) amortir
(GER) an Nutzwert *m* verlieren;
abschreiben; abwerten, herabsetzen *v*; im
Preis/Wert *m* fallen *v*
(JAP) 減価見積りをする、減価償却を求
める、価格を下げる、価値が下がる
(RUS) ТЕРЯТЬ ЦЕННОСТЬ;
ПОДВЕРГАТЬСЯ АМОРТИЗАЦИИ

depreciated cost
(CHIN) 折余成本
(FRE) coût amorti
(GER) Buch- *m*, Restbuchwert *m*
(JAP) 減価償却対象原価
(RUS) ИСХОДНАЯ СТОИМОСТЬ АКТИВА
МИНУС АМОРТИЗАЦИЯ

depreciation
(CHIN) 贬值，折旧
(FRE) dépréciation, amortissement
(GER) Wertminderung *f*, -verlust *m*, -
rückgang *m*; Abschreibung *f* (Steuern);
Währungsabwertung *f* (Währung);
Kursverlust *m*
(JAP) 価値低減、減価償却
(RUS) АМОРТИЗАЦИЯ; СНИЖЕНИЕ
ЦЕННОСТИ

depreciation recapture
(CHIN) 折旧回收
(FRE) reprise de dépréciation,
(C) récupération d'amortissement
(GER) Nachholbesteuerung *f*,
Nachversteuerung *f* von Abschreibungen *fpl*
(JAP) 減価償却額再徴収
(RUS) ВОЗВРАТ УТРАЧЕННОЙ
СТОИМОСТИ

depreciation reserve
(CHIN) 折旧准备
(FRE) réserve pour provision
d'amortissement
(GER) Wertminderungs- *f*,
Abschreibungsreserve *f*; Rücklagen *fpl* für
Abschreibungen *fpl*
(JAP) 減価償却積立金・準備金

112

(RUS) РЕЗЕРВ НА АМОРТИЗАЦИЮ

depression
(CHIN) 萧条，衰退
(FRE) dépression, conjoncture défavorable
(GER) Depression *f*, Talsohle *f*
(JAP) 不景気、不況
(RUS) ДЕПРЕССИЯ

depth interview
(CHIN) 现场顾客深度调查
(FRE) entretien en profondeur
(GER) offenes Interview *n*; Intensiv-Interview *n*
(JAP) 深層テスト、深層面接
(RUS) УГЛУБЛЕННОЕ СОБЕСЕДОВАНИЕ

deregulation
(CHIN) 解除管制
(FRE) déréglementation, dérégulation
(GER) De- *f*, Entregulierung *f*, Liberalisierung *f*; Abschaffung *f* von beschränkenden Bestimmungen *fpl*
(JAP) 規制撤廃、規制緩和
(RUS) ОТМЕНА РЕГУЛИРОВАНИЯ; СНЯТИЕ ОГРАНИЧЕНИЙ

derived demand
(CHIN) 衍生需求，引伸需求
(FRE) demande dérivée
(GER) abgeleitete Nachfrage *f*, nichtautonome Nachfrage *f*, sekundäre Nachfrage *f*, abgeleiteter Bedarf *f*
(JAP) 派生需要、間接需要
(RUS) ПРОИЗВОДНЫЙ СПРОС

descent
(CHIN) 无遗嘱遗产
(FRE) hérédité, succession héréditaire, transmission héréditaire, (C) descendance
(GER) Niedergang *m*, Abstieg *m*
(JAP) 下降、相続
(RUS) ОПУСКАНИЕ; СНИЖЕНИЕ

description
(CHIN) 描述，说明
(FRE) description, désignation
(GER) Beschreibung *f*, Darstellung *f*
(JAP) 記述、説明書
(RUS) ОПИСАНИЕ; НАИМЕНОВАНИЕ

descriptive memorandum
(CHIN) 叙述性备忘录
(FRE) note descriptives
(GER) beschreibender Schriftsatz *m*, Vermerk *m*; Kurzprospekt *m*
(JAP) 説明的備忘録
(RUS) ОПИСАТЕЛЬНЫЙ МЕМОРАНДУМ, ПРОТОКОЛ

descriptive statistics
(CHIN) 叙述性统计
(FRE) statistiques descriptives
(GER) beschreibende Statistik *f*
(JAP) 記述統計学
(RUS) ОПИСАТЕЛЬНАЯ СТАТИСТИКА

desk
(CHIN) 工作台，服务台，部
(FRE) bureau, réception (front-)
(GER) Schreib- *m*, Arbeitstisch *m*; Schalter *m*
(JAP) 編集部、編集主任
(RUS) РАБОЧЕЕ МЕСТО; ПОДРАЗДЕЛЕНИЕ ОРГАНИЗАЦИИ

desktop publishing
(CHIN) 桌面计算机排版系统
(FRE) publication assistée par ordinateur (PAO), (C) éditique
(GER) Desktop-Publishing *n*
(JAP) デスクトップパブリッシング
(RUS) «НАСТОЛЬНОЕ ИЗДАТЕЛЬСТВО», ИСПОЛЬЗОВАНИЕ КОМПЬЮТЕРА ДЛЯ СОЗДАНИЯ ОФИЦИАЛЬНЫХ БЛАНКОВ И Т. П.

destination file (network)
目标文件
(FRE) fichier cible (réseau)
(GER) Zieldatei *f* (Netzwerk *n*)
(JAP) 宛先ファイル、宛先ネットワーク）
(RUS) ВЫХОДНОЙ ФАЙЛ

detail person
(CHIN) 营销代表，推销员
(FRE) représentant, (C) personne-ressource
(GER) Perfektionist *m*, detailorientierte Person *f*
(JAP) プロパー、販売店支援担当者

(RUS) ЛИЦО , В ЗАДАЧУ КОТОРОГО
ВХОДИТ ОБСЛУХИВАНИЕ КЛИЕНТОВ,
«ВНИМАНИЕ К ДЕТАЛЯМ»

devaluation
(CHIN) 货币贬值
(FRE) dévaluation
(GER) Abwertung *f*, Entwertung *f*
(JAP) 平価切下げ
(RUS) ДЕВАЛЬВАЦИЯ

developer
(CHIN) 开发商
(FRE) développeur
(GER) Erschließungsunternehmen *n*, -
gesellschaft *f*; Bauträger *m*
(RUS) РАЗРАБОТЧИК; ЗАСТРОЙЩИК

development
(CHIN) 开发
(FRE) développement
(GER) Entwicklung *f*; Erschließung *f*;
Bauvorhaben *n*
(JAP) 開発、開発した地区(土地)
(RUS) РАЗВИТИЕ; РАЗРАБОТКА;
ЗАСТРОЙКА

developmental drilling program
(CHIN) 开发性开采项目
(FRE) programme de forage
développemental, (C) programme de forage
en zone productive
(GER) Entwicklungsbohrprogramm *n*
(RUS) ПРОГРАММА РАЗВИТИЯ
НЕФТЕРОЖДЕНИЯ

development stage enterprise
(CHIN) 草创阶段企业
(FRE) entreprise au stade de développement
(GER) junges Unternehmen *n*,
aufstrebendes Unternehmen *n*
(JAP) 発展段階企業、成長途上企業
(RUS) ПРЕДПРИЯТИЕ НА СТАДИИ
СТАНОВЛЕНИЯ

deviation policy
(CHIN) 脱规政策
(FRE) politique des écarts
(GER) Abweichungsrichtlinien *m*
(RUS) ПОЛИТИКА РЕАГИРОВАНИЯ
КОМПАНИИ НА ОТКЛОНЕНИЯ ОТ

ПРИНЯТЫХ НОРМ ПОВЕДЕНИЯ

devise
(CHIN) 不动产遗赠，发明
(FRE) legs de biens réels, disposer par
testament, léguer, legs
(GER) testamentarische Übertragung *f* von
Grundbesitz *m*, Immobilienlegat *n*,
Vererbung *f* unbeweglichen Nachlasses *m*
(JAP) (不動産の)遺贈、遺贈財産
(RUS) ИЗМЫШЛЯТЬ; ЗАВЕЩАТЬ

diagonal expansion
(CHIN) 派生产品扩展
(FRE) expansion diagonale
(GER) diagonale Expansion *f*, diagonales
Wachstum *n*
(JAP) 対角線的拡張
(RUS) «ДИАГОНАЛЬНОЕ» РАСШИРЕНИЕ

dialup
(CHIN) 拨号
(FRE) numéroter, appeler un abonné,
(C) composition, (C) ligne commutée
(GER) Einwahl *f*
(JAP) ダイアルアップ、電話回線接続
(RUS) ВРЕМЕННАЯ СВЯЗЬ МЕЖДУ
КОМПЬЮТЕРАМИ ПОСРЕДСТВОМ
НАБОРА ТЕЛЕФОННОГО НОМЕРА ЧЕРЕЗ
МОДЕМ

diary
(CHIN) 日记
(FRE) agenda, journal
(GER) Notiz- *n*, Tagebuch *n*,
Terminkalender *m*
(JAP) 日誌、日記
(RUS) ДНЕВНИК; ХРОНОЛОГИЧЕСКИЙ
ОТЧЕТ

differential advantage
(CHIN) 差别优势
(FRE) avantage différentiel
(GER) Differentialvorteil *m*
(JAP) 特異性による優位
(RUS) ПРЕИМУЩЕСТВО ПО РАЗНИЦЕ
ЦЕН

differential analysis
(CHIN) 差异分析

114

(FRE) analyse différentielle
(GER) Diffentialanalyse *f*
(JAP) 微分分析
(RUS) ДИФФЕРЕНЦИАЛЬНЫЙ АНАЛИЗ

differentiation strategy

(CHIN) 差別策略
(FRE) stratégie de différentiation, (C) différentiation du produit
(GER) Differenzierungsstrategie *f*
(JAP) 差別化戦略
(RUS) СТРАТЕГИЯ ДИФФЕРЕНЦИАЦИИ

digits deleted

(CHIN) 被删除数字
(FRE) chiffres effacés
(GER) gelöschte Ziffern *fpl*
(JAP) 削除された桁数
(RUS) ИСКЛЮЧЕННЫЕ РАЗРЯДЫ (числа)

dilution

(CHIN) 冲淡，稀释
(FRE) dilution
(GER) Verwässerung *f*, Verdünnung *f*
(JAP) 希釈（例：労働希釈）、希釈化
（１株当りの利益などの）
(RUS) «РАСТВОРЕНИЕ» КОНТРОЛЯ и ДОХОДОВ (при выпуске новых акций); РАЗБАВЛЕНИЕ

diminishing-balance method

(CHIN) 余额递减折旧法
(FRE) méthode de l'amortissement dégressif
(GER) degressive Abschreibung *f*, Buchwertabschreibung *f*
(JAP) 定率減価償却法
(RUS) СОКРАЩАЮЩИЙСЯ (УМЕНЬШАЮЩИЙСЯ) БАЛАНС

diplomacy

(CHIN) 外交，外交手腕
(FRE) diplomatie
(GER) Diplomatie *f*
(JAP) 外交、駆引き
(RUS) ДИПЛОМАТИЯ

direct access

(CHIN) 直接存取，直接作业
(FRE) accès direct

(GER) direkter Zugriff *m*, Direktzugriff *m*
(JAP) 直接アクセス
(RUS) ПРЯМОЙ ДОСТУП

direct-action advertising

(CHIN) 直接行动广告
(FRE) publicité à action directe
(GER) Direktwerbung *f*
(JAP) 直接行動広告
(RUS) МЕТОД МАРКЕТИНГА, КОГДА ТОВАР РАСПРОСТРОНЯЕТСЯ ТОЛЬКО ЧЕРЕЗ РЕКЛАМУ

direct charge-off method

(CHIN) 直接冲销法
(FRE) méthode de passation directe par pertes et profits
(GER) Direktabschreibungsmethode *f*
(JAP) 損失直接処理方式
(RUS) МЕТОД ПРЯМОГО СПИСАНИЯ

direct cost

(CHIN) 直接成本
(FRE) coût direct
(GER) Einzelkosten *pl*, direkte Kosten *pl*
(JAP) 直接費
(RUS) ПРЯМЫЕ ЗАТРАТЫ, ИЗДЕРЖКИ

direct costing

(CHIN) 直接成本法
(FRE) méthode des coûts variables
(GER) Direct Costing *n*; Grenzplankosten- *f*, Proportionalkostenrechnung *f*
(JAP) 直接原価計算
(RUS) УЧЕТ ПО ПРЯМОЙ СЕБЕСТОИМОСТИ

direct financing lease

(CHIN) 直接融资租赁
(FRE) contrat de location financement
(GER) Direktfinanzierungsleasing *n*, Barfinanzierungsleasing *n*
(JAP) 直接金融型リース
(RUS) АРЕНДА С ПРЯМЫМ ФИНАНСИРОВАНИЕМ

direct investment

(CHIN) 直接投资
(FRE) investissement direct

(GER) Direktinvestition *f*;
Beteiligungsinvestition *f*
(JAP) 直接投資
(RUS) ПРЯМЫЕ ИНВЕСТИЦИИ

direct labor
(CHIN) 直接人工成本
(FRE) main d'œuvre directe
Fertigungslohn *m*; Lohneinzelkosten *pl*
(JAP) 直接労働
(RUS) ПРЯМЫЕ ТРУДОЗАТРАТЫ

direct liability
(CHIN) 直接负债
(FRE) responsabilité directe
(GER) primäre Haftung *f*; unbestimmte und
unbedingte Verbindlichkeit *f*
(JAP) 直接債務、確定負債
(RUS) НЕПОСРЕДСТВЕННАЯ
ОТВЕТСТВЕННОСТЬ

direct marketing
(CHIN) 直接营销
(FRE) marketing direct
(GER) Direktabsatz *m*, Direktvertrieb *m*
(JAP) 直接販売、直接マーケティング
(RUS) ПРЯМОЙ МАРКЕТИНГ

direct material
(CHIN) 直接原料成本
(FRE) matière première
(GER) Einzelkosten- *n*, Produktionsmaterial
n, Materialeinzelkosten *pl*,
Fertigungsmaterialkosten *pl*; Rohstoffe *mpl*
(JAP) 直接材料
(RUS) ПРЯМЫЕ МАТЕРИАЛЬНЫЕ
ЗАТРАТЫ

direct overhead
(CHIN) 直接管理费用
(FRE) frais fixes directs
(GER) direkte Gemeinkosten *pl*
(JAP) 直接間接費
(RUS) ПРЯМЫЕ НАКЛАДНЫЕ РАСХОДЫ

direct production
(CHIN) 直接生产
(FRE) production directe
(GER) direkte Herstellung *f*

(JAP) 直産
(RUS) ПРЯМОЕ ПРОИЗВОДСТВО

direct-reduction mortgage
(CHIN) 本息同时扣除抵押贷款
(FRE) hypothèque de réduction directe
(GER) Tilgungshypothek *f*; Hypothek *f* mit
direkter Tilgung *f*
(JAP) 直接減価償却法
(RUS) ЗАКЛАДНАЯ С ПРЯМЫМ
СНИЖЕНИЕМ

direct response advertising
(CHIN) 直接反应广告
(FRE) publicité à réponse directe, (C)
publicité directe
(GER) Direktwerbung *f*
(JAP) 直接反応広告
(RUS) РЕКЛАМА С НЕПОСРЕДСТВЕННЫМ
ЗАПРОСОМ ОТВЕТА; МЕТОД
МАРКЕТИНГА, КОГДА ТОВАР
РАСПРОСТРОНЯЕТСЯ ТОЛЬКО ЧЕРЕЗ
РЕКЛАМУ

direct sales
(CHIN) 直接销售
(FRE) ventes directes
(GER) Direktverkauf *m*, -absatz *m*,
-vertrieb *m*
(JAP) 直売
(RUS) ПРЯМАЯ ПРОДАЖА

direct verdict
(CHIN) 直接裁决
(FRE) verdict imposé
(GER) Urteil *n* auf Anweisung *f*, (Spruch
der Geschworenen gemäß juristischer
Anweisung des Berufsrichters)
(JAP) 指示評決
(RUS) РЕШЕНИЕ (ВЕРДИКТ) (присяжных)
ПО УКАЗАНИЯМ СУДЬИ

director
(CHIN) 董事，主任，
管理者
(FRE) directeur,administrateur
(GER) Direktor *m*
Vorstandsmitglied *n*
(JAP) 取締役、重役、理事
(RUS) ДИРЕКТОР; РЕЖИССЕР

directorate

(CHIN) 董事会，理事会

(FRE) directorat

(GER) Direktorium *n*, Direktorat *n*, Vorstand *m*

(JAP) 重役会、役員会、理事会、管理職

(RUS) СОВЕТ (КОЛЛЕГИЯ) ДИРЕКТОРОВ

disability benefit

(CHIN) 伤残恤养金

(FRE) prestations d'invalidité

(GER) Invaliden- *f*, Invaliditätsrente *f*, Erwerbsunfähigkeitsleistung *f*

(JAP) 廃疾給付、労働不能給付

(RUS) ВЫПЛАТА ПО НЕТРУДОСПОСОБНОСТИ

disability buy-out insurance

(CHIN) 伤残买断保险

(FRE) assurance-rachat de parts d'associés en cas d'invalidité

(GER) Erwerbs- *f* bzw. Arbeitsunfähigkeitsablöseversicherung *f*

(JAP) 廃疾買取保険

(RUS) СТРАХОВАНИЕ НА СЛУЧАЙ НЕОБХОДИМОСТИ ВЫКУПА ДОЛИ НЕТРУДОСПОСОБНОГО ПАРТНЁРА

disability income insurance

(CHIN) 伤残收入保险

(FRE) garantie des revenus d'invalidité, (C) assurance invalidité

(GER) Einkommensversicherung *f* bei Erwerbs- *f* bzw. Arbeitsunfähigkeit

(JAP) 廃疾所得補償保険、就業不能時所得補償保険

(RUS) СТРАХОВАНИЕ ДОХОДА НА СЛУЧАЙ НЕТРУДОСПОСОБНОСТИ

disaffirm

(CHIN) 反驳，否认

(FRE) se rétracter, revenir sur, renoncer, (C) rejecter

(GER) nicht einhalten, nicht anerkennen *v*; zurückweisen, aufheben, ablehnen *v*

(JAP) 〜を破棄する、〜を拒否する

(RUS) ОТКАЗ ОТ РАННЕГО ПОДТВЕРЖДЕНИЯ, СОГЛАСИЯ

disbursement

(CHIN) 支出，付款

(FRE) décaissement, déboursement

(GER) Auszahlung *f*, ausgezahlter Betrag *m*, Aufwendung *f*

(JAP) 支出、支出金、出費

(RUS) ВЫПЛАТА ДЕНЕГ, ПОГАШЕНИЕ ДОЛГА ПО ЭТАПАМ

discharge

(CHIN) 卸货，解除，释放

(FRE) décharge, contre-passation d'une opération, (C) quittance

(GER) Entlastung *f*; Freispruch *m*; Begleichung *f*, Abgeltung *f*; Entlassung *f*, Kündigung *f* (durch Arbeitgeber *m*); Erfüllung *f*

(JAP) 免除、解除、解雇、履行、免責

(RUS) УВОЛЬНЕНИЕ; ПРИКАЗНОЕ ПОЛОЖЕНИЕ; ИСПОЛНЕНИЕ

discharge in bankruptcy

(CHIN) 解除破产债务

(FRE) réhabilitation, (C) décharge de faillite

(GER) Freistellung *f* bzw. Entlastung *f* eines Konkursschuldners *m*; Konkursaufhebung *f*

(JAP) 破産の取消、破産の免責

(RUS) СУДЕБНЫЙ ПРИКАЗ, УТВЕРЖДАЮЩИЙ БАНКРОТСТВО

discharge in lien

(CHIN) 解除留置权

(FRE) mainlevée du privilège

(GER) Erfüllung *f* bzw. Beendigung *f* bzw. Aufhebung *f* eines Pfandrechts *n*

(JAP) 担保権の取消、先取特権の取消

(RUS) ИСПОЛНЕНИЕ ПО ПРАВУ УДЕРЖАНИЯ

disciplinary layoff

(CHIN) 惩戒性临时解雇

(FRE) suspension

(GER) disziplinarische Entlassung *f*

(JAP) 懲戒停職

(RUS) ДИСЦИПЛИНАРНОЕ ВРЕМЕННОЕ ОТСТРАНЕНИЕ ОТ РАБОТЫ

disclaimer

(CHIN) 弃权，否认，不承认，不认领

(FRE) renonciation, acte de renonciation
(GER) Verzicht *m*; Verzichterklärung *f*;
Freizeichnungsklausel *f*,
Haftungsausschlusserklärung *f*
(JAP) 拒否、放棄、否認、放棄声明書、
否認声明書
(RUS) ОТКАЗ (от права)

disclosure
(CHIN) 揭示，透露，表述
(GER) Offenlegung *f*, Mitteilung *f*
(JAP) 開示、公開
(RUS) РАСКРЫТИЕ; ОБНАРУЖЕНИЕ;
СООБЩЕНИЕ

discontinuance of plan
(CHIN) 计划中断
(FRE) suppression du plan, (C) suppression
du régime
(GER) Planaufhebung *f*, -abbruch *m*
(JAP) 計画停止、計画中止
(RUS) ПРЕКРАЩЕНИЕ СЛЕДОВАНИЯ
ПЛАНУ

discontinued operation
(CHIN) 停产，停售
(FRE) exploitation interrompue
(GER) aufgegebener Betriebsbereich *n*
(JAP) 廃止事業、廃止部門
(RUS) ПРЕКРАЩЕНИЕ ДЕЯТЕЛЬНОСТИ,
ОПЕРАЦИИ

discount
(CHIN) 贴现，折扣
(FRE) réduction, rabais, décote, ristourne,
discompte, escompte, discompter
(GER) Nachlass *m*, Skonto *m/n*, Rabatt *m*,
Disagio *n*; Bankdiskont *m*; Abgeld *n*;
Abschlag *m*
(JAP) 割引額、割引する
(RUS) ДИСКОНТ, СКИДКА; УЧЕТ
ВЕКСЕЛЯ; ЗАЧЕТ ТРЕБОВАНИЙ

discount bond
(CHIN) 贴现债券
(FRE) obligation vendue à perte,
(C) obligation à escompte
(GER) Anleihe *f* mit Kurs *m* unter
Nennwert *m*, Disagio-Obligation *f*; Anleihe
f mit Zinszahlung *f* bei Fälligkeit *f*,
abgezinste Anleihe *f*

(JAP) 割引債券
(RUS) ОБЛИГАЦИЯ С ЦЕНОЙ НИЖЕ
НОМИНАЛА

discount broker
(CHIN) 票据贴现经纪人
(FRE) courtier d'escompte, (C) courtier
exécutant
(GER) Diskontmakler *m*, Wechselhändler *m*
(JAP) 手形割引仲買人、
手形割引ブローカー
(RUS) ДИСКОНТНЫЙ БРОКЕР

discounted cash flow
(CHIN) 折现现金流量
(FRE) actualisation des flux financiers,
bénéfices nets actualisés, techniques
d'actualisation (C) valeur actualisée des
flux de trésorerie
(GER) diskontierter Einnahmeüberschuss
m, Discounted Cash Flow
(JAP) 割引キャッシュフロー
(RUS) ДИСКОНТИРОВАННЫЙ ПОТОК
НАЛИЧНОСТИ

discounting the news
(CHIN) 根据预期消息开价
(FRE) intégrer instantanément dans les prix
le flux d'informations sur les sociétés,
(C) actualisation anticipée
(GER) Nachrichten *fpl* unberücksichtigt
lassen *v*
(JAP) ニュース予想による株式価格付け
(RUS) В ОЖИДАНИИСТАВИТЬ НА
ПОДЪЁМ ИЛИ ПАДЕНИЕ ЦЕНЫ АКЦИЙ
КОМПАНИИ В КАЧЕСТВЕ РЕАКЦИИ НА
ХОРОЩИЕ ИЛИ ПЛОХИЕ О НЕЙ
НОВОСТИ

discount points
(CHIN) 贴现点数
(FRE) points d'escompte
(GER) Diskontpunkt *m*
(JAP) ディスカウントポイント
(RUS) УЧЕТНЫЕ ПУНКТЫ

discount rate
(CHIN) 贴现率
(FRE) taux de réduction, taux d'escompte
(GER) Diskontsatz *m*, -faktor *m*;
Abzinsungssatzfaktor *m*, Bankdiskontrate *f*

(JAP) 公定歩合、手形割引歩合
(RUS) УЧЕТНАЯ СТАВКА

discount window

(CHIN) 贴现贷款业务窗口
(GER) Diskontfenster *n*,
Rediskontierungsstelle *f* (Zentralbank)
(JAP) 割引窓口
(RUS) «УЧЕТНОЕ ОКНО», буквально
МЕСТО В ЦЕНТРАЛЬНОМ БАНКЕ, ГДЕ
БАНКИ ПОДАЮТ ЗАЯВКИ НА ЗАЙМЫ ПО
УЧЁТНОЙ СТАВКЕ

discount yield

(CHIN) 贴现收益率
(FRE) rendement de l'escompte
(GER) Diskontertrag *m*
(JAP) 割引利回り
(RUS) (ГОДОВАЯ) ДОХОДНОСТЬ
ДИСКОНТНОЙ ЦЕННОЙ БУМАГИ

discovery

(CHIN) 发现，披露
(FRE) garantie subséquente, découverte
(GER) Beweisermittlung *n*, Discovery-
Verfahren *n*
(JAP) 証拠開示手続き
(RUS) ОТКРЫТИЕ; РАСКРЫТИЕ;
ОБНАРУЖЕНИЕ

discovery sampling

(CHIN) 发现采样
(FRE) échantillonnage de la découverte
(GER) Probeerhebung *f*, Voremittlung *f*
(JAP) 発見のための抽出法

discrepancy

(CHIN) 不一致，差异
(FRE) contradiction, différence, (C) écart
(GER) Diskrepanz *f*, Unstimmigkeit *f*,
Unregelmäßigkeit *f*
(JAP) 食い違い、不一致
(RUS) РАСХОЖДЕНИЕ,
НЕСООТВЕТСТВИЕ

discretion

(CHIN) 自行处理
(FRE) discrétion
(GER) Ermessen *n*, Diskretion *f*,
Verschwiegenheit *f*

(JAP) 自由裁量、裁量権
(RUS) СВОБОДА ДЕЙСТВИЙ; ПРАВО
ДЕЙСТВИЯ ПО УСМОТРЕНИЮ

discretionary cost

(CHIN) 任意性成本，自定成本
(FRE) coût discrétionnaire
(GER) ermessensbedingte Kosten *pl*
(JAP) 裁量原価
(RUS) ЗАТРАТЫ ПО УСМОТРЕНИЮ

discretionary income

(CHIN) 可自由支配的收入
(FRE) revenu discrétionnaire
(GER) verfügbares Einkommen *n*,
Nettoeinkommen *f*
(JAP) 裁量所得
(RUS) ЧАСТЬ ДОХОДА ЛИЦА ПОСЛЕ
УДОВЛЕТВОРЕНИЯ ПЕРВООЧЕРЕДНЫХ
ПОТРЕБНОСТЕЙ

discretionary policy

(CHIN) 可自由处理的政策
(FRE) politique discrétionnaire
(GER) Ermessensrichtlinie *f*, -grundsatz *m*
(JAP) 裁量政策
(RUS) ПОЛИТИКА ПРЕДОСТАВЛЕНИЕ
ОГОВОРЕННОЙ СВОБОДЫ ДЕЙСТВИЙ

discretionary spending power

(CHIN) 收入中可自由支配的购买力
(FRE) pouvoir de dépense discrétionnaire
(GER) verfügbare Kaufkraft *f*
(JAP) 裁量支出力
(RUS) ПОЛНОМОЧИЕ НА
РАСХОДОВАНИЕ ПО УСМОТРЕНИЮ

discrimination

(CHIN) 歧视，区别
(FRE) discrimination
(GER) Diskriminierung *f*, Benachteiligung *f*
(JAP) 差別、差別待遇
(RUS) ДИСКРИМИНАЦИЯ; НЕРАВЕНСТВО
В ПРАВАХ

diseconomies

(CHIN) 不经济，成本的增加
(FRE) déséconomies
(GER) Nachteile *mpl*, Zusatzkosten *pl*
(JAP) 不経済

(RUS) ОТРИЦАТЕЛЬНЫЙ ВНЕШНИЙ ЭФФЕКТ ЭКОНОМИЧЕСКОЙ ДЕЯТЕЛЬНОСТИ

dishonor

(CHIN) 拒绝付款，拒绝承兑

(FRE) refuser de payer, ne pas honorer

(GER) Annahme *f* verweigern, nicht einlösen *v*

(JAP) 不渡り、支払拒絶、引受拒否

(RUS) БЕСЧЕСТИЕ; ОТКАЗ В ПРИЕМЕ ДОКУМЕНТА; ПРОСРОЧКА ОПЛАТЫ ПО СЧЕТУ

disinflation

(CHIN) 通货收缩，反通货膨胀

(FRE) désinflation

(GER) Desinflation *f*

(JAP) ディスインフレーション、ディスインフレ政策

(RUS) ДЕФЛЯЦИЯ

disintermediation

(CHIN) 不干预

(FRE) désintermédiation

(GER) Einlagenabzug *m*; Einlagenumschichtung *f* (auf höherverzinsliche Kurzläufer); Ausweichen *n* auf andere Quellen*fpl*

(JAP) 金融機関仲介離れ、非仲介

(RUS) ОТЛИВ ДЕНЕЖНЫХ РЕСУРСОВ ИЗ КРЕДИТНО-ФИНАНСОВЫХ УЧРЕЖДЕНИЙ НА НЕОРГАНИЗОВАННЫЙ РЫНОК ССУДНОГО КАПИТАЛА

disjoint events

(CHIN) 不相交事件

(FRE) événements disjoints

(GER) zusammenhanglose Ereignisse *npl*

(JAP) ばらばらの出来事、支離滅裂な出来事

(RUS) НЕСОГЛАСУЕМЫЕ СОБЫТИЯ

disk

(CHIN) 磁盘

(FRE) disque

(GER) Diskette *f*, Magnetplatte *f*

(JAP) ディスク

(RUS) ДИСК

disk drive

(CHIN) 磁盘机，磁盘驱动器

(FRE) lecteur

(GER) Disketten- *n*, Plattenlaufwerk *n*

(JAP) ディスクドライブ

(RUS) ДИСКОВОД

dismissal

(CHIN) 免职，解雇，开除

(GER) Abberufung *f*; Entlassung *f*; Kündigung *f*; Absetzung *f*; Abweisung *f* (Klage)

(JAP) 解雇、却下、放棄

(RUS) ОТКЛОНЕНИЕ ИСКА; ПРЕКРАЩЕНИЕ ДЕЛА; УВОЛЬНЕНИЕ

dispatcher

(CHIN) 调度员，发送人

(FRE) répartiteur

(GER) Expedient *m*; Vermittlung *f*; Expedition *f*

(JAP) 発信人、発車係、発送者

(RUS) ДИСПЕТЧЕР; ДОСТАВЩИК

disposable income

(CHIN) 可支配收入

(FRE) revenu disponible, (C) revenu alinable

(GER) verfügbares Einkommen *n*

(JAP) 可処分所得

(RUS) ДОХОД НАСЕЛЕНИЯ ПОСЛЕ УПЛАТЫ НАЛОГОВ

dispossess

(CHIN) 驱逐，剥夺，撵走

(FRE) déposséder

(GER) Besitz *m* entziehen, von der Nutzung *f* ausschließen, enteignen *v*

(JAP) 財産を)～から取り上げる、奪う

(RUS) ЛИШАТЬ ВЛАДЕНИЯ; ВЫСЕЛЯТЬ

dispossess proceedings

(CHIN) 驱逐行动

(FRE) procédure de dépossession

(GER) Räumungsklage *f*, Exmissionsverfahren *n*

(JAP) 明渡し略式手続、明渡し請求訴訟

(RUS) РАЗБИРАТЕЛЬСТВО ПО ЛИШЕНИЮ ВЛАДЕНИЯ

dissolution
(CHIN) 解除，解体，溶解
(FRE) dissolution
(GER) Auflösung *f*; Entflechtung *f* (Kartell)
(JAP) 解散、解除
(RUS) РАСТОРЖЕНИЕ, ПРЕКРАЩЕНИЕ
(договора); РОСПУСК, ЛИКВИДАЦИЯ
(компании)

distressed property
(CHIN) 被扣押财产
(FRE) propriété en difficulté
(GER) Anwesen *n* in Notlage *f*
(JAP) 差押不動産物件
(RUS) ИМУЩЕСТВО ЛИЦА, ТЕРЯЮЩЕГО
ПРАВА НА ЕГО ВЫКУП ИЗ-ЗА
НЕДОСТАТОЧНОГО ДОХОДА

distribution
(CHIN) 分配，分布，分销，推销，流通，
配载
(FRE) distribution, répartition
(GER) Vertrieb *m*, Absatz *m*; Ausschüttung
f; Verteilung *f*
(JAP) 分配、分布、流通
(RUS) СБЫТ, РАСПРЕДЕЛЕНИЕ;
РАЗМЕЩЕНИЕ (бумаг на рынке)

distribution allowance
(CHIN) 分销折扣
(FRE) allocation de la distribution
(GER) Absatznachlass *m*,
Vertriebszuschuss *m*
(JAP) 流通引当金、
製造元による価格割引
(RUS) СКИДКА, ПРЕДОСТАВЛЕННАЯ
ПРОИЗВОДИТЕЛЕМ ДИСТРИБУТОРУ ИЛИ
ОПТОВИКУ НА ВОЗМЕЩЕНИЕ
РАСХОДОВ ПО СБЫТУ ТОВАРА

distribution cost analysis
(CHIN) 分配成本分析，推销费用分析
(FRE) analyse des coûts de distribution
(GER) Vertriebskostenanalyse *f*, -
untersuchung *f*
(JAP) 流通経費分析
(RUS) АНАЛИЗ ЗАТРАТ НА
РАСПРОСТРАНЕНИЕ, РАЗМЕЩЕНИЕ

distributor
(CHIN) 经销者，发行人，批发商

(FRE) distributeur
(GER) Groß- *m*, Vertragshändler *m*,
Vertreiber *m*, Vertriebsstelle *f*,
-gesellschaft *f*
(JAP) 小売業者、販売業者
**(RUS) АГЕНТ ПО СБЫТУ,
ДИСТРИБУТОР**

diversification
(CHIN) 多样化，分散经营
(FRE) diversification
(GER) Diversifizierung *f*, Diversifikation *f*,
Streuung *f*
(JAP) 多角経営、分散投資
(RUS) ДИВЕРСИФИКАЦИЯ

diversified company
(CHIN) 多种经营公司
(FRE) société diversifiée
(GER) diversifiziertes Unternehmen *n*
(JAP) 多角経営企業
(RUS) ДИВЕРСИФИЦИРОВАННАЯ
КОМПАНИЯ

divestiture
(CHIN) 剥夺
(FRE) désengagement, démembrement,
démantèlement, dépossession
(GER) Veräußerung *f*, Ausgliederung *f*;
Abtrennung *f*, Entziehung *f*, Zwangsverkauf
m; Zerschlagung *f*
(JAP) 子会社の売却、投資の撤収、
企業分割
(RUS) ЛИШЕНИЕ ПРАВ,
СОБСТВЕННОСТИ, ПОЛНОМОЧИЙ

dividend
(CHIN) 红利，股利，股息
(FRE) dividende
(GER) Dividende *f*,
Gewinnausschüttung *f*
(JAP) 配当(金)、公債利息

dividend addition
(CHIN) 股息附加
(FRE) ajout de dividendes
(GER) Bonus *m* (Versicherung)
(JAP) 追加配当
(RUS) ОПЛАТА УВЕЛИЧЕНИЯ
НОМИНАЛЬНОЙ СТОИМОСТИ

СТРАХОВОГО ПОЛИСА ЗА СЧЁТ
ВЫПЛАЧЕННЫХ ПО НЕМУ ДИВИДЕНДОВ

dividend exclusion

(CHIN) 股息不予计列
(FRE) exclusion de dividendes
(GER) Dividendenfreibetrag *m*
(JAP) 控除配当
(RUS) ИСКЛЮЧЕНИЕ ДИВИДЕНДОВ ИЗ
НАЛОГООБЛОЖЕНИЯ

dividend payout ratio

(CHIN) 股息分配率
(FRE) taux de paiement d'un dividende
(GER) Dividendenausschüttungssatz *m*
(JAP) 配当性向、配当支出割合
(RUS) ОТНОШЕНИЕ ВЫПЛАТЫ
ДИВИДЕНДОВ К ПРИБЫЛИ

dividend reinvestment plan

(CHIN) 股息再投资计划
(FRE) programme de capitalisation des
dividendes, (C) régime de capitalisation des
dividendes
(GER) Dividendenwiederanlageplan *m*
(JAP) 配当再投資制度
(RUS) ПРОГРАММА
РЕИНВЕСТИРОВАНИЯ ДИВИДЕНДОВ

dividend requirement

(CHIN) 派息要求
(FRE) besoins en dividendes, (C) bénéfices
nécessaires à l'émission d'un dividende
(GER) Dividendenbedarf *m*
(JAP) 配当必要額
(RUS) СУММА ГОДОВОГО ДОХОДА,
НЕОБХОДИМАЯ ДЛЯ ВЫПЛАТЫ
ДИВИДЕНДОВ

dividend rollover plan

(CHIN) 股息贷款计划
(FRE) plan de réemploi des dividendes,
(C) régime de roulement de dividends
(GER) Dividenden-Rollover-Plan *m*
(JAP) 配当借換え制度
(RUS) МЕТОД КУПЛИ АКЦИЙ В ПЕРИОД
ВЫПЛАТЫ ДИВИДЕНДОВ

dividends payable

(CHIN) 应付未付股息
(FRE) dividendes à payer

(GER) zahlbare Dividenden *fpl*
(JAP) 未払配当金、支払配当金
(RUS) ДИВИДЕНДЫ, ПОДЛЕЖАЩИЕ
УПЛАТЕ

division of labor

(CHIN) 分工
(FRE) division du travail
(GER) Arbeitsteilung *f*
(JAP) 分業
(RUS) РАЗДЕЛЕНИЕ ТРУДА

docking

(CHIN) 缺勤费
(FRE) diminuer (le salaire), (C) amende,
(C) coupure de salaire
(GER) Lohnkürzung *f*
(JAP) ドッキング、結合
(RUS) СТЫКОВКА; ПОСТАНОВКА К
ПРИЧАЛУ

docking station

(CHIN) 坞站
(FRE) station d'accueil
(GER) Andockstation *f*
(JAP) ドッキングステーション
(RUS) ПУЛЬТ ПОДКЛЮЧЕНИЯ

documentary evidence

(CHIN) 书面证据，证明文件
(FRE) document probant
(GER) Urkundenbeweis *m*
(JAP) 証拠書類、証書
(RUS) ДОКУМЕНТАЛЬНО
ПОДТВЕРЖДЕННЫЕ ДОКАЗАТЕЛЬСТВА

documentation

(CHIN) 提示单证，证明文件
(FRE) documentation
(GER) Dokumentation *f*, Dokumentierung *f*,
Belegung *f*; Dokumente *npl*, Unterlagen *fpl*
(JAP) 文書添付、証拠書類提出
(RUS) ДОКУМЕНТАЦИЯ

doing business as (DBA)

(CHIN) 假定商业名称
(GER) Geschäfte *npl* führend unter dem
Namen *m*, Auftreten *n* im Geschäftsverkehr
m unter dem Namen *m*
(JAP) ～の名前で事業経営中

(RUS) ДЕЛОВОЙ ПСЕВДОНИМ

dollar cost averaging
(CHIN) 美元成本平均
(FRE) moyenner une position, (C) coût moyen des actions achetées par sommes fixes
(GER) Dollar-Durchschnittskostenverfahren *n*
(JAP) 定期定額買い、ドルコスト平均法
(RUS) ПОЭТАПНОЕ РЕГУЛЯРНОЕ ИНВЕСТИРОВАНИЕ

dollar drain
(CHIN) 美元枯竭
(FRE) drainage du dollar
(GER) Dollarschwund *m*, Abfluss *m* von Dollars *mpl*
(JAP) ドル流出
(RUS) УТЕЧКА ДОЛЛАРОВ

dollar unit sampling (DUS)
(CHIN) 美元单位采样 (DUS)
(FRE) échantillonnage avec probabilité proportionnelle au capital restant dû, (C) sondage par unités monétaires
(GER) Stichproben- bzw. Auswahlverfahren *n* zur Ermittlung *f* des oberen Fehlerwertes *m* in einem Prüffeld (Dollar) *n*, wertbezogenes Stichproben- *n* bzw. Auswahlverfahren (Dollar) *n*
(JAP) ユニットドル価抽出
(RUS) ВЫБОРКА В ДОЛЛАРОВОМ ПЕРЕСЧЕТЕ

dollar value LIFO
(CHIN) 美元币值后进先出法
(FRE) dernier entré premier sorti, avec indexation, (C) deps avec indexation
(GER) Dollar-Value-Lifo-Methode *f*
(JAP) ドル価先入先出法
(RUS) МЕТОД УЧЕТА «ПОСЛЕДНИМ ПРИШЕЛ, ПЕРВЫМ УШЕЛ» (LIFO) В ДОЛЛАРОВОМ ВЫРАЖЕНИИ

domain name system
(CHIN) 域名系统
(FRE) système de nom de domaine
(GER) Domainnamensystem *n*
(JAP) ドメイン名システム

(RUS) СИСТЕМА ИМЕНОВАНИЯ ДОМЕНОВ

domestic corporation
(CHIN) 国内公司
(FRE) société nationale
(GER) inländisches Unternehmen *n*, inländische Körperschaft *f*, (US-einzelstaatlich zugelassene Gesellschaft *f*)
(JAP) 国内企業、国内法人
(RUS) ОТЕЧЕСТВЕННАЯ КОМПАНИЯ

domicile
(CHIN) 住所，期票支付场所
(FRE) domicile
(GER) Domizil *n*; Wohnsitz *m*, Wohnort *m*; Firmen- *m*, Unternehmenssitz *m*
(JAP) 住所、手形支払場所
(RUS) ПОСТОЯННЫЙ или ЮРИДИЧЕСКИЙ АДРЕС; МЕСТО ПЛАТЕЖА (по векселю); ДОМИЦИЛЬ

dominant tenement
(CHIN) 主要地产
(FRE) fonds dominant
(GER) herrschendes Grundstück *n*, herrschende Dienstbarkeit *f*
(JAP) 要役地
(RUS) ЗЕМЛЯ, ВЫИГРЫВАЮЩАЯ В СЛУЧАЕ СЕРВИТУТА НА ПРИЛЕГАЮЩУЮ НЕДВИЖИМОСТЬ

donated stock
(CHIN) 捐赠股份
(FRE) action à titre de don
(GER) (von Gesellschaftern bzw. Aktionaren in eine Unternehmung eingebrachte Aktien, die im Rahmen der Kapitalbeschaffung weiterveräußert werden)
(JAP) 贈与株式
(RUS) ОПЛАЧЕННАЯ АКЦИЯ, БЕСПЛАТНО ПЕРЕДАННАЯ ЭМИТЕНТУ

donated surplus
(CHIN) 捐赠盈余
(FRE) excédent à titre de don
(GER) (von Gesellschaftern bzw. Aktionären eingebrachte Vermögenswerte)
(JAP) 贈与剰余金

(RUS) ЧАСТЬ КАПИТАЛА, ПЕРЕДАННАЯ КОМПАНИИ БЕЗВОЗМЕЗДНО

donor

(CHIN) 捐款人，捐赠人
(FRE) donateur
(GER) Vollmachtgeber *m*; Schenkungsgeber *m*; Treuhandgeber *m*; Geberland *n*, -nation *f*
(JAP) 贈与者、遺贈者
(RUS) ДОНОР; ЖЕРТВОВАТЕЛЬ

double click

(CHIN) 双击
(FRE) double-cliquer, cliquer deux fois
(GER) doppelklicken *v*
(JAP) ダブルクリック
(RUS) ДВОЙНОЙ ЩЕЛЧОК ПРИ НАЖАТИИ КЛАВИШИ

double declining balance

(CHIN) 双倍余额递减法
(FRE) amortissement dégressif à taux double
(GER) degressive Doppelratenabschreibung *f*
(JAP) 倍額定率法、二重漸減残高
(RUS) ВДВОЙНЕ СНИЖАЮЩИЙСЯ БАЛАНС

double-digit inflation

(CHIN) 两位数的通货膨胀
(FRE) inflation à deux chiffres
(GER) zweistellige Inflation *f*
(JAP) 二桁のインフレ
(RUS) ИНФЛЯЦИЯ С ГОДОВЫМИ ТЕМПАМИ, ВЫРАЖАЮЩИМИСЯ ДВУЗНАЧНЫМИ ПРОЦЕНТАМИ

double-dipping

(CHIN) 双重职业
(FRE) cumul, (C) double deduction
(GER) Double Dipping *n*, Doppelt-Verdienen *n*,
(JAP) （年金と給料の）二重取り
(RUS) СОСТОЯНИЕ, КОГДА ВОЕННОСЛУЖАЩИЙ ИЛИ ГОСУДАРСТВЕННЫЙ СЛУЖАЩИЙ ОДНОВРЕМЕННО РАБОТАЮТ И В ГРАЖДАНСКОМ СЕКТОРЕ

double-entry accounting

(CHIN) 复式会计
(FRE) comptabilité en partie double
(GER) doppeltes Buchführungssystem *n*
(JAP) 複式簿記
(RUS) ДВОЙНАЯ БУХГАЛТЕРИЯ

double precision

(CHIN) 双精度
(FRE) double précision
(GER) doppelte Genauigkeit *f*; Rechnen *n* mit doppelter Stellenzahl *f*
(JAP) 倍精度
(RUS) УДВОЕННАЯ ТОЧНОСТЬ

double taxation

(CHIN) 双重征税
(FRE) double imposition
(GER) Doppelbesteuerung *f*
(JAP) 二重課税
(RUS) ДВОЙНОЕ НАЛОГООБЛОЖЕНИЕ

double time

(CHIN) 双倍加班费
(FRE) double du temps, (C) double tarif, (C) heures majorées de 100 %
(GER) doppelter Lohn *m*
(JAP) 倍額支給、賃金の倍額料金
(RUS) УДВОЕННАЯ ПОЧАСОВАЯ СТАВКА ЗА СВЕРХУРОЧНУЮ РАБОТУ

double (treble) damages

(CHIN) 双倍（三倍）损失补偿
(FRE) double (triple) des dommages et intérêts
(GER) doppelter (dreifacher) Schadensersatz *m*
(JAP) 倍額（3倍額）損害賠償
(RUS) УДВОЕННЫЕ (УТРОЕННЫЕ) ВЫПЛАТЫ ЗА НАНЕСЕНИЕ УЩЕРБА

dower

(CHIN) 亡夫遗产
(FRE) douaire
(GER) Witwenrente *f*, Witwenanteil *m*, Mitgift *f*
(JAP) 寡婦産
(RUS) ВДОВЬЯ ЧАСТЬ НАСЛЕДСТВА

download

(CHIN) 下载

(FRE) télécharger

(GER) herunterladen, downloaden *v*

(RUS) ЗАГРУЖАТЬ, ПЕРЕСЫЛАТЬ (ПО ЛИНИИ СВЯЗИ)

downpayment

(CHIN) 预付款，分期付款定金

(FRE) acompte

(GER) Anzahlung *f*

(JAP) 頭金、手付金

(RUS) ПЕРВЫЙ ВЗНОС

downscale

(CHIN) 缩减规模

(FRE) réduction de la production

(GER) verringern, reduzieren *v*

(JAP) 規模を縮小する、小型化する

(RUS) СНИЖЕНИЕ МАСШТАБА; УМЕНЬШЕНИЕ

downside risk

(CHIN) 下降风险

(FRE) risque à la baisse

(GER) Risiko *n* des Kursrückgangs *m* bzw. Abschwungs *m*, Baisse-Risiko *n*

(JAP) 可能損失額

(RUS) РИСК СНИЖЕНИЯ СТОИМОСТИ ЦЕННОЙ БУМАГИ

downstream

(CHIN) 后续程序

(FRE) en amont

(GER) nachgeschaltet, nachgelagert, nachfolgend, unterhalb *adj*

(JAP) 下流部門 （の）

(RUS) ФИН. ПОТОКИ ОТ МАТЕРИНСКОЙ КОМПАНИИ К ДОЧЕРНЕЙ

down tick

(CHIN) 向下赊购

(FRE) légère diminution, négociation d'un titre à un cours légèrement inférieur à celui de la négociation précédente,

(C) négociation à un cours inférieur

(GER) leichter Kursabfall *m*; Kursabschlag *m*; leicht abfallende Tendenz *f*

(JAP) 前回の引値より安い取引株価がつく相場の動き

(RUS) ПРОДАЖА ЦЕННЫХ БУМАГ ПО ЦЕНАМ НИЖЕ, ЧЕМ ЦЕНЫ ПРЕДЫДУЩЕЙ СДЕЛКИ

downtime

(CHIN) 准备时间，停工时间

(FRE) indisponibilité

(JAP) 非稼動時間、作業中止時間

(RUS) ПРОСТОЙ

downturn

(CHIN) 下跌，下降趋势

(FRE) ralentissement

(GER) Abschwung *m*, (Konjunktur)rückgang *m*, Rezession *f*, Konjunkturabschwächung *f*

(JAP) (景気などの)下降、沈滞

(RUS) ЭКОНОМИЧЕСКИЙ СПАД

downzoning

(CHIN) 下降分带

(FRE) fait de réduire la taille d'un terrain, (C) zonage réduit

(GER) Flächennutzungsreduzierung *f*

(JAP) ゾーンを小さくする

(RUS) ПЕРЕ- ЗОНИРОВАНИЕ С ЦЕЛЬЮ СНИЖЕНИЯ ИНТЕНСИВНОСТИ ИСПОЛЬЗОВАНИЯ НАДЕЛА

dowry

(CHIN) 嫁妆

(FRE) fonds dotal, dot

(GER) Aussteuer *f*, Mitgift *f*; Erbanteil *m* der Witwe *f*, Nießbrauchrecht *m*

(JAP) 結婚持参金

(RUS) ПРИДАНОЕ

Dow theory

(CHIN) 道氏理论

(FRE) théorie de dow

(GER) Dow-Theorie *f*

(JAP) ダウ理論

(RUS) ТЕОРИЯ ДОУ

draft

(CHIN) 汇票，付款通知，草案，选拔

(FRE) effet, traite, projet

(GER) Entwurf *m*; Tratte *f*; Wechsel *m*; Zahlungsanweisung *f*

(JAP) 為替手形、支払指図書

(RUS) ПРОЕКТ; ЧЕРНОВИК; ПЕРЕВОДНОЙ
ВЕКСЕЛЬ; ТРАТТА

draining reserves
(CHIN) 外流储备
(FRE) réduire les réserves, (C) réserve de
drainage
(GER) Reserven *fpl* bzw. Rücklagen *fpl*
abschöpfen *v*, Liquidität *f* abschöpfen *v*
(JAP) 準備金の枯渇・流出
(RUS) ИЗЪЯТИЕ РЕЗЕРВОВ

draw
(CHIN) 支取，提款，预支佣金，
借款
(FRE) tirer
(GER) ziehen (Wechsel *m*); abheben (Geld
n); beziehen (Gehalt *n*/Pension *f*)
(JAP) 為替手形振出し
(RUS) СОСТАВЛЯТЬ, ОФОРМЛЯТЬ;
СНИМАТЬ (со счета); ВЫПИСЫВАТЬ,
ВЫСТАВЛЯТЬ (чек, тратту); ВЫТЯГИВАТЬ

draw tool
(CHIN) 画线工具
(FRE) outil de dessin
(GER) Freihandzeichenwerkzeug *n*
(JAP) 描画ツール、画像作成ツール
(RUS) ПРОГРАММА РИСОВАНИЯ,
ЧЕРЧЕНИЯ

drawee
(CHIN) 汇票受票人，付款人
(FRE) tiré
(GER) Bezogener *m*, Trassat *m*
(JAP) (\為替手形の)支払人、(約束手形
の)受取人
(RUS) ТРАССАТ

drawer
(CHIN) 出票人
(FRE) tireur
(GER) Aussteller *m*, Trassant *m*
(JAP) 為替手形振出人
(RUS) ТРАССАНТ; ЧЕКОДАТЕЛЬ;
ВЕКСЕЛЕДАТЕЛЬ

drawing account
(CHIN) 提款账户，提存账户
(FRE) compte de triage

(GER) Kontokorrentkonto *n*, laufendes
Konto *n*
(JAP) 引出金勘定
(RUS) РАСХОДНЫЙ СЧЕТ

drive
(CHIN) 驱动，推动
(FRE) lecteur
(GER) Laufwerk *n*
(JAP) 駆動、駆動装置、ドライブ
(RUS) ДИСКОВОД

**drop-down menu (pull-down
menu)**
(CHIN) 下拉式选项屏 (下拉选单)
(FRE) menu déroulant
(GER) Drop-Down-Menü (Pull-Down-
Menü) *n*
(JAP) ドロップダウンメニュー（プルダ
ウンメニュー）
(RUS) ПУЛ-ДАУН МЕНЮ,
СПУСКАЮЩЕЕСЯ МЕНЮ

drop-shipping
(CHIN) 直接运输，直达货运
(FRE) envoi commercial facturé à un
grossiste mais expédié directement au
détaillant, (C) expédition directe,
(C) expédition sur demande
(GER) Direkt(be)lieferung *f*,
Streckengeschäft *n*
(JAP) 生産者直送、製造元直送
(RUS) ПРЯМАЯ ДОСТАВКА ОТ
ИЗГОТОВИТЕЛЯ ПОТРЕБИТЕЛЮ (по
заказу через оптового торговца)

dry goods
(CHIN) 绸缎，呢绒类，
布匹织物类
(FRE) biens non durables
(GER) Trockenware *f*; Kurzwaren *fpl*
(JAP) 〔英〕穀類、〔米〕織物類
(RUS) СУХИЕ ГРУЗЫ

dual contract
(CHIN) 复式合约
(FRE) double contrat
(GER) Doppelvertrag *m*
(JAP) 二重契約
(RUS) ДВОЙНОЙ КОНТРАКТ, ДОГОВОР

due bill

(CHIN) 到期票据，借据
(FRE) facture à payer
(GER) fälliger Wechsel *m*; fällige
Rechnung *f*; Schuldverschreibung *f*;
Verpflichtungserklärung *f* (über Lieferung *f*
von Wertpapieren *npl*)
(JAP) 借用証書、有価証券引渡し書
(RUS) СЧЕТ С НАСТУПИВШИМ СРОКОМ
ОПЛАТЫ

due-on-sale clause

(CHIN) 销售后贷款立即到位条款
(FRE) clause de paiement à la vente
(GER) Fällig-bei-Verkauf-Klausel *f*
(JAP) 売却時返済条項
(RUS) УСЛОВИЕ, ПО КОТОРОМУ
КРЕДИТОР МОЖЕТ ПОТРЕБОВАТЬ
ПОГАШЕНИЯ ИПОТЕЧНОГО КРЕДИТА,
ЕСЛИ ЗАЛОГОВАЯ СОБСТВЕННОСТЬ
ПРОДАНА

dummy

(CHIN) 虚假物，虚拟
(FRE) factice, (C) prête-nom
(GER) Strohmann *m*; Attrappe *f*
(JAP) ダミー、模造品
(RUS) ПОДСТАВНОЕ ЛИЦО; МАНЕКЕН;
«КУКЛА»

dumping

(CHIN) 倾销
(FRE) dumping
(GER) Dumping *n*, Preisschleuderei *f*
(JAP) ダンピング、不当廉売
(RUS) ДЕМПИНГ

dun

(CHIN) 讨债，催债
(FRE) presser, harceler, (C) exiger un
paiement en retard
(GER) Mahnung *f*
(JAP) 借金の催促をする、借金の督促
(RUS) ТРЕБОВАНИЕ УПЛАТЫ ОТ

ПРОСРОЧИВШЕГО ДОЛЖНИКА

duplex copying (printing)

(CHIN) 双面拷贝 （打印）
(FRE) copie recto-verso (impression)
(GER) zweiseitiges Kopieren (Drucken)
(JAP) デュプレックスコピー
（両面印刷）
(RUS) ДУПЛЕКСНОЕ ПЕРЕПИСЫВАНИЕ
(РАСПЕЧАТКА)

duplication of benefits

(CHIN) 福利重叠
(FRE) duplication des prestations
(GER) doppelte Leistungen *fpl*
(JAP) 重複手当
(RUS) ДУБЛИРОВАНИЕ ВЫГОД, ЛЬГОТ

duress

(CHIN) 强迫，胁迫
(FRE) contrainte
(GER) Nötigung *f*, Drohung *f*, Druck *m*,
Zwang *m*
(JAP) 強迫、強要
(RUS) ПРИНУЖДЕНИЕ

dutch auction

(CHIN) 荷兰式拍卖
(FRE) vente au rabais
(GER) Holländische Auktion *f*;
Abwärtsversteigerung *f*
(JAP) 競り下げ競売、逆競り
(RUS) «ГОЛЛАНДСКИЙ» АУКЦИОН
(начиная с заведомо завышенной цены)

duty

(CHIN) 税，关税，责任
(FRE) obligation
(GER) Zoll *m*, Abgabe *f*; Steuer *f*, Taxe *f*
(JAP) 任務、課税、(複数の場合)関税
(RUS) ДОЛГ; ОБЯЗАННОСТЬ; НАЛОГ;
СБОР; ТАМОЖЕННАЯ ПОШЛИНА

E

each way

(CHIN) 买卖双方个别负担之约定

(FRE) dans chaque sens, (C) double commission

(GER) hin und zurück *adj*

(JAP) 手数料各自払い、ブローカーの売買上の

(RUS) »В ОБЕ СТОРОНЫ»; КОМИССИОННЫЕ БРОКЕРА, ВОВЛЕЧЁННОГО КАК В ПОКУПКУ, ТАК И В ПРОДАЖУ ОПРЕДЕЛЁННЫХ ЦЕННЫХ БУМАГ

early retirement

(CHIN) 提早退休

(FRE) retraite anticipée, (C) préretraite

(GER) vorzeitige Rückzahlung *f* einer Anleihe *f*; vorzeitige Verrentung *f*; Frühpensionierung *f*, Vorruhestand *m*

(JAP) 早期退職

(RUS) РАНИИЙ, ДОСРОЧНЫЙ ВЫХОД НА ПЕНСИЮ

early retirement benefits

(CHIN) 提前退休金

(FRE) prestations de retraite anticipée, (C) prestations de préretraite

(GER) Vorruhestandsleistungen *fpl*

(JAP) 早期退職手当

(RUS) ЛЬГОТЫ, ВЫПЛАТЫ ПРИ РАННЕМ, ДОСРОЧНОМ ВЫХОДЕ НА ПЕНСИЮ

early withdrawal penalty

CHIN) 提前支取罚款

(FRE) pénalité pour retraite anticipée

(GER) Strafe *f* für vorzeitige Geldentnahme *f*

(JAP) 退職前引出罰則金

(RUS) ШТРАФ ЗА ДОСРОЧНОЕ ИЗЪЯТИЕ ИНВЕСТИЦИЙ С ФИКС. СРОКОМ

earned income

(CHIN) 劳力收入

(FRE) revenu perçu/touché, (C) revenu gagné

(GER) realisierte Gewinne *mpl*; Erwerbseinkünfte *fpl*, -einkommen *n*, Arbeitsverdienst *m*, Einkünfte *pl* aus selbständiger und unselbständiger Arbeit *f*

(JAP) 勤労所得、稼得所得

(RUS) ЗАРАБОТАННЫЙ ДОХОД

earnest money

(CHIN) 定金，保证金

(FRE) arrhes, (C) dépôt de garantie

(GER) Bietungsgarantie *f*, -bürgschaft *f*

(JAP) 手付金、保証金

(RUS) АВАНСОВАЯ ОПЛАТА ПРИ ЗАКЛЮЧЕНИИ КОНТРАКТА

earnings and profits

(CHIN) 收入及收益

(FRE) revenus et bénéfices, (C) bénéfices

(GER) Erträge *mpl* und Gewinne *mpl*

(JAP) 収益

(RUS) ДОХОД И ПРИБЫЛЬ

earnings before taxes

(CHIN) 税前收益

(FRE) revenus avant impôt

(GER) Gewinn *m* vor Steuern *fpl*, Bruttoergebnis *n*

(JAP) 税引前収益額、税引前所得額

(RUS) ДОХОД ДО УПЛАТЫ НАЛОГОВ

earnings per share

(CHIN) 每股收益

(FRE) bénéfice par action

(GER) Gewinn *m* je Aktie *f*, Aktienrendite *f*, Aktienertrag *m*, Ergebnis *n* je Aktie *f*

(JAP) 一株当り収益

(RUS) ДОХОД НА ОДНУ АКЦИЮ

earnings report

(CHIN) 收益报告

(FRE) rapport des gains, (C) rapport sur les bénéfices

(GER) Gewinn- und Verlustrechnung *f*, Ertragsbericht *m*

(JAP) 利益報告書

(RUS) ОТЧЕТ О ПРИБЫЛЯХ И УБЫТКАХ

easement

(CHIN) 地役权

(FRE) servitude

(GER) (Grund)dienstbarkeit *f*,
Nutzungsrecht *n*, Realservitut *n*

(JAP) 地役権
　　（土地の採光権や通行権など）

(RUS) ПРАВО ПРОХОДА, ПРОВЕДЕНИЯ
КОММУНИКАЦИОННЫХ ЛИНИЙ И Т. П.
ПО ЧУЖОЙ ЗЕМЛЕ

easy money

(CHIN) 放松银根，低利贷款，低息货币

(FRE) argent facilement gagné, (C) détente
monétaire, (C) crédit facile

(GER) leichtes Geld *n*

(JAP) 低金利の金、悪銭

(RUS) «ДЕШЕВЫЕ ДЕНЬГИ»;
СТИМУЛИРОВАНИЕ ЭКОНОМИЧЕСКОГО
РОСТА СНИЖЕНИЕМ ПРОЦ. СТАВКИ

econometrics

(CHIN) 计量经济学

(FRE) économétrie

(GER) Ökonometrie *f*

(JAP) 計量経済学

(RUS) ЭКОНОМЕТРИКА

economic

(CHIN) 经济的，经济学的

(FRE) économique

(GER) volkswirtschaftlich; ökonomisch;
konjunturell *adj*

(JAP) 経済の、経済学上の

(RUS) ЭКОНОМИЧЕСКИЙ

economic analysis

(CHIN) 经济分析

(FRE) analyse économique

(GER) Wirtschaftlichkeitsanalyse *f*,
Wirtschaftlichkeitsstudie *f*, -analyse *f*,
Konjunkturanalyse *f*

(JAP) 経済分析

(RUS) ЭКОНОМИЧЕСКИЙ
АНАЛИЗ

economic base

(CHIN) 经济基础

(FRE) base économique, (C) fondation
économique

(GER) wirtschaftliche Grundlage *f*;
Wirtschaftsbasis *f*

(JAP) 経済基盤、経済的基盤

(RUS) ЭКОНОМИЧЕСКАЯ ОСНОВА, БАЗА

economic depreciation

(CHIN) 经济性贬值，
由外在原因引起的地产贬值

(FRE) dépréciation économique,
(C) dévaluation économique

(GER) wirtschaftliche Wertminderung *f*

(JAP) 経済的減価

(RUS) ЭКОНОМИЧЕСКАЯ АМОРТИЗАЦИЯ

economic freedom

(CHIN) 经济自由

(FRE) liberté économique

(GER) wirtschaftliche Freiheit *f*,
Gewerbefreiheit *f*

(JAP) 経済的自由

(RUS) ЭКОНОМИЧЕСКАЯ СВОБОДА

economic growth

(CHIN) 经济增长

(FRE) croissance économique

(GER) Wirtschafts- *n*,
Konjunkturwachstum *n*

(JAP) 経済成長

(RUS) ЭКОНОМИЧЕСКИЙ РОСТ

economic growth rate

(CHIN) 经济增长率

(FRE) taux de croissance économique

(GER) Wirtschaftswachstumsrate *f*

(JAP) 経済成長率

(RUS) ТЕМПЫ ЭКОНОМИЧЕСКОГО
РОСТА

economic indicators

(CHIN) 经济指标

(FRE) indicateurs économiques

(GER) Konjunktur- *mpl*,
Wirtschaftsindikatoren *mpl*,
Wirtschaftsbarometer *m*

(JAP) 経済指標

(RUS) ЭКОНОМИЧЕСКИЕ ИНДИКАТОРЫ,
ПОКАЗАТЕЛИ

economic life

(CHIN) 经济寿命

(FRE) vie économique
(GER) wirtschaftliche Nutzungsdauer *f*
(JAP) 経済的耐用年数、経済的寿命
(RUS) ПОЛЕЗНЫЙ ИЛИ ПРИБЫЛЬНЫЙ
ПЕРИОД ИМУЩЕСТВА

economic loss

(CHIN) 经济损失
(FRE) perte économique
(GER) Vermögenseinbuße *f*, wirtschaftliche
Einbuße *f*, wirtschaftlicher Schaden *m*
(JAP) 経済的損失
(RUS) УРОВЕНЬ ПРИБЫЛИ,
НЕДОСТАТОЧНЫЙ ДЛЯ ПРОДОЛЖЕНИЯ
ПРОИЗВОДСТВА

economic rent

(CHIN) 经济租金
(FRE) loyer économique
(GER) Kostenmiete *f*, Ertragsmiete *f*;
Grundrente *f*, wirtschaftliche Rente *f*
(JAP) 経済地代、(家主にとって)採算の
合う家賃
(RUS) ДИФФЕРЕНЦИАЛЬНАЯ РЕНТА

economics

(CHIN) 经济学
(FRE) économie
(GER) Volkswirtschaftslehre *f*;
Wirtschaftswissenschaften *fpl*
(JAP) 経済学
(RUS) ЭКОНОМИКА; ЭКОНОМИЧЕСКАЯ
НАУКА

economic sanctions

(CHIN) 经济制裁
(FRE) sanctions économiques
(GER) Wirtschaftssanktionen *fpl*
(JAP) 経済的制裁
(RUS) ЭКОНОМИЧЕСКИЕ САНКЦИИ

economic system

(CHIN) 经济制度
(FRE) système économique
(GER) Wirtschaftssystem *n*
(JAP) 経済体制
(RUS) ЭКОНОМИЧЕСКАЯ СИСТЕМА

economic value

(CHIN) 经济价值

(FRE) valeur économique
(GER) wirtschaftlicher Wert *m*; Handels- *m*,
Marktwert *m*
(JAP) 経済価値
(RUS) ЭКОНОМИЧЕСКАЯ ЦЕННОСТЬ

economies of scale

(CHIN) 规模经济
(FRE) économies d'échelles
(GER) Größenvorteile *mpl*,
Massenproduktionsvorteile *mpl*,
Skaleneffekt *m*, Größen- *f*,
Kostendegression *f*
(JAP) 規模の経済
(RUS) ЭКОНОМИЯ ОТ РОСТА
МАСШТАБА ПРОИЗВОДСТВА

economist

(CHIN) 经济学家
(FRE) économiste
(GER) Volkswirt *m*
Wirtschaftswissenschaftler *m*, Ökonom *m*
(JAP) 経済学者、経済専門家
(RUS) ЭКОНОМИСТ

economy

(CHIN) 经济
(FRE) économie
(GER) Volkswirtschaft *f*, Konjunktur *f*;
Wirtschaftlichkeit *f*; Sparsamkeit *f*
(RUS) ЭКОНОМИКА; ЭКОНОМИЯ

edit

(CHIN) 编辑
(FRE) modifier, éditer
(GER) bearbeiten, editieren *v*
(JAP) 編集、編集する
(RUS) РЕДАКТИРОВАНИЕ

effective date

(CHIN) 生效日期，有效日期
(GER) Stichtag *m*, Zeitpunkt *m* des
Inkrafttretens *n*, Gültigkeitsdatum *n*
(JAP) 発効期日、有効日
(RUS) ДАТА НАЧАЛА ДЕЙСТВИЯ

effective debt

(CHIN) 有效债务
(FRE) dettes effectives, (C) dette totale
d'une entreprise

(GER) effektive Schulden *pl*
(JAP) 有効負債
(RUS) СУММАРНАЯ ЗАДОЛЖЕННОСТЬ КОМПАНИИ

effective net worth
(CHIN) 有效资产净值
(FRE) valeur nette
(GER) effektives Nettovermögen *n*
(JAP) 有効純資産
(RUS) РЕАЛЬНАЯ ЧИСТАЯ СТОИМОСТЬ КОМПАНИИ

effective rate
(CHIN) 实际利率
(FRE) taux effectif, (C) taux en vigueur
(GER) effektiver Zinssatz *m*, Effektivverzinsung *f*
(JAP) 実効レート、実勢相場
(RUS) РЕАЛЬНАЯ ПРОЦЕНТНАЯ СТАВКА

effective tax rate
(CHIN) 实际税率
(FRE) taux d'imposition effectif, (C) taux d'imposition en vigueur
(GER) effektiver Steuersatz *m*
(JAP) 実効税率
(RUS) РЕАЛЬНАЯ СТАВКА НАЛОГООБЛОЖЕНИЯ

efficiency
(CHIN) 有效性，效率
(FRE) efficacité, (C) efficience
(GER) Effizienz *f*, Wirksamkeit *f*; Leistungsfähigkeit *f*; Produktivität *f*; Rentabilität *f*; Wirtschaftlichkeit *f*
(JAP) 能率、効率、有効性
(RUS) ПРОИЗВОДИТЕЛЬНОСТЬ; ЭФФЕКТИВНОСТЬ; К.П.Д.

efficient market
(CHIN) 有效市场
(FRE) marché efficace, (C) marché efficient
(GER) effizienter *m* bzw. leistungsfähiger Markt *m*
(JAP) 効率的市場
(RUS) РАЦИОНАЛЬНЫЙ РЫНОК, ТЕОРИЯ, СОГЛАСНО КОТОРОЙ РЫНОЧНАЯ ЦЕНА ОТРАЖАЕТЗНАНИЯ И ОЖИДАНИЯ ВСЕХ ИНВЕСТОРОВ

efficient portfolio
(CHIN) 有效有价证券
(FRE) portefeuille efficace, (C) portefeuille efficient
(GER) effizienter Wertpapierbestand *m*, effizientes Portefeuille *n*
(JAP) 効率的ポートフォリオ
(RUS) ПОРТФЕЛЬ ЦЕННЫХ БУМАГ, ПРИНОСЯЩИЙ МАКСИМАЛЬНЫЙ ДОХОД ПРИ ОПРЕДЕЛЁННОМ РИСКЕ, ИЛИ С МИНИМАЛЬНЫМ РИСКОМ ДЛЯ ДОСТИЖЕНИЯ ОПРЕДЕЛЁННОГО УРОВНЯ ДОХОДА

eject
(CHIN) 退出，弹出
(FRE) éjecter
(GER) ausstoßen, auswerfen *v*
(JAP) 取り出す、イジェクトする、追い出す、立ち退かせる
(RUS) ИЗГОНЯТЬ; ВЫДАВАТЬ

ejectment
(CHIN) 驱逐，收回不动产(地产占有权)诉讼
(FRE) expulsion
(GER) Räumung *f*, Vertreibung *f* aus dem Besitz *m*; gesetzliches Recht *n* zur Wiederbeschaffung *f* von Immobilien *fpl*
(JAP) 妨害排除訴訟、不動産占有回復訴訟
(RUS) ОТВЕРЖЕНИЕ; ВЫСЕЛЕГИЕ

elasticity of supply and demand
(CHIN) 供求弹性
(FRE) élasticité de l'offre et de la demande
(GER) Angebots- *f* und Nachfrageelastizität *f*
(JAP) 需要と供給の弾力性
(RUS) ЭЛАСТИЧНОСТЬ, ГИБКОСТЬ СПРОСА И ПРЕДЛОЖЕНИЯ

elect
(CHIN) 选择
(FRE) élire
(GER) wählen *v*
(JAP) 当選した、選ぶ、決める、選挙する
(RUS) ИЗБИРАТЬ

electronic mail (email)

(CHIN) 电子邮件（EMAIL）

(FRE) message électronique (e-mail),
(C) courrier électronique (courriel)

(GER) elektronischer Briefverkehr *m*, E-Mail *f*

(JAP) 電子メール（Eメール）

(RUS) ЭЛЕКТРОННАЯ ПОЧТА

eligibility requirements

(CHIN) 资格要求

(FRE) critères d'admissibilité

(GER) Zulassungsanforderungen *fpl*, -voraussetzungen *fpl*; Berechtigungsnachweis *m*, -erfordernisse *npl*; Qualfikations- *fpl*, Aufnahmebedingungen *fpl*

(JAP) 資格要件

(RUS) ТРЕБОВАНИЯ ПРИГОДНОСТИ, СООТВЕТСТВИЯ

eligible paper

(CHIN) 合法证券

(FRE) papier escomptable

(GER) diskont- und lombardfähiges Wertpapier *n*; (zentral)bankfähiger Wechsel *m*; bankfähiges bzw. diskontfähiges Papier *n*

(JAP) 適格手形

(RUS) ПРИЕМЛИМЫЙ ДОКУМЕНТ

email address

(CHIN) 电子邮件地址

(FRE) adresse e-mail

(GER) E-Mail-Adresse *f*

(JAP) 電子メールアドレス

(RUS) АДРЕС ЭЛЕКТРОННОЙ ПОЧТЫ

emancipation

(CHIN) 自立，解放，释放

(FRE) émancipation

(GER) Emanzipation *f*, Gleichberechtigung *f*

(JAP) （束縛・因習・身分制度からの）解放

(RUS) ЭМАНСИПАЦИЯ

embargo

(CHIN) 封港，禁运

(FRE) embargo

(GER) Embargo *n*, Nachrichten- *f*, Handelssperre *f*

(JAP) 輸出禁止、通商禁止

(RUS) ЭМБАРГО

embed

(CHIN) 嵌入

(FRE) intégrer, (C) incorporer

(GER) einbetten *v*

(JAP) 埋め込む、組み込む、はめ込む

(RUS) ВСТАВЛЯТЬ

embezzlement

(CHIN) 侵吞，贪污，监守自盗，挪用公款

(FRE) détournement de fonds, (C) détournement de biens

(GER) Unterschlagung *f*; Veruntreuung *f*, Hinterziehung *f*

(JAP) 使いこみ、横領

(RUS) ХИЩЕНИЕ; РАСТРАТА

emblement

(CHIN) 耕作的庄稼，庄稼收益

(FRE) emblavage (n, m), (C) récoltes sur pied

(GER) Ernteertrag *m*, Feldfrüchte *fpl*

(JAP) 勤労果実、作物収得権、人工耕作物

(RUS) ПРАВО АРЕНДАТОРА СОБРАТЬ ВЫРАЩЕННЫЙ ИМ УРОЖАЙ ДАЖЕ ЕСЛИ СРОК АРЕНДЫ ИСТЁК ДО СРОКА СБОРА УРОЖАЯ

eminent domain

(CHIN) 征用权，国家征用私产权

(FRE) domaine éminent, (C) pouvoir d'expropriation

(GER) Enteignungsbefugnis *f* des Staates *m* (im öffentlichen Interesse *n*), Enteignungsrecht *n*

(JAP) 収用権

(RUS) ПРАВО ГОСУДАРСТВА НА ИЗЪЯТИЕ ЧАСТНОЙ СОБСТВЕННОСТИ ДЛЯ ОБЩЕГО ПОЛЬЗОВАНИЯ С ПОЛНОЙ КОМПЕНСАЦИЕЙ СТОИМОСТИ ВЛАДЕЛЬЦУ

employee

(CHIN) 职工，雇员，员工

(FRE) salarié, (C) employé

(GER) Arbeitnehmer *m*, Beschäftigter *m*,
Angestellter *m*
(JAP) 従業員、雇い人、
使用人
(RUS) РАБОТНИК (наемный)

employee association

(CHIN) 雇员协会
(FRE) association de salariés,
(C) association d'employés
(GER) Arbeitnehmervereinigung *f*, -
verband *m*
(JAP) 従業員組合
(RUS) СОЮЗ РАБОТНИКОВ

employee benefits

(CHIN) 员工福利
(FRE) avantages salariaux
(GER) Sozialleistungen *fpl*,
Versorgungsleistungen *fpl*,
Nebenleistungen *fpl*
(JAP) 被用者給付、従業員福利
(RUS) ПРИЧИТАЮЩИЕСЯ РАБОТНИКУ
ЛЬГОТЫ И ВЫПЛАТЫ

employee contributions

(CHIN) 雇员醵出金，员工摊款
(FRE) cotisations salariales, (C) cotisations
des employés
(GER) Arbeitnehmerbeiträge *mpl*,
Arbeitnehmeranteile *mpl*
(JAP) 従業員負担金
(RUS) ВЗНОС РАБОТНИКА

employee profit sharing

(CHIN) 员工福利分享
(FRE) participation des salariés aux
résultats de l'entreprise, (C) intéressement
des employés
(GER) Gewinnbeteiligung *f* von
Arbeitnehmern *mpl*, Mitarbeiterbeteiligung
f am Gewinn *m*
(JAP) 従業員利益共有制度
(RUS) РАЗДЕЛЕНИЕ ПРИБЫЛИ С
РАБОТНИКАМИ

employee stock option

(CHIN) 职工认股权
(FRE) option d'achat d'action des salariés,
(C) actionnariat des salariés

(GER) Belegschaftsaktienprogramm *n*,
Optionsplan *m* für Mitarbeiter *pl*
(JAP) 従業員自社株購入制度
(RUS) ЛЬГОТНОЕ ПРАВО РАБОТНИКА НА
ПРИОБРЕТЕНИЕ АКЦИЙ КОМПАНИИ

employee stock ownership plan (ESOP)

(CHIN) 职工股票所有权计划
(FRE) programme d'actionnariat,
(C) régime d'actionnariat des salariés
(JAP) 従業員持株制度、
従業員株式所有制度
(RUS) ПРОГРАММА ПООЩРЕНИЯ
ПОКУПКИ АКЦИЙ КОМПСНИИ ЕЁ
РАБОТНИКАМИ

employer

(CHIN) 雇主，业主
(FRE) employeur
(GER) Arbeitgeber *m*, Unternehmer *m*,
Dienstgeber *m*
(JAP) 事業主、雇主、雇用者
(RUS) РАБОТОДАТЕЛЬ

employer interference

(CHIN) 雇主干涉
(FRE) intervention de l'employcur,
(C) immixtion de l'employeur
(GER) unlautere Arbeitgebermethoden *fpl*
(JAP) 雇用者介入
(RUS) ВМЕШАТЕЛЬСТВО
РАБОТОДАТЕЛЯ

employment agency

(CHIN) 职业介绍所
(FRE) agence pour l'emploi, (C) bureau de
placement
(GER) Stellen- *f*,
Arbeitsvermittlungsbüro *n*,
(JAP) 職業紹介所、職業安定所
(RUS) АГЕНТСТВО ПО
ТРУДОУСТРОЙСТВУ

employment contract

(CHIN) 聘约，雇用合同
(FRE) contrat de travail
(GER) Arbeits- *m*, Dienst- *m*,
Beschäftigungsvertrag *m*
(JAP) 雇用契約
(RUS) ДОГОВОР О НАЙМЕ

enable
(CHIN) 启动，允许，使能，激活
(FRE) activer
(GER) aktivieren, einschalten, freigeben *v*
(JAP) 可能にする、使用可能にする
(RUS) ПОЗВОЛЯТЬ

enabling clause
(CHIN) 授权法案
(FRE) disposition habilitante, (C) clause d'autorisation
(JAP) 権限賦与条項、授権条項
(RUS) ПУНКТ НОВОГО ЗАКОНОДАТЕЛЬНОГО ДОКУМЕНТА, ДАЮЩИЙ ПРАВО ВЛАСТЯМ НА ВВЕДЕНИЕ ЕГО В СИЛУ

encoding
(CHIN) 加密
(FRE) codage, (C) encodage
(GER) Codierung *f*, Verschlüsselung *f*, Chiffrierung *f*
(JAP) コード化
(RUS) КОДИРОВАНИЕ

encroach
(CHIN) 侵占，侵犯
(FRE) entamer (vtr), avoir recours à (vintr), (C) empiéter, (C) prélever
(GER) beeinträchtigen, eingreifen, schmälern; missbrauchen *v*; in Anspruch nehmen; unberechtigt eindringen *v*
(JAP) 侵入する、侵害する
(RUS) ВТОРГАТЬСЯ; ПОСЯГАТЬ

encroachment
(CHIN) 侵占，侵犯
(FRE) recours à, (C) empiètement, (C) prélèvement sur quelque chose
(GER) Beeinträchtigung *f*, Eingriff *m*, Übergriff *m*; Behinderung *f*; Schmälerung *f*
(JAP) 権利の不法拡張、侵略、侵害、不法侵入
(RUS) ВТОРЖЕНИЕ

encryption
(CHIN) 加密
(FRE) cryptage, (C) chiffrement
(GER) Datenverschlüsselung *f*, Kodierung *f*, Chiffrierung *f*

(JAP) 暗号化、コード化
(RUS) КОДИРОВАНИЕ; СОКРЫТИЕ СОДЕРЖАНИЯ

encumbrance
(CHIN) 债权，财产置留权
(FRE) charge hypothècaire servitudes, (C) droit réel sur un bien, (C) engagement
(GER) Grundstücksbelastung *f*, dingliche Belastung *f*, hypothekarische Belastung *f*
(JAP) （財産上の）負担、債務（抵当権など）
(RUS) ОБЯЗАТЕЛЬСТВО С ОБЕСПЕЧЕНИЕМ ИМУЩЕСТВОМ ЗАКЛАДНАЯ

end of month
(CHIN) 月底
(FRE) fin de mois
(GER) Monatsende *n*, Monatsultimo *m*
(JAP) 月末
(RUS) КОНЕЦ МЕСЯЦА

end user
(CHIN) 最终用户
(FRE) utilisateur final
(GER) Endbenutzer *m*, -anwender *m*
(JAP) エンドユーザー、最終利用者
(RUS) КОНЕЧНЫЙ ПОЛЬЗОВАТЕЛЬ; ЧЕЛОВЕК, ПРИМЕНЯЮЩИЙ ЭВМ ДЛЯ РЕШЕНИЯ СОБСТВЕННЫХ ЗАДАЧ

endorsement or indorsement
(CHIN) 背书
(FRE) endos, endossement, (C) aval
(JAP) 裏書、保証
(RUS) ПЕРЕДАТОЧНАЯ или ПОДТВЕРЖДАЮЩАЯ ПОДПИСЬ или НАДПИСЬ; ИНДОССАМЕНТ

endowment
(CHIN) 捐赠，捐款
(FRE) dotation, (C) capital terme
(GER) Stiftung *f*, Zuwendung *f*; Dotation *f*, Dotierung *f*
(JAP) 基金の寄付行為、寄贈、遺贈、養老資金、基本財産
(RUS) ДАРЕНИЕ; ПОЖЕРТВОВАНИЕ

energy tax credit

(CHIN) 能源税信贷

(FRE) crédit de la taxe sur l'énergie,
(C) crédit d'impôt pour l'énergie

(GER) Energiesteuerfreibetrag *m*,
Energiesteuervergünstigung *f*

(JAP) エネルギー税控除

(RUS) НАЛОГОВЫЙ КРЕДИТ
ЭНЕРГОПОТРЕБЛЕНИЯ

enjoin

(CHIN) 责成，指示

(FRE) enjoindre à, exiger, (C) enjoindre

(GER) mahnen, warnen, vorschreiben;
(gerichtlich) anordnen, untersagen *v*

(JAP) 命じる、差し止める、禁止する

(RUS) ТРЕБОВАТЬ; РАСПОРЯЖАТЬСЯ

enterprise

(CHIN) 企业，事业，公司

(FRE) entreprise

(GER) Unternehmen *n*, Firma *f*, Betrieb *m*,
Geschäft *n*; Wirtschaftsunternehmen *n*

(JAP) 企業、事業

(RUS) ПРЕДПРИЯТИЕ

enterprise zone

(CHIN) 保税区

(FRE) zone d'encouragement à
l'implantation d'entreprises, (C) zone
d'entreprise

(GER) Industriegebiet *n*, Gewerbegebiet *n*

(JAP) 企業地域、企業地区

(RUS) ЗОНА ПРЕДПРИНИМАТЕЛЬСТВА

entity

(CHIN) 实体，机构

(FRE) entité

(GER) Rechtssubjekt *n*, -träger *m*,
juristische Person *f*; Organisation *f*;
Unternehmen *n*; Institution *f*

(JAP) 企業、実在物

(RUS) ЛИЦО (чаще, юридическое);
ОРГАНИЗАЦИЯ

entreprenuer

(CHIN) 企业家

(FRE) entrepreneur

(GER) Unternehmer *m*, Betriebsinhaber *m*

(JAP) 企業家、実業家

(RUS) ПРЕДПРИНИМАТЕЛЬ

entry-level job

(CHIN) 入门性工作

(FRE) poste de premier niveau, (C) poste de
débutant

(GER) Berufseinsteigerstelle *f*

(JAP) 新米の仕事、初歩的な仕事入社
段階の仕事

(RUS) РАБОТА НА НАЧАЛЬНОМ
УРОВНЕ

environmental impact satement (EIS)

(CHIN) 环境影响报告

(FRE) notice d'impact sur l'environnement,
(C) dossier d'impact sur l'environnement

(GER) Umweltgutachten *n*

(JAP) 環境影響報告書

(RUS) ЭКОЛОГИЧЕСКОЕ ЗАКЛЮЧЕНИЕ

EOM dating

(CHIN) 月底付账法

(FRE) datation EOM, (C) facturation
différée à la fin du mois

(GER) EOM-Datierung *f*, Datierung *f* auf
das Monatsende *n*

(JAP) EOM日付、月末日付

(RUS) СИСТЕМА, ПРИ КОТОРОЙ ВСЕ
ПОКУПКИ, СДЕЛАННЫЕ НА 25-Е ЧИСЛО
ОДНОГО МЕСЯЦА, ПОДЛЕЖАТ ОПЛАТЕ
В ТЕЧЕНИИ 30 ДНЕЙ ОТ КОНЦА
СЛЕДУЮЩЕГО МЕСЯЦА

equalization board

(CHIN) 统一地税委员会

(FRE) equalization board, (C) conseil de
régularisation

(GER) Ausgleichsstelle *f*,
Steuerausgleichsrat *m*

(JAP) 査定平準局

(RUS) АДМИНИСТРАТИВНЫЙ ОРГАН ПО
ВЫРАВНИВАНИЮ НАЛОГООБЛОЖЕНИЯ

equal opportunity employer

(CHIN) 倡导就业机会均等的雇主

(FRE) entreprise équitable en matière
d'emploi, (C) employeur offrant l'égalité
professionnelle

(GER) (Arbeitgeber *m*, der
Chancengleichheit *f* unterstützt)

(JAP) 機会均等主義雇用主

(RUS) РАБОТОДАТЕЛЬ БЕЗ
ДИСКРИМИНАЦИИ

equal protection of the laws
(CHIN) 法律平等保护权
(FRE) protection égale devant la loi, (C)
protection égale des lois
(GER) Gleichheit *f* vor dem Gesetz *n*
(JAP) 法律の均等保護
(RUS) РАВНАЯ ЗАЩИТА ЗАКОНОМ

equilibrium
(CHIN) 平衡，均衡
(FRE) équilibre
(GER) Gleichgewicht *n*,
Gleichgewichtszustand *m*
(JAP) 均衡、平衡
(RUS) РАВНОВЕСИЕ

equilibrium price
(CHIN) 均衡价格
(FRE) prix d'équilibre
(GER) Gleichgewichtspreis *m*;
ausgeglichener Kurs *m*
(JAP) 均衡価格
(RUS) ЦЕНА РАВНОВЕСИЯ

equilibrium quantity
(CHIN) 均衡数量
(FRE) quantité d'équilibre
(GER) Gleichgewichtsmenge *f*
(JAP) 均衡量
(RUS) РАВНОВЕСНОЕ КОЛИЧЕСТВО

equipment
(CHIN) 设备，装备，器材
(FRE) équipement, matériel, mobilier
(GER) Ausrüstung *f*, Geräte *npl*,
Ausstattung *f*, Einrichtung *f*, Anlagen *fpl*
(JAP) 備品、設備、施設、装置
(RUS) ОБОРУДОВАНИЕ

equipment leasing
(CHIN) 设备租赁
(FRE) crédit-bail mobilier, (C) location
d'équipement
(GER) Investitionsgüter-Leasing *n*,
Gerätevermietung *f*
(JAP) 設備・備品リース

(RUS) СДАЧА ОБОРУДОВАНИЯ В
АРЕНДУ

equipment trust bond
(CHIN) 设备信托债券
(FRE) obligation de fiducie pour l'achat de
matériel, (C) titre garanti par nantissement
de matériel
(GER) Schuldverschreibung *f* mit dinglicher
Sicherheit *f*
(JAP) 設備信託債券
(RUS) ДОВЕРИТЕЛЬНАЯ ОБЛИГАЦИЯ НА
ОБОРУДОВАНИЕ

equitable
(CHIN) 公正的，公平的
(FRE) équitable
(GER) gerecht, recht und billig, fair *adj*
(JAP) 公平な、公正な、衡平法の
(RUS) СПРАВЕДЛИВЫЙ,
БЕСПРИСТРАСТНЫЙ

equitable distribution
(CHIN) 公平分配
(FRE) distribution équitable
(GER) gerechte Verteilung *f*, ausgewogene
Aufteilung *f*
(JAP) 公平な分配
(RUS) СПРАВЕДЛИВОЕ РАСПРЕДЕЛЕНИЕ

equity
(CHIN) 权益，产权，股权，股票，证券
(FRE) valeur nette d'une participation,
apport, équité, (C) capitaux propres
(GER) Billigkeit *f*; Gleichheit *f*, Fairness *f*;
Stammaktie *f*, Nettoanteil *m*,
Beteiligungspapier *n*; Eigen- *n*,
Firmenkapital *n*, Gesellschaftsvermögen *n*;
Eigentumsrecht *n*
(JAP) 株式、財産物件の純粋価格、純
資産価値
(RUS) КАПИТАЛ (компании);
СОБСТВЕННЫЙ КАПИТАЛ

equity financing
(CHIN) 增股筹资
(FRE) financement par émission d'action,
(C) financement par actions
(GER) Aktien- *f*, Eigenfinanzierung *f*;
Finanzierung *f* mit Eigenkapital *n*;

Kapitalbeschaffung *f* durch Aktienemission *f*
(JAP) 持分金融（新株発行を伴う企業の資金調達のこと）
(RUS) МОБИЛИЗАЦИЯ КАПИТАЛА ПУТЕМ ВЫПУСКА АКЦИЙ

equity method
(CHIN) 净值法，产权法
(FRE) méthode de la mise en équivalence
(GER) Equity-Methode *f*, Eigenkapitalanteilmethode *f*, Bewertung *f* von Beteiligungen *fpl* beim Konzernabschluss *m* nach der Equity-Methode
(JAP) 持分法
(RUS) МЕТОДИКА НА ОСНОВЕ ОЦЕНКИ КАПИТАЛА (БУХГ.)

equity of redemption
(CHIN) 衡平偿还权
(FRE) droit de rachat, droit hypothécaire de rachat
(GER) Löschungsanspruch *m*, Ablösungsrecht *n*, Rückkaufsrecht *n*
(JAP) 衡平法上の受戻権
(RUS) ПРАВО ВЫКУПА ЗАЛОЖЕННОГО ИМУЩЕСТВА

equity REIT
(CHIN) 业主权
(FRE) part de SCPI, (C) société de placement immobilier
(GER) Immobilienfonds *m*, der produktive Immobilien *fpl* besitzt und betreibt; Immobilienfonds *m*, der Renditeimmobilien *fpl* betreibt
(JAP) 不動産投資信託
(RUS) ИНВЕСТИЦИОННЫЙ ФОНД, ВКЛАДЫВАЮЩИЙ СРЕДСТВА В НЕДВИЖИМОСТЬ (REIT),КОТОРЫЙ ВСТУПАЕТ ВО ВЛАДЕНИЕ ТОЙ НЕДВИЖИМОСТЬЮ, В КОТОРУЮ ОН ВКЛАДЫВАЕТ ИНВЕСТИЦИИ

equivalent taxable yield
(CHIN) 约当可征税收益
(FRE) rendement imposable équivalent
(GER) Rendite *f* nach Steuern *fpl*
(JAP) 課税対象等価利回り
(RUS) СРАВНЕНИЕ ДОХОДА ОТ НАЛОГООБЛАГАЕМЫХ И СВОБОДНЫХ ОТ НАЛАГА ОБЛИГАЦИЙ

erase
(CHIN) 清除，删除
(FRE) effacer
(GER) löschen, radieren *v*
(JAP) 消去する、消去
(RUS) СТИРАТЬ

error
(CHIN) 错误，差错
(FRE) erreur
(GER) Fehler *m*; Irrtum *m*
(JAP) 過失、誤差、エラ・
(RUS) ОШИБКА

error message
(CHIN) 错误信息
(FRE) message d'erreur
(JAP) エラー・メッセージ
(RUS) СООБЩЕНИЕ ОБ ОШИБКЕ

escalator clause
(CHIN) 调整条款
(FRE) clause de révision, clause de garantie éventuelle, clause d'échelle mobile des salaires, (C) clause de variation de prix
(GER) Preisgleit- *f*, Wertsicherungs- *f*, Steigerungsklausel *f*; Not-, Gleit-Indexklausel *f*; Gleitlohnklausel *f*
(JAP) エスカレーター条項、均等変動条項
(RUS) УСЛОВИЕ КОНТРАКТА, ПОЗВОЛЯЮЩЕЕ УЧИТЫВАТЬ РОСТ ИЗДЕРЖЕК (ЦЕН)

escape key (esc)
(CHIN) 换码键
(GER) Escape-Taste *f*, Rücksprungtaste *f*, (esc)
(JAP) エスケープキー、Esc キー
(RUS) КЛАВИША ВЫХОДА

escheat
(CHIN) 无继承人的财产，产业归公
(FRE) déshérence (n, f), tomber en déshérence (vintr), (C) droit de naufrage, tomber en déshérence

(GER) Heimfallsrecht *n*; Erbenlosigkeit *f*,
Heimfall *m* an den Staat *m*, Staatserbrecht
m; herrenloses heimgefallenes Gut *n*
(JAP) 復帰財産、
復帰によって没収する
(RUS) ПЕРЕДАЧА БЕСХОЗНОЙ
СОБСТВЕННОСТИ ГОСУДА
РСТВУ

escrow

(CHIN) 附条件委付盖印契约(由第三者保
存，待条件完成
后即交受让人的契据)
(FRE) compte bloquè, (C) convention
d'entiercement
(GER) Sequestration *f*; Aufbewahrung *f*
durch Dritten *m*, bei einem Treuhänder *m*
vorläufig hinterlegte Werte *mpl*
(JAP) 条件付捺印証書、第三者寄託
（財産）、エスクロウ
(RUS) КОНТРАКТ, ДОКУМЕНТ или
СРЕДСТВА НА ХРАНЕНИИ У ТРЕТЬЕГО
ЛИЦА КАК ГАРАНТИЯ (выполнения чего-
либо)

escrow agent

(CHIN) 委付代理
(FRE) dépositaire légal
(GER) Sequester *m*; Treuhänder *m*
(JAP) 条件付捺印証書受託者
(RUS) ЛИЦО, ХРАНЯЩЕЕ ДОКУМЕНТ или
СРЕДСТВА КАК ГАРАНТИЮ

espionage

(CHIN) 间谍活动
(FRE) espionnage
(GER) Spionage *f*,
Spionagetätigkeit *f*
(JAP) スパイ行為、諜報活動
(RUS) ШПИОНАЖ

essential industry

(CHIN) 基础产业，主要产业
(FRE) industrie de première nécéssité,
industrie incontournable, (C) industrie
essentielle
(GER) Hauptindustrie- *m*,
Schlüsselindustriezweig *m*
(JAP) 基幹産業
(RUS) БАЗОВАЯ ОТРАСЛЬ

estate

(CHIN) 财产，房地产，所有权
(FRE) bien, propriété, patrimoine (m),
(C) succession
(GER) Nachlass *m*, Hinterlassenschaft *f*;
Anwesen *n*, Landgut *n*; Vermögen *n*;
Immobilien *fpl*, Grundbesitz *m*
(JAP) 不動産(権)、財産(権)
(RUS) ВЛАДЕНИЕ; ИМУЩЕСТВО ВО
ВЛАДЕНИИ; УСАДЬБА

estate in reversion

(CHIN) 可期待继承的遗产
(FRE) bien substitué, (C) succession
restituée
(GER) eingesetzte Liegenschaft *f*;
Heimfallgut *n*
(JAP) 復帰不動産権
(RUS) ИМУЩЕСТВО, ПРАВА НА
КОТОРОЕ ПЕРЕЙДУТ ОБРАТНО К
ПЕРВОНАЧАЛЬНОМУ СОБСТВЕННИКУ

estate in severalty

(CHIN) 独占的不动产
(FRE) domaine en possession individuelle,
(C) succession individuelle
(GER) Sondereigentum *n*
(JAP) 単独保有財産権（資産）
(RUS) НЕРАЗДЕЛЕННОЕ ВЛАДЕНИЕ
ИМУЩЕСТВОМ

estate planning

(CHIN) 财产规划
(FRE) gestion du patrimoine,
(C) planification successorale
(GER) Nachlassplanung *f*, -regelung *f*, -
vorsorge *f*
(JAP) 資産計画
(RUS) РАЗДЕЛ ПРАВА,
ЗАНИМАЮЩИЙСЯ ВОПРОСАМИ
ВЛАДЕНИЯ И НАСЛЕДОВАНИЯ ЛИЧНОЙ
СОБСТВЕННОСТИ

estate tax

(CHIN) 遗产税
(FRE) impôt sur la fortune, (C) impôt sur
les successions
(GER) Erbschafts- *f*, Nachlasssteuer *f*;
Vermögenssteuer *f*; Grundsteuer *f*
(JAP) 相続税、遺産税
(RUS) НАЛОГ НА НАСЛЕДСТВО

estimate

(CHIN) 估计，预计

(FRE) devis, (C) estimé, (C) estimation, (C) prévision

(GER) Schätzung *f*; Kostenvoranschlag *m*, Veranschlagung *f*; Schätzwert *m*

(JAP) 予測する、見積（書）

(RUS) ОЦЕНКА; СМЕТА

estimated tax

(CHIN) 估计·税款

(FRE) impôts estimés, (C) impôts estimatifs

(GER) Steuervorauszahlung *f*, geschätzter Steuerbetrag *m*

(JAP) 見積税

(RUS) ОЦЕНОЧНЫЙ НАЛОГ НА БУДУЩИЙ ПЕРИОД

estimator

(CHIN) 估价员，概算员

(FRE) estimateur, (C) évaluateur

(GER) Schätzer *m*, Kalkulator *m*, Taxator *m*; Schätzfunktion *f*, Schätzgröße *f*

(JAP) 見積人、推定量・値

(RUS) ОЦЕНЩИК

estoppel

(CHIN) 禁止翻供

(FRE) forclusion, préclusion, (C) estoppel

(GER) Rechtsverwirkung *f*, rechtshemmender Einwand *m*, Unzulässigkeit *f* der Rechtsausübung *f*, Präklusion *f*, Hinderungsgrund *m*

(JAP) 禁反言

(RUS) ЛИШЕНИЕ ПРАВА ВОЗРАЖЕНИЯ

estoppel certificate

(CHIN) 禁止翻供证明

(FRE) certificat de préclusion, (C) attestation pour préclusion

(GER) Verwirkungs- *f*, Verfallsklausel *f*

(JAP) 禁反言証書

(RUS) ПОДПИСАННОЕ ЗАЁМЩИКОМ О СУММЕ ЗАЙМА

estovers

(CHIN) 必需品

(FRE) affouage, (C) droit d'utilisation de bois de mine pour l'entretien

(GER) Holznutzung *f*, Holzungsrecht *n*; Holzanteil *m*, Holzgerechtigkeit *f*

(JAP) 必要物（離婚扶助料など）、必要物収取権

(RUS) ПРАВА АРЕНДАТОРА ИСПОЛЬЗОВАТЬ ЛЕС, РАСТУЩИЙ НА ТЕРРИТОРИИ ДАННОЙ СОБСТВЕННОСТИ, ДЛЯ НАДЛЕЖАЩЕГО УХОДА ЗА НЕЙ

ethical, ethics

(CHIN) 道德，伦理

(FRE) éthique, code de déontologie, (C) déontologie

(GER) ethisch, moralisch, sittlich *adj*; Ethik *f*, Moral *f*, Sittenlehre *f*, Sittenkodex *m*

(JAP) 道徳上の、倫理上の、道徳、倫理

(RUS) ЭТИЧЕСКИЙ; ЭТИКА

euro

(CHIN) 欧元

(FRE) euro

(GER) Euro *m*

(JAP) ユーロ（通貨単位）

(RUS) ЕВРО

European Common Market

(CHIN) 欧洲共同市场

(FRE) Marché Commun Européen

(GER) Gemeinsamer Europäischer Markt *m*; Europäische Gemeinschaft (EG) *f*

(JAP) 欧州共同市場

(RUS) ЕВРОПЕЙСКИЙ ОБЩИЙ РЫНОК

European Economic Community (EEC)

(CHIN) 欧洲经济共同体（EEC）

(FRE) Communauté Economique Européenne (CEE)

(GER) Europäische Wirtschaftsgemeinschaft *f*

(JAP) 欧州経済共同体

(RUS) ЕВРОПЕЙСКОЕ ЭКОНОМИЧЕСКОЕ СООБЩЕСТВО (ЕЭС)

eviction

(CHIN) 收回租地，逐出

(FRE) expulsion, éviction

(GER) Zwangsräumung *f*; Enteignung *f*, Aberkennung *f* des Besitzrechts *n*; Ausweisung *f*; Besitzentsetzung *f*

(JAP) 追い立て、立ち退き
(RUS) ВЫСЕЛЕНИЕ

eviction, actual
(CHIN) 实际驱逐
(FRE) éviction, effective, (C) expulsion, réelle
(GER) faktische Zwangsräumung *f*; faktische Exmission *f*
(JAP) 現実の追い立て
(RUS) ФАКТИЧЕСКОЕ ВЫСЕЛЕНИЕ

eviction, constructive
(CHIN) 推定驱逐
(FRE) éviction, constructive, (C) expulsion, déguisée
(GER) konstruktive Zwangsräumung *f*
(JAP) 擬制の追い立て
(RUS) ФОРМАЛЬНАЯ ЭВИКЦИЯ (действия арендодателя, фактически лишающие арендатора возможности пользования арендованным объектом)

eviction, partial
(CHIN) 部分驱逐
(FRE) éviction, partielle, (C) expulsion, partielle
(GER) Teilräumung *f*
(JAP) 部分的追い立て
(RUS) ЧАСТИЧНОЕ ВЫСЕЛЕНИЕ

evidence of title
(CHIN) 所有权证明
(FRE) titre, certificat, (C) preuve de titre
(GER) Eigentumsnachweis *m*
(JAP) 権利書
(RUS) ДОКУМЕНТ ПОДТВЕРЖДАЮЩИЙ ПРАВО СОБСТВЕННОСТИ

exact interest
(CHIN) 实计利息，抽息
(FRE) intérêt exact
(GER) exakte Zinsen *mpl*, (Zinsen bezogen auf 365 Tage)
(JAP) 完全利子、完全利息、正確な金利
(RUS) ТОЧНАЯ ПРОЦЕНТНАЯ СТАВКА

"except for" opinion
(CHIN) 查账附注意见

(FRE) opinion (n, f) avec réserve, (C) opinion « à l'exception de »
(GER) eingeschränkter Bestätigungsvermerk *m*
(JAP) 監査人による監査不可意見(書)
(RUS) ЗАКЛЮЧЕНИЕ АУДИТОРА С ИСКЛЮЧАЮЩЕЙ ОГОВОРКОЙ

excess profits tax
(CHIN) 超额利得税
(FRE) impôt sur les bénéfices exceptionnels, impôt sur les bénéfices extraordinaires
(GER) Mehr- *f*, Übergewinnsteuer *f*, Gewinnabführungssteuer *f*
(JAP) 超過利得税、超過利潤税
(RUS) НАЛОГ НА СВЕРХПРИБЫЛЬ

excess reserves
(CHIN) 超额储备金
(FRE) fonds de réserves spéciales, (C) couverture excédentaire, (C) réserve extraordinaire
(GER) Überschussreserve *f*, andere (Gewinn)rücklagen *fpl*, außerordentliche Reserve *f*
(JAP) 銀行の)過剰準備、過剰準備金
(RUS) ИЗБЫТОЧНЫЕ РЕЗЕРВЫ

exchange
(CHIN) 交换，交易，汇票，交易所
(FRE) échange, change, (C) monnaie étrangère, (C) bourse, (C) opération de change
(GER) Tausch *m*, Umtausch *m*; Tauschgeschäft *n*; Effekten- oder Warenbörse *f* (Börse), Wertpapiermarkt *m*
(JAP) 為替、取引所
(RUS) ОБМЕН; БИРЖА; ОБМЕН ВАЛЮТЫ

exchange control
(CHIN) 外汇管制
(FRE) réglementation des changes, contrôle des changes
(GER) Devisenbewirtschaftung *f*, Währungs-, Devisenkontrolle *f*, Devisenrestriktionen *fpl*
(JAP) 為替管理
(RUS) ГОСУДАРСТВЕННЫЙ КОНТРОЛЬ ОБМЕНА ВАЛЮТЫ

exchange rate

(CHIN) 汇率，汇价

(FRE) taux de change

(GER) Wechsel- *m*, Devisen- *m*, Valutakurs *m*

(JAP) 為替相場、為替レート

(RUS) ВАЛЮТНЫЙ КУРС

excise tax

(CHIN) 消费税，货物税

(FRE) taxe d'accise

(GER) Verbrauchs- *f*, Konsum- *f*, Warensteuer *f*, Verbrauchsabgabe *f*

(JAP) 物品税、国内消費税

(RUS) АКЦИЗНЫЙ НАЛОГ

exclusion

(CHIN) 排斥，排除

(FRE) exclusion

(GER) Ausschließung *f*, Ausschluss *m*

(JAP) 除外、免責、控除金額

(RUS) ИСКЛЮЧЕНИЕ

exclusion clause

(CHIN) (保险契约中声明) 的除外条款

(FRE) clause d'exclusion

exculpatory

(CHIN) 抗辩，辩护

(FRE) à décharge, (C) disculpatoire

(GER) Entlastungs-, entlastend *adj*

(JAP) 弁明の無罪を証明する

(RUS) ОПРАВДЫВАЮЩИЙ; СНИМАЮЩИЙ ВИНУ; РЕАБИЛИТИРУЮЩИЙ

ex-dividend date

(CHIN) 除息日期

(FRE) date de l'ex-dividende, date du coupon détaché

(GER) Ex-Dividendendatum *n*

(JAP) 配当落ち期日

(RUS) ДАТА ПОТЕРИ АКЦИЕЙ ПРАВА НА ДИВИДЕНД

execute

(CHIN) 履行，实施，执行，转让

(FRE) exécuter

(GER) ausführen; ausfertigen; unterzeichnen (z.B. Dokument);
vollstrecken (z.B. Testament); abwickeln *v*

(JAP) 履行する、実行する、執行する、作成する

(RUS) ВЫПОЛНИТЬ; ПРИВЕСТИ В ИСПОЛНЕНИЕ

executed

(CHIN) 已履行

(FRE) exécuté(e)

(GER) ausgefertigt; ausgeführt, erfüllt *adj*

(JAP) 履行された、実行された

(RUS) ВЫПОЛНЕННЫЙ; КАЗНЕННЫЙ

executed contract

(CHIN) 已履行合同

(FRE) contrat exécuté

(GER) erfüllter Vertrag *m*

(JAP) 履行契約

(RUS) ИСПОЛНЕННЫЙ (ВЫПОЛНЕННЫЙ) ДОГОВОР

execution

(CHIN) 实行，执行，履行，签名生效

(FRE) exécution

(GER) Vollstreckung *f*; Durchführung *f*, Erfüllung *f*; Ausfertigung *f*, Unterzeichnung *f*; Vollziehung *f*

(JAP) 執行、実行、強制執行

(RUS) ИСПОЛНЕНИЕ

executive

(CHIN) 执行的，行政的，主管人员，经理

(FRE) exécutif, directeur, cadre, (C) de gestion, (C) de direction

(GER) Führungskraft *f*; leitender Angestellter *m*, Mitglied *n* der Unternehmensleitung *f*

(JAP) 幹部役員、行政部

(RUS) ИСПОЛНИТЕЛЬНЫЙ

executive committee

(CHIN) 执行委员会

(FRE) comité exécutif, (C) directoire, (C) conseil de direction

(GER) Leitungsausschuss *m*, -gremium *n*; geschäftsführendes Komitee *m*; Vollzugs-, Exekutivausschuss *m*

(JAP) 実行委員会、執行委員会

(RUS) ИСПОЛНИТЕЛЬНЫЙ КОМИТЕТ

executive perquisites

(CHIN) 公司高级主管人员待遇

(FRE) accessoires de rémunération des cadres, (C) avantages indirects des cadres

(GER) Nebeneinkünfte *fpl* bzw. Sondervergütung *f* für Führungskräfte *fpl*

(JAP) 役員の役得、役員への優遇措置

(RUS) ПРИВИЛЕГИИ РУКОВОДЯЩЕГО СОСТАВА

executor

(CHIN) 执行者，遗嘱执行人

(FRE) exécuteur

(GER) Testamentsvollstrecker *m*, Nachlass-*m*, Erbschaftsverwalter *m*; Ausführender *m*

(JAP) 遺言執行者

(RUS) ИСПОЛНИТЕЛЬ ЗАВЕЩАНИЯ, ДУШЕПРИКАЗЧИК

executory

(CHIN) 待执行的

(FRE) exécutoire

(GER) zu erfüllen, unvollzogen, vollziehend, vollstreckend, vollstreckbar, ausübend, erfüllungsbedürftig *adj*

(JAP) 行政上の、未履行の

(RUS) ПОДЛЕЖАЩИЙ ИСПОЛНЕНИЮ

exemption

(CHIN) 免税，豁免，免税额，除外

(FRE) exemption, exonération

(GER) Freibetrag *m*, Steuerfreibetrag *m*; Befreiung *f*, Entbindung *f*, Ausnahmegenemigung *f*, Freistellung *f*

(JAP) 免除、免税、適用免除

(RUS) ОСВОБОЖДЕНИЕ (от уплаты налога), ЛЬГОТА

exempt securities

(CHIN) 免办登记证券

(FRE) titre/valeur exonérée, (C) titres exempts

(GER) von Börsenvorschriften *fpl* befreite Wertpapiere *npl*

(JAP) 免除証券

(RUS) ЦЕННЫЕ БУМАГИ, НА КОТОРЫЕ НЕ РАСПРОСТРАНЯЮТСЯ НЕКОТОРЫЕ ОБЯЗАТЕЛЬНЫЕ ПРАВИЛА

exercise

(CHIN) 运用，履行，实习

(FRE) exercer, lever, exercice, levée

(GER) Anwenden, ausüben, geltend machen *v*; Ausübung *f* (z.B. Optionen)

(JAP) 行使、用いる

(RUS) ПОЛЬЗОВАТЬСЯ (властью, правом)

exit interview

(CHIN) 离职面谈

(FRE) entretien de fin d'emploi, (C) entrevue de départ

(GER) Entlassungs- *n*, Abschlussgespräch *n*

(JAP) 出口インタビュー

(RUS) ОПРОС «НА ВЫХОДЕ», Т. Е. ОПРОС РАБОТНИКОВ, ПОКИДАЮЩИХ КОМПАНИЮ

ex-legal

(CHIN) 未印法律意见的债券

(FRE) ex-légal, (C) sans avis juridique

(GER) Kommunalobligation *f* ohne Rechtsgutachten *n* einer Anwaltssozietät *f*

(JAP) 不法の、不法行為上の、非合法な

(RUS) МУНИЦИПАЛЬНАЯ ОБЛИГАЦИЯ БЕЗ ЮРИДИЧЕСКОГО ЗАКЛЮЧЕНИЯ

expandable

(CHIN) 可扩充的

(FRE) extensible

(GER) ausbaufähig, erweiterungsfähig *adj*

(JAP) 拡張可能な

(RUS) РАСШИРЯЕМЫЙ

expansion

(CHIN) 扩建，扩张

(FRE) expansion, développement

(GER) Expansion *f*; Ausweitung *f*, Ausdehnung *f*; Zunahme *f*, Vergrößerung *f*, Wachstum *n*

(JAP) 拡大、発展

(RUS) РАСШИРЕНИЕ; РАЗВИТИЕ

expected value

(CHIN) 预期值，期望值

(FRE) valeur probable, espérance mathématique, (C) valeur attendue

(GER) Erwartungswert *n*, erwarteter Nutzen *m*

(JAP) 期待値

(RUS) ОЖИДАЕМАЯ ВЕЛИЧИНА

expense

(CHIN) 经费，花费
(FRE) dépense
(GER) Unkosten *pl*, Ausgaben *fpl*,
Aufwendungen *fpl*; Spesen *pl*, Auslagen *fpl*
(JAP) 費用、支払
(RUS) РАСХОД; ЗАТРАТА

expense account

(CHIN) 费用账户，支出账户
(FRE) compte de dépenses, compte de frais
(GER) Spesen- *n*, Ausgabenkonto *n*,
(JAP) 経費勘定
(RUS) СЧЕТ НА СЛУЖЕБНЫЕ РАСХОДЫ

expense budget

(CHIN) 费用预算
(FRE) budget des dépenses, (C) budget des
frais
(GER) Spesen- *n*, Aufwandsbudget *n*,
Unkostenetat *m*
(JAP) 経費予算
(RUS) БЮДЖЕТ РАСХОДОВ

experience rating

(CHIN) 经验定额，经验费率
(FRE) tarification ajustable, (C) tarification
personnalisée, (C) tarification selon les
résultats techniques
(GER) (Prämienfestsetzung (durch eine
Versicherung) auf der Grundlage der beim
Versicherungsnehmer festgestellten
Schadenshäufigkeit)
(JAP) 経験料率法

expense ratio

(CHIN) 费用比率
(FRE) rapport des frais, généraux aux
primes, (C) ratio de dépenses
(GER) Verhältnis *n* von Aufwand *m* zu
Umsatzerlös *m*, Kostensatz *m*,
Aufwendungs- *f*, Kostenquote *f*;
Unkostenanteil *m*
(JAP) 管理費率、経費率
(RUS) ОТНОШЕНИЕ РАСХОДОВ
АКЦИОНЕРОВ ВЗАИМНОГО ФОНДА К
ОБЩЕЙ СУММЕ КАПИТАЛОВЛОЖЕНИЙ

expense report

(CHIN) 费用报告

(FRE) état des frais de déplacement,
(C) note de frais
(GER) Spesenabrechnung *f*
(JAP) 経費報告書
(RUS) ОТЧЕТ ПО РАСХОДАМ

experience refund

(CHIN) 再保经验退还金
(FRE) remboursement statistique,
(C) bonification
(GER) Erfahrungswerte *mpl* für
Rückerstattungen *fpl*
(JAP) 経験料率法による保険料金の返済
(RUS) ВОЗВРАТ СТРАХОВОЙ
КОМПАНИЕЙ ЧАСТИ СТРАХОВОГО
ВЗНОСА, ЕСЛИ ПОТЕРИ КОМПАНИИ
ОКАЗЫВАЮТСЯ НИЖЕ
ЗАСТРАХОВАННОГО УРОВНЯ

expert power

(CHIN) 专家权威
(FRE) pouvoir de l'expert
(GER) Macht *f* kraft Wissen *n* und
Fähigkeiten *fpl*
(RUS) ЭКСПЕРТНОЕ ПРЕИМУЩЕСТВО

expiration

(CHIN) 到期，有效期，终止
(FRE) limite, date limite,
(C) expiration
(GER) Ablauf *m*, Erlöschen *n* durch
Zeitablauf *m*; Fälligwerden *n*;
Außerkrafttreten *n*, Verfall *m*, Ende *n*
(JAP) 満了、満期、期間経過
(RUS) ИСТЕЧЕНИЕ (срока)

expiration notice

(CHIN) 到期通知
(FRE) avis de limite d'exercice, (C) avis
d'expiration
(GER) Verfallsbescheid *m*;
Benachrichtigung *f* über Fristablauf *m*
(JAP) 満期通知、有効期間終了通知
(RUS) УВЕДОМЛЕНИЕ ОБ ИСТЕЧЕНИИ
(срока)

exploitation

(CHIN) 剥削，开发，利用
(FRE) exploitation
(GER) Ausbeutung *f*, Ausnutzung *f*;
Auswertung *f*, Verwertung *f*; Abbau *m*,

143

Gewinnung *f*; Nutzung *f*, Verwertung *f*;
Bewirtschaftung *f*
(JAP) 搾取、不法利用
(RUS) ЭКСПЛУАТАЦИЯ;
ИСПОЛЬЗОВАНИЕ

exponential smoothing
(CHIN) 指数平滑法
(FRE) lissage exponentiel
(GER) exponentielle Glättung *f*,
exponentielles Glätten *n* (Bedarfsprognose)
(JAP) 指数平滑法
(RUS) ЭКСПОНЕНЦИАЛЬНОЕ
СГЛАЖИВАНИЕ

export
(CHIN) 出口，出口额，出口商品
(FRE) export, exporter, (C) exportation
(GER) Export *m*, Ausfuhr *f*
(JAP) 輸出、輸出する
(RUS) ЭКСПОРТ

Export-Import Bank (EXIMBANK)
(CHIN) 美国进出口银行（EXIM）
(FRE) Banque d'Import Export, (C) Banque
Import-Export
(GER) Export-Import-Bank *f*, Eximbank *f*,
Auslandskreditinstitut *n*
(JAP) 輸出入銀行
(RUS) ЭКСПОРТНО-ИМПОРТНЫЙ БАНК
(ЭКСИМБАНК)

exposure
(CHIN) 风险，揭露，广告暴露程度，
方位
(FRE) exposition aux risques, (C) exposé
(GER) Risiko *n*, Gefahrenpotential *n*,
Gefährdung *f*, Aussetzung *f*; offene
Position *f*
(JAP) 摘発、曝露、エクスポージャー
（融資者や投資者のリスクに曝される
程度）
(RUS) ПОДВЕРЖЕННОСТЬ (влиянию,
воздействию); ЭКСПОЗИЦИЯ

exposure draft
(CHIN) 征询意见稿
(FRE) exposé-sondage
(GER) Arbeits- *n*, Diskussionspapier *n*,
Entwurf *m*

(JAP) 公開草案
(RUS) ПРЕДВАРИТЕЛЬНЫЙ ПРОЕКТ

express
(CHIN) 表达，快运汇，捷运公司
(FRE) express(e), (C) exprès, (C) express
(GER) ausdrücklich, bestimmt; eilig
adj; Eilzustellung *f*, -post *f*
(JAP) 特別の、急行(便)の
(RUS) СРОЧНЫЙ; КУРЬЕРСКИЙ (почте)

express authority
(CHIN) 明示权限
(FRE) autorité expresse, (C) autorisation
expresse
(GER) ausdrückliche Genehmigung *f* bzw
Vollmacht *f*, ausdrückliche
Vertretungsmacht *f*
(JAP) 明示的権限
(RUS) ПРЯМЫЕ (ЯВНО ОГОВОРЕННЫЕ)
ПОЛНОМОЧИЯ

express contract
(CHIN) 明示合同
(FRE) contrat express, (C) contrat de
transport
(GER) ausdrücklicher Vertrag *m*
(JAP) 明示的契約
(RUS) ТОЧНО ОГОВОРЕННЫЙ ИЛИ
ОПИСАННЫЙ ДОГОВОР

extended coverage
(CHIN) 扩展保险范围
(FRE) couverture élargie, (C) garantie
risques annexes
(GER) erweiterter bzw. zusätzlicher
Versicherungsschutz *m*, erweiterte
Deckung *f*
(JAP) 拡張担保
(RUS) РАСШИРЕННОЕ ПОКРЫТИЕ

extended coverage endorsement
(CHIN) 扩展保险范围批单
(FRE) avenant de couverture
supplémentaire, (C) endossement de
garantie risques annexes
(GER) Nachtrag *m* über erweiterten
Versicherungsschutz *m*, Zusatz *m* über
erweiterte Deckung *f*
(JAP) 拡張担保裏書き

extension
(CHIN) 延期，扩展，延长期
(FRE) prolongation, (C) prorogation, (C)
délai, (C) multiplication
(GER) Nebenstelle *f*, Nebenanschluss *m*,
Durchwahl *f* (Telefon); Fristverlängerung *f*
(Termin); Zahlungsaufschub *m*, Stundung *f*;
Erneuerung *f* (Kredit); Erweiterung *f*,
Vergrößerung *f*, Ausdehnung *f*
(JAP) 延長、延期
(RUS) ПРОДОЛЖЕНИЕ; ПРОДЛЕНИЕ

extension of time for filing
(CHIN) 延长报税截止期
(FRE) prolongation des délais de
déclaration d'impôts, (C) prorogation du
délai de production de la déclaration de
revenus
(GER) Fristverlängerung *f* bis zur
Einreichung *f*, Nachfrist *f* bis zur
Einreichung *f*
(JAP) 提出期限延長
(RUS) ПРОДЛЕНИЕ СРОКА
ПРЕДСТАВЛЕНИЯ ДОКУМЕНТОВ

extenuating circumstances
(CHIN) 可斟酌的情形，情有可原
(FRE) circonstances atténuantes
(GER) (straf)mildernde Umstände *mpl*
(JAP) 酌量すべき事情、軽減事由
(RUS) СМЯГЧАЮЩИЕ ОБСТОЯТЕЛЬСТВА

external audit
(CHIN) 外界审计
(FRE) audit externe, contrôle externe,
(C) vérification externe
externe bzw. außerbetriebliche Revision *f*,
Buchprüfung *f* durch einen unabhängigen
Wirtschaftsprüfer *m*
(JAP) 外部監査
(RUS) ВНЕШНИЙ, НЕЗАВИСИМЫЙ
АУДИТ

external documents
(CHIN) 外部文件
(FRE) documents externes
(GER) externe Unterlagen *fpl*

(JAP) 外部資料
(RUS) ВНЕШНИЕ ДОКУМЕНТЫ

external funds
(CHIN) 外部资金
(FRE) fonds externe
(GER) externes Kapital *n*; Fremdmittel *npl*
(JAP) 外部資金
(RUS) ВНЕШНЕ ФИНАНСИРОВАНИЕ

external report
(CHIN) 对外报告
(FRE) rapport externe
(GER) externer Bericht *m*
(JAP) 社外報告（書）、外部の報告
(RUS) ДОКЛАД, ПРЕДНАЗНАЧЕННЫЙ
ДЛЯ РАСПРОСТРАНЕНИЯ ЗА
ПРЕДЕЛАМИ КОМПАНИИ

extractive industry
(CHIN) 采掘工业，提炼工业
(FRE) industrie minière, (C) industrie
extractive
(GER) Grundstoffgewinnungsindustrie *f*,
Abbauwirtschaft *f*, Rohstoffindustrie *f*,
Urproduktionsbetriebe *mpl*
(JAP) 採掘産業
(RUS) ДОБЫВАЮЩАЯ (СЫРЬЕВАЯ)
ПРОМЫШЛЕННОСТЬ
(из сырья)

extra dividend
(CHIN) 特别红利，额外股息
(FRE) dividende supplémentaire
(GER) Sonder- *f*, Zusatzdividende *f*;
Bonus *m*
(JAP) 特別配当
(RUS) ДОПОЛНИТЕЛЬНЫЙ ДИВИДЕНД

extraordinary dividends
(CHIN) 非经常性股息
(FRE) dividendes extraordinaires
(GER) außerordentliche Dividenden *f*
(JAP) 臨時配当
(RUS) ИСКЛЮЧИТЕЛЬНЫЙ ДИВИДЕНД

extraordinary item
(CHIN) 特殊项目，非经常性项目
(FRE) poste extraordinaire

(GER) außerordentlicher Posten *m*,
Sonderposten *m*,
Rechnungsabgrenzungsposten *m*,
Fremdposten *m*
(JAP) 臨時項目
(RUS) НЕОБЫЧНОЕ ТРЕБОВАНИЕ

extrapolation
(CHIN) 外推法
(FRE) extrapolation
(GER) Extrapolation *f*, Hochrechnung *f*
(JAP) 外挿法、補外法
(RUS) ЭКСТРАПОЛЯЦИЯ

F

fabricator
(CHIN) 装配工
(FRE) transformateur, (C) finisseur
(GER) Hersteller *m*, Fabrikant *m*
(JAP) 組立製造業者、加工業者
(RUS) ИЗГОТОВИТЕЛЬ

face amount
(CHIN) 面额
(FRE) montant de la garantie, capital assuré,
(C) valeur nominale
(GER) Nenn- *m*, Nominalwert *m*, Nenn- *m*,
Nominalbetrag *m*
(JAP) 額面、額面価額
(RUS) НОМИНАЛЬНАЯ СУММА

face interest rate
(CHIN) 票面利率
(FRE) taux d'intérêt facial, (C) taux
d'intérêt nominal
(GER) Einstandszinssatz *m*
(JAP) 額面金利
(RUS) НОМИНАЛЬНАЯ ПРОЦЕНТНАЯ
СТАВКА

face value
(CHIN) 面值
(FRE) valeur nominale
(GER) Nenn- *m*, Nominalwert *m*, Nenn- *m*,
Nominalbetrag *m*, Pariwert *m*;
Versicherungssumme *f*, -wert *m*
(JAP) 額面価額、表面価値
(RUS) НОМИНАЛЬНАЯ СТОИМОСТЬ,
ЦЕННОСТЬ

facility
(CHIN) 熟练，设备，工具，
便利
(FRE) installation, bâtiment,
(C) installations
(GER) Einrichtung *f*; (Betriebs)anlage *f*, -
stätte *f*, Werk *n*
(JAP) 施設、設備
(RUS) ПРОИЗВОДСТВЕННЫЕ
МОЩНОСТИ; ПРЕДПРИЯТИЕ, ОБЪЕКТ
(производственный, технологический и т.п.)

facsimile
(CHIN) 传真
(FRE) fac-similé, (C) télécopie
(GER) Faksimile *n*, Telefax *n*
(JAP) 複写、ファックス
(RUS) ФАКСИМИЛЕ

factor analysis
(CHIN) 因素分析
(FRE) analyse factorielle
(GER) Faktor(en)analyse *f*,
Einflussanalyse *f*
(JAP) 因子分析、要因分析
(RUS) ФАКТОРНЫЙ АНАЛИЗ

factorial
(CHIN) 阶乘积，析因，阶乘
(FRE) factorielle
(GER) faktoriell
(JAP) 階乗の、問屋の、階乗
(RUS) ФАКТОРИАЛ

factoring
(CHIN) 财务代理商，托收信贷行
(FRE) affacturage
(GER) Factoring *n*, Warenbevorschussung
f, Debitorenverkauf *m*, Auf- *m*, Verkauf *m*
von Forderungen *fpl*, Absatzfinanzierung *f*
(JAP) 売掛債権買取
(RUS) ФАКТОРИНГ (фин.)

factory overhead
(CHIN) 间接制造费用
(FRE) frais (n, m) général de fabrication,
(C) coûts indirects de production, frais
généraux de fabrication
(GER) Werksgemeinkosten *pl*, fixe
Kosten *pl*
(JAP) 製造間接費、工場諸経費
(RUS) ЗАВОДСКИЕ НАКЛАДНЫЕ
РАСХОДЫ

fail to deliver
(CHIN) 未能支付

(FRE) défaut de livraison, (C) titre non
livré
(GER) Nichterfüllung *f*, -lieferung *f*,
Lieferversagen *n*
(JAP) 引渡不履行
(RUS) НЕПРЕДСТАВЛЕНИЕ;
НЕПОСТАВКА; НЕВЫПОЛНЕНИЕ

fail to receive
(CHIN) 未能接收
(FRE) réception en suspens, (C) titre non
reçu
(GER) Empfangs- *n*, Abnahmeversagen *n*
(JAP) 引取不履行
(RUS) НЕПОЛУЧЕНИЕ

failure analysis
(CHIN) 失败分析
(FRE) analyse des défaillances
(GER) Fehler- *f*; Störungs- *f*,
Schadensanalyse *f*
(JAP) 不良分析
(RUS) АНАЛИЗ НЕУДАЧ

fair market rent
(CHIN) 公平市场租金
(FRE) loyer d'un logement mis sur le
marché à un tarif modéré, (C) loyer selon le
marché
(GER) angemessener bzw. marktgängiger
Mietspreis *m*
(JAP) 公正市場賃貸料
(RUS) ОБОСНОВАННАЯ РЫНОЧНАЯ
АРЕНДНАЯ ПЛАТА

fair market value
(CHIN) 公平市价
(FRE) valeur vénale, (C) juste valeur de
marché
(GER) angemessener bzw. gängiger
Marktpreis *m*, üblicher Marktwert *m*, Zeit-
m, Verkehrswert *m*
(JAP) 公正市場価格
(RUS) ОБОСНОВАННАЯ РЫНОЧНАЯ
СТОИМОСТЬ

fair rate of return
(CHIN) 公平报酬率
(FRE) équilibre (n, m) budgétaire, (C) taux
de rendement équitable

(GER) angemessene Verzinsung *f*,
angemessener Ertragssatz *m*, angemessene
Ertragsrate *f*
(JAP) 適性収益率
(RUS) ОБОСНОВАННЫЙ УРОВЕНЬ
ДОХОДА

fair trade
(CHIN) 互惠贸易，公平交易
(FRE) de commerce équitable
(GER) lauterer Handel *m*
(JAP) 公正取引、互恵貿易
(RUS) ТОРГОВЛЯ НА
ОСНОВЕ ВЗАИМНОЙ
ВЫГОДЫ

fallback option
(CHIN) 后备选择权
(FRE) option de repli, (C) option de
rechange
(GER) Ersatz- *m*, Alternativplan *m*,
Ausweichmöglichkeit *f*
(JAP) 最低補償オプション
(RUS) АЛЬТЕРНАТИВНЫЙ ПЛАН НА
СЛУЧАЙ НЕУДАЧИ ПЕРВОГАЧАЛЬНОГО
ПЛАНА

fallen building clause
(CHIN) 倒坍房屋条款
(FRE) clause d'annulation de l'assurance en
cas d'effondrement du bâtiment pour des
raisons non couvertes, (C) clause de
ommages non couverts
(GER) Einsturzklausel *f*
(JAP) 倒壊建物約款
(RUS) ОГОВОРКА СТРАХОВОГО
КОНТРАКТА ИСКЛЮЧАЮЩАЯ
СТРАХОВОЕ ПОКРЫТИЕ СТРОЕНИЯ В
СЛУЧАЕ, ЕСЛИ БОЛЬШАЯ ЕГО ЧАСТЬ
ПОТЕРПИТ РАЗРУШЕНИЕ ПО
ПРИЧИНАМ, НЕОГОВОРЕННЫМ В
КОНТРАКТЕ

false advertising
(CHIN) 虚假广告
(FRE) publicité mensongère, (C) publicité
trompeuse
(GER) irreführende Werbung *f*
(JAP) 虚偽広告、不良広告
(RUS) ВВОДЯЩАЯ В ЗАБЛУЖДЕНИЕ
РЕКЛАМА

family income policy

(CHIN) 家庭收入保险单

(FRE) assurance de rente familiale,
(C) police de revenu familial

(GER) Familienvorsorgeversicherung *f*

(JAP) 家族所得保険

(RUS) КОМБИНИРОВАННОЕ
СТРАХОВАНИЕ ЖИЗНИ, ПОЗВОЛЯЮЩЕЕ
СЕМЬЕ С МАЛЕНЬКИМИ ДЕТЬМИ
ПОЛУЧАТЬ ДОПОЛНИТЕЛЬНЫЙ ДОХОД

family life cycle

(CHIN) 家庭寿命周期

(FRE) cycle de vie familial, (C) cycle de vie
de la famille

(GER) Familienlebenszyklus *m*

(JAP) 家族生活周期、
家族のライフリイクル

(RUS) ЦИКЛ СЕМЕЙНОЙ ЖИЗНИ
(совместного существования)

family of funds

(CHIN) 基金组合

(FRE) famille de fonds

(GER) (Investment)fondsfamilie *f*

(JAP) 資金群、資金グループ

(RUS) ГРУППА ВЗАИМНЫХ ФОНДОВ под
единым управлением

FAQ (frequently asked questions)

(CHIN) 常见问题（经常问到的问题）

(FRE) forum aux questions, questions
fréquemment posées, (C) foire aux
questions

(GER) häufig gestellte Fragen *fpl*, FAQ

(JAP) よく出される質問と、それに対す
る回答をまとめたファイル、FAQ

(RUS) ЧАСТО ВСТАЮЩИЕ
ВОПРОСЫ

farm surplus

(CHIN) 剩余农产品

(FRE) excédent agricole, (C) surplus
agricole

(GER) Agrarüberschuss *m*,
landwirtschaftliche
Überproduktion *f*

(JAP) 余剰農産物、農産物余剰

(RUS) ИЗЛИШЕК
СЕЛЬСКОХОЗЯЙСТВЕННОГО
ПРОДУКТА

fascism

(CHIN) 法西斯主义

(FRE) fascisme

(GER) Faschismus *m*

(JAP) ファシズム

(RUS) ФАШИЗМ

fast tracking

(CHIN) 快速培养

(FRE) avancement rapide,
(C) construction en régime
accléré

(GER) Fast Tracking *n*, rascher
Aufstiegspfad *m*

(RUS) БЫСТРОЕ ПРОДВИЖЕНИЕ
НЕКОТОРЫХ РАБОТНИКОВ ПО
СЛУЖБЕ

fatal error

(CHIN) 致命错误

(FRE) erreur fatale

(GER) schwerer Fehler *m*

(JAP) 致命的誤り

(RUS) ФАТАЛЬНАЯ ОШИБКАБ Т. Е.
ОШИБКА, ПРИ КОТОРОЙ НЕВОЗМОЖНО
ПРОДОЛЖЕНИЕ ВЫПОЛНЕНИЯ
ПРОГРАММЫ

faulty installation

(CHIN) 有缺陷的安装

(FRE) installation défectueuse

(GER) fehlerhafte Installation

favorable trade balance

(CHIN) 贸易顺差

(FRE) balance commerciale excédentaire,
balance commerciale favorable,
(C) balance commerciale positive

(GER) aktive bzw. positive Handelsbilanz *f*

(JAP) 貿易収支の黒字、輸出超過

(RUS) ПОЛОЖИТЕЛЬНЫЙ ТОРГОВЫЙ
БАЛАНС

feasibility study

(CHIN) 可行性研究

(FRE) étude de faisabilité

(GER) Durchführbarkeits- *f*,
Machbarkeitsstudie *f*; Vorstudie *f*; Projekt-
f, Planungsstudie *f*

(RUS) ТЕХНИКО-ЭКОНОМИЧЕСКОЕ
ОБОСНОВАНИЕ (ТЭО)

featherbedding

(CHIN) 额外雇工，强迫雇用

(FRE) subventionnement excessif,
(C) maintien d'emplois fictifs, (C)
limitation du rendement de la production
(GER) Überbesetzung *f* von Arbeitsplätzen
mpl, personelle Überbesetzung *f*
(JAP) 水増雇用

(RUS) ПРАВИЛВ, ТРЕБУЮЩИЕ ОПЛАТЫ
НЕНУЖНОГО ИЛИ НЕВЫПОЛНЕННОГО
ТРУДА

federal deficit

(CHIN) 联邦赤字

(FRE) déficit budgétaire, déficit public, (C)
déficit fédéral
(GER) (Staats)haushaltsdefizit *n*, Fehlbetrag
m im Bundeshaushalt *m*
(JAP) 財政赤字、国家赤字
(RUS) ФЕДЕРАЛЬНЫЙ ДЕФИЦИТ

**Federal Deposit Insurance Corporation
(FDIC)**

(CHIN) 联邦储蓄保险公司（FDIC）

(FRE) organisme garantissant la sécurité
des dépôts dans les banques qui en sont
membres, (C) Société d'assurance-dépôts
du Canada (SADC)
(GER) FDIC *f*, (US-Bundesversicherung für
Bankeinlagen)
(JAP) 連邦預金保険会社
(RUS) ФЕДЕРАЛЬНАЯ КОРПОРАЦИЯ
СТРАХОВАНИЯ ВКЛАДОВ
(ФКСВ)

federal funds

(CHIN) 联邦资金

(FRE) fonds fédéraux
(GER) Tagesgeld *n*, Sichteinlagen *fpl* bei
der Landeszentralbank *f*;
Zentralbankguthaben *n*
(JAP) (連邦準備銀行の)準備金
(RUS) ФЕДЕРАЛЬНЫЕ ФОНДЫ

federal funds rate

(CHIN) 联邦资金利率

(FRE) taux de fonds fédéraux
(GER) Tagesgeldsatz *m*, -kurs *m* für
Staatsanleihen *fpl*, (US-Interbanken-
Geldmarktzinssatz)
(JAP) 準備金利率

(RUS) ПРОЦЕНТНАЯ СТАВКА ПО
ФЕДЕРАЛЬНЫМ ФОНДАМ

Federal Reserve Bank

(CHIN) 联邦储备银行

(FRE) Banque de la Réserve Fédérale,
(C) Réserve Fédérale
(GER) Federal Reserve Bank *f*, US-
Notenbank *f*, (eine der 12 regionalen
Banken des US-Zentralbankensystems)
(JAP) 連邦準備銀行
(RUS) ФЕДЕРАЛЬНЫЙ РЕЗЕРВНЫЙ
БАНК

Federal Reserve Board (FRB)

(CHIN) 联邦储备局（FRB）

(FRE) Conseil de la Réserve Fédérale
(GER) Zentralbankvorstand *m*;
Landeszentralbankrat *m*
(JAP) 連邦準備制度理事会
(RUS) ФЕДЕРАЛЬНАЯ РЕЗЕРВНАЯ
КОЛЛЕГИЯ (ФРК)

Federal Reserve System (FED)

(CHIN) 联邦储备系统

(FRE) Système de Réserve Fédérale
(GER) Federal Reserve System *n*,
(US-Landeszentralbankwesen)
(JAP) 連邦準備制度
(RUS) ФЕДЕРАЛЬНАЯ РЕЗЕРВНАЯ
СИСТЕМА (ФРС)

Federal Savings and Loan Association

(CHIN) 联邦储备及贷款协会

(FRE) société d'épargne et de crédit, caisse
d'épargne logement, (C) institution fédérale
d'épargne et de prêts
(GER) Federal Savings and Loan
Association *f*, Bundesspar- und
Darlehensverein *m*, (bausparkassenähnliche
Institution des Bundes)
(JAP) 連邦貯蓄貸付協会
(RUS) ФЕДЕРАЛЬНАЯ ССУДО-
СБЕРЕГАТЕЛЬНАЯ АССОЦИАЦИЯ

Fed wire

(CHIN) 联邦储蓄银行通讯网络

(FRE) Fed wire (transfert de fonds entre
banques gerées par le réseau de
télécommunications du système de réserve
fédérale), (C) ransfert bancaire

150

(GER) elektronisches Clearing- und Kommunikationssystem *n* des Zentralbankvorstands *m*
(JAP) 連邦準備銀行間通信システム
(RUS) СИСТЕМА ЭЛЕКТРОННОЙ СВЯЗИ ФЕДЕРАЛЬНОЙ РЕЗЕРВНОЙ СИСТЕМЫ

fee
(CHIN) 费，费用，手续费，税，小账
(FRE) propriété inconditionnelle, droits, honoraires, redevance, prestation, commission, (C) frais, honoraires
(GER) Honorar *n*; Abgabe *f*, Gebühr *f*; Provision *f*; Vergütung *f*
(JAP) 報酬、手数料、料金（入会金など、相続不動産権
(RUS) ГОНОРАР; СБОР

feeder lines
(CHIN) 补给线
(FRE) lignes secondaires, (C) réseau de transport
(GER) Zubringerlinien *fpl*
(JAP) 分配線、支線
(RUS) ФИДЕРНЫЕ ЛИНИИ; ПУТИ «ПОДПИТКИ»

fee simple or fee simple absolute
(CHIN) 土地绝对所有权
(FRE) propriété inconditionnelle, (C) pleine propriété, propriété inconditionnelle
(GER) bedingungsloses Eigentum *n*, Eigentum *n* frei von Grundschulden *fpl*, unbelastetes Eigentum *n*
(JAP) 無条件相続不動産権、単純不動産権
(RUS) ПОЛНОЕ или АБСОЛЮТНОЕ ПРАВО СОБСТВЕННОСТИ НА НЕДВИЖИМОСТЬ

FHA motgage loan
(CHIN) 由联邦房屋管理局提供保险的抵押贷款
(FRE) placement hypothécaire de l'association des établissements financiers, prêt hypothécaire de l'association des établissements financiers, (C) hypothèque garantie par le gouvernement fédéral
(GER) Hypothekendarlehen *n*, -kredit *m* der FHA (Federal Housing Association = Bundesstelle für Wohnungsbau)

(RUS) ИПОТЕЧНЫЙ КРЕДИТ ОТ ФЕДЕРАЛЬНОЙ ЖИЛИЩНОЙ АДМИНИСТРАЦИИ

fidelity bond
(CHIN) 忠实保证，员工信用保证
(FRE) assurance patronale contre la négligence oul a malhonnêteté éventuelle d'employés, (C) assurance contre les détournements
(GER) Kaution *f* gegen Veruntreuung *f*
(JAP) 身元保証保険、信用保険
(RUS) ПУНКТ ДЕЛОВОГО СТРАХОВАНИЯ, ПОКРЫВАЮЩИЙ НЕЧЕСТНЫЕ ДЕЙСТВИЯ ОГОВОРЕННЫХ ДОЛЖНОСТНЫХ ЛИЦ

fiduciary
(CHIN) 信托的，信托者
(FRE) mandataire, (C) fiduciaire
(GER) treuhänderisch, fiduziarisch, anvertraut; ungedeckt *adj*; Treuhänder *m*, (Vermögens)verwalter *m*
(JAP) 受託者（の）、被信託者（の）、信託された
(RUS) ДОВЕРЕННОЕ ЛИЦО, ФИДУЦИАРИЙ

fiduciary bond
(CHIN) 受托人保证
(FRE) caution de bonne exécution de mandat, (C) caution du fiduciaire
(GER) Kautionsverpflichtung *f*
(JAP) 受託者保証書
(RUS) ДОВЕРИТЕЛЬНЫЕ, НЕОБЕСПЕЧЕННЫЕ ОБЛИГАЦИИ

field staff
(CHIN) 现场工作人员
(FRE) personnel d'exécution, personnel de terrain, (C) personnel itinérant, (C) personnel roulant
(GER) Außendienstmitarbeiter *mpl*, -personal *n*
(JAP) 現地スタッフ、現場スタッフ
(RUS) ЛИНЕЙНЫЙ ПЕРСОНАЛ; РАБОТНИКИ НА МЕСТАХ

field theory of motivation
(CHIN) 现场激励理论

(FRE) théorie de la motivation, (C) théorie
de l'influence du milieu sur la motivation
(GER) Feldtheorie *f* der Motivation *f*
(JAP) 人間動機付け現場理論
(RUS) «ПОЛЕВАЯ» ТЕОРИЯ
СТИМУЛИРОВАНИЯ,
ОСНОВАННАЯ НА ПРОИЗВОДСТВЕННОЙ
АТМОСФЕРЕ

file

(CHIN) 文件，档案
(FRE) faire du classement , classer, fichier,
déposer, intente, remplir
(GER) Akte *f*, Unterlage *f*; Ablage *f*; Datei *f*
(JAP) 書類とじ、提出する
(RUS) ПАПКА (с делом); ФАЙЛ; СДАВАТЬ
ДОКУМЕНТЫ; ПОДАВАТЬ (ИСК)

file backup

(CHIN) 文件备份
(FRE) sauvegarde de fichier
(GER) Dateisicherung *f*
(JAP) ファイルバックアップ
(RUS) РЕЗЕРВ ФАЙЛА

file extension

(CHIN) 文件扩充
(FRE) extension de fichier, (C) extension de
nom de fichier
(GER) Dateinamenserweiterung *f*,
Namenssuffix *n*
(JAP) ファイル拡張子
(RUS) МЕТКА ФАЙЛА

file format

(CHIN) 文件格式
(FRE) format de fichier
(GER) Dateiformat *n*
(JAP) ファイル形式
(RUS) ФОРМАТ ФАЙЛА

file transfer protocol (FTP)

(CHIN) 文件传输协议 （FTP）
(FRE) protocole de transfert de fichiers,
protocole FTP
(GER) Dateiübertragungsprotokoll *n*, File-
Transfer-Protocol *n* (FTP)
(JAP) ファイル転送プロトコル
(RUS) ПРОТОКОЛ ПЕРЕДАЧИ
ФАЙЛОВ

fill or kill (FOK)

(CHIN) 指令立即买卖某一证券，成交或
取消 （FOK）
(FRE) « exécuter sinon annuler » immédiat,
(C) ordre exécuter sinon annuler
(GER) ausüben oder aufgeben *v* (Börse);
alles-oder-nichts *adj*; Auftrag *m* zur
sofortigen Ausführung *f*
(JAP) 即時実行注文
(RUS) ПРИКАЗ НЕМЕДЛЕННОГО
ИСПОЛНЕНИЯ (брокеру)

filtering down

(CHIN) 最终渗透
(FRE) se répercuter, (C) nivellement par le
bas
(GER) allmähliches Herunterkommen *n*
(RUS) ПРОЦЕСС, В РЕЗУЛЬТАТЕ
КОТОРОГО ЖИЛОЙ КОМПЛЕКС ИЛИ
РАЙОН ЗАСЕЛЯЕТСЯ БОЛЕЕ БЕДНЫМИ
ЖИЛЬЦАМИ

final assembly

(CHIN) 总装，最后装配
(FRE) assemblage final, (C) poste de
montage final
(GER) End- *f*, Fertigmontage *f*
(RUS) КОНЕЧНАЯ СБОРКА

finance charge

(CHIN) 信贷延期费
(FRE) frais financier
(GER) Finanzierungskosten *pl*, -gebühr *f*, -
aufwand *m*
(JAP) 融資手数料、金融費用
(RUS) ПЛАТА ЗА КРЕДИТ

finance company

(CHIN) 信贷公司，金融公司
(FRE) société financière, (C) société de
crédit à la consommation   .
(GER) Finanz(ierungs)gesellschaft *f*, -träger
m, Kredit- *n*, Finanzinstitut *n*
(JAP) 金融会社
(RUS) ФИНАНСОВАЯ КОМПАНИЯ

financial accounting

(CHIN) 财务会计
(FRE) comptabilité financière
(GER) Finanzbuchhaltung *f*, -wesen *n*,
Geschäftsbuchhaltung *f*, Rechnungswesen *n*

(JAP) 財務会計
(RUS) ФИНАНСОВЫЙ УЧЕТ

financial advertising
(CHIN) 财务广告
(FRE) publicité financière
(GER) Finanzwerbung *f*
(JAP) 金融広告
(RUS) ФИНАНСОВАЯ РЕКЛАМА

financial future
(CHIN) 金融期货
(FRE) instrument financier à terme,
(C) contrat à terme normalisé d'instrument financier
(GER) Finanzterminkontrakt *m*; finanzielle Zukunft *f*
(JAP) 金融先物
(RUS) ФИНАНСОВЫЕ ФЬЮЧЕРСЫ

financial insitution
(CHIN) 金融机构
(FRE) établissement financier,
(C) institution financière
(GER) Kredit- *n*; Finanz(ierungs)institut *n*, Geldinstitut *n*
(JAP) 金融機関
(RUS) ФИНАНСОВОЕ УЧРЕЖДЕНИЕ

financial intermediary
(CHIN) 金融中介
(FRE) intermédiaire financier
(GER) Finanzmittler *m*, -makler *m*; Geld- und Kapitalvermittler *m*; intermediäres Finanzinstitut *n*, Finanzintermediär *m*
(JAP) 信用仲介機関、金融仲介機関
(RUS) ФИНАНСОВЫЙ ПОСРЕДНИК

financial lease
(CHIN) 金融租赁
(FRE) bail financier, (C) opération de crédit-bail
(GER) Finanz(ierungs)-Leasing *n*; Maschinenpachtvertrag *m*
(JAP) ファイナンスリース、金融リース
(RUS) ФИНАНСОВАЯ АРЕНДА

financial management rate of return (FMRR)
(CHIN) 金融管理回报率（FMRR）

(FRE) taux de rentabilité de la gestion financière, (C) taux de rendement de gestion financière
(GER) Finanzverwaltungsertragsrate *f*
(JAP) 財務管理収益率、財テク収益率
(RUS) МЕТОД ИЗМЕРЕНИЯ ДОХОДНОСТИ НЕДВИЖИМОСТИ

financial market
(CHIN) 金融市场
(FRE) marché financier
(GER) Finanz- *m*, Kreditmarkt *m*, Geldmarkt *m*; Finanzwirtschaft *f*
(JAP) 金融市場、金融筋
(RUS) ФИНАНСОВЫЙ РЫНОК

financial position
(CHIN) 财务状况
(FRE) position financière, situation financière
(GER) Finanz- *f*, Vermögenslage *f*; Vermögens- und Kapitalübersicht *f*
(JAP) 金融状態、財政状態
(RUS) ФИНАНСОВАЯ ПОЗИЦИЯ, СИТУАЦИЯ

financial pyramid
(CHIN) 财务金字塔风险结构
(FRE) pyramide (n, f) financière
(GER) Finanzpyramide *f*
(JAP) 金融ピラミッド
(RUS) ФИНАНСОВАЯ ПИРАМИДА

financial statement
(CHIN) 财务报表
(FRE) état financier, déclaration financière
(GER) Abschluss *m*, Bilanz(abschluss) *m*, Finanzaufstellung *f*, Finanzbericht *m*, Vermögensaufstellung *f*
(JAP) 財務諸表
(RUS) ФИНАНСОВЫЙ ОТЧЕТ

financial stucture
(CHIN) 财务结构
(FRE) structure financière, structure du capital
(GER) Finanz- *f*, Geld- und Kreditsystem *n*; Finanzierungsstruktur *f*; Finanz- *f*, Vermögens- *f*, Kapitalstruktur *f*
(JAP) 金融組織、財務構造

financial supermarket
(CHIN) 金融超市
(FRE) « supermarché » de la finance, (C) supermarché financier
(GER) Finanz-Supermarkt *m*
(JAP) 金融スーパーマーケット
(RUS) ФИНАНСОВЫЙ СУПЕРМАРКЕТ

financing
(CHIN) 融资，筹资
(FRE) financement
(GER) Finanzierung *f*, Kapitalbeschaffung *f*; finanzielle Mittel *npl*
(JAP) 融資、資金調達
(RUS) ФИНАНСИРОВАНИЕ

finder's fee
(CHIN) 中间人佣金
(FRE) commission de démarcheur, (C) commission d'introduction, (C) honoraires de recherche
(GER) Vermittlungsprovision *f*; Maklerprovision *f*
(JAP) 仲介手数料
(RUS) КОМИССИЯ ПОСРЕДНИКА

finished goods
(CHIN) 制成品
(FRE) produits finis
(GER) Fertigerzeugnisse *npl*, -güter *npl*, -waren *fpl*, Endprodukte *npl*
(JAP) 加工品、完成品
(RUS) ГОТОВЫЕ ИЗДЕЛИЯ

fire insurance
(CHIN) 火灾保险
(FRE) assurance incendie, (C) assurance contre l'incendie
(GER) Feuerversicherung *f*
(JAP) 火災保険
(RUS) СТРАХОВАНИЕ ОТ ПОЖАРА

firm
(CHIN) 公司，商号，厂商
(FRE) entreprise, société, (C) firme, entreprise, société, (C) compagnie
(GER) Firma *f*, Betrieb *m*
(JAP) 会社、企業、商社

firm commitment
(CHIN) 债券的总额承受，包销承诺，包销
(FRE) prise ferme, souscription intégrale, (C) promesse de prêt
(GER) feste Übernahme *f*, vollständige Zeichnung *f*; verbindliche Zusage *f*, bzw. Verpflichtung *f*
(JAP) 真剣にかかわり合うこと、確定約束
(RUS) ТВЕРДОЕ ОБЯЗАТЕЛЬСТВО

firm offer
(CHIN) 实盘，确盘
(FRE) offre ferme
(GER) verbindliches Angebot *n*, bzw. Offerte *f*, Festangebot *n*
(JAP) 回答期限付売買申し込み、確定的申し込み、確定価格提示
(RUS) ТВЕРДОЕ ПРЕДЛОЖЕНИЕ

firm order
(CHIN) 确定订货
(FRE) commande (n, f) ferme
(GER) Festauftrag *m*, -bestellung *f*
(JAP) 期限指定注文、確定注文
(RUS) ТВЕРДЫЙ ЗАКАЗ

firm quote
(CHIN) 确定报价
(FRE) devis, (C) devis final
(GER) verbindliche Kursnotierung *f*; verbindliches (Preis)angebot *n*
(JAP) 確約値段
(RUS) ТВЕРДАЯ КОТИРОВКА

first in, first out (FIFO)
(CHIN) 先进先出（FIFO）
(FRE) premier entré premier sorti
(GER) Fifo, FIFO-Methode *f*, Zuerstentnahme *f* des älteren Bestands *m*, Zuerstbehandlung *f* der älteren Aufträge *mpl*
(JAP) 先入先出法
(RUS) РАСХОДОВАНИЕ ЗАПАСОВ В ПОРЯДКЕ ПОСТУПЛЕНИЯ

first lien
(CHIN) 最先留置权
(FRE) privilège de premier rang,
(C) premier droit de rétention
(GER) erstrangiges Pfandrecht *n*
(JAP) 第 1 順位の留置権・先取権
(RUS) ПЕРВЫЙ ЗАЛОГ ОПРЕДЕЛЁННОГО
ИМУЩЕСТВА

first-line management
(CHIN) 基层管理部门
(FRE) maîtrise, (C) cadres de terrain
(GER) unterste Leitungsebene *f*, unterste
Managementsebene *f*
(JAP) 最優秀の経営、第一線の経営
(RUS) РУКОВОДСТВО НИЗШЕГО ЗВЕНА

first mortgage
(CHIN) 第一抵押权
(FRE) première hypothèque, (C) prêt sur
hypothèque de premier rang
(GER) erste bzw. bevorrechtigte Hypothek *f*
(JAP) 第一抵当
(RUS) ПЕРВАЯ ИПОТЕКА

first-year depreciation
(CHIN) 第一年折旧
(FRE) amortissement (de la première année
(GER) Abschreibung *f* im ersten Jahr *n*
bzw. im Anschaffungsjahr *n*
(JAP) 初年度減価償却
(RUS) АМОРТИЗАЦИЯ ПЕРВОГО ГОДА

fiscal
(CHIN) 财政的，国库的，会计的
(FRE) fiscal
(GER) fiskalisch; steuerlich;
steuerrechtlich; finanzwirtschaftlich, -
politisch *adj*
(JAP) 国庫の、財政の、会計の
(RUS) ФИСКАЛЬНЫЙ; НАЛОГОВО-
БЮДЖЕТНЫЙ

fiscal agent
(CHIN) 财务代理人
(FRE) représentant fiscal, (C) agent
financier
(GER) Zahl(ungs)agent *m*;
Fiskusvertreter *m*
(JAP) 財務代理人、財務代理機関
(RUS) ФИСКАЛЬНОЕ ДЕЙСТВУЮЩЕЕ
ЛИЦО

fiscalist
(CHIN) 主张政府影响经济运行的经济学家
(FRE) fiscaliste
(GER) Fiskalist *m*, Finanzmensch *m*
(JAP) フィスカリスト、財政主義者
(RUS) ЭКОНОМИСТ, НАСТАИВАЮЩИЙ
НА РЕГУЛИРОВАНИИ ЭКОНОМИКИ
ПУТЁМ ИЗМЕНЕНИЯ НАЛОГОВ

fiscal policy
(CHIN) 财政政策
(FRE) politique budgétaire, (C) politique
fiscal
(GER) Fiskal- *f*, Steuer- *f*, Finanzpolitik *f*
(JAP) 財政政策
(RUS) ФИСКАЛЬНАЯ, НАЛОГОВО-
БЮДЖЕТНАЯ ПОЛИТИКА

fixation
(CHIN) 固定，决定
(FRE) fixation, (C) détermination
(GER) Fixierung *f*, Festsetzung *f*,
Festlegung *f*
(RUS) УСТАНОВЛЕНИЕ ЦЕНЫ ТОВАРА

fixed annuity
(CHIN) 固定年金
(FRE) rente fixe
(GER) feste Rentenzahlung *f*, feste
Annuität *f*
(JAP) 定額型年金
(RUS) ФИКСИРОВАННЫЙ АННУИТЕТ

fixed asset
(CHIN) 固定资产
(FRE) actif immobilisé,
(C) immobilisations, (C) actif immobilisé
corporel
(GER) Inventar *n*; Anlagevermögen *n*;
Anlagegut *n*, -gegenstand *m*,
Sachvermögen *n*, -anlage *f*
(JAP) 固定資産
(RUS) ОСНОВНОЙ ФОНД

fixed benefits
(CHIN) 固定福利
(FRE) prestation fixe, (C) prestations
déterminées

(GER) feste Leistungen *fpl*, festgelegte Nebenleistungen *fpl*
(JAP) 固定給付
(RUS) ФИКСИРОВАННЫЕ ЛЬГОТЫ

fixed charge
(CHIN) 固定费用，固定支出
(FRE) frais fixes, (C) charge fixe
(GER) Fest- *pl*, Fixkosten *pl*; feste, fixe Gebühr *f*
(JAP) 確定負債、固定担保
(RUS) ФИКСИРОВАННАЯ ОПЛАТА, СБОР

fixed-charge coverage
(CHIN) 固定费用负担保障
(FRE) couverture des frais fixes, (C) ratio de couverture des charges fixes
(GER) Fixkostendeckung *f*
(JAP) 固定担保補償(範囲)
(RUS) ОТНОШЕНИЕ ПРИБЫЛИ ДО ВЫПЛАТЫ ПРОЦЕНТОВ К ПРОЦЕНТАМ ПО ОБЛИГАЦИЯМ И ДРУГИМ ОЛГОСРОЧНЫМ ЗАДОЛЖЕННОСТЯМ

fixed cost
(CHIN) 固定成本
(FRE) coût fixe, coût constant, (C) frais fixes
(GER) Fix- *pl*, Festkosten *pl*
(JAP) 固定原価、固定費用
(RUS) ФИКСИРОВАННАЯ СТОИМОСТЬ

fixed fee
(CHIN) 固定收费
(FRE) droit fixe
(GER) feste Gebühr *f*
(JAP) 固定料金
(RUS) ФИКСИРОВАННЫЙ ГОНОРАР, СБОР

fixed income
(CHIN) 固定收入
(FRE) revenu fixe
(GER) festes Einkommen *n*; fester Ertrag *m* Rentenertrag *m*; festverzinslich *adj*
(JAP) 固定収入、定額所得
(RUS) ФИКСИРОВАННЫЙ ДОХОД

fixed income statement
(CHIN) 固定收入损益表
(FRE) état de revenus fixes

(GER) Auszug *m* über festverzinsliche Kapitalanlagen *fpl*
(JAP) 固定所得計算書
(RUS) ОТЧЕТ О ФИКСИРОВАННОМ ДОХОДЕ

fixed-point number
(CHIN) 定点数
(FRE) nombre à virgule fixe
(GER) Festkommazahl *f*
(JAP) 固定少数点数
(RUS) ЧИСЛО С «ФИКСИРОВАННОЙ» ЗАПЯТОЙ

fixed premium
(CHIN) 固定保费
(FRE) prime forfaitaire, (C) prime du change
(GER) Fest- *f*, Pauschalprämie *f*
(JAP) 固定保険料
(RUS) ФИКСИРОВАННАЯ СТРАХОВАЯ ПРЕМИЯ

fixed-price contract
(CHIN) 固定价格合同
(FRE) marché à prix ferme, (C) contrat à forfait
(GER) Festpreisvertrag *m*, -kontrakt *m*
(JAP) 固定価格契約
(RUS) ДОГОВОР (КОНТРАКТ) С ФИКСИРОВАННОЙ ЦЕНОЙ

fixed-rate loan
(CHIN) 固定利率贷款
(FRE) prêt à taux fixe
(GER) Festzinsdarlehen *n*, -kredit *m*, zinsgebundener Kredit *m*; festverzinsliche Anleihe *f*
(JAP) 固定金利融資
(RUS) ЗАЕМ (КРЕДИТ) ПОД ФИКСИРОВАННЫЕ ПРОЦЕНТЫ

fixture
(CHIN) 过时货，装置物
(FRE) immeuble par destination, (C) agencement
(GER) Inventarstück *n*, feste Anlage *f*, Einbauteil *n*
(JAP) 備品
(RUS) НЕОТДЕЛИМАЯ (без ущерба) ЧАСТЬ НЕДВИЖИМОСТИ

flanker brand

(CHIN) 延展品牌

(FRE) marque défensive

(GER) flankierende Marke *f*

(JAP) いんちきブランド、いんちき商標

(RUS) НОВАЯ ТОРГОВАЯ МАРКА
ПРОИЗВОДИТЕЛЯ, КОТОРЫЙ УЖЕ
ИМЕЕТ ТОВАРЫ В ДАННОЙ КАТЕГОРИИ

flash memory

(CHIN) 快速[闪]存储器

(FRE) mémoire flash

(GER) Flash-Kartenspeicher *m*

(JAP) フラッシュメモリー

(RUS) БЛИЦ-ПАМЯТЬ

flat

(CHIN) 半坦，平展的，恰好，价格平稳，
无息的

(FRE) fixe, sans intérêt, plat, sans position,
position d'équilibre, inchangé, (C) sans
intérêts courus

(GER) pauschal; flau, lustlos (Börse) *adj*

(JAP) (市場が)不振の、均一な

(RUS) ЕДИНООБРАЗНЫЙ,
ОКОНЧАТЕЛЬНЫЙ

flat rate

(CHIN) 统一费率，定额

(FRE) tarif fixe, (C) taux uniforme, taux
fixe

(GER) Pauschale *f*, Einheitstarif *m*, -satz *m*;
Pauschalsatz *m*, -preis *m*, Pauschal-,
Einheitsgebühr *f*; Grundgebühr *f*; Fest-,
Grundpreis *m*

(JAP) 均一料金、定率

(RUS) ЕДИНАЯ СТАВКА

flat scale

(CHIN) 统一工时费

(FRE) échelle uniforme, (C) échelle
salariale fixe

(GER) Pauschalskala *f*

(JAP) 定率

(RUS) ЕДИНАЯ ШКАЛА

flat tax

(CHIN) 单一税率

(FRE) taux uniforme dc l'impôt, impôt à
taux uniforme, (C) taxe uniforme

(GER) Einheitssteuer *f*, Pauschalsteuer *f*,
Steuerpauschalierung *f*

(JAP) 一律課税、均等税

(RUS) НАЛОГ ПО ЕДИНОЙ СТАВКЕ

flexible budget

(CHIN) 弹性预算

(FRE) budget variable, budget flexible

(GER) flexibles Budget *n*, elastischer
Etat *m*

(JAP) 弾力性予算、変動予算

(RUS) ГИБКИЙ БЮДЖЕТ

flexible-payment mortgage (FPM)

(CHIN) 弹性付款抵押贷款（FPM）

(FRE) emprunt immobilier à échéances
variables, (C) prêt hypothécaire à
versements flexibles

(GER) flexible Hypothek *f*

(JAP) 弾性支払住宅ローン変動支払住宅
ローン

(RUS) ИПОТЕКА С ГИБКОЙ СХЕМОЙ
ОПЛАТЫ

flextime

(CHIN) 弹性工作制

(FRE) horaires flexibles, horaires à la carte,
(C) horaire variable

(GER) Gleitzeit *f*; gleitende Arbeitszeit *f*

(JAP) フレックスタイム、
伸縮的労働時間

(RUS) ГИБКИЙ РАБОЧИЙ ДЕНЬ

flight to quality

(CHIN) 追求投资质量

(FRE) ruée vers les titres de qualité, (C)
mouvement des capitaux vers les titres de
grande qualité

(GER) Flucht *f* zu Qualität *f*, Flucht *f* in
sichere Werte *mpl* bzw. sichere Anlagen *fpl*

(JAP) （危険投資から）安全投資への資
金の流れ

(RUS) «БЕГСТВО В КАЧЕСТВО», Т.Е.
УТЕЧКА КАПИТАЛА В МЕНЕЕ
РИСКОВАННЫЕ ИНВЕСТИЦИИ

float

(CHIN) 浮动，发行，创立

(FRE) moyens de paiment en cours, fonds
en transit, lancer, emettre, flottant, (C) titre

de premier ordre, instrument à taux variable
(GER) Floaten *n*, Floating *n*; Inkassi *n*; Wertstellungsgewinn *m*; nicht plazierter Teil *m* einer Wertpapieremission *f*; im Einzug *m* befindliche Schecks *mpl*, schwebende Überweisungen *fpl*; Pufferzeit *f*; freigegebener Wechselkurs *m*
(JAP) 変動、変動相場制、浮動証券、起債する
(RUS) «ПЛАВАТЬ»; ВРЕМЯ МЕЖДУ ПРЕДЪЯВЛЕНИЕМ И ОПЛАТОЙ ЧЕКА (КЛИРИНГА)

floater
(CHIN) 证券保险
(FRE) garantie à tous endroits
(GER) Gründer *m* (einer Gesellschaft *f*); offene Police *f*, Abschreibepolice *f* (Versicherung); variabel verzinsliche Wertpapiere *fpl*; erstklassiges Inhaberpapier *n*
(JAP) (会社設立の)発起人、包括保険、浮動証券
(RUS) ОБЛИГАЦИЯ С ПЛАВАЮЩЕЙ СТАВКОЙ; ПОЛИС СТРАХОВАНИЯ ИМУЩЕСТВА, НАХОДЯЩЕГОСЯ В РАЗНЫХ МЕСТАХ

floating debt
(CHIN) 流动负债
(FRE) dette flottante, (C) passif à court terme
(GER) kurzfristige Verbindlichkeiten *fpl*, schwebende bzw. unfundierte Schuld(en) *f(pl)*
(JAP) 一時借入金、流動負債、変動負債
(RUS) «ПЛАВАЮЩИЙ» ДОЛГ

floating currency exchange rate
(CHIN) 浮动货币汇率
(FRE) taux de change flottant, (C) taux de change de monnaie flottante
(GER) gleitender Währungskurs *m*
(JAP) 浮動通貨交換レート
(RUS) ПЛАВАЮЩИЙ ВАЛЮТНЫЙ КУРС

floating exchange rate
(CHIN) 浮动汇率
(FRE) taux de change flottant

(GER) gleitender Wechsel- *m* bzw. Devisenkurs *m*
(JAP) 浮動為替相場(レート)
(RUS) ПЛАВАЮЩИЙ ОБМЕННЫЙ (ВАЛЮТНЫЙ) КУРС

floating-point number
(CHIN) 浮点数
(FRE) nombre à virgule flottante
(GER) Gleitkommazahl *f*, Fließkommazahl *f*
(JAP) 浮動小数点数
(RUS) ЧИСЛО С «ПЛАВАЮЩЕЙ» ЗАПЯТОЙ

floating-rate note
(CHIN) 浮动利率票据
(FRE) effet à taux flottant, (C) obligation à taux variable
(GER) variabel verzinsliche Anleihe *f*, Schuldverschreibung *f* mit schwankendem Zinssatz *m*
(JAP) 変動金利手形、変動利付債
(RUS) ОБЛИГАЦИЯ С ПЛАВАЮЩЕЙ СТАВКОЙ

floating securities
(CHIN) 浮动证券
(FRE) valeurs à revenu variable, titres à revenu variable, (C) titres flottants
(GER) Gesamtschuld *f*, auswechselbare (Kredit)sicherheit *f*
(JAP) 浮動証券
(RUS) ПЛАВАЮЩИЕ ЦЕННЫЕ БУМАГИ

floating supply
(CHIN) 流动供应
(FRE) flottant
(GER) Umlaufmaterial *n*, angebotenes Material *n* (Börse); laufendes Angebot *n*
(JAP) 短期在庫品、短期供給品
(RUS) ПЛАВАЮЩЕЕ ПРЕДЛОЖЕНИЕ

flood insurance
(CHIN) 水灾险
(FRE) assurance contre les inondations
(GER) Überschwemmungs- *f*, Hochwasserversicherung *f*
(JAP) 洪水保険
(RUS) СТРАХОВАНИЕ ОТ НАВОДНЕНИЙ

floor loan

(CHIN) 最低贷款额

(FRE) prêt minimum

(GER) Mindestdarlehen *n*

(JAP) 最低融資

(RUS) МИНИМАЛЬНАЯ СУММА КРЕДИТ

floor plan

(CHIN) 楼层布局

(FRE) plan, (C) financement des stocks,
(C) plan de boutique

(GER) Grundriss *m*; Raumaufteilungsplan
m; Finanzierung *f* eincs Warenlagers *n*

(JAP) 間取図、床配置図、見取り図、
平面図

(RUS) ПЛАН, ЧЕРТЁЖ ЭТАЖА

floor plan insurance

(CHIN) 铺面保险

(FRE) régime à seuil défini, (C) assurance
des stocks remis en nantissement de prêt

(GER) Versicherung *f* zur Finanzierung *f*
eines Warenlagers *n*

(JAP) 担保商品保険、
ディスプレイ用保険

(RUS) СТРАХОВАНИЕ ЗАЛОГА, КОГДА
ЗАЛОГОМ ЯВЛЯЕТСЯ ИМУЩЕСТВО,
РАЗМЕЩЁННОЕ НА ТОРГОВЫХ
ПЛОЩАДЯХ

flotation (floatation) cost

(CHIN) 发行成本

(FRE) frais d'émission

(GER) Begebungs- *pl*, Emissionskosten *pl*
eines Wertpapiers *n*;
Börseneinführungskosten *pl*

(JAP) 証券発行費用、設立費用

(RUS) СТОИМОСТЬ ВЫПУСКА НОВЫХ
АКЦИЙ, ОБЛИГАЦИЙ

flowchart

(CHIN) 流程图，程序表

(FRE) graphique d'évolution,
organigramme, (C) diagramme de flux,
(C) graphique d'acheminemcnt,
organigramme, (C) schéma de procédé

(GER) Flußdiagramm *n*

(JAP) フローチャート、生産工程一覧表、
業務運行表

(RUS) СХЕМА АЛГОРИТМА

flow of funds

(CHIN) 资金流量

(FRE) flux financier, mouvement de fonds,
(C) afflux de fonds, flux financiers

(GER) Geldstrom *m*, Kapitalfluss *m*

(JAP) 資金循環

(RUS) ПОТОК СРЕДСТВ

fluctuation

(CHIN) 变动，浮动，起伏

(FRE) fluctuation

(GER) Schwankung *f*, Fluktuation *f*,
Bewegung *f*, (Preis)ausschlag *m*

(JAP) 変動、騰落

(RUS) КОЛЕБАНИЕ; ФЛЮКТУАЦИЯ

fluctuation limit

(CHIN) 浮动限幅

(FRE) limite de fluctuation

(GER) Schwankungs- *f*,
Fluktuationsgrenze *f*

(JAP) 変動限界

(RUS) ПРЕДЕЛ КОЛЕБАНИЙ

flush (left/right)

(CHIN) (左/右边)排齐

(FRE) aligné (à gauche/à droite),
(C) justification à gauche/droite

(GER) (links-/rechts)bündig *adj*

(JAP) 左寄せ・左揃え、右寄せ・右揃え

(RUS) ВЫРАВНИВАНИЕ СТРОК;
РАЗМЕЩЕНИЕ ТЕКСТА ТАК, ЧТО ВСЕ
СТРОКИ (КРОМЕ ПЕРВЫХ СТРОК
АБЗАЦЕВ) ИМЕЮТ ОДИНАКОВУЮ
ДЛИНУ И НАЧИНАЮТСЯ НА ОДНОМ
УРОВНЕ С ПРАВОЙ ИЛИ С ЛЕВОЙ
СТОРОНЫ

follow-up letter

(CHIN) 后续营销信

(FRE) lettre de relance, (C) avis de relance

(GER) Nachfass- *m*, Folgebrief *m*,
Erinnerungsschreiben *n*

(JAP) 追いかけ状、続報

(RUS) НАПОМИНАЮЩЕЕ ПИСЬМО

font

(CHIN) 字型，字体，字模

(FRE) police, (C) police de caractères

(GER) Schriftart *f*

(JAP) フォント、字体
(RUS) ШРИФТ

footing
(CHIN) 总结，结算，英尺，合计
(FRE) addition, (C) situation
(GER) Kolonnenaddition *f*, Addieren *n*
einzelner Posten *mpl*; Grundlage *f*
(JAP) 立場、入会金、合計（額）
(RUS) ИТОГОВАЯ ЦИФРА В КОЛОНКЕ

footnote
(CHIN) 脚注
(FRE) note de bas de page, (C) note en bas
de page
(GER) Fußnote *f*
(JAP) 脚注
(RUS) ССЫЛКА

forced page break
(CHIN) 强制换页
(FRE) saut de page forcé
(GER) erzwungener Seitenumbruch *m*
(JAP) 強制的ページ区切り
(RUS) ВЫНУЖДЕННЫЙ РАЗДЕЛИТЕЛЬ
СТРАНИЦЫ

forced sale
(CHIN) 强制出售，迫卖
(FRE) vente forcée
(GER) Zwangsverwertung *f*, -verkauf *m*
(JAP) 公売、強制売却
(RUS) ВЫНУЖДЕННАЯ ПРОДАЖА

forced saving
(CHIN) 强制储蓄
(FRE) épargne forcée
(GER) Zwangssparen *n*
(JAP) 強制貯蓄
(RUS) ВЫНУЖДЕННЫЕ
СБЕРЕЖЕНИЯ

forecasting
(CHIN) 预测
(FRE) prévision, (C) prévisions financières
(GER) Prognosenstellung *f*,
Prognostizierung *f*, Voraussage *f*
(JAP) 予測、予想
(RUS) ПРОГНОЗИРОВАНИЕ;
ПРЕДСКАЗАНИЕ

foreclosure
(CHIN) 取消抵押品赎回权
(FRE) forclusion, (C) jugement
hypothécaire
(GER) Vollstreckung *f* aus einem
Grundpfandrecht *n*, Liegenschaftspfändung
f; Wettbewerbsausschluss *m* (Kartell);
Rechtsausschließung *f*, Präklusion *f*
(JAP) 抵当流れ、請戻権喪失
(RUS) ЛИШЕНИЕ ПРАВА ВЫКУПА
ЗАЛОЖЕННОГО ИМУЩЕСТВА

foreign corporation
(CHIN) 外国公司
(FRE) société établie dans un autre état,
(C) société étrangère
(GER) ausländische Gesellschaft *f*
(JAP) 外国企業
(RUS) ИНОСТРАННАЯ КОМПАНИЯ

foreign direct investment
(CHIN) 国外直接投资
(FRE) investissement (n, m) direct à
l'étranger, (C) investissement direct
étranger
(GER) ausländische Direktinvestition *f*,
Auslandsinvestition *f*
(JAP) 直接国外投資
(RUS) ПРЯМАЯ ЗАРУБЕЖНАЯ
ИНВЕСТИЦИЯ

foreign exchange
(CHIN) 外汇
(FRE) devises étrangères, (C) monnaie
étrangère, (C) devises, (C) opération de
change
(GER) Fremdwährung *f*, ausländische
Währung *f*, Devisen *pl*, Valuta *pl*;
Auslandsbörse *f*, Devisenmarkt *m*;
Sichtguthaben *npl* in inländischer Währung
f bei ausländischen Banken *fpl*
(JAP) 外国為替、外国為替取引
(RUS) ИНОСТРАННАЯ ВАЛЮТА

foreign income
(CHIN) 国外收入
(FRE) revenu de source étrangère,
(C) revenus de provenance étrangère
(GER) Einkünfte *fpl* aus dem Ausland *n*
(JAP) 外国所得
(RUS) ЗАРУБЕЖНЫЙ ДОХОД

foreign investment

(CHIN) 国外投资，外商投资
(FRE) investissement à l'étranger,
(C) investissement étranger
(GER) Auslandsinvestition f,
Auslandsanlage f
(JAP) 国外投資、海外投資
(RUS) ЗАРУБЕЖНАЯ
ИНВЕСТИЦИЯ

foreign trade zone

(CHIN) 外贸区
(FRE) zone de commerce extérieur,
(C) zone franche
(GER) Freihandelszone f
(JAP) 外国貿易地帯
(RUS) ЗАРУБЕЖНАЯ ТОРГОВАЯ
ЗОНА

forfeiture

(CHIN) 没收，罚款
(FRE) déchéance
(GER) Verwirkung f, Rechts- f,
Anspruchsverwirkung f
(JAP) (財産の)没収、失権、（契約の）
失効
(RUS) ПОТЕРЯ, УТРАТА, ЛИШЕНИЕ (прав,
имущества); ШТРАФ; КОНФИСКАЦИЯ

forgery

(CHIN) 伪造签字或文件
(FRE) faux (n, m) en écriture, falsification,
contrefaçon
(GER) Fälschung f; Falsifikat n
(JAP) 偽造、文書偽造、贋造、捏造、
改竄、偽造物
(RUS) ПОДДЕЛКА

format

(CHIN) 格式，格式化
(FRE) format
(GER) formaticren, aufbereiten v
(JAP) フォーマット、書式、形式
(RUS) ФОРМАТ

formula investing

(CHIN) 公式投资，方案投资
(FRE) formule forfaitaire de placement,
ordre de placement automatique,
(C) formule de placement

(GER) Kapitalanlage f mit festen
Mischungsverhältnis n von Aktien fpl und
fest verzinsten Wertpapieren npl
(JAP) フォーミュラ投資方法
(RUS) ИНВЕСТИРОВАНИЕ ПО
ФОРМУЛЕ

fortuitous loss

(CHIN) 意外损失
(FRE) perte fortuite
(GER) unvorhergesehener Verlust m,
Zufallsverlust m
(JAP) 偶然損失、偶発的損失
(RUS) СЛУЧАЙНЫЙ УЩЕРБ, ПОТЕРЯ

forward

(CHIN) 远期，期货
(FRE) faire suivre, (C) à terme, report
(GER) weiterbefördern, -leiten, vortragen v
(JAP) 先物の、前方の、先の、送る、
発送する
(RUS) ЭКСПЕДИРОВАТЬ; ПРЕДСТАВЛЯТЬ;
АВАНСИРОВАТЬ

forward contract

(CHIN) 期货合同，远期合同
(FRE) contrat à terme, (C) contrat à terme
de gré à gré
(GER) Terminkontrakt m, -abschluss m, -
geschäft n
(RUS) ФОРВАРДНЫЙ КОНТРАКТ

forwarding company

(CHIN) 转运公司
(FRE) entreprise de transport,
(C) groupeur
(GER) Speditions-, Transportgesellschaft f,
Frachtführer m
(JAP) 運送業者
(RUS) КОМПАНИЯ – ЭКСПЕДИТОР

forward integration

(CHIN) 远期合并
(FRE) intégration en aval, integration
descendante
(GER) Vorwärtsintegration f, vertikales
Betriebswachstum n
(JAP) 製品・サービスの拡張(統合)、
前向きの統合
(RUS) ФОРВАРДНАЯ ИНТЕГРАЦИЯ

161

forward pricing
(CHIN) 远期定价
(FRE) tarification à terme, (C) prix à terme
(GER) geplante Preisfestsetzung *f*;
Terminpreis *m*
(JAP) 先物価格付け
(RUS) ФОРВАРДНОЕ ЦЕНООБРАЗОВАНИЕ

forward stock
(CHIN) 待售商品，期货证券
(FRE) articles utilisés pour la mise en scène
des vitrines, (C) marchandise protégée
contre le vol
(GER) Lagervorrat *m* (in der
Verkaufsabteilung *f*)
(JAP) 先物株式
(RUS) ФОРВАРДНЫЕ АКЦИИ

for your information (FYI)
(CHIN) 仅供参考（FYI）
(FRE) pour information, pour votre
information
(GER) zur Kenntnisnahme *f*
(JAP) ご参考のため
(RUS) К ВАШЕМУ СВЕДЕНИЮ

foul bill of lading
(CHIN) 不洁提单
(FRE) connaissement avec réserve
(GER) unreines bzw. eingeschränktes
Konnossement *n*
(JAP) 故障付き船荷証券
(RUS) КОНОСАМЕНТ НА
ПОВРЕЖДЁННЫЙ ИЛИ
НЕДОПОСТАВЛЕННЫЙ
ТОВАР

401(k) plan
(CHIN) 401（K）方案
(FRE) plan 401 (k), (C) régime d'épargne
par réduction de salaire
(GER) 401 (K) Plan *m* (betrieblicher
steuerbegünstigter Rentenplan)
(JAP) 米国の企業年金制度
(RUS) СХЕМА ПЕНСИОННЫХ
СБЕРЕЖЕНИЙ 401(K)

fourth market
(CHIN) 第四市场
(FRE) quatrième marché

(GER) Markt *m* für nicht notierte
Wertpapiere *npl*; Interbankenmarkt *m* für
Wertpapiere *npl*
(JAP) 第四市場
(RUS) «ЧЕТВЕРТЫЙ» РЫНОК (прямая
торговля крупными партиями ценных
бумаг)

fractional share
(CHIN) 零星股份，
不足额股份
(FRE) fraction d'action
(GER) Bruchteilsaktie *f*, Teilaktie *f*,
gestückelte Aktie *f*
(JAP) 端株
(RUS) ЧАСТИЧНАЯ (ДРОБНАЯ) АКЦИЯ

frame rate
(CHIN) 帧速率
(FRE) fréquence de trame, (C) taux de
trame, (C) vitesse de défilement d'images
(GER) Bildwiederholrate *f*, -frequenz *f*
(JAP) フレームレート、フレーム率、
画面書換速度
(RUS) ЧАСТОТА КАДРОВ

franchise
(CHIN) 免赔额，特许证书，特许权，
选举权
(FRE) franchise
(GER) Konzession *f*,
Gründungsbescheinigung *f* einer AG;
Franchise *f*, Alleinvertretung *f*; Franchise-
Unternehmen *n*
(JAP) 営業特権、一手販売権、
フランチャイズ
(RUS) ФРАНШИЗА; ЛИЦЕНЗИЯ
ИНДИВИДУАЛЬНЫМ ЛИЦАМ НА
ЗАНЯТИЕ ЗАЛИЦЕНЗИРОВАННЫМ
ВИДОМ ДЕЯТЕЛЬНОСТИ ПО МЕТОДУ И
ПРИ ПОДДЕРЖКЕ ЛИЦЕНЗИРУЮЩЕЙ
КОМПАНИИ

franchise tax
(CHIN) 特许经营税，专卖税
(FRE) impôt de franchise,
(C) droit de monopole
(GER) Konzessionsabgabe *f*,
-steuer *f*
(JAP) 免許税、特許税
(RUS) ФРАНШИЗНЫЙ НАЛОГ

frank

(CHIN) 免费邮寄，邮资先付
(FRE) affranchissement, prépayé,
(C) exonération de frais de poste
(GER) Portofreiheit *f*, Franko- *m*,
Freivermerk *m*
(JAP) 率直な、無料配達郵便物
(RUS) ФРАНКИРОВАТЬ
ПИСЬМО

fraud

(CHIN) 欺骗，欺诈
(FRE) fraude, escroquerie
(GER) Betrug *m*, Schwindel *m*;
Irreführung *f*
(JAP) 詐欺、不正行為
(RUS) МОШЕННИЧЕСТВО; ОБМАН

fraudulent misrepresentation

(CHIN) 虚假的陈述
(FRE) assertion inexacte et frauduleuse,
(C) fausse déclaration intentionnelle
(GER) wissentlich falsche Darstellung *f*,
Vorspiegelung *f* falscher Tatsachen *fpl*,
arglistige Täuschung *f*
(JAP) 詐欺的不実表示
(RUS) МОШЕННИЧЕСКОЕ ВВЕДЕНИЕ В
ЗАБЛУЖДЕНИЕ

free alongside ship (FAS)

(CHIN) 船边交货价，靠船价
(FRE) franco à quai, (C) franco le long du
bateau
(GER) frei längsseits *adj* Schiff im
Abgangshafen
(JAP) 船側渡し
(RUS) «ФРАНКО ВДОЛЬ СУДНА»

free and clear

(CHIN) 自由处理
(FRE) libre de toute süretésans hypothèque,
(C) quitte et libre
(GER) schuldenfrei, frei und unbelastet *adj*
(JAP) (不動産が)抵当に入っていない、
留置権がつけられていない
(RUS) ТИТУЛ НА СОБСТВЕННОСТЬ БЕЗ
ОБЯЗАТЕЛЬСТВ

free and open market

(CHIN) 自由开放市场

(FRE) marché libre, (C) marche libre et
sans restriction de territoire

(GER) freier und offener Markt *m*,
Wettbewerbsmarkt *m*
(JAP) 自由開放市場
(RUS) СВОБОДНЫЙ И ОТКРЫТЫЙ
РЫНОК

free enterprise

(CHIN) 自由企业
(FRE) libre entreprise
(GER) freie Marktwirtschaft *f*,
Unternehmerfreiheit *f*
(JAP) 自由企業、自由企業体制
(RUS) СВОБОДНОЕ
ПРЕДПРИНИМАТЕЛЬСТВО

freehold (estate)

(CHIN) （地产）自由保有权
(FRE) propriété (n, f) foncière perpétuelle et
libre, (C) franc-fief, (C) tenure franche
(GER) Allod *n*; Eigenland *n*,
(Grund)eigentum *n*
(JAP) 自由保有権、自由保有不動産
(RUS) БЕЗУСЛОВНОЕ ПРАВО НА
НЕДВИЖИМОСТЬ

free market

(CHIN) 自由市场
(FRE) marché libre
(GER) freier und offener Markt *m*, freie
Marktwirtschaft *f*
(JAP) 自由市場、実勢市場
(RUS) СВОБОДНЫЙ РЫНОК

free on board (FOB)

(CHIN) 离岸价格（FOB）
(FRE) franco à bord
(GER) frei an Bord (fob), frei Schiff im
Abgangshafen *adj*
(JAP) 本船渡し
(RUS) Ф.О.Б. – ФРАНКО – БОРТ

free port

(CHIN) 自由港，免税港
(FRE) port franc
(GER) freier Hafen *m*, Freihafen *m*
(JAP) 自由港
(RUS) ФРАНКО-ПОРТ

freight insurance
(CHIN) 运费保险
(FRE) assurance du fret
(GER) Fracht- *f*,
Gütertransportversicherung *f*
(JAP) 運賃保険
(RUS) СТРАХОВАНИЕ
ГРУЗА

frequency
(CHIN) 次数，频率，频数，
广告频率
(FRE) fréquence
(GER) Häufigkeit *f*
(JAP) 頻度、度数
(RUS) ЧАСТОТА

frictional unemployment
(CHIN) 短期失业
(FRE) chômage frictionnel, chômage de
mobilité
(GER) Fluktuationsarbeitslosigkeit *f*
(JAP) 摩擦的失業
(RUS) ЧАСТИЧНАЯ БЕЗРАБОТИЦА

friendly suit
(CHIN) 友好诉讼
(FRE) transaction amiable, (C) poursuite à
l'amiable
(GER) Klage *f* ohne feindliche Absicht *f*;
Klage *f* zur Regulierung *f* oder
Feststellung *f*
(JAP) 友誼的訴訟
(RUS) «ДРУЖЕСКИЙ ИСК» (по соглашению
сторон)

frontage
(CHIN) 前面或正面的长度
(FRE) devanture
(GER) Anlieger *m*, Angrenzer *m*;
Straßenfront *f*, Frontlänge *f*
(JAP) （建物・地所の）正面（幅）、
向き、臨界地、隣接地
(RUS) УЧАСТОК С ГРАНИЦЕЙ ПО РЕКЕ,
ДОРОГЕ

front-end load
(CHIN) 前端负载
(FRE) droit d'entrée, commission d'entrée,
(C) frais prélevés à l'acquisition

(GER) hohe Anfangskosten *pl*, hohe
Anfangsbelastung *f*; Eintrittsgebühr *f*
(Börse)
(JAP) 先取り手数料、当初販売手数料
(RUS) РАЗОВЫЙ КОМИССИОННЫЙ СБОР

front foot
(CHIN) 前面长度
(FRE) longueur de la façade, (C) pied avant
(GER) Straßenfrontlänge, -breite *f*
(JAP) 間口幅
(RUS) ИЗМЕРЕНИЕ ДЛЯ ОЦЕНКИ ЗАТРАТ
НА БЛАГОУСТРОЙСТВО

front money
(CHIN) 预付定金
(FRE) capital initial, capital de départ,
(C) capitaux de lancement
(GER) Anfangskapital *n*
(JAP) 仲買人への前払い金、前貸し金
(RUS) ДЕНЬГИ, НЕОБХОДИМЫЕ ДЛЯ
НАЧАЛА ПРЕДПРИЯТИЯ

front office
(CHIN) 董事会，理事会，全体决策人员
(FRE) front-office, (C) salle des marchés
(GER) Rezeption *f*, Vorzimmer *n*;
Börsenraum *m*, Front Office *n*
(JAP) 本部、総務室
(RUS) СОВОКУПНОСТЬ ОФФИСОВ
РУКОВОДСТВА КОМПАНИИ

frozen account
(CHIN) 冻结账户
(FRE) compte gelé
(GER) eingefrorenes Konto *n*, Sperrkonto *n*
(JAP) 凍結勘定
(RUS) ЗАМОРОЖЕННЫЙ СЧЕТ

F statistic
(CHIN) F 值统计
(FRE) statistisque *F*, (C) loi
(GER) *F*-Statistik *f*
(JAP) Ｆ－統計
(RUS) СТАТИСТИКА F

fulfillment
(CHIN) 履行，完成
(FRE) exécution, (C) gestion optimale des
commandes

(GER) Erfüllung *f*, Ausführung *f*,
Vollziehung *f*, Durchführung *f*
(JAP) 履行、実現
(RUS) ВЫПОЛНЕНИЕ; ИСПОЛНЕНИЕ

full coverage
(CHIN) 完全承保，全面保险
(FRE) couverture totale
(GER) volle Deckung *f*, volle
Risikoübernahme *f*
(JAP) 完全適用範囲
(RUS) ПОЛНОЕ ПОКРЫТИЕ

full disclosure
(CHIN) 财务公开
(FRE) révélation totale d'une information,
(C) principe de bonne information, (C)
exposé complet
(GER) vollständige Offenlegung *f*
(JAP) 完全開示
(RUS) ПОЛНОЕ РАЗГЛАШЕНИЕ,
ПРЕДОСТАВЛЕНИЕ СВЕДЕНИЙ

full faith and credit
(CHIN) 市政信用
(FRE) foi et crédit attaché aux actes publics,
aux registres et procédures judiciaires
émanant de chaque autre état, (C) pleine foi
(GER) (gegenseitige Anerkennung von
Gesetzen und Gerichtsentscheidungen
zwischen den US-Gliedstaaten)
(JAP) 全面的信用と信頼
(RUS) ОБЕСПЕЧЕНИЕ
ГОСУДАРСТВЕННЫХ ИЛИ
МУНИЦИПАЛЬНЫХ ОБЛИГАЦИЙ ВСЕМИ
ДОХОДАМИ И ЗАЙМАМИ ЭМИТЕНТА

full screen display
(CHIN) 全屏幕显示
(FRE) affichage plein écran
(GER) Vollbildschirmanzeige
(JAP) 全画面表示、全画面ディスプレイ
(RUS) ПОЛНОЭКРАННЫЙ ПРОСМОТР,
ПОКАЗ

full-service broker
(CHIN) 全面服务经纪人
(FRE) courtier traditionnel, (C) courtier à
services complets
(GER) Universalbroker *m*

(JAP) 完全サービス提供ブローカー
(RUS) БРОКЕР ПОЛНОГО ДИАПАЗОНА
УСЛУГ

**fully diluted earnings per (common)
share**
(CHIN) 全面冲淡每（普通）股赢利
(FRE) bénéfice par action entièrement dilué,
(C) bénéfice dilué par action (ordinaire)
(GER) Gewinn *m* je (Stamm)aktie *f* unter
Berücksichtigung *f* möglicher
Wandelrechte *npl*
(JAP) (普通株)1 株当たり完全稀釈収益
(RUS) ПРИБЫЛЬ КОМПАНИИ НА ОДНУ
АКЦИЮ (исчисляемая на все уже
существующие и планируемые акции)

fully paid policy
(CHIN) 完全付清保单
(FRE) police entièrement payée, (C) police
acquittée
(GER) vollständig eingezahlte Police *f*
(JAP) 全額払込保険
(RUS) ПОЛНОСТЬЮ ОПЛАЧЕННЫЙ
ПОЛИС

functional authority
(CHIN) 职能权力
(FRE) autorité fonctionnelle, pouvoir
fonctionnel
(GER) funktionelle Autorität *f* bzw.
Weisungsrecht *n*
(JAP) 職能権限
(RUS) ФУНКЦИОНАЛЬНЫЕ
ПОЛНОМОЧИЯ

functional currency
(CHIN) 功能性货币
(FRE) devise fonctionnelle, (C) monnaie
fonctionnelle
(GER) wirtschaftlich maßgebende Währung
f; gesetzliches Zahlungsmittel *n*
(JAP) 機能通貨
(RUS) ФУНКЦИОНАЛЬНАЯ ВАЛЮТА

functional obsolescence
(CHIN) 功能性萎缩
(FRE) obsolescence fonctionnelle, vétusté
fonctionnelle
(GER) funktionelles Veralten *n*; technisch-
wirtschaftliche Veraltung *f*

(JAP) 機能的陳腐化
(RUS) ФУНКЦИОНАЛЬНОЕ УСТАРЕНИЕ

fuctional organization
(CHIN) 职能部门
(FRE) organisation fonctionnelle,
organisation horizontale
(GER) funktionelle Organisation *f*
(JAP) 職能組織、機能組織
(RUS) ФУНКЦИОНАЛЬНАЯ
ОРГАНИЗАЦИЯ

function key
(CHIN) 功能键
(FRE) touche de fonction, (C) touche
fonction
(GER) Funktionstaste *f*
(JAP) 機能キー、ファンクションキー
(RUS) ФУНКЦИОНАЛЬНАЯ КЛАВИША

fund accounting
(CHIN) 基金会计
(FRE) valorisation de fonds,
(C) comptabilité par fonds
(GER) Fund Accounting *n*,
Rechenschaftslegung *f* über
zweckgebundene Mittel *npl*
(JAP) 資金会計
(RUS) СИСТЕМА УЧЁТА
НЕКОММЕРЧЕСКИХ ОРГАНИЗАЦИЙ

fundamental analysis
(CHIN) 基本分析
(FRE) analyse fondamentale
(GER) Fundamentalanalyse *f*;
Grundanalyse *f*
(JAP) 基礎分析
(RUS) БАЗОВЫЙ АНАЛИЗ

funded debt
(CHIN) 长期债务
(FRE) dette consolidée, (C) dette à long
terme
(GER) finanzierte Schuld(en) *f(pl)*;
konsolidierte Kredite *mpl*; langfristige
Kredite *mpl*; Anleiheschuld *f*, langfristige
Staatsanleihe *f*
(JAP) 長期借入金、長期債務
(RUS) КОНСОЛИДИРОВАННЫЙ
ДОЛГ

funded pension plan
(CHIN) 设有基金的退休计划
(FRE) plan de retraite par capitalisation, (C)
régime de retraite par capitalisation
(GER) über Fondseinzahlungen *fpl*
gedeckte Pensionskasse *f*; kapitalgedecktes
Altersversorgunssystem *n*
(JAP) 長期年金制
(RUS) ОБЕСПЕЧЕННАЯ ПЕНСИОННАЯ
ПРОГРАММА

funding
(CHIN) 筹集资金，债务转期
(FRE) financement constitution d'un fonds
capitalisation, (C) refinancement d'une
dette
(GER) Finanzierung *f*, Ausstattung *f* mit
Mitteln *npl*, Finanzausstattung *f*
(JAP) 長期公債投資、基金繰り入れ、資
金操作
(RUS) ФИНАНСИРОВАНИЕ; ВЫДЕЛЕНИЕ
СРЕДСТВ

fund-raising
(CHIN) 资金筹措
(FRE) collecte de fonds, (C) campagne de
financement
(GER) Geld- *f*, Mittelbeschaffung *f*
(JAP) 資金調達
(RUS) СБОР СРЕДСТВ

furlough
(CHIN) 休假
(FRE) absence autorisée par l'employeur,
congé, (C) accorder un congé
(GER) Beurlaubung *f*; Urlaubsschein *m*
(JAP) 賜暇、休暇
(RUS) ОТПУСК; УВОЛЬНЕНИЕ (армия)

future interest
(CHIN) 将来利息
(FRE) droits futurs, intérêts à terme,
(C) droit différé
(GER) zukünftiger Anspruch *m*,
Anwartschaft *f*
(JAP) 将来権
(RUS) ФЬЮЧЕРСКАЯ СТАВКА ПРОЦЕНТА

futures contract
(CHIN) 期货合同

(FRE) contrat à terme, (C) contrat à terme normalisé, (C) marché de contrats à terme
(GER) Terminkontrakt *m*, -geschäft *n*, -vertrag *m*
(JAP) 先物取引(契約)
(RUS) КОНТРАКТ С ФЬЮЧЕРСАМИ

futures market
(CHIN) 期货市场
(FRE) marché à terme
(GER) Termin(kontrakt)markt *m*, Markt *m* für Termingeschäfte *npl*; Terminbörse *f*
(JAP) 先物市場
(RUS) ФЬЮЧЕРСКИЙ РЫНОК

G

gain
(CHIN) 收益，利益，利润，增加
(FRE) plus-value, (C) bénéfice, (C) profit, (C) gain
(GER) Wertzuwachs *m*, -steigerung *f*; Ertrag *m*, Gewinn *m*; Kursgewinn *m*; Vorteil *m*, Nutzen *m*
(JAP) 所得、利益
(RUS) ПРИБЫЛЬ; ПОВЫШЕНИЕ ЦЕНЫ, ВАЛЮТНОГО КУРСА

gain contingency
(CHIN) 收益可能性
(FRE) profit éventuel
(GER) Eventualgewinn *m*
(JAP) 利益の偶発性
(RUS) ВОЗМОЖНОСТЬ БЛАГОПРИЯТНОГО, ПРИБЫЛЬНОГО ИСХОДА

galloping inflation
(CHIN) 急剧的通货膨胀
(FRE) inflation galopante
(GER) galoppierende Inflation *f*
(JAP) 急進のインフレ
(RUS) ГАЛОПИРУЮЩАЯ ИНФЛЯЦИЯ

game card
(CHIN) 游戏卡
(FRE) carte de jeu
(GER) Spiele-Steckkarte *f*
(JAP) ゲームカード
(RUS) КАРТА ЗАГРУЗКИ ИГРЫ

gaming
(CHIN) 博弈，赌博
(FRE) jeu d'argent, (C) jeu
(GER) Glücksspiel *n*
(JAP) 賭博、ギャンブル、賭け
(RUS) ТЕОРИЯ ДЕЛОВЫХ ИГР

gap
(CHIN) 亏空，不足，短缺
(FRE) écart
(GER) Lücke *f*, Diskrepanz *f*; Wartezeit *f* (Versicherung)
(JAP) ギャップ、ずれ、格差、欠陥、間隙
(RUS) ПРОБЕЛ; РАЗРЫВ

gap loan
(CHIN) 缺口资金贷款
(FRE) prêt complémentaire, (C) crédit d'anticipation
(GER) Überbrückungsdarlehen *n*, -kredit *m*
(JAP) ギャップローン
(RUS) КРЕДИТ НА ПОКРЫТИЕ НЕХВАТКИ ФИНАНСОВЫХ РЕСУРСОВ

garnish
(CHIN) 装饰，修饰，扣押
(FRE) faire pratiquer une saisie-arrêt, (C) pratiquer une saisie-arrêt
(GER) Drittschuldnerpfändung *f* vornehmen lassen; pfänden; vorladen *v*
(JAP) 差押える
(RUS) ВРУЧИТЬ ТРЕТЬЕМУ ЛИЦУ ПРИКАЗ СУДА О НАЛОЖЕНИИ АРЕСТА НА ИМЕЮЩЕЕСЯ У НЕГО ИМУЩЕСТВО ДОЛЖНИКА

garnishee
(CHIN) 第三债务人，传讯，扣押
(FRE) tiers saisi
(GER) Pfändungsschuldner *m*, Drittschuldner *m*; Vorgeladener *m*
(JAP) 第三債務者
(RUS) ЛИЦО, КОТОРОМУ ВРУЧАЕТСЯ ПРИКАЗ СУДА

garnishment
(CHIN) 扣押被告财产的通知，扣押令
(FRE) saisie-arrêt
(GER) Pfändung *f* eines Drittschuldners *m*; Forderungspfändung *f*, Zahlungsverbot *n* an Drittschuldner *m*, Beschlagnahme *f* einer Forde rung *f*; Pfändungs- und Überweisungsbeschluss *m*; gerichtliche Vorladung *f*
(JAP) 債権差押え、差押え通知
(RUS) НАЛОЖЕНИЕ АРЕСТА НА ИМУЩЕСТВО ТРЕТЬЕГО ЛИЦА

gender analysis
(CHIN) 性别分析
(FRE) présentation des données en fonction du sexe
(GER) geschlechtsspezifische Analyse *f*
(JAP) 性別分析
(RUS) АНАЛИЗ ПО ПОЛОВОМУ ПРИЗНАКУ

general contractor
(CHIN) 总合同
(FRE) entreprise générale, entrepreneur général, (C) maître d'œuvre, (C) maître des travaux
(GER) Generalunternehmer *m*
(JAP) 一般請負人
(RUS) ГЕНЕРАЛЬНЫЙ ПОДРЯДЧИК

general equilibrium analysis
(CHIN) 一般均衡分析
(FRE) analyse de l'équilibre général
(GER) allgemeine Gleichgewichtsanalyse *f*
(JAP) 一般均衡分析
(RUS) АНАЛИЗ ОБЩЕГО РАВНОВЕСИЯ

general expense
(CHIN) 一般费用，日用开支，杂费
(FRE) frais général
(GER) General- *pl*, Allgemeinkosten *pl*, allgemeine Unkosten *pl*
(JAP) 一般営業費、一般経費
(RUS) ОБЩИЕ РАСХОДЫ

general fund
(CHIN) 普通基金
(FRE) caisse générale, (C) fonds d'administration générale
(GER) allgemeine Rücklage *f*; allgemeine Kasse *f*, öffentliches Vermögen *n*, allgemeine Etatmittel *npl*
(JAP) 一般資金、一般財源
(RUS) НЕЦЕЛЕВОЙ ФОНД ФОНД НА РАЗНЫЕ РАСХОДЫ

generalist
(CHIN) 多面手，通才
(FRE) généraliste
(GER) Generalist *m*
(JAP) 一般職、ゼネラリスト
(RUS) СПЕЦИАЛИСТ ШИРОКОГО ПРОФИЛЯ; ЧЕЛОВЕК С ШИРОКИМ КРУГОМ ИНТЕРЕСОВ

general journal
(CHIN) 普通日记账，普通分录账
(FRE) journal général
(GER) Sammeljournal *n*
(JAP) 一般仕訳帳
(RUS) ОБЩАЯ КНИГА ЗАПИСЕЙ

general ledger
(CHIN) 总分类账
(FRE) grand livre, (C) grand livre général
(GER) Hauptbuch *n*
(JAP) 総勘定元帳、一般元帳
(RUS) ОСНОВНАЯ БУХГАЛТЕРСКАЯ КНИГА КОМПАНИИ

general liability insurance
(CHIN) 一般责任险
(FRE) assurance responsabilité civile
(GER) allgemeine Haftpflichtversicherung *f*
(JAP) 総合賠償責任保険
(RUS) ГЕНЕРАЛЬНОЕ СТРАХОВАНИЕ ОТВЕТСТВЕННОСТИ

general lien
(CHIN) 一般留置权
(FRE) privilège général
(GER) allgemeines Zurückbehaltungsrecht *n* bzw. Pfandrecht *n*
(JAP) (不動産を除く)すべての物品に対する先取り特権
(RUS) ОБЩЕЕ ПРАВО УДЕРЖАНИЯ

generally accepted accounting principles
(CHIN) 公认会计原则
(FRE) principes comptables généralement employés, (C) principes comptables généralement reconnus
(GER) allgemein annerkannte Grundsätze *mpl* ordnungsgemäßer Rechnungslegung *f*
(JAP) 一般に受け入れられている会計原則
(RUS) ОБЩЕПРИНЯТЫЕ ПРАВИЛА БУХГАЛТЕРСКОГО УЧЕТА

general obligation bond
(CHIN) 普通责任债务
(FRE) emprunt de collectivité locale
(GER) Kommunalobligation *f*

(JAP) 一般財源債、一般公債
(RUS) ОБЛИГАЦИИ С БЕЗУСЛОВНОЙ
ГАРАНТИЕЙ

general partner
(CHIN) 普通合伙人
(FRE) associé, (C) associé gérant
(GER) Vollhafter *m*; Komplementär *m*;
unbeschränkt haftender bzw. persönlich
haftender Gesellschafter *m*
(JAP) 無限責任社員、一般社員
(RUS) ПОЛНЫЙ ПАРТНЕР

general revenue
(CHIN) 一般收入
(FRE) recettes fiscales générales,
(C) revenus généraux
(GER) allgemeine Steuermittel *npl*
(RUS) ОБЩИЕ ДОХОДЫ

general revenue sharing
(CHIN) 一般收入分享
(FRE) partage des recettes fiscales
générales, (C) partage des revenus
généraux
(GER) (vertikaler) Steuer- *m*,
Finanzausgleich *m*
(JAP) (JAP) 一般交付金、一般目的財務
補助制度
(RUS) РАЗДЕЛЕНИЕ ОБЩИХ ДОХОДОВ

general scheme
(CHIN) 一般投递流程
(FRE) régime général, (C) projet général
(GER) allgemeines System *n*, allgemeine
Regelung *f*, allgemeiner Aufbau *m*
(JAP) 一般的構想
(RUS) ОБЩАЯ СХЕМА ДОСТАВКИ
ПОЧТЫ В МЕСТНЫЕ ПОЧТОВЫЕ
ОТДЕЛЕНИЯ

general strike
(CHIN) 总罢工
(FRE) grève générale
(GER) Generalstreik *m*
(JAP) ゼネスト、総同盟罷業
(RUS) ВСЕОБЩАЯ ЗАБАСТОВКА

general warranty deed
(CHIN) 全面保证书

(FRE) acte de transfert avec clause de
garantie, (C) acte de garantie générale
(GER) allgemeine
Grundstücksübertragungsurkunde *f*
(JAP) 無債権土地譲渡証書、全般的瑕疵
担保証書
(RUS) ДОКУМЕНТ ОБ ОБЩЕЙ ГАРАНТИИ

generation-skipping transfer
(CHIN) 隔代财产转移
(FRE) don ou mutation sautant une ou
plusieurs generations, (C) transfert sautant
une génération
(GER) generationsüberspringende
(Eigentums)übertragung *f*
(JAP) 世代を飛び越えた譲渡
(RUS) ПЕРЕДАЧА «С ПРОПУСКОМ
ПОКОЛЕНИЯ»

generic appeal
(CHIN) 泛指广告
(FRE) communication collective, (C) attrait
générique
(GER) generische bzw. gattungspezifische
Anziehungskraft *f*
(JAP) (一般的な商品としての魅力)
(RUS) ОБОБЩЕННАЯ АПЕЛЛЯЦИЯ,
ПРОТЕСТ

generic bond
(CHIN) 一般债券
(FRE) obligation générique
(GER) generische Schuldverschreibung *f*,
Gattungsobligation *f*
(JAP) 一般債券
(RUS) ОБЩАЯ ОБЛИГАЦИЯ

generic market
(CHIN) 广泛市场
(FRE) marché générique
(GER) generischer Markt *m*
(JAP) 一般市場
(RUS) ШИРОКАЯ ГРУППА
ПОТРЕБИТЕЛЕЙ СО СХОЖИМИ
НУЖДАМИ; РАЗЛИЧНЫЕ
ПРОИЗВОДИТЕЛИ, УДОВЛЕТВОРЯЮЩИЕ
ЭТИ НУЖДЫ

gentrification
(CHIN) 住宅区阶层上移
(FRE) gentrification,

(C) embourgeoisement
(GER) Gentrifizierung *f*, Sozialsanierung *f* eines Stadtteils *m*
(JAP) (スラムなどの) 高級化
(RUS) ПОВЫШЕНИЕ СТАТУСА; «ОБЛАГОРАЖИВАНИЕ»

geodemography
(CHIN) 地域人口统计学
(FRE) géodémographie, (C) géo-démographie
(GER) Geodemographie *f*
(JAP) 地球人口統計学
(RUS) ГЕОДЕМОГРАФИЯ

gift
(CHIN) 礼品，赠品，授予权，赠送
(FRE) don, donation
(GER) Schenkung *f*, Zuwendung *f*, Spende *f*
(JAP) 贈与
(RUS) ПОДАРОК; ДАРЕНИЕ

gift deed
(CHIN) 赠与行为
(FRE) acte de donation entre vifs, (C) acte de don
(GER) Schenkungsurkunde *f*
(JAP) 贈与証書
(RUS) ДАРСТВЕННЫЙ ДОКУМЕНТ

gift tax
(CHIN) 赠与税
(FRE) impôt sur les donations, droit sur les donations, droit de mutation à titre gratuit, (C) impôt sur les dons
(JAP) 贈与税
(RUS) НАЛОГ НА ДАРЕНИЯ

girth
(CHIN) 横梁
(FRE) circonférence, largeur
(GER) Umfang *m*
(JAP) 周囲の寸法、太さ、胴回り
(RUS) ОБХВАТ, РАЗМЕР ПОДПРУГА

glamor stock
(CHIN) 热门股票
(FRE) valeur vedette
(GER) stark gefragte Aktie *f* spekulativen Charakters *m*, Börsenliebling *m*

(JAP) 花形株、投資家魅了株
(RUS) ПРИВЛЕКАТЕЛЬНЫЕ РОСТОМ ДОХОДНОСТИ И Т. П. АКЦИИ

glut
(CHIN) 供过于求
(FRE) encombrement, surabondance, (C) goulot d'étranglement, (C) encombrement du marché
(GER) Schwemme *f*, Überhang *m*
(JAP) 過多、供給過剰、過剰生産
(RUS) ПЕРЕНАСЫЩЕНИЕ РЫНКА

goal
(CHIN) 终点，目标，标的
(FRE) objectif, (C) but
(GER) Ziel *n*, Zielpunkt *m*, -stellung, -setzung *f*
(JAP) 目標、目的
(RUS) ЦЕЛЬ; ЗАДАЧА

goal congruence
(CHIN) 目标一致性
(FRE) congruence des objectifs
(GER) Zielübereinstimmung *f*, -kongruenz *f*
(JAP) 目標一致
(RUS) СОВМЕСТИМОСТЬ ЗАДАЧ

goal programming
(CHIN) 目标规划
(FRE) programmation des objectifs, (C) programmation des efforts
(GER) Zielprogrammierung *f*
(JAP) 目標の計画
(RUS) ФОРМА ЛИНЕЙНОГО ПРОГРАММИРОВАНИЯ, ПОЗВОЛЯЮЩАЯ УЧИТЫВАТЬ ДОСТИЖЕНИЕ МНОГИХ, ЧАСТО КОНФЛИКТУЮЩИХ, ЦЕЛЕЙ

goal setting
(CHIN) 目标设定
définition des objectifs, détermination des objectifs, établissement des objectifs
(GER) Zielsetzung *f*
(JAP) 目標設定
(RUS) ПОСТАНОВКА ЗАДАЧИ

go-between
(CHIN) 中间人，经纪人
(FRE) intermédiaire

(GER) Mittelsmann *m*, Zwischenträger *m*, Unterhändler *m*, Vermittler *m*, Verbindungsmann *m*; Mittler *m*, Schlichter *m*

(JAP) 仲介者、媒介者

(RUS) ПОСРЕДНИК

going-concern value

(CHIN) 继续经营条款

(FRE) valeur de la continuité de l'exploitation, (C) valeur d'exploitation

(GER) aktueller Unternehmenswert *m*

(RUS) СТОИМОСТЬ КОМПАНИИ КАК ДЕЙСТВУЮЩЕГО ПРЕДПРИЯТИЯ (АКТИВЫ ПЛЮС ДЕНЕЖНАЯ ОЦЕНКА ПРЕСТИЖА)

going long

(CHIN) 买空

(FRE) prendre une position longue, (C) achat spéculatif

(GER) Long-Position *f* einnehmen *v* (Börse), Erwerb *m* von Wertpapieren *npl* bzw. Terminkontrakten *mpl*, Haussespekulation *f*

(JAP) 見込み買い、思惑買い

(RUS) ПОКУПКА ЦЕННЫХ БУМАГ ИЛИ ТОВАРОВ СО СПЕКУЛЯЦИОННЫМИ ИЛИ ИНВЕСТИЦИОННЫМИ ЦЕЛЯМИ; СОЗДАНИЕ ДЛИННОЙ ПОЗИЦИИ

going private

(CHIN) 私人投资，不公开买卖

(FRE) privatisation, (C) rachat privé

(GER) Aktien *fpl* vom Publikum *n* zurückkaufen *v*

(JAP) 株式非公開化

(RUS) ПРЕВРАЩЕНИЕ ПУБЛИЧНОЙ КОМПАНИИ В ЧАСТНУЮ

going public

(CHIN) 公众投资，公开买卖

(FRE) nationalisation, (C) émission publique d'actions

(GER) Gang *m* an die Börse *f*, (Unternehmen in) Publikumsgesellschaft *f* umwandeln *v*

(JAP) 株式公開化

(RUS) ПРЕВРАЩЕНИЕ ЧАСТНОЙ КОМПАНИИ В ПУБЛИЧНУЮ

going short

(CHIN) 卖空

(FRE) prendre une position courte, (C) vente à découvert

(GER) Baissespekulation *f*; Baisseposition *f* einnehmen, Leerverkauf *m*, Wertpapiere *npl*/Terminkontrakte *mpl* leerverkaufen (Börse)

(JAP) 思惑売り

(RUS) ПРОДАЖА АЦЦИЙ ИЛИ ТОВАРОВ, КОТОРЫХ НЕТ У ПРОДАВЦА; СОЗДАНИЕ КОРОТКОЙ ПОЗИЦИИ

goldbrick

(CHIN) 假金砖，赝品，假货

(FRE) flâner, (C) attrape-nigaud

(GER) wertlose Wertpapiere *npl*, zweifelhafte Spekulation *f*

(JAP) 見かけ倒しの、にせ物

(RUS) ПРЕНЕБРЕГАТЬ СВОИМИ ПОРУЧЕНИЯМИ

goldbug

(CHIN) 臭财主，主张金本位者

(FRE) analyste spécialisé dans les valeurs aurifères, (C) amateur d'or

(GER) Befürworter *m* der Goldwährung *f*, Verfechter *m* des Goldstandards *n*

(JAP) 金本位制支持者、黄金狂

(RUS) АНАЛИТИК , ПРЕДПОЧИТАЮЩИЙ ВЛОЖЕНИЕ СРЕДСТВ В ЗОЛОТА

golden handcuffs

(CHIN) 以公司股票吸引主要员工的方法

(FRE) primes (versées à intervalles réguliers à un cadre pour le dissuader de partir), (C) cage dorée

(GER) goldene Handschellen *fpl*, goldene Fesseln *fpl*; (finanzieller Anreiz zum Zweck der engeren Bindung von Mitarbeitern)

(JAP) 黄金の手錠
（転職防止のための給料上の特別優遇措置のこと）

(RUS) «ЗОЛОТЫЕ НАРУЧНИКИ»: МЕТОД УДЕРЖАНИЯ КЛЮЧЕВЫХ РАБОТНИКОВ КОМПАНИИ ПОСРЕДСТВОМ ПРЕДЛОЖЕНИЯ ИМ ОПЦИОНА НА ПОКУПКУ АКЦИЙ

golden handshake

(CHIN) 提前退休奖励计划

(FRE) indemnité de départ, (C) prime de départ

(GER) hohe Abfindung *f*, goldener Handschlag *m*
(JAP) （定年前の退職者に支払う）特別報酬、割増退職金
(RUS) «ЗОЛОТОЕ РУКОПОЖАТИЕ»: ВЫПЛАТА ПРИ УВОЛЬНЕНИИ ИЛИ ДОСРОЧНОМ УХОДЕ НА ПЕНСИЮ

golden parachute
(CHIN) 公司高层福利合同
(FRE) prime de licenciement, (C) parachute doré
(GER) (Abfindungszahlungen an einen vorzeitig zum Ausscheiden aus seinem Vertrag gezwungenen Spitzenmanager); Golden Parachute *m*, vertragliche Großabfindung *f*
(JAP) ゴールデンパラシュート（経営者の高額退職金を受ける旨の雇用契約）
(RUS) «ЗОЛОТОЙ ПАРАШЮТ»: СОГЛАШЕНИЕ О ПОЛУЧЕНИИ ВЫПЛАТЫ ПРИ УВОЛЬНЕНИИ

gold fixing
(CHIN) 议定金价
(FRE) cotation de l'or, (C) détermination du prix de l'or
(GER) Goldfixing *n*, Festsetzung *f* des Goldpreises *mpl*
(JAP) 金の建値決定、（ロンドン金市場の）金価格、
(RUS) ЕЖЕДНЕВНАЯ ФИКСАЦИЯ ЦЕНЫ ЗОЛОТА

gold mutual fund
(CHIN) 黄金互助资金
(FRE) fonds (n, m) commun de placement dont le portefeuille est investi principalement en valeurs liées à l'or, (C) fonds commun de placement d'or
(GER) Gold(investment)fonds *m*
(JAP) 金鉱採掘会社投資信託
(RUS) ЗОЛОТОЙ ИНВЕСТИЦИОННЫЙ ФОНД

gold standard
(CHIN) 金本位
(FRE) étalon-or
(GER) Goldwährung *f*, -standard *m*
(JAP) 金本位制
(RUS) ЗОЛОТОЙ СТАНДАРТ

good delivery
(CHIN) 完好交货
(FRE) de bonne livraison
(GER) einwandfreie Übergabe *f*, rechtzeitige Lieferung *f*
(JAP) 適法受渡し、適格受渡し証券の合格調達
(RUS) ПОСТАВКА В СООТВЕТСТВИИ С УСЛОВИЯМИ КОНТРАКТА

good faith
(CHIN) 信誉
(FRE) bonne foi
(GER) Redlichkeit *f*, Gutgläubigkeit *f*
(JAP) 誠実、誠意、善意
(RUS) ДОБРОСОВЕСТНОСТЬ

good-faith deposit
(CHIN) 意向订金，善意保证金
(FRE) garantie de bonne foi, (C) dépôt de bonne foi
(GER) Sicherheitshinterlegung *f*, Einzahlung *f* in gutem Glauben *m*
(JAP) 手付金
(RUS) ДОБРОСОВЕСТНЫЙ ДЕПОЗИТ

good money
(CHIN) 高薪，巨款
(FRE) bonne monnaie, (C) fonds garantis
(GER) gutes Geld *n*; sofort verfügbares Geld *n*
(JAP) 高賃金、良貨
(RUS) ЧИСТЫЕ ДЕНЬГИ

goodness-of-fit test
(CHIN) 适合性检验
(FRE) test d'ajustement statistique
(GER) Anpassungstest *m*, Test *m* zur Güte *f* der Anpassung *f*
(JAP) 適合度検定
(RUS) ПРАКТИЧЕСКОЕ ИСПЫТАНИЕ ФУНКЦИИ РАСПРЕДЕЛЕНИЯ (СТАТ.)

goods
(CHIN) 货物，商品，货品
(FRE) marchandises, (C) biens, marchandises

(GER) Güter *npl*, (Handels)waren *fpl*, -artikel *mpl*, Erzeugnisse *npl*, bewegliche Gegenstände *mpl*
(JAP) 財貨、商品
(RUS) ТОВАРЫ

goods and services
(CHIN) 商品与劳务
(FRE) biens et services, (C) produits et services
(GER) Waren *fpl* und Dienstleistungen *fpl*
(JAP) 物品とサービス
(RUS) ТОВАРЫ И ОБСЛУЖИВАНИЕ

good-till-canceled order (GTC)
(CHIN) 按指定价格进行交易（GTC）
(FRE) ordre GTC, (C) ordre à révocation
(GER) Auftrag *m* bis auf Widerruf *m*, GTC
(JAP) 取消しまで有効な注文
(RUS) ЗАКАЗ (ПРИКАЗ БРОКЕРУ) С ПРАВОМ ОТМЕНЫ

good title
(CHIN) 有效的所有权
(FRE) titre de propriété non équivoque, (C) titre valable
(GER) gültiger Rechtsanspruch *m*, einwandfreier Rechtstitel *m*
(JAP) 無傷の権利、良権原
(RUS) ЗАКОННЫЙ ПРАВОВОЙ ТИТУЛ

goodwill
(CHIN) 商誉，信誉
(FRE) fonds de commerce, biens incorporels, (C) cote d'estime, (C) achalandage, fonds commercial
(GER) Firmenwert *m*; Wohlwollen *n*, Kulanz *f*
(JAP) のれん、(店の)株、営業権
(RUS) ДЕЛОВАЯ РЕПУТАЦИЯ ДОБРОЖЕЛАТЕЛЬНОСТИ

grace period
(CHIN) 宽限期，优惠期
(FRE) délai de paiement (en cas de renouvellement)
(GER) Nachfrist *f*, Zahlungsaufschub *m*; tilgungsfreie Zeit *f*, Tilgungsaufschub *m*
(JAP) (払込)猶予期間
(RUS) ЛЬГОТНЫЙ СРОК, СРОК ОТСРОЧКИ ПЛАТЕЖЕЙ

graduated lease
(CHIN) 分级租赁
(FRE) loyer progressif, (C) bail progressif
(GER) gestaffelter Leasing-Vertrag *m*
(JAP) 賃貸料累進型リース
(RUS) ПРОГРЕССИВНАЯ АРЕНДА

graduated payment mortgage (GPM)
(CHIN) 分级支付抵押贷款（GPM）
(FRE) hypothèque à paiements échelonnés, (C) prêt à mensualités progressives
(GER) Hypothek *f* mit gestaffelten (aber steigenden) Tilgungsleistungen *fpl*
(JAP) 累進返済方式抵当
(RUS) ПРОГРЕССИВНАЯ ИПОТЕКА

graduated wage
(CHIN) 分级工资
(FRE) salaire évolutif, salaire progressif
(GER) gestaffelter Lohn *m*, Staffellohn *m*
(JAP) 累進式賃金
(RUS) ПРОГРЕССИВНАЯ ЗАРАБОТНАЯ ПЛАТА

graft
(CHIN) 贪污，受贿
(FRE) concussion, corruption de fonctionnaires, (C) greffage
(GER) Schiebung *f*, Schmiergeld *n*; Heilung *f* eines Mangels *m* bei der Hypothekenbestellung *f*
(JAP) 不正利得、汚職（事件）、収賄（事件）
(RUS) ВЗЯТКА; ВЗЯТОЧНИЧЕСТВО

grandfather clause
(CHIN) 不追溯条款
(FRE) clause des droits acquis, (C) clause de protection des droits acquis
(GER) Besitzstandsklausel *f*, Befähigungsnachweisklausel *f*
(JAP) 祖父条項、グランドファーザー条項
(RUS) ПОЛОЖЕНИЕ В НОВОМ ЗАКОНОДАТЕЛЬСТВЕ, ИСКЛЮЧАЮЩЕЕ ЕГО ДЕЙСТВИЕ НА ТЕ ПРЕДПРИЯТИЯ, КОТОРЫЕ УЖЕ ВОВЛЕЧЕНЫ В

ДЕЯТЕЛЬНОСТЬ ОГОВОРЕННУЮ В ДАННОМ ЗАКОНОДАТЕЛЬСТВЕ

grant
(CHIN) 许可，授予，让予，转让证书
(FRE) subvention, allocation, cession
(GER) Gewährleistung *f*; Erteilung *f*; Bewilligung *f*, Genehmigung *f*, Zuschuss *m*, Subvention *f*
(JAP) 補助（金）、交付（金）、譲与
(RUS) ГРАНТ; ПЕРЕДАЧА ПРАВА СОБСТВЕННОСТИ; ДАРЕНИЕ; ОТЧУЖДЕНИЕ

grantee
(CHIN) 被授与者，受让人
(FRE) concessionnaire, (C) titulaire de lettres
(GER) Rechtsnachfolger *m*; Käufer *m*, Erwerber *m*; Empfänger *m*, Berechtigter *m*; Begünstigter *m*; Lizenznehmer *m*; Zessionär *m*; Käufer *m* einer Option *f*
(JAP) 譲受人、被譲与者
(RUS) ЛИЦО, ПОЛУЧАЮЩЕЕ ПРАВО СОБСТВЕННОСТИ

grantor
(CHIN) 授与者，转让人
(FRE) concédant, donateur
(GER) Veräußerer *m*, Rechtsvorgänger *m*; Treugeber *m*; Lizenzgeber *m*; Zedent *m*; Übertragender *m*, Verleiher *m*; Verkäufer *m* einer Option *f*, Stillhalter *m*
(JAP) 譲与者
(RUS) ЛИЦО, ПЕРЕДАЮЩЕЕ ПРАВО СОБСТВЕННОСТИ

grantor trust
(CHIN) 转让人信托
(FRE) « trust » où l'apporteur des biens se réserve un droit de réversion future sur ces biens, (C) fiducie de cédant
(GER) Treuhandverhältnis *n*, Treuhänderschaft *f* mit Treugeberrechten *npl*
(JAP) 贈与信託
(RUS) ПЕРЕДАЧА В ДОВЕРИТЕЛЬНУЮ СОБСТВЕННОСТЬ

graph
(CHIN) 图，图形

(FRE) graphique
(GER) Grafik *m*, Schaubild *n*, Diagramm *n*
(JAP) 図、図表、グラフ
(RUS) ДИАГРАММА, ГРАФИК

graphics card
(CHIN) 图形卡
(FRE) carte graphique, (C) carte de mémoire graphique
(GER) Grafikkarte *f*
(JAP) グラフィックスカード、図形カード
(RUS) КАРТА КОМПЬЮТЕРИОЙ ГРАФИКИ

gratis
(CHIN) 无偿
(FRE) gratuit, gratis
(GER) gratis, kostenlos, frei *adj*
(JAP) 無料で
(RUS) БЕЗ ОПЛАТЫ

gratuitous
(CHIN) 无偿的
(FRE) gratuit, bénévole, (C) injustifié, (C) à titre gratuit
(GER) unentgeltlich, frei, kostenlos, ohne Gegenleistung *f*, umsonst *adj*
(JAP) 無料の、無償の
(RUS) БЕСПЛАТНЫЙ

gratuity
(CHIN) 小账，赏金，抚恤金
(FRE) pourboire, gratification
(GER) Trinkgeld *n*; Gratifikation *f*,
(JAP) 祝儀、チップ
(RUS) ДЕНЕЖНОЕ ВОЗНАГРАЖДЕНИЕ; ЧАЕВЫЕ

graveyard market
(CHIN) 濒死股市
(FRE) marché mort, (C) marché suicidaire
(GER) Baissemarkt *m* (bei dem die Kurse *mfp* ins Uferlose *n* stürzen)
(JAP) 墓場市場、活気のない市場
(RUS) МЕРТВЫЙ РЫНОК

graveyard shift
(CHIN) 夜班
(FRE) équipe de nuit

(GER) (zweite) Nachtschicht *f* (0.00 – 8.00
Uhr)
(JAP) 深夜勤務、第三次作業
(RUS) НОЧНАЯ СМЕНА

gray scale
(CHIN) 灰度
(FRE) échelle de gris
(GER) Grauton- *f*, Graustufenskala *f*
(JAP) グレイスケール、無彩色スケール
(RUS) ШКАЛА ЯРКОСТИ

Great Depression
(CHIN) 大萧条
(FRE) grande dépression
(GER) Große Depression *f*,
Weltwirtschaftskrise *f*
(JAP) 大恐慌
(RUS) «ВЕЛИКАЯ ДЕПРЕССИЯ»

greenmail
(CHIN) 绿色收购，被收购公司以市场价
转让股票的安排
(FRE) greenmail, (C) chantage à l'opa
(GER) Greenmail *f*; (erpresserischer)
(Rück)kauf *m* eines Aktienpakets *n* (meist
beachtlich über Kurswert *m*);
Übernahmeangebot *n* (zum erhöhten
Preis *n*)
(JAP) グリーンメール、
株式買い戻し工作
(RUS) «ЗЕЛЕНЫЙ ШАНТАЖ»: ПОКУПКА
АКЦИЙ КОМПАНИИ – ОБЪЕКТА
ПОГЛОЩЕНИЯ

gross
(CHIN) 全体，总计，毛额，毛重
(FRE) douze douzaines, grosse, (C) brut
(GER) brutto *adj*
(JAP) 全体の、総額の
(RUS) БРУТТО

gross amount
(CHIN) 总额，总计
(FRE) montant brut, (C) montant
brut facturation brute
(GER) Bruttobetrag *m*
(JAP) 総額
(RUS) СУММА БРУТТО

gross billing
(CHIN) 总通讯费
(FRE) facturation brute
(GER) Bruttofakturierung *f*; -
rechnungsstellung *f*
(JAP) 総額請求
(RUS) ВЫСТАВЛЕНИЕ СЧЕТОВ БРУТТО

gross earnings
(CHIN) 总收入，毛利
(FRE) recette brute, (C) salaire brut
(GER) Brutto(arbeits)einkommen *n*, -
verdienst *m*, -einkünfte *fpl*; Bruttoerlös *m*, -
gewinn *m*
(JAP) 総収益、総収入
(RUS) ВАЛОВЫЙ ЗАРОБОТОК

gross estate
(CHIN) 总资产
(FRE) succession brute, valeur brute de
succession, (C) actif brut d'une succession
(GER) Bruttovermögen *n*, Bruttonachlass *m*
(Erbschaft)
(JAP) 総財産、総不動産、総遺産
(RUS) ИМУЩЕСТВО, СОБСТВЕННОСТЬ
ДО ВЫЧЕТА ЗАДОЛЖЕННОСТЕЙ

gross income
(CHIN) 总收入
(FRE) produit brut, revenu brut
(GER) Bruttoerlös *m*; Bruttoeinkommen *n*, -
verdienst *m*, Gesamteinkommen *n*,
Bruttoeinkünfte, -einnahmen *fpl*;
Roheinkommen *n* (Marketing)
(JAP) 総所得、総収入
(RUS) ВАЛОВЫЙ ДОХОД

gross leasable area
(CHIN) 可出租总面积
(FRE) surface commerciale utile,
(C) surface locative brute
(GER) zu vermietende bzw. leasingfähige
Bruttofläche *f*
(JAP) 総賃貸契約地域
(RUS) ОБЩАЯ ПЛОЩАДЬ ДЛЯ АРЕНДЫ

gross lease
(CHIN) 全包出租
(FRE) loyer brut, (C) bail tous frais
compris

(GER) Bruttoleasing *n*
(JAP) 費用貸主持ちの賃貸借契約
(RUS) АРЕНДА , ПРИ КОТОРОЙ
АРЕНДОДАТЕЛЬ ОПЛАЧИВАЕТ
ВСЕ ОПЕРАЦИОННЫЕ
РАСХОДЫ

gross national debt
(CHIN) 国民负债总额
(FRE) dette nationale brute
(GER) Staatsschuld *f*, Nationalschuld *f*;
Bruttosumme *f* der Schulden *pl* des
Bundes *m*
(JAP) 国債総額
(RUS) ОБЩАЯ ГОСУДАРСТВЕННАЯ
ЗАДОЛЖЕННОСТЬ

gross national expenditure
(CHIN) 国民支出总值
(FRE) dépense nationale brute
(GER) Bruttoausgaben *fpl*
(JAP) 国民総支出
(RUS) ОБЩИЕ ГОСУДАРСТВЕННЫЕ
РАСХОДЫ

**gross national product
(GNP)**
(CHIN) 国民生产总值
(FRE) produit national brut (PNB),
(C) production nationale brute (PNB)
(GER) Bruttosozialprodukt *n*
(JAP) 国民総生産
(RUS) ВАЛОВЫЙ НАЦИОНАЛЬНЫЙ
ПРОДУКТ (ВНП)

gross profit
(CHIN) 毛利润，总利润
(FRE) bénéfice brut, (C) marge bénéficiaire
brute
(GER) Bruttoertrag, -gewinn *m*, Rohertrag,
-profit *m*
(JAP) 総利益、総利潤
(RUS) БРУТТО – ПРИБЫЛЬ

gross profit method
(CHIN) 毛利法，总利润法
(FRE) méthode du bénéfice brut
(GER) Vorratsbewertung *f* anhand des
Rohgewinns *m*
(JAP) 総益法
(RUS) МЕТОДИКА ОЦЕНКИ ЗАПАСОВ НА
КОНЕЦ ОТЧЁТНОГО ПЕРИОДА

gross profit ratio
(CHIN) 毛利率，总利润比率
(FRE) ratio de bénéfice brut, (C) ratio de la
marge bénéficiaire brute
(GER) Rohgewinnquotient *m*, Bruttogewinn
m dividiert durch Nettoerlöse *mpl*
(JAP) 粗利益率、粗利潤率
(RUS) ПРИ ПРОДАЖЕ – ОТНОШЕНИЕ
МЕЖДУ ПРИБЫЛЬЮ И ЦЕНОЙ

gross rating point (GRP)
(CHIN) 按毛费率计算（GRP）
(FRE) indicateur de pression des médias,
(C) point de couverture brute
(GER) Bruttoreichweite *f* (Medien)
(JAP) 総視聴率
(RUS) СУММА ВСЕХ РЕЙТИНГОВ ЗА
ОПРЕДЕЛЁННЫЙ ПЕРИОД

gross rent multiplier (GRM)
(CHIN) 毛租金倍数（GRM）
(FRE) multiplicateur de loyer brut,
(C) multiplicateur du revenu brut
(GER) Bruttomietemultiplikator *m*
(JAP) 総賃貸料乗数
(RUS) ОБОБЩЕННЫЙ КОЭФФИЦИЕНТ
СТАВОК АРЕНДНОЙ ПЛАТЫ

gross revenue
(CHIN) 收入总额
(FRE) revenu brut, (C) chiffre d'affaires
brut
(GER) Bruttoeinkünfte *m*; Rohertrag *m*,
Bruttoeinnahmen *fpl*
(JAP) 総収入、総収益
(RUS) ОБЩИЙ (БРУТТО) ДОХОД

gross ton
(CHIN) 英吨
(FRE) tonne anglaise, tonne Washington,
(C) tonne de jauge
(GER) Bruttoregistertonne *f*
(JAP) 英トン（２２４０ポンド）
(RUS) ТОННА БРУТТО

gross weight
(CHIN) 总重，毛重，全重
(FRE) poids brut
(GER) Bruttogewicht *n*, Gesamtgewicht *n*
(JAP) 総重量、風袋込み重量
(RUS) ВЕС БРУТТО

ground lease

(CHIN) 地契

(FRE) bail foncier, (C) bail à construction

(GER) Baupacht *f*, Grundstückspacht *f*

(JAP) 土地賃貸し、土地賃貸借

(RUS) АРЕНДА ЗЕМЛИ

ground rent

(CHIN) 地租

(FRE) rente foncière, (C) charge foncière,
(C) redevance emphytéotique, (C) canon,
rente foncière

(GER) Grund- *f*, Bodenrente *f*, Grundpacht *f*,
Erbbauzins *m*, Pacht- *m*, Grund- *m*,
Bodenzins *m*

(JAP) (英)地代、借地料

(RUS) АРЕНДНАЯ ПЛАТА ЗА ЗЕМЛЮ

group credit insurance

(CHIN) 团体信用保险

(FRE) assurance crédit collective

(GER) Kollektivkreditversicherung *f*,
Kollektivlebensversicherung *f* für
Kreditnehmer *mpl* ausstehender
Darlehen *npl*

(JAP) 団体信用保険

(RUS) ГРУППОВОЕ СТРАХОВАНИЕ
КРЕДИТА

group disability insurance

(CHIN) 团体伤残险

(FRE) assurance invalidité de groupe,
assurance invalidité collective

(GER) Sammelunfallversicherung *f*

(JAP) 団体廃疾保険

(RUS) ГРУППОВОЕ СТРАХОВАНИЕ ПО
НЕТРУДОСПОСОБНОСТИ

group health insurance

(CHIN) 团体健康保险

(FRE) assurance groupe maladies,
(C) assurance maladie collective

(GER) Gruppenkrankenversicherung *f*

(JAP) 団体健康保険

(RUS) ГРУППОВОЕ МЕДИЦИНСКОЕ
СТРАХОВАНИЕ

group life insurance

(CHIN) 团体人寿保险

(FRE) assurance groupe sur la vie,
(C) assurance vie collective

(GER) Gruppen- *f*, Kollektiv- *f*,
Sammellebensversicherung *f*

(JAP) 団体生命保険

(RUS) ГРУППОВОЕ СТРАХОВАНИЕ
ЖИЗНИ

growing-equity mortgage (GEM)

(CHIN) 不断增长产权长期抵押贷款

(FRE) hypothèque à capital croissant,
(C) prêt hypothécaire à mensualités
progressives

(GER) Hypothek *f* mit zunehmendem
Eigenkapitalbetrag *m*

(JAP) 持分成長担保

(RUS) ИПОТЕЧНЫЙ КРЕДИТ С
ВОЗРАСТАНИЕМ ПЛАТЕЖЕЙ ЗА СЧЁТ
ПОГАШЕНИЕ СУММЫ ДОЛГА

growth fund

(CHIN) 发展基金

(FRE) fonds commun de placement (FCP),
(C) fonds de croissance

(GER) Wachstumsfonds *m*,
Thesaurierungsfonds *m*

(JAP) 成長型投資信託ファンド

(RUS) ФОНД, ВКЛАДЫВАЮЩИЙ
СРЕДСТВА В АКЦИИ, КУРС КОТОРЫХ
РАСТЕТ ДЛИТЕЛЬНОЕ ВРЕМЯ И БЫСТРЕЕ
АКЦИЙ ДРУГИХ КОМПАНИЙ

growth rate

(CHIN) 增长率，成长率

(FRE) taux de croissance

(GER) Wachstums- *f*, Zuwachs- *f*,
Steigerungs- *f*, Expansionsrate *f*

(JAP) 成長率、増加率

(RUS) ТЕМПЫ РОСТА

growth stock

(CHIN) 增长股份，成长股

(FRE) actions d'avenir,actions
de croissance, (C) valeur
d'avenir

(GER) Wachstumsaktie *f*

(JAP) 成長株式

(RUS) «АКЦИЯ РОСТА», АКЦИИ, КУРС
КОТОРЫХ РАСТЕТ ДЛИТЕЛЬНОЕ ВРЕМЯ
И БЫСТРЕЕ АКЦИЙ ДРУГИХ КОМПАНИЙ

guarantee

(CHIN) 保证，担保，保证书

(FRE) garantie

(GER) Garantie *f*, Gewährleistung *f*,
Zusicherung *f*; Bürgschaft *f*, Absicherung *f*,
Sicherheit *f*; Kaution *f*
(JAP) 保証、担保（物件）、被保証人、
保証する
(RUS) ГАРАНТИРУЕМОЕ ЛИЦО

guaranteed annual wage (GAW)

(CHIN) 年保证工资
(FRE) salaire annuel garanti
(GER) garantierter jährlicher Mindestlohn *n*,
garantiertes Jahreseinkommen *m*
(JAP) 保証年間賃金
(RUS) ГАРАНТИРОВАННАЯ ГОДОВАЯ
ЗАРАБОТНАЯ ПЛАТА

guaranteed bond

(CHIN) 担保债券
(FRE) obligation garantie, (C) obligation
cautionnée par un tiers
(GER) Schuldverschreibung *f* mit Kapital- *f*
und Dividendengarantie *f*; durch Bürgschaft
f gesicherte bzw. garantierte
Schuldverschreibung *f*, gesicherte
Obligation *f*
(JAP) (元金利子支払などの)保証債券、
保証付債券
(RUS) ГАРАНТИРОВАННЫЕ ОБЛИГАЦИИ

guaranteed income contract (GIC)

(CHIN) 保证收入合同（GIC）
(FRE) contrat de revenu garanti
(GER) Versicherung *f* mit garantiertem
Einkommen *n*, Vertrag *m* mit garantierter
Verzinsung *f*
(JAP) 所得保証契約
(RUS) КОНТРАКТ С ГАРАНТИРОВАННЫМ
ДОХОДОМ

guaranteed insurability

(CHIN) 保证可保险性
(FRE) assurabilité garantie, (C) garantie
d'assurabilité
(GER) garantierte Versicherbarkeit *f*,
garantierte Versicherungsfähigkeit *f*
(JAP) 保証被保険性
(RUS) ГАРАНТИРУЕМАЯ СТРАХУЕМОСТЬ

guaranteed mortgage

(CHIN) 保证抵押贷款
(FRE) créance hypothécaire garantie,

(C) prêt hypothécaire garanti
(GER) Hypothek *f* mit voller
Haftungssumme *f*
(JAP) 保証担保
(RUS) ГАРАНТИРОВАННЫЙ ИПОТЕЧНЫЙ
КРЕДИТ

guaranteed security

(CHIN) 保证证券
(FRE) titre garanti, valeur garantie
(GER) Wertpapier *n* mit
Dividendengarantie *f*
(JAP) 保証証券
(RUS) ГАРАНТИРОВАННАЯ ЦЕННАЯ
БУМАГА

guaranteed letter

(CHIN) 保证书
(FRE) lettre de garantie
(GER) Garantiebrief *m*, -schein *m;*
Garantieerklärungsschreiben *n*
(JAP) 保証レター
(RUS) ГАРАНТИРОВАННЫЙ ВЕКСЕЛЬ;
ГАРАНТИЙНОЕ ПИСЬМО

guarantee of signature

(CHIN) 签字真实性保证
(FRE) légalisation de signature
(GER) Garantie *f* der Unterschrift *f*;
Schuldnerqualität *f*
(JAP) 署名保証
(RUS) ГАРАНТИЯ (СЕРТИФИКАТ)
ПОДПИСИ

guarantor

(CHIN) 保证人，担保人
(FRE) garant, (C) caution
(GER) Garantiegeber *m*; Bürge *m*,
Bürgschaftsträger *m*; Sicherungsgeber *m*;
Avalist *m*, Garant *m*
(JAP) 保証人、引受人
(RUS) ГАРАНТИРУЮЩЕЕ ЛИЦО

guaranty

(CHIN) 保证书，抵押品
(FRE) caution, garantie, (C) sûreté
(GER) Qualitätssicherung *f*; Kaution *f*,
Bürgschaft(surkunde) *f*, Garantie *f*,
Sicherheit *f*, Gewährleistung *f*; Aval *n/m*,
Garantieschein *m*
(JAP) 保証契約、保証行為、担保
(RUS) ГАРАНТИЯ

guardian

(CHIN) 管理人，监护人
(FRE) tuteur, curateur, (C) conservateur
(GER) Vormund *m*, Sorge- *m*,
Erziehungsberechtiger *m*; Kurator *m*,
Verwahrer *m*
(JAP) 後見人、保護者、監視者
(RUS) ОПЕКУН; ПОПЕЧИТЕЛЬ

guardian deed

(CHIN) 监护人行为
(FRE) acte de tutelle, (C) acte de curatelle
(GER) Zessionsurkunde *f* des
Vormunds *m*
(JAP) 後見人捺印証書
(RUS) ДОКУМЕНТ О ПОПЕЧИТЕЛЬСТВЕ

guideline lives

(CHIN) 标准使用年限
(FRE) dépréciation de vétusté, (C) durée
amortissable
(GER) Abschreibungstabellen *fpl*
(RUS) ПРИНЦИПЫ ИСЧИСЛЕНИЯ СРОК
ГОДНОСТИ ЗДАНИЙ

guild

(CHIN) 行会，同业公会
(FRE) association, corporation, cercle,
(C) guilde
(GER) Zunft *f*, Innung *f*, Gilde *f*;
Fachschaft *f*
(JAP) ギルド、同業組合
(RUS) ГИЛЬДИЯ; ОРГАНИЗАЦИЯ, СОЮЗ

H

habendum

(CHIN) 受让人及受让地产定义条款

(FRE) clause de désignation (du bénéficiaire), (C) habendum

(GER) (Auflassungsklausel, dingliche Übertragungsklausel)

(JAP) 物権表示条項

(RUS) ЧАСТЬ ДОКУМЕНТА НАЗЫВАЮЩАЯ ТОГО, КТО ПОЛУЧАЕТ ДАР, И ОПИСЫВАЕТ ПЕРЕДАВАЕМОЕ ИМУЩЕСТВО

hacker

(CHIN) 骇客，计算机程序专家

(FRE) pirate informatique, hacker, (C) bidouilleur

(GER) Hacker *m*

(JAP) ハッカー、コンピュータへの不法侵入者

(RUS) «ХАКЕР» (компьютерный специалист, незаконно вторгающийся в чужие программы)

half duplex

(CHIN) 半双向

(FRE) semi-duplex, (C) bidirectionnel à l'alternat

(GER) Wechselverkehr *m*, Halbduplex *n/m*

(JAP) 半二重（伝送方式）

(RUS) ПОЛОВИНА ДВУХКВАРТИРНОГО ДОМА

half-life

(CHIN) 半衰期，半减期

(FRE) demi-vie

(GER) Zeitraum *m* vor Rückzahlung *f* der Hälfte *f* einer Anleihe *f*; Halbwertzeit *f*

(JAP) 半减期

(RUS) ПОЛОВИНА СРОКА

halo effect

(CHIN) 光环效应

(FRE) effet de halo

(GER) Halo- *m*, Lichthofeffekt *m*

(JAP) ハロー効果、後光（背光）効果

(RUS) «ЭФФЕКТ ОРЕОЛА», МНЕНИЕ О ЧЕЛОВЕКЕ, СФОРМИРОВАННОЕ НА ОСНОВЕ ОДНОГО ФАКТОРА ИЛИ СЛУЧАЯ

hammering the market

(CHIN) 大量抛售股票

(FRE) vendre à découvert, (C) matraquer le marché

(GER) Kurs *m* durch Leerverkäufe *mpl* nach unten drücken; Baisseangriffe *mpl* durchführen

(JAP) マーケットの売りたたき

(RUS) АКТИВНАЯ ПРОДАЖА АКЦИЙ СПЕКУЛЯНТАМИ (ожидающими падения конъюнктуры)

handling allowance

(CHIN) 产品整理折扣

(FRE) réduction des frais de manutention, (C) rabais de manutention, remise pour manutention

(GER) Bearbeitungspauschale *f*

(JAP) 取扱い準備金、取扱い費

(RUS) СКИДКА ПРОИЗВОДИТЕЛЯ ОПТОВИКУ, ЕСЛИ ТОВАР ТРЕБУЕТ ОСОБОГО ОБРАЩЕНИЯ

hangout

(CHIN) 贷款余额

(FRE) reliquat, (C) solde d'un prêt à l'échéance

(GER) beliebter Treffpunkt *m*

(JAP) 溜まり場、低級娯楽場所

(RUS) ОСТАТОК ЗАДОЛЖЕННОСТИ ЗА ИМУЩЕСТВО НА МОМЕНТ, КОГДА ИСТЁК СРОК ЕГО АРЕНДЫ

hard cash

(CHIN) 硬币，现金

(FRE) espèces sonnantes et trébuchantes, argent liquide, numéraire

(GER) Bargeld *n*, Hart- *n*, Münzgeld *n*, klingende Münze *f*

(JAP) 正金、硬貨

(RUS) МОНЕТЫ; НАЛИЧНОСТЬ

hard currency

(CHIN) 硬通货，硬币，紧俏货币

(FRE) devise forte, (C) monnaie forte
(GER) harte, stabile Währung *f*,
Hartwährung *f*
(JAP) 硬貨、交換可能通貨、
ハードカレンシー
(RUS) ТВЕРДАЯ ВАЛЮТА,
КОНВЕРТИРУЕМАЯ ВАЛЮТА

hard disk
(CHIN) 硬盘
(FRE) disque dur
(GER) Festplatte *f*
(JAP) ハードディスク
(RUS) ЖЁСТКИЙ ДИСК

hard dollars
(CHIN) 实际付款
(FRE) dollars sonnants et trébuchants ,
(C) argent sonnant
(GER) harte Dollar *mpl*
(JAP) 実際の現金による支払
(RUS) РЕАЛЬНАЯ ОПЛАТА КЛИЕНТОМ
ИЛИ ИНВЕСТОРОМ

hard drive
(CHIN) 硬盘驱动器
(FRE) disque dur
(GER) Festplattenlaufwerk *n*
(JAP) ハードドライブ
(RUS) ЖЁСТКИЙ ДИСК

hard goods
(CHIN) 耐用货物
(FRE) biens durables, (C) bien de
consommation durable
(GER) Gebrauchsgüter *npl*,
langlebige Güter *npl*; devisenstarke
Waren *fpl*
(JAP) 耐久財、ハードグッヅ
(RUS) ТОВАРЫ ДЛИТЕЛЬНОГО
ПОЛЬЗОВАНИЯ

hard money
(CHIN) 硬币，现金，硬通货，紧俏货币
(FRE) monnaie forte, (C) argent liquide
(GER) harte bzw. starke Währung *f*; frei
konvertierbares Geld *n*
(JAP) 硬貨、現金
(RUS) ДЕНЬГИ В МОНЕТАХ; «ТВЕРДАЯ»
ВАЛЮТА

hard return
(CHIN) 硬回车
(FRE) retour chariot
(GER) erzwungener Zeilenumbruch *m*
(JAP) ハードリターン
(RUS) ВОЗВРАТ КАРЕТКИ

hardware
(CHIN) 硬件
(FRE) matériel
(GER) Hardware *f*
(JAP) ハードウェア
(RUS) ОБОРУДОВАНИЕ АППАРАТНЫЕ
СРЕДСТВА

hardwired
(CHIN) 电路的，硬连线的
(FRE) câblé
(JAP) ハードワイヤード、配線による
(RUS) АППАРАТНЫЙ, ЗАШИТЫЙ;
РЕАЛИЗОВАННЫЙ АППАРАТНЫМИ
СРЕДСТВАМИ

hash total
(CHIN) 混列总量
(FRE) total mêlé, total de contrôle
(GER) festverdrahtet *adj*
(GER) Kontroll- *f*, Prüfsumme *f*,
Stapelzwischensumme *f*
(JAP) ハッシュ合計、検査和
(RUS) КОНТРОЛЬНАЯ СУММА

hatch
(CHIN) 阴影线
(FRE) hachurer
(GER) schraffieren *v*
(JAP) ハッチ

hazard insurance
(CHIN) 危害保险
(FRE) assurance tous risques, (C) assurance
risques
(GER) Risikoversicherung *f*
(JAP) 危険保険
(RUS) СТРАХОВАНИЕ РИСКА

head and shoulders
(CHIN) 头肩形
(FRE) tête-et-epaules

(GER) einsame Spitze *f*, haushoch
überlegen *adj*
(JAP) ヘッドアンドショルダー、
三山天井、三尊
(RUS) «ГОЛОВА И ПЛЕЧИ» (ФИГУРА
ДВИЖЕНИЯ ЦЕН В АНАЛИЗЕ, КОГДА
СТАБИЛЬНЫЙ УРОВЕНЬ СМЕНЯЕТСЯ
ПОДЪЕМОМ И СНОВА ВОЗВРАЩАЕТСЯ К
УРОВНЮ, БЛИЗКОМУ К ИСХОДНОМУ)

header
(CHIN) 标题，报头
(FRE) en-tête
(GER) Dateikopf *m*, Kopfzeile *f*
(JAP) 見出し、ヘッダー、見出し部
(RUS) ЗАГОЛОВОК; ШАПКА

headhunter
(CHIN) 私人职业介绍所
(FRE) chasseur de tête , (C) agence de
recrutement de cadres, conseil en
recrutement de cadres
(GER) Talentsucher *m*, Kopfjäger *m*,
Abwerber *m*
(JAP) 人材スカウト会社(の社員)、
ヘッドハンター（会社）、
人材引き抜き係
(RUS) «ОХОТНИК ЗА ГОЛОВАМИ»
(АКТИВНЫЙ ВЕРБОВЩИК
СОТРУДНИКОВ)

head of household
(CHIN) 户主
(FRE) chef de famille, (C) chef de ménage
(GER) Haushaltsvorstand *m*,
Familienoberhaupt *n*
(JAP) 世帯主
(RUS) ГЛАВА СЕМЬИ

health maintenance organization (HMO)
(CHIN) 健康维护组织 （HMO）
(FRE) HMO (health maintenance
organization) (centre de santé),
(C) organisme d'assurance maladie
(GER) Health Maintenance Organization
(HMO) *f*, (Art der privaten
Krankenversicherung in USA)
(JAP) 健康維持機構
(RUS) ПЛАН ПРЕДОПЛАЧЕННОГО
ГРУППОВОГО МЕДИЦИНСКОГО

СТРАХОВАНИЯ, КЛИЕНТЫ КОГОРОГО
ПОЛЬЗУЮТСЯ УСЛУГАМИ ТОЛЬКО
УЧАВСТВУЮЩИХ В ПЛАНЕ
СПЕЦИАЛИСТОВ

hearing
(CHIN) 听证
(FRE) audience audience , (C) audition,
instruction
(GER) Anhörung *f* (vor Gericht)
(JAP) 聴取会、審問、聴覚、
(RUS) СЛУШАНИЕ ДЕЛА (суд.)

heavy industry
(CHIN) 重工业
(FRE) industrie lourde
(GER) Schwerindustrie *f*
(JAP) 重工業
(RUS) ТЯЖЕЛАЯ ПРОМЫШЛЕННОСТЬ

hectare
(CHIN) 公顷
(FRE) hectare
(GER) Hektar *m*
(JAP) ヘクタール
(RUS) ГЕКТАР

hedge
(CHIN) 对冲买卖，套期保值
(FRE) couverture, (C) garantie de cours
(GER) Sicherungsgeschäft *n* (Börse);
Deckungsgeschäft *n*, Geschäft *n* mit
Gegendeckung *f*; Kursdeckungsgeschäft *m*
(JAP) 売り（買い）つなぎ、両掛け
(RUS) ХЕДЖ (СРОЧНАЯ БИРЖЕВАЯ
СДЕЛКА ДЛЯ ПОДСТРАХОВКИ)

heirs
(CHIN) 继承人
(FRE) héritiers, légataires
(GER) Erben *mpl/fpl*
(JAP) 相続人、法定相続人、継承者
(RUS) НАСЛЕДНИКИ

heirs and assigns
(CHIN) 继承人和受让人
(FRE) héritiers et ayants droit , (C) ayants
droits
(GER) Erben *mpl/fpl* und
Abtretungsempfänger *mpl*

(JAP) 相続人ならびに譲受人
(RUS) НАСЛЕДНИКИ И ПОЛУЧАТЕЛИ ПЕРЕДАННЫХ ПРАВ

help index
(CHIN) 求助信息索引
(FRE) index de l'aide
(GER) Hilfe-Index *m*
(JAP) ヘルプ索引
(RUS) КАРТОТЕКА ПОДСКАЗОК

help screen
(CHIN) 求助屏幕
(FRE) écran d'aide
(GER) Hilfebildschirm *m*
(JAP) ヘルプ画面、ヘルプスクリーン
(RUS) ЭКРАН ПОДСКАЗКИ

help wizard
(CHIN) 求助向导系统
(FRE) assistant
(GER) Hilfeassistent *m*
(JAP) ヘルプウィザード
(RUS) ИНСТРУМЕНТ ПОДСКАЗКИ

heterogeneous
(CHIN) 异质，多元
(FRE) hétèrogène
(GER) heterogen *adj*
(JAP) 異質の
(RUS) НЕОДНОРОДНЫЙ

heuristic
(CHIN) 启发式
(FRE) heuristique
(GER) heuristisch *adj*
(JAP) ヒューリスティック、
発見にやくだつ、発見的
(RUS) ЭВРИСТИЧЕСКИЙ

hidden agenda
(CHIN) 隐蔽日程
(FRE) ordre du jour cache, (C) intentions non déclarées
(GER) Hintergedanke *m*, versteckte Absicht *f*
(JAP) 隠れた処理事項
(RUS) СКРЫТЫЕ НАМЕРЕНИЯ

hidden asset
(CHIN) 隐匿资产
(FRE) réserve latente, réserve pour mémoire, (C) plus-value latente
(GER) stille Reserven *fpl*
(JAP) 含み資産
(RUS) СКРЫТЫЕ АКТИВЫ

hidden inflation
(CHIN) 隐蔽性通货膨胀
(FRE) inflation larvée, inflation masquée , (C) inflation camouflée
(GER) versteckte Inflation *f*
(JAP) 隠れたインフレ、
隠されたインフレ
(RUS) СКРЫТАЯ ИНФЛЯЦИЯ

hidden tax
(CHIN) 隐蔽税收
(FRE) impôt déguisé, (C) impôts indirects
(GER) versteckte Steuer *f*
(JAP) 隠れた税金
(RUS) СКРЫТОЕ НАЛОГООБЛОЖЕНИЕ

hierarchy
(CHIN) 分层，等级制度，级别，系统
(FRE)hiérarchie
(GER) Hierarchie *f*
(JAP) ヒエラルキー、階級制度
(RUS) ИЕРАРХИЯ

high credit
(CHIN) 高档信贷
(FRE) plafond des prêts en cours
(GER) Kredithöchstbetrag *m*
(JAP) 高い信用、ハイクレジット
(RUS) МАКСИМАЛЬНЫЙ РАЗМЕР КРЕДИТА

highest and best use
(CHIN) 最佳利用
(FRE) notion de « highest and best use », usage optimal, utilisation optimale, utilisation qui permet d'obtenir le plus grand gain monétaire sous forme de loyer ou de valeur en capital
(GER) höchster und bester Einsatz *m*
(JAP) 最高最善の使用（用途）

(RUS) ИСПОЛЬЗОВАНИЕ НЕДВИЖИМОСТИ ДЛЯ НАИБОЛЬШЕЙ ДОХОДНОСТИ (при оценке)

high flyer
(CHIN) 价格飞涨的存货，投机性股票
(FRE) valeur en forte hausse, (C) valeur volatile, employé prometteur
(GER) hochspekulative Aktie *f*; Wertpapier *n* mit sehr hohem Kursanstieg *m*
(JAP) 高値株、ハイフライヤー
(RUS) СПЕКУЛЯТИВНЫЕ АКЦИИ

high-grade bond
(CHIN) 高级债券
(FRE) obligation « high grade » (fourchette haute de l'échelle alphabétique de notation), (C) obligation sûre
(GER) erstklassige Schuldverschreibung *f*
(JAP) 優良証券、優良債券
(RUS) ОБЛИГАЦИЯ ВЫСОКОГО РЕЙТИНГА

high-involvement model
(CHIN) 高难度模型
(FRE) modèle a forte participation des consommateurs, (C) modèle à degré d'implication élevé
(GER) Modell *n* mit hoher Beteiligung *f*
(JAP) 係わりの高いモデル
(RUS) СХЕМА С БОЛЬШИМ ЛИЧНЫМ УЧАСТИЕМ

highlight
(CHIN) 增亮，加亮
(FRE) surligner, mettre en surbrillance
(GER) hervorheben, markieren *v*
(JAP) 強調表示、強調表示する
(RUS) ВЫДЕЛЯТЬ (ЦВЕТОМ И Т. П.)

high resolution
(CHIN) 高分辨率
(FRE) haute résolution
(GER) hohe Auflösung *f*
(JAP) 高解像度、高レゾリューション
(RUS) ВЫСОКОЕ РАЗРЕШЕНИЕ

high-speed
(CHIN) 高速
(FRE) haute vitesse

(GER) Hochgeschwindigkeits-
(JAP) 高速度
(RUS) ВЫСОКОСКОРОСТНОЙ

highs
(CHIN) 股票冲高值
(FRE) hauts, (C) cours maximum
(GER) Höchststand *m*, Höchstkurs *m*
(JAP) 高値
(RUS) АКЦИИ, ЦЕНЫ КОТОРЫХ НА ПРОТЯЖЕНИИ ГОДА ДОСТИГАЛИ УРОВНЯ ВЫШЕ СРЕДНЕГО

high technology
(CHIN) 高技术
(FRE) perfectionné de pointe, qui a recours a une technologie de pointe
(GER) High-Tech *f*; Spitzentechnologie *f*
(JAP) ハイテク、高度技術、高度先端技術
(RUS) НАУКОЕМКАЯ ТЕХНОЛОГИЯ

high-tech stock
(CHIN) 高技术公司股票
(FRE) actions high-tech
(GER) High-Tech-Aktie *f*
(JAP) ハイテク株
(RUS) АКЦИИ КОМПАНИЙ НАУКОЕМКОЙ СФЕРЫ

historical cost
(CHIN) 历史成本，实际成本
(FRE) coût historique
(GER) historische Kosten *pl*
(JAP) 実際原価、歴史的原価
(RUS) ПЕРВОНАЧАЛЬНАЯ СТОИМОСТЬ АКТИВА

historical structure
(CHIN) 历史结构
(FRE) structure historique
(GER) historische Struktur *f*
(JAP) 歴史的構造物、歴史的組織
(RUS) СТРОЕНИЕ, ОБЛАДАЮЩЕЕ ИСТОРИЧЕСКОЙ ЦЕННОСТЬЮ

historical yield
(CHIN) 历史产率，实际收益率
(FRE) rendement historique

185

(GER) historischer Ertrag *m*
(JAP) 歴史的步留、歴史的生産高
(RUS) ДОХОДНОСТЬ
ИНВЕСТИЦИОННОГО ФОНДА В
ПРОШЛОМ

hit list
(CHIN)目标客户名单
(FRE) liste, (C) clientèle cible
(GER) Hitliste *f*
(JAP) 対象物リスト、人気リスト、
ヒットリスト
(RUS) ПЕРЕЧЕНЬ ЦЕЛЕЙ

hit the bricks
(CHIN) 员工罢工
(FRE) se mettre en grève (US),
(C) employés en grève
(GER) streiken *v*
(JAP) ストライキをする
(RUS) БАСТОВАТЬ ПРОТИВ
РАБОТОДАТЕЛЕЙ

hobby loss
(CHIN) 由非盈利性爱好引起的损失,
嗜好损失
(FRE) déficit sur loccupation d'agrément
(GER) Verlust *m* aus Freizeitaktivitäten *fpl*
(Steuer)
(JAP) ホビーロス、趣味（道楽）
による損失条項
(RUS) НЕ ВЫЧИТАЕМЫЕ ИЗ
НАЛОГООБЛОЖЕНИЯ ЛИЧНЫЕ
РАСХОДЫ (в отличие от деловых)

holdback
(CHIN) 暂欠, 暂时扣发
(FRE) retenue, (C) retenue de garantie
(GER) zurückbehaltener Teil *m* der
Vertragssumme *f*
(JAP) 停止遅延、阻止、保留物
(RUS) ЗАДЕРЖИВАТЬ, УДЕРЖИВАТЬ

holdback pay
(CHIN) 暂欠工资
(FRE) retenue sur salaire, (C) salaire retenu
(GER) Lohnrückstand *m*, einbehaltener
Verdienst *m*
(JAP) 支払保留賃金

(RUS) ЗАДЕРЖКА ОПЛАТЫ

holder in due course
(CHIN) 正当持票人
(FRE) porteur de bonne foi porteur
légitime, (C) détenteur régulier
(GER) rechtmäßiger Inhaber *m*,
legitimierter Inhaber *m*
(JAP) 正当所持人
(RUS) ДЕРЖАТЕЛЬ ФИНАНСОВОГО
ИНСТРУМЕНТА, ПОЛУЧИВШИЙ ЕГО ПО
ОБЪЯВЛЕННОЙ СТОИМОСТИ, БЕЗ
ОГОВОРОК

holder of record
(CHIN) 记录在案的公司证券拥有人
(FRE) détenteur à la date de cloture,
(C) porteur inscrit à la date de clôture des
registres
(GER) eingetragener Wertpapierinhaber *m*
(JAP) 記録保持者
(RUS) ЗАРЕГИСТРИРОВАННЫЙ
ДЕРЖАТЕЛЬ, ВЛАДЕЛЕЦ

hold-harmless agreements
(CHIN) 免损害协议
(FRE) contrats de non responsabilité,
(C) accords de sauvegarde
(GER) Vereinbarungen *fpl* über die
Freistellung *f* von der Haftung *f*
(JAP) 賠償責任免除特約
(RUS) СОГЛАШЕНИЕ ОБ
ОСВОБОЖДЕНИИ ОТ ПОТЕНЦИАЛЬНОЙ
ОТВЕТСТВЕННОСТИ

hold harmless clause
(CHIN) 免损害条款
(FRE) clause de non responsabilité,
(C) clause de sauvegarde
(GER) Schadloshaltungsklausel *f*;
Freizeichnungs- *f*,
Haftungsausschlussklausel *f*
(JAP) 賠償責任免除条項
(RUS) ПОЛОЖЕНИЕ КОНТРАКТА,
СОГЛАСНО КОТОРОГО ОДНА СТОРОНА
ЗАЩИЩИЕТ ДРУГУЮ ОТ
ПОТЕНЦИАЛЬНОЙ ОТВЕТСТВЕННОСТИ

holding
(CHIN) 把握, 占有, 存款, 所有物
(FRE) holding

(GER) Holding *f*, Beteiligung *f*, Besitz *m*
(JAP) 支持、保有、所有
(RUS) ХОЛДИНГ

holding company
(CHIN) 控股公司
(FRE) holding, société de portefeuille
(GER) Holding-Gesellschaft *f*, Kontroll-, Beteiligungsgesellschaft *f*; Holding *f*
(JAP) 親会社、持ち株会社
(RUS) ХОЛДИНГОВАЯ КОМПАНИЯ

holding fee
(CHIN) 储存费，保管费
(FRE) coût de detention, (C) frais d'attente
(GER) Bestandskosten *pl*
(JAP) 保有手数料
(RUS) СБОР ЗА УЧАСТИЕ В КАПИТАЛЕ

holding period
(CHIN) 持有期间
(FRE) durée de detention, (C) période d'attente
(GER) Eigentums-, Besitzdauer *f*, Haltezeit *f*, Haltefrist *f*; Sperrfrist *f*
(JAP) 保有期間
(RUS) СРОК ВЛАДЕНИЯ АКТИВАМИ

holdover tenant
(CHIN) 赖住租户
(FRE) locataire demeurant dans les lieux après l'expiration ou la résiliation du bail, (C) locataire en souffrance
(GER) Mieter *m* der bei Ablauf *m* des Mietvertrags *m* die Immobilie *f* nicht räumt
(JAP) 保有期間満了後占有者
(RUS) АРЕНДАТОР, СОХРАНЯЮЩИЙ АРЕНДУЕМЫЙ ОБЪЕКТ ПО ОКОНЧАНИИ СРОКА АРЕНДЫ

home key
(CHIN) (光标)返回原址键
(FRE) touche début
(GER) Hometaste *f*
(JAP) ホームキー
(RUS) КЛАВИША ВОЗВРАТА К НАЧАЛУ ЭКРАНА (ЛЕВОМУ ВЕРХНЕМУ УГЛУ ЭКРАНА ДИСПЛЕЯ)

homeowner's association
(CHIN) 屋主协会
(FRE) association de propriétaires
(GER) Eigenheimbesitzerverband *m*
(JAP) 住宅所有者協会
АССОЦИАЦИЯ, СОЮЗ ДОМОВЛАДЕЛЬЦЕВ

homeowner's equity account
(CHIN) 屋主产权账户
(FRE) compte capitaux, balance des opérations en capital, compte capital, compte de capital, (C) compte de capital des propriétaires
(GER) Kreditlinienkonto *n* für Eigenheimbesitzer *m*
(JAP) 住宅所有者持分勘定
(RUS) КРЕДИТ, ПРЕДОСТАВЛЯЕМЫЙ ДОМОВЛАДЕЛЬЦУ ПОД ОБЕСПЕЧЕНИЕ НЕДВИЖИМОСТЬЮ

homeowner's policy
(CHIN) 屋主保险单
(FRE) assurance habitation, (C) assurance des propriétaires occupants
(GER) Police *f* für Eigenheimbesitzer *mpl*
(JAP) 住宅所有者保険証券 (または約款)
(RUS) СТРАХОВОЙ ПОЛИС ДОМОВЛАДЕЛЬЦА

homeowner warranty program (HOW)
(CHIN) 屋主担保计划（HOW）
(FRE) « homeowner warranty program » (programme de garantie des nouvelles constructions), (C) programme de garantie pour les propriétaires
(GER) Garantieprogramm *n* für Eigenheimbesitzer *mpl*
(JAP) 住宅所有者保証プログラム
(RUS) ПРОГРАММА ГАРАНТИЙ И СТРАХОВАНИЯ, ПРЕДЛАГАЕМАЯ ДОМОСТРОИТЕЛЯМИ

home page
(CHIN) 主页，起始页
(FRE) page d'accueil
(GER) Einstiegsseite *f*, Homepage *f*, Startseite *f*
(JAP) ホームページ
(RUS) БАЗОВАЯ СТРАНИЦА САЙТА

homestead
(CHIN) 家宅，宅地
(FRE) bien de famille propriété familiale,
(C) bien-fonds de famille
(GER) Eigenheim *n*; Gehöft *n*; Heimstätte *f*
(JAP) 家屋敷
(RUS) ЖИЛИЩЕ С ПРИЛЕГАЮЩИМ
УЧАСТКОМ

homestead tax exemption
(CHIN) 宅地税务免除
(FRE) exonération pour la résidence
principale, (C) exonération d'impôt pour
bien-fonds de famille
(GER) Steuerbefreiung *f* bzw.
Steuerfreibetrag *m* für Eigenheim *n*
(JAP) 不動産税免除
(RUS) НАЛОГОВЫЕ ЛЬГОТЫ НА МЕСТО
ПОСТОЯННОГО ПРОЖИВАНИЯ

homogeneous
(CHIN) 同质的，同种类的
(FRE) homogène
(GER) homogen *adj*
(JAP) 同質的な、均質的な
(RUS) ОДНОРОДНЫЙ

homogeneous oligopoly
(CHIN) 同质垄断
(FRE) oligopole homogène
(GER) homogenes Oligopol *n*
(JAP) 同質的寡占
(RUS) ОДНОРОДНАЯ ОЛИГОПОЛИЯ
(частичная монополия)

honor
(CHIN) 承付，承兑，付款，荣誉
(FRE) honneur, distinction
(GER) Ehre *f*; Auszeichnung *f*;
erfüllen, einhalten *v*
(JAP) 引き受けて支払う、引き受ける、
支払う
(RUS) ПРИЗНАВАТЬ; УВАЖАТЬ;
СОБЛЮДАТЬ

honorarium
(CHIN) 报酬金
(FRE) honoraries, (C) cachetier
(GER) Honorar *n*

(JAP) 謝礼金
(RUS) ГОНОРАР

horizontal analysis
(CHIN) 横向分析
(FRE) analyse horizontale
(GER) Horizontalanalyse *f*
(JAP) 水平分析
(RUS) ГОРИЗОНТАЛЬНЫЙ АНАЛИЗ

horizontal channel integration
(CHIN) 横向企业合并
(FRE) intégration horizontale,
(C) intégration horizontale des concurrents
(GER) horizontale Eingliederung *f* bzw.
Zusammenlegung *f*; Verschmelzung *f* von
Konkurrenzunternehmen bzw. *npl*/
von gleichartigen Unternehmen *npl*
(JAP) 水平チャンネル統合
(RUS) ИНТЕГРАЦИЯ ПО
ГОРИЗОНТАЛЬНЫМ КАНАЛАМ (компаний,
занимающихся одинаковой деятельностью)

horizontal combination
(CHIN) 横向合并，同业联合
(FRE) concentration horizontale intégration
horizontale
(GER) horizontaler Zusammenschluss *m*,
horizontaler Konzern *m*,
Horizontalverflechtung *f*
(JAP) 水平結合
(RUS) СЛИЯНИЕ ПО ГОРИЗОНТАЛЬНЫМ
КАНАЛАМ (см. выше)

horizontal expansion
(CHIN) 横向发展
(FRE) expansion horizontale
(GER) horizontales Wachstum *n*,
horizontale Expansion *f*
(JAP) 水平拡張
(RUS) ГОРИЗОНТАЛЬНОЕ РАСШИРЕНИЕ,
РАЗВИТИЕ (см. Выше)

horizontal merger
(CHIN) 横向合并，同行业合并
(FRE) fusion horizontale
(GER) horizontale Fusion *f*,
Zusammenschluss *m* von
Konkurrenzunternehmen *npl*
(JAP) 水平合併

(RUS) ГОРИЗОНТАЛЬНОЕ СЛИЯНИЕ (см. выше)

horizontal specialization

(CHIN) 横向专业分工
(FRE) spécialisation horizontale
(GER) horizontale Spezialisierung *f*
(JAP) 水平特殊化
(RUS) ГОРИЗОНТАЛЬНАЯ СПЕЦИАЛИЗАЦИЯ (см. выше)

horizontal union

(CHIN)同业工会，行业工会
(FRE) syndicat de corps de métier,
(C) syndicat horizontal
(GER) Berufs- *f*, Fachgewerkschaft *f*
(JAP) 水平合併、水平団結
(RUS) ГОРИЗОНТАЛЬНЫЙ ПРОФСОЮЗ (см. выше)

host computer

(CHIN) 主机
(FRE) ordinateur hôte
(GER) Verarbeitungsrechner *m*, Gastcomputer *m*, Hostrechner *m*
(RUS) ГЛАВНАЯ ВЫЧИСЛИТЕЛЬНАЯ МАШИНА

hot cargo

(CHIN) 热门货物
(FRE) articles interdits
(GER) Güter *npl* eines bestreikten Unternehmens *n*
(JAP) 盗品貨物、密輸貨物、ホットカーゴ
(RUS) ТОВАР ПРОИЗВОДИТЕЛЯ, НАХОДЯЩЕГОСЯ В КОНФЛИКТЕ С ПРОФСОЮЗОМ

hot issue

(CHIN) 热门股票
(FRE) question brûlante, problèmeaigu, problème controversé, émission d'actions vedettes, émission d'actions très côtées, (C) émission populaire
(GER) Spekulationswert *m*, heisse Emission *f*; überzeichnetes Papier *n*
(JAP) 人気新銘柄、緊急問題、注目材料
(RUS) АКЦИИ НОВОГО ВЫПУСКА, ПОЛЬЗУЮЩИЕСЯ ПОВЫШЕННЫМ СПРОСОМ

hot stock

(CHIN) 热门股票
(FRE) action dont le cours bondit des son premier jour de cotation en bours, (C) titre volé, titre populaire
(GER) spekulative Aktie *f*, spekulatives Wertpapier *m*
高人気の新規発売株
(RUS) (ТОЖЕ, ЧТО И HOT ISSUE) УКРАДЕННЫЙ ТОВАР

house

(CHIN) 场所，机构，号子
(FRE) maison, demeure, habitation, (C) établissement
(GER) Kammer *f*; Abgeordnetenhaus *n*, Parlament *n*
(JAP) 家屋、住宅
(RUS) ДОМ; ПАЛАТА

house account

(CHIN) 大客户
(FRE) compte maison, (C) compte de membre
(GER) Hauskonto *n*
(JAP) 社内勘定
(RUS) СЧЕТ В ШТАБ-КВАРТИРЕ БРОКЕРСКОЙ ФИРМЫ

house to house

(CHIN) 挨户服务
(FRE) domicile-domicile, (C) porte à porte
(GER) Haus-zu-Haus *adj*
(JAP) 戸ごとの、家から家へ
(RUS) ДОСТАВКА ОТ ДВЕРИ ОТПРАВЛЯЮЩЕГО К ДВЕРИ ПОЛУЧАЮЩЕГО

house-to-house sampling

(CHIN) 挨家挨户派发样品
(GER) Stichprobennahme *f* von Haus-zu-Haus
(JAP) 家をまわって抽出見本をとる
(RUS) РАСПРОСТРАНЕНИЕ ОБРАЗЦОВ ТОВАРА ПО СЕМЬЯМ ДЛЯ ИЗУЧЕНИЯ ПОТЕНЦИАЛЬНОГО СПРОСА

house-to-house selling

(CHIN) 挨家挨户推销
(FRE) vente en porte à porte, (C) vente de porte à porte

(GER) von Haus-zu-Haus Direktverkauf *m* durch Vertreter *m*, Verkauf *m* durch Hausierer *m*
(JAP) 家をまわっつって販売
(RUS) ПРОДАЖА «ПО ДОМАМ»

housing bond
(CHIN) 住宅债券
(FRE) obligation immobilière, (C) obligation finançant la construction d'immeubles
(GER) von der örtlichen Wohnungsbehörde *f* begebene Obligation *f*
(JAP) 住宅証券、住宅債券
(RUS) ЖИЛИЩНАЯ ОБЛИГАЦИЯ

housing code
(CHIN) 住宅建设规范
(FRE) code de l'habitation, (C) code du logement
(GER) baupolizeiliche Verordnung *f*
(JAP) 住宅基準法規
(RUS) КОДЕКС ЖИЛИЩНЫХ НОРМ

housing starts
(CHIN) 新开工住宅数
(FRE) nombre de logement mis en chantier, (C) mises en chantier d'habitations
(GER) neue Wohnungsbauten *mpl*, Wohnungsneubauten *mpl*
(JAP) 住宅着工件数
(RUS) ЭКОНОМИЧЕСКИЙ ПОКАЗАТЕЛЬ КОЛИЧЕСТВА НОВЫХ ЗАСТРОЕК ЗА ОПРЕДЕЛЁННЫЙ ПЕРИОД ВРЕМЕНИ

huckster
(CHIN) 沿街贩卖者
(FRE) publicitaire (qui travaille pour la radio et la télévision), (C) mercanti, colporteur
(GER) Straßenhändler *m*; Profitmacher *m*
(JAP) 行商人、宣伝屋、強引なセールスマン
(RUS) НЕЧЕСТНЫЙ ТОРГОВЕЦ, ТОЛКАЧ

human factors
(CHIN) 人为因素
(FRE) facteurs humains
(GER) menschliche Faktoren *mpl*, menschliche Seite *f*
(JAP) 人的要素、人的要因

(RUS) ЧЕЛОВЕЧЕСКИЙ ФАКТОР

human relations
(CHIN) 人事关系，人际关系
(FRE) relations humaines
(GER) zwischenmenschliche Beziehungen *fpl*; Personalabteilung *f*
(JAP) 人的関係論、ヒューマンリレーションズ
(RUS) ОТНОШЕНИЯ МЕЖДУ ЛЮДЬМИ

human resource accounting
(CHIN) 人力资源会计
(FRE) gestion des ressources humaines, (C) comptabilité des ressources humaines
(GER) Erfassung *f* des betrieblichen Humanvermögens *n*
(JAP) 人的資源会計
(RUS) УЧЕТ ЛЮДСКИХ РЕСУРСОВ

human resources
(CHIN) 人力资源
(FRE) ressources humaines
(GER) Personalwesen *n*, Humanvermögen *n*, HR *fpl*
(JAP) 人的資源
(RUS) ЛЮДСКИЕ РЕСУРСЫ

human resources management (HRM)
(CHIN) 人力资源管理（HRM）
(FRE) gestion des ressources humaines
(GER) Personalmanagement *n*, -leitung *f*
(JAP) 人的資源管理
(RUS) РАСПОРЯЖЕНИЕ ЛЮДСКИМИ РЕСУРСАМИ

hurdle rate
(CHIN) 设定利率
(FRE) taux de rendement minimal
(GER) erwartete Mindestrendite *f*; Basisvergütung *f*
(JAP) 投資の期待率収益
(RUS) МИНИМАЛЬНО ПРИЕМЛЕМЫЙ УРОВЕНЬ ДОХОДА

hush money
(CHIN) 贿赂，贿赂金
(FRE) prix du silence
(GER) Schweigegeld *n*, Bestechungsgeld *n*

(JAP) 口止め料
(RUS) ПЛАТА, ВЗЯТКА ЗА
МОЛЧАНИЕ

hybrid annuity
(CHIN) 混合年金
(FRE) rente mixte, (C) rente viagère
hybride
(GER) Hybridrentenprodukt *n*, gemischte
Annuität *f*
(JAP) 混合型確定年金、
複合確定年金
(RUS) ГИБРИДНЫЙ
АННУИТЕТ

hyperinflation
(CHIN) 恶性通货膨胀
(FRE) hyperinflation, (C) inflation
galopante
(GER) Hyperinflation *f*
(JAP) 超インフレーション、
ハイパーインフレーション
(RUS) ГИПЕРИНФЛЯЦИЯ

hyperlink
(CHIN) 超级链接
(FRE) lien hypertexte
(GER) Hyperlink *m*, Querverweis *m*
(RUS) ДОСТУП К КАНАЛУ
СВЯЗИ

hypertext
(CHIN) 超文本
(FRE) hypertexte
(GER) Hypertext *m*
(JAP) ハイパーテキスト
(RUS) ГИПЕРТЕКСТ

hypothecate
(CHIN) 抵押，担保
(FRE) hypothéquer
(GER) verpfänden, (mit einer Hypothek *f*)
belasten, beleihen; lombardieren *v*
(JAP) （不動産等を）担保にいれる
(RUS) ИМЕТЬ ИПОТЕЧНЫЕ ОТНОШЕНИЯ

hypothesis
(CHIN)假设，猜测，前提
(FRE) hypothèse
(GER) Hypothese *f*, Annahme *f*
(JAP) 仮定、仮説、前提
(RUS) ГИПОТЕЗА

hypothesis testing
(CHIN) 假设检验
(FRE) vérification des hypothèses, test
d'hypothèse
(GER) Hypothesenuntersuchung *m*
(JAP) 仮説テスト
(RUS) ПРОВЕРКА, ИСПЫТАНИЕ
ГИПОТЕЗЫ

I

icon
(CHIN) 图标
(FRE) icône
(GER) Symbol *n*
(JAP) アイコン
(RUS) ПИКТОГРАММА (компьют.)

ideal capacity
(CHIN) 理想生产能力
(FRE) capacité idéale
(GER) Betriebs- *n*, Kapazitätsoptimum *n*
(JAP) 理想能力、収容力
(RUS) ИДЕАЛЬНАЯ МОЩНОСТЬ

idle capacity
(CHIN) 闲置生产能力
(FRE) capital improductif, capacité de production inutilisée
(GER) ungenutzte Kapazität *f*, Unterauslastung *f*, Leerkapazität *f*
(JAP) 遊休能力
(RUS) ПРОСТАИВАЮЩАЯ МОЩНОСТЬ

illegal dividend
(CHIN) 非法分红
(FRE) dividende illégal
(GER) unrechtmäßiger Gewinnanteil *m*
(JAP) 不法配当
(RUS) НЕЗАКОННЫЙ ДИВИДЕНД

illiquid
(CHIN) 资金周转困难的公司，非流动资产
(FRE) non liquide, non disponible, immobilisé
(GER) illiquide, nicht flüssig; schwer handelbar *adj*
(JAP) 非流動的、流動資産に欠けている
(RUS) НЕЛИКВИДНЫЙ

image
(CHIN) 图象，影象，映象
(FRE) image
(GER) Abbildung *f*, Bild *n*
(JAP) 画像、像、イメージ
(RUS) ОБРАЗ, ИЗОБРАЖЕНИЕ

image advertising
(CHIN) 形象广告
(FRE) publicité institutionnelle, publicité de prestige, (C) publicité d'entreprise
(GER) Imagewerbung *f*, Repräsentationswerbung *f*
(JAP) イメージ広告
(RUS) РЕКЛАМА, НАПРАВЛЕННАЯ НА СОЗДАНИЕИМИДЖА

image definition
(CHIN) 图象定义
(FRE) définition d'image
(GER) Bildschärfe *f*
(JAP) 画像定義
(RUS) ОПИСАНИЕ ИЗОБРАЖЕНИЯ

image file
(CHIN) 图象文件
(FRE) dossier d'image
(GER) Bilddatei *f*
(JAP) 画像ファイル
(RUS) ЗАГРУЗОЧНЫЙ МОДУЛЬ, ФАЙЛ ОБРАЗА ЗАДАЧИ

impacted area
(CHIN) 受影响地区
(FRE) zone touchée
(GER) betroffenes Gebiet *n* bzw. Bereich *m*
(JAP) インパクトエリア、衝撃を受ける地域または範囲
(RUS) ЗОНА ВОЗДЕЙСТВИЯ, ПОРАЖЕНИЯ

impaired capital
(CHIN) 资本不足，削弱的资本
(FRE) quasi-contrat
(GER) (durch Verlust *m*) gemindertes Kapital *n*, nicht gedecktes Kapital *n*
(JAP) 減殺資本
(RUS) , УМЕНЬШИВШИЙСЯ ПО СРАВНЕНИЮ С ОБЪЯВЛЕННЫМ

impasse
(CHIN) 僵局
(FRE) impasse

(GER) Sackgasse *f*, Pattsituation *f*,
ausweglose Situation *f*
(JAP) 袋小路、難局、窮境
(RUS) ТУПИКОВАЯ СИТУАЦИЯ

imperfect market
(CHIN) 不完全市场
(FRE) marché imparfait
(GER) imperfekter Market *m*
(JAP) 不完全市場
(RUS) НЕСОВЕРШЕННЫЙ РЫНОК

imperialism
(CHIN) 帝国主义
(FRE) imperialisme
(GER) Imperialismus *m*
(JAP) 帝国主義
(RUS) ИМПЕРИАЛИЗМ

implied
(CHIN) 默示的
(FRE) implicite
(GER) stillschweigend zugesichert,
impliziert *adj*; unterstellt *adj*
(JAP) 含蓄された、言外の
(RUS) ПОДРАЗУМЕВАЕМЫЙ; НЕЯВНЫЙ

implied contract
(CHIN) 默约，默示合同
(FRE) contrat tacite
(GER) stillschweigend bzw. konkludent
abgeschlossener Vertrag *m*
(JAP) 黙示的契約
(RUS) ПОДРАЗУМЕВАЕМАЯ
ДОГОВОРЕННОСТЬ

implied easement
(CHIN) 默示地役权
(FRE) servitude implicite
(GER) übernommene
dienstbarkeitsähnliche Verpflichtung *f*
(JAP) 黙示的地役権
(RUS) ПОДРАЗУМЕВАЕМОЕ ПРАВО
ПРОХОДА И Т. П. ПО ЧУЖОЙ ЗЕМЛЕ

implied in fact contract
(CHIN) 事实上默认的合同
(FRE) contrat implicite dans les faits
(GER) auf einem gemeinsamen Konsens *m*
basierender stillschweigender Vertrag *m*

(JAP) 黙示的実際契約
(RUS) ФАКТИЧЕСКИЙ, НО НЕ
ОФОРМЛЕННЫЙ ДОГОВОР

implied warranty
(CHIN) 默示担保
(FRE) garantie implicite
(GER) stillschweigende Garantie *f*,
implizierte Gewährleistung *f*,
Anscheinsgarantie *f*
(JAP) 黙示的保証
(RUS) ПОДРАЗУМЕВАЕМАЯ ГАРАНТИЯ

import
(CHIN) 进口，输入
(FRE) importer
(GER) import *m*, Einfuhr *f*
(JAP) 輸入
(RUS) ИМПОРТ

import quota
(CHIN) 进口配额
(FRE) contingent d'importation, quota
d'importation
(GER) import- *n*, Einfuhrkontingent *n*,
Import- *f*, Einfuhrquote *f*
(JAP) 輸入割当
(RUS) ИМПОРТНАЯ КВОТА

imposition
(CHIN) 缴税，税款
(FRE) imposition
(GER) Auferlegung *f*, Verhängung *f*
(JAP) 賦課、課税、負担
(RUS) ОБЛОЖЕНИЕ (НАЛОГОМ),
НАВЯЗЫВАНИЕ

impound
(CHIN) 扣押，没收
(FRE) confisquer, saisir, faire deposer au
greffe
(GER) beschlagnahmen, pfänden,
sicherstellen, einziehen, in gerichtliche
Verwahrung *f* nehmen *v*
(JAP) 押収する、没収する
(RUS) ЗАДЕРЖИВАТЬ; ИЗЫМАТЬ

impound account
(CHIN) 储备金账户
(FRE) compte saisi

(GER) Treuhandkonto *n*,
Hinterlegungskonto *n*
(JAP) 口座を押収する
(RUS) ЗАДЕРЖАННЫЙ СЧЕТ

imprest fund, imprest system
(CHIN) 定额储备金，定额备用金制
(FRE) fonds de caisse a montant fixe,
comptabilité de prévision
(GER) Kleine Kasse *f*, fester Kassenbestand
m, Sonderfonds *m*, Spesen-,
Vorschusskonto *n*;
Kassenvorschusssystem *n*
(JAP) 定額前渡し資金、定額（資金）前
渡し制
(RUS) СЧЕТ, ОСТАТОК НА КОТОРОМ
ДОЛЖЕН РАВНЯТЬСЯ ОГОВОРЕННОЙ
СУММЕ; СИСТЕМА ОГОВОРЕННЫХ
СУММ

improved land
(CHIN) 熟地，已开发土地
(FRE) terrain viabilisé
(GER) kultiviertes bzw. erschlossenes
Land *n*
(JAP) 改良された土地
(RUS) БЛАГОУСТРОЕННЫЙ,
ОЗЕЛЕНЕННЫЙ ЗЕМЕЛЬНЫЙ УЧАСТОК

improvement
(CHIN) 改良，改善
(FRE) embellissement
(GER) Verbesserung *f*, Steigerung *f*
(JAP) 改良、増進
(RUS) УСОВЕРШЕНСТВОВАНИЕ;
МОДЕРНИЗАЦИЯ

improvements and betterments insurance
(CHIN) 装修改建保险
(FRE) garantie pour améliorations locatives
(GER) Versicherung *f* für (vom Mieter
durchgeführte) Werterhaltungs- und
Wertsteigerungsmaßnahmen *fpl*
(JAP) 改良設備保険
(RUS) СТРАХОВАНИЕ
БЛАГОУСТРОЙСТВА И
СОВЕРШЕНСТВОВАНИЯ

imputed cost
(CHIN)假设成本，归宿成本，估算成本
(FRE) coût implicite, coût imputé

(GER) kalkulatorische Kosten *pl*, nicht
erfasste Kosten *pl*
(JAP) 帰属原価
(RUS) ВМЕНЁННЫЕ ИЗДЕРЖКИ

imputed income
(CHIN) 应计收入，估算收入
(FRE) revenu impute, loyer imputé
(GER) geschätztes bzw. zurechenbares
Einkommen *n*
(JAP) 帰属所得
(RUS) ВМЕНЁННЫЙ ДОХОД

imputed interest
(CHIN) 应计利息，估算利息
(FRE) intérêt implicite
(GER) fiktive Zinsen *mpl*,
zurechenbare Zinsen *mpl*; unterstellte
Zinsen *mpl*
(JAP) 帰属利子
(RUS) ВМЕНЁННЫЕ ПРОЦЕНТЫ

**imputed value or imputed
income**
(CHIN) 估算价值或估算收入
(FRE) revenu imputé
(GER) veranschlagter Wert *m*,
steuerlich angerechneter Wert *m*
(JAP) 帰属価値または帰属所得
(RUS) ВМЕНЁННАЯ СТОИМОСТЬ

inactive stock or inactive bond
(CHIN) 呆滞股票或呆滞证券
(FRE) titre inactive, action inactive
(GER) tote, flaue, selten gehandelte Aktie *f*
oder Obligation *f*, Aktie *f* bzw. Obligation *f*
mit geringen Umsätzen *mpl*
(JAP) 不活発株、不人気株、
または不人気債券
(RUS) НЕХОДОВАЯ АКЦИЯ или
НЕХОДОВАЯ ОБЛИГАЦИЯ

inadvertently
(CHIN) 疏忽的，非有意的
(FRE) par inadvertance
(GER) versehentlich, ungewollt,
unbeabsichtigt *adj*
(JAP) 不注意に
(RUS) НЕПРЕДНАМЕРЕННО; ПО
НЕДОСМОТРУ

incapacity

(CHIN) 无能，丧失能力

(FRE) incapacité

(GER) (Rechts-, Geschäfts)unfähigkeit *f*, Invalidität *f*

(JAP) 無能、無力、無能力

(RUS) НЕСПОСОБНОСТЬ; НЕПРИГОДНОСТЬНЕПРАВОСПОСОБНОСТЬ

incentive fee

(CHIN) 奖励费

(FRE) prime d'incitation

(GER) Erfolgs-, Anreizhonorar *n*; Anreizprämie *f* (Marketing)

(JAP) 奨励報酬

(RUS) ПООЩРИТЕЛЬНАЯ ПРЕМИЯ

incentive pay

(CHIN) 奖金

(FRE) prime de rendement

(GER) Entlohnung *f* auf Leistungsgrundlage *f*, Leistungs- *m*, Erfolgslohn *m*

(JAP) 報酬金、奨励金

(RUS) ПООЩРИТЕЛЬНАЯ ОПЛАТА

incentive wage plan

(CHIN) 奖励工资计划

(FRE) plan de prime au rendement, (C) régime de rémunération au rendement

(GER) Leistungslohnsystem *n*, leistungsabhängige Lohnform *f*

(JAP) 奨励賃金制、奨励金計画

(RUS) СХЕМА ПРОГРЕССИВНОЙ ЗАРАБОТНОЙ ПЛАТЫ

incentive stock option (ISO)

(CHIN) 奖励性股票认购权 （ISO）

(FRE) option d'achat d'actions, plan d'option

(GER) Aktien-Incentive-Programm *n*, Aktienanreizplan *m*

(JAP) 自社株奨励購入権

(RUS) ПРАВО НА ПОКУПКУ АКЦИЙ КОМПАНИИ (работником) ПО ОГОВОРЕННОЙ ЦЕНЕ, БЕЗ НАЛОГА

inchoate

(CHIN) 空白汇票

(FRE) en puissance, incomplet,

(C) imparfait

(GER) entstehend, im Entstehen begriffen; nicht vollendet, unausgereift, rudimentär *adj*

(JAP) 未終結の

(RUS) НЕ ЗАКОНЧЕННЫЙ; НЕЗАВЕРШЕННЫЙ; НЕ ОФОРМЛЕННЫЙ ОКОНЧАТЕЛЬНО

incidental damages

(CHIN) 附带损失，杂项损失

(FRE) dommages accessoires

(GER) Schadenersatz *m* für Aufwendungen *fpl* bei Vertragserfüllung *f*; Ersatz *m* beiläufig entstandener Schäden *mpl*

(JAP) 偶発損害賠償金

(RUS) НЕИЗБЕЖНО ПОСЛЕДОВАВШИЙ УЩЕРБ

income

(CHIN) 收入，收益，所得

(FRE) revenu

(GER) Einkommen *n*, Bezüge *mpl*, Verdienst *m*; Ertrag *m*; Einkünfte *pl*, Einnahmen *pl*; Gewinn *m*

(JAP) 所得、収益

(RUS) ДОХОД

income accounts

(CHIN) 收益账户，损益账户

(FRE) comptes de produits

(GER) Einkommenskonto *n*; Ertrags- *n*, Ergebnis-*n*, Erlöskonto *n*; Aufwendungen *fpl* und Erträge *mpl*

(JAP) 収入勘定、所得勘定

(RUS) СЧЁТ ДОХОДОВ

income approach

(CHIN) 收入法，收益法

(FRE) méthode de détermination du revenu

(GER) Ertragsansatz *m*, einkunftsbasierter Ansatz *m*

(JAP) 所得接近方

(RUS) МЕТОД ОЦЕНКИ НЕДВИЖИМОСТИ ПУТЁМ ОЦЕНКИ ПОТЕНЦИАЛЬНОГОДОХОДА ОТ ЕЁ ИСПОЛЬЗОВАНИЯ

income averaging

(CHIN) 收入平均法

(FRE) moyenne du revenu, établissement de la moyenne du revenu
(GER) Durchschnittsbesteuerung *f*; Einkommensverteilung *f* auf mehrere Jahre *npl*, Berechnung *f* des Durchschnittsatzes *m*
(JAP) 所得平均化
(RUS) МЕТОД РАСПРЕДЕЛЕНИЯ ФЕРМЕРСКОГО ДОХОДА ТЕКУЩЕГО ГОДА НА ПРЕДЫДУЩИЕ ТРИ ГОДА

income bond
(CHIN) 收益债券
(FRE) obligation à intérêt conditionnel
(GER) Gewinnschuldverschreibung *f*, -obligation *f*, Besserungsschein *n*, Obligation *f* mit Gewinnbeteiligung *f*
(JAP) 収益債券、収益社債
(RUS) ДОХОДНАЯ ОБЛИГАЦИЯ, Т. Е. ТА, ПО КОТОРОЙ ВЫПЛАЧИВАЮТСЯ ПРОЦЕНТЫ ТОЛЬКО ПРИ НАЛИЧИИ ПРИБЫЛИ У КОМПАНИИ

income effect
(CHIN) 收入效应
(FRE) effet de revenu
(GER) Einkommenseffekt *m*
(JAP) 所得効果
(RUS) ЭФФЕКТ ДОХОДА

income group
(CHIN) 收入组别
(FRE) tranche de salaries, tranche de revenus
(GER) Einkommensklasse *f*, -gruppe *f*, -stufe *f*
(JAP) 所得階層、所得層
(RUS) ГРУППА НАСЕЛЕНИЯ, ИМЕЮЩЕГО ОДИНАКОВЫЙ ДОХОД

income in respect of a decedent
(CHIN) 死者的持续收入
(FRE) revenus relatifs au défunt
(GER) Einkommen *n* unter Berücksichtigung *f* einesVerstorbenen *m*, vom Erblasser *m* erwirtschaftetes aber nicht versteuertes Einkommen *n*
(JAP) 死亡者に係わる所得
(RUS) ДОХОД, ПРИЧИТАВШИЙСЯ УМЕРШЕМУ ПОСЛЕ СМЕРТИ

income property
(CHIN) 收入财产
(FRE) immobilier de rapport
(GER) Renditeobjekt *n*
(JAP) 利益財産、収益財産
(RUS) ДОХОДНАЯ СОБСТВЕННОСТЬ

income redistribution
(CHIN) 收入再分配
(FRE) redistribution des revenus
(GER) Einkommensumschichtung *f*, -umverteilung *f*
(JAP) 所得再分配
(RUS) ПЕРЕРАСПРЕДЕЛЕНИЕ ДОХОДОВ

income replacement
(CHIN) 折合收入
(FRE) remplacement de revenu
(GER) Einkommensersatz *m*
(JAP) 代替所得
(RUS) ЗАМЕНА ИСТОЧНИКА ДОХОДА

income splitting
(CHIN) 收入分析
(FRE) fractionnement du revenu
(GER) Splitting *n*, Einkommensaufteilung *f*,
(JAP) 所得分割法
(RUS) РАЗДЕЛЕНИЕ ДОХОДА

income statement
(CHIN) 收益表，损益表
(FRE) compte d'exploitation
(GER) Gewinn- *f* und Verlustrechnung *f*, Ergebnis- *f*, Erfolgsrechnung *f*, Erfolgsbilanz *f*, Aufwands- *f* und Ertragsrechnung *f*; Einkommensnachweis *m*
(JAP) 所得計算書、損益計算書
(RUS) ОТЧЕТ О ДОХОДЕ

income stream
(CHIN) 收入流
(FRE) flux de revenus
(GER) Einnahmequelle *f*
(JAP) 所得流れ
(RUS) ПОТОК ДОХОДОВ

income tax
(CHIN) 所得税
(FRE) impôt sur le revenu

(GER) Einkommensteuer f
(JAP) 所得税
(RUS) ПОДОХОДНЫЙ НАЛОГ

income tax return

(CHIN) 所得税报税单
(FRE) déclaration de revenus
(GER) Einkommens- f,
Lohnsteuererklärung f
(JAP) 所得税申告、所得税申告書
(RUS) ДЕКЛАРАЦИЯ ПОДОХОДНОГО
НАЛОГА

incompatible

(CHIN) 不相容的，不兼容的
(FRE) incompatible
(GER) nicht kompatibel adj
(JAP) 互換性がない
(RUS) НЕСОВМЕСТИМЫЙ

incompetent

(CHIN) 无管辖权，无能力
(FRE) incompetent, non qualifié
(GER) unfähig, inkompetent; nicht
zuständig; unzulässig adj
(JAP) 無能力な、証言能力のない、
禁治産者
(RUS) НЕКОМПЕТЕНТНЫЙ

incontestable clause

(CHIN) 不可抗辩条款
(FRE) clause d'incontestabilité
(GER) Unanfechtbarkeitsklausel f
(JAP) 不可争条項
(RUS) НЕОСПОРИМОЕ ПОЛОЖЕНИЕ,
КЛАУЗУЛА (В ДОГОВОРЕ)

inconvertible money

(CHIN) 不能兑现的货币，不兑换货币
(FRE) monnaie inconvertible
(GER) Papiergeld n, Banknoten fpl,
Notenumlauf m
(JAP) 不兑换貨幣
(RUS) НЕКОНВЕРТИРУЕМАЯ ВАЛЮТА

incorporate

(CHIN) 注册公司，附加
(FRE) Incorporer, organiser, constituer, (C)
constituer en société

(GER) (als Kapitalgesellschaft f) gründen,
als AG eintragen, als juristische Person f
eintragen; eingemeinden v (Ortschaft)
(JAP) 法人を設立する、組み込む
(RUS) ИНКОРПОРИРОВАТЬ; ПОЛУЧАТЬ
ПРАВА ЮРИДИЧЕСКОГО ЛИЦА;
ВКЛЮЧАТЬ В СОСТАВ

incorporation

(CHIN) 成立公司，登记，有限公司
(FRE) incorporation, constitution,
(C) constitution en société
(GER) Errichtung f, Gründung f (einer
juristischen Person f);
Gesellschaftsgründung f, Eintragung f (als
AG f; im Handelsregister n);
Eingemeindung f (Ortschaft)
(JAP) 合併、会社設立、会社
(RUS) РЕГИСТРАЦИЯ ЮРИДИЧЕСКОГО
ЛИЦА, КОРПОРАЦИИ; ВКЛЮЧЕНИЕ В
СОСТАВ ЮРИДИЧЕСКОГО ЛИЦА

inncorporeal property

(CHIN) 无形财产
(FRE) bien incorporel
(GER) immaterielles Eigentum m bzw.
Vermögen n
(JAP) 無体財産
(RUS) НЕМАТЕРИАЛЬНАЯ
СОБСТВЕННОСТЬ

incremental analysis

(CHIN) 增量分析
(FRE) analyse marginaliste
(GER) Zuwachsanalyse f
(JAP) 増分分析
(RUS) ПРИРОСТНОЙ АНАЛИЗ

incremental cash flow

(CHIN) 增加现金流动
(FRE) cash-flow marginal, (C) flux de
trésorerie marginal
(GER) Cashflowzuwachs m, -zunahme f
(JAP) 増分キャッシュフロー
(RUS) ПРИРОСТНОЕ ДВИЖЕНИЕ
НАЛИЧНОСТИ

incremental spending

(CHIN) 增量花费
(FRE) dépenses incrémentielle
(GER) Mehrausgaben pl, Zusatzausgaben pl

(JAP) 増分支出
(RUS) ПРИРОСТНЫЕ РАСХОДЫ

incurable depreciation
(CHIN) 不可挽回的折旧
(FRE) dépréciation incurable
(GER) nicht kompensierbare
Wertminderung *f*
(JAP) 矯正不能減価償却
(RUS) НЕОБРАТИМАЯ АМОРТИЗАЦИЯ

indemnify
(CHIN) 补偿，赔偿，使免于受罚，保护
(FRE) indemniser, dédommager, compenser
(GER) schadlos halten; entschädigen,
abfinden; Schadensersatz *m* leisten *v*
(JAP) 補償する、弁償する
(RUS) ГАРАНТИРОВАТЬ ВОЗМЕЩЕНИЕ
ВРЕДА, УЩЕРБА

indemnity
(CHIN) 赔偿，赔偿金，赔款
(FRE) indemnisation, indemnité
(GER) Abfindung *f*, Entschädigung *f*;
Schadenersatz *m*; Schadloshaltung *f*;
Leistung *f* (Versicherung); Indemnität *f*
(JAP) 損害賠償、弁償金
(RUS) ГАРАНТИЯ ВОЗМЕЩЕНИЯ УЩЕРБА,
УБЫТКОВ

indent
(CHIN) 缩进编排
(FRE) décaler, mettre en retrait
(GER) einrücken *v*
(JAP) インデント、字下げすること
(RUS) ОТСТУП

indenture
(CHIN) 双联合同，契约
(FRE) engagement contractuel
(GER) mehrseitig errichtete
Vertragsurkunde *f*; Lehrbrief *m*
(JAP) 契約書、証書
(RUS) ДОКУМЕНТ, КОНТРАКТ, ДОГОВОР

independence
(CHIN) 独立，自主权
(FRE) indépendance
(GER) Selbständigkeit *f*, Unabhängigkeit *f*
(JAP) 独立、自立

(RUS) НЕЗАВИСИМОСТЬ

independent adjuster
(CHIN) 独立理赔员
(FRE) expert libre, (C) expert en sinistre
indépendant
(GER) selbständiger
Regulierungsbeauftragter *m*
(JAP) 独立調停人、独立損害査定人
(RUS) НЕЗАВИСИМЫЙ ОЦЕНЩИК

independent contractor
(CHIN) 独立承包商
(FRE) travailleur indépendant, indépendant
(GER) selbständiger (Sub)unternehmer *m*
(JAP) 請負人、独立契約者
(RUS) НЕЗАВИСИМЫЙ ПОДРЯДЧИК

independent store
(CHIN) 独立商店
(FRE) magasin indépendant
(GER) selbständiges
Einzelhandelsgeschäft *n*
(JAP) 独立店舗
(RUS) НЕЗАВИСИМЫЙ МАГАЗИН

independent union
(CHIN) 独立工会
(FRE) syndicat indépendant
(GER) unabhängige Gewerkschaft *f*
(JAP) 独立労働組合、単独組合
(RUS) НЕЗАВИСИМЫЙ ПРОФСОЮЗ

independent variables
(CHIN) 自变量
(FRE) variable indépendante, variable
explicative, variable active
(GER) unabhängige Variablen *fpl*
(JAP) 独立変数、自変数
(RUS) НЕЗАВИСИМЫЕ ПЕРЕМЕННЫЕ

indeterminate premium life insurance
(CHIN) 无定额保费人寿保险
(FRE) assurance-vie à prime indéterminée
(GER) Todesfallversicherung *f* mit
unbestimmter Prämie *f*
(JAP) 不確定保険料生命保険
(RUS) СТРАХОВАНИЕ ЖИЗНИ С
НЕФИКСИРОВАННОЙ СТРАХОВОЙ
ПРЕМИЕЙ

index

(CHIN) 指数，指标，目录
(FRE) indice
(GER) Index *m*, Richtzahl *f*;
Stichwortverzeichnis *n*
(JAP) 指数、目録、索引
(RUS) УКАЗАТЕЛЬ; ПОКАЗАТЕЛЬ;
ИНДЕКС; ИНДИКАТОР

indexation

(CHIN) 指数化
(FRE) indexation
(GER) Indexierung *f*
(JAP) インデックス化、指数化
(RUS) ИНДЕКСАЦИЯ

index basis

(CHIN) 指数基准
(FRE) base indicielle
(GER) Indexbasis *f*
(JAP) 指数基準
(RUS) БАЗА ИНДЕКСАЦИИ

indexed life insurance

(CHIN) 指数化人寿保险
(FRE) assurance vie à capital indexé
(GER) dynamische
Lebensversicherung *f*
(JAP) 指数化された生命保険
(RUS) ИНДЕКСИРОВАННОЕ
СТРАХОВАНИЕ ЖИЗНИ

indexed loan

(CHIN) 指数化货款
(FRE) emprunt indexé
(GER) Indexanleihe *f*, Anleihe *f* mit
Indexklausel *f*
(JAP) 指数化された貸付金、指数化され
た融資
(RUS) ИНДЕКСИРОВАННЫЙ КРЕДИТ

index fund

(CHIN) 指数证券投资基金
(FRE) fonds à gestion indicielle, fonds
indiciel
(GER) Indexfonds *m*, an einen Aktienindex
m gekoppelter Investmentfonds *m*
(JAP) 物価指数資金
(RUS) ИНДЕКСИРОВАННЫЙ ФОНД

indexing

(CHIN) 指数调整
(FRE) indexation
(GER) Indexierung *f*, Indexbindung *f*;
Katalogisierung *f*
(JAP) インデクシング
(RUS) ИНДЕКСАЦИЯ

index lease

(CHIN) 指数租赁
(FRE) loyer indexé
(GER) indexgebundene Miete *f*
(JAP) インデックスリース
(RUS) ИНДЕКСИРОВАННАЯ
АРЕНДА

index options

(CHIN) 股票指数选择权
(FRE) options sur indice
(GER) Aktienindexoptionen *fpl*
(JAP) 株価指数オプション
(RUS) ИНДЕКСНЫЕ ОПЦИОНЫ

indirect cost

(CHIN) 间接成本
(FRE) élément indirect du coût de revient,
(C) charge indirecte
(GER) indirekte Kosten *pl*
(JAP) 間接費
(RUS) КОСВЕННЫЕ РАСХОДЫ

indirect labor

(CHIN) 间接人工成本
(FRE) élément indirect du coût de revient
de main d'œuvre, (C) coût de main d'œuvre
indirecte
(GER) Lohn- *pl*, Fertigungsgemeinkosten
pl, Gemeinkostenlöhne *mpl*
(JAP) 間接労働
(RUS) КОСВЕННЫЕ ТРУДОЗАТРАТЫ

indirect overhead

(CHIN) 间接费用
(FRE) frais généraux indirects
(GER) indirekte
Gemeinbetriebskosten *pl*
(JAP) 間接諸経費
(RUS) КОСВЕННЫЕ НАКЛАДНЫЕ
РАСХОДЫ

indirect production
(CHIN) 间接生产
(FRE) production indirecte
(GER) Umweg- *f*, mittelbare Produktion *f*
(JAP) 間接生産
(RUS) КОСВЕННОЕ ПРОИЗВОДСТВО

individual bargaining
(CHIN) 个别谈判，个别议价
(FRE) marchandage sur les salaires,
(C) négociation individuelle
(GER) Einzeltarifvertrag *m*, -verhandlung *f*
(JAP) 個別交渉、個人交渉
(RUS) ИНДИВИДУАЛЬНОЕ ТРУДОВОЕ
СОГЛАШЕНИЕ (не через профсоюз)

individual life insurance
(CHIN) 个人人寿保险
(FRE) assurance vie individuelle
(GER) Einzellebensversicherung *f*,
Individualversicherung *f*
(JAP) 個人生命保険
(RUS) ИНДИВИДУАЛЬНОЕ
СТРАХОВАНИЕ ЖИЗНИ

individual retirement account (IRA)
(CHIN) 个人退休金账户 （IRA）
(FRE) plan d'épargne retraite personnel,
(C) régime d'épargne
(GER) individueller Rentensparplan *m*,
steuerbegünstigtes Sparkonto *n* zur
Alterssicherung *f*
(JAP) 個人退職積立勘定
(RUS) ИНДИВИДУАЛЬНЫЙ
ПЕНСИОННЫЙ СЧЕТ

inductive reasoning
(CHIN) 归纳推理
(FRE) raisonnement inductif
(GER) induktive Beweisführung *f*
(JAP) 帰納的推理
(RUS) ИНДУКТИВНОЕ РАССУЖДЕНИЕ

industrial
(CHIN) 工业的，工业股票，工业公司
(FRE) industriel
(GER) industriell *adj*
(JAP) 産業の、工業の、工業用の
(RUS) ПРОМЫШЛЕННЫЙ

industrial advertising
(CHIN) 工业广告
(FRE) publicité industrielle
(GER) Industriewerbung *f*
(JAP) 産業広告
(RUS) ПРОМЫШЛЕННАЯ РЕКЛАМА

industrial consumer
(CHIN) 工业消费者
(FRE) consommateur industriel
(GER) gewerblicher Abnehmer *m*, Groß- *m*,
Industrieabnehmer *m*
(JAP) 産業消費者、工業消費者
(RUS) ПРОМЫШЛЕННЫЙ ПОТРЕБИТЕЛЬ

industrial engineer
(CHIN) 工业工程师
(FRE) ingénieur industriel, ingénieur en
organisation
(GER) Betriebs- *m*; Wirtschaftsingenieur *m*
(JAP) 産業（または工業）技師、産業
（または工業）エンジニア
(RUS) ИНЖЕНЕР – ТЕХНОЛОГ

industrial fatigue
(CHIN) 工业性疲劳
(FRE) fatigue industrielle
(GER) Ermüdung *f* im Betrieb *m*,
industrielle Ermüdung *f*
(JAP) 産業的疲労
(RUS) ПРОФЕССИОНАЛЬНАЯ
УСТАЛОСТЬ

industrial goods
(CHIN) 工业品，工业用品
(FRE) biens industriels
(GER) Industrieprodukte *npl*, -güter *npl*,
Güter *npl* der gewerblichen Wirtschaft *f*
(JAP) 生産財、工業生品
(RUS) ПРОМЫШЛЕННЫЕ
ТОВАРЫ

industrialist
(CHIN) 实业家，企业家
(FRE) industriel
(GER) Fabrikant *m*, Industrieller *m*,
Unternehmer *m*
(JAP) 産業経営者、実業家、工業家
(RUS) ПРОМЫШЛЕННИК

industrial park
(CHIN) 工业区
(FRE) zone industrielle
(GER) Industriepark *m*, Gewerbegebiet *n*
(JAP) 工業団地
(RUS) ПРОМЫШЛЕННАЯ ЗОНА

industrial production
(CHIN) 工业生产
(FRE) production industrielle
(GER) Industrieproduktion *f*, industrielle Produktion *f*
(JAP) 工業生産、工業生産額
(RUS) ПРОМЫШЛЕННОЕ ПРОИЗВОДСТВО

industrial property
(CHIN) 工业产权
(FRE) propriété industrielle
(GER) Industriegrundstück *n*, gewerblich genutztes Grundstück *n*; gewerbliches Schutzrecht *n* (Patent)
(JAP) 工業所有権
(RUS) ПРОМЫШЛЕННАЯ СОБСТВЕННОСТЬ

industrial psychology
(CHIN) 工业心理学
(FRE) psychologie industrielle
(GER) Arbeits- *f*, Betriebspsychologie *f*
(JAP) 産業心理学
(RUS) ПРОФЕССИОНАЛЬНАЯ ПСИХОЛОГИЯ

industrial relations
(CHIN) 企业关系
(FRE) relations entre le patronat et les salariés, (C) relations professionnelles
(GER) industrielle Arbeitsbeziehungen *fpl*; Arbeitgeber-Arbeitnehmer-Beziehungen *fpl*; Beziehungen *fpl* zwischen Betrieb *m* und überbetrieblichen Institutionen *fpl*, Beziehungen *fpl* zwischen Tarifpartnern *fpl*
(JAP) 労使関係
(RUS) ОТНОШЕНИЯ НА ПРОИЗВОДСТВЕ

Industrial Revolution
(CHIN) 工业革命
(FRE) révolution industrielle
(GER) Industrielle Revolution *f*
(JAP) 産業革命

(RUS) ПРОМЫШЛЕННАЯ РЕВОЛЮЦИЯ

industrial union
(CHIN) 工会
(FRE) syndicat d'industrie
(GER) Industriegewerkschaft *f*, wirtschaftszweiggebundene Gewerkschaft *f*; Einheitsgewerkschaft *f*; Berufs- *m*, Fachverband *m*
(JAP) 産業別組合、産業別労働組合
(RUS) ПРОМЫШЛЕННЫЙ СОЮЗ; СОЮЗ ПРОИЗВОДИТЕЛЕЙ

industry
(CHIN) 工业，实业，行业，产业
(FRE) industrie
(GER) Industrie *f*, Wirtschaftszweig *m*, Branche *f*
(JAP) 産業、工業
(RUS) ПРОМЫШЛЕННОСТЬ; ОТРАСЛЬ

industry standard
(CHIN) 工业标准
(FRE) pratique courante, norme de fait
(GER) Industrienorm *f*, Industriestandard *m*
(JAP) 産業基準
(RUS) ОТРАСЛЕВОЙ СТАНДАРТ

inefficiency in the market
(CHIN) 无效率市场
(FRE) inefficacité sur le marché
(GER) Marktineffizienz *f*
(JAP) 市場における非能率（低能率）
(RUS) НЕЭФФЕКТИВНОСТЬ НА РЫНКЕ

infant industry argument
(CHIN) 幼稚工业保护说
(FRE) argument sur les industries émergentes
(GER) Infant-Industrievertrag *m*, (GER) Infant-Industrieargument *n*
(JAP) 幼稚産業合意
(RUS) АРГУМЕНТ ЗАЩИТЫ МОЛОДЫХ ОТРАСЛЕЙ

inferential statistics
(CHIN) 推理统计
(FRE) statistique inférentielle
(GER) induktive Statistik *f*; Inferenzstatistik *f*

(JAP) 推論的統計、推測的統計
(RUS) ДЕДУКТИВНАЯ СТАТИСТИКА

inferior good
(CHIN) 低档货，次品
(FRE) biens inférieurs, biens de giffen, bas produits
(GER) billige Ersatzgüter *npl*, minderwertige Ware *f*
(JAP) 劣等財、低級財、下級品
(RUS) ТОВАР , ПОТРЕБЛЕНИЕ КОТОРОГО НЕ РАСТЁТ С РОСТОМ ДОХОДОВ НАСЕЛЕНИЯ

inferred authority
(CHIN) 递补职权
(FRE) autorité déduite
(GER) abgeleitete (Vertretungs)vollmacht *f*
(JAP) 推測された権威
(RUS) ПОДРАЗУМЕВАЕМЫЕ ПОЛНОМОЧИЯ

inflation
(CHIN) 通货膨胀
(GER) Inflation *f*, Teuerung *f*
(JAP) インフレ
(RUS) ИНФЛЯЦИЯ

inflation accounting
(CHIN) 通货膨胀会计
(FRE) comptabilité d'inflation
(GER) inflationsbereinigte Rechnungslegung *f*
(JAP) インフレ会計
(RUS) УЧЕТ ИНФЛЯЦИИ В БУХГАЛТЕРСКОЙ ОТЧЕТНОСТИ

inflationary gap
(CHIN) 通货膨胀差额
(FRE) écart inflationniste
(GER) inflatorische Lücke *f*, Inflationslücke *f*
(JAP) インフレギャップ
(RUS) ИНФЛЯЦИОННЫЙ РАЗРЫВ

inflationary spiral
(CHIN) 螺旋式通货膨胀
(FRE) spirale inflationniste
(GER) Inflationsschraube *f*, Inflations-, Preisspirale *f*, Lohn-Preis-Spirale *f*

(JAP) 螺旋状の物価上昇
(RUS) СПИРАЛЬ ИНФЛЯЦИИ

inflation endorsement
(CHIN) 通货膨胀附加条款
(FRE) avenant de protection contre l'inflation
(GER) Inflationsnachtrag *m*, Inflationsklausel *f*
(JAP) （物保険の）インフレ裏書（条項）
(RUS) ИНФЛЯЦИОННЫЙ ИНДОССАМЕНТ

inflation rate
(CHIN) 通货膨胀率
(FRE) taux d'inflation
(GER) Inflations- *f*, Teuerungsrate *f*
(JAP) インフレ率
(RUS) ТЕМП, УРОВЕНЬ ИНФЛЯЦИИ

informal leader
(CHIN) 非正式领袖
(FRE) chef informel
(GER) inoffizielle Führungspersönlichkeit *f*
(JAP) インフォーマルリーダー、非公式リーダー
(RUS) НЕФОРМАЛЬНЫЙ ЛИДЕР

information flow
(CHIN) 信息流程，信息流
(FRE) flux d'informations
(GER) Informationsfluss *m*
(JAP) 情報の流れ
(RUS) ПОТОК ИНФОРМАЦИИ

information page
(CHIN) 信息页
(FRE) page d'informations
(GER) Informationsseite *f*
(JAP) インフォーメーション呼び出し
(RUS) СПРАВОЧНАЯ СТРАНИЦА ПАМЯТИ

information return
(CHIN) 信息申报表
(FRE) retour d'informations
(GER) Rücksendung *f* von Information *f*
(JAP) 支払調書
(RUS) ОДИН ИЗ ВИДОВ ДЕКЛАРАЦИЙ ДЛЯ НАЛОГОВОГО ВЕДОМСТВА,

КОТОРЫЙ ДАЁТ ИНФОРМАЦИЮ ОБ
ИЗМЕНЕНИИ НАЛОГОВОГО СТАТУСА

infrastructure
(CHIN) 基础设施
(FRE) infrastructure
(GER) Infrastruktur *f*
(JAP) 下部構造、下部組織、経済基盤
(RUS) ИНФРАСТРУКТУРА

infringement
(CHIN) 违约，侵犯，违反
(FRE) violation
(GER) Beeinträchtigung *f*; Rechtsbruch *m*,
Verletzung *f* eines gewerblichen
Schutzrechts *n* (Patent)
(JAP) 権利侵害、法規違反
(RUS) НАРУШЕНИЕ (прав, закона)

ingress and egress
(CHIN) 入境及出境权
(FRE) entrées et sorties
(GER) Eintritt *m* und Ausgang *m*; Recht *n*
der freien Zufahrt *f*
(JAP) 土地家屋への出入り、
家屋出入り権
(RUS) ПРАВО ВХОДА И ВЫХОДА

inherent explosion clause
(CHIN) 固有爆炸因素保险条款
(FRE) clause d'explosion inhérente
(GER) mitversicherte bzw. immanente
Explosionsklausel *f*
(JAP) (物保険の)特定立地
(工場などの）爆発危険条項
(RUS) ОГОВОРКА СТРАХОВОГО ПОЛИСА
НА СЛУЧАЙ ВЗРЫВА

inherit
(CHIN) 继承
(FRE) hériter
(GER) erben, beerben *v*
(JAP) 相続する
(RUS) НАСЛЕДОВАТЬ

inheritance
(CHIN) 继承权
(FRE) héritage
(GER) Erbschaft *f*, Erbe *n*, Erbteil *m*,
Hinterlassenschaft *f*; Vererbung *f*

(JAP) 物的財産（法定）相続、法定不動
産相続
(RUS) НАСЛЕДСТВО

inheritance tax
(CHIN) 遗产税
(FRE) droits de succession
(GER) Erbschaftssteuer *f*
(JAP) 遺産相続税、遺産取得税、相続税
(RUS) НАЛОГ НА НАСЛЕДСТВО

in-house
(CHIN) 内部的，对内的
(FRE) interne
(GER) innerbetrieblich, betriebs-, konzern-,
firmenintern *adj*
(JAP) 社内の
(RUS) ШТАТНЫЙ (работник, специалист)

initial public offering (IPO)
(CHIN) 原始公开股（IPO）
(FRE) introduction en bourse, (C) premier
appel public à l'épargne
(GER) Börsengang *m*, öffentliche
Erstemission *f*, Aktienneuemission *f*
(JAP) 新規株式公募
(RUS) ПЕРВОНАЧАЛЬНОЕ ОТКРЫТОЕ
ПРЕДЛОЖЕНИЕ АКЦИЙ

initiative
(CHIN) 积极性
(FRE) initiative
(GER) Initiative *f*, Anregung *f*,
Veranlassung *f*, Anstoß *m*
(JAP) 率先の、率先、発議権
(RUS) ИНИЦИАТИВА

injunction
(CHIN) 禁令
(FRE) injonction
(GER) einstweilige gerichtliche
Verfügung *f*, gerichtliche Anordnung *f*
(JAP) 強制命令、差止め命令、禁止命令
(RUS) СУДЕБНЫЙ ЗАПРЕТ

injunction bond
(CHIN) 禁令保证金
(FRE) injonction
(GER) Verpflichtung *f* zur
Sicherheitsleistung *f*

203

(JAP) 差止命令債務証書
(RUS) ГАРАНТИЯ ЗАПРЕТА

injury independent of all other means

(CHIN) 独立工伤
(FRE) risque couvert indépendamment des autres
(GER) von allen anderen Einwirkungen *fpl* unabhängige Verletzung *f*
(JAP) 全ての他の手段から独立した権利侵害
(RUS) УЩЕРБ, ВРЕД САМ ПО СЕБЕ (вне зависимости от других обстоятельств)

inland carrier

(CHIN) 内陆承运人
(FRE) transporteur routier
(GER) Inland- *m*, Binnenfrachtführer *m*, Inlandspediteur *m*
(JAP) 内地運送業者
(RUS) НАЗЕМНЫЙ ПЕРЕВОЗЧИК

inner city

(CHIN) 内陆城市
(FRE) centre bâti, ville intérieure,
(C) milieu urbain
(GER) Inner City *f*, verarmte Innenstadtgebiete *f*
(JAP) 都会の中の中心市街地、大都会の既成市街地
(RUS) РАЙОНЫ ОКОЛО ЦЕНТРА ГОРОДА

innovation

(CHIN) 革新，创新，竞争
(FRE) innovation
(GER) Innovation *f*, Neuerung *f*
(JAP) 新規軸、革新、技術革新
(RUS) НОВАТОРСТВО; ОБНОВЛЕНИЕ

in perpetuity

(CHIN) 永久所有权
(FRE) à perpétuité, perpetuel
(GER) auf unbegrenzte Zeit *f*, für alle Zeiten *fpl*, auf ewig *adj*
(JAP) 永久に、終期の定めなく
(RUS) БЕЗ ОГРАНИЧЕНИЯ ВРЕМЕНИ; НАВСЕГДА

input

(CHIN) 输入

(FRE) entrée
(GER) Eingabe *f*
(JAP) 入力
(RUS) ВВОД, ВХОДНАЯ ИНФОРМАЦИЯ , ВХОДНОЙ СИГНАЛ, ВВОДИТЬ, ПОДАВАТЬ НА ВХОД

input field

(CHIN) 输入字段，输入区
(FRE) zone de saisie
(GER) Eingabefeld *n*
(JAP) 入力フィールド
(RUS) ПОЛЕ ВВОДА

input mask

(CHIN) 输入掩码
(FRE) masque de saisie
(GER) Eingabemaske *f*
(JAP) 入力フィールド
(RUS) МАСКА ВВОДА

input-output device

(CHIN) 输入-输出设备
(FRE) unité périphérique d'entrée/sortie,
(C) périphérique d'entrée/sortie
(GER) Ein-Ausgabe-Gerät *n*, peripheres Gerät *m*
(JAP) 入出力装置
(RUS) УСТРОЙСТВО ВВОДА-ВЫВОДА

inside information

(CHIN) 内部消息
(FRE) information privilégiée
(GER) Insiderkenntnis *f*, -information *f*
(JAP) 内部情報
(RUS) ВНУТРЕННЯЯ ИНФОРМАЦИЯ КОМПАНИИ

inside lot

(CHIN) 中间地段
(FRE) terrain intérieur
(GER) innen gelegenes Grundstück *n*, von anderen Bauplätzen *mpl* umgebenes Grundstück *n*
(JAP) 中敷地
(RUS) ЗЕМЕЛЬНЫЙ УЧАСТОК ВНУТРИ ДРУГОГО УЧАСТКА

insider

(CHIN) 内线，内部人员

(FRE) initié
(GER) Insider *m*, Eingeweihter *m*
(JAP) インサイダー、内部者
(RUS) «СВОЙ ЧЕЛОВЕК»; ИНСАЙДЕР

insolvency
(CHIN) 无力还债，破产
(FRE) insolvabilité
(GER) Insolvenz *f*, Illiquidität *f*,
Zahlungsunfähigkeit *f*, Überschuldung *f*;
Bankrott *m*, Konkurs *m*
(JAP) 債務超過、支払不能、破産
(RUS) НЕПЛАТЕЖЕСПОСОБНОСТЬ

insolvency clause
(CHIN) 破产条款
(FRE) clause d'insolvabilité
(GER) Insolvenzklausel *f*
(JAP) 債務超過条項
(RUS) ОГОВОРКА О
НЕПЛАТЕЖЕСПОСОБНОСТИ

inspection
(CHIN) 检查，检验
(FRE) inspection
(GER) Einsichtnahme *f*; Inspektion *f*,
Besichtigung *f*, (Über)prüfung *f*;
Abnahme(prüfung) *f*; Kontrolle *f*, Aufsicht *f*
(JAP) 審査、検査、点検
(RUS) ИНСПЕКЦИЯ; ОСМОТР; ПРОВЕРКА

installation
(CHIN) 安装
(FRE) installation
(GER) Installierung *f*, Installation *f*
(JAP) インストレーション、
導入、設置
(RUS) УСТАНОВКА

installment
(CHIN) 分期付款
(FRE) accompte, versement, (C) versement
échelonné
(GER) Rate *f*, Raten- *f*; Teilzahlung *f*;
Abschlagszahlung *f*; (Teil)lieferung *f*; Folge
f, Fortsetzung *f*
(JAP) 割賦払い、割賦払金、
月賦
(RUS) ЧАСТЬ, ДОЛЯ (оплаты, погашения
долга)

installment contract
(CHIN) 分期付款契约
(FRE) vente de biens à exécutions
successives
(GER) Ratenvereinbarung *f*, Abzahlungs-
m, Teilzahlungsvertrag *m*, Ratenvertrag *m*;
Teillieferungsvertrag *m*
(JAP) 賦払契約
(RUS) ДОГОВОР С ОПЛАТОЙ В
РАССРОЧКУ

installment sale
(CHIN) 分期付款销售
(FRE) vente à tempérament
(GER) Verkauf *m* auf Ratenzahlung *f*
(JAP) 月賦販売、割賦売上
(RUS) ПОТРЕБИТЕЛЬСКИЙ КРЕДИТ,
ВЫПЛАЧИВАЕМЫЙ ДОЛЯМИ; ПРОДАЖА
В РАССРОЧКУ

institutional investor
(CHIN) 投资法团，投资机构
(FRE) investisseur institutionnel
(GER) institutioneller (Kapital)anleger *m*
(JAP) 機関投資家
(RUS) ИНСТИТУЦИОНАЛЬНЫЙ
ИНВЕСТОР

institutional lender
(CHIN) 机构借款人
(FRE) établissement de crédit
(GER) institutioneller Kredit- *m*,
Darlehensgeber *m*; Kapitalsammelstelle *f*
(JAP) 機関貸手
(RUS) ИНСТИТУЦИОНАЛЬНЫЙ
КРЕДИТОР

instrument
(CHIN) 有价证券票据，工具，文件，
证书，契约
(FRE) instrument, effet, titre, acte juridique
(GER) Urkunde *f*; Schriftstück *n*, Papier *n*,
Dokument *n*; Rechtsakt *m*, Rechtsgeschäft
n; Instrument *n*
(JAP) 証書、証券、手段
(RUS) ИНСТРУМЕНТ; ДОКУМЕНТ

instrumentalities of transportation
(CHIN) 运输工具
(FRE) instrumentalités de transport
(GER) Transporteinrichtungen *fpl*

(JAP) 移動（輸送）方法、手段
(RUS) ТРАНСПОРТНЫЕ ОРГАНИЗАЦИИ

instrumentalitity

(CHIN) 手段，工具，债券，票据，
文件，契约
(FRE) instrumentalité
(GER) Mitwirkung *f*, Zweckdienlichkeit *f*,
Nützlichkeit *f*
(JAP) 道具、手段
(RUS) ОРГАНИЗАЦИЯ; АГЕНТСТВО

insurability

(CHIN) 可保险性
(FRE) assurabilité
(GER) Versicherbarkeit *f*,
Versicherungsfähigkeit *f*
(JAP) 保険適合性
(RUS) СТРАХУЕМОСТЬ

insurable interest

(CHIN) 可保险利益
(FRE) intérêt assurable
(GER) Versicherungsinteresse *n*,
versicherbares Interesse *n*
(JAP) 被保険利益
(RUS) СТРАХУЕМЫЙ ИНТЕРЕС

insurable title

(CHIN) 可保险产权
(FRE) bien assurable
(GER) versicherbares Risiko *n* an
Eigentumsrechten *npl*
(JAP) 保険可能権原、権利証書
(RUS) СТРАХУЕМЫЙ ПРАВОВОЙ ТИТУЛ

insurance

(CHIN) 保险，保单，保费，投保
(FRE) assurance
(GER) Versicherung *f*,
Versicherungswesen *n*
(JAP) 保険、保険契約
(RUS) СТРАХОВАНИЕ

insurance company (insurer)

(CHIN) 保险公司（保险人）
(FRE) compagnie d'assurance (assureur)
(GER) Versicherungsgesellschaft *f*, -anstalt
f, Versicherungskonzern *m*, -träger *m*
(Versicherer *m*)

(JAP) 保険会社（保険者）
(RUS) СТРАХОВАЯ КОМПАНИЯ
(СТРАХОВЩИК)

insurance contract

(CHIN) 保险合同
(FRE) contrat d'assurance
(GER) Versicherungsvertrag *m*
(JAP) 保険契約、保険契約書
(RUS) ДОГОВОР СТРАХОВАНИЯ

insurance coverage

(CHIN) 保险范围
(FRE) couverture-assurance
(GER) Versicherungsschutz *m*, -deckung *f*,
Versicherungsumfang *m*
(JAP) 保険担保
(RUS) СТРАХОВОЕ ПОКРЫТИЕ

insurance settlement

(CHIN) 保险处理
(FRE) réglement d'assurance
(GER) (von der Versicherung *f* ausbezahlte)
Abfindungssumme *f*
(JAP) 保険金解決、保険金決済
(RUS) РЕШЕНИЕ СТРАХОВОГО СПОРА

insured

(CHIN) 被保险人
(FRE) assuré(e)
(GER) Versicherter *m*, Versicherungs- *m*,
Deckungsnehmer *m*; versichert *adj*
(JAP) 被保険者、保険契約者
(RUS) ЗАСТРАХОВАННОЕ ЛИЦО;
СТРАХОВАТЕЛЬ

insured account

(CHIN) 被保险人账户
(FRE) compte assuré
(GER) versichertes Konto *n*
(JAP) 保険金額
(RUS) ЗАСТРАХОВАННЫЙ СЧЕТ

insurgent

(CHIN) 反叛者
(FRE) insurgé
(GER) Aufständischer *m*, Rebell *m*,
Aufrührer *m*
(JAP) 反者、暴徒、造反分子
(RUS) ВОССТАВШАЯ СТОРОНА

intangible asset

(CHIN) 无形资产

(FRE) bien immatériel

(GER) immaterielle Aktiva *npl*,
Immaterialgüter *npl*, immaterielles
Vermögen *n*

(JAP) 無形資産、無体資産 （特許権、
商標権など）

(RUS) НЕМАТЕРИАЛЬНЫЙ АКТИВ

intangible reward

(CHIN) 无形报酬

(FRE) compensation intangible

(GER) immaterielle Belohnung *f*

(JAP) 無形報酬

(RUS) НЕМАТЕРИАЛЬНОЕ
ВОЗНАГРАЖДЕНИЕ

intangible value

(CHIN) 无形价值

(FRE) valeur incorporelle

(GER) immaterieller Wert *m*; Geldwert *m*

(JAP) 無形価額

(RUS) НЕМАТЕРИАЛЬНАЯ ЦЕННОСТЬ

integrated circuit

(CHIN) 集成电路

(FRE) circuit intégré

(GER) integrierter Schaltkreis *m*, IC-
Baustein *m* (EDV)

(JAP) 集積回路、ＩＣ

(RUS) ИНТЕГРАЛЬНАЯ СХЕМА,
МИКРОСХЕМА

integration, backward

(CHIN) 反向联合

(FRE) intégration en amont

(GER) Rückwärtsintegration *f*, vertikale
Integration *f* einer vorgelagerten
Produktionsstufe *f*

(JAP) 後方統合、後向きの統合

(RUS) ИНТЕГРАЦИЯ
ПРОИЗВОДСТВЕННОГО ПРОЦЕССА

integration, forward

(CHIN) 前向联合

(FRE) intégration en aval

(GER) Vorwärtsintegration *f*, vertikales
Betriebswachstum *n* mit Angliederung *f*

einer nachgelagerten Produktionsstufe *f*

(JAP) 順方向統合

(RUS) ИНТЕГРАЦИЯ ДЛЯ РАСШИРЕНИЯ
ПОЛЯ ДЕЯТЕЛЬНОСТИ

integration, horizontal

(CHIN) 横向联合

(FRE) intégration horizontale

(GER) horizontale Integration *f*,
Verschmelzung *f* von Konkurrenzfirmen *fpl*

(JAP) 水平統合

(RUS) ГОРИЗОНТАЛЬНАЯ ИНТЕГРАЦИЯ

integration, vertical

(CHIN) 竖向联合

(FRE) intégration verticale

(GER) vertikale Integration *f*, vertikaler
Zusammenschluss *m*

(JAP) 縦の統合

(RUS) ВЕРТИКАЛЬНАЯ ИНТЕГРАЦИЯ

integrity

(CHIN) 完全性，完整性，诚实，正直

(FRE) intégrité

(GER) Integrität *f*, Rechtschaffenheit *f*,
Redlichkeit *f*; Datengenauigkeit *f*, -
intaktheit *f* (EDV)

(JAP) 完全性、インテグリティー

(RUS) ЧЕСТНОСТЬ; ПОРЯДОЧНОСТЬ;
ЦЕЛЬНОСТЬ

interactive

(CHIN) 交互式的，人机对话的

(FRE) intéractif

(GER) interaktiv *adj*

(JAP) 対話形の、会話形の、
インターアクティブの

(RUS) ДИАЛОГОВЫЙ, ИНТЕРАКТИВНЫЙ

interactive system

(CHIN) 交互式系统

(FRE) système interactif

(GER) interaktives System *n* (EDV)

(JAP) 対話形システム

(RUS) ИНТЕРАКТИВНАЯ (ДИАЛОГОВАЯ)
СИСТЕМА

interest

(CHIN) 利息，利益，权益，股权，产权

(FRE) intérêt, risque

(GER) Zins(fuß/-satz) *m*; Anteilsrecht *n*; Nutzungsrecht *n*; Beteiligung *f*; Interesse *n*, Vorteil *m*, Nutzen *m*
(JAP) 利害関係、利権、利子
(RUS) ПРОЦЕНТЫ; ИНТЕРЕС

interest group
(CHIN) 利益集团
(FRE) groupe d'intérêt
(GER) Interessengruppe *f*, -verband *m*, -gemeinschaft *f*
(JAP) 利益集団、利益者集団、インタレストグループ
(RUS) ГРУППА, ОБЪЕДИНЁННАЯ ОБЩИМИ ИНТЕРЕСАМИ

interest-only loan
(CHIN) 只付利息的贷款
(FRE) prêt hypothécaire non amorti
(GER) tilgungsfreies Darlehen *n*
(JAP) 当座の支払債務が利子のみで元金の支払は据置かれる方式の貸付金（融資）
(RUS) ССУДА С ОПЛАТОЙ ТОЛЬКО ПРОЦЕНТОВ

interest rate
(CHIN) 利率
(FRE) taux d'intérêt
(GER) Zinssatz *m*, -fuß *m*, Verzinsung *f*, Kreditzins *m*
(JAP) 利子率、利率
(RUS) ПРОЦЕНТНАЯ СТАВКА

interest sensitive policies
(CHIN) 利率敏感保险单
(FRE) polices sensibles à l'intérêt,
(C) polices sensibles aux fluctuations des taux d'intérêt
(GER) zinsempfindliche Politik *f*, zinsreagible Policen *fpl*
(JAP) 金利連動型保険証券
(RUS) ВИД СТРАХОВОГО ПОЛИСА С ВЫПЛАТОЙ ПРОЦЕНТОВ

interface
(CHIN) 界面
(FRE) interface
(GER) Schnittstelle *f*
(EDV)

(JAP) インターフェイス、接続器、相異なる装置を接続するための仲介装置、
(RUS) ИНТЕРФЕЙС; СОПРЯЖЕНИЕ

interim audit
(CHIN) 年中审计，期中审计
(FRE) contrôle intermédiaire des comptes
(GER) Zwischenprüfung *f*, in der Berichtszeit *f* vorgenommene Revision *f*
(JAP) 中間監査、期中監査
(RUS) ПРОМЕЖУТОЧНЫЙ АУДИТ

interim financing
(CHIN) 中期贷款
(FRE) financement provisoire
(GER) Zwischen- *f*, Überbrückungsfinanzierung *f*
(JAP) 中間資金調達
(RUS) ПРОМЕЖУТОЧНОЕ ФИНАНСИРОВАНИЕ

interim statement
(CHIN) 期中报表
(FRE) bilan intérimaire
(GER) Zwischenbilanz *f*, -abschluss *m*
(JAP) 中間計算書
(RUS) ПРОМЕЖУТОЧНЫЙ ОТЧЕТ

interindustry competition
(CHIN) 产业部门间竞争，工业间竞争
(FRE) concurrence entre les industries
(GER) Wettbewerb *m* zwischen unterschiedlichen Industriezweigen *mpl*
(JAP) 産業間競争
(RUS) МЕЖОТРАСЛЕВАЯ КОНКУРЕНЦИЯ

interlocking directorate
(CHIN) 交叉董事会，互兼董事
(FRE) administrateur de liaison
(GER) Überkreuzverflechtung *f*, -mandat *n*, Schachtelaufsichtsrat *m*
(JAP) 兼任重役会
(RUS) ОБЪЕДИНЕННОЕ УПРАВЛЕНИЕ

interlocutory decree
(CHIN) 临时判决
(FRE) décret extraordinaire
(GER) Zwischenurteil *n*, -entscheid *m*, einstweilige Entscheidung *f*, vorläufiges Urteil *n*

(JAP) 中間判決、暫定的判決
(RUS) ПРОМЕЖУТОЧНОЕ,
НЕОКОНЧАТЕЛЬНОЕ ПОСТАНОВЛЕНИЕ
СУДА

intermediary
(CHIN) 中间人，居间人
(FRE) intermédiaire
(GER) Vermittler *m*, Zwischenhändler *m*
(JAP) 中間の、媒介の、仲介者
(RUS) ПОСРЕДНИК

intermediate goods
(CHIN) 中间货物，中间产品
(FRE) biens intermédiaires
(GER) Zwischenerzeugnisse *npl*, -produkte
npl, Halbfabrikate *npl*, Halbfertigware *f*
(JAP) 中間財
(RUS) ПРОМЕЖУТОЧНЫЕ ТОВАРЫ

intermediate term
(CHIN) 中期
(FRE) moyen terme
(GER) Mittelfristig *adj*
(JAP) 中期
(RUS) СРЕДНИЙ ПЕРИОД

intermediation
(CHIN) 中介作用，媒介作用
(FRE) intermédiation
(GER) Geldanlage *f* über Banken *fpl* bzw.
Finanzinstitute *npl*; Vermittlung *f*
(JAP) 仲介、中継売買
(RUS) ПОСРЕДНИЧЕСТВО

intermittent production
(CHIN) 间歇性生产
(FRE) régime de fonctionnement
discontinu, (C) système de production
intermittente
(GER) zeitweiser Betrieb *m*,
Stoßproduktion *f*
(JAP) 断続生産
(RUS) ПЕРЕМЕЖАЮЩЕЕСЯ
ПРОИЗВОДСТВО, Т. Е. ПРОИЗВОДСТВО
РАЗЛИЧНОЙ ПРОДУКЦИИ НА ОДНОЙ
ЛИНИИ

internal audit
(CHIN) 内部审计

(FRE) audit interne
(GER) interne Revision *f*, innerbetriebliche
Buch- *f* bzw. Rechnungsprüfung *f*
(JAP) 内部監査
(RUS) ВНУТРЕННИЙ АУДИТ

internal check
(CHIN) 内部检查，内部审核
(FRE) contrôle interne, (C) autocontrôle
(GER) interne Prüfung *f*
(JAP) 内部牽制
(RUS) ВНУТРЕННЯЯ ПРОВЕРКА

internal control
(CHIN) 内部控制，内部管理
(FRE) contrôle interne
(GER) interne Kontrolle *f*; interne Aufsicht
f, betriebseigene Überwachung *f*; interne
Steuerung *f* (EDV)
(JAP) 内部統制
(RUS) ВНУТРЕННИЙ КОНТРОЛЬ

internal expansion
(CHIN) 内部资产扩充
(FRE) expansion interne
(GER) internes Wachstum *n*
(JAP) 内部膨張、内部拡大
(RUS) ВНУТРЕННЕЕ РАСШИРЕНИЕ

internal financing
(CHIN) 内部融资
(FRE) autofinancement, financement
interne, cash-flow, financement par fonds
propres
(GER) Innen- *f*, Selbst- *f*,
Eigenmittelfinanzicrung *f*
(JAP) 内部金融
(RUS) ВНУТРЕННЕЕ ФИНАНСИРОВАНИЕ

internal memory
(CHIN) 内存(储器)
(FRE) mémoire interne
(GER) Arbeitsspeicher *m*, interner
Speicher *m*
(JAP) 内部記憶装置、内部メモリー
(RUS) ОПЕРАТИВНАЯ ПАМЯТЬ

internal modem
(CHIN) 内置式调制解调器
(FRE) modem interne

209

(GER) internes Modem *n*, Steckkarten-Modem *m*
(JAP) 内臓モデム
(RUS) ВНУТРЕННИЙ МОДЕМ

internal rate of return (IRR)
(CHIN) 内部利润率（IRR）
(FRE) taux de rentabilité interne
(GER) interner Zinsfuß *m*, kalkulatorische Zinsen *mpl*
(JAP) 内部収益率
(RUS) ВНУТРЕННЯЯ РЕНТАБЕЛЬНОСТЬ

Internal Revenue Service (IRS)
(CHIN) 美国税务总局（IRS）
(FRE) FISC, la direction générale des impôts, (C) ministère du revenu
(GER) IRS *f*, (US-Bundessteuerbehörde *f*)
(JAP) 米国内国歳入庁
(RUS) НАЛОГОВОЕ УПРАВЛЕНИЕ (США)

International Bank for Reconstruction and Development (IBRD)
(CHIN) 国际开发银行
(FRE) Banque Internationale pour la Reconstruction et le Développement
(GER) Internationale Bank *f* für Wiederaufbau *m* und Entwicklung *f*
(JAP) 国際復興開発銀行
(RUS) МЕЖДУНАРОДНЫЙ БАНК РЕКОНСТРУКЦИИ И РАЗВИТИЯ (МБРР)

international cartel
(CHIN) 国际卡特尔
(FRE) cartel international
(GER) internationales Kartell *n*
(JAP) 国際カルテル
(RUS) МЕЖДУНАРОДНЫЙ КАРТЕЛЬ

international law
(CHIN) 国际法
(FRE) droit international
(GER) internationals Recht *n*, fölkerrecht *n*
(JAP) 国際法
(RUS) МЕЖДУНАРОДНОЕ ПРАВО

International Monetary Fund (IMF)
(CHIN) 国际货币基金
(FRE) Fonds Monétaire International

(GER) Internationaler Währungsfonds *m*, IWF *m*
(JAP) 国際通貨基金
(RUS) МЕЖДУНАРОДНЫЙ ВАЛЮТНЫЙ ФОНД (МВФ)

International Monetary Market (IMM)
(CHIN) 国际货币市场
(FRE) Marché Monétaire International
(GER) internationaler Geldmarkt *m*
(JAP) 国際通貨市場
(RUS) МИРОВОЙ ВАЛЮТНЫЙ РЫНОК

international union
(CHIN) 国际联盟
(FRE) union internationale
(GER) internationaler Verband *m*
(JAP) 国際的連盟、国際的組合
(RUS) МЕЖДУНАРОДНЫЙ СОЮЗ

internet
(CHIN) 互联网
(FRE) internet
(GER) Internet *n* (EDV)
(JAP) インターネット
(RUS) ИНТЕРНЕТ; ВСЕМИРНАЯ СЕТЬ КОМПЬЮТЕРНОЙ СВЯЗИ

internet protocol (IP) address
(CHIN) 互联网协议（IP）地址
(FRE) adresse IP
(GER) IP-Adresse *f*, Internetprotokolladresse *f*
(JAP) インターネット プロトコルアドレス、ＩＰ住所
(RUS) АДРЕС МЕЖСЕТЕВОГО ПРОТОКОЛА

internet service provider
(CHIN) 互联网服务提供商
(FRE) fournisseur d'accès à internet
(GER) Internet-Dienstanbieter *m*, Anbieter *m* von Internetdiensten *mpl*
(JAP) インターネットサービス提供者
(RUS) ПОСТАВЩИК УСЛУГ ИНТЕРНЕТА

interperiod income tax allocation
(CHIN) 年度间所得税分配

(FRE) ventilation des impôts de l'exercice sur le revenu, (C) méthode du report d'impôts
(GER) periodengerechte Einkommenssteuerverbuchung *f*
(JAP) 所得課税の期間を跨っての配分
(RUS) ПРОМЕЖУТОЧНОЕ АССИГНОВАНИЕ ДОХОДОВ

interpleader
(CHIN) 相互诉讼者
(FRE) action pétitoire, (C) action pétitoire
(GER) Streitverkündigung *f* zur Verweisung *f* auf den Prätendentenstreit *m*; Einwand *m* der mangelnden Passivlegitimation *f*
(JAP) 競合権利者確定手続
(RUS) ВОЗБУЖДЕНИЕ ПРОЦЕССА ДЛЯ ОПРЕДЕЛЕНИЯ ПРАВ ТРЕТЬИХ ЛИЦ

interpolation
(CHIN) 插值法
(FRE) interpolation
(GER) Einschub *m*, Interpolation *f*, Einschaltung *f*, Erweiterung *f*
(JAP) 加筆、改竄、挿入
(RUS) ИНТЕРПОЛЯЦИЯ

interpreter
(CHIN) 口译，翻译
(FRE) interprète
(GER) Dolmetscher *m*; Lochschriftenübersetzer *m* (EDV)
(JAP) 解釈者、通訳、通訳官

(RUS) УСТНЫЙ ПЕРЕВОДЧИК

interrogatories
(CHIN) 询问
(FRE) questions échangées entre les parties
(GER) schriftliche unter Eid zu beantwortende Befragung *f*
(JAP) 質問、質問書
(RUS) ПИСЬМЕННЫЙ ОПРОС СТОРОН или СВИДЕТЕЛЕЙ

interval scale
(CHIN) 区间尺度
(FRE) échelle par intervalles
(GER) Intervallskala *f*
(JAP) 間隔尺度、単位尺度

(RUS) ШКАЛА ВРЕМЕННЫХ ИНТЕРВАЛОВ

interview
(CHIN) 访谈，面谈
(FRE) entretien
(GER) Befragung *f*, Vernehmung *f* (Recht); Vorstellungsgespräch *n*
(JAP) 会見、面談、面接
(RUS) ИНТЕРВЬЮ; ОПРОС

interview, structured
(CHIN) 正式面谈
(FRE) entretien structuré
(GER) strukturiertes Vorstellungsgespräch *n*
(JAP) 定形会見（面談、面接）
(RUS) СТРУКТУРИРОВАННЫЙ ОПРОС

interview, unstructured
(CHIN) 非正式面谈
(FRE) entretien non structuré
(GER) unstrukturiertes Vorstellungsgespräch *n*
(JAP) 非定形会見（面談、面接）
(RUS) НЕСТРУКТУРИРОВАННЫЙ ОПРОС

interviewer bias
(CHIN) 调查者偏倚
(FRE) polarization de l'interviewer
(GER) Voreingenommenheit *f* des Befragers *m*
(JAP) 会見の基本
(RUS) ИСХОДНАЯ ПОЗИЦИЯ ОПРАШИВАЮЩЕГО

intestate
(CHIN) 未留下遗嘱的，无遗嘱死亡者
(FRE) intestat
(GER) Intestaterblasser *m*
(JAP) 州間
(RUS) УМЕРШИЙ БЕЗ ЗАВЕЩАНИЯ

in the money
(CHIN) 资金充裕，较现值有利
(FRE) en dedans
(GER) im Geld *n*, bei Kasse *f* (Kaufoption) mit Abschlusspreis *m* unter dem Marktpreis *m* des Wertpapiers *n*
(JAP) 金持ちで、インザマネーで

211

(RUS) «ПРИ ДЕНЬГАХ»

in the tank
(CHIN) 缺乏客观性
(FRE) orienté
(GER) im Eimer *m*
(JAP) インザタンク、市価の急落
(RUS) НЕОБЪЕКТИВНОСТЬ

intraperiod tax allocation
(CHIN) 期内所得税分摊
(FRE) ventilation des impôts de l'exercice
(GER) Aufteilung *f* angefallener Steuern *fpl*
auf die verschiedenen
Veranlagungszeiträume *mpl*
(JAP) 所得課税の期間内配分
(RUS) РАСПРЕДЕЛЕНИЕ НАЛОГА
ДАННОГО ГОДА В РАЗНЫХ ЧАСТЯХ
ОТЧЁТНОСТИ

intrinsic value
(CHIN) 本质价，固有价值
(FRE) valeur intrinsèque
(GER) innerer Wert *m*,
Eigenwert *m*; Substanzwert *m*
 (Börse); Anlagewert *m*;
Materialwert *m*
(JAP) 本源的価値、真性価値、
本質価値
(RUS) НЕОТЪЕМЛЕМАЯ ЦЕННОСТЬ

inure
(CHIN) 生效，适用
(FRE) assurer, s'assurer
(GER) wirksam werden, in Kraft *f* treten; in
Gebrauch *m* kommen *v*
(JAP) 保証する、に保険をつける、
を保険に入れる
(RUS) СТРАХОВАТЬ

inventory
(CHIN) 库存，盘点，商品目录，清单
(FRE) inventaire, (C) stocks, inventaire
(GER) Inventur *f*, Bestandsaufnahme *f*;
Inventar *n*, Inventarliste *f*,
Bestandsnachweis *m*; Vorrat *m*,
Lagerbestand *m*
(JAP) 棚卸資産、在庫品、在庫調べ
(RUS) ИНВЕНТАРЬ; МАТЕРИАЛЬНЫЕ
ЗАПАСЫ

inventory certificate
(CHIN) 库存证书
(FRE) déclaration d'inventaire
(GER) Inventar- *f*,
Bestandprüfungsbescheinigung *f*
(JAP) 棚卸証明書
(RUS) СЕРТИФИКАТ, СПРАВКА О
НАЛИЧИИ МАТЕРИАЛЬНЫХ ЗАПАСОВ

inventory control
(CHIN) 库存控制
(FRE) contrôle des stocks
(GER) Bestandskontrolle *f*
(JAP) 在庫管理、在庫品管理、棚卸管理
(RUS) КОНТРОЛЬ НАЛИЧИЯ
МАТЕРИАЛЬНЫХ ЗАПАСОВ

inventory financing
(CHIN) 以存货融通资金
(FRE) financement sur stocks
(GER) Lagerfinanzierung *f*
(JAP) 在庫品金融
(RUS) ФИНАНСИРОВАНИЕ ТОВАРНЫХ
ЗАПАСОВ

inventory planning
(CHIN) 库存规划
(FRE) contrôle des stocks, (C) contrôle des
stocks
(GER) Lager- *f*, Bestandsplanung *f*
(JAP) 在庫計画
(RUS) ПЛАНИРОВАНИЕ МАТЕРИАЛЬНЫХ
ЗАПАСОВ

inventory shortage (shrinkage)
(CHIN) 存货盘亏，存货短缺
(FRE) écart sur stock
(GER) Lagerdefizit *n*, Inventar- *n*, Lager-
m, Bestandsfehlbetrag *m*, Lager- *f*,
Bestandsknappheit *f* (Bestandsverlust *m*,-
schwund *m*)
(JAP) 在庫不足
(RUS) ДЕФИЦИТ (СОКРАЩЕНИЕ)
МАТЕРИАЛЬНЫХ ЗАПАСОВ

inventory turnover
(CHIN) 存货周转
(FRE) rotation des stocks
(GER) Lagerumschlag *m*, -umsatz *m*
(JAP) 棚卸資産回転率

inverse condemnation
(CHIN) 反向谴责
(FRE) arrêt infirmatif de jugement
(GER) enteignungsgleicher Eingriff *m*
(RUS) ИСК ЗЕМЛЕВЛАДЕЛЬЦА О
КОМПЕНСАЦИИ ЗА ЗЕМЛЮ,
ОТОБРАННУЮ ДЛЯ ОБЩЕСТВЕННОГО
ПОЛЬЗОВАНИЯ

inverted yield curve
(CHIN) 反向产率曲线
(FRE) courbe de rendement inversée
(GER) inverse Zinsstruktur *f*,
Zinsinversion *f*
(JAP) 逆利回り曲線
(RUS) «ПЕРЕВЕРНУТАЯ» (ОБРАТНАЯ)
КРИВАЯ ДОХОДНОСТИ

invest
(CHIN) 投资，投入
(FRE) investir
(GER) investieren, Investitionen *fpl*
vornehmen *v*
(JAP) 投資する、運用する、授ける
(RUS) ИНВЕСТИРОВАТЬ

investment
(CHIN) 投资，投入资本，资本
(FRE) placement
(GER) Investition *f*, Anlage *f*; Kapital- *f*,
Vermögensanlage *f*
(JAP) 投資
(RUS) ИНВЕСТИЦИЯ,
КАПИТАЛОВЛОЖЕНИЕ

investment advisory service
(CHIN) 投资咨询服务
(FRE) conseil en placement
(GER) Wertpapier- *f* und Anlageberatung *f*,
Anlageberatungsdienst *m*
(JAP) 投資顧問サービス
(RUS) СЛУЖБА КОНСУЛЬТАЦИИ
ИНВЕСТОРОВ

investment banker
(CHIN) 投资银行家
(FRE) banquier d'affaires
(GER) Investment Banker *m*
(JAP) 投資金融業者

investment club
(CHIN) 投资俱乐部
(FRE) club d'investissement, club
d'actionnaires
(GER) Investmentclub *m*, Verein *m* für
Kapitalanlageinteressenten *mpl*
(JAP) 投資クラブ
(RUS) ИНВЕСТИЦИОННЫЙ «КЛУБ»;
ГРУППА СОВМЕСТНО ДЕЙСТВУЮЩИХ
ИНВЕСТОРОВ

investment company
(CHIN) 投资公司
(FRE) société d'investissement
(GER) Investment- *f*,
Kapitalanlagegesellschaft *f*
(JAP) 投資会社、投資信託会社
(RUS) ИНВЕСТИЦИОННАЯ КОМПАНИЯ

investment counsel
(CHIN) 投资顾问
(FRE) conseiller en placement
(GER) Anlage- *m*, Effektenberater *m*
(JAP) 投資相談
(RUS) ИНВЕСТИЦИОННЫЙ СОВЕТНИК,
КОНСУЛЬТАНТ

investment grade
(CHIN) 投资等级
(FRE) sans risque
(GER) Investment-Güte *n*, -Grade *n*
(JAP) 投資等級
(RUS) ЦЕННЫЕ БУМАГИ,
РЕКОМЕНДУЕМЫЕ К ПОКУПКЕ

investment interest expense
(CHIN) 投资利息支出
(FRE) intérêt payé de placement
(GER) Zinsaufwand *m* für Investitionen *fpl*
(JAP) 投資利息費用
(RUS) РАСХОДЫ НА СОДЕРЖАНИЕ
ПОРТФЕЛЯ ИНВЕСТИЦИЙ

investment life cycle
(CHIN) 投资循环期
(FRE) cycle de vie d'investissement
(GER) Lebenszyklus *m* einer Investition *f*
(JAP) 投資寿命

213

(RUS) ЖИЗНЕННЫЙ ЦИКЛ ИНВЕСТИЦИИ

investment strategy
(CHIN) 投资策略
(FRE) stratégie d'investissement
(GER) Investitionsstrategie *f*,
Anlagepolitik *f*
(JAP) 投資戦略
(RUS) СТРАТЕГИЯ ИНВЕСТИЦИЙ

investment trust
(CHIN) 投资信托
(FRE) fonds d'investissement
(GER) Investmentgesellschaft *f*,
Investmenttrust *m*,
Effektenfinanzierungsgesellschaft *f*
(JAP) 投資信託
(RUS) ИНВЕСТИЦИОННЫЙ ТРАСТ

investor relations department
(CHIN) 投资人联络部
(FRE) service des relations avec les
investisseurs
(GER) Abteilung *f* für Anlegerbetreuung *f*
bzw. Aktionärspflege *f*
(JAP) 投資家関係担当部課
(RUS) ОТДЕЛ ВЗАИМООТНОШЕНИЙ С
ИНВЕСТОРАМИ

invoice
(CHIN) 发票，货物托运单
(FRE) facture
(GER) Rechnung *f*, Faktura *f*; berechnen;
fakturieren, in Rechnung *f* stellen *v*
(JAP) 仕入状、請求書
(RUS) СЧЕТ-ФАКТУРА

involuntary conversion
(CHIN) 非自愿转换
(FRE) conversion forcée
(GER) Zwangskonvertierung *f*
(JAP) 強制交換
(RUS) ПРИНУДИТЕЛЬНОЕ
КОНВЕРТИРОВАНИЕ, ПРЕОБРАЗОВАНИЕ

involuntary lien
(CHIN) 非自愿留置
(FRE) hypothèque non volontaire
(GER) Zwangspfandrecht *n*
(JAP) 強制留置権、強制先取特権

(RUS) ПРИНУДИТЕЛЬНОЕ УСЛОВИЕ
ЗАЛОГА

involuntary trust
(CHIN) 非自愿信托
(FRE) fiducie par détermination de la loi,
fiducie par interprétation, fiducie judiciaire,
trust implicitement consenti
(GER) gesetzliches
Treuhandverhältnis *n*
(JAP) 強制信託
(RUS) ТРАСТ, ПРИЗНАННЫЙ СУДОМ НА
ОСНОВЕ ОТНОШЕНИЙ МЕЖДУ
СТОРОНАМИ

involuntary unemployment
(CHIN) 非自愿失业
(FRE) chômage involontaire
(GER) unfreiwillige Arbeitslosigkeit *f*
(JAP) 非自発的失業
(RUS) ВЫНУЖДЕННАЯ
БЕЗРАБОТИЦА

Inwood annuity factor
(CHIN) 因伍德年金因子
(FRE) facteur d'annuité inwood, facteur de
récupération du capital
(GER) Inwood-Annuitätenfaktor *m*,
Inwood-Rentenfaktor *m*
(JAP) インウッド年金要素、
インウッド年金要因
(RUS) КОЭФФИЦИЕНТ АННУИТЕТА
ИНВУДА

iota
(CHIN) 很小数量，极微小
(FRE) iota
(GER) Kleinigkeit *f*
(JAP) 少量、微量
(RUS) ЙОТА; МАЛАЯ
ВЕЛИЧИНА

irregulars
(CHIN) 不合格品，劣品
(FRE) articles de deuxiéme qualité, articles
de qualité moyenne
(GER) minderwertige Produkte *npl*, zweite
Wahl *f*
(JAP) 傷物、規則外の品
(RUS) НЕРЕГУЛЯРНЫЕ
КЛИЕНТЫ

irreparable harm, irreparable damage

(CHIN) 不可弥补的伤害，不可弥补的损坏

(FRE) préjudice irréparable
(GER) nicht wieder gutzumachender Schaden *m*
(JAP) 回復不能の損害
(RUS) НЕПОПРАВИМЫЙ ВРЕД, УЩЕРБ

irretrievable

(CHIN) 无法检索的
(FRE) irrécupérable
(GER) nicht wiederfindbar, nicht abrufbar *adj*
(JAP) 検索不能な
(RUS) НЕ ПОДЛЕЖАЩИЙ ВОССТАНОВЛЕНИЮ

irrevocable

(CHIN) 不可撤消的
(FRE) irrévocable
(GER) unwiderruflich, unumstößlich, *adj*
(JAP) 取消不能な、撤回不能
(RUS) БЕЗВОЗВРАТНЫЙ

irrevocable trust

(CHIN) 不可撤消信托
(FRE) fiducie irrévocable
(GER) unwiderrufliche Treuhandbestellung *f*; unwiderrufliche Stiftung *f*
(JAP) 取消不能信託
(RUS) ТРАСТ, НЕ ПОДЛЕЖАЩИЙ ИЗМЕНЕНИЮ

issue

(CHIN) 开发，发行，争议的问题，纠纷
(FRE) émission, émettre, mettre en circulation, descendance en ligne directe, point en litige, (C) mise en circulation, point en litige
(FRE) émis et en circulation
(GER) Frage *f*, Problem *n*, Streitpunkt *m*, Angelegenheit *f*; Ausstellung *f*, Ausfertigung *f*; Erteilung *f*; Begebung *f*, Emission *f*, Ausgabe *f* von Wertpapieren *npl*; Ausgabe *f* von Banknoten *fpl*; Auflage *f*; Erlass *m*

(JAP) 出す、振り出し、問題
(RUS) ВОПРОС; ПОЗИЦИЯ; ИЗДАНИЕ; ЭМИССИЯ

issued and outstanding

(CHIN) 发行在外的股票
(GER) begeben und im Umlauf *m* befindlich (Börse)
(JAP) 振出済みで未払いの
(RUS) ВЫПУЩЕННЫЕ АКЦИИ, НЕ ВЫКУПЛЕННЫЕ САМОЙ КОМПАНИЕЙ

issuer

(CHIN) 开证银行，证券发行者
(FRE) émetteur
(GER) Emittent *m*, Aussteller *m*
(JAP) 発行者、振出人
(RUS) ЭМИТЕНТ ЦЕННЫХ БУМАГ

itemized deductions

(CHIN) 法定扣减项目
(FRE) déductions fiscals accordées aux particuliers
(GER) Einzelabzug *m*, aufgegliederte bzw. einzeln aufgeführte Abzugsbeträge *mpl* (Steuer); Einzelabschlag *m*
(JAP) 項目別控除額、明細控除額
(RUS) ВЫЧЕТЫ ПО ОТДЕЛЬНЫМ ПОЗИЦИЯМ

iteration

(CHIN) 重复操作，重复运算
(FRE) itération, processus iterative, méthode itérative
(GER) Iteration *f*, Iterationsmethode *f*, -verfahren *n*; Schritt *m*
(JAP) 反復
(RUS) ИТЕРАЦИЯ

itinerant worker

(CHIN) 流动工人
(FRE) travailleur migrant, (C) travailleur itinérant
(GER) Wanderarbeiter *m*; Saisonarbeiter *m*
渡り労働者、移動労働者
(RUS) РАБОТНИК БЕЗ ПОСТОЯННОГО МЕСТА РАБОТЫ

J

jawboning
(CHIN) 赊买，借贷
(FRE) persuasion morale
(GER) wirtschaftspolitische
"Seelenmassage" *f*, Maßhalteappell *m*
(JAP) ジョーボーニング、
強制的説得工作
(RUS) ОКАЗАНИЕ ДАВЛЕНИЯ «С ВЕРХУ»

J-curve
(CHIN) J 曲线
(FRE) courbe en J
(GER) J-Kurve *f*
(JAP) J カーブ
(RUS) КРИВАЯ «J» (КРИВАЯ ОБОРОТА
МЕЖДУНАРОДНОЙ ТОРГОВЛИ)

job
(CHIN) 工作，职位，任务，批发
(FRE) travail, emploi
(GER) Beschäftigung *f*, Beruf *m*, Posten *m*,
Tätigkeit *f*; Arbeitsplatz *m*, -stelle *f*;
Aufgabe *f*, Pflicht *f*
(JAP) 仕事、職務
(RUS) РАБОТА; ДОЛЖНОСТЬ

job bank
(CHIN) 工作职位资料库
(FRE) banque de l'emploi
(GER) Arbeitsplatz-Datenbank *f* (EDV);
Stellen-, Arbeitsvermittlung *f*
(JAP) 人材銀行、ジョブバンク
(RUS) БАЗА ДАННЫХ ВАКАНТНЫХ
ДОЛЖНОСТЕЙ

jobber
(CHIN) 计件工，临时工，股票公司，
批发商
(FRE) jobber, (C) tâcheron, ouvrier à la
tâche, revendeur
(GER) Groß- *m*, Zwischenhändler *m*;
Jobber *m*, Börsenmakler *m*, Aktien- *m*,
Effekten- *m*, Eigen- *m*, Wertpapierhändler
m (Börse); Gelegenheitsarbeiter *m*,
Tagelöhner *m*

(JAP) 仲買人、手間賃人夫
(RUS) МЕЛКИЙ ОПТОВЫЙ ТОРГОВЕЦ

job classification
(CHIN) 职业分类
(FRE) classification des emplois
(GER) Arbeits(platz)klassifizierung *f*, -
bewertung *f*, Stelleneinstufung *f*
(JAP) 職階制、職務分類
(RUS) КЛАССИФИКАЦИЯ ВИДОВ РАБОТ,
ДОЛЖНОСТЕЙ

job cost sheet
(CHIN) 分批成本单
(FRE) fiche de coût de revient
(GER) (Auftrags)kostensammelblatt *n*
(JAP) 個別原価計算書、
作業指図書別原価計算表
(RUS) ТАБЛИЦА СТОИМОСТИ
ВЫПОЛНЕНИЯ РАБОТ

job depth
(CHIN) 工作深度
(FRE) étendue du poste
(GER) Freiheitsgrad *m* im
Aufgabenbereich *m*
(JAP) 作業深度
(RUS) СЛОЖНОСТЬ РАБОТЫ

job description
(CHIN) 职责
(FRE) description de poste
(GER) Stellenbeschreibung *f*, Berufsbild *n*
(JAP) 職務(職種)記載書、職務説明書
(RUS) ДОЛЖНОСТНЫЕ ОБЯЗАННОСТИ

job evaluation
(CHIN) 工作评价
(FRE) evaluation des tâches
(GER) Arbeitsbewertung *f*,
Leistungsbewertung *f*
(JAP) 職務評価
(RUS) ОЦЕНКА ВЫПОЛНЕННОЙ РАБОТЫ

job jumper

(CHIN) 跳槽者

(FRE) job-hopper, job-zappeur (connotation négative)

(GER) Job Hopper *m*, (Person, die häufig die Arbeitsstelle wechselt)

(JAP) 職場を転々と変える人

(RUS) ЛИЦО, МЕНЯЮЩЕЕ ОДНУ РАБОТУ НА ДРУГУЮ

job lot

(CHIN) 分批出售，批量

(GER) Partieware *f*, Kleinserie *f*, Warenposten *mpl* zweiter Wahl *f*, Restposten *mpl*; weniger als die handelsübliche

Schlussmenge *f*

(JAP) 取引口、込み売りの廉価品、規格はずれ品

(RUS) КОНТРАКТ НА ВЫПОЛНЕНИЕ ЧАСТИ РАБОТЫ

job order

(CHIN) 分批工作通知单，订货，定单

(FRE) bon de commande

(GER) Arbeitungsanweisung *f*, Herstellungs- *m*, Arbeitsauftrag *m*; Werks- *m*, Innenauftrag *m*

(JAP) (作業員に対する)作業指令票、作業票

(RUS) ЗАКАЗ НА ВЫПОЛНЕНИЕ РАБОТЫ

job placement

(CHIN) 工作安排

(FRE) placement

(GER) Arbeitsvermittlung *f*, Stellenzuweisung *f*

(JAP) 職業紹介、就業斡旋、作業の配置、

(RUS) РАСПРЕДЕЛЕНИЕ ЛЮДЕЙ ПО ВИДАМ РАБОТЫ; НАЗНАЧЕНИЕ НА ДОЛЖНОСТЬ

job rotation

(CHIN) 工作轮换

(FRE) rotation des postes

(GER) innerbetrieblicher Arbeitsplatzwechsel *m*, Arbeitsplatzrotation *f*

(JAP) 職場の配置転換

(RUS) «РОТАЦИЯ» ПО РАЗНЫМ ВИДАМ РАБОТ

job satisfaction

(CHIN) 工作满意度

(FRE) satisfaction professionnelle

(GER) Zufriedenheit *f* am Arbeitsplatz *m*

(JAP) 仕事の満足度

(RUS) УДОВЛЕТВОРЕНИЕ ОТ РАБОТЫ

job security

(CHIN) 工作稳定性

(FRE) securite d'emploi

(GER) Arbeitsplatzsicherheit *f*

(JAP) 雇用保証

(RUS) НАДЕЖНОСТЬ ЗАНЯТОСТИ НА РАБОТЕ

job sharing

(CHIN) 工作共享

(FRE) partage de poste

(GER) Arbeitsplatz- *f*, Stellenteilung *f*, Job Sharing *n*

(JAP) 仕事分配

(RUS) РАЗДЕЛЕНИЕ ДОЛЖНОСТНЫХ ОБЯЗАННОСТЕЙ МЕЖДУ ДВУМЯ СОТРУДНИКАМИ

job shop

(CHIN) 小批量生产厂家

(FRE) atelier travaillant a la commande, (C) atelier multigamme

(GER) Betrieb *m* mit Auftragsfertigung *f*, Zulieferbetrieb *m*; Auftrags- *f*, Einzelfertigung *f*

(JAP) ジョブショップ　(短期雇用契約で働く人を斡旋する職業紹介機関)

(RUS) ПРЕДПРИЯТИЕ, РАБОТАЮЩЕЕ НА ЗАКАЗ

job specification

(CHIN) 工作说明书，操作规程

(FRE) description de l'emploi

(GER) Arbeitsplatzanforderungsprofil *n*, Arbeitsplatzspezifizierung *f*

(JAP) 職場(職務)の明細書または説明書

(RUS) КВАЛИФИКАЦИОННЫЕ

job ticket

(CHIN) 工作卡片

(FRE) fiche de travail

(GER) Akkordzettel *m*, -karte *f*,
Arbeitszettel *m*, Auftragsticket *n*,
Laufkarte *f*

(JAP) 作業票 (労働者に対して配布される)

(RUS) НАПРАВЛЕНИЕ НА РАБОТУ

joint account

(CHIN) 共同账户

(FRE) compte joint, (C) compte collectif,
état d'une société en participation

(GER) Gemeinschaftskonto *n*, gemeinsames
Konto *n*

(JAP) 共同勘定、共同口座、

(RUS) ОБЩИЙ, СОВМЕСТНЫЙ СЧЕТ

joint and several liability

(CHIN) 连带责任

(FRE) responsabilité solidaire et indivise

(FRE) responsabilité conjointe et solidaire

(GER) gesamtschuldnerische Haftung *f*,
Gesamt- *f*, Solidarhaftung *f*

(JAP) 連帯的債務

(RUS) ПОЛНАЯ ОТВЕТСТВЕННОСТЬ
КАЖДОГО УЧАСТНИКА ДОГОВОРА ЗА
ВСЮ СУММУ ЗАЙМА

joint and survivor annuity

(CHIN) 联合生存者年金

(FRE) rente sur deux têtes réversible

(GER) (gemeinsame) Überlebensrente *f*,
Partnerrente *f*

(JAP) 共同生存者年金

(RUS) ПОЖИЗНЕННЫЙ АННУИТЕТ В
ПОЛЬЗУ ДВУХ И БОЛЕЕ ЛИЦ (до смерти
последнего)

joint fare, joint rate

(CHIN) 联合票价

(FRE) tarif commun

(GER) Sammeltarif *m*; Verbundstarif *m*;
kombinierter Frachttarif *m*

(JAP) 結合運賃、結合料率

(RUS) ОБЩАЯ ПЛАТА, ОБЩАЯ СТАВКА

joint liability

(CHIN) 连带责任，共同负责

(FRE) responsabilité conjointe

(GER) Gesamt- *f*, Solidarschuld *f*,
Solidarhaftung *f*; gesamtschuldnerische
Haftung *f*, Gesamthaftung *f*

(JAP) 共同責任

(RUS) СОВМЕСТНАЯ
ОТВЕТСТВЕННОСТЬ

jointly and severally

(CHIN) 共同及个别责任者

(FRE) conjointement et solidairement

(GER) gesamtschuldnerisch *adj*

(JAP) 連帯的に

(RUS) СОВМЕСТНО И РАЗДЕЛЬНО

joint product cost

(CHIN) 联产品成本

(FRE) coût incorporable total, (C) coût du
produit lié

(GER) Kosten *pl* der Kuppelprodukte *npl*

(JAP) 共同製品原価

joint return

(CHIN) 联合税务申报

(FRE) déclaration commune

(GER) gemeinsame Steuererklärung *f*

(JAP) 共同申告

(RUS) СОВМЕСТНАЯ НАЛОГОВАЯ
ДЕКЛАРАЦИЯ (МУЖА И ЖЕНЫ)

joint stock company

(CHIN) 股份公司

(FRE) société par actions

(GER) (Gesellschaft in Form einer
körperschaftlich organisierten)
Personengesellschaft *f*, Aktiengesellschaft *f*;
Kommanditgesellschaft *f* auf Aktien *fpl*

(JAP) 法人格のない株式会社[株式社団]、
(英)株式会社

(RUS) АКЦИОНЕРНОЕ ОБЩЕСТВО

joint tenancy

(CHIN) 联合租借，共有不动产权

(FRE) tendance commune

(GER) Gesamt(hands)eigentum *n*,
gesamthändnerisches Eigentum *n*, Eigentum
n zur gesamten Hand *f*

(JAP) 合有不動産権
(RUS) СОВМЕСТНОЕ ВЛАДЕНИЕ

joint venture
(CHIN) 合资企业
(FRE) opération en commun, entreprise commune, coentreprise, joint venture,société commune, société en participation
(GER) Joint Venture *n*
(JAP) 合弁事業、
ジョイントベンチャー
(RUS) СОВМЕСТНОЕ ПРЕДПРИЯТИЕ

journal
(CHIN) 日记账，流水账，分类账
(FRE) livre de comptejournal, (C) journal général
(GER) Fachzeitschrift *f*; Tagebuch *n*, Journal *n*, Logbuch *n*
(JAP) 仕訳帳
(RUS) ЖУРНАЛ; ПРОТОКОЛ; ДНЕВНИК

journal entry
(CHIN) 分录，流水分录
(FRE) ecriture comptable passation d'ecriture
(GER) Journaleintrag *f*; Tagebucheintrag *f*
(JAP) 仕訳記入
(RUS) ЗАПИСЬ В ЖУРНАЛЕ, ПРОТОКОЛЕ, ДНЕВНИКЕ

journalize
(CHIN) 分录
(FRE) journaliser
(GER) ins Journal *n* bzw. Hauptbuch *n* eintragen, ein Journal *n* bzw. Tagebuch *n* führen
(JAP) (勘定を)仕訳する、
を仕訳帳に記入する
(RUS) ВЕСТИ ЗАПИСИ В ЖУРНАЛЕ, ПРОТОКОЛЕ, ДНЕВНИКЕ

journal voucher
(CHIN) 分录凭单
(FRE) pièce justificative
(GER) Journal- *m*, Buchungs- *m*, Kassenbeleg *m*
(JAP) 仕訳伝票

(RUS) «КНИЖНЫЙ» ВАУЧЕР; СВИДЕТЕЛЬСТВО; ПОДТВЕРЖДЕНИЕ

journeyman
(CHIN) 伙计，短工
(FRE) compagnon
(GER) Tagelöhner *m*, Handwerksgeselle *m*
(JAP) 職人、(平凡な仕事分野の)熟練者、下働きをする人
(RUS) КВАЛИФИЦИРОВАННЫЙ РАБОЧИЙ

judgment
(CHIN) 审判，裁决
(FRE) jugement
(GER) Gerichtsurteil *n*, Richterspruch *m*
(JAP) 判決、判断
(RUS) ПРИГОВОР; СУДЕБНОЕ РЕШЕНИЕ

judgment creditor
(CHIN) 胜诉债权人
(FRE) créancier autorisé, créancier en vertu d'un jugement
(GER) Vollstreckungs- *m*, Pfändungsgläubiger *m*, Gläubiger *m* mit vollstreckbarem Titel *m*, gerichtlich festgestellter Gläubiger *m*
(JAP) 判決債権者
(RUS) КРЕДИТОР, В ПОЛЬЗУ КОТОРОГО ВЫНЕСЕНО РЕШЕНИЕ О ВЗИМАНИИ ДОЛГА

judgment debtor
(CHIN) 败诉债务人
(FRE) débiteur d'une créance exécutoire, débiteur en vertu d'un jugement
(GER) Vollstreckungs- *m*, Urteilsschuldner *m*
(JAP) 判決債務者
(RUS) ДОЛЖНИК, ПРОТИВ КОТОРОГО ВЫНЕСЕНО СУДЕБНОЕ РЕШЕНИЕ

judgment lien
(CHIN) 判决留置权
(FRE) nantissement en vertu d'un jugement
(GER) Zwangshypothek *f*, gerichtlich festgestelltes Zurückbehaltungsrecht *n*, Grundstückspfandrecht *n*,
(JAP) 判決先取特権
(RUS) ЗАЛОГОВОЕ ПРАВО В СИЛУ СУДЕБНОГО РЕШЕНИЯ

judgment proof

(CHIN) 无能力还债者

(FRE) individu n'ayant pas les moyens de faire face aux conséquences d'une éventuelle condamnation en responsabilité

(GER) unpfändbar, nicht der Zwangsvollstreckung *f* unterliegend *adj*

(JAP) 紙切れ判決、判決執行不能の

(RUS) ДОКАЗАТЕЛЬСТВА В ОБОСНОВАНИЕ СУДЕБНОГО РЕШЕНИЯ

judgment sample

(CHIN) 审计决定

(FRE) échantillon discrétionnaire

(GER) subjektiv ausgewählte Stichprobe *f*, Urteilsstichprobe *f*

(JAP) 有意見本

(RUS) ВЫБОРКА ДЛЯ АУДИТА И ПРОВЕРКИ

judicial bond

(CHIN) 司法保证

(FRE) obligation judiciaire

(GER) Kaution *f* bzw. Sicherheitsleistung *f* bei Gericht *n*

(JAP) 裁判保障

(RUS) ОПЛАТА ЗА РАССМОТРЕНИЕ В СУДАХ РАЗНОГО УРОВНЯ

judicial foreclosure or judicial sale

(CHIN) 司法没收或法院判决的拍卖

(FRE) saisie judiciaire ou vente judiciaire

(GER) Zwangsversteigerung *f*, gerichtliche Versteigerung *f* oderVeräußerung *f*; gerichtlich angeordnete Vollstreckung *f* oder gerichtlich angeordneter Verkauf *m*

(JAP) 司法上の譲渡抵当実行手続き、または司法上の売却

(RUS) КОНФИСКАЦИЯ ЗАЛОЖЕННОГО ИМУЩЕСТВА или ЕГО ПРОДАЖА ПО РЕШЕНИЮ СУДА

jumbo certificate of deposit

(CHIN) 巨额存款证明

(FRE) certificat de très grand depot, (C) certificat de dépôt négociable

(GER) Einlagenzertifikat *n* mit einer Einlage *f* von mehr als $100.000

(JAP) ジャンボ預金証書

(RUS) ДЕПОЗИТНЫЙ СЕРТИФИКАТ С НОМИНАЛОМ 100 000 долл. ИЛИ ВЫШЕ

junior issue

(CHIN) 后序发行，低级证券

(FRE) émission de deuxième rang,

(C) émission de second rang

(GER) Ausgabe *f* geringen Rangs *m*, nachrangige Emission *f*, junge Aktien *fpl*

(JAP) 下位証券

(RUS) «МЛАДШИЕ» ЦЕННЫЕ БУМАГИ (ПОГАШЕНИЕ ОБЯЗАТЕЛЬСТВ ПО КОТОРЫМ ПРОИСХОДИТ ПОСЛЕ УДОВЛЕТВОРЕНИЯ ОБЯЗАТЕЛЬСТВ ПО «СТАРШИМ» БУМАГАМ)

junior lien

(CHIN) 低级留置权

(FRE) nantissement de second rang, privilège de second rang, (C) nantissement de second rang

(GER) nachrangiges bzw. jüngeres Pfandrecht *n*

(JAP) 下位先取権、下位留置権

(RUS) МЛАДШЕЕ (второе, третье) ПРАВО УДЕРЖАНИЯ ИМУЩЕСТВА ЗА ДОЛГИ

junior mortgage

(CHIN) 低级抵押权

(FRE) prêt sur hypothèque de rang subsequent, titre de rang inférieur, valeur de deuxième rang, titre de second rang,

(C) hypothèque de rang subséquent, hypothèque de rang inférieur

(GER) nachrangige bzw. zweite Hypothek *f*

(JAP) 後順位抵当

(RUS) «МЛАДШАЯ» (вторая, третья) ИПОТЕКА, ЗАКЛАДНАЯ

junior partner

(CHIN) 低级合伙人

(FRE) jeune associe(e), (C) associé en second

(GER) Juniorpartner *m*, Juniorteilhabe *m*

(JAP) 下級社員

(RUS) МЛАДШИЙ ПАРТНЕР

junior security

(CHIN) 次级证券

(FRE) titre de second rang

(GER) nachrangige Sicherheit *f*,
nachrangige Anleihe *f*
(JAP) 下位証券、下位担保
(RUS) «МЛАДШАЯ» ЦЕННАЯ БУМАГА (с
меньшими правами на активы эмитента)

junk bond
(CHIN) 垃圾债券
(FRE) obligation a haut rendement mais a
haut risque, junk bond
(GER) (hochverzinsliches) Risikopapier *n*,
Schundobligation *f*, ungesicherter
Schuldschein *m*, Spekulationsobligation *f*
(JAP) ジャンクボンド、ジャンク債
(RUS) ОБЛИГАЦИЯ СПЕКУЛЯТИВНОГО
РЕЙТИНГА

jurisdiction
(CHIN) 管辖权，司法权
(FRE) juridiction
(GER) Gerichtsbarkeit *f*, Gerichtsstand *m*
(JAP) 裁判権、管轄権、管轄区域
(RUS) ЮРИСДИКЦИЯ; ПОДСУДНОСТЬ

jurisprudence
(CHIN) 裁决，国际裁决
(FRE) jurisprudence
(GER) Rechtswissenschaften *fpl*,
Jurisprudenz *f*
(JAP) 法律学、法理学
(RUS) ЮРИСПРУДЕНЦИЯ;
ЗАКОНОВЕДЕНИЕ

jury
(CHIN) 陪审团

(FRE) jury
(GER) Geschworene *pl*,
Geschworenenausschuss *m*, Schwurgericht
n; Jury *f*
(JAP) 陪審
(RUS) ПРИСЯЖНЫЕ; СУД ПРИСЯЖНЫХ;
ЖЮРИ (конкурса)

just compensation
(CHIN) 正当补偿，合理补偿
(FRE) compensation juste
(GER) angemessene
Entschädigung *f*
(JAP) 当然の（正当な）補償
(RUS) СПРАВЕДЛИВАЯ
КОМПЕНСАЦИЯ

justifiable
(CHIN) 公正的，合理的
(FRE) justifable
(GER) vertretbar, berechtigt, gerechtfertigt;
entschuldbar *adj*
(JAP) 正当と認められる、もっともな
(RUS) ДОПУСТИМЫЙ; УВАЖИТЕЛЬНЫЙ;
ДОСТОЙНЫЙ ОПРАВДАНИЯ

justified price
(CHIN) 合理价格
(FRE) juste prix
(GER) gerechtfertigter Preis *n*, fairer
Preis *m*
(JAP) 正当だと認められた価格
(RUS) ОБОСНОВАННАЯ
(РЕАЛИСТИЧНАЯ)
РЫНОЧНАЯ ЦЕН

K

Keogh plan
(CHIN) 吉奥老年金计划
(FRE) plan de retraite « Keogh », (C)
régime de retraite pour travailleurs
autonomes
(GER) Keogh-Plan *m*, steuerbegünstigter
Pensionsplan *m* für Selbständige *pl*
(JAP) キオプラン、
米国の自営業者退職年金制度
(RUS) ПЛАН КЕОГ (ПЛАН ПЕНСИОННЫХ
СБЕРЕЖЕНИЙ для РАБОТНИКОВ МЕЛКИХ
КОМПАНИЙ И лицРАБОТАЮЩИХ
САМОСТОЯТЕЛЬНО)

key
(CHIN) 键，关键字，密钥
(FRE) touche
(GER) Taste *f*; Schlüssel-; Haupt-
(JAP) キー
(RUS) КЛАВИША

key-area evaluation
(CHIN) 关键领域评估理论
(FRE) evaluation des secteurs clés
(GER) Bewertung *f* der Hauptbereiche *mpl*
(JAP) 重要地域評価
(RUS) ОЦЕНКА КЛЮЧЕВОЙ
ЗОНЫ

keyboard
(CHIN) 键盘
(FRE) clavier
(GER) Tastatur *f*
(JAP) キーボード
(RUS) КЛАВИАТУРА

key person life and health insurance
(CHIN) 企业主管人员人寿及健康保险
(FRE) assurance-vie collaborateurs et
assurance maladie, (C) assurance vie et
assurance maladie collaborateurs
(GER) Lebens- *f* und Krankenversicherung *f*
für leitende Angestellte *mpl* eines
Unternehmens *n*
(JAP) 経営者保険、企業幹部保険

(RUS) СТРАХОВАНИЕ ЖИЗНИ И
ЗДОРОВЬЯ КЛЮЧЕВОГО (ВЕДУЩЕГО)
РАБОТНИКА

kickback
(CHIN) 回扣，佣金
(FRE) dessous-de-table (n,m, fam), pot-de-
vin (C) ristourne
(GER) Schmiergeld *n*; Kickback-Geschäft
n; geheime Provision *f*
(JAP) 不当手数料、
(賃金などの)ピンはね、返答
(RUS) ВЗЯТКА

kicker
(CHIN) 附加好处
(FRE) avantage (n,m)
(GER) Zusatzgebühr *f*, Aufschlag *m*;
zusätzliche Darlehensvergütung *f*
(JAP) 追加的コスト、インセンティブ
(証券などに付随する追加的特権)、
以外な結末
(RUS) ДОПОЛНИТЕЛЬНАЯ
ХАРАКТЕРИСТИКА, ПОВЫШАЮЩАЯ
ПРИВЛЕКАТЕЛЬНОСТЬ ОБЛИГАЦИИ

kiddie tax
(CHIN) 儿童税务责任
(FRE) impôt sur le revenu fractionné
(GER) (Tarifvorschrift, wonach auf die
passiven Einkünfte eines Kindes unter 14
Jahren der Grenzsteuersatz der Eltern
anzuwenden ist)
(JAP) 14歳未満の未成年者の投資収入に
対する税金（親が申告する）
(RUS) НАЛОГ НА НЕ ЗАРАБОТАННЫЙ
ДОХОД (свыше определенной суммы)
РЕБЕНКА ДО 14 ЛЕТ

killing
(CHIN) 赚大钱，大发利市
(FRE) grosse somme d'argent gagnée
rapidement
(GER) ungewöhnlich hoher
Spekulationsgewinn *m*

(JAP) 殺すこと、（株などでの）ぼろも
うけ、大もうけ
(RUS) СОРВАТЬ «КУШ»

kiting
(CHIN) 开空头支票，挪用
(FRE) tirage en l'air, tirage a découvert,
(C) détournement par virements bancaires
Wechselreiterei *f*; Bereitstellung *f*
(JAP)（小切手の）過振り、
融通手形（空手形）を振り出すこと
(RUS) ИСПОЛЬЗОВАНИЕ ФИКТИВНЫХ
ЧЕКОВ; ПОДДЕЛКА СУММЫ ЧЕКА;
ВЗВИНЧИВАНИЕ ЦЕН

know-how
(CHIN) 专有技术，诀窍
(FRE) savoir-faire
(GER) Know-How *n*, Fachwissen *n*
(JAP) ノウハウ、実際的な知識、技術
(RUS) «НОУ-ХАУ»;
ПРОИЗВОДСТВЕННЫЕ (ФИРМЕННЫЕ)
СЕКРЕТЫ

knowledge intensive
(CHIN) 知识密集型
(FRE) (C) forte concentration
d'expertise forte concentration
d'expertise
(GER) wissensintensiv *adj*,
umfassende Kenntnisse *fpl*
erfordernd
(JAP) 知識集中的な、知識集約的な
(RUS) НАУКОЕМКИЙ

know-your-customer rule
(CHIN) 了解客户需要规则
(FRE) règle de la connaissance du client
(GER) Know-Your-Customer-Prinzip *n*,
Kenne- Deinen-Kunden-Prinzip *n*
(JAP) 顧客を良く知るという原則
(RUS) ПРАВИЛО «ЗНАЙ СВОЕГО
КЛИЕНТА»

kudos
(CHIN) 奖赏，赞扬
(FRE) kudos (sorte de points de
récompense)
(GER) Lob *n* für gute Leistung *f*
(JAP) 栄光、名声、賞賛
(RUS) СЛАВА;
ВЫСОКАЯ РЕПУТАЦИЯ

L

labeling laws
(CHIN) 标签法
(FRE) lois sur l'étiquettage
(GER) Etikettierungsgesetze *fpl*
(JAP) 法律のラベルを付けること
(RUS) ЗАКОН О НАДЛЕЖАЩЕЙ
МАРКИРОВКЕ ТОВАРОВ

labor
(CHIN) 劳工，人力，工人
(FRE) travail, main d'oeuvre, ouvriers
(GER) Arbeit *f*; Arbeiterschaft *f*, -nehmer *pl*
(JAP) 労働、労力
(RUS) НАЕМНЫЙ ТРУД; РАБОТА

labor agreement
(CHIN) 劳资协议
(FRE) convention collective
(GER) Tarif- *m*, Kollektiv- *m*,
Arbeitsvertrag *m*, Lohnabsprache *f*,
Tarifabkommen *n*
(JAP) 労働協約
(RUS) ТРУДОВОЕ СОГЛАШЕНИЕ

labor dispute
(CHIN) 劳资纠纷
(FRE) conflit du travail
(GER) Arbeitskampf *n*, Tarif- *m*,
Arbeitskonflikt *m*, arbeitsrechtliche
Auseinandersetzung *f*
(JAP) 労働争議
(RUS) ТРУДОВОЙ СПОР

labor force
(CHIN) 劳动力
(FRE) effectifs, population active
(GER) Arbeitskräfte *fpl*, -kräftepotenzial *n*;
Erwerbsbevölkerung *f*,
(JAP) 労働人口、労働力
(RUS) РАБОЧАЯ СИЛА

labor intensive
(CHIN) 劳动密集型
(FRE) qui dépend d'une main d'oeuvre
considérable, (C) non-capitalistique

(GER) arbeits-, personalintensiv,
arbeitsaufwändig *adj*
(JAP) 労働集約的
(RUS) ТРУДОЕМКИЙ

labor mobility
(CHIN) 劳力流动性
(FRE) mobilité de la main d'oeuvre
(GER) Arbeits(kräfte)mobilität *f*,
(Bereitwilligkeit von Arbeitskräften, den
Arbeitsplatz *m* zu wechseln)
(JAP) 労働の移動性、労働移動性
(RUS) МОБИЛЬНОСТЬ ТРУДА, РАБОЧЕЙ
СИЛЫ

labor piracy
(CHIN) 引诱工人跳槽，挖角
(FRE) piratage de main d'oeuvre
(GER) Abwerbung *f* von Arbeitskräften *fpl*
(JAP) 労働争奪
(RUS) «ПИРАТСКОЕ» ПЕРЕМАНИВАНИЕ
РАБОТНИКОВ

labor pool
(CHIN) 劳动人口库
(FRE) main d'œuvre, (C) bassin de
travailleurs
(GER) Arbeitskräftereserve *f*, -potenzial *n*
Markt *m* freier Arbeitskräfte *fpl*
(JAP) 労働プール
(RUS) ФОНД РАБОЧЕЙ СИЛЫ

labor union
(CHIN) 工会，工人联合会
(FRE) syndicat
(GER) Gewerkschaft *f*
(JAP) 労働組合
(RUS) ПРОФСОЮЗ

laches
(CHIN) 因延误而丧失履行合约的权利
(FRE) délai préjudiciable, (C) inertie
(JAP) 権利行使の懈怠
(RUS) ПРОСРОЧКА; ПРЕСТУПНАЯ
ХАЛАТНОСТЬ

lading

(CHIN) 装载，装船
(FRE) chargement, embarquement, mise à bord
(JAP) 荷を積むこと、船積み
(RUS) ОТПРАВЛЕННЫЙ ГРУЗ, ФРАХТ

lagging indicator

(CHIN) 滞后指标
(FRE) indicateur retardé
(GER) Spätindikator m, verzögerter Indikator m
(JAP) 遅行指標
(RUS) ОТСТАЮЩИЙ ПОКАЗАТЕЛЬ

LAN
(local area network)

(CHIN) lan（局域网）
(FRE) LAN (réseau local d'entreprise, rle)
(GER) LAN n
(JAP) ラン、構内ネットワーク、LAN
(RUS) ЛВС: ЛОКАЛЬНАЯ ВЫЧИСЛИТЕЛЬНАЯ СЕТЬ

land

(CHIN) 地产，土地
(FRE) terre, (C) terrain, (C) pays, terre
(GER) Land n, Grund m und Boden m
(JAP) 陸、陸地、土地
(RUS) ЗЕМЛЯ; ЗЕМЕЛЬНЫЙ НАДЕЛ, УЧАСТОК

land banking

(CHIN) 购买准备将来使用的土地
(FRE) crédit foncier, (C) banque foncière
(GER) spekulativer Erwerb m von Grund m und Boden m für spätere Nutzung f; Land-Banking n; Bodenbevorratung f
(JAP) 土地抵当貸銀行業、
土地担保貸銀行業、
(RUS) ПОКУПКА ЗЕМЛИ ДЛЯ БУДУЩЕГО ПОЛЬЗОВАНИЯ

land contract

(CHIN) 土地合约
(FRE) contrat foncier, (C) contrat d'occupation de propriété
(GER) Grundstückskaufkontrakt m, -überlassungsvertrag m
(JAP) 土地延べ払い契約

(RUS) ДОГОВОР О ЗЕМЛЕПОЛЬЗОВАНИИ

land development

(CHIN) 土地开发
(FRE) aménagement du paysage, (C) lotissement
(GER) Erschließung f von Grundstücken npl, Grundstücksentwicklung f, Flächennutzung f, Baulanderschließung f
(JAP) 土地開発
(RUS) ЗАСТРОЙКА ЗЕМЕЛЬНОГО УЧАСТКА; БЛАГОУСТРОЙСТВО

landlocked

(CHIN) 内陆土地，内陆国
(FRE) Enclave, sans littoral
(GER) Binnen- adj
(JAP) 陸地に囲まれた、内陸の
(RUS) БЕЗ ВЫХОДА К МОРЮ

landlord

(CHIN) 地主
(FRE) propriétaire foncier, (C) propriétaire
(GER) Vermieter m, Mietsherr m; Grundbesitzer m; Guts- m, Grundherr m; Hausbesitzer m, -herr m
(JAP) 地主、家主、アパート経営者
(RUS) ЗЕМЛЕВЛАДЕЛЕЦ; ВЛАДЕЛЕЦ НЕДВИЖИМОСТИ

landmark

(CHIN) 界标
(FRE) amer terrestre, point de repère, (C) point d'intérêt
(GER) Grenzstein m; Wegpunkt m; Sehenswürdigkeit f, Wahrzeichen n
(JAP) 陸標、陸上の目印、
歴史的建造物
(RUS) ОРИЕНТИР; ВЕХА; ПРИМЕЧАТЕЛЬНЫЙ ОБЪЕКТ

landscape (format)

(CHIN) 横向（格式）
(FRE) paysage (format), (C) format à l'italienne
(GER) Querformat n
(JAP) 横向き（形式）
(RUS) ГОРИЗОНАЛЬНЫЙ - О РАСПОЛОЖЕНИИ ТЕКСТА ИЛИ ИЗОБРАЖЕНИЯ НА БУМАГЕ, ПРИ КОТОРОМ ГОРИЗОНАЛЬНОЕ

land trust
(CHIN) 土地信托
(FRE) titre de propriété bénéficiaire, fiducie
foncière
(GER) Grundstückstreuhand *f*;
Grundstücksgenossenschaft *f*
(JAP) 土地信託
(RUS) ЗЕМЕЛЬНЫЙ ТРАСТ

land-use intensity
(CHIN) 土地使用密度
(FRE) intensité de l'utilisation des sols,
(C) densité de l'affectation du sol
(GER) Intensität *f* der Boden- *f* bzw.
Flächennutzung *f*
(JAP) 土地利用集約度
(RUS) ИНТЕНСИВНОСТЬ
ЗЕМЛЕПОЛЬЗОВАНИЯ

land-use planning
(CHIN) 土地使用规划
(FRE) établissement d'un plan d'occupation
des sols, (C) aménagement de l'espace
(GER) Boden- *m*, Flächennutzungsplan *m*;
Raumplanung *f*; Bauleitplanung *f*
(JAP) 土地利用計画
(RUS) ПЛАНИРОВАНИЕ
ЗЕМЛЕПОЛЬЗОВАНИЯ

land-use regulation
(CHIN) 土地使用规定
(FRE) aménagement du territoire,
(C) politique d'occupation des sols
(GER) Grundstücksnutzungsvorschrift *f*
(JAP) 土地利用規制
(RUS) РЕГУЛИРОВАНИЕ
ЗЕМЛЕПОЛЬЗОВАНИЯ

land-use succession
(CHIN) 土地使用继承
(FRE) nouvelle utilisation d'un terrain,
(C) nouvelle vocation d'un secteur
(GER) Grundstücksnutzungswechsel *m*,
Nachfolge *m* in der Grundstücksnutzung *f*
(JAP) 土地利用相続（権）
(RUS) ПРЕЕМСТВЕННОСТЬ
ЗЕМЛЕПОЛЬЗОВАНИЯ

lapping
(CHIN) 挪后补前，截留，移用
(FRE) rodage, abrasage, (C) fraude par
report différés
(GER) Fälschen *n* von Buchungsunterlagen
fpl durch Aufschieben *n* von
Kasseneingängen *mpl*, Aufschieben *n* von
Kasseneinnahmen *fpl*, verzögerte Buchung *f*
von Kundengeldern *npl*
(JAP) たらい回し（売掛金の）
(RUS) СОКРЫТИЕ НЕДОСТАЧИ ПУТЁМ
ЗАДЕРЖКИ ПРОВОДКИ

lapse
(CHIN) 过期失效，作废，终止
(FRE) déchéance, laps
(JAP) 保険契約の失効、
権利特権の消滅、失効
(RUS) УПУЩЕНИЕ; ИСТЕЧЕНИЕ;
ПРЕКРАЩЕНИЕ СТРАХОВОГО
ПОКРЫТИЯ ИЗ-ЗА НЕУПЛАТЫ

lapsing schedule
(CHIN) 固定资产增减明细表
(FRE) calendrier de déchéance
(GER) Kostenverteilungsschema *n*,
Abschreibungsaufgliederung *f* nach
Zugangsjahren *npl*
(JAP) 固定資産増減明細表
(RUS) ГРАФИК ИСТЕЧЕНИЯ СРОКОВ

last in, first out (LIFO)
(CHIN) 后进先出（LIFO）
(FRE) dernier entré premier sorti
(GER) Lifo-Methode *f*, -Verfahren *n*,
Zuerstentnahme *f* der neueren Bestände *mpl*
(JAP) 後入先出法
(RUS) УЧЕТ «ПРИШЕЛ ПОСЛЕДНИМ,
ОБСЛУЖЕН ПЕРВЫМ», РАСХОДОВАНИЕ
ТОВАРНЫХ ЗАПАСОВ В ПОРЯДКЕ,
ОБРАТНОМ ПОСТУПЛЕНИЮ

last sale
(CHIN) 最近销售，当天收盘价
(FRE) dernière vente
(GER) letzter Verkauf *m* (Börse)
(JAP) 最終売上げ
(RUS) ПОСЛЕДНЯЯ
ЗАРЕГИСТРИРОВАННАЯ РЕАЛИЗАЦИЯ
(ценной бумаги)

latent defect

(CHIN) 潜在缺陷

(FRE) défaut latent défaut caché, vice latent, vice caché, (C) vice rédhibitoire

(GER) verborgener Fehler *m*, latenter Mangel *m*

(JAP) 潜在欠陷

(RUS) СКРЫТЫЙ ИЗЪЯН, ДЕФЕКТ

latitude

(CHIN) 活动余地

(FRE) latitude

(GER) Breite *f*, Weite *f*; Bewegungsfreiheit *f*, Rahmen *m* bzw. Handlungsspielraum *m* (Gericht)

(JAP) 緯度、自由の範囲、許容度

(RUS) ДОПУСТИМАЯ ШИРОТА толкования

law

(CHIN) 法律，法令，规律，法则

(FRE) loi, droit

(GER) Recht *n*; Gesetz *n*; Rechtswissenschaften *f*

(JAP) 法、法律、法令

(RUS) ЗАКОН; ПРАВО

law of diminishing returns

(CHIN) 报酬递减律

(FRE) loi du rendement decroissant, loi du rendement non-proportionnel

(GER) Gesetz *n* vom abnehmenden Ertragszuwachs *m*

(JAP) 収穫逓減の法則

(RUS) ЗАКОН СНИЖЕНИЯ РЕНТАБЕЛЬНОСТИ

law of increasing costs

(CHIN) 成本递增法则

(FRE) loi de la hausse des coûts, (C) loi des coûts à la hausse

(GER) Gesetz *n* der steigenden Kosten *pl*

(JAP) 生産費漸増の法則

(RUS) ЗАКОН РОСТА СЕБЕСТОИМОСТИ

law of large numbers

(CHIN) 大数法则

(FRE) loi des grands nombres

(GER) Gesetz *n* der großen Zahlen *fpl*

(JAP) （統計）大数の法則

(RUS) ЗАКОН БОЛЬШИХ ЧИСЕЛ

law of supply and demand

(CHIN) 供求法则

(FRE) loi de l'offre et de la demande

(GER) Gesetz *n* von Angebot *n* und Nachfrage *f*

(JAP) 供給と需要の法則

(RUS) ЗАКОН СПРОСА И ПРЕДЛОЖЕНИЯ

lay off

(CHIN) 解雇，暂时停业

(FRE) licencier, mettre en chômage technique, (C) mise à pied

(GER) entlassen, freisetzen, (Personal) abbauen *v*

(JAP) レイオフ、一時解雇、一時的強制休業

(RUS) УВОЛЬНЕНИЕ РАБОТНИКОВ (в связи с сокращением производства)

leader

(CHIN) 领导者，大户，特价品，先导指数

(FRE) chef, dirigeant, leader, (C) numéro un, (C) meneur

(GER) Führer *m*; Vorreiter *m*; Spitzenwert *m*, führender Wert *m* (Börse); Lockartikel *m*; Frühindikator *m*; Leitartikel *m*

(JAP) 指揮者、指導者

(RUS) ЛИДЕР; ВЕДУЩЕЕ ЛИЦО

leader pricing

(CHIN) 特价品定价政策

(FRE) vente a perte

(GER) Preispolitik *f* für Lockangebote *npl*

(JAP) 花形銘柄価格決定

(RUS) СНИЖЕНИЕ ЦЕН НА ВЕДУЩИЕ ТОВАРЫ С ЦЕЛЬЮ ПРИВЛЕЧЕНИЯ ПОКУПАТЕЛЕЙ

leading indicators

(CHIN) 主要指标

(FRE) principaux indicateurs économiques, (C) indicateurs de tendance

(GER) Konjunkturbarometer *n* (US)

(JAP) 先駆指標、先行指標

(RUS) ОПЕРЕЖАЮЩИЕ ИНДИКАТОРЫ

lead time

(CHIN) 生产准备时间，订货至交货时间

(FRE) délai de démarrage, délai de mise en route, délai de miise en marche, (C) délai d'exécution
(GER) Vorlaufzeit *f*, -frist *f*
(JAP) リードタイム、準備期間

lease
(CHIN) 租约，租赁
(FRE) bail, location
(JAP) 借受証、借用契約、貸借契約期間
(RUS) АРЕНДА; СДАЧА В АРЕНДУ

leasehold
(CHIN) 租赁物，租借期，租约
(FRE) bail, location à bail, (C) propriété louée à bail, (C) immeuble donné à bail
(GER) Miet- *m*, Pachtbesitz *m*; Erbpachtvertrag *m*, Erbbaurecht *n*, Erbpacht *f*
(JAP) 賃借権、定期賃借権
(RUS) АРЕНДОВАННАЯ СОБСТВЕННОСТЬ

leasehold improvement
(CHIN) 租赁物改良
(FRE) amélioration apportée par le locataire
(GER) Werterhöhungen *fpl* während der Miet-*f* bzw. Pachtzeit *f*, Investitionen *fpl* in gemietete Anlagen *fpl*
(JAP) 借地借家加工改良費
(RUS) БЛАГОУСТРОЙСТВО, СОВЕРШЕНСТВОВАНИЕ АРЕНДОВАННОЙ СОБСТВЕННОСТИ

leasehold insurance
(CHIN) 租赁物保险
(FRE) assurance de remboursement de capital
(GER) Pachtgutversicherung *f*; Pachtausfallversicherung *f*
(JAP) 賃貸保険
(RUS) СТРАХОВАНИЕ АРЕНДОВАННОЙ СОБСТВЕННОСТИ

leasehold mortgage
(CHIN) 租借抵押
(FRE) hypothèque sur tenure libre
(GER) Verpfändung *f* eines Pachtanspruchs *m* bzw. Pachtgrundstücks *n*, Grundpfandrecht *n* auf ein Pachtgrundstück *n*

(JAP) 賃貸抵当、賃貸抵当権
(RUS) ИПОТЕКА НА АРЕНДОВАННУЮ СОБСТВЕННОСТЬ

leasehold value
(CHIN) 租借价值
(FRE) valeur d'une propriété louée
(GER) Pachtgrundstückswert *m*
(JAP) 賃貸価値
(RUS) ЦЕННОСТЬ АРЕНДОВАННОЙ СОБСТВЕННОСТИ

lease with option to purchase
(CHIN) 有权购买的租赁
(FRE) bail avec option d'achat
(GER) Mietvertrag *m* mit Kaufoption *f*
(JAP) 購買選択権付き賃貸
(RUS) АРЕНДА С ВОЗМОЖНОСТЬЮ ВЫКУПА

least-effort principle
(CHIN) 最省力原则
(FRE) principe du moindre effort, (C) loi du moindre d'effort
(GER) Prinzip *n* des geringsten Aufwands *m*
(JAP) 最小努力の原理
(RUS) ПРИНЦИП «НАИМЕНЬШИХ УСИЛИЙ»

leave of absence
(CHIN) 获准假期
(FRE) autorisation d'absence, congé autorisé
(GER) Sonderurlaub *m*, unbezahlte Arbeitsbefreiung *f*
(JAP) 休職（休暇、休学）許可
(RUS) ОТПУСК за собственный счет

ledger
(CHIN) 分类账，明细账
(FRE) grand-livre
(GER) Hauptbuch *n*; Register *n*
(JAP) 元帳、台帳
(RUS) БУХГАЛТЕРСКАЯ КНИГА; ГРОССБУХ

legal entity
(CHIN) 合法组织，法定单位
(FRE) personne morale

(GER) Rechtspersönlichkeit *f*, juristische Person *f*
(JAP) 法的実体、法的組織体
(RUS) ЮРИДИЧЕСКОЕ ЛИЦО

legal investment
(CHIN) 合法投资
(FRE) placement légal
(GER) mündelsichere Kapitalanlage *f*
(JAP) 法的投資
(RUS) ЗАКОННАЯ ИНВЕСТИЦИЯ

legal list
(CHIN) 合法证券
(FRE) valeurs sûres
(GER) Liste *f* mündelsicherer Wertpapiere *npl*
(JAP) 法定銘柄
(RUS) СПИСОК ВЫСОКОКАЧЕСТВЕННЫХ ЦЕННЫХ БУМАГ, ОДОБРЕННЫХ К ПОКУПКЕ ФИДУЦИАРНЫМИ УЧРЕЖДЕНИЯМИ

legal monopoly
(CHIN) 合法垄断
(FRE) monopole légal
(GER) gesetzliches Monopol *n*
(JAP) 合法的独占、法定独占
(RUS) ЗАКОННАЯ МОНОПОЛИЯ

legal name
(CHIN) 依法登记的名称
(FRE) nom légal
(GER) gesetzlicher Name *m*
(JAP) （正式）氏名
(RUS) ЮРИДИЧЕСКОЕ НАЗВАНИЕ

legal notice
(CHIN) 法律通知
(FRE) annonce légale, (C) avis légal
(GER) gesetzlich vorgeschriebene Kündigungsfrist *f*; gesetzliche Mitteilung *f*; rechtlicher Hinweis *m*
(JAP) 適法な通知

legal opinion
(CHIN) 法律意见，律师意见，法律说明
(FRE) avis juridique
(GER) Rechtsgutachten *n*

(JAP) 裁判官（裁判所）の意見（評価，判定）
(RUS) УДОСТОВЕРЕНИЕ ЗАКОННОСТИ

legal right
(CHIN) 合法权利
(FRE) droit en common law, (C) droit reconnu par la loi
(GER) gesetzliches Recht *n*, dingliches Recht *n*, Rechtsanspruch *m*
(JAP) 法的権利
(RUS) ЮРИДИЧЕСКОЕ ПРАВО

legal tender
(CHIN) 法定货币
(FRE) cours légal, monnaie légale
(GER) gesetzliches Zahlungsmittel *n*
(JAP) 法定通貨、本位貨幣
(RUS) ЗАКОННОЕ СРЕДСТВО ПЛАТЕЖА

legal wrong
(CHIN) 侵权
(FRE) atteinte au droit reconnu par la loi
(GER) Rechtsverletzung *f*
(JAP) 法的な誤り、法的不正
(RUS) НАРУШЕНИЕ ЗАКОННОГО ПРАВА

legatee
(CHIN) 遗嘱接受人
(FRE) légataire, (C) légataire de biens personnels
(GER) Vermächtnisnehmer *m*, Erbe *m*, Legatar *m*
(JAP) 遺産受取人、被遺贈者
(RUS) ЛЕГАТАРИЙ; НАСЛЕДНИК ПО ЗАВЕЩАНИЮ

lender
(CHIN) 出借人，出租人，放款人，债权人
(FRE) prêteur
(GER) Darlehens- *m*, Kredit- *m*, Geldgeber *m*
(JAP) （コール資金の)出し手、貸方
(RUS) КРЕДИТОР; ЗАИМОДАВЕЦ

lessee
(CHIN) 承租人，承租方，租户
(FRE) locataire (à bail)

229

(GER) Mieter *m*, Pächter *m*;
Leasingnehmer *m*
(JAP) 賃借人
(RUS) АРЕНДАТОР; СЪЕМЩИК

lessor
(CHIN) 出租人，出租方
(FRE) bailleur
(GER) Vermieter *m*, Verpächter *m*;
Leasinggeber *m*, Leasingfirma *f*
(JAP) 賃貸人、貸主
(RUS) АРЕНДОДАТЕЛЬ

less than carload (L/C)
(CHIN) 零担货运（L/C）
(FRE) de détail, (C) expédition de détail
(GER) (Waggon)teilladung *f*, Stückgut *n*
(JAP) 一両分の貨車より少ない
(RUS) МЕНЬШЕ ОДНОЙ ЗАГРУЗКИ
ТРАНСПОРТНОГО СРЕДСТВА

letter of intent
(CHIN) 意向书
(FRE) lettre d'intention
(GER) Absichts- *f*, Bereitschaftserklärung *f*,
Auftragszusicherung *f*; Vorvertrag *m*
(JAP) 契約意図表明書
(RUS) ПРОТОКОЛ О НАМЕРЕНИЯХ

letter stock
(CHIN) 非注册股票
(FRE) valeur a negociabilité restreinte,
actions non cotees
(GER) nicht-börsengängige Aktien *f*
(JAP) 投資目的確認書付株式、
売却制限株式
(RUS) АКЦИИ, НЕ
ЗАРЕГИСТРИРОВАННЫЕ В КОМИССИИ
ПО ЦЕННЫМ БУМАГАМ И ИХ ОБМЕНУ
(SEC), ВСЛЕДСТВИИ ЧЕГО ОНИ НЕ
МОГУТ ОТКРЫТО ОБМЕНИВАТЬСЯ

level debt service
(CHIN) 均衡还债
(FRE) service de la dette à niveau égal, (C)
charges de remboursement égales
(GER) konstanter Schuldendienst *m*
(JAP) 負債均等化サービス
(RUS) РАВНОМЕРНО РАСПРЕДЕЛЕННОЕ
ОБСЛУЖИВАНИЕ ДОЛГА

level out
(CHIN) 平衡，稳定
(FRE) se stabilizer, s'équilibrer, (C) niveler
(GER) ausgleichen, abflachen, sich
einpendeln *v*
(JAP) 均等にする、均一化する
(RUS) ВЫРАВНИВАТЬ; ВЫРАВНИВАТЬСЯ

level-payment income stream
(CHIN) 平衡支付收入流
(FRE) revenus constants
(GER) (Leib)rente *f*, Einnahmequelle *f* mit
gleichbleibenden Beträgen *mpl*
(JAP) 定額年金の定期的支払い
(RUS) РАВНОМЕРНОЕ ПОСТУПЛЕНИЕ
ДОХОДОВ

level-payment mortgage
(CHIN) 平衡支付抵押贷款
(FRE) prêt à mensualités constantes
(GER) Tilgungs- *f*, Annuitätenhypothek *f*
(JAP) 定額支払抵当
(RUS) ИПОТЕКА С РАВНОМЕРНОЙ
УПЛАТОЙ

level premium
(CHIN) 平均保险费
(FRE) prime constante, prime nivelée
(GER) gleichbleibende Prämie *f*
(JAP) 平準保険料
(RUS) РАВНОМЕРНАЯ ОПЛАТА
СТРАХОВОЙ ПРЕМИИ

leverage
(CHIN) 杠杆作用，借贷机会，浮动
股息
(FRE) effet de levier, ratio d'endettement,
ratio de levier, (C) levier d'exploitation,
niveau d'endettement, effet de levier
financier
(GER) Hebelwirkung *f*, -effekt *m*, Leverage
n; Verschuldungsgrad *m*; (verdeckte)
Beeinflussung *f*, Verhältnis *n* Eigen- zu
Fremdkapital *n*; Verhältnis *n* von
Obligationen *fpl* zu Stammaktien *fpl*
(JAP) レバリッジ、影響力
(RUS) СРЕДСТВА ВОЗДЕЙСТВИЯ

leveraged buyout (LBO)
(CHIN) 融资买断

230

(FRE) rachat d'entreprise financé par
l'endettement, (C) acquisition par emprunt
(GER) Leveraged Buyout *m*,
Unternehmenserwerb *m* unter Ausnutzung *f*
des Leverage-Effekts *m*, durch Aufnahme *f*
von Fremdmitteln *npl* finanzierte
Übernahme *f*, fremdfinanzierter Firmenkauf
m, fremdfinanziertes Übernahmeangebot *n*
(JAP) レバリッジ・バイアウト,
LBO 式企業買収
(RUS) ПРИОБРЕТЕНИЕ КОМПАНИИ В
КРЕДИТ С ЗАЛОГОМ АКТИВОВ
ЗАКУПАЕМОЙ КОМПАНИИ

leveraged company
(CHIN) 负债较高的公司
(FRE) société endettée, (C) société à fort
levier financier
(GER) Unternehmen *n* mit (hohem)
Fremdkapitalanteil *m*
(JAP) レバレッジド会社　　（利益を見越
して資金を借り入れた）
(RUS) КОМПАНИЯ С ВЫСОКОЙ ДОЛЕЙ
ДОЛГОСРОЧНОГО КРЕДИТА

leveraged lease
(CHIN) 融资租赁
(FRE) bail à effet de levier, (C) bail adossé
(GER) fremdfinanziertes Leasing *n*, durch
Leihkapital *n* finanziertes Leasing *n*
(JAP) レバレッジド・リース
(RUS) АРЕНДА АКТИВА, ЧАСТИЧНО
ПРИОБРЕТЕННОГО В КРЕДИТ

levy
(CHIN) 征税，征集，征税额，扣押
(FRE) prélèvement, (C) imposition,
prélèvement
(GER) Abgabe *f*, Steuer *f*, Beitrag *m*,
(Steuer- *f*, Zoll)erhebung *f*; Pfändung *f*,
Beschlagnahme *f*
(JAP) 課税、徴税
(RUS) ОБЛОЖЕНИЕ; ВЗИМАНИЕ

liability
(CHIN) 负债，义务，债务
(FRE) responsabilité, (C) élément depassif,
(C) dette, responsabilité
(GER) Haftung *f*; Verbindlichkeit *f*,
Zahlungsverpflichtung *f*, Schuld *f*;
Leistungspflicht *f*

(JAP) 責任、負担義務、
負担額
(RUS) ОБЯЗАТЕЛЬСТВО

liability, business exposures
(CHIN) 商业风险责任
(FRE) responsabilité sur l'exposition
financière
(GER) Haftung *f* für Geschäftsrisiken *npl*
(JAP) 事業の経済的リスクの責任\
（負債）
(RUS) ОТВЕТСТВЕННОСТЬ КАК
РЕЗУЛЬТАТ ДЕЛОВЫХ ОПЕРАЦИЙ

liability, civil
(CHIN) 民事责任
(FRE) responsabilité civile
(GER) zivilrechtliche Haftung *f*
(JAP) 民事責任
(RUS) ГРАЖДАНСКАЯ
ОТВЕТСТВЕННОСТЬ

liability, criminal
(CHIN) 刑事责任
(FRE) responsabilité criminelle
(GER) strafrechtliche Haftung *f*
(JAP) 刑事責任
(RUS) УГОЛОВНАЯ ОТВЕТСТВЕННОСТЬ

liability dividend
(CHIN) 负债股利
(FRE) dividende sur un poste passif, (C)
dividende responsabilité
(GER) Dividende *f* in Form *f* von
Schuldurkunden *fpl*, durch Ausgabe *f* von
Schuldverschreibungen *fpl* gezahlte
Dividende *f*
(JAP) 責任配当
(RUS) ДИВИДЕНД С УЧЕТОМ
ОТВЕТСТВЕННОСТИ

liability insurance
(CHIN) 责任保险
(FRE) assurance de responsabilité
(GER) Haftpflicht- *f*,
Schadenersatzversicherung *f*
(JAP) （賠償）責任保険、
損害賠償保険、
(RUS) СТРАХОВАНИЕ
ОТВЕТСТВЕННОСТИ

liability, legal
(CHIN) 法律责任
(FRE) responsabilité de droit commun,
(C) responsabilité civile
(GER) gesetzliche Haftpflicht *f* bzw.
Haftung *f*
(JAP) 法定責任
(RUS) ОТВЕТСТВЕННОСТЬ ПО ЗАКОНУ

liability, professional
(CHIN) 职业责任
(FRE) responsabilité professionnelle
(GER) Berufshaftpflicht *f*
(JAP) 專門職業責任
(RUS) ПРОФЕССИОНАЛЬНАЯ
ОТВЕТСТВЕННОСТЬ

liable
(CHIN) 应负责任
(FRE) responsible
(GER) haftbar, haftend, haftungsfähig;
verantwortlich, verpflichtet *adj*
(JAP) (法律上の、または負債・
損害などに対し) 責任がある、(…する)
義務がある、(返済に)当てられる
(RUS) ОТВЕТСТВЕННЫЙ; ОБЯЗАННЫЙ

libel
(CHIN) 诽谤，侮辱，中伤
(FRE) diffamation, (C) libelle
(GER) Verleumdung *f*, üble Nachrede *f*
(JAP) 文書誹毀、文書誹毀罪
(RUS) ЖАЛОБА; ИСКОВОЕ ЗАЯВЛЕНИЕ;
КЛЕВЕТА; ОЧЕРНЕНИЕ

license
(CHIN) 许可证，特许证，认可，授权
(FRE) licence, (C) permis
(GER) Genehmigung *f*, Erlaubnis *f*,
Bewilligung *f*, Zulassung *f*, Konzession *f*;
Lizenz *f*; Berechtigungsnachweis *m*
(JAP) 許可（書）、認可（書）、
免許（状）、使用許（書）
(RUS) ЛИЦЕНЗИЯ

license bond
(CHIN) 许可保证金
(FRE) assurance caution
(GER) Konzessionssicherheitsleistung *f*

(JAP) 免許(認可)債券、認可証債務証書
(RUS) ГАРАНТИЯ НАЛИЧИЯ
НЕОБХОДИМЫХ ЛИЦЕНЗИЙ

licensee
(CHIN) 买方，受证人，被许可人
(FRE) titulaire d'une licence, (C) licencié,
fabricant licencié
(GER) Konzessionsinhaber *m*,
Konzessionär *m*; Lizenzinhaber *m*, -nehmer
m; Nutzungsberechtigter *m*
(JAP) 許可(認可、許諾、
免許)を受けた者、被許可者
(RUS) ЛИЦЕНЗИАТ; ДЕРЖАТЕЛЬ
ЛИЦЕНЗИИ

license law
(CHIN) 执业法，牌照法
(FRE) loi sur les professions avec licence,
(C) loi sur les professions
(GER) Konzessionsrecht *n*
(JAP) 免許法
(RUS) ЛИЦЕНЗИОННОЕ ПРАВО

licensing examination
(CHIN) 执照考试
(FRE) examen professionnel
(GER) Lizenz- *f*;
Konzessionsantragsprüfung *f*
(JAP) 免許(認可、許諾)審査
(RUS) ЭКСПЕРТИЗА ПРИ ПОЛУЧЕНИИ
ЛИЦЕНЗИИ

lien
(CHIN) 留置权，扣押权
(FRE) privilege, droit de rétention,
(C) sûreté réelle
(GER) Pfandrecht *n*, -sicherheit *f*,
Zurückbehaltungsrecht *n*,
Grundstücksbelastung *f*
(JAP) 先取特権、留置権

life cycle
(CHIN) 寿命周期，耐用年数
(FRE) cycle de vie
(GER) Lebenszyklus *m*
(JAP) ライフサイクル、
生活循環
(RUS) ЖИЗНЕННЫЙ ЦИКЛ; СРОК
СЛУЖБЫ

life estate

(CHIN) 终身产业

(FRE) droit de propriété viager, (C) biens en viager

(GER) (Liegenschafts- *m*, Grundstücks)nießbrauch *m*

(JAP) 生涯不動産権

(RUS) ВЛАДЕНИЕ СОБСТВЕННОСТЬЮ НА СРОК ЖИЗНИ ВЛАДЕЛЬЦА

life expectancy

(CHIN) 平均寿命， 预期使用期限

(FRE) espérance de vie, durée utile

(GER) Lebenserwartung *f*; erwartete Nutzungsdauer *f*

(JAP) 平均余命、平均余命数

(RUS) СРЕДНЯЯ ПРОДОЛЖИТЕЛЬНОСТЬ ЖИЗНИ

life tenant

(CHIN) 终身受益人

(FRE) usufruitier, propriétaire viager, (C) titulaire de jouissance à vie

(GER) Nießbraucher *m* auf Lebenszeit *f*; Mieter *m* bzw. Pächter *m* auf Lebenszeit *f*

(JAP) 終身借地人、終身財産使用権者

(RUS) АРЕНДАТОР, СЪЕМЩИК НА ВСЮ ЖИЗНЬ

lighterage

(CHIN) 驳船费

(FRE) transport par barge, aconage, frais d'allège, (C) transport par allège

(GER) Leichtern *n*; Leichtergebühr *f*; Löschungsgebühr *f*, Leichtergeld *n*, -kosten *pl*

(JAP) はしけ運搬、はしけ(使用)料

(RUS) ПОГРУЗКА И РАЗГРУЗКА СУДОВ ПОСРЕДСТВОМ ЛИХТЕРОВ; ПЛАТА ЗА ПОЛЬЗОВАНИЕ ЛИХТЕРОМ

like-kind property

(CHIN) 同类财产

(FRE) biens de même nature, (C) échange de biens de même nature

(GER) gleichartiger Vermögenswert *m*

(JAP) 同種類の財産（所有物、不動産）、特性（属性、固有性）

(RUS) НАЛОГОВАЯ КАТЕГОРИЯ ДЛЯ ОБОЗНАЧЕНИЯ СОБСТВЕННОСТИ ОДНОГ КЛАССА

limited audit

(CHIN) 有限审计

(FRE) audit limitèe, (C) vérification restreinte

(GER) abgekürzte bzw. begrenzte (Buch)prüfung *f*

(JAP) 限定監査

(RUS) ОГРАНИЧЕННЫЙ АУДИТ

limited company

(CHIN) 有限公司

(FRE) société à responsabilité limitée

(GER) Gesellschaft *f* mit beschränkter Haftung *f*

(JAP) 有限責任会社

(RUS) КОМПАНИЯ С ОГРАНИЧЕННОЙ ОТВЕТСТВЕННОСТЬЮ

limited distribution

(CHIN) 限额分配

(FRE) distribution limitée, (C) distribution restreinte

(GER) begrenzter Vertrieb *m*; begrenzte Verteilung *f*; beschränkte Ausschüttung *f* (Dividende)

(JAP) 限定分配（配給、配当、分布）

(RUS) ОГРАНИЧЕННЫЙ СБЫТ

limited liability

(CHIN) 有限责任

(FRE) responsabilité limité

(GER) begrenzte Haftung *f*, Haftungsbeschränkung *f*

(JAP) 有限責任

(RUS) ОГРАНИЧЕННАЯ ОТВЕТСТВЕННОСТЬ

limited occupancy agreement

(CHIN) 有限占用协议

(FRE) contrat d'occupation limité

(GER) beschränkte Nutzungvereinbarung *f*; begrenzte Inanspruchnahmevereinbarung

(JAP) 限定占有居住の合意、限定居住の合意

(RUS) СОГЛАШЕНИЕ ОБ ОГРАНИЧЕННОЙ АРЕНДЕ

limited or special partner

(CHIN) 有限或特殊合伙人

(FRE) commanditaire, (C) associé passif

(GER) Teilhafter *m*, Kommanditist *m*,
Kommanditär *m*, beschränkt haftender
Gesellschafter *m*
(JAP) 有限責任社員、有限責任組合員
(RUS) ПАРТНЕР С ОГРАНИЧЕННОЙ
ОТВЕТСТВЕННОСТЬЮ; ПАРТНЕР НА
ОСОБЫХ ПРАВАХ

limited partnership

(CHIN) 有限合伙企业
(FRE) société en commandite, (C) société
en commandite simple
(GER) Kommanditgesellschaft *f*,
Teilhaberschaft *f* mit beschränkter Haftung
f, begrenzt haftende Teilhaberschaft *f*
(JAP) 有限責任会社、有限責任組合、
合資会社、
(RUS) ТОВАРИЩЕСТВО С
ОГРАНИЧЕННОЙ
ОТВЕТСТВЕННОСТЬЮ

limited payment life insurance

(CHIN) 限期交费终身保单
(FRE) assurance vie à cotisation limitée,
(C) assurance vie à primes temporaires
(GER) begrenzte Lebensversicherung *f*,
Lebensversicherung *f* mit abgekürzter
Prämien- *f* bzw. Beitragszahlung(sdauer) *f*
(JAP) 有限払込み生命保険
(RUS) ПОЖИЗНЕННОЕ СТРАХОВАНИЕ С
ОГРАНИЧЕННЫМ ПЕРИОДОМ УПЛАТЫ
ВЗНОСОВ

limit order

(CHIN) 限价定单，限制性定单
(FRE) ordre limite, (C) ordre à cours limité
(GER) Limit-Order *f*, Limitauftrag *m*
(Börse)
(JAP) 指値付き注文
(RUS) ЛИМИТИРОВАННЫЙ ЗАКАЗ

limit up, limit down

(CHIN) 升达限幅，降至限幅
(FRE) limite supérieure, limite inférieure,
(C) limite à la hausse, limite à la baisse
(GER) zugestandene minimale/maximale
Preisschwankung *f* pro (Börsen)tag *m*
(JAP) ストップ高、
ストップ安
(RUS) ОГРАНИЧЕНИЕ ЦЕНЫ «СВЕРХУ»
или «СНИЗУ»

line

(CHIN) 生产线，航线，行业，生意种类，
限度
(FRE) ligne, (C) gamme, (C) hiérarchique
(GER) Linie *f*; Fertigungs- *n*,
Lieferprogramm *n*; Sparte *f*; Leitung *f*
(EDV)
(RUS) ЛИНИЯ; ЛИНЕЙНЫЙ

line and staff organization

(CHIN) 条块式组织结构
(FRE) structure mixte, (C) structure
hiérarchique
(GER) Stablinienorganisation *f*
(JAP) ラインスタッフ組織、
参謀部制直系組織
(RUS) ЛИНЕЙНЫЙ ТИВ РАСПРЕДЕЛЕНИЯ
ПОЛНОМОЧИЙ

line authority

(CHIN) 生产线主管
(FRE) pouvoir hiérarchique, autorité
hiérarchique
(GER) dienstliche Befehlsgewalt *f*;
Linienvollmacht *f*, Produktionsautorität *f*
(JAP) ラインの権威（権限、当局）
(RUS) ЛИНЕЙНЫЕ ПОЛНОМОЧИЯ

line control

(CHIN) 生产控制，组织控制
(FRE) gestion de lignes
(GER) (Daten)übertragungs- *f*,
Leitungssteuerung *f*; Linienkontrolle *f*
(JAP) ライン管理、ライン制御
(RUS) ЛИНЕЙНЫЙ КОНТРОЛЬ

line extension

(CHIN) 产品扩展
(FRE) extension de ligne, (C) extension de
gamme
(GER) Nebenstelle *f*; Linien- *fpl*, Sortiment-
f, Programmerweiterung *f*
(JAP) ライン拡張
(RUS) РАСШИРЕНИЕ ЛИНИИ (кредита)

line function

(CHIN) 生产功能
(FRE) fonction hiérarchique, (C) ligne
organique hiérarchique
(GER) Linienfunktion *f*, direkte Funktion *f*

(JAP) ライン機能
(RUS) ЛИНЕЙНАЯ ФУНКЦИЯ

line management
(CHIN) 生产线管理，直线管理
(FRE) cadres, (C) chefs directs
(GER) Fachgebietsleitung *f*, Linienführung
f, -verwaltung *f*, -management *n*
(JAP) ライン経営、ライン管理
(RUS) ЛИНЕЙНОЕ РУКОВОДСТВО

line of credit
(CHIN) 信用额度
(FRE) ligne (n, f) de crédit
(GER) Kreditlinie *f*, Kredit- *f*,
Beleihungsgrenze *f*, Kreditrahmen *m*
(JAP) 信用限度
(RUS) КРЕДИТНАЯ ЛИНИЯ (ПОТОЛОК, В
ПРЕДЕЛАХ КОТОРОГО ЗАЁМЩИК
МОЖЕТ БРАТЬ КРЕДИТ)

line organization
(CHIN) 生产组织
(FRE) structure hiérarchique
(GER) Linienorganisation *f*
(JAP) 直系組織、ライン組織
(RUS) ЛИНЕЙНАЯ ОРГАНИЗАЦИЯ

line pitch
(CHIN) 线间距
(FRE) espacement des lignes,
(C) argumentaire, boniment
(GER) Zeilenabstand *m*
(RUS) ИНТЕРВАЛ СТРОК

line printer
(CHIN) 行式打印机
(FRE) imprimante ligne à ligne
(JAP) 行ピッチ
(JAP) ラインプリンター
(RUS) СТРОЧНОЕ ПЕЧАТАЮЩЕЕ
УСТРОЙСТВО; СТРОЧНЫЙ ПРИНТЕР

link
(CHIN) 链接，链路
(FRE) lien
(GER) Link *m*, Verknüpfung *f* (Internet),
Verbindung *f*, Zwischenglied *n*
(JAP) 相互連絡、リンクする、連結する
(RUS) УКАЗАТЕЛЬ СВЯЗИ, ССЫЛКА

linked object
(CHIN) 链接对象
(FRE) objet lié
(GER) verknüpftes Objekt *n*
(JAP) リンク（相互連結）
したオブジェクト
(RUS) МЕТОД РАСПРЕДЕЛЕНИЯ
ФЕРМЕРСКОГО ДОХОДА
ТЕКУЩЕГО ГОДА НА
ПРЕДЫДУЩИЕ ТРИ ГОДА

liquid asset
(CHIN) 流动资产
(FRE) fonds liquide, (C) liquidités
(GER) liquide Mittel *npl*, sofort einlösbares
bzw. flüssiges Guthaben *n*;
Umlaufvermögen *n*
(JAP) 流動資産
(RUS) ЛИКВИДНЫЙ АКТИВ, ОБОРОТНЫЙ
КАПИТАЛ

liquidate
(CHIN) 清算，变线，平仓
(FRE) liquider, mobiliser
(GER) flüssig machen, verwerten *v*; tilgen,
zurückzahlen, abtragen, begleichen
(Schulden) *v*; abwickeln, liquidieren;
auflösen (Geschäft) *v*
(JAP) 清算する、支払う、弁済する
(RUS) ЛИКВИДИРОВАТЬ

liquidated damages
(CHIN) 清偿损失额，赔偿金
(FRE) dommages-intérêts liquidés,
(C) indemnité de résiliation
(GER) bezifferter Schadensersatz *m*,
(vertraglich) festgesetzte Schadenssumme *f*,
(im voraus festgelegter) pauschalierter
Schadensersatz *m*
(JAP) 確定賠償額
(RUS) ЗАРАНЕЕ ОЦЕНЕННЫЕ УБЫТКИ
ОДНОЙ СТОРОНЫ В СЛУЧАЕ
НАРУШЕНИЯ КОНТРАКТА ДРУГОЙ
СТОРОНОЙ

liquidated debt
(CHIN) 已清算债务额
(FRE) dette amortie
(GER) bezahlte bzw. getilgte Schuld *f*
(JAP) 確定額債務
(RUS) ПОГАШЕННЫЙ ДОЛГ

liquidated value
(CHIN) 已清算价值
(FRE) valeur de liquidation
(GER) Liquidationswert *m*, -erlös *m*,
Veräußerungswert *m*
(JAP) 清算価額
(RUS) СТОИМОСТЬ ПРИ ЛИКВИДАЦИИ

liquidation
(CHIN) 清盘，清算，结清，变现，清理
(FRE) liquidation, mobilisation
(GER) Abwicklung *f*, Liquidation *f*;
Verwertung *f*, Verflüssigung *f* eines
Vermögenswerts *m*; Tilgung *f*; Abrechnung
f; Abwicklung *f*, Auflösung *f*
(JAP) 清算、換金、解散
(RUS) ЛИКВИДАЦИЯ;
ПОГАШЕНИЕ

liquidation dividend
(CHIN) 清算分摊额
(FRE) dividende de liquidation, (C) boni de
liquidation
(GER) Schluss- *f*, Vergleichsquote *f*,
Schlussdividende *f*; Liquidations- *f* bzw.
Konkursquote *f*
(JAP) 清算配当
(RUS) ДИВИДЕНД ПРИ ЛИКВИДАЦИИ

liquid crystal display (LCD)
(CHIN) 液晶显示器
(FRE) écran à cristaux liquides
(GER) Flüssigkristallanzeige *f*, LCD-
Anzeige *f*
(JAP) 液晶ディスプレイ、LCD
(RUS) ДИСПЛЕЙ НА ЖИДКИХ
КРИСТАЛЛАХ

liquidity
(CHIN) 周转率，流动性，变现能力
(FRE) liquidité
(GER) Liquidität *f*, Flüssigkeit *f*,
Zahlungsfähigkeit *f*
(JAP) 流動性、換金性
(RUS) ЛИКВИДНОСТЬ

liquidity preference
(CHIN) 流动偏好
(FRE) préférence pour la liquidité,
(C) liquidité du marché

(GER) Liquiditätsneigung *f*, -präferenz *f*,
Liquiditätsstreben *n*
(JAP) 流動性選好
(RUS) ПРЕДПОЧТЕНИЕ ЛИКВИДНОСТИ

liquidity ratio
(CHIN) 现金周转率，清算比率
(FRE) ration de liquidité, coefficient de
liquidité
(GER) Liquiditätsgrad *m*, Deckungsgrad *m*;
Liquiditätskennzahl *f*, -quote *f*, -ziffer *f*,
-koeffizient *m*
(JAP) 流動性比率
(RUS) КОЭФФИЦИЕНТ ЛИКВИДНОСТИ

list
(CHIN) 一览表，价目表，清单，名单
(FRE) liste
(GER) Liste *f*, Aufstellung *f*
(RUS) СПИСОК; ПЕРЕЧЕНЬ; ВКЛЮЧАТЬ В
СПИСОК

listed options
(CHIN) 上市期权
(FRE) option négociable, (C) option
standardisée
(GER) börsennotierte bzw. börsengängige
Optionen *fpl*
(JAP) 上場オプション
(RUS) ОПЦИОНЫ, ДОПУЩЕННЫЕ К
ТОРГАМ НА БИРЖЕ

listed security
(CHIN) 上市证券
(FRE) valeur admise à la cote officielle,
valeur inscrite à la cote officielle, (C) titres
inscrits à la bourse
(GER) (börsen)notiertes bzw.
börsengängiges Wertpapier *n*
(JAP) 上場株式（証券）
(RUS) ЦЕННЫЕ БУМАГИ, ВХОДЯЩИЕ В
ЛИСТИНГ, Т. Е. ДОПУЩЕННЫЕ К
ОБРАЩЕНИЮ НА ФОНДОВОЙ БИРЖЕ

listing
(CHIN) 上市，挂牌
(FRE) admission à la cote officielle,
(C) inscription
(GER) (Börsen)zulassung *f*, -notierung *f*
(von Wertpapieren); amtliche Notierung *f*;
Grundstücksmaklervertrag *m* (Immobilien)

(JAP) 不動産業者の土地家屋仲介権（契
約）、(証券の）場、表・名簿などの作
成、表・名簿などに記載されること
(RUS) ЛИСТИНГ, УСТАНОВЛЕНИЕ
СООТВЕТСТВИЯ ЦЕННОЙ БУМАГИ
ОПРЕДЕЛЁННЫМ КРИТЕРИЯМ ДЛЯ
ДОПУСКА К ТОРГАМ НА БИРЖЕ

listing agent, listing broker
(CHIN) 上市代理，上市经纪人
(FRE) agent contractant, (C) courtier
contractant
(GER) Immobilien- m,
Grundstücksmakler m
(JAP) （不動産取扱物件の）
リスト掲載仲介業者、上場代理人、
上場ブローカー
(RUS) АГЕНТ ПО ТОРГОВЛЕ
НЕДВИЖИМОСТЬЮ ПРОДАЮЩЕЙ
СТОРОНЫ

listing requirements
(CHIN) 上市要求
(GER) Zulassungsvorschriften fpl,
Bedingungen fpl für die Börseneinführung f
(JAP) 上場審査基準
(RUS) ТРЕБОВАНИЯ ДЛЯ ДОПУСКА К
ТОРГАМ НА БИРЖЕ

list price
(CHIN) 价目表价格，批发价
(FRE) prix courant, prix usual, prix de
catalogue
(GER) Listen- m, Katalogpreis m
(JAP) 表示価格
(RUS) ПРЕЙСКУРАНТНАЯ,
ОПУБЛИКОВАННАЯ или
РЕКЛАМИРУЕМАЯ ЦЕНА

litigant
(CHIN) 诉讼
(FRE) partic, (C) litigant
(GER) Prozesspartei f, prozessführende
Partei f
(JAP) 訴訟当事者
(RUS) ТЯЖУЩАЯСЯ СТОРОНА, СТОРОНА
В СУДОПРОИЗВОДСТВЕ

litigation
(CHIN) 诉讼，争论
(FRE) action en justice

(GER) Rechtsstreit m, Prozess m (Gericht)
(JAP) 訴訟
(RUS) ТЯЖБА; СУДЕБНЫЙ СПОР,
ПРОЦЕСС

living trust
(CHIN) 生前信托，有效信托
(FRE) fiducie non testamentaire, fiducie
entre vifs
(GER) Treuhandverhältnis n zu Lebzeiten
fpl des Verfügenden m, lebenslängliche
Treuhandverwaltung f
(JAP) 生前信託
(RUS) ПРИЖИЗНЕННЫЙ ТРАСТ

load
(CHIN) 装船，加载，加收额外费用
(FRE) charge, chargement, (C) frais
d'acquisition
(GER) Ladung f; Belastung f; Aufschlag m;
Gewicht n; laden (Software) v
(JAP) 付加料、保険料に付加する
(RUS) ГРУЗ; КОМИССИЯ НА ПОКУПКУ
АКЦИЙ ОТКРЫТОГО
ИНВЕСТИЦИОННОГО ФОНДА

load fund
(CHIN) 加收交易费的互助基金
(FRE) fonds commun de placement à droit
d'entrée, (C) fonds avec frais d'acquisition
(GER) Investmentfonds m mit
Gebührenberechnung f beim Anteilskauf m
bzw. -verkauf m
(JAP) ロードファンド、手数料負荷投資
信託（ミューチュアルファンドなど）
(RUS) СОВМЕСТНЫЙ
ИНВЕСТИЦИОННЫЙ ФОНД,
ВЗИМАЮЩИЙ КОМИССИИ С СУММЫ
СВОИХ АКЦИЙ ПРИ СДЕСКАХ С НИМИ
ИНВЕСТОРОВ

loan
(CHIN) 贷款，借款
(FRE) prêt, emprunt
(GER) Kredit m, Darlehen n
(JAP) 貸付、借入、融資、ローン
(RUS) ЗАЕМ; ССУДА; КРЕДИТ

loan application
(CHIN) 贷款申请书
(FRE) demande de prêt

(GER) Kredit- *m*, Darlehensantrag *m*

(JAP) 貸付申込み、融資申込み、ローン申込み

(RUS) ЗАЯВКА НА ПОЛУЧЕНИЕ КРЕДИТА, ЗАЙМА

loan committee

(CHIN) 贷款委员会

(FRE) comité des prêts, (C) comité d'approbation des prêts

(GER) Kreditausschuss *m*

(JAP) 貸付委員会、融資委員会

(RUS) ССУДНЫЙ КОМИТЕТ

loan-to-value ratio (LTV)

(CHIN) 借款价值比率（LTV）

(FRE) rapport entre le capital, estant dû et la valeur du bien financé, (C) quotité de financement

(GER) Beleihungsquote *f*, -satz *m*

(JAP) 評価価格融資率

(RUS) ОТНОШЕНИЕ РАЗМЕРА КРЕДИТА К ЦЕННОСТИ КРЕДИТУЕМОГО ОБЪЕКТА

loan value

(CHIN) 借款价值

(FRE) valeur hypothécable, (C) valeur d'emprunt

(GER) Beleihungs- *m*, Lombardwert *m*

(JAP) 貸付価値

(RUS) РАЗМЕР КРЕДИТА

lobbyist

(CHIN) 院外活动集团成员

(FRE) démarcheur, agent d'affaires, (C) lobbyiste

(GER) Lobbyist *m*

(JAP) ロビイスト、院外活動家

(RUS) ЛОББИСТ

lock box

(CHIN) 银行存款箱

(FRE) serrure, (C) boîte postale scellée

(GER) Schließfach *n*; verschließbare Kassette *f*

(JAP) ロックボックス、鍵付の箱

(RUS) »ЗАПЕРТЫЙ ЯЩИК«, БАНКОВСКАЯ УСЛУГА ПО ПОЛУЧЕНИЮ И ПЕРЕДАЧЕ ПЛАТЁЖНОЙ КОРРЕСПОНДЕНЦИИ КОМПАНИИ ЧЕРЕЗ ОТДЕЛЬНЫЙ ПОЧТОВЫЙ ЯЩИК, И ПО

ОСУЩЕСТВЛЕНИЮ НА ЭТОЙ ОСНОВЕ ЗАЧИСЛЕНИЙ НА СЧЁТ И СПИСАНИЙ С НЕГО

locked in

(CHIN) 被锁住，锁定，套牢

(FRE) enfermé à l'intérieur, (C) bloqué

(GER) gesichert; festgelegt, festgeschrieben *adj*

(JAP) 固定した、確定した

(RUS) ЗАМОРОЖЕННЫЙ, ЗАФИКСИРОВАННЫЙ

lockout

(CHIN) 封闭工厂

(FRE) lock-out, contre-grève, grève patronale

(GER) Aussperrung *f* (u.a. auch von Streikenden); Ausschluss *m*; Sperre *f* (EDV)

(JAP) 労働者締め出し、工場閉鎖、事業所閉鎖、ロックアウト

(RUS) БЛОКИРОВКА, ЗАХВАТ; ЛОКАУТ, Т. Е. БЛОКАДА РУКОВОДСТВОМ ДОПУСКА К РАБОЧИМ МЕСТАМ ДО РАЗРЕШЕНИЯ ТРУДОВОГО СПОРА

lock-up option

(CHIN) 封存选择权

(FRE) option d'achat privilégiée

(GER) Festschreibungs- *f*, Festlegungsoption *f*

(JAP) (JAP) 固定オプション、ロックアップ・オプション

(RUS) ПРЕДОСТАВЛЕНИЕ ПРАВА ПРИОБРЕТЕНИЯ ПАКЕТА ДОЧЕРНЕЙ КОМПАНИИ, КОТОРОЙ ГРОЗИТ ЗАХВАТ

logic diagram

(CHIN) 逻辑图

(FRE) diagramme logique, (C) schéma logique

(GER) Schaltplan *m*

(JAP) 論理図

(RUS) ЛОГИЧЕСКАЯ БЛОК-СХЕМА

log in (log on)

(CHIN) 注册（登录）

(FRE) log in, ouverture de session

(GER) einloggen, anmelden *v* (Computer)

(JAP) ログイン（ログオン）、接続開始、ネットワークシステムにアクセスする

(RUS) ВХОД В СИСТЕМУ, ЛОГОН

login identification (login ID)
(CHIN) 注册标识 （注册 id）
(FRE) ID de login, identifiant, (C) ID de connexion
(GER) Anmeldename *m*, Anmelde-ID *f*
(JAP) ID をログインする
(RUS) ИДЕНТИФИКАЦИЯ ПРИ ВХОДЕ В СИСТЕМУ

logo
(CHIN) 徽标，标志
(FRE) logo
(GER) Logo *n*, Erkennungssymbol *n*, Firmenzeichen *n*
(JAP) ロゴ、社名・商品名などを図案化した文字、ロゴマーク
(RUS) ЛОГОТИП; ЯЗЫК ПРОГРАММИРОВАНИЯ, РАЗРАБОТАННЫЙ С ЦЕЛЬЮ ОБУЧЕНИЯ ДЕТЕЙ

log off
(CHIN) 注销
(FRE) fermeture de session
(GER) ausloggen, abmelden *v* (Computer)
(JAP) ログオフする、コンピューターの使用を終了する
(RUS) ВЫХОД ИЗ СИСТЕМЫ

long bond
(CHIN) 长期债券
(FRE) obligation à long terme, obligation à longue échéance
(GER) Langläufer *m*, langfristige Schuldverschreibung *f*, langlaufender Rentenwert *m*
(JAP) 長期債券
(RUS) ДОЛГОСРОЧНАЯ ОБЛИГАЦИЯ, СРОКОМ БОЛЕЕ 10 ЛЕТ

long coupon
(CHIN) 长期息票
(FRE) coupon à long terme
(GER) langfristiger Zinsschein *m*
(JAP) 長期クーポン
(RUS) ДОЛГОСРОЧНАЯ ОБЛИГАЦИЯ

longevity pay
(CHIN) 按资历增加的工资
(FRE) prime d'ancienneté
(GER) nach Dauer *f* der Betriebszugehörigkeit *f* gestaffelte Gehaltszulage *f*
(JAP) 年功加給、年功加俸
(RUS) ПЛАТА ЗА ВЫСЛУГУ ЛЕТ

long position
(CHIN) 进远期货，多头，买超，多头市场
(FRE) position longue
(GER) Überbestand *m*; Long-Position *f*, Hausse-Position *f*
(JAP) 買い超、買持ちポジション、ロングポジション
(RUS) ДЛИННАЯ ПОЗИЦИЯ (В КОТОРОЙ НАХОДИТСЯ УЧАСТНИК ТОРГОВОЙ СДЕЛКИ, КУПИВШИЙ БОЛЬШЕ ЦЕННЫХ БУМАГ, ЧЕМ ПРОДАЛ)

long-range planning
(CHIN) 远景规划
(FRE) planification à longue portée
(GER) Langzeitplanung *f*, langfristige Planung *f*
(JAP) 長期計画
(RUS) ДОЛГОСРОЧНОЕ ПЛАНИРОВАНИЕ

long-term debt or long-term liability
(CHIN) 长期债务 或长期负债
(FRE) dette à long terme
(GER) langfristige Schuldtitel *mpl* oder langfristige Verschuldung *f*
(JAP) 長期借入金または長期債務
(RUS) ДОЛГОСРОЧНЫЙ ДОЛГ или ДОЛГОСРОЧНОЕ ОБЯЗАТЕЛЬСТВО

long-term gain (loss)
(CHIN) 长期收益 （损失）
(FRE) gain (perte) à long terme, (C) bénéfice (perte) à long terme
(GER) langfristiger Gewinn *m* (Verlust *m*)
(JAP) 長期収益 （損失）
(RUS) ДОЛГОСРОЧНАЯ ПРИБЫЛЬ (УБЫТОК)

long-term trend
(CHIN) 长期趋势

(FRE) tendance à long terme
(GER) langfristiger Trend *m*,
Langzeittrend *m*
(JAP) 長期的趨勢
(RUS) ДОЛГОСРОЧНАЯ
ТЕНДЕНЦИЯ

long-wave cycle
(CHIN) 长周期
(FRE) cycle long, cycle de Kondratieff,
(C) cycle à grandes ondes
(GER) Kondratieff-Zyklus *m*
(JAP) 長期波動循環
(RUS) ЦИКЛ КОНДРАТЬЕВА, СОГЛАСНО
КОТОРОМУ ЭКОНОМИКИ ЗАПАДНЫХ
СТРАН ПОДВЕРЖЕННЫ ОСОБО
ДЛИТЕЛЬНЫМ ЦИКЛИЧЕСКИМ
КОЛЕБАНИЯМ 50-60 ЛЕТ

loop
(CHIN) 环，环路，循环
(FRE) boucle
(GER) Schleife *f*
(JAP) 輪、輪形のもの、環
(RUS) ПЕТЛЯ; ЦИКЛ, Т. Е. КОНСТРУКЦИЯ
ПРОГРАММЫ, ОБЕСПЕЧИВАЮЩАЯ
ПОВТОРЕНИЕ ГРУППЫ ОПЕРАЦИЙ

loophole
(CHIN) 漏洞
(FRE) vide juridique
(GER) (Gesetzes)lücke *f*
(JAP) 空気抜き、抜け穴
(RUS) ЛАЗЕЙКА; УЛОВКА

loose rein
(CHIN) 放松型管理
(FRE) rêne laché
(GER) freier Lauf *m*, lockere Zügel *mpl*
(JAP) 統制を緩める
(RUS) ОСЛАБЛЕНИЕ УПРАВЛЕНИЕ;
УПРАВЛЕНИЕ «НА ДЛИННОМ
ПОВОДКЕ»

loss
(CHIN) 损失，亏损，错过
(FRE) perte
(GER) Verlust *m*, Einbuße *f*, Ausfall *m*
(JAP) 欠損、損失、穴（欠損）
(RUS) ПОТЕРЯ; УТРАТА; УБЫТОК

loss adjustment expense
(CHIN) 理算费用
(FRE) dépense de règlement des sinistres,
(C) ajustement de perte
(GER) Schadenregulierungskosten *pl*
(JAP) 損失修正（調整、補正）費用
(RUS) РАСХОД НА КОМПЕНСАЦИЮ
УБЫТКА

loss carryback
(CHIN) 回计亏损
(FRE) report déficitaire sur les exercices
précédents
(GER) Verlustrücktrag *m*
(JAP) 繰戻欠損金
(RUS) ОБРАТНЫЙ ПЕРЕНОС УБЫТКА (для
учета в налогообложении за предшествующие
годы)

loss carryforward
(CHIN) 计入后期亏损
(FRE) déficit reportable, report déficitaire
sur les exercices ultérieurs, (C) report de
perte en avant
(GER) Verlustvortrag *m*
(JAP) 繰越欠損金
(RUS) ПЕРЕНОС УБЫТКА «ВПЕРЕД» (для
учета в последующем налогообложении)

loss contingency
(CHIN) 或有损失
(FRE) perte éventuelle
(GER) Verlustrücklage *f*
(JAP) 損失偶発事件
(RUS) НЕПРЕДВИДЕННЫЙ УБЫТОК

loss leader
(CHIN) 亏本出售，特廉商品
(FRE) produit d'appel, (C) produit
d'attraction
(GER) Lockvogel *m*, -artikel *m*, -ware *f*
(JAP) 目玉商品、おとり商品
(RUS) ТОВАР, ПРОДАЮЩИЙСЯ ПО
ЗАНИЖЕННОЙ ЦЕНЕ ДЛЯ ПРИВЛЕЧЕНИЯ
ПОКУПАТЕЛЕЙ

loss of income insurance
(CHIN) 收入损失保险
(FRE) assurance privation de revenus,
(C) assurance en cas de perte de revenu

(GER) Einkommensausfallversicherung *f*,
(Versicherung zur Kompensation von
Einkommensverlusten)
(JAP) 所得損失保険
(RUS) СТРАХОВАНИЕ ОТ УТРАТЫ
ДОХОДА

loss ratio
(CHIN) 损失率，赔款率
(FRE) rapport sinistres-primes
(GER) Schadenshäufigkeit *f*, -quote *f*
(Versicherung); Verhältnis der
Pämieneinnahmen *fpl* zur Gesamtsumme *f*
der erbrachten Versicherungsleistungen *fpl*
(JAP) 損害率
(RUS) КОЭФФИЦИЕНТ УБЫТКОВ

lot and block
(CHIN) 分块土地定位法
(FRE) lot et bloc, (C) certificat de
localisation
(GER) Blockparzellierung *f*
(JAP) ロット・アンド・ブロック、
一口と大口（の株）
(RUS) МЕТОД ЛОКАЛИЗАЦИИ УЧАСТКА
ЗЕМЛИ

lot line
(CHIN) 地块边界线
(FRE) ligne d'arpentage
(GER) Grundstücksgrenze *f*
(JAP) 用地境界線
(RUS) ГРАНИЦА ЗЕМЕЛЬНОГО УЧАСТКА

lottery
(CHIN) 彩票
(FRE) à lots, (C) loterie
(GER) Lotterie *f*, Ausspielung *f*, Verlosung
f, Gewinnspiel *n*; Losverfahren *n*
(JAP) 抽選、富くじ
(RUS) ЛОТЕРЕЯ

low
(CHIN) 证券最低价
(FRE) bas, peu élevé
(GER) Tiefstand *m*, -punkt *m*
(JAP) 低い、安い
(RUS) НИЗКИЙ; САМАЯ НИЗКАЯ ЦЕНА
КОГДА-ЛИБО УПЛАЧЕННАЯ ЗА ЦЕННУЮ
БУМАГУ

lower case character/letter
(CHIN) 小写字符/字母
(FRE) minuscule, (C) lettre minuscule
(GER) Kleinbuchstabe *m*
(JAP) 下段文字、小文字
(RUS) ЗНАК/БУКВА В НИЖНЕМ РЕГИСТРЕ

lower-involvement model
(CHIN) 低参与模型
(FRE) modèle d'implication réduite
(GER) Modell *n* der geringeren
Einmischung *f* bzw. Beteiligung *f*
(JAP) 係わり合いの少ないモデル
(RUS) МОДЕЛЬ МАЛОЙ ВОВЛЕЧЕННОСТИ

lower of cost or market
(CHIN) 以成本或市价低者为准
(FRE) prix coûtant ou prix du marché,
(C) méthode d'évaluation au plus petit du
coût ou de la valeur du marché
(GER) Niederstwert *m*
(JAP) 原価又は市価の低いほう
(RUS) МЕТОД УЧЁТА ЗАПАСОВ, ПРИ
КОТОРОМ АКТИВ УЧИТЫВАЕТСЯ ИЛИ
ПО СЕБЕСТОИМОСТИ, ИЛИ ПО
РЫНОЧНОЙ ЦЕНЕ – СМОТРЯ КАКАЯ ИЗ
НИХ НИЖЕ

low-grade
(CHIN) 低等，次品
(FRE) qualité inférieure
(GER) minderwertig, von minderer
Qualität *f*
(JAP) 低等級、低品位、低格付け
(RUS) НИЗКОСОРТНЫЙ;
НИЗКОКАЧЕСТВЕННЫЙ

low resolution
(CHIN) 低分辨率
(FRE) faible résolution
(GER) geringe Auflösung *f*
(JAP) 低解像度
(RUS) НИЗКАЯ РАЗРЕШАЮЩАЯ
СПОСОБНОСТЬ, РЕЗОЛЮЦИЯ

low-tech
(CHIN) 低技术产品
(FRE) techniques traditionnelles
(GER) Low-Tech, technisch einfach
ausgestattet *adj*

(JAP) ローテク（低レベルの工業技術）
(RUS) НИЗКОТЕХНОЛОГИЧНЫЙ
ПРОДУКТ

lump sum

(CHIN) 总价，总计，总数
(FRE) somme forfaitaire
(GER) Pauschalbetrag *m*, -summe *f*,
Pauschale *f*
(JAP) 一括、一括払い、総金額
(RUS) ЕДИНОВРЕМЕННАЯ СУММА

lumpsum distribution

(CHIN) 一次性总付
(FRE) distribution forfaitaire
(GER) Pauschal(aus)zahlung *f*,
Ausschüttung *f* in einer Summe *f* (z.B.
Dividende, Abfindung)
(JAP) 一括配賦、一括分配

(RUS) ЕДИНОВРЕМЕННАЯ ВЫПЛАТА
БЕНЕФИЦИАРИЮ ВСЕЙ СУММЫ

lump-sum purchase

(CHIN) 整套购买，整批购买
(FRE) achat à payer en une seule fois,
(C) achat à prix forfaitaire
(GER) Globalkauf *m*
(JAP) 一括購入
(RUS) ПОКУПКА С ЕДИНОВРЕМЕННОЙ
УПЛАТОЙ

luxury tax

(CHIN) 奢侈品税
(FRE) taxe sur les produits de luxe, (C) taxe
de luxe
(GER) Luxussteuer *f*
(JAP) ぜいたく品税，奢侈税
(RUS) НАЛОГ НА ПРЕДМЕТЫ РОСКОШИ

M

macro
(CHIN) 宏(功能，指令)
(FRE) macro, (C) macro-instruction, macrocommande
(GER) Makro *n*, Makrobefehl *m*
(JAP) マクロ
(RUS) МАКРОКОМАНДА

macroeconomics
(CHIN) 宏观经济学
(FRE) macroéconomie
(GER) Makroökonomik *f*, Makroökonomie *f*
(JAP) 巨視的経済学、マクロ経済学
(RUS) МАКРОЭКОНОМИКА

macroenvironment
(CHIN) 宏观环境
(FRE) macroenvironnement
(GER) Makrostruktur *f*, -umfeld *n*
(JAP) 巨視的環境
(RUS) СОВОКУПНОСТЬ НАЦИОНАЛЬНЫХ И МЕЖДУНАРОДНЫХ МАКРОЭКОНОМИЧЕСКИХ СИЛ

magnetic card
(CHIN) 磁卡
(FRE) carte magnétique
(GER) Magnetkarte *f*
(JAP) 磁気カード
(RUS) МАГНИТНАЯ КАРТА

magnetic strip
(CHIN) 磁条
(FRE) bande magnétique
(GER) Magnetstreifen *m*
(JAP) 磁気ストリップ
(RUS) МАГНИТНАЯ ПОЛОСКА

mailbox
(CHIN) 信箱区，邮箱
(FRE) boîte aux letters, (C) boîte aux lettres électronique
(GER) Mailbox *f*, (elektronischer) Briefkasten *m*
(JAP)（電子メールの）メールボックス、ポスト
(RUS) ПОЧТОВЫЙ ЯЩИК

mail fraud
(CHIN) 邮寄诈骗
(FRE) fraude postale
(GER) betrügerische Postbenutzung *f*
(JAP) 郵便物詐欺
(RUS) МОШЕННИЧЕСТВО С ПОЧТОВЫМИ ПЕРЕВОДАМИ

mailing list
(CHIN) 邮寄清单
(FRE) liste de publipostage, liste de diffusion, (C) liste d'adresses
(GER) Adressen- *f*, Verteilerliste *f*, Anschriftenverzeichnis *n*
(JAP) 郵送リスト、郵送一覧表
(RUS) СПИСОК ДЛЯ РАССЫЛКИ

mainframe
(CHIN) 大型计算机；主机；主机柜；底盘
(FRE) processeur central, gros ordinateur, (C) ordinateur central
(GER) Großrechner m, Mainframe *m*
(JAP) メーンフレーム、大型汎用コンピューター
(RUS) БАЗОВОЕ ВЫЧИСЛИТЕЛЬНОЕ УСТРОЙСТВО

main menu
(CHIN) 主选项屏[菜单，选单]
(FRE) menu principal
(GER) Hauptmenü *n*
(JAP) メインメニュー
(RUS) БАЗОВОЕ МЕНЮ

maintenance
(CHIN) 维护，维修
(FRE) maintenance, entretien
(GER) Pflege *f*, Betreuung *f*; Wartung *f*, Instandhaltung *f* (u.a. Software,

243

Computer); Kontoführung
(Rechnungswesen); Versorgung *f*, Unterhalt
m (Recht)
(JAP) 維持、扶養、生計
(RUS) ОБСЛУЖИВАНИЕ (кредита);
ТЕХОБСЛУЖИВАНИЕ

maintenance bond
(CHIN) 维修契约，维修保证
(FRE) garantie de maintenance
(GER) Leistungsgarantie *f*,
Mängelgewährleistungsbürgschaft *f*,
Garantieversprechen *n*;
Unterhaltszusage *f*
(JAP) 扶養保証
(RUS) ДОКУМЕНТ ГАРАНТИИ КАЧЕСТВА
ВЫПОЛНЕНИЯ РАБОТ, ДАННЫЙ
ПОДРЯДЧИКОМ

maintenance fee
(CHIN) 维修费，维持费
(FRE) frais de maintenance, (C) frais de
gestion
(GER) Kontoführungsgebühr *f*,
Wartungsgebühr *f*, Instandhaltungs- *pl*,
Unterhaltskosten *pl*
(JAP) 維持費、管理費
(RUS) СБОР ЗА ОБСЛУЖИВАНИЕ;
ЕЖЕГОДНАЯ КОМИССИЯ

maintenance method
(CHIN) 维修期
(FRE) méthode de maintenance,
(C) méthode de conservation des abonnés
(GER) (Abonnenten)erhaltungsprinzip *n*
(JAP) 維持法、管理法
(RUS) СПОСОБ ОБСЛУЖИВАНИЯ

majority
(CHIN) 多数
(FRE) majorité
(GER) Mehrheit *f*, -zahl *f*, Majorität *f*;
Volljährigkeit *f*, Mündigkeit *f*;
Stimmenmehrheit *f* (Abstimmung)
(JAP) 過半数、大多数
(RUS) БОЛЬШИНСТВО

majority shareholder
(CHIN) 多数股持有人
(FRE) actionnaire majoritaire

(GER) Mehrheitsaktionär *m*, Inhaber *m* der
Kapitalanteilsmehrheit *f*,
(JAP) 株主の過半数

maker
(CHIN) 制造商，出票人，制单人
(FRE) fabricant, constructeur
(GER) Hersteller *m*, Erzeuger *m*, Produzent
m; Aussteller *m*, (Wechsel)geber *m*
(JAP) 製作者、メーカー、
製造業者
(RUS) ИЗГОТОВИТЕЛЬ

make-work
(CHIN) 无价值工作
(FRE) travail artificial, (C) embauche
inutile
(GER) Arbeitsbeschaffungsmaßnahmen *fpl*,
Beschäftigungsprogramm *n*
(RUS) БЕСПОЛЕЗНАЯ РАБОТА,
СОЗДАННАЯ ДЛЯ ПОВЫШЕНИЯ
ЗАНЯТОСТИ

malicious mischief
(CHIN) 恶意伤害
(FRE) acte de malveillance, (C) dommage
par acte de malveillance
(GER) vorsätzlicher Unfug *m*; mutwilliges
Übel *n*
(JAP) 故意の器物損壊
(RUS) ЗЛОУМЫШЛЕННЫЙ ВРЕД

malingerer
(CHIN) 装病逃差的人
(FRE) faux malade
(GER) Simulant *m*
(JAP) （任務回避のために）
仮病を使う者
(RUS) СИМУЛЯНТ

malingering
(CHIN) 装病，开小差
(FRE) simulation, (C) sinistrose
(GER) krankstellen, simulieren *v*;
Simulation *f*, Krankstellen *n*
(JAP) 仮病を使うこと
(RUS) СИМУЛЯЦИЯ

mall
(CHIN) 封闭式购物中心

(FRE) galerie marchande, (C) centre commercial
(GER) Einkaufszentrum *n*, Mall *m*
(JAP) モール、プロムナード風商店街、ショッピングセンター
(RUS) ТОРГОВЫЙ ЦЕНТР

malpractice
(CHIN) 渎职，违法行为
(FRE) faute professionnelle, (C) incurie professionnelle
(GER) Amtsmissbrauch *m*; Berufsvergehen *n*; Kunstfehler *m*
(JAP) 医療過誤、弁護過誤、（専門の）業務過誤
(RUS) НЕДОБРОСОВЕСТНАЯ ПРАКТИКА; ЗЛОУПОТРЕБЛЕНИЕ ДОВЕРИЕМ

manage
(CHIN) 管理，经营
(FRE) gérer
(GER) führen, leiten, lenken, managen, verwalten *v*
(JAP) 管理する、運営（経営）する、監督する
(RUS) УПРАВЛЯТЬ; РУКОВОДИТЬ; СПРАВЛЯТЬСЯ

managed account
(CHIN) 管理账户，经营账户
(FRE) compte géré
(GER) treuhänderisch verwaltetes Konto
(JAP) 管理会計
(RUS) УПРАВЛЯЕМЫЙ СЧЕТ

managed currency
(CHIN) 管理货币，管理通货
(FRE) devise contrôlée, devise dirigée, (C) monnaie dirigée
(GER) kontrollierte bzw. manipulierte Währung *f*
(JAP) 管理通貨、統制貨幣
(RUS) УПРАВЛЯЕМАЯ ВАЛЮТА

managed economy
(CHIN) 管制经济，计划经济
(FRE) économie dirigée
(GER) Verwaltungs- *f*, Planwirtschaft *f*
(JAP) 管理経済
(RUS) УПРАВЛЯЕМАЯ ЭКОНОМИКА

management
(CHIN) 管理，主管，管理当局
(FRE) gestion, direction
(GER) Unternehmensführung *f*, -leitung *f*, Management *n*, Geschäftsführung *f*, -leitung *f*
(JAP) 経営、管理、経営者側
(RUS) УПРАВЛЕНИЕ; РУКОВОДСТВО

management agreement
(CHIN) 管理协议
(FRE) location-gérance, (C) accord de gestion
(GER) Geschäftsführungs- *m*, Managementvertrag *m*
(JAP) 経営委託契約
(RUS) СОГЛАШЕНИЕ ОБ УПРАВЛЕНИИ; РУКОВОДСТВЕ

management audit
(CHIN) 经营审计
(FRE) contrôle de gestion, (C) vérification de gestion
(GER) Geschäftsprüfung *f*, Prüfung *f* der Ablaufsysteme *npl* einer Unternehmung *f*
(JAP) 経営監査
(RUS) АУДИТ РУКОВОДСТВА

management by crisis
(CHIN) 危机管理
(FRE) gestion par évaluation des problèmes, (C) gestion réactive
(GER) Management *n* nach dem Krisenprinzip *n*
(JAP) 危機による管理
(RUS) МЕТОД УПРАВЛЕНИЯ, ПРИ КОТОРОМ СООТВЕТСТВУЮЩИЕ МЕРЫ ПРИНИМАЮТСЯ ТОЛЬКО ПОСЛЕ ВОЗНИКНОВЕНИЯ КРИЗИСНОЙ СИТУАЦИИ

management by exception
(CHIN) 例外事件管理
(FRE) direction par exceptions, (C) gestion par l'exception
(GER) Geschäftsführung *f* bzw. Management *n* nach dem Ausnahmeprinzip *n*
(JAP) 例外による管理
(RUS) МЕТОД УПРАВЛЕНИЯ , ПРИ КОТОРОМ КОРРЕКТИРУЮТСЯ

ОТКЛОНЕНИЯ ОТ ЗАРАНЕЕ
ОПРЕДЕЛЁННОЙ НОРМЫ

management by objective (MBO)
(CHIN) 目标管理（MBO）
(FRE) gestion par objectifs
(GER) zielgesteuerte Unternehmensführung
f, Management *n* durch Zielsetzung *f* bzw.
Zielvorgaben *fpl*
(JAP) 目的による管理
(RUS) МЕТОД УПРАВЛЕНИЯ,
ОСНОВАННЫЙ НА СОГЛАСОВАНИИ
ЦЕЛЕЙ РУКОВОДСТВА И
ПОДЧИНЁННЫХ

management by walking around (MBWA)
(CHIN) 注重人际交流的管理方法
（MBWA）
(FRE) gestion sur le terrain
(GER) Management *n* durch die Pflege *f*
persönlicher Kontakte *mpl*
(JAP) 歩き回り管理、視察案内型経営
(RUS) МЕТОД УПРАВЛЕНИЯ,
ОСНОВАННЫЙ НА ЛИЧНОМ
ПРИСУТСТВИИ РУКОВОДИТЕЛЯ И
ЛИЧНОМ КОНТАКТЕ С ПОДЧИНЁННЫМИ

management consultant
(CHIN) 经营顾问，业务顾问
(FRE) conseiller en gestion,
(GER) Unternehmensberater *m*
(JAP) 経営コンサルタント、マネジメン
トコンサルタント
(RUS) КОНСУЛЬТАНТ ПО
МЕНЕДЖМЕНТУ

management cycle
(CHIN) 管理循环
(FRE) cycle de gestion
(GER) Managementzyklus *m*
(JAP) 管理サイクル
(RUS) ЦИКЛ УПРАВЛЕНИЯ,
РУКОВОДСТВА

management fee
(CHIN) 管理费
(FRE) frais de gestion,
(GER) Kontoführungs- *f*; Konsortialgebühr
f, Konsortialführungsprovision *f*;
Verwaltungsgebühr *f*;
Geschäftsführungshonorar *n*

(JAP) 幹事手数料
(RUS) КОМИССИОННЫЕ ЗА УПРАВЛЕНИЕ

management game
(CHIN) 管理训练
(FRE) simulation de geston, (C) jeu de
simulation
(GER) (Betriebs)planspiel *n*
(JAP) 経営管理ゲーム
(RUS) ДЕЛОВАЯ ИГРА

management guide
(CHIN) 管理指导手册
(FRE) guide de gestion
(GER) Richtlinie *f* für die Geschäftsführung
f, Managementhandbuch *n*
(JAP) 経営管理ガイド
(RUS) РУКОВОДСТВО ПО УПРАВЛЕНИЮ

management information system (MIS)
(CHIN) 管理信息系统（MIS）
(FRE) système d'informations de gestion
(JAP) 経営情報システム、
経営情報管理制度
(RUS) СИСТЕМА ОБЕСПЕЧЕНИЯ
РУКОВОДСТВА НЕОБХОДИМОЙ
ИНФОРМАЦИЕЙ

management prerogative
(CHIN) 管理特权
(FRE) prérogative de gestion,
(C) prérogative de direction
(GER) Vorrecht *n* der
Geschäftsleitung *f*
(JAP) 経営特権
(RUS) ПРЕРОГАТИВА РУКОВОДСТВА

management ratio
(CHIN) 管理人员比例
(FRE) ratio cadres/salaries, ratio de gestion
(GER) betriebswirtschaftliche Kennzahl *f*,
Wirtschaftsführungskennziffer *f*, Verhältnis
n der leitenden Angestellten *mpl* zur
Belegschaft *f*
(JAP) 経営比率
(RUS) КОЛИЧЕСТВО РУКОВОДИТЕЛЕЙ
НА 1000 РАБОТНИКОВ

management science
(CHIN) 管理科学
(FRE) science de la gestion
(GER) Managementlehre *f*

(JAP) 経営科学
(RUS) НАУКА О РУКОВОДСТВЕ

management style
(CHIN) 管理风格
(FRE) mode de gestion, (C) style de gestion
(GER) Führungsstil *m*
(JAP) 経営スタイル、経営様式
(RUS) СТИЛЬ РУКОВОДСТВА

management system
(CHIN) 管理系统
(FRE) système de direction
(GER) Management- *n*, Führungssystem *n*
(JAP) 経営システム、管理システム

manager
(CHIN) 经理
(FRE) directeur, gérant, administrateur, gestionnaire, (C) chef de service
(GER) Geschäftsführer *m*, Manager *m*, Unternehmensleiter *m*; Führungskraft *f*; Konsortialführer *m*, Abteilungs- *m*, Filial- *m*, Spartenleiter *m*; Verwalter *m*, Vorsteher *m*
(JAP) 支配人、経営者、部長
(RUS) РУКОВОДИТЕЛЬ; МЕНЕДЖЕР

managerial accounting
(CHIN) 管理会计
(FRE) comptabilité de gestion
(GER) Kosten- *f* und Leistungsrechnung *f*, (innerbetriebliches Rechnungswesen)
(JAP) 管理会計
(RUS) ИСПОЛЬЗОВАНИЕ ФИНАНСОВОЙ ОТЧЁТНОСТИ ДЛЯ ПРИНЯТИЯ ИНФОРМИРОВАННЫХ РЕШЕНИЙ РУКОВОДСТВОМ

managerial grid
(CHIN) 管理人员领导行为分类方法
(FRE) grille de gestion
(GER) Verhaltensgitter *n*
(JAP) 経営グリッド、
経営管理の配列網
(RUS) ТАБЛИЦА КЛАССИФИКАЦИИ СТИЛЕЙ РУКОВОДСТВА, ОСНОВАННАЯ НА БАЛАНСЕ ЗАБОТ О ЛЮДЯХ И ПРОИЗВОДСТВЕ (81 ВЗМОЖНЫХ ВАРИАНТОВ)

mandate
(CHIN) 授权书，委托书，委托
(FRE) mandat
(GER) Mandat *n*; Vollmacht *f*, Ermächtigung *f*; Anordnung *f*, Weisung *f*
(JAP) 指令、職務執行令状、依託
（代理）
(RUS) МАНДАТ; ПОЛНОМОЧИЕ

mandatory copy
(CHIN) 命令副本
(FRE) exemplaire obligatoire, (C) copie obligatoire
(GER) Pflichtwerbetext *m*
(JAP) 強制的コピー
(RUS) ЗАЩИТА ОТ КОПИРОВАНИЯ МУЗЫКАЛЬНЫХ ФАЙЛОВ

man-hour
(CHIN) 人时
(FRE) heure homme, (C) heure-personne
(GER) Mannstunde *f*, Arbeitsstunde *f*
(JAP) （延べ）労働時間、工数
(RUS) ЧЕЛОВЕКО-ЧАС

manifest
(CHIN) 舱单，装货单，声明
(FRE) manifeste, (C) déclaration
(GER) (Ladungs)manifest *n*, -verzeichnis *n*, Lade- *f*, Frachtliste *f*; Passagierliste *f*; öffentliche Erklärung *f*; Kundgebung *f*
(JAP) 宣言、声明書、積荷目録
(RUS) ПРОЯВЛЯТЬСЯ, ОБНАРУЖИВАТЬСЯ; МАНИФЕСТ; ЗАЯВЛЕНИЕ; ДЕКЛАРАЦИЯ СУДОВОГО ГРУЗА

manipulation
(CHIN) 操纵，篡改，控制，操作，处理
(FRE) manipulation
(GER) Beeinflussung *f*, Manipulation *f*, Manipulierung *f*
(JAP) 巧妙な取扱い、市場操作、あやつり相場
(RUS) МАНИПУЛЯЦИЯ; МАНИПУЛИРОВАНИЕ

manual
(CHIN) 手册，指南，手工操作的
FRE) manuel

(GER) Handbuch *n*, Betriebsanleitung *f*,
Dienstvorschrift *f*; Gebrauchsanweisung *f*
von Hand *f*, manuell, handwerklich *adj*
(JAP) 手の、提要、手引き
(RUS) РУЧНОЙ

manual skill

(CHIN) 手工技巧
(FRE) compétences manuelles, (C) habileté
manuelle
(GER) Handfertigkeit *f*, handwerkliches
Können *n*
(JAP) 器用さ（技能、技術、わざ）
(RUS) МАСТЕРСТВО, УМЕНИЕ

manufacture

(CHIN) 制造商，厂家
(FRE) fabrication, (C) manufacture
(GER) Fertigung *f*, Produktion *f*,
Herstellung *f*, Fabrikation *f*; Erzeugnis *n*,
Produkt *n*, Fabrikat *n*
(JAP) 製造（する）、生産（する）
(RUS) ИЗГОТОВЛЕНИЕ; ПРОИЗВОДСТВО

manufacturing cost

(CHIN) 制造成本
(FRE) coût de fabrication
(GER) Fertigungs- *pl*, Herstellungs- *pl*,
Produktions- *pl*, Fabrikationskosten *pl*
(JAP) 製造原価、製造費
(RUS) ЦЕНА ПРОИЗВОДСТВА

manufacturing inventory

(CHIN) 生产库存
(FRE) inventaire de fabrication, (C) stocks
de fabrication
(GER) (Lager)bestände *mpl* im
Fertigungsbereich *m*, Fabrikbestände *mpl*
(JAP) 製造棚卸資産（在庫、在庫品）
(RUS) ПРОИЗВОДСТВЕННЫЕ
МАТЕРИАЛЬНЫЕ ЗАПАСЫ

manufacturing order

(CHIN) 生产指令，制造任务书
(FRE) commande de fabrication, (C) ordre
de fabrication
(GER) Fertigungs- *m*, Fabrik- *m*, Werk- *m*,
Produktionsauftrag *m*
(JAP) 製造指図書
(RUS) ЗАКАЗ НА ИЗГОТОВЛЕНИЕ

MAP

(CHIN) 地图，示意图
(FRE) MAP (technique de simulation de
gestion)
(GER) Managementsimulationstechnik
(JAP) 地図、図

margin

(CHIN) 保证金，价差，边缘，余额，
押金，毛利
(FRE) marge
(GER) Handelsspanne *f*; Gewinnspanne *f*;
Bruttogewinn *m*; Deckungsbeitrag *m*;
Einschuss *m*, Marge *f*; (Seiten)rand *m*
(Format)
(JAP) 限界、最低収益点、差額、
（株式の）証拠金
(RUS) МАРЖА; МИНИМАЛЬНО
ПРИЕМЛЕМЫЙ УРОВЕНЬ; РАЗНИЦА

margin account

(CHIN) 保证金账户，边际账户
(FRE) compte sur marge, compte de
couverture
(GER) Hinterlegungs- *n*, Einschuss- *n*,
Lombardkonto *n*, Effektenkreditkonto *n*
(JAP) 証拠金勘定

marginal cost

(CHIN) 边际成本
(FRE) coût marginal, (C) coût marginal
(GER) Grenzkosten *pl*, relevante Kosten *pl*,
Grenzbelastung *f*, an der Grenze *f* der
Wirtschaftlichkeit *f* liegender Aufwand *m*
(JAP) 限界原価、限界費用
(RUS) ПРЕДЕЛЬНАЯ СТОИМОСТЬ

marginal cost curve

(CHIN) 边际成本区线
(FRE) courbe des coûts marginaux,
(C) courbe du coût marginal
(GER) Grenzkostenkurve *f*
(JAP) 限界費用曲線
(RUS) КРИВАЯ ПРЕДЕЛЬНОЙ
СТОИМОСТИ

marginal efficiency of capital

(CHIN) 资本边际效率
(FRE) efficacité marginale, (C) èfficacité
marginale du capital

(GER) Grenzleistungsfähigkeit *f* des
Kapitals *n*
(JAP) 資本の限界効率
(RUS) ПРЕДЕЛЬНАЯ ЭФФЕКТИВНОСТЬ
КАПИТАЛА

marginal producer
(CHIN) 边际生产者
(FRE) producteur marginal
(GER) Grenzproduzent *m*, -betrieb *m*,
Betrieb *m* an der Grenze *f* der
Rentabilität *f*
(JAP) 限界生産者
(RUS) ПРОИЗВОДИТЕЛЬ, С ТРУДОМ
СВОДЯЩИЙ КОНЦЫ С
КОНЦАМИ

marginal propensity to consume (MPC)
(CHIN) 边际消费倾向 （MPC）
(FRE) propension marginale à consommer
(GER) marginale Konsumquote *f*
(JAP) 限界消費性向
(RUS) ПРЕДЕЛЬНАЯ СКЛОННОСТЬ К
ПОТРЕБЛЕНИЮ

marginal propensity to invest
(CHIN) 边际投资倾向
(FRE) propension marginale à investir
(GER) marginale Investitionsquote *f*
(JAP) 限界投資性向
(RUS) ПРЕДЕЛЬНАЯ СКЛОННОСТЬ К
ИНВЕСТИРОВАНИЮ

marginal propensity to save (MPS)
(CHIN) 边际储蓄倾向 (MPS)
(FRE) propension marginale à économiser,
(C) propension marginale à épargner
(GER) marginale Sparquote *f*
(RUS) ПРЕДЕЛЬНАЯ СКЛОННОСТЬ К
СБЕРЕЖЕНИЮ

marginal property
(CHIN) 边际财产
(FRE) propriété marginale
(GER) an der Grenze *f* der
Wirtschaftlichkeit *f* liegender Grundbesitz
m (Immobilien)
(JAP) 限界財産、限界所有物、
限界不動産
(RUS) ПРЕДЕЛЬНАЯ
СОБСТВЕННОСТЬ

marginal revenue
(CHIN) 边际收入
(FRE) revenu marginal
(GER) Grenzerlös *m*, -ertrag *m*,
-einnahmen *fpl*
(JAP) 限界収入
(RUS) ПРЕДЕЛЬНЫЙ ДОХОД

marginal tax rate
(CHIN) 边际税率
(FRE) taux marginal d'imposition
(GER) Grenz- *m*,
Höchststeuersatz *m*
(JAP) 限界税率
(RUS) ПРЕДЕЛЬНАЯ СТАВКА
НАЛОГООБЛОЖЕНИЯ

marginal utility
(CHIN) 边际效用
(FRE) utilité marginale
(GER) Grenznutzen *m*
(JAP) 限界効用
(RUS) ПРЕДЕЛЬНАЯ ПОЛЕЗНОСТЬ

margin call
(CHIN) 交纳保证金通知
(FRE) appel de couverture, appel de marge,
appel de garantie,
(GER) Nach- *f*, Einschuss(auf)forderung *f*
(JAP) 追加証拠金
(RUS) ТРЕБОВАНИЕ
ГАРАНТИЙНОГОВЗНОСА,
ДОПОЛНИТЕЛЬНОГО ОБЕСПЕЧЕНИЯ

margin of profit
(CHIN) 利润边际
(FRE) marge de profit
(GER) Gewinn- *f*, Verdienst- *f*,
Handelsspanne *f*, Gewinnmarge *f*,
Ertragsgrenze *f*
(JAP) 利ざや、採算
(RUS) МАРЖА ПРИБЫЛИ

margin of safety
(CHIN) 安全边际
(FRE) marge de sécurité
(GER) Sicherheitszuschlag *m*, -spielraum
m, Sicherheitsfaktor *m*, -koeffizient *m*
(JAP) 安全余裕率
(RUS) ЗАПАС ПРОЧНОСТИ

margins

(CHIN) 保证金，价差，边缘，余额，押金

(FRE) marges

(GER) Margen *fpl*, Gewinn- *mpl*, Handelsspannen *fpl*

(JAP) 利ざや、証拠金、限界収益点

(RUS) ПОЛЯ; КРАЙНИЕ ПРЕДЕЛЫ

marital deduction

(CHIN) 配偶扣除

(FRE) déduction basée sur la situation matrimoniale, (C) déduction pour conjoint

(GER) Steuerermäßigung *f* für Verheiratete *pl*, Steuerabzug *m* für Ehepaare *npl*

(JAP) 婚姻控除

(RUS) СУПРУЖЕСКАЯ НАЛОГОВАЯ СКИДКА

markdown

(CHIN) 减价，降价

(FRE) baisser, (C) démarque

(GER) Preissenkung *f*, -ermäßigung *f*, Preisnachlass *m*, Rabatt *m*; Kurs- *m*, Wertabschlag *m*; Kalkulationsabschlag *m*

(JAP) マークダウン、価格引下げ、値段引き下げ

(RUS) ВЕЛИЧИНА СКИДКИ

market

(CHIN) 市场，市价，商业中心，销售，推销

(FRE) marché

(GER) Markt *m*, Absatzgebiet *n*; Handelsplatz *m*, Wirtschaftsgebiet *n*; Nachfrage *f*; Börse *f*; vermarkten, auf den Markt *m* bringen, handeln *v*

(JAP) 市場、売買、市価

(RUS) РЫНОК

marketablility

(CHIN) 可销性，适销性

(FRE) possibilité de commercialization

(GER) Verkehrsfähigkeit *f*; Marktgängigkeit *f*, Verkäuflichkeit *f*, Absetzbarkeit *f*; Markt- *f*, Börsenfähigkeit *f*, Börsengängigkeit *f*

(JAP) 市場性

(RUS) ПРИГОДНОСТЬ К ПРОДАЖЕ НА РЫНКЕ

marketable securities

(CHIN) 有价证券，可转让政权

(FRE) valeurs négociables

(GER) börsengängige, -fähige, marktfähige Wertpapiere *npl*; Wertpapiere *npl* des Umlaufvermögens *n*

(JAP) 有価証券、市場性のある証券

(RUS) ЛЕГКО РЕАЛИЗУЕМЫЕ ЦЕННЫЕ БУМАГИ

marketable title

(CHIN) 适销证券，可转让产权

(FRE) titre négociable

(GER) vollgültiger Rechtstitel *m*, rechtsmängelfreier Grundbesitz *m*; gerichtlich festgestellter Eigentumsanspruch *m*

(JAP) 売買に適する権利

(RUS) ЛЕГКО РЕАЛИЗУЕМЫЙ ПРАВОВОЙ ТИТУЛ

market aggregation

(CHIN) 市场统合，统一市场

(FRE) regroupement de marchés

(GER) Marktaggregation *f*

(JAP) 市場合算

(RUS) РЫНОЧНОЕ НАКОПЛЕНИЕ

market analysis

(CHIN) 市场分析

(FRE) analyse du marché

(GER) Marktanalyse *f*

(JAP) 市場分析

(RUS) РЫНОЧНЫЙ АНАЛИЗ

market area

(CHIN) 市场区域

(FRE) marché debouche, (C) secteur de marché

(GER) Absatz- *n*, Verkaufs- *n*, Vertriebsgebiet *n*; Wirtschaftsraum *m*

(JAP) 市場地域

(RUS) ЗОНА РЫНКА

market basket

(CHIN) 市场指标性商品组合

(FRE) panier de la menagerie, (C) éventail de biens

(GER) Warenkorb *m*

(RUS) «РЫНОЧНАЯ КОРЗИНА»

market comparison approach
(CHIN) 市场比较法
(FRE) technique des données du marché
(GER) Marktvergleichsansatz *m*
(JAP) 市場比較手法
(RUS) ОДИН ИЗ ТРЁХ МЕТОДОВ ОЦЕНКИ
НЕДВИЖИМОСТИ, ОСНОВАННЫЙ НА
СОПОСТАВЛЕНИИИ ЦЕН НА ПОДОБНУЮ
СОБСТВЕННОСТЬ

market demand
(CHIN) 市场需求
(FRE) demande du marché
(GER) Marktnachfrage *f*, -bedarf *m*,
Nachfrage *f* am Markt *m*
(JAP) 市場需要
(RUS) РЫНОЧНЫЙ СПРОС

market development index
(CHIN) 市场发展指数
(FRE) indice de développement du marché
(GER) Marktausschöpfungsindex *m*
(JAP) 市場開発指数
(RUS) ИНДЕКС РАЗВИТИЯ РЫНКА

market economy
(CHIN) 市场经济
(FRE) économie de marché
(GER) Markt- *f*, Wettbewerbswirtschaft *f*,
freie Marktwirtschaft *f*
(JAP) 市場経済
(RUS) РЫНОЧНАЯ ЭКОНОМИКА

market equilibrium
(CHIN) 市场供需平衡
(FRE) équilibre du marché
(GER) Marktgleichgewicht *n*,
marktwirtschaftliches Gleichgewicht *n*
(JAP) 市場均衡
(RUS) РАВНОВЕСИЕ РЫНКА

market index
(CHIN) 市价指数
(FRE) indice du marché
(JAP) 市場指数
(RUS) РЫНОЧНЫЙ ПОКАЗАТЕЛЬ,
ИНДЕКС

marketing
(CHIN) 营销，市场销售

(FRE) marketing, mercatique,
commercialisation
(GER) Marketing *n*, Absatz- *n*,
Vertriebswesen *n*,
Vermarktung *f*
(JAP) マーケティング、市場取引
(RUS) МАРКЕТИНГ; СБЫТ; РЕКЛАМА,
ПРОДВИЖЕНИЕ ТОВАРА

marketing concept
(CHIN) 营销观点，市场学概念
(FRE) concept de marketing, (C) stratégie
commerciale
(GER) Vermarktungs- *n*, Marketing-
Konzept *n*
(JAP) マーケティングコンセプト、マー
ケティング志向
(RUS) ПРИНЦИП МАРКЕТИНГА

marketing director
(CHIN) 市场部经理
(FRE) directeur du marketing, directeur des
études de marché, (C) directeur commercial
(GER) Vertriebsleiter *m*, -direktor *m*
(JAP) 市場担当取締役、市場担当理事
(RUS) ДИРЕКТОР ПО МАРКЕТИНГУ

marketing information system
(CHIN) 市场营销信息系统
(FRE) système d'information marketing
(GER) Marketing-Informationssystem *n*
(JAP) マーケティング戦略情報システム、
市場情報システム
(RUS) СИСТЕМА ИНФОРМАЦИИ
МАРКЕТИНГА

marketing mix
(CHIN) 营销组合
(FRE) marchéage, marketing mix
(GER) Marketing-Mix *n*, Marktplan *m*,
Vermarktungsmischstrategie *f*
(JAP) マーケティングミックス
(RUS) СОВОКУПНОСТЬ ЧЕТЫРЁХ
ЭЛЕМЕНТОВ, НЕОБХОДИМЫХ ДЛЯ
УДАЧНОГО СБЫТА: ПРОДУКТ, ЦЕНА,
МЕСТО СБЫТА И УСИЛИЯ ПО
ПРОДВИЖЕНИЮ

marketing plan
(CHIN) 营销计划
(FRE) plan marketing, (C) stratégie

commerciale
(GER) Marketing-Plan *m*, Absatzplanung *f*,
Vertriebsplan *m*
(JAP) マーケティング計画
(RUS) ПЛАН СБЫТА НА РЫНКЕ; ПЛАН
МАРКЕТИНГА

marketing research
(CHIN) 市场研究
(FRE) recherche commerciale
(GER) Marketing- *f*, Absatz- *f*,
Verkaufsforschung *f*
(JAP) マーケティング調査、市場調査
(RUS) ИЗУЧЕНИЕ ПРОДВИЖЕНИЯ
ТОВАРА ОТ ПРОИЗВОДИТЕЛЯ К
ПОТРЕБИТЕЛЮ

market letter
(CHIN) 市场简报，行情通报
(FRE) lettre commerciale, (C) circulaire
(GER) Börsenbrief *m*, täglicher
Marktbericht *m*
(JAP) 市場案内、市況レポート
(RUS) КОНЪЮНКТУРНЫЙ ОБЗОР

market order
(CHIN) 市场指令
(FRE) ordre au mieux, (C) ordre au prix du
marché
(GER) Bestens- *m*, Billigstauftrag *m*,
Bestens-Order *f*, Verkaufsauftrag *m* zum
Marktpreis *m*; Billigstauftrag *m*
(JAP) 成行き注文、
市価取引注文

market penetration
(CHIN) 市场渗透
(FRE) pénétration du marché
(GER) Marktdurchdringung *f*
(JAP) 市場浸透
(RUS) ВЫХОД НА РЫНОК

market price
(CHIN) 市价，时价，
市场价格
(FRE) prix du marché, cours
(GER) Markt- *m*, Tageswert *m*, Markt- *m*,
Tageskurs *m*; letzter Kurs *m* (Börse)
(JAP) 市場価格、相場、時価
(RUS) РЫНОЧНАЯ ЦЕНА

market rent
(CHIN) 市面租金
(FRE) loyer selon le marché
(GER) Marktmiete *f*
(JAP) 市場超過利潤
(RUS) ЫНОЧНАЯ
АРЕНДНАЯ ПЛАТА

market research
(CHIN) 市场调查
(FRE) étude de marché
(GER) Marktforschung *f*
(JAP) 市場調査
(RUS) ИЗУЧЕНИЕ РЫНКА,
КОНЪЮНКТУРЫ

market segmentation
(CHIN) 区隔市场
(FRE) segmentation du marché
(GER) Marktsegmentierung *f*
(JAP) 市場細分化
(RUS) СЕГМЕНТАЦИЯ РЫНКА

market share
(CHIN) 市场份额 占有率
(FRE) part de marché
(GER) Marktanteil *m*
(JAP) マーケットシェア、市場占拠率、
市場占有率
(RUS) ДОЛЯ В СБЫТЕ НА РЫНКЕ

market system
(CHIN) 市场体制，销售系统
(FRE) système de marché
(GER) Marktsystem *n*
(JAP) 市場組織
(RUS) РЫНОЧНАЯ СИСТЕМА

market test
(CHIN) 市场试验
(FRE) test de marché
(GER) Markttest *m*
(JAP) 市場試験
ПРОВЕРКА РЫНКОМ

market timing
(CHIN) 营销时机
(FRE) détermination du moment
propice

(GER) Markt-Timing *n*, (versuchte) Wahl *f*
des richtigen Zeitpunkts *m* beim
Effektenkauf *m* bzw. -verkauf *m*
(JAP) 市場タイミング
(RUS) ВЫБОР ВРЕМЕНИ ОПЕРАЦИЙ НА
РЫНКЕ

market value
(CHIN) 市场价值
(FRE) valeur marchande, valeur boursière
(GER) Markt- *m*, Tages- *m*, Zeit- *m*,
Verkehrswert *m*; realisierbarer
Verkaufswert *m*; Kurswert *m*, Notierung *f*,
Tageskurs *m* (Börse)
(JAP) 市場価格
(RUS) РЫНОЧНАЯ СТОИМОСТЬ

market value clause
(CHIN) 市场价值条款
(FRE) clause de valeur marchande, clause
de valeur boursière
(GER) Marktwert- *f*, Zeitwertklausel *f*
(JAP) 市場価格条項
(RUS) ОГОВОРКА О РЫНОЧНОЙ
СТОИМОСТИ

mark to the market
(CHIN) 逐日盯市
(FRE) évaluation à la valeur de marché
(GER) Options- und Terminkontrakte *mpl*
täglich bewerten *v*
(JAP) 市場価格条項
(JAP) 値洗い
(RUS) ПРАКТИКА ЕЖЕДНЕВНОЙ
ПЕРЕОЦЕНКИ ПОРТФЕЛЯ ИНВЕСТИЦИЙ
ПО ТЕКУЩЕМУСОСТОЯНИЮ ЦЕН НА
РЫНКЕ

markup
(CHIN) 加价, 加利
(FRE) majoration, (C) marge sur coût
d'achat
(GER) (Preis)aufschlag *m*,
Gewinnaufschlag *m*; Höherbewertung *f*,
Kursaufschlag *m* (Börse)
(JAP) 値上げ
(RUS) ПОДНЯТИЕ ЦЕНЫ; НАЦЕНКА

marriage penalty
(CHIN) 婚姻税务加重

(FRE) pénalité en raison de la situation
matrimoniale, (C) pénalité fiscale pour les
couples mariés
(GER) höhere Einkommensteuerbelastung *f*
bei doppelt verdienenden Ehepaaren *npl*
(JAP) 婚姻罰金
(RUS) НАКАЗАНИЕ ЗА СУПРУЖЕСТВО
(особенность налогообложения, когда супруги
вместе платят более высокий налог, чем
платили бы по отдельности)

Marxism
(CHIN) 马克思主义
(FRE) marxisme
(GER) Marxismus *m*
(JAP) マルクス主義
(RUS) МАРКСИЗМ

mask
(CHIN) 掩模, 掩码, 屏蔽
(FRE) masque
(GER) Maske *f*, Schablone *f*
(JAP) マスク
(RUS) МАСКА; КОМБИНАЦИЯ РАЗРЯДОВ

mass appeal
(CHIN) 集体诉讼
(FRE) appel de masse, (C) attrait populaire
(GER) Massenanreiz *m*
(JAP) 大衆の心を捉える（魅了する）
(RUS) ПРИВЛЕКАТЕЛЬНОСТЬ ДЛЯ МАСС

mass communication
(CHIN) 大众广告
(FRE) communication de masse
(GER) Massenkommunikation *f*
(JAP) 大衆伝達、マスコミ
(RUS) СРЕДСТВА МАССОВОЙ СВЯЗИ

mass media
(CHIN) 大众媒体
(FRE) mass medias, (C) média de masse
(GER) Massenmedien *pl*
(JAP) マスメディア、大衆媒体
(RUS) СРЕДСТВА МАССОВОЙ
ИНФОРМАЦИИ (СМИ)

mass production
(CHIN) 大批量生产

(FRE) production de masse, (C) production continue
(GER) Massenfertigung *f*, -herstellung *f*, -produktion *f*, -erzeugung *f*, Serienproduktion *f*, Fließbandfertigung *f*, Großfabrikation *f*
(RUS) МАССОВОЕ ПРОИЗВОДСТВО

master boot record

(CHIN) 主引导记录
(FRE) enregistrement d'initialisation principal, (C) enregistrement d'amorçage maître
(GER) Hauptstartsatz *m*
(JAP) マスタ起動記録

master lease

(CHIN) 主租约
(FRE) bail principal
(GER) Hauptmiet- *m*, Hauptpachtvertrag *m*
(JAP) マスターリース、基本賃借権
(RUS) ГЛАВНЫЙ ДОГОВОР АРЕНДЫ

master limited partnership

(CHIN) 主要有限合伙企业
(FRE) société en commandite principale, (C) société en commandite simple
(GER) öffentliche gehandelte Kommandit- *f* bzw. Personengesellschaft *f*
(JAP) 基本有限会社
(RUS) ТОВАРИЩЕСТВО С ОДНИМ ГЛАВНЫМ И ПАРТНЁРОМ И С ПАРТНЁРАМИ С ОГРАНИЧЕННОЙ ОТВЕТСТВЕННОСТЬЮ

master plan

(CHIN) 主要计划，主规划图，总体计划
(FRE) plan directeur, (C) plan de situation
(GER) Gesamt- *m*, Hauptplan *m*
(JAP) マスタープラン、基本計画
(RUS) ОСНОВНОЙ ПЛАН

master policy

(CHIN) 主保险单，总保单
(FRE) police de base
(GER) Haupt- *f*, Gruppen- *f*, Rahmenpolice *f*, Stammversicherungsschein *m*
(JAP) 一括保険証券
(RUS) ГЕНЕРАЛЬНАЯ ПОЛИТИКА

master-servant rule

(CHIN) 主仆规则
(FRE) règle maître-serviteur
(GER) Dienstregelverhältnis *n*
(JAP) 雇用規則、雇用関係規則
(RUS) ПРАВИЛО «ХОЗЯИН – СЛУГА», Т. Е. РАБОТОДАТЕЛЬ НЕСЁТ ОТВЕТСТВЕННОСТЬ ЗА УЩЕРБ, НАНЕСЁННЫЙ РАБОТНИКАМИ В РЕЗУЛЬТАТЕ ПРОЦЕССА ПРОИЗВОДСТВА

masthead

(CHIN) 桅顶，旗杆之顶
(FRE) cartouche de titre, (C) générique
(GER) Titelleiste *f*, -zeile *f*; Impressum *n*, Druckvermerk *m*
(JAP) 発行人欄、マストの先端
(RUS) НАЗВАНИЕ ГАЗЕТЫ (НА ПЕРВОЙ СТРАНИЦЕ), СВЕДЕНИЯ О ЕЁ РЕДАКТОРЕ, ПОДПИСКЕ И Т. П., РАСПОЛОЖЕННЫЕ НА ПЕРВОЙ СТРАНИЦЕ

matching principle

(CHIN) 收支对应原则
(GER) Prinzip *n* der sachlichen Abgrenzung *f*, Grundsatz *m* der Periodenabgrenzung *f*
(JAP) 対応の原則
(RUS) ПРИНЦИП УЧЁТА ИЗДЕРЖЕК ПО МЕРЕ ПОСТУПЛЕНИЯ ДОХОДА, НА СОЗДАНИЕ КОТОРОГО ПОШЛИ ЭТИ ИЗДЕРЖКИ

material

(CHIN) 原料，材料，物资，实质性的
(FRE) matériel
(GER) Material *n*, Werkstoff *m*, Baustoff *m*; wesentlich; rechtserheblich *adj* (Recht)
(JAP) 材料、資料、原料
(RUS) МАТЕРИАЛ; ДОКУМЕНТ; МАТЕРИАЛЬНЫЙ; СУЩЕСТВЕННЫЙ

material fact

(CHIN) 重要事实
(FRE) fait matériel
(GER) wesentliche Tatsache *f*
(JAP) 重要な事実
(RUS) СУЩЕСТВЕННЫЙ ФАКТ (необходимое условие договора, контракта)

materiality
(CHIN) 物质性，重要性，实质性
(FRE) matérialité, (C) importance relative
(GER) (Prinzip *n* der) Wesentlichkeit *f*,
Wesentlichkeitsgrundsatz *m*; Erheblichkeit *f*
(JAP) 重要性
(RUS) МАТЕРИАЛЬНОСТЬ;
СУЩЕСТВЕННОСТЬ

material man
(CHIN) 建材供应商
(FRE) fournisseur du materiel,
(C) responsable du matériel
(GER) Baustoffhändler *m*,
Materiallieferant *m*
(JAP) 資材供給業者
(RUS) РЕАЛЬНЫЙ ЧЕЛОВЕК

materials handling
(CHIN) 原料管理，材料搬运
(FRE) manipulation des matières,
(C) manutention
(GER) Transport- *n*, Förderwesen *n*,
Materialtransport *m*, -wirtschaft *f*
(JAP) 資材取扱い
(RUS) ПОГРУЗО-РАЗГРУЗОЧНЫЕ;
ОПЕРАЦИИ; ВНУТРИЗАВОДСКОЙ
ТРАНСПОРТ; ОБРАЩЕНИЕ С
МАТЕРИАЛАМИ

materials management
(CHIN) 物料管理，物资管理
(GER) Materialwirtschaft *f*, Steuerung *f* des
Materialflusses *m*, Lagerwirtschaft *f*,
Materialverwaltung *f*, Logistik *f*
(JAP) 原材料の管理
(RUS) УПРАВЛЕНИЕ МАТЕРИАЛЬНЫМИ
ЗАПАСАМИ

matrix
(CHIN) 矩阵，真值表
(FRE) matrice
(GER) Matrix *f*; Matrize *f*; Rastermuster *n*
(JAP) マトリックス、母体、原版
(RUS) МАТРИЦА; ТАБЛИЦА

matrix organization
(CHIN) 矩阵式组织结构
(FRE) organisation matricielle,
(C) structure matricielle

(GER) Matrixorganisation *f*
(JAP) マトリックス編成（組織、体制、
機構）
(RUS) МАТРИЧНАЯ ОРГАНИЗАЦИЯ

matured endowment
(CHIN) 到期证券或保险金
(FRE) assurance à capital différé venue à
échéance
(GER) fällige Auszahlung *f*
(JAP) 満期になった基金（養老資金、
養老保険）
(RUS) ДАРЕНИЕ С НАСТУПИВШИМ
СРОКОМ ПОГАШЕНИЯ

mature economy
(CHIN) 成熟经济
(FRE) économie en pleine maturité,
(C) économie mature
(GER) ausgereifte Volkswirtschaft *f*
(JAP) 成熟経済
(RUS) ЭКОНОМИКА С НИЗКИМ
ПРИРОСТОМ НАСЕЛЕНИЯ И НИЗКИМ
УРОВНЕМ ЭКОНОМИЧЕСКОГО РОСТА

maturity
(CHIN) 到期，偿还日，期限
(FRE) maturité, (C) échéance
(GER) Laufzeit *f*, Fristigkeit *f*; Ablauf *m*;
Fälligkeit *f*
(JAP) 成熟、満期、成熟期
(RUS) СРОК (ДОЛГОВОГО
ОБЯЗАТЕЛЬСТВА); НАСТУПЛЕНИЕ
СРОКА

maturity date
(CHIN) 到期日
(FRE) date d'échéance, (C) échéance
(GER) Fälligkeitsdatum *n*, -termin *m*, -tag
m; Rückzahlungstermin *m*
(JAP) 満期日、支払期日、返済日
(RUS) ДАТА НАСТУПЛЕНИЯ СРОКА

maximize
(CHIN) 最大化
(FRE) optimiser, (C) maximiser
(GER) auf Bildschirmgröße *f* vergrößern
(EDV), maximieren *v*
(JAP) 最大限にする、最大化する、極大
化する

maximum capacity
(CHIN) 最大产能
(FRE) capacité maximale, (C) capacité
théorique
(GER) Höchstkapazität *f*, Produktions- *n*,
Betriebsmaximum *n*, Belastungsgrenze *f*
(JAP) 最大能力、最大容量、
最大収容能力
(RUS) МАКСИМАЛЬНАЯ МОЩНОСТЬ

M-CATS
(CHIN) 市政应计证券证明
(GER) steuerfreies Kommunalzertifikat *n*
mit Zinsansammlung *f*
(JAP) 医学大学入学テスト
(RUS) МУНИЦИПАЛЬНЫЕ ЦЕННЫЕ
БУМАГИ, ВЫПУЩЕННЫЕ
КАЗНАЧЕЙСТВОМ США И ПРОДАННЫЕ
НАМНОГО НИЖЕ НОМИНАЛЬНОЙ
СТОИМОСТИ

mean, arithmetic
(CHIN) 算数平均值
(FRE) moyen arithmétique
(GER) arithmetisches Mittel *n*,
arithmetischer Mittelwert *m*
(JAP) 算術平均
(RUS) СРЕДНЕАРИФМЕТИЧЕСКОЕ

mean, geometric
(CHIN) 几何平均值
(FRE) moyen géométrique
(GER) geometrischer Mittelwert *m*
(JAP) 幾何平均
(RUS) СРЕДНЕГЕОМЕТРИЧЕСКОЕ

mean return
(CHIN) 平均回报
(FRE) rendement attendu, (C) rendement
moyen
(GER) Durchschnittsrendite *f*
(JAP) 平均利益
(RUS) СРЕДНЯЯ ОКУПАЕМОСТЬ,
ПРИБЫЛЬНОСТЬ

mechanic's lien
(CHIN) 技工留置权
(FRE) privilège immobilier special,
privilège du constructeur, (C) privilège sur
les immeubles
(GER) gewerbliches Zurückbehaltungsrecht
n, gesetzliches Bauhandwerkerpfandrecht *n*
(JAP) 建築工事に関するリーエン
（先取権）
(RUS) ЗАЛОГОВОЕ ПРАВО
ИСПОЛНИТЕЛЯ РАБОТЫ КАК ГАРАНТИЯ
ЕЁ ОПЛАТЫ

mechanization
(CHIN) 机械化
(FRE) mécanisation
(GER) Automatisierung *f*, Mechanisierung *f*
(JAP) 機械化
(RUS) МЕХАНИЗАЦИЯ

media
(CHIN) 媒体，媒介
(FRE) medias, (C) media
(GER) Medien *pl*; Werbeträger *mpl*,
Reklamemittel *npl*; Datenträger *mpl*
(Computer); Mittel *npl*
(JAP) 媒体、手段、情報伝達媒体、
(RUS) СРЕДСТВА МАССОВОЙ
ИНФОРМАЦИИ (СМИ)

media buy
(CHIN) 广告时段购买
(FRE) achat d'espaces, (C) achat-média
(GER) Media-Einkauf *m*, Streuplanung *f*;
Medienwerbung *f*
(JAP) メディア買い、メディア購買、
媒体購入
(RUS) ПОКУПКА ВРЕМЕНИ И МЕСТА В
СМИ ДЛЯ РАЗМЕЩЕНИЯ РЕКЛАМЫ

media buyer
(CHIN) 广告时段购买人
(FRE) acheteur d'espaces, (C) acheteur-
média
(GER) Streu- *m*, Mediaplaner *m*
(JAP) メディアバイヤー、
媒体セールス担当
(RUS) ПОКУПАТЕЛЬ ВРЕМЕНИ И МЕСТА
В СМИ ДЛЯ РАЗМЕЩЕНИЯ РЕКЛАМЫ

media option
(CHIN) 广告手段选择
(FRE) option de média
(GER) Medienwahl *f*
(JAP) メディアオプション

256

(RUS) ВЫБОР СМИ ДЛЯ РАЗМЕЩЕНИЯ РЕКЛАМЫ

media plan

(CHIN) 广告手段计划者
(FRE) plan média
(GER) Media- *m*, Streu- *m*, Werbe- *m*, Belegungsplan *m*
(JAP) 媒体計画
ПЛАН И СПОЛЬЗОВАНИЯ СМИ ДЛЯ РЕКЛАМЫ

media planner

(CHIN) 仲裁，调解
(FRE) médiaplaneur, (C) responsable du plan médias
(GER) Streu- *m*, Mediaplaner *m*, Streufachmann *m*
(JAP) メディアプランナー、メディア計画者
(RUS) ОТВЕТСТВЕННЫЙ ЗА ПЛАНИРОВАНИЕ И РАЗМЕЩЕНИЕ РЕКЛАМЫ В СМИ

media player

(CHIN) 媒体播放器
(FRE) lecteur multimedia, (C) diffuseur de médias
(GER) Medien-Wiedergabeeinrichtung *f*
(JAP) ミディアプレイヤー

mediation

(CHIN) 广告影响度
(FRE) médiation
(GER) Schlichtung *f*, (Ver)mittlung *f* (Recht); Güteverfahren *n*
(JAP) 仲介、調停、仲裁
(RUS) ПОСРЕДНИЧЕСТВО

media weight

(CHIN) 医疗检查
(FRE) poids des médias, (C) influence des médias
(GER) Gesamtwerbeaufwand *m*
(JAP) メディアウェイト
(RUS) ШИРОТА РАСПРОСТРАНЕНИЯ РЕКЛАМЫ ПОСРЕДСТВОМ СМИ, ВЫРАЖЕННАЯ В КОЛИЧЕСТВЕ ЗРИТЕЛЕЙ, ЧИТАТЕЛЕЙ И Т. П.

medical examination

(CHIN) 医疗检查
(FRE) examen médical
(GER) ärztliche Untersuchung *f*
(JAP) 身体検査、健康診断
(RUS) МЕДИЦИНСКИЙ ОСМОТР

medium

(CHIN) 中等，媒介，工具
(FRE) medium, moyen de communication, (C) intermédiaire
(GER) Mittel *n*, Medium *n*; Mittel- *adj*
(JAP) 中間の、中間物、媒体、手段
(RUS) ПОСРЕДНИК; СРЕДА

medium of exchange

(CHIN) 交换媒介
(FRE) moyen d'échange, (C) instrument d'échange
(GER) Tausch- *n*, Zahlungsmittel *n*
(JAP) 交換手段
(RUS) СРЕДСТВО ОБРАЩЕНИЯ

medium-term bond

(CHIN) 中期债券
(FRE) obligation à moyen terme
(GER) Kassenobligation *f*, mittelfristige Obligation *f* bzw. Anleihe *f*; mittelfristiges Darlehen *n*
(JAP) 中期債券
(RUS) СРЕДНЕСРОЧНАЯ ОБЛИГАЦИЯ

meeting of the minds

(CHIN) 合同条款经由各方同意
(FRE) accord de volonté, (C) accord des parties
(GER) Willenseinigung *f*, Übereinstimmung *f* der Willenserklärung *f*, gemeinsamer Rechtsgeschäftswille *m*
(JAP) 意見の一致、見解の完全な一致
(RUS) СОГЛАШЕНИЕ ВСЕХ УЧАСТВУЮЩИХ СТОРОН С УСЛОВИЯМИ КОНТРАКТА

megabucks

(CHIN) 百万美元
(FRE) films à gros budget, (C) somme d'argent considérable
(GER) Mega-Geldsumme *f*

(JAP) 100万ドル、大金、何百万ドルも
の金
(RUS) МИЛЛИОННЫЕ СУММЫ, БОЛЬШИЕ
ДЕНЬГИ

member bank
(CHIN) 会员银行
(FRE) banque membre de la Réserve
Fédérale
(GER) Mitgliedsbank *f* (dem US-Federal
Reserve System angeschlossene Bank)
(JAP) 会員銀行、加盟銀行、組合銀行
(RUS) БАНК – ЧЛЕН ФЕДЕРАЛЬНОЙ
РЕЗЕРВНОЙ СИСТЕМЫ США

member firm or member corporation
(CHIN) 会员公司
(FRE) société member, (C) firme membre
(GER) zugelassene Börsenmaklerfirma *f*
(JAP) 会員業者または会社
(RUS) ФИРМА или КОРПОРАЦИЯ – ЧЛЕН
БИРЖИ

memorandum
(CHIN) 备忘录，纪要，摘要 通知单
(FRE) memorandum, (C) note de service
(GER) Memorandum *n*; Aktennotiz *f*, -
vermerk *m*; Memo *n*, Mitteilung *f*
(JAP) メモ、覚書き、売買覚書き
(RUS) МЕМОРАНДУМ; СЛУЖЕБНАЯ
ЗАПИСКА

memory
(CHIN) 记忆，记录，存储；存储器，内
存
(FRE) mémoire
(GER) (Daten)speicher *m* (EDV)
(JAP) 記憶（力）、記憶の範囲、
記憶装置；) 記憶装置、メモリー
(RUS) ПАМЯТЬ

menial
(CHIN) 卑下的，不体面的工作
(FRE) ingrat, subalterne
(GER) niedrig, untergeordnet, einfach *adj*
(JAP) 卑しい、下賎な、みすぼらしい
(RUS) РУЧНОЙ (труд)

menu bar
(CHIN) 选项栏[条，区，行]

(FRE) barre de menu, (C) barre de menus
(GER) Menüleiste *f*
(JAP) メニューバー
(RUS) ЛИНЕЙКА МЕНЮ

mercantile
(CHIN) 商业的
(FRE) commercial, (C) mercantile
(GER) kaufmännisch, merkantil,
Handels- *adj*
(JAP) 商人の、商業の、商売の
(RUS) ТОРГОВЫЙ

mercantile agency
(CHIN) 商业征信所
(FRE) agence commerciale, (C) organisme
de petit commerce
(GER) Kreditauskunftei *f*;
Handelsvertretung *f*, -agentur *f*
(JAP) 商事代理
(RUS) ОРГАНИЗАЦИЯ, ПОСТАВЛЯЮЩАЯ
СВОИМ КЛИЕНТАМ ИНФОРМАЦИЮ О
РАЗЛИЧНЫХ ФИРМАХ И КОМПАНИЯХ

mercantile law
(CHIN) 商法
(FRE) droit commercial
(GER) Handelsrecht *n*
(JAP) 商事法、商業法、商法
(RUS) ЗАКОН О ТОРГОВЛЕ

mercantilism
(CHIN) 重商主义，商业习惯
(FRE) mercantilisme
(GER) Merkantilismus *m*
(JAP) マーカンティリズム、
重商主義、商業本位
(RUS) МЕРКАНТИЛИЗМ

merchandise
(CHIN) 商品，经商，推销
(FRE) marchandises
(GER) Handelsware *f*,
-güter *npl*,
-artikel *mpl*
(JAP) 商品、物品、製品
(RUS) РОЗНИЧНЫЙ ТОВАР

merchandise allowance
(CHIN) 商品折扣

(FRE) redevance-marchandises,
(C) indemnité de mise en valeur
(GER) Warenrabatt *m*
(JAP) 商品準備金、商品引当金、
商品控除
(RUS) НАДБАВКА НА РАСХОДЫ,
СВЯЗАННЫЕ С ВОЗВРАТОМ
НЕКАЧЕСТВЕННОГО И Т.П. ТОВАРА

merchandise broker
(CHIN) 商品经纪人
(FRE) courtier agissant pour le compte
d'acheteurs de merchandises, (C) courtier
en marchandises
(GER) Handels- *m*, Waren- *m*,
Produktenmakler *m*
(JAP) 商品ブローカー、商品仲介業者
(RUS) ТОВАРНЫЙ БРОКЕР

merchandise control
(CHIN) 商品控制
(FRE) contrôle des marchandises
(GER) Warenkontrolle *f*
(JAP) 商品管理、商品統制
(RUS) УПРАВЛЕНИЕ ДВИЖЕНИЕМ
ТОВАРОВ

merchandising
(CHIN) 商品学，商品销售
(FRE) marchandisage, commercialisation
(GER) Merchandising *n*, Verkaufspolitik *f*,
-förderung *f*
(JAP) 取引、商品化計画、流通業
(RUS) УСИЛИЯ ПО ПРОДВИЖЕНИЮ
ТОВАРА, ВКЛЮЧАЯ РЕКЛАМУ,
ГАРАНТИИ, ОФОРМЛЕНИЕ ДИСПЛЕЕВ,
РАСПРОДАЖИ И Т. П.

merchandising director
(CHIN) 商品销售主管
(FRE) directeur du marchandisage
(GER) Leiter *m* der
Verkaufsförderungsabteilung *f*
(JAP) マーチャンダイジング担当取締役、
商品化計画担当取締役
(RUS) ДИРЕКТОР ПО ДВИЖЕНИЮ
ТОВАРОВ

merchandising service
(CHIN) 商品服务
(FRE) service du marchandisage

(GER) Vertriebs- und Verkaufstätigkeit *f*
(JAP) マーチャンダイジングサービス
(RUS) УСЛУГИ ПО СБЫТУ ТОВАРОВ

merchantable
(CHIN) 有销路的，可销售的
(FRE) marchand
(JAP) 市場性のある、市場向きの
(RUS) ПРИГОДНЫЙ К КУПЛЕ – ПРОДАЖЕ
ТОВАР

merchant bank
(CHIN) 商业银行
(FRE) banque d'affaires, banque
'investissement, (C) banque marchande
(GER) Geschäfts- *f*, Handels- *f*;
Investmentbank *f* (US)
(JAP) マーチャントバンク、
証券引受銀行
(RUS) ТОРГОВЫЙ БАНК

merge
(CHIN) 合并
(FRE) fusionner
(GER) fusionieren, verschmelzen,
vereinigen, zusammenlegen, -schließen *v*
(JAP) 合併（併合）する、結合する、
吸収される
(RUS) СЛИВАТЬСЯ: ОБЪЕДИНЯТЬСЯ

merger
(CHIN) 合并，兼并
(FRE) fusion
(GER) Fusion *f*, Fusionierung *f*,
Unternehmenszusammenschluss *m*,
Vereinigung *f*, Konzernbildung *f*,
Verschmelzung *f*, Kapitalverflechtung *f*
(JAP) 合同、吸収合併、合併する人
（もの）
(RUS) СЛИЯНИЕ, ОБЪЕДИНЕНИЕ
(компаний)

merit increase
(CHIN) 功绩报酬上涨
(FRE) augmentation au mérite,
(C) augmentation de
(GER) leistungsbezogene Gehaltssteigerung
f, Leistungszulage *f*
(JAP) 価値（業績，長所）の増大

(RUS) ПРИБАВКА К ЗАРАБОТНОЙ ПЛАТЕ
ЗА ПОВЫШЕНИЕ КВАЛИФИКАЦИИ

merit rating
(CHIN) 等级税率
(FRE) notation du personnel
(GER) Leistungsbeurteilung *f*, -einstufung *f*,
-bewertung *f*
(JAP) 人事考査、勤務評定、能力考査
(RUS) ОЦЕНКА КВАЛИФИКАЦИИ ;
(ПЕРЕ)АТТЕСТАЦИЯ

meter rate
(CHIN) 电表计费率
(FRE) métré
(GER) Tarif *m* für Normalverbraucher *mpl*,
Zählerpreis *m*
(JAP) メーター料金（代金）、
計測料金
(RUS) ТАРИФ ОПЛАТЫ ПО
СЧЕТЧИКУ

metes and bounds
(CHIN) 地产边界
(FRE) projection horizontale,
(C) bornes et limites
(GER) (natürliche) Grenzlinien *fpl*;
Maß *n* und Ziel *n*
(JAP) 境界、境界線、境界石
(RUS) ГРАНИЦЫ ЗЕМЕЛЬНОГО УЧАСТКА
С УКАЗАНИЕМ КРАЙНИХ ТОЧЕК И
УГЛОВ

methods-time measurement (MTM)
(CHIN) 时间计量方法（MTM）
(FRE) méthode MTM, (C) méthode des
temps mesurés
(GER) Methoden-Zeitermittlung *f*, MTM-
Verfahren *n*
(JAP) 時間測定方法
(RUS) ХРОНОМЕТРАЖ ТРУДОВЫХ
ОПЕРАЦИЙ

metrication
(CHIN) 公制，米制
(FRE) metrication, (C) conversion au
système métrique
(GER) Metrikation *f*; Einführung *f* des
metrischen Systems *n*
(RUS) ПЕРЕВОД В МЕТРИЧЕСКУЮ
СИСТЕМУ

metric system
(CHIN) 公制，十进位制
(FRE) système métrique
(GER) metrisches System *n*
(JAP) メートル法
(RUS) МЕТРИЧЕСКАЯ СИСТЕМА

metropolitan area
(CHIN) 大都会区
(FRE) zone métropolitaine, (C) région
métropolitaine
(GER) Ballungsgebiet *n*
(JAP) 大都市圏、首都圏
(RUS) ЗОНА ВОКРУГ крупного города
с пригородами

microeconomics
(CHIN) 微观经济学
(FRE) microéconomie
(GER) Mikroökonomie *f*, Mikroökonomik *f*
(JAP) 微視的経済学、ミクロ経済学
(RUS) МИКРОЭКОНОМИКА

micromotion study
(CHIN) 微动研究
(FRE) étude des micromouvements
(GER) Mikrobewegungsstudie *f*
(JAP) 微少時間の微細動作研究、微細動
作分析
(RUS) ИССЛЕДОВАНИЕ МИКРОСДВИГОВ

midcareer plateau
(CHIN) 职业升迁障碍
(FRE) pallier de milieu de carrière, (C) mi-
carrière
(GER) Plateau *n* in der Mitte *f* der Karriere *f*
(JAP) 履歴半ばの安定状態、経歴半ばの
停滞期（状態）
(RUS) ПЛАТО, ЗАМЕДЛЕНИЕ РОСТА В
СЕРЕДИНЕ КАРЬЕРЫ

middle management
(CHIN) 中级管理层
(FRE) cadres moyens, (C) cadres
intermédiaires
(GER) mittleres Management *n*, mittlere
Leitungs- *f* bzw. Führungsebene *f*
(JAP) 中間管理者、中間管理層、
ミドルマネージメント

(RUS) СРЕДНЕЕ АДМИНИСТРАТИВНОЕ ЗВЕНО

midnight deadline
(CHIN) 零时 截止时间
(FRE) date-limite de minuit, (C) échéance à minuit
(GER) Schlusstermin *m* Mitternacht *f*
(JAP) 真夜中締切り、午前 0 時締切り
(RUS) КРАЙНИЙ СРОК, НАСТУПАЮЩИЙ В ПОЛНОЧЬ НА ДАТУ КРАЙНЕГО СРОКА

migrate
(CHIN) 迁移
(FRE) migrer, (C) passer d'un système à l'autre
(GER) (auf ein anderes System) übergehen, migrieren; umstellen *v*
(JAP) （ファイルなどを）移動させる
(RUS) МИГРИРОВАТЬ, ПЕРЕСЕЛЯТЬСЯ

migratory worker
(CHIN) 流动工人
(FRE) travailleur migrant
(GER) Wander- *m*, Saisonarbeiter *m*
(JAP) 季節労働者
(RUS) РАБОЧИЙ-ОТХОДНИК

military-industrial complex
(CHIN) 军队-企业关系
(FRE) complexe militaire-industriel
(GER) militärischer Industriekomplex *m*
(JAP) 軍産複合体制
(RUS) ВОЕННО-ПРОМЫШЛЕННЫЙ КОМПЛЕКС

milking
(CHIN) 利用局势谋取私利
(FRE) écrémage, (C) tirer profit au maximum d'une situation
(GER) Ausbeutung *f*, Schröpfen *n*
(JAP) 搾乳、搾り出すこと、搾取すること、（情報などを）
(RUS) ПОБОРЫ

milking strategy
(CHIN) 操纵市场从中谋利
(FRE) stratégie d'écrémage
(GER) Ausbeutungsstrategie *f*
(JAP) 搾乳戦略

(RUS) СТРАТЕГИЯ ПОБОРОВ

millage rate
(CHIN) 按英里里程计算运费率
(FRE) taux exprimé en millièmes
(GER) Grundsteuersatz *m*, Gemeindesteuersatz *m*
(JAP) 1 ドル当たり 1000 分の 1 の課税率

millionaire
(CHIN) 百万富翁
(FRE) millionaire
(GER) Millionär *m*
(JAP) 百万長者、大金持ち、大富豪
(RUS) МИЛЛИОНЕР

millionaire on paper
(CHIN) 名义百万富翁
(FRE) millionnaire sur le papier, (C) millionnaire théorique
(GER) Millionär *m* auf dem Papier *n*
(JAP) 紙の上だけの百万長者、名目だけの百万長者
(RUS) «БУМАЖНЫЙ» МИЛЛИОНЕР

mineral rights
(CHIN) 采矿权
(FRE) droits miniers, redevance minière
(GER) Schürf- *npl*, Mineralgewinnungsrechte *npl*
(JAP) 鉱業（採掘）権
(RUS) ПРАВА НА НЕДРА

minimax principle
(CHIN) 极大极小原则
(FRE) principe minimax
(GER) Minimax-Prinzip *n*
(RUS) ПРИНЦИП МИНИМАКС, Т. Е. ПРИНЦИП ПРИНЯТИЯ РЕШЕНИЙ НА ОСНОВЕ МИНИМАЛЬНЫХ ПОТЕРЬ В СЛУЧАЕ НЕБЛАГОПРИЯТНОГО ИСХОДА

minimize
(CHIN) 最小化
(FRE) réduire
(GER) (Fenster) verkleinern (EDV); minimieren *v*
(JAP) アイコン化する、ミニマイズ
(RUS) СВОДИТЬ К МИНИМУМУ, УМЕНЬШАТЬ

minimum lease payments

(CHIN) 最低租金

(FRE) paiements minimaux exigibles en vertu d'un bail

(GER) Mindestleasingzahlungen *fpl*

(JAP) 最低額リース支払

(RUS) МИНИМАЛЬНАЯ АРЕНДНАЯ ПЛАТА

minimum lot area

(CHIN) 最小地段面积

(FRE) zone minimale de lot,

(C) plus petit terrain à bâtir

(GER) Mindestgrundstücksgebiet *n*

(JAP) 最小区画地域

(RUS) МИНИМАЛЬНАЯ РАЗРЕШЁННАЯ ПЛОЩАДЬ ЗЕМЕЛЬНОГО УЧАСТКА, НАДЕЛА

minimum pension liability

(CHIN) 最低养老金责任

(FRE) engagement de retraite minimum

(GER) Mindestpensionsverpflichtung *f*

(JAP) 最低年金債務

(RUS) СОСТОЯНИЕ ПЕНСИОННОГО ПЛАНА, КОГДА ПЕНСИОННЫЕ ОБЯЗАТЕЛЬСТВА ПРЕВЫШАЮТ СРЕДНЮЮ СТОИМОСТЬ ЕГО АКТИВОВ

minimum permium deposit plan

(CHIN) 最低保险费储蓄计划

(FRE) régime de dépôt de primes minimum

(GER) Mindestprämieneinzahlungsplan *m*

(JAP) 最低保険料供託金方式

(RUS) ПЛАН ДЕПОНИРОВАНИЯ С МИНИМАЛЬНОЙ ВЫПЛАТОЙ

minimum wage

(CHIN) 最低工资

(FRE) salaire minimum

(GER) Mindestlohn *m*

(JAP) 最低賃金

(RUS) МИНИМАЛЬНАЯ ЗАРАБОТНАЯ ПЛАТА

minor

(CHIN) 未成年人

(FRE) mineur

(GER) Minderjähriger *m*, Unmündiger *m*

(JAP) 未成年者、少数の、重要でない

(RUS) МЕЛКИЙ; НЕСОВЕРШЕННОЛЕТНИЙ

minority interest or minority investment

(CHIN) 少数权益或少数投资

(FRE) participation minoritaire,

(C) part des actionnaires minoritaires

(GER) Minderheitsbeteiligung *f*, -besitz *m*, Minoritätsbeteiligung *f*

(JAP) 少数株主持分、少数株主権、またはマイノリティー投資

(RUS) УЧАСТИЕ В КАПИТАЛЕ или ИНВЕСТИЦИЯ БЕЗ КОНТРОЛЬНОГО ПАКЕТА

mintage

(CHIN) 造币，铸币权，硬币

(FRE) monnayage, frappe (de monnaie),

(C) droit de monnayage

(GER) Prägegebühr *f*; Münzen *fpl*; Ausprägung *f*, Ausmünzung *f*

(JAP) 貨幣鋳造、造幣

(RUS) ЧЕКАНКА МОНЕТЫ

minutes

(CHIN) 会议记录

(FRE) minutes

(GER) Protokoll *n*, Sitzungsprotokoll *n*

(JAP) 議事録

(RUS) ПРОТОКОЛ (собрания, заседания)

misdemeanor

(CHIN) 不端行为

(FRE) délit,

(C) infraction

(GER) Vergehen *n*, Ordnungwidrigkeit *f*; Fehlverhalten *n*

(JAP) 軽罪

(RUS) ПРОСТУПОК

mismanagement

(CHIN) 管理不善

(FRE) mauvaise gestion, (C) abus de biens sociaux

(GER) Misswirtschaft *f*; schlechte Betriebs- *f*, Unternehmens- *f*, Geschäftsführung *f*

(JAP) 管理（経営）を誤ること、管理失敗

(RUS) НЕКАЧЕСТВЕННОЕ, ОШИБОЧНОЕ РУКОВОДСТВО

misrepresentation
(CHIN) 错误报道，歪曲
(FRE) manoeuvres frauduleuses,
(C) information fausse ou trompeuse
(GER) falsche Darstellung *f*; Irreführung *f*,
Vorspiegelung *f* falscher Tatsachen *fpl*
(JAP) 不実表示、虚偽の表示

misstatement of age
(CHIN) 慌报年龄
(FRE) déclaration d'âge érronée
(GER) falsche Altersangabe *f*
(JAP) 年齢の誤った陳述、
年齢の偽りの申立て
(RUS) НЕПРАВИЛЬНОЕ УКАЗАНИЕ
ВОЗРАСТА

mistake
(CHIN) 错误
(FRE) erreur
(GER) Irrtum *m*, Fehler *m*, Versehen *n*
(JAP) 誤り、間違い、誤解
(RUS) ОШИБКА

mistake of law
(CHIN) 引用法律不当
(FRE) erreur de droit
(GER) Rechtsirrtum *m*
(JAP) 法律の錯誤
(RUS) ОШИБКА В ПРАВЕ; ЮРИДИЧЕСКАЯ
ОШИБКА

mitigation of damages
(CHIN) 减轻损失，
减少损害费
(FRE) réduction des dommages-intérêts
(GER) Schadensminderung *f*
(JAP) 損害賠償額の軽減
(RUS) УМЕНЬШЕНИЕ СУММЫ
ВЗЫСКИВАЕМЫХ УБЫТКОВ

mix
(CHIN) 组合，组成，结构，
混合
(FRE) mélange, (C) composition,
(C) mixage
(GER) Mischung *f*, Zusammensetzung *f*
(JAP) 混ぜる、混合、混乱
(RUS) СМЕСЬ; АССОРТИМЕНТ

mixed economy
(CHIN) 混合经济
(FRE) économie mixte
(GER) Mischwirtschaft *f*, gemischte
Wirtschaftsform *f*
(RUS) СМЕШАННАЯ
ЭКОНОМИКА

mixed perils
(CHIN) 混合危险
(FRE) risques mixtes
(GER) Mischwirtschaft *f*, gemischte
Wirtschaftsform *f*
(GER) gemischtes Risiko *n*
(JAP) 混合危険（保険）
(RUS) СМЕШАННЫЕ РИСКИ

mixed signals
(CHIN) 混乱信息
(GER) unklare Signale *npl*
(JAP) 混合信号、混沌とした合図、まち
まちの市況
(RUS) НЕЯСНЫЕ НАМЁКИ, СИГНАЛЫ

mode
(CHIN) 模式，方式，样式，时尚，状况
(FRE) mode
(GER) Methode *f*, Verfahren *n*, Modus *m*;
Betriebsart *f* (EDV)
(JAP) 方法、様式、モード
(RUS) РЕЖИМ, СПОСОБ

modeling
(CHIN) 模拟，模型化，成型
(FRE) modélisation
(GER) Modellbildung *f*, Modellicrung *f*,
Modellplanung *f*
(JAP) モデリング、モデル化、模型製作
(RUS) МОДЕЛИРОВАНИЕ

modeling language
(CHIN) 模型化语言，模拟语言
(FRE) langage de modélisation
(GER) Modellierungssprache *f* (EDV)
(JAP) モデル化言語
(RUS) ЯЗЫК МОДЕЛИРОВАНИЯ

model unit
(CHIN) 样板单位
(FRE) unité modèle

(GER) (Bau)muster *n*
(JAP) モデル単位、モデル装置
(RUS) ОБРАЗЦОВАЯ, ПОКАЗАТЕЛЬНАЯ КВАРТИРА или ОБЪЕКТ

modern portfolio theory (MPT)
(CHIN) 现代投资组合理论（MPT）
(GER) moderne Portfolio- *f* bzw. Portefeuille-Theorie *f*
(RUS) ТЕОРИЯ СОВРЕМЕННОГО ПОРТФЕЛЯ

modified accrual
(CHIN) 修正权责会计法
(FRE) comptabilité de caisse modifiée
(GER) modifizierte Abgrenzungsposten *mpl*
(JAP) 修正未収支勘定
(RUS), БУХГАЛТЕРСКИЙ МЕТОД, ПРИМЕНЯЕМЫЙ ПРАВИТЕЛЬСТВОМ, ПРИ КОТОРОМ ПОСТУПЛЕНИЯ УЧИТЫВАЮТСЯ ТОЛЬКО ПРИ ИХ НАЛИЧИИ И ВОЗМОЖНОСТИ ОЦЕНКИ

modified life insurance
(CHIN) 修正人寿保险
(FRE) assurance vie modifiée
(GER) abgeänderte Lebensversicherung *f*
(JAP) 修正生命保険
(RUS) МОДИФИЦИРОВАННОЕ СТРАХОВАНИЕ ЖИЗНИ

modified union shop
(CHIN) 重建的全工会成员工厂
(FRE) atelier syndical modifié, (C) atelier syndical imparfait
(GER) gewerkschaftspflichtiger Betrieb *m* mit Beschränkung *f* auf neue Betriebsmitglieder *npl*, Betrieb *m* mit modifizierter Gewerkschaftsbindung *f*
(JAP) 修正ユニオンショップ
(RUS) МОДИФИЦИРОВАННАЯ ПРОФСОЮЗНАЯ ЯЧЕЙКА

module
(CHIN) 模块，组件
(FRE) module
(GER) (Programm)baustein *m* (EDV), Modul *n*; Bauelement *n*, Bauteil *n*
(JAP) モジュール、交換可能な構成部分
(RUS) МОДУЛЬ

mom and pop store
(CHIN) 小零售商店
(FRE) boutique familiale, petit magasin familial, (C) commerce de vente au détail familial
(GER) Tante-Emma-Laden *m*
(JAP) 夫婦経営商店、小規模小売店
(RUS) (мелкое торговое предприятие в семейном владении

momentum
(CHIN) 价格变动速度，势力，力量
(FRE) momentum, force vive, élan, force d'impulsion
(GER) Eigendynamik *f*,
(JAP) はずみ、勢い、運動量
(RUS) ИНЕРЦИЯ; НАБРАННЫЙ РАЗГОН

monetarist
(CHIN) 货币学派
(FRE) monétariste
(GER) Monetarist *m*
(JAP) マネタリスト、通貨主義者
(RUS) МОНЕТАРИСТ; ПРИВЕРЖЕНЕЦ ТЕОРИЙ МОНЕТАРИЗМА

monetary
(CHIN) 货币的，金融的
(FRE) monétaire
(GER) monetär, geldwirtschaftlich *adj*
(JAP) 貨幣の、通貨の、金融上の
(RUS) ДЕНЕЖНЫЙ

monetary item
(CHIN) 货币项目，金融项目
(FRE) élément monétaire
(GER) Geldposten *m*, monetärer Posten *m*
(JAP) 金銭項目
(RUS) АКТИВ В ДЕНЕЖНОМ ВЫРАЖЕНИИ

monetary reserve
(CHIN) 货币储备
(FRE) réserve monétaire
(GER) Währungsreserve *f*
(JAP) 通貨準備金
(RUS) ДЕНЕЖНЫЕ РЕЗЕРВЫ

monetary standard
(CHIN) 货币本位

(FRE) étalon monétaire
(GER) Münzfuß *m*, -standard *m*,
Währungsstandard *m*, -einheit *f*
(JAP) 貨幣標準
(RUS) ДЕНЕЖНЫЙ СТАНДАРТ

money
(CHIN) 钱，现金，货币，款项
(FRE) argent, monnaie
(GER) Geld *n*
(JAP) 金、通貨
(RUS) ДЕНЬГИ

money illusion
(CHIN) 货币幻觉
(FRE) illusion monétaire
(GER) Geldillusion *f*, Geldschleier *m*
(JAP) 貨幣錯覚、マネーイリュージョン
(RUS) «ДЕНЕЖНАЯ ИЛЛЮЗИЯ»

money income
(CHIN) 货币收入，现金收入
(FRE) revenu financier
(GER) Geldeinkommen *n*, -einnahmen *fpl*
(JAP) 貨幣所得
(RUS) ДЕНЕЖНЫЙ ДОХОД

money market
(CHIN) 金融市场，货币市场
(FRE) marché monétaire, marché financier
(GER) Geldmarkt *m*, Finanzplatz *m*; Markt
m für kurzfristige Gelder *npl*, Markt *m* für
Tagesgeld *n*
(JAP) マネーマーケット、（短期）
金融市場
(RUS) ДЕНЕЖНЫЙ РЫНОК (РЫНОК
КРАТКОСРОЧНЫХ КАПИТАЛОВ В
ФОРМЕ КРЕДИТОВ И ЦЕННЫХ БУМАГ
СРОКОМ ОБЫЧНО ДО 90 ДНЕЙ)

money market fund
(CHIN) 用在短期资金市场投资的资金
(FRE) fonds commun de placement
(GER) Geldmarkt(investment)fonds *m*
(JAP) 短期金融資産ファンド、
短期金融資産投資信託
(RUS) СОВМЕСТНЫЙ ФОНД,
ВКЛАДЫВАЮЩИЙ СРЕДСТВА В ЦЕННЫЕ
БУМАГИ ДЕНЕЖНОГО РЫНКА

money supply
(CHIN) 货币供应量，货币发行量
(FRE) masse monétaire
(GER) Geldmenge *f*, -angebot *m*, -
versorgung *f*
(JAP) マネーサプライ、通貨供給量、
貨幣供給量
(RUS) ПРЕДЛОЖЕНИЕ ДЕНЕГ НА РЫНКЕ

monopolist
(CHIN) 垄断者，独占的
(FRE) monopoleur, (C) monopolisateur
(JAP) 独占者、独占論者、独占企業
(RUS) МОНОПОЛИСТ

monopoly
(CHIN) 垄断
(FRE) monopole
(GER) Monopol *n*, Monopolstellung *f*
Alleinherstellungs- *n*,
Ausschließlichkeitsrecht *n*;
Alleinvertriebsrecht *n*, -verkaufsrecht *n*,
alleiniges Handelsrecht *n*
(JAP) 独占、独占権、独占企業
(RUS) МОНОПОЛИЯ

monopoly price
(CHIN) 垄断价格
(FRE) prix de monopole,
(C) prix monopolistique
(GER) Monopolpreis *m*
(JAP) 独占価格
(RUS) МОНОПОЛЬНАЯ ЦЕНА

monopsony
(CHIN) 买主垄断，统购，专买
(FRE) monopsone
(GER) Nachfragemonopol *n*, Monopson *n*
(JAP) 需要独占、購買者独占、買手独占
(RUS) МОНОПСОНИЯ; МОНОПОЛИЯ
ПОКУПАТЕЛЯ

monthly compounding of interest
(CHIN) 按月复计利息
(FRE) regroupement mensuel des interest,
(C) calcul mensuel de l'intérêt composé
(GER) monatliche Zinsberechnung *f*,
monatliche Aufzinsung *f*
(JAP) 毎月利子を福利計算すること

monthly investment plan
(CHIN) 按月投资计划
(FRE) plan d'investissement mensuel,
(C) régime d'investissement mensuel
(GER) monatlicher Investitionsplan *m*
(JAP) 月次利子計画
(RUS) ПЛАН ЕЖЕМЕСЯЧНЫХ
ИНВЕСТИЦИЙ

month-to-month tenancy
(CHIN) 按月租赁
(FRE) location mois par mois, (C) location
au mois
(GER) sich monatlich verlängerndes Miet-
n bzw. Pachtverhältnis *n*; Vermietung *f* auf
Monatsbasis *f*
(JAP) 月決め借用（借家人、居住人）
(RUS) ПОМЕСЯЧНАЯ АРЕНДА ЖИЛЬЯ

monument
(CHIN) 界标，界石
(FRE) monument
(GER) Monument *n*, Denkmal *n*
(JAP) 記念建造物、モニュメント、
重要遺物
(RUS) МЕЖЕВОЙ ЗНАК

moonlighting
(CHIN) 兼职工作
(FRE) travail au noir, cumul d'emplois
(GER) Ausübung *f* einer Nebentätigkeit *f*;
Schwarzarbeit *f*
(JAP) 夜間副業をすること
(RUS) ВТОРАЯ РАБОТА; ПРИРАБОТОК

morale
(CHIN) 士气，道德
(FRE) moral
(GER) (Arbeits)moral *f*
(JAP) 士気、風紀
(RUS) МОРАЛЬНОЕ СОСТОЯНИЕ, ДУХ

moral hazard
(CHIN) 品行危险
(FRE) risque moral, (C) risque subjectif
(GER) Risiko *n* falscher Angaben *fpl* des
Versicherten *m*, subjektives

(Versicherungs)risiko *n*, Risiko *n*
unehrlichen bzw. fahrlässigen Verhaltens *n*
(JAP) 道徳的危険、モラル・ハザード
(RUS) МОРАЛЬНАЯ УГРОЗА

moral law
(CHIN) 道德准则
(FRE) loi morale
(GER) Sittengesetz *n*
(JAP) 道徳律
(RUS) НРАВСТВЕННЫЙ ЗАКОН

moral obligation bond
(CHIN) 义务债券
(FRE) obligation morale
(GER) Anleihe *f* eines Bundesstaats *m*
(JAP) 道義的支払保証債券
(RUS) МУНИЦИПАЛЬНАЯ ОБЛИГАЦИЯ,
ОБЕСПЕЧЕННАЯ МОРАЛЬНЫМ
ОБЯЗАТЕЛЬСТВОМ ПРАВИТЕЛЬСТВА

moral suasion
(CHIN) 道德劝告
(FRE) persuasion morale
(GER) Seelenmassage *f*, Wirtschaftspolitik *f*
des gütlichen Zuredens *n*, Maßhalteappell *m*
(JAP) 道徳に訴える勧告、道徳的勧告
(RUS) МЕРЫ МОРАЛЬНОГО
ПРИНУЖДЕНИЯ

moratorium
(CHIN) 延期偿付，延缓履行
(FRE) moratoire
(GER) Moratorium *n*, Stillhalteabkommen
n; Stundung *f*, Zahlungsaufschub *m*
(JAP) 支払停止、支払猶予、
支払猶予期間
(RUS) МОРАТОРИЙ

mortality table
(CHIN) 死亡统计表
(FRE) table de mortalité
(GER) Sterblichkeitstabelle *f*
(JAP) 死亡表、死亡率統計表
(RUS) ТАБЛИЦА СМЕРТНОСТИ

mortgage
(CHIN) 典当，抵押，抵押权
(FRE) crédit immobilier, prêt immobilier,
hypothèque, (C) prêt hypothécaire

(GER) Hypothek *f*, Grundpfandrecht *n*,
Grundschuldbrief *m*, Immobilienpfandrecht
n, hypothekarische Belastung *f*
(JAP) 譲渡抵当権、抵当権、
抵当に入れる
(RUS) ИПОТЕКА; ЗАКЛАДНАЯ

mortgage assumption
(CHIN) 抵押责任
(FRE) acceptation d'hypothèque,
(C) prise en charge de prêt
hypothécaire
(GER) Hypothekenübernahme *f*
(JAP) 抵当権引受け
(RUS) ПРИНЯТИЕ НА СЕБЕ ИПОТЕЧНЫХ
ОБЯЗАТЕЛЬСТВ (ОБЫЧНО ПРИ ПОКУПКЕ
ЗЕМЕЛЬНОГО УЧАСТКА) ПРОДАВЦА

mortgage-backed certificate
(CHIN) 抵押权证书
(FRE) certificat garanti par des créances
hypothécaires
(GER) hypothekengesicherter gesicherter
Anteilsschein *m*
(JAP) モーゲージ担保証書
(RUS) СЕРТИФИКАТ, ОБЕСПЕЧЕННЫЙ
ПУЛОМ ИПОТЕК

mortgage-backed security
(CHIN) 抵押证券
(FRE) titre garanti par des créances
hypothécaires
(GER) hypothekengesichertes Wertpapier *n*;
grundpfandrechtliche Absicherung *f*
(JAP) モーゲージ担保証券
(RUS) ЦЕННАЯ БУМАГА, ОБЕСПЕЧЕННАЯ
ПУЛОМ ИПОТЕК

mortgage banker
(CHIN) 经营抵押业务的银行家
(FRE) banquier hypothécaire, (C) société de
prêt hypothécaire
(GER) Hypothekenbanker *m*
(JAP) 譲渡抵当権金融会社、抵当銀行
(RUS) ИПОТЕЧНЫЙ БАНКИР

mortgage bond
(CHIN) 抵押债券
(FRE) obligation hypothécaire,
(C) lettre de gage

(GER) hypothekarisch gesicherte
Schuldverschreibung *f*, hypothekarische
Obligation *f*, Grundpfandbrief *m*,
Grundschuldverschreibung *f*,
Hypothekenpfandbrief *m*
(JAP) モーゲージ付債券、担保付き債券
(RUS) ИПОТЕЧНАЯ ОБЛИГАЦИЯ

mortgage broker
(CHIN) 抵押经纪人
(FRE) courtier en prêts hypothécaires
(GER) Hypothekenmakler *m*, -vermittler *m*
(JAP) モーゲージブローカー、
譲渡抵当権仲買人
(RUS) ИПОТЕЧНЫЙ БРОКЕР

mortgage commitment
(CHIN) 抵押承诺
(FRE) lettre d'entente, (C) engagement de
prêt hypothécaire
(GER) Hypotheken(kredit)zusage *f*;
hypothekarische Verpflichtung *f*
(JAP) 譲渡抵当権売買約定（約束）
(RUS) ДОГОВОР О ВЫДАЧЕ ИПОТЕЧНОГО
КРЕДИТА В БУДУЩЕМ

mortgage constant
(CHIN) 抵押常数
(FRE) constante hypothécaire
(GER) Hypothekenkonstante *f*
(JAP) モーゲージ定数（常数）
(RUS) ИПОТЕЧНАЯ КОНСТАНТА6
СООТНОШЕНИЕ МЕЖДУ ГОДОВЫМ
ОБСЛУЖИВАНИЕ ДОЛГА И ОСНОВНОЙ
СУММОЙ ДОЛГА

mortgage correspondent
(CHIN) 收费抵押服务经纪人
(FRE) correspondant hypothécaire
(GER) Person *f* die ein Hypothekendarlehen
n abbezahlt
(JAP) モーゲージ通信者（取引先）、
抵当権取引店
(RUS) ПОСРЕДНИК, ОКАЗЫВАЮЩИЙ
ПЛАТНЫЕ УСЛУГИ ПО ОБСЛУЖИВАНИЮ
ИПОТЕЧНОЙ ЗАДОЛЖЕННОСТИ

mortgage debt
(CHIN) 抵押债务
(FRE) dette hypothécaire

(GER) Hypothekenschuld *f*,
hypothekarische Belastung *f*
(JAP) 不動産抵当負債、抵当借
(RUS) ЗАДОЛЖЕННОСТЬ ПО ЗАКЛАДНОЙ,
ИПОТЕЧНАЯ ЗАДОЛЖЕННОСТЬ

mortgage discount
(CHIN) 抵押折扣
(FRE) escompte sur hypothèque, (C) remise
sur prêt hypothécaire
(GER) Hypothekendamnum *n*, -disagio *n*
(JAP) 抵当割引
(RUS) ВЫЧЕТ ЗАЁМЩИКОМ ИЗ
ОСНОВНОЙ СУММОЙ ИПОТЕКИ В ЕЁ
НАЧАЛЕ

mortgagee
(CHIN) 承受抵押者，受抵押人
(FRE) créancier hypothécaire
(GER) Hypothekeninhaber *m*, Hypothekar
m, (Grund)pfandgläubiger *m*,
Hypothekengläubiger *m*, -besitzer *m*
(JAP) 譲渡抵当権者、
抵当債券者
(RUS) КРЕДИТОР ПО ИПОТЕЧНОМУ
ЗАЛОГУ; ЗАЛОГОДЕРЖАТЕЛЬ

mortgage insurance
(CHIN) 抵押保险
(FRE) assurance hypothécaire
(GER) Hypothekenversicherung *f*
(JAP) 抵当保険
(RUS) СТРАХОВАНИЕ ИПОТЕЧНОГО
ЗАЛОГА

mortgage insurance policy
(CHIN) 抵押保险单
(FRE) police d'assurance hypothécaire
(GER) Hypothekenversicherungspolice *f*
(JAP) 抵当保険証券、抵当保険証書、
抵当保険契約
(RUS) ПОЛИС СТРАХОВАНИЯ
ИПОТЕЧНОГО ЗАЛОГА

mortgage lien
(CHIN) 抵押留置权
(FRE) gage hypothécaire
(GER) Hypotheken- *n*, Grundpfandrecht *n*
(JAP) 抵当リーエン、抵当先取権、
抵当留置権

(RUS) ПРАВО УДЕРЖАНИЯ
ЗАЛОЖЕННОЙ НЕДВИЖИМОСТИ В
СЛУЧАЕ НЕВЫПОЛНЕНИЯ ДОЛГОВЫХ
ОБЯЗАТЕЛЬСТВ

mortgage out
(CHIN) 超额抵押融资
(FRE) obtenir un prêt qui couvre plus que
nécessaire
(GER) voll finanzieren *v*
(JAP) 譲渡抵当権アウト、
モーゲージアウト
(RUS) ПОЛУЧЕНИЕ БОЛЬШЕЙ СУММЫ
КРЕДИТА, ЧЕМ ТРЕБУЕТСЯ ДЛЯ
ЗАВЕРШЕНИЯ СТРОИТЕЛЬСТВА

mortgage relief
(CHIN) 抵押解除
(FRE) main levee, (C) exonération
hypothécaire
(GER) hypothekarische Entlastung *f*,
steuerliche Anerkennung *f* von
Hypothekenzinsen *mpl*
(JAP) 抵当救済、抵当除去
(RUS) ОСВОБОЖДЕНИЕ ОТ ИПОТЕЧНЫХ
ОБЯЗАТЕЛЬСТВ

mortgage servicing
(CHIN) 抵押管理
(FRE) administration de la créance
hypothécaire
(GER) Bedienung *f* eines
Hypothekenkredits *m*, Zins- und
Tilgungszahlung *f* eines
Hypothekenkredits *m*
(JAP) 抵当ローンの提供
(RUS) ОБСЛУЖИВАНИЕ ДОЛГА ПО
ЗАКЛАДНОЙ

mortgagor
(CHIN) 抵押人
(FRE) débiteur hypothécaire
(GER) Hypotheken- *m*, Grundschuldner *m*,
Hypothekennehmer *m*
(JAP) 抵当権設定者
(RUS) ДОЛЖНИК ПО ИПОТЕЧНОМУ
ЗАЛОГУ

motion study
(CHIN) 动作研究
(FRE) étude des mouvements

(GER) Bewegungs- *f*, Arbeitsstudie *f*
(RUS) ИЗУЧЕНИЕ ЭФФЕКТИВНОСТИ
ОТДЕЛЬНЫХ МАНИПУЛЯЦИЙ,
НЕОБХОДИМЫХ ДЛЯ ПРОЦЕССА
ПРОИЗВОДСТВА

motivation
(CHIN) 动机，动力，促动因素，激励
(FRE) motivation
(GER) Motivation *f*, Beweggrund *m*,
Antrieb *m*, Leistungsbereitschaft *f*
(RUS) МОТИВАЦИЯ, ВНУТРЕННЕЕ
ПОБУЖДЕНИЕ

motor freight
(CHIN) 汽车运费
(FRE) camionnage
(GER) per LKW *m*, Straßentransport *m*
(JAP) 自動車貨物、自動車運送賃
(RUS) ПЕРЕВОЗКА ГРУЗА
АВТОТРАНСПОРТОМ

mouse
(CHIN) 鼠标器
(FRE) souris
(GER) Maus *f* (Computer)
(JAP) マウス
(RUS) МЫШЬ (УСТРОЙСТВО ВВОДА
КООРДИНАТ)

mouse pad
(CHIN) 鼠标垫
(FRE) tapis de souris
(GER) Mausunterlage *f*, Mauspad *n*
(Computer)
(JAP) マウスパッド
(RUS) КОВРИК ДЛЯ МЫШИ

movement
(CHIN) 价格变动
(FRE) mouvement
(GER) (Waren)bewegung *f*, Versand *m*,
Beförderung *f*, Umsatz *m*; Tätigkeit *f*,
Handlung *f*; Kursbewegung *f* (Börse)
(JAP) 動き、変動、動向
(RUS) ДВИЖЕНИЕ; ПЕРЕМЕЩЕНИЕ

mover and shaker
(CHIN) 具有超常影响力的人
(FRE) personne ayant un impact
remarquable sur une entreprise

(GER) Mover-und-Shaker *m*, Hans-Dampf-
in-allen-Gassen *m*
(JAP) 実力者、有力者、大者
(RUS) ЧЕЛОВЕК, ОКАЗЫВАЮЩИЙ
БОЛЬШОЕ ВЛИЯНИЕ

moving average
(CHIN) 移动平均数，移动均值
(FRE) moyenne mobile
(GER) gleitender Mittelwert *m* bzw.
Durchschnitt *m*, gleitendes Mittel *n*
(JAP) 移動平均
(RUS) ПОДВИЖНАЯ СРЕДНЯЯ ЦЕНА
ЦЕННЫХ БУМАГ ИЛИ ЗАПАСОВ

muckraker
(CHIN) 政商腐败揭露者
(FRE) journaliste à l'affut des
scandales
(GER) Sensations- *m*,
Skandalmacher *m*
(JAP) 醜聞あさり、醜聞を暴く人、
醜聞記事を記載する新聞雑誌
(RUS) ЧЕЛОВЕК, ПОСТАВИВШИЙ СВОЕЙ
ЗАДАЧЕЙ РАЗОБЛАЧАТЬ КОРРУПЦИЮ

multibuyer
(CHIN) 多次购买者
(FRE) multi-acheteur
(GER) Mehrfachkäufer *m*
(JAP) 複数バイヤー、
多数購入者
(RUS) ЧАСТЫЙ, АКТИВНЫЙ
ПОКУПАТЕЛЬ

multicasting
(CHIN) 多投影，多映射
(FRE) diffusion multiple
(GER) Mehrfachsendung *f*
(JAP) マルチキャスティング
(RUS) МЕТОД ПЕРЕДАЧИ
ИНФОРМАЦИИ ОТ ОДНОГО
ИСТОЧНИКА К ГРУППЕ
ПОЛУЧАТЕЛЕЙ

multicollinearity
(CHIN) 多边共线性
(FRE) multicollinéarité
(GER) Multikollinearität *f*
(JAP) 多数共直線性

(RUS) МНОЖЕСТВЕННАЯ
КОЛИНЕАРНОСТЬ

multiemployer bargaining
(CHIN) 多雇主谈判
(FRE) négociations multi-employeurs
(GER) Tarifverhandlungen *fpl* auf
Verbandsebene *f*
(JAP) 統一団体交渉
(RUS) ПЕРЕГОВОРЫ МЕЖДУ
АССОЦИАЦИЕЙ РАБОТОДАТЕЛЕЙ И
ТРУДОВЫМ СОЮЗОМ

multifunction
(CHIN) 多功能
(FRE) multi-fonctions
(GER) Mehrfachfunktion *f*; Mehr-,
Multifunktions-
(JAP) 多重機能
(RUS) МНОГОФУНКЦИОНАЛЬНЫЙ

multimedia
(CHIN) 多媒体
(FRE) multimédia
(GER) Multimedia *f*
(JAP)（多様な伝達手段・宣伝媒体を持
つ）マルチメディア、多元媒体
(RUS) ДВА ИЛИ БОЛЬШЕ СМИ;
КОМПЬЮТЕРНЫЕ ПРИЛОЖЕНИЯ,
ВКЛЮЧАЮЩИЕ В СЕБЯ ТЕКСТ,
ГРАФИКУ ВЫСОКОГО РАЗРЕШЕНИЯ,
МУЛЬТИПЛИКАЦИЮ,
ЗВУК И Т. П.

multinational corporation (MNC)
(CHIN) 跨国公司（MNC）
(FRE) entreprise multinationale, société
multinationale
(GER) multinationales Unternehmen *n* bzw.
Konzern *m*
(JAP) 多国籍企業
(RUS) МЕЖДУНАРОДНАЯ
КОРПОРАЦИЯ

multiple
(CHIN) 多种，复合
(FRE) multiple
(GER) mehrfach *adj*
(JAP) 多数の、多量の、複合の
(RUS) МНОЖЕСТВЕННЫЙ; КРАТНЫЙ;
ОТНОШЕНИЕ ЦЕНЫ К ДОХОДУ

multiple listing
(CHIN) 多家房产公司信息登记
(FRE) contrat avec inscription au service
inter-agences
(GER) Notierung *f* an mehreren Börsen *fpl*;
Mehrfachvergabe *f* von Immobilien *fpl* an
mehrere Makler *mpl/fpl*,
Maklerkartell *n*
(JAP) 複数リスト
(RUS) МНОЖЕСТВЕННАЯ КОТИРОВКА
ЦЕННОЙ БУМАГИ

multiple locations forms
(CHIN) 多址财产保险单
(FRE) projet à emplacements multiples
(GER) Mehrfachstandortformulare *npl*
(JAP) 複数所在地書式
(RUS) СТРАХОВОЕ ПОКРЫТИЕ
СОБСТВЕННОСТИ, НАХОДЯЩЕЙСЯ В
РАЗНЫХ МЕСТАХ

multiple-management plan
(CHIN) 多方参加管理计划
(FRE) plan de direction multiple,
(C) régime à direction polyvalente
(GER) System *n* der mehrstufigen
Betriebsführung *f*, System *n* der mehrfachen
Führungsgremien *npl*
(JAP) 複合経営計画、複層管理計画、
多角経営計画
(RUS) ПЛАН КОЛЛЕКТИВНОГО
РУКОВОДСТВА

multiple-peril insurance
(CHIN) 多种风险保险
(GER) kombinierte Versicherung *f*,
Versicherung *f* gegen mehrere
Gefahren *fpl*
(JAP) 複合危機保険
(RUS) СТРАХОВАНИЕ РАЗЛИЧНЫХ
РИСКОВ

multiple regression
(CHIN) 复合回归分析
(FRE) régression multiple
(GER) Mehrfachregression *f*, multiple
Regression *f*
(JAP) 多重回帰
(RUS) МНОЖЕСТВЕННАЯ
РЕГРЕССИЯ

multiple retirement ages
(CHIN) 复合退休年龄
(FRE) âges multiples de départ à la retraite
(GER) unterschiedliche Pensionsalter *npl*
(JAP) 複合退職年齡
(RUS) ШКАЛА ВОЗРАСТА ВЫХОДА НА ПЕНСИЮ

multiple shop
(CHIN) 联号商店
(FRE) magasin à secteurs multiples
(GER) Filialladen *m*, -geschäft *n*,
(JAP) 連鎖店、チェーンストア
(RUS) ТРУДОВОЙ СОЮЗ, ВКЛЮЧАЮЩИЙ КАК СПЕЦИАЛИСТОВ, ТАК И НЕКВАЛИФИЦИРОВАННЫХ РАБОТНИКОВ

multiplier
(CHIN) 乘数
(FRE) multiplicateur
(GER) Multiplikator *m*
(JAP) 乘数
(RUS) МУЛЬТИПЛИКАТОР

multiuser
(CHIN) 多用户
(FRE) multi-utilisateurs
(GER) Mehrbenutzer *m*; Mehrbenutzer-, Mehrplatz- *adj*
(JAP) マルチユーザー、多数利用者
(RUS) МНОГОПОЛЬЗОВАТЕЛЬСКИЙ, ДЛЯ МНОГИХ ПОЛЬЗОВАТЕЛЕЙ

municipal bond
(CHIN) 市政公债
(FRE) obligation de collectivité locale, (C) obligation municipale
(GER) Kommunalobligation *f*
(JAP) 地方債
(RUS) МУНИЦИПАЛЬНАЯ ОБЛИГАЦИЯ

municipal revenue bond
(CHIN) 市政收入债券
(FRE) obligation municipale
(GER) Kommunalschatzanweisung *f*, -obligation *f*
(JAP) 市特定財源債、地方特定財源債券
(RUS) МУНИЦИПАЛЬНАЯ ОБЛИГАЦИЯ С ВЫПЛАТОЙ ИЗ ДОХОДОВ ОТ

ФИНАНСИРУЕМЫХ ПРОЕКТОВ

muniments of title
(CHIN) 产权契据
(FRE) titre
(GER) Grundstücksurkunde *f*, Grundeigentumsurkunde *f*
(JAP) 不動産権利証書
(RUS) ДОКУМЕНТАЛЬНОЕ ПОДТВЕРЖДЕНИЕ ПРАВОВОГО ТИТУЛА

mutual association
(CHIN) 互助储蓄贷款协会
(FRE) association mutuelle
(GER) Gegenseitigkeitsverband *m*, Vereinigung *f* bzw. Verein *m* auf Gegenseitigkeit *f*
(JAP) 相互組合、相互協会
(RUS) ВЗАИМНАЯ ССУДО-СБЕРЕГАТЕЛЬНАЯ АССОЦИАЦИЯ

mutual company
(CHIN) 合股公司
(FRE) société mutuelle
(GER) Gegenseitigkeitsgesellschaft *f*, Versicherungsverein *m* auf Gegenseitigkeit *f*
(JAP) 相互会社
(RUS) ВЗАИМНАЯ КОМПАНИЯ

mutual fund
(CHIN) 互助基金，共同基金
(FRE) fonds commun de placement
(GER) (offener) Investment fonds *m*; Kapitalanlage- *f*, Investmentgesellschaft *f*, Anlagefonds *m*
(JAP) ミューチュアルファンド、オープンエンド型投資資金、投資信託
(RUS) СОВМЕСТНЫЙ ФОНД, ИНВЕСТИЦИОННАЯ КОМПАНИЯ ОТКРЫТОГО ТИПА

mutual insurance company
(CHIN) 相互保险公司
(FRE) mutuelle de société
(GER) Versicherungsverein *m* auf Gegenseitigkeit *f* (VVaG)
(JAP) 相互保険会社
(RUS) КОМПАНИЯ ВЗАИМНОГО СТРАХОВАНИЯ

mutuality of contract
(CHIN) 合同双方关系
(FRE) réciprocité de contrat
(GER) Vertragsgegenseitigkeit *f*,

Gegenseitigkeit *f* eines Vertrags *m*
(JAP) 契約の相互性
(RUS) ВЗАИМНОСТЬ ОБЯЗАТЕЛЬСТВ ПО
ДОГОВОРУ, КОНТРАКТУ

N

naked option
(CHIN) 无保证期权
(FRE) option d'achat vendue à découvert, (C) option non couverte
(GER) ungesicherte bzw. ungedeckte Option *f*, Nacktoption *f*
(JAP) ネーキッドオプション、無権利オプションファンド
(RUS) НЕ ЗАЩИЩЕННЫЙ ОПЦИОН (бирж.)

naked position
(CHIN) 无担保部位
(FRE) position non couverte
(GER) ungesicherte bzw. ungedeckte Position *f*
(JAP) ネーキッドポジション、無権利所有
(RUS) НЕ ЗАЩИЩЕННАЯ ПОЗИЦИЯ (бирж.)

named peril policy
(CHIN) 指定危险保险单
(FRE) assurance risque nominative, (C) police à risques désignés
(GER) Versicherung *f* gegen benannte Risiken *npl*
(JAP) 特定危険保険
(RUS) СТРАХОВОЙ ПОЛИС С КОНКРЕТНЫМ РИСКОМ – ОБЪЕКТОМ СТРАХОВАНИЯ

name position bond
(CHIN) 记名职位忠诚保险
(FRE) cautionnement énumératif du personnel, (C) assurance contre les détournements
(GER) Kautionsversicherung *f* des Arbeitgebers *m* gegen Veruntreuung *f* der Angestellten *mpl*
(JAP) 記名式地位身元信用債権

name schedule bond
(CIIN) 在册雇员忠诚保险
(FRE) cautionnement énumératif

dupersonnel, (C) assurance contre les détournements
(GER) Kautionsversicherung *f* des Arbeitgebers *m* gegen interne Veruntreuung *f* (wobei die Namen der gedeckten Angestellten und die Deckungsbeträge auflistet sind)
(JAP) 記名式明細書付信用債権
(RUS) ПУНКТ ДЕЛОВОГО СТРАХОВАНИЯ, ПОКРЫВАЮЩИЙ НЕЧЕСТНЫЕ ДЕЙСТВИЯ ОГОВОРЕННЫХ ДОЛЖНОСТНЫХ ЛИЦ

nationalization
(CHIN) 国有化
(FRE) nationalisation
(GER) Verstaatlichung *f*, Nationalisierung *f*
(JAP) 国有化、国民化、国営
(RUS) НАЦИОНАЛИЗАЦИЯ

national wealth
(CHIN) 国民财富
(FRE) richesse nationale
(GER) Volksvermögen *n*
(JAP) 国富
(RUS) НАЦИОНАЛЬНОЕ БОГАТСТВО

natural business year
(CHIN) 自然营业年度
(FRE) exercice cyclique, (C) année normale d'exploitation
(GER) normales Geschäftsjahr *n*
(JAP) 自然営業年度、自然年度
(RUS) КАЛЕНДАРНЫЙ ДЕЛОВОЙ ГОД

natural monopoly
(CHIN) 自然垄断
(FRE) monopole naturel
(GER) natürliches Monopol *n*
(JAP) 自然独占
(RUS) ЕСТЕСТВЕННАЯ МОНОПОЛИЯ

natural resources
(CHIN) 自然资源
(FRE) ressources naturelles

(GER) Boden- *mpl*, Naturschätze *mpl*,
Rohstoffe *fpl*
(JAP) 天然資源、自然資源（土地、
鉱物、水）
(RUS) ПРИРОДНЫЕ РЕСУРСЫ

navigation
(CHIN) 导航
(FRE) navigation
(GER) Navigation *f*, (auch EDV)
(JAP) ナビゲーション、移動
(RUS) НАВИГАЦИЯ

near money
(CHIN) 类货币，准货币
(FRE) quasi-monnaie
(GER) Quasigeld *n*, Geldsubstitut *n*, -
surrogat *n*, geldähnliche Forderungen *fpl*,
Beinahgeld *n*, leicht liquidierbare Einlagen
fpl
(JAP) ニヤーマネー、近似通貨、準貨幣
(RUS) «ПОЧТИ ДЕНЬГИ» (высоколиквидные
активы)

need satisfaction
(CHIN) 需要得到满足
(FRE) satisfaction des besoins,
(C) réalisation d'un besoin
(GER) Bedürfnisbefriedigung *f*
(JAP) ニーズ充足、必要充足
(RUS) УДОВЛЕТВОРЕНИЕ ПОТРЕБНОСТИ

negative amortization
(CHIN) 负摊还
(FRE) amortissement négatif
(GER) Negativamortisierung *f*
(JAP) (借入元本の) 負の償却、
逆償還
(RUS) ОТРИЦАТЕЛЬНАЯ (ОБРАТНАЯ)
АМОРТИЗАЦИЯ

negative carry
(CHIN) 账面赔本
(FRE) coût de maintien négatif, report
négatif, (C) portage négatif
(GER) Nettobestandhaltekosten *pl*
(JAP) ネガティブキャリー
(RUS) СИТУАЦИЯ, КОГДА СТОИМОСТЬ
ФИНАНСИРОВАНИЯ ЦЕННЫХ БУМАГ
ВЫШЕ ДОХОДА ОТ НИХ

negative cash flow
(CHIN) 负现金流量
(FRE) flux de trésorerie
négatif
(GER) negativer Cashflow *m*,
Einnahmeunterdeckung *f*
(JAP) マイナスキャッシュフロー、
現金流出
(RUS) ПРЕВЫШЕНИЕ НАЛИЧНЫХ
ВЫПЛАТ НАД ПОСТУПЛЕНИЯМИ

negative correlation
(CHIN) 负相关
(FRE) corrélation negative, corrélation
inverse
(GER) negative Korrelation *f*
(JAP) 逆相関、負の相関
(RUS) ОТРИЦАТЕЛЬНАЯ КОРРЕЛЯЦИЯ

negative income tax
(CHIN) 负所得税
(FRE) impôt négatif (sur le revenu)
(GER) negative Einkommensteuer *f*
(JAP) 負の所得税、逆所得税
(RUS) ОТРИЦАТЕЛЬНЫЙ ПОДОХОДНЫЙ
НАЛОГ, ПРЕДЛОЖЕННАЯ СИСТЕМА, ПРИ
КОТОРОЙ ЛИЦА С ДОХОДОМ НИЖЕ
ОПРЕДЕЛЕННОГО УРОВНЯ ПОЛУЧАЛИ
БЫ ВЫПЛАТЫ

negative working capital
(CHIN) 负周转资金，负运用资本
(FRE) fonds de roulement négatif, fonds
de roulement déficitaire
(GER) negatives Betriebskapital *n*
(JAP) 負の営業資本、負の運転資本
(RUS) ОТРИЦАТЕЛЬНЫЙ ОБОРОТНЫЙ
КАПИТАЛ

negligence
(CHIN) 疏忽
(FRE) négligence
(GER) Fahrlässigkeit *f*, fahrlässiges
Verschulden *n*; Unachtsamkeit *f*,
Nachlässigkeit *f*, Versehen *n*;
Vernachlässigung *f*; Verletzung *f* der
Sorgfaltspflicht *f*; fahrlässiges Verhalten *n*
(RUS) НЕБРЕЖНОСТЬ, ХАЛАТНОСТЬ

negotiable
(CHIN) 可议付的，可转让的

(FRE) négociable, à débattre
(GER) frei übertragbar, abtretbar; begebbar, verkehrs-, handelsfähig, verkäuflich, veräußerlich *adj*; börsenfähig *adj*
(JAP) 怠慢、不注意な行為、過失
(RUS) СВОБОДНООБРАЩАЮЩИЙСЯ, ОБОРОТНЫЙ

negotiable certificate of deposit
(CHIN) 可转让存款单
(FRE) certificat de dépôt négociable, (C) certificat négociable de dépôt
(GER) begebbares bzw. übertragbares Einlagenzertifikat *n*, handelbarer Hinterlegungsschein *n* für Zeiteinlagen *fpl*
(JAP) 譲渡可能定期預金証書
(RUS) СВОБОДНО ОБРАЩАЮЩИЙСЯ ДЕПОЗИТНЫЙ СЕРТИФИКАТ

negotiable instrument
(CHIN) 可转让票据
(FRE) instrument négociable, (C) titre négociable
(GER) begebbares bzw. übertragbares Wertpapier *n*, verkehrs- bzw. handelsfähiges Papier *n*; umlauffähiges Wertpapier *n*
(JAP) 流通証券
(RUS) ОБРАЩАЮЩИЙСЯ КРЕДИТНО-ФИНАНСОВЫЙ ДОКУМЕНТ

negotiable order of withdrawal (NOW)
(CHIN) 能开可转让支付命令的活期存款账户（NOW）
(FRE) compte-chèques rémunéré, compte à vue rémunéré, (C) retrait négociable tiré d'un compte-chèques rémunéré
(GER) übertragbare Auszahlungsanweisung *f* bzw. Abhebungsauftrag *m*
(JAP) 譲渡可能払戻し指図
(RUS) ОБРАЩАЮЩИЙСЯ ПРИКАЗ ОБ ИЗЪЯТИИ СРЕДСТВ

negotiated market price
(CHIN) 议价市场价格
(FRE) prix de marché négocié
(GER) ausgehandelter Marktpreis *m*
(JAP) 相対市場価格、顧客市場価格
(RUS) ДОГОВОРНАЯ РЫНОЧНАЯ ЦЕНА (МЕЖДУ ПРАВИТЕЛЬСТВОМ И ПРОИЗВОДИТЕЛЕМ)

negotiated price
(CHIN) 议付价
(FRE) prix négocié
(GER) ausgehandelter Preis *m*
(JAP) 相対価格、交渉価格
(RUS) ДОГОВОРНАЯ ЦЕНА

negotiation
(CHIN) 谈判，协商，议付
(FRE) négotiation
(GER) Verhandlung *f*; Begebung *f* von Wertpapieren *npl*; Übertragung *f*
(JAP) 交渉、商議、取引
(RUS) ПЕРЕГОВОРЫ; ОБСУЖДЕНИЕ

neighborhood store
(CHIN) 社区商店
(FRE) magasin de quartier, magasin de proximité
(GER) Nachbarschaftsladen *m*, Tante-Emma-Laden *m*
(JAP) 近所の店、近隣の店舗
(RUS) МЕСТНЫЙ МАГАЗИН

neoclassical economics
(CHIN) 新古典经济学
(FRE) économie néoclassique
(GER) neoklassische Volkswirtschaftslehre *f*
(JAP) 新古典派経済学
(RUS) НЕОКЛАССИЧЕСКАЯ ЭКОНОМИКА

nepotism
(CHIN) 任人唯亲
(FRE) népotisme
(GER) Nepotismus *m*, Vetternwirtschaft *f*
(JAP) 縁者びいき、親族登用、縁故者のコネ
(RUS) СЕМЕЙСТВЕННОСТЬ; НЕПОТИЗМ

nest egg
(CHIN) 储备金
(FRE) bas de laine, pécule
(GER) Spargroschen *m*, Rücklage *f*, finanzielles Polster *n*
(JAP) 種銭、予備金、蓄え
(RUS) ДЕНЬГИ, ОТЛОЖЕННЫЕ НА ЧЁРНЫЙ ДЕНЬ

net

(CHIN) 纯净，净价，净额，净得

(FRE) net

(GER) netto, frei von Abzügen *mpl*, rein *adj*

(JAP) 正味の、正価の、最終的な

(RUS) НЕТТО; ЧИСТЫЙ

net assets

(CHIN) 净资产

(FRE) actif net

(GER) Netto- *m*, Reinvermögen *n*;
Forderungssalden *npl*; Rücklagen *fpl* und
Gewinn *m*

(JAP) 純財産、純資産

(RUS) НЕТТО – АКТИВЫ

net asset value (NAV)

(CHIN) 资产净值（NAV）

(FRE) valeur d'actif net

(GER) Nettovermögens- *m*,
Nettoanlagewert *m*; Teilreproduktionswert
m; Substanzwert *m*; Liquidations- *m*,
Inventarwert *m*

(JAP) 純資産価値

(RUS) СТОИМОСТЬ ЧИСТЫХ АКТИВОВ (в
расчете на одну акцию)

net book value

(CHIN) 账面净值

(FRE) valeur comptable nette

(GER) Netto- *m*, Restbuchwert *m*;
Abnutzungswert *m*; fortgeführte
Anschaffungskosten *pl*

(JAP) 正味帳簿価額

(RUS) АМОРТИЗИРОВАННАЯ
СТОИМОСТЬ

net contribution

(CHIN) 净贡献额

(FRE) contribution nette

(GER) Nettoeinzahlung *f*, -leistung *f*, -
beitrag *m*

(JAP) 正味掛金、正味拠出金、
正味分担金

(RUS) ЧИСТЫЙ ВКЛАД

net cost

(CHIN) 净价，实价，净成本

(FRE) prix de revient, (C) coût net

(GER) Nettokosten *pl*; Selb stkostenpreis *m*

(JAP) 純原価

(RUS) ЧИСТАЯ СТОИМОСТЬ

net current assets

(CHIN) 净流动资产

(FRE) actif circulant net, (C) fonds de
roulement

(GER) Nettoumlaufvermögen *n*,
Liquiditätsüberschuss *m*,
Betriebskapital *n*

(JAP) 正味流動資産

(RUS) ЧИСТЫЕ ТЕКУЩИЕ АКТИВЫ

net income

(CHIN) 净收入

(FRE) produit net, revenu net,
(C) bénéfice net

(GER) Netto- *m*, Reingewinn *m*, Netto- *m*,
Reinertrag *m*, Nettoe innahmen *fpl*; Netto-
m, Reinverdienst *m*

(JAP) 純所得、純利益、純益

(RUS) ЧИСТЫЙ ДОХОД

net income per share of common stock

(CHIN) 普通股每股净收入

(FRE) revenu net par action ordinaire,
(C) bénéfice net par action ordinaire

(GER) Nettogewinn *m* je Stammaktie *f*

(JAP) 普通株の一株（一口）
当たりの純益

(RUS) ЧИСТЫЙ ДОХОД НА ОДНУ
ПРОСТУЮ АКЦИЮ

net leasable area

(CHIN) 可租赁净面积

(FRE) surface locative nette

(GER) Nettopacht- *f*, Nettomietfläche *f*

(JAP) 純賃借可能地域

(RUS) «ЧИСТАЯ» АРЕНДУЕМАЯ
ПЛОЩАДЬ

net lease

(CHIN) 纯租赁

(FRE) contrat de louage inconditionnel,
(C) bail hors frais d'entretien

(GER) Nettopacht- *m*, Nettomiet- *m*, Netto-
Leasingvertrag *m*; Miete *f* plus sämtliche
Kosten *pl*

(JAP) ネットリース（賃借人が諸経費を
負担する賃貸借契約）

(RUS) НЕТТО – АРЕНДА (арендатор оплачивает все текущие расходы)

net listing
(CHIN) 净标价
(FRE) contrat de courtage avec rémunération différée
(GER) Grundstücksmaklervertrag *m* mit Nettoangebot *n*, Mehrerlös *m* als Maklerprovision *f*, (Grundstücks- bzw. Immobilienmaklervertrag, bei dem die Provision aus der Differenz zwischen Verkaufspreis und Nettopreis an den Verkäuferbesteht)
(JAP) 手取額指定仲介
(RUS) БРОКЕРСКИЙ ДОГОВОР, ПО КОТОРОМУ брокер получает комиссию, ЕСЛИ продажнАЯ ценА ПРЕВЫШАЕТ опредесннУЮ величинУ)

net loss
(CHIN) 损失净额
(FRE) perte nette
(GER) Netto- *m*, Reinverlust *m*, Bilanzverlust *m*, Jahresfehlbetrag *m*, Barverlust *m*
(JAP) 純損失、正味支払保険金
(RUS) ЧИСТЫЕ УБЫТКИ

net national product
(CHIN) 国民生产净值
(FRE) produit national net
(GER) Nettosozialprodukt *n*
(JAP) 国民純生産、純国民生産物
(RUS) ЧИСТЫЙ НАЦИОНАЛЬНЫЙ ПРОДУКТ

net operating income (NOI)
(CHIN) 营业净收益（NOI）
(FRE) revenu net d'exploitation
(GER) Nettobetriebs- *fpl*, Betriebsreineinnahmen *fpl*; Nettobetriebsgewinn *m*
(JAP) 純営業収益
(RUS) ЧИСТЫЙ ОПЕРАЦИОННЫЙ ДОХОД

net operating loss (NOL)
(CHIN) 营业净损失（NOL）
(FRE) pertes d'exploitation nettes, (C) perte nette d'exploitation
(GER) Nettobetriebsverlust *m*

(JAP) 純営業損失
(RUS) ЧИСТЫЙ ОПЕРАЦИОННЫЙ УБЫТОК

net present value (NPV)
(CHIN) 净现值（NPV）
(FRE) valeur actuelle nette, (C) valeur actualisée nette
(GER) Kapital- *m*, Barwert *m*, aktualisierter Wert *m*
(JAP) 純現在価値
(RUS) ЧИСТАЯ ТЕКУЩАЯ ЦЕННОСТЬ

net proceeds
(CHIN) 净收入，实得额
(FRE) produit net
(GER) Netto- *m*, Reinerlös *m*, Netto- *m*, Reinertrag *m*, Auszahlung *f*
(JAP) 正味売上高、純売上高、純手取金
(RUS) НЕТТО –ВЫРУЧКА (от продажи)

net profit
(CHIN) 净利，纯利润
(FRE) bénéfice net, (C) résultat net
(GER) Netto- *m*, Reingewinn *m*, Jahresüberschuss *m*, Bilanzgewinn *m*
(JAP) 純益
(RUS) ЧИСТАЯ ПРИБЫЛЬ

net profit margin
(CHIN) 纯利润率，净利率
(FRE) marge commerciale nette, (C) marge bénéficiaire nette
(GER) Nettoumsatzrendite *f*
(JAP) 売上純利益限界
(RUS) ПРЕДЕЛ ЧИСТОЙ ПРИБЫЛИ (отношение нетто-прибыли к нетто-продажам)

net purchases
(CHIN) 购货净额
(FRE) acquisitions nettes   achats nets, (C) achats nets
(GER) Nettoeinkaufswert *m*
(JAP) 純仕入高、純購入高、正味仕入高
(RUS) ЧИСТЫЕ ЗАКУПКИ

net quick assets
(CHIN) 速动资产净额
(FRE) liquidités nettes

(GER) Nettoumlaufvermögen *n*,
Betriebskapital *n*
(JAP) 正味当座資産
(RUS) ЧИСТЫЕ ЛИКВИДНЫЕ АКТИВЫ

net rate

(CHIN) 净比例，净费率

(FRE) taux net, (C) rendement net
(GER) Nettorisikoprämie *f*, Bedarfsprämie
f; Nettorate *f*, -satz *m*; Nettozinssatz *m*
(JAP) 正味料率
(RUS) ЧИСТАЯ СТАВКА

net realizable value

(CHIN) 可变现净值

(FRE) valeur réalisable nette, (C) valeur de
réalisation nette
(GER) Netto-Realisationswert *m*,
realisierbarer Nettowert *m*; realisierbarer
Verkaufswert *m*
(JAP) (資産評価の) 正味実現可能価額
(RUS) ЧИСТАЯ РЕАЛИЗУЕМАЯ
СТОИМОСТЬ

net sales

(CHIN) 净销售额

(FRE) ventes nettes, (C) chiffre d'affaires
net
(GER) Nettoauftragseingang *m*, Netto- *m*,
Reinumsatz *m*
(JAP) 正(JAP) 味売上高、純売上高
(RUS) НЕТТО – ПРОДАЖИ

net surfing

(CHIN) 网上浏览

(FRE) navigation sur le net, (C) surf
(GER) im Internet *n* surfen *v*
(JAP) ネットサーフィン

net transaction

(CHIN) 净交易

(FRE) transaction nette transaction nette
(GER) Nettotransaktion *f*
(JAP) 正味取引
(RUS) НЕТТО – ТРАНЗАКЦИЯ (СДЕЛКА)

network
(CHIN) 网络
(FRE) réseau
(GER) Netz(werk) *n*,

(JAP) ネットワーク
(RUS) СЕТЬ ЭВМ ИЛИ СЕТЬ ПЕРЕДАЧИ
ДАННЫХ

network administrator
(CHIN) 网络管理员
(FRE) administrateur réseau,
(C) administrateur de réseau
(GER) Netzverwalter *m*
(JAP) ネットワーク管理者、
ネットワークアドミニストレーター
(RUS) СПЕЦИАЛИСТ ПО
ОБСЛУЖИВАНИЮ СЕТЕЙ

networking
(CHIN) 联网
(FRE) travail en réseau, mise en réseau,
(C) réseautage
(GER) Knüpfen *n* von Kontakten *mpl*,
Beziehungspflege *f*, Networking *n*;
Vernetzung *f*, Netzwerkbetrieb *m* (EDV)
(JAP) ネットワーキング、
ネットワーク作り
(RUS) СОЗДАНИЕ СЕТЕЙ;
ИСПОЛЬЗОВАНИЕ СВЯЗЕЙ

net yield
(CHIN) 净收益，净产量
(FRE) rendement net
(GER) Nettorendite *f*, Effektivverzinsung *f*,
effektive Rendite *f*; Netto- *m*, Reinertrag *m*,
Netto- *m*, Reinerlös *m*
(JAP) 純利回り、税引利回り
(RUS) НЕТТО – ДОХОД

new issue
(CHIN) 股票等的初次上市发行
(FRE) nouvelle émission
(GER) Neuemission *f*, -begebung *f*;
Neuauflage *f*, -ausgabe *f*
(JAP) 新規発売
(RUS) НОВАЯ ЭМИССИЯ

new money
(CHIN) 新货币
(FRE) crédit de restructuration, argent
frais
(GER) neues Geld *n*; Neukredit *m*
(JAP) ニューマネー、新規貨幣、
新規資金

278

(RUS) СУММА ДОПОЛНИТЕЛЬНОГО
ДОЛГОСРОЧНОГО ФИНАНСИРОВАНИЯ,
ПРЕВЫШАЮЩАЯ СУММУ
РЕФИНАНСИРОВАНИЯ

newspaper syndicate

(CHIN) 新闻联合组织
(FRE) agence de presse, (C) consortium de
journaux
(GER) Zeitungssyndikat *n*
(JAP) ニュースペーパーシンジケート、
新聞企業連合、新聞記事配給業者
(RUS) ГАЗЕТНЫЙ СИНДИКАТ

new town

(CHIN) 新城镇
(FRE) ville nouvelle, nouveaux quartiers,
(C) ville neuve
(GER) Satellitenstadt *f*, Trabantenstadt *f*
(JAP) ニュータウン、新都市、
大住宅団地
(RUS) НОВЫЙ ГОРОД

niche

(CHIN) 恰当的地方，活动范围
(FRE) créneau, niche
(GER) Nische *f*
(JAP) ニッチ、特定市場分野、市場のす
き間
(RUS) НИША

night letter

(CHIN) 夜间书信电报
(FRE) lettre de nuit, (C) téléposte
(GER) Nachttelegramm *n*,
Brieftelegramm *n*
(JAP) 夜間（発送）電報、overnight
telegram の旧称
(RUS) МЕТОД ДОСТАВКИ
КОРРЕПОНДЕНЦИИ АДРЕССАТУ НА
СЛЕДУЮЩИЙ ДЕНЬ

node

(CHIN) 节点，结点
(FRE) noeud
(GER) Knoten *m*, Knotenpunkt *f*
(JAP) ノード、節点、
結節点
(RUS) УЗЕЛ СЕТИ ПЕРЕДАЧИ ДАННЫХ
ИЛИ СЕТИ ЭВМ

no-growth

(CHIN) 无增长
(FRE) croissance zero, croissance nulle
(GER) Nullwachstum *n*;
wachstumsneutral *adj*
(JAP) ゼロ成長
(RUS) ОТСУТСТВИЕ РОСТА

no-load fund

(CHIN) 无负担基金
(FRE) fonds sans frais d'acquisition: fonds
qui ne prélèvent pas une commission
(GER) gebührenfreier Investmentfonds *m*,
Investmentsfonds *m* ohne
Ausgabeaufschlag *m*
(JAP) ノーロードファンド、
（手数料無料の）
ミューチュアルファンド、
直売ミューチュアルファンド
(RUS) ВЗАИМНЫЙ ИНВЕСТИЦИОННЫЙ
ФОНД, ПРОДАЮЩИЙ СВОИ АКЦИИ
ИНВЕСТОРАМ БЕЗ КОМИССИОННЫХ

nominal account

(CHIN) 名义账户
(FRE) compte d'exploitation générale,
(C) compte nominal
(GER) Erfolgs- *n*, Sachkonto *n*, totes Konto
n; Aufwand- *n* und Ertragskonto *n*
(JAP) 名目勘定、仮勘定
(RUS) НОМИНАЛЬНЫЙ СЧЕТ; СЧЁТ
ПРИХОДОВ И РАСХОДОВ

nominal damages

(CHIN) 象征性损失
(FRE) dommages-intérêts
symboliques
(GER) nomineller Schadensersatz *m*;
nomineller Schaden *m*
(JAP) 名目的損害賠償金
(RUS) НОМИНАЛЬНЫЙ УЩЕРБ

nominal interest rate

(CHIN) 名义利率，虚利率
(FRE) taux d'intérêt nominal
(GER) Nominalzinssatz *m*, -verzinsung *f*
(JAP) 表面金利、名目金利,
表面利子率
(RUS) НОМИНАЛЬНАЯ ПРОЦЕНТНАЯ
СТАВКА

nominal scale

(CHIN) 名义规模

(FRE) échelle nominale, échelle principale

(GER) nomineller Maßstab *m*

(JAP) 名義尺度

(RUS) НОМИНАЛЬНАЯ ШКАЛА

nominal wage

(CHIN) 名义工资

(FRE) salaire nominal, (C) rémunération nominale

(GER) Nominallohn *m*

(JAP) 名目賃金

(RUS) НОМИНАЛЬНАЯ ЗАРАБОТНАЯ ПЛАТА

nominal yield

(CHIN) 名义收益

(FRE) taux nominal, (C) rendement nominal

(GER) Nominalverzinsung *f*

(JAP) 名目利回り

(RUS) НОМИНАЛЬНЫЙ ДОХОД

nominee

(CHIN) 被提名人

(FRE) candidat, nominé, personne nommée, prête-nom, intermédiaire, (C) propriétaire apparent

(GER) Kandidat *m*, benannte *f*; Bevollmächtigter *m*; Strohmann *m*; Leibrenten- *m*, Zuschussempfänger *m*

(JAP) 推薦された人、

候補に指名された人、受取人、名義人

(RUS) УСЛОВНЫЙ ВЛАДЕЛЕЦ, Т.Е. ФИЗИЧЕСКОЕ ИЛИ ЮРИДИЧЕСКОЕ ЛИЦО НА ЧЬЁ ИМЯ ЗАРЕГИСТРИРОВАНЫ ЦЕННЫЕ БУМАГИ ПРИ СОВЕРШЕНИИ С НИМИ ТРАСТОВЫХ ОПЕРАЦИЙ В ИНТЕРЕСАХ РЕАЛЬНОГО ВЛАДЕЛЬЦА

noncallable

(CHIN) 到期偿还优先股票或债券

(FRE) qui ne peut pas être amorti(e) par anticipation, (C) non remboursable par anticipation

(GER) unkündbar, nicht (vorzeitig) kündbar *adj*

(JAP) （債券が）繰上げ償還のできない、満期償還の

(RUS) ОБЛИГАЦИЯ, НЕ ПОГАШАЕМАЯ ДОСРОЧНО

noncompetitive bid

(CHIN) 非竞争性招标

(FRE) offre non compétitive,(C) appel d'offres restreint

(GER) Angebot *n* unter Ausschluss *m* der Konkurrenz *f*; nicht wettbewerbsfähiges Angebot *n*

(JAP) 非競争入札

(RUS) НЕКОНКУРЕНТНОЕ ТЕНДЕРНОЕ ПРЕДЛОЖЕНИЕ (ЗАЯВКА)

nonconforming use

(CHIN) 不符合规定的土地使用

(FRE) utilisation non conforme

(GER) nicht vertragsgemäße Verwendung *f*; nicht vorschriftsmäßige Benutzung *f*

(JAP) 不適合利用

(RUS) НЕПРЕДУСМОТРЕННОЕ ИСПОЛЬЗОВАНИЕ

noncontestability clause

(CHIN) 无争议性条款

(FRE) clause d'incontestabilité, (C) clause de non-contestabilité

(GER) Unanfechtbarkeitsklausel *f*

(JAP) 不可争条項

(RUS) ОГОВОРКА О НЕОСПОРИМОСТИ

noncumulative preferred stock

(CHIN) 非累积优先股

(FRE) action privilégiée non cumulative, (C) action de priorité à dividende non cumulatif

(GER) nichtkumulative Vorzugsaktie *f*, Vorzugsaktie *f* ohne Dividenden- *m* bzw. Nachbezugsrecht *n*, Vorzugsaktie *f* ohne kumulativen Dividendenanspruch *m*, Vorzugsaktie *f*

(JAP) 非累積型優先株式

(RUS) ПРИВИЛЕГИРОВАННАЯ АКЦИЯ, ПО КОТОРОЙ ДИВИДЕНД НЕ НАКАПЛИВАЕТСЯ

noncurrent asset

(CHIN) 非流动资产

(FRE) actif non exigible, (C) actif à long terme

(GER) langfristige Vermögensteile *npl*

(JAP) 非流動資産、固定資産
(RUS) АКТИВ, НЕ УЧАСТВУЮЩИЙ В ФИНАНСОВЫХ ОПЕРАЦИЯХ КОМПАНИИ В ТЕЧЕНИИ ЦЕЛОГО ДЕЛОВОГО ЦИКЛА (ГОДА)

nondeductibility of employer contributions
(CHIN) 不可扣除性雇主贡献额
(FRE) indéductabilité des cotisations de l'employeur, (C) non-déductibilité des cotisations salariales
(GER) Nichtabzugsfähigkeit *f* von Arbeitgeberbeiträgen *mpl*
(JAP) 控除不可能雇用者分担金
（企業拠出金）、
非控除雇用者分担金
(RUS) НЕВОЗМОЖНОСТЬ СПИСАНИЯ ВЗНОСОВ РАБОТОДАТЕЛЯ

nondiscretionary trust
(CHIN) 非自主信托
(FRE) fiducie non discrétionnaire, (C) fiducie sans pouvoirs discrétionnaires
(GER) Treuhandverwaltung *f* mit strengen Anlagevorschriften *fpl*, (Investmentfonds mit nur teilweise emittierten Anteilen und dessen Wertpapierbestand nicht verändert werden darf)
(JAP) 限定信託
(RUS) ТРАСТ, КОТОРЫЙ МОЖЕТ ПРИОБРЕТАТЬ ТОЛЬКО ЗАРАНЕЕ ОГОВОРЕННЫЕ ЦЕННЫЕ БУМАГИ

nondisturbance clause
(CHIN) 非变动条款
(FRE) garantie de jouissance paisible,
(C) clause de non-perturbation
(GER) Nichtbeeinträchtigungsklausel *f*
(JAP) 権利不侵害条項
(RUS) ОГОВОРКА О НЕВМЕШАТЕЛЬСТВЕ, О ПРОДОЛЖЕНИИ ДЕЯТЕЛЬНОСТИ

nondurable goods
(CHIN) 非耐用品
(FRE) produits périssables, (C) biens non durables
(GER) (kurzlebige) Verbrauchs- *npl* bzw. Konsumgüter *npl*
(JAP) 非耐久財、非耐久消費財

(RUS) ТОВАРЫ НЕДЛИТЕЛЬНОГО ПОЛЬЗОВАНИЯ

nonformatted
(CHIN) 非格式化的
(FRE) non formatté, (C) non structuré
(GER) formatfrei, unformatiert *adj*
(JAP) 書式化されていない
(RUS) НЕФОРМАТИРОВАННЫЙ

nonglare
(CHIN) 不闪光的
(FRE) non éblouissant
blendfrei *adj*
(JAP) ノングレア、反射防止
(RUS) АНТИБЛИКОВЫЙ

nonmember bank
(CHIN) 非会员银行
(FRE) banque non membre de la chambre de compensation, (C) banque hors de la chambre de compensation
(GER) Nichtmitgliedsbank *f* (des US-Federal Reserve Systems), nicht dem US-Zentralbanksystem *n* angeschlossene Bank *f*
(JAP) 非加盟銀行、組合外銀行、
ノンメンバーバンク
(RUS) БАНК, НЕ ЯВЛЯЮЩИЙСЯ ЧЛЕНОМ ФЕДЕРАЛЬНОЙ РЕЗЕРВНОЙ СИСТЕМЫ США

nonmember firm
(CHIN) 非会员公司
(FRE) entreprise non membre,
(C) forme sous-participante
(GER) Nichtbörsenmitgliedsunternehmen*n*
(JAP) 非会員会社、組合外商会
(RUS) БРОКЕРСКАЯ ФИРМА, НЕ ЯВЛЯЮЩАЯСЯ ЧЛЕНОМ БИРЖИ

nonmonetary item
(CHIN) 非货币性项目
(FRE) élément non monétaire
(GER) Sachgut *n*
(JAP) 非貨幣項目
(RUS) НЕ ДЕНЕЖНАЯ СТАТЬЯ

nonnegotiable instrument
(CHIN) 不可转让票据

(FRE) instrument non négociable, (C) titre
non négociable
(GER) nicht übertragbares Papier *n*
(JAP) 譲渡不能証券
(RUS) НЕ ОБРАЩАЮЩИЙСЯ КРЕДИТНО-
ФИНАНСОВЫЙ ИНСТРУМЕНТ

nonoperating expense (revenue)

(CHIN) 非营业费用（收入）

(FRE) charges diverses [produit divers],
(C) charges diverses (revenus divers)
(GER) betriebsfremde Aufwendungen *fpl*
(Einkünfte *fpl*)
(JAP) 営業外費用（収益）
(RUS) НЕЭКСПЛУАТАЦИОННЫЙ РАСХОД
(ДОХОД)

nonparametric statistics

(CHIN) 非参数统计

(FRE) statistiques non paramétriques
(GER) parameterfreie Statistik *f*
(JAP) ノンパラメトリック統計
(RUS) НЕПАРАМЕТРИЧЕСКАЯ
СТАТИСТИКА

nonperformance

(CHIN) 不履行，不清偿

(FRE) défaut d'exéction, (C) non-
exécution
(GER) Nichterfüllung *f*, -leistung *f*,
Unterlassung *f*
(JAP) 不履行
(RUS) НЕВЫПОЛНЕНИЕ

nonproductive

(CHIN) 非生产性的

(FRE) improductif, (C) non
productif
(GER) nicht-produktiv *adj*
(JAP) 非生産的
(RUS) НЕПРОДУКТИВНЫЙ

nonproductive loan

(CHIN) 非生产性贷款

(FRE) emprunt non productif, (C) prêt-
problème
(GER) nicht-produktives Darlehen *n*
(JAP) 非生産的融資
(RUS) НЕПРОИЗВОДИТЕЛЬНЫЙ
КРЕДИТ

nonprofit accounting

(CHIN) 非营利会计

(FRE) comptabilité des organismes à but
non lucratif, (C) comptabilité à but non
lucratif
(GER) nicht-gewinnorientierte
Buchführung *f*
(JAP) 非営利会計
(RUS) СИСТЕМА УЧЕТА
НЕКОММЕРЧЕСКИХ
ОРГАНИЗАЦИЙ

nonprofit corporation

(CHIN) 非营利性公司

(FRE) association à but non lucratif,
(C) société à but non lucratif
(GER) gemeinnütziges Unternehmen *n*
(JAP) 非営利会社、非営利企業
(RUS) НЕКОММЕРЧЕСКАЯ КОРПОРАЦИЯ,

nonpublic information

(CHIN) 不公开资料

(FRE) informations non publiques,
(C) resnseignements confidentiels
(GER) nicht öffentlich zugängliche
Information *f*; nicht für die Öffentlichkeit *f*
bestimmte Informationen *fpl*
(JAP) 非公開情報
(RUS) ВНУТРЕННЯЯ ИНФОРМАЦИЯ

nonrecourse

(CHIN) 无追索权

(FRE) sans recours à forfait, (C) sans
recours
(GER) regresslos *adj*
(JAP) ノンリコース、
第二次的請求権放棄の
(RUS) БЕЗ ПРАВА ОБОРОТА, РЕГРЕССА

nonrecurring charge

(CHIN) 临时性费用

(FRE) frais extraordinaire,
(C) frais non périodiques
(GER) einmalige Gebühr *f*;
außerordentlicher Aufwand *m*
(JAP) 臨時経費
(RUS) ЕДИНИЧНЫЙ СБОР

nonrefundable

(CHIN) 不退款的

(FRE) non-remboursable, perdu
(GER) nicht zurückzahlbar, nicht erstattungsfähig *adj*
(JAP) 返金不可の、払戻し不能の
(RUS) ОГРАНИЧЕНИЕ ПРАВА ЭМИТЕНТА ОБЛИГАЦИЙ ПОГАШАТЬ ЗАЕМ ЗА СЧЕТ НОВОГО ЗАЙМА

nonrefundable fee or nonrefundable deposit
(CHIN) 不退还的收费或不退还的定金
(FRE) acompte non remboursable, dépôt non remboursable, (C) frais non remboursables
(GER) nicht erstattungsfähige Gebühr *f* (oder Einlage *f*)
(JAP) 払戻し不能手数料、
払戻し不能予約金
(RUS) НЕ ВОЗВРАЩАЕМАЯ ОПЛАТА или НЕ ВОЗВРАЩАЕМЫЙ ПЕРВЫЙ ВЗНОС

nonrenewable natural resources
(CHIN) 不能再生的能源
(FRE) ressources non renouvelables, (C) ressources naturelles non renouvelables
(GER) nicht erneuerbare natürliche Ressourcen *fpl*, nicht erneuerbare Rohstoffe *mpl*
(JAP) 再生不能の天然資源
(RUS) НЕВОЗОБНОВЛЯЕМЫЕ ПРИРОДНЫЕ РЕСУРСЫ

nonstock corporation
(CHIN) 非股份公司
(FRE) société civile, société de droit civil, (C) société sans actions
(GER) rechtsfähiger Verein *m*, gemeinnützige Institution *f*
(JAP) 非株式法人
(RUS) КОМПАНИЯ БЕЗ АКЦИОНЕРНОГО КАПИТАЛА

nonstore retailing
(CHIN) 无商品销售
(FRE) vente hors magasin, (C) vente au détail hors boutique
(GER) Einzelhandelsaktivität *f* ohne Laden *m*
(JAP) 無店舗販売
(RUS) РОЗНИЧНАЯ ТОРГОВЛЯ НЕ ЧЕРЕЗ МАГАЗИН

nonvoting stock
(CHIN) 无投票选举权的股票
(FRE) sans droit de vote, (C) action sans droit de vote
(GER) stimmrechtslose Aktie *f*
(JAP) 無議決権株
(RUS) АКЦИИ БЕЗ ПРАВА ГОЛОСА

no-par stock
(CHIN) 无面额股票
(FRE) action sans valeur nominale
(GER) nennwertlose Aktie *f*, Quotenaktie *f*
(JAP) 無額面株、額面未詳株
(RUS) АКЦИИ БЕЗ ФИКСИРОВАННОГО НОМИНАЛА

norm
(CHIN) 定额，标准，典型
(FRE) norme
(GER) Norm *f*, Standard *m*, Maßstab *m*
(JAP) 標準、ノルマ、責任生産量
(RUS) НОРМА; СТАНДАРТ

normal price
(CHIN) 正常价格，标准价格
(FRE) prix normal
(GER) Normal- *m*, Gleichgewichtspreis *m*
(JAP) 正常価格、平準価格
(RUS) НОРМАЛЬНАЯ ЦЕНА

normal profit
(CHIN) 正常利润
(FRE) benefice normal
(GER) Normalgewinn *m*, -profit *m*
(JAP) 正常利潤、正常利益
(RUS) НОРМАЛЬНАЯ ПРИБЫЛЬ

normal retirement age
(CHIN) 正常退休年龄
(FRE) âge normal de départ à la retraite, (C) âge de la retraite normale
(GER) normales Rentenalter *n*
(JAP) 通常退職年齢
(RUS) НОРМАЛЬНЫЙ ПЕНСИОННЫЙ ВОЗРАСТ

normal wear and tear
(CHIN) 正常损耗
(FRE) usure normale

(GER) normale Abnutzung *f*, normaler Verschleiß *m*

(JAP) 正常損耗、通常の摩滅

(RUS) НОРМАЛЬНЫЙ ИЗНОС

normative economics

(CHIN) 规范经济学

(FRE) économie normative

(GER) normative Volkswirtschaftslehre *f*, normative Wirtschaftswissenschaften *f*

(JAP) 規範的経済学

(RUS) НОРМАТИВНАЯ ЭКОНОМИКА

no-strike clause

(CHIN) 不罢工条款

(FRE) clause de paix sociale, obligation de paix sociale, (C) clause d'interdiction de grève

(GER) Streikverbotsklausel *f*

(JAP) 非ストライキ条項、非同盟罷業条項

(RUS) ОГОВОРКА ОБ ОТКАЗЕ ОТ ЗАБАСТОВОК

notarize

(CHIN) 公证

(FRE) certifier, authentifier, (C) notarier

(GER) notariell beglaubigen, notariell beurkunden, notariell bestätigen *v*

(JAP) <証書・契約などを> (公証人を通して)公証する、証明させる

(RUS) ЗАВЕРИТЬ НОТАРИАЛЬНО

note

(CHIN) 纸币，票据，借据，注释，照会

(FRE) billet, (C) obligation

(GER) Mitteilung *f*; Aufzeichnung *f*, Notiz *f*; Nachricht *f*; Vermerk *m*; Anmerkung *f*, Fußnote *f*; Geldschein *m*, Banknote *f*; Anleihe *f*, Schuldverschreibung *f*; Solawechsel *m*

(JAP) 覚書、ノート、手形

(RUS) ПРИМЕЧАНИЕ; ИЗВЕЩЕНИЕ; УВЕДОМЛЕНИЕ; БАНКНОТА; КРАТКОСРОЧНАЯ ЦЕННАЯ БУМАГА

notebook computer

(CHIN) 笔记本式计算机

(FRE) notebook, (C) ordinateur bloc-notes

(GER) Notebook-Computer *m*

(JAP) ノート（型）パソコン、ノートブックサイズの携帯コンピューター

(RUS) НОУТБУК

note payable

(CHIN) 应付票据

(FRE) effet à payer, (C) billet à payer

(GER) Schuldwechsel *m*, Wechselverbindlichkeit *f*; Schuldscheinverbindlichtkeit *f*

(JAP) 支払手形

(RUS) ВЕКСЕЛЬ К ОПЛАТЕ

note receivable

(CHIN) 应收票据

(FRE) effet à recevoir

(GER) ausstehender Schuldschein *m*, Wechselforderung *f*, Besitzwechsel *m*; Schuldscheinforderung *f*

(JAP) 受取手形

(RUS) ВЕКСЕЛЬ К ПОЛУЧЕНИЮ

not for profit

(CHIN) 非营利

(FRE) à but non lucratif, (C) sans but lucratif

(GER) gemeinnützig *adj*

(JAP) 非営利、非営利の

(RUS) НЕ ДЛЯ ПОЛУЧЕНИЯ ПРИБЫЛИ

notice

(CHIN) 通知书，布告，注意

(FRE) avis, notification

(GER) Ankündigung *f*, Bekanntmachung *f*, Erklärung *f*; Bescheid *m*; Kündigung *f*; Information *f*; Aufmerksamkeit *f*; Warnung *f*

(JAP) 通知、通告、通知書

(RUS) УВЕДОМЛЕНИЕ; ИЗВЕЩЕНИЕ

notice of cancellation clause

(CHIN) 撤销通知条款

(FRE) clause d'avis de résiliation

(GER) Vertragskündigungsklausel *f*

(JAP) 解約予告条項、解約通知条項

(RUS) ОГОВОРКА ОБ ОБЯЗАТЕЛЬНОСТИ УВЕДОМЛЕНИЯ ОБ ОТМЕНЕ, ПРЕКРАЩЕНИИ

notice of default

(CHIN) 违约通知

(FRE) avis de défaut

(GER) Inzugversetzung *f*, Anzeige *f* der Nichterfüllung *f*

(JAP) 債務不履行通知

(RUS) УВЕДОМЛЕНИЕ О НАРУШЕНИИ

notice to quit

(CHIN) 解雇通知

(FRE) avis de congé

(GER) (Dienst- *f* bzw.Miet)kündigung *f*, Aufkündigung *f*

(JAP) 解約予告、辞職勧告

(RUS) ЗАЯВЛЕНИЕ ОБ УВОЛЬНЕНИИ

not rated (NR)

(CHIN) 未评级 （NR）

(FRE) fonds qui n'est pas noté, (C) non coté

(GER) ohne Rating *n*, ohne Klassifizierung *f*, ohne Bewertung *f*

(JAP) 見積もられなかった、
評価されなかった、
課税評価されていない

(RUS) БЕЗ РЕЙТИНГА

novation

(CHIN) 更新，代替

(FRE) novation

(GER) Novation *f*, Umschuldung *f*, Schuldumwandlung *f*,

(JAP) (債務・契約などの)更改、更新、刷新、革新

(RUS) НОВАЦИЯ;
НОВОВВЕДЕНИЕ

NSF (not sufficient funds)

(CHIN) 存款不足

(FRE) insuffisance de fonds en depot, (C) sans provision

(GER) ohne ausreichende Deckung *f*, kein ausreichendes Guthaben *n*

(JAP) 資金不足、残高不足

(RUS) НЕОБЕСПЕЧЕННЫЙ ЧЕК

nuisance

(CHIN) 小额，低税

(FRE) impôt vexatoire, (C) nuisance

(GER) Belästigung *f*, Ärgernis *n*, Störung *f*

(JAP) 迷惑な人・物・こと・行為など、生活妨害

(RUS) НЕУДОБСТВО, ПОМЕХА

null and void

(CHIN) 无效，作废

(FRE) nul et non avenu

(GER) nichtig, rechtsunwirksam, kraftlos, ungültig *adj*

(JAP) (法律上)無効の

(RUS) НЕ ИМЕЮЩИЙ ЮРИДИЧЕСКОЙ СИЛЫ; НЕДЕЙСТВИТЕЛЬНЫЙ

num lock key

(CHIN) 数字锁定键

(FRE) touche verr. maj., (C) touche verrouillage numérique

(GER) Num-Taste *f*, Zahlensperrtaste *f* (Tastatur)

(JAP) 数値ロックキー

(RUS) КЛАВИША "ЦИФР"; КЛАВИША ПЕРЕКЛЮЧЕНИЯ И ФИКСАЦИИ РЕГИСТРА ВСПОМОГАТЕЛЬНОЙ КЛАВИАТУРЫ

O

objective
(CHIN) 目标，客观的
(FRE) objectif
(GER) Ziel *n*, Zielvorstellung *f*, Zweck *m*
(JAP) 目的、客観的な、目的の
(RUS) ЦЕЛЬ, ЗАДАЧ; ОБЪЕКТИВНЫЙ

objective value
(CHIN) 客观价值
(FRE) valeur objective, (C) valeur d'échange
(GER) objektiver Wert *m*
(JAP) 客観的価値、客観価値説
(RUS) ОБЪЕКТИВНАЯ ЦЕННОСТЬ

obligation bond
(CHIN) 责任债券
(FRE) obligation
(GER) Anleiheschuld *f*
(JAP) 公債、社債
(RUS) ТИП ИПОТЕЧНОЙ ОБЛИГАЦИИ, У КОТОРОЙ НОМИНАЛЬНАЯ СТОИМОСТЬ ПРЕВЫШАЕТ СТОИМОСТЬ ЗАЛОЖЕННОЙ НЕДВИЖИМОСТИ

obligee
(CHIN) 权利人，债权人
(FRE) obligataire, (C) obligé
(GER) Gläubiger *m*, Forderungsberechtigter *m*, Bürgschaftsbegünstigter *m*
(JAP) 債権者
(RUS) лицо, по отношению к которому имеются обязательства

obligor
(CHIN) 义务人，债务人
(FRE) caution, débiteur, (C) obligeant
(GER) Schuldner *m*, Verpflichteter *m*
(JAP) 債務者
(RUS) лицо, принявшее на себя обязательство

observation test
(CHIN) 观察测验
(FRE) essai d'observation, (C) exercice d'observation
(GER) Beobachtungstest *m*

(JAP) 立会検査
(RUS) ПРОВЕРКА НАБЛЮДЕНИЕМ

obsolescence
(CHIN) 废弃
(FRE) obsolescence
(GER) technisches Veralten *n*, technisch-wirtschaftliche Überalterung *f*
(JAP) 老朽、衰微、旧式化
(RUS) УСТАРЕВАНИЕ, МОРАЛЬНЫЙ ИЗНОС

occupancy level
(CHIN) 租出率
(FRE) niveau d'occupation
(GER) Auslastungs- *f*, Belegungsrate *f*, Belegungsgrad *m*
(JAP) 居住・財産占有・（所有物の）利用の程度・度合
(RUS) УРОВЕНЬ ЗАНЯТОСТИ (например, в гостинице); АРЕНДЫ (жилья)

occupancy, occupant
(CHIN) 占有，居住
(FRE) occupation, occupant
(GER) Belegung *f*, Inanspruchnahme *f*; Besitz *m*; Aneignung *f*; Inhaber *m*, Besitzer *m*; Nutzer *m*, Bewohner *m*, Insasse *m*
(JAP) 財産占有、使用；占有者、現住者
(RUS) ВЛАДЕНИЕ; ПРОЖИВАНИЕ; ЖИЛЕЦ; СЪЕМЩИК

occupation
(CHIN) 占用，职业，开业
(FRE) métier, emploi, (C) poste
(GER) Tätigkeit *f*, Beruf *m*, Beschäftigung *f*, Berufs- *f*, Erwerbstätigkeit *f*; Besetzung *f*
(JAP) 業務、仕事、職業
(RUS) РОД ЗАНЯТИЙ; ПРОФЕССИЯ

occupational analysis
(CHIN) 职业分析
(FRE) analyse de profession, (C) analyse d'un poste
(GER) Arbeitsplatzanalyse *f*
(JAP) 職業分析

286

occupational disease
(CHIN) 职业病
(FRE) maladie professionelle
(GER) Berufskrankheit *f*
(JAP) 職業的疾病、職業病、
業務上の疾病
(RUS) ПРОФЕССИОНАЛЬНОЕ
ЗАБОЛЕВАНИЕ

occupational group
(CHIN) 职业类别
(FRE) groupe professionnel, (C) catégorie socioprofessionnelle
(GER) Berufsgruppe *f*
(JAP) 職業集団
(RUS) ПРОФЕССИОНАЛЬНАЯ
ГРУППА

occupational hazard
(CHIN) 职业危险
(FRE) risque du métier, (C) risque professionnel
(GER) Berufsrisiko *n*, Risiko *n* am Arbeitsplatz *m*
(JAP) 職業上の危険
(RUS) ПРОФЕССИОНАЛЬНАЯ
ОПАСНОСТЬ

odd lot
(CHIN) 零星股票，零星交易
(FRE) lot dépareillé, (C) lot de taille anormale
(GER) Bruchschluss *m*, Paket *n* von weniger als 100 Aktien *fpl* (Börse); ungerade Menge *f*, weniger als die handelsübliche Menge *f*, Restpartie *f*, -posten *m*
(JAP) 半端もの、端数、端株
(RUS) БИРЖЕВАЯ СДЕЛКА С БЛОКОМ ЦЕННЫХ БУМАГ МЕНЕЕ 100 ШТУК

odd page
(CHIN) 奇数页
(FRE) page impaire, (C) belle page
(GER) ungerade Seite *f*
(JAP) 奇数ページ
(RUS) НЕЧЁТНАЯ СТРАНИЦА

odd-value pricing
(CHIN) 临时计价，奇零定价法
(FRE) prix magique, (C) fixation d'un prix non arrondi
(GER) Preisauszeichnung *f* mit ungeraden Zahlen *fpl*, Auszeichnung *f* mit einem gebrochenen Preis *m*
(JAP) 端数価格設定
(RUS) УСТАНОВЛЕНИЕ ЦЕН НА 1 ЦЕНТ НИЖЕ КРУГЛОЙ ЦЕНЫ (НАПР. 1.99)

offer
(CHIN) 发盘，出价，报价，提供，给予，要约
(FRE) offre
(GER) Angebot *n*, Offerte *f*; Briefkurs *m* (Börse)
(JAP) 申し出る、売りに出す、売買の申込み
(RUS) ПРЕДЛОЖЕНИЕ

offer and acceptance
(CHIN) 报盘及接受
(FRE) offre et acceptation
(GER) Angebot *n* und Annahme *f*
(JAP) 申し込みと引受け
(RUS) ПРЕДЛОЖЕНИЕ И ЕГО ПРИНЯТИЕ

offeree
(CHIN) 接盘人，受盘人
(FRE) destinataire de l'offre, (C) société visée
(GER) Angebotsadressat *m*, Empfänger *m* eines Angebots *n*
(JAP) 申込みの相手方、被申込人
(RUS) ЛИЦО, КОТОРОМУ ДЕЛАЕТСЯ ПРЕДЛОЖЕНИЕ

offerer
(CHIN) 发盘人，报价人
(FRE) personne qui fait une offre, (C) société offrante
(GER) Anbieter *m*, Offerent *m*, Angebotssteller *m*
(JAP) 申込者
(RUS) ЛИЦО, ДЕЛАЮЩЕЕ ПРЕДЛОЖЕНИЕ

offering date
(CHIN) 报价日期

(FRE) date de mise sur le marché, (C) date de l'offre
(GER) Emissions- *n*, Zeichnungs- *n*, Ausgabedatum *n*
(JAP) 申込期日
(RUS) ДАТА НАЧАЛА ПУБЛИЧНОЙ ПРОДАЖИ НОВЫХ АКЦИЙ

offering price
(CHIN) 报出价格
(FRE) prix d'offre, (C) cours vendeur
(GER) Emissions- *m*, Zeichnungskurs *m*; Angebots- *m*, Submissions preis *m*
(JAP) 申込価格
(RUS) НАЧАЛЬНАЯ ЦЕНА ПУБЛИЧНОЙ ПРОДАЖИ НОВЫХ АКЦИЙ

office management
(CHIN) 办公室管理
(FRE) organisation des bureaux, (C) gestion de bureau
(GER) Büroverwaltung *f*, -leitung *f*
(JAP) 事務管理
(RUS) РУКОВОДСТВО ДЕЛОВОЙ КОНТОРОЙ

official exchange rate
(CHIN) 法定汇率，官方汇率
(FRE) cours officiel, (C) taux de change officiel
(GER) amtlicher bzw. offizieller Wechselkurs *m*
(JAP) 公定為替相場、公定交換比率
(RUS) ОФИЦИАЛЬНЫЙ ВАЛЮТНЫЙ КУРС

off-line
(CHIN) 脱机
(FRE) hors ligne
(GER) nicht angeschlossen, offline *adj*
(JAP) オフライン、非直結
(RUS) АВТОНОМНЫЙ, НЕПОДКЛЮЧЁННЫЙ

off peak
(CHIN) 非高峰
(FRE) pendant les heures creuses, (C) période creuse
(GER) außerhalb der Hauptsaison *f* bzw. Hauptverkehrszeit *f*, außerhalb der Stoßzeit *f* bzw. Spitzenbelastungszeit *f*

(JAP) オフピーク、混雑していない時間帯
(RUS) ВНЕПИКОВЫЙ

off-price
(CHIN) 低价
(FRE) à prix réduits, (C) prix inférieur au marché
(GER) zum Preis *m* unter dem der Konkurrenz *f*, zum Ausverkaufspreis *m*, Off-Price *m*
(JAP) 割引販売の、安売りの
(RUS) УЦЕНКА

off-sale date
(CHIN) 从货架撤下日期
(FRE) date de retrait de la vente, (C) date de compilation des revenus du kiosque à journaux
(GER) Verkaufsende *n* (Datum, an dem der Verkauf endet)
(JAP) 売残品引き取り日
(RUS) ДАТА ОТЧЁТА ГАЗЕТНОГО КИОСКА СВОЕМУ РАСПРОСТРАНИТЕЛЮ

offset
(CHIN) 抵消，冲销，对冲，补偿，平仓
(FRE) compensation, dédommagement, (C) annuler
(GER) Aufrechnung *f*, Gegenposten *m*, Verrechnung *f*, Kompensierung *f*, anrechnen *v*; aufrechnen, in Gegenrechnung *f* bringen *v*; ausgleichen, aufwiegen *v*
(JAP) 差引勘定の等しいもの、埋め合わせ、釣り合う
(RUS) ЗАЧЕТ; КОМПЕНСАЦИЯ

offshore
(CHIN) 近岸，境外
(FRE) offshore, (C) extraterritorial
(GER) offshore *adj*, (z.B. Bankgeschäfte außerhalb der nationalen Grenzen bzw. der Währungsgesetzgebung eines Landes)
(JAP) 海外の、沖合で、国外での
(RUS) ОФФШОРНЫЙ

off-site cost
(CHIN) 间接成本，间接费用
(FRE) coût externe

(GER) Kosten *pl* außerhalb der Baustelle *f*
bzw. des Standortes *m*
(JAP) オフサイトコスト、
敷地外での価格
(RUS) ИЗДЕРЖКИ, ПОНЕСЁННЫЕ ВНЕ
СТРОИТЕЛЬНОЙ ПЛОЩАДКИ, НО
СВЯЗАННЫЕ СО СТРОИТЕЛЬСТВОМ

off the balance sheet
(CHIN) 未在资产负债表中列出的交易
(FRE) hors bilan, (C) non compris dans le
bilan
(GER) außerhalb der Bilanzaufstellung *f*
liegend, bilanzunwirksam, ohne Belastung *f*
der Bilanzstruktur *f adj*
(JAP) 貸借対照表外の
(RUS) ВНЕБАЛАНСОВЫЙ;
ЗАБАЛАНСОВЫЙ

off the books
(CHIN) 账外
(FRE) transparent, au noir, (C) non inscrit
dans ls livres
(GER) inoffiziell, formlos *adj*
(JAP) 記録から消されて、
（法律などが）廃止されて、
除名されて
(RUS) НЕ ПРОВОДИМЫЙ ПО
БУХГАЛТЕРСКИМ КНИГАМ

off time
(CHIN) 非服务时间，时间外
(FRE) période de repos, période
d'immobilisation, (C) temps d'arrêt
(GER) außerhalb der Arbeits- *f*, Betriebszeit
f; Sperrzeit *f*
(JAP) 暇な時間、閑散時、不景気な時
(RUS) НЕРАБОЧЕЕ ВРЕМЯ

oil and gas lease
(CHIN) 油气租赁
(FRE) location à bail de terres pour le
forage de pétrole et de gaz, (C) droit
pétrolier
(GER) Vertrag *m* über Öl- und
Gasbohrrechte *npl*
(JAP) オイルガスリース、石油・ガスを
採掘する権利を与える借地契約
(RUS) АРЕНДА НЕФТЕГАЗОВОГО
МЕСТОРОЖДЕНИЯ

oligopoly
(CHIN) 卖主寡头垄断
(FRE) oligopole
(GER) Oligopol *n*
(JAP) 少数独占、寡占
(RUS) ОЛИГОПОЛИЯ

ombudsman
(CHIN) 巡查官，
机构内负责听取意见的人
(FRE) médiateur de la république,
(C) protecteur du citoyen
(GER) Ombudsmann *m*, Beschwerdestelle *f*,
Vertrauensperson *f*
(JAP) オンブズマン
(RUS) УПОЛНОМОЧЕННЫЙ ПО РАБОТЕ С
ЖАЛОБАМИ (на банки, госучреждения)

omitted dividend
(CHIN) 略去的分红
(FRE) dividende omis
(GER) ausgefallene Dividende *f*
(JAP) 無配
(RUS) ПРОПУЩЕННЫЙ
(НЕВЫПЛАЧЕННЫЙ) ДИВИДЕНД

on account
(CHIN) 赊账，记账
(FRE) à credit, à valoir sur
(GER) gegen Kredit *m*, auf Rechnung *f*
(JAP) 掛売り、内払い、信用で
(RUS) ЧАСТИЧНЫЙ ПЛАТЕЖ В СЧЕТ
ПОГАШЕНИЯ

onboard computer
(CHIN) 机载计算机
(FRE) ordinateur embarqué,
(C) ordinateur de bord
(GER) Bordrechner *m*
(JAP) 搭載コンピューター
(RUS) БОРТОВОЙ КОМПЬЮТЕР

on demand
(CHIN) 即期，见票即付
(FRE) sur demande, requis, sollicité
(GER) auf Verlangen *n*, auf Wunsch *m*; bei
Vorlage *f*, bei Vorzeigen *n*, bei Sicht *f*
(JAP) 要求払いで、一覧払いで、
参着払いで、
(RUS) ПО ТРЕБОВАНИЮ

one-cent sale

(CHIN) 名义出售，白送

(FRE) vente à un cent, (C) vente de débarras

(GER) One-Cent-Verkauf, (Verkauf von zwei Produkten zum Preis von einem plus einem Cent)

(JAP) １銭セール

(RUS) СИМВОЛИЧЕСКАЯ ПРОДАЖА (ЗА 1 ЦЕНТ)

one-hundred-percent location

(CHIN) 销售额最高的店面

(FRE) emplacement à cent pour cent, (C) emplacement optimal

(GER) hundertprozentiger Standort *m*

(JAP) 百分率所在地

(RUS) МЕСТО, ГДЕ ТОРГОВОЕ ПРЕДПРИЯТИЕ МОЖЕТ ДОСТИГНУТЬ НАИВЫСШЕЙ ЭФФЕКТИВНОСТИ

one-minute manager

(CHIN) 过分简单化的经理

(FRE) le manager minute, (C) comment gérer en une minute

(GER) One-Minute-Manager *m*

(JAP)「ワン・ミニット・マネージャー」（本のタイトル）

(RUS) НАЗВАНИЕ ПОПУЛЯРНОЙ КНИГИ К, БЛАНШАРДА И С. ДЖОНСОНА; УПРОЩЕНИЕ СЛОЖНЫХ УПРАВЛЕНЧЕСКИХ СИТУАЦИЙ

one-time buyer

(CHIN) 一次性购买者

(FRE) acheteur d'un jour

(GER) Einmalkäufer *m*, einmaliger Käufer *m*

(JAP) 単発購入者

(RUS) РАЗОВЫЙ ПОКУПАТЕЛЬ

one-time rate

(CHIN) 一次性费率

(FRE) prix de base

(GER) Einmaltarif *m*

(JAP) 単発料金

(RUS) РАЗОВАЯ СТАВКА

on-line

(CHIN) 线上，在线，联机

(FRE) en ligne

(GER) angeschlossen, online *adj*

(JAP) オンライン、直結

(RUS) ПОДКЛЮЧЁННЫЙ; ИНТЕРАКТИВНЫЙ, ДИАЛОГОВЫЙ

on-line data base

(CHIN) 在线数据库

(FRE) base de données en ligne,(C) banque de données en ligne

(GER) Online-Datenbank *f*

(JAP) オンラインデータベース

(RUS) ИНТЕРАКТИВНАЯ БАЗА ДАННЫХ

on order

(CHIN) 已订货物，在订购中

(FRE) en cours de commande, commandé

(GER) in Bestellung *f*, bestellt; in Auftrag *m* gegeben

(JAP) (品物が)発注済みの、注文中の

(RUS) ЗАКАЗАННЫЙ, НО ЕЩЁ НЕ ПОЛУЧЕННЫЙ ТОВАР

on-sale date

(CHIN) 上市日

(FRE) date de parution

(GER) Verkaufsbeginn *m*, (Datum, an dem der Verkauf beginnt)

(JAP) 販売日

(RUS) ДАТУ ДОСТАВКИ НОВЫХ ПЕЧАТНЫХ ИЗДАНИЙ В ГАЗЕТНЫЙ КИОСК

on speculation (on spec)

(CHIN) 投机活动（ON SPEC）

(FRE) non commandé, (C) spéculatif

(GER) spekulationsweise *adj*

(JAP) 投機で

(RUS) РАБОТА, ВЫПОЛНЕННАЯ БЕЗ ЗАКАЗА И КОТОРАЯ БУДЕТ ОПЛАЧЕНА ТОЛЬКО ЕСЛИ КЛИЕНТ ЕЙ ВОСПОЛЬЗУЕТСЯ

on-the-job training (OJT)

(CHIN) 在职培训（OJT）

(FRE) formation sur le tas, (C) formation sur le tas

(GER) Ausbildung *f* am Arbeitsplatz *m*, innerbetriebliche Ausbildung *f*

(JAP) 職場内教育、職場内訓練、職場訓練

(RUS) ОБУЧЕНИЕ БЕЗ ОТРЫВА ОТ
ПРОИЗВОДСТВА

open
(CHIN) 未结清的，自由开放的，公开的，
开信用证
(FRE) ouvert
(GER) offen, geöffnet; eröffnet; frei;
ungelöst, ungeklärt; aufrichtig,
aufgeschlossen, zugänglich *adj*
(JAP) 開いた、開放した、公開の、
未定の
(RUS) ОТКРЫВАТЬ; ОТКРЫТЫЙ

open account
(CHIN) 未清账户，
往来账户
(FRE) compte ouvert, compte courant
(GER) offene Rechnung *f*; Kontokorrent *n*;
offenes Konto *n*
(JAP) オープン勘定、掛売買勘定、
掛売買取引、未決算勘定
(RUS) ОТКРЫТЫЙ СЧЕТ

open bid
(CHIN) 公开招标
(FRE) adjudication ouverte, (C) soumission
ouverte
(GER) offenes Angebot *n*
(JAP) 公開入札
(RUS) ТЕНДЕРНАЯ ЗАЯВКА С ОТКРЫТОЙ
К ПОНИЖЕНИЮ ЦЕНОЙ ПРОЕКТА

open dating
(CHIN) 注明期限
(FRE) date d'ouverture, (C) date
d'expiration
(GER) offene Volkswirtschaft *f*
(JAP) 日付表示制度、（食品の）鮮度保
証期限の表示
(RUS) УКАЗАНИЕ СРОКА ХРАНЕНИЯ НА
ПРОДУКТАХ ПИТАНИЯ

open distribution
(CHIN) 开发式分销
(FRE) distribution ouverte
(JAP) オープンディストリビューション
(RUS) ПРОДАЖА ОДИНАКОВОГО
ТОВАРА НА ОДНОЙ ТЕРРИТОРИИ
РАЗНЫМИ ПРОДАВЦАМИ

open-door policy
(CHIN) 门户开放政策
(FRE) politique de la porte ouverte
(GER) Politik *f* der offenen Tür *f*
(JAP) 門戸開放政策、自由貿易政策、
オープンドア方式
(RUS) ПОЛИТИКА ОТКРЫТЫХ ДВЕРЕЙ

open economy
(CHIN) 开放经济
(FRE) économie ouverte
(GER) offene Volkswirtschaft
(JAP) 開放経済
(RUS) ОТКРЫТАЯ ЭКОНОМИКА

open-end
(CHIN) 开放，开口，公开
(FRE) ouvert, (C) aléatoire, ouvert
(GER) mit offener Laufzeit *f*; unbegrenzt,
unbeschränkt, unbefristet, offen *adj*
(JAP) (担保、契約などが)開放式の、
資本額の可変的な、無期限の
(RUS) ОТКРЫТОГО ТИПА

open-end lease
(CHIN) 开口租赁
(FRE) bail ouvert, (C) crédit-bail aléatoire
(GER) Miet- *m* bzw. Pachtvertrag *m* mit
offener Laufzeit *f*; offenes Leasing *f*
(JAP) リース物件の交換自由なリース
(RUS) ОТКРЫТАЯ АРЕНДА , С
ДОПОЛНИТЕЛЬНОЙ ПОСЛЕДНЕЙ
ВЫПЛАТОЙ, ПОКРЫВАЮЩЕЙ
ВОЗМОЖНЫЙ УЩЕРБ, НАНЕСЁННЫЙ
СОБСТВЕННОСТИ

open-end management company
(CHIN) 开放式管理公司
(FRE) société de gestion ouverte
(GER) offenes Managementunternehmen *n*,
offene Verwaltungsgesellschaft *f*
(JAP) 開放型経営会社
(RUS) УПРАВЛЕНЧЕСКАЯ КОМПАНИЯ
ОТКРЫТОГО ТИПА

open-end mortgage
(CHIN) 开放抵押
(FRE) prêt hypothécaire à capital variable,
(C) prêt hypothécaire avec droit de
remboursement anticipé

(GER) nicht voll valutierte Hypothek f,
offene Hypothek f
(JAP) 開放型担保付き社債
(RUS) ОТКРЫТАЯ ИПОТЕКА , С
ВОЗМОЖНОСТЬЮ УВЕЛИЧЕНИЯ СУММЫ
ЗАЙМА

open house

(CHIN) 公开展示
(FRE) jour d'accueil, portes ouvertes,
(C) visite libre
(GER) Tag m der offenen Tür f
(JAP) 一般公開、工場公開、自宅開放、
(RUS) ДЕНЬ ОТКРЫТЫХ ДВЕРЕЙ

open housing

(CHIN) 开放房屋
(FRE) « open housing » (accès égalitaire au
logement), (C) complexe immobilier non
discriminatoire
(GER) Diskriminierungsverbot f bei
Vermietung f, Wohnungwahl f ohne
Diskrimierung f
(JAP) 公正住宅販売政策
(RUS) ВОЗМОЖНОСТЬ ПОКУПКИ ИЛИ
СНЯТИЯ В АРЕНДУ ЖИЛЬЯ ЛИЦАМИ
ЛЮБОЙ РАССЫ ИЛИ РЕЛИГИИ
БЕЗИСКРИМИНАЦИИ

opening

(CHIN) 开业，开盘，出售，开始，机会，
开放
(FRE) ouverture
(GER) offene Arbeitsstelle f; Eröffnung f,
Inbetriebnahme f; Beginn m der
Börsensitzung f
(JAP) 開く（あける）こと、始まり、
［証券］寄り付き
(RUS) (RUS) ЦЕНА ЦЕННЫХ
БУМАГ НА НАЧПЛО ДНЯ ТОРГОВ;
ПРЕДСТАВЛЯЮЩАЯСЯ
ВОЗМОЖНОСТЬ

open interest

(CHIN) 未结清权益，空盘量
(FRE) position ouverte
(GER) offene bzw. ungedeckte Positionen
fpl; offenes Interesse n
(JAP) オープンインタレスト、
（売り手側の／買手側の）
建玉

(RUS) ОБЩАЯ СУММА
НЕРЕАЛИЗОВАННЫХ КОНТРАКТОВ НА
БИРЖЕ

open listing

(CHIN) 公开地产代理权
(FRE) contrat de courtage immobilier non
exclusif
(GER) Maklervertrag m ohne
Alleinverkaufsrecht n, (Verkaufsauftrag an
mehrere Makler)
(JAP) 開放式委任契約
(RUS) ОТКРЫТАЯ КОТИРОВКА

open-market rates

(CHIN) 公开市场汇率
(FRE) bours du marché libre, (C) taux
déterminés par le marché
(GER) Offenmarktsätze mpl
(JAP) 市中金利
(RUS) ПРОЦЕНТНЫЕ СТАВКИ СВОБОДНО
ОБРАЩАЮЩИХСЯ НА РЫНКЕ ЦЕННЫХ
БУМАГ

open mortgage

(CHIN) 可加抵押
(FRE) prêt hypothécaire remboursable par
anticipation, (C) prêt hypothécaire ouvert
(GER) offene Hypothek f
(JAP) 総括抵当権
(RUS) ИПОТЕКА, СРОЧНАЯ К
ПОГАШЕНИЮ ИЛИ ПРОСРОЧЕННАЯ

open order

(CHIN) 开口定单，未完成定单
(FRE) ordre ouvert, ordre à révocation,
(C) ordre permanent
(GER) noch nicht ausgeführter bzw. noch
unerledigter Auftrag m
(JAP) 見計らい注文、市価注文、無条件
注文、保留注文
(RUS) НЕВЫПОЛНЕННЫЙ ПРИКАЗ К
ПОКУПКЕ ИЛИ ПРОДАЖЕ НА БИРЖЕ

open outcry

(CHIN) 公开喊价
(FRE) cotation à la criée
(GER) offener Zuruf m, (Ermittlung von
Kontraktpreisen auf dem Börsenparkett)
JAP) オープンアウトクライ方式、公開
セリ売買方式

(RUS) СВОБОДНЫЙ БИРЖЕВОЙ ТОРГ
(голосом, без аукционера)

open shop
(CHIN) 开放制工厂或商店
(FRE) entreprise ne pratiquant pas le
monopole d'embauche, (C) atelier ouvert
(GER) Beschäftigung *f* ohne Pflicht zu
Gewerkschaftszugehörigkeit *f*, nicht
gewerkschaftspflichtiger Betrieb *m*
(JAP) オープンショップ、労働組合への
加入が任意で、それが雇用の条件には
ならない事業所・
企業またはその労使間協定
(RUS) ПРЕДПРИЯТИЕ, НАНИМАЮЩЕЕ
КАК ЧЛЕНОВ, ТАК И НЕ ЧЛЕНОВ
ПРОФСОЮЗА

open space
(CHIN) 开放空间
(FRE) espace libre, (C) espace ouvert
(GER) unbebautes Gelände *n*, freie Fläche *f*
(JAP) オープンスペース、空地、広場
(RUS) ОТКРЫТОЕ ПРОСТРАНСТВО,
ОСТАВЛЕННОЕ НЕЗАСТРОЕННЫМ ДЛЯ
ОБЩЕГО ПОЛЬЗОВАНИЯ

open stock
(CHIN) 期初存款，期初存货
(FRE) stock disponible
(GER) ständig vorrätige Ware *f*
(JAP) バラ買いできる補充商品、
セット商品
(RUS) ОТКРЫТЫЙ К ПОКУПКЕ
ТОВАРНЫЙ ЗАПАС

open-to-buy
(CHIN) 可购限额，准购定额
(FRE) (méthode du) point de
réapprovisionnement, (C) droit aux achats
(GER) Einkaufsbudget *n* für bestimmten
Zeitraum *m*
(JAP) 購買余力、発注残高
(RUS) ОТКРЫТЫЙ МЕТОД ЗАКУПКИ
ТОВАРНЫХ ЗАПАСОВ РОЗНИЧНЫМ
ПРОДАВЦОМ

open union
(CHIN) 开放式工会
(FRE) syndicat ouvert, (C) sybdicat ouvert
(GER) Gewerkschaft *f* ohne

Mitgliedssperre *f*
(JAP) 公開組合
(RUS) ПРОФСОЮЗ БЕЗ ОГРАНИЧЕНИЯ
ЧЛЕНСТВА

operand
(CHIN) 操作数，基数
(FRE) opérande
(GER) Operand *m*, Rechengröße *f*;
Datenteil *n* (EDV)
(JAP) 演算数
(RUS) ОПЕРАНД

operating cycle
(CHIN) 营业周期，经营周期
(FRE) cycle d'exploitation
(GER) Betriebszyklus *m*, Geschäfts- *m*,
Betriebskreislauf *m*, Arbeitsperiode *f*;
Ablaufprogramm *n* (EDV)
(JAP) 営業周期
(RUS) РАБОЧИЙ, ОПЕРАЦИОННЫЙ ЦИКЛ

operating expense
(CHIN) 营业费用，使用费
(FRE) frais d'exploitation, (C) dépense
d'exploitation
(GER) betriebliche Aufwendungen *fpl*,
Betriebsausgaben *fpl*, -kosten *pl*
(JAP) 営業費用、作業費用、運転費用
(RUS) ЭКСПЛУАТАЦИОННЫЕ РАСХОДЫ

operating lease
(CHIN) 经营性租赁，营业租赁
(FRE) bail d'exploitation
(GER) Operate-Leasingvertrag *m*
(JAP) 営業リース
(RUS) ЭКСПЛУАТАЦИОННАЯ АРЕНДА
БЕЗ ОБСЛУЖИВАНИЯ ОБОРУДОВАНИЯ

operating loss
(CHIN) 营业亏损，经营亏损
(FRE) bail d'exploitation
(FRE) perte d'exploitation
(GER) Betriebsverlust *m*, operativer
Verlust *m*
(JAP) 営業損失、操業損失、業務損失

operating profit (loss)
(CHIN) 营业利润(损失)
(FRE) bénéfice d'exploitation (perte)

(GER) Betriebs- *m*, Geschäftsgewinn *m*,
(JAP) 営業利潤（損失）、操業利潤
（損失）、業務利益（損失）
(RUS) ОПЕРАЦИОННАЯ ПРИБЫЛЬ
(УБЫТОК)

operating ratio
(CHIN) 开工率，经营比率
(FRE) coefficient d'exploitation
(GER) betriebswirtschaftliche Kennzahl *f*,
(Kennzahl zur Bestimmung der Ertragskraft
bzw. Wirtschaftlichkeit einer
Unternehmung)
(JAP) 営業比率、操業度、操業率
(RUS) ОПЕРАЦИОННЫЙ КОЭФФИЦИЕНТ,
СООТНОШЕНИЕ ДОХОДОВ К ЗАТРАТАМ

operating system
(CHIN) 操作系统
(FRE) système d'exploitation
(GER) Betriebssystem *n*
(JAP) オペレーティングシステム、
基本ソフトウエア
(RUS) ОПЕРАЦИОННАЯ СИСТЕМА

operational audit
(CHIN) 业务审计，营业核查
(FRE) audit opérationnel, (C) vérification
de gestion
(GER) Innenrevision *f*, Prüfung *f* der
Ablaufsysteme *n* einer Unternehmung *f*
(JAP) 業務監査
(RUS) АНАЛИЗ ПРОИЗВОДСТВЕННОГО
ПРОЦЕССА ДЛЯ ЕГО УЛУЧШЕНИЯ

operational control
(CHIN) 营业管理
(FRE) contrôle opérationnel, (C) contrôle
d'exploitation
(GER) Betriebskontrolle *f*; laufende
Überwachung *f* der Betriebsabläufe *mpl*
(JAP) 運転統制、作業統制、業務管理
(RUS) ОПЕРАТИВНЫЙ КОНТРОЛЬ,
УПРАВЛЕНИЕ

operation mode
(CHIN) 操作模式
(FRE) mode de fonctionnement,
(C) programme opérationnel
(GER) Arbeitsweise *f*, Betriebsart *f*

(JAP) 操作モード
(RUS) ОПЕРАЦИОННЫЙ РЕЖИМ

operations research (OR)
(CHIN) 运筹学习(OR)
(FRE) recherches opérationnelles
(GER) Operations Research *n*,
Unternehmens- *f*, Verfahrensforschung *f*,
Optimalplanung *f*
(JAP) 作戦研究、経営研究
(RUS) РАЗРАБОТКА МАТЕМАТИЧЕСКИХ
МОДЕЛЕЙ ПОСТОРЯЮЩИХСЯ
ОПЕРАЦИЙ

operator
(CHIN) 运算符，操作员，操作
(FRE) opérateur, (C) exploitant
(GER) Bediener *m*, Benutzer *m*, Betreiber *m*
(JAP) 操作員、演算子、
オペレーター
(RUS) ОПЕРАТОР

opinion
(CHIN) 意见
(FRE) opinion
(GER) Meinung *f*, Auffassung *f*, Ansicht *f*,
Überzeugung *f*, Standpunkt *m*; Gutachten *n*;
Aussage *f*; Ermessen *n*
(JAP) 意見、見解、世論
(RUS) МНЕНИЕ; ТОЧКА ЗРЕНИЯ;
ЗАКЛЮЧЕНИЕ АДВОКАТА

opinion leader
(CHIN) 意见领导人
(FRE) préconisateur, (C) prescripteur
(GER) Meinungsführer *m*
(JAP) 世論指導者、世論の担い手、世論
形成者
(RUS) ЛИЦО, ОКАЗЫВАЮЩЕЕ СИЛЬНОЕ
ВЛИЯНИЕ НА МНЕНИЕ ДРУГИХ

opinion of title
(CHIN) 产权意见
(FRE) certificat de titre, (C) certificat de
propriété
(GER) Eigentumsnachweis *m*,
Übertragungsbestätigung *f*
(JAP) 不動産権原の弁護士意見書
(RUS) ЗАКЛЮЧЕНИЕ АДВОКАТА О
ПРАВОВОМ ТИТУЛ

opportunity cost

(CHIN) 机会成本

(FRE) coût d'opportunité, coût de renoncement, (C) coût de renonciation

(GER) Opportunitäts- pl, Warte- pl, Alternativkosten pl

(JAP) 機会費用、機会原価

(RUS) АЛЬТЕРНАТИВНЫЕ ИЗДЕРЖКИ

optical character recognition (OCR)

(CHIN) 光学字符识别（OCR）

(FRE) reconnaissance des caractères optiques, (C) reconnaissance optique de caractères

(GER) optische Zeichenerkennung f

(JAP) 光学式文字認識

(RUS) ОПТИЧЕСКОЕ РАСПОЗНАВАНИЕ ЗНАКОВ

optical fiber

(CHIN) 光导纤维，光纤

(FRE) fibre optique

(GER) Lichtwellenfaser m, Glasfaser m

(JAP) 光ファイバー、光学繊維、オプティカルファイバー

(RUS) ОПТИЧЕСКОЕ ВОЛОКНО

optimum capacity

(CHIN) 最适生产能力

(FRE) capacité optimale

(GER) optimale Kapazität f, Höchstkapazität f

(JAP) 最適能力

(RUS) ОПТИМАЛЬНАЯ МОЩНОСТЬ, ЗАГРУЗКА

option

(CHIN) 期权，选择权，约束力，优先购买权

(FRE) option, prime Wahl f, Möglichkeit f, Alternative f; Option f, Vorverkaufsrecht n; Extra n; Option f (Börse)

(JAP) 選択権、（売付買付）選択権、選択

(RUS) ОПЦИОН; ВАРИАНТ ВЫБОРА

optional modes of settlement

(CHIN) 人寿险赔偿方式选择

(FRE) moyens de règlement facultatifs, (C) mode de règlement optionnel

(GER) Wahlrecht n beim Empfang m der Versicherungsleistung f, wahlweise Schadensregulierung f

(JAP) （保険金などの）支払い選択条項

(RUS) ВАРИАНТЫ УЛАЖИВАНИЯ, ДОСТИЖЕНИЯ ДОГОВОРЕННОСТИ

option holder

(CHIN) 选择权持有人

(FRE) acheteur de l'option, détenteur d'option

(GER) Optionsinhaber m

(JAP) オプション保有者

(RUS) ДЕРЖАТЕЛЬ ОПЦИОНА

oral contract

(CHIN) 口头协议

(FRE) contrat oral, (C) entente verbale

(GER) mündlicher Vertrag m, mündliche Absprache f

(JAP) 口頭による契約、口約束

(RUS) УСТНАЯ ДОГОВОРЕННОСТЬ

orange goods

(CHIN) 橙类消费物品

(FRE) biens de consommation intermédiaires, (C) biens remplacés occasionnellement

(GER) Konsumgüter npl mit mittlerer Lebensdauer f

(JAP) オレンジ商品

(RUS) ТОВАРЫ СРЕДНЕГО СРОКА ПОЛЬЗОВАНИЯ (НАПР. ОДЕЖДА)

or better

(CHIN) 或者更好价格

(FRE) ou mieux

(GER) (zum Kurs m) oder besser adj

(JAP) 〔株式〕指値かまたはそれ以上で

(RUS) «ИЛИ ЛУЧШЕ» (оговорка в документе)

order

(CHIN) 秩序，订货，定单，抬头人，汇票，指示

(FRE) ordre, (C) commande, ordre

(GER) Auftrag m, Bestellung f; Verfügung f, Weisung f (Recht); Anforderung f;

Anweisung *f*, Aufforderung *f*, Befehl *m*;
Erlass *m* (Recht); Ordnung *f*, Zustand *m*;
Reihenfolge *f*
(JAP) 注文、受注（為替・手形の）
受注高、指図
(RUS) ЗАКАЗ; ПРИКАЗ; ПОРЯДОК;
ПОСЛЕДОВАТЕЛЬНОСТЬ

order bill of lading
(CHIN) 指定人提单
(FRE) connaissement à l'ordre, (C) lettre
de voiture à ordre, (C) connaissement à
ordre
(GER) Orderkonnossement *n*, -frachtbrief *m*,
-ladeschein *m*
(JAP) 指図式船荷証券
(RUS) ОРДЕРНЫЙ КОНОСАМЕНТ

order card
(CHIN) 订购卡
(FRE) fiche de commande, (C) bon de
commande
(GER) Auftrags- *f*, Bestellkarte *f*
(JAP) 注文カード、作業指図書
(RUS) БЛАНК ЗАКАЗА, ОТПЕЧАТАННАЯ
НА ОТКРЫТКЕ ДЛЯ ОТВЕТА НА
ПРЕДЛОЖЕНИЕ ТОВАРА, УСЛУГИ

order entry
(CHIN) 定单内容记录
(FRE) entrée de commande
(GER) Bestellungseingabe *f*, Auftrags- *f*,
Ordererfassung *f*
(JAP) 注文入力、受注、
オーダーエントリー
(RUS) ВЗЯТИЕ, ОФОРМЛЕНИЕ ЗАКАЗА
ПОТРЕБИТЕЛЯ

order flow pattern
(CHIN) 定单流动模式
(FRE) schéma de circulation des
commandes, (C) processus de traitement de
commande
(GER) Bestell- *f*, Auftragseingangsstruktur *f*,
Bestell- *f*, Auftragszugangsverhalten *n*
(JAP) 受注（注文）の流れパターン、受
注フローパターン
(RUS) ТЕНДЕНЦИЯ ПОСТУПЛЕНИЯ
ЗАКАЗА

order form
(CHIN) 定货单，定单格式
(FRE) bon de commande
(GER) Bestell- *n*, Auftragsformular *n*,
Bestellzettel *m*
(JAP) 注文書式、注文用紙
(RUS) БЛАНК ЗАКАЗА

order number
(CHIN) 定单编号
(FRE) numéro de commande
(GER) Bestell- *f*, Auftragsnummer *f*,
Artikelnummer *f*
(JAP) 注文番号
(RUS) НОМЕР ЗАКАЗА

order paper
(CHIN) 指示票据，记名票据
(FRE) effet à ordre
(GER) Orderpapier *n*; Tagesordnung *f*,
Tages- *n*, Sitzungsprogramm *n*
(JAP) 注文書類、注文控え帳
(RUS) ДОКУМЕНТ ЗАКАЗА, ПРИКАЗА

order-point system
(CHIN) 定货点系统
(FRE) méthode du point de commande
(GER) Bestellpunktsystem *n*
(JAP) 発注点方式
(RUS) СИСТЕМА АВТОМАТИЧЕСКОГО
ПОПОЛНЕНИЯ МАТЕРИАЛЬНЫХ
ЗАПАСОВ, КОГДА ОНИ ДОСТИГАЮТ
ОПРЕДЕЛЁННОГО УРОВНЯ

order regulation
(CHIN) 定货规定
(FRE) règlement sur l'ordre,
(C) réglementation des commandes
(GER) Bestell- *f*, Auftragsregelung *f*
(JAP) 注文の規則
(RUS) РЕГУЛИРОВАНИЕ ЗАКАЗОВ,
ПРИКАЗОВ

ordinal scale
(CHIN) 顺序量表
(GER) Ordinalskala *f*
(JAP) 順序尺度
(RUS) ПОРЯДКОВАЯ ШКАЛА

ordinance

(CHIN) 法令，条例，法规，布告

(FRE) ordonnance, décrêt, ordre,
(C) règlement

(GER) Verordnung *f*, Verfügung *f*,
Regelung *m*

(JAP) 法令、布告、命令

(RUS) УКАЗ; ДЕКРЕТ

ordinary and necessary business expense

(CHIN) 普通及必要的商业开支

(FRE) frais professionnel ordinaire et
nécessaire, (C) dépense d'exploitation
ordinaire et nécessaire

(GER) ordentliche und notwendige
(Geschäfts)ausgaben *fpl*

(JAP) 通常必要な営業費

(RUS) «ОБЫЧНЫЕ И НЕОБХОДИМЫЕ
ДЕЛОВЫЕ РАСХОДЫ»

ordinary annuity

(CHIN) 普通年金

(FRE) annuité de capitalisation, (C) rente
de la grande branche

(GER) nachschüssige Rente *f*,
Postnumerando-Rente *f*

(JAP) 普通年金

(RUS) ОБЫЧНЫЙ АННУИТЕТ

ordinary course of business

(CHIN) 正常业务程序

(FRE) cours normal des négociations,
(C) cours normal des affaires

(GER) normaler Geschäftsgang *m*, normaler
–verlauf *m*, -ablauf *m*

(JAP) 普通の業務過程

(RUS) «В ОБЫЧНОМ ПОРЯДКЕ ДЕЛ»

ordinary gain or ordinary income

(CHIN) 正常收益或收入

(FRE) revenu ordinaire

(GER) Normaleinkommen *n*, ordentliches
Einkommen *n*, normale Einkünfte *fpl*

(JAP) 経常収入、経常利益、通常所得

(RUS) ОБЫЧНАЯ ПРИБЫЛЬ или ОБЫЧНЫЙ
ДОХОД

ordinary interest

(CHIN) 正常利息

(FRE) intérêt ordinaire

(GER) gewöhnlicher bzw. normaler Zins *m*,
(auf der Basis *f* von 360 Tagen berechnet er
Zins)

(JAP) 通常利息、通常利子、通常金利

(RUS) ОБЫЧНЫЙ ПРОЦЕНТ (рассчитанный
на основе года в 360 дней)

ordinary loss

(CHIN) 正常损失

(FRE) perte ordinaire

(GER) Verluste *mpl* außer
Kapitalverlusten *mpl*

(JAP) 経常損失

(RUS) ОБЫЧНЫЙ УБЫТОК

ordinary payroll exclusion endorsement

(CHIN) 正常工资单免列认可

(FRE) avenant d'exclusion salaires
ordinaires, (C) exclusion approuvée de la
liste de paie

(GER) Nachtrag *m* zur
Betriebsunterbrechungsversicherung *f* laut
dem Arbeiter *mpl* und niedrigere
Angestellte *mpl* von Zahlungen *fpl*
ausgeschlossen warden

(JAP) 通常給料除外指示

(RUS) УТВЕРЖДЕНИЕ ИСКЛЮЧЕНИЯ ИЗ
ОБЫЧНОГО ФОНДА ЗАРАБОТНОЙ
ПЛАТЫ

organization

(CHIN) 组织，机构，体制，编制，建制，
机关

(FRE) organisation, organisme

(GER) Organisation *f*, Struktur *f*, Aufbau *m*,
Gefüge *n*; Gründung *f*

(JAP) 組織、機構、協会

(RUS) ОРГАНИЗАЦИЯ

organizational behavior

(CHIN) 组织行为

(FRE) (C) comportement organisationnel

(GER) Organisationsverhalten *n*

(JAP) 組織行動

(RUS) ОРГАНИЗАЦИОННОЕ ПОВЕДЕНИЕ

organizational chart

(CHIN) 组织机构图

(FRE) organigramme

(GER) Organigramm *n*

(JAP) 組織図、会社構成図
(RUS) ОРГАНИЗАЦИОННАЯ СХЕМА

organization cost
(CHIN) 开办成本，组织费用
(FRE) frais de constitution
(GER) Gründungskosten *pl*
(JAP) 創業費
(RUS) РАСХОДЫ НА СОЗДАНИЕ
ПРЕДПРИЯТИЯ

organization development
(CHIN) 组织改进
(FRE) développement des organisations,
(C) développement organisationnel
(GER) Organisations- *f*,
Betriebsentwicklung *f*
(JAP) 組織開発
(RUS) ОРГАНИЗАЦИОННОЕ РАЗВИТИЕ

organization planning
(CHIN) 组织计划
(FRE) planification de l'organisation,
(C) planification organisationnelle
(GER) Organisationsplanung *f*
(JAP) 組織計画
(RUS) ОРГАНИЗАЦИОННОЕ
ПЛАНИРОВАНИЕ

organization structure
(CHIN) 组织结构
(FRE) structure, structure de l'entreprise,
structure organique, (C) structure
organisationnelle
(GER) Organisationsstruktur *f*
(JAP) 組織構造
(RUS) ОРГАНИЗАЦИОННАЯ СТРУКТУРА

organized labor
(CHIN) 有组织的劳动力
(FRE) mouvement syndical
(GER) gewerkschaftlich organisierte
Arbeitnehmerschaft *f*
(JAP) 組織労働
(RUS) ТРУДОВАЯ СИЛА,
ОРГАНИЗОВАННАЯ В ПРОФСОЮЗЫ

orientation
(CHIN) 定向，方向性
(FRE) orientation

(GER) Orientierung *f*, Einarbeitung *f*,
(Arbeitsplatz)einweisung *f*
(JAP) オリエンテーション、（新入社員
などの）指導、方向付け
(RUS) ОРИЕНТАЦИЯ

original cost
(CHIN) 原始成本，最初成本
(FRE) coût initial, (C) coût historique
(GER) Anschaffungskosten *pl*, usprüngliche
Kosten *pl*
(JAP) 取得原価、仕入原価
(RUS) ИСХОДНАЯ СТОИМОСТЬ

original entry
(CHIN) 原始记入账
(FRE) écriture de journal, (C) écriture
originaire
(GER) ursprüngliche Buchung *f*,
Erstaufzeichnung *f*
(JAP) 初記入、原始記入
(RUS) ИСХОДНАЯ ПОЗИЦИЯ

original issue discount (OID)
(CHIN) 原始发行股票折扣(OID)
(FRE) prime d'émission, (C) obligation à
prime d'émission
(GER) Emissionsdisagio *n*;
Abzinsungsbetrag *m*
(JAP) 発売時割引
(RUS) СКИДКА С НОМИНАЛЬНОЙ ЦЕНЫ
(ценной бумаги в момент выпуска)

original maturity
(CHIN) 原定偿还期
(FRE) échéance initiale, durée de crédit
initiale, (C) échéance originale
(GER) ursprüngliche Laufzeit *f*
(JAP) オリジナルマチュリティ、
当初満期
(RUS) ПЕРВОНАЧАЛЬНЫЙ СРОК
ПОГАШЕНИЯ ЦЕННОЙ БУМАГИ

original order
(CHIN) 原定单
(FRE) commande initiale
(GER) ursprünglicher Auftrag *m*
(JAP) 最初の注文
(RUS) ИСХОДНЫЙ, ПЕРВОНАЧАЛЬНЫЙ
ЗАКАЗ (ПРИКАЗ)

origination fee

(CHIN) 开办费

(FRE) frais de constitution,
(C) commission sur prêt
(GER) Krediträumungsgebühr,
(Gewährungsgebühr für
Hypthekendarlehen)
(JAP) 融資開始手数料、
融資取組み手数料
(RUS) ПЛАТА БАНКУ ВО ВРЕМЯ
ИНИЦИАЦИИ КРЕДИТА

originator

(CHIN) 创始人，原始承销人

(FRE) autorité d'origine, expéditeur,
donneur d'ordre, (C) initiateur
(GER) Auftraggeber *m*
(JAP) 創作者、創始者、原資産所有者
(RUS) ИНИЦИАТОР ОПЕРАЦИЙ

other income

(CHIN) 其它收入

(FRE) produit divers, recettes diverses,
(C) autres revenus
(GER) sonstige Einkünfte *fpl*, anderes
Einkommen *n*
(JAP) 雑所得、雑益、営業外所得
(RUS) ПРОЧИЕ ДОХОДЫ (не от обычных
операций)

other insurance clause

(CHIN) 其它保险条款

(FRE) clause de pluralité d'assurance,
(C) autre clause d'assurance
(GER)
Versicherungsüberschneidungsklausel*f*
(JAP) 他保険条項
(RUS) ОГОВОРКА О СУЩЕСТВОВАНИИ
ПАРАЛЛЕЛЬНОГО СТРАХОВАНИЯ

other people's money

(CHIN) 借入款

(FRE) l'argent des autres, (C) l'argent
d'autrui
(GER) Geld *n* anderer Parteien *fpl*
(JAP) 借入金
(RUS) ЗАЕМНЫЕ СРЕДСТВА

outbid

(CHIN) 抬高出价

(FRE) enchérir sur, (C) surenchérir
(GER) überbieten *v*
(JAP) 高値をつける、せりに勝つ
(RUS) ВЫИГРАТЬ ТЕНДЕР

outcry market

(CHIN) 喊价成交，拍卖市场

(FRE) marché aux enchères,
(C) marché à la criée
(GER) Auktionsmarkt *m*
(JAP) 競売市場
(RUS) РЫНОК ТОРГОВЛИ БЕЗ
АУКЦИОНЕРА (бирж.)

outline view

(CHIN) 大纲视图

(FRE) mode plan, (C) vision sommaire
(GER) Überblickansicht *f*
(JAP) 概観図

out of the money

(CHIN) 认购价格

(FRE) en dehors, (C) hors du cours
(GER) aus dem Geld *n adj*
(JAP) アウトオブザマネー
(RUS) ОПЦИОН С ЦЕНОЙ ИСПОЛНЕНИЯ
НИЖЕ ТЕКУЩЕЙ ЦЕНЫ В СЛУЧАЕ
ОПЦИОНА НА ПРОДАЖУ И ВЫШЕ
ТЕКУЩЕЙ ЦЕНЫ В СЛУЧАЕ ОПЦИОНА
НА ПОКУПКУ

outlet store

(CHIN) 代销店

(FRE) point de vente
(GER) Werks-*f*, Fabrikverkaufstelle *f*
(JAP) アウトレット店、販売店、在庫処
分店、直売店
(RUS) ФИРМЕННЫЙ МАГАЗИН
РОЗНИЧНОЙ ТОРГОВЛИ

outside director

(CHIN) 外部董事,
不参与管理的董事

(FRE) administrateur externe
(GER) externes Vorstandsmitglied *n*,
(Vorstandsmitglied, das nicht gleichzeitig
Mitglied der Geschäftsleitung ist)
(JAP) 外部重役、社外重役、社外取締役
(RUS) ПРИГЛАШЕННЫЙ
ДИРЕКТОР

outsourcing

(CHIN) 外协

(FRE) externalisation, (C) impartition

(GER) Oursourcing *n*, Fremdleistungsbezug *m*, -vergabe *f*, Auslagerung *f*

(JAP) 外部調達、外注、外部委託

(RUS) ПЕРЕДАЧА РАБОТЫ ТРЕТЬИМ ЛИЦАМ

outstanding

(CHIN) 应付未付，未清

(FRE) en suspens, dû, en souffrance, en circulation, en cours

(GER) im Umlauf *m* befindlich, umlaufend; ausstehend, ausständig, unbeglichen, fällig *adj*

(JAP) 未決済の、未払いの、
（pl.）未払い負債

(RUS) НЕОПЛАЧЕННЫЙ; НЕ ПРЕДЪЯВЛЕННЫЙ К ПЛАТЕЖУ; В ОБРАЩЕНИИ; ВЫДАЮЩИЙСЯ

outstanding balance

(CHIN) 未付差额

(FRE) solde à découvert, (C) solde en souffrance, (C) solde impayé

(GER) ausstehende Schuld *f*, Forderung *f*

(JAP) 未済残高、未払残高、融資残高

(RUS) ТЕКУЩАЯ ЗАДОЛЖЕННОСТЬ

outstanding capital stock

(CHIN) 净发股本

(FRE) capital-actions en circulation, (C) actions en circulation

(GER) ausstehende Aktien *fpl*, ausstehendes Aktienkapital *n*

(JAP) 株式発行高、資本金現在高

(RUS) АКЦИИ В ОБРАЩЕНИИ

overage

(CHIN) 超额，超过部分，溢数

(FRE) excédent, surplus

(GER) Bestandsüberschuss *m*; Mehrbetrag *m*; Mengenüberschreitung *f*

(JAP) 規定年齢を超えた、適齢を過ぎた、過多量

(RUS) ИЗБЫТОК; ИЗЛИШЕК

overall expenses method

(CHIN) 总费用方法

(FRE) méthode des dépenses générales, (C) méthode du total des frais

(GER) Gesamtkostenmethode *f*

(JAP) 総費用方式

(RUS) МЕТОД АНАЛИЗА ПО ОБЩИМ РАСХОДАМ

overall rate of return

(CHIN) 总回报率

(FRE) taux de retour, (C) taux de rendement global

(GER) Unternehmensrentabilität *f*

(JAP) 総収益率

(RUS) ОБЩИЙ УРОВЕНЬ ДОХОДНОСТИ

over-and-short

(CHIN) 溢缺

(FRE) recouvrement, (C) surplus et déficit de caisse

(GER) Kassendifferenz-

(JAP) 過不足の

(RUS) «СВЕРХ ИЛИ В НЕДОСТАЧЕ», РАЗНИЦА МЕЖДУ ЗАРЕГИСТРИРОВАННЫМИ ЦИФРАМИ ПРОДАЖ И РЕЗУЛЬТАТАМИ АУДИТА

overbooked

(CHIN) 订座超出

(FRE) surréservé, (C) surréservation

(GER) überbucht, überbelegt; übertariflich verdienen *adj*

(JAP) 超過予約である、オーバーブッキング

(RUS) ПОДПИСКА СВЕРХ ПРЕДЛАГАЕМОЙ СУММЫ （бирж.）; ПРОДАЖА (мест или билетов) СВЕРХ ВОЗМОЖНОСТИ

overbought

(CHIN) 多头，买空，超买

(FRE) surévalué, suracheté

(GER) überkauft *adj*, Überhang *m* an aufpositionen *fpl*

(JAP) 過剰買いの

(RUS) ХАРАКТЕРИЗУЮЩИЙСЯ ЧРЕЗМЕРНО ВЫСОКИМ КУРСОМ

overcharge

(CHIN) 收费过多

(FRE) faire payer trop cher, survendre, (C) trop-perçu

(GER) zuviel berechnen *v*; Berechnung *f* eines überhöhten Preises *m*
 (JAP) 不当な値段、不当な要求、
(RUS) ЗАВЫШЕННАЯ ЦЕНА

overflow
(CHIN) 超溢
(FRE) dépassement de capacité, (C) débord
(GER) Überschuss *m*; Überlauf *m*, Bereichsüberschreitung *f*
(JAP) 過多、過剰、オーバーフロー
(RUS) ПЕРЕПОЛНЕНИЕ

overhang
(CHIN) 悬置
(FRE) surplomb, (C) offre excédentaire
(GER) Überhang *m*
(JAP) 張り出す、突き出る、余剰の
(RUS) ЗНАЧИТЕЛЬНЫЙ ЗАПАС ЦЕННЫХ БУМАГ, КОТОРЫЙОКАЖЕТ ЦЕНОВОЕ ДАВЛЕНИЕ В СЛУЧАЕ ПОСТУПЛЕНИЯ НА РЫНОК

overhead
(CHIN) 制造费用，间接费用
(FRE) charge opérationnelle, frais généraux, (C) coûts indirects, (C) charges indirectes
(GER) Gemeinkosten *pl*
(JAP) 諸掛込みの、諸経費、間接費
(RUS) НАКЛАДНЫЕ РАСХОДЫ

overheating
(CHIN) 过热
(FRE) surchauffe
(GER) (Konjunktur)überhitzung *f*
(JAP) （景気の）過熱
(RUS) ЧРЕЗМЕРНОЕ УСКОРЕНИЕ ЭКОНОМИЧЕСКОГО РАЗВИТИЯ

overimprovement
(CHIN) 改善过度
(FRE) amélioration excessive, (C) suramélioration
(GER) übermäßige Verbesserungsmaßnahmen *fpl*
(JAP) 過剰改良
(RUS) ИЗЛИШНЕЕ УЛУЧШЕНИЕ

overissue
(CHIN) 溢发，超额发行

(FRE) surémission, (C) invendu
(GER) Überemission *f*, Überhangemission *f*
(JAP) （通貨、証券の）過大発行
(RUS) ВЫПУСК АКЦИЙ СВЕРХ УСТАВНОЙ СУММЫ

overkill
(CHIN) 过度推销
(FRE) promotion excessive
(GER) Übermaß *n*, Overkill *m*
(JAP) やり過ぎ、行き過ぎ、オーバーキル
(RUS) ПЕРЕСТАРАТЬСЯ

overpayment
(CHIN) 多付，超付
(FRE) trop-perçu
(GER) Überbezahlung *f*
(JAP) 払い過ぎ、支払超過
(RUS) ПЕРЕПЛАТА

overproduction
(CHIN) 生产过剩
(FRE) surproduction
(GER) Überproduktion *f*
(JAP) 生産過剰、過剰生産
(RUS) ПЕРЕПРОИЗВОДСТВО

override
(CHIN) 代理佣金
(FRE) commission indirecte, (C) dérogation, (C) passer outreà, (C) avoir la priorité sur, (C) commission indirecte
(GER) Zulage *f*, Gratifikation *f*, Absatzprovision *f*; Tantieme *f*, Ertragsbeteiligung *f*; Übersteuerung *f*, Beeinflussung *f*; außer Kraft *f* setzen, aufheben, annullieren *v*; neutralisieren, übersteuern *v*; überlappen *v*
(JAP) 無視する、無効にする、
（売上・利益に応じた）
コミッション、歩合
(RUS) ОТМЕНЯТЬ, ДАТЬ КОМАНДУ БОЛЕЕ ВЫСОКОГО УРОВНЯ

overrun
(CHIN) 超过，超出
(FRE) excédent, surplus, (C) excédent de commande
(GER) (Kosten- *f*, Zeit)überschreitung *f*; Überschuss *m*, Überhang *m*, -produktion *f*

(JAP)（予算、見積もりを）超過する、
見積もり超過額、過剰支出額
(RUS) ПЕРЕПРОИЗВОДСТВО

over (short)

(CHIN) 超出（短缺）

(FRE) recouvrement, (C) surplus (déficit)

(GER) darüber (darunter) adj

(JAP) ~以上、~より多く
（~以下、～より少なく）

(RUS) ПРЕВЫШЕНИЕ (НЕДОСТАТОК)

over the counter (OTC)

(CHIN) 直接交易（OTC）

(FRE) hors cote

(GER) außerbörslich adj; frei
verkäuflich adj

(JAP)（株券、証券などが）（取引所を
通さずに）直接売買された、店頭売買

(RUS) ВНЕБИРЖЕВОЙ РЫНОК ЦЕННЫХ
БУМАГ; ПРОДАЖА ЛЕКАРСТВ БЕЗ
рецепта)

over-the-counter retailing

(CHIN) 直接零售

(FRE) vente libre, (C) vente au comptoir

(GER) Thekenverkauf m, offener
Verkauf m

(JAP) 店頭小売り

(RUS) ОТКРЫТАЯ РОЗНИЧНАЯ ПРОДАЖА
(без ограничений)

overtime

(CHIN) 加班，超时

(FRE) heures supplémentaires

(GER) Überstunden fpl, Mehrarbeitszeit f

(JAP) 残業時間、超過勤務時間、
残業手当

(RUS) СВЕРХУРОЧНОЕ ВРЕМЯ

overtrading

(CHIN) 超额经营

(FRE) emballement de l'activité d'une
entreprise (au-delà des limites de son
capital), (C) surtransiger

(GER) Liquiditätsschwierigkeiten fpl,
übermäßiger Kreditkauf m;
Überspekulation f

(JAP) 資金超過取引

(RUS) ИЗБЫТОЧНАЯ, ЧРЕЗМЕРНАЯ
ТОРГОВЛЯ

overvalued

(CHIN) 计值过高的

(FRE) surestimé, surévalué

(GER) überbewertet adj

(JAP) 過大評価の

(RUS) ПЕРЕОЦЕНЕННЫЙ (ОЦЕНЕННЫЙ
ВЫШЕ СТОИМОСТИ)

overwrite

(CHIN) 重写，覆写

(FRE) écraser

(GER) überschreiben v

(RUS) ЗАТИРАТЬ, ЗАПИСЫВАТЬ ДАННЫЕ
В ОБЛАСТЬ НОСИТЕЛЯ, ЗАНЯТУЮ
ДРУГИМИ ДАННЫМИ

owner-operator

(CHIN) 物主-操作人

(FRE) propriétaire exploitant
Eigenbewirtschaftung f

(RUS) ВЛАДЕЛЕЦ – ИСПОЛНИТЕЛЬ

ownership

(CHIN) 所有权

(FRE) propriété, (C) droit de propriété

(GER) Inhaberschaft f, Besitz m

(JAP) 所有権

ownership form

(CHIN) 所有权形式

(FRE) ropriété, (C) méthode d'exercice du
droit de propriété

(GER) Besitzart f

(JAP) 所有形態

P

pacesetter
(CHIN) 模范，标兵
(FRE) meneur
(GER) Akkordrichtarbeiter *m*;
Akkordbrecher *m*
(JAP) (仕事の)進度設定者
(RUS) ЛИЦО, ТОВАР И Т. П., ЗАДАЮЩИЕ
РИТМ

package
(CHIN) 统包价格，整批，一揽子
(FRE) ensemble, contrat, global, colis,
paquet, (C) emballage
(GER) Paket *n*, Päckchen *n*; (Ver)packung
f; Baugruppe *f* (Zusammenbau);
Verhandlungsergebnis *n*
(Lohnverhandlungen); Maßnahmenbündel *n*
(JAP) 荷造り、一括、小包
(RUS) ПАКЕТ; УПАКОВКА; КОМПЛЕКТ

package band
(CHIN) 包装条广告
(FRE) bande publicitaire, (C) publicité
autour de l'emballage
(GER) Packungsbanderole *f*,
Packungsstreifen *m* (mit
Sonderangebotsaufdrucken)
(JAP) パッケージバンド
(RUS) ДОПОЛНИТЕЛЬНЫЙ ОБОДОК НА
УПАКОВКЕ, СОДЕРЖАЩИЙ РЕКЛАМУ,
ОБЬЯВЛЕНИЯ И Т. П.

package code
(CHIN) 包装代码
(FRE) code de suivi, (C) code des
emballages
(GER) Packungscode *m*
(JAP) パッケージコード
(RUS) СИСТЕМА ИДЕНТИФИКАЦИИ
КАЖДОЙ ПОСЫЛКИ ПРИ ТОРГОВЛЕ
ПОЧТОЙ

package design
(CHIN) 包装设计
(FRE) conditionnement
(GER) Verpackungsdesign *n*
(JAP) パッケージデザイン、

包装デザイン
(RUS) КОНСТРУКЦИЯ УПАКОВКИ

packaged goods
(CHIN) 包装货物
(FRE) marchandises), emballées,
marchandises conditionnées, (C) biens
emballés
(GER) abgepackte Ware *f*, Stückgut *n*
(JAP) 包装品
(RUS) РАСФАСОВАННЫЕ ТОВАРЫ

package mortgage
(CHIN) 一揽子抵押贷款
(FRE) prêt (n, m) multiple, (C) prêt
hypothécaire rehaussé par collatéral
(GER) zubehörerfassende Hypothek *f*
(JAP) 包括抵当
(RUS) КОМБИНИРОВАННАЯ ИПОТЕКА

packing list
(CHIN) 包装物详单，装箱单
(FRE) liste de colisage, (C) prêt multiple
bordereau d'expédition
(GER) Pack- *f*, Versandliste *f*
(JAP) 荷造目録、包装明細書
(RUS) УПАКОВОЧНЫЙ ЛИСТ

padding
(CHIN) 填料，虚报账目
(FRE) remplissage), rembourrage
(GER) Füllmaterial *n*; Polsterung *f*;
Fälschung *f* von Buchungsunterlagen *fpl*
(JAP) 詰め物用の材料、詰め物、
（帳簿上の）不正な経費
(RUS) ПОДСТИЛКА;
РАЗДУВАНИЕ

page break
(CHIN) 分页符
(FRE) saut de page
(GER) Seitenumbruch *m*
(EDV)
(JAP) 改ページ、ページの区切り
(RUS) РАЗДЕЛИТЕЛЬ
СТРАНИЦЫ

page down
(CHIN) 页下移，版面往下移
(FRE) défilement vers le bas, (C) touche page suivante
(GER) nach unten blättern *v* (EDV)
(JAP) 次のページへ
(RUS) КЛАВИША «СТРАНИЦА ВНИЗ»

page format
(CHIN) 页格式
(FRE) format de la page, (C) format de page
(GER) Seitenformat *n* (EDV)
(JAP) ページ形式
(RUS) ФОРМАТ СТРАНИЦЫ

page up
(CHIN) 页上移，版面往上移
(FRE) défilement vers le haut
(GER) nach oben blättern *v* (EDV)
(JAP) 前のページへ
(RUS) КЛАВИША «СТРАНИЦА ВВЕРХ»

pagination
(CHIN) 标页码，分页
(FRE) pagination
(GER) Seitennummerierung *f*, -zählung *f* (EDV)
(RUS) РАЗДЕЛЕНИЕ ДОКУМЕНТА НА СТРАНИЦЫ

paid in advance
(CHIN) 已提前支付
(FRE) payé par avance, (C) payé à l'avance
(GER) voraus-, vorabbezahlt *adj*
(JAP) 前払いした
(RUS) ПРЕДОПЛАТА

paid-in capital
(CHIN) 实收资本，缴入资本
capital versé, capital libéré, (C) capital d'apport
(GER) einbezahltes Kapital *n*
(JAP) 払込資金
(RUS) ОПЛАЧЕННАЯ ЧАСТЬ КАПИТАЛА

paid-in surplus
(CHIN) 缴入盈余，盈余
(FRE) primes d'émission d'actions,
(C) surplus d'apport
(GER) Agio *n*, Aufgeld *n*, Agiorücklage *f*

(JAP) 払込剰余金
(RUS) ОПЛАЧЕННЫЙ ИЗЛИШЕК КАПИТАЛА

paid status
(CHIN) 支付情况
(FRE) état des paiements, (C) payé
(GER) Zahlungsstand *m*
(JAP) 支払済み状態、
支払済みステータス
(RUS) ОПЛАЧЕННЫЙ ЗАКАЗ

paintbrush
(CHIN) 画笔
(FRE) pinceau
(GER) Malpinsel *m*
(JAP) 絵筆、ペンキ用のはけ、
ペントブラシュ
(RUS) ПРОГРАММА РИСОВАНИЯ

painting the tape
(CHIN) 托市
(FRE) fait d'effectuer une serie d'operations qui sont affichees publiquement sur des ecrans en vue de donner, pour un instrument financier determine, une impression d'activite ou de mouvement de son cours, (C) transactions artificielles fréquentes
(GER) Kursbetrug *m* begehen, (durch Scheingeschäfte den Eindruck des regen Handels eines Wertpapiers erwecken)
(JAP) 証券偽装取引
(RUS) НЕЛЕГАЛЬНАЯ ПРАКТИКА КУПЛИ-ПРОДАЖИ ЦЕННЫХ БУМАГ С ЦЕЛЬЮ СОЗДАНИЯ ВИДИМОСТИ АКТИВНОЙ ТОРГОВЛИ И ПРИВЛЕЧЕНИЯ ИНВЕСТИТОРОВ

palmtop
(CHIN) 掌上型
(FRE) ordinateur (portable) format calculette, (C) ordinateur de poche
(GER) Palmtop *m*, Handcomputer *m*
(JAP) パームトップ、
手の平に載せて使える小型の
(RUS) РУЧНОЕ ЭВМ

paper
(CHIN) 钞票，纸币，票据，
证券，汇票，支票

(FRE) papier, billet
(GER) Vortrag *m*, Referat *n*; Wertpapier *n*
(JAP) 手形、紙幣、（pl.）書類
(RUS) БУМАГА; ДОКУМЕНТ

paper gold
(CHIN) 纸黄金
(GER) Papiergold *n*, Sonderziehungsrecht *n*
(JAP) ペーパー・ゴールド（IMF の特別引出権）
(RUS) СЕРТИФИКАТ ОБМЕНЫ НА ЗОЛОТО

paper jam
(CHIN) 卡纸
(FRE) bourrage (de papier)
(GER) Papierstau *m*
(JAP) 紙詰まり
(RUS) ЗАМЯТИЕ БУМАГИ В ПЕЧАТАЮЩЕМ УСТРОЙСТВЕ

paper money
(CHIN) 纸币，钞票，票据，支票
(FRE) papier-monnaie
(GER) Papiergeld *n*, Banknoten *fpl*
(JAP) 紙幣
(RUS) БУМАЖНЫЕ ДЕНЬГИ

paper profit (loss)
(CHIN) 账面利润（损失）
(FRE) profit fictif, (C) profit (perte) non réalisé(e)
(GER) Buchgewinn *m* (-verlust *m*), (rechnerischer bzw. nicht realisierter Kursgewinn oder -verlust)
(JAP) 紙上利益（損失）、架空利益（損失）、見込利益（損失）
(RUS) БУМАЖНАЯ (НЕРЕАЛИЗОВАННАЯ) ПРИБЫЛЬ (УБЫТОК)

par
(CHIN) 面额，平价，同等地位，平均的
(FRE) pair
(GER) Nennwert *m*, Pari *m*
(JAP) 額面価格、平価、為替平価
(RUS) ПАРИТЕТ; НОМИНАЛЬНАЯ СТОИМОСТЬ

paralegal
(CHIN) 律师的专职助手

(FRE) adjoint juridique, (C) parajuridique, (C) technicien juridique
(GER) Rechtsanwaltsgehilfe *m*, (-in *f*)
(JAP) 弁護士補助員
(RUS) РАБОТНИК ЮРИДИЧЕСКОЙ ФИРМЫ, НЕ ЯВЛЯЮЩИЙСЯ ПРОФЕССИОНАЛЬНЫМ ЮРИСТОМ И ВЫПОЛНЯЮЩИЙ ВСПОМОГАТЕЛЬНЫЕ ФУНКЦИИ

parallel connection
(CHIN) 并联连接
(FRE) connexion parallèle, (C) couplage en parallèle
(GER) Parallelschaltung *f*
(JAP) パラレル接続、並列接続
(RUS) ПАРАЛЛЕЛЬНАЯ СВЯЗЬ

parallel processing
(CHIN) 平行处理
(FRE) traitement en parallèle, (C) traitement parallèle
(GER) Simultanverarbeitung *f*
(JAP) 並列処理、並行処理、パラレルプロセシング

parameter
(CHIN) 参数，数据
(FRE) parameter
(GER) Parameter *m*
(JAP) パラメーター、媒介変数、補助変数
(RUS) ПАРАМЕТР

par bond
(CHIN) 平价债券
(FRE) obligation émise au pair, (C) obligation au pair
(GER) Pariobligation *f*
(JAP) 額面売買債券、額面価格債券
(RUS) ОБЛИГАЦИЯ, ВЫПУСКАЕМАЯ ИЛИ ПРОДАВАЕМАЯ ПО НОМИНАЛЬНОЙ СТОИМОСТИ

parcel
(CHIN) 包裹，邮包
(FRE) paquet, colis
(GER) Paket *n*; Parzelle *f*, Grundstück *n*; Partie *f*
(JAP) 一口の取引、一組、～を分配する

(RUS) БЛОК АКЦИЙ; ЗЕМЕЛЬНЫЙ НАДЕЛ; ПАКЕТ

parent company
(CHIN) 母公司，总公司
(FRE) maison mère
(GER) Mutter- f, Dachgesellschaft f, Stammhaus
(JAP) 親会社
(RUS) МАТЕРИНСКАЯ КОМПАНИЯ

parity
(CHIN) 平价，比价
(FRE) parité
(GER) Parität f, amtlicher Wechselkurs m, Umrechnungskurs m; Gleichwertigkeit f, Gleichheit f
(JAP) （品質、等級、価格などの）同等、平衡価格、等価
(RUS) ПАРИТЕТ; РАВЕНСТВО; ПАРНОСТЬ

parity check
(CHIN) 奇偶校验
(FRE) contrôle par parité, (C) contrôle de parité
(GER) Paritätsprüfung f, -kontrolle f
(JAP) パリティチェック、奇遇検査
(RUS) КОНТРОЛЬ ПАРНОСТИ

parity price
(CHIN) 平价，对等价格
(FRE) prix à parité, cours au pair, (C) prix de parité
(GER) Paritäts- m, Parikurs m; Paritätspreis m
(JAP) パリティ価格、平価
(RUS) ПАРИТЕТНАЯ ЦЕНА

parking
(CHIN) 安全投资
(FRE) mise en attente,
(C) stationnement
(GER) Parken n
(JAP) 駐車場
(RUS) ВРЕМЕННОЕ ПОМЕЩЕНИЕ СРЕДСТВ; АВТОСТОЯНКА; ВЫЖИДАНИЕ

parliament procedure
(CHIN) 正式程序
(FRE) procédure parlementaires

(GER) parlamentarische Geschäftsordnung f, parlamentarisches Verfahren n
(JAP) 議会手続き
(RUS) ПАРЛАМЕНТСКАЯ ПРОЦЕДУРА

partial delivery
(CHIN) 部分交货，局部交割
(FRE) livraison partielle
(GER) Teillieferung f
(JAP) 一部受渡し、分割出荷
(RUS) ЧАСТИЧНАЯ ПОСТАВКА

partial-equilibrium analysis
(CHIN) 部分均衡分析
(FRE) analyse de l'équilibre partiel
(GER) partielle Gleichgewichtsanalyse f
(JAP) 部分均衡分析
(RUS) АНАЛИЗ ЧАСТИЧНОГО РАВНОВЕСИЯ

partial release
(CHIN) 部分解除索赔权
(FRE) libération partielle
(GER) Teilfreigabe f
(JAP) 抵当一部解除、段階的解除
(RUS) ЧАСТИЧНЫЙ ВЫПУСК

partial taking
(CHIN) 部分获得
(FRE) prise partielle, (C) acquisition partielle
(GER) Teilfreistellung f
(JAP) 土地の一部収用
(RUS) ПРИОБРЕТЕНИЕ ЧАСТИ СОБСТВЕННОСТИ

participating insurance
(CHIN) 参与保险，分享保险
(FRE) assurance-vie avec participation aux bénéfices
(GER) Versicherung f mit Selbstbehalt m; Versicherung f mit Gewinnbeteiligung f
(JAP) 利益配当付き保険
(RUS) СТРАХОВАНИЕ С ВЫПЛАТОЙ ДИВИДЕНДОВ

participating policy
(CHIN) 分享保单
(FRE) politique avec participation,
(C) contrat d'assurance avec participation

306

(GER) gewinnbeteiligte
Versicherungspolice *f*, Versicherungspolice
f mit Gewinnbeteiligung *f*
(JAP) 利益配当付き保険証書
(RUS) СТРАХОВОЙ ПОЛИС С ВЫПЛАТОЙ
ДИВИДЕНДОВ

participating preferred stock
(CHIN) 共享优先股
(FRE) action privilégiée de participation,
(C) actions participatives
(GER) Vorzugsaktie *f* mit zusätzlicher
Gewinnbeteiligung *f*, partizipierende
Vorzugsaktie *f*
(JAP) 参加優先株式
(RUS) ПРИВИЛЕГИРОВАННЫЕ АКЦИИ,
ДАЮЩИЕ ПРАВО НА
ДОПОЛНИТЕЛЬНЫЙ ДИВИДЕНД
УЧАСТИЯ

participation certificate
(CHIN) 参与权益证书
(FRE) certificat de participation, (C) bon de
participation
(GER) Anteilsschein *m*, Teilobligation *f*,
Dividendenpapier *n*
(JAP) 参加証書
(RUS) СЕРТИФИКАТ УЧАСТИЯ

participation loan
(CHIN) 参与贷款，共同
(FRE) prêt hypothécaire avec participation,
(C) crédit consortial, crédit syndical
(GER) Konsortialkredit *m*
(JAP) 協調融資、参加貸付け
(RUS) СОВМЕСТНАЯ ССУДА
(НЕСКОЛЬКИХ БАНКОВ ОДНОМУ
ЗАЁМЩИКУ)

participative budgeting
(CHIN) 职工参与型预算制
(FRE) gestion budgétaire participative
(GER) partizipative Finanzplanung *f* bzw.
Haushaltsaufstellung *f*
(JAP) 参加型予算編成
(RUS) УЧАСТИЕ КЛЮЧЕВЫХ
РАБОТНИКОВ КОМПАНИИ В
ПЛАНИРОВАНИИ ЕЁ БЮДЖЕТА

participative leadership
(CHIN) 参与型领导方法

(FRE) direction participative, (C) direction
d'un groupe avec participation
(GER) partizipative Unternehmensführung *f*
(JAP) 参加型指導者、参加型指導
（統率、指揮）
(RUS) ПООЩРЕНИЕ УЧАСТИЯ РЯДОВЫХ
РАБОТНИКОВ В ПРИНЯТИИ РЕШЕНИЙ

partition
(CHIN) 划分，分割，分配
(FRE) partition, (C) partage,
(C) cloisonnage
(GER) Grundstücksteilung *f*, Parzellierung
f; Trenn- *f*, Zwischenwand *f*; Unterteilung *f*,
Untergliederung *f*; Abschottung *f*;
Programmbereich *m* (EDV)
(JAP) 分割、部分、仕切り
(RUS) РАЗДЕЛЯТЬ; ВЫДЕЛЯТЬ;
РАЗДЕЛЕНИЕ; ВЫДЕЛЕНИЕ;
ПЕРЕГОРОДКА

partner
(CHIN) 合伙人，合伙董事
(FRE) associé, partenaire
(GER) Gesellschafter *m*; Teilhaber *m*,
(Geschäfts)partner *m*, Mitinhaber *m*;
Sozius *m*
(JAP) 仲間、共同出資者、パートナー
(RUS) ПАРТНЕР

partnership
(CHIN) 合伙关系，合伙企业，合股
(FRE) association, partenariat, (C) société,
association, partenariat
(GER) Personengesellschaft *f*; Sozietät *f*,
Teilhaberschaft *f*; Partnerschaft *f*;
Mitbeteiligung *f*
(JAP) 共同、協力、共同経営
(RUS) ТОВАРИЩЕСТВО; ПАРТНЕРСТВО

part-time
(CHIN) 兼任
(FRE) temps partiel
(GER) Teilzeit-
(JAP) パートタイムの、非常勤の
(RUS) НА ПОЛ СТАВКИ

par value
(CHIN) 票面价值
(FRE) valeur au pair, valeur nominale

(GER) Nennwert *m*, Nominal- *m*,
Pariwert *m*
(JAP) 為替平価、額面価額
(RUS) ПАРИТЕТ, НОМИНАЛ,
НОМИНАЛЬНАЯ ВЕЛИЧИНА

passed dividend
(CHIN) 过期未付的股息
(FRE) excercice (n, m) conclu sans payer de
dividende, (C) dividende non déclaré
(GER) rückständige Dividende *f*,
Dividendenausfall *m*
(JAP)（未払いの）保留配当、
見送り配当、無配
(RUS) ПРОПУЩЕННЫЙ ДИВИДЕНД

passenger mile
(CHIN) 旅客里程
(FRE) passager-mille
(GER) Passagiermeile *f*
(JAP) 旅客マイル
(RUS) ПАССАЖИРО – МИЛЯ

passive activities
(CHIN) 被动管理
(FRE) activités passives
(GER) passive Tätigkeiten *fpl*
(JAP) 受動的の活動
(RUS) ПАССИВНЫЕ ОПЕРАЦИИ

passive income (loss)
(CHIN) 被动收入（损失）
(FRE) revenu passif, (C) revenus (pertes)
hors exploitation
(GER) Einkünfte *fpl* (Verluste *mpl*) aus
Kapitalvermögen *npl*
(JAP) 受動的所得（損失）

passive investor
(CHIN) 被动投资人
(FRE) investisseur passif
(GER) passiver Investor *m*
(JAP) 受動的投資家
(RUS) ПАССИВНЫЙ ИНВЕСТОР

passport
(CHIN) 护照
(FRE) passeport
(GER) Reisepass *m*

(JAP) 旅券、パスポート、（比喩的に）
保障

pass-through security
(CHIN) 转嫁证券
(FRE) titre garanti par des créances
hypothécaires, (C) titre avec flux identiques
(GER) Wertpapier *n* mit laufenden
Zinszahlungen *fpl*
(JAP) パススルー証券
(RUS) ЦЕННЫЕ БУМАГИ , ПОЛУЧАЮЩИЕ
ДОХОД ОТ ДРУГИХ КРЕДИТНО-
ФИНАНСОВЫХ ИНСТРУМЕНТОВ

password
(CHIN) 通行口令，密码
(FRE) mot de passe
(GER) Passwort *n*, Kennwort *n*
(JAP) パスワード、合い言葉、暗証番号
(RUS) ПАРОЛЬ

paste
(CHIN) 粘贴
(FRE) coler, (C) coller
(GER) einfügen *v* (EDV)
(JAP) 貼り付ける、ペースト
(RUS) ПРИКЛЕИВАТЬ

past service benefit
(CHIN) 过去服务年资收益
(FRE) prestation de services rendus,
(C) prestation préretraite au survivant
(GER) Anwartschaft *f* bzw.
Leistungsanspruch *m* aus der Vordienstzeit *f*
(JAP) 過去勤務給付、過去勤務年金
(RUS) ЛЬГОТЫ ЗА
ПРЕДШЕСТВОВАВШУЮ СЛУЖБУ

patent
(CHIN) 专利，专利权
(FRE) brevet
(GER) Patent *n*; patentieren *v*
(JAP) 特許、特許権、土地譲渡証書
(RUS) ПАТЕНТ; ПАТЕНТОВАТЬ

patent infringement
(CHIN) 侵犯专利权
(FRE) violation de brevet, (C) contrefaçon
de brevet
(GER) Patentverletzung *f*

(JAP) 特許権侵害
(RUS) НАРУШЕНИЕ ПАТЕНТНЫХ ПРАВ

patent monopoly
(CHIN) 专利独占
(FRE) monopole sur un brevet,
(C) monopole de brevet
(GER) Patentmonopol *n*
(JAP) 特許権独占、専売特許
(RUS) ПАТЕНТНАЯ МОНОПОЛИЯ

patent of invention
(CHIN) 发明专利
(FRE) brevet d'invention
(GER) Erfindungspatent *n*
(JAP) 発明特許
(RUS) ПАТЕНТ НА ИЗОБРЕТЕНИЕ

patent pending
(CHIN) 专利申请
(FRE) demande de brevet déposée, (C)
brevet en instance
(GER) Patent *n* angemeldet, schwebende
bzw. anhängige Patentanmeldung *f*,
laufendes Patentverfahren *n*
(JAP) 特許出願中
(RUS) ЗАЯВКА НА ПАТЕНТ ПОДАНА

patent warfare
(CHIN) 专利战
(FRE) guerre des brevets
(GER) Patentkrieg *m*
(JAP) 特許争い
(RUS) «ПАТЕНТНАЯ ВОЙНА»

paternalism
(CHIN) 家长式作风，
温和的干涉主义
(FRE) paternalisme
(GER) Paternalismus *m*
(JAP) 父権主義、父権的干渉（統制）、
パターナリズム

path
(CHIN) 路径，通路
(FRE) chemin, (C) chemin d'accès
(GER) Pfad *m*
(JAP) パス、経路
(RUS) МАРШРУТ

patronage dividend and rebate
(CHIN) 赞助人红利及回扣
(FRE) ristourne et rabais, (C) Ristourne
(GER) Kundenrückvergütung *f*
und -rabatt *m*
(JAP) 利益配当および割引(払戻し、
リベート、割戻し)
(RUS) ДИВИДЕНД (ПРЕМИЯ) И СКИДКА
ОПТОВИКА РОЗНИЧНОМУ ПРОДАВЦУ

pauper
(CHIN) 穷人，乞丐
(FRE) personne indigente
(GER) Armer *m*, verarmte Person *f*
(JAP) 救貧法受給者
НИЩИЙ; НЕСОСТОЯТЕЛЬНЫЙ ДОЛЖНИК

pay
(CHIN) 支付，付款，偿还，工资
(FRE) salaire, paie
(GER) Lohn *m*, Gehalt *n*, Bezüge *mpl*
(JAP) 支給、給料、支払う
(RUS) ЗАПЛАТИТЬ, ОПЛАТИТЬ; ОПЛАТА

payables
(CHIN) 应付款
(FRE) factures à payer, (C) comptes
fournisseurs
(GER) Kreditoren *mpl*, Verbindlichkeiten
fpl
(JAP) 支払債務、買入債務、掛金
(RUS) ДЕБЕТ; СЧЕТА К ОПЛАТЕ

pay as you go
(CHIN) 分期付款，按成收费
(FRE) prélèvement de l'impôt à la source
(GER) aus laufenden Erträgen bezahlen *v*
(JAP) 現金支払主義
(RUS) ВЫПЛАТА ПЕНСИЙ ИЗ ТЕКУЩИХ
ДОХОДОВ

payback period
(CHIN) 偿付期
(FRE) période de remboursement, (C) délai
de récupération
(GER) Amortisationszeit *f*, -periode *f*,
Tilgungszeit *m*; Wiedergewinnungszeit *f*
(JAP) 返済期間、資本回収期間、
払戻期間

(RUS) СРОК ПОГАШЕНИЯ

paycheck
(CHIN) 工资 支票
(FRE) chèque de paie, (C) salaire
(GER) Lohn- *m*, Gehaltsscheck *m*
(JAP) 給料、俸給、給与
(RUS) ЗАРПЛАТА, ВЫДАВАЕМАЯ ЧЕКОМ

payday
(CHIN) 发薪日，结算日
(FRE) jour de paie
(GER) Zahltag *m*
(JAP) 給料日、俸給日、支払日
(RUS) ДЕНЬ ЗАРАБОТНОЙ ПЛАТЫ

payee
(CHIN) 受款人，收款人
(FRE) bénéficiaire, porteur
(GER) Zahlungsempfänger *m*,
-berechtigter *m*; Wechselnehmer *m*,
Remittent *m*
(JAP) 被支払人、受取人
(RUS) ПОЛУЧАТЕЛЬ ПЛАТЕЖА

payer
(CHIN) 付款人
(FRE) payeur, tireur
(GER) (Ein)zahler *m*;
Zahlungspflichtiger *m*
支払人、払渡人
(RUS) ПЛАТЕЛЬЩИК

paying agent
(CHIN) 代付人
(FRE) office de paiement,
(C) domicile de paiement
(GER) Zahlstelle *f*
支払代理人
(RUS) ПЛАТЕЖНЫЙ АГЕНТ

payload
(CHIN) 工资负担，付运费的货物
(FRE) charge utile
(GER) Nutzlast *f*, Ladegewicht *n*; Arbeits-
pl, Lohnkosten *pl*, -summe *f*
(JAP) 給金負担高、有料荷重
(RUS) ПОЛЕЗНЫЙ ГРУЗ;
КОММЕРЧЕСКАЯ НАГРУЗКА;
ОПЛАЧИВАЕМЫЙ ГРУЗ

payment bond
(CHIN) 付款债券
(FRE) cautionnement vis à vis des tiers,
(C) garantie de paiement
(GER) Zahlungsbürgschaft *f*, -garantie *f*,
Sicherheitsleistung *f*
支払保証、返還保証証券、払込み債
(RUS) ОБЯЗАТЕЛЬСТВО ОПЛАТЫ

payment date
(CHIN) 付款日期
(FRE) date de paiement
(GER) Zahlungs- *m*, Tilgungstermin *m*
(JAP) 支払期日
(RUS) ДАТА ПЛАТЕЖА

payment in due course
(CHIN) 期满兑付
(FRE) paiement dans les délais impartis,
(C) paiement dans les délais prévus
(GER) Zahlung *f* bei Fälligkeit *f*,
ordnungsgemäße Zahlung *f*
(JAP) 満期払い
(RUS) ОПЛАТА В НАДЛЕЖАЩЕЕ ВРЕМЯ

payment method
(CHIN) 支付方法，付款方法
(FRE) méthode de paiement, (C) mode de
paiement
(GER) Zahlungsweg *m*, -art *f*, -methode *f*
(JAP) 支払方法、料金設定、返済方法
(RUS) СПОСОБ ОПЛАТЫ, РАСЧЕТОВ

payola
(CHIN) 贿赂，收买
(FRE) methode consistant a soudoyer les
programmateurs pour qu'ils passent tres
frequemment le disque qu'on veut lancer
(GER) Bestechung *f*; Schmiergeld *n*
(JAP) リベート、贿赂
(RUS) СРЫТАЯ ИЛИ КОСВЕННАЯ
ОПЛАТА (за услугу)

payout
(CHIN) 偿付，补偿
(FRE) paiement, règlement,
(C) récupération
(GER) Dividendenzahlung *f*; Rendite *f*;
Amortisation *f*; (Gewinn)ausschüttung *f*;
Barregulierung *f* (Versicherung)

(JAP) 支払（金）、（投資の）回収、
配当（金）、元金回収
(RUS) ПРИБЫЛЬ ОТ ИНВЕСТИЦИЙ,
РАВНАЯ ПЕРВОНАЧАЛЬНОМУ
ВЛОЖЕНИЮ

payout ratio
(CHIN) 股息支付率，股利发放率
(FRE) payout ratio, (C) ratio de
récupération
(GER) Ausschüttungskennzahl f, -quote f,
Dividendendeckung f, Auszahlungskurs m
(JAP) 配当性向、
配当支払率
(RUS) КОЭФФИЦИЕНТ ВЫПЛАТЫ
ПРИБЫЛИ В ФОРМЕ ДИВИДЕНДОВ

pay period
(CHIN) 工资支付期，
工资结算期
(FRE) période de paie
(GER) Zahlungszeitraum m, Lohn- f,
Gehaltsperiode f, Bezugszeitraum m
(JAP) 給与期間
(RUS) СРОК ОПЛАТЫ

payroll
(CHIN) 工资单
(FRE) liste du personnel, (C) liste de
paie
(GER) Lohn- f und Gehaltsliste f;
Lohnkonto n; Gehaltsabrechnung f
(JAP) 給与、給料、支払台帳、
賃金支払帳、給与者名簿
(RUS) ВЕДОМОСТЬ НАЧИСЛЕНИЯ
ЗАРАБОТНОЙ ПЛАТЫ

payroll deduction
(CHIN) 工薪扣款
(FRE) déduction sur le traitement déduction
sur le salaire
(GER) Lohn- mpl und Gehaltsabzüge mpl
(JAP) 賃金控除
(RUS) СПИСАНИЕ ФОНДА ЗАРАБОТНОЙ
ПЛАТЫ

payroll savings plan
(CHIN) 工资储蓄计划
(FRE) régime d'épargne automatique,
(C) mode d'épargne sur le salaire

(GER) Lohnsparplan m, (Programm zum
Erwerb von Sparschuldverschreibungen
durch freiwilligen Lohnabzug)
(JAP) 給料天引き貯金プラン
(RUS) ПРОГРАММА СБЕРЕЖЕНИЙ ИЗ
ЗАРАБОТНОЙ ПЛАТЫ

payroll tax
(CHIN) 工薪税
(FRE) impôt sur la masse salariale,
(C) impôt sur les salaries
(GER) Lohnsummensteuer f,
Arbeitgeberbeiträge mpl zur
Sozialversicherung f (US)
給与税、賃金税
(RUS) НАЛОГ НА ЗАРАБОТНУЮ ПЛАТУ

peak
(CHIN) 最高，高峰
(FRE) maximum, (C) arc, (C) pointe,
(C) sommet
(GER) Höchststand m; Gipfelwert m,
Scheitelpunkt m; Hauptbelastung f
(JAP) 景気の山
(RUS) ПИК; ВЫСШАЯ ТОЧКА

peak period
(CHIN) 高峰期间
(FRE) période de pointe
(GER) Spitzenzeit f, Hauptumsatz- f,
Hauptbelastungs- f,
Hauptverkehrszeit f
(JAP) 最高期間、ピーク時

peculation
(CHIN) 盗用公款
(FRE) détournement des biens
(GER) Unterschlagung f, Unterschleif m,
Veruntreuung f
(JAP) 公金横領、受託金横領者
(RUS) НЕЗАКОННОЕ РАСПОРЯЖЕНИЕ
ЧУЖОЙ СОБСТВЕННОСТЬЮ

pecuniary
(CHIN) 金钱的
(FRE) pécuniaire
(GER) finanziell, monetär, geldlich adj
(JAP) 金銭（上）の、財政（上）の、
罰金を課せるべき
(RUS) ДЕНЕЖНЫЙ; ФИНАНСОВЫЙ

peg
(CHIN) 固定
(FRE) fixer, stabiliser, (C) stabiliser le prix d'un titre
(GER) (Währung, Preise) stützen, festsetzen *v*
(JAP) 釘付けにする、（株の売買によって高騰・低落を）安定させる、(為替相場の騰落を)抑える
(RUS) ФИКСАЦИЯ ЦЕНЫ НА ОПРЕДЕЛЁННОМ УРОВНЕ

penalty
(CHIN) 罚款
(FRE) amende, (C) pénalité
(GER) Vertrags- *f*, Konventionalstrafe *f*, Strafgeld *n*
(JAP) 罰金、違約金
(RUS) НАКАЗАНИЕ; ШТРАФ

penny stock
(CHIN) 便士股票，低价股票
(FRE) action d'une valeur de moins d'un dollar,
(C) actions cotées en cents
(GER) Billigaktien *fpl*, Kleinaktien *fpl*, (unter einem Dollar gehandelte Aktie, sehr billige (Spekulations)aktie)
(JAP) ペニー株、投機的低位株、投機的安物株
(RUS) «КОПЕЕЧНАЯ» АКЦИЯ (с рыночной ценой менее 1 долл.)

pension fund
(CHIN) 抚恤基金，退休基金
(FRE) caisse de retraite, (C) régime de retraite
(GER) Pensions- *f*, Rentenkasse *f*
(JAP) 年金基金、恩給基金

peon
(CHIN) 日工，散工
(FRE) peon, (C) domestique
(GER) arbeitsverpflichteter Schuldner *m*, Schuldknecht *m*
(JAP) 日雇い人、日雇い労働者
(RUS) ПЕОН; РАБ

people intensive
(CHIN) 人工密集型

(FRE) à forte intensité de main d'oeuvre,
(C) prédominance de main-d'œuvre
(GER) personalintensiv *adj*
(JAP) 人手集約的な
(RUS) ТРУДОЕМКИЙ

per capita
(CHIN) 人均
(FRE) par personne, par tête
(GER) pro Kopf *m*, pro Person *f*
(JAP) 一人当たり、頭割りで

per-capita debt
(CHIN) 人均负债
(FRE) dette par tête
(GER) Pro-Kopf-Verschuldung *f*
(JAP) 一人当たりの負債
(RUS) ЗАДОЛЖЕННОСТЬ НА ДУШУ НАСЕЛЕНИЯ

percentage lease
(CHIN) 分成租约
(FRE) loyer correspondant à un certain pourcentage du chiffres d'affaires
(GER) Umsatzmietvertrag *m*, -pachtvertrag *m*
(JAP) 歩合制リース、歩合制賃貸借率
(RUS) АРЕНДА С ОПЛАТОЙ НА ОСНОВЕ ПРОЦЕНТОВ ОТ ДОХОДА или ВЫРУЧКИ

percentage-of-completion method
(CHIN) 按完成进度报税法
(FRE) méthode du pourcentage d'achèvement, (C) méthode d'estimation fondée sur le chiffre d'affaires
(GER) Methode *f* der Bewertung *f* nach prozentualem Beendigungsfortschritt *m*, (steuerliche Gewinnermittlungsmethode, bei der die aus langfristigen Verträgen resultierenden Gewinne anteilig zu der prozentualen Fertigstellung des Projektes berücksichtigt werden)
(JAP) 工事進行比率法、工事進行基準法
(RUS) МЕТОДИКА УЧЕТА ИСХОДЯ ИЗ ПРОЦЕНТА ВЫПОЛНЕНИЯ

percentage-of-sales method
(CHIN) 销售百分比法
(FRE) méthode d'estimation fondée sur le pourcentage du chiffre d'affaires
(GER) Umsatzprovision(smethode) *f*

(JAP) 売上比率法
(RUS) МЕТОДИКА УЧЕТА ИСХОДЯ ОТ ПРОЦЕНТА СБЫТА

percent, percentage
(CHIN) 百分比
(FRE) pour cent, pourcentage
(GER) Prozent *n*, Prozentsatz *m*, -anteil *m*
(JAP) パーセント、百分率
(RUS) ПРОЦЕНТ, ПРОЦЕНТНОЕ СООТНОШЕНИЕ

percolation test
(CHIN) 渗透测试
(FRE) test de percolation, (C) test de perméabilité
(GER) Perkolationstest *m*
(JAP) 浸透試験
(RUS) ИСПЫТАНИЕ ФИЛЬТРАЦИОННОЙ СПОСОБНОСТИ (ПОЧВЫ)

per diem
(CHIN) 每日津贴
(FRE) prix de journée, per diem, (C) par jour
(GER) Tagespauschale *f*, -satz *m*
(JAP) 毎日当り、１日当り
(RUS) СУТОЧНЫЕ

perfect competition
(CHIN) 完全竞争
(FRE) concurrence parfaite
(GER) vollständige Konkurrenz *f*
(JAP) 完全競争
(RUS) СОВЕРШЕННАЯ КОНКУРЕНЦИЯ

perfect (pure) monopoly
(CHIN) 完全垄断
(FRE) monopole parfait
(GER) perfektes (reines) Monopol *n*
(JAP) 完全独占（＝ABSOLUTE MONOPOLY）
(RUS) СОВЕРШЕННАЯ (ЧИСТАЯ) МОНОПОЛИЯ

perfected
(CHIN) 完美的
(FRE) complet, perfectionné), (C) rendu opposable, (C) mis en état
(GER) ausgereift, vollendet *adj*

(JAP) 大成された、完成された
(RUS) УСОВЕРШЕНСТВОВАННЫЙ

performance
(CHIN) 履行，完成，业绩，表现，清偿
(FRE) performance, exécution, résultats, (C) rendement
(GER) Leistung *f*; Abschneiden *n*, Erfüllung *f*; Performance *f*
(JAP) 遂行、履行、成績、業績
(RUS) ПОКАЗАТЕЛИ РАБОТЫ, ИСПОЛНЕНИЯ; ЭКСПЛУАТАЦИОННЫЕ КАЧЕСТВА

performance bond
(CHIN) 履约保证金
(FRE) garantie de bonne fin, (C) cautionnement définitif, (C) cautionnement d'exécution
(GER) Leistungs- *f*, Erfüllungsgarantie *f*, Gewährleistungsbürgschaft *f*, Leistungsversprechen *n*, Bietungsgarantie *f*
(JAP) 契約履行保証，契約保証保険
(RUS) ГАРАНТИЯ КАЧЕСТВА ИСПОЛНЕНИЯ

performance fund
(CHIN) 营业基金
(FRE) fonds hautement spéculatif
(GER) Leistungs- *m*, Wachstumsfonds *m*
(JAP) パフォーマンスファンド
(RUS) СОВМЕСТНЫЙ ФОНД, СОЗДАННЫЙ ДЛЯ ПРИРОСТ КАПИТАЛА (А НЕ ВЫПЛАТЫ ДИВИДЕНДОВ)

performance stock
(CHIN) 绩优股
(FRE) valeur à forte croissance, (C) valeur d'avenir
(GER) Wachstumsaktie *f*, -wert *m*
(JAP) 業績株
(RUS) АКЦИИ СБЫСТРО РАСТУЩЕЙ ЦЕНОЙ

period
(CHIN) 会计期，时期，周期，有效期
(FRE) période
(GER) Periode *f*, Zeitraum *m*, Laufzeit *f*
(JAP) 期間
(RUS) СРОК

313

period expense, period cost
(CHIN) 期间费用，期间成本
(FRE) coût de période
(GER) Periodenkosten *pl*, zeitabhängige Kosten *pl*
(JAP) 期間費用、期間原価
(RUS) ПЕРИОДИЧЕСКИЕ ЗАТРАТЫ, РАСХОДЫ

periodic inventory method
(CHIN) 定期盘存法
(FRE) méthode d'inventaire périodique, (C) inventaire périodique
(GER) Stichtagsinventurmethode *f*
(JAP) 定期的棚卸法
(RUS) МЕТОДИКА ПЕРИОДИЧЕСКОГО УЧЕТА МАТЕРИАЛЬНЫХ ЗАПАСОВ

peripheral device
(CHIN) 外围设备，外部设备
(FRE) périphérique
(GER) Peripheriegerät *n*
(JAP) 周辺機器、周辺装置
(RUS) ПЕРЕФИРИЙНОЕ УСТРОЙСТВО

permanent difference
(CHIN) 恒差，永久差别
(FRE) écart permanent
(GER) Dauerabweichung *f*
(JAP) 永久差異
(RUS) ПОСТОЯННАЯ РАЗНИЦА

permanent financing
(CHIN) 长期融资，长期抵押贷款
(FRE) financement permanent
(GER) Dauerfinanzierung *f*
(JAP) 永久貸出し、永久的資金調達
(RUS) ПОСТОЯННОЕ (ДОЛГОСРОЧНОЕ) ФИНАНСИРОВАНИЕ

permit
(CHIN) 许可证，执照，许可
(FRE) permis
(GER) Genehmigung *f*, Zulassung *f*, Erlaubnis *f*; Lizenz *f*, Konzession
(JAP) 許す、許可、許可証
(RUS) РАЗРЕШИТЬ; РАЗРЕШЕНИЕ

permit bond
(CHIN) 许可证押金

(FRE) assurance caution
(GER) Lizenzkaution *f*
(JAP) 保証を許可する
(RUS) ОБЯЗАТЕЛЬСТВО ВЫПОЛНЕНИЯ ОПЕРАЦИЙ, НА КОТОРЫЕ ВЫДАНО РАЗРЕШЕНИЕ

permutations
(CHIN) 变更，交换，彻底改变
(FRE) permutations
(GER) Permutation *f*, Umsetzung *f*, Vertauschung *f*
(JAP) 順列、置換、並べ換え
(RUS) ПЕРЕСТАНОВКИ

perpetual inventory
(CHIN) 永续盘存
(FRE) inventaire permanent, stock stratégique
(GER) permanent geführte Inventur *f*, Bestandsfortschreibung *f*
(JAP) 継続棚卸、恒久的棚卸
(RUS) СИСТЕМА НЕПРЕРЫВНОГО УЧЕТА (ИНВЕНТАРИЗАЦИИ) ЗАПАСОВ

perpetuity
(CHIN) 永久，永久财产，终身年金
(FRE) rente perpétuelle, (C) perpétuité
(GER) Dauerzustand *m*; (Rente *f*) auf Lebenszeit *f*
(JAP) 永続、終身年金、永久所有
(RUS) БЕССРОЧНОЕ ВЛАДЕНИЕ; ПОЖИЗНЕННАЯ РЕНТА

perquisite (perk)
(CHIN) 津贴，奖金，额外收入
(FRE) avantage en nature, (C) avantage indirect
(GER) Nebenleistung *f*, Sondervergütung *f*, -zulage *f*, Vergünstigung *f*, Nebenbezüge *mpl*
(JAP) （定収入、給料、賃金以外の）付加給与、特別給付
(RUS) ДОПОЛНИТЕЛЬНАЯ ЛЬГОТА, ПРИВИЛЕГИЯ, ВЫПЛАТА

person
(CHIN) 人，本人，法人
(FRE) personne
(GER) Person *f*

(JAP) 人、自然人、人間、個人
(RUS) ЛИЦО

personal data sheet
(CHIN) 个人资料
(FRE) fiche de renseignements personnels,
(C) feuille de renseignements personnels
(GER) Personalbogen *m*
(JAP) 個人データ表
(RUS) ЛИЧНАЯ УЧЕТНАЯ
КАРТОЧКА

personal digital assistant (PDA)
(CHIN) 个人数字助理（PDA）
(FRE) assistant numérique personnel
(GER) PDA *m*, persönlicher digitaler
Assistent *m*
(JAP) パーソナルデジタルアシスタント、
携帯情報端末
(RUS) ЭЛЕКТРОННЫЙ ОРГАНАЙЗЕР

personal financial statement
(CHIN) 个人财务报表
(FRE) situation financière personnelle, (C)
états financiers personnels
(GER) persönliche Vermögensaufstellung *f*
(JAP) 個人の財産状況報告書
(RUS) ПЕРСОНАЛЬНЫЙ ФИНАНСОВЫЙ
ОТЧЕТ

personal holding company (PHC)
(CHIN) 个人持股公司（PHC）
(FRE) holding personnelle, (C) société
personnelle du portefeuille
(GER) kleine Holding *f*, personenbezogene
Holdinggesellschaft *f*
(JAP) 個人持ち株会社
(RUS) ЛИЧНЫЙ ХОЛДИНГ, Т. Е.
КОРПОРАЦИЯ, КОТОРАЯ ПОЛУЧАЕТ
БОЛЕЕ 60 % ПРИБЫЛИ ОТ ДИВИДЕНДОВ,
ПРОЦЕНТОВ И Т. П. И 50 % АКЦИЙ
КОТОРОЙ ВЛАДЕЮТ 5 ИЛИ МЕНЕЕ
ЛИЦ

personal income
(CHIN) 个人收入
(FRE) revenu personnel
(GER) persönliches Einkommen *n*,
Privateinkünfte *pl*
(JAP) 個人所得
(RUS) ЛИЧНЫЙ ДОХОД

personal influence
(CHIN) 个人影响
(FRE) influence personnelle
(GER) persönlicher Einfluss *m*
(JAP) パーソナルインフルエンス、
個人的影響
(RUS) ЛИЧНОЕ ВЛИЯНИЕ

personal injury
(CHIN) 个人伤害
(FRE) dommage corporel
(GER) Personenschaden *m*
(JAP) 人身傷害、人体損傷、個人的権利
に対する被害
(RUS) ТРАВМА; ЛИЧНЫЙ УЩЕРБ

personal liability
(CHIN) 个人责任
(FRE) responsabilité personnelle
(GER) persönliche Haftung *f*,
Individualhaftung *f*
(JAP) 人的責任、個人的責任、
個人的負債
(RUS) ЛИЧНАЯ ОТВЕТСТВЕННОСТЬ

personal property
(CHIN) 个人财产
(FRE) biens personnels, (C) bien meuble
(GER) bewegliches (Privat)eigentum *n*, -
vermögen *n*, persönliches Eigentum
(JAP) 人的財産（権）、動産、個人財産
(RUS) ЛИЧНАЯ СОБСТВЕННОСТЬ

personal property floater
(CHIN) 私人财产总括
(FRE) tous risques flottants sur biens
personnels, (C) risques flottants sur biens
mobiliers
(GER) Abschreibepolice *f* über
Privateigentum *n*
(JAP) 動産包括保険、動産包括保険証券
(RUS) СТРАХОВОЕ ПОКРЫТИЕ ВСЕЙ
ЛИЧНОЙ СОБСТВЕННОСТИ,
НЕЗАВИСИМО ОТ ЕЁ НАХОЖДЕНИЯ

personal selling
(CHIN) 个人推销
(FRE) ventes personnelles
(GER) Haustür- *m*, Direktverkauf *m*,
persönlicher Verkauf *m* durch Vertreter *mpl*

(JAP) 対個人販売、人的販売、
(RUS) ЛИЧНАЯ ПРОДАЖА

personnel
(CHIN) 人员，人事
(GER) (Betriebs)personal *n*, Mitarbeiter *mpl*, Beschäftigte *mpl*, Belegschaft *f*
(RUS) ПЕРСОНАЛ; ШТАТ; КАДРЫ

personnel department
(CHIN) 人事部门
(FRE) service du personnel
(GER) Personalabteilung *f*
(JAP) （会社の）人事課
(RUS) ОТДЕЛ КАДРОВ

petition
(CHIN) 请求，请求书
(FRE) demande, (C) pétition
(GER) Petition *f*, Bittschrift *f*, Gesuch *n*, Eingabe *f*; Klage *f*, (Verfahrens)antrag *m*
(JAP) 請願（書）、陳情（書）、申請する
(RUS) ПЕТИЦИЯ; ПРОШЕНИЕ; ХОДАТАЙСТВО

petty cash fund
(CHIN) 零用现金基金
(FRE) fond de petite caisse, (C) fonds de caisse
(GER) kleine Kasse *f*, Nebenkasse *f*, Spesenkasse *f*, Portokassenfonds *m*
(JAP) 小口現金、小払い用現金
(RUS) ФОНД МЕЛКОЙ НАЛИЧНОСТИ

Phillip's curve
(CHIN) 菲利浦斯曲线
(FRE) courbe de Phillip
(GER) Phillips-Kurve *f*
(JAP) フィリップス曲線
(RUS) КРИВАЯ ФИЛЛИПСА
(взаимодействия инфляции и безработицы)

physical commodity
(CHIN) 实物商品
(FRE) marchandises physiques, (C) biens physiques
(GER) Effektivware *f* (Terminbörse)
(JAP) 実物商品

(RUS) МАТЕРИАЛЬНЫЙ (ФИЗИЧЕСКИЙ) ТОВАР, ИМУЩЕСТВО

physical depreciation
(CHIN) 实际折旧，实物折旧，有形损耗
(FRE) dépréciation), amortissement, (C) dépréciation physique
(GER) kalkulatorische Abschreibung *f*, verbrauchsbedingte Wertminderung *f*
(JAP) 物質的減価、物量的減価、物理的減価
(RUS) ФИЗИЧЕСКАЯ АМОРТИЗАЦИЯ

physical examination
(CHIN) 实物检查
(FRE) examen physique, (C) inspection des biens
(GER) Musterung *f*, (ärztliche) Untersuchung *f*
(JAP) 身体検査、健康診断
(RUS) МЕДИЦИНСКИЙ ОСМОТР

physical inventory
(CHIN) 实地盘存
(FRE) inventaire physique
(GER) Warenbestand *f*, -vorräte *mpl*
(JAP) 現物棚卸、実地棚卸、実在庫量
(RUS) ФАКТИЧЕСКИЕ МАТЕРИАЛЬНЫЕ ЗАПАСЫ

picketing
(CHIN) 站在公共建筑物前表示抗议的示威群众
(GER) Aufstellung *f* von Streikposten *mpl*, Bestreiken *n*
(JAP) ピケを張る
(RUS) ПИКЕТИРОВАНИЕ

picture format
(CHIN) 图片格式
(FRE) format d'image
(GER) Bildformat *n*
(JAP) ピクチャフォーマット、ピクチャ形式

piece rate
(CHIN) 计件工资，论件计
(FRE) salaire à la pièce, salaire à la tâche
(GER) Stück- *m*, Akkordlohnsatz *m*

(JAP) 単価、出来高払い、請負単価
(RUS) ПОШТУЧНАЯ СТАВКА ПОЧТОВЫХ УСЛУГ

piece work
(CHIN) 计件工作
(GER) Akkordarbeit *f*, Stückakkord *m*, -arbeit *f*
(JAP) 出来高（払いの）仕事、請負仕事、賃仕事
(RUS) СДЕЛЬНАЯ РАБОТА

pie chart
(CHIN) 圆形分析图
(FRE) graphique à secteurs camembert
(GER) Kreisdiagramm *n*
(JAP) 円グラフ、円分グラフ，パイ図表
(RUS) СЕКТОРНАЯ ДИАГРАММА

pier to house
(CHIN) 码头到仓库运输
(FRE) quai à domicile
(GER) Transport *m* vom Ladehafen *m* zum Werk *n* des Empfängers *m*
(JAP) 埠頭（桟橋）から戸口へ
(RUS) ОТ ПРИЧАЛА ДО ПРЕДПРИЯТИЯ

piggyback loan
(CHIN) 寄生贷款
(FRE) prêt multiple, (C) prêt jumelé
(GER) Huckepackdarlehen *n*
(JAP) ピギーバックローン
(RUS) КОМБИНИРОВАНИЕ СТРОИТЕЛЬНОЙ И ОБЫЧНОЙ ССУДЫ; ЗАЙМ, КОТОРЫЙ НАХОДЯТСЯ В РУКАХ НЕСКОЛЬКИХ СУБОРДИНИРОВАННЫХ КРЕДИТОРОВ

pilot plan
(CHIN) 新产品试制计划
(FRE) plan pilote, (C) plan expérimental
(GER) Pilot- *n*, Versuchswerk *n*, -anstalt *f*, Musteranlage *f*
(JAP) パイロットプラン、実験的計画、試験的計画
(RUS) ПРЕДВАРИТЕЛЬНЫЙ ПЛАН

pin money
(CHIN) 零用钱
(GER) Taschengeld *n*, Nadelgeld *n*; Heim-*m*, Saisonarbeiterlohn *m*
(JAP) 小額の金、はした金
(RUS) «ДЕНЬГИ НА КАРМАННЫЕ РАСХОДЫ» (МЕЛКИЕ ВЫПЛАТЫ)

pipeline
(CHIN) 管道
(FRE) pipeline, (C) filière
(GER) Pipeline *f*
(JAP) パイプライン、輸送管路、流通経路
(RUS) В СТАДИИ РАЗРАБОТКИКОНВЕЕРНАЯ ОБРАБОТКА (ПРОГР.)

pitch
(CHIN) 孔距，间距，声调
(FRE) pas, espacement
(GER) Abstand *m*, Höhe *f*
(JAP) ピッチ、（文字、行などの）送り
(RUS) ШАГ, ЧИСЛО ЗНАКОВ, ПЕЧАТАЕМЫХ ИЛИ ПЕРФОРИРУЕМЫХ НА ЕДИНИЦУ ДЛИНЫ

pixel/picture element
(CHIN) 象素/象元
(FRE) pixel
(GER) Bildelement *n*
(JAP) ピクセル、画素
(RUS) ПИКСЕЛ, ЭЛЕМЕНТ ИЗОБРАЖЕНИЯ

pixel image
(CHIN) 象素映象
(FRE) image pixel
(GER) Bildpunktabbild *n*
(JAP) ピクセルイメージ、ピクセル画像
(RUS) ИЗОБРАЖЕНИЕ, РАЗЛОЖЕННОЕ НА ЭЛЕМЕНТЫ

placement test
(CHIN) 招工测试
(FRE) test d'orientation
(GER) Einstufungstest *m*
(JAP) 就職試験、従業員の採用試験、（人員）配置テスト
(RUS) ТЕСТ ДЛЯ ПОДБОРКИ НАИБОЛЕЕ ПОДХОДЯЩЕЙ РАБОТЫ

place utility

(CHIN) 商品摆放效应

(FRE) avantage du lieu

(GER) Klartext *m*

(JAP) 場所効果

(RUS) РАЗМЕЩЕНИЕ ТОВАРА В
УДОЬНЫХ ДЛЯ ПОТРЕБИТЕЛЯ МЕСТАХ

plain text

(CHIN) 明文；纯文本

(FRE) texte en clair

(GER) Klartext *m*

(JAP) 普通テキスト

(RUS) НЕЗАШИФРОВАННЫЙ ТЕКСТ

plaintiff

(CHIN) 原告

(FRE) plaignant, (C) demandeur

(GER) Kläger *m*, Klagepartei *f*,
Antragsteller *m*

(JAP) 訴訟人、原告、起訴人

(RUS) ИСТЕЦ

plan

(CHIN) 计划，规划，方案，方法，制度

(FRE) plan, projet

(GER) Plan *m*, Vorhaben *n*

(JAP) (物事を進める)計画、案、制度
（年金などの必要資金の）

(RUS) ПЛАН; ПРОГРАММА;
ПЛАНИРОВАТЬ

plan B

(CHIN) 备用计划

(FRE) plan B

(GER) Alternativ- *m*, Ausweichplan *n*

(JAP) 計画B

(RUS) РЕЗЕРВНЫЙ, ЗАПАСНОЙ ПЛАН

planned economy

(CHIN) 计划经济

(FRE) économie planifiée

(GER) Planwirtschaft *f*

(JAP) 計画的経済

(RUS) ПЛАНОВАЯ ЭКОНОМИКА

plant

(CHIN) 工厂，车间，设备，固定资产

(FRE) matériel, usine, (C) usine

(GER) Werk *n*, Betrieb *m*, Betriebsstätte *f*,
Fabrik *f*

(JAP) 植物、作物、施設

(RUS) ЗАВОД; ПРОМЫШЛЕННАЯ
УСТАНОВКА; НАСАЖДАТЬ, ВНЕДРЯТЬ

plat

(CHIN) 绘制土地图，规划

(FRE) lotissement

(GER) (Bau)grundstück *n*, Stück *n* Land *n*

(JAP) 小さな地面（地所）、図面

(RUS) КАРТА ЗЕМЕЛЬНОГО УЧАСТКА

plat book

(CHIN) 土地使用图

(FRE) cadastre, (C) registre des
lotissements

(GER) Grundbuch *n*, Kataster *n*

(JAP) プラットブック、地所台帳、
土地登録簿

(RUS) КНИГА ЗЕМЕЛЬНОГО УЧЕТА

pleading

(CHIN) 抗辩，承认

(FRE) plaidant

(GER) anwaltliche Prozessführung;
schriftsätzliche Vorbereitung der
mündlichen Verhandlung *f*; Schriftsatz,
Plädieren *m*

(JAP) 訴答、訴訟手続き、申立書

(RUS) ЗАЯВЛЕНИЕ (В СУДЕ)

pledge

(CHIN) 典当，抵押，抵押权

(FRE) gage, garantie, (C) bien transporté en
garantie, (C) promesse de don

(GER) Verpfändung *f*; Pfandsache *f*;
Versprechen *n*; Bürgschaft *f*, Sicherheit *f*;
Pfandgegenstand *m*

(JAP) 誓約、担保

(RUS) ЗАЛОГ; ОБЕСПЕЧЕНИЕ (КРЕДИТА)

plot

(CHIN) 地块，图谋，绘图

(FRE) parcelle de terrain, lopin de terre,
comploter, conspirer, dresser le plan de
faire le levé de tracer

(GER) Grundstück *n*, Gelände *n*; grafische
Darstellung *f*, Diagramm *n*; Plan *m*,
Verschwörung *f*

(JAP) 陰謀、計画、構想
(RUS) ЗЕМЕЛЬНЫЙ УЧАСТОК; ЧЕРТИТЬ; ПЛАНИРОВАТЬ

plot plan
(CHIN) 土地使用规划
(FRE) parcelle de terrain, (C) plan d'ensemble
(GER) Flur- *m*, Grundstücksplan *m*
(RUS) ПЛАН ЗЕМЕЛЬНОГО УЧАСТКА

plottage value
(CHIN) 地块整合价值
(FRE) plus-value, (C) valeur de groupement
(GER) Grundstückswert *m*, lagemäßig gestiegener Wert *m*
(JAP) 敷地価値、合筆価額
(RUS) УВЕЛИЧЕНИЕ СТОИМОСТИ НАДЕЛА ИЗ-ЗА ОБЪЕДИНЕНИЯ МЕЛКИХ УЧАСТКОВ В ОДИН КРУПНЫЙ

plotter
(CHIN) 绘图机
(FRE) traceur, (C) traceur à commande numérique
(GER) Plotter *m*, Kurvenschreiber *m* (EDV); Intrigant *m*, Verschwörer *m*, Anstifter *m*
(JAP) 陰謀者、地図（図面）製作者
(RUS) ПЛАНИРОВЩИК; ГРАФОПОСТРОИТЕЛЬ (ПЛОТТЕР)

plow back
(CHIN) 再投资
(FRE) bénéfices réinvestis
(GER) einbehalten, reinvestieren, wieder anlegen, thesaurieren *v*
(JAP) （資本などを）再投資する
(RUS) РЕИНВЕСТИРОВАНИЕ ПРИБЫЛИ В ОСНОВНЫЕ ФОНДЫ

plus tick
(CHIN) 证券价格上涨符号
(FRE) négociation à un cours supérieur
(GER) Aufwärts-Kursschwankung *f*
(JAP) 景気の上昇、前回より高い出来値
(RUS) ОБОЗНАЧЕНИЕ ПОСЛЕДНЕЙ ВО ВРЕМЕНИ СДЕЛКИ (с ценными бумагами)

pocket computer
(CHIN) 袖珍型计算机

(FRE) ordinateur de poche
(GER) Taschencomputer *m*
(JAP) ポケットコンピューター
(RUS) КАРМАННОЕ ЭВУ

point
(CHIN) 地点，细目，条款
(FRE) point
(GER) Punkt *m*, Prozentpunkt *m*; Platz *m*, Stelle *f*; Hinweis *m*; Kernpunkt *m*, Hauptfrage *f*
(JAP) ［商業］刻み、ポイント
(RUS) ТОЧКА; «ПУНКТ» (бирж.)

point chart
(CHIN) 点图，散点图
(FRE) nuage de points, (C) graphique à points
(GER) Punktdiagramm *n*
(JAP) 点図表、ポイントチャート
(RUS) ТОЧЕЧНАЯ СХЕМА

poison pill
(CHIN) 毒丸计划
(FRE) pilule empoisonnée, (C) pastille empoisonnée
(GER) Anti-Übernahme-Strategie *f*, Stimmrechtsbeschränkung *f* zur Übernahmeabwehr *f*
(JAP) ［金融］ポイズンピル防衛戦略
(RUS) «ГОРЬКАЯ ТАБЛЕТКА» (прием принятия повышенных обязательств во избежание поглощения)

Poisson distribution
(CHIN) 泊松分布
(FRE) loi de Poisson, (C) distribution de Poisson
(GER) Gesetz *n* der seltenen Ereignisse *npl*
(JAP) ポワソン分布
(RUS) ПУАССОНОВО РАСПРЕДЕЛЕНИЕ

police power
(CHIN) 警察权力
(FRE) pouvoir de police
(GER) Polizeigewalt *f*, -befugnis *f*
(RUS) ПОЛНОМОЧИЯ НА ВЫПОЛНЕНИЕ ПОЛИЦЕЙСКИХ, НАДЗОРНЫХ ФУНКЦИЙ

policy holder

(CHIN) 保险客户，投保人

(FRE) assuré, (C) souscripteur

(GER) Versicherter *m*,
Versicherungsnehmer *m*, Policeninhaber *m*

(JAP) 保険契約者

(RUS) ДЕРЖАТЕЛЬ СТРАХОВОГО
ПОЛИСА; СТРАХОВАТЕЛЬ

policy loan

(CHIN) 保险单贷款

(FRE) prêt sur contrat d'assurance

(GER) Policendarlehen *n*, -beleihung *f*

(JAP) 保険証券貸付、契約者貸付

(RUS) КРЕДИТ ПОД СТРАХОВОЙ ПОЛИС

pollution

(CHIN) 污染

(FRE) pollution

(GER) (Umwelt)verschmutzung *f*, -
belastung *f*

(JAP) 汚染、汚すこと

(RUS) ЗАГРЯЗНЕНИЕ

pool

(CHIN) 集合基金，联营

(FRE) groupement, pool, (C) bassin

(GER) Pool *m*, Zusammenschluss *m* von
Investoren *mpl*, Fonds *m*; Vereinigung *f*;
Konsortium *n*; Interessengemeinschaft *f*,
Kartell *n* höherer Ordnung *f*; Vorrats- *m*,
Teilbestand *m*; Versicherungspool *m*

(JAP) 企業連合、割り当てカルテル、
プール

(RUS) ПУЛ; ОБЪЕДИНЕНИЕ

pooling of interests

(CHIN) 合并经营，利益共享

(FRE) fusion, unification, (C) mise en
commun d'intérêts

(GER) Interessenvereinigung *f*, -
gemeinschaft *f*, -zusammenführung *f*

(JAP) 持分プーリング法

(RUS) «ПУЛИНГ»; ОБЪЕДИНЕНИЕ
ИНТЕРЕСОВ

portal-to-portal pay

(CHIN) 门对门旅费全包

(FRE) salaire applicable aux heures totales
de presence, (C) salaire à la demarcation

(GER) Vergütung *f* für die Zeit *f* vom
Betreten *n* bis zum Verlassen *n* des Betriebs
m; Betriebsanwesenheitsvergütung *f* (vom
Werktor bis zum Arbeitsplatz und zurück,
Bergwerk)

(JAP) 拘束時間賃金

(RUS) ОПЛАТА ДОСТАВКИ «ОТ ТОЧКИ
ДО ТОЧКИ»

portfolio

(CHIN) 业务责任，有价证券，资财，
投资搭配

(FRE) portefeuille

(GER) Portefeuille *n*, Portfolio *n*, Aktien-
m, Effekten- *m*, Wertpapierbestand *m*

(JAP) ポートフォリオ（各種の金融資産
の集合）、有価証券明細書

(RUS) ПОРТФЕЛЬ (ЦЕННЫХ БУМАГ)

portfolio beta score

(CHIN) 有价证券贝塔值

(FRE) coefficient beta de portefeuille, (C)
pointage bêta du portefeuille

(GER) Portefeuille-Betakoeffizient *m*

(JAP) ポートフォリオのベータスコア

(RUS) ОЦЕНКА РИСКА ПОРТФЕЛЯ
ЦЕННЫХ БУМАГ ПОСРЕДСТВОМ БЕТА-
КОЭФФИЦИЕНТА

portfolio income

(CHIN) 证券收入

(FRE) revenu de portefeuille

(GER) Portefeuilleerträge *mpl*,
Portfolioeinkommen *n*

(JAP) ポートフォリオの収入

(RUS) ДОХОД ОТ ПОРТФЕЛЯ ЦЕННЫХ
БУМАГ

portfolio manger

(CHIN) 有价证券管理人

(FRE) gestionnaire de portefeuille

(GER) Portefeuille- *m*, Portfolioverwalter *m*

(JAP) ポートフォリオマネジャー、
資産管理担当者

(RUS) ОТВЕТСТВЕННЫЙ ЗА
УПРАВЛЕНИЕ ИНВЕСТИЦИЯМИ
КЛИЕНТА

portfolio reinsurance

(CHIN) 有价证券再保险

(FRE) réassurance de portefeuille
(GER) Portfeuille- *f*,
Portfoliorückversicherung *f*
(JAP) ポートフォリオ再保険
(RUS) ПОВТОРНОЕ СТРАХОВАНИЕ
ПОРТФЕЛЯ ЦЕННЫХ БУМАГ

portfolio theory

(CHIN) 投资 搭配理论
(FRE) théorie du portefeuille
(GER) Portfeuille- *f*,
Portfoliorückversicherung *f*
(JAP) ポートフォリオ理論
(RUS) ТЕОРИЯ РАЗМЕЩЕНИЯ
ИНВЕСТИЦИЙ

port of entry

(CHIN) 进口港
(FRE) port d'entrée
(GER) Einlauf- *m*, Löschhafen *m*
(JAP) 輸入港、手続港、通関港
(RUS) ПОРТ ВВОЗА (ТАМОЖЕННОЙ
ОБРАБОТКИ)

portrait (format)

(CHIN) 纵向 (格式)
(FRE) portrait (format), (C) format vertical
(GER) Hochformat *n*
(JAP) 横向き (形式)
(RUS) ВЕРТИКАЛЬНЫЙ - О
РАСПОЛОЖЕНИИ ТЕКСТА ИЛИ
ИЗОБРАЖЕНИЯ НА БУМАГЕ, ПРИ
КОТОРОМ ВЕРТИКАЛЬНОЕ
НАПРАВЛЕНИЕ СОВПАДАЕТ С
ШИРОКОЙ СТОРОНОЙ ЛИСТА

position

(CHIN) 位置，金融头寸，期货进货，
额度
(FRE) état, situation, position
(GER) Stelle *f*, Position *f*, Posten *m*;
Meinung *f*
(JAP) 位置、適所、為替持高
(RUS) ПОЗИЦИЯ, ПОЛОЖЕНИЕ

positioning

(CHIN) 定位
(FRE) positionnement
(GER) Platzierung *f*, Positionierung *f*
(JAP) 位置付け、位置決め

(RUS) РАЗМЕЩЕНИЕ; ОПРЕДЕЛЕНИЕ
ПОЗИЦИИ

positive confirmation

(CHIN) 正向确认
(FRE) confirmation positive
(GER) positives Bestätigung *f*
(JAP) 積極的確認
(RUS) ПОЛОЖИТЕЛЬНОЕ
ПОДТВЕРЖДЕНИЕ

positive leverage

(CHIN) 正借贷投资收益
(FRE) effet de levier financier positif
(GER) positiver Leverage-Effekt *m*
(JAP) 正のレバレッジ
(RUS) ПРИВЛЕЧЕНИЕ ЗАЁМНЫХ
СРЕДСТВ ДЛЯ УВЕЛИЧЕНИЯ
ДОХОДНОСТИ ИНВЕСТИЦИЙ

positive yield curve

(CHIN) 正产出曲线
(FRE) courbe de rendement ascendante,
courbe de rendement positive
(GER) positive Rendite- *f*, Ertragskurve *f*
(JAP) 正の利回り曲線
(RUS) ПОЛОЖИТЕЛЬНАЯ КРИВАЯ
ДОХОДНОСТИ

possession

(CHIN) 保有，拥有
(FRE) possession, jouissance
(GER) Besitz *m*, Eigentum *n*
(JAP) 所有、占有、
所有物
(RUS) ВЛАДЕНИЕ

post closing trial balance

(CHIN) 结账后试算表
(FRE) balance de vérification après clôture
(GER) Rohbilanz *f* ohne Aufwand *m* und
Ertrag *m*
(JAP) 締切り後試算表、繰越試算表
(RUS) ПРЕДВАРИТЕЛЫІЫЙ БАЛАНС
ПОСЛЕ ЗАКРЫТИЯ СЧЁТА

posting

(CHIN) 过账；贴出，显出，记入
(FRE) affichage, enregistrement, écriture
comptable, écriture, inscription

321

(GER) Versendung *f*; Buchung *f*,
Eintragung *f*; Versetzung *f*; Posting *n*
(Internet)
(JAP) 記帳、転記;) 転記すること、
記入する
(RUS) ВЫВЕШИВАНИЕ (ОБЪЯВЛЕНИЯ);
ПРОВОДКА ПО БУХГАЛТЕРСКИМ
КНИГАМ

poverty
(CHIN) 贫困
(FRE) pauvreté
(GER) Armut *f*, Mittellosigkeit *f*,
Bedürftigkeit *f*
(JAP) 貧乏
(RUS) БЕДНОСТЬ; НИЩЕТА

power connection
(CHIN) 电源连接
(FRE) connexion d'alimentation,
(C) alimentation
(GER) Strom- *m*, Netzanschluss *m*
(JAP) 電源接続

power down
(CHIN) 电源关闭，掉电
(FRE) coupure de courant, (C) mise hors
tension
(GER) ab-, ausschalten, runterfahren
(Computer) *v*
(JAP) 電源を切る、パワーをさげる、出
力をさげる
(RUS) ВЫКЛЮЧЕНИЕ ПИТАНИЯ

power of attorney
(CHIN) 委托书，律师代理权
(FRE) procuration
(GER) (Handlungs- *f*, Prozess)vollmacht *f*,
Prokura *f*, Ermächtigung *f*
(JAP) 委任状、委任権
（委任状にもとづく）代理権
(RUS) ДОВЕРЕННОСТЬ

power of sale
(CHIN) 销售权
(FRE) pouvoir de vendre, pouvoir de vente
(GER) Verkaufsvollmacht *f*
(JAP) 売却権
(RUS) ПРАВО НА ПРОДАЖУ (ПО
ЗАКЛАДНОЙ ИЛИ ДОВЕРИТЕЛЬНОМУ

ФОНДУ, В СЛУЧАЕ НЕВЫПОЛНЕНИЯ
УСЛОВИЙ)

power surge
(CHIN) 权力高峰
(FRE) montée en puissance, (C) saute de
puissance
(GER) Spannungsstoß *m*
(JAP) サージ電圧、サージ電流
(RUS) ВСПЛЕСК НАПРЯЖЕНИЯ В СЕТИ

power up
(CHIN) 加电
(FRE) mettre sous tension, (C) mise sous
tension
(GER) an, einschalten, hochfahren
(Computer) *v*
(JAP) 電源を入れる、パワーを上げる、
出力をあげる
(RUS) ВКЛЮЧЕНИЕ ПИТАНИЯ

practical capacity
(CHIN) 实际生产能力
(FRE) capacité pratique, (C) capacité
pratique de production
(GER) praktisch realisierbare Kapazität *f*
(JAP) 実際的生産能力、実用容量、
実用生産能力
(RUS) ПРАКТИЧЕСКАЯ
ПРОИЗВОДСТВЕННАЯ МОЩНОСТЬ

pre-bill
(CHIN) 事前账单
(FRE) préfacturer
(GER) vorfakturieren *n*
(JAP) 予備請求、前もって請求する
(RUS) (ВЫСТАВЛЯТЬ)
ПРЕДВАРИТЕЛЬНЫЙ СЧЕТ

precautionary motive
(CHIN) 预防动机
(FRE) motif de précaution
(GER) Vorsichtsmotiv *n*
(JAP) 警戒的動機、事前対応的動機
(RUS) ИЗ СООБРАЖЕНИЙ
ПРЕДОСТОРОЖНОСТИ

preclosing
(CHIN) 结账前
(GER) Probe- *f*, Rohbilanz *f*

(JAP) 締め切り前の

precompute
(CHIN) 预先计算
(FRE) précalculer
(GER) vorausberechnen *v*
(JAP) あらかじめ演算する
(RUS) ПРЕДВАРИТЕЛЬНЫЙ ПОДСЧЕТ

prediction
(CHIN) 预测，推测
(FRE) prédiction
(GER) Vorhersage *f*, Voraussage *f*;
Prophezeiung *f*
(JAP) 予測、予報
(RUS) ПРЕДСКАЗАНИЕ; ПРОГНОЗ

preemptive rights
(CHIN) 优先认购权
(FRE) droits préférentiels de souscription
(GER) Vorkaufs- *npl*, Bezugsrechte *npl*
(JAP) （優先的）新株引受権、先買い権
(RUS) ПРЕИМУЩЕСТВЕННОЕ ПРАВО
(существующих акционеров на вновь
выпускаемые акции)

preexisting use
(CHIN) 已存在使用权
(FRE) utilisation preexistante, (C) usage
préexistant
(GER) vorbestehender Nutzen *m*
(JAP) すでに存在している使用
(RUS) ПРЕЖДЕПОЛЬЗОВАНИЕ

prefabricated
(CHIN) 预制的
(FRE) préfabriqué
(GER) vorgefertigt, in Fertigbauweise *f*
hergestellt *v*; Fertigteil-
(JAP) 前もって作り上られた（製造され
た）、作成済みの、プレハブの
(RUS) СБОРНЫЙ

preferential rehiring
(CHIN) 优先再雇用
(FRE) réemploi préférentiel,
(C) réembauchage préférentiel
(GER) Bevorzugung *f* bei der
Wiedereinstellung *f*

(JAP) 優先的再雇用
(RUS) ПОВТОРНЫЙ ПРИЕМ НА РАБОТУ
ЛИЦ, уволенных ИЗ-ЗА НЕЗАКОННОЙ
ДИСКРИМИНАЦИИ

preferred dividend
(CHIN) 优先股息
(FRE) dividende prioritaire, dividende
privilegie, dividende preferentiel
(GER) Vorzugsdividende *f*, Dividende *f* auf
Vorzugsaktien *fpl*
(JAP) 優先配当
(RUS) ДИВИДЕНД ПО
ПРИВИЛЕГИРОВАННЫМ АКЦИЯМ

preferred dividend coverage
(CHIN) 优先股总收入
(FRE) couverture de dividende prioritaire,
couverture de dividende privilegie,
couverture de dividende preferentiel
(GER) Vorzugsdividendendeckung *f*
(JAP) 優先配当適用率
(RUS) ПОКРЫТИЕ ДИВИДЕНДА ПО
ПРИВИЛЕГИРОВАННЫМ АКЦИЯМ

preferred stock
(CHIN) 优先股
(FRE) actions privilégiées, actions de
priorité
(GER) Vorzugsaktie *f*
(JAP) 優先株
(RUS) ПРИВИЛЕГИРОВАННАЯ АКЦИЯ

prelease
(CHIN) 预租赁
(FRE) prélocation
(GER) vor Abschluss *m* des Leasing- *m*,
Pacht- *m*, Mietvertrags *m*
(JAP) 建築開始以前に結ぶ賃貸借契約、
賃貸借契約を建築前に結ぶ
(RUS) АРЕНДА ПЛОЩАДЕЙ, ЕЩЁ НЕ
СДАННЫХ В ЭКСПЛУАТАЦИЮ

preliminary prospectus
(CHIN) 初步募股书
(FRE) prospectus préliminaire,
(C) prospectus proviso ire
(GER) vorläufiger (Emissions)prospekt *m*
(JAP) 予備設立趣意書、仮目論見書
(RUS) ПРЕДВАРИТЕЛЬНЫЙ ПРОСПЕКТ

premises
(CHIN) 前序
(FRE) locaux, lieux
(GER) (Betriebs)grundstück *n*; Geschäfts-*mpl*, Gewerberäume *mpl*
(JAP) （建物を含めた）土地、〔法律〕
（理由付けの）前提
(RUS) ТЕРРИТОРИЯ (ЗДАНИЕ,
ПОМЕЩЕНИЕ) ПРЕДПРИЯТИЯ ;ВВОДНАЯ
ЧАСТЬ ДОГОВОРА

premium
(CHIN) 保险费，溢价，奖金
(FRE) prime
(GER) Prämie *f*, Zulage *f*, Bonifikation *f*;
Zuschlag *m*; Zuschuss *m*; Agio *n*, Aufgeld
n, Aufpreis *m*; Versicherungsprämie *f*,
Beitrag *m*
(JAP) 割増し価格、保険料、手数料
(RUS) ПРЕМИЯ; НАДБАВКА; МАРЖА

premium bond
(CHIN) 有奖公债，溢价债券
(FRE) obligation à lot, (C) obligation cotée
à prime
(GER) Prämienschuldverschreibung *f*, -pfandbrief *m*, -anleihe *f*, Losanleihe *f*
(JAP) 割増金付き債権
(RUS) ОБЛИГАЦИЯ с рыночной ценой выше
номинальной

premium income
(CHIN) 保险费收入
(FRE) recette de prime, (C) primes echoes
(GER) Prämien- *fpl*, Beitragsaufkommen *n*,
Prämieneinnahme *f*, Beitragseingang *m*
(JAP) 保険料収入
(RUS) ПРЕМИАЛЬНЫЙ ДОХОД

premium pay
(CHIN) 加班费，奖金
(FRE) salaire majoré, (C) indemnité
compensatrice
(GER) Lohnzuschlag *m*, -zulage *f*,
Sondervergütung *f*
(JAP) 奨励給、奨励給与
(RUS) ПРЕМИАЛЬНАЯ ОПЛАТА

premium rate
(CHIN) 保险费率

(FRE) taux de salaire majoré, taux de prime,
(C) tarif majoré
(GER) Prämien- *f*, Beitragsrate *f*, Prämien-*m*, Beitragssatz *m*; Überstundenzuschlag *m*
(JAP) 保険料率
(RUS) ПРЕМИАЛЬНАЯ СТАВКА

prenuptial agreement
(CHIN) 婚前协议
(FRE) contrat de mariage
(GER) Vorehevertrag *m*
(JAP) 結婚前の同意契約
(RUS) СОГЛАШЕНИЕ (ФИНАНСОВОЕ)
ПЕРЕД ВСТУПЛЕНИЕМ В БРАК

prepaid
(CHIN) 已预付，先付的
(FRE) prépayé
(GER) vorausbezahlt *adj*
(JAP) 前払いした
(RUS) ПРЕДОПЛАЧЕННЫЙ

prepaid expense
(CHIN) 预付费用
(FRE) charge constatée d'avance,
(C) charge reportée
(GER) (aktive)
Rechnungsabgrenzungsposten *npl*;
transitorische Aktiva *npl*, vorausbezahlte
Aufwendungen *fpl*
(JAP) 前払経費
(RUS) ПРЕДОПЛАЧЕННЫЕ РАСХОДЫ

prepaid-interest
(CHIN) 预付利息
(FRE) Intérêt payé d'avance
(GER) vorausbezahlte Zinsen *mpl*
(JAP) 前払利息
(RUS) ПРЕДВАРИТЕЛЬНО
ВЫПЛАЧЕННЫЙ ПРОЦЕНТ

prepayment
(CHIN) 预付，先付
(FRE) paiement à l'avance
(GER) Vorauszahlung *f*, Vorkasse *f*;
Zahlung *f* vor Fälligkeit *f*, vorzeitige
Rückzahlung *f*
(JAP) 満期前支払い、中途償還、
前払金
(RUS) ПРЕДОПЛАТА

prepayment clause

(CHIN) 预付条款

(FRE) clause de remboursement par anticipation

(GER) Vorfälligkeitsklausel *f*

(JAP) 中途償還条項、前払金条項

(RUS) ОГОВОРКА О ПРЕДОПЛАТЕ

prepayment penalty

(CHIN) 提前偿付罚金

(FRE) Indemnité de remboursement par anticipation

(GER) Aufschlag *m* für vorzeitige Tilgung *f*; Belastung *f* wegen vorzeitiger Tilgung *f*

(JAP) 前払い罰則手数料

(RUS) ШТРАФ (ОПЛАТА) ЗА ДОСРОЧНОЕ ПОГАШЕНИЕ ССУДЫ

prepayment privilege

(CHIN) 预付权利

(FRE) privilège de prépaiement, (C) droit de remboursement par anticipation

(GER) vorzeitiges Tilgungsprivileg *n*

(JAP) 前払い特典（特権）

(RUS) ЛЬГОТА ЗА ПРЕДОПЛАТУ

prerogative

(CHIN) 特权，君权

(FRE) prérogative, (C) bénéfice

(GER) Vorrecht *n*, Privileg *n*

(JAP) 地位、職務に与えられる）特権、特典

(RUS) ПРЕРОГАТИВА; ИСКЛЮЧИТЕЛЬНОЕ ПРАВО

presale

(CHIN) 预售

(FRE) pré-vente, (C) vente par anticipation

(GER) vor Verkauf(sabschluss) *m*

(JAP) プレセール、セール前特別セール

(RUS) ПРОБНАЯ ПРОДАЖА

prescription

(CHIN) 规定，时效，处方

(FRE) prescription

(GER) Verordnung *f*, Vorschrift *f*; Ersitzung *f*; Verjährung *f*; (Medikamenten)rezept *n*

(JAP) 命令（指示、規定）すること、〔法律〕（取得）時効

(RUS) ПРАВО ДАВНОСТИ; РЕЦЕПТ НА ЛЕКАРСТВО; ПРЕДПИСАНИЕ

presentation

(CHIN) 交兑，议付

(FRE) présentation

(GER) Vorlage *f*, Überreichung *f*; Aufmachung *f*, Gestaltung *f*, Darbietung *f*, Präsentation *f*, Vorstellung *f*, Vorführung *f*;

(JAP) プレゼンテーション、提出、提示

(RUS) ПРЕЗЕНТАЦИЯ; ДОКЛАД; СООБЩЕНИЕ

present fairly

(CHIN) 现时公平资料

(FRE) présenter fidèlement

(GER) fair bzw. ehrlich darstellen *v*

(JAP) …を正しく示す、…を公平に提示する

(RUS) ЧЕСТНО ИЗВЕСТИТЬ, ДОЛОЖИТЬ

present value

(CHIN) 现值

(FRE) valeur actuelle, (C) valeur actualisée

(GER) Gegenwartswert *m*, Tages- *m*, Zeitwert *m*, aktueller Wert *m*

(JAP) 現在価値、現在価格、現在価額

(RUS) ПРИВЕДЁННАЯ СТОИМОСТЬ

present value of 1

(CHIN) 一元现值

(FRE) valeur actuelle de 1

(GER) Gegenwartswert *m* von 1

(JAP) １の現価

(RUS) ПРИВЕДЁННВЯ СТОИМОСТЬ ЕДИНИЦЫ

present value of annuity

(CHIN) 年金现值

(FRE) valeur actualisée d'une rente

(GER) Rentenbarwert *m*

(JAP) 年金の現在価値、年金現価

(RUS) ПРИВЕДЁННАЯ СТОИМОСТЬ АННУИТЕТА

president

(CHIN) 总裁，总经理，会长，行长

(FRE) président

(GER) Präsident *m*, President *m*; Staatspräsident *m*

(JAP) 社長、会長、総裁、長官、頭取、
級長
(RUS) ПРЕЗИДЕНТ

presold issue
(CHIN) 预售一空的政府债券
(FRE) titre prévendu, (C) émission vendue
par anticipation
(GER) im Voraus verkaufte Emission *f*,
(Emission, die noch vor Bekanntgabe des
Preises oder der Ertragsrate ausverkauft
wird)
(JAP) 事前売却済公債発行
(RUS) ВЫПУСК ОБЛИГАЦИЙ,
ПОЛНОСТЬЮ ПРОДАННЫЙ ДО
ПУБЛИЧНОГО ОБЪЯВЛЕНИЯ ЕГО ЦЕНЫ
И ПРОЦЕНТА

press kit
(CHIN) 公司就某一事件向媒体发放的信
息资料
(FRE) dossier de presse, (C) cahier de
presse
(JAP) 記者会見時に配る資料一式、宣伝
資料
(RUS) НАБОРДОКУМЕНТОВ ДЛЯ
ПОМЕЩЕНИЯ В ПРЕССЕ

prestige advertising
(CHIN) 形象提升广告
(FRE) publicité de prestige
(GER) Prestige- *f*, Vertrauens- *f*,
Sympathie- *f*, Repräsentationswerbung *f*
(JAP) 評判の高い広告、有名な広告、立
派な広告
(RUS) РЕКЛАМАНАПРАВЛЕННАЯ НА
ПОДНЯТИЕ ПРЕСТИЖА КОМПАНИИ И ЕЁ
ПРОДУКЦИИ И УСЛУГ

prestige pricing
(CHIN) 威信性高价策略
(FRE) prix de prestige, (C) établissement
d'un prix de prestige
(GER) Festsetzung *f* von
Prestigepreisen *mpl*
(JAP) 名声価格
(RUS) ЦЕНООБРАЗОВАНИЕ С УЧЕТОМ
ПРЕСТИЖА, РЕПУТАЦИИ

pretax earnings
(CHIN) 税前收入

(FRE) gains avant impôt, (C) bénéfices
avant impôts
(GER) Einnahmen *fpl* vor Steuern *fpl*
(JAP) 課税前の収入、税込所得
(RUS) ДОХОД, ПОСТУПЛЕНИЯ ДО
УПЛАТЫ НАЛОГОВ

pretax rate of return
(CHIN) 税前回报率
(FRE) taux de rendement avant impôt
(GER) Rendite *f* vor Steuern *fpl*
(JAP) 税込み収益率、税引き前収益率
(RUS) ДОХОД ПО ФИНАНСОВОМУ
АКТИВУ ДО ВЫЧЕТА НАЛОГОВ

preventive maintenance
(CHIN) 预防性维护
(FRE) maintenance préventive,
(C) entretien préventif
(GER) vorbeugende Wartung *f*
(JAP) 予防保全、予防保守、予防整備
(RUS) ПРОФИЛАКТИЧЕСКОЕ
ОБСЛУЖИВАНИЕ

price elasticity
(CHIN) 价格弹性
(FRE) élasticité des prix, (C) élasticité prix
de la demande
(GER) Preiselastizität *f*
(JAP) 価格弾力性
(RUS) ЦЕНОВАЯ ЭЛАСТИЧНОСТЬ

price-fixing
(CHIN) 价格管制，定价，限价，
价格垄断
(FRE) contrôle des prix, (C) fixation des
prix
(GER) Preisabsprache *f*; vertikale
Preisbindung *f*; Tariffestsetzung *f*,
Preisfestlegung *f*
(JAP) 価格の固定、価格協定
(RUS) ПРЕСТУПНЫЙ СГОВОР С ЦЕЛЬЮ
ВЛИЮНИЯ НА ЦЕНУ

price index
(CHIN) 价格指数
(FRE) indice des prix
(GER) Preisindex *m*; Lebenshaltungindex *m*
(JAP) 物価指数、価格指数
(RUS) ИНДЕКС ЦЕН

price lining
(CHIN) 底价
(FRE) limitation de la gamme des prix
(GER) Festsetzung *f* von Einheitspreisen
mpl; Einheitspreissystem *n*
(JAP) 価格ライン
(RUS) УСТАНОВЛЕНИЕ ОПРЕДЕЛЁННЫХ
ЦЕН НА ТОВАР, КОТОРЫЕ НЕ
МЕНЯЮТСЯ НА ПРОТЯЖЕНИИ
ДЛИТЕЛЬНОГО ВРЕМЕНИ. А ИЗМЕНЕНИЯ
РЫНОЧНЫХ УСЛОВИЙ ОТРАЖАЮТСЯ
НА ИЗМЕНЕНИЕ КАЧЕСТВА ИЛИ
КОЛИЧЕСТВА ПРЕДЛАГАЕМОГО ПО
ЭТОЙ ЦЕНЕ ТОВАРА

price stabilization
(CHIN) 稳定物价
(FRE) stabilisation des prix,
(C) régularisation d'un cours
(GER) Preisstabilisierung *f*, -beruhigung *f*;
Kursstabilisierung *f*
(JAP) 価格安定、価格安定化
(RUS) СТАБИЛИЗАЦИЯ ЦЕН

price support
(CHIN) 价格补贴
(FRE) soutien des prix
(GER) Preisstützung *f*; Kursstützung *f*
(JAP) 価格支持、価格維持
(RUS) ЦЕНОВАЯ ПОДДЕРЖКА
ПРОИЗВОДИТЕЛЕЙ ГОСУДАРСТВОМ

price system
(CHIN) 价格制度，价格体制
(FRE) systéme de prix, système tarifaire,
(C) régime des prix
(GER) Preissystem *n*,
Preisfestsetzungswesen *n*
(JAP) 価格制度、価格体制
(RUS) СИСТЕМА ЦЕНООБРАЗОВАНИЯ

price war
(CHIN) 价格战
(FRE) guerre des prix
(GER) Preiskrieg *m*
(JAP) 価格戦、値引き競争
(RUS) ЦЕНОВАЯ КОНКУРЕНЦИЯ

pricey
(CHIN) 昂贵的，高价的，价格离谱的
(FRE) cher, coûteux

(GER) teuer, kostspielig *adj*
(JAP) 高価な、値段の高い
(RUS) МАКСИМАЛЬНО ВЫСОКАЯ ЦЕНА;
ЯВНО ЗАНИЖЕННАЯ или ЗАВЫШЕННАЯ
ЦЕНА ценной бумаги ПРИ ТОРГОВЛЕ НА
БИРЖЕ

pricing below market
(CHIN) 低于市场价格的定价政策
(FRE) tarification inférieure au marché,
(C) prix inférieur au marché
(GER) Preisfestsetzung *f* unter dem
Marktpreis *m*
(JAP) 市場価格以下の値付け
(RUS) НАЗНАЧЕНИЕ ЦЕНЫ НИЖЕ
РЫНОЧНОЙ

primary boycott
(CHIN) 一级抵制，初级抵制
(FRE) boycottage primaire
(GER) unmittelbarer Boykott *m*
(JAP) 一次的ボイコット
(RUS) БОЙКОТ ПРОФСОЮЗОМ ТОВАРОВ
ИЛИ УСЛУГ КОМПАНИИ (с которой он
находится в конфликте)

primary demand
(CHIN) 初级需求
(FRE) demande primaire, (C) demande
générique
(GER) Primärbedarf *m*, -nachfrage *f*
(JAP) 第一次需要、基本的需要
(RUS) СПРОС НА ТОВАРЫ ПЕРВОЙ
НЕОБХОДИМОСТИ

primary distribution
(CHIN) 股票或债券初次上市发行，
初次分配
(FRE) distribution primaire, (C) placement
d'une émission nouvelle
(GER) Neuemission *f*, Erstvertrieb *m* einer
Aktie *f*; Primärvertrieb *m*
(JAP) 第一次分売
(RUS) ПЕРВИЧНОЕ РАСПРЕДЕЛЕНИЕ,
РАЗМЕЩЕНИЕ (ценных бумаг)

primary earnings per (common) share
(CHIN) 基本每股（普通股）收益
(FRE) bénéfices premiers par action
(GER) tatsächlicher bzw. ungeminderter
Gewinn *m* je (Stamm)aktie *f*

327

(JAP) 1株当りの本源的収益
(RUS) ДОХОДЫ КОМПАНИИ НА ОДНУ
ПРОСТУЮ АКЦИЮ (после выплаты налогов
и привилегированных дивидендов)

primary lease
(CHIN) 主要租赁
(FRE) bail principal
(GER) Hauptmietvertrag *m*, -pachtvertrag *m*
(JAP) 第一次賃借権、第一次リース
(RUS) ПЕРВОНАЧАЛЬНАЯ АРЕНДА

primary market
(CHIN) 初级市场，原始市场，主要市场
(FRE) marché primaire
(GER) Primärmarkt *m*, Markt *m* für
Neuemissionen *fpl*; Neuemissionsmarkt *m*
(JAP) 主要市場、一次市場
(RUS) ПЕРВИЧНЫЙ РЫНОК

primary market area
(CHIN) 报纸目标发行区，主要销售区
(FRE) marché principal, (C) secteur de
marché primaire
(GER) Primärmarktbereich *m*
(JAP) 主要市場地域、一次市場地域
(RUS) ЗОНА ПЕРВИЧНОГО РЫНКА

primary package
(CHIN) 主包装
(FRE) emballage primaire
(GER) Grundverpackung *f*
(JAP) プライマリーパッケージ
(RUS) ЕДИНИЧНАЯ УПАКОВКА ТОВАРА

prime paper
(CHIN) 最佳票据，无风险票据
(FRE) papier commercial de la plus haute
qualité, (C) papier commercial de premier
plan
(GER) erstklassiges Geldmarkt- *n*, Handels-
n, Wertpapier *n*, Primapapier *n*
(JAP) 優良手形(RUS) ПЕРВОКЛАССНАЯ
ЦЕННАЯ БУМАГА

prime rate
(CHIN) 基本贷款利率，优惠利率
(FRE) taux d'escompte bancaire
préférentiel, (C) taux préférentiel

(GER) Prime Rate *f*, Leitzins *m* von US-
Banken *fpl*, Kreditzins *m* für erste Adressen
fpl; Basiszinssatz *m*, Basiszinsfuß
(JAP) プライムレート、最優遇貸出金利
(RUS) ПРАЙМ – РЕЙТ (ставка по кредитам
первоклассным заемщикам)

prime tenant
(CHIN) 主要租户
(FRE) locataire principal
(GER) Hauptmieter *m*, -pächter *m*
(JAP) 主要賃借人
(RUS) ПЕРВОКЛАССНЫЙ АРЕНДАТОР,
СЪЕМЩИК

principal
(CHIN) 主要的，本金的
(FRE) mandant, commettant, capital,
principal,(C) directeur non associé,
(C) contrepartiste
(GER) Auftraggeber *m*; Kapitalsumme *f*;
Darlehens- *m*, Kreditbetrag *m*, Darlehens *f*, -
Kreditsumme *f*; Kapital *n*;
Hauptverpflichteter *m*; Eigenhändler *m*;
Geschäftsherr *m*
(RUS) ОСНОВНАЯ СУММА (займа,
кредита); ПРИНЦИПАЛ (основной участник
или партнер)

principal amount
(CHIN) 本金
(FRE) montant principal, (C) capital
(GER) Hautp- *m*, Kapital- *m*;
Darlehensbetrag *m*
(JAP) 元金、元本金額
(RUS) ОСНОВНАЯ СУММА

principal and interest payment (P&I)
(CHIN) 本息付款（P&I）
(FRE) paiement du capital et des intérêts,
(C) remboursement du capital et des intérêts
(GER) Kapital- *f* und Zinszahlung *f*
(JAP) 元利払い
(RUS) ОПЛАТА ОСНОВНОЙ СУММЫ И
ПРОЦЕНТОВ

**principal, interest, taxes, and insurance
payment (PITI)**
(CHIN) 本金，利息，税务，保险支付
（PITI）

(C) remboursement du capital, des intérêts
et de l'assurance
(GER) Kapital- *f*, Zinsen- *f*, Steuer- *f* und
Versicherungszahlung *f*
(JAP) 元利税金および保険料払い
(RUS) ОПЛАТА ОСНОВНОЙ СУММЫ,
ПРОЦЕНТОВ, НАЛОГОВ И
СТРАХОВАНИЯ

principal residence
(CHIN) 主要居住地
(FRE) résidence principale
(GER) Hauptwohnsitz *m*, erster Wohnsitz *f*
(JAP) 主たる住居（住所）
(RUS) ОСНОВНОЕ МЕСТО ПРОЖИВАНИЯ

principal stock holder
(CHIN) 主要持股人
(FRE) actionnaire principal
(GER) Haupt- *m*, Großaktionär *m*
(JAP) 主要株主
(RUS) ОСНОВНОЙ АКЦИОНЕР

principal sum
(CHIN) 本金，本金额
(FRE) somme principale, (C) capital
(GER) Hauptsumme *f*, Kapitalbetrag *m*
(JAP) 元金、（保険契約に基づいた）
支払金
(RUS) ОСНОВНАЯ СУММА (в частности,
сумма для выплаты бенефициару страхового
полиса)

printer
(CHIN) 打印机
(FRE) imprimante
(GER) Drucker *m*
(JAP) プリンター、印刷機
(RUS) ПРИНТЕР

printout
(CHIN) 打印输出，印出
(FRE) sortie sur imprimante, impression,
(C) liste des résultats
(GER) Ausdruck *m*
(JAP) プリントアウト、印刷、プリンタ
ーで印刷されたもの
(RUS) РАСПЕЧАТКА

prior period adjustment

上期调整
(FRE) ajustement sur exercices antérieurs
(GER) Ergebnisberichtigung *f* früherer
Jahre *npl*, Berichtigung *f* des
Vorjahresergebnisses *n*,
Berichtigungsfortschreibung *f*
(JAP) 前期損益修正、過年度損益修正
(RUS) КОРРЕКТИРОВКА НА
ПРЕДШЕСТВОВАВШИЙ ПЕРИОД

prior-preferred stock
(CHIN) 最优先股
(FRE) actions privilégiées de premier rang
(GER) erststellige Vorzugsaktie *f*
(JAP) 前期優先株
(RUS) ОСОБО ПРИВИЛЕГИРОВАННЫЕ
АКЦИИ

prior service cost
(CHIN) 前期服务成本
(FRE) charge financière représentée par la
prise en compte dans le calcul des droits des
salariés de leurs années d'activité au sein de
l'entreprise avant la création du plan,
(C) coût des services passés
(GER) Aufwendungen *fpl* für
Rentenfondsbeiträge *mpl* für
Betriebszugehörigkeit *f* vor einem
bestimmten Datum *n*; Aufwendungen *fpl*
aus rückwirkenden Planänderungen *fpl*
(JAP) 事前業務コスト、過去勤務費用、
過去勤務債務
(RUS) СУММА, НЕОБХОДИМАЯ ДЛЯ
ВНЕСЕНИЯ В ПЕНСИОННЫЙ ФОНД ДО
ОПРЕДЕЛЁННОЙ ДАТЫ

privacy laws
(CHIN) 隐私法
(FRE) lois sur le respect de la vie privée,
(C) lois sur la vie privée
(GER) Datenschutzgesetze *npl*, Gesetze *npl*
zum Schutz *m* der Privatssphäre *f*
(JAP) プライバシー法、
私生活の権利に関係する法
(RUS) ЗАКОНЫ О ПРАВАХ ЛИЧНОСТИ НА
ОБЕСПЕЧЕНИЕ СЕКРЕТНОСТИ

private cost
(CHIN) 私人开支
(FRE) coût (n, m) privé
(GER) private Kosten *pl*, Privatausgaben *fpl*

(JAP) 私的費用
(RUS) ЛИЧНАЯ СТОИМОСТЬ

private limited partnership
(CHIN) 私营有限公司
(FRE) société à responsabilité limitée,
(C) propriété limitée privée
(GER) Kommanditgesellschaft *f*
(JAP) 私的有限責任合資会社、小さな合資会社
(RUS) ЗАКРЫТОЕ ОГРАНИЧЕННОЕ ТОВАРИЩЕСТВО

private mortgage insurance
(CHIN) 私营抵押保险
(FRE) assurance hypothécaire privée,
(C) assurance prêt hypothécaire privée
(GER) Restschuldversicherung *f*
(JAP) 民間抵当保険、自家抵当保険
(RUS) ЛИЧНОЕ СТРАХОВАНИЕ ИПОТЕЧНОГО ЗАЛОГА

private offering or private placement
(CHIN) 不公开出售或直接销售
(FRE) placement privé
(GER) private Platzierung *f*, nicht öffentlich begebene Emission *f*
(JAP) （債券などの）私募、プライベートプレースメント、私募発行、第三者割当て

privatization
(CHIN) 私有化
(FRE) privatisation
(GER) Privatisierung *f*
(JAP) 民営化
(RUS) ПРИВАТИЗАЦИЯ

privity
(CHIN) 当事人关系
(FRE) rapport uridique, (C) participation de l'assureur
(GER) Interessengemeinschaft *f*; Rechtsgemeinschaft *f*; Mitwissen *n*
(JAP) 〔法律〕当事者間の関係
(RUS) ИМУЩЕСТВЕННЫЕ ОТНОШЕНИЯ ЛИЦ

prize broker
(CHIN) 以奖品换广告经纪人

(FRE) courtier d'échange, (C) courtier de contrat-échange
(GER) Prämienhändler *m*
(RUS) ОТВЕТСТВЕННЫЙ ЗА ОРГАНИЗАЦИЮ ОБМЕНА ТОВАРОВ И УСЛУГ ФИРМЫ НА РАЗМЕЩЕНИЕ РЕКЛАМЫ В СМИ

probate
(CHIN) 遗嘱检验，检验
(FRE) valider, homologuer, (C) vérification
(GER) gerichtliche Bestätigung *f* der Gültigkeit *f* eines Testaments n; Testamentsvollstreckungszeugnis *n*
(JAP) （遺言の）検認をする、検認済みの遺言書、保護観察に付す
(RUS) ПРОВЕРЯТЬ, ДОКАЗЫВАТЬ ПОДЛИННОСТЬ, ДЕЙСТВИТЕЛЬНОСТЬ

probationary employee
(CHIN) 试用期雇员，记过雇员
(FRE) salarié à l'essai
(GER) Mitarbeiter *m* auf Probe *f*
(JAP) 試用従業員、見習い従業員
(RUS) РАБОТНИК С ИСПЫТАТЕЛЬНЫМ СРОКОМ

proceeds
(CHIN) 进行，前往，收益，收入
(FRE) recette, (C) produit, (C) revenus, (C) prix de réalisation de biens sinistrés
(GER) Erlös *m*, Einkünfte *fpl*, Erträge *mpl*, Einnahmen *fpl*; Gewinn *m*; Gegenwert *m*
(JAP) 収入、売上金、売上高
(RUS) ВЫРУЧКА; ПОСТУПЛЕНИЯ

proceeds from resale
(CHIN) 重售收益
(FRE) produit de revente
(GER) Erlös *m* bzw. Gewinn *m* vom Wiederverkauf *m*
(JAP) 再販の売上高
(RUS) ВЫРУЧКА ОТ ПЕРЕПРОДАЖИ

processor upgrade
(CHIN) 处理器升级
(FRE) mise à niveau du processeur
(GER) Prozessoraufrüstung *f*, -Upgrade *m*
(JAP) 処理装置 （プロセサー）の品質改良

(RUS) МОДЕРНИЗАЦИЯ ПРОЦЕССОРА

procurement
(CHIN) 采购，获得，供货合同
(FRE) approvisionnement, (C) acquisition
(GER) Beschaffung *f*, Besorgung *f*, Bezug *m*, Erwerb *m*
(JAP) 調達、獲得、買い上げ
(RUS) ПРИОБРЕТЕНИЕ

procurring cause
(CHIN) 成事归因
(FRE) cause efficiente, (C) cause justifiant une commission
(GER) Hauptursache *f*
(JAP) 購買成立原因（住宅などの売買成立の結果をもたらした原因となった人）
(RUS) ПОБУДИТЕЛЬНАЯ ПРИЧИНА

produce
(CHIN) 生产，产物，产生
(FRE) produits, (C) fruits et légumes
(GER) fertigen, produzieren, herstellen, erzeugen *v*; vorlegen, vorzeigen; erzielen *v*
(JAP) 生み出す、作り出す、製造する
(RUS) ПРОИЗВОДИТЬ; ИЗГОТАВЛИВАТЬ

producer cooperative
(CHIN) 厂商合作组织
(FRE) coopérative de production, (C) coopérative de producteurs
(GER) Erzeugergenossenschaft *f*, Produktionsgemeinschaft *f*
(JAP) 生産者協同組合、製作者協同組合
(RUS) ПРОИЗВОДСТВЕННЫЙ КООПЕРАТИВ

producer goods
(CHIN) 生产资料，生产物资，机器设备
(FRE) biens de production
(GER) Produktionsgüter *npl*
(JAP) 生産財（消費財の生産を助ける財、機械、原料品など）
(RUS) ТОВАРЫ ПРОИЗВОДИТЕЛЯ

product
(CHIN) 产品，产物，成果
(FRE) produit
(GER) Produkt *n*, Erzeugnis *n*
(JAP) 生産物、生産品、製品

(RUS) ПРОДУКЦИЯ; ИЗДЕЛИЕ; ПРОИЗВЕДЕНИЕ (чисел)

production
(CHIN) 生产，产品，制造品
(FRE) production
(GER) Produktion *f*, Fertigung *f*, Herstellung *f*; Ertrag *m*, Ausbringung *f*; Vorlage *f*
(JAP) 生産、産出、製造、製作

production control
(CHIN) 生产控制，生产管理
(FRE) direction de la production
(GER) Fertigungs- *f*, Produktionskontrolle *f*, Fertigungs- *f*, Produktionssteuerung *f*
(JAP) 生産管理、工程管理
(RUS) ПРОИЗВОДСТВЕННЫЙ КОНТРОЛЬ

production-oriented organization
(CHIN) 以生产为主的企业
(FRE) organisation axée sur la production
(GER) produktions- bzw. fertigungsorientierte Organisation *f*
(JAP) 生産志向組織（機構、体制）
(RUS) ОРГАНИЗАЦИЯ С ПРОИЗВОДСТВЕННОЙ ОРИЕНТАЦИЕЙ

production-possibility curve
(CHIN) 生产—可能性曲线
(FRE) courbe de possibilité de production
(GER) Produktionsmöglichkeitenkurve *f*
(JAP) 生産可能性曲線
(RUS) КРИВАЯ ПРОИЗВОДСТВЕННЫХ ВОЗМОЖНОСТЕЙ

production rate
(CHIN) 生产率
(FRE) taux de production
(GER) Fertigungs- *f*, Produktionsrate *n*
(JAP) 生産率
(RUS) ТЕМПЫ ПРОИЗВОДСТВА; ПРОЦЕНТНАЯ СТАВКА (сертификатов)

production worker
(CHIN) 生产工人
(FRE) agent de fabrication, (C) travailleur de production, (C) main-d'œuvre directe
(GER) Produktionsarbeiter *m*, Industriearbeiter *m*

(JAP) 生産労働者
(RUS) ПРОИЗВОДСТВЕННЫЙ РАБОЧИЙ

productivity
(CHIN) 生产率，生产能力，多产
(FRE) productivité
(GER) Produktivität *f*
(JAP) 生産性、生産力
(RUS) ПРОИЗВОДИТЕЛЬНОСТЬ

product liability
(CHIN) 品责任
(FRE) responsabilité du produit
(GER) Produkthaftung *f*, -haftpflicht *f*
(JAP) 製造物責任
(RUS) ОТВЕТСТВЕННОСТЬ ЗА
ПРОДУКЦИЮ

product liability Insurance
(CHIN) 产品责任保险
(FRE) assurance de responsabilité du
produit
(GER) Produkthaftpflichtversicherung *f*
(JAP) 製造物責任保険
(RUS) СТРАХОВАНИЕ
ОТВЕТСТВЕННОСТИ ЗА ПРОДУКЦИЮ

product life cycle
(CHIN) 产品寿命周期
(FRE) cycle de vie du produit
(GER) Produktlebenszyklus *m*
(JAP) 製品寿命、
プロダクトライフサイクル
(RUS) ЖИЗНЕННЫЙ ЦИКЛ ИЗДЕЛИЯ

product line
(CHIN) 生产线，产品系列
(FRE) ligne de produits, (C) gamme de
produits
(GER) Produktlinie *f*
(JAP) プロダクトライン、製品種目
(RUS) ВИД ПРОДУКЦИИ

product mix
(CHIN) 产品结构，产品搭配
(FRE) assortiment de produits
(GER) Produktmix *m*; Warenkorb *m*
(JAP) 複合生産物、製品組合せ
(RUS) СМЕСЬ ИЗДЕЛИЙ

profession
(CHIN) 专门职业，专业，工种
(FRE) profession
(GER) Beruf *m*; Berufsstand *m*
(JAP) 職業（特に知的職業）、公言、
（集合的）同業者仲間
(RUS) ПРОФЕССИЯ

profit
(CHIN) 赢利，利润，收入
(FRE) bénéfice, profit
(GER) Profit *m*, Gewinn *m*, Ertrag *m*;
Vorteil *m*, Nutzen *m*
(JAP) 利益、収益、利潤
(RUS) ПРИБЫЛЬ

profitability
(CHIN) 有利性，赢利性，获利能力
(FRE) rentabilité
(GER) Rentabilität *f*, Wirtschaftlichkeit *f*,
Profitabilität *f*
(JAP) 収益性、利潤性
(RUS) ПРИБЫЛЬНОСТЬ

profit and loss statemnt (P&L)
(CHIN) 损益表（P&L）
(FRE) compte de résultat, (C) état des
resultants
(JAP) 損益計算書
(RUS) ОТЧЕТ О ПРИБЫЛЯХ И УБЫТКАХ

profit center
(CHIN) 利润中心，
盈利部门
(FRE) centre de profit
(GER) Profitcenter *m*,
(Unternehmensbereich mit eigener
Ergebnisverantwortung)
(JAP) プロフィットセンター、
利益中心点、利益責任単位
(RUS) СЕГМЕНТ КОМПАНИИ,
ПРИНОСЯЩИЙ ПРИБЫЛЬ

profiteer
(CHIN) 贪图暴利者，奸商
(FRE) profiteur
(GER) Profitgeier *m*, -jäger *m*, Geschäfte-
m, Gewinnmacher *m*, Schieber *m*,
Preistreiber *m*

(JAP) 不当利得者、暴利商人、
暴利を貪る
(RUS) СПЕКУЛЯНТ

profit margin
(CHIN) 利润边际
(FRE) marge bénéficiaire, (C) ratio de
marge bénéficiaire
(GER) Ertrags- *f*, Gewinnspanne *f*, -marge *f*
(JAP) 利鞘、利潤差額、利益率
(RUS) МАРЖА ПРИБЫЛИ (прибыль в
процентах к реализации продукции или
капиталу)

profit motive
(CHIN) 利润动机
(FRE) motivation par le profit
(GER) Gewinnmotiv *n*
(JAP) 利潤動機、営利主義
(RUS) ЗАИНТЕРЕСОВАННОСТЬ В
ПОЛУЧЕНИИ ПРИБЫЛИ

profits and commissions form
(CHIN) 利润及提成险
(FRE) formulaire des bénéfices et
commissions
(GER) Gewinn- *n* und Provisionsformular *n*
(Versicherung)
(JAP) 利益・手数料書式
(RUS) СТРАХОВОЕ ПОКРЫТИЕ
ВОЗМОЖНЫХ ПРИБЫЛИ И
КОМИССИОННЫХ ОТ РЕАЛИЗАЦИИ
ТОВАРА

profit-sharing plan
(CHIN) 利润分享计划
(FRE) plan (n, m) de participation aux
bénéfices, (C) régime d'intéressement
(GER) Gewinn- *m*,
Erfolgsbeteiligungsplan *m*
(JAP) 利益分配制度
(RUS) ПРОГРАММА УЧАСТИЯ В
ПРИБЫЛЯХ

profit squeeze
(CHIN) 套取利润，利润压缩
(FRE) compression des bénéfices, (C)
difficulté à maintenir les profits
(GER) Gewinn- *m*, Profitdruck *m*
(JAP) 利潤圧縮

(RUS) ТРУДНОСТИ В ДОСТИЖЕНИИ
ПРОШЛОГО УРОВНЯ ПРИБЫЛИ

profit system
(CHIN) 利润制度
(FRE) système de bénéfice, (C) système
motivé par l'appât des benefices
(GER) Gewinnsystem *n*
(JAP) 利潤制度
(RUS) СИСТЕМА НА ОСНОВЕ ПРИБЫЛИ

profit taking
(CHIN) 获利回吐，套购谋利
(FRE) prise de bénéfices, vente bénéficiaire,
vente avec bénéfices
(GER) Gewinnmitnahme *f*, -realisierung *f*, -
sicherung *f*
(JAP) 利食い、利潤獲得

program budgeting
(CHIN) 方案预算编制
(FRE) budgétisation de programme,
(C) rationalisation des choix budgétaires
(GER) Programmbudgetierung *f*
(JAP) プログラム予算を計上する
(RUS) ФИНАНСИРОВАНИЕ ПРОГРАММЫ

programmer
(CHIN) 编程员
(FRE) programmeur
(GER) Programmierer *m*
(JAP) プログラム作成者、プログラマー
(RUS) ПРОГРАММИСТ

programming language
(CHIN) 编程语言
(FRE) langage de programmation
(GER) Programmiersprache *f*
(JAP) プログラミング言語
(RUS) ЯЗЫК ПРОГРАМИРОВАНИЯ

program trade
(CHIN) 集团股票交易
(FRE) transaction déclenchée par
ordinateur, (C) achat ou vente de tous les
titres d'un programme ou d'un indice
(GER) Programmhandel *m*
(JAP) プログラム売買

(RUS) КУПЛЯ-ПРОДАЖА ВСЕХ АКЦИЙ В ОПРЕДЕЛЁННОЙ КАТЕГОРИИ

progressive tax
(CHIN) 累进税
(FRE) impôt progressif
(GER) progressive Steuer *f*, gestaffelte Steuer *f*
(JAP) 累進税
(RUS) ПРОГРЕССИВНЫЙ НАЛОГ

progress payments
(CHIN) 施工分期付款，按进度付款
(FRE) paiement roportionnel (à l'avancement des travaux, (C) avances échelonnées
(GER) Abschlags- *f*, Fortschrittszahlung *f*, anteilige Zahlung *f*
(JAP) 分割払い
(RUS) ПЕРИОДИЧЕСКИЕ ПЛАТЕЖИ ПО МЕРЕ ВЫПОЛНЕНИЯ ПРОЕКТА

projected benefit obligation
(CHIN) 预期福利责任
(FRE) obligation au titre des prestations rejetées
(GER) Anwartschaftsbarwert *m* unter Berücksichtigung *f* künftiger Gehaltssteigerungen *fpl*
(JAP) 予測給付債務
(RUS) ПРОГНОЗИРУЕМЫЕ ОБЯЗАТЕЛЬСТВА ПО ЛЬГОТАМ

projected (pro forma) financial statement
(CHIN) 预期（预计）财务报表
(FRE) état pro forma des résultats, (C) états financiers pro forma
(GER) (pro forma) Plan- *f*, Vorschaubilanz *f*
(JAP) 見積財務諸表
(RUS) ПРЕДВАРИТЕЛЬНЫЙ («ФОРМАЛЬНЫЙ») ФИНАНСОВЫЙ ОТЧЕТ

projection
(CHIN) 预测
(FRE) projection, prévision
(GER) Hochrechnung *f*, Prognose *f*, Vorausschau *f*
(JAP) 予測、見積り、投出
(RUS) ПРОГНОЗ; ПРЕДСКАЗАНИЕ

promissory note
(CHIN) 本票，期票，借据
(FRE) billet à ordre, effet à ordre
(GER) Sola- *m*, Eigenwechsel *m*, Schuldschein *m*, -verschreibung *f*
(JAP) 約束手形
(RUS) ПРОСТОЙ ВЕКСЕЛЬ

promotional allowance
(CHIN) 推销津贴，促销津贴
(FRE) remise promotionnelle
(GER) Verkaufsförderungsbonus *m*; Werberabatt *m*
(JAP) 促進割引、販売促進引当金
(RUS) ВЫДЕЛЕНИЕ СРЕДСТВ НА РОСТ (заработной платы работников)

promotion mix
(CHIN) 推广组合，促销组合
(FRE) mix des communications, (C) gamme de promotions
(GER) Verkaufsförderungs- *m*, Werbemix *m*
(JAP) プロモーションミックス
(RUS) НАБОР УСИЛИЙ ДЛЯ ПРОДВИЖЕНИЯ НА РЫНКЕ

proof of loss
(CHIN) 损失证明
(FRE) preuve du dommage, (C) preuve de sinistre
(GER) Schadens- *m*, Verlustnachweis *m*
(JAP) 損害証明、損失証明
(RUS) ДОКАЗАТЕЛЬСТВО (СВИДЕТЕЛЬСТВО) УБЫТКА

property
(CHIN) 财产，地产
(FRE) propriété, biens immobiliers
(GER) Besitz *m*, Eigentum *n*, Habe *f*; Immobilie *f*, Grundbesitz *m*, Liegenschaft *f*, Grund *m* und Boden *m*; Vermögensgegenstand *m*; Eigenschaft *f*, Merkmal *n*
(JAP) 財産、所有物、所有権
(RUS) СОБСТВЕННОСТЬ; ИМУЩЕСТВО

property line
(CHIN) 地产边界线
(FRE) ligne séparative, limite

334

(GER) Eigentumsgrenze *f*
(JAP) 土地の境界線
(RUS) ГРАНИЦА ЗЕМЕЛЬНОГО НАДЕЛА

property management

(CHIN) 财产管理
(FRE) gérance d'immeuble, (C) gestion de biens immobiliers, (C) gestion d'immeubles
(GER) Immobilien- *f*, Objekt- *f*, Gebäudeverwaltung *f*
(JAP) 財産管理、不動産管理
(RUS) УПРАВЛЕНИЕ СОБСТВЕННОСТЬЮ

property report

(CHIN) 财产报告
(FRE) rapport de propriété, (C) rapport sur les biens immobiliers
(GER) Liegenschaftsbericht *m* (bei Verkauf von mehr als 50 Parzellen)
(JAP) 財産報告
(RUS) ОТЧЕТ О ПРОДАЖЕ КРУПНОЙ ЗЕМЕЛЬНОЙ СОБСТВЕННОСТИ

property rights

(CHIN) 财产权，产权
(FRE) droits de propriété, (C) droits afférents à des biens immobiliers
(GER) Eigentumsrechte *npl*, dingliche Rechte *npl*
(JAP) 財産権
(RUS) ПРАВА СОБСТВЕННОСТИ

property tax

(CHIN) 财产税
(FRE) taxe foncière, impôt foncier
(GER) Grundstücks- *f*, Liegenschafts- *f*, Grundsteuer *f*
(JAP) 財産税、固定資産税、不動産税
(RUS) НАЛОГ НА СОБСТВЕННОСТЬ (землю и недвижимость)

proprietary interest

(CHIN) 专利，业主权益
(FRE) intérêt patrimonial
(GER) Eigentumsrechte *fpl* und eigentumsähnliche Rechte *npl*
(JAP) 所有権、持分、独占的所有権
(RUS) ХОЗЯЙСКАЯ ЗАИНТЕРЕСОВАННОСТЬ

proprietary lease

(CHIN) 产权租赁
(FRE) bail de coopérative
(GER) Hauptmietvertrag *m*, -pachtvertrag *m*, (Pacht- bzw. Mietverhältnis direkt mit dem Eigentümer)
(JAP) 所有者賃貸借契約
(RUS) АРЕНДА У СОБСТВЕННИКА

proprietorship

(CHIN) 独资企业，资本净值，所有制
(FRE) entreprise individuelle
(GER) Eigentum *n*; Eigentumsrecht *n*; Eigentumsverhältnisse *npl*
(JAP) 所有主持分、個人企業、正味財産
(RUS) ПРАВО СОБСТВЕННОСТИ

prorate

(CHIN) 按比例分配
(FRE) calculer au prorata
(GER) anteilsmäßig umlegen, anteilig zuordnen *v*
(JAP) 〜を比例配分する
(RUS) ПРОПОРЦИОНАЛЬНО

prospect

(CHIN) 潜在的顾客，前景
(FRE) perspective, client eventual, prospect,
(C) client potentiel, client éventuel
(GER) Interessent *m*, potenzieller Kunde *m*; Aussicht *f*, Erwartung *f*, Ausblick *m*
(RUS) ПЕРСПЕКТИВА; ВОЗМОЖНЫЙ КЛИЕНТ

prospective rating

(CHIN) 预期评级
(FRE) tarification prospective
(GER) voraussichtliche Bewertung *f*, voraussichtliches Rating *n*
(JAP) 予想料率算定
(RUS) УСТАНОВЛЕНИЕ СТРАХОВЫХ СТАВОК НА ОСНОВЕ ПРЕДЫДУЩЕГО ОПЫТА

prospectus

(CHIN) 说明书，计划书
(FRE) appel à la souscription publique,
(C) prospectus

(GER) Emissions- *m*, Börsenprospekt *m*,
Subskriptionsanzeige *f*
(JAP) 創立趣意書、目論見書
(RUS) ПРОСПЕКТ (ЭМИССИИ ЦЕННЫХ
БУМАГ)

protected file
(CHIN) 保护文件
(FRE) fichier protégé
(GER) geschützte Datei *f*
(JAP) 保護ファイル
(RUS) ЗАЩИЩЁННЫЙ ФАЙЛ

protectionism
(CHIN) 保护主义
(FRE) protectionisme
(GER) Protektionismus *m*,
Schutzzollpolitik *f*
(JAP) 保護貿易主義、保護政策
(RUS) ПРОТЕКЦИОНИЗМ

protocol
(CHIN) 协议书，协定草案
(FRE) protocole
(GER) Protokoll *n*
(JAP) 条約原案、条約議定書、
　（国家間の）補足協約
(RUS) ПРОТОКОЛ; ПРОЦЕДУРНЫЕ
ПРАВИЛА

proviso
(CHIN) 但书，限制性条款
(FRE) condition, stipulation, (C) clause
conditionnelle
(GER) vertragliche Bedingung *f*; Vorbehalt
m, Bedingung *f*, Maßgabe *f*, Einschränkung
f
(JAP) 但し書き、条件
(RUS) ОГОВОРКА (в законе или договоре)

proxy
(CHIN) 代理人，代表，委托书，授权书
(FRE) mandataire
(GER) (Stell)vertreter *m*,
Stimmrechtsbevollmächtigter *m*,
(Handlungs- *f*, Vertretungs)vollmacht *f*
(JAP) 代理、代理権、代理人
(RUS) ДОВЕРЕННОСТЬ (на голосование);
ДОВЕРЕННОЕ ЛИЦО (для
голосования)

proxy fight
(CHIN) 委托书争夺
(FRE) course aux procurations
(GER) Kampf *m* um Stimmrechte *npl*
(JAP) 代理戦争、委任状投票決戦
(RUS) БОРЬБА ЗА ГОЛОСА
АКЦИОНЕРОВ

proxy statement
(CHIN) 委托书
(FRE) circulaire de sollicitation de
procurations
(GER) Vollmachtsformular *n*, -anweisung *f*,
Bevollmächtigung *f*
(JAP) 委任状
(RUS) ДОКУМЕНТ О ПРЕДСТОЯЩЕМ
ЕЖЕГОДНОМ СОБРАНИИ АКЦИОНЕРОВ

prudence
(CHIN) 慎重，谨慎
(FRE) prudence
(GER) Überlegtheit *f*, Sorgfalt *f*, Umsicht *f*,
Besonnenheit *f*, Klugheit *f*, Vorsicht *f*,
Bedachtsamkeit *f*
(JAP) 賢明さ、慎重
(RUS) БЛАГОРАЗУМИЕ (финан.)

psychic income
(CHIN) 心理收入，精神收益
(FRE) revenu psychique, (C) revenus autres
que monétaires
(GER) hellseherisches Einkommen *n*
(JAP) 心理的収入
(RUS) «ПСИХОЛОГИЧЕСКИЙ» ДОХОД
(ДОХОД В НЕДЕНЕЖНОЙ ФОРМЕ)

public accounting
(CHIN) 公众会计，公共会计
(FRE) expertise comptable,
(C) comptabilité publique
(GER) öffentliches Rechnungs- *n*,
Prüfungswesen *n*; öffentlicher
Rechenschaftsbericht *m*
(JAP) 公認会計士会計報告、公会計
(RUS) БУХГАЛТЕРСКОЕ ОБСЛУЖИВАНИЕ

public domain
(CHIN) 公有财产
(FRE) domaine public
(GER) Staatseigentum *n*, öffentliches
Eigentum *m*; Staatsdomäne *f*

(JAP) 公有、社会の共有財産、公物
(RUS) СФЕРА ГОСУДАРСТВЕННОГО
ВЛАДЕНИЯ

public employee
(CHIN) 公务员
(FRE) agent public, (C) fonctionnaire
(GER) Beschäftigter *m* im öffentlichen
Dienst *m*, Staatsangestellter *m*
(JAP) 公務員
(RUS) ГОСУДАРСТВЕННЫЙ РАБОТНИК

public file
(CHIN) 公共文件
(FRE) fichier public
(GER) öffentliche Datei *f*
(RUS) ФАЙЛ ОБЩЕГО ПОЛЬЗОВАНИЯ

publicly held
(CHIN) 公众持股公司
(FRE) publiquement tenu
(GER) staatlich *adj*; im Besitz *m* der
öffentlichen Hand *f*
(JAP) 公共所有の

public record
(CHIN) 土地公开记录，
法庭公开记录
(FRE) archives publiques
(GER) öffentliche Urkunde *f*
(JAP) 公文書、公記録
(RUS) ОТКРЫТЫЕ АРХИВЫ

public relations (PR)
(CHIN) 公共关系（PR）
(FRE) relations publiques
(GER) Public Relations *pl*; PR-Arbeit *f*,
Öffentlichkeitsarbeit *f*
(JAP) 広報、宣伝活動、ピーアール
(RUS) связи С ОБЩЕСТВЕННОСТЬЮ ;
прсдставительские функции
(фирмы)

public sale
(CHIN) 公卖，拍卖，专卖
(FRE) vente publique
(GER) Auktion *f*, öffentliche
Versteigerung *f*
(JAP) 公開売却
(RUS) ПУБЛИЧНАЯ
ПРОДАЖА

public use
(CHIN) 公共使用
(FRE) usage public, utilisation publique
(GER) öffentlicher Gebrauch *m*,
Gemeingebrauch *m*, Verwendung *f* im
öffentlichen Interesse *n*
(JAP) 公用
(RUS) ОБЩЕСТВЕННОЕ ПОЛЬЗОВАНИЕ

public works
(CHIN) 公共项目
(FRE) travaux publics
(GER) öffentliche Bauvorhaben *npl*,
öffentliche Arbeiten *fpl*
(JAP) 公共（土木）工事、公共事業
(RUS) ОБЩЕСТВЕННЫЕ РАБОТЫ

puffing
(CHIN) 哄抬
(FRE) (publicité) tapageuse
(GER) Marktschreierei *f*, übertriebene
Werbung *f*, Preistreiberei *f*
(JAP) 値を競り上げること
(RUS) САМОВОСХВАЛЕНИЕ,
ПРЕУВЕЛИЧЕНИЕ

pull-down menu
(CHIN) 下拉式选单
(FRE) menu déroulant
(GER) Pull-Down Menü *n* (EDV)
(RUS) ПУЛ-ДАУН МЕНЮ,
СПУСКАЮЩЕЕСЯ МЕНЮ

pump priming
(CHIN) 刺激经济政策
(FRE) mesure de relance,
(C) aide financière de démarrage
(GER) (Wirtschafts- *f*,
Konjunktur)ankurbelung *f*
(JAP) 景気刺激、景気刺激策、
経済振興策
（公共投資による）
(RUS) ЭКОНОМИЧЕСКОЕ
СТИМУЛИРОВАНИЕ ПУТЁМ
ПОВЫШЕНИЯ ГОСУДАРСТВЕННЫХ
РАСХОДОВ И СНИЖЕНИЯ НАЛОГОВ

punch list
(CHIN) 修正项目
(FRE) liste des malfaçons apparentes
(GER) Mängelliste *f*; Lochkartenliste *f*
(JAP) 未決済事項の表

punitive damages
(CHIN) 惩罚性损害赔偿
(FRE) dommages-intérêts punitifs
(GER) tatsächlicher Schaden *m* zuzüglich Zivilstrafe *f*, Schadensersatz *m* mit Strafcharakter *m*
(JAP) 懲罰的損害賠償
(RUS) ШТРАФНЫЕ УБЫТКИ

purchase
(CHIN) 买，购买，采购，议付
(FRE) achat, rachat
(GER) Kauf *m*, Erwerb *m*, Anschaffung *f*, Einkauf *m*
(JAP) 購入、買入れ、買いけつ
(RUS) ПРИОБРЕТЕНИЕ; ПОКУПКА

purchase journal
(CHIN) 采购分录账
(FRE) livre des achats, journal des achats
(GER) Einkaufsbuch *n*, -journal *n*, Wareneingangsbuch *n*
(JAP) 仕入帳、仕入仕訳帳
(RUS) ЖУРНАЛ УЧЕТА ПРИОБРЕТЕНИЙ

purchase money mortgage
(CHIN) 购买财产担保
(FRE) hypothèque garantissant le prix d'achat, (C) prêt hypothécaire accordé par le vendeur
(GER) Restkaufpreis- *f*, Restgeldhypothek *f*
(JAP) 購入代金抵当
(RUS) ИПОТЕКА ДЛЯ ПОЛУЧЕНИЯ ДЕНЕГ НА ПРИОБРЕТЕНИЕ

purchase order
(CHIN) 购货定单，定货单
(FRE) bon de commande, ordre d'achat
(GER) (Kauf- *m*, Bestell)auftrag *m*, Bestellung *f*
(JAP) 買付注文、購入注文
(RUS) ПРИКАЗ О ПРИОБРЕТЕНИИ; ЗАКАЗ

purchasing power
(CHIN) 购买力
(FRE) pouvoir d'achat
(GER) Kaufkraft *f*
(JAP) 購買力

pure competition
(CHIN) 纯粹竞争，完全竞争
(FRE) concurrence pure
(GER) reiner bzw. unverfälschter Wettbewerb *m f*
(JAP) 純粹競争
(RUS) ЧИСТАЯ КОНКУРЕНЦИЯ

pure capitalism
(CHIN) 纯资本主义
(FRE) capitalisme pur
(GER) reiner Kapitalismus *m*
(JAP) 純粹資本主義
(RUS) ЧИСТЫЙ КАПИТАЛИЗМ

pure-market economy
(CHIN) 完全市场经济
(FRE) économie pure de marché,
(C) économie de marché pure
(GER) reine bzw. unverfälschte Marktwirtschaft *f*
(JAP) 純粹市場経済
(RUS) ЭКОНОМИКА ЧИСТОГО РЫНКА

purge
(CHIN) 清除
(FRE) éliminer, vider, (C) purge
(GER) löschen, entfernen *v*; nicht benötigte Daten *pl* entfernen (EDV) *v*
(RUS) ЧИСТИТЬ, ПРОИЗВОДИТЬ ЧИСТКУ ДИСКОВОЙ ПАМЯТИ, УНИЧТОЖАЯ НЕНУЖНЫЕ ФАЙЛЫ

push money (PM)
(CHIN) 推销奖金
(FRE) prime au vendeur, (C) gratification à la force de vente
(GER) Verkaufsprämie *f*; Schmiergeld *n*
(JAP) 特別報奨金
(RUS) ДЕНЬГИ НА ПРОДВИЖЕНИЕ ТОВАРА

put option
(CHIN) 卖期货的权利，
出售选择权
(FRE) option de vente
(GER) Verkaufsoption *f*, Rückprämie *f*, -prämiengeschäft *n*

(JAP) 解消（売り・延期）選択権、
プットオプション
(RUS) ОПЦИОН ПУТ, ОПЦИОН
ПРОДАВЦА

put to seller
(CHIN) 卖方出售权
(FRE) exercice de l'option de vente,
(C) option de vente exercée
(GER) erforderliche Abnahme *f* durch den
Verkäufer *m* (Verkaufsoption)
(JAP) 「プット・ツー・セラー」
〔プットオプションを行使するさいに
使われる表現〕
(RUS) ИСПОЛНЕНИЕ ОПЦИОНА ПУТ

p value
(CHIN) *p* 值
(FRE) valeur *P*
(GER) *p*-Wert m

(JAP) *p* 価値
(RUS) величина «p»

pyramiding
(CHIN) 金字塔式控制股权
(FRE) vente pyramidale, vente suspendue,
système pyramidal de distribution
(GER) Kaskadenbesteuerung *f*; Erwerb *m*
einer Reihe *f* von Mehrheitsbeteiligungen *pl*
an Holdings *fpl*,
Unternehmensbeherrschung *f* durch
Holdings *fpl*; Aktiennachkauf *m* bei
steigendem Kurs *m*, Anhäufung *f* durch
Aktiennachkauf *m*
(JAP) 株式の買（売）乗せ、
利乗せすること、漸増すること
(RUS) ПРИОБРЕТЕНИЕ
ДОПОЛНИТЕЛЬНЫХ ЦЕННЫХ БУМАГ
ИЛИ ТОВАРОВ ПУТЁМ ПРОДАЖИ
«БУМАЖНОЙ» (НЕРЕАЛИЗОВАННОЙ)
ПРИБЫЛИ

Q

qualified endorsement

(CHIN) 条件背书，限制背书

(FRE) endossement spécifiant les limites de la responsabilité de l'endosseur,
(C) endossement conditionnel, (C) endos sous réserve
(GER) eingeschränktes bzw. bedingtes Indossament *n*, Indossament *n* ohne Obligo *n*, beschränktes Giro *n*
(JAP) 限定裏書
(RUS) ОГРАНИЧЕННЫЙ ИНДОССАМЕНТ

qualified opinion

(CHIN) 限定意见，保留意见

(FRE) opinion avec réserves
(GER) eingeschränktes Testat *n*; Stellungnahme *f* mit Vorbehalt *m*, Meinung *f* mit Vorbehalt *m*
(JAP) 限定意見
(RUS) КВАЛИФИЦИРОВАННОЕ МНЕНИЕ

qualified plan or qualified trust

(CHIN) 附条件老年金计划或附条件信托

(FRE) plan d'épargne salariale, (C) régime ou fiducie admissible
(GER) steuerlich begünstigter Gewinnbeteiligungs- *m*, Pensionsplan *m*
(JAP) 受給資格制度（あるいは信託）
(RUS) ПРОГРАММА УЧАСТИЯ В ПРИБЫЛЯХ ИЛИ ПЕНСИОННЫХ СБЕРЕЖЕНИЙ, ПОПАДАЮЩАЯ ПОД НАЛОГОВЫЕ ЛЬГОТЫ

qualified terminable interest property (Q-TIP) trust

(CHIN) 附条件可终止利息财产

（Q-TIP）信托

(FRE) fiducie QTIP , (C) fiducie admissible payable annuellement au conjoint survivant
(GER) Q-TIP Fonds *m*, Fonds *m* der nach dem Tod *m* eines der Ehegatten *pl* einen stetigen Fluss *m* an Einkünften *fpl* durch jährliche Auszahlungen *fpl* bringt
(JAP) 受給資格期限付利子財産信託
(RUS) ПОЖИЗНЕННЫЙ ТРАСТ С ВЫПЛАТОЙ ВСЕХ ДОХОДОВ КАК МИНИМУМ РАЗ В ГОД

qualitative analysis

(CHIN) 定性分析

(FRE) analyse qualitative
(GER) qualitative Analyse *f*
(JAP) 定性分析
(RUS) КАЧЕСТВЕННЫЙ АНАЛИЗ

qualitative research

(CHIN) 定性研究

(FRE) études qualitatives, (C) recherche qualitative
(GER) qualitative Forschung *f*
(JAP) 定性調査
(RUS) ИССЛЕДОВАНИЕ КАЧЕСТВЕННЫХ ПАРАМЕТРОВ ВЛИЯНИЯ РЕКЛАМЫ НА АУДИТОРИЮ

quality

(CHIN) 质量，品质，优质的，高级的

(FRE) qualité
(GER) Qualität *f*, Güte *f*; Beschaffenheit *f*, Eigenschaft *f*
(JAP) 品質、質
(RUS) КАЧЕСТВО; СВОЙСТВО

quality control

(CHIN) 质量管理，品质控制

(FRE) contrôle de qualité
(GER) Qualitäts- *f*, Gütekontrolle *f*
(JAP) 品質管理
(RUS) КОНТРОЛЬ КАЧЕСТВА

quality engineering

(CHIN) 质量工程

(FRE) technique de gestion de la qualité, (C) évaluation de concept
(GER) Qualitätstechnik *f*
(JAP) 品質工学
(RUS) ИНЖИНЕРНЫЙ КОНТРОЛЬ КАЧЕСТВА

quantitative analysis

(CHIN) 定量分析

(FRE) analyse quantitative
(GER) qantitative Analyse *f*
(JAP) 定量分析、量的分析

340

quantitative research

(CHIN) 定量研究
(FRE) études quantitatives
(GER) quantitative Forschung *f*
(JAP) 定量調査、数量調査
(RUS) ИССЛЕДОВАНИЕ
КОЛИЧЕСТВЕННЫХ ПАРАМЕТРОВ
ВЛИЯНИЯ РЕКЛАМЫ НА АУДИТОРИЮ

quantity discount

(CHIN) 数量折扣
(FRE) rabais sur achats en grande quantité,
(C) remise sur quantité
(GER) Mengenrabatt *m*, Nachlass *m* bzw.
Rabatt *m* bei Mengenabnahme *f*
(JAP) 数量割引
(RUS) СКИДКА С ОБЪЁМА

quarterly

(CHIN) 季度的
(FRE) Trimestriel , par trimestre
(GER) vierteljährlich, quartalsweise *adj*;
Quartals-,
(JAP) 毎期の、年4回の、四半期の、
季刊誌
(RUS) КВАРТАЛЬНЫЙ

quasi contract

(CHIN) 准契约，准合同
(FRE) quasi-contrat
(GER) vertragsähnliches Verhältnis *n*
(JAP) 準契約
(RUS) КВАЗИКОНТРАКТ

query

(CHIN) 查询；询问程序
(FRE) requite
(GER) Frage *f*, Such- *f*, Abfrage *f*
(JAP) 問合せ、照会、照会文
(RUS) ЗАПРОС

queue

(CHIN) 队列，排队
(FRE) file
(GER) (Warte)schlange *f* (auch EDV)
(JAP) 待ち行列、キュー
(RUS) ОЧЕРЕДЬ, СТРУКТУРА ДАННЫХ
ДЛЯ ХРАНЕНИЯ СПИСКА ОБЙЕКТОВ,

quick asset

(CHIN) 速动资产，可兑现资产
(FRE) actif liquide , (C) actif disponible et
réalisable
(GER) Umlaufvermögen *n*, leicht
realisierbare Aktiva *pl*; flüssige Mittel *npl*
und Forderungen *fpl*; Liquidität *f* ersten
Grades *m*
(JAP) 当座資産
(RUS) НАЛИЧНОСТЬ ИЛИ
ВЫСОКОЛИКВИДНЫЕ АКТИВЫ

quick ratio

(CHIN) 速动比率，偿付力比率
(FRE) taux de liquidité, (C) ratio de
liquidité relative
(GER) Liquiditäts- *n*,
Flüssigkeitsverhältnis *n*, Verhältnis *n* des
Umlaufvermögens *n* zu den laufenden
Verbindlichkeiten *fpl*, Liquidität *f* zweiten
Grades *m*
(JAP) 当座比率
(RUS) КОЭФФИЦИЕНТ БЫСТРОТЫ
ПОКРЫТИЯ ЛИКВИДНЫМИ
АКТИВАМИ

quiet enjoyment

(CHIN) 安静享受权
(FRE) clause de paisible jouissance ,
(C) jouissance paisible
(GER) ungestörter Besitzgenuss *m*,
ungestörter Besitz *m*
(JAP) 平穏享有権
(RUS) ПРАВО НА СПОКОЙНЫЕ УСЛОВИЯ
ПОЛЬЗОВАНИЕ ПРЕДМЕТОМ АРЕНДЫ
(например, жильем)

quiet title suit

(CHIN) 不活跃产权诉讼
(FRE) action en validation du titre de
propriété, (C) confirmation de droit
immobilier
(GER) Eigentumsfeststellungsklage *f*,
-verfahren *n*
(JAP) 権原確認訴訟、
土地所有権保全訴訟
(RUS) СУДЕБНОЕ РАССМОТРЕНИЕ
СПОРА О ПРАВОВОМ ТИТУЛЕ С
УЧАСТИЕМ СПОРЯЩИХ
СТОРОН

341

quitclaim deed

(CHIN) 放弃权利契约

(FRE) acte de transfert d'un droit ou d'un titre par voie de renonciation mais sans garantie de validité, (C) acte de renonciation à des droits

(GER) Grundstücksübertragungsurkunde *f*, Verzichtserklärung *f*, Zessionsurkunde *f*, Auflassungs- *m*, Überlassungsvertrag *m*

(JAP) 権利放棄型捺印証書、
無担保譲渡証書

(RUS) ДОКУМЕНТ ОБ ОТКАЗЕ ОТ ПРЕТЕНЗИЙ

quorum

(CHIN) 必须到法庭的法定人数

(FRE) quorum

(GER) Quorum *n*, beschlussfähige Mehrheit *f*

(JAP) 定足数、（合議などの）要員数

(RUS) КВОРУМ

quota

(CHIN) 配额，限额，指标

(FRE) quota

(GER) Quote *f*, Kontingent *n*, Soll *n*; Quantum *n*, Pensum *n*; Stückzahl *f*; Verteilungsschlüssel *m*; Mengengrenze *f*

(JAP) 一定割合、割当数、枠

(RUS) КВОТА

quota sample

(CHIN) 定额样本

(FRE) échantillon de population par groupes homogènes, (C) échantillon de quota

(GER) Quotenstichprobe *f*, Stichprobenanalyse *f*

(JAP) 割当標本

(RUS) НЕОБХОДИМОЕ КОЛИЧЕСТВО ВЫБОРКИ

quotation

(CHIN) 价，行情，估价表

(FRE) référence, devis, cours,

(GER) (Preis)angebot *n*, Kosten(vor)anschlag *m*; Preisangabe *f*; Kurs- *f*, Effekten- *f*, Preisnotierung *f*; Prämienmitteilung *f*

(JAP) 相場、時価、見積

(RUS) ЦИТАТА; КОТИРОВКА

quo warranto

(CHIN) 责问某人根据什么行使职权的令状

(FRE) quo warranto

(GER) Klage *f* bzw. Verfahren *n* wegen Amtsanmaßung *f*

(JAP) 権限開示令状

(RUS) РАССЛЕДОВАНИЕ ПРАВОМЕРНОСТИ ПРИТЯЗАНИЯ НА ДОЛЖНОСТЬ, ПРИВИЛЕГИЮ, ПРАВО

qwerty keyboard

(CHIN) qwerty 键盘

(FRE) clavier qwerty

 (GER) QWERTY Tastatur *f* (Englisch) (EDV)

(RUS) КЛАВИАТУРА СО СТАНДАРТНЫМ АМЕРИКАНСКИМ РАСПОЛОЖЕНИЕМ ТЕКСТОВЫХ КЛАВИШ (НАЗВАНИЕ ПРОИСХОДИТ ОТ ЛИТЕР, РАСПОЛОЖЕННЫХ СЛЕВА В ПЕРВОМ РЯДУ)

R

racket
(CHIN) 诈骗，敲诈
(FRE) racket, (C) combine
(GER) Gaunerei *f*, Betrügerei *f*, Schwindel *m*, Masche *f*
(JAP) 不正な金儲け、密売
(RUS) РЭКЕТ, ПРЕСТУПНОЕ ВЫМОГАТЕЛЬСТВО

rag content
(CHIN) 纸中棉花纤维含量百分比
(FRE) teneur en drilles, (C) teneur en chiffons
(GER) Haderngehalt *m*
(JAP) ぼろ含有量
(RUS) СОДЕРЖАНИЕ ХЛОПКОВОГО ВОЛОКОНА В БУМАГЕ; ПОКАЗАТЕЛЬ КАЧЕСТВА

raider
(CHIN) 袭击者，市场扰乱者
(FRE) raider, (C) attaquant
(GER) Übernahme-Geier *m*, Freibeuter *m*, Plünderer *m*
(JAP) （株買占めで会社を）乗っ取る人、不正摘発者
(RUS) «НАЛЕТЧИК»; «РЕЙДЕР» (лицо, активно скупающее акции для получения контрольного пакета)

rain insurance
(CHIN) 雨淋险
(FRE) assurance contre la pluie
(GER) Regen- *f*, Schlechtwetterversicherung *f*
(JAP) 雨害保険
(RUS) СТРАХОВАНИЕ ОТ НЕБЛАГОПРИЯТНЫХ ПОГОДНЫХ УСЛОВИЙ

raised check
(CHIN) 涂改金额的支票，伪造支票
(FRE) chèque en relief
(GER) Scheck *m* mit geprägtem Betragsfeld *n* (zur Vermeidung von Abänderung)
(JAP) 変造小切手

(RUS) ЧЕК С ВЫПУКЛОЙ НАДПИСЬЮ (ДЛЯ ПРЕДОТВРАЩЕНИЯ ПОДДЕЛКИ)

rally
(CHIN) 回升
(FRE) reprise, (C) reprise boursière
(GER) (Markt- *f*, Kurs)erholung *f*, Auftrieb *m*, Preisaufschwung *m* (Börse); erholen, aufholen *v* (Börse)
(JAP) 盛り返し、回復する
(RUS) РЕЗКОЕ ПОВЫШЕНИЕ КУРСА ЦЕННЫХ БУМАГ или ТОВАРНЫХ ЦЕН; ВОССТАНОВЛЕНИЕ ПОСЛЕ СПАДА

random access memory (RAM)
(CHIN) 随机存取存储器 (RAM)
(FRE) mémoire vive
(GER) RAM, Direktzugriffsspeicher *m*
(JAP) ランダムアクセス記憶装置、ランダムアクセスメモリー、RAM
(RUS) ОПЕРАТИВНАЯ ПАМЯТЬ (ОЗУ)

random-digit dialing
(CHIN) 随机拨号选择
(FRE) composition aléatoire
(GER) Wählen *n* nach Zufallszahlen *fpl*
(JAP) ランダムディジタルダイヤリング
(RUS) ПРОИЗВОЛЬНЫЙ НАБОР ТЕЛЕФОННЫХ НОМЕРОВ (МЕТОД ТЕЛЕФОННОГО ИАРКЕТИНГА)

random-number generator
(CHIN) 随机号码发生器
(FRE) générateur de nombres aléatoires
(GER) Zufallszahlengenerator *m*
(JAP) 乱数発生器
(RUS) ГЕНЕРАТОР СЛУЧАЙНЫХ ЧИСЕЛ (вычисл.)

random sample
(CHIN) 随机样本
(FRE) échantillon aléatoire
(GER) (Zufalls)stichprobe *f*, -probe *f*
(JAP) ランダムサンプル、任意抽出見本
(RUS) СЛУЧАЙНАЯ ВЫБОРКА

random walk

(CHIN) 随机运动

(FRE) théorie du cheminement aléatoire

(GER) Zufallsweg *m*, zufallsbedingte Kursentwicklung *f*; Irrfahrt *f*

(JAP) 〔統計〕乱歩、（経済）千鳥足（理論）、ランダムウォーク（法）

(RUS) ТЕОРИЯ ДВИЖЕНИЯ КУРСА ЦЕННЫХ БУМАГ, СОГЛАСНО КОТОЙ ПРОЩЛЫЕ ДВИЖЕНИЕ ЦЕН НЕ ЯВЛЯЕТСЯ ИНДИКАТОРОМ БУДУЩЕГО

range

(CHIN) 全距，范围，规模，范围，值域，量程

(FRE) étendue, série, gamme, éventail

(GER) Bereich *m*, Umfang *m*, Spannweite *f*, Schwankungsbreite *f*, Spielraum *m*; Angebot *n*, Auswahl *f*, Sortiment *n*, Produkt- *f*, Angebotspalette *f*

(JAP) 範囲、区域、限界

(RUS) ДИАПАЗОН; РАЗБРОС (ЦЕН)

rank-and file

(CHIN) 一般付费工会成员

(FRE) base (d'un syndicat), (C) personnel subalterne

(GER) Basis *f*, breite Masse *f*; Belegschaft *f*

(JAP) 一般人、一般庶民、一般社員

(RUS) ЧЛЕН, НЕ ЗАНИМАЮЩИЙ НИКАКОЙ ДОЛЖНОСТИ

ratable

(CHIN) 可估价的

(FRE) tarifiable

(GER) anteilig, verhältnismäßig *adj*; veranlagungspflichtig *adj*; abgabe-, umlagepflichtig, schätzbar *adj*

(JAP) 評価しうる、（英）課税しうる

(RUS) ПРОПОРЦИОНАЛЬНЫЙ; ОБЛАГАЕМЫЙ НАЛОГОМ

rate

(CHIN) 率，比例，价格，费用，定额，行情

(FRE) Taux, tarif

(GER) beurteilen *v*; verdienen *v*; festsetzen *v*

(JAP) 割合、歩合、評価する

(RUS) СТАВКА; ТЕМП РОСТА; УРОВЕНЬ

rate base

(CHIN) 运价率基数，收费标准

(FRE) base de tarification

(GER) Tarif- *f*; Bemessungsgrundlage *f*; Steuerbasis *f*; Richtsatz *m*

(JAP) 料金算定基準

(RUS) ОГРАНИЧЕНИЕ УРОВНЯ ПРИБЫЛЬНОСТИ РЕГУЛИРУЕМЫХ ОТРАСЛЕЙ

rate card

(CHIN) 价目牌

(FRE) carte tarif, (C) avis de tarification

(GER) Anzeigenpreisliste *f*, Preistafel *f*

(JAP) 料金表

(RUS) ИНФОРМАЦИЯ О РАСХОДАХ НА КАЖДЫЙ РЕКЛАМНЫЙ ОБЪЕКТ

rated policy

(CHIN) 标准保单

(FRE) police tarifiée

(GER) Versicherung *f* zu erhöhter Prämie *f*

(JAP) 評定保険証券

(RUS) СТРАХОВОЙ ПОЛИС С ПОВЫШЕННОЙ ПРЕМИАЛЬНОЙ ВЫПЛАТОЙ ИЗ-ЗА СОСТОЯНИЯ ЗДОРОВЬЯ, ВРЕДНЫХ ПРИВЫЧЕК ИЛИ ОПАСНОЙ ПРОФЕССИИ СТРАХУЕМОГО

rates and classifications

(CHIN) 费率及分类

(FRE) tarifs et classifications

(GER) Gebühren *fpl* und Einstufungen *fpl*

(JAP) 料率と等級

(RUS) СТАВКИ И КЛАССИФИКАЦИИ

rate setting

(CHIN) 劳动定额，工资定额

(FRE) tarification

(GER) Festsetzung *f* von Abgabepreisen *mpl*; Festsetzung *f* von Lohnsätzen *mpl*, Tarifgestaltung *f*; Prämien- *f*, Gebührenfestsetzung *f* (Versicherung)

(JAP) 賃率設定

(RUS) УСТАНОВЛЕНИЕ ТАРИФНОЙ СТАВКИ КОММУНАЛЬНЫХ УСЛУГ

ratification

(CHIN) 批准，通过

(FRE) ratification

(GER) Ratifikation *f*, Genehmigung *f*,
Anerkennung *f*
(JAP) 承認、認可、批准
(RUS) РАТИФИКАЦИЯ

rating

(CHIN) 评价，评级

(FRE) notation, (C) contrôle des résultats,
(C) cote, (C) classement selon le mérite
(GER) Leistungsbewertung *f*;
Kreditfähigkeit *f*, -würdigkeit *f*;
Klassifizierung *f*, Wertpapiereinstufung *f*;
Bemessung *f*, Beurteilung *f*
(JAP) 格付け、評価、採点
(RUS) РЕЙТИНГ; УСЛОВНАЯ
КОЛИЧЕСТВЕННАЯ ОЦЕНКА

ratio analysis

(CHIN) 比率分析

(FRE) méthodes des ratios, (C) analyse au
moyen de ratios
(GER) Kennziffernanalyse *f*,
Kennzahlenanalyse *f*; Bilanzanalyse *f*
(JAP) 比率分析
(RUS) КРЕДИТНЫЙ (ИНВЕСТИЦИОННЫЙ)
АНАЛИЗ ПО СООТНОШЕНИЯМ МЕЖДУ
ФИНАНСОВЫМИ ПОКАЗАТЕЛЯМИ

rationing

(CHIN) 配额
(FRE) rationnement
(GER) Rationierung *f*
(JAP) 配給（の）
(RUS) РАЦИОНИРОВАНИЕ (ТОВАРОВ);
КАРТОЧНАЯ СИСТЕМА

ratio scale

(CHIN) 比率尺度，等比量表
(FRE) échelle de rapports, échelle de
variations relatives
(GER) einfach-logarithmischer Maßstab *m*,
Verhältnismaßstab *m*
(JAP) 比例尺度
(RUS) ШКАЛА СООТНОШЕНИЙ

raw data

(CHIN) 原始数据
(FRE) données brutes
(GER) Rohdaten *pl*; Originaldaten *pl*,
Urdaten *pl*

(JAP) 生データ
(RUS) НЕОБРАБОТАННЫЕ ДАННЫЕ

raw land

(CHIN) 生地，未开发士地
(FRE) terrain nu
(GER) unerschlossenes Land *n*, unbebaute
Grundstücke *npl*
(JAP) 未開発地
(RUS) НЕОБРАБОТАННАЯ ЗЕМЛЯ;
ЦЕЛИНА

raw material

(CHIN) 原料
(FRE) matières premières
(GER) Roh- *fpl*, Grundstoffe *mpl*
(JAP) 原料
(RUS) СЫРЬЕ; СЫРЬЕВОЙ МАТЕРИАЛ

reading the tape

(CHIN) 监视股票价格涨落
(FRE) lecture de la bande, (C) lecture du
téléscripteur
(GER) Verfolgen *n* der Börsenticker *mpl*
(JAP) テープ読み取り
(RUS) ЧТЕНИЕ БЕГУЩЕЙ СТРОКИ (БИРЖ.)

readjustment

(CHIN) 再调整
(FRE) rajustement
(GER) (wirtschaftliche) Sanierung *f*,
Neuordnung *f*, Reorganisation *f*; Korrektur *f*,
Neuregelung *f*, Nachregelung *f*,
Neuanpassung *f*
(JAP) 再調整、財政建て直し
(RUS) КОРРЕКТИРОВКА

read-only

(CHIN) 只读
(FRE) lecture seule
(GER) schreibgeschützt *adj* (EDV)
(JAP) 読取り専用
(RUS) НЕИЗМЕНЯЕМЫЙ (О ДАННЫХ,
ИЗМЕНЕНИЕ КОТОРЫХ ЗАПРЕЩЕНО
ИЛИ ФИЗИЧЕСКИ НЕ- ВОЗМОЖНО

real

(CHIN) 真实的，实际的
(FRE) réel, (C) valeur
(GER) real, wirklich, echt, tatsächlich *adj*

(JAP) 本当の、実在する、実際の
(RUS) РЕАЛЬНЫЙ, СУЩЕСТВУЮЩИЙ; НЕДВИЖИМЫЙ

real account

(CHIN) 真实账户，实账
(FRE) compte de valeurs
(GER) Bestands- *n*, Bilanzkonto *n*, Sachkonto *n*
(JAP) 実在勘定、実体勘定
(RUS) РЕАЛЬНЫЙ СЧЕТ

real earnings

(CHIN) 实际收益
(FRE) revenu réel
(GER) Realeinkommen *n*, -lohn *m*
(JAP) 実質所得、実質収入
(RUS) ЗАРАБОТНАЯ ПЛАТА И ДРУГИЕ ЗАРАБОТКИ, СКОРРЕКТИРОВАННЫЕ НА ИНФЛЯЦИЮ

real estate

(CHIN) 房地产，不动产
(FRE) immobilier
(GER) Immobilien *fpl*, Grundbesitz *m*, Grundeigentum *n*, Grundvermögen *n*, Grund *m* und Boden *m*, Liegenschaft *f*
(JAP) 不動産
(RUS) НЕДВИЖИМОСТЬ

real estate investment trust (REIT)

(CHIN) 房地产投资信托 (REIT)
(FRE) société de placement immobilier
(GER) Immobilienfonds *m*, Immobilieninvestmentgesellschaft *f*
(JAP) 不動産投資信託
(RUS) ТРАСТ, ПЕЦИАЛИЗИРУЮЩИЙСЯ НА ИНВЕСТИЦИЯХ В НЕДВИЖИМОСТЬ, ИПОТЕКИ

real estate market

(CHIN) 房地产市场
(FRE) marché immobilier
(GER) Immobilienmarkt *m*, Grundstücksmarkt *m*
(JAP) 不動産市場
(RUS) РЫНОК НЕДВИЖИМОСТИ

real estate owned (REO)

(CHIN) 备用房地产 （REO）
(FRE) regroupement des propriétés
(GER) Grundeigentumsübernahme *f* aufgrund von Zahlungsunfähigkeit *f* bzw. Zwangsvollstreckung *f*
(JAP) 所有されている不動産
(RUS) НЕДВИЖИМОСТЬ ВО ВЛАДЕНИИ

real income

(CHIN) 实际收入
(FRE) revenu réel
(GER) Real- *n*, Effektiveinkommen *n*
(JAP) 実質所得
(RUS) «РЕАЛЬНЫЙ» ДОХОД
(скорректированный на уровень цен)

real interest rate

(CHIN) 实际利率
(FRE) taux d'intérêt réel
(GER) Real- *m*, Effektivzins *m*, Realverzinsung *f*
(JAP) 実質利子率、実質金利
(RUS) РЕАЛЬНЫЕ ПРОЦЕНТНЫЕ СТАВКИ
(текущие ставки за вычетом темпов роста цен)

realized gain

(CHIN) 实现收益
(FRE) bénéfice réalisé
(GER) realisierte Gewinne *mpl*
(JAP) 実現収益
(RUS) РЕАЛИЗОВАННАЯ ПРИБЫЛЬ

real property

(CHIN) 不动产，房地产
(FRE) propriété immobilière
(GER) Immobilien *fpl*, Grundbesitz *m*, -eigentum *n*, -vermögen *n*, Liegenschaft *f*
(JAP) 不動産、物的財産
(RUS) ЗЕМЛЯ С ПОСТРОЙКАМИ И РАСТИТЕЛЬНОСТЬЮ НА НЕЙ

real rate of return

(CHIN) 实际回报率
(FRE) taux de rendement réel
(GER) effektive Ertragsrate *f*, effektive Rendite *f*, effektive Kapitalverzinsung *f*
(JAP) 実勢利益率
(RUS) РЕАЛЬНАЯ СТАВКА ДОХОДА
(скорректированная на темпы роста цен)

realtor

(CHIN) 房地产经纪人

(FRE) courtier immobilier

(GER) Immobilien- *m*, rundstücksmakler *m*

(JAP) 公認不動産業者〔商標〕

(RUS) АГЕНТ ПО ОПЕРАЦИЯМ С НЕДВИЖИМОСТЬЮ

real value of money

(CHIN) 实际货币价值

(FRE) valeur réelle de l'argent

(GER) Realkaufkraft *f*, effektive Kaufkraft *f* des Geldes *n*

(JAP) 貨幣の実質価値

(RUS) РЕАЛЬНАЯ ЦЕНА ДЕНЕГ

real wages

(CHIN) 实际工资

(FRE) salaire réel

(GER) Reallohn *m*

(JAP) 実質賃金

(RUS) РЕАЛЬНАЯ ЗАРАБОТНАЯ ПЛАТА

reappraisal lease

(CHIN) 重估租赁

(FRE) révision du loyer, (C) nouvelle appréciation du loyer

(GER) Miet- *m*, Pachtvertrag *m* mit periodischer Neubewertung *f*

(JAP) 再評価リース

(RUS) АРЕНДА С ПЕРИОДИЧЕСКИМ ПЕРЕСМОТРОМ ПЛАТЫ

reasonable person

(CHIN) 通情达理之人

(FRE) personne raisonnable

(GER) vernünftige Person *f*

(JAP) 道理をわきまえた人

(RUS) РАЗУМНОЕ ЛИЦО

reassessment

(CHIN) 更正

(FRE) réexamen, réévaluation, (C) avis de redressement, (C) avis de nouvelle cotisation

(GER) Neubewertung *f*; Neuveranlagung *f*, -festsetzung *f*; Bereinigung *f*; Umwertung *f*

(JAP) 再評価、再検討

(RUS) ПЕРЕСМОТР, ПРЕОЦЕНКА

rebate

(CHIN) 回扣，折扣，退税

(FRE) rabais, ristourne, (C) abattement, rabais, ristourne

(GER) Preisnachlass *m*, Rabatt *m*; Abzug *m*, Abschlag *m*; Rückvergütung *f*, Erstattung *f*; Provisionsbeteiligung *f* durch den Versicherungsmakler *m*

(JAP) 割戻し、払い戻し、リベート

(RUS) СКИДКА С ЦЕНЫ; ВОЗВРАТ ЧАСТИ УПЛАЧЕННЫХ ДЕНЕГ

reboot

(CHIN) 再引导，重新启动

(FRE) réinitialisation, réinitialiser

(GER) Neustart *m*; neu starten *v* (Computer)

(JAP) リブート、再起動、リブートする

(RUS) ПЕРЕЗАГРУЗКА

recall

(CHIN) 收回, 复检，二次呼叫

(FRE) rappel, rappeler, (C) offre de reprise

(GER) Rückruf *m*; Wiedereinstellung *f*, rückrufen; abberufen *v*

(JAP) リコール、

　（欠陥商品などの）回収、撤回

(RUS) ОТОЗВАТЬ; ОТЗЫВ; ОТМЕНА

recall campaign

(CHIN) 产品收回广告

(FRE) campagne de rappel

(GER) Rückrufaktion *f*

(JAP) 回収キャンペーン

(RUS) КАМПАНИЯ ПО ОТЗЫВУ

recall study

(CHIN) 产品收回研究

(FRE) étude de mémorisation

(GER) Rückrufstudie *f*

(JAP) リコール研究

(RUS) ИЗУЧЕНИЕ ПРИЧИН ОТЗЫВА

recapitalization

(CHIN) 资本重组

(FRE) recapitalisation, changement de la structure financière, (C) refonte de capital

(GER) Neukapitalisierung *f*, Kapitalerhöhung *f*, Kapitalumschichtung *f*, -umstrukturierung *f*

(JAP) 資本修正、資本再編成
(RUS) РЕКАПИТАЛИЗАЦИЯ

recapture

(CHIN) 回收，收复，归公
(FRE) saisie, (C) reprise
(GER) Nachholbesteuerung *f*; Rücknahme *f*
rückversicherter Risiken *npl*
(Versicherung); Enteignung *f*;
Wiedergewinnung *f*, Rückeroberung *f*
(JAP) 再捕獲、再収集
(RUS) ВОССТАНОВЛЕНИЕ РАНЕЕ
ОТМЕНЕННЫХ (НАЛОГОВЫХ) ЛЬГОТ

recapture rate

(CHIN) 回收率
(FRE) taux de reprise
(GER) Rückgewinnungsrate *f*
(JAP) 再捕獲率
(RUS) УРОВЕНЬ ВОЗМЕЩЕНИЯ
ИНВЕСТИЦИЙ В УБЫВАЮЩИЕ РЕСУРСЫ

recasting a debt

(CHIN) 债务重新安排
(FRE) refonte d'un prêt
(GER) eine Schuld *f* umgestalten bzw. neu
kalkulieren *v*
(JAP) 負債を再計算すること
(RUS) КОРРЕКТИРОВКА УСЛОВИЙ
КРЕДИТА, ЗАЙМА

receipt, receipt book

(CHIN) 收据，收款凭单簿
(FRE) reçu, carnet de quittances
(GER) Quittung *f*, Beleg *m*;
Quittungsbuch *n*
(JAP) 受取り、領収証、受取証、
受取台帳
(RUS) РАСПИСКА (ЧЕК О ПОЛУЧЕНИИ
ПЛАТЫ), КНИЖКА ДЛЯ РАСПИСОК

receivables turnover

(CHIN) 应收款周转率
(FRE) ratio de rotation des comptes clients
(GER) Forderungsumschlag *m*,
Umschlagsgeschwindigkeit *f* bzw. -
häufigkeit *f* der Forderungen *fpl*
(JAP) 受取勘定回転率
(RUS) ОБОРОТ СЧЕТОВ К
ПОЛУЧЕНИЮ

receiver

(CHIN) 清算人，收款人
(FRE) administrateur judiciaire,(C) syndic
(GER) Empfänger *m*, Adressat *m*; Sequester,
vorläufiger Konkursverwalter *m*,
Zwangsverwalter *m*
(JAP) 受取人、領収者、会計係
(RUS) ПОЛУЧАТЕЛЬ; ЛИЦО,
НАЗНАЧЕННОЕ СУДОМ ДЛЯ
ПРОВЕДЕНИЯ ЛИКВИДАЦИИ
ОБАНКРОТИВШЕЙСЯ КОМПАНИИ

receiver's certificate

(CHIN) 清算人借款证
(FRE) titre de liquidateur judiciaire,
(C) certificat de syndic
(GER) Verpfändungsurkunde *f* über
Zwangsverwaltungsgut *n*
(JAP) 管財人証明書
(RUS) СЕРТИФИКАТ, СВИДЕТЕЛЬСТВО
ПОЛУЧАТЕЛЯ

receivership

(CHIN) 财力清算，清算管理
(FRE) règlement judiciaire, (C) fonction de
syndic de faillite
(GER) Konkurs- *f*, Zwangsverwaltung *f*;
Verwaltung *f* durch
Grundpfandgläubiger *m*
(JAP) 受取係、収入係
(RUS) СТАТУС ЛИЦА, НАЗНАЧЕННОГО
УПРАВЛЯТЬ БАНКРОТОМ или
ОСПАРИВАЕМЫМ ИМУЩЕСТВОМ

receiving clerk

(CHIN) 收货员，收料员，验收员
(FRE) réceptionniste
(GER) Warenannahmebevollmächtiger *m*,
Angestellter *m* im Wareneingang *m*
(RUS) СЕКРЕТАРЬ (СУДА)

receiving record

(CHIN) 收货记录
(FRE) registre de réception
(GER) (Waren)eingangsmeldung *f*
(JAP) 受取記録、領収記録
(RUS) ДОКУМЕНТАЦИЯ ПОЛУЧЕНИЯ
ДОКУМЕНТА ИЛИ ИМУЩЕСТВА

recession

(CHIN) 经济衰退

(FRE) récession
(GER) Rezession *f*, Konjunkturrückgang *m*,
Flaute *f*, Abschwung *m*,
Konjunkturschwäche *f*
(JAP) 景気後退、不景気、
リセッション
(RUS) СПАД

reciprocal buying

(CHIN) 相互购买
(FRE) achats réciproques
(GER) wechselseitige Lieferbeziehungen *fpl*
(JAP) 相互購買
(RUS) ВСТРЕЧНЫЕ ПОКУПКИ

reciprocity

(CHIN) 互惠，交换
(FRE) réciprocité, (C) réciprocité d'achats
(GER) Reziprozität *f*; Gegenseitigkeit *f*,
Wechselseitigkeit *f*
(JAP) 互恵主義、相互利益、交換再保険
(RUS) ВЗАИМНОСТЬ

reckoning

(CHIN) 计算，估算
(FRE) calcul, compte, (C) comptage
(GER) Kalkulation *f*, Aus- *f*, Berechnung *f*;
Schätzung *f*
(JAP) 計算、集計、勘定
(RUS) СООБРАЖЕНИЯ; ОБОСНОВАНИЯ

recognition

(CHIN) 确认
(FRE) reconnaissance
(GER) Anerkennung *f*, Bestätigung *f*;
Geltung *f*
(JAP) 認可、承認、表彰
(RUS) ПРИЗНАНИЕ

recognized gain

(CHIN) 公认收益
(FRE) revenu imposable
(GER) anerkannter Gewinn *m*
(JAP) 認識利益
(RUS) УЧТЕННАЯ ПРИБЫЛЬ

recompense

(CHIN) 偿还，补偿，赔偿
(FRE) récompense

(GER) Belohnung *f*; Entgelt *n*;
Entschädigung *f*, Wiedergutmachung *f*
(JAP) 賠償、償い、補償
(RUS) КОМПЕНСИРОВАТЬ; ВОЗМЕСТИТЬ

reconciliation

(CHIN) 调节，调停，调和
(FRE) rapprochement, (C) réconciliation
(GER) Versöhnung *f*; Schlichtung *f*,
Beilegung *f*; Abstimmung *f*
(JAP) 和解、調停、調和
(RUS) ПРИМИРЕНИЕ, УЛАЖИВАНИЕ

reconditioning property

(CHIN) 维修财产
(FRE) remise à neuf de biens
(GER) Instandsetzung *f* von Grundbesitz *m*
(JAP) 財産の修理
(RUS) ВОССТАНОВЛЕНИЕ КАЧЕСТВА
ИМУЩЕСТВА

reconsign

(CHIN) 再委托，再托卖
(FRE) réexpédition
(GER) umleiten, weiterleiten, mit einer
neuen Adresse *f* versehen, umadressieren *v*
(JAP) 〜を再委託する
(RUS) ИЗМЕНИТЬ УСЛОВИЯ
КОНСИГНАЦИИ В ПРОЦЕССЕ ДОСТАВКИ

reconveyance

(CHIN) 再转让
(FRE) rétrocession
(GER) Rückübertragung *f*, -abtreteung *f*, -
übereignung *f*
(JAP) 再讓渡、前所有者に返還
(RUS) ОБРАТНАЯ ПЕРЕДАЧА ПРАВОВОГО
ТИТУЛА

record

(CHIN) 记录，记载项目
(FRE) dossier, registre
(GER) Aufzeichnung *f*; Akte *f*, Urkunde *f*;
Dokument *n*; Nachweis *m*, Beleg *m*;
Protokoll *n*, Niederschrift *f*; Verzeichnis *n*;
Datensatz *m* (EDV); Rekord *m*,
Spitzenleistung *f*
(JAP) 記録、登記、登録
(RUS) ЗАПИСЬ; ДОКУМЕНТ;
АКТ

recorder point

(CHIN) 记录点

(FRE) point d'enregistrement

(GER) Aufzeichnungs- *m*,
Dokumentierpunkt *m*

(JAP) レコーダーポイント

(RUS) ПРИМЕЧАНИЕ В ПРОТОКОЛЕ (суд.)

recording

(CHIN) 入账，记录

(FRE) enregistrement

(GER) Eintragung *f*, Aufzeichnung *f*,
Registrierung *f*, Protokollierung *f*;
Verbuchung *f*

(JAP) 記録、記載

(RUS) ЗАПИСЬ

records management

(CHIN) 账目管理

(FRE) gestion des dossiers, gestion des
registres

(GER) Dokumenten- *f*, Aktenverwaltung *f*

(JAP) 記録情報管理

(RUS) ВЕДЕНИЕ ЗАПИСЕЙ, АРХИВОВ

recoup, recoupment

(CHIN) 补偿，赔偿，扣除

(FRE) récupération

(GER) zurückgewinnen, zurückerlangen,
wettmachen, wieder hereinholen,
ausgleichen *v*; entschädigen *v*;
Entschädigung *f*, Ersetzung *f*; Minderung *f*,
Schadloshaltung *f*; Zurückgewinnung *f*

(JAP) 損害を回復する、損失を）取り戻
す、弁償する、賠償、控除

(RUS) КОМПЕНСИРОВАТЬ, ВОЗМЕЩАТЬ;
КОМПЕНСАЦИЯ, ВОЗМЕЩЕНИЕ

recourse

(CHIN) 索赔，追索

(FRE) recours

(GER) Regress *m*, Rückanspruch *m*;
Rückgriff *m*

(JAP) （手形・小切手などの）遡及
（権）、償還請求（権）、償還

(RUS) ПРАВО ОБОРОТА (РЕГРЕССА)

recourse loan

(CHIN) 索赔贷款，偿还贷款

(FRE) prêt avec clause de recours

(GER) Darlehen *n* mit Regress *m*

(JAP) リコースローン、
償還準備貸付（金）

(RUS) ССУДА С ПРАВОМ РЕГРЕССА

recover

(CHIN) 恢复

(FRE) récupérer

(GER) wiederherstellen *v*; beheben *v*

(JAP) 回復する、取り戻す

(RUS) ВОССТАНАВЛИВАТЬ

recovery

(CHIN) 追索，追赔，收回，恢复

(FRE) recouvrement, redressement,
récupération, (C) reprise sur réduction de
valeur, recouvrement

(GER) Aufschwung *m*, Erholung *f*, Anstieg
m, Wiederbelebung *f*

(JAP) 改修、回復

(RUS) «ВЫЗДОРОВЛЕНИЕ»: ПОВЫШЕНИЕ
ЭКОНОМИЧЕСКОЙ АКТИВНОСТИ;
ПОЛУЧЕНИЕ СПИСАННОГО ДОЛГА

recovery fund

(CHIN) 追偿基金

(FRE) fonds recouvrés

(GER) Fonds *m* für Ausgleichszahlungen
fpl (bei von Immobilienmaklern
verursachten Rechtsverletzungen)

(JAP) 回復資金

(RUS) ФОНД НА ВОССТАНОВЛЕНИЕ (при
наступлении неблагоприятных
обстоятельств)

recovery of basis

(CHIN) 基本成本收回

(FRE) récupération de coût

(GER) Rückgewinnung *f* der Basis *f*

(JAP) 基準の回復

(RUS) ОБРАТНОЕ ПОЛУЧЕНИЕ БАЗОВОЙ
СУММЫ

recruitment

(CHIN) 招聘，征收

(FRE) recrutement

(GER) Anwerbung *f*,
Rekrutierung *f*

(JAP) 採用、補充、募集

(RUS) НАБОР РАБОТНИКОВ;
ВЕРБОВКА

recruitment bonus

(CHIN) 招聘奖金

(FRE) prime de recrutement

(GER) Anwerbeprämie *f*

(JAP) 採用ボーナス

(RUS) ПРЕМИЯ ЗА ПРИВЛЕЧЕНИЕ РАБОТНИКА

recycle bin

(CHIN) 回收站

(FRE) corbeille de recyclage

(GER) Recylingbehälter *m*

(JAP) ごみ箱

(RUS) КОРЗИНА ДЛЯ СБОРА ВТОРСЫРЬЯ

recycling

(CHIN) 回收，再循环

(FRE) recyclage

(GER) Recycling *n*, Wiederaufbereitung *f*; Rückführung *f* von Geldmitteln *npl*

(JAP) 再生利用、再循環

(RUS) ПЕРЕРАБОТКА ВТОРСЫРЬЯ

redeem

(CHIN) 赎回，偿还，履行，兑现

(FRE) réaliser, échanger, amortir, se libérer, rembourser, (C) racheter, (C) purger

(GER) Tilgen, abtragen *v*; ablösen, amortisieren zurückzahlen; zurückkaufen *v*

(JAP) 買戻す、質受けする、還する

(RUS) ВЫКУПИТЬ; ПОГАСИТЬ (ЗАЕМ)

redemption

(CHIN) 赎买，抵消，弥补，偿还

(FRE) rachat, amortissement, remboursement

(GER) Tilgung *f*; Rückzahlung *f*, Amortisierung *f*; Einlösung *f*

(JAP) 買戻し、償還、償却

(RUS) ПОГАШЕНИЕ КРЕДИТА или ЦЕННЫХ БУМАГ

redemption period

(CHIN) 赎回期，偿还期

(FRE) période de remboursement, (C) période de rachat

(GER) Tilgungsdauer *f*; Laufzeit *f*, Einlösungsfrist *f*

(JAP) 償還期間、買戻し期間

(RUS) ПЕРИОД ПОГАШЕНИЯ

redevelop

(CHIN) 再开发

(FRE) mettre en valeur

(GER) sanieren *v*

(JAP) 再開発する

(RUS) ПОВТОРНАЯ ЗАСТРОЙКА

rediscount

(CHIN) 现贴现，转贴现

(FRE) réescompte

(GER) Rediskont *m*, Rediskontierung *f*

(JAP) 再割引する、再割引

(RUS) ПЕРЕУЧЁТ ВЕКСЕЛЕЙ

rediscount rate

(CHIN) 再贴现率

(FRE) taux de réescompte

(GER) Rediskontsatz *m*

(JAP) 再割引率、再割引利率

(RUS) ПЕРЕУЧЁТНАЯ СТАВКА; СТАВКА, ПО КОТОРОЙ ФЕДЕРАЛЬНЫЙ БАНК ДАЕТ КРЕДИТЫ УЧАСТВУЮЩИМ БАНКАМ

redlining

(CHIN) 基于种族原因的贷款限制

(FRE) discrimination, (C) exclusion systématique

(GER) willkürlicher Ausschluss *m* von (Bank)kunden *mpl*

(JAP) 銀行・保険会社による）特別警戒地区指定、融資・保険契約指し止め地区指定

(RUS) ДИСКРИМИНАЦИЯ В ВЫДЕЛЕНИИ ИПОТЕЧНЫХ ЗАЙМОВ В ОТНОШЕНИИ ОПРЕДЕЛЕННЫХ РАЙОНОВ

red tape

(CHIN) 红章，官僚主义

(FRE) formalités administratives, (C) bureaucratie

(GER) Papierkrieg *m*, Bürokratie *f*

(JAP) 官僚的形式主義、繁文縟礼

(RUS) БЮРОКРАТИЯ, ПРОВОЛОЧКА

reduced rate

(CHIN) 降低费率

(FRE) taux réduit

(GER) ermäßigter Satz *m* bzw. Tarif *m*

(JAP) 割引料金

(RUS) СНИЖЕННАЯ СТАВКА

reduction certificate

(CHIN) 贷款余额证明

(FRE) certificat de réduction

(GER) Aufstellung *f* der Hypothekenrestsumme *f*

(JAP) 値引保証書

(RUS) ДОКУМЕНТ, ПОДТВЕРЖДАЮЩИЙ СУММУ ЗАДОЛЖЕННОСТИ ПО ИПОТЕКЕ

referee

(CHIN) 仲裁人，公断人，鉴定人

(FRE) référant, (C) arbitre, (C) recommandataire

(GER) Schlichter *m*, Schiedsrichter *m*; Sachverständiger *m*, Gutachter *m*

(JAP) 仲裁人、裁決者、審判員

(RUS) СУДЬЯ, АРБИТР

referral

(CHIN) 转介

(FRE) référence, (C) indication de client

(GER) Überweisung *f*; Rechtsstreitverweisung *f*

(JAP) 参照、照会

(RUS) РЕКОМЕНДАЦИЯ СПЕЦИАЛИСТА, ВОЗМОЖНОГО КЛИЕНТА И Т. П.

refinance

(CHIN) 再筹措资金

(FRE) refinancer

(GER) Refinanzieren, umfinanzieren, neu finanzieren, umschulden *v*

(JAP) 財政を立て直す、資金を補充する、リファイナンス

(RUS) РЕФИНАНСИРОВАНИЕ

reformation

(CHIN) 改革，改良，改善，调整

(FRE) reformation

(GER) Reformation *f*, Umgestaltung *f*, Erneuerung *f*; Umgründung *f*

(JAP) 再構成、改良

(RUS) ИСПРАВЛЕНИЕ ДОКУМЕНТА ПО РЕШЕНИЮ СУДА

refresh

(CHIN) 刷新；重新整理

(FRE) rafraîchier, actualiser

(GER) auffrischen, aktualisieren *v* (EDV)

(JAP) リフレッシュする、復元する、

再生する

(RUS) ОБНОВЛЯТЬ, ВОССТАНАВЛИВАТЬ, РЕГЕНЕРИРОВАТЬ

refunding

(CHIN) 再融资，举债还债，发行新债券取代旧债券

(FRE) remboursement

(GER) Umfinanzierung *f*; Umschuldung *f*; Rückzahlung *f*, Erstattung *f*

(JAP) （金）の返済、償還、払戻し

(RUS) ВОЗВРАТ ДЕНЕГ ПОКУПАТЕЛЮ ПРИ ВОЗВРАТЕ ТОВАРА; ПОВТОРНОЕ ФИНАНСИРОВАНИЕ

refund

(CHIN) 偿还，退款

(FRE) rembourser

(GER) Rückerstattung *f*, -vergütung *f*

(JAP) 返済する、払い戻す、返済

(RUS) ВОЗВРАТИТЬ ДЕНЬГИ; РЕФИНАНСИРОВАТЬ

registered bond

(CHIN) 登记债券，记名债券

(FRE) obligation nominative

(GER) Namensschuldverschreibung *f*, -obligation *f*, Namenspfandbrief *m*, auf den Namen *m* lautende Schuldverschreibung *f*

(JAP) 記名式債券、登録式債券

(RUS) ИМЕННАЯ ОБЛИГАЦИЯ

registered check

(CHIN) 记名支票

(FRE) traite bancaire

(GER) Bankscheck *m*

(JAP) 登録小切手

(RUS) ЗАРЕГИСТРИРОВАННЫЙ ЧЕК

registered company

(CHIN) 法人公司，注册公司

(FRE) société inscrite au registre du commerce, (C) société enregistrée

(GER) eingetragenes Unternehmen *n*

(JAP) 登録会社

(RUS) ЗАРЕГИСТРИРОВАННАЯ КОМПАНИЯ

registered investment company

(CHIN) 注册投资公司

(FRE) société de placement enregistrée
(GER) eingetragene Investment- *f* bzw.
Kapitalanlagegesellschaft *f*
(JAP) 登録投資会社
(RUS) ЗАРЕГИСТРИРОВАННАЯ
ИНВЕСТИЦИОННАЯ КОМПАНИЯ

registered representative (RR)
(CHIN) 登记代表
(FRE) représentant agréé
(GER) amtlich zugelassener Vertreter *m*
eines Brokers *m*, Börsenauftragsnehmer *m*
(JAP) （株式取引所の会員証券会社の従
業員である）登録代理人
(RUS) ЗАРЕГИСТРИРОВАННЫЙ
ПРЕДСТАВИТЕЛЬ

registered security
(CHIN) 记名债券
(FRE) titre nominatif
(GER) Namens- *n*, Rektapapier *n*,
Namenstitel *m*
(JAP) 記名証券
(RUS) ИМЕННЫЕ ЦЕННЫЕ БУМАГИ

registrar
(CHIN) 注册官，
登记股票转让的信托公司
(FRE) officier de l'état civil, (C) registraire
(GER) Urkundsbeamter *m*, Standesbeamter
m; Registerstelle *f*, Führer *m* des
Aktionärsregisters *n*
(JAP) 登記係、公認の記録係、
株式名簿係
(RUS) РЕГИСТРАТОР (АКЦИЙ)

registration
(CHIN) 注册，登记，挂号
(FRE) enregistrement, immatriculation, (C)
inscription, immatriculation
(GER) Anmeldung *f*, Registrierung *f*,
amtliche Eintragung *f*, Beurkundung *f*;
Erfassung *f*; Börsenanmeldung *f*
(JAP) 記録、登録、登記
(RUS) РЕГИСТРАЦИЯ (ЦЕННЫХ БУМАГ)

registration statement
(CHIN) 注册上市申请书
(FRE) déclaration d'immatriculation

(GER) Anmeldeerklärung *f*,
Eintragungsbekanntmachung *f* (Börse);
Gründungs- *f*, Eröffnungsbilanz *f*
(JAP) 登録届出書
(RUS) РЕГИСТРАЦИОННЫЙ ДОКУМЕНТ

registry of deeds
(CHIN) 契约登记处
(FRE) registre des actes
(GER) Grundbuchamt *n*
(JAP) 捺印証書の登録（登記）、権利書
の登記
(RUS) РЕЕСТР ЮРИДИЧЕСКИХ
ДОКУМЕНТОВ

regression analysis
(CHIN) 同归分析
(FRE) analyse de régression
(GER) Regressionsanalyse *f*
(JAP) 回帰分析
(RUS) РЕГРЕССИВНЫЙ АНАЛИЗ

regression line
(CHIN) 回归线
(FRE) droite de régression
(GER) Regressionsgerade *f*, -linie *f*
(JAP) 回帰直線
(RUS) УРОВЕНЬ ОТСЧЕТА РЕГРЕССИИ

regressive tax
(CHIN) 递减税
(FRE) impôt dégressif
(GER) regressive Steuer *f*
(JAP) 累退税
(RUS) РЕГРЕССИВНЫЙ НАЛОГ

regular-way delivery (and settlement)
(CHIN) 正常交货（常规结算）
(FRE) règlement dans les délais prévus par
la bourse
(GER) Lieferung *f* am vierten Tag *m* (und
Regelerfüllung *f*) (Börse)
(JAP) 通常受渡し（および決済、清算）
(RUS) ОБЫЧНОЕ ВЫПОЛНЕНИЕ (И
ОКОНЧАТЕЛЬНЫЙ РАСЧЕТ)

regulated commodities
(CHIN) 管制商品
(FRE) marchandises réglementées

(GER) den Marktbestimmungen *fpl*
unterliegende Güter *npl*
(JAP) 統制商品
(RUS) РЕГУЛИРУЕМЫЕ ТОВАРЫ

regulated industry
(CHIN) 管制工业
(FRE) industrie réglementée
(GER) öffentlich regulierte Branche *m*,
staatlich kontrollierter Industriezweig *m*
(JAP) 統制された産業、統制産業
(RUS) РЕГУЛИРУЕМАЯ ОТРАСЛЬ

regulated investment company
(CHIN) 管制投资公司
(FRE) société de placement réglementée
(GER) steuerbegünstigte Investment- *f* bzw.
Kapitalanlagegesellschaft *f*
(JAP) 統制投資会社
(RUS) РЕГУЛИРУЕМАЯ
ИНВЕСТИЦИОННАЯ КОМПАНИЯ

regulation
(CHIN) 规章，条例，管理，控制，调整
(FRE) réglement, (C) réglementation
(GER) Verordnung *f*, Vorschrift *f*,
Bestimmung *f*, Regelung *f*, Festlegung *f*,
Festsetzung *f*
(JAP) 調整、調節、規則
(RUS) РЕГУЛИРОВАНИЕ; ПРАВИЛО;
НОРМА

regulatory agency
(CHIN) 管理机构
(FRE) organisme de réglementation
(GER) Regulierungs- *f*, Ordnungs- *f*,
Aufsichts- *f*, Kontroll- *f*,
Überwachungsbehörde *f*
(JAP) 監督官庁、規制機関
(RUS) РЕГУЛИРУЮЩИЙ ОРГАН

rehabilitation
(CHIN) 修复，恢复
(FRE) réhabilitation
(GER) Rehabilitation *f*, Wiederherstellung *f*,
-einsetzung *f*; Sanierung *f*
(JAP) 更生、再建、復興
(RUS) ОЗДОРОВЛЕНИЕ, РЕАБИЛИТАЦИЯ,
ВОССТАНОВЛЕНИЕ (также в правах)

reindustrialization
(CHIN) 再工业化
(FRE) réindustrialisation
(GER) Reindustrialisierung *f*
(JAP) 再工業化
(RUS) РЕИНДУСТРИАЛИЗАЦИЯ

reinstatement
(CHIN) 续保，复职，复原，恢复权利
(FRE) Rétablissement, réintégration,
(C) paiement de rétablissement
(GER) Wiedereinsetzung *f*, -anstellung *f*,
Wiederinkraftsetzung *f*
(JAP) 復権、回復、契約復活
(RUS) ВОССТАНОВЛЕНИЕ (на прежней
позиции)

reinsurance
(CHIN) 再保险，分保
(FRE) réassurance
(GER) Rückversicherung *f*, Reassekuranz *f*,
Zweitrisikoversicherung *f*, Rückdeckung *f*
(JAP) 再保険
(RUS) ПОВТОРНОЕ СТРАХОВАНИЕ,
ПЕРЕСТРАХОВАНИЕ

reinvestment privilege
(CHIN) 再投资特权
(FRE) privilège de réinvestissement
(GER) Wiederanlageprivileg *n*, -recht *n*
(JAP) 再投資特権
(RUS) РЕИНВЕСТИЦИОННАЯ
ПРИВИЛЕГИЯ

reinvestment rate
(CHIN) 再投资率
(FRE) taux de réinvestissement
(GER) Reinvestitionsrate *f*
(JAP) 再投資収益率
(RUS) СТЕПЕНЬ РЕИНВЕСТИЦИИ

related party transaction
(CHIN) 集团内交易
(FRE) opération entre deux personnes
apparentées, (C) transaction
intéressée
(GER) Transaktion *f* zwischen
nahestehenden Parteien *fpl*
(JAP) 関連当事者取引

(RUS) ТРАНЗАКЦИЯ МЕЖДУ ДВУМЯ СТОРОНАМИ, ОДНА ИЗ КОТОРЫХ ИМЕЕТ ЗНАЧИТЕЛЬНОЕ ВЛИЯНИЕ НА ДРУГУЮ

release
(CHIN) 解除，免除，卸货，放行，放弃，宣布
(FRE) libération, libérer, (C) renonciation, (C) parution, (C) déclenchement, (C) lancement, (C) mise en vente
(GER) Freigabe *f*; Veröffentlichung *f*; Verlautbarung *f*; Verzichtserklärung *f*; Abfindungserklärung *f*; (Haft)entlassung *f*; Auflösung *f*; Version *f*
(JAP) 開放、解除、放免、譲渡
(RUS) ВЫПУСТИТЬ; ОСВОБОДИТЬ

release clause
(CHIN) 解除条款
(FRE) clause de remboursement de prêt hypothécaire
(GER) Erlass- *f*, Freigabeklausel *f*
(JAP) 免除条項、解除条項、譲渡条項
(RUS) УСЛОВИЕ ИПОТЕКИ О ВОЗВРАТЕ ЗАЛОГОВОЙ СОБСТВЕННОСТИ ПО МЕРЕ ВЫПОЛНЕНИЯ ПЛАТЕЖЕЙ

relevance
(CHIN) 相关
(FRE) pertinence
(GER) Relevanz *fm*
(JAP) （当面する問題どの）関連性
(RUS) ЗНАЧИМОСТЬ; ОБОСНОВАННОСТЬ; РЕЛЕВАНТНОСТЬ

reliability
(CHIN) 可信性，可靠性
(FRE) fiabilité
(GER) Zuverlässigkeit *f*, Verlässlichkeit *f*; Ausfall- *f*, Betriebssicherheit *f*
(JAP) 信頼性
(RUS) НАДЕЖНОСТЬ

relocate
(CHIN) 重新安置
(FRE) transférer, muter, (C) délocaliser
(GER) umziehen, (Standort *m*) wechseln, umsiedeln *v*; verlagern *v*
(JAP) 移転する（させる）
(RUS) ПЕРЕМЕЩЕНИЕ (на новое место)

remainder
(CHIN) 剩余财产
(FRE) solde, reste
(GER) Restbestand *m*, -menge *f*,-posten *m*
(JAP) 残り、残り物
(RUS) ОСТАТОК; ПОСЛЕДУЮЩЕЕ ИМУЩЕСТВЕННОЕ ПРАВО

remainderman
(CHIN) 剩余财产受益人
(FRE) titulaire du droit réversible, (C) appelé, (C) héritier substitué
(GER) Anfalls- *m*, Anwartschaftsberechtigter *m*; Nacherbe *m*
(JAP) 残余権者
(RUS) СУБЪЕКТ ПОСЛЕДУЮЩЕГО ИМУЩЕСТВЕННОГО ПРАВА

remedy
(CHIN) 补救，赔偿，贴水
(FRE) réparation
(GER) Abhilfe *f*, Hilfsmittel *n*; Rechtsmittel *n*, -behelf *m*
(JAP) 救済方法、賠償、弁償
(RUS) ИСПРАВЛЕНИЕ; СРЕДСТВО ЗАЩИТЫ ПРАВА

remit
(CHIN) 汇款，免除，提交，移交
(FRE) attribution, (C) remise
(GER) einreichen *v*; aufschieben *v*; überweisen, Zahlung *f* leisten *v*; erlassen (Schuld) *v*
(JAP) 支払う、罪などを免除する、軽減する
(RUS) ПЕРЕДАТЬ, ПЕРЕВОДИТЬ, ПЕРЕЧИСЛЯТЬ ФОНДЫ

remit rate
(CHIN) 免除率
(FRE) taux de remise
(GER) Überweisungs- *f*, Weiterleitungsrate *f*
(JAP) 支払い率
(RUS) СТАВКА ЗА ПЕРЕВОД

remonetization
(CHIN) 再货币化
(FRE) remonétisation

(GER) Remonetisierung *f*,
Wiederinkurssetzung *f*
(JAP) 再び通貨とすること
(RUS) РЕМОНЕТИЗАЦИЯ; ВОЗВРАТ К
ТОВАРНО-ДЕНЕЖНЫМ ОТНОШЕНИЯМ

remote access
(CHIN) 远程存取，远程访问
(FRE) accès à distance
(GER) Fernzugriff *m*
(JAP) 遠隔アクセス、
リモートアクセスする
(RUS) ДИСТАНЦИОННЫЙ ДОСТУП

remuneration
(CHIN) 薪酬，报酬，补偿
(FRE) Rémunération, salaire
(GER) Entschädigung *f*; Belohnung *f*;
Vergütung *f*, Bezahlung *f*; Honorar *n*;
Tantieme *f*
(JAP) 給料、報酬、報償
(RUS) ВОЗНАГРАЖДЕНИЕ;
КОМПЕНСАЦИЯ; ОПЛАТА

renegotiate
(CHIN) 再谈判，重新协商
(FRE) renégocier
(GER) neu aushandeln, neu verhandeln;
weiterbegeben, wiederverkaufen *v*
(JAP) 再交渉する
(RUS) ПРОВЕСТИ ПОВТОРНЫЕ
ПЕРЕГОВОРЫ; ИЗМЕНИТЬ УСЛОВИЯ

renegotiated rate mortgage (RRM)
(CHIN) 利率重订抵押贷款（RRM）
(FRE) prêt hypothécaire à taux renégocié,
(C) prêt hypothécaire avec paiement
forfaitaire
(GER) neuverhandelte Hypothek *f*
(JAP) 再調整金利モーゲージ
(RUS) ИПОТЕКА С ПЕРЕСМОТРЕННОЙ
СТАВКОЙ

renewable natural resource
(CHIN) 可再生自然能源
(FRE) ressources naturelles renouvelables
(GER) erneuerbare natürliche Ressourcen
fpl, erneuerbarer Rohstoff *m*
(JAP) 再生可能天然資源
(RUS) ВОЗОБНОВЛЯЕМЫЕ

ПРИРОДНЫЕ РЕСУРСЫ

renewal option
(CHIN) 可续期选择权
(FRE) option de renouvellement
(GER) Verlängerungsoption *f*
(JAP) 更新選択権、更新選択肢
(RUS) ВОЗМОЖНОСТЬ ВОЗОБНОВЛЕНИЯ;
ПРОДЛЕНИЯ

rent
(CHIN) 租，租金，房租，承租，期款
(FRE) loyer
(GER) Miete *f*, Pacht *f*, Pachtzins *m*, Miet- *f*,
Pachtgebühr *f*
(JAP) 家賃、賃借（賃貸）する
(RUS) РЕНТА; АРЕНДНАЯ ПЛАТА;
ПРОКАТ (имущества)

rentable area
(CHIN) 可租赁面积
(FRE) secteur locatif
(GER) vermietbare Fläche *f*
(JAP) 賃貸可能面積
(RUS) СДАВАЕМАЯ В НАЕМ ПЛОЩАДЬ

rental rate
(CHIN) 租率
(FRE) taux de location
(GER) Leihgebühr *f*; Miet- *m*, Pachtpreis *m*
(JAP) 賃貸料、レンタル料、賃料率
(RUS) СТАВКА АРЕНДНОЙ ПЛАТЫ;
СТАВКА ПРОКАТА

rent control
(CHIN) 租金控制
(FRE) contrôle des loyers
(GER) Mietpreisbindung *f*, -regelung *f*, -
kontrolle *f*, Mieterschutz *m*
(JAP) 家賃統制、地代家賃統制
(RUS) PFRJYJLFNTKMYSQ КОНТРОЛЬ
СТАВКИ АРЕНДЫ

rent-free period
(CHIN) 租金免付期
(FRE) période de gratuité, (C) délai de
gratuité
(GER) miet- bzw. pachtfreie Zeitraum *m*
(JAP) 家賃無料期間
(RUS) ПЕРИОД БЕЗ УПЛАТЫ ЗА АРЕНДУ

356

rent-up period

(CHIN) 租金上涨期

(GER) Zeitspanne *f* bis zur kompletten Vermietung *f* (bei neuen Gebäuden)

(JAP) レントアップ期間

(RUS) ПЕРИОД ДО ПОЛНОЙ СДАЧИ В АРЕНДЫ ВСЕХ ПЛОЩАДЕЙ НОВОГО ЗДАНИЯ

reopener clause

(CHIN) 重开谈判条款

(FRE) clause de réouverture

(GER) Revisionsklausel *f*; Offenhalteklausel *f*

(JAP) （契約条項の）交渉再開条項

(RUS) ОГОВОРКА О ПЕРЕСМОТРЕ КОЛЛЕКТИВНОГО ТРУДОВОГО СОГЛАШЕНИЯ

reorganization

(CHIN) 改组

(FRE) réorganisation

(GER) Um- *f*, Restrukturierung *f*, Neu- *f*, Re- *f*, Umorganisation *f*, Sanierung *f*; Vergleichsverfahren *n*

(JAP) 再組織、再編成、〔金融〕再建

(RUS) РЕОРГАНИЗАЦИЯ

repairs

(CHIN) 修理，修补，修缮

(FRE) réparations

(GER) Reparaturen *fpl*, Instandhaltungs- *fpl*, Wartungsarbeiten *fpl*

(JAP) 修繕作業

(RUS) РЕМОНТ

repatriation

(CHIN) 收回，返回

(FRE) rapatriement

(GER) Repatriierung *f*, Wiedereinbürgerung *f*; Heim- *f*, Rückführung *f*, -verlagerung *f*, -übertragung *f*

(JAP) （手形などの）再提出、再提示

(RUS) РЕПАТРИАЦИЯ (КАПИТАЛА)

replace

(CHIN) 替换，代换，置换

(FRE) remplacer

(GER) eustauschen, ersetzen *v*

(JAP) 置換する、置き換わる、更新

(RUS) ЗАМЕЩАТЬ, ВОЗВРАЩАТЬ

replacement cost

(CHIN) 重置费用，重置成本

(FRE) coût de remplacement

(GER) Wiederbeschaffungskosten *pl*

(JAP) 再取得価格、取替費用

(RUS) ЗАМЕЩЁННАЯ СТОИМОСТЬ

replacement cost accounting

(CHIN) 重置成本会计

(FRE) comptabilité des coûts de remplacement

(GER) Wiederbeschaffungskostenrechnung *f*, Rechnungslegung *f* zu den Wiederbeschaffungskosten *pl*

(JAP) 取替原価会計

(RUS) УЧЕТ ПО ЗАМЕЩЕННОЙ СТОИМОСТИ

replacement reserve

(CHIN) 重置储备金

(FRE) réserve de remplacement

(GER) Wiederbeschaffungsrücklage *f*, Rückstellung *f* für Wiederanschaffungen *fpl*

(JAP) 補充引当金、設備更新準備金

(RUS) РЕЗЕРВ НА ЗАМЕНУ

replevin

(CHIN) 没收物的发还

(FRE) levée d'une saisie, saisie-revendication, (C) recouvrement en replevin

(GER) Pfandfreigabe *f*, -auslösung *f*, Einlösung *f* gegen Sicherheitsleistung *f*; Wiedererlangen *n* eines gepfändeten Gegenstands *m*; Aufhebung *f* der Beschlagnahme *f*; Klage *f* auf Herausgabe *f*

(JAP) 動産占有回復訴訟

(RUS) ИСК О ВОЗВРАЩЕНИИ НЕЗАКОННО УДЕРЖАННОЙ СОБСТВЕННОСТИ

reporting currency

(CHIN) 申报货币

(FRE) monnaie de présentation des états financiers

(GER) Bilanz- *f*, Rechnungslegungswährung *f*

(JAP) 報告通貨

(RUS) УЧЕТНАЯ ВАЛЮТА

357

repressive tax
(CHIN) 抑制性税收
(FRE) taxe répressive
(GER) repressive Steuer *f*, Steuer *f* mit negativen Leistungsanreizen *mpl*
(JAP) 抑制的課税
(RUS) РЕПРЕССИВНЫЙ НАЛОГ

reproduction cost
(CHIN) 复制成本，再生产成本
(FRE) coût de reconstitution
(GER) Reproduktions- *pl*, Neufertigungskosten *pl*
(JAP) 再生産費、再生産費用、（機械設備などの）再取得原価
(RUS) СТОИМОСТЬ ВОСПРОИЗВОДСТВА

repudiation
(CHIN) 拒绝，废弃，拒付
(FRE) répudiation
(GER) Zahlungs- *f*, Leistungs- *f*, Erfüllungsverweigerung *f*; Repudiation *f*; Zurückweisung *f*, Ablehnung *f*; Verstoßung *f*
(JAP) 拒否、債務履行の拒否、国債（公債）の支払拒否
(RUS) ОТКАЗ; АННУЛИРОВАНИЕ; РАСТОРЖЕНИЕ

repurchase agreement (REPO; RP)
(CHIN) 证券重购买协议，购回协定（REPO；RP）
(FRE) opération de réméré, opération de prise en pension, (C) pension sur titres
(GER) (Wertpapier)pensionsgeschäft *n*; Rückkaufvertrag *m*, -geschäft *n*, -vereinbarung *f*, vertraglich vereinbarte Rücknahme *f*
(JAP) 買戻し約定
(RUS) СОГЛАШЕНИЕ О ПРОДАЖЕ И ОБРАТНОЙ ПОКУПКЕ (РЕПО)

reputation
(CHIN) 信誉，声望
(FRE) réputation
(GER) Ruf *m*, Ansehen *n*, Name *m*, Leumund *m*
(JAP) 評判
(RUS) РЕПУТАЦИЯ; ПРЕСТИЖ

request for proposal (RFP)
(CHIN) 征询报价，征询方案
(FRE) appel d'offres
(GER) Aufforderung *f* zur Angebotsabgabe *f*; Ausschreibung *f*
(JAP) 見積依頼（書）、提案依頼（書）
(RUS) ЗАПРОС НА ПОДАЧУ ПРЕДЛОЖЕНИЙ, ЗАЯВОК

required rate of return
(CHIN) 应得报酬率
(FRE) taux de rendement exigé
(GER) erforderliche (Invstitions)rendite *f*
(JAP) 必要収益率、最低所要利益率
(RUS) ТРЕБУЕМЫЙ (ИНВЕСТОРОМ) УРОВЕНЬ ДОХОДА

requisition
(CHIN) 申请书，请款单，领料单
(FRE) demande, (C) demande d'achat
(GER) Material- *f*, Bestellanforderung *f*
(JAP) 請求、請求（書）、注文（書）
(RUS) РЕКВИЗИЦИЯ; ФОРМАЛЬНОЕ ПИСЬМЕННОЕ ТРЕБОВАНИЕ

resale proceeds
(CHIN) 重售收入
(FRE) produit de la revente
(GER) Wiederverkaufserlös *m*, -gewinn *m*
(JAP) 譲渡収入、公開収入
(RUS) ВЫРУЧКА ОТ ПОВТОРНОЙ ПРОДАЖИ

rescission
(CHIN) 解约，撤销，废除，解除
(FRE) annulation, résiliation, abrogation, (C) résolution
(GER) Rücktritt *m*, Widerruf *m*, Anfechtung *f*; Aufhebung *f*, Annullierung *f*, Außerkraftsetzung *f*, Nichtigkeitserklärung *f*, Stornierung *f*; Wandelung *f*
(JAP) 無効にすること、契約解除、計上予算撤回
(RUS) АННУЛИРОВАНИЕ; РАСТОРЖЕНИЕ

research
(CHIN) 研究，分析，考察，调查
(FRE) recherche
(GER) Forschung *f*

358

(JAP) 研究（する）、調査（する）
(RUS) ИССЛЕДОВАНИЕ; ИССЛЕДОВАТЬ

research and development (R&D)
(CHIN) 研究和发展，研制（R&D）
(FRE) recherche et développement
(GER) Forschung *f* und Entwicklung *f*, F&E
(JAP) 研究開発
(RUS) ИССЛЕДОВАНИЯ И РАЗРАБОТКИ (ИР)

research department
(CHIN) 研究部门
(FRE) service de recherche
(GER) Forschungsabteilung *f*
(JAP) 研究部門
(RUS) ИССЛЕДОВАТЕЛЬСКИЙ ОТДЕЛ

research intensive
(CHIN) 研究密集型
(FRE) activité à prédominance de recherche
(GER) forschungsintensiv *adj*
(JAP) 研究集約的
(RUS) НАУКОЕМКИЙ; ТРЕБУЮЩИЙ БОЛЬШОГО ОБЪЕМА ИССЛЕДОВАНИЙ

reserve
(CHIN) 储备，准备金，保存
(FRE) réserve
(GER) Rücklage *f*, Reserve *f*, Vorrat *m*; Rückstellung *f*; Sperrbetrag *m*; Deckungskapital *n*
(JAP) 保存、予備（品）、準備金
(RUS) РЕЗЕРВ; СОЗДАВАТЬ РЕЗЕРВЫ; СОХРАНЯТЬ (за собой право)

reserve fund
(CHIN) 储备基金，后备基金
(FRE) fonds de réserve
(GER) Rücklagen- *m*, Rückstellungsfonds *m*; (Kapital)reserve *f*
(JAP) 積立金
(RUS) РЕЗЕРВНЫЙ ФОНД

reserve requirement
(CHIN) 准备金规定，储备要求
(FRE) réserve obligatoire
(GER) Reserveanforderungen *fpl*, -soll *n*, -vorschriften *fpl* Rückstellungs- *m*, Reservebedarf *m*,

(JAP) 準備預金規定
(RUS) ТРЕБОВАНИЕ О НАЛИЧИИ РЕЗЕРВОВ

reserve-stock control
(CHIN) 库存储备控制
(FRE) contrôle des stocks de réserve
(GER) Mindest(sicherheits)-bestandssteuerung *f*
(JAP) 予約株式統制
(RUS) МЕТОД КОНТРОЛЯ ЗА УРОВНЕМ ЗАПАСОВ, УЧИТЫВАЮЩИЙ ВРЕМЯ, НЕОБХОДИМОЕ ДЛЯ ИХ ПОПОЛНЕНИЯ

reset
(CHIN) 复位
(FRE) réinitialiser
(GER) rücksetzen *v* (EDV)
(JAP) リセットする、規定値にもどす
(RUS) СБРОС; ВОЗВРАТ В ИСХОДНОЕ СОСТОЯНИЕ

resident buyer
(CHIN) 常驻采购员
(FRE) acheteur à la commission
(GER) Einkaufsagent *m* im Einkaufsland *m*, im Ausland *n*, inlädischer Einkaufsvertreter *m*
(JAP) 駐在仕入人
(RUS) ПОКУПАТЕЛЬ – РЕЗИДЕНТ

resident buying office
(CHIN) 常驻采购办公室
(FRE) bureau des achats à la commission
(GER) im Ausland befindliches Einkaufsbüro *n*
(JAP) 駐在仕入事務所
(RUS) МЕСТНЫЙ ОТДЕЛ ЗАКУПОК

residential
(CHIN) 住宅
(FRE) résidentiel
(GER) Wohn-
(JAP) 住宅の、居住の
(RUS) ЖИЛИЩНЫЙ

residential broker
(CHIN) 住宅地产经纪人
(FRE) courtier résidentiel

(GER) Immobilienmakler *m* für
Wohnobjekte *npl*
(JAP) 住宅ブローカー、住宅仲介業者
(RUS) БРОКЕР ПО ЖИЛИЩНОМУ
ИМУЩЕСТВУ

residential district
(CHIN) 住宅区
(FRE) district résidentiel
(GER) Wohngebiet *n*, -gegend *f*, -viertel *n*, -
bezirk *m*
(JAP) 住宅区域、住宅地域
(RUS) ЖИЛОЙ РАЙОН, ЗОНА

residential energy credit
(CHIN) 住宅能源信贷
(FRE) crédit pour l'énergie résidentielle
(GER) Freibetrag *m* für Aufwendungen *fpl*
zwecks Energieeinsparung *f*
(JAP) 住宅エネルギー貸付け（融資）
(RUS) КРЕДИТ НА ПОТРЕБЛЕНИЕ
ЭНЕРГИИ В ЖИЛИЩНОМ КОМПЛЕКСЕ

residential service contract
(CHIN) 住宅服务合同
(FRE) contrat de service résidentiel
(GER) Wartungs- *m*,
Dienstleistungsrahmen- *m*, Dienstvertrag *m*
für Wohngebäude *npl*
(JAP) 住宅サービス契約
(RUS) КОНТРАКТ ОБСЛУЖИВАНИЯ
ЖИЛОГО ФОНДА

residual value
(CHIN) 余值，残值，剩余成本
(FRE) valeur résiduelle
(GER) Restwert *m*, -anlagewert *m*;
Restpreis *m*; Veräußerungswert *m*,
Schrottwert *m*
(JAP) 残存価値、残存価額
(RUS) ОСТАТОЧНАЯ СТОИМОСТЬ

resolution
(CHIN) 决心，果断，决议，解决
(FRE) résolution
(GER) Beschluss *m*, Resolution *f*;
Aufhebung *f*; Lösung *f*; Auflösung *f* (EDV)
(JAP) 決議
(RUS) РЕЗОЛЮЦИЯ; РЕШЕНИЕ;
РАЗРЕШЕНИЕ

resource
(CHIN) 资源，物资，财力，资产
(FRE) ressource
(GER) Betriebs- *n*, Produktionsmittel *n*;
Rohstoff *m*, Ressource *fpl*
(RUS) РЕСУРС; ЗАПАС

respondent
(CHIN) 答辩者，被告
(FRE) répondant
(GER) Beklagter *m*, Antragsgegner *m*;
Versuchsperson *f*
(JAP) 応答する人、回答者、被告
（特に離婚訴訟の）
(RUS) ОТВЕТЧИК; АДРЕСАТ

response
(CHIN) 回应，反应
(FRE) réponse
(GER) Antwort *f*, Reaktion *f*; Rückmeldung
f; Erwiderung *f*; Stellungnahme *f*;
Klagebeantwortung *f*
(JAP) 応答、回答
(RUS) ОТВЕТ; РЕАКЦИЯ

response projection
(CHIN) 反应预测
(FRE) prévisions sur le taux de réponses
(GER) Rücklaufprognose *f*
(JAP) 応答の予測、回答見積
(RUS) ПРОГНОЗ РЕАКЦИИ

restitution
(CHIN) 退回，归还，赔偿，恢复
(FRE) réparation, (C) action en résolution
(GER) Entschädigung *f*, Rückerstattung *f*,
Wiedergutmachung *f*, Restitution *f*;
Wiedergabe *f* (EDV)
(JAP) （損害の）賠償、補償、回復
(RUS) ВОССТАНОВЛЕНИЕ
(ПЕРВОНАЧАЛЬНОГО) ПОЛОЖЕНИЯ;
РЕСТИТУЦИЯ

restraint of trade
(CHIN) 贸易限制
(FRE) restriction de concurrence
(GER) wettbewerbsbeschränkendes
Verhalten *n*, Behinderung *f* bzw.
Einschränkung *f* des Handels *m*
(JAP) 取引の制限

(RUS) ОГРАНИЧЕНИЕ СВОБОДЫ
ТОРГОВЛИ

restraint on alienation

(CHIN) 转让限制

 (FRE) restriction du droit d'aliénation,
(C) interdiction d'aliéncr
(GER) Veräußerungsverbot *n*
(JAP) 讓渡制限
(RUS) ОГРАНИЧЕНИЕ НА ПЕРЕВОД ДЕЛ
ЗАГРАНИЦУ

restricted surplus

(CHIN) 限制性盈余

(FRE) bénéfices non répartis sujets à
restrictions
(GER) nicht ausschüttungsfähiger
Gewinnvortrag *m*
(JAP) 制限付き余剰金
(RUS) ОГРАНИЧЕННЫЙ ИЗЛИШЕК

restriction

(CHIN) 限制，限定，约束，管制

(FRE) restriction, (C) interdiction
(GER) Beschränkung *f*, Begrenzung *f*,
Einschränkung *f*; Befristung *f*; Restriktion *f*,
Nebenbedingung *f*; Vorbehalt *m*
(JAP) 規制、限定、制限
(RUS) ОГРАНИЧЕНИЕ

restrictive covenant

(CHIN) 限制贸易契约

(FRE) clause restrictive d'un contrat de prêt
(GER) Konkurrenz- *f*, Wettbewerbsklausel
f; Wettbcwcrbsbeschränkung *f*,
einschränkende Abmachung *f*, vertragliche
Bcschränkung *f*
(JAP) 制限契約
(RUS) ОГРАНИЧИВАЮЩЕЕ УСЛОВИЕ

retail

(CHIN) 零售，零售的
(FRE) vente au détail
(GER) Einzelhandel *m*
(JAP) 小売
(RUS) РОЗНИЧНАЯ ТОРГОВЛЯ, РОЗНИЦА

retail credit

(CHIN) 零售信用
(FRE) crédit à la consommation

(GER) Privatkunden- *m*, Konsumenten- *m*,
Einzelhandelskredit *m*
(JAP) 小売信用
(RUS) КРЕДИТ ПОТРЕБИТЕЛЮ ОТ
РОЗНИЧНОГО ПРОДАВЦА

retail display allowance

(CHIN) 零售商品展示回扣

(FRE) allocation linéaire
(GER) Auslagen- *m*, Dekorationsrabatt *m*,
Displayvergütung *f* im Einzelhandel *m*
(JAP) 小売陳列割引
(RUS) ДОБАВКА НА ДЕМОНСТРАЦИЮ
РОЗНИЧНЫХ ТОВАРОВ

retailer's service program

(CHIN) 零售商服务项目

(FRE) programme de services au détaillant
(GER) Dienstleistungsprogramm *n* für
Einzelhändler *mpl*
(JAP) 小売サービスプログラム
(RUS) ПОМОЩЬ РОЗНИЧНОМУ
ПРОДАВЦУ В ПРОДВИЖЕНИИ ТОВАРА
СО СТОРОНЫ ОПТОВИКА,
ПРОИЗВОДИТЕЛЯ

retail inventory method

(CHIN) 零售价盘存法

(FRE) méthode de l'inventaire au prix de
détail
(GER) (Inventar)kostenberechnung-
smethode *f*
(JAP) 小売棚卸し法
(RUS) СПОСОБ УЧЕТА ПО ЗАПАСАМ
РОЗНИ́Ч́ЫХ ТОВАРОВ

retail outlet

(CHIN) 零售销路

(FRE) magasin de détail
(GER) Einzelhandelsgeschäft *n*, -
verkaufsstelle *f*, Ladengeschäft *n*
(JAP) 小売販売店
(RUS) ТОРГОВАЯ ТОЧКА РОЗНИЧНОЙ
ТОРГОВЛИ

retail rate

(CHIN) 零售商广告费率

(FRE) tarif publicitaire pour les détaillants
(GER) Anzeigenpreis *m* für Einzelhändler
mpl; An- *m* und Verkaufskurse *mpl* für
Sorten *fpl* (US)

(JAP) 小売レート
(RUS) СТАВКА РОЗНИЧНОЙ ТОРГОВЛИ

retaining
(CHIN) 保留，保持
(FRE) retenue
(GER) zurückbehaltend *adj*
(JAP) 保有（保持）すること、
損続させること、（弁護しなどを）
雇っておくこと
(RUS) СОХРАНЕНИЕ; УДЕРЖИВАНИЕ

retained earnings
(CHIN) 保留盈余，留存收益
(FRE) bénéfices non répartis
(GER) einbehaltene bzw. unverteilte
Gewinne *mpl*, thesaurierte Gewinne *mpl*
(JAP) 利益積立金、任意積立金、
社内保留利益金
(RUS) ЧИСТАЯ ПРИБЫЛЬ, НЕ
РАСПРЕДЕЛЕННАЯ МЕЖДУ
АКЦИОНЕРАМИ

retained earnings appropriated
(CHIN) 已分配留存收益
(FRE) bénéfices non répartis appropriés
(GER) einbehaltene Gewinne *mpl*, freie
Rücklage *f*, zweckgebunden *adj*
(JAP) 処分済み保留利益
(RUS) ВЫДЕЛЕННАЯ НА ТЕКУЩИЕ ЦЕЛИ
НЕРАСПРЕДЕЛЕННАЯ ПРИБЫЛЬ

retained earnings statement
(CHIN) 留存收益表
(FRE) état des bénéfices non répartis
(GER) Bilanz *f* thesaurierter
Gewinne *mpl*
(JAP) 保留利益計算書
(RUS) ДОКУМЕНТ ОБ ИЗМЕНЕНИИ
СУММЫ НЕРАСПРЕДЕЛЕННОЙ
ПРИБЫЛИ

retaliatory eviction
(CHIN) 报复性驱逐
(FRE) expulsion de représailles
(GER) Retorsions- *f*,
Vergeltungszwangsräumung *f*
(JAP) 報復的追立て
(RUS) ВЫСЕЛЕНИЕ В ПОРЯДКЕ
ВОЗМЕЗДИЯ

retire
(CHIN) 兑清票据，赎票，付清，退休
(FRE) prendre sa retraite
(GER) in den Ruhestand *m* gehen,
pensionieren *v*; außer Betrieb *m* nehmen,
einziehen *v*; ausscheiden *v*; einlösen *v*;
zurückzahlen *v*
(JAP) 退く、退職する、廃物にする
(RUS) ВЫЙТИ НА ПЕНСИЮ; ПОГАСИТЬ
(ценные бумаги)

retirement
(CHIN) 赎票，退休金，退股，偿还
(FRE) retraite
(GER) Ausscheiden *n*; Pensionierung *f*,
Ruhestand *m*; Abgang *m*; Entlassung *f*;
Einzug *m*; Rückkauf *m*, Tilgung *f*
(JAP) 退職、年金、（債券などの）
回収・満期償還
(RUS) ВЫХОД НА ПЕНСИЮ; ПОГАШЕНИЕ
ЦЕННЫХ БУМАГ

retirement age
(CHIN) 退休年龄
(FRE) âge de la retraite
(GER) Pensions- *n*, Renten- *n*,
Ruhestandsalter *n*, pensionsfähiges Alter *n*
(JAP) 退職年齢
(RUS) ПЕНСИОННЫЙ
ВОЗРАСТ

reitrement fund
(CHIN) 退休基金
(FRE) caisse de retraite
(GER) Pensions- *m*, Rentenfonds *m*,
Pensions- *f*, Rentenkasse *f*
(JAP) 退職基金、退職資金
(RUS) ПЕНСИОННЫЙ ФОНД

retirement income
(CHIN) 退休收入
(FRE) pension de retraite
(GER) Renten- *n*, Pensionseinkommen *n*,
Ruhestandsgehalt *n*, Pensionsbezüge *mpl*
(JAP) 退職所得
(RUS) ПЕНСИОННЫЙ ДОХОД

retirement plan
(CHIN) 退休计划
(FRE) régime de retraite

(GER) Rentenspar- *m*, Pensionsplan *m*, Rentenversicherung *f*, Pensionssystem *n*
(JAP) 退職金制度
(RUS) ПРОГРАММА ПЕНСИОННЫХ СБЕРЕЖЕНИЙ

retroactive
(CHIN) 追溯，追加
(FRE) rétroactif
(GER) Rückwirkend *adj*
(JAP) 遡及する、（過去のある時期に）さかのぼって、逆戻りの
(RUS) ИМЕЮЩИЙ ОБРАТНУЮ СИЛУ

retroactive adjustment
(CHIN) 追溯调整
(FRE) ajustement rétroactif
(GER) rückwirkende Berichtigung *f* bzw. Anpassung *f*
(JAP) 遡及調整
(RUS) КОРРЕКТИРОВКА С ОБРАТНОЙ СИЛОЙ

return
(CHIN) 退货，报酬，收益，赢利
(FRE) rendement, rapport
(GER) Steuererklärung *f*; Umkehr *f*, Heimkehr *f*; Ertrag *m*, Rendite *f*; Verzinsung *f*; Bruttoumsatzerlös *m*; Rücksendung *f*; Rücksprung *m* (EDV)
(JAP) 収益、返品、返却する
(RUS) ВОЗВРАЩАТЬ; ДОХОД, ПРИБЫЛЬ, ОКУПАЕМОСТЬ

return of capital
(CHIN) 资本收益率
(FRE) remboursement du capital
(GER) Kapitalrückzahlung *f*, -rückfluss *m*
(JAP) 資本収益、資本利益
(RUS) КОЭФФИЦИЕНТ ДОХОДНОСТИ КАПИТАЛА

return on equity
(CHIN) 权益报酬率
(FRE) taux de rendement des capitaux propres
(GER) Eigenkapitalrendite *f*, -ertrag *m*, Verzinsung *f* des Eigenkapitals *n*
(JAP) 株式資本利益

(RUS) КОЭФФИЦИЕНТ ДОХОДНОСТИ АКЦИОНЕРНОГО КАПИТАЛА

return on invested capital
(CHIN) 投入资本收益率，投资报酬率
(FRE) taux de rendement du capital investi
(GER) Investitionskapitalrendite *f*, Kapitalverzinsung *f*
(JAP) 投資資本利益
(RUS) КОЭФФИЦИЕНТ ДОХОДНОСТИ ИНВЕСТИРОВАННОГО КАПИТАЛА

return on pension plan assets
(CHIN) 老年金计划资产回报率
(FRE) rendement de l'actif du régime de retraite
(GER) Ertrag *m* bzw. Rendite *f* aus Pensionskassenvermögen *n*
(JAP) 年金計画資産利益
(RUS) КОЭФФИЦИЕНТ ДОХОДНОСТИ АКТИВОВ ПЕНСИОННОГО ФОНДА

return on sales
(CHIN) 销售利润率
(FRE) retour sur ventes, (C) rentabilité commerciale
(GER) Umsatzrendite *f*
(JAP) 売上利益
(RUS) ДОХОДНОСТЬ ПРОДАЖ

returns
(CHIN) 退货，报酬，收益
(FRE) bénéfices, (C) rendements
(GER) Rücksendungen *fpl*; Rückwaren *fpl*, Retouren *fpl*
(JAP) 総売上高、利回り、収益
(RUS) ДОХОДЫ; ПРИБЫЛЬ; ОТЧЁТЫ; (НАЛОГОВЫЕ) ДЕКЛАРАЦИИ

revaluation
(CHIN) 重估价值，再评价
(FRE) réévaluation
(GER) Neu- *f*, Nach- *f*, Umbewertung *f*, Neuberechnung *f*; Wertberichtigung *f*
(JAP) 平価切上げ、再評価
(RUS) ПЕРЕОЦЕНКА; РЕВАЛЬВАЦИЯ (ВАЛЮТЫ)

revenue
(CHIN) 收入，收益

(FRE) revenus, recettes
(GER) Einnahmen *fpl*, Einkommen *n*,
Einkünfte *pl*; Ertrag *m*, Umsatzerlös *m*;
Steueraufkommen *n*
(JAP) （国家の）歳入、収益、収入
(RUS) ДОХОДЫ; ПОСТУПЛЕНИЯ

revenue anticipation note (RAN)

(CHIN) 收入预期票据（RAN）
(FRE) obligation émise par une collectivité
publique dans l'attente de rentrées non
fiscales
(GER) (kurzfristige) mit erwarteten
Aufkommen *npl* beglichene Anleihe *f*
(JAP) 収入予想証券
(RUS) КРАТКОСРОЧНОЕ ДОЛГОВОЕ
ОБЯЗАТЕЛЬСТВО (местной власти)

revenue bond

(CHIN) 收益债券
(FRE) obligation à intérêt conditionnel
(GER) kurzfristige Schatzanweisung *f* bzw.
Kommunalanleihe *f* Ertragsobligation *f*,
(Anleihe, deren Schuldendienst aus dem
Ertrag bestimmter Steuern zu leisten ist)
(JAP) 収益担保債、歳入担保債、
特定財源債
(RUS) МУНИЦИПАЛЬНЫЕ ОБЛИГАЦИИ С
ВЫПЛАТАМИ ИЗ ДОХОДОВ

revenue ruling

(CHIN) 收入裁决
(FRE) jugement du ministère du revenu
(GER) Auslegung *f* des Steuerrechts *n*
durch die IRS
(JAP) 内国歳入規則
(RUS) ОФИЦИАЛЬНОЕ РЕШЕНИЕ О
ПРИМЕНИМОСТИ НАЛОГООБЛОЖЕНИЯ
К КОНКРЕТНЫМ ДОХОДАМ

reversal

(CHIN) 反向
(FRE) écriture de contrepassation, jugement
renversé
(GER) Wende *f*, Kehrtwendung *f*,
Umschwung *m*; Rückbuchung *f*;
Stornierung *f*, Rückbelastung *f*
(JAP) 反転、逆転、
転換
(RUS) ИЗМЕНЕНИЕ; ОТМЕНА;
ПОВОРОТ НА 180 ГРАДУСОВ

reverse annuity mortgage (RAM)

(CHIN) 反向年金抵押 （RAM）
(FRE) prêt hypothécaire à rente viagère
inversée
(GER) Hypothek *f* auf
Rentenversicherungsbasis *f*
(JAP) （年齢方式）逆住宅ローン
(RUS) ОБРАТНАЯ РЕНТНАЯ
ИПОТЕКА

reverse leverage

(CHIN) 反向影响
(FRE) effet de levier inverse
(GER) umgekehrte Hebelwirkung *f*
(JAP) 逆梃率、負の梃率効果
(RUS) ОБРАТНЫЙ ЛЕВЕРИДЖ

reverse split

(CHIN) 并股
(FRE) regroupement d'actions
(GER) Aktienzusammenlegung *f*
(JAP) 逆記入
(RUS) ОБРАТНЫЙ СПЛИТ

reversing entry

(CHIN) 反向分录，转回分录
(FRE) écriture de contrepassation
(GER) Gegenbuchung *f*, -eintrag *m*,
Rückbuchung *f*, Stornobuchung *f*
(RUS) ПОЗИЦИЯ
РЕВЕРСИРОВАНИЯ

reversion

(CHIN) 回复，修正
(FRE) restitution
(GER) Anwartschaft *f*, Rückfallrecht *n*,
Heimfall *m*; Rückkehr *f*,
Umkehr *f*
(JAP) 復帰権、財産復帰
(RUS) РЕВЕРСИРОВАНИЕ;
ПРЕОБРАЗОВАНИЕ

reversionary factor

(CHIN) 反向因子
(FRE) facteur réversible
(GER) Anpassungsfaktor *m*
(JAP) 復帰権の要因、
復帰権的ファクター
(RUS) КОЭФФИЦИЕНТ
ПРЕОБРАЗОВАНИЯ

reversionary interest
(CHIN) 可享有的利益
(FRE) droit réversif
(GER) Anwartschafts- *n*, Rückfallrecht *n*,
Rückfall- *m*, Heimfallanspruch *m*;
Nacherbschaftsrecht *n*
(JAP) 復帰権的権利
(RUS) ЗАИНТЕРЕСОВАННОСТЬ
СУБЪЕКТА ПОСЛЕДУЮЩЕГО
ИМУЩЕСТВЕННОГО ПРАВА

reversionary value
(CHIN) 应继承的价值
(FRE) valeur réversible
(GER) Rückfallswert *m*
(JAP) 復帰権的価値
(RUS) ОЦЕНОЧНАЯ ЦЕННОСТЬ
СОБСТВЕННОСТИ ПО ИСТЕЧЕНИИ
ОПРЕДЕЛЁННОГО ПЕРИОДА

review
(CHIN) 再检查，分析考察，审查
(FRE) révision
(GER) Überprüfung *f*, Durchsicht *f*;
Rückblick *m*; Rezension *f*; Übersicht *f*
(JAP) 批評、再考、再検討、審査
(RUS) ОБЗОР; РАССМОТРЕНИЕ; АНАЛИЗ

revocable trust
(CHIN) 可取消信托
(FRE) fiducie révocable
(GER) widerrufliche Treuhandbestellung *f*,
kündbare Stiftung *f*
(JAP) 撤回可能信託、
取消可能信託
(RUS) ОТЗЫВНОЙ ТРАСТ

revocation
(CHIN) 取消，废除，撤回，撤销
(FRE) révocation
(GER) Widerruf *m*, Zurückziehung *f*,
Aufhebung *f*, Aufkündigung *f*, Entziehung *f*;
Annulierung *f*
(JAP) 撤回、取消、破棄
(RUS) ОТЗЫВ; ОТМЕНА;
АННУЛИРОВАНИЕ

revolving charge account
(CHIN) 循环费用账户

(FRE) compte d'achats à crédit
renouvelable, (C) compte d'achats à crédit
permanent
(GER) revolvierendes Kunden- *n*,
Anschreibungskonto *n*
(JAP) 回転売掛金勘定
(RUS) СЧЁТ, КОТОРЫЙ НЕ ТРЕБУЕТСЯ
ПОЛНОСТЬЮ ВЫПЛАЧИВАТЬ, НО
СЛЕДУЕТ ДЕЛАТЬ ПЕРИОДИЧЕСКИЕ
ПЛАТЕЖИ

revolving credit
(CHIN) 周转信贷
(FRE) crédit renouvelable
(GER) revolvierender Kredit *m*, kurzfristig
finanzierter Kredit *n*
(JAP) 回転信用、回転信用状
(RUS) АВТОМАТИЧЕСКИ
ВОЗОБНОВЛЯЕМЫЙ КРЕДИТ

revolving fund
(CHIN) 周转基金
(FRE) fonds renouvelable
(GER) revolvierender Fonds *m*,
Umlauffonds *m*
(JAP) 回転基金、回転資金、
リヴォルビング基金
(RUS) ОБОРОТНЫЙ ФОНД

rezoning
(CHIN) 重新分区
(FRE) rectification d'un zonage
(GER) Änderung *f* des
Flächennutzungsplans *m*
(JAP) 再区分（の）、区分変更（の）
(RUS) ИЗМЕНЕНИЕ ЗОНИРОВАНИЯ

rich
(CHIN) 价格太高的证券，
太高的利率，富有
(FRE) riche
(GER) reich, wohlhabend, vermögend *adj*
(JAP) 金持ちの、富んだ、豊富な
(RUS) БОГАТЫЙ; БОГАТСТВО

rich text format (RTF)
(CHIN) 多信息文本格式（RTF）
(FRE) format RTF
(GER) Volltextformat *n* (EDV)

(JAP) リッチテキストフォーマット、
RTF フォーマット

rider
(CHIN) 批单，追加条款，附则
(FRE) avenant, annexe, (C) resquilleur,
avenant
(GER) Anhang *m*, Zusatz *m*; Zusatzklausel
f; Policenzusatz *m*; Nebenbestimmung *f*
(JAP) 添書き、追加条項、付加条項
(RUS) НОВАЯ, ДОПОЛНИТЕЛЬНАЯ
СТАТЬЯ СТРАХОВОГО ПОЛИСА

right of first refusal
(CHIN) 优先购买权
(FRE) droit de préférence, (C) droit de
première offre
(GER) Vorkaufsrecht *n*
(JAP) 最優先引受権行使の拒絶、第一先
買権行使の拒絶
(RUS) ПРАВО ПЕРВОГО ОТКАЗА

right of redemption
(CHIN) 赎买权，买回权
(FRE) droit de rachat
(GER) Ablöse- *n*, Tilgungs- *n*, Rückkaufs-
n, Rückerwerbsrecht *n*
(JAP) 買戻し権、取戻し権
(RUS) ПРАВО ВЕРНУТЬ СОБСТВЕННОСТЬ
ПО УПЛАТЕ ДОЛГА

right of rescission
(CHIN) 解约权，撤销权
(FRE) droit de résolution
(GER) Rücktritts- *n*, Aufhebungs- *n*,
Anfechtungsrecht *n*
(JAP) 解約権、撤回
(RUS) ПРАВО ОТКАЗА ОТ
ПОТРЕБИТЕЛЬСКОГО КРЕДИТА (без
штрафа)

right of return
(CHIN) 退货权
(FRE) droit de retour
(GER) Rückgabe- *n*, Remissionsrecht *n*
(JAP) 返却権、帰還権、買戻し請求権
(RUS) ПРАВО ВОЗВРАТА

right of survivorship
(CHIN) 承继权

(FRE) gain de survie
(GER) Anwachsungsrecht *n*
(JAP) 生存者権、残存者取得権
(RUS) ПРАВО (ВЫЖИВШЕГО) СУПРУГА

right-of-way
(CHIN) 过境权，地段权
(FRE) droit de passage, (C) servitude
(GER) Wege- *n*, Begehungsrecht *n*,
(JAP) 先行権、優先通行権、通行権
(RUS) ПРАВО ПРОХОДА, ПРОЕЗДА

risk
(CHIN) 危险，风险，保险种类，保险
(FRE) risque
(GER) Risiko *n*, Gefahr *f*
(JAP) リスク、危険、危険負担
(RUS) РИСК; РИСКОВАТЬ

risk-adjusted discount rate
(CHIN) 按风险调整贴现率
(FRE) taux d'actualisation à risques
pondérés
(GER) risikobereinigter Diskontsatz *m*
(JAP) 危険調整割引率
(RUS) ПРОЦЕНТНАЯ СТАВКА С
КОРРЕКЦИЕЙ НА РИСК

risk arbitrage
(CHIN) 风险套利
(FRE) arbitrage risque
(GER) riskantes Arbitragegeschäft *n*,
Risikoarbitrage *f*
(JAP) リスクアービトラージ、
危険鞘取り売買
(RUS) РИСКОВЫЙ АРБИТРАЖ

risk averse
(CHIN) 不愿承担风险，风险反感
(FRE) peu enclin vers le risque
(GER) risikoscheu *adj*
(JAP) リスク回避的な
(RUS) НЕ РАСПОЛОЖЕННЫЙ К РИСКУ

risk management
(CHIN) 风险管理
(FRE) gestion des risques
(GER) Risikomanagement *n*
(JAP) リスクマネジメント、危機管理

(RUS) УПРАВЛЕНИЕ РИСКОМ

rolling stock

(CHIN) 轮式运输设备

(FRE) matériel roulant

(GER) rollendes Material *n*, rollendes Inventar *n*, Schienenfahrzeuge *npl*, Fahrzeugpark *m*

(JAP) （鉄道の）車両、貨物自動車

(RUS) ПОДВИЖНОЙ СОСТАВ (железнод.)

rollover

(CHIN) 以新债券代替旧债券，纳税递延交易

(FRE) reconduction, (C) disposition de roulement,(C) renouvelable

(GER) Erneuerung *f* eines Kredits *m*, Verlängerung *f*

(JAP) 回転、乗り換え、借り換え

(RUS) РОЛЛОВЕР; ПЕРЕВОД СРЕДСТВ ИЗ ОДНОЙ ФОРМЫ ИНВЕСТИЦИЙ В ДРУГУЮ

rollover loan

(CHIN) 展期贷款，循环贷款

(FRE) prêt renouvelable

(GER) Rollover-Kredit *m*, revolvierender Kredit *m*

(JAP) 回転貸付、ロールオーバーローン

(RUS) РОЛЛОВЕРНЫЙ КРЕДИТ

ROM (read-only memory)

(CHIN) ROM （只读存储器）

(FRE) mémoire morte

(GER) Festwertspeicher *m*, Nur-Lese-Speicher *m*

(JAP) ROM、ロム、読出し専用メモリー

(RUS) ПОСТОЯННОЕ ЗАПОМИНАЮЩЕЕ УСТРОЙСТВО (ПЗУ)

rotating shift

(CHIN) 轮班

(FRE) roulement des postes, équipe tournante

(GER) Wechselschicht *f*, periodische Schicht *f*

(JAP) 交替制、輪番

(RUS) ВАХТА

roundhouse

(CHIN) 圆形机车库

(FRE) rotonde

(GER) Bahnbetriebswerk *n*

(JAP) 転写台付き機関車、（後甲板の）後部船室

(RUS) ЛОКОМОТИВНОЕ ДЕПО С ПОВОРОТНЫМ КРУГОМ

round lot

(CHIN) 整数批量，整份

(FRE) lot régulier, (C) lot de taille normale

(GER) voller Börsenschluss *m*; Handelseinheit *f*; 100 Stück Aktien *fpl*; volles Aktienpaket *n*

(JAP) 最低取引単位、まとまった株数

(RUS) СТАНДАРТНАЯ СДЕЛКА (бирж.)

royalty

(CHIN) 专利税，版权税

(FRE) redevance

(GER) Tantieme *f*; Patentabgabe *f*; Lizenzgebühr *f*

(JAP) ロイヤルティ、使用料、許諾料、印税

(RUS) РОЯЛТИ; КОМПЕНСАЦИЯ ЗА ИСПОЛЬЗОВАНИЕ ИСКЛЮЧИТЕЛЬНОГО ПРАВА; ПЛАТА ЗА РАЗРАБОТКУ МИНЕРАЛЬНЫХ РЕСУРСОВ

royalty trust

(CHIN) 特许权信托有效，运货，循环，流动，连续，经营

(FRE) fiducie de redevance

(GER) Lizenztrust *m*

(JAP) 使用料信託

(RUS) ТРАСТ С УПЛАТОЙ РОЯЛТИ

run

(CHIN) 有效，运货，循环，流动，连续，经营

(FRE) exécuter, retrait simultané de fonds

(GER) Maschinenlauf *m*; Arbeitsgang *m*, Zyklus *m*; Fahrt *f*; Andrang *m*, Ansturm *m*, hohe Nachfrage *f*; Run (Börse); (Programm)durchlauf *m* (EDV)

(JAP) 経営する、（契約などを）継続する、有効である

367

(RUS) СПИСОК (ценных бумаг с текущими ценами); ТИРАЖ; ПРОГОН; «НАБЕГ» (на банк)

rundown

(CHIN) 逐项核对

(FRE) Relevé, sommaire

(GER) detaillierte Übersicht *f*; Geschäftsauflösung *f*, Stilllegung *f*; heruntergekommen, heruntergewirtschaftet, verfallen *adj*

(JAP) (情報などの）要約、まとめ、〔証券〕最終値相場表要約

(RUS) ОБЗОР; КРАТКИЙ ПЕРЕЧЕНЬ

run of paper (ROP)

(CHIN) 报纸广告位置（ROP）

(FRE) position libre, (C) emplacement indéterminé

(GER) Anzeigenplatzierung *f* nach Wahl *f* des Verlegers *m*, ohne Platzvereinbarung *f*

(JAP) （新聞・雑誌の広告の）掲載位置編集者一任

(RUS) МЕСТОРАСПОЛОЖЕНИЕ РЕКЛАМЫ НА ПОЛОСАХ ГАЗЕТНЫХ СТРАНИЦ

run with the land

(CHIN) 对土地所有人产生影响的权利或限制

(FRE) être rattaché au bien-fonds

(GER) auf einem Grundstück *n* lasten, dinglich mit dem Grundstück *n* verbunden sein

(JAP) 土地とともに移転する

(RUS) ПЕРЕХОД УСЛОВИЙ ПРИ ПЕРЕХОДЕ ВЛАДЕНИЯ ЗЕМЛЕЙ

rural

(CHIN) 农村的

(FRE) rural

(GER) ländlich *adj*

(JAP) 田舎の

(RUS) СЕЛЬСКИЙ

rurban

(CHIN) 郊外住宅区的

(FRE) rurbain

(GER) periurban *adj*

(JAP) 田園都市の

(RUS) РАЙОНЫ НА ГРАНИЦЕ БОЛЬШИХ ГОРОДОВ, ПОПАДАЮЩИЕ ПОД ГОРОДСКУЮ ЗАСТРОЙКУ

S

sabotage
(CHIN) 罢工，怠工，破坏
(FRE) sabotage
(GER) Sabotage *f*
(JAP) サボタージュ、妨害（する）、
破壊（する）
(RUS) САБОТАЖ

safe harbor rule
(CHIN) 避风港规则
(FRE) règle de la base sécurisée , règle de
la sphère de sécurité, (C) règles refuge
(GER) Safe-Harbor-Regel *f*
(JAP) 安全港ルール、承認領域ルール、
安全ルール
(RUS) НАЛОГОВОЕ УБЕЖЕЩЕ

safekeeping
(CHIN) 保管费
(FRE) garde
(GER) Verwahrung *f*, Hinterlegung *f*,
sicherer Gewahrsam *m*
(JAP) 保管
(RUS) БЕЗОПАСНОЕ ХРАНЕНИЕ
ЦЕННОСТЕЙ (БАНКОМ)

safety commission
(CHIN) 安全委员会
(FRE) commission de securité
(GER) Sicherheitsausschuss *m*,
Arbeitsschutzkomitee *n*
(JAP) 安全手数料
(RUS) КОМИССИЯ ПО БЕЗОПАСТНОСТИ
(ПРОИЗВОДСТВА)

safety margin
(CHIN) 安全幅度
(FRE) marge de securité
(GER) Sicherheitsspanne *f*, -marge *f*
(JAP) 安全マージン
(RUS) ГАРАНТИЙНЫЙ РЕЗЕРВ

salariat
(CHIN) 薪水阶层
(FRE) prolétariat, classe ouvrière

(GER) Mittelklasse *f*, Angestellte *mpl*
(JAP) 俸給生活者階級、サラリーマン
(RUS) РАБОЧИЙ КЛАСС

salary
(CHIN) 工资，薪金，薪水
(FRE) salaire, rémunération
(GER) Gehalt *n*, Verdienst *m*
(JAP) 俸給、給料、月給
(RUS) ЖАЛОВАНИЕ, ОКЛАД

salary reduction plan
(CHIN) 工资调低计划
(FRE) régime d'épargne par réduction de
salaire
(GER) Gehaltskürzungsplan *m*, -
senkungsplan *m*
(JAP) 俸給減少計画
(RUS) ПЛАН, ПОЗВОЛЯЮЩИЙ
РАБОТНИКАМ ИНВЕСТИРОВАТЬ ЧАСТЬ
СВОЕЙ ЗАРАБОТНОЙ ПЛАТЫ ПО
СВОЕМУ УСМОТРЕНИЮ

sale
(CHIN) 销货，大减价，交易
(FRE) vente
(GER) Verkauf *m*, Absatz *m*, Veräußerung *f*
(JAP) 販売、売却、売渡し
(RUS) ПРОДАЖА; РАСПРОДАЖА

sale and leaseback
(CHIN) 出售与回租
(FRE) cession-bail, vente et cession-bail
(GER) Verkauf *m* bei gleichzeitiger
Rückvermietung *f* an Verkäufer *m*, Verkauf
m mit Rückmiete *f*
(JAP) リース契約付き売却
(RUS) ПРОДАЖА С ПОСЛЕДУЮЩЕЙ
АРЕНДОЙ

sale or exchange
(CHIN) 出售或交换
(FRE) vente ou echange
(GER) (Ver)kauf *m* mit Umtauschrecht *n*
(JAP) 売却あるいは交換
(RUS) РАСПОРЯЖЕНИЕ
СОБСТВЕННОСТЬЮ НА ОСНОВЕ
ОБМЕНЫ (А НЕ ДАРЕНИЯ, НАПР.)

sales analyst

(CHIN) 销售分析家

(FRE) analyste des ventes

(GER) Absatzanalytiker *m*

(JAP) 売上分析者

(RUS) АНАЛИТИК ПО СБЫТУ

sales budget

(CHIN) 销售额预估

(FRE) budget commercial, budget des ventes

(GER) Absatz- *n*,Verkaufsbudget *n*

(JAP) 販売予算

(RUS) БЮДЖЕТ ПРОДАЖ, СБЫТА

sales charge

(CHIN) 销售费

(FRE) droits d'entrée, commission d'entrée, redevance d'entrée, (C) frais de placement

(GER) Verkaufsgebühr *f*

(JAP) 売費用

(RUS) КОМИССИОННЫЙ СБОР (БРОКЕРА)

sales contract

(CHIN) 销售合同

(FRE) contrat de vente

(GER) Kaufvertrag *m*

(JAP) 販売契約

(RUS) ДОГОВОР О ПРОДАЖЕ

sales effectiveness test

(CHIN) 推销效果测试

(FRE) test d'efficacité des ventes

(GER) Verkaufswirksamkeitstest *m*

(JAP) 販売効果テスト

(RUS) ПРОВЕРКА ЭФФЕКТИВНОСТИ СБЫТА

sales incentive

(CHIN) 销售奖励

(FRE) stimulant de vente

(GER) Verkaufsanreiz *m*

(JAP) 売上奨励手当

(RUS) СТИМУЛИРОВАНИЕ СБЫТА

sales journal

(CHIN) 销售日记账

(FRE) journal de vente, livre de vente

(GER) Verkaufsjournal *n*, Warenausgangsbuch *n*

(JAP) 売上仕訳帳、売上帳

(RUS) КНИГА УЧЕТА ПРОДАЖ

sales letter

(CHIN) 推销信函

(FRE) lettre de vente, lettre publicitaire

(GER) Werbebrief *m*, -schreiben *n*

(JAP) 売込み状

(RUS) ИЗВЕЩЕНИЕ О ПРОДАЖЕ

salesperson

(CHIN) 推销员

(FRE) commercial, representant, vendeur

(GER) Verkäufer(in) *f/m*

(JAP) 販売店員、売り子

(RUS) ПРОДАВЕЦ: ЧЕЛОВЕК, ПРОДАЮЩИЙ ТОВАРЫ И УСЛУГИ

sales portfolio

(CHIN) 推销参考资料

(FRE) portefeuille des ventes, argumentaire

(GER) Verkaufsportefeuille *n*, -portfolio *n*, -bestand *m*

(JAP) 売上高明細表

(RUS) НАБОР ВСПОМАГАТЕЛЬНЫХ МАТЕРИАЛОВ ЧЕЛОВЕКА, ПРОДАЮЩЕГО ТОВАРЫ И УСЛУГИ

sales promotion

(CHIN) 推销，促销

(FRE) promotion des ventes

(GER) Absatz- *f*, Verkaufs- *f*, Vertriebsförderung *f*, Absatzwerbung *f*

(JAP) 販売促進

(RUS) ПРОДВИЖЕНИЕ ПРОДАЖ, СБЫТА

sales returns and allowances

(CHIN) 销售退货与折扣

(FRE) ristournes et remises sur vente, retours et réductions sur ventes

(GER) Rücksendungen *fpl* und Nachlässe *mpl*

(JAP) 返品調整引当金

(RUS) СЧЁТ ДЛЯ УЧЁТА СКИДОК И ВОЗВРАТА НЕКАЧЕСТВЕННОЙ И НЕПОДХОДЯЩЕЙ ПОКУПАТЕЛЮ ПРОДУКЦИИ

sales revenue

(CHIN) 销售收入

(FRE) revenu des ventes, chiffre d'affaires
(GER) Umsatz- *m*, Verkaufserlös *m*,
Umsatz- *fpl*, Verkaufseinnahmen *fpl*
(JAP) 売上収益、総売上高

sales tax

(CHIN) 销售税
(FRE) taxe sur les ventes, taxe de vente
(GER) Umsatz- *f*, Verkaufssteuer *f*; (etwa:)
MWst
(JAP) （英）物品税、(米)物品販売税、
売上税
(RUS) НАЛОГ НА ПРОДАЖИ

sales type lease

(CHIN) 销售形式的租赁
(GER) Sales Type Lease *m*, (Leasingvertrag,
bei dem der Händler bzw. Produzent
gleichzeitig als Leasinggeber fungiert)
(JAP) 販売型リース
(RUS) ВИД БУХГАЛТЕРСКОГО УЧЁТА
АРЕНДОДАТЕЛЯ

salvage value

(CHIN) 残余价值，折余值
(FRE) recuperabilité, évaleur de
récupération
(GER) Schrottwert *m*; Restbuchwert *m*
(Buchwesen); Veräußerungs- *m*,
Realisierungswert *m*
(JAP) 救出財貨価格（売却金）
(RUS)
ОСТАТОЧНАЯ ,ЛИКВИДАЦИОННАЯ
СТОИМОСТЬ

sample buyer

(CHIN) 样品购买者
(FRE) consommateur d'echantillons
(GER) Musterkäufer *m*
(JAP) 見本購入者
(RUS) ПОКУПАТЕЛЬ ПРОБНОГО
КОЛИЧЕСТВА ТОВАРА

sampling

(CHIN) 采样，抽样
(FRE) echantillonnage
(GER) Probenahme *f*; Stichproben- *f*,
Musterentnahme *f*, Musterziehung *f*
(JAP) サンプリング、見本抽出、
抜取り
(RUS) ОТБОР ОБРАЗЦОВ; ВЫБОРКА

sandwich lease

(CHIN) 分租
(FRE) sous-loyer, ésous-location
(GER) Sandwich-Leasing *n*
(JAP) （不動産）原貸借、
サンドイッチリース
(RUS) СДАЧА АРЕНДУЕМОЙ
СОБСТВЕННОСТИ В АРЕНДУ

satellite communication

(CHIN) 卫星通讯
(FRE) communications par satellite,
télécommunication par satellite
(GER) Satellitenkommunikation *f*
(JAP) 衛星通信
(RUS) СПУТНИКОВАЯ СВЯЗЬ

satisfaction of a debt

(CHIN) 债务偿还
(FRE) satisfaction des créances, équittance
(GER) Erfüllung *f* eines Darlehens *n*,
Tilgung *f* einer Schuld *f*
(JAP) 負債の償還、負債の弁済、
負債の弁済証書
(RUS) ПОГАШЕНИЕ КРЕДИТА, ЗАЙМА

satisfaction piece

(CHIN) 偿付单
(FRE) enquête de satisfaction, équittance
du prêt hypothécaire
(GER) Schuldbegleichungsurkunde *f*;
löschungsfähige Quittung *f*
(JAP) 債務履行証書、返済証書
(RUS) ДОКУИЕНТ, ПОДТВЕРЖДАЮЩИЙ
ПОГАШЕНИЕ ДОЛГА

savings bond

(CHIN) 储蓄公债
(FRE) bon d'épargne,obligation d'épargne
(GER) Sparanleihe *f*; Sparbrief *m*,
Sparzertifikat *n*; Schatzbrief *m*
(JAP) 貯蓄債券、貯蓄公債
(RUS) СБЕРЕГАТЕЛЬНАЯ ОБЛИГАЦИЯ

savings element

(CHIN) 人寿保险现值
(FRE) élément d'épargne, valeur monétaire
d'une police d'assurance vie
(GER) Sparanteil *m*, -beitrag *m*,
Kapitalanteil *m*

(JAP) (生命保険の)貯蓄要素
(RUS) КОМПОНЕНТ СБЕРЕЖЕНИЙ
СТРАХОВОГО ПОЛИСА

savings rate
(CHIN) 储蓄利率
(FRE) taux d'epargne, propension à
l'épargne
(GER) Sparquote *f*, volkswirtschaftliche
Sparrate *f*
(JAP) 貯蓄率
(RUS) УРОВЕНЬ СБЕРЕЖЕНИЙ

scab
(CHIN) 非工会工人，破坏罢工者，无赖
(FRE) jaune, briseur de grève, briseur de
grève
(GER) Streikbrecher *m*
(JAP) 労働組合非加入者、スト破り
(RUS) ШТРЕЙКБРЕХЕР

scalage
(CHIN) 缩减率，损耗率
(FRE) remise pour caution de freinte,
remise sur freinte
(GER) Schwundgeld *n*
(JAP) （縮み、漏れなどの恐れのある品
物の値段の）差引率
(RUS) ДОПУЩЕНИЕ НА УТРЯСКУ И
УТЕЧКУ ТОВАРА

scale
(CHIN) 尺度，规模，比率，比例 标度，
规模，刻度
(FRE) échelle
(GER) Skala *f*, Maßstab *m*; Rahmen *m*
(JAP) 目盛、尺度、指数、等級; 位取り、
目盛、物差し
(RUS) ШКАЛА; МАСШТАБ, СТАВКА
ЗАРАБОТНОЙ ПЛАТЫ

scale order
(CHIN) 比例定单
(FRE) ordre echelonne, ordre à
échelle
(GER) gestaffelter Auftrag *m*, (Auftrag an
den Makler bestimmte Anteile zu
unterschiedlichen Preisen zu verkaufen
bzw. kaufen
(JAP) 刻み注文

(RUS) ПРИКАЗ О ПОЭТАПНОЙ ПОКУПКЕ
АКЦИЙ ПО МЕРЕ СНИЖЕНИЯ ЦЕНЫ

scale relationship
(CHIN) 比例关系
(FRE) relation hierarchisee, comparaison à
l'échelle
(GER) Skalenbeziehung *f*
(JAP) 関係（係わり合い、結びつき、
取引先など）を天秤にかける
(RUS) СООТНОШЕНИЕ ШКАЛ

scalper
(CHIN) 投机商，投机倒把者
(FRE) spéculateur à la journée, trafiqueur
de billets
(GER) Spekulant *m*, spekulativer Händler *m*
(JAP) 株券を素早く売買してわずかな利
鞘を稼ぐ人、ダフ屋
(RUS) СПЕКУЛЯНТ НА ПЕРЕПРОДАЖЕ

scanner
(CHIN) 扫描器[仪]，扫描程序
(FRE) scanner, numériseur
(GER) Scanner *m*, Abtastgerät *n*
(JAP) スキャナー、走査器
(RUS) СКАНИРУЮЩЕЕ УСТРОЙСТВО

scarcity, scarcity value
(CHIN) 缺货，资源匮乏，不足，缺乏
(FRE) manque, penurie, valeur de rareté,
(C) rareté
(GER) Streu- *n*, Korrelationsdiagramm *n*
(JAP) 欠乏、不足；稀少価値
(RUS) РЕДКОСТЬ СТОИМОСТЬ РЕДКОСТИ

scatter diagram
(CHIN) 分散示意图
(FRE) diagramme de dispersion
(GER) Korrelationsdiagramm
(JAP) 散布図
(RUS) КОРРЕЛЯЦИОННАЯ ДИАГРАММА

scatter plan
(CHIN) 分散计划
(FRE) plan de dispersion, calendrier de
diffusion de la publicité
(GER) Gießkannenplan *m*, Mediaplan *m*
nach dem Gießkannenprinzip *n*

(JAP) 散布図面

(RUS) ПЛАН РАЗМЕЩЕНИЯ РЕКЛАМЫ ВО ВРЕМЯ РАЗЛИЧНЫХ РАДИО И ТЕЛЕПЕРЕДАЧ

scenic easement

(CHIN) 保持原貌地役权

(FRE) servitude

(GER) Wegerecht *n* aus landschaftlichen Gründen *mpl*

(JAP) 景観地役権

(RUS) БРЕМЯ СОХРАНЕНИЯ ПРИРОДНОГО СОСТОЯНИЯ ЗЕМЛИ

schedule

(CHIN) 计划表，日程表，明细表，安排，附表

(FRE) programme, planning, calendrier, horaire

(GER) Zeitplan *m*; Programm *n*; Verzeichnis *n*, Liste *f*, Aufstellung *f*; Flug-*m*, Fahrplan *m*

(JAP) 一覧表、時間表、予定、予定する、表をつくる

(RUS) ГРАФИК; ОПИСЬ; ПЕРЕЧЕНЬ; ПЛАН

scheduling

(CHIN) 调度

(FRE) planification, programmation, ordonnancement, établissement du calendrier

(GER) Terminierung *f*; Disposition *f*; Prozessplanung *f*

(JAP) 日程計画

(RUS) ПОСТРОЕНИЕ ГРАФИКА, ПЛАНИРОВАНИЕ

scheduled production

(CHIN) 计划生产

(FRE) production planifiee, production systématique

(GER) geplante Produktion *f*

(JAP) 計画された生産品（高、額）

(RUS) ПРОИЗВОДСТВО ПО ГРАФИКУ

scope of employment

(CHIN) 雇用范围

(FRE) sciemment , en connaissance de cause, connaissance de faits pertinents

(FRE) étendue du poste

(GER) Aufgabenkreis *m*

(JAP) 雇用範囲

(RUS) ПЕРЕЧЕНЬ ВЫПОЛНЕННЫХ ЗАДАЧ ВО ВРЕМЯ НАХОЖДЕНИИ В ДОЛЖНОСТИ

scorched-earth defense

(CHIN) 防止恶意收购的焦土政策

(FRE) defense de la terre brulée

(GER) (Verteidigungs)strategie *f* der verbrannten Erde *f*

(JAP) 焦土防御（策）

(RUS) ЗАЩИТА ОТ ПОГЛАЩЕНИЯ ПУТЁМ ИЗБАВЛЕНИЯ ОТ НАИБОЛЕЕ ЦЕННОЙ ДОЧЕРНЕЙ КОМПАНИИ

screen filter

(CHIN) 屏幕过滤器

(FRE) filtre d'écran

(GER) Bildschirmfilter *f* (Computer)

(RUS) ЭКРАННЫЙ ФИЛЬТР

screen saver

(CHIN) 屏幕保护程序

(FRE) economiseur d'ecran

(GER) Bildschirmschoner *f* (Computer)

(JAP) スクリーンセーバー

(RUS) ЭКРАННАЯ ЗАЩИТА

scrip

(CHIN) 股票临时收据，暂时股票，股单，准股票

(FRE) titre provisoire, certificat provisoire

(GER) Interim- *m*, Zwischen- *m*, Bezugsschein *m*

(JAP) 仮株券、仮証券、仮債券

(RUS) ВРЕМЕННОЕ СВИДЕТЕЛЬСТВО НА АКЦИЮ ИЛИ ОБЛИГАЦИЮ; ЛЮБАЯ ЦЕННАЯ БУМАГА

scroll down

(CHIN) 下卷[滚]，向下卷动

(FRE) déplacement vers le bas, défiler vers le bas

(GER) nach unten rollen, zurückrollen *v* (EDV)

(JAP) スクロールダウン

(RUS) ПЕРЕМЕЩЕНИЕ, ПРОСМАТРИВАНИЕ ВНИЗ СТРАНИЦЫ

scroll up

(CHIN) 上卷[滚], 向上卷动

(FRE) déplacement vers le haut, défiler vers le haut

(GER) nach oben rollen *v* (EDV)

(JAP) スクロールアップ

(RUS) ПЕРЕМЕЩЕНИЕ, ПРОСМАТРИВАНИЕ ВВЕРХ СТРАНИЦЫ

seal

(CHIN) 印章, 封印, 保证, 批准

(FRE) sceau , cachet, label

(GER) Siegel *n*, Plombe *f*, Stempel *m*; versiegeln; mit einem Siegel *n* versehen, plombieren *v*

(JAP) 印、封印、印章、印証、確証 （保証、契約）のしるし

(RUS) ПЕЧАТЬ; СТАВИТЬ ПЕЧАТЬ; ПЛОМБИРОВАТЬ

sealed bid

(CHIN) 密封投标

(FRE) prix de soumission, soumission approuvée

(GER) versiegeltes Submissionsangebot *n*

(JAP) 封縅入札

(RUS) СЕКРЕТНАЯ ТЕНДЕРНАЯ ЗАЯВКА

seal of approval

(CHIN) 同意盖章

(FRE) label de qualité

(GER) Gütesiegel *n*

(JAP) 承認の印章

(RUS) СВИДЕТЕЛЬСТВО ОДОБРЕНИЯ

search engine

(CHIN) 搜索引擎

(FRE) moteur de recherche

(GER) Suchmaschine *f*

(JAP) サーチエンジン、検索エンジン

(RUS) ИНСТРУМЕНТ, ПРОГРАММА ПОИСКА

seasonal adjustment

(CHIN) 季节性调整

(FRE) correction des variations saisonnières

(GER) Saisonbereinigung *f*, -ausgleich *m*

(JAP) 季節調整

(RUS) ПОПРАВКА НА ВРЕМЯ ГОДА

seasonality

(CHIN) 季节性

(FRE) caractère saisonnier

(GER) Saisonbedingtheit *f*

(JAP) 季節性

(RUS) СЕЗОННЫЙ ХАРАКТЕР; СЕЗОННОСТЬ

seasoned issue

(CHIN) 稳妥证券发行

(FRE) titre acclimaté

(GER) favorisierte Emission *f*

(JAP) 確実証券

(RUS) ОБЛИГАЦИИ ПОЛЬЗУЮЩИЕСЯ СПРОСОМ

seasoned loan

(CHIN) 稳妥贷款

(FRE) prêt bonifié

(GER) Darlehen *n* mit Erfahrungswerten *mpl*

(JAP) 堅実融資

(RUS) ЗАЙМ, ПО КОТОРОМУ УЖЕ БЫЛО ПОЛУЧЕНО НЕСКОЛЬКО ПЛАТЕЖЕЙ

seat

(CHIN) 席位

(FRE) siège

(GER) Sitz *m*; Börsensitz *m*; Mandat *n*

(JAP) 所在地、（証券取引所などの）会員券、議席、役職

(RUS) МЕСТО (на бирже); ШТАБ-КВАРТИРА; МЕСТО ПРЕБЫВАНИЯ

secondary boycott

(CHIN) 二级抵制, 次级抵制

(FRE) boycottage secondaire

(GER) indirekter Boykott *m*

(RUS) БОЙКОТ ТОВАРОВ И УСЛУГ, КОСВЕННО СВЯЗАННЫХ С РАБОТОДАТЕЛЕМ, ПРОТИВ КОТОРОГО ОН НАЦЕЛЕН

secondary distribution

(CHIN) 证券二次发行, 第二次分配

(FRE) distribution secondaire

(GER) Wertpapierangebot *n* im Sekundärmarkt *m*; Sekundärverteilung *f*

(JAP) (既発行証券の)第二次分売

(RUS) ВТОРИЧНОЕ РАЗМЕЩЕНИЕ (ПРЕДЛОЖЕНИЕ) (ценных бумаг)

secondary market
(CHIN) 次级市场，二级市场
(FRE) marché secondaire
(GER) Sekundär- *m*, Neben- *m*, Zweitmarkt *m*; Rückversicherungsmarkt *m*
(JAP) 流通市場、第二次市場
(RUS) ВТОРИЧНЫЙ РЫНОК

secondary mortgage market
(CHIN) 二级抵押市场
(FRE) marché hypothécaire secondaire
(GER) Markt *m* für nachrangige Hypotheken *fpl*
(JAP) 第二次抵当市場
(RUS) ВТОРИЧНЫЙ ИПОТЕЧНЫЙ РЫНОК

second lien or second mortgage
(CHIN) 第二留置权或第二抵押权
(FRE) hypothèque secondaire, prêt hypothécaire de second rang
(GER) nachrangiges Pfandrecht *n*, zweitrangige Hypothek *f*, Zweithypothek *f*
(JAP) 二番抵当、第二順位抵当
(RUS) ВТОРИЧНЫЙ ЗАЛОГ или ВТОРАЯ ИПОТЕКА

second mortgage lending
(CHIN) 第二抵押借贷
(FRE) prêt hypothécaire secondaire, octroi de prêt hypothécaire de second rang
(GER) Zweithypothekengeschäft *n*
(JAP) 二番抵当貸付
(RUS) КРЕДИТОВАНИЕ ПОД ВТОРИЧНУЮ ИПОТЕКУ

second-preferred stock
(CHIN) 第二优先股
(FRE) seconde action privilégiée, actions privilégiées de second rang
(GER) Vorzugsaktien *fpl* zweiter Klasse *f*
(JAP) 低位優先株
(RUS) ВТОРИЧНЫЕ ПРИВИЛЕГИРОВАННЫЕ АКЦИИ, УСТУПАЮЩИЕ ДРУГИМ ПРИВИЛЕГИРОВАННЫМ АКЦИЯМ (в правах на дивиденды и активы при ликвидации)

sector
(CHIN) 部门，成分，段，区
(FRE) secteur

(GER) Sektor *m*, Bereich *m*
(JAP) 部門、産業部門、セクター
(RUS) СЕКТОР; ОТРАСЛЬ

secured bond
(CHIN) 抵押债券，担保债券
(FRE) obligation cautionnée, obligation garantie
(GER) gesicherte Schuldverschreibung *f*, pfandgesicherte Obligation *f*
(JAP) 担保付き社債、担保付き債券
(RUS) ОБЕСПЕЧЕННАЯ ОБЛИГАЦИЯ (например, ипотекой)

secured debt
(CHIN) 担保债务
(FRE) créance garantie
(GER) dinglich gesicherte Forderung *f*
(JAP) 担保付き負債
(RUS) ОБЕСПЕЧЕННЫЙ КРЕДИТ

secured transaction
(CHIN) 担保交易
(FRE) transaction garantie, transaction sécurisée
(GER) Kreditgeschäft *n* mit Zugriffsrecht *n* des Gläubigers *m*, Sicherungsgeschäft
(JAP) 担保付き取引
(RUS) ОБЕСПЕЧЕННАЯ СДЕЛКА

securities
(CHIN) 证券
(FRE) titres, valeurs, titres de placement, valeurs mobilières
(GER) Wertpapiere *npl*, Effekten *pl*; Sicherheiten *fpl*
(JAP) 証券、有価証券
(RUS) ЦЕННЫЕ БУМАГИ

securities analyst
(CHIN) 证券分析家，股市专家
(FRE) analyste financier, analyste des valeurs
(GER) Wertpapieranalyst *m*
(JAP) 証券分析家、証券アナリスト
(RUS) АНАЛИТИК ЦЕННЫХ БУМАГ

securities and commodities exchanges
(CHIN) 证券及商品交换

(FRE) échanges de valeurs mobilières et de biens, bourse
(GER) Wertpapier- und Warenbörsen *fpl*
(JAP) 証券商品取引所
(RUS) ФОНДОВЫЕ И ТОВАРНЫЕ БИРЖИ

Securities and Exchange Commission (SEC)
(CHIN) 证券交易委员会（SEC）
(FRE) commission américaine des opérations de bourse, commission des valeurs mobilières
(GER) SEC *f*, US-Börsenaufsichtsbehörde *f*
(JAP) 〔米〕証券取引委員会
(RUS) КОМИССИЯ ПО ЦЕННЫМ БУМАГАМ (США)

securities loan
(CHIN) 证券贷款
(FRE) prêt de titres
(GER) Effektenkredit *m*, Wertpapierdarlehen *n*
(JAP) 証券担保貸出し、証券金融、証券貸付け
(RUS) ССУДА ЦЕННЫМИ БУМАГАМИ

security
(CHIN) 保证，担保
(FRE) garantie, caution, cautionnement, nantissement, garant, sécurité, titre de placement
(GER) Wertpapier *n*; Sicherheit *f*; Sicherung *f*, Bürgschaft *f*, Garantie *f*
(JAP) 保証、担保、（通常 pl.）有価証券
(RUS) БЕЗОПАСНОСТЬ; ОБЕСПЕЧЕНИЕ; ЦЕННАЯ БУМАГА

security deposit
(CHIN) 保证金
(FRE) dépôt de garantie
(GER) Kaution *f*, Sicherheitsleistung *f*
(JAP) 敷金
(RUS) ЗАЛОГ

security interest
(CHIN) 物权担保，抵押权益
(FRE) privilège, intérêts remis en nantissement de prêt

(GER) Sicherungsrecht *n*; Sicherheitsinteresse *n*
(JAP) 〔法律〕先取特権、担保権
(RUS) ПРАВО КРЕДИТОРА ВСТУПИТЬ ВО ВЛАДЕНИЕ СОБСТВЕННОСТЬ, ПРЕДЛОЖЕННОЙ КАК ОБЕСПЕЧЕНИЕ

security rating
(CHIN) 证券评级
(FRE) degré de sécurité, cote d'un titre
(GER) Sicherheitseinstufung *f*; Wertpapier- *f*, Effektenbewertung *f*
(JAP) 担保評価・格付け
(RUS) РЕЙТИНГИ ЦЕННЫХ БУМАГ

seed money
(CHIN) 种子基金，创办基金
(FRE) capital initial, capitaux de lancement
(GER) Startkapital *n*, Gründungskapital *n*
(JAP) （新事業の）元手、着手資金、投機的資金
(RUS) ПЕРВИЧНОЕ ВЛОЖЕНИЕ КАПИТАЛА

segmentation strategy
(CHIN) 分割策略
(FRE) stratégie de segmentation
(JAP) 分割戦略、市場分断戦略
(RUS) СТРАТЕГИЯ СЕГМЕНТАЦИИ (рынка)

segment margin
(CHIN) 部门利润边际
(FRE) marge sectorielle, (C) résultat sectoriel
(GER) Segmentspanne *f*
(JAP) 事業区分別利ざや、セグメントマージン
(RUS) МАРЖА СЕГМЕНТА, МЕРА ОЦЕНКИ ФИНАНСОВОГО СОСТОЯНИЯ СЕГМЕНТА ДЕЛОВОГО ПРЕДПРИЯТИЯ

segment reporting
(CHIN) 分部财务报告
(FRE) analyse par secteur d'activité, (C) publication d'informations sectorielles
(GER) Erstellung *f* von Ergebnisberichten *mpl* nach Geschäftsbereichen *mpl*
(JAP) 事業区分別損益報告、セグメントリポート
(RUS) ОТЧЕТНОСТЬ ПО СЕГМЕНТАМ

segregation of duties

(CHIN) 职责划分

(FRE) séparation des pouvoirs,
(C) cloisonnement des tâches

(GER) Aufgabentrennung *f*

(JAP) 任務の分割化、関税の区分化

(RUS) РАЗДЕЛЕНИЕ ОБЯЗАННОСТЕЙ

seisin

(CHIN) 依法占有

(FRE) saisine

(GER) Grundbesitz *m* in freiem und
unbeschränktem Eigentum *n*;
Inbesitznahme *f* eines Grundstücks *n*

(JAP) （土地の）占有（権）、所有
（権）

(RUS) ВСТУПЛЕНИЕ ВО ВЛАДЕНИЕ

select

(CHIN) 选择

(FRE) selectionner, (C) choisir

(GER) ansteuern, auswählen, markieren *v*
(EDV)

(JAP) 選択する、選択

(RUS) ВЫБИРАТЬ, ВЫДЕЛЯТЬ, ОПЕРАЦИЯ,
УКАЗЫВАЮЩАЯ ФРАГМЕНТ ТЕКСТА
ИЛИ ЭЛЕМЕНТ ИЗОБРАЖЕНИЯ, НАД
КОТОРЫМ ВЫПОЛНЯЕТСЯ СЛЕДУЮЩАЯ
ОПЕРАЦИЯ

selective credit control

(CHIN) 选择性信贷控制

(FRE) contrôle sélectif du crédit, (C)
contrôle du crédit sélectif

(GER) Kreditlenkung *f*, selektive
Kreditkontrolle *f*

(JAP) 選択的信用統制、選択的信用調整

(RUS) СЕЛЕКТИВНЫЙ КРЕДИТНЫЙ
КОНТРОЛЬ

selective distribution

(CHIN) 选择性分销

(FRE) distribution sélective

(GER) Vertrieb *m* durch ausgewählte
Händler *mpl*

(JAP) 選択的販売経路、選択的販売

(RUS) СЕЛЕКТИВНОЕ (ВЫБОРОЧНОЕ)
РАЗМЕЩЕНИЕ, РАСПРЕДЕЛЕНИЕ

self-amortizing mortgage

(CHIN) 自摊销抵押贷款

(FRE) crédit auto-amortissable, (C) prêt
hypothécaire avec paiement forfaitaire

(GER) selbsttilgende Hypothek *f*

(JAP) 自己償還的抵当貸付

(RUS) ИПОТЕКА, ВЫПЛАЧЕВАЕМАЯ
ПОСРЕДСТВОМ ПЕРИОДИЧЕСКИХ
ВЫПЛАТ ПРОЦЕНТА И ОСНОВНОЙ
СУММЫ

self-directed IRA

(CHIN) 自己管理的个人退休金账户

(FRE) plan d'épargne retraite auto-géré,
(C) régime d'épargne-retraite autogéré

(GER) selbst verwaltetes IRA *n* (privates
US-Rentenkonto)

(JAP) 自己決定個人退職積立勘定
（IRA）

(RUS) ИНДИВИДУАЛЬНЫЙ
ПЕНСИОННЫЙ СЧЕТ ПОД ЛИЧНЫМ
КОНТРОЛЕМ

self employed

(CHIN) 自雇

(FRE) indépendant qui travaille à son
compte, (C) travailleur autonome

(GER) selbständig, freiberuflich,
-schaffend *adj*

(JAP) 自営業の、自営業者の

(RUS) ИНДИВИДУАЛЬНЫЙ
ПРЕДПРИНИМАТЕЛЬ

self-help

(CHIN) 自助

(FRE) effort personnel, auto-assistance,
(C) initiative personnelle

(GER) Selbsthilfe *f*

(JAP) 自助、自助努力、ルフヘルプ

(RUS) САМОПОМОЩЬ

self insurance

(CHIN) 自保

(FRE) auto-assurance

(GER) Eigen- *f*, Selbstversicherung *f*

(JAP) 自家保険、自己保険

(RUS) СТРАХОВАНИЕ СОБСТВЕННЫМИ
СИЛАМИ

self-tender offer

(CHIN) 自投标股票回购

(FRE) proposition de rachat présentée par
une entreprise à ses actionnaires, (C) offre

publique d'achat
(GER) Rückkauf *m* eigener Anteile *mpl*
(JAP) 自己株式公開買付け制度
(RUS) ПРЕДЛОЖЕНИЕ КОМПАНИЕЙ
ВЫКУПА СВОИХ АКЦИЙ ОТ
АКЦИОНЕРОВ

seller's market
(CHIN) 卖方市场
(FRE) marché à la hausse, (C) marché
favorable au vendeur
(GER) Verkäufermarkt *m*
(JAP) 売手市場
(RUS) «РЫНОК ПРОДАВЦОВ» (где
продавцы диктуют условия в силу
превышения спроса над предложением)

sell-in
(CHIN) 经销，销售
(FRE) vendre au distributeur, (C) vendre à
profit
(GER) an den Markt *m* abgeben *v*
(JAP) 売り込む
(RUS) ПРОДАТЬ ДЛЯ ПОЛУЧЕНИЯ
ПРИБЫЛИ

selling agent or selling broker
(CHIN) 代销商，销售经纪人
(FRE) agent de vente, (C) courtier de vente
(GER) Verkaufskommissionär *m* oder
Verkaufsmakler *m*; Vertriebsgesellschaft *f*
(JAP) 販売代理店、販売仲買人
(RUS) АГЕНТ или БРОКЕР ПО ПРОДАЖЕ

selling climax
(CHIN) 抛售顶点，成交高潮
(FRE) f(FRE) orte baisse du prix des
actions dû à des ventes massives, (C) point
culminant de la vente
(GER) Verkaufshöhepunkt *m*
(JAP) セリングクライマックス
(RUS) КУЛЬМИНАЦИЯ ПРОДАЖ (резкое
падение цен на фондовой бирже)

selling short
(CHIN) 卖空
(FRE) vendre à découvert
(GER) Leerverkauf *m*, Baissespekulation *f*
(JAP) 空売り
(RUS) КОРОТКАЯ ПРОДАЖА

sell-off
(CHIN) 廉价清货，大量抛售
(FRE) solde liquidation
(GER) Glattstellungsverkauf *m*, Liquidation
f, Abstoßung *f*
(JAP) 売崩し
(RUS) СБРОС, АКТИВНАЯ РАСПРОДАЖА
(бумаг или товаров)

semiannual
(CHIN) 半年期
(FRE) semestriel
(GER) halbjährlich *adj*
(JAP) 半年の、半期の、半年ごとの
(RUS) ПОЛУГОДОВОЙ

semiconductor
(CHIN) 半导体
(FRE) semi-conducteur
(GER) Halbleiter *m*
(JAP) セミコンダクター、半導体
(RUS) ПОЛУПРОВОДНИК

semimonthly
(CHIN) 半月的
(FRE) bimensuel
(GER) halbmonatlich *adj*
(JAP) 月二回の、半月ごと
(RUS) ДВАЖДЫ В МЕСЯЦ

semivariable costs
(CHIN) 半变动成本，
混合成本
(FRE) coûts semi-variables
(GER) halbvariable Kosten *pl*
(JAP) 半変動費
(RUS) ИЗДЕРЖКИ, РЕАГИРУЮЩИЕ НА
ИЗМЕНЕНИЕ ОБЪЁМА, НО
НЕПРОПОРЦИОНАЛЬНО ЭТОМУ
ИЗМЕНЕНИЮ

senior debt
(CHIN) 优先债务
(FRE) dette senior, (C) créance prioritaire
(GER) vorrangige Verbindlichkeiten *fpl*,
vorrangiger Schuldtitel *m*
(JAP) 優位弁済債務、上位債務
(RUS) «СТАРШИЙ» ДОЛГ (кредиты и
облигации с преимущественным правом на
активы при ликвидации)

senior refunding

(CHIN) 优先偿还

(FRE) remboursement senior,
(C) remboursement prioritaire

(GER) vorrangige Umschuldung *f*,
bevorrechtigte Umfinanzierung *f*

(JAP) 優位（上位、優先）償還、優位
（上位、優先）払戻し

(RUS) РЕФИНАНСИРОВАНИЕ ЦЕННЫХ
БУМАГ бумагами с большим сроком
погашения

senior security

(CHIN) 优先股，主要担保

(FRE) titre prioritaire

(GER) vorrangiges Wertpapier *n*, mit
Vorrechten *npl* ausgestattetes Wertpapier *n*

(JAP) 優位（上位、優先）担保（保証、
抵当、証券（*pl*）

(RUS) СТАРШАЯ ЦЕННАЯ БУМАГА с
преимущественным правом на активы при
ликвидации

sensitive market

(CHIN) 敏感市场

(FRE) marché sensible

(GER) empfindliche reagierende Börse *f*

(JAP) 不安定市場

(RUS) «ЧУТКИЙ» РЫНОК, РЫНОК, ЧУТКО
РЕАГИРУЮЩИЙ НА ОТРИЦАТЕЛЬНУЮ
ИЛИ ПОЛОЖИТЕЛЬНУЮ ИНФОРМАЦИЮ

sensitivity training

(CHIN) 敏感性训练

(FRE) formation psychosociale,
(C) formation sur la sensibilité

(GER) Sensibilitäts-Training *n*

(JAP) グループ研究、
人間関係セミナー

(RUS) ИЗУЧЕНИЕ РЕАКЦИИ НА
ИНФОРМАЦИЮ НА ПОДОПЫТНОЙ
ГРУППЕ

sentiment indicators

(CHIN) 市场行情指标

(FRE) indicateurs de la psychologie,
(C) indicateurs de sentiment

(GER) Stimmungsindikatoren *mpl*

(JAP) センチメント指標

(RUS) ИНДИКАТОРЫ НАСТРОЕНИЯ
(инвесторов)

separate property

(CHIN) 特有财产，可单独支配的财产

(FRE) biens propres

(GER) Privatvermögen *n* (der
Gesellschafter einer Personengesellschaft);
getrenntes Vermögen *n* (von Ehegatten)

(JAP) 特有財産

(RUS) СОБСТВЕННОСТЬ В РАЗТДЕЛЬНОМ
ВЛАДЕНИИ СУПРУГОВ

serial bond

(CHIN) 序列债券，分期偿还债券

(FRE) obligation échéant en série

(GER) Serienanleihe *f*

(JAP) 連続償還債券

(RUS) СЕРИЙНЫЕ ОБЛИГАЦИИ

series bond

(CHIN) 系列债券

(FRE) obligation en série

(GER) Anleihe *f* aus der gleichen Reihe *f*

(JAP) 連続発行債券

(RUS) ГРУППА ОБЛИГАЦИЙ,
ВЫПУЩЕННЫХ ПОД ОДНИМ
КОНТРАКТОМ

serial port

(CHIN) 串行端口，串行出入口

(GER) serieller Anschluss *m*

(JAP) シリアルポート

(RUS) ПОСЛЕДОВАТЕЛЬНЫЙ ПОРТ

server

(CHIN) 服务器，服务模块

(FRE) serveur

(GER) Server *m* (Internet)

(JAP) サーバー

(RUS) СЕРВЕР, СЛУЖЕБНЫЙ ПРОЦЕССОР,
ОБСЛУЖИВАЮЩЕЕ УСТРОЙСТВО

service

(CHIN) 服务，业务，公共事业，
公营机构，检修

(FRE) service

(GER) Dienstleistung *f*, Service *m*; Wartung
f, Unterhaltung *f*; Kundendienst *m*;
Bedienung *f*, Zinsendienst *m*; Zustellung *f*

(JAP) 役務、客扱い、サービス業

(RUS) УСЛУГА; ОБСЛУЖИВАНИЕ;
ОБСЛУЖИВАНИЕ ЗАЙМА

service bureau

(CHIN) 服务机构

(FRE) société de services, (C) service bureau

(GER) Serviceunternehmen *n*; DV-Dienstleistungsunternehmen *n*

(JAP) サービスビューロ、サービス機関

(RUS) БЮРО УСЛУГ

service club

(CHIN) 服务性社团

(FRE) club philantropique

(GER) gemeinnütziger Verein *m*

(JAP) 奉仕クラブ、福祉団体

(RUS) ОБЪЕДИНЕНИЕ ДЛЯ ОКАЗАНИЯ ОБЩЕСТВЕННЫХ УСЛУГ И УСЛУГ СВОИМ ЧЛЕНАМ

service department

(CHIN) 服务部门

(FRE) section auxiliaire

(GER) Kundendienstabteilung *f*

(JAP) サービス部門、サービス係

(RUS) ОТДЕЛ ОБСЛУЖИВАНИЯ, СЕРВИСА

service economy

(CHIN) 服务经济

(FRE) société de services, (C) économie des services

(GER) Dienstleistungsgesellschaft *f*

(JAP) サービス経済、奉仕経済

(RUS) ЭКОНОМИКА СВЫСОКОЙ ДОЛЕЙ СЕКТОРА ОБСЛУЖИВАНИЯ

service fee

(CHIN) 服务费

(FRE) prestation de services, (C) frais de gestion

(GER) Kontoführungsgebühr *f*; Bearbeitungsgebühr *f*; Dienstleistungsgebühr *f*

(JAP) 手数料、サービス料金

(RUS) ПЛАТА (СБОР) ЗА ОБСЛУЖИВАНИЕ

service worker

(CHIN) 服务人员

(FRE) personnel de service

(GER) Beschäftigter *m* in einem Dienstleistungsbetrieb *m*

(JAP) サービス業労働者、～業従事者

(RUS) РАБОТНИК СЕРВИСНОЙ СЛУЖБЫ

servicing

(CHIN) 日常维修，贷款服务

(FRE) entretien, (C) entretien courant

(GER) Wartung *f*, Instandhaltung *f*; Kundendienst *m*

(JAP) 供給、サービス

(RUS) ОБСЛУЖИВАНИЕ; ОБСЛУЖИВАНИЕ ДОЛГА

setback

(CHIN) 挫折，倒退

(FRE) tassement, repli, (C) fléchissement, recul

(GER) Rückschlag *m*; Einbruch *m*; Fehlschlag *m*

(JAP) 頓挫、セットバック

(RUS) ОТКАТ НАЗАД; НЕУДАЧА

setoff

(CHIN) 抵消

(FRE) déduire, (C) écriture inverse

(GER) Aufrechnung *f*, Gegenforderung *f*; Ausgleich *m*, Kompensation *f*

(JAP) 債務の差引、（損失等の）埋め合わせ、相殺する

(RUS) ЗАЧЕТ; КОНТРПРЕТЕНЗИЯ

settle

(CHIN) 解决，结算，偿付，定居

(FRE) fixer, déterminer, régler

(GER) Glattstellen *v*; regeln, klären *v*; bereinigen *v*

(JAP) 清算する、決算する、安定させる

(RUS) УРЕГУЛИРОВАТЬ; УЛАДИТЬ

settlement

(CHIN) 决算，结算，解决，处理

(FRE) règlement

(GER) Schlichtung *f*, Vergleich *m*; Abfindung *f*; Abwicklung *f*; Abrechnung *f* (Börse); Glattstellung *f*; Regulierung *f* (Versicherung)

(JAP) 解决、支払い、清算

(RUS) РАСЧЕТ; УЛАЖИВАНИЕ; ОКОНЧАТЕЛЬНОЕ ОФОРМЛЕНИЕ

settlement date

(CHIN) 决算日期

(FRE) date de règlement
(GER) Abrechnungs- *m*, Kurstermin *m*,
Fälligkeitstag *m*
(JAP) 決算日、決済日、勘定日
(RUS) ДЕНЬ ОКОНЧАТЕЛЬНОГО
РАССЧЁТА И ПЕРЕДАЧИ БУМАГ

settlor
(CHIN) 财产授与人
(FRE) disposant, (C) constituant
(GER) Treugeber *m*, Stifter *m*
(JAP) 設定者、財産譲渡者
(RUS) ДОВЕРИТЕЛЬ; ЛИЦО,
СОВЕРШАЮЩЕЕ АКТ РАСПОРЯЖЕНИЯ
ИМУЩЕСТВОМ

severalty
(CHIN) 土地的个人拥有权
(FRE) possession individuelle
 (GER) Bruchteilseigentum *n*, -vermögen *n*
(JAP) （財産の）単独保有、
単独土地保有
(RUS) ВЛАДЕНИЕ СОБСТВЕННОСТЬЮ В
КАЧЕСТВЕ ИНДИВИДУАЛЬНОГО
ВЛАДЕЛЬЦА

severance damages
(CHIN) 分割损害
(FRE) coût de remplacement, (C)
dommages-intérêts de cession
(GER) Entschädigung *f* bei Entlassung *f*
(JAP) 残地損失
(RUS) УЩЕРБ ОТ РАЗДЕЛЕНИЯ
(СОБСТВЕННОСТИ)

severance pay
(CHIN) 解雇金，遣散费
(FRE) iindemnité de licenciement,
(C) indemnité de cessation d'emploi
(GER) Entlassungsabfindung *f*,
Abfindungszahlung *f*
(JAP) 解雇手当、退職金
(RUS) ВЫХОДНОЕ ПОСОБИЕ

sexual harassment
(CHIN) 性骚扰
(FRE) harcèlement sexuel
(GER) sexuelle Belästigung *f*
(JAP) 性的嫌がらせ、
セクハラ

(RUS) СЕКСУАЛЬНОЕ
ДОМОГАТЕЛЬСТВО

shakedown
(CHIN) 试航，试验
(FRE) accomodation, (C) débourrer
(GER) Umstrukturierung *f*; Erpressung *f*
強奪、ゆすり、徹底的捜索
(RUS) ПРИСПОСАБЛИВАНИЕ;
ВЫМОГАТЕЛЬСТВО (под угрозой)

shakeout
(CHIN) 股票市场的暴跌，景气的消退
(FRE) dégraissage, (C) changement des
conditions du marché
(GER) Gesundschrumpfung *f*;
Herausdrängung *f* schwächerer Spekulanten
mpl; natürliche Auslese *f*
(JAP) 淘汰、（株などの）暴落、
小投資家の淘汰、
組織の合理化・刷新
(RUS) ИЗМЕНЕНИЕ РЫНОЧНЫХ
УСЛОВИЙ, ПРИВОДЯЩЕЕ К
УСТРАНЕНИЮ СЛАБЫХ УЧАСТНИКОВ

shakeup
(CHIN) [公司机构等的]大改革，大变动
(FRE) remaniement, restructuration
(GER) Reorganisation *f*, Umbesetzung *f*;
Umstrukturierung *f*
(JAP) （人事・組織の）大整理、再編成
(RUS) РЕЗКОЕ ИЗМЕНЕНИЕ СТРУКТУРЫ
И РУКОВОДСТВА ОРГАНИЗАЦИИ

share
(CHIN) 股，股份，股票，股权，份额，
分配
(FRE) action, titre, part
(GER) Anteil *m*, Beteiligung *f*,
Beteiligungs *n*, Aktie *f*
(JAP) 割当て、分担、共有権、株式、共
有する、分配する
(RUS) ДОЛЯ; АКЦИЯ

sharecropper
(CHIN) 小佃农
(FRE) métayer
(GER) Landarbeiter *m* auf Naturalbasis *f*,
Farmpächter *m*
(JAP) シェアクロッパー、分益小作人

(RUS) КРЕСТЬЯНИН – ИЗДОЛЬЩИК

shared-appreciation mortgage (SAM)

(CHIN) 分成增值抵押 （SAM）

(FRE) prêt hypothécaire avec participation à la plus-value

(GER) Hypothek *f* mit Gewinnbeteiligung *f* des Gläubigers *m*

(JAP) 抵当物件増加分共有条件貸付け、SAM 方式抵当貸付け

(RUS) ДЕШЕВАЯ ИПОТЕКА когда заемщик должен поделиться с кредитором доходом от РОСТА СТОИМОСТИ СОБСТВЕННОСТИ

shared drive

(CHIN) 共享驱动器

(FRE) lecteur partage

(GER) gemeinsames Laufwerk *n* (Computer)

(JAP) 共用ドライブ、共用駆動装置

(RUS) ДИСКОВОД СОВМЕСТНОГО ПОЛЬЗОВАНИЯ

shared-equity mortgage

(CHIN) 分成股本抵押

(FRE) prêt hypothécaire avec participation à la plus-value

(GER) Hypothek *f* mit Anteilskapitalbeteiligung *f*

(JAP) 抵当物件エクイティ共有条件貸付け

(RUS) ИПОТЕКА С ПРАВОМ КРЕДИТОРА НА ЧАСТЬ ДОХОДА ОТ ПОСЛЕДУЮЩЕЙ ПРОДАЖИ СОБСТВЕННОСТИ

shareholder

(CHIN) 股东，股票持有人

(FRE) actionnaire

(GER) Aktionär *m*; Anteilseigner *m*, -inhaber *m*; Gesellschafter *m*

(JAP) 株主

(RUS) АКЦИОНЕР

shareholder's equity

(CHIN) 股东权益

(FRE) capitaux propres, fonds propres, avoir des actionnaires

(GER) Eigenkapital *n* des Gesellschafters *m*

(JAP) 自己資本

(RUS) АКЦИОНЕРНЫЙ КАПИТАЛ (все активы минус все пассивы)

shares authorized

(CHIN) 核准股票

(FRE) actions autorisées

(GER) genehmigte Aktien *fpl*

(JAP) 授権株式数、授権株式

(RUS) ЧИСЛО АКЦИЙ СОГЛАСНО УСТАВУ

shareware

(CHIN) 共享软件，共用软件

(FRE) logiciel en libre essai, (C) partagiciel

(GER) Shareware *f*

(JAP) シェアウェア

(RUS) ПАКЕТ КОЛЛЕКТИВНОГО ПОЛЬЗОВАНИЯ

shark repellent

(CHIN) 防止被收购的拒鲨行动

(FRE) pilule empoisonnée, mesures anti-OPA

(GER) Übernahmeabwehrklausel *f*

(JAP) 企業買収防御策、会社乗っ取り屋防御策

(RUS) МЕРЫ ПО ЗАЩИТЕ ОТ ВРАЖДЕБНОГО ПОГЛОЩЕНИЯ

shark watcher

(CHIN) 监视收购活动的公司

(FRE) détecteur de requin, (C) entreprise surveillant les acquisitions

(GER) Shark Watcher *m*

(JAP) 企業買収対応監視専門家

(RUS) ФИРМА, СПЕЦИАЛИЗИРУЮЩАЯСЯ НА РАННЕМ ПРОГНОЗИРОВАНИИ ПОПЫТОК ПОГЛОЩЕНИЯ

sheet feeder

(CHIN) 供[送]纸器

(FRE) dispositif d'alimentation feuille a feuille, (C) chargeur feuille à feuille

(GER) Einzelblattzuführung *f* (z.B. Fax)

(JAP) シートフィーダー

(RUS) УСТРОЙСТВО АВТОПОДАЧИ СТРАНИЦ БУМАГИ

shell corporation

(CHIN) 空壳公司

(FRE) société fictive, (C) société à actif nominal

(GER) Dachgesellschaft *f*;
Mantelunternehmen *n*
(JAP) ペーパーカンパニー、幽霊会社、
架空会社
(RUS) КОМПАНИЯ – ПРИКРЫТИЕ

shift

(CHIN) 转让，转移，改变，替换，换班
(FRE) poste, équipe, (C) quart de travail
(GER) Verlagerung *f*, Verlegung *f*,
Umgruppierung *f*; Schicht *f*; Wandel *m*,
Wechsel *m*
(JAP) 移る、変動、交替（交代）
(RUS) ИЗМЕНЯТЬСЯ, СДВИГАТЬСЯ;
СМЕНА; СДВИГ

shift differential

(CHIN) 班次补助，值班津贴
(FRE) supplément d'équipe, prime
d'équipe, (C) prime de poste
(GER) Schichtzulage *f*
(JAP) 交代勤務手当
(RUS) НАДБАВКА ЗА РАБОТУ В
НЕУДОБНУЮ (НАПР., НОЧНУЮ) СМЕНУ

shift key

(CHIN) 换档键
(FRE) touche « majuscules »
(GER) Umschalttaste *f* (Tastatur)
(JAP) シフトキー
(RUS) КЛАВИША
СМЕНЫ РЕГИСТРА

shift lock

(CHIN) 换档锁
(FRE) verrouillage des majuscules,
(C) touche de verrouillage de motion
(GER) Umschaltsperre *f* (Tastatur)
(JAP) シフトロック
(RUS) ФИКСАЦИЯ РЕГИСТРА

shop

(CHIN) 商店，车间，工厂
(FRE) magasin, (C) boutique, magasiner, ,
(C) acheter
(GER) Laden *m*; Werkstatt *f*
(JAP) （米）仕事場、作業所、工場、
（英）商店
(RUS) МАГАЗИН; ПРОИЗВОДСТВЕННОЕ
ПОМЕЩЕНИЕ; ОФИС БРОКЕРА;

ПРОФСОЮЗНАЯ ЯЧЕЙКА; ХОДИТЬ ЗА
ПОКУПКАМИ; ПРИЦЕНИВАТЬСЯ

shopper

(CHIN) 买东西的顾客，购物人
(FRE) acheteur, (C) client
(GER) Käufer *m*, Einkäufer *m*
(JAP) 買物客、買物代理人
(RUS) ПОКУПАТЕЛЬ

shopping service

(CHIN) 采购服务
(FRE) service d'achat
(GER) Einkaufsservice *m*
(JAP) ショッピングサービス
(RUS) УСЛУГИ ПО ПРИОБРЕТЕНИЮ
ТОВАРОВ

short bond

(CHIN) 短期债券
(FRE) obligation à courte échéance,
(C) obligation à court terme
(GER) kurzfristige Anleihe *f*
(JAP) 短期債券、短期社債
(RUS) КРАТКОСРОЧНАЯ ОБЛИГАЦИЯ

short covering

(CHIN) 抛空补回，空头补进
(FRE) couverture de position,
(C) couverture de position à découvert
(GER) Deckungskauf *m* zum Ausgleich *n*
eines Leerverkaufs *m*
(JAP) 買戻し
(RUS) ЗАЧЕТ КОРОТКОЙ ПОЗИЦИИ
(бирж.)

shortfall

(CHIN) 不足，亏空
(FRE) insuffisance, manque, (C) manque à
gagner
(GER) Defizit *n*, Fehlbetrag *m*,
Deckungslücke *f*
(JAP) 短期投資利益
(RUS) НЕХВАТКА; НЕДОСТАТОК;
ДЕФИЦИТ

short form

(CHIN) 简式
(FRE) connaissement abrégé,
(C) formulaire abrégé
(GER) Kurzform *f*

(JAP) 短文書式、簡易型
(RUS) СОКРАЩЕННАЯ ФОРМА

short interest

(CHIN) 空头净额

(FRE) opérations à découvert, (C) nombre total d'actions vendues à découvert

(GER) Baisse-Engagement *n*, Baisse-Position *f*

(JAP) 空売り総額、空売りされたまま買い戻されていない株式

(RUS) КОРОТКАЯ ПРОДАЖА ЗАИМСТВОВАННЫХ АКЦИЙ

short position

(CHIN) 空头

(FRE) position courte, (C) position à découvert

(GER) Baisse-Position *f*, Leerverkauf-Position *f*

(JAP) ショートポジション、売持ち

(RUS) КОРОТКАЯ ПОЗИЦИЯ

short-sale rule

(CHIN) 卖空规则

(FRE) régle de la vente à découvert

(GER) Leerverkaufsregel *f*

(JAP) 空売り規定、短期見越し売却規定

(RUS) ПРАВИЛО (Комиссии по ценным бумагам и биржам), ПО КОТОРОМУ КОРОТКИЕ ПРОДАЖИ ДОПУСТИМЫ ЛИШЬ ПРИ ПОДЪЕМЕ КОНЪЮНКТУРЫ (бирж.)

short squeeze

(CHIN) 空头轧平，杀空头

(FRE) short squeeze, (C) achat couvrant la position à découvert

(GER) Zwingung *f* zum Deckungskauf *m*

(JAP) 踏み上げ

(RUS) КОРОТКОЕ СЖАТИЕ (ситуация резкого подъема цен) (бирж.)

short term

(CHIN) 短期

(FRE) court terme

(GER) kurzfristig *adj*

(JAP) 短期

(RUS) КРАТКОСРОЧНЫЙ

short-term capital gain (loss)

(CHIN) 短期资本收益 损失）

(FRE) gain (perte) de capital à court terme

(GER) Spekulationsgewinn *m* (-verlust *m*)

(JAP) 短期資本売却収益 （損失）

(RUS) КРАТКОСРОЧНАЯ КАПИТАЛЬНАЯ ПРИБЫЛЬ (УБЫТОК)

short-term debt or short-term liability

(CHIN) 短期债务 或短期负债

(FRE) dette à court terme, (C) créance à court terme, dette à court terme

(GER) kurzfristiger Schuldtitel *m* bzw. kurzfristige Verbindlichkeit *f*

(JAP) 短期国債、短期負債、短期借入金

(RUS) КРАТКОСРОЧНЫЙ ДОЛГ (до 1 года)

shrinkage

(CHIN) 价值下降，收缩，损耗

(FRE) pertes, casse, (C) resserrement du crédit

(GER) Minderung *f*, Schwund *m*, Schrumpfung *f*

(JAP) 収縮、縮小 （量）、減少

(RUS) СЖАТИЕ; СОКРАЩЕНИЕ; УСАДКА

shut down

(CHIN) 关机

(FRE) arrêt, (C) interruption de service

(GER) abschalten *v*

(JAP) 一時閉店、操業休止、（工場）閉鎖;
シャットダウン、遮断

(RUS) ОСТАНОВКА (принудительная); ПРЕКРАЩЕНИЕ; ВЫКЛЮЧЕНИЕ

shutdown

(CHIN) 停业，停工

(FRE) fermeture

(GER) Betriebsschließung *f*; Außerbetriebnahme *f*

sight draft

(CHIN) 即期汇票

(FRE) traite à vue

(GER) Sichttratte *f*, -wechsel *m*

(JAP) 一覧払為替手形

(RUS) ТРАТТА С ОПЛАТОЙ ПО ПРЕДЪЯВЛЕНИИ

sign off
(CHIN) 结束指令
(FRE) fermer une session
(GER) abmelden *v*
(JAP) サインオフ
(RUS) ВХОД В СИСТЕМУ, ЛОГОН

sign on
(CHIN) 开始指令
(FRE) ouvrir une session
(GER) anmelden *v*
(JAP) サインオン

silent partner
(CHIN) 隱名合伙人
(FRE) associé, commanditaire, bailleur de fonds, (C) associé passif
(GER) stiller Teilhaber *m*
(JAP) 匿名社員、裏参加者
(RUS) «МОЛЧАЛИВЫЙ» ПАРТНЕР (внешний пай, но не принимающий активного участия в делах товарищества)

silver standard
(CHIN) 银本位
(FRE) étalon argent, (C) norme d'argent
(GER) Silberwährung *f*
(JAP) 銀本位制
(RUS) СЕРЕБРЯНЫЙ СТАНДАРТ

SIMM (single in-line memory module)
(CHIN) SIMM (单列直插式内存模块)
(FRE) module SIMM, (C) module de mémoire à simple rangée de connexions
(GER) SIMM-Speichermodul *n* (Computer)
(JAP) SIMM、シングル・インライン・メモリーモジュール

simple interest
(CHIN) 单利
(FRE) intérêt simple
(GER) einfacher Zins *m*
(JAP) 单利
(RUS) ПРОСТЫЕ ПРОЦЕНТЫ

simple trust
(CHIN) 简单信托，单纯信托
(FRE) simple fiducie

(GER) Thesaurierungsfonds *m*, einfache Treuhandverwaltung *f*, nur Zinsen *mpl* ausschüttende Stiftung *f*
(JAP) 単純信託
(RUS) ПРОСТОЙ ТРАСТ

simple yield
(CHIN) 简单收益
(FRE) rendement simple
(GER) einfache Rendite *f*
(JAP) 単純利回り
(RUS) ПРОСТОЙ ПРОЦЕНТНЫЙ ДОХОД ПО ЦЕННЫМ БУМАГАМ

simulation
(CHIN) 模拟，模仿，仿真，伪装
(FRE) simulation
(GER) Simulation *f*
(JAP) 擬態、模擬実験、シミュレーション
(RUS) ИМИТАЦИЯ; МОДЕЛИРОВАНИЕ

single-entry bookkeeping
(CHIN) 单式簿记
(FRE) comptabilité en partie simple
(GER) einfache Buchführung *f*
(JAP) 単式簿記
(RUS) ПРОСТАЯ БУХГАЛТЕРИЯ

single premium life insurance
(CHIN) 一次性付清保费的人寿保险
(FRE) assurance vie à prime unique, (C) assurance vie à prime unique
(GER) Einmalprämienlebensversicherung *f*
(JAP) 一時払い保険料生命保険
(RUS) ПОЛИС СТРАХОВАНИЯ ЖИЗНИ С УПЛАТОЙ РАЗОВОЙ ПРЕМИИ В НАЧАЛЕ

sinking fund
(CHIN) 累积基金，偿债基金
fonds d'amortissement, caisse d'amortissement
(GER) Tilgungs- *m*, Amortisationsfonds *m*
(JAP) 減債基金、債券償還基金、負債償却積立金
(RUS) ФОНД ПОГАШЕНИЯ (ОБЛИГАЦИЙ)

site
(CHIN) 地点，现场，位置，工地

(FRE) terrain, (C) site
(GER) Standort *m*, Stelle *f*, Platz *m*;
Grundstück *n*
(JAP) 用地、現場、所在地
(RUS) УЧАСТОК; ПЛОЩАДКА; ОБЪЕКТ

site audit
(CHIN) 就地审计
(FRE) audit de site
(GER) Standortprüfung *f*
(JAP) 現場監査
(RUS) АУДИТ НА МЕСТЕ

sit-down strike
(CHIN) 闭厂停产罢工
(FRE) grève sur le tas, (C) grève à
l'italienne
(GER) Sitzstreik *m*
(JAP) 座り込みスト
(RUS) СИДЯЧАЯ ЗАБАСТОВКА

skill intensive
(CHIN) 技术密集型
(FRE) à forte demande en compétences,
(C) travail hautement spécialisé
(GER) Geschick *n* erfordernd *adj*
(JAP) 技術集約的、技術集中的
(RUS) ТРЕБУЮЩИЙ ВЫСОКИХ ЗАТРАТ
квалифицированного труда

skill obsolescence
(CHIN) 过时的技能
(FRE) obsolescence des compétences,
(C) travail désuet
(GER) Veralterung von Fähigkeiten *fpl*
(JAP) 技術老朽化
(RUS) УСТАРЕВАНИЕ НАВЫКОВ

slack
(CHIN) 萧条期，淡季，松弛的
(FRE) calme, (C) marge
(GER) Flaute *f*; Puffer *m*; Spielraum *m*
(JAP) 不振な、不景気な、不活発に
(RUS) ОСЛАБЛЕНИЕ, СОКРАЩЕНИЕ
АКТИВНОСТИ

slander
(CHIN) 诽谤，诋毁
(FRE) calomnier, diffamer
(GER) Verleumdung *f*, üble Nachrede *f*

(JAP) 中傷、名誉毀損、悪口
(RUS) УСТНАЯ КЛЕВЕТА

sleeper
(CHIN) 爆冷门的股票
(FRE) titre dormant, (C) titre oublié
(GER) Artikel *m* mit unerkanntem
Absatzpotential *n*
(JAP) スリーパー、
後にヒットする商品、大穴
(RUS) ЦЕННАЯ БУМАГА С ВЫСОКИМ
ПОТЕНЦИАЛОМ, НО НЕ
ПОЛЬЗУЮЩАЯСЯ ВЫСОКИМ
СПРОСОМ

sleeping beauty
(CHIN) 潜在收购目标
(FRE) belle endormie, (C) entreprise
susceptible de faire l'objet d'une acquisition
(GER) potentielles
Übernahmeunternehmen *n*
(JAP) 眠り姫
(RUS) «СПЯЩАЯ КРАСАВИЦА»
(потенциальный объект поглощения без
предложений)

slowdown
(CHIN) 需求下降，放慢
(FRE) grève perlée, (C) ralentissement
(GER) Verlangsamung *f*, Abschwächung *f*;
Konjunkturabkühlung *f*
(JAP) 操短、怠業
(RUS) ЗАМЕДЛЕНИЕ; СНИЖЕНИЕ
АКТИВНОСТИ

slump
(CHIN) 价格狂跌，市场萧条
(FRE) effondrement, crise
(GER) Rezession *f*, (Kurs)einbruch *m*, -
verfall *m*, Wirtschaftskrise *f*
(JAP) スランプ、暴落、景気沈滞
(RUS) ДЕПРЕССИЯ, СПАД

small business
(CHIN) 小型企业
(FRE) petite entreprise
(GER) mittel- und kleinständische
Unternehmen *npl*; Kleinbetrieb *m*
(JAP) 小企業、中小企業
(RUS) МАЛОЕ ПРЕДПРИЯТИЕ; МЕЛКИЙ
БИЗНЕС

small investor

(CHIN) 小型投资者

(FRE) petit porteur, (C) petit investisseur

(GER) Klein- *m*, Privatanleger *m*

(JAP) 小投資家、小口投資家

(RUS) МЕЛКИЙ (РОЗНИЧНЫЙ) ИНВЕСТОР

smoke clause

(CHIN) 烟雾险条款

(FRE) clause couvrant les dommages dus à la fumée

(GER) Rauchklausel *f*

(JAP) 〔保険〕煙害条項

(RUS) ПОЛОЖЕНИЕ СТРАХОВОГО ПОЛИСА ОБ УРОНЕ, НАНЕСЁННОМ ДЫМОМ

smokestack industry

(CHIN) 冒烟工业，重工业

(FRE) industrie de transformation en produits de base

(GER) Schornsteinindustrie *f*

(JAP) 煙突産業、構造不況産業、旧技術の既存産業、重厚長大型の旧式産業

(RUS) КРУПНАЯ ПРОМЫШЛЕННОСТЬ

snowballing

(CHIN) 滚雪球式业务增长

(FRE) effet boule de neige, (C) boule de neige

(GER) Lawinenartige Entwicklung *f*, Schneeballeffekt *m*

(JAP) 雪だるま式に大きくする（拡大する）

(RUS) «ЭФФЕКТ СНЕЖНОГО КОМА», БЫСТРЫЙ РОСТ ДЕЛОВОЙ АКТИВНОСТИ

social insurance

(CHIN) 社会保险

(FRE) sécurité sociale, assurance sociale

(GER) Sozialversicherung *f*

(JAP) 社会保険

(RUS) СОЦИАЛЬНОЕ СТРАХОВАНИЕ

socialism

(CHIN) 社会主义

(FRE) socialisme

(GER) Sozialismus *m*

(JAP) 社会主義

(RUS) СОЦИАЛИЗМ

socially conscious investor

(CHIN) 有社会责任感的投资者

(FRE) investisseur responsable, (C) investisseur socialement responsable

(GER) sozialverantwortlicher Anleger *m*

(JAP) 社会意識型投資家

(RUS) СОЦИАЛЬНО СОЗНАТЕЛЬНЫЙ ИНВЕСТОР

social responsibility

(CHIN) 社会责任

(FRE) responsabilité sociale

(GER) soziale Verantwortung *f*

(JAP) 社会的責任

(RUS) СОЦИАЛЬНАЯ ОТВЕТСТВЕННОСТЬ

soft currency

(CHIN) 软币，软性货币

(FRE) devise faible, monnaie faible

(GER) weiche Währung *f*

(JAP) 軟貨、弱体通貨

(RUS) СЛАБАЯ (МЯГКАЯ) ВАЛЮТА

soft goods

(CHIN) 纺织品，软货物，非耐用品

(FRE) biens non durables

(GER) kurzlebige Konsumgüter *npl*

(RUS) СЛАБО ПРОДАЮЩИЕСЯ ТОВАРЫ

soft market

(CHIN) 疲软的市场

(FRE) marché faible

(GER) rückläufig tendierender Aktienmarkt *m*

(JAP) 軟調市況

(RUS) СЛАБЫЙ (ВЯЛЫЙ) РЫНОК

soft money

(CHIN) 软币，汇票

(FRE) (C) fonds non réglementés

(GER) Banknoten *fpl*

(JAP) 軟貨、紙幣、不換紙幣、

(RUS) «МЯГКИЕ» ДЕНЬГИ (обычно, в избирательной компании без указания источников)

soft spot
(CHIN) 不景气企业
(FRE) endroit faible, (C) point faible
(GER) Schwachstelle *f*
(JAP) 弱点、不利な立場（地位、状態）
(RUS) УЯЗВИМАЯ ПОЗИЦИЯ; СЛАБОСТЬ

soil bank
(CHIN) 土地银行
(FRE) programme volontaire de
conservation des sols mis en place en 1956
(GER) Bodenreserve *f*; subventionierte
Anbaukontingentierung *f*
 (JAP) 土壤銀行
(RUS) СЕЛЬСКОХОЗЯЙСТВЕННАЯ
ПРОГРАММА ВЫПЛАТЫ ФЕРМЕРАМ
ДЕНЕГ ЗА НЕИСПОЛЬЗОВАНИЕ ЗЕМЛИ

sole proprietorship
(CHIN) 独资企业，独资经营
(FRE) entreprise individuelle
(GER) Einzelfirma *f*, -unternehmen *n*, -
inhaberschaft *f*
(JAP) 個人営業、個人店主
(RUS) ЕДИНОЛИЧНОЕ ВЛАДЕНИЕ

solvency
(CHIN) 偿付能力，支付能力
(FRE) solvabilité
(GER) Solvenz *f*, Zahlungsfähigkeit *f*,
Liquidität *f*
(JAP) 支払能力、弁済能力、資力
(RUS) ПЛАТЕЖЕСПОСОБНОСТЬ

source
(CHIN) 根据，来源，出处，
销售渠道
(FRE) source
(GER) Quelle *f*, Ursprung *m*, Herkunft *f*
(JAP) 原因、源泉、利子や配当を払う人、
資料
(RUS) ИСТОЧНИК

source evaluation
(CHIN) 销售渠道评估
(FRE) évaluation des sources
(GER) Herkunftsbewertung *f*
(JAP) 資料評価
(RUS) ОЦЕНКА ИСТОЧНИКОВ

sources of funds
(CHIN) 资金来源
(FRE) sources de fonds
(GER) Mittelherkunft *f*
(JAP) 資金源
(RUS) ИСТОЧНИКИ ФИНАНСИРОВАНИЯ

source worksheet
(CHIN) 源工作底稿，源表
(FRE) feuille de travail source, (C) feuille
de travail de la source
(GER) Ursprungstabelle *f*
(JAP) ソースワークシート
(RUS) ИНСТРУМЕНТ ОЦЕНКИ
ПОГРЕШНОСТИ ИЗМЕРЕНИЯ
ОТДЕЛЬНОЙ ВЕЛИЧИНЫ ИЛИ
ИСТОЧНИКА ОШИБКИ

sovereign risk
(CHIN) 政治风险，政府风险，
主权国风险
(FRE) risque d'insolvabilité de l'état
emprunteur
(GER) Länderrisiko *n*
(JAP) ソブリンリスク、国家主権直結機
関への信用供与リスク
(RUS) Риск отказа иностранного
правительства выполнять принятые
обязательства

space bar
(CHIN) 空格键
(FRE) barre d'espace, (C) barre
d'espacement
(GER) Leertaste *f* (Tastatur)
(JAP) スペースバー
(RUS) КЛАВИША ПРОБЕЛА

spamming
(CHIN) 滥言
(FRE) envoi a des destinataires multiples
de messages parfois publicitaires
encombrant abusivement les boites aux
lettres
(GER) Spamming *n*
(JAP) スパミング、
スパム
(RUS) РАССЫЛКА НЕВОСТРЕБОВАННЫХ
ЭЛЕКТРОННЫХ СООБЩЕНИЙ
(СПЭМ)

span of control
(CHIN) 管理幅度
(FRE) aire de contrôle
(GER) Kontrollspanne *f*; Leitungsspanne *f*
(JAP) 管理限界
(RUS) ОБЪЕМ, ДИАПАЗОН КОНТРОЛЯ

special agent
(CHIN) 特别助理，特别调查员
(FRE) agent spécial, (C) représentant spécial
(GER) Sonderbevollmächtiger *m*
(JAP) 特別捜査官、特別代理人
(RUS) АГЕНТ ПО ОСОБЫМ ПОРУЧЕНИЯМ

special assignment
(CHIN) 特别任务
(FRE) mission spéciale, (C) affectation spéciale
(GER) Sonderaufgabe *f*
(JAP) 特別任務、特別割当て、
（財産、権利などの）特別譲渡
(RUS) ОСОБОЕ ПОРУЧЕНИЕ

special delivery
(CHIN) 专递
(FRE) envoi en exprès, (C) livraison spéciale
(GER) Sonderzustellung *f*, -lieferung *f*
(JAP) 速達、速達便、速達郵便
(RUS) ДОСТАВКА НА ОСОБЫХ УСЛОВИЯХ

special drawing rights (SDR)
(CHIN) 特别提款权（SDR）
(FRE) droits de tirage spéciaux
(GER) Sonderziehungsrechte *npl*
(JAP) 特別引出権
(RUS) СПЕЦИАЛЬНЫЕ ПРАВА ЗАИМСТВОВАНИЯ (СДР) (денежная единица на основе корзины ведущих валют)

special handling
(CHIN) 特别处理服务
(FRE) opération spécifique de manutention, (C) manutention spéciale
(GER) Sonderbearbeitung *f*
(JAP) 特殊取扱い
(RUS) ОСОБОЕ ОБРАЩЕНИЕ

specialist
(CHIN) 专家，交易所经纪人
(FRE) spécialiste
(GER) Fachmann *m*, Experte *m*, Sachverständiger *m*
(JAP) 専門家、スペシャリスト
(RUS) СПЕЦИАЛИСТ

special purchase
(CHIN) 专项采购
(FRE) acquisition spéciale
(GER) Sonderkauf *m*
(JAP) 特別購入
(RUS) СПЕЦИАЛИЗИРОВАННАЯ ЗАКУПКА

special situation
(CHIN) 特殊情况
(FRE) situation spéciale
(GER) besondere Lage *f*
(JAP) 特別な状況
(RUS) ОСОБАЯ СИТУАЦИЯ; ОСОБЫЕ ОБСТОЯТЕЛЬСТВА

specialty advertising
(CHIN) 特色宣传广告
(FRE) publicité par objet
(GER) Werbung *f* für Spezialartikel *m*
(JAP) 特製品（名産品、特産品）広告、高級専門品の広告
(RUS) СПЕЦИАЛИЗИРОВАННАЯ РЕКЛАМА

specialty goods
(CHIN) 特色物品，特殊商品
(FRE) produits spécialisés, (C) produits de spécialité
(GER) Spezialprodukte *npl*
(JAP) 専門品
(RUS) СПЕЦИЛИЗИРОВАННЫЕ ТОВАРЫ

specialty retailer
(CHIN) 特色商品零售商
(FRE) détaillant spécialisé
(GER) Einzelhandel *m* für Spezialartikel *mpl*
(JAP) （特選品を扱う）専門小売店
(RUS) СПЕЦИАЛИЗИРОВАННЫЙ РОЗНИЧНЫЙ ТОРГОВЕЦ

specialty selling
(CHIN) 特色商品销售
(FRE) vente spécialisée
(GER) Verkauf *m* von Spezialartikeln *mpl*
(JAP) 特選品販売
(RUS) СПЕЦИАЛИЗИРОВАННАЯ
ПРОДАЖА

specialty shop
(CHIN) 特色商店
(FRE) magasin spécialisé, (C) boutique spécialisée
(GER) Fachgeschäft *n* für Spezialartikel *mpl*
(JAP) 専門店
(RUS) СПЕЦИАЛИЗИРОВАННЫЙ
МАГАЗИН, ЦЕХ

special-use permit
(CHIN) 专用许可证
(FRE) permis à usage spécialisé
(GER) Sondergenehmigung *f*, -erlaubnis *f*
(JAP) 特別使用許可
(RUS) РАЗРЕШЕНИЕ НА ОСОБОЕ
ПОЛЬЗОВАНИЕ

special warranty deed
(CHIN) 特别保证契约
(FRE) acte de garantie spécial, (C) garantie spéciale
(GER) Sonderbürgschafturkunde, -rechtsgarantie
(JAP) 特別権原担保捺印証書
(RUS) КУПЧАЯ С ОСОБОЙ ГАРАНТИЕЙ

specie
(CHIN) 铸币，硬币，现金
(FRE) espèces
(GER) Münz- *n*, Hartgeld *n*
(JAP) 正金、正貨
(RUS) ВИД, РАЗНОВИДНОСТЬ; МОНЕТА
ИЗ БЛАГОРОДНЫХ МЕТАЛЛОВ

specification
(CHIN) 规格，说明，技术要求
(FRE) stipulation
(GER) Spezifikation *f*
(JAP) (通常 *pl.*)仕様書、明細（書）、
特許説明書
(RUS) ТЕХНИЧЕСКИЕ УСЛОВИЯ

specific identification
(CHIN) 个别鉴定法
(FRE) identification spécifique
(GER) Sonderkennzeichnung *f*
(RUS) ИНВЕНТАРНЫЙ МЕТОД
КОНКРЕТНОГО ОБОЗНАЧЕНИЯ

specific performance
(CHIN) 个别行为
(FRE) performance spécifique,
(C) exécution en nature
(GER) spezifische Performance *f*;
spezifische Vertragserfüllung *f*
(JAP) 〔法律〕特定履行
(RUS) КОНКРЕТНЫЕ, ОСОБЫЕ
ПОКАЗАТЕЛИ

specific subsidy
(CHIN) 个别补贴
(FRE) assistance spécifique,
(C) subvention particulière
(GER) spezifische Subvention *f*;
Sondersubvention *f*
(JAP) 特定補助金
(RUS) ЦЕЛЕВАЯ СУБСИДИЯ

speculative risk
(CHIN) 投机风险
(FRE) risque spéculatif
(GER) Spekulationsrisiko *n*
(JAP) 投機的リスク
(RUS) СПЕКУЛЯТИВНЫЙ РИСК

speech recognition
(CHIN) 语音识别
(FRE) reconnaissance vocale
(GER) Spracherkennung *f*
(JAP) 音声認識
(RUS) РАСПОЗНОВАНИЕ ГОЛОСА, РЕЧИ

speedup
(CHIN) 加速
(FRE) accélération, (C) cadence infernale
(GER) Beschleunigung *f*; Steigerung *f*
(JAP) 生産増加
(RUS) УСКОРЕНИЕ

spell checker
(CHIN) 拼写检查程序
(FRE) correcteur orthographique

(GER) Rechtschreibhilfe *f* (EDV)
(JAP) スペルチェッカー
(RUS) СПЕЛЛЕР

spending money
(CHIN) 零用钱，花费
(FRE) argent de poche
(GER) frei verfügbares Geld *n*
(JAP) 小遣銭、現金
(RUS) ДЕНЬГИ НА РАСХОДЫ

spendthrift trust
(CHIN) 规定受益人不得自由处理的信托资产
(FRE) fiducie à participation, (C) fiducie insaisissable protégée
(GER) Unterhaltfonds *m*
(JAP) 消費者信託
(RUS) ТРАСТ ДЛЯ ОБЕСПЕЧЕНИЯ БЕНЕФИЦИАРИЯ С ГАРАНТИЕЙ ПРОТИВ НЕРАЗУМНОГО ИСПОЛЬЗОВАНИЯ СРЕДСТВ

spider chart
(CHIN) 蛛网图
(FRE) graphique en toile d'araignce
(GER) Spinnendiagramm *n*
(JAP) スパイダー図表

spillover
(CHIN) 溢出，溢出物
(FRE) déversement, (C) retombées
(GER) Anschlussverkäufe *pl* (Börse); Nebenwirkung *f*; Überlauf *m* (EDV)
(JAP) あふれること、過剰、豊富
(RUS) ВЛИЯНИЕ ЭКОНОМИЧЕСКОЙ ДЕЯТЕЛЬНОСТИ НА НЕУЧАСТВУЮЩИХ В НЕЙ СУБЪЕКТОВ

spin-off
(CHIN) 母公司收回子公司全部股本使之脱离的作法，让产易股，折产为投
(FRE) produit dérivé, retombée, (C) essaimage
(GER) Nebenprodukt *n*, -ergebnis *n*; Ausgliederung *f*, Ausgründung *f*, Firmcnableger *m*
(JAP) スピンオフ、副産物

(RUS) СПИН-ОФ, СОЗДАНИЕ НОВОЙ КОМПАНИИ НА ОСНОВЕ СТРУКТУРНОГО ПОДРАЗДЕЛЕНИЯ СТАРОЙ КОМПАНИИ

splintered authority
(CHIN) 意见纷纭的管理机关
(FRE) autorité fractionnée, (C) autorité divisée
(GER) Splitterbehörde *f*
(JAP) 分裂した権威
(RUS) РАЗДЕЛЁННЫЕ ПОЛНОМОЧИЯ

split
(CHIN) 分割，分摊，分股
(FRE) division fractionnement
(GER) (Aktien)split *m*; Spaltung *f*, Teilung *f*, Split *m*
(JAP) 分割する、分配する、分割、分裂
(RUS) СПЛИТ, РАЗБИВКА АКЦИЙ НА НЕСКОЛЬКО БУМАГ (с меньшим номиналом)

split commission
(CHIN) 佣金平分
(FRE) commission fractionnéecommission partagée
(GER) geteilte Provision *f*
(JAP) 分割手数料
(RUS) КОМИССИОННЫЕ, ПОДЕЛЕННЫЕ МЕЖДУ ДВУМЯ БРОКЕРАМИ

split shift
(CHIN) 间断工时
(FRE) poste fractionné
(GER) geteilte Schicht *f*
(JAP) 分割勤務、分割シフト
(RUS) РАЗБИТАЯ РАБОЧАЯ СМЕНА

spokesperson
(CHIN) 发言人
(FRE) porte-parole
(GER) Sprecher *m*
(JAP) 代弁者、スポークスパーソン
(RUS) ПРЕСС-СЕКРЕТАРЬ (для общения со СМИ)

sponsor
(CHIN) 保证人，担保人，主持人，主办人
(FRE) sponsor, (C) commanditaire

(GER) Sponsor *m*; Bürge *m*; Schirmherr *m*
(JAP) スポンサー、出資者、保証人、
出資する
(RUS) СПОНСОР

spot check
(CHIN) 抽样，抽查，现场检查
(FRE) contrôle ponctuel, contrôle par
sondage, (C) vérification faite à intervalles
réguliers, (C) sondage au hasard
(GER) Stichprobe *f*, unerwartete
Kassenprüfung *f*
(JAP) 無作為抽出検査、抜き打ち検査
(RUS) ЧЕК «СПОТ» (с немедленной наличной
оплатой)

spot commodity
(CHIN) 现货，现货商品
(FRE) contrat au comptant
(GER) Lokoware *f*, Kassaware *f*
(JAP) スポット商品、現物商品、
直物商品
(RUS) ФИЗИЧЕСКИЙ (НАЛИЧНЫЙ) ТОВАР
(на товарной бирже)

spot delivery month
(CHIN) 当场交货月份
(FRE) mois de livraison immédiate
(GER) sofortiger Lieferungsmonat *m*
(JAP) 現場渡し（現物渡し、直渡し）
限月
(RUS) БЛИЖАЙШИЙ МЕСЯЦ ПОСТАВКИ
(в торговле на товарной бирже)

spot market
(CHIN) 现货交易市场
(FRE) marché au comptant, (C) marché
instantané
(GER) Lokomarkt *m*, Kassamarkt *m*,
Barverkehrs- *m*, Kassahandel *m*
(JAP) 現金取引市場、現物市場、
スポット市場
(RUS) РЫНОК «СПОТ», РЫНОК
НАЛИЧНОСТИ

spot price
(CHIN) 现货价格
(FRE) prix au comptant
(GER) Kassakurs *m*, Loko- *m*, Kassapreis *m*
(JAP) スポット価格、現物価格

(RUS) НАЛИЧНАЯ ЦЕНА

spot zoning
(CHIN) 现场土地重划
(FRE) ciblage d'un terrain, (C) zonage
individuel
(GER) Baudispens *m*,
Bauausnahmegenehmigung *f*
(JAP) スポット地帯制（地域制、
区域制）
(RUS) ЗОНИРОВАНИЕ ПО ОТДЕЛЬНЫМ
КЛАССАМ УЧАСТКОВ

spread
(CHIN) 分录过账，赢利，差幅，跨栏目
广告
(FRE) différence, écart
(GER) Spanne *f*, Differenz *f*, Marge *f*,
Aufschlag *m*; Bandbreite *f*,
Schwankungsbreite *f*, Streuung *f*; Stellage *f*,
Stellgeschäft *n*
(JAP) 広がり、マージン、値開き
(RUS) СПРЕД – РАЗНИЦА МЕЖДУ
ЦЕНАМИ, КУРСАМИ, СТАВКАМ; МАРЖА

spreading agreement
(CHIN) 分散担保协议
(FRE) accord d'élargissement
(GER) Spreading-Vereinbarung *f*
(JAP) 抵当権追加設定契約
(RUS) ДОГОВОР УВЕЛИЧЕНИЯ ЗАЛОГА

spread sheet
(CHIN) 电子表格
(FRE) feuille de calcul, tableur
(GER) Kalkulationstabelle *f* (EDV)
(JAP) スプレッドシート
(RUS) ЭЛЕКТРОННАЯ ТАБЛИЦА

squatter's rights
(CHIN) 斯夸特权利
(FRE) droits des squatters, (C) droits des
squatteurs
(GER) Ersitzungsrechte *npl*
(JAP) 不法占拠者の権利、（土地）
占有者の権利
(RUS) ПОЛУЧЕНИЕ ПРАВОВОГО ТИТУЛА
НА ИСПОЛЬЗУЕМУЮ ЗЕМЛЮ ЧЕРЕЗ
ОПРЕДЕЛЕННЫЙ СРОК
(при соблюдении оговоренных
условий)

squeeze

(CHIN) 压榨，挤兑，剥削，回扣，使缩减，夹回

(FRE) resserrement, (C) resserrement de crédit, (C) tableau à colonnes empilées

(GER) Geldknappheit *f*, Liquiditätsmangel *m*; Engpass *m*, Klemme *f*

(JAP) 絞めつける、不正手数料、収賄

(RUS) ТЯЖЕЛОЕ ПОЛОЖЕНИЕ

stabilization

(CHIN) 稳定，稳定作用，安全

(FRE) stabilisation

(GER) Sabilisierung *f*

(JAP) 安定、安定させること、安定化

(RUS) СТАБИЛИЗАЦИЯ

stacked column chart

(CHIN) 堆积柱形图

(FRE) diagramme a colonnes cumulées

(GER) gestapeltes Säulendiagramm *n*

(JAP) スタックカラム図表、連続カラム図表

(RUS) СТЕКОВАЯ СТОЛБИКОВАЯ ДИАГРАММА

staggered election

(CHIN) 交错选举

(FRE) élection décalée, (C) élection étalée

(GER) gestaffelte Wahl *f*

(JAP) ずらし任期選挙、期差任期選挙

(RUS) МНОГОСТАДИЙНЫЕ ВЫБОРЫ

staggering maturities

(CHIN) 证券交错到期

(FRE) étalement des échéances, (C) échéances étalées

(GER) Fälligkeitenstaffelung *f*

(JAP) 満期分散

(RUS) ДИВЕРСИФИКАЦИЯ ОБЛИГАЦИОННОГО ПОРТФЕЛЯ ПО СРОКАМ

stagnation

(CHIN) 停滞，萧条，不景气

(FRE) stagnation

(GER) Stagnation *f*, Flaute *f*

(JAP) 停滞、不景気、不振

(RUS) ЗАСТОЙ

stake

(CHIN) 投机股本

(FRE) part, participation, (C) enjeu

(GER) Beteiligung *f*, Einlage *f*, Stake *m*

(JAP) 賭け金、（金銭上、仕事上の）利害関係、関与

(RUS) СТАВКА; «ЗАСТОЛБИТЬ»

stand-alone system

(CHIN) 独立系统

(FRE) système autonome, (C) système indépendant

(GER) separates System *n*, Stand-Alone-System *n*

(JAP) 独立制度、無比のシステム

(RUS) АВТОНОМНАЯ СИСТЕМА

standard

(CHIN) 标准，规则，定额，本位

(FRE) standard, norme, niveau

(GER) Standard *m*, Norm *f*, Maßstab *m*, Richtwert *m*

(JAP) 基準、規範、標準規格品

(RUS) СТАНДАРТ; НОРМА; СТАНДАРТНЫЙ; ОБЩЕПРИНЯТЫЙ

standard cost

(CHIN) 标准成本

(FRE) coût standard

(GER) Standard- *pl*, Plan- *pl*, Richtkosten *pl*

(JAP) 標準原価

(RUS) СТАНДАРТНАЯ СТОИМОСТЬ

standard deduction

(CHIN) 标准扣除额

(FRE) déduction standard, (C) déduction forfaitaire

(GER) Freibetrag *m*, (Pauschalbeträge für bestimmte Aufwendungen des US-Steuerpflichtigen)

(JAP) 標準控除

(RUS) СТАНДАРТНЫЕ СУММЫ ДОХОДА, НЕ ОБЛАГАЕМЫЕ НАЛОГОМ

standard deviation

(CHIN) 标准偏差

(FRE) déviation standard, (C) écart-type empirique

(GER) Normalabweichung *f*, mittlere quadratische Abweichung *f*
(JAP) 標準偏差
(RUS) СТАНДАРТНОЕ ОТКЛОНЕНИЕ

standard industrial classification (SIC) system
(CHIN) 标准产业分类（SIC）系统
(FRE) système de classification type des industries, (C) système de classement industriel normalisé
(GER) SIC, Branchenklassifikation *f*
(JAP) 標準産業分類制度
(RUS) СИСТЕМА СТАНДАРТНОЙ ПРОМЫШЛЕННОЙ КЛАССИФИКАЦИИ

standard of living
(CHIN) 生活水准
(FRE) niveau de vie
(GER) Lebensstandard *m*
(JAP) 生活水準
(RUS) ЖИЗНЕННЫЙ УРОВЕНЬ

standard time
(CHIN) 标准时间
(FRE) temps de référence, (C) heure normale
(GER) Vorgabe- *f*, Normal- *f*, Standardzeit *f*
(JAP) 標準時、標準時間
(RUS) СТАНДАРТНОЕ (ПОЯСНОЕ) ВРЕМЯ

standard wage rate
(CHIN) 标准工资率
(FRE) salaire standard, (C) taux de salaire standard
(GER) Normallohn *m*, Tariflohn(satz) *m*
(JAP) 標準賃金率
(RUS) СТАНДАРТНАЯ СТАВКА ЗАРАБОТНОЙ ПЛАТЫ

standby
(CHIN) 备用，辅助
(FRE) veille, (C) attente
(GER) In Bereitschaft *f*; einsatzbereit *adj*
(JAP) スタンドバイ、代替物、交代要員
(RUS) РЕЗЕРВИРОВАНИЕ

standby fee
(CHIN) 候补押金

(FRE) frais de mise en attente, (C) commission de confirmation
(GER) Bereitstellungsgebühr *f*
(JAP) 代替物料金、交替要員手数料、キャンセル待ち料金
(RUS) ПЛАТА ЗА РЕЗЕРВИРОВАНИЕ КРЕДИТА

standby loan
(CHIN) 备用贷款
(FRE) prêt conditionnel, (C) prêt à modalités déterminées
(GER) Kreditbereitstellung *f*
(JAP) 準備融資
(RUS) РЕЗЕРВНЫЙ (ГАРАНТИРОВАННЫЙ) ЗАЕМ, КРЕДИТ

standing order
(CHIN) 标准定单
(FRE) virement automatique, (C) office
(GER) Dauerauftrag *m*; Zahlungsauftrag *m*
(JAP) 継続注文、継続指図書
(RUS) ПОСТОЯННОЕ ПОРУЧЕНИЕ

staple stock
(CHIN) 大路货，大宗货物
(FRE) actions de base, (C) stock constant
(GER) Stapelware *f*
(JAP) 主要株式
(RUS) ЗАПАС ОСНОВНЫХ ТОВАРОВ

start-up
(CHIN) 新创企业
(FRE) start-up, (C) entreprise en démarrage
(GER) Neugründung *f*, Jungunternehmen *n*; Inbetriebnahme *f*; Anlaufzeit *f*; Wiederanlauf *m*
(JAP) 運転（活動、操業）開始、運転始動、新規事業開始の
(RUS) ПУСК (в эксплуатацию); СОЗДАНИЕ (новой компании)

start-up screen
(CHIN) 启动屏幕
(FRE) ecran de demarrage
(GER) Einschalt-Bildschirm *m* (Computer)
(JAP) スタートアップスクリーン、始動画面
(RUS) УСТАНОВОЧНЫЙ ЭКРАН

stated value

(CHIN) 设定价值

(FRE) valeur fixée, (C) valeur attribuée

(GER) Bilanz- *m*, Nennwert *m*, ausgewiesener Wert *m* nennwertloser Aktien *pl*

(JAP) 表示価格、表記価格

(RUS) ОБЪЯВЛЕННАЯ СТОИМОСТЬ АКЦИИ

statement

(CHIN) 账单，报表，财务报告，清账，陈述

(FRE) exposé, compte-rendu, communiqué, (C) énoncé, (C) bilan

(GER) Kontoauszug *m*; Aussage *f*, Erklärung *f*, Mitteilung *f*, Verlautbarung *f*; Bilanz *f*, Aufstellung *f*; Angabe *f*, Darstellung *f*

(JAP) 声明、申告、計算書

(RUS) ЗАЯВЛЕНИЕ; ОТЧЕТ; СПРАВКА

statement of affairs

(CHIN) 业务报告，财产状况说明书

(FRE) bilan de liquidation

(GER) Konkurs- *f*, Liquidationsbilanz *f*, Vermögensaufstellung *f*

(JAP) 業績報告書、資産負債表

(RUS) ОТЧЕТ О СОСТОЯНИИ ДЕЛ

statement of condition

(CHIN) 状况表，借贷对照表

(FRE) relevé des conditions, (C) bilan

(GER) Bank- *f*, Tagesbilanz *f*, Tagesbericht *m*

(JAP) 貸借対照表、~条件の明示、営業報告書

(RUS) ДОКУМЕНТ О ФИНАНСОВОМ СОСТОЯНИИ (банка, компании)

statement of partners' capital

(CHIN) 合伙人资金报表

(FRE) état du capital des partenaires, (C) bilan de l'actif net des associés

(GER) Aufstellung *f* der Partnereinlagen *fpl*

(JAP) パートナーの資本計算書

(RUS) ОБЪЯВЛЕННЫЙ КАПИТАЛ ПАРТНЕРОВ

static anaylsis

(CHIN) 静态分析

(FRE) analyse statique

(GER) statische Analyse *f*

(JAP) 静態分析、静学分析

(RUS) СТАТИЧЕСКИЙ АНАЛИЗ

static budget

(CHIN) 静态预算

(FRE) budget statique

(GER) starres Budget *n*

(JAP) 静態予算

(RUS) «СТАТИЧНЫЙ» БЮДЖЕТ

static risk

(CHIN) 固定风险

(FRE) risque statique

(GER) statisches Risiko *n*

(JAP) 静態的リスク

(RUS) «СТАТИЧНЫЙ» РИСК

statistic

(CHIN) 统计的，统计学的

(FRE) statistique

(GER) Statistik *f*

(JAP) 統計の、統計的の、統計値

(RUS) СТАТИСТИЧЕСКИЙ

statistical inference

(CHIN) 统计性推论

(FRE) inférence statistique, induction statistique

(GER) statistische Inferenz *f*, statistisches Schließen *n*, statistische Kausalforschung *f*

(JAP) 推測統計、統計的推論、統計的推理

(RUS) ВЫВОДЫ ИЗ СТАТИСТИКИ

statistically significant

(CHIN) 有统计学意义的

(FRE) significatif, significatif statistiquement

(GER) von statistischer Bedeutung *f*

(JAP) 統計的に重要な

(RUS) СТАТИСТИЧЕСКАЯ ЗНАЧИМОСТЬ

statistical sampling

(CHIN) 统计抽样

(FRE) échantillonnage statistique

(GER) statistisches Stichprobenverfahren *n*
(JAP) 統計（的）標本抽出
(RUS) СТАТИСТИЧЕСКАЯ ВЫБОРКА

statistics

(CHIN) 统计，统计学
(FRE) statistique, statistiques
(GER) Statistik *f*; Statistiken *fpl*,
Erhebungen *fpl*; statistische Daten *pl*
(JAP) 統計学、統計、統計表
(RUS) СТАТИСТИКА: ОТЧЕТНОСТЬ

status

(CHIN) 效力，情况，地位，资格
(FRE) position, statut, (C) état
(GER) Status *m*, Lage *f*, Zustand *m*; soziale
Stellung *f*, Rang *m*
(JAP) 地位、資格、情勢
(RUS) СТАТУС; СОСТОЯНИЕ (гражданское)

status bar

(CHIN) 状态栏
(FRE) barre d'état
(GER) Statuszeile *f*, -leiste *f*
(JAP) ステータスバー
(RUS) СТАТУСНАЯ ЛИНЕЙКА

status symbol

(CHIN) 地位标志
(FRE) symbole social
(GER) Statussymbol *n*
(JAP) 地位の象徴、身分の象徴、
権威の象徴
(RUS) СИМВОЛ, ПРИЗНАК
СТАТУСА

statute

(CHIN) 章程，法规，条例
(FRE) loi, ordonnance
(GER) Gesetz *n*, Gesetzesvorschrift *f*;
Satzung *f*, Statut *n*
(JAP) 制定法、法令、規則
(RUS) СТАТУТ (международный); ЗАКОН;
УСТАВ

statute of frauds

(CHIN) 反欺骗法
(FRE) loi « statute of frauds », (C) loi sur
les contrats écrits

(GER) Gesetz *n* zur Vermeidung *f* von
Arglist *f* und Betrug *m*
(JAP) 詐欺防止法
(RUS) ЗАКОН О ПОДСУДНОСТИ ИСКОВ
ПО ОПРЕДЕЛЕННЫМ ВИДАМ
ДОГОВОРОВ

statute of limitations

(CHIN) 法定追索期限，诉讼时效法
(FRE) prescription, (C) délai de
prescription
(GER) Verjährungsfrist *f*
(JAP) 出訴期限法
(RUS) ЗАКОН ОБ ИСКОВОЙ ДАВНОСТИ

statutory audit

(CHIN) 法定审计
(FRE) contrôle légal des comptes,
(C) vérification légale
(GER) Pflichtprüfung *f*, vorgeschriebene
Abschlussprüfung *f*
(JAP) 法定監査
(RUS) ОБЯЗАТЕЛЬНЫЙ (по закону) АУДИТ

statutory merger

(CHIN) 法定合并
(FRE) fusion en vertu d'une loi, (C) fusion
légale
(GER) gesetzliche Fusion *f*
(JAP) 法定合併
(RUS) ОБЯЗАТЕЛЬНОЕ (по закону)
СЛИЯНИЕ

statutory notice

(CHIN) 法定通知
(FRE) loi codifiée, (C) avis
légal
(GER) gesetzliche Kündigungsfrist *f*
(JAP) 法定通知期間
(RUS) ОБЯЗАТЕЛЬНОЕ (по закону)
ИЗВЕЩЕНИЕ, УВЕДОМЛЕНИЕ

statutory voting

(CHIN) 法定投票
(FRE) système légal d'élection, (C) vote
cumulatif
(GER) gesetzesmäßige Stimmenabgabe *f*
(JAP) 法定投票
(RUS) ОБЯЗАТЕЛЬНОЕ
ГОЛОСОВАНИЕ

staying power

(CHIN) 持久力，耐久性

(FRE) résistance

(GER) Ausdauer *f*, Durchstehvermögen *n*, Standfestigkeit *f*

(JAP) 持久力、耐久力、スタミナ

(RUS) «ВЫНОСЛИВОСТЬ» инвестора

steady-growth method

(CHIN) 均衡增长法

(FRE) méthode de croissance continue, (C) méthode de la croissance constante

(GER) Methode *f* stetigen Wachstums *n*

(JAP) 恒常的成長模型、均衡成長模型

(RUS) МЕТОД УСТОЙЧИВОГО РОСТА

steering

(CHIN) 非法限制某一族裔团体获得住房

(FRE) ségrégation résidentielle ethnique, (C) discrimination locative

(GER) Lenkung *f*, Steuerung *f*

(JAP) かじをとる、操縦する、導く

(RUS) НАПРАВЛЕНИЕ; УПРАВЛЕНИЕ

stepped-up basis

(CHIN) 税基上调

(FRE) base verticale

(GER) Erhöhte Grundlage *f*

(JAP) 漸増した基準、向上した基準 （標準）

(RUS) СТУПЕНЧАТАЯ ОСНОВА

stipend, stipendiary

(CHIN) 薪水，定期生活津贴

(FRE) traitement, appointements, rémunéré, (C) personne qui reçoit une rémunération

(GER) Stipendium *n* ; Stipendiat(in) *m/f*

(JAP) 固定給、俸給、定期的な支払金

(RUS) СТИПЕНДИЯ; ЖАЛОВАНИЕ; РЕГУЛЯРНО ВЫПЛАЧИВАЕМЫЙ

stipulation

(CHIN) 规定，条款，条件

(GER) Vertragsbestimmung *f*, Abmachung *f*, Klausel *f*, Vereinbarung *f*, Verpflichtung *f*, Bedingung *f*, Auflage *f*, Vorschrift *f*

(JAP) 合意、条項、約定

(RUS) УСЛОВИЕ ДОГОВОРА, КОНТРАКТА

stochastic

(CHIN) 随机的

(FRE) stochastique

(GER) Wahrscheinlichkeits-; stochastisch, zufällig *adj*

(JAP) 確立的な、確立論的な

(RUS) СТОХАСТИЧЕСКИЙ

stock

(CHIN) 股份，股票，证券，库存，存料

(FRE) action, stock, (C) titre

(GER) Aktie *f*, Wertpapier *n*; Aktienkapital *n*; Vorräte *mpl*, Lager- *npl*, Warenbestände *mpl*

(JAP) 株式、株式資本、在庫品

(RUS) АКЦИИ; ЦЕННЫЕ БУМАГИ; ЗАПАСЫ; ЗАПАСАТЬ

stockbroker

(CHIN) 股票经纪人

(FRE) agent de change, société de bourse, (C) courtier en valeurs mobilières

(GER) Wertpapier- *m*, Effekten-*m*, Börsenmakler *m*, Wertpapier- *m*, Effektenhändler *m*

(JAP) 株式仲買人

(RUS) ФОНДОВЫЙ БРОКЕР

stock certificate

(CHIN) 股票，股权证

(FRE) titre, (C) certificat d'action

(GER) Aktienzertifikat *n*, -schein *m*, -urkunde *f*

(JAP) 株券、株式証券

(RUS) ДОКУМЕНТ, ПОДТВЕРЖДАЮЩИЙ ДЕПОНИРОВАНИЕ АКЦИЙ

stock dividend

(CHIN) 股息，股利

(FRE) dividende en action

(GER) Dividende *f* in Form *f* von Aktien *fpl*, Kapitalbonus *m*, Kapitalprämie *f*, Zusatzaktie *f*

(JAP) 株式配当

(RUS) ДИВИДЕНД ПО АКЦИЯМ

stock exchange

(CHIN) 股票交易所，证券交易

(FRE) bourse

(GER) Wertpapier- *f*, Effektenbörse *f*

397

(JAP) 株式取引所、証券取引所、
株式取引
(RUS) ФОНДОВАЯ БИРЖА

stockholder
(CHIN) 股东
(FRE) actionnaire
(GER) Aktionär *m*, Anteilsinhaber *m*,
Aktienbesitzer *m*; Grossist *m*, Lagerhalter *m*
(JAP) 株主、家畜所有者
(RUS) АКЦИОНЕР

stockholder of record
(CHIN) 注册股东
(FRE) actionnaire enregistré,
(C) actionnaire nominatif
(GER) eingetragener Aktionär *m*,
Namensaktionär *m*, Inhaber *m* von
Namensaktien *fpl*
(JAP) 登録株主
(RUS) ЗАРЕГИСТРИРОВАННЫЙ
АКЦИОНЕР

stockholder's derivative action
(CHIN) 股东派生诉讼
(FRE) action oblique de l'actionnaire,
(C) action en justice intentée par un
actionnaire
(GER) Aktionärsklage *f*
(JAP) 株主代表訴訟
(RUS) СУДЕБНЫЙ ИСК АКЦИОНЕРОВ,
ПОДДАННЫЙ ИМИ ОТ ЛИЦА
КОРПОРАЦИИ ПРОТИВ СУБЪЕКТОВ,
НАНЁСШИХ УРОН КОРПОРАЦИИ

stockholder's equity
(CHIN) 股东股本
(FRE) capitaux propres, fonds propres,
avoir des actionnaires
(GER) Eigenkapital *n*; Aktien- *n*,
Anteilskapital *n*
(JAP) 株主持分、自己資本、
純資産、
(RUS) СРЕДСТВА АКЦИОНЕРОВ
КОМПАНИИ

stock index future
(CHIN) 股票指数期货
(FRE) contrat financier à terme sur indice
boursier

(GER) Aktien- *m*,
Effektenindexterminkontrakt *m*
(JAP) 株価指数先物
(RUS) ФЬЮЧЕРСКИЙ КОНТРАКТ НА
ОСНОВЕ ФОНДОВЫХ ИНДЕКСОВ

stock insurance company
(CHIN) 股票保险公司
(FRE) société d'assurance par actions
(GER) Versicherungsaktiengesellschaft *f*
(JAP) 株式保険会社
(RUS) АКЦИОНЕРНАЯ СТРАХОВАЯ
КОМПАНИЯ

stock jobbing
(CHIN) 证券批发
(FRE) agiotage
(GER) Agio- *n*, Effektengeschäft *n*,
Spekulationsgeschäft *n*, Aktienspekulation *f*
(JAP) 株の仲買
(RUS) ПРОВЕДЕНИЕ СДЕЛКОК С
ЦЕННЫМИ БУМАГАМИ

stock ledger
(CHIN) 股东名册，存货分类账
(FRE) liste d'actionnaires
(GER) Aktienbuch *n*, Aktien- *n*,
Aktionärsverzeichnis *n*; Lagerbuch *n*
(RUS) КНИГА УЧЕТА АКЦИЙ

stock market
(CHIN) 股市，证券市场
(FRE) marché boursier
(GER) Aktien- *m*, Wertpapier- *m*,
Effektenmarkt *m*
(JAP) 株式市場、株式取引所、株式市況
(RUS) ФОНДОВЫЙ РЫНОК

stock option
(CHIN) 认股权，股票购买权
(FRE) stock-option, option sur titre,
(C) option d'achat d'action
(GER) Aktienoption *f*, Aktienbezugsrecht *n*
(JAP) 自社株購入権、社員持ち株制度、
ストックオプション
(RUS) ПРАВО НА ПОЛУЧЕНИЕ, ВЫКУП
АКЦИЙ; ФОНДОВЫЙ ОПЦИОН

stockout cost
(CHIN) 缺货成本

(FRE) coût de rupture, coût de rupture de stock
(GER) Fehlmengenkosten *pl*
(JAP) 品切れ損失
(RUS) ИЗДЕРЖКИ ИСТОЩЕНИЯ ЗАПАСОВ

stockpile

(CHIN) 储存，囤储
(FRE) dépôt, réserves
(GER) Vorrat *m*, Reserve *f*, Lagerbestand *m*
(JAP) 備蓄、貯蔵（する）
(RUS) НАКАПЛИВАТЬ; КОПИТЬ

stock power

(CHIN) 股票转让授权书
(FRE) pouvoir pour le transfert et la vente d'actions
(GER) Vollmacht *f* zur Übertragung *f* von Aktien *fpl*
(JAP) 株式名義書換委任状、
株式譲渡委任状
(RUS) ДОВЕРЕННОСТЬ НА ПЕРЕДАЧУ ПРАВ СОБСТВЕННОСТИ НА ЦЕННУЮ БУМАГУ

stock record

(CHIN) 股票记录
(FRE) comptabilité-matière, (C) fiche de stock
(GER) Aktienregister *n*, -kurszettel *m*
(JAP) 株式元帳、在庫記録
(RUS) ДОКУМЕНТ УЧЕТА АКЦИЙ

stockroom

(CHIN) 商品陈列室，商品储藏室
(FRE) dépôt, entrepôt, magasin
(GER) Lager *n*, Lager- *m*, Vorratsraum *m*
(JAP) 貯蔵室、商品見本展示室、倉庫
(RUS) СКЛАД; ХРАНИЛИЩЕ

stock symbol

(CHIN) 股票代号
(FRE) symbole de téléscripteur
(GER) Aktiensymbol *n*
(JAP) 株式銘柄
(RUS) СТАНДАРТНЫЙ СИМВОЛ ЦЕННОЙ БУМАГИ

stock turnover

(CHIN) 存货周转率，证券交易额

(FRE) mouvement des stocks, rotation des stocks
(GER) Lagerumschlag *m*, Umschlagsgeschwindigkeit *f*
(JAP) 在庫品回転率、商品回転率
(RUS) ОБОРОТ МАТЕРИАЛЬНЫХ ЗАПАСОВ

stonewalling

(CHIN) 拒绝承认，拒绝合作
(FRE) obstructionnisme, (C) refus de coopérer
(GER) Obstruktionspolitik betreiben *v*
(JAP) 議事妨害、（調査、投票などを）意識的に妨害すること、強固な拒否
(RUS) ОТМАЛЧИВАНИЕ; ИСКУССТВЕННАЯ ЗАДЕРЖКА; ЗАТЯГИВАНИЕ

stool pigeon

(CHIN) 间谍，线人
(FRE) mouchard, (C) indicateur, (C) délateur
(GER) Lockvogel *m*, Köder *m*
(JAP) おとりに使うハト、（警察の）スパイ、おとり
(RUS) ДОНОЩИК; «СТУКАЧ»

stop clause

(CHIN) 终止合同条款
(FRE) clause d'arrêt, (C) clause de variation de prix
(GER) Schwellenklausel *f*
(JAP) （契約の）終止条項
(RUS) ПРИ ЛИЗИНГЕ, УРОВЕНЬ ОПЕРАЦИОННЫХ РАСХОДОВ, ПРИ КОТОРОМ АРЕНДАТОР ДОЛЖЕН БРАТЬ НА СЕБЯ ИХ ОПЛАТУ

stop-loss reinsurance

(CHIN) 停止损失再保险
(FRE) réassurance de vente stop, (C) réassurance en excédent de pourcentage de sinistres
(GER) Jahresüberschadenrück-versicherung *f*, Gesamtschadenexzeden-tenversicherung *f*
(JAP) 超過損害再保険
(RUS) ПЕРЕСТРАХОВКА УБЫТКОВ СВЕРХ ОГОВОРЕННОЙ СУММЫ

stop order

(CHIN) 预定低点抛售，限额定单，
中止命令

(FRE) ordre stop, (C) interdiction
d'opérations sur valeurs

(GER) Schecksperre *f*, Sperre *f* einer
Aktienemission *f*; Stop-Order *f*

(JAP) 逆指値注文、差止め命令、
取引停止命令

(RUS) ПРИКАЗ «СТОП» (приказ продавать
или покупать по достижении ценой
определенного уровня)

stop payment

(CHIN) 止付，停付

(FRE) opposition, (C) faire opposition à un
chèque

(GER) Zahlungssperre *f*,
Auszahlungsverbot *n*, Zahlung *f* einstellen *v*

(JAP) 支払停止指図、支払いを停止する

(RUS) ПРИКАЗ БАНКУ (ОТ ЛИЦА
ВЫПИСАВШЕГО ЧЕК) НЕ СОВЕРШАТЬ
ПЛАТЁЖ ПО ЧЕКУ

store

(CHIN) 货仓，储存，商店

(FRE) , provision, réserve, magasin

(GER) Geschäft *n*, Laden *m*

(JAP) 商店、貯える、保管する

(RUS) МАГАЗИН; СКЛАД;
ХРАНИТЬ

store brand

(CHIN) 商店自名产品

(FRE) marque de magasin, (C) marque de
distributeur

(GER) Hausmarke *f*

(JAP) 自社ブランド、
ストアブランド商品

(RUS) ТОВАРНАЯ МАРКА

straddle

(CHIN) 限价套利，股票买卖选择权

(FRE) ordre lié, (C) option double

(GER) Straddle *m*, Stellagegeschäft *n*

(JAP) またぐ、複合オプション、
複合選択付き取引

(RUS) «СТРЭДДЛ», СДЕЛКА с
одновременной покупкой и продажей одного
и того же товара (БИРЖ.)

straight bill of lading

(CHIN) 直接提单，记名提单

(FRE) connaissement nominatif,
(C) connaissement direct

(GER) Namenskonnossement *n*,
Rektakonnossement *n*, nicht übertragbarer
Ladeschein *m*

(JAP) 記名式船荷証券、
記名式積み荷証券

(RUS) ПРЯМОЙ КОНОСАМЕНТ

straight-line method of depreciation

(CHIN) 直线折旧法，平均折旧法

(FRE) méthode d'amortissement linéaire

(GER) lineare Abschreibung *f*

(JAP) 直線法式減価償却、
定額法式減価償却

(RUS) МЕТОД УЧЕТА ОБЫЧНОЙ (НЕ
УСКОРЕННОЙ) АМОРТИЗАЦИИ

straight-line production

(CHIN) 直线生产

(FRE) production linéaire

(GER) gleichbleibende Produktion *f*

(JAP) 直線法式生産高

(RUS) КОНВЕЕРНОЕ ПРОИЗВОДСТВО

straight time

(CHIN) 单纯记时

(FRE) plein temps

(GER) normale Arbeitszeit *f*

(JAP) 正規就業時間

(RUS) УРОЧНОЕ ВРЕМЯ

straphanger

(CHIN) 拉着吊环站立的乘客，
乘车上下班的人

(FRE) voyageur debout

(GER) Stehplatzinhaber *m*

(JAP) つり革につかまっている乗客
（通勤客）

(RUS) ЛИЦО, ПОЛЬЗУЮЩЕЕСЯ
ОБЩЕСТВЕННЫМ ТРАНСПОРТОМ
(ОСОБЕННО СТОЯ)

strategic planning

(CHIN) 战略规划

(FRE) planification stratégique

(GER) strategische Planung *f*

(JAP) 戦略計画
(RUS) СТРАТЕГИЧЕСКОЕ
ПЛАНИРОВАНИЕ

strategy
(CHIN) 战略，策略
(FRE) stratégie
(GER) Strategic *f*, Politik *f*
(JAP) 戦略、策略、計画
(RUS) СТРАТЕГИЯ

stratified random sampling
(CHIN) 分层随机抽样
(FRE) échantillonnage aléatoire stratifié
(GER) geschichtete Zufallsprobennahme *f*
(JAP) 層化任意抽出
(RUS) РАССЛОЕННАЯ ПРОИЗВОЛЬНАЯ
ВЫБОРКА

straw boss
(CHIN) 临时领导
(FRE) chef d'équipe
(GER) Pro-Forma-Vorgesetzter *m*
(JAP) 職長代理、監督代行者
(RUS) ЗАМЕСТИТЕЛЬ МАСТЕРА;
БРИГАДИР

straw man
(CHIN) 稻草人，假想敌，身无分文的人
(FRE) prête-nom
(GER) Strohmann *m*, Marionette *f*
(JAP) 頼りない人、つまらない問題、
無資力者、偽証者
(RUS) ПОДСТАВНОЕ ЛИЦО

street name
(CHIN) 记在经纪人名下的客户证券
(FRE) nom du courtier
(GER) Scheinfirma *f*; Straßenname *m*
(JAP) 〔証券〕仲買人名義
(RUS) НОМИНАЛЬНЫЙ ИНВЕСТОР

stretchout
(CHIN) 无偿加班，展期
(FRE) surcharge, allongement
(GER) Streckung *f*, Produktionssteigerung *f*
(ohne entsprechende Sachkostenerhöhung)
(JAP) 引き延ばし、労働強化

(RUS) РАСТЯГИВАНИЕ; ВЫНУЖДЕНИЕ
ВЫПОЛНЯТЬ ДОПОЛНИТЕЛЬНУЮ
РАБОТУ БЕЗ ОПЛАТЫ

strike
(CHIN) 定价，定约，罢工
(FRE) grève
(GER) Streik *m*, Arbeitsniederlegung *f*
(JAP) ストライキ、同盟罷業、品質優良
(RUS) ЗАБАСТОВКА

strike benefits
(CHIN) 罢工期间福利
(FRE) allocations de grève, indemnités de
grève
(GER) Streikgeld *n*, Streikunterstützung *f*
(JAP) ストライキ手当
(RUS) ПРОФСОЮЗНЫЕ ВЫПЛАТЫ
БАСТУЮЩИМ РАБОТНИКАМ

strikebreaker
(CHIN) 罢工期间由管理层雇用的人手
(FRE) briseur de grève
(GER) Streikbrecher *m*
(JAP) スト破り、スキャップ
(RUS) ШТРЕЙКБРЕХЕР

strike notice
(CHIN) 罢工通知
(FRE) avis de grève
(GER) Streikankündigung *f*
(JAP) スト通告、ストライキ通告
(RUS) УВЕДОМЛЕНИЕ О ПРЕДСТОЯЩЕЙ
ЗАБАСТОВКЕ

strike pay
(CHIN) 罢工工资
(FRE) allocation de grève
(GER) Streikzahlungen *fpl*, -beihilfe *f*
(JAP) 罷業手当、ストライキ手当
(RUS) ПРОФСОЮЗНЫЕ ВЫПЛАТЫ
БАСТУЮЩИМ

strike price
(CHIN) 成交价格
(FRE) prix d'exercice
(GER) Basispreis *m*; Emissionskurs *m*;
Abrechnungskurs *m*; Zuschlagskurs *m*,
Zuschlags- *m*, Einstiegspreis *m*
(JAP) =STRIKING PRICE 、
権利行使価格

(RUS) ЦЕНА ИСПОЛНЕНИЯ ПРИКАЗА
БРОКЕРУ (бирж.)

strike vote
(CHIN) 罢工投票
(FRE) vote de grève
(GER) Streik- f, Urabstimmung f
(JAP) スト権確立投票
(RUS) ГОЛОСОВАНИЕ О ЗАБАСТОВКЕ

strip
(CHIN) 债券分开出售
(FRE) coupon détaché, coupure,
(C) obligation coupons détachés
(GER) Strip m (Börse); Stellagegeschäft n
mit Kaufoption f; Streifen m;
Streifenanzeige f
(RUS) ПОЛОСА

structural inflation
(CHIN) 结构性通货膨胀
(FRE) inflation structurelle
(GER) strukturelle Inflation f
(JAP) 構造的インフレーション
(RUS) СТРУКТУРНАЯ
ИНФЛЯЦИЯ

structural unemployment
(CHIN) 结构性失业
(FRE) chômage structurel, (C) emploi
structural
(GER) strukturelle Arbeitslosigkeit f,
strukturbedingte Arbeitslosigkeit f
(JAP) 構造的失業
(RUS) СТРУКТУРНАЯ БЕЗРАБОТИЦА

structure
(CHIN) 结构，体制，构成，
构造
(FRE) structure
(GER) Struktur f
(JAP) 構造、組織、建造物
(RUS) СТРУКТУРА

subcontractor
(CHIN) 分包商
(FRE) sous-traitant
(GER) Subunternehmer m
(JAP) 下請負人、下請会社、
下請契約人

(RUS) СУБПОДРЯДЧИК

subdirectory
(CHIN) 子目录
(FRE) sous-répertoire
(GER) Unterverzeichnis n
(JAP) サブディレクトリー
(RUS) ПОДКАТАЛОГ

subdivider
(CHIN) 土地分块出售者
(FRE) sous-diviseur, (C) subdiviseur
(GER) Bauunternehmer m im Stand m der
Parzellierung f
(JAP) 区分するもの
(RUS) РАЗДЕЛИТЕЛЬ

subdividing
(CHIN) 土地分块
(FRE) sous-division
(GER) unterteilen, untergliedern n
(JAP) 細分すること、分割すること
(RUS) ПОДРАЗДЕЛЕНИЕ

subdivision
(CHIN) 用于建房的地块
(FRE) subdivision, sous-division
(GER) Unterteilung f, Untergliederung f;
Parzellierung f
(JAP) 再分割、一区分、分譲地
(RUS) ПОДРАЗДЕЛЕНИЕ; ОТДЕЛ

subject to mortgage
(CHIN) 尚待抵押贷款
(FRE) hypothéqué, (C) assujetti à un prët
hypothécaire existent
(GER) hypothekengebunden adj
(JAP) 譲渡抵当に左右される
（に従う）
(RUS) УСЛОВИЕ ПОКУПКИ
ЗАЛОЖЕННОЙ ЗЕМЛИ

sublease
(CHIN) 转租
(FRE) sous-location
(GER) Untervermietung f,
Untermietervertrag m
(JAP) （不動産）転貸借
(RUS) СДАЧА АРЕНДУЕМОЙ
СОБСТВЕННОСТИ В АРЕНДУ

402

sublet

(CHIN) 转租，分租
(FRE) sous-louer
(GER) Unter-, weitervermieten *v*
(JAP) 転貸する、
転貸用の物件
(RUS) СУБАРЕНДА

subliminal advertising

(CHIN) 潜性广告
(FRE) publicité subliminale
(GER) unterschwellige Werbung *f*,
Schleichwerbung *f*
(JAP) サブリミナル広告、閾下広告
(RUS) АССОЦИАТИВНАЯ РЕКЛАМА

submarginal

(CHIN) 低于边际的
(FRE) submarginal, sous-marginal
(GER) nicht kostendeckend, nicht rentabel
adj
(JAP) 限度以下の、必要最低基準以下の、
耕作に適さない
(RUS) НИЖЕ УСТАНОВЛЕННОГО
ПРЕДЕЛА, МАРЖИ

suboptimize

(CHIN) 未发挥最大潜力
(FRE) sous-optimiser
(GER) suboptimieren *v*
(JAP) 次善の状態にする
(RUS) НЕПОЛНАЯ
ОПТИМИЗАЦИЯ

subordinated

(CHIN) 次等的，附属的
(FRE) subordonné
(GER) nachrangig *adj*
(JAP) 〔金融〕劣後した、後順位の、
下位におかれた
(RUS) ПОДЧИНЕННЫЙ

subordinate debt

(CHIN) 次要债务
(FRE) dette subordonnée, (C) créance de
rang inférieur
(GER) nachrangiger Schuldtitel *m*
(JAP) 劣位弁済債務
(RUS) ВТОРОСТЕПЕННЫЙ
ДОЛГ

subordination

(CHIN) 次要，附属，从属
(FRE) subordination
(GER) Nachrangigkeit *f*, Unterordnung *f*;
Gehorsam *m*
(JAP) 従属関係、債券劣後、劣後化
(RUS) ПОДЧИНЕНИЕ; СУБОРДИНАЦИЯ

subpoena

(CHIN) 传票
(FRE) citation, assignation, (C) citation à
comparaître
(GER) Ladung *f*, Vor- *f*, Zeugenladung *f*
(unter Strafandrohung bei Nichterscheinen)
(JAP) 罰則付き召還令状
(RUS) ВЫЗОВ В СУД; ПОВЕСТКА О ЯВКЕ
В СУД

subrogation

(CHIN) 代位求偿权，权益转让
(FRE) subrogation, (C) subrogation de
créance
(GER) Subrogation *f*; Gläubigerwechsel *m*,
Forderungsübergang *m*, Übergang *m* von
Ersatzansprüchen *mpl*; Eintritt *m* in Rechte
npl
(JAP) ～の代わりをすること、
理をすること、～に代位弁済
（請求）する
(RUS) ПРОДАЖА КРЕДИТА; ПЕРЕДАЧА
ПРАВА

subroutine

(CHIN) 子程序
(FRE) sous-programme
(GER) Unterprogramm *n* (EDV)
(JAP) サブルーチン
(RUS) ПОДПРОГРАММА (вычисл.)

subscript

(CHIN) 下标,下标，脚注
(FRE) indice, indice inférieur, (C) indiçage
(GER) Subskript *n*; Index *m*; Indexliste *f*;
(GER) indizieren *v*, tiefer gestellt *adj*
(EDV)
(JAP) 下付きの、下付き文字; 添字、
添字を
(RUS) ИНДЕКС, ВЫРАЖЕНИЕ,
УКАЗЫВАЮЩЕЕ НОМЕР ЭЛЕМЕНТА
МАССИВ; НИЖНИЙ ИНДЕКС

subscripted variable

(CHIN) 带下标的变量

(FRE) variable souscrite, (C) variable indicée

(GER) indizierte Variable *f*

(JAP) 下付き変数

(RUS) ИНДЕКСИРОВАННАЯ ПЕРЕМЕННАЯ

subscription

(CHIN) 认股，定购，签署，订阅

(FRE) souscription, (C) abonnement

(GER) (Anteils)zeichnung *f*;Abonnement *n*; Unterschriftsleistung *f*, Unterzeichnung *f*

(JAP) 寄付申込み、申込み、株式応募、引受け

(RUS) ПОДПИСКА

subscription price

(CHIN) 订价，认定价

(FRE) prix de souscription

(GER) Begebungs- *m*, Zeichnungs- *m*, Bezugspreis *m*

(JAP) (株式などの)応募価格、売り出し価格

(RUS) ЦЕНА ПОДПИСКИ; ЦЕНА БУМАГИ ПРИ ЕЕ ЭМИССИИ

subscription privilege

(CHIN) 认股优先权

(FRE) privilège de souscription

(GER) Bezugsrecht *n*, Bezugsberechtigung *f*

(JAP) 新株引受け特権、新株応募特権

(RUS) ПРИВИЛЕГИЯ ПОДПИСКИ

subscription right

(CHIN) 认股权

(FRE) droit de souscription

(GER) Bezugs- *n*, Zeichnungsrecht *n*

(JAP) 新株引受け権、（株式の）優先応募権

(RUS) ПРАВО ПОДПИСКИ

subsequent event

(CHIN) 后发事件，结账后发生的事项

(FRE) evenement ultérieur, C) événement postérieur à la clôture de l'exercice

(GER) Folgeereignis *n*

(JAP) 続いて起こる出来事（事件、成行き）

(RUS) ПОСЛЕДУЮЩЕЕ СОБЫТИЕ

subsidiary

(CHIN) 附属公司，子公司，分行，辅助的

(FRE) filiale

(GER) Tochtergesellschaft *f*, -unternehmen *n*, Konzerntochter *f*; Filiale *f*

(JAP) 補助の、従属的な、子会社、同族会社、

(RUS) ФИЛИАЛ; ДОЧЕРНЯЯ КОМПАНИЯ

subsidiary company

(CHIN) 附属公司，子公司

(FRE) filiale

(GER) Tochter- *f*, Konzern- *f*, Untergesellschaft *f*

(JAP) 従属会社、子会社、＝ AFFILIATED COMPANY

(RUS) ДОЧЕРНЯЯ КОМПАНИЯ

subsidiary ledger

(CHIN) 明细分类账

(FRE) grand-livre auxiliaire

(GER) Nebenbuch *n*, Skontration *f*, Hilfsbuch *n*

(JAP) 補助元帳、

(RUS) ГРОССБУХ ДОЧЕРНЕЙ КОМПАНИИ

subsidy

(CHIN) 补助金，津贴，奖励金

(FRE) subvention

(GER) Subvention *f*, Zuschuss *m*, Beihilfe *f*

(JAP) 補助金、価格調整補給金、輸出補助金

(RUS) СУБСИДИЯ

subsistence

(CHIN) 维持生活

(FRE) subsistance

(GER) Subsistenz *f*, Auskommen *n*, Unterhalt *m*

(JAP) 生活、生計費、存在

(RUS) СРЕДСТВА К СУЩЕСТВОВАНИЮ; ПРОЖИТОЧНЫЙ МИНИМУМ

substitution

(CHIN) 代替，取代，替换，代位

(FRE) substitution

(GER) Ersatz *m*, Vertretung *f*, Substitution *f*

(JAP) 取換え、代替、代用品

(RUS) СУБСТИТУЦИЯ, ЗАМЕЩЕНИЕ

substitution effect

(CHIN) 替代效应

(FRE) effet de substitution

(GER) Substitutionseffekt *m*

(JAP) 代替効果

(RUS) ЭФФЕКТ ЗАМЕЩЕНИЯ

substitution law

(CHIN) 替代法则

(FRE) loi de substitution

(GER) Gesetz *n* der Ersatzkäufe *mpl*

(JAP) 代替調剤法

(RUS) ЗАКОН СУБСТИТУЦИИ

substitution slope

(CHIN) 替代斜率

(FRE) pente de substitution

(GER) Substitutionslinie *f*

(JAP) 交替勾配（傾斜）

(RUS) НАКЛОННАЯ СУБСТИТУЦИИ

subtenant

(CHIN) 转租人，次承租人

(FRE) sous-locataire

(GER) Untermieter *m*, -pächter *m*

(JAP) 又借り人、転借人、下級小作人

(RUS) СУБАРЕНДАТОР

subtotal

(CHIN) 合计

(FRE) sous-total

(GER) Zwischensumme *f*, Teilsaldo *m*, -ergebnis *n*

(JAP) 一部分の合計、完全に近い

(RUS) ПРОМЕЖУТОЧНЫЙ ИТОГ

suggested retail price

(CHIN) 建议零售价

(FRE) prix de vente conseillé, (C) prix de détail suggéré

(GER) empfohlener Richtpreis *m*

(JAP) 提案小売価格

(RUS) ПРЕДЛАГАЕМАЯ (ПРОИЗВОДИТЕЛЕМ) РОЗНИЧНАЯ ЦЕНА

suggestion system

(CHIN) 职工建议系统

(FRE) système de suggestions

(GER) Vorschlagswesen *n* (für Mitarbeiter)

(JAP) 提案制度

(RUS) СИСТЕМА ПООЩРЕНИЯ ПРЕДЛОЖЕНИЙ ОТ РАБОТНИКОВ

suicide clause

(CHIN) 人寿保险中的自杀条款

(FRE) clause de suicide, (C) clause suicide

(GER) Selbstmordklausel *f*

(JAP) 自殺条項

(RUS) ОГОВОРКА О САМОУБИЙСТВЕ В ПОЛИСЕ СТРАХОВАНИЯ ЖИЗНИ

suite

(CHIN) 套；(程序)组

(FRE) suite, progiciel, (C) poursuite

(GER) Programmpaket *n*

(JAP) スーツ（パッケージソフト）

(RUS) КОМПЛЕКТ ПРОГРАММ

summons

(CHIN) 传讯，传票

(FRE) assignation à comparaître, citation à comparaître,(C) assignation de témoin

(GER) (gerichtliche) Vorladung *f*, Ladungsschreiben *n*, Vorladungsbefehl *m*

(JAP) 呼出状、召喚状、召還令状

(RUS) ВЫЗОВ В СУД

sunset industry

(CHIN) 夕阳工业

(FRE) industrie déclinante, (C) secteur d'activité en decline

(GER) absterbender Industriezweig *m*

(JAP) 斜陽産業

(RUS) ЗРЕЛАЯ ОТРАСЛЬ УСТАРЕВАЮЩИХ ТОВАРОВ

sunset provision

(CHIN) 法律或法规有效期条款

(FRE) disposition de temporisation, (C) disposition de temporisation

(GER) Sunset-Klausel *f*

(JAP) サンセット条項

(RUS) УСЛОВИЕ ЗАКОНА или ПРАВИЛА,
ОГОВАРИВАЮЩЕЕ СРОК ПРЕКРАЩЕНИЯ
ЕГО ДЕЙСТВИЯ

superfund

(CHIN) 联邦政府设立用于清理危险性污
染的基金

(FRE) superfund (fond d'indemnisation)

(GER) Superfund *m*, (Entschädigungsfonds
für Umweltschäden)

(JAP) スーパーファンド、
有害物質除去基金

(RUS) ФОНД, УСТАНОВЛЕННЫЙ
ПРАВИТЕЛЬСТВОМ НА ОЧИСТКУ
ОКРУЖАЮЩЕЙ СРЕДЫ

superintendent

(CHIN) 总督，总监

(FRE) superintendant, (C) contremaître
général, (C) chef de service

(GER) Abteilungsleiter *m*, Betriebsleiter *m*;
Oberaufseher *m*, Inspektor *m*

(JAP) 指導監督者、管理者

(RUS) ЗАВЕДУЮЩИЙ, УПРАВЛЯЮЩИЙ

supermarket

(CHIN) 超级市场

(FRE) supermarché

(GER) Supermarkt *m*

(JAP) スーパーマーケット

(RUS) «СУПЕРМАРКЕТ»;
УНИВЕРСАЛЬНЫЙ МАГАЗИН

super NOW account

(CHIN) 存款额越高利息越高的一
种银行账户

(FRE) compte à vue rémunéré, (C) compte-
chèques rémunéré

(GER) Super Now Account *n*,
höherverzinsliches Kontokorrentkonto *n*

(JAP) スーパーナウアカウント

(RUS) БАНКОВСКИЙ СЧЁТ ДО
ВОСТРЕБОВАНИЯ, ПО КОТОРОМУ
ВЫПЛАЧИВАЮТСЯ ПРОЦЕНТЫ

supersaver fare

(CHIN) 超储费

(FRE) catégorie de tarif supersaver,
(C) tarif super économique

(GER) Billigflugpreis *m*

(JAP) 特別割引料金

(RUS) СВЕРХЭКОНОМИЧНАЯ ПЛАТА ЗА
ПРОЕЗД, ПЕРЕВОЗКУ

superscript

(CHIN) 上标

(FRE) indice supérieur, (C) lettre
supérieure

(GER) Exponent *m*, hochgestellte Schrift *f*
(EDV)

上付き文字、肩文字、上添字

(RUS) ВЕРХНИЙ ИНДЕКС

super sinker bond

(CHIN) 超跌价债券

(FRE) obligation à terme, (C) obligation
avec amortissement

(GER) Super Sinker Bond *m*, Anleihe *f* mit
langfristigem Kupon *m* aber kurzer
Laufzeit *f*

(JAP) スーパーシンカーボンド

(RUS) ОБЛИГАЦИЯ С УРОВНЕМ
КУПОНА, РАВНЫМ СТАВКАМ ПО
ДОЛГОСРОЧНЫМ ОБЛИГАЦИЯМ
(но погашаемая гораздо раньше)

superstore

(CHIN) 超级市场，超级商店

(FRE) hypermarché, grande surface

(GER) Super- *m*, Verbrauchermarkt *m*

(JAP) スーパーストア

(RUS) КРУПНЫЙ МАГАЗИН

supplemental agreement

(CHIN) 补充协议

(FRE) contrat complémentaire,
(C) accord supplémentaire

(GER) Zusatzabkommen *n*

(JAP) 補足契約書

(RUS) ДОПОЛНИТЕЛЬНОЕ
СОГЛАШЕНИЕ

supplier

(CHIN) 供应商,
供货人

(FRE) fournisseur

(GER) Lieferant *m*, Zulieferer *m*;
Auftragnehmer *m*

(JAP) 供給者

(RUS) ПОСТАВЩИК

supply

(CHIN) 供应，提供

(FRE) fournir, (C) offre

(GER) Angebot *n*; Lieferung *f*, Versorgung *f*

(JAP) 供給する、供給、供給物

(RUS) ПРЕДЛОЖЕНИЕ; ПОСТАВКА; НАЛИЧИЕ ТОВАРА

supply price

(CHIN) 供货价

(FRE) prix de l'offre, (C) prix d'offre

(GER) Angebotspreis *m*; Lieferpreis *m*

(JAP) 供給価格

(RUS) ЦЕНА ПРЕДЛОЖЕНИЯ

supply-side economics

(CHIN) 供应经济学派

(FRE) économie de l'offre, (C) politique économique de l'offre

(GER) angebotsorientierte Wirtschaftspolitik *f*, Supply Side Economics *pl*

(JAP) 供給サイド経済、供給側経済

(RUS) ЭКОНОМИКА ПРЕДЛОЖЕНИЯ (теория)

support level

(CHIN) 支持价

(FRE) niveau de support

(GER) Supportschwelle *f*, -niveau *n*, -level *n*

(JAP) サポートレベル

(RUS) УРОВЕНЬ ПОДДЕРЖКИ

surcharge

(CHIN) 超载，额外费用，附加税

(FRE) surtaxe, supplément, majoration, (C) frais supplémentaires

(GER) Aufpreis *m*, Aufschlag *m*, Zuschlag *m*, Aufgeld *n*; Mehrbelastung *f*; Zusatzgebühr *f*

(JAP) 追加税（金）、追加料金、付加金、追徴金

(RUS) НАДБАВКА К ЦЕНЕ

surety bond

(CHIN) 担保债券，担保书

(FRE) acte de cautionnement, acte de caution, obligation de garantie,

(C) assurance-cautionnement

(GER) Kaution *f*, Kautionsurkunde *f*, Bürgschein *m*, Sicherheit *f*; Bürgschaftserklärung *f*; Garantieschein *m*

(JAP) 保証状、保証書

(RUS) ГАРАНТИЙНАЯ ОБЛИГАЦИЯ

surge protector

(CHIN) 浪涌保护器

(FRE) parasurtenseur

(GER) Spannungsableiter *m*

(JAP) サージプロテクター、サージ保安器

(RUS) УСТРОЙСТВО ЗАЩИТЫ ОТ СКАЧКОВ НАПРЯЖЕНИЯ В СЕТИ

surplus

(CHIN) 盈余，剩余物资，贸易顺差

(FRE) surplus , excédent

(GER) Überschuss *m*, Mehrbetrag *m*, Gewinnreserve *f*

(JAP) 超過金、余剰、付加資本

(RUS) ИЗЛИШЕК; ИЗБЫТОК

surrender

(CHIN) 交出，提交，放弃，缴纳，退保

(FRE) rachat, (C) reddition

(GER) Übergabe *f*, Auslieferung *f*, Aushändigung *f*, Überlassung *f*; Kapitulation *f*; Rückgabe *f*

(JAP) 譲渡する、放棄する、期限切れ以前に放棄する

(RUS) СДАЧА; КАПИТУЛЯЦИЯ

surrender, life insurance

(CHIN) 人寿保险退保

(FRE) rachat d'assurance vie, (C) rachat

(GER) Rückkauf *m* einer Lebensversicherung *f*

(JAP) 生命保険を解約する、生命保険の解約

(RUS) ДОСРОЧНОЕ РАСТОРЖЕНИЕ ДОГОВОРА О СТРАХОВАНИИ ЖИЗНИ

surtax

(CHIN) 附加税

(FRE) surtaxe

(GER) Zusatzsteuer *f*, Ergänzungsabgabe *f*, Steuerzuschlag *m*

(JAP) （米）付加税、割増税、〜に付加
税を課す
(RUS) ДОБАВОЧНЫЙ ПОДОХОДНЫЙ
НАЛОГ

survey
(CHIN) 勘查，鉴定，检验，评论
(FRE) expertise, étude, enquête,
(C) sondage, étude
(GER) Umfrage *f*, Erhebung *f*,
Meinungsbefragung *f*, -umfrage *f*;
Übersicht *f*; Vermessung *f*
(JAP) 測量する、調査する、検分する、
査察
(RUS) ОБЗОР; ОБСЛЕДОВАНИЕ;
РАЗВЕДКА

survey area
(CHIN) 勘查地区
(FRE) zone d'étude, (C) région du sondage
(GER) Vermessungsgebiet *n*;
Umfragebereich *m*
(JAP) 測量地域、検分地域
(RUS) ОБСЛЕДУЕМАЯ
(РАЗВЕДЫВАЕМАЯ) ПЛОЩАДЬ, ЗОНА

surveyor
(CHIN) 鉴定师，公证人，海关验货员
(FRE) expert, (C) sondeur
(GER) Landvermesser *m*
(JAP) 測量士、測量技師、検査員
(RUS) ИНСПЕКТОР; ЭКСПЕРТ;
ГЕОДЕЗИСТ

survivorship
(CHIN) 生存
(FRE) droit du survivant, (C) survie
(GER) Überlebensfall *m*
(JAP) 生存者への権利の帰属、
生存者財産権、生き残り
(RUS) ВЫЖИВАНИЕ

suspended trading
(CHIN) 中断贸易
(FRE) cotation réservée, (C) suspension de
cotation
(GER) Aussetzen *n* des Handels *m* (Börse)
(JAP) 保留取引、売買停止
(RUS) ПРИОСТАНОВКА ТОРГОВЛИ
(бирж.)

suspense account
(CHIN) 暂记账，悬账
(FRE) compte d'ordre, (C) compte
d'attente
(GER) Zwischen- *n*, Interimskonto *n*,
Durchgangs- *n*, Übergangskonto *n*
(JAP) 仮勘定、未決算勘定
(RUS) ПРОМЕЖУТОЧНЫЙ СЧЕТ

suspension
(CHIN) 停止支付，中止，暂停营业
(FRE) suspension
(GER) zeitweiliges Berufsausübungsverbot
n; einstweilige bzw, vorübergehende
Aussetzung *f*; vorübergehende Schließung *f*;
zeitweilige Beurlaubung *f*
(JAP) 宙ぶらりんの状態、一時停止、
停止
(RUS) ПРИОСТАНОВЛЕНИЕ;
ПРЕРЫВАНИЕ; ПОДВЕСКА (техн.)

swap
(CHIN) 掉换，交换，互惠信贷
(FRE) swaper, (C) permutation
(GER) Swap *m*, Swapgeschäft *n*;
Devisenreportgeschäft *n*;
Devisentauschgeschäft *n*; Tauschgeschäft *n*;
(JAP) 交換する、（為替を）スワップ取
引する、スワップ、（物々）交換
(RUS) «СВОП»; ОБМЕН (бирж.)

sweepstakes
(CHIN) 彩票
(FRE) lotteries promotionnelles,
(C) sweepstake
(GER) Preisausschreiben *n*
(JAP) 賞金レース、総賭け勝負、投機
(RUS) ЛОТЕРЕЯ

sweetener
(CHIN) 证券附加特点
(FRE) avantage
(GER) Zusätzlicher Anreiz *m*;
Schmiergeld *n*
(JAP) スイトナー、賄賂
(RUS) «ПОДСЛАСТИТЕЛЬНАЯ»
ХАРАКТЕРИСТИКА (ценной бумаги, товара)

swing shift
(CHIN) 小夜班[下午 4-12 时的值班]

(FRE) équipe qui travaille de 16 heures à minuit, (C) poste de rèleve
(GER) Sonderschicht *f*
(JAP) （三交代制の）第二次夜勤、半夜勤、午後交代
(RUS) СМЕНА ПЕРЕД ПОЛНОЧНОЙ СМЕНОЙ

switching
(CHIN) 转手
(FRE) arbitrage de portefeuille, (C) transfert
(GER) Umschichtung *f*; Umlagerung *f*
(JAP) 切換え、スウィッチ、むち打ち
(RUS) ПЕРЕКЛЮЧЕНИЕ

symbol bar
(CHIN) 符号栏
(FRE) barre des symboles
(GER) Symbolleiste *f* (EDV)
(JAP) シンボルバー、記号バー

sympathetic strike
(CHIN) 同情性罢工
(FRE) grève de solidarité
(GER) Solidaritäts- *m*, Sympathiestreik *m*
(JAP) 同情ストライキ
(RUS) ЗАБАСТОВКА ДЛЯ ДЕМОНСТРАЦИИ СОЛИДАРНОСТИ

syndicate
(CHIN) 辛迪加，企业组合垄断，财团
(FRE) syndicat, groupement,(C) syndicat financier
(GER) Syndikat *n*; Konsortium *n*; Verkaufs- *n*, Absatzkartell *n*; Versicherergruppe *f*
(JAP) 企業連合、シンジケート、公社債募集、引受団体
(RUS) СИНДИКАТ; КОНСОРЦИУМ

syndication
(CHIN) 辛迪加组织
(FRE) syndication
(GER) Syndizierung *f*, Platzierung *f* eines Konsortialkredits *m*; Syndikats- *f*, Konsortialbildung *f*
(JAP) シンジケートを結成すること
(RUS) ОБЪЕДИНЕНИЕ В СИНДИКАТ; СИНДИКАЦИЯ

syndicator
(CHIN) 财团投资人
(FRE) instigateur de syndicat d'investisseurs
(GER) Syndizierer *m*
(JAP) シンジケート運営者
(RUS) ИНИЦИАТОР ОБЪЕДИНЕНИЯ В СИНДИКАТ, СИНДИКАЦИИ

synergy
(CHIN) 协同，企业合并后的协力优势
(FRE) synergie
(GER) Synergie *f*
(JAP) 相乗作用、共力作用
(RUS) СИНЕРГИЗМ; ЭФФЕКТ ВЗАИМОДЕЙСТВИЯ БОЛЬШЕ СУММЫ ЭФФЕКТОВ ЧАСТЕЙ

system
(CHIN) 系统，制度，体系，系统，体制
(FRE) système
(GER) System *n* ; (GER) Anlage *f*, Netz *n*, System *n*
(JAP) 系、組織、機構；システム、組織、体系、系
(RUS) СИСТЕМА; СИСТЕМНЫЙ

system administrator
(CHIN) 系统管理员
(FRE) administrateur système, (C) administrateur du système
(GER) Systemverwalter *m*
(JAP) システム管理者
(RUS) СПЕЦИАЛИСТ ПО ОБСЛУЖИВАНИЮ СИСТЕМ

systematic risk
(CHIN) 无法避免的风险
(FRE) risque systématique
(GER) systematisches Risiko *n*
(JAP) 体系的リスク
(RUS) СИСТЕМАТИЧЕСКИЙ РИСК

systematic sampling
(CHIN) 系统性抽样
(FRE) échantillonnage systématique
(GER) systematische Stichprobennahme *f*
(JAP) 組織的抽出、系統抽出
(RUS) СИСТЕМАТИЧЕСКАЯ ВЫБОРКА

T

tab key
(CHIN) 制表键
(FRE) touche de tabulation
(GER) Tabulatortaste *f*, Tab-Taste
(Tastatur)
(JAP) タブキー
(RUS) КЛАВИША ТАБУЛЯЦИИ

table column
(CHIN) 表格列
(FRE) colonne de tableau
(GER) Tabellenspalte *f*
(JAP) 表の欄，表のカラム、目録欄
(RUS) СТОЛБЕЦ ТАБЛИЦЫ

table field
(CHIN) 表栏，表域
(FRE) champ de tableau
(GER) Tabellenfeld *n*
(JAP) 表のフィールド
(RUS) ПОЛЕ ТАБЛИЦЫ

T-account
(CHIN) T 形账户
(FRE) compte en T, (C) compte en T
(GER) T-Konto *n*
(JAP) T 字型勘定
(RUS) СЧЕТ В ФОРМЕ БУКВЫ «Т»
(с именем заявителя сверху и двумя
колонками для дебета и кредита)

tactic
(CHIN) 战术
(FRE) tactique
(GER) Taktik *f*
(JAP) 戦法、兵法、方策
(RUS) ТАКТИКА

tag sale
(CHIN) 自家旧货售卖
(FRE) vente-débarras
(GER) Garagenverkauf *m*
(JAP) ガレージセール
(RUS) ПРОДАЖА ДОМАШНЕГО

ИМУЩЕСТВА ВЛАДЕЛЬЦЕМ ИЗ СВОЕГО
ДОМА

take
(CHIN) 拿，取，获得
(FRE) prendre
(GER) nehmen, entgegennehmen *v*;
(Risiko) tragen, eingehen *v*; bekommen *v*;
verkraften, ertragen *v*
(JAP) 受納する、採用する、売上高
(RUS) ПРИНЯТЬ; ВЗЯТЬ; ПРИЕМ

take a bath, take a beating
(CHIN) 投资失败，遭受巨大损失
(FRE) enregistrer de lourdes pertes,
(C) subir une perte colossale
(GER) baden gehen, schwere Verluste *mpl*
erleiden *v*
(JAP) 破産する、大損する
(RUS) ПОНЕСТИ БОЛЬШИЕ УБЫТКИ (по
спекулятивной сделке)

take a flier
(CHIN) 冒险行事，投机
(FRE) spéculer, (C) prendre un risque,
(C) spéculer
(GER) spekulative Effektentransaktion *f*
durchführen *v*; spekulieren *v*
(JAP) 一か八か賭けてみる、やまを張る、
高飛びする
(RUS) СПЕКУЛИРОВАТЬ, СОВЕРШАТЬ
ЗАВЕДОМО РИСКОВАННУЮ
СДЕЛКУ

take a position
(CHIN) 购买股票
(FRE) prendre une position, (C) détenir une
position acheteur
(GER) eine Wertpapierposition *f* erwerben
v; eine Stellung *f* einnehmen *v*
(JAP) 買い持ちをする、
ポジションを持つ
(RUS) ОТКРЫТЬ ПОЗИЦИЮ (купить акции
компании с целью долгосрочных
инвестиций)

take-home pay

(CHIN) 净剩工资

(FRE) gain net, salaire net

(GER) Nettoverdienst *m*, -gehalt *n*

(JAP) （税金などを差し引いた）手取り賃金（給与）

(RUS) ФАКТИЧЕСКАЯ (ЧИСТАЯ) ЗАРАБОТНАЯ ПЛАТА (минус налоги, страхование и т.п.)

takeoff

(CHIN) 起飞，稳定

(FRE) déduire, rabattre, (C) décollage

(GER) (wirtschaftlicher) Aufstieg *m*; Anlauf *m*; Start *m*, Abflug *m*

(JAP) テイクオフ、離陸

(RUS) СТАРТ; ВЗЛЁТ,

take-out loan, take-out financing

(CHIN) 取代贷款，取代融资

(FRE) prêt postconstruction, financement postconstruction, (C) financement permanent

(GER) langfristige Immobilienfinanzierung *f* nach Bauabschluss *m*

(JAP) 〔金融〕テークアウト建設 融資、長期不動産担保金融

(RUS) ДОЛГОСРОЧНЫЙ ИПОТЕЧНЫЙ КРЕДИТ ДЛЯ РЕФИНАНСИРОВАНИЯ КРАТКОСРОЧНОГО

takeover

(CHIN) 收购，合并

(FRE) prise de participation

(GER) (Betriebs- *f*, Geschäfts)übernahme *f*, Aufkauf *m*; Machtergreifung *f*

(JAP) 奪取、企業経営権買収、乗っ取り

(RUS) ПОГЛОЩЕНИЕ; ПОКУПКА КОНТРОЛЬНОГО ПАКЕТА АКЦИЙ КОМПАНИИ

taking

(CHIN) 取得土地

(FRE) prise, (C) acquisition d'un terrain

(GER) Inbesitznahme *f*; Festnahme *f*; Entnahme *f*; Abnahme *f*

(JAP) 取ること、捕獲、売上高

(RUS) ВЗЯТИЕ; ОВЛАДЕНИЕ; ПРИЕМ

taking delivery

(CHIN) 接收货物

(FRE) prendre livraison, (C) réception

(GER) Abnahme *f* einer Lieferung *f*

(JAP) 荷取り

(RUS) ПОЛУЧЕНИЕ ДОСТАВКИ

taking inventory

(CHIN) 盘存，盘货

(FRE) établir l'inventaire, (C) prise d'inventaire

(GER) Bestandsaufnahme *f*, Inventur *f*

(JAP) 在庫品調べ、棚卸し

(RUS) ИНВЕНТАРИЗАЦИЯ

tally

(CHIN) 点数，理货，记账，标签

(FRE) pointage, inventaire

(GER) Zählung *f*, Aufstellung *f*, Strichliste *f*; Frachtliste *f*; Zähler *m*; Gegenrechnung *f*

(JAP) 割賦、割印、一致、計算

(RUS) СЧЕТ; ИТОГ; СХОЖДЕНИЕ РЕЗУЛЬТАТОВ

tangible asset

(CHIN) 有形资产，实际资产

(FRE) actif corporel, valeurs matérielles, (C) bien corporel

(GER) materieller Vermögensgegenstand *m*, Sachanlage *f*, Sachwert *m*

(JAP) 有形資産、有体財産

(RUS) МАТЕРИАЛЬНЫЙ АКТИВ

tangible personal property

(CHIN) 有形个人财产

(FRE) biens meubles personnels, (C) bien meuble corporel

(GER) persönliches Sachanlagevermögen *n*

(JAP) 有形（有体）個人財産、有形（有体）人的財産

(RUS) ЛИЧНАЯ МАТЕРИАЛЬНАЯ СОБСТВЕННОСТЬ

tank car

(CHIN) 油罐车

(FRE) camion citerne, (C) wagon-citerne

(GER) Tankwagen *m*, Kesselwagen *m*

(JAP) タンク車、油槽車、水槽車

411

(RUS) ЦИСТЕРНА

tape
(CHIN) 磁带，胶带，录音带
(FRE) bande, (C) téléscripteur
(GER) Börsenticker *m*, Lochstreifen *m*;
Band *n*
(JAP) テープ、テープ録音（録画）する、
（巻尺で）測る
(RUS) ЛЕНТА (в т.ч. биржевая);
ЗАПИСЫВАТЬ НА ЛЕНТУ, ПЛЕНКУ

target audience
(CHIN) 目标听众
(FRE) audience cible, (C) auditoire cible
(GER) Zielpublikum *n*
(JAP) 対象会衆、大衆、聴衆
(RUS) ЦЕЛЕВАЯ АУДИТОРИЯ

target file
(CHIN) 目标文件
(FRE) fichier cible
(GER) Zieldatei *f*
(JAP) 目標ファイル

target group index (TGI)
(CHIN) 目标群组指数 （TGI）
(FRE) tarif douanier, droit de douane
(GER) Zielgruppenindex *m*
(JAP) 目標（対象）グループ指数
(RUS) ИНДЕКС ЦЕЛЕВЫХ ГРУПП

target market
(CHIN) 目标市场
(FRE) marché cible
(GER) Zielmarkt *m*
(JAP) 目標市場
(RUS) ЦЕЛЕВОЙ РЫНОК

target price
(CHIN) 目标价格，标准价格
(FRE) prix cible
(GER) Richtpreis *m*; Zielpreis *m*
(JAP) 目標価格
(RUS) КОНТРОЛЬНАЯ ЦЕНА

tariff
(CHIN) 关税率，运费率，票价
(FRE) tarif
(GER) Zoll *m*; Zolltarif *m*; Preisverzeichnis

n, -liste *f*; Gebührenordnung *f*, -tarif *f*
(JAP) 関税、関税率、関税表
(RUS) ТАРИФ

tariff war
(CHIN) 关税战
(FRE) guerre des tarifs, guerre tarifaire
(GER) Handelskrieg *m*
(JAP) 関税戦、関税戦争、
(RUS) «ВОЙНА ТАРИФОВ»

task force
(CHIN) 工作组
(FRE) groupe d'intervention, (C) groupe de travail
(GER) Arbeits- *f*, Projekt- *f*, Einsatzgruppe *f*; Arbeitsausschuss *m*; Sonder- *f*, Spezialeinheit *f*; Einsatzkommando *n*
(JAP) タスクフォース、特別作業班、特別委員会
(RUS) СПЕЦИАЛЬНОЕ ПОДРАЗДЕЛЕНИЕ (с особой задачей)

task group
(CHIN) 任务小组
(FRE) groupe de travail
(GER) Arbeitsgruppe *f*
(RUS) СПЕЦИАЛЬНАЯ ГРУППА (с особой задачей)

task list
(CHIN) 任务列表
(FRE) liste des tâches
(GER) Aufgabenliste *f*
(JAP) タスクリスト
(RUS) СПИСОК ЗАДАЧ

task management
(CHIN) 任务管理
(FRE) gestion des tâches
(GER) Aufgaben *f*; Prozessverwaltung *f*
(JAP) 課業管理
(RUS) ЦЕЛЕВОЕ УПРАВЛЕНИЕ

task manager
(CHIN) 任务管理器
(FRE) gestionnaire des tâches
(GER) Aufgabenverwalter *f* (Computer)
(JAP) タスクマネジャー

(RUS) ПРОГРАММА УПРАВЛЕНИЯ
ЗАДАЧАМИ

tax

(CHIN) 税，税款，支付，评定

(FRE) impôt, taxe, (C) tax

(GER) Steuer *f*

(JAP) 税金、重荷、課税する

(RUS) НАЛОГ; ВЗИМАТЬ или ОБЛАГАТЬ
НАЛОГОМ

tax abatement

(CHIN) 减税

(FRE) exonération d'impôts, exonération
fiscale, (C) abattement d'impôt

(GER) Steuernachlass *m*, -erleichterung *f*,
-ermäßigung *f*

(JAP) 減税　　（＝ TAX CUT, TAX
REDUCTION）

(RUS) СНИЖЕНИЕ НАЛОГА; НАЛОГОВАЯ
ЛЬГОТА

taxable income

(CHIN) 应税收入

(FRE) revenu imposable

(GER) steuerpflichtiges Einkommen *n*, zu
versteuernde Einkünfte *fpl*

(JAP) 課税所得

(RUS) НАЛОГООБЛАГАЕМЫЙ ДОХОД

taxable year

(CHIN) 应税年度

(FRE) année d'imposition

(GER) Steuer- *n*, Wirtschafts- *n*,
Veranlagungsjahr *n*

(JAP) 課税年度　　（＝ FISCAL YEAR）

(RUS) НАЛОГОВЫЙ ГОД (год для
начисления налогов; совпадает либо с
календарным, либо с финансовым)

tax and loan account

(CHIN) 税收与借款账户

(FRE) compte courant du tresor aupres des
grandes banques, (C) compte de déductions
à la source

(GER) Konto *n* der Federal Reserve Bank *f*
bei den Geschäftsbanken *fpl*

(JAP) （米）租税国債勘定、
租税公債勘定

(RUS) СЧЕТ ДЛЯ УПЛАТЫ НАЛОГА И
РАСЧЕТОВ ПО КРЕДИТУ

tax anticipation bill (TAB)

(CHIN) 先期交税债券 （TAB）

(FRE) bon du trésor,(C) obligation garantie
par les recettes fiscales prévues

(GER) Steuergutschein *m* (von US-
Treasury)

(JAP) 租税準備証券、納税証券

(RUS) НАЛОГОВЫЙ ВЕКСЕЛЬ
(выпускаемый Мин. финансов США)

tax anticipation note (TAN)

(CHIN) 税收预期票据 （TAN）

(FRE) bon (n, m) garanti par les recettes
fiscales prévues

(GER) Steuergutschein *m* (von US-
Bundesstaat oder einer Kommune)

(JAP) 税収見返り手形

(RUS) НАЛОГОВЫЕ
ОБЛИГАЦИИ

taxation, interest on dividends

(CHIN) 股息税

(FRE) Imposition, intérêts sur les
dividendes, (C) intérêt sur les dividendes
imposées

(GER) Besteuerung *f* der
Dividendenzinsen *mpl*

(JAP) 配当利子課税

(RUS) ОБЛОЖЕНИЕ НАЛОГОМ
ПРОЦЕНТОВ НА ДИВИДЕНДЫ

tax base

(CHIN) 计税基础

(FRE) assiette fiscale

(GER) Steuerbemessungsgrundlage *f*

(JAP) 課税基准、税基盤

(RUS) НАЛОГОВАЯ БАЗА (сумма для
вычисления налога)

tax bracket

(CHIN) 税收等级

(FRE) tranche d'imposition, fourchette
d'imposition

(GER) Steuerklasse *f*

(JAP) 税率等級

(RUS) СТУПЕНЬ НАЛОГОВОЙ ШКАЛЫ
(при прогрессивном
налогообложении)

tax credit

(CHIN) 税收抵免

(FRE) aide fiscale, avoir fiscal, (C) crédit d'impôt
(GER) Steuergutschrift *f*, -freibetrag *m*; Steueranrechnung *f*
(JAP) 税額控除
(RUS) НАЛОГОВЫЙ КРЕДИТ

tax deductible
(CHIN) 免税，税务扣减
(FRE) déductible des impôts, (C) admis en déduction d'impôt
(GER) steuerlich abzugsfähig, steuerlich absetzbar *adj*
(RUS) СТАТЬСЯ, ВЫЧИТАЕМАЯ ИЗ НАЛОГООБЛАГАЕМОЙ СУММЫ

tax deduction
(CHIN) 税额扣减，免税，减税
(FRE) déduction fiscale
(GER) Steuerabzug *m*
(JAP) 課税控除、課税控除額、租税控除
(RUS) ВЫЧЕТ ИЗ НАЛОГООБЛАГАЕМОЙ СУММЫ

tax deed
(CHIN) 税务契据
(FRE) acte de transfert pour taxes, (C) acte d'adjudication
(GER) Grunderwerbsurkunde *f* beim Kauf *m* eines zwecks Steuerrückständen *mpl* zwangsversteigerten Grundvermögens *n*
(JAP) 公売証書
(RUS) СВИДЕТЕЛЬСТВО О ВЛАДЕНИИ ЗЕМЛЕЙ, ИЗЪЯТОЙ ЗА НЕУПЛАТУ НАЛОГОВ

tax deferred
(CHIN) 递延税务
(FRE) imposition différée
(GER) mit Steueraufschub *m*, steuerlich gestundet *adj*
(JAP) 課税猶予の、納税猶予の
(RUS) ОТЛОЖЕННОЕ НАЛОГООБЛОЖЕНИЕ

tax evasion
(CHIN) 逃税，偷税
(FRE) fraude fiscale, evasion fiscale, (C) évasion fiscale
(GER) Steuerhinterziehung *f*
(JAP) 脱税

(RUS) УКЛОНЕНИЕ ОТ УПЛАТЫ НАЛОГОВ

tax-exempt property
(CHIN) 免税财产
(FRE) propriété exempte d'impôts, (C) bien exempt de taxe
(GER) steuerbefreites Eigentum *n* bzw. Vermögen *n*
(JAP) 免税財産、免税資産
(RUS) СОБСТВЕННОСТЬ, ДОХОД ОТ КОТОРОЙ НЕ ОБЛАГАЕТСЯ НАЛОГОМ

tax-exempt security
(CHIN) 免税证券
(FRE) titre à intérêt non imposable, (C) titre exempt d'impôt
(GER) steuerbefreites Wertpapier *n*
(JAP) 免税証券
(RUS) ЦЕННАЯ БУМАГА, ДОХОД ПО КОТОРОЙ НЕ ОБЛАГАЕТСЯ НАЛОГОМ

tax foreclosure
(CHIN) 因未交税而取消赎回权的没收财产
(FRE) saisie fiscale, (C) action en forclusion
(GER) Steuerpfändung *f*
(JAP) 税金抵当流れ、タックスフォークロージャー
(RUS) ИЗЪЯТИЕ И ПРОДАЖА ИМУЩЕСТВА ЗА НЕУПЛАТУ НАЛОГОВ

tax-free exchange
(CHIN) 免税资产交换
(FRE) échange exempt d'impôt, (C) transaction exempte de taxe
(GER) steuerfreier Tausch *m* (einer Immobilie für eine andere der gleichen Art)
(JAP) 非課税為替、免税為替
(RUS) ПЕРЕДАЧА СОБСТВЕННОСТИ, ОСОБО ИСКЛЮЧЕННАЯ ИЗ ОБЛОЖЕНИЯ НАЛОГОМ

tax impact
(CHIN) 税赋影响
(FRE) incidence fiscale, (C) impact fiscal
(GER) Steuerwirkung *f*
(JAP) 租税効果
(RUS) ВЛИЯНИЕ, ВОЗДЕЙСТВИЕ НАЛОГА

tax incentive

(CHIN) 税收鼓励

(FRE) incitation fiscale, avantage fiscal, (C) encouragement fiscal

(GER) steuerlicher Anreiz *m*

(JAP) 税制上の優遇措置、租税誘引

(RUS) НАЛОГОВАЯ ПОЛИТИКА, НАЦЕЛЕННАЯ НА СТИМУЛИРОВАНИЕ ОПРЕДЕЛЕННОГО ВИДА ДЕЯТЕЛЬНОСТИ

tax incidence

(CHIN) 课税归宿，纳税负担

(FRE) incidence fiscale, incidence de l'impôt, (C) incidence

(GER) Steuerinzidenz *f*, -last *f*, -anfall *m*

(JAP) 税負担、租税の帰着

(RUS) СФЕРА ДЕЙСТВИЯ (РЕАЛЬНОЕ ВОЗДЕЙСТВИЕ) НАЛОГОВ

tax lien

(CHIN) 课税扣押权

(FRE) droit de rétention, (C) privilège fiscal

(GER) Pfandrecht *n* der Steuerbehörde *f*

(JAP) 租税先取特権

(RUS) ПРАВО УДЕРЖАНИЯ В СИЛУ НАЛОГОВОЙ ЗАДОЛЖЕННОСТИ

tax loss carryback (carryforward)

(CHIN) 赋税亏损转回（结转）

(FRE) report en arrière des déficits fiscaux, (C) report de perte fiscale

(GER) steuerlicher Verlustrücktrag *m* (-vortrag *m*)

(JAP) 租税の損金遡及
　（租税の損金繰越）

(RUS) ПЕРЕНОС УБЫТКА ДЛЯ ПОКРЫТИЯ ИЗ ПОШЛОЙ или БУДУЩЕЙ ПРИБЫЛИ, В ЦЕЛЯХ СНИЖЕНИЯ НАЛОГОВОГО БРЕМЕНИ

tax map

(CHIN) 土地税务图

(FRE) carte d'imposition foncière

(GER) Grundstückssteuerverzeichnis *n*

(JAP) 租税地図

(RUS) СХЕМА НАЛОГООБЛОЖЕНИЯ

taxpayer

(CHIN) 纳税人

(FRE) contribuable

(GER) Steuerzahler *m*

(JAP) 納税者

(RUS) НАЛОГОПЛАТЕЛЬЩИК

tax planning

(CHIN) 计划避税

(FRE) gestion fiscale, (C) planification fiscale

(GER) Steuerplanung *f*

(JAP) 税金計画、租税計画

(RUS) ПЛАНИРОВАНИЕ НАЛОГОВ

tax preference item

(CHIN) 优惠税率项目

(FRE) élément bénéficiant d'un traitement fiscal préférentiel, (C) traitement fiscal préférentiel

(GER) steuerlich begünstigte Einkommensposition *f*

(JAP) 税金優先権項目

(RUS) ПОЗИЦИИ, УЧИТЫВАЕМЫЕ ПРИ РАСЧЕТЕ АЛЬТЕРНАТИВНОГО МИНИМАЛЬНОГО НАЛОГА

tax rate

(CHIN) 税率

(FRE) taux d'imposition

(GER) Steuersatz *m*, -tarif *m*, Abgabenquote *f*

(JAP) 税率、課税率

(RUS) СТАВКА НАЛОГООБЛОЖЕНИЯ

tax return

(CHIN) 税单，纳税申报表

(FRE) déclaration de revenu, feuille d'impôt, (C) remboursement d'impôt

(GER) Steuererklärung *f*

(JAP) 納税申告書、税務申告

(RUS) БЛАНК (И) ДЛЯ ОФОРМЛЕНИЯ НАЛОГОВОЙ ОТЧЕТНОСТИ; НАЛОГОВАЯ ДЕКЛАРАЦИЯ

tax roll

(CHIN) 税率，税款清册

(FRE) rôle d'impôt, rôle des contributions, (C) rôle d'imposition

(GER) Steuerliste *f*, -kataster *n*, Veranlagungsliste *f*

(JAP) 課税台帳

(RUS) УЧЕТ (ГОСУДАРСТВЕННЫЙ) НАЛОГОПЛАТЕЛЬЩИКОВ И НАЛОГООБЛАГАЕМОЙ СОБСТВЕННОСТИ

tax sale

(CHIN) 欠税财产的拍卖

(FRE) vente d'une propriété pour défaut de paiement des impôts, (C) vente pour défaut de paiement de l'impôt foncier

(GER) Steuerzwangsverkauf m, (Zwangsversteigerung zur Deckung von Steuerschulden)

(JAP) 滞納処分公売、公売、兑換処分

(RUS) ПРОДАЖА СОБСТВЕННОСТИ ЗА НЕУПЛАТУ НАЛОГОВ

tax selling

(CHIN) 纳税抛售

(FRE) vente de titres dans un but fiscal, (C) vente de titres à perte

(GER) steuerlich motivierter Verkauf m von Aktien fpl

(JAP) 税金対策として証券売却

(RUS) ПРОДАЖА СОБСТВЕННОСТИ (например, ценных бумаг) ДЛЯ УМЕНЬШЕНИЯ НАЛОГОВОГО БРЕМЕНИ

tax shelter

(CHIN) 避税办法

(FRE) avantage fiscal, (C) abri fiscal

(GER) Nichtbesteuerung f, Steueroase f

(JAP) タックスシェルター、税金回避手段

(RUS) НАЛОГОВАЯ ЗАЩИТА (средство исключения или уменьшения налогового бремени)

tax stop

(CHIN) 纳税停止线

(FRE) clause d'arrêt des versements, (C) impôt foncier maximum

(GER) Grundstückssteuerausgleichsklausel f

(JAP) 税金を止める

(RUS) ПРИКАЗ «СТОП» (бирж.) (из соображений сокращения налогового бремени)

tax straddle

(CHIN) 税收套购

(FRE) straddle, stellage, (C) option double fiscale

(GER) Gewinntransferierung f ins nächste Jahr n zur Steuervermeidung f

(JAP) 税金ストラドル

(RUS) НАЛОГОВЫЙ «СТРЭДДЛ» (из соображений сокращения налогового бремени)

tax wedge

(CHIN) 税务原因

(FRE) écart fiscal, coin fiscal, (C) conséquence d'une taxe sur la vente d'un bien

(GER) Steuerkeil m

(JAP) タックスウェッジ

(RUS) НАЛОГОВЫЙ «КЛИН» (влияние налоговых соображений на выбор между операциями)

team building

(CHIN) 团队建设

(FRE) création d'un esprit d'équipe, (C) consolidation d'équipe

(GER) Teambildung f, -aufbau m, Mannschaftsbildung f

(JAP) チーム構築、チーム協力

(RUS) ПОСТРОЕНИЕ КОЛЛЕКТИВА

team management

(CHIN) 团队管理

(FRE) gestion d'équipe

(GER) Teammanagement n

(JAP) チーム管理

(RUS) РУКОВОДСТВО КОЛЛЕКТИВОМ

teaser ad

(CHIN) 含蓄而令人好奇的广告

(FRE) aguiche, teaser

(GER) Lockwerbung f

(JAP) 賞金（賞品）などで購買者の気を引く広告、誘導広告

(RUS) «ЗАВЛЕКАТЕЛЬНАЯ» РЕКЛАМА, Т. Е. ИНТЕРЕСНАЯ РЕКЛАМА, НЕ ДАЮЩАЯ ПОЛНОЙ ИНФОРМАЦИИ О ПРОДУКТЕ ИЛИ РЕКЛАМОДЕТЕЛЕ

teaser rate

(CHIN) 最初利率

(FRE) taux amorce

(GER) Lock-Zinssatz m

(JAP) ティーザーレート、
借手誘導のための変動金利モー ゲージ
の導入時のレート
(RUS) «ЗАВЛЕКАТЕЛЬНАЯ» СТАВКА,
ВРЕМЕННО НИЗКАЯ ПРОЦЕНТНАЯ
СТАВКА

technical analysis

(CHIN) 技术分析
(FRE) analyse sur graphiques
(GER) technische Analyse *f*
(JAP) 技術的分析
(RUS) ТЕХНИЧЕСКИЙ АНАЛИЗ

technical rally

(CHIN) 技术性回升
(FRE) reprise boursière technique
(GER) markttechnische Erholung *f*
(JAP) （相場の）自律的反発、
人為的回復、アヤ戻し
(RUS) ВСПЛЕСК ЦЕН НА ФИНАНСОВОМ
РЫНКЕ ВО ВРЕМЯ ТЕНДЕНЦИИ К
ПОНИЖЕНИЮ

technological obsolescence

(CHIN) 技术陈旧
(FRE) vétusté technologique, (C)
obsolescence technologique
(GER) technische Überalterung *f* bzw.
Veraltung *f*
(JAP) 技術的老朽、技術的陳腐化
(RUS) ТЕХНИЧЕСКОЕ УСТАРЕВАНИЕ

technological unemployment

(CHIN) 技术性失业
(FRE) chômage technique, (C) chômage
technologique
(GER) technologische Arbeitslosigkeit *f*
 (JAP) 技術的失業
(RUS) БЕЗРАБОТИЦА, ВЫЗВАННАЯ
ИЗМЕНЕНИЯМИ ТЕХНОЛОГИЙ

technology

(CHIN) 技术，工艺，
术语
(FRE) technologie
(GER) Technologie *f*
(JAP) 科学技術、応用技術、
テクノロジー
(RUS) ТЕХНОЛОГИЯ

telecommunications

(CHIN) 电讯
(FRE) télécommunications
(GER) Telekommunikation *f*,
Nachrichtentechnik *f*,
Fernmeldewesen *n*
(JAP) 遠距離通信、電気通信学
(RUS) ТЕЛЕКОММУНИКАЦИЯ; СРЕДСТВА
СВЯЗИ

telemarketing

(CHIN) 电话营销
(FRE) télémarketing
(GER) Telemarketing *n*
(JAP) テレマーケティング、
電話による販売・広告活動
(RUS) ПРОДАЖА ПО ТЕЛЕФОНУ

telephone switching

(CHIN) 通过电话转移互助基金资产
(FRE) commutation téléphonique
(GER) Fernsprechvermittlung *f*
(JAP) 電話交換
(RUS) ПЕРЕБРОСКА ИНВЕСТИЦИЙ ПО
ТЕЛЕФОНУ

template

(CHIN) 模板
(FRE) réglette, modèle, (C) gabarit
(GER) Dokumentvorlage *f* (EDV)
(JAP) 型板、テンプレート
(RUS) ШАБЛОН; ОБРАЗЕЦ

tenancy

(CHIN) 租赁，租期，租借权
(FRE) location
(GER) Miet- *n*, Pachtverhältnis *n*; Miet- *f*,
Pachtdauer *f*
(JAP) （土地、家屋などの）保有、占有、
借用権
(RUS) ПРОЖИВАНИЕ; ЗАСЕЛЕНИЕ

tenancy at sufferance

(CHIN) 过期租赁
(FRE) occupation tolérée, (C) tenance par
tolérance
(GER) (nach Ablauf der Miet- bzw.
Pachtzeit) jederzeit kündbarer Miet- bzw.
Pachtvertrag *m*, stillschweigend
verlängertes Miet- *n* bzw. Pachtverhältnis *n*

(JAP) 黙認不動産権
(RUS) АРЕНДНОЕ ВЛАДЕНИЕ С
МОЛЧАЛИВОГО СОГЛАСИЯ
СОБСТВЕННИКА

tenancy at will

(CHIN) 意愿性租赁
(FRE) bail à titre précaire, (C) location à
discrétion
(GER) jederzeit kündbares Miet- n bzw.
Pachtverhältnis n
(JAP) 任意不動産権
(RUS) АРЕНДА БЕЗ ОПРЕДЕЛЕННОГО
СРОКА, БЕССРОЧНАЯ

tenancy by the entirety

(CHIN) 整体租赁
(FRE) propriété indivise, propriété en
indivision, propriété conjointe,
(C) copropriété des conjoints avec gain de
survie
(GER) Gesamthandeigentum n,
Gütergemeinschaft f
(JAP) 夫婦全部保有（不動産権）
(RUS) СОВМЕСТНОЕ ПРАВО СУПРУГОВ
НА НЕДВИЖИМУЮ СОБСТВЕННОСТЬ

tenancy for years

(CHIN) 固定期限租赁
(FRE) location en années
(GER) auf Jahre npl begrenztes Miet- n bzw.
Pachtverhältnis n
(JAP) 定期不動産権
(RUS) ВРЕМЕННОЕ ВЛАДЕНИЕ
АРЕНДУЕМОЙ СОБСТВЕННОСТЬЮ

tenancy in common

(CHIN) 共同租赁
(FRE) propriété en commun,
(C) copropriété indivise
(GER) Miteigentum n nach Bruchteilen fpl,
Gemeinschaftseigentum n
(JAP) 共有不動産権、共有財産権
(RUS) ОБЩЕЕ (СОВМЕСТНОЕ) ВЛАДЕНИЕ
СОБСТВЕННОСТЬЮ

tenancy in severalty

(CHIN) 单独租赁
(FRE) occupation individuelle
(GER) alleinberechtiges Miet- n bzw.
Pachtverhältnis

(JAP) 単独保有不動産権、
単独保有財産権
(RUS) САМОСТОЯТЕЛЬНОЕ ВЛАДЕНИЕ
СОБСТВЕННОСТЬЮ

tenant

(CHIN) 承租人，租户，房客，租借
(FRE) locataire
(GER) Mieter m, Pächter m
(JAP) 借家人、
暫定的不動産権保有者、貸借人
(RUS) ВЛАДЕЛЕЦ, АРЕНДАТОР
НЕДВИЖИМОСТИ

tenant finish-out allowance

(CHIN) 租户整改折扣
(FRE) allocation pour travaux
d'aménagement du locataire commercial,
(C) allocation pour améliorations
(GER) Bewilligung f für
Mieterumbauten mpl
(JAP) テナント終了引当金
(RUS) ВЫПЛАТЫ АРЕНДАТОРУ НА
МЕЛКОЕ ПЕРЕОБОРУДОВАНИЕ
ПОМЕЩЕНИЯ ПОД СВОИ НУЖДЫ

tender

(CHIN) 投标，清偿，提出，投标书
(FRE) offre, proposition, soumission
(GER) Angebot n, Offerte f;
Submissionsangebot n;
Zeichnungsangebot n
(JAP) 提供（物・する）、入札、
賠償金、請負見積書
(RUS) ТЕНДЕР; ЗАПРОС НА
ПОКУПКУ

tender of delivery

(CHIN) 提供运送服务
(FRE) offre de livraison
(GER) Lieferangebot n
(JAP) 引渡し賠償金
(RUS) ТЕНДЕР НА ПОСТАВКУ,
ДОСТАВКУ

tender offer

(CHIN) 收购股权，招标，提出要约
(FRE) offre par adjudication adjudication,
procédure des appels d'offres, (C) offre
publique d'achat

(GER) Zeichnungsangebot *n*, Tender-
Offerte *f*, Ausschreibungsangebot *n*;
Übernahmeangebot *n*
(JAP) 株式公開買付け、
テンダーオファー
(RUS) ПРЕДЛОЖЕНИЕ О ПОКУПКЕ

tenure
(CHIN) 占用，占有，使用期
(FRE) inamovibilité occupation, possession
(C) permanence
(GER) Dienst- *f*, Amtszeit *f*; Besitz *m*
(JAP) 保有期間、保有条件、終身在任権
(RUS) ВЛАДЕНИЕ НЕДВИЖИМОСТЬЮ;
ПРЕБЫВАНИЕ (в должности)

tenure in land
(CHIN) 土地占有
(FRE) tenure foncière, (C) mode de
détention d'un domaine foncier
(GER) Landbesitz *m*
(JAP) 土地保留期間
(RUS) ЗЕМЛЕВЛАДЕНИЕ

term
(CHIN) 期限，条款，约定，术语，
结账期
(FRE) terme
(GER) Dauer *f*, Zeitraum *m*; Laufzeit *f*, Frist
f; Amts- *f*, Legislaturperiode *f*
(JAP) 期間、期限、 *(pl.)* （支払・契約
などの）条件
(RUS) СРОК; ТЕРМИН; ВЫРАЖЕНИЕ

term, amortization
(CHIN) 摊还期
(FRE) durée, amortissement, (C)
(GER) Tilgungsfrist *f*; Tilgungsbedingung *f*
(JAP) 債務償還期限、債務償還約定日
(RUS) СРОК АМОРТИЗАЦИИ

term certificate
(CHIN) 定期存款证明
(FRE) certificat à long terme
(GER) Einlagen- *n*,
Depositenzertifikat *n*
(JAP) 期限付き証券、
定期預金証書
(RUS) СРОЧНЫЙ СЕРТИФИКАТ

termination benefits
(CHIN) 解雇福利
(FRE) prestations de pré- retraite,
(C) certificat de dépôt à terme
(GER) Entlassungsabfindung *f*
(JAP) 満期給付、満期給付額
(RUS) ЛЬГОТЫ, ВЫГОДЫ ПРИ
ПРЕКРАЩЕНИИ

term life insurance
(CHIN) 定期人手保险
(FRE) assurance temporaire
GER) auf Zeit abgeschlossene
Todesfallversicherung *f*
(JAP) 定期生命保険
(RUS) СРОЧНОЕ СТРАХОВАНИЕ ЖИЗНИ

term loan
(CHIN) 定期贷款
(FRE) emprunt à terme, (C) crédit à long
terme
(GER) befristeter Kredit *m* bzw. Darlehen *n*
(JAP) タームローン
(RUS) СРОЧНЫЙ КРЕДИТ

terms
(CHIN) 条款
(FRE) durée), termes conditions,
(C) modalités
(GER) Bedingungen *fpl*, Konditionen *fpl*;
Ausstattung *f*, Modalitäten *fpl*
(JAP) 条件、条項、料金
(RUS) УСЛОВИЯ, ПОЛОЖЕНИЯ (договора)

test
(CHIN) 检验，测试，测验方法
(FRE) test, épreuve, examen,
(C) essai
(GER) Test *m*; Versuch *m*
(JAP) 試験、を試す
(RUS) ПРОВЕРКА, ИСПЫТАНИЕ; ТЕСТ

testament
(CHIN) 遗嘱
(FRE) testament
(GER) Testament *n*, letztwillige
Verfügung *f*
(JAP) 遺言、遺言書、立証
(RUS) ЗАВЕЩАНИЕ

419

testamentary trust

(CHIN) 遺囑信托

(FRE) fiducie (n, f) testamentaire

(GER) testamentarischer Trust *m*, Nachlassstiftung *f*, letztwillige Treuhandbestellung *f*

(JAP) 遺言信託

(RUS) ТРАСТ ПО ЗАВЕЩАНИЮ ДОВЕРИТЕЛЯ

testate

(CHIN) 有遺囑的

(FRE) ayant testé

(GER) unter Hinterlassung *f* eines Testaments *n*

(JAP) 有効な遺言を残して

(RUS) ОСТАВЛЯТЬ ПО ЗАВЕЩАНИЮ

testator

(CHIN) 立有遺囑的人

(FRE) testateur

(GER) Erblasser *m*, Testator *m*

(JAP) 遺言者

(RUS) ЗАВЕЩАТЕЛЬ

testcheck

(CHIN) 抽査，抽査法

(FRE) sondage, échantillonnage statistique

(GER) stichprobenweise prüfen *v*

(JAP) テストチェック

(RUS) ПРОВЕРКА ИСПЫТАНИЕМ

testimonial

奖金，纪念品，证明书，鉴定书

(FRE) témoignage

(GER) Zeugnis *n*, Testat *n*, Empfehlung *f*

(JAP) 証明書（の）、証拠（の）

(RUS) АТТЕСТАТ; СВИДЕТЕЛЬСТВО; УДОСТОВЕРЕНИЕ

testimonium

(CHIN) 援引条款

(FRE) de signature

(GER) Schlussklausel *f*, Beglaubigungsvermerk *m*

(JAP) 証明、証拠、宣誓証言

(RUS) ЗАКЛЮЧИТЕЛЬНАЯ ЧАСТЬ (с подписями и адресами) ЮРИДИЧЕСКОГО ДОКУМЕНТА

test market

(CHIN) 试销市场

(FRE) marché témoin, marché test

(GER) Test- *m*, Versuchsmarkt *m*

(JAP) テストマーケット、試験市場、試験販売

(RUS) ПРОБНЫЙ РЫНОК

test statistic

(CHIN) 调查统计

(FRE) fonction des observations, (C) test d'hypothèse

(GER) Versuchsstatistik *f*, Prüfgröße *f*

(JAP) 検定統計

(RUS) ПРОБНАЯ СТАТИСТИКА

text editing

(CHIN) 正文[文本]编辑

(FRE) édition de texte, (C) édition

(GER) Textbearbeitung *f* (EDV)

(JAP) テキスト編集

(RUS) РЕДАКТИРОВАНИЕ ТЕКСТА

text processing

(CHIN) 正文[文本]处理

(FRE) traitement de texte

(GER) Textverarbeitung *f* (EDV)

(JAP) テキスト処理

(RUS) ОБРАБОТКА ТЕКСТОВ

text wrap

(CHIN) 正文[文本]围绕

(FRE) mots non coupés, (C) intégration de texte

(GER) Textumlauf *m* (EDV)

(JAP) テキストラップ、テキスト折返し

thin market

(CHIN) 滞呆市场，清淡市场

(FRE) marché étroit, marché serré

(GER) schwacher Markt *m*

third market

(CHIN) 第三市场

(FRE) troisième marché, marché hors bourse

(GER) Drittmarkt *m*; ungeregelter Freiverkehr *m*

(JAP) 閑散な市況、手薄な市況、

420

薄商い市場
(RUS) ВЯЛЫЙ РЫНОК

third party
(CHIN) 第三方，第三者
(FRE) tiers
(GER) Dritter *m*
(JAP) 第三者、第三政党、
サードパーティ
(RUS) «ТРЕТИЙ" РЫНОК; ВНЕБИРЖЕВОЙ
РЫНОК
(RUS) ТРЕТЬЯ СТОРОНА; ТРЕТЬЕ ЛИЦО

third-party check
(CHIN) 第三者支票
(FRE) lettre de change, (C) vérification
d'un tiers
(GER) Scheck *m* zugunsten einer dritten
Person *f*
 (JAP) 第三者小切手
(RUS) КОНТРОЛЬ ТРЕТЬЕЙ СТОРОНЫ

third-party sale
(CHIN) 第三者销售
(FRE) vente par un intermédiaire, (C) vente
réalisée par un tiers
(GER) Verkauf *m* über eine dritte Partei *f*
(JAP) 第三者販売
(RUS) ПРОДАЖА ТРЕТЬЕЙ СТОРОНОЙ или
ТРЕТЬЕЙ СТОРОНЕ

threshold-point ordering
(CHIN) 起点订购
(FRE) commande à seuil, (C) commande
minimum pour répondre à la demande
(GER) Schwellenpunktbestellsystem *n*
(JAP) 限界点注文
(RUS) ЗАКАЗ (ПРИКАЗ НА ПОКУПКУ)
С НАЗНАЧЕНИЕМ КРАЙНЕЙ ТОЧКИ

thrift insitution
(CHIN) 储蓄机构
(FRE) caisse d'épargne, (C) établissement
d'épargne
(GER) Sparkasse *f* und
Kreditgenossenschaft *f* (US);
Sparvereinigung *f*; Bausparkasse *f*
(JAP) 貯蓄金融機関
(RUS) СБЕРЕГАТЕЛЬНОЕ
УЧРЕЖДЕНИЕ

thrifty
(CHIN) 廉价的
(FRE) précoce, (C) économe
(GER) sparsam *adj*
(JAP) 節約する、倹約的な
(RUS) БЕРЕЖЛИВЫЙ, ЭКОНОМНЫЙ

through rate
(CHIN) 联运运费，直达运价
(FRE) tarif direct, prix de bout en bout,
(C) taux télégraphique
(GER) Durchfracht- *m*, Durchgangstarif *m*
(JAP) スルーレート、通し運賃、
通し値段
(RUS) ПОЛНЫЙ ТАРИФ

tick
(CHIN) 信用，赊欠，赊销，赊购
(FRE) crédit, (C) pointer
(GER) Abhakungszeichen *n*, Haken *m*;
Kredit *m*; Kurs- *m*, Preisveränderung *f*
(JAP) 目盛、小さな印、点 チック
(RUS) ИЗМЕНЕНИЕ БИРЖЕВОЙ ЦЕНЫ

ticker
(CHIN) 股票行情自动收录器
(FRE) données historique des transactions,
(C) téléscripteur
(GER) Börsenticker *m*,
Kursübermittlungsanlage *f*
(JAP) ティッカー、株式相場表示板
(RUS) УСТРОЙСТВО ОПЕРАТИВНОЙ
ВЫДАЧИ ФИН. ИНФОРМАЦИИ; БЕГУЩАЯ
СТРОКА

tie-in promotion
(CHIN) 联合推销
(FRE) promotion collective
(GER) Anknüpfungs- *f*,
Kombinationswerbung *f*
(RUS) СОВМЕСТНОЕ ПРОДВИЖЕНИЕ (на
рынок)

tight market
(CHIN) 供不应求的市场
(FRE) marché étroit, marché
 serré
(GER) enger Markt *m*
(JAP) 逼迫市場、逼迫市況

tight money
(CHIN) 收紧银根
(FRE)
(GER) knappes Geld *n*
(JAP) 金融引締め、金融逼迫、金詰まり
(RUS) НЕЖВАТКА ДЕНЕГ, СЛОЖНОСТИ В ПОЛУЧЕНИИ КРЕДИТОВ

tight ship
(CHIN) 严格的规章制度
(FRE) gestion rigoureuse, (C) gestion serrée
(GER) straffe Organisation *f*
(JAP) 統制のとれた会社（組織、機関）
(RUS) ЖЕСТКАЯ ОРГАНИЗАЦИЯ

till
(CHIN) 备用现金，钱柜
(FRE) caisse, (C) tiroir-caisse
(GER) Ladenkasse *f*, Geldfach *n*
(JAP) (英)レジ、キャッシュドローアー、（帳場の）銭箱
(RUS) КАССА

time-and-a-half
(CHIN) 一点五倍加班费
(FRE) majoration de moitié, salaire horaire majoré de moitié, (C) salaire majoré de 50 %
(GER) 50%-iger Lohnzuschlag *m* (bei Nacht- und Feiertagsarbeit)
(JAP) ５割増の超過勤務手当
(RUS) ПОЛУТОРНЫЙ, С 50-ПРОЦЕНТНОЙ НАДБАВКОЙ

time card
(CHIN) 工时卡
(FRE) feuille de présence
(GER) Zeitkarte *f*, Istzeit-Meldung *f*
(JAP) 就業時間記録カード、作業時間票
(RUS) КАРТОЧКА РЕГИСТРАЦИИ ПРИХОДА И УХОДА РАБОТНИКОВ

time deposit
(CHIN) 定期存款
(FRE) dépôt à terme, (C) dépôt à terme fixe
(JAP) 有期預金、定期預金

(RUS) СРОЧНЫЙ ДЕПОЗИТ

time draft
(CHIN) 定期汇票，远期汇票
(FRE) traite à terme, (C) traite à échéance
(GER) Termin- *f*, Festgeldeinlage *f*
(GER) Terminwechsel *m*; Zielwechsel *m*
(JAP) 一覧後定期払手形、定期払為替手形、定期払約束手形
(RUS) СРОЧНАЯ ТРАТТА; ПЕРЕВОДНОЙ ВЕКСЕЛЬ С ФИКСИРОВАННЫМ СРОКОМ

time is of the essence
(CHIN) 强调时间要素的重要性，时限
(FRE) le temps est une condition essentielle
(GER) Fristeinhaltung *f* ist wesentlich für die Vertragserfüllung *f*; zeitsensibel *adj*
(JAP) 時間は重要である、期限厳守
(RUS) С ЖЕСТКИМ УЧЕТОМ ВРЕМЕНИ, СРОКОВ

time management
(CHIN) 时间管理
(FRE) gestion du temps de travail, (C) gestion de temps
(GER) Zeiteinteilung *f*, -management *f*
(JAP) 時間管理
(RUS) ЭФФЕКТИВНОСТЬ ИСПОЛЬЗОВАНИЯ ВРЕМЕНИ

time series analysis
(CHIN) 时序分析
(FRE) analyse de séries chronologiques
(GER) Zeitreihenanalyse *f*
(JAP) タイムシリーズ分析、時系列分析
(RUS) АНАЛИЗ ВРЕМЕННЫХ РЯДОВ

time series data
(CHIN) 时序数据
(FRE) données par séries de temps
(GER) Zeitreihendaten *pl*
(JAP) 時系列資料、タイムシリーズデータ
(RUS) ДАННЫЕ ВРЕМЕННЫХ РЯДОВ

time-sharing
(CHIN) 分时
(FRE) partage de temps, temps partagé

422

(GER) Time Sharing *n*; Nutzung *f* eines anteilsmäßigen und zeitlich begrenzten Rechtstitels *m*; Mehrbenutzersystem *n*
(JAP) タイムシェアリング
(RUS) ВЛАДЕНИЕ СОБСТВЕННОСТЬЮ В РЕЖИМЕ РАЗДЕЛЕНИЯ ВРЕМЕНИ

timetable
(CHIN) 时间表，时刻表
(FRE) horaire, emploi du temps,
(C) indicateur
(GER) Zeitplan *m*
(JAP) 計画表，時間表、予定表
(RUS) РАСПИСАНИЕ, ГРАФИК

time value
(CHIN) 时间价值
(FRE) valeur temporelle, (C) valeur temps
(GER) Zeitwert *m*
(JAP) 時間的価値
(RUS) ВРЕМЕННАЯ (СРОЧНАЯ) СТОИМОСТЬ (опциона)

tip
(CHIN) 小费，内幕消息，暗示，劝告
(FRE) pourboire, (C) conseil
(GER) Trinkgeld *n*; Ratschlag *m*; Spitze *f*
(JAP) チップ、警告暗示、内密の情報 （予想、助言、警告）
(RUS) ИНФОРМАЦИЯ, ПОДСКАЗКА; ЧАЕВЫЕ

title
(CHIN) 产权，权利，所有权，科目，名称
(FRE) titre, (C) désignation
(GER) Eigentumsrecht *n*, (Rechts)titel *m*, Rechtsanspruch *m*, Anrecht *n*; Eigentums- *f*, Besitzurkunde *f*
(JAP) 所有権、権原証書、敬称、表題
(RUS) ЗАКОННОЕ ПРАВО ВЛАДЕНИЯ; ПРАВОВОЙ ТИТУЛ

title bar
(CHIN) 标题栏 [条]
(FRE) barre des titres
(GER) Titelleiste *f*, Überschriftsleiste *f* (EDV)
(JAP) タイトルバー
(RUS) ЗАГОЛОВОК ОКНА

title company
(CHIN) 产权调查公司
(FRE) societe d'acquisitions immobilieres, (C) émetteur de titre de propriété
(GER) Rechtstitelversicherungsgesellschaft *f*
(JAP) 権原保険会社
(RUS) КОМПАНИЯ, ПРОВЕРЯЮЩАЯ ПРАВА НА НЕДВИЖИМОСТЬ

title defect
(CHIN) 产权缺陷
(FRE) défaut de titre, (C) titre de propriété non déterminé
(GER) mit Mangel *m* behafteter Rechtstitel *m*
(JAP) 権原の欠陥、権原の瑕疵、権原の欠如
(RUS) ДЕФЕКТ (уязвимое место) ПРАВОВОГО ТИТУЛА

title insurance
(CHIN) 产权保险
(FRE) assurance de titre de propriété, (C) contrat d'assurance des titres de propriété
(GER) Rechtstitelversicherung *f*
(JAP) 権原保険、所有権保証
(RUS) СТРАХОВАНИЕ ПРАВОВОГО ТИТУЛА

title report
(CHIN) 产权报告
(FRE) état du titre, (C) rapport d'introduction
(GER) Rechtstitelreport *n*, -bericht *m*, (Ergebnis der Prüfung der Rechtsbeständigkeit von Eigentumsrechten)
(JAP) 不動産所有権報告書、権原報告書
(RUS) ЗАКЛЮЧЕНИЕ ПО ПРОВЕРКЕ ПРАВОВОГО ТИТУЛА

title screen
(CHIN) 标题屏幕
(FRE) écran de titre, (C) écran d'introduction
(GER) Titelbildschirm *m*
(JAP) タイトルスクリーン、タイトル画面

(RUS) ТИТУЛЬНАЯ СТРАНИЦА КОМПЬЮРЕНОЙ ИГРЫ, СОДЕРЖАЩАЯ ЕЁ НАЗВАНИЕ И ДР. ИНФОРМАЦИЮ

title search

(CHIN) 产权搜索

(FRE) recherche de titres

(GER) Rechtstitelüberprüfung *f*, (Überprüfung der Rechtsbeständigkeit von Eigentumsrechten)

(JAP) 不動産所有権調査

(RUS) ПРОВЕРКА ПРАВОВОГО ТИТУЛА ПО АРХИВАМ

title theory

(CHIN) 产权理论

(FRE) théorie de la propriété, (C) théorie sur la possession du titre de propriété

(GER) Rechtstiteltheorie *f*, (Lehre vom treuhänderischen Eigentumsübergang auf den Hypothekengläubiger)

(JAP) 所有権理論

(RUS) ТЕОРИЯ ИПОТЕЧНОГО ЗАКОНА ОТНОСИТЕЛЬНО ПРЕЕМСТВЕННОСТИ ПРАВА ВЛАДЕНИЯ

toggle key

(CHIN) 切换键

(FRE) touche de basculement, (C) touche à bascule

(GER) Kipptaste *f*, Toggle-Taste *f*

(JAP) トグルキー

(RUS) КЛЮЧ, КЛАВИША ПЕРЕКЛЮЧЕНИЯ

tokenism

(CHIN) 象征主义

(FRE) tokenisme, cause politique, (C) geste symbolique

(GER) Tokenismus *m*, Alibipolitik *f*

(JAP) 名目主義、形式主義

(RUS) ФОРМАЛЬНЫЙ ПОДХОД К ВЫПОЛНЕНИЮ ТРЕБОВАНИЯ, СОЗДАНИЕ ВИДИМОСТИ

toll

(CHIN) 通行税，过境税，长途电话费，服务费

(FRE) péage, coût

(GER) Gebühr *f*, Abgabe *f*, Maut *f*, Zoll *m*

(JAP) 使用料、サービス料、（通例単数形）（事後・災害などの）代償、犠牲者数

(RUS) ПЛАТА; ПОШЛИНА; СБОР; РЕЗУЛЬТАТ

tombstone ad

(CHIN) 证券发行广告

(FRE) pierre tombale (se dit d'une annonce saturée de texte, ne faisant que très peu de place au visuel et manquant très nettement de créativité), (C) annonce de placement

(GER) Emissionsanzeige *f*

(JAP) ツームストーン広告、墓碑広告

(RUS) ОБЪЯВЛЕНИЕ В ГАЗЕТЕ О ПУБЛИЧНОЙ ПРОДАЖЕ ВЫПУСКА ЦЕННЫХ БУМАГ (получило название из-за внешней схожести с колонкой некрологов)

toner cartridge

(CHIN) 墨粉盒

(FRE) toner, (C) cartouche d'encre

(GER) Tonerkassette *f*, -kartusche *f* (Drucker)

(JAP) トーナーカートリッジ

(RUS) ТОННЕРНЫЙ КАРТРИДЖ

tool bar

(CHIN) 工具栏

(FRE) barre d'outils

(GER) Werkzeugleiste *f* (EDV)

(JAP) ツールバー

(RUS) ЗОНА ИНДИКАЦИИ

tool box

(CHIN) 工具箱

(FRE) boîteà outils

(GER) Toolbox *f*, Werkzeugkasten *f*

(JAP) ツールボックス

(RUS) ИНСТРУМЕНТАРИЙ

topping out

(CHIN) 市场或证券达到顶点

(FRE) plafonnement, (C) prix plafond

(GER) Höchststand *m* erreichen *v*

(JAP) 上げ止まり

(RUS) ДОСТИЖЕНИЕ ЦЕНОЙ СВОЕГО ПИКА

tort

(CHIN) 侵权

(FRE) préjudice, dommage, acte dommageable, (C) acte délictuel

(GER) Delikt *n*, unerlaubte Handlung *f*

(JAP) 不法行為

(RUS) ГРАЖДАНСКОЕ ПРАВОНАРУШЕНИЕ; ДЕЛИКТ

total capitalization

(CHIN) 总资本结构

(FRE) capitalisation totale

(GER) Gesamtkapitalisierung *f*

(JAP) 総資本化、総資産化、総額資本組入れ

(RUS) ПОЛНАЯ КАПИТАЛИЗАЦИЯ

total loss

(CHIN) 总亏损，亏损总额，全损险

(FRE) perte totale, sinistre total

(GER) Totalschaden *m*; Totalverlust *m*

(JAP) （保険で）全損

(RUS) ПОЛНЫЕ УБЫТКИ

total paid

(CHIN) 总付款

(FRE) total versé, (C) paiement total

(GER) insamt bezahlt *adj*; bezahlte Endsumme *f*

(JAP) 支払済み総額

(RUS) ИТОГ ОПЛАТЫ, ВЫПЛАТ

total volume

(CHIN) 总额，总量

(FRE) volume total, volume utile

(GER) Gesamtvolumen *n*

(JAP) 総取引高

(RUS) ИТОГОВЫЙ (ПОЛНЫЙ) ОБЪЕМ

touch screen

(CHIN) 触摸屏

(FRE) écran tactile

(GER) Berührungsbildschirm *m* (Computer)

(RUS) СЕНСОРНЫЙ ЭКРАН

trace, tracer

(CHIN) 追踪，追询书

(FRE) trace, traceur, (C) repérer, (C) agent de relance

(GER) (mit)verfolgen; nachzeichnen; verrechnen *v*; Lauf- *n*, Suchzettel *m*

(JAP) 跡をつける、複写する、跡、紛失物捜査照会状、転写（透写）用具

(RUS) ЛОКАЛИЗОВАТЬ; ЗАПРОС О ЛОКАЛИЗАЦИИ (ПОТЕРЯННОЙ ПАРТИИ ТОВАРА)

trackage

(CHIN) 铁路轨道使用费

(FRE) droit (n, m) de circulation, (C) circulation

(GER) Streckengeschäft *n*, -benutzungsrecht *n*, -benutzungsgebühr *f*

(JAP) 鉄道の総線路、軌道使用料

(RUS) ОТСЛЕЖИВАНИЕ; ПРЕДЫСТОРИЯ

trackball

(CHIN) 跟踪球

(FRE) boule roulante, boule de commande

(GER) Rollkugel *f*, Trackball-Gerät *n*

(JAP) トラックボール

(RUS) ОТСЛЕЖИВАЮЩИЙ ШАРИК

tract

(CHIN) 一片土地

(FRE) terrain

(GER) Landstrich *m*; Abhandlung *f*

(JAP) 地帯、領域、住宅団地、宅地

(RUS) ЧАСТЬ БОЛЕЕ КРУПНОГО ЗЕМЕЛЬНОГО УЧАСТКА

trade

(CHIN) 贸易，商业，交易，买卖，行业

(FRE) commerce, affaires, (C) transaction, (C) échange

(GER) Handel *m*; Gewerbe *n*

(JAP) 商業、職業、貿易する、（物々）交換する

(RUS) ТОРГОВЛЯ; СДЕЛКА (с ценными бумагами)

trade acceptance

(CHIN) 商业承兑汇票

(FRE) acceptation commerciale

(GER) Waren- *m*, Kunden- *m*,Wechselakzept *m*, Waren- *m*, Handelswechsel *m*; Außenhandelsakzept *n*

(JAP) 商業引受手形、貿易引受手形、
引受荷為替手形
(RUS) ТОРГОВЫЙ АКЦЕПТ –
ПЕРЕВОДНОЙ ВЕКСЕЛЬ,
ВЫСТАВЛЕННЫЙ НА ЭКСПОРТЕРА или
ИМПОРТЕРА

trade advertising
(CHIN) 消费品广告
(FRE) publicité professionnelle
(GER) Fachwerbung *f*
(JAP) 業者向け広告、産業広告、
流通広告
(RUS) ТОРГОВАЯ РЕКЛАМА

trade agreement
(CHIN) 贸易协议
(FRE) accord commercial
(GER) Handelsabkommen *n*, -vertrag *m*, -
vereinbarung *f*
(JAP) 貿易協約
(RUS) ТОРГОВОЕ СОГЛАШЕНИЕ

trade barrier
(CHIN) 贸易壁垒
(FRE) barrière commerciale
(GER) Handelsschranke *f*
(JAP) 貿易障害
(RUS) ТОРГОВЫЙ БАРЬЕР

trade credit
(CHIN) 贸易赊账，商业信用
(FRE) crédit fournisseur, crédit commercial
(GER) Handels- *m*, Warenkredit *m*
(JAP) 企業間信用、貿易信用、商業信用
状
(RUS) ТОРГОВЫЙ, КОММЕРЧЕСКИЙ
КРЕДИТ

trade date
(CHIN) 交易日期，成交日期
(FRE) jour de la transaction, date de la
transaction
(GER) Schlusstag *m*, Transaktionsdatum *n*
(JAP) 取引日、約定日
(RUS) ДАТА ЗАКЛЮЧЕНИЯ или
ИСПОЛНЕНИЯ СДЕЛКИ

trade deficit (surplus)
(CHIN) 贸易赤字（盈余）

(FRE) balance commerciale déficitaire,
déficit, (C) déficit commercial (surplus)
(GER) Außenhandelsdefizit *n*
(-überschuss *m*)
(JAP) 貿易収支の赤字、
（貿易収支の黒字）
(RUS) ТОРГОВЫЙ ДЕФИЦИТ (ИЗЛИШЕК)

trade fixture
(CHIN) 工商业设备，贸易设施
objet fixé en vue de l'exploitation d'un
commerce
(GER) gewerbliche Einbauten *mpl*
(JAP) 営業用備品
(RUS) КОМПОНЕНТ ТОРГОВЛИ

trade magazine
(CHIN) 贸易杂志
(FRE) journal professionnel, revue
professionnelle, (C) magazine spécialisé
(GER) Fachzeitschrift *f*
(JAP) 業界誌
(RUS) ПРОФЕССИОНАЛЬНЫЙ ЖУРНАЛ

trademark
(CHIN) 商标
(FRE) marque, marquecommerciale,
(C) marque de commerce
(GER) Warenzeichen *n*, Schutzmarke *f*
(JAP) 登録商標、商標、トレードマーク
(RUS) ТОВАРНЫЙ ЗНАК

trade-off
(CHIN) 卖掉，换掉
(FRE) compromis, substituabilité), (C) troc
(GER) Tradeoff *m*, Gegen-
n, Tauschgeschäft *n*; Austauschbeziehung *f*;
Kompromiss *m*
(JAP) 相殺取引、相殺協定、
トレードオフ
(RUS) КОММЕРЧЕСКИЙ
КОМПРОМИСС

trade rate
(CHIN) 同业汇率
(FRE) taux commercial, (C) prix spécial
aux grossistes
(GER) Handelspreis *m*
(JAP) 業者間料金
(RUS) УРОВЕНЬ ТОРГОВЛИ

trader

(CHIN) 贸易商，交易员，商船

(FRE) commerçant, marchand, négociant, opérateur, (C) délégué en bourse, (C) spéculateur habituel, (C) négociateur

(GER) Wertpapierhändler *m*; Gewerbetreibender *m*; Händler *m*, Kaufmann *m*

(JAP) 貿易業者、トレーダー、株の売買人、株式証券業

(RUS) БИРЖЕВОЙ МАКЛЕР

trade secret

(CHIN) 商业秘密，行业秘密

(FRE) secret commercial, secret des affaires, (C) secret de commerce

(GER) Geschäfts- *n*, Betriebsgeheimnis *n*

(JAP) 企業秘密、営業秘密、取引上の秘密

(RUS) КОММЕРЧЕСКАЯ ТАЙНА

trade show

(CHIN) 商业展览

(FRE) salon, salonprofessionnel, exposition professionnelle, (C) foire commerciale trade union syndicat

(GER) Fachmesse *f*, Trade Show *f*

(JAP) 商業展示会

(RUS) СПЕЦИАЛИЗИРОВАННАЯ ВЫСТАВКА

trade union

(CHIN) 工会，行业工会

(FRE) syndicat

(GER) Gewerkschaft *f*

(JAP) 労働組合

(RUS) ПРОФСОЮЗ

trading authorization

(CHIN) 贸易委托书

(FRE) autorisation de négocier

(GER) Handelserlaubnis *f*; Gewerbeerlaubnis *f*

(JAP) 取引認可証、取引権限委任書

(RUS) РАЗРЕШЕНИЕ НА ИСПОЛНЕНИЕ СДЕЛКИ (бирж.)

trading post

(CHIN) 交易所，商站

(FRE) parquet, corbeille, (C) poste pour la traite

(GER) Börsenstand *m*; Handelsposten *m*, -niederlassung *f*, -stützpunkt *m*

(JAP) 貿易所、交易場、銘柄の取引ポスト

(RUS) ТОРГОВЫЙ ПОСТ (бирж.)

trading range

(CHIN) 成交价格幅度

(FRE) écart de prix, fourchette de cotation, (C) variation

(GER) gehandelter Kursbereich *m*, Kursspanne *f*

(JAP) 取引限度、値動き幅

(RUS) РАЗБРОС, КОЛЕБАНИЕ ЦЕН

trading stamp

(CHIN) 购货赠券，商品券

(FRE) timbre, (C) timbre-prime,(C) point-épargne

(GER) Rabattmarke *f*, -sparmarke *f*

(JAP) 商品引換スタンプ、商品券、クーポン券

(RUS) ПООЩРИТЕЛЬНЫЕ МАРКИ (КУПОНЫ) ОТ ПРОДАВЦА ПОКУПАТЕЛЮ, КОТОРЫЕ МОЖНО ОБМЕНЯТЬ НА ТОВАРЫ

trading unit

(CHIN) 交易单位

(FRE) quotité de négociation, unité de négociation, lot

(GER) Börsenschluss *m*, Handelseinheit *f*

(JAP) （株式の）取引単位、売買単位

(RUS) ТОРГОВАЯ ЕДИНИЦА

traditional economy

(CHIN) 传统经济

(FRE) économie traditionnelle

(GER) traditionelles Wirtschaftssystem *n*

(JAP) 伝統経済

(RUS) ТРАДИЦИОННАЯ ЭКОНОМИКА

tramp

(CHIN) 不定期货船

(FRE) navire de charge libre, navire hors conférence, (C) navire marchand

(GER) Trampschiff *n*, -dampfer *m*; Landstreicher *m*

(JAP) 不定期船、移動労働者、渡り職人
(RUS) «ТРАМП», ТОРГОВОЕ СУДНО БЕЗ
ФИКСИРОВАННОГО РАСПИСАНИЯ
РЕЙСОВ

transaction
(CHIN) 交易，业务，会计事项
(FRE) affaire, opération, (C) transaction
(GER) Transaktion f, Abschluss m,
Abwicklung f, Vorgang m, Geschäft n
(JAP) （業務・交渉・活動などの）執行、
取引、売買
(RUS) ТРАНЗАКЦИЯ; СДЕЛКА; ОПЕРАЦИЯ

transaction cost
(CHIN) 交易费用，交易成本
(FRE) frais de bourse, (C) frais de
transaction
(GER) Transaktionskosten pl
(JAP) 取引費用、取引コスト
(RUS) ОПЕРАЦИОННАЯ ИЗДЕРЖКА

transfer agent
(CHIN) 过户代理人
(FRE) agent (n, m) de transfert
(GER) Transferagent m;
Umschreibungsstelle f Transferstelle f,
Bevollmächtiger m für den Verkauf m von
Aktien fpl
(JAP) 証券代行、証券代理人、
名義書換代理人
(RUS) АГЕНТ ПО ТРАНСФЕРТАМ

transfer development rights
(CHIN) 转让开发权
(FRE) transfert des droits d'aménagement,
transfert des droits de développement,
TDA
(GER) Übertragung f von
Erschließungsrechten npl
(JAP) 開発権を譲渡する
(RUS) ПРАВА НА ОСВОЕНИЕ
ПЕРЕДАВАЕМОЙ НЕДВИЖИМОСТИ

transfer payment
(CHIN) 转账性支付，转付款项
(FRE) paiement de transfert
(GER) Transfer- f, Übertragungszahlung f,
Einkommensübertragung f
(JAP) 移転支払、譲渡支払、移転支出

(RUS) ПЕРЕВОДНОЙ (ТРАНСФЕРТНЫЙ)
ПЛАТЕЖ

transfer price
(CHIN) 转让价
(FRE) prix (n, m) de transfert
(GER) Transfer- m, Übertragungspreis m
(JAP) 移転価格、振替価格、譲渡価格
(RUS) ТРАНСФЕРТНАЯ ЦЕНА

transfer tax
(CHIN) 转让税
(FRE) droits de succession, (C) taxe de
transaction
(GER) Wertpapierumsatzsteuer f;
Erbschaftssteuer f
(JAP) 資産移転税、資産取引税
(RUS) НАЛОГ НА ПЕРЕДАЧУ
СОБСТВЕННОСТИ

translate
(CHIN) 翻译，折算，换算
(FRE) traduire
(GER) übersetzen, übertragen;
konvertieren; umsetzen; umcodieren v
(JAP) 移す、転換する、外貨に換算する
(RUS) ПЕРЕВОДИТЬ (одну валюту в другую)

transmit a virus
(CHIN) 传输病毒
(FRE) transmettre un virus
(GER) Virus m übertragen v
(JAP) ウィルスを送信する
(RUS) ПЕРЕДАВАТЬ, ПОСЫЛАТЬ
КОМПЬЮТЕРНЫЙ ВИРУС

transmittal letter
(CHIN) 转让信
(FRE) engagement de vente, (C) lettre de
transmission
(GER) Begleit- n, Überweisungsschreiben n
(JAP) 譲渡状
(RUS) СОПРОВОДИТЕЛЬНОЕ ПИСЬМО

transnational
(CHIN) 跨国的
(FRE) transnational, (C) société
transnationale transportation transport
(GER) transnational,
grenzüberschreitend adj

(JAP) 超国家的
(RUS) ТРАНСНАЦИОНАЛЬНАЯ (компания)

transportation

(CHIN) 运输，运输业，货运，交通
(FRE) transport
(GER) Transport *m*, Beförderung *f*;
Versand *m*
(JAP) 運送、輸送手段、交通機関
(RUS) ТРАНСПОРТИРОВАНИЕ

treason

(CHIN) 叛逆，背信弃义
(FRE) trahison
(GER) Verrat *m*
(JAP) （国家、政府に対する）大逆
（罪）、反逆（罪）、国事犯（罪）
(RUS) ИЗМЕНА; ПРЕДАТЕЛЬСТВО

treasurer

(CHIN) 司库，财务主任，出纳员
(FRE) trésorier
(GER) Finanzdirektor *m*, Leiter *m* der
Finanzabteilung *f*
(JAP) 会計係、財務部長、財務担当者
(RUS) КАЗНАЧЕЙ; ФИНАНСОВЫЙ
РУКОВОДИТЕЛЬ

tree diagram

(CHIN) 树形图
(FRE) arbre, (C) dendrogramme
(GER) Baumdiagramm *n*
(JAP) 樹形図、枝分かれ図
(RUS) ДРЕВОВИДНАЯ СХЕМА

trend

(CHIN) 趋势，倾向，动向
(FRE) tendance
(GER) Trend *m*
(JAP) 動勢、傾向、トレンド
(RUS) ТЕНДЕНЦИЯ РАЗВИТИЯ; ТРЕНД

trend chart

(CHIN) 趋势图
(FRE) graphique de tendance, (C) tableau
des tendances
(GER) Trenddiagramm *n*
(JAP) 傾向図表
(RUS) СХЕМА РАЗВИТИЯ ТЕНДЕНЦИИ

trend line

(CHIN) 经济趋势线
(FRE) ligne de tendance, (C) courbe de
tendance
(GER) Trendlinie *f*, -kurve *f*
(JAP) 趨勢線
(RUS) КРИВАЯ ТРЕНДА

trespass

(CHIN) 非法侵入，非法侵害
(FRE) intrusion, (C) atteinte
(GER) Besitz- *f*, Eigentumsstörung *f*,
Hausfriedensbruch *m*
(JAP) 不法侵害、立ち入り、不法侵入
(RUS) НАРУШАТЬ ПРАВО ВЛАДЕНИЯ,
ПОСЯГАТЬ НА ЧТО-ЛИБО

trial and error

(CHIN) 检误，反复性试验
(FRE) essai et erreur, approximation
(GER) systematisches Probieren *n* (durch
Versuch *m* und Irrtum *m*)
(JAP) 試行錯誤
(RUS) МЕТОД ПРОБ И ОШИБОК

trial balance

(CHIN) 试算法，
总账平衡法
(FRE) balance d'inventaire,
(C) balance de vérification
(GER) Roh- *f*, Saldenbilanz *f*
(JAP) 試算表
(RUS) ПРОБНЫЙ БАЛАНС

trial offer

(CHIN) 试发盘
(FRE) offre d'essai
(GER) Test- *n*, Probe- *n*,
Versuchsangebot *n*
(JAP) 試供品
(RUS) ПРОБНОЕ ПРЕДЛОЖЕНИЕ

trial subscriber

(CHIN) 试用用户
(FRE) souscripteur d'essai, (C) abonné
d'essai
(GER) Probeabonnent *m*
(JAP) ためし購読者
(RUS) ПРОБНЫЙ ПОДПИСЧИК

trigger point

(CHIN) 触发点

(FRE) prix-gachette, (C) point critique

(GER) Schwellenpunkt *m*; Ereignispunkt *m*;
Einsatzpunkt *m* (von Schadenhaftung)

(JAP) 引き金点、トリガーポイント

(RUS) КРИТИЧЕСКАЯ ТОЧКА

trigger price

(CHIN) 触发价格，基准价格

(FRE) prix-gachette, (C) prix de
déclenchement

(GER) Schwellenpreis *m*

(JAP) トリガー価格、引き金価格

(RUS) ТРИГГЕР – ЦЕНА: МИНИМАЛЬНАЯ
ЦЕНА ПО ТОВАРНОМУ СОГЛАШЕНИЮ

triple-net lease

(CHIN) 净租赁

(FRE) bail hors frais d'entretien

(GER) Triple-Net-Mietvertrag *m*,
Nettomietvertrag *m* mit Umlage *f* aller
Kosten *pl*

(JAP) 三重ネットリース

(RUS) АРЕНДА, ГДЕ АРЕНДАТОР
ОПЛАЧИВАЕТ ПОЛНОСТЬЮ ВСЕ
РАСХОДЫ И ИЗДЕРЖКИ (в т.ч. по
закладной)

Trojan horse

(CHIN) 特洛伊木马，欺骗软件，
欺骗程序

(FRE) cheval de troie

(GER) Trojanisches Pferd *n* (EDV)

(JAP) トロイの木馬
（破壊的プログラム）

(RUS) ТРОЯНСКИЙ КОНЬ

troubled debt restructuring

(CHIN) 滞还债款重整

(FRE) restructuration de la
dette

(GER) Umschuldung *f* von
Problemschulden *fpl*

(JAP) 不良債権の再編成

(RUS) РЕСТРУКТУРИРОВАНИЕ
НЕИСПРАВНОГО ДОЛГА

troubleshooter

(CHIN) 发现和解决问题的人

(FRE) médiateur, expert troubleshooting
dépannage

(GER) Fehler- *m*, Störungssucher *m*;
Krisenmanager *m*

(JAP) 調停者、仲裁者、修理係

(RUS) ЛИЦО, ЗАНИМАЮЩЕЕСЯ
ПОИСКОМ И ИСПРАВЛЕНИЕМ
НЕИСПРАВНОСТЕЙ

troubleshooting

(CHIN) 故障寻找

(FRE) dépannage

(GER) Fehlersuche *f*

(JAP) 傷害解析、トラブルシューチング

(RUS) ПОИСК И ИСПРАВЛЕНИЕМ
НЕИСПРАВНОСТЕЙ

trough

(CHIN) 衰退谷底

(FRE) creux, (C) creux saisonnier

(GER) Talsohle *f*, Konjunkturtief *n*,
Tiefpunkt *m*

(JAP) 景気の谷

(RUS) ДНО, НИЗШАЯ ТОЧКА ДЕЛОВОГО
ЦИКЛА

true lease

(CHIN) 正式租约

(FRE) bail à juste valeur marchande,
(C) opération de crédit- bailtrue to scale à
l'échelle

(GER) echter Miet- *m*, Pachtvertrag *m*

(JAP) 真正リース

(RUS) ФАКТИЧЕСКАЯ АРЕНДА

true to scale

(CHIN) 标度正确的

(FRE) rectifiez pour mesurer

(GER) maßstabgetreu *adj*

(JAP) 目盛どおり、基準どおり、スケー
ルに一致する

(RUS) СООТВЕТСТВУЮЩИЙ МАСШТАБУ

truncation

(CHIN) 切断，剪断

(FRE) troncation, (C) troncature,
(C) non-échange de chèques

(GER) Abschneiden *n*, Abbruch *m*,
Kürzung *f*

(JAP) 先端を切ること

(RUS) УСЕЧЕНИЕ; ОТБРАСЫВАНИЕ

trust

(CHIN) 信托，委托，联合垄断，信用
(FRE) trust, (C) fiducie, (C) fidéicommis
(GER) Trust *m*, Konzern *m*, Kartell *n*;
Stiftung *f*; Treuhandverhältnis *n*, Treuhand
f; Fondsvermögen *n*
(JAP) 信託財産（物件）、企業連合、
信託
(RUS) ТРАСТ. РАСПОРЯЖЕНИЕ
ИМУЩЕСТВОМ НА ПРАВАХ
ДОВЕРИТЕЛЬНОЙ СОБСТВЕННОСТИ

trust account

(CHIN) 信托账户，托管财产
(FRE) compte en fidéicommis
(GER) Treuhandkonto *n*; Nachlasskonto *n*
(JAP) 信託勘定
(RUS) ДОВЕРИТЕЛЬНЫЙ СЧЕТ, ТРАСТ-
СЧЁТ

trust certificate

(CHIN) 委托证书，信托证券
(FRE) certificat de placement en fiducie,
(C) titre de propriété bénéficiaire
(GER) Treuhandzertifikat *n*
(JAP) 信託証券
(RUS) СВИДЕТЕЛЬСТВО О ПЕРЕДАЧЕ В
ДОВЕРИТЕЛЬНУЮ СОБСТВЕННОСТЬ

trust company

(CHIN) 信托公司
(FRE) société de gestion, (C) compagnie de
fidéicommis
(GER) Treuhandbank *f*;
Treuhandgesellschaft *f*;
Verwaltungsgesellschaft *f*
(JAP) 信託会社
(RUS) ТРАСТОВАЯ КОМПАНИЯ
(специализирующаяся на операциях по
доверенности)

trust deed

(CHIN) 信托契约，委托书
(FRE) acte de fidéicommis, (C) acte de
fiducie
(GER) Treuhandvertrag *m*;
Sicherungsübereignung *f*;
Stiftungsurkunde *f*
(JAP) 信託証書

(RUS) ДОКУМЕНТ ОБ УЧРЕЖДЕНИИ
ДОВЕРИТЕЛЬНОЙ СОБСТВЕННОСТИ

trust, discretionary

(CHIN) 任意決定信托
(FRE) fiducie discrétionnaire
(GER) Treuhandverhältnis *n* mit
uneingeschränkter
Ermessensbefugnis *f*
(JAP) 裁量信託
(RUS) ТРАСТ, ДАЮЩИЙ ДОВЕРЕННОМУ
ЛИЦУ СВОБОДУ В РАСПОРЯЖЕНИИ
ИМУЩЕСТВОМ

trustee

(CHIN) 托管人，受托人
(FRE) syndic
(GER) Treuhänder *m*;
Vermögensverwalter *m*, -pfleger *m*
(JAP) 役員、理事、受託者
(RUS) ДОВЕРИТЕЛЬНЫЙ СОБСТВЕННИК,
ОПЕКУН

trustee in bankruptcy

(CHIN) 破产管理人
(FRE) syndic de faillite
(GER) Konkursverwalter *m*, -verwaltung *f*
(JAP) 破産管財人
(RUS) УПРАВЛЯЮЩИЙ ПРИ
ЛИКВИДАЦИИ ПО БАНКРОТСТВУ

trust fund

(CHIN) 信托基金
(FRE) fonds en fidéicommis, (C) caisse
centrale, fonds de dépôt
(GER) Trustfonds *m*; Treuhandvermögen *n*,
Treuhänderfonds *m*
(JAP) 信託資金、信託基金、
信託財産
(RUS) ТРАСТОВЫЙ ФОНД

trust, general management

(CHIN) 普通管理信托
(FRE) trust, aux pouvoirs discrétionnaires,
(C) direction générale de fiducie
(GER) Investmentgesellschaft *f* mit breit
gestreutem Wertpapierportfeuille *n*
(JAP) 一般管理投資信託
(RUS) ТРАСТ, ДАЮЩИЙ ДОВЕРЕННОМУ
ЛИЦУ СВОБОДУ В РАСПОРЯЖЕНИИ
ИМУЩЕСТВОМ

trustor

(CHIN) 信托人，财产授予者

(FRE) cédant (n, m), (C) constituant

(GER) Treugeber *m*

(JAP) 信託設定者

(RUS) ДОВЕРИТЕЛЬ

truth in lending act

(CHIN) 贷款真实法案

(FRE) loi en vigueur aux états-unis qui précise les obligations de divulgation aux conditions du credit *T*

(GER) Gesetz *n* zur wahrheitsgemäßen Kreditkostenangabe *f*, (US-Konsumentenkreditgesetz)

(JAP) 貸付け条件表示制定法

(RUS) ЗАКОН, ОБЯЗЫВАЮЩИЙ КРЕДИТОРОВ НАЗЫВАТЬ ИСТИННУЮ ПРОЦЕНТНУЮ СТАВКУ

T statistic

(CHIN) T 统计

(FRE) score normalisé, (C) loi *T*

(GER) *T*-Statistik *f*

(JAP) T 統計量

(RUS) СТАТИСТИКА «T»

turkey

(CHIN) 失败的投资

(FRE) mauvais placement

(GER) verlustbringende Kapitalanlage *f*; Flop *m*

(JAP) 七面鳥、役に立たない人（もの）、愚か者

(RUS) РАЗОЧАРОВЫВАЮЩАЯ ОПЕРАЦИЯ или СДЕЛКА

turnaround

(CHIN) 周转

(FRE) traitement), (C) redressement

(GER) Markt- *f*, Trendwende *f*, Umschwung *m*

(JAP) 一つの仕事（工程、作業）をやり終えるのに必要な時間、投資期間、（相場の）上げ方向への転換

(RUS) РЕЗКАЯ ПЕРЕМЕНА

turnaround time

(CHIN) 周转时间

(FRE) délai d'exécution

(GER) Umschlag- *f*, Erledigungszeit *f* (einer Aufgabe)

(JAP) 転換時間、投資期間、納期

(RUS) ВРЕМЯ, ТРЕБУЮЩЕЕСЯ ДЛЯ НАЧАЛА И ЗАВЕРШЕНИЯ ПРОЕКТА

turnkey

(CHIN) 统包方式，'交钥匙'方式

(FRE) clé en main

(GER) schlüsselfertig *adj*

(JAP) ターンキー方式

(RUS) «ПОД КЛЮЧ»

turn off

(CHIN) 断开，关断

(FRE) désactiver, (C) arrêt

(GER) abschalten *v*

(JAP) スイッチを切る、オフにする、消す

(RUS) ВЫКЛЮЧАТЬ

turn on

(CHIN) 接通，开启

(FRE) activer, (C) mise en marche

(GER) anschalten *v*

(JAP) スイッチを入れる、オンにする、作動させる

(RUS) ВКЛЮЧАТЬ

turnover

(CHIN) 营业额，周转额，销售额

(FRE) chiffre d'affaires, rotation

(GER) Umsatz *m*, Absatz *m*, Handelsvolumen *n*; (Arbeitskräfte)wechsel *m*

(JAP) 転換、売上高、回転率

(RUS) ОБОРОТ

twisting

(CHIN) 翘曲，扭曲

(FRE) reprise), (C) reprise d'assurance

(GER) Drehung *f*, Wendung *f*; Windung *f*

(JAP) 生命保険の乗り換え契約取り、ツイスティング

(RUS) НЕЧЕСТНАЯ ПРАКТИКА

two percent rule
(CHIN) 百分之二规则
(FRE) règle des deux pour cent
(GER) Zweiprozent-Regel *f*
(JAP) ２パーセントの法則

two-tailed test
(CHIN) 双边假设性检验
(FRE) test bilatéral, test statistique bilatéral
(GER) zweiseitiger Test *m*
(RUS) «ПРАВИЛО ДВУХ ПРОЦЕНТОВ»
(JAP) 〔統計〕両側検定
(RUS) ДВОЙСТВЕННОЕ ИСПЫТАНИЕ

tycoon
(CHIN) 工商巨头，大亨
(FRE) magnat de l'industrie, ponte,

(C) magnat
(GER) Großkapitalist *m*, -unternehmer *m*, Industriemagnat *m*
(JAP) 巨頭、大立て者、大君
(RUS) МАГНАТ

typeface
(CHIN) 字样
(FRE) oeil de caractère, caractère), (C) type de caractères
(GER) Schriftart *f* (EDV)
(JAP) 字形、書体、タイプフェース
(RUS) ТИП ШРИФТА

type-over mode
(CHIN) 改写模式
(FRE) type de saisie dans lequel le nouveau texte frappé se substitue à l'ancien, (C) mode refrappe
(GER) Überschreibmodus *m* (EDV)
(JAP) 上書きモード
(RUS) РЕЖИМ ЗАПЕЧАТЫВАНИЯ

U

umbrella liability insurance
(CHIN) 总括责任险
(FRE) assurance responsabilité civile
complémentaire et excédentaire,
(C) assurance parapluie
(GER) Pauschal-Haftpflichtversicherung *f*
(JAP) 包括的損害賠償保険、
包括的責任保険
(RUS) ВСЕОБЪЕМЛЮЩЕЕ СТРАХОВАНИЕ
ОТВЕТСТВЕННОСТИ

unappropriated retained earnings
(CHIN) 未分配保留收益
(FRE) bénéfices non répartis non affectés
(GER) freie Rücklage *f*, nicht
zweckgebunde Erträge *mpl*
(JAP) 未処理保留利益、未処理保留所得
(RUS) НЕ РАСПИСАННЫЙ
НЕРАСПРЕДЕЛЕННЫЙ ДОХОД

unbalanced growth
(CHIN) 不平衡增长
(FRE) croissance déséquilibrée
(GER) unausgeglichenes Wachstum *n*
(JAP) 不均衡成長、不均斉成長
(RUS) НЕСБАЛАНСИРОВАННЫЙ РОСТ

unbiased estimator
(CHIN) 无偏估计
(FRE) estimateur sans biais
(GER) unbefangener Schätzer *m*;
tendenzfreie Schätzfunktion *f*
(JAP) 不偏推定量
(RUS) НЕПРЕДВЗЯТЫЙ, ОБЪЕКТИВНЫЙ
ОЦЕНЩИК

uncollected funds
(CHIN) 未结清资金
(FRE) fonds non encaissés, fonds non
perçus, (C) sommes non reçues
(GER) nicht eingezogene Gelder *npl* bzw.
Mittel *npl*
(JAP) 取立未済資金
(RUS) НЕ ИНКАССИРОВАННЫЕ
СРЕДСТВА

uncollectible
(CHIN) 无法兑付的，无法收取的

(FRE) irrécouvrable, irréccupérable,
(C) créance irrécouvrable
(GER) nicht einziehbar *adj*; uneinbringliche
Forderung *f*
(JAP) 収集不可能の、回収できない
(RUS) НЕ ПОДДАЮЩИЙСЯ ВЗЫСКАНИЮ,
БЕЗНАДЁЖНЫЙ

unconsolidated subsidiary
(CHIN) 不合并计算的子公司
(FRE) entreprise non consolidée, (C) filiale
non consolidée
(GER) nicht konsolidierte
Tochtergesellschaft *f*
(JAP) 非連結子会社
(RUS) НЕКОНСОЛИДИРОВАННЫЙ
ФИЛИАЛ, ДОЧЕРНЯЯ КОМПАНИЯ

underapplied overhead
(CHIN) 少分配的制造费用
(FRE) coûts indirects sous imputés
(GER) Gemeinkostenunterdeckung *f*
(JAP) 過少賦課間接費
(RUS) НЕ ПОЛНОСТЬЮ УЧТЕННЫЕ
НАКЛАДНЫЕ РАСХОДЫ

undercapaliztion
(CHIN) 资本不足，投资不足
(FRE) sous-capitalisation
(GER) Unterkapitalisierung *f*,
unzureichende Kapitalausstattung *f*
(JAP) 不十分な資本供給、過少出資
(RUS) НЕПОЛНАЯ, НЕДОСТАТОЧНАЯ
КАПИТАЛИЗАЦИЯ

underclass
(CHIN) 社会地层
(FRE) sous-prolétariat,quart-monde,
(C) gens peu fortunés
(GER) Unterklasse *f*
(JAP) 底辺層、下層階級
(RUS) НЕСТАНДАРТНЫЙ; НИЗКОГО
КАЧЕСТВА; НЕПРИВИЛЕГИРОВАННЫЙ
КЛАСС

underemployed
(CHIN) 高能低就
(FRE) sous-employé

434

(GER) nicht ausgelastet (Kapazität, Arbeitskraft) *adj*
(JAP) 不完全就業の、（機械・設備など
が）十分に活用（利用）されていない
RUS) НЕ ПОЛНОСТЬЮ ЗАНЯТЫЙ

underground economy
(CHIN) 地下经济
(FRE) économie souterraine, (C) économie parallèle
(GER) Schattenwirtschaft *f*
(JAP) アングラ経済、地下経済
(RUS) «ПОДПОЛЬНАЯ», ТЕНЕВАЯ ЭКОНОМИКА

underinsured
(CHIN) 保险不足
(FRE) sous-assuré
 (JAP) 付保険価額過少の、一部保険の
(RUS) НЕДОСТАТОЧНО ПОКРЫТЫЙ СТРАХОВАНИЕМ

underline
(CHIN) 下划线
(FRE) sousligner
(GER) unterstreichen *v*
(JAP) アンダーライン、下線、
下線を引く
(RUS) ПОДЧЁРКИВАТЬ

underlying debt
(CHIN) 第一债务
(FRE) hypothèque prioritaire, créance prioritaire, (C) dette sous-jacente
(GER) zugrundeliegendes Schuld *f*
(JAP) 優先債務、第一債務
(RUS) СТАРШИЙ ДОЛГ

underlying mortgage
(CHIN) 第一担保抵押
(FRE) hypothèque sous-jacente,
(C) hypothèque de priorité
(GER) zugrundeliegende Hypothek *f*
(JAP) 優位抵当、第一担保
(RUS) БАЗОВАЯ, ИСХОДНЛЯ ИПОТЕКА

underlying security
(CHIN) 抵押担保
(FRE) titre sous-jacent, (C) valeur support de l'option
(GER) zugrundeliegendes Wertpapier *n*

(JAP) 基礎有価証券、原有価証券、対象
有価証券
(RUS) ЦЕННАЯ БУМАГА, ЛЕЖАЩАЯ В ОСНОВЕ ФЬЮЧЕРСКИХ И ОПЦИОННЫХ КОНТАКТОВ

underpay
(CHIN) 支付不足
(FRE) sous-rémunération, (C) salaire inadéquat
(GER) unterbezahlen, schlecht bezahlen *v*
(JAP) （人に）賃金を十分に払わない
(RUS) НЕДОСТАТОЧНАЯ, ЗАНИЖЕННАЯ ЗАРАБОТНАЯ ПЛАТА; НЕДОПЛАЧИВАТЬ

under the counter
(CHIN) 私下交易，贿赂
(FRE) clandestin, (C) au noir
(GER) schwarz (verkaufen, zahlen) *adj*
(JAP) 不法に取引される（禁制品など）
内密の、非合法の
(RUS) «ИЗ-ПОД ПРИЛАВКА» - НЕЗАКОННАЯ, СКРЫТАЯ НЕОФИЦИАЛЬНАЯ ТОРГОВЛЯ

undervalued
(CHIN) 估值偏低
(FRE) sous-évalué
(GER) unterbewertet *adj*
(JAP) 過少評価された、
価格が減じられた、軽視された
(RUS) НЕДООЦЕНЕННЫЙ; С ЗАНИЖЕННОЙ ЦЕНОЙ

underwriter
(CHIN) 保险商，包销商，承销人
(FRE) assureur, souscripteur,
(C) souscripteur
(GER) Bürge *m*; Garant *m*; Emissionsbank *f*; Konsorte *m*, Konsortialmitglied *n*; Versicherer *m*, Versicherungsgeber *m*, -träger *m*
(JAP) 保険業者、証券引受業者
(RUS) СТРАХОВЩИК; ГАРАНТ РАЗМЕЩЕНИЯ (ЗАЙМА И Т. П.),
(RUS) АНДЕРРАЙТЕР

underwriting spread
(CHIN) 承保差额
(FRE) prime d'émission, (C) écart de prise ferme
(GER) Konsortialspanne *f*

(JAP) 引受手数料
(RUS) ГАРАНТИЙНЫЙ СПРЕД (разница между ценой, выплаченной заемщику гарантами, и ценой предложения на рынке)

undiscounted
(CHIN) 未打折扣
(FRE) non actualisè, (C) non escompté
(GER) nicht diskontiert *adj*
(JAP) 割引なしの
(RUS) БЕЗ ДИСКОНТА; БЕЗ СКИДКИ

undivided interest
(CHIN) 不可分割的利益
(FRE) intérêt indivis
(GER) ungeteilter Zins *m*; Nutznießung *f* zur gesamten Hand *f*
(JAP) 不可分権
(RUS) НЕРАСПРЕДЕЛЁННЫЕ ПРОЦЕНТЫ

undivided profit
(CHIN) 未分利润
(FRE) bénéfice non distribué, (C) droits indivis, (C) bénéfices non répartis
(GER) ungeteilter Gewinn *m*
(JAP) 未処理利益、未配当利益、未分配利益
(RUS) НЕРАСПРЕДЕЛЁННАЯ ПРИБЫЛЬ

undue influence
(CHIN) 不当影响
(FRE) abus d'influence, (C) abus d'autorité
(GER) unzulässige Beeinflussung *f*
(JAP) 不当威圧、不適切な影響、不当な圧力
(RUS) НЕЗАКОННОЕ ВЛИЯНИЕ

unearned discount
(CHIN) 未获折扣，未得贴现
(FRE) escompte comptabilisé d'avance, (C) intérêt payé d'avance
(GER) transitorische Diskonterträge *mpl*, abgegrenztes Disagio *n*
(JAP) 不労割引
(RUS) НЕ ПОЛОЖЕННАЯ СКИДКА, ДИСКОНТ

unearned income (revenue)
(CHIN) 非营业收入（收益）
(FRE) revenus non professionnels, rentes, (C) produit comptabilisé d'avance,

(C) produit d'exploitation
(GER) Besitzeinkommen *n*, (leistungslose Einkünfte *fpl*)
(JAP) 不労所得　　（前受け収益）
(RUS) НЕ ЗАРАБОТАННЫЙ ДОХОД (РЕНТНЫЕ ДОХОДЫ, ДОХОДЫ С ЦЕННЫХ БУМАГ)

unearned increment
(CHIN) 自然增值
(FRE) plus-value
(GER) nicht erdienter Wertzuwachs *m*
(JAP) （財産、特に土地の）自然増加、不労増加、未稼得増加
(RUS) НЕ ЗАРАБОТАННЫЙ ПРИРОСТ

unearned interest
(CHIN) 已收到但未实现的利息
(FRE) intérêt perçu d'avance, (C) intérêt à courir
(GER) transitorische Zinserträge *mpl*
(JAP) 未経過利子
(RUS) НЕ ЗАРАБОТАННЫЕ ПРОЦЕНТЫ

unearned premium
(CHIN) 未满期保险费
(FRE) prime non-acquise
(GER) Entgeltübertrag *m*, Prämienübertrag *m*
(JAP) 未経過保険料、未収保険料、
(RUS) НЕ ЗАРАБОТАННАЯ ПРЕМИЯ

unemployable
(CHIN) 无法就业的
(FRE) inemployable, (C) inapte à l'emploi
(GER) nicht vermittelbar, arbeitsuntauglich *adj*; nicht verwendbar *adj*
(JAP) 雇用不能な、雇用に適さない
(RUS) НЕТРУДОСПОСОБНЫЙ

unemployed labor force
(CHIN) 失业劳动力
(FRE) les chômeurs, les sans-emplois), (C) travailleurs sans emploi
(GER) arbeitslose Arbeitskräfte *fpl*
(JAP) 失業労働者
(RUS) НЕЗАНЯТАЯ (БЕЗРАБОТНАЯ) РАБОЧАЯ СИЛА

unemployment
(CHIN) 失业，未就业，无工作
(FRE) chômage

(GER) Arbeits- *f*, Erwerbslosigkeit *f*
(JAP) 失業、失業者数
(RUS) БЕЗРАБОТИЦА

unencumbered property
(CHIN) 未支配财产，未承担债务财产
(FRE) propriété libre de toute hypothèque,
bien libre de toute hypothèque, (C) biens
non grevés
(GER) unbelastetes Grundstück *n*;
lastenfreies Vermögen *n*
(JAP) 抵当に入っていない財産
（不動産）
(RUS) СОБСТВЕННОСТЬ, СВОБОДНАЯ ОТ
ПРИТЯЗАНИЙ ДРУГИХ ЛИЦ

unexpired cost
(CHIN) 未抵消成本，未耗成本
(FRE) coût restant à couvrir, (C) coût non
absorbé
(GER) nicht erfolgswirksame Kosten *pl*
(JAP) 未消費原価
(RUS) НЕ ИСТЕКШИЙ СРОК УЧЕТА
РАСХОДОВ

unfair competition
(CHIN) 不公平竞争
(FRE) concurrence déloyale
(GER) unlauterer Wettbewerb *m*
(JAP) 不正競争、不公正競争
(RUS) НЕЧЕСТНАЯ КОНКУРЕНЦИЯ

unfavorable balance of trade
(CHIN) 贸易逆差
(FRE) balance commerciale défavorable,
(C) balance commerciale négative
(GER) defizitäre Handelsbilanz *f*, passive
Leistungsbilanz *f*
(JAP) 貿易収支の赤字、
輸入超過
(RUS) НЕБЛАГОПРИЯТНЫЙ ТОРГОВЫЙ
БАЛАНС

unfreeze
(CHIN) 解除限制
(FRE) débloquer
(GER) (Geld) freigeben;
auftauen *v*
(JAP) （資金・予算・施策などの）
凍結を解除する
(RUS) «РАЗМОРОЗИТЬ»

unified estate and gift tax
(CHIN) 统一遗产税和赠与税
(FRE) impôt unifié sur les droits de
succession et les donations, (C) impôt
consolidé sur les dons et les
successions
(GER) einheitliche Erbschafts- *f* und
Schenkungssteuer *f*
(JAP) 統一遺産贈与税
(RUS) НАЛОГ НА ПЕРЕДАЧУ
СОБСТВЕННОСТИ ПОСЛЕ СМЕРТИ ИЛИ
НА ДАРЕНИЕ

unilateral contract
(CHIN) 单边契约
(FRE) contrat unilatéral
(GER) einseitiger Vertrag *m*
(JAP) 一方的契約、片務契約
(RUS) ОДНОСТОРОННИЙ ДОГОВОР,
КОНТРАКТ

unimproved property
(CHIN) 未作改进的财产
(FRE) terrain non bâti, (C) terrain nu
(GER) nicht erschlossener Grundbesitz *m*,
unbebauter Grund und Boden *m*
(JAP) 改良のない不動産
(RUS) НЕБЛАГОУСТРОЕННАЯ
СОБСТВЕННОСТЬ

unincorporated association
(CHIN) 未注册协会
(FRE) association non constituée en société,
(C) association sans personnalité morale
(GER) nicht eingetragener Verein *m*
(JAP) 法人組織になっていない協会
（組合）
(RUS) НЕ ИНКОРПОРИРОВАННАЯ
АССОЦИАЦИЯ

unique impairment
(CHIN) 独特损害
(FRE) déficience unique, (C) dégradation
unique
(GER) einzigartige Schädigung *f* bzw.
Beeinträchtigung *f*
(JAP) 一意的損傷、
一意的損減
(RUS) УНИКАЛЬНОЕ ПОВРЕЖДЕНИЕ

unissued stock
(CHIN) 未发行股票

(FRE) titre non encore émis, (C) titre non émis, (C) actions non émises
(GER) genehmigte, noch nicht emittierte Aktie *f*
(JAP) 未発行株
(RUS) НЕ ВЫПУЩЕННЫЙ АКЦИОНЕРНЫЙ КАПИТАЛ

unit
(CHIN) 单位，单元
(FRE) unité
(GER) Anteil *m*, Einheit *f*, Stück *n*, Element *n*; Gerät *n*, Teil *m*; Werksabteilung *f*; Bestandteil *m*; Zertifikat *n*, Fondsanteil *m*
(JAP) 一個、構成単位、一定量
(RUS) ЕДИНИЦА; ПОДРАЗДЕЛЕНИЕ

unitary elasticity
(CHIN) 单一弹性
(FRE) élasticité égale à l'unité, élasticité unitaire
(GER) Elastizität *f* =1
(JAP) 弾力性 1
(RUS) ЕДИНИЧНАЯ ЭЛАСТИЧНОСТЬ

unit-labor cost
(CHIN) 单位劳动成本
(FRE) coût unitaire de travail
(GER) Lohnstückkosten *pl*, Lohnkosten *pl* je Ausbringungseinheit *f*
(JAP) 単位労働コスト
(RUS) СЕБЕСТОИМОСТЬ В ТРУДОЗАТРАТАХ

unit of trading
(CHIN) 成交单位
(FRE) unité de négociation, (C) quotité de négociation
(GER) Handelsgröße *f*, -einheit *f*, Börsenschluss *m*, Schlusseinheit *f* (Börse); Kontraktgröße *f* (Options-, Terminkontrakt), Mindestbetrag *m* (eines Abschlusses bei Wertpapieren)
(JAP) 売買単位、取引単位
(RUS) ЕДИНИЦА ТОРГОВЛИ (КОНТРАКТА)

units-of-production method
(CHIN) 生产单位折旧法
(FRE) méthode des unités de production
(GER) leistungsbezogene bzw. leistungsproportionale Methode *f*

(JAP)（減価償却法での）生産高比例法
(RUS) СПОСОБ УЧЕТА В ЕДИНИЦАХ ПРОИЗВОДСТВА

unity of command
(CHIN) 统一指挥
(FRE) unité de commandement
(GER) Einliniensystem *n*, Einheit *f* der Auftragserteilung *f*
(JAP) 命令の統一性
(RUS) ЦЕЛЬНОСТЬ УПРАВЛЕНИЯ

universal life insurance
(CHIN) 综合人寿保险
(FRE) assurance vie universelle
(GER) Universallebensversicherung *f*
(JAP) ユニバーサル生命保険
(RUS) УНИВЕРСАЛЬНОЕ СТРАХОВАНИЕ ЖИЗНИ

universal product code (UPC)
(CHIN) 通用商品代码 （UPC）
(FRE) code barres, (C) code universel de produit (CUP)
(GER) UPC-Code *m*
(JAP)（米）統一商品コード
(RUS) УНИВЕРСАЛЬНЫЙ КОД ИЗДЕЛИЙ

unlisted security
(CHIN) 非挂牌证券
(FRE) valeur du second marché, (C) titres non cotés
(GER) Freiverkehrswert *m*, nicht börsennotiertes Wertpapier *n*
(JAP) 非上場証券
(RUS) ЦЕННЫЕ БУМАГИ БЕЗ КОТИРОВКИ НА ОСНОВНОЙ

unloading
(CHIN) 卸货，抛售，倾销，支持
(FRE) déchargement
(GER) Niedrigpreisverkauf *m*; Abladen *n*, Entladen *n*, Ausladen *n*; Abstoßen *n* von Wertpapieren *npl*, Glattstellung *f*
(JAP) 積荷降ろし、処分、売り抜け
(RUS) «СБРОС» НА РЫНОК ФИНАНСОВЫХ ИНСТРУМЕНТОВ, ВАЛЮТЫ; РАЗГРУЗКА

unoccupancy
(CHIN) 空置
(FRE) inhabitation

(GER) Unterbrechung *f* der Gebäudenutzung *f*
(JAP) 非居住、非占有、非占有期間
(RUS) НЕПОЛНЫЙ СЪЕМ ЖИЛЬЯ

unpaid dividend
(CHIN) 未付利息
(FRE) dividende non versé, (C) dividende impayé
(GER) ausgeschüttete aber noch nicht ausgezahlte Dividende *f*
(JAP) 未払配当金
(RUS) НЕВЫПЛАЧЕННЫЙ ДИВИДЕНД

unrealized profit (loss)
(CHIN) 未实现利润（损失）
(FRE) bénéfice manqué, profit manqué, (C) bénéfice (perte) non réalisé(e)
(GER) nicht realisierter Gewinn *m* (Verlust)
(JAP) 未実現利益　（未実現損失）
(RUS) НЕРЕАЛИЗОВАННАЯ ПРИБЫЛЬ (УБЫТОК)

unrecorded deed
(CHIN) 未列契据
(FRE) acte de cession non enregistré, acte de transfert non enregistré
(GER) nicht amtlich eingetragene Urkunde *f*
(JAP) 未登録証書
(RUS) НЕ ДОКУМЕНТИРОВАННАЯ СДЕЛКА

unrecoverable
(CHIN) 不可恢复的
(FRE) irrémédiable
(GER) nicht wiederherstellbar *adj*; unbehebbar *adj*; unwiederbringlich; *adj*
(JAP) 回復不能の
(RUS) НЕИСПРАВИМЫЙ, НЕВОССТОНАВЛИВАЕМЫЙ

unrecovered cost
(CHIN) 未收回成本
(FRE) valeur nette comptable, (C) coût non couvert
(GER) Restbuchwert *m*
(JAP) 未記録原価
(RUS) НЕВОЗВРАЩЕННЫЕ ИЗДЕРЖКИ

unsecured debt
(CHIN) 无担保债务

(FRE) créance chirographaire, créance sans garantie
(GER) ungesicherte Forderungen *fpl*, ungesicherter bzw. nicht gedeckter Schuldtitel *f*
(JAP) 無担保負債、無担保債務
(RUS) НЕОБЕСПЕЧЕННЫЙ ДОЛГ

unskilled
(CHIN) 不熟练的
(FRE) non qualifié, non spécialisé
(GER) ungelernt, unqualifiziert *adj*
(JAP) 未熟練の、不熟練の
(RUS) НЕКВАЛИФИЦИРОВАННЫЙ

unwind a trade
(CHIN) 反向交易
(FRE) dénouer une position, (C) dénouer une transaction
(GER) einen Abschluss *m* kompensieren *v* (Börse)
(JAP) 逆取引によって証券取引を手仕舞う
(RUS) «ЗАКРЫТЬ» ТОРГОВУЮ ПОЗИЦИЮ

update
(CHIN) 更新; 更改，更新
(FRE) mise à jour, actualisation, actualiser
(GER) aktualisieren, fortschreiben *v*; auf den neuesten Stand *m* bringen *v*, Aktualisierung *f*
(JAP) 更新する、書き換える、アップデートする; 最新のものにする、アップデートする、改正する
(RUS) ОБНОВИТЬ; МОДЕРНИЗИРОВАТЬ

up front
(CHIN) 即付现金，坦率的
(FRE) à l'avance, franc, direct, (C) d'avance
(GER) im voraus *adj*
(JAP) 経営陣、先払いとして、原始投下資本として
(RUS) (ПЛАТА) ВПЕРЕД

upgrade
(CHIN) 升级，更新
(FRE) mettre à niveau
(GER) aufrüsten, ausbauen *v*
(JAP) アップグレードする、性能（機能、効果、品質、価値）を高める
(RUS) МОДЕРНИЗИРОВАТЬ, РАСШИРИТЬ

439

upgrade software
(CHIN) 升级 软件
(FRE) mise à niveau logiciel
(GER) Aufrüstungs- f, Upgrade-Software f
(JAP) ソフトをアップグレードする
(RUS) МОДЕРНИЗИРОВАТЬ, РАСШИРИТЬ ПРОГРАМНОЕ ОБЕСПЕЧЕНИЕ

upgrading
(CHIN) 提高，改进，提高等级
(FRE) mettre à niveau, (C) avancement temporaire, (C) formation complémentaire, (C) mise à niveau, (C) amélioration
(GER) Höhergruppierung f, Höherstufung f, Stellenanhebung f; Modernisierung f, Nachrüstung f
(JAP) 格上げすること、品質を高めること、効果（性能）を高めること
(RUS) СОВЕРШЕНСТВОВАНИЕ; МОДЕРНИЗАЦИЯ

upkeep
(CHIN) 保养，维修，管理
(FRE) entretien, (C) impenses
(GER) Wartung f, Instandhaltung f
(JAP) 維持、扶養、維持費
(RUS) СОДЕРЖАНИЕ; УХОД

upload
(CHIN) 上载
(FRE) téléchargement
(GER) hochladen f
(JAP) アップロード、アップロードする
(RUS) ЗАТРУЖАТЬ

upper case letter
(CHIN) 大写字母
(FRE) lettre majuscule
(GER) Großbuchstabe m
(JAP) 上段文字、大文字
(RUS) БУКВА ВЕРХНЕГО РЕГИСТРА

upright format
(CHIN) 垂直格式
(FRE) format droit
(GER) Hochformat n (EDV)
(JAP) アップライトフォーマット、直立様式
(RUS) ВЕРТИКАЛЬНЫЙ ФОРМАТ

upside potential
(CHIN) 股票的可能上涨幅度

(FRE) potentiel de hausse, (C) potentiel
(GER) Kurssteigerungspotential n
(JAP) 上限の能力、上昇する可能性
(RUS) ПОТЕНЦИАЛ ДВИЖЕНИЯ ЦЕНЫ НА ПОВЫШЕНИЕ (по прогнозу)

upswing
(CHIN) 好转，增加
(FRE) mouvement vers la hausse,
(C) tendance à la hausse
(GER) Konjunkturaufschwung m, Erholung f, Belebung f
(JAP) 著しい増加（向上、上昇、発展）
(RUS) ПОДЪЕМ (цен, конъюнктуры)

up tick
(CHIN) 交易价上涨，股票报升
(FRE) légère augmentation, (C) négociation à un cours supérieur
(GER) leichter Kursanstieg m, Aktie f mit leicht steigender Tendenz f
(JAP) （需要・供給の）増大、上向き、（事業・景気の）上昇機運
(RUS) «ПЛЮС ТИК» (обозначение последней во времени биржевой сделки по цене выше предыдущей сделки)

uptrend
(CHIN) 上升趋势
(FRE) tendance à la hausse
(GER) Aufwärtstrend m, steigende Tendenz f
(JAP) （特に経済発展の）上昇傾向、好転、上向き
(RUS) ТЕНДЕНЦИЯ НА ПОВЫШЕНИЕ (движения цены)

upwardly mobile
(CHIN) 上移阶层
(FRE) qui a la possibilité de s'élever dans la société, (C) ascendant
(GER) aufstrebend adj; aufsteigend adj
(JAP) 社会的金銭的に上向き移動の、将来有望な
(RUS) ПОДВИЖНЫЙ В НАПРАВЛЕНИИ ВВЕРХ

urban
(CHIN) 城市的，都市的
(FRE) urbain
(GER) städtisch adj
(JAP) 都市の、都会の、都会風の

440

(RUS) ГОРОДСКОЙ; УРБАНИСТИЧЕСКИЙ

urban renewal
(CHIN) 城市再开发
(FRE) rénovations urbaines
(GER) Stadtsanierung *f*, -erneuerung *f*
(JAP) 都市再開発
(RUS) ГОРОДСКОЕ ОБНОВЛЕНИЕ, ВОЗРОЖДЕНИЕ

useful life
(CHIN) 有用年限，可用寿命
(FRE) durée de vie économique, (C) durée de vie utile
(GER) Nutzungsdauer *f*, wirtschaftliche Lebensdauer *f*
(JAP) 耐用年数
(RUS) СРОК СЛУЖБЫ

user
(CHIN) 用户
(FRE) utilisateur
(GER) Anwender *m*, Benutzer *m*
(JAP) ユーザー、使用者、利用者
(RUS) ПОЛЬЗОВАТЕЛЬ

user authorization
(CHIN) 用户特许文件
(FRE) autorisation d'utilisateur
(GER) Benutzerberechtigung *f*
(JAP) ユーザー許可
(RUS) РАЗРЕШЕНИЕ НА ИСПОЛЬЗОВАНИЕ ПРОГРАМ ПОЛЬЗОВАТЕЛЕМ

user manual
(CHIN) 用户手册
(FRE) manuel d'utilisateur
(GER) Benutzerhandbuch *n*
(JAP) ユーザーのための手引き、ユーザーマニュアル

(RUS) РУКОВОДСТВО ДЛЯ ПОЛЬЗОВАТЕЛЯ

usufructuary right
(CHIN) 用益权，使用权
(FRE) droit d'usufruit
(GER) Nießbrauch *m*, Nutzungsrecht *n*
(JAP) 使用権
(RUS) ПРАВО ЛИЦА НА ИСПОЛЬЗОВАНИЕ НЕ ПРИНАДЛЕЖАЩЕЙ ЕМУ СОБСТВЕННОСТИ

usury
(CHIN) 高利贷
(FRE) usure
(GER) Wucher *m*
高利貸し、高利、
法定利率超過利子
(RUS) РОСТОВЩИЧЕСТВО

utility
(CHIN) 共用事业，共用设施，效用
(FRE) service public, utilitaire
(GER) Öffentliche Werke *npl*, Versorgungsbetrieb *m*; Nutzen *m*; Nützlichkeit *f*; Dienstprogramm *n* (EDV)
有用性、公益事業（電気・ガス・水道などの）、公益事業株（債券）、公共施設
(RUS) ЭНЕРГОНОСИТЕЛЬ; КОММУНИКАЦИИ; ПОЛЕЗНОСТЬ

utility easement
(CHIN) 共用设施的地役权
(FRE) servitude d'utilité publique, (C) servitude
(GER) Wegerecht *n* für öffentliche Versorgungseinrichtungen *fpl*
公共施設地役権、
公益事業地役権
(RUS) СЕРВИТУТ В ПОЛЬЗУ КОММУНАЛЬНОЙ СЛУЖБЫ

V

vacancy rate

(CHIN) 闲置率，空房率

(FRE) taux de vacance

(GER) Vakanz *f*, offene (freie) Stelle *f*; freie Wohnungen *fpl*

(JAP) 求人率、空き室率

(RUS) УРОВЕНЬ ВАКАНСИЙ; УРОВЕНЬ НЕЗАНЯТОГО ЖИЛЬЯ

vacant

(CHIN) 空置，空闲

(FRE) vacant

(GER) frei, offen, unbesetzt; leerstehend, unbewohnt, unvermietet *adj*

(JAP) 空の、使用されていない、無住の

(RUS) СВОБОДНЫЙ; НЕЗАНЯТЫЙ; ВАКАНТНЫЙ

vacant land

(CHIN) 土地闲置

(FRE) terrain libre, (C) terrain vague

(GER) unbebautes Land *n*

(JAP) 空閑地

(RUS) НЕЗАНЯТАЯ ЗЕМЛЯ

vacate

(CHIN) 取消，辞职

(FRE) quitter, libérer, annuler, (C) évacuer, (C) donner mainlevée de

(GER) aufheben, annullieren; frei machen; räumen, verlassen; aufgeben *v*

(JAP) （家・部屋・席などを）明け渡す、空ける、（職・地位などを）退く

(RUS) ОСВОБОЖДАТЬ, ПОКИДАТЬ, ОСТАВЛЯТЬ; АННУЛИРОВАТЬ

valid

(CHIN) 有效的，有根据的

(FRE) valide, valable

(GER) (rechts)gültig, geltend, bindend, rechtswirksam, -kräftig *adj*

(RUS) ДЕЙСТВИТЕЛЬНЫЙ; ИМЕЮЩИЙ СИЛУ

valuable consideration

(CHIN) 有价值的对偿物

(FRE) à titre lucratif, onéreux, (C) contrepartie de valeur

(GER) geldwerte Gegenleistung *f*, entgeltliche Leistung *f*

(JAP) 〔法律〕有価約因、対価

(RUS) СУММА ВОЗНАГРАЖДЕНИ, УПЛАЧИВАЕМАЯ ОДНОЙ СТОРОНОЙ СДЕЛКИ ДРУГОЙ (В ОБМЕН НА ОБЯЗАТЕЛЬСТВО ЧТО-ЛИБО СДЕЛАТЬ)

valuable papers (records) insurance

(CHIN) 有价证券（档案）保险

(FRE) assurance sur les titres et valeurs, (C) assurance pour documents précieux

(GER) Versicherung *f* wichtiger Urkunden *fpl* (Dokumente)

(JAP) 有価証券保険

(RUS) СТРАХОВАНИЕ ВАЖНЫХ БУМАГ (ДОКУМЕНТОВ)

valuation

(CHIN) 估价，评价

(FRE) évalutation, estimation, expertise

(GER) Bewertung *f*, Wertbestimmung *f*

(JAP) （物の）（金銭的）評価、価値判断、評価額、生命保険証券の現価評価

(RUS) ОЦЕНКА

value

(CHIN) 价值，估价

(FRE) valeur

(GER) Wert *m*; Wertstellung *f*; Nutzen *m*

(JAP) 価値、価格、評価価格

(RUS) СТОИМОСТЬ; ЦЕННОСТЬ; ЦЕНА; ВЕЛИЧИНА

value-added tax

(CHIN) 增值税

(FRE) taxe à la valeur ajoutée

(GER) Mehrwertsteuer *f*

(JAP) 付加価値税

(RUS) НАЛОГ НА ДОБАВЛЕННУЮ СТОИМОСТЬ (НДС)

value date
(CHIN) 起息日，交割日
(FRE) date de valeur
(GER) Wertstellungsdatum *n*, -termin *m*;
Verbuchungstag *m*, Valutatag *m*;
Valutierungstermin *m*
(JAP) 為替資金引渡日
(RUS) ДАТА ВАЛЮТИРОВАНИЯ; СРОК
ВЕКСЕЛЯ

value in exchange
(CHIN) 交換价值
(FRE) valeur d'échange, contre-valeur
(GER) Tauschwert *m*
(JAP) 交換価値（＝EXCHANGE
VALUE）
(RUS) МЕНОВАЯ СТОИМОСТЬ

value line investment survey
(CHIN) 价值线投资调查
(FRE) le value line investment survey est
un service d'information et de notation
influent et très respecté dans le domaine du
placement aux États-Unis, (C) analyse des
placements value line
(GER) Investitionsuntersuchung *f* zur
Wertlinie *f*
(JAP) ヴァリューライン投機調査
(RUS) СЛУЖБА АНАЛИЗА ИНВЕСТИЦИЙ
(ПОД НАЗВАНИЕМ Value Line)

variable
(CHIN) 变量
(FRE) variable
(GER) Variable *f*; Einflussgröße *f*;
beweglich (Zins) *adj*
(JAP) 変わりやすい、変数、可変
(RUS) ПЕРЕМЕННАЯ (ВЕЛИЧИНА)

variable annuity
(CHIN) 可变年金
(FRE) rente variable
(GER) private Rentenversicherung *f* mit
variablen Leistungen *fpl*
(JAP) 変動年金
(RUS) ПЛАВАЮЩАЯ РЕНТА

variable cost
(CHIN) 可变成本
(FRE) coût variable, (C) frais variables

(GER) variable Kosten *pl*
(JAP) 変動費、変動費用
(RUS) ПЕРЕМЕННАЯ
ЗАТРАТА

variable interest rate
(CHIN) 可变利率
(FRE) taux d'intérêt variable
(GER) variabler Zinssatz *m*
(JAP) 変動金利
(RUS) ПЛАВАЮЩАЯ ПРОЦЕНТНАЯ
СТАВКА

variable life insurance
(CHIN) 变额人寿保险
(FRE) assurance vie investie en actions,
(C) assurance sur la vie à capital variable
(GER) fondsgebundene
Lebensversicherung *f*
(JAP) 変額生命保険
(RUS) СТРАХОВАНИЕ ЖИЗНИ С
ИНВЕСТИЦИЕЙ ЧАСТИ ГОДОВОЙ
ПРЕМИИ В
ФИНАНСОВЫЕ АКТИВЫ

variable pricing
(CHIN) 差别定价
(FRE) tarification variable,
(C) détermination de prix variable
(GER) variable Preisgebung *f*
(JAP) 変動価格設定
(RUS) ПЛАВАЮЩЕЕ ЦЕНООБРАЗОВАНИЕ

variable-rate mortgage (VRM)
(CHIN) 可变利率抵押贷款
(FRE) prêt immobilier à taux variable,
(C) prêt hypothécaire à taux variable
(GER) variabel verzinsliche
Hypothek *f*
(JAP) 変動金利型抵当
(RUS) ИПОТЕКА С ПЛАВАЮЩЕЙ
СТАВКОЙ

variables sampling
(CHIN) 变量采样
(FRE) échantillonnage des variables,
(C) sondage de variables
(GER) Variablenauswahl *f*
(JAP) 変動見本抽出
(RUS) ВЫБОРКА ПЕРЕМЕННЫХ ВЕЛИЧИН
(для анализа)

variance
(CHIN) 差异，出入，方差
(FRE) variance, écart
(GER) Abweichung *f*, Varianz *f*; Differenz *f*
zwischen Ist- und Planleistung
(JAP) 変動、差異、分散、齟齬、
適用除外措置
(RUS) РАЗНИЦА; ОТКЛОНЕНИЕ

variety store
(CHIN) 杂货店
(FRE) grand magasin, (C) magasin
populaire
(GER) Gemischtwarengeschäft *n*,
Kramladen *n*
(JAP) 雑貨店、安物雑貨店
(RUS) УНИВЕРСАЛЬНЫЙ МАГАЗИН

velocity
(CHIN) 速度，周转率，流通速度
(FRE) vitesse, (C) vélocité
(GER) Geschwindigkeit *f*, Schnelligkeit *f*
(JAP) 速度
(RUS) СКОРОСТЬ ОБРАЩЕНИЯ ДЕНЕГ

vendee
(CHIN) 受货人，买方
(FRE) acquéreur), (C) acheteur
(GER) Erwerber *m*, Käufer *m*
(JAP) 買手、買主、引受人
(RUS) ПОКУПАТЕЛЬ (по отношению к
продавцу)

vendor
(CHIN) 卖主，商贩
(FRE) vendeur, (C) fournisseur
(GER) Verkäufer *m*, Vendor *m*,
Veräußerer *m*
(JAP) 売手、売主、譲渡人、自動販売機
(RUS) ПРОДАВЕЦ; ПОСТАВЩИК

vendor's lien
(CHIN) 卖主留置权
(FRE) privilège du vendeur, (C) vente
suspensive
(GER) Eigentumsvorbehalt *m* des
Verkäufers *m*
(JAP) 売手先取権、売手留置権
(RUS) ПРАВО УДЕРЖАНИЯ,
ПРИНАДЛЕЖАЩЕЕ ПРОДАВЦУ

venture
(CHIN) 商业冒险，短期投机
(FRE) entreprise
(GER) Unternehmensneugründung *f*;
Wagnis *n*, Risiko *n*
(JAP) 投機、投機の対象になるもの、
依託販売積送品
(RUS) КОММЕРЧЕСКОЕ ПРЕДПРИЯТИЕ

venture capital
(CHIN) 投机资本
(FRE) capital-risque, (C) capital de risque
(GER) Risiko- *n*, Wagniskapital *n*
(JAP) 危険負担資本、投機資本
(RUS) «РИСКОВЫЙ», ВЕНЧУРНЫЙ
КАПИТАЛ

venture team
(CHIN) 冒险小组
(FRE) équipe commando, (C) équipe
responsable de l'entreprise
(GER) Venture-Team *n*,
Unternehmensgruppe *f*
(JAP) ベンチャーチーム
(RUS) КОЛЛЕКТИВ ВЕНЧУРНЫХ
ИНВЕСТОРОВ

verbations
(CHIN) 语言学上的词汇
(FRE) verbalisations, (C) comptes rendus
textuels
(GER) Verbationen *fpl*
(RUS) УСТНЫЕ, СЛОВЕСНЫЕ
ДОКАЗАТЕЛЬСТВА

vertical analysis
(CHIN) 垂直分析，纵向分析
(FRE) analyse verticale
(GER) vertikale Analyse *f*
(JAP) 垂直分析
(RUS) ВЕРТИКАЛЬНЫЙ АНАЛИЗ

vertical discount
(CHIN) 纵向时段广告折扣
(FRE) réduction accordée pour publicité
multiple, (C) remise verticale
(GER) vertikaler Rabatt *m*, Rabatt *m* für
Werbung *f* einer bestimmten Häufigkeit *f*
(JAP) 垂直割引
(RUS) ВЕРТИКАЛЬНЫЙ ДИСКОНТ

vertical management structure

(CHIN) 垂直管理结构

(FRE) structure de gestion, (C) structure de direction verticale verticale

(GER) vertikale Führungs- *f* bzw. Managementstruktur *f*

(JAP) 垂直経営層

(RUS) ВЕРТИКАЛЬНАЯ СТРУКТУРА РУКОВОДСТВА

vertical promotion

(CHIN) 垂直提升

(FRE) promotion verticale

(GER) vertikale Beförderung *f*

(JAP) 垂直昇進

(RUS) ПОВЫШЕНИЕ В ДОЛЖНОСТИ; ПРОДВИЖЕНИЕ «ПО ВЕРТИКАЛИ»

vertical specialization

(CHIN) 纵向专业化管理

(FRE) spécialisation verticale

(GER) vertikale Spezialisierung *f*

(JAP) 垂直的分業

(RUS) ВЕРТИКАЛЬНАЯ СПЕЦИАЛИЗАЦИЯ

vertical union

(CHIN) 产业工会

(FRE) confédération syndicale, (C) syndicat industriel, (C) syndicat vertical

(GER) Industrie- *f*, Fachgewerkschaft *f*

(JAP) 産業別労働組合 （＝INDUSTRIAL UNION）

(RUS) ВЕРТИКАЛЬНОЕ ОБЪЕДИНЕНИЕ

vested interest

(CHIN) 既得利益

(FRE) droit acquis, capital investi, intérêt

(GER) feststehendes bzw. gesichertes Recht *n*; wohlerworbene Rechte *npl*; Besitzstand *m*; Sonderprivilegien *npl*;

(JAP) 既得権、終身権利、

一国の商業や金融活動を支配する人々（団体など）

(RUS) ЛИЧНЫЙ ИНТЕРЕС; ЗАКРЕПЛЁННОЕ ЗА КЕМ-ЛИБО ПРАВО (УЧАСТИЯ И Т. П.)

vesting

(CHIN) 授权

(FRE) droits, (C) acquisition

(GER) Erwerb *m* unverfallbarer Anwartschaften *fpl* aus einer betrieblichen Alterversorgung *f* oder einem Gewinnbeteiligungsplan *m*; Eigentumsübertragung *f*, Verleihung *f*

(JAP) 受領権、年金付与、授けられる

(RUS) ВВЕДЕНИЕ ВО ВЛАДЕНИЕ; НАДЕЛЕНИЕ ПРАВАМИ, ПОЛНОМОЧИЯМИ

vicarious liability

(CHIN) 转承责任,

替代责任

(FRE) responsabilité du fait d'autrui, responsabilité du cautionnement, (C) responsabilité du fait d'autrui

(GER) Haftung *f* für fremdes Verschulden *n*, stellvertretende Haftung *f*

(RUS) ПЕРЕНЕСЕННАЯ (на другое лицо) ОТВЕТСТВЕННОСТЬ

vice-president

(CHIN) 副总裁

(FRE) vice-président

(GER) Vize-Präsident *m*, Vice President *m*

(JAP) 副大統領、副総裁、副社長

(RUS) ВИЦЕ-ПРЕЗИДЕНТ

video conference

(CHIN) 电视会议

(FRE) visioconférence

(GER) Videokonferenz *f*

(JAP) テレビ会議

(RUS) ВИДЕО-КОНФЕРЕНЦИЯ

video graphics board

(CHIN) 视频图形板

(FRE) carte graphique vidéo

(GER) Videografikkarte *f*

(JAP) ビデオグラフィックス基板

(RUS) ПЛАТА ВИДЕО-ГРАФИКИ

violation

(CHIN) 违反, 违背

(FRE) violation, (C) abus

(GER) (Rechts)verletzung *f*, Verstoß *m*, Übertretung *f*, Zuwiderhandlung *f*

(JAP) 違反、侵害、邪魔

(RUS) НАРУШЕНИЕ (условия, обязательства, закона)

virtual memory
(CHIN) 虚拟存储器
(FRE) mémoire virtuelle
(GER) virtueller Arbeitsspeicher *m*
(Computer)
(JAP) 仮想記憶装置
(RUS) ВИРТУАЛЬНАЯ ПАМЯТЬ

visual interface
(CHIN) 可视界面
(FRE) interface visuelle
(GER) visuelle Schnittstelle *f*, Bildschirm-
Benutzeroberfläche *f* (Computer)
(JAP) ビジュアルインターフェース
(RUS) ВИЗУАЛЬНЫЙ ИНТЕРФЕЙС
(ДИСПЛЕЙ)

vocational guidance
(CHIN) 职业指南
(FRE) orientation professionnelle
(GER) Berufsberatung *f*
(JAP) 職業指導、就職指導
(RUS) ПРОФОРИЕНТАЦИЯ

vocational rehabilitation
(CHIN) 恢复就业资格
(FRE) réhabilitation professionnelle
(GER) berufliche Rehabilitation *f*,
Umschulung *f*, Wiedereingliederung *f* in
den Arbeitsprozess *m*
(JAP) 職業的復帰
(RUS) ПОВЫШЕНИЕ КВАЛИФИКАЦИИ

voice mail
(CHIN) 语音邮件
(FRE) messagerie vocale
(GER) Sprachspeicher *m*, Voicemail *n*
(JAP) 音声メール
(RUS) РЕЧЕВАЯ КОРРЕСПОНДЕНЦИЯ

voice recognition
(CHIN) 声音识别
(FRE) reconnaissance vocale
(GER) Spracherkennung *f*
(JAP) 音声認識
(RUS) РАСПОЗНАВАНИЕ РЕЧИ

voidable
(CHIN) 可撤销的，可取消的

(FRE) annulable, (C) résiliable, (C) nul
(GER) anfechtbar, aufhebbar,
annullierbar *adj*
(JAP) 無（無効、無益）にできる、
取消可能な、
〔法律〕無効にできる
(RUS) ОТМЕНЯЕМЫЙ, АННУЛИРУЕМЫЙ

volatile
(CHIN) 易变的，反复无常的
(FRE) volatil(e)
(GER) unstetig, unbeständig, veränderlich,
schwankend *adj*
(JAP) 激しく変動する、揮発性の
(RUS) НЕУСТОЙЧИВЫЙ

volume
(CHIN) 体积，容积，容量，数额
(FRE) volume
(GER) Volumen *n*, Umfang *m*
(JAP) 量、（しばしば pl.）大量、
売上高
(RUS) ОБЪЕМ; СУММА; ТОМ

volume discount
(CHIN) 大数量折扣
(FRE) remise sur la quantité, (C) ristourne
(GER) Mengenrabatt *m*
(JAP) 数量割引
(RUS) СКИДКА ЗА ОБЪЕМ

volume merchandise allowance
(CHIN) 大额商品减价
(FRE) ristourne accordée sur les volumes
d'achat des marchandises, (C) indemnité de
mise en valeur
(GER) Mengenrabatt *m*, Bewilligung *f* für
mengenmäßige Abnahme *f*
(JAP) 大量購入割引
(RUS) ПОПРАВКА НА ОБЪЕМ ТОВАРА

voluntary accumulation plan
(CHIN) 自愿购储计划
(FRE) plan d'accumulation en FCP avec
versements libres, (C) régime
d'accumulation volontaire
(GER) freiwilliger Spar- *m* bzw.
Anlageplan *m*
(JAP) 任意型継続投資プラン

(RUS) ДОБРОВОЛЬНОЕ НАКОПЛЕНИЕ ВЗАИМНОГО ФОНДА

voluntary bankruptcy

(CHIN) 自愿申请破产，自动倒闭
(FRE) faillite volontaire
(GER) freiwilliger Konkurs *m*,
(Konkursverfahren, das auf Antrag des
Gemeinschuldners eröffnet wird)
(JAP) 自己破産
(RUS) ДОБРОВОЛЬНОЕ БАНКРОТСТВО

voluntary conveyance

(CHIN) 无偿让与，
自愿转让
(FRE) cession volontaire, (C) transfert de
possession volontaire
(GER) freiwillige Übereignung *f* bzw.
Veräußerung *f*
(JAP) 無償譲渡
(RUS) ДОБРОВОЛЬНАЯ ПЕРЕДАЧА
(ПРАВОВОГО ТИТУЛА)

voluntary lien

(CHIN) 自愿留置权
(FRE) hypothéque volontaire,
(C) privilège volontaire
(GER) freiwilliges
Pfandrecht *n*
(JAP) 自発的留
(RUS) ДОБРОВОЛЬНОЕ ПРАВО
УДЕРЖАНИЯ

voting right

(CHIN) 投票权
(FRE) droit de vote
(GER) Stimm- *n*, Wahlrecht *n*
(JAP) 議決権、投票権
(RUS) ПРАВО ГОЛОСА

voting stock

(CHIN) 有投票权股
(FRE) action donnant droit au vote,
(C) titre comportant droit de vote
(GER) stimmberechtigte Aktie *f*;
stimmberechtigtes Aktienkapital *n*
(JAP) 議決権株、議決権行使株
(RUS) АКЦИИ С ПРАВОМ ГОЛОСА

voting trust certificate

(CHIN) 授权信托证书
(FRE) certificat de placement en fiducie
portant sur des redevances et comportant
droit de vote, (C) certificat de placement en
fiducie avec droit de vote
(GER) Stimmbindungszertifikat *n*
(JAP) 議決権信託証書
(RUS) СЕРТИФИКАТ УЧАСТИЯ В
«ГОЛОСУЮЩЕМ» ТРАСТЕ

voucher

(CHIN) 传票，凭单，收据
(FRE) bon, reçu, récépissé, pièce comptable,
(C) document commercial, (C) pièce
justificative
(GER) Beleg *m*, Quittung *f*; Gutschein *m*,
Bon *m*
(JAP) 保証人、証拠物件、証憑書類、
伝票
(RUS) РАСПИСКА; ГАРАНТИЯ; ВАУЧЕР

voucher register

(CHIN) 进货登记簿
(FRE) livre comptable, registre comptable,
(C) journal des pièces justificatives
(GER) Belegregister *n*, -verzeichnis *n*
(JAP) 支払伝票記入帳
(RUS) РЕЕСТР ГАРАНТИЙНЫХ БУМАГ,
ВАУЧЕРОВ

447

wage
(CHIN) 工资，工资基金，雇佣
(FRE) salaire, paie
(GER) Lohn *m*, Entgelt *n*, Verdienst *m*
(JAP) （通例 pl.）賃金、給料、報償
(RUS) ЗАРАБОТНАЯ ПЛАТА; СТАВКА
ОПЛАТЫ

wage assignment
(CHIN) 工资转让
(FRE) retenue sur salaire, (C) cession de
paie
(GER) Lohnabtretung *f*
(JAP) 給料控除
(RUS) НАЗНАЧЕНИЕ (СТАВКИ)
ЗАРАБОТНОЙ ПЛАТЫ

wage bracket
(CHIN) 工资等级
(FRE) fourchette de salaire, (C) fourchette
salariale
(GER) Lohngruppe *f*, -klasse *f*
(JAP) 賃金範囲
(RUS) РАЗРЯД ЗАРАБОТНОЙ ПЛАТЫ

wage ceiling
(CHIN) 最高工资限额
(FRE) salaire plafonné, (C) salaire limite
(GER) Höchstlohn *m*
(JAP) 賃金のシーリング設定
(RUS) ПРЕДЕЛ ЗАРАБОТНОЙ ПЛАТЫ

wage control
(CHIN) 工资控制，工资管理
(FRE) freinage des salaires, (C) contrôle des
salaires
(GER) Lohnreglementierung *f*,
-begrenzung *f*
(JAP) 賃金統制
(RUS) КОНТРОЛЬ ЗАРАБОТНОЙ ПЛАТЫ

wage floor
(CHIN) 工资最低额
(FRE) plancher des salaires, (C) salaire
minimum

(GER) Grundlohn *m*, Mindestlohn *m*
(JAP) 最低賃金
(RUS) БАЗИСНАЯ ЗАРАБОТНАЯ ПЛАТА

wage freeze
(CHIN) 工资冻结
(FRE) gel des salaires, blocage des salaires
(GER) Lohnstopp *m*
(JAP) 賃金凍結
(RUS) ЗАМОРАЖИВАНИЕ ЗАРАБОТНОЙ
ПЛАТЫ

wage incentive
(CHIN) 奖励工资
(FRE) prime, (C) rémunération au
rendement
(GER) Lohnanreiz *m*
(JAP) 能率給、奨励給
(RUS) ПРОГРЕССИВНАЯ ЗАРАБОТНАЯ
ПЛАТА

wage-push inflation
(CHIN) 工资推动通货膨胀
(FRE) inflation provoquée par la hausse des
salaires, (C) inflation des salaires
(GER) Lohndruckinflation *f*
(JAP) 賃金インフレーション
(RUS) РОСТ ЗАРАБОТНОЙ ПЛАТЫ ПОД
ВОЗДЕЙСТВИЕМ ИНФЛЯЦИИ

wage rate
(CHIN) 工资率，工资标准
(FRE) taux des salaires
(GER) Arbeitslohn *m*; Lohnsatz *m*,
-tarif *m*
(JAP) 賃率、賃金率
(RUS) СТАВКА ЗАРАБОТНОЙ ПЛАТЫ

wage scale
(CHIN) 工资等级
(FRE) échelle des salaires
(GER) Lohnskala *f*, -tabelle
(JAP) 賃金一覧表、賃金階梯表
(RUS) ШКАЛА ЗАРАБОТНОЙ
ПЛАТЫ

wage stabilization

(CHIN) 工资稳定化

(FRE) blocage des salaires, (C) stabilisation des salaires

(GER) Lohnstabilisierung *f*

(JAP) 賃金安定化

(RUS) СТАБИЛИЗАЦИЯ ЗАРАБОТНОЙ ПЛАТЫ

waiver

(CHIN) 放弃，免除，弃权书

(FRE) abandon, dérogation, renonciation, (C) exonération, (C) renonciation

(GER) Verzichterklärung *f*, Forderungsverzicht *m*; Ausnahmegenehmigung *f*

(JAP) 権利放棄、権利放棄証書

(RUS) ОТКАЗ (от права, требования, привилегии)

walkout

(CHIN) 罢工，同盟罢工

(FRE) grève (surprise), (C) débrayage

(GER) Arbeitsniederlegung *f*

(JAP) ストライキをする

(RUS) ЗАБАСТОВКА; ОТКАЗ РАБОТАТЬ

wallflower

(CHIN) 不受投资者青睐的股票

(FRE) titre délaissé par les investisseurs, (C) tapisserie

(GER) Mauerblümchen *n*

(JAP) 人気の落ちた銘柄

(RUS) ЦЕННАЯ БУМАГА, НЕ ПОПУЛЯРНАЯ СРЕДИ ИНВЕСТОРОВ (бирж)

wallpaper

(CHIN) 壁[墙]纸

(FRE) image de fond d'écran

(GER) Tapete *f*

(JAP) 壁紙

(RUS) НЕ ИМЕЮЩИЕ ЦЕННОСТИ ЦЕННЫЕ БУМАГИ;ПРОСТЫНЯ

ware

(CHIN) 商品，产品，货物

(FRE) marchandise, article, produit

(C) biens semblables

(GER) Waren *fpl*, Erzeugnisse *npl*,

Artikel *mpl*

(JAP) （通例～S）商品、製品

(RUS) ТОВАР, ИЗДЕЛИЯ

warehouse

(CHIN) 仓库，货仓，货栈

(FRE) entrepôt, dépôt

(GER) Lager *n*, -haus *n*, -halle *f*; Depot *n*

(JAP) 倉庫、商品保管所

(RUS) СКЛАД; ХРАНИЛИЩЕ

warm boot/start

(CHIN) 热引导[启动]

(FRE) démarrage à chaud

(GER) Warmstart *m*

(JAP) ウォームブート

(RUS) ПЕРЕЗАПУСК ИЗ ПАМЯТИ

warranty

(CHIN) 保证书，保函，保证条款

(FRE) garantie

(GER) Garantie *f*; Gewährleistung *f*; Garantieerklärung *f*; Zusicherung *f*; Bürgschaft *f*

(JAP) 保証、瑕疵担保責任、保証書

(RUS) ГАРАНТИЯ; ПОРУЧИТЕЛЬСТВО

warranty deed

(CHIN) 担保契约

(FRE) acte de transfert avec clause de garantie, (C) acte translatif de garantie

(GER) Rechtsgarantie *f*, Bürgschaftsurkunde *f*; Gewährleistungsvertrag *m*

(JAP) 権原担保捺印証書

(RUS) ДОКУМЕНТ ГАРАНТИИ

warranty of habitability

(CHIN) 可居住保证

(FRE) garantie d'habitabilité

(GER) Gewährleistung *f* der Bewohnbarkeit *f*

(JAP) 居住性保証

(RUS) ГАРАНТИЯ ПРИГОДНОСТИ К ПРОЖИВАНИЮ

warranty of merchantability

(CHIN) 商品可销售性保证

(FRE) garantie de qualité marchande

449

(GER) Gewährleistung *f* der marktgängigen Qualität *f*
(RUS) ГАРАНТИЯ ПРИГОДНОСТИ К ПРОДАЖЕ

wash sale

(CHIN) 虚假交易，欺诈交易
(FRE) transaction fictive, (C) vente fictive
(GER) (Börsen)scheingeschäft *n*
(JAP) 仮想売買、なれ合い売買
(RUS) КУПЛЯ ЦЕННОЙ БУМАГИ С ПРОДАЖЕЙ ЧЕРЕЗ ОЧЕНЬ КОРОТКОЕ ВРЕМЯ

waste

(CHIN) 废料，浪费，滥用损耗
(FRE) déchets, gaspillage, perte, étérioration, dégradation
(GER) Abfall *m*, Ausschuss *m*; Müll *m*, Schrott *m*; Verschwendung *f*
(JAP) 浪費する、屑、廃棄物
(RUS) ОТХОДЫ; НАПРАСНАЯ ТРАТА

wasting asset

(CHIN) 消耗资产，减耗资产
(FRE) actif dégradable, (C) bien consomptive
(GER) Wirtschaftsgut *n* mit begrenzter Nutzungsdauer *f*, kurzlebiger Vermögenswert *m*, Abnutzungsgut *n*; abbaufähige etriebsfläche *f*, Abbauland *n*
(JAP) 消耗性資産、減耗資産
(RUS) УБЫВАЮЩИЙ АКТИВ

watch list

(CHIN) 观察名单
(FRE) liste sous contrôle, (C) liste de titres sous surveillance
(GER) Watch List *f*, (persönliche) Wertpapierzusammenstellung *f* zur Verfolgung *f* von Kursveränderungen *fpl*
(JAP) 要注意人物リスト、
警戒事項一覧表
(RUS) СПИСОК (ценных бумаг), ЗА КОТОРЫМИ ВЕДЕТСЯ НАБЛЮДЕНИЕ

watered stock

(CHIN) 掺水股票，虚假
(FRE) titres dilués, (C) actions diluées
(GER) verwässerte Aktie *f*

(JAP) 水増し株、架空資本
(RUS) ДУТАЯ АКЦИЯ

waybill

(CHIN) 运货单，路程单
(FRE) connaissement, (C) bordereau
(GER) Frachtbrief *m*, Frachtkonnossement *n*, Warenbegleitschein *m*; Luftfrachtbrief *m*; Ladungsverzeichnis *n*; Passagierliste *f*
(JAP) 貨物引換証、貨物送状
(RUS) ПУТЕВОЙ ЛИСТ; НАКЛАДНАЯ

weakest link theory

(CHIN) 最薄弱环节理论
(FRE) théorie du maillon faible
(GER) Theorie *f* des schwächsten Glieds *n*
(JAP) 最弱リンク説
(RUS) ТЕОРИЯ СЛАБОГО ЗВЕНА

weak market

(CHIN) 疲软市场
(FRE) marché en baisse, marché baissier
(GER) schwacher Markt *m*; Kursabschwächung *f*
(JAP) 軟弱市況、下向市場
(RUS) «СЛАБЫЙ» РЫНОК (характеризуемый преобладанием продавцов и понижением цен)

wear and tear

(CHIN) 损耗，磨损
(FRE) usure
(GER) Abnutzung *f*, Verschleiß *m*; Abschreibung *f* für Wertminderung *f*
(JAP) すり切れ、いたみ、磨滅
(RUS) ИЗНОС (оборудования)

wearout factor

(CHIN) 失效因素
(FRE) facteur d'usure
(GER) Abnutzungsfaktor *m*
(JAP) 磨滅要素、損耗要素
(RUS) КОЭФФИЦИЕНТ ИЗНОСА

web browser

(CHIN) 万维网浏览器
(FRE) navigateur web
(GER) Web-Browser *m*
(JAP) ウェブブラウザー
(RUS) БРАУЗЕР

web server

(CHIN) 万维网服务器

(FRE) serveur web

(GER) Web-Server *m*

(JAP) ウェブサーバー

(RUS) УЗЕЛ ЛОКАЛЬНОЙ СЕТИ, СВЯЗЫВАЮЩИЙ ПОЛЬЗОВАТЕЛЯ С ИНТЕРНЕТОМ

welfare state

(CHIN) 福利国家

(FRE) état providence

(GER) Sozialstaat *m*

(JAP) 福祉国家

(RUS) ГОСУДАРСТВО, ГДЕ БОЛЬШОЕ ЧИСЛО ЛЮДЕЙ ЖИВЕТ НА ПОСОБИЯ

when issued

(CHIN) 虚股交易，假若发行

(FRE) titre vendu avant son émission

(GER) bei Begebung *f*, bei Emission *f*

(JAP) (株式・債券が)発効日決済取引の、発効日取引の

(RUS) «КОГДА И ЕСЛИ БУДЕТ ВЫПУЩЕН»

whipsawed

(CHIN) 遭受双重损失

(FRE) qui a fait une spéculation malheureuse à la bourse, (C) surenchère

(GER) doppelten Verlust *m* erleidend *adj*

(JAP) 〔証券〕二重損をした

(RUS) ЛИЦО, ПОНЕСШЕЕ ДВОЙНОЙ УБЫТОК (купившее по высокой цене и продавшее по низкой)

white goods

(CHIN) 大型家用电器，白色货物

(FRE) appareils ménagers, (C) produits blancs

(GER) weiße Ware *f*, Haushaltsgeräte *npl*

(JAP) 白布製家庭用品、（白く塗った）大型家庭用品、白物

(RUS) БЫТОВАЯ ТЕХНИКА

white knight

(CHIN) 白衣骑士策略，恶意收购解救人

(FRE) chevalier blanc

(GER) Retter *m* in der Not *f*

(JAP) 白馬の騎士、企業買収の危機にある会社を救済するために介入する第三の企業

(RUS) КОМПАНИЯ, ДЕЛАЮЩАЯ ПРЕДЛОЖЕНИЕ О ПРИОБРЕТЕНИИ ФИРМЕ, ЯВЛЯЮЩЕЙСЯ ОБЪЕКТОМ НЕЖЕЛАТЕЛЬНОГО ПОГЛОЩЕНИЯ

white paper

(CHIN) 白皮书

(FRE) livre blanc, (C) document de présentation technique

(GER) Weißbuch *n*

(JAP) 白書、公式報告書

(RUS) ПРАВИТЕЛЬСТВЕННЫЙ ДОКУМЕНТ

whole life insurance

(CHIN) 终身人寿保险

(FRE) assurance décès, (C) assurance vie entière

(GER) Todesfallversicherung *f*

(JAP) 終身生命保険 （＝ORDINARY LIFE INSURANCE）

(RUS) СТРАХОВАНИЕ ЖИЗНИ ВПЛОТЬ ДО СМЕРТИ

whole loan

(CHIN) 成套贷款

(FRE) prêt unique, (C) prêt partiel

(GER) Gesamtdarlehen *n*

(JAP) 全部の貸付（部分に対して）

(RUS) ЦЕЛЬНАЯ ССУДА

wholesaler

(CHIN) 批发商

(FRE) grossiste, marchand en gros

(GER) Großhändler *m*, Großhandelsbetrieb *m*

(JAP) 卸売業者、卸取次店

(RUS) ОПТОВЫЙ ТОРГОВЕЦ

widget

(CHIN) 小机械，装饰物

(FRE) widget, objet graphique, (C) gadget

(GER) Gerät *n*, Vorrichtung *f*

(JAP) 小さな機械装置、まだ名のつかないもの、ウィジェット

(RUS) ГИПОТЕТИЧЕСКИЙ ПРИМЕР

widow-and-orphan stock

(CHIN) 高回报低风险的股票

(FRE) valeur sûre, (C) titre à dividende élevé

(GER) Witwen- und Waisenpapiere *npl*, (mündelsichere Wert- bzw. Anlagepapiere)

(JAP) 安定配当株

(RUS) «АКЦИИ ВДОВ И СИРОТ» (с высоким доходом и малым рисом)

wildcat drilling

(CHIN) 不可靠的开采

(FRE) forage sauvage (d'exploration, de reconnaissance, de recherche), forage d'exploration

(GER) Erdölversuchsbohrung *f*

(JAP) 無謀な試掘井

(RUS) БУРЕНИЕ СКВАЖИН НА НЕФТЬ И ГАЗ НА УДАЧУ

wildcat strike

(CHIN) 未经工会批准的罢工

(FRE) grève sauvage

(GER) wilder Streik *m*

(JAP) 山猫争議、山猫スト

(RUS) ЗАБАСТОВКА БЕЗ СОГЛАСОВАНИЯ С ПРОФСОЮЗОМ или В НАРУШЕНИЕ ОГОВОРКИ ОБ ОТКАЗЕ ОТ ЗАБАСТОВОК

will

(CHIN) 遗嘱

(FRE) testament

(GER) Testament *n*, letzter Wille *m*, letztwillige Verfügung *f*

(JAP) 意図、遺言書、意思できめる

(RUS) ВОЛЯ; ВОЛЕИЗЪЯВЛЕНИЕ; ЗАВЕЩАНИЕ

windfall profit

(CHIN) 意外利润，暴利

(FRE) bénéfice exceptionnel, (C) profit imprévu

(GER) unerwarteter Profit *m*, Überraschungsgewinn *m*

(JAP) 超過利潤、棚ぼた式利益、意外の利潤

(RUS) СЛУЧАЙНАЯ ПРИБЫЛЬ

winding up

(CHIN) 倒闭，停业，清理，结束

(FRE) liquidation, (C) liquidation des biens

(GER) Abwicklung *f*, Liquidation *f*, Auflösung *f*, Schließung *f*

(JAP) 終了、整理解散、企業閉鎖

(RUS) РОСПУСК; ПРЕКРАЩЕНИЕ ДЕЯТЕЛЬНОСТИ; ЗАВЕРШЕНИЕ

window

(CHIN) 业务，橱窗，窗口；窗口

(FRE) créneau, escompte officiel, vitrine, fenêtre

(GER) Fenster *n*; Schalter *m*

(JAP) 陳列窓、接触の手段、時間（帯）；) ウィンドウ、窓

(RUS) ОКНО; ВРЕМЕННОЕ УЛУЧШЕНИЕ КОНЪЮНКТУРЫ

windows application

(CHIN) windows 应用程序

(FRE) application windows

(GER) Windows-Anwendung *f*

(JAP) ウィンドウズアのプリケーション、ウィンドウズ用アプリケーション

(RUS) ПРОГРАММА, РАБОТАЮЩАЯ ПОД УПРАВЛЕНИЕМ СИСТЕМЫ Windows

wipeout

(CHIN) 抹去，消除

(FRE) éliminer, (C) suppression complète

(GER) Vernichtung *f*, Zerstörung *f*, Ausrottung *f*

(JAP) 大敗、大破、惨敗

(RUS) УНИЧТОЖЕНИЕ

wire house

(CHIN) 联网经纪公司

(FRE) maison de commission, (C) maison de courtage électronique

(GER) große Maklerfirma *f*, Brokerfirma *f*

(JAP) ワイヤハウス

(RUS) БРОКЕРСКАЯ ФИРМА, ИМЕЮЩАЯ ПРЯМЫЕ ЛИНИИ СВЯЗИ СО СВОИМИ ОТДЕЛЕНИЯМИ

withdrawal

(CHIN) 提款，退股，撤销，收回

(FRE) retrait

(GER) Abberufung *f*; Rücktritt *m*, -zug *m*; Austritt *m*; Entnahme *f*; Abhebung *f* (Konto)

(JAP) 取消し、撤回、引出した金

(RUS) СНЯТИЕ СО СЧЕТА; ПРОДАЖА ДОЛИ УЧАСТИЯ

withdrawal plan
(CHIN) 提款计划
(FRE) plan de retrait
(GER) Entnahmeplan *m*; Rückzugsplan *m*
(JAP) 引出しプラン
(RUS) ПЛАН СИТЕМАТИЧЕСКОГО СНЯТИЯ СРЕДСТВ ИЗ ВЗАИМНОГО ФОНДА

withholding
(CHIN) 税款扣除
(FRE) retenue sur le traitement, retenue sur le salaire, (C) rétention, (C) refus
(GER) Abzug *m*, Einbehaltung *f*, Bestcuerung *f*
(JAP) 源泉徴収、天引き
(RUS) УДЕРЖИВАТЬ ВО ВЛАДЕНИИ; ВЫЧИТАТЬ; УТАИВАТЬ (ИНФОРМАЦИЮ)

withholding tax
(CHIN) 扣除税，预提税
(FRE) impôt retenu à la source, retenue fiscale, (C) retenue d'impôt
(GER) Quellensteuer *f*
(JAP) 源泉徴収税、源泉課税
(RUS) НАЛОГ ПУТЕМ ВЫЧЕТОВ (УДЕРЖАНИЙ)

without recourse
(CHIN) 无追索权，无偿还义务
(FRE) sans recours
(GER) ohne Regress *m*
(JAP) 親会社のリスク引受けなし
(RUS) БЕЗОБОРОТНО

wizard
(CHIN) 向导，范例
(FRE) assistant
(GER) Assistent *m* (EDV)
(JAP) ウィザード（プログラム名）、名人

word processing
(CHIN) 文字处理
(FRE) traitement de texte
(GER) Textverarbeitung *f* (EDV)
(JAP) ワードプロセッシング、文書処理

(RUS) ОБРАБОТКА ТЕКСТОВ

word wrapping
(CHIN) 字绕回，自动换行
(FRE) saisie au kilomètre, retour à la ligne automatique
(GER) Fließtext *m* (EDV)
(JAP) ワードラップすること
(RUS) ПЕРЕХОД НА НОВУЮ СТРОКУ

work force
(CHIN) 劳动力
(FRE) main-d'oeuvre, (C) population active
(GER) Personal *m*; Belegschaft *f*, Arbeitskräfte *fpl*
(JAP) 全従業員、全労働人口
(RUS) РАБОЧАЯ СИЛА

working capital
(CHIN) 运用资本，周转资金，流动现金
(FRE) fonds de roulement
(GER) Betriebs- *n*, Umlaufkapital *n*; Nettoumlaufvermögen *n*
(JAP) 営業資本、運転資本、流動資産
(RUS) ОБОРОТНЫЙ КАПИТАЛ

work in progress
(CHIN) 在制品，未完工程
(FRE) travail en cours
(GER) in Bearbeitung *f* befindlicher Auftrag *m*; unfertige Erzeugnisse *npl*
(JAP) 仕掛品（＝WORK IN PROCESS）
(RUS) НЕЗАВЕРШЕННАЯ РАБОТА

workload
(CHIN) 工作量，工作负荷
(FRE) travail à effectuer, charge de travail
(GER) Arbeitsbelastung *f*, -pensum *n*
(JAP) 作業負荷、標準仕事量
(RUS) РАБОЧАЯ ПЛГРУЗКА

work order
(CHIN) 工作单，任务单
(FRE) bon de commande, (C) bon de travail, (C) ordre de fabrication
(GER) Arbeitsauftrag *m*
(JAP) 製造指図書、工程経路、作業工程
(RUS) ЗАКАЗ НА ПРОИЗВОДСТВО

workout

(CHIN) 双方努力

(FRE) arrangement, (C) sauvetage
(GER) (Schuld)umwandlung *f*; Entwicklung
f eines Kompromisses *m*
(JAP) （運動競技の）練習、運動能力適
正検査、試験
(RUS) РАЗМИНКА, ПРОБНАЯ РАБОТА

work permit

(CHIN) 工作许可证

(FRE) permis de travail
(GER) Arbeitserlaubnis *f*, -genehmigung *f*
(JAP) 就労許可、労働許可
(RUS) РАЗРЕШЕНИЕ НА РАБОТУ

worksheet

(CHIN) 加工单，记工单；工作表，
工作单
(FRE) feuille de travail, tableur, (C) fiche
technique
(GER) Arbeitsblatt *n*
(JAP) 作業票、〔会計〕清算表; (JAP)
ワークシート
(RUS) РАБОЧАЯ ВЕДОМОСТЬ, СХЕМА

work simplification

(CHIN) 工作程序简化

(FRE) simplification du travail, (C)
rationalisation du travail
(GER) Arbeitsvereinfachung *f*
(JAP) 業務簡素化、作業簡素化
(RUS) УПРОЩЕНИЕ ХАРАКТЕРА РАБОТЫ

work station

(CHIN) 工作站

(FRE) poste de travail, station de travail
(GER) Arbeitsplatz *m*, -station *f*
(JAP) ワークステーション
(RUS) РАБОЧЕЕ МЕСТО

work stoppage

(CHIN) 停工

(FRE) cessation du travail, (C) arrêt de
travail
(GER) Arbeitsunterbrechung *f*, -
niederlegung *f*
(JAP) 作業停止

(RUS) ПРЕКРАЩЕНИЕ (ОСТАНОВКА)
РАБОТЫ

work week

(CHIN) 工作周

(FRE) semaine de travail
(GER) Arbeitswoche *f*
(JAP) 週労働日数（時間）
(RUS) РАБОЧАЯ НЕДЕЛЯ

World Bank

(CHIN) 世界银行

(FRE) Banque Mondiale
(GER) Weltbank *f*, Internationale Bank *f* für
Wiederaufbau *m* und Entwicklung *f*
(JAP) 世界銀行
(RUS) МЕЖДУНАРОДНЫЙ БАНК
РЕКОНСТРУКЦИИ И РАЗВИТИЯ

world wide web (www)

(CHIN) 万维网

(FRE) le web, la toile
(GER) World-Wide Web *n* (WWW)
(JAP) WWW、ワールドワイドウェブ
(RUS) ИНТЕРНЕТ

WORM

(CHIN) 一种复制保护程序；蠕虫

(FRE) ver
(GER) Wurm *m*
(JAP) WORM （Write Once, Read Many）
（光ディスクの一種）、ワーム
(RUS) ИНФОРМАЦИОННЫЙ НОСИТЕЛЬ С
ОДНОКРАТНОЙ ЗАПИСЬЮ

worth

(CHIN) 资本，价值，财富

(FRE) valeur
(GER) Wert *m*
(JAP) の値打ちがある、有用性、
（金銭的な）価値
(RUS) ЦЕННОСТЬ, СТОИМОСТЬ

wraparound mortgage

(CHIN) 环绕抵押贷款

(FRE) hypothéque intégrante, hypothéque
complémentaire, (C) prêt hypothécaire
intégrant
(GER) zweite Hypothek *f* einschließlich des
Restbetrags *m* aus der ersten Hypothek *f*

(JAP) 包括抵当権
(RUS) ВТОРИЧНАЯ ИПОТЕКА

wraparound type
(CHIN) 回绕类型
(FRE) type en bouclage
(GER) bildumhüllender Textdruck *m*
(JAP) 循環タイプ、
ラップアラウンドタイプ
(RUS) ВВОД ТЕКСТА С ПЕРЕХОДОМ НА НОВУЮ СТРОКУ

writ
(CHIN) 令状，传票，法令，文书
(FRE) ordonnance, (C) acte judiciaire, (C) bref
(GER) gerichtliche Anordnung *f*, Gerichtsbeschluss *m*, gerichtlicher Verfügung *m*
(JAP) 令状
(RUS) СУДЕБНЫЙ ПРИКАЗ; ПРЕДПИСАНИЕ

write error
(CHIN) 写入错误
(FRE) erreur en écriture
(GER) Schreibfehler *m*
(JAP) 書込み誤り
(RUS) ОШИБКА ЗАПИСИ

write-protected
(CHIN) 写保护
(FRE) protégé en écriture
(GER) schreibgeschützt *adj*
(RUS) С ЗАЩИТОЙ ОТ ЗАПИСИ

writer
(CHIN) 卖方，开票人，签署人
(FRE) vendeur, souscripteur

(GER) Aussteller *m*; Versicherer *m*; Verkäufer *m* einer Option *f*; Verfasser *m*
(JAP) 〔証券〕売り手
(RUS) ПРОДАВЕЦ ОПЦИОНА; ЛИЦО, ПРИНИМАЮЩЕЕ НА СЕБЯ СТРАХОВОЙ РИСК

write-up
(CHIN) 增记，增值，补写
(FRE) augmenter, valoriser
(GER) Presseartikel *m*; Höherbewertung *f*, Zuschreibung *f*
(JAP) 評価増し
(RUS) ПОВЫШЕНИЕ ЦЕНЫ

writing naked
(CHIN) 卖出非补进期权
(FRE) option d'achat à découvert
(GER) ungedeckter Verkauf *m*
(JAP) 無約因契約
(RUS) ПРОДАЖА НЕЗАЩИЩЁННОГО ОПЦИОНА

writ of error
(CHIN) 检误船票
(FRE) recours pour erreur de droit, (C) procédure d'appel
(GER) Revisionsbeschluss *m*
(JAP) 誤審令状
(RUS) СУДЕБНЫЙ ПРИКАЗ О ПЕРЕСМОТРЕ ДЕЛА

written-down value
(CHIN) 折旧后价值
(FRE) valeur amortie, (C) méthode de la valeur comptable
(GER) Restwert *m*, Nettobuchwert *m*
(RUS) ПОНИЖЕННАЯ СТОИМОСТЬ

XYZ

x-coordinate
(CHIN) x-坐标
(FRE) coordonnée x
(GER) X-Achse *f*, Abszissenwert *m*
(JAP) X 座標
(RUS) X-КООРДИНАТА

y-coordinate
 (CHIN) y-坐标
(FRE) coordonnée y
(GER) Y-Achse *f*, Ordinatenwert *m*
(JAP) Y 座標
(RUS) Y-КООРДИНАТА

year-end
(CHIN) 年终
(FRE) de fin d'exercice, (C) clôture de l'exercice
(GER) Jahresende n, zum Jahresende *n*
(JAP) 年末（の）、歳末（の）
(RUS) КОНЕЦ ГОДА; ОКОНЧАНИЕ ГОДА

year-end dividend
(CHIN) 年终股息
(FRE) dividende final, solde de dividende, (C) dividence de clôture
(GER) (Jahres)abschlussdividende *f*
(JAP) 年度末配当
(RUS) ДИВИДЕНД НА КОНЕЦ ГОДА

year-to-date (YTD)
(CHIN) 年初至当前日 （YTD）
(FRE) depuis le début de l'année en cours, (C) cumul annuel jusqu'à ce jour
(GER) seit Jahresanfang *m*
(JAP) 当会計年度の初めから今日（現在）まで、累計、過去１年間
(RUS) ЗА ИСТЕКШИЙ ГОД

yellow dog contract
(CHIN) 黄狗契约
(FRE) contrat de jaune
(GER) Arbeitsvertrag *m* mit Verbot *n* des Gewerkschaftsbeitritts *m*
(JAP) 黄犬契約

(RUS) СОГЛАШЕНИЕ О ПРИЕМЕ НА РАБОТУ С ОБЯЗАТЕЛЬСТВОМ РАБОТНИКА НЕ ВСТУПАТЬ В ПРОФСОЮЗ (с увольнением в случае вступления)

yellow goods
(CHIN) 非消耗性家居用品
(FRE) biens de consommation durables, (C) biens durables
(GER) Gebrauchsgüter *npl*, langlebige Konsumgüter *npl*
(JAP) イエローグッズ
（利幅の大きい耐久消費財）
(RUS) »ЖЁЛТЫЕ ТОВАРЫ», Т. Е. ПОТРЕБИТЕЛЬСКИЕ ТОВАРЫ ДЛИТЕЛЬНОГО ПОЛЬЗОВАНИЯ

yellow sheets
(CHIN) 债券交易每日通报
(FRE) « feuilles jaunes », « yellow sheets », (C) rapports jaunes
(GER) Yellow Sheet, Kursblatt *n* (Anleihe)
(JAP) 警察記録 （＝RAP SHEET）
(RUS) «ЖЕЛТЫЕ ЛИСТЫ» – ЕЖЕДНЕВНАЯ ПУБЛИКАЦИЯ О ЦЕНАХ ОБЛИГАЦИЙ

yield
(CHIN) 盈利，收益，盈利率，产量
(FRE) rapport, rendement
(GER) Rendite *f*; Steueraufkommen *n*; Ausbeute *f*, Ertrag *m*, Ergebnis *n*
(JAP) 産（出）する、譲る、歩留、利回り
(RUS) ДОХОД (в частности, по ценным бумагам) В ФОРМЕ ПРОЦЕНТНОЙ СТАВКИ

yield curve
(CHIN) 收益率曲线
(FRE) courbe des taux, (C) courbe de rendement
(GER) Zinsertragskurve *f*
(JAP) イールドカーブ、利回曲線
(RUS) КРИВАЯ ДОХОДНОСТИ

yield equivalence
(CHIN) 约当利率
(FRE) équivalence de taux, (C) rendement équivalent
(GER) Ertragsäquivalenz *f*
(JAP) 利回等価、歩留等価
(RUS) РАВЕНСТВО В ДОХОДНОСТИ

yield spread
(CHIN) 收益率差价
(FRE) écart de taux, (C) écart de rendement
(GER) Renditenspanne *f*
(JAP) 利回格差、利回り幅
(RUS) РАЗНИЦА В ДОХОДНОСТИ (различных типов ценных бумаг)

yield to average life
(CHIN) 平均年限收益率
(FRE) taux de rendement à la durée de vie moyenne, taux de rendement à l'échéance moyenne, (C) rendement selon la durée de vie moyenne
(GER) Rendite *f* auf durchschnittliche Laufzeit *f*
(JAP) 平均寿命利回り
(RUS) ДОХОДНОСТЬ ОБЛИГАЦИИ, РАССЧИТАННАЯ ОТНОСИТЕЛЬНО СРЕДНЕГО СРОКА ЕЕ ПОГАШЕНИЯ

yield to call
(CHIN) 至通知债券收益率
(FRE) taux de rendement à l'échéance intermédiaire, taux de rendement en cas de remboursement anticipé par l'émetteur, (C) rendement à la date d'appel, (C) rendement à la date de remboursement par anticipation
(GER) Rendite *f* einer kündbaren Anleihe *f*
(JAP) 繰上償還利回り
(RUS) ДОХОДНОСТЬ ОБЛИГАЦИИ, РАССЧИТАННАЯ ОТНОСИТЕЛЬНО ПЕРВОЙ ВОЗМОЖНОЙ ДАТЫ ПОГАШЕНИЯ

yield-to-mature (YTM)
(CHIN) 到期收益 （YTM）
(FRE) rendement (n, m) à maturité, (C) taux de rendement actuariel
(GER) Rückzahlungsrendite *f*
(JAP) 満期利回り

(RUS) ДОХОДНО ПО ЦЕННОЙ БУМАГЕ (В ПРОЦЕНТАХ), РАССЧИТАННЫЙ НА ДАТУ ПОГАШЕНИЯ

yo-yo stock
"悠悠" 股票
(FRE) action volatile, (C) titre yoyo
(GER) Wertpapier *n* mit starken Kursschwankungen *fpl*
(JAP) ヨーヨー株、乱高下する株
(RUS) ЦЕННАЯ БУМАГА С КРАЙНЕ НЕУСТОЙЧИВЫМ КУРСОМ

zero-base budgeting (ZBB)
(CHIN) 零基预算 （ZBB）
(FRE) budget base zéro
(GER) Null-Basis-Budgetierung *f*, ZBB-Planung *f*
(JAP) ゼロベース予算
(RUS) БЮДЖЕТЫ С НУЛЕВОЙ БАЗОЙ

zero coupon bond
(CHIN) 无息票债券
(FRE) fonds d'état libres d'intérêt nominal, (C) obligation coupon zéro (FELIN)
(GER) Nullkupon-Anleihe *f*; Nullprozenter *m*
(JAP) ゼロクーポン （方式の） 割引債券
(RUS) ОБЛИГАЦИЯ С НУЛЕВЫМИ КУПОНАМИ (БЕЗ ВЫПЛАТЫ ПРОЦЕНТОВ)

zero economic growth
(CHIN) 经济无增长
(FRE) croissance zéro, croissance nulle, (C) croissance économique zéro, (C) zégisme
(GER) Nullwirtschaftswachstum *n*
(JAP) ゼロ経済成長
(RUS) НУЛЕВОЙ ЭКОНОМИЧЕСКИЙ РОСТ

zero lot line
(CHIN) 零地界线
(FRE) limite de terrain zéro, (C) ligne d'arpentage zéro
(GER) Grundstücksnulllinie- *f*, -nullgrenze *f*
(JAP) ゼロ敷地線
(RUS) ОТСЧЕТНАЯ ГРАНИЦА ЗЕМЕЛЬНОГО УЧАСТКА

zero population growth (ZPG)

(CHIN) 人口无增长 （ZPG）

(FRE) accroissement démographique nul,
croissance zéro, croissance nulle,
(C) stagnation de la population
(GER) Null-Bevölkerungswachstum *n*,
(JAP) 人口ゼロ成長
(RUS) НУЛЕВОЙ ПРИРОСТ НАСЕЛЕНИЯ

zero-sum game

(CHIN) 零和游戏

(FRE) jeu à somme nulle
(GER) Nullsummenspiel *n*
(JAP) ゼロ和ゲーム
(RUS) ИГРА С НУЛЕВЫМ ИТОГОМ,
НИЧЬЯ

zone of employment

(CHIN) 工作区

(FRE) zone d'emploi
(GER) Bereich *m* der
Arbeitsstätte *f*
(JAP) 雇用地带、雇用地域、
雇用領域
(RUS) З(RUS) ОНА ЗАНЯТОСТИ

zoning

(CHIN) 分区

(FRE) zonage
(GER) Gebiets- *f*, Flächenaufteilung *f*;
Bauleitplanung *f*
(JAP) 区画割の、建築規制、ゾーニング
(RUS) РАЙОНИРОВАНИЕ

zoning map

(CHIN) 区划图

(FRE) plan de zonage
(GER) Flächenaufteilungskarte *f*
(JAP) ゾーニングマップ、用途地域図
(RUS) КАРТА РАЙОНИРОВАНИЯ

zoning ordinance

(CHIN) 市区划分法令

(FRE) règlement de zonage
(GER) Baunutzungsverordnung *f*,
Flächennutzungssatzung *f*
(JAP) 土地利用規制条例
(RUS) ПРИКАЗ, ПОСТАНОВЛЕНИЕ О
РАЙОНИРОВАНИИ

zoom function

(CHIN) 缩放功能

(FRE) fonction de zoom
(GER) Zoomfunktion *f*
(JAP) ズーム機能
(RUS) ФУНКЦИЯ ИЗМЕНЕНИЯ
МАСШТАБА ИЗОБРАЖЕНИЯ

z score

(CHIN) Z 值

(FRE) z-score), (C) note z
(GER) Z-Punkt *m*
(JAP) 標準得点、ゼロ平均得点
(RUS) МОДЕЛЬ, РАЗРАБОТАННАЯ
ДЛЯ ВЫЯВЛЕНИЯ КОМПАНИИ,
КОТОРОЙ ГРОЗЯТ ФИНАНСОВЫЕ
ТРУДНОСТИ, ПО ЕЕ
ОТЧЕТНОСТИ

Order Form

Fax orders (Send this form): (301) 424-2518.
Telephone orders: Call 1(800) 822-3213 (in Maryland: (301)424-7737)
E-mail orders: spbooks@aol.com or: books@schreiberpublishing.com
Mail orders to:
Schreiber Publishing, 51 Monroe St., Suite 101, Rockville MD 20850 USA

Please send the following books, programs, and/or a free catalog. I under-stand that I may
return any of them for a full refund, for any reason, no questions asked:

The Translator's Handbook 5th Revised Edition - $25.95
Spanish Business Dictionary - Multicultural Spanish - $24.95
German Business Dictionary - $24.95
French (France and Canada) Business Dictionary - $24.95
Chinese Business Dictionary - $24.95
Japanese Business Dictionary - $24.95
Russian Business Dictionary - $24.95
**Global Business Dictionary (English, French, German, Chinese,
Russian, Japanese)** - $33.95
Spanish Chemical and Pharmaceutical Glossary - $29.95
The Translator's Self-Training Program (circle the language/s of your
choice): Spanish French   German   Japanese Chinese   Italian
Portuguese   Russian   Arabic   Hebrew - $69.00
The Translator's Self-Training Program Spanish Medical - $69.00
The Translator's Self-Training Program Spanish Legal - $69.00
The Translator's Self-Training Program - German Patents - $69.00
The Translator's Self-Training Program - Japanese Patents - $69.00
Multicultural Spanish Dictionary - How Spanish Differs from
Country to Country - $24.95
21st Century American English Compendium - The "Odds and Ends"
of American English Usage - $24.95
Dictionary of Medicine French/English - Over one million words of
medical terminology - $179.50

Name: _____

Address: _____

City: _____ State: _____ Zip: _____

Telephone: _____ e-mail: _____

Sales tax: Please add 5% sales tax in Maryland
Shipping (est.): $4 for the first book and $2.00 for each additional product
International: $ $9 for the first book, and $5 for each additional book
Payment: Cheque   Credit card: Visa   MasterCard

Card number: _____

Name on card: _____ Exp. Date: __/__